2000 IBC Handbook
Structural Provisions

S.K. Ghosh, Ph.D.
R. Chittenden, S.E.

2000 IBC Handbook—Structural Provisions

Publication Date: July 2001
Second printing: November 2002

ISBN 1-58001-041-5

ICBO
5360 Workman Mill Rd. Whittier, CA 90601-2298
www.icbo.org
The World's Leading Source in Code Publications

Comments regarding this publication are welcome and will be considered in future revisions. Send to: products@icbo.org.

PRINTED IN THE U.S.A.

Preface

Internationally, code officials recognize the need for a modern, up-to-date building code addressing the design and installation of building systems through requirements emphasizing performance. The 2000 *International Building Code* (IBC) is designed to meet those needs through model code regulations that safeguard the public health and safety in all communities, large and small.

This comprehensive code establishes minimum regulations for building systems using prescriptive and performance-based provisions. It is founded on broad-based principles that make possible the use of alternate materials and new, improved design methodologies.

The changes in the structural provisions of the 2000 *International Building Code* when compared to previous editions of the model codes (*Uniform Building Code, National Building Code, Standard Building Code*) creates the need for a comprehensive work that expands on many of the new or improved provisions. This book, the *2000 IBC Handbook—Structural Provisions,* does just that. By helping code users understand and apply the structural provisions (Chapters 16 through 23) of the 2000 IBC, this handbook is a valuable resource for those who design, review, inspect or construct buildings or other structures regulated by the 2000 IBC. Although it will prove useful to a broad range of individuals, it was written primarily so that architects, engineers, and code officials can easily understand the IBC's provisions and gain insight into their underlying basis and intent. To that end, the handbook's numerous figures, tables, and examples help clarify and illustrate the proper application of many code provisions.

The *2000 IBC Handbook—Structural Provisions* covers four major structural categories:

- Structural design and loading provisions of Chapter 16
- Special inspection, testing and structural observation provisions of Chapter 17
- Foundation and soil provisions of Chapter 18
- Specific structural material provisions for concrete, masonry, steel and wood in Chapters 19 through 23

As an added benefit to readers, ICBO has included a CD-ROM containing the complete handbook as well as a variety of helpful resource documents such as FEMA 302 and 303 (1997 NEHRP), the *UBC-IBC Structural Comparison & Cross Reference,* and the *2000 IBC Structural Q&A Application Guide.*

Acknowledgements

Appreciation goes to the authors, S.K. Ghosh, Ph.D., and Robert Chittenden, S.E., both of whom have extensive knowledge, expertise, and experience in the development of many of the structural provisions of the 2000 IBC. Dr. Ghosh authored the introductory chapter, and chapters 16 and 19 of this handbook; Mr. Chittenden authored Chapters 17, 18, 20, 21, 22 and 23.

Dr. Ghosh would like to acknowledge the significant contributions of Madhu Khuntia, Ph.D., and Susan Dowty, S.E., his colleagues at S.K. Ghosh Associates, Inc. Dr. Khuntia contributed two of the examples, developed or modified many of the figures, and more than once extensively reviewed Chapters 16 and 19 manuscripts. Ms. Dowty contributed the initial version of the discussion on Section 1913.

A special tip of the hat goes to John Henry, P.E., ICBO Senior Staff Engineer, for his technical review of the handbook and to Mark Johnson, ICBO Director of Publications and Product Development, for general oversight of this project. ICBO would also like to express appreciation to Jerry Neville, P.E., and Tom Campbell, P.E., for reviewing the original document and to Alan Carr, S.E., for creating the index.

This publication was produced by a team of talented and highly qualified people who put in many hours of effort. Thanks to Marje Cates, David Jamieson and Kim Akhavan for editing; Mary Bridges for designing both the publication and CD-ROM; Yolanda Nickoley and Alberto Herrera for typesetting; and Mike Tamai for creating the illustrations and figures.

Foreword

The 2000 *International Building Code* (IBC) represents the state-of-the-art in building safety technology. Participation and input from various sectors of government, industry, academia and others reflect the inclusive process under which the development of the IBC took place. This intensive process has resulted in a superior code document that adopts by reference the latest consensus design standards and specifications.

The *2000 IBC Handbook—Structural Provisions* contains the most recent information on the Structural Provisions as they pertain to the 2000 IBC. The scope and treatment of the various provisions of the code presented in this handbook will benefit designers, students and code officials alike. In addition to explanations for the code provisions, the handbook chronicles the history behind many of these provisions. The *2000 IBC Handbook* represents the most thorough, comprehensive coverage of the IBC Structural Provisions to date.

A unique feature of this handbook is the inclusion of a CD-ROM containing essential references that support the IBC. While no single reference can hope to replace the code or substitute for on-the-job experience, the *2000 IBC Handbook* comes as close as possible, providing in-depth coverage in a consistent and coherent manner.

It is the wish of its developers, the *International Conference of Building Officials*, that this handbook facilitate a uniform and objective approach to code enforcement and compliance. The *2000 IBC Handbook* goes a long way toward accomplishing this goal. Those familiar with one of the three earlier regional model codes (UBC, NBC, or SBC) will find this publication a most useful transitional guide.

As a member of the design community and one who is intimately familiar with structural codes and standards, I am pleased to be a part of the historic movement toward code consolidation under the International Code Council (ICC) and applaud the efforts of the nation's three model code groups.

Farzad Naeim, Ph.D., P.E.
Editor of the *Seismic Handbook*
Director of Research and Development, John A. Martin and Associates

Foreword

TABLE OF CONTENTS

INTRODUCTION

This introduction provides a brief background on the current (2001) situation concerning building codes in this country, including the development of the *International Building Code*™.

Existing Model Codes

The building codes of most legal jurisdictions within the United States are based on one of three model codes: the BOCA *National Building Code* (BOCA/NBC)[1] published by the Building Officials and Code Administrators International, Country Club Hills, Illinois; the *Uniform Building Code*™ (UBC)[2] published by the International Conference of Building Officials (ICBO), Whittier, California; and the *Standard Building Code* (SBC)[3] published by the Southern Building Code Congress International (SBCCI), Birmingham, Alabama. Figure 1 shows the approximate areas of influence of each model code—areas in which each is typically adopted.

The 1993 edition of the BOCA/NBC, the 1994 edition of the UBC, and the 1994 edition of the SBC were organized into a common code format established by the Council of American Building Officials (CABO). The new format established common chapter designations for the three model building codes published in the United States. For example, structural design requirements have since been in Chapter 16 of all three model codes so they would all be organized by subject in a similar manner; that would then facilitate the comparison process in creating a single code.

There has traditionally been a difference in the way standards have been adopted into the UBC and the other two model codes. The BOCA/NBC and SBC have adopted standards by reference, reproducing only such portions as are likely to be frequently used by building officials, making few, if any, modifications in the process. The UBC, on the other hand, has adopted standards by both transcription and by reference. Frequently used standards such as material design standards are reproduced in the code itself, while the other standards are transcribed as UBC Standards. Modifications, sometimes significant ones, have often been made during this process of adoption.

International Building Code

At the end of 1994, the three existing model code groups together formed the International Code Council (ICC) with the express purpose of developing a single set of construction codes for the entire country. Included in this family of International Codes is the 2000 *International Building Code* (IBC), which represents a major step in a cooperative effort to bring national uniformity to building codes. The development of the IBC is schematically illustrated in Figure 2.

Five technical subcommittees (Fire Safety, Structural, Occupancies, Means of Egress, and General) were formed in 1996 by the International Code Council. The intent of the technical subcommittees was to develop a working draft of a comprehensive building code that is consistent with and inclusive of the scope and content of the existing model building codes.

The technical content of the latest building codes promulgated by BOCA, ICBO, and SBCCI was the nucleus for the development of the working draft. Other sources of relevant technical information were also considered. While there were a great many similarities among the three codes, careful consideration was given to identified differences. The technical subcommittees used certain principles as guidance in the resolution of technical differences. The principles were based on the intent to establish provisions consistent with the scope of a building code that adequately protects public health, safety, and welfare; provisions that do not increase construction costs unnecessarily; provisions that do not restrict the use of new materials, products or methods of construction; and provisions that do not give preferential treatment to particular types or classes of materials, products or methods of construction. The Working Draft was published in May 1997.

To assess the views of building code users, the building industry, and all other interested parties, a public forum was held in August 1997 in Denver, Colorado, where the technical subcommittees considered close to 3,000 submitted public comments to determine the content of the First Draft, which was published in November 1997. The ICC subsequently appointed five hearing subcommittees responsible for the same IBC chapters as the five technical subcommittees. These five subcommittees held public hearings in April 1998 in Alexandria, Virginia, using ICC code development procedures, except that successful assembly votes replaced committee recommendations for text revisions in the Final Draft. Over 2,000 code changes were processed. The Final Draft was published in July 1998.

The five ICC subcommittees held public hearings for a second time in March 1999 in Costa Mesa, California, to consider proposed changes to the Final Draft. The changes were processed using ICC code development procedures; any assembly action was also recorded. The committee recommendations and assembly actions were published by the ICC. The recommendations were subject to challenge (or so-called Public Comment). The challenges submitted were published by the ICC and then considered at a Joint Annual Business Meeting of the three model code groups in St. Louis in September 1999. At that meeting the challenged committee recommendations from Costa Mesa were either ratified or overturned by action of the memberships of the three model code groups. Unchallenged recommendations were automatically ratified. The final membership action from St. Louis is reflected in the 2000 edition of the IBC.

The topic of adoption of standards by reference rather than transcription was the subject of lengthy debates within the IBC Structural Subcommittee. The IBC chose to emulate the BOCA and SBCCI practice of adopting standards by reference. This caused a fundamental change in operating procedure for the ICBO membership.

Map of Building Code Influence

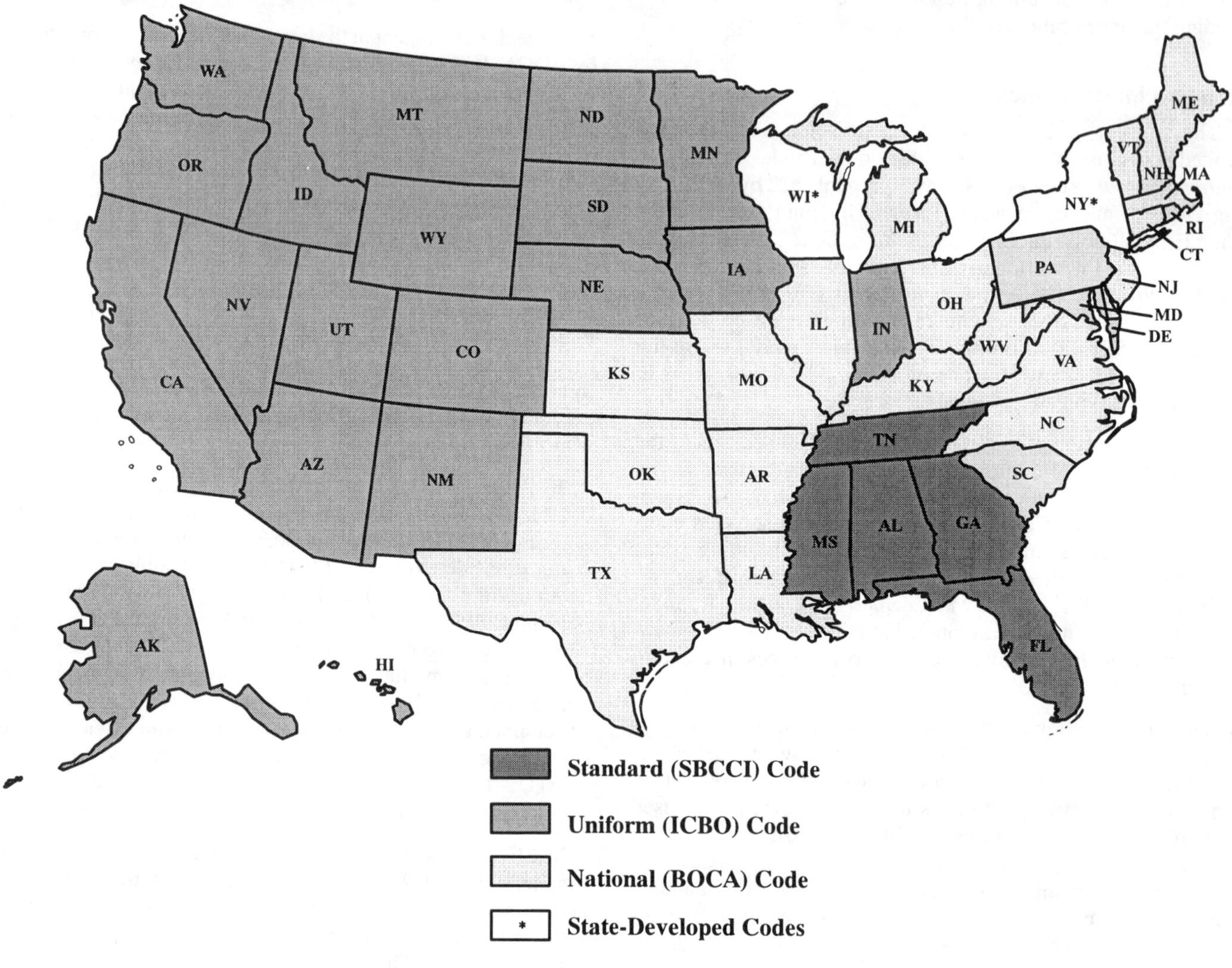

Prepared by the National Conference of States on Building Codes and Standards as of January 2001

APPROXIMATE AREAS OF INFLUENCE OF EACH MODEL CODE PRIOR TO PUBLICATION OF THE IBC

FIGURE 1

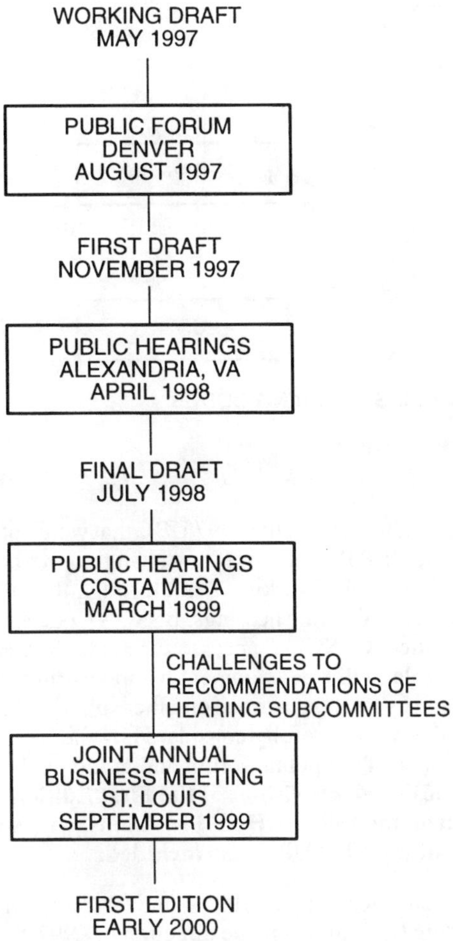

DEVELOPMENT OF INTERNATIONAL BUILDING CODE

FIGURE 2

Primary arguments against transcribing standards have been that the practice increases the length of the code and that, more important, provisions of the referenced standards become subject to change through the code change process. Legal ramifications of transcribing only portions of a standard into the code have also been pointed out: Code users may rely on the code alone for what they need when they should be relying on the standard. The Portland Cement Association has developed an inspection manual for concrete for the BOCA/NBC, the SBC, and the UBC.[4]

Structural Design (Chapter 16): Nonseismic

Chapter 16 of all three model codes, including the IBC, addresses the design requirements for various types of loads and, also very important, addresses the design load combinations.

The BOCA/NBC and the SBC have traditionally adopted the provisions of the latest available edition of ASCE 7 (previously ANSI A58.1)[5] for nonseismic loads. There are sometimes variations to this. The SBC, for example, also allows the design of low-rise metal buildings by the Metal Building Manufacturers Association manual.[6] Rather substantive modifications to the ASCE 7 provisions have often been made in the UBC. A case in point: the wind-load provisions of the 1997 UBC, which are simplified versions of the corresponding provisions of ASCE 7-88.

The 2000 IBC has chosen to make ASCE 7-98 the basis of all provisions related to nonseismic loads.

Structural Design (Chapter 16): Seismic

Until recently, seismic design provisions in U.S. building codes followed a certain pattern (Figure 3). Provisions were first proposed by the Structural Engineers Association of California (SEAOC) in its *Recommended Lateral Force Requirements*[7] (commonly referred to as the Blue Book), then adopted by ICBO in its *Uniform Building Code*. The UBC provisions were then adopted (often with modifications) by the American National Standards Institute (ANSI) Standard A58.1, which, in turn, was adopted by the other two model codes: the BOCA/NBC and the SBC. Thus, the seismic design provisions of all three model codes were based on the SEAOC Blue Book provisions, although a time lag was sometimes involved. The latest available editions of the BOCA/NBC and the SBC at a particular time might be based on an older edition of the Blue Book than the then-latest edition of the UBC.

A departure from the above pattern was initiated in 1972 when the National Science Foundation and the National Bureau of Standards (now the National Institute of Standards and Technology) decided to jointly sponsor a Cooperative Program in Building Practices for Disaster Mitigation. Under that program, the Applied Technology Council (ATC) developed a document entitled *Tentative Provisions for the Development of Seismic Regulations for Buildings*.[8] This document, published in 1978 and commonly referred to as ATC 3-06, underwent a thorough review by the building community in ensuing years. Trial designs were conducted to establish the technical validity of the new provisions and to assess their impact. A new entity, the Building Seismic Safety Council (BSSC), was created under the auspices of the National Institute of Building Sciences (NIBS) to administer and oversee the trial design effort. The trial designs indicated the need for certain modifications to the original ATC 3-06 document. The modifications were made. The resulting document was the first edition, dated 1985, of the NEHRP (National Earthquake Hazards Reduction Program) *Recommended Provisions for the Development of Seismic Regulations for New Buildings*.[9] Under continued federal funding, this document has been updated every three years; the 1988, 1991, 1994 and 1997 editions of the NEHRP Provisions have been issued by the Building Seismic Safety Council (Figure 4). The 2000 edition of the NEHRP Provisions is currently under development.

In 1980, the SEAOC Seismology Committee undertook the task of developing an ATC-based revision of their Blue Book. This extensive effort resulted in the 1988 edition of the SEAOC Blue Book[7], which was then adopted into the 1988 edition of the UBC (Figure 4). Changes from the 1988 to the 1991 and from the 1991 to the 1994 editions of the UBC were minor. There were major revisions to the seismic code provisions between the 1994 and 1997 editions of the UBC,which were due to a code change under development since 1993 by the SEAOC Seismology Committee and its ad hoc subcommittees on strength design and strong ground motions. Numerous significant revisions were incorporated into their code change proposal to reflect the lessons learned from the Northridge and Kobe earthquakes. Also, recognizing that the IBC would be based on existing model codes, SEAOC evaluated the basis of the seismic provisions in the BOCA/NBC and the SBC to determine if convergence of the

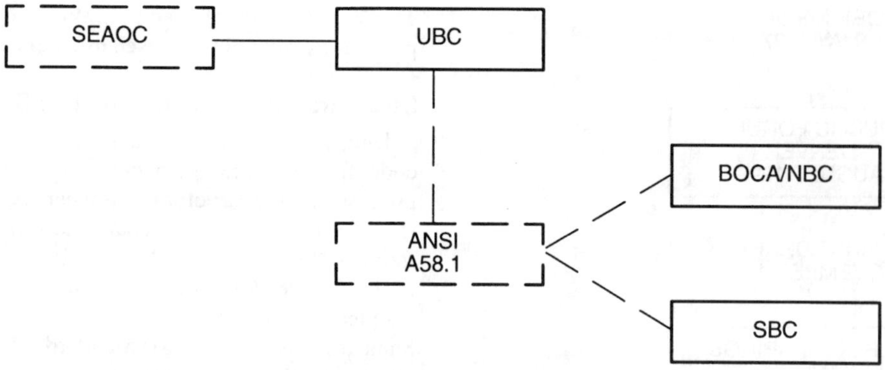

ORIGIN OF SEISMIC DESIGN PROVISIONS IN U.S. BUILDING CODES

FIGURE 3

seismic provisions was possible. As a result, significant concepts consistent with the seismic provisions in these other two model codes were incorporated into SEAOC's code change proposal. These changes, sometimes in modified forms, were included in Appendix C to the 1996 SEAOC Blue Book and in the 1999 SEAOC Blue Book.

The BOCA/NBC and the SBC, which traditionally adopted the seismic provisions of the ANSI A58.1 (now ASCE 7) Standard, adopted seismic design provisions based on the 1991 NEHRP Provisions in 1993 and 1994, respectively. This is because the seismic provisions of the national loading standard had fallen behind the times. The 1988 edition of the ASCE/ANSI Standard, published in 1990, still had seismic design provisions based on the 1979 UBC. Requirements based on the 1991 NEHRP Provisions were retained in the 1996 edition of the BOCA/NBC and the 1997 edition of the SBC. The 1994 NEHRP Provisions did not become the basis of the seismic design provisions of the 1996 BOCA/NBC or the 1997 SBC. However, seismic design provisions based on the 1994 NEHRP Provisions were adopted into the 1995 edition of the ASCE 7 Standard. Both the 1996 edition of the BOCA/NBC and the 1997 edition of the SBC permit seismic design by ASCE 7-95. The seismic design provisions of the 1999 edition of the BOCA/NBC remain the same as those of the 1996 edition. Similarly, the seismic design provisions of the 1999 edition of the SBC remain the same as those of the 1997 edition. Table 1 summarizes seismic design provisions of the model codes.

The seismic design provisions of the IBC were treated separately from the rest of the structural provisions in the code development process. In 1996, the IBC Code Development Committee agreed in concept for the IBC to be based on the 1997 edition of the NEHRP Provisions, which was being developed after the last edition of the UBC (1997) had been published. A Code Resource Development Committee (CRDC), funded by the Federal Emergency Management Agency (FEMA), was formed under the direction of the Building Seismic Safety Council (BSSC) to generate seismic code provisions based on the 1997 edition of the NEHRP Provisions, for incorporation into the 2000 IBC. This effort was successful and the CRDC submittal was accepted by the IBC Code Development Committee for inclusion in the IBC. The seismic design provisions of the Working Draft were thus based on the 1997 NEHRP Provisions, but also included a number of features of the 1997 UBC that were not included in the 1997 NEHRP Provisions. Many changes have been made to the provisions of the Working Draft through the public forum and the two sets of public hearings. BSSC's Code Resource Support Committee (CRSC), a successor group to the CRDC, played an active role in this development by sponsoring changes of their own and by taking positions on other submitted changes—positions that were carefully considered by the IBC Structural Subcommittee at the public forum and at the public hearings. **The seismic design provisions of the First Edition of the IBC are based on the 1997 NEHRP Provisions, with some of the features of the 1997 UBC also included.**

The changes from the 1994 to the 1997 edition of the *Uniform Building Code* took it in the direction of 1997 NEHRP and IBC. However, there are still substantial differences between the seismic design provisions of the 1997 UBC and those of the 2000 IBC. The treatment of ground motion parameters in seismic design is entirely different in the two documents. Another major difference is discussed below.

The 2000 IBC uses Seismic Design Categories (SDC) to determine permissible structural systems, limitations on height and irregularity, the type of lateral force analysis that must be performed, the level of detailing for structural members and joints that are part of the lateral-force-resisting system and for the components that are not. The 1997 UBC, as in prior editions of the code, uses the seismic zone in which a structure is located for all these purposes. The SDC is a function of occupancy (called Seismic Use Group in the 2000 IBC and the 1997 NEHRP Provisions) and of soil-modified seismic risk at the site of the structure.

In 1978, when ATC 3-06, the predecessor document to the NEHRP Provisions, made the level of detailing (and other restrictions concerning permissible structural system, height, irregularity, and analysis procedure) a function of occupancy, that was a major departure from UBC practice, which was continued in all the NEHRP Provisions through the 1994 edition. Now, in the 2000 IBC and the 1997 NEHRP Provisions, the level of detailing and the other restrictions have been made a function of the soil characteristics at the site of the structure. This is a further major departure from UBC practice and indeed from current seismic design practice across the country.

Structural Design (Chapter 16): Load Combinations

Design load combinations of all three model codes have progressively become inordinately complex, primarily because of an emphasis on modernizing the seismic regulations in each of those codes over the past decade. The advancement in the understanding of seismic structural response has brought about changes in design philosophy which, in turn, has resulted in changes in load combinations that must be used when earthquake forces are considered. The complexity continues into the 2000 IBC. The design load combinations of ASCE 7, if and when adopted, have been subject to so many modifications that confusion has not abated. A reader seeking clarity may benefit from consulting References 10-12. Some of the current confusion should dissipate as the IBC eventually replaces the existing model codes.

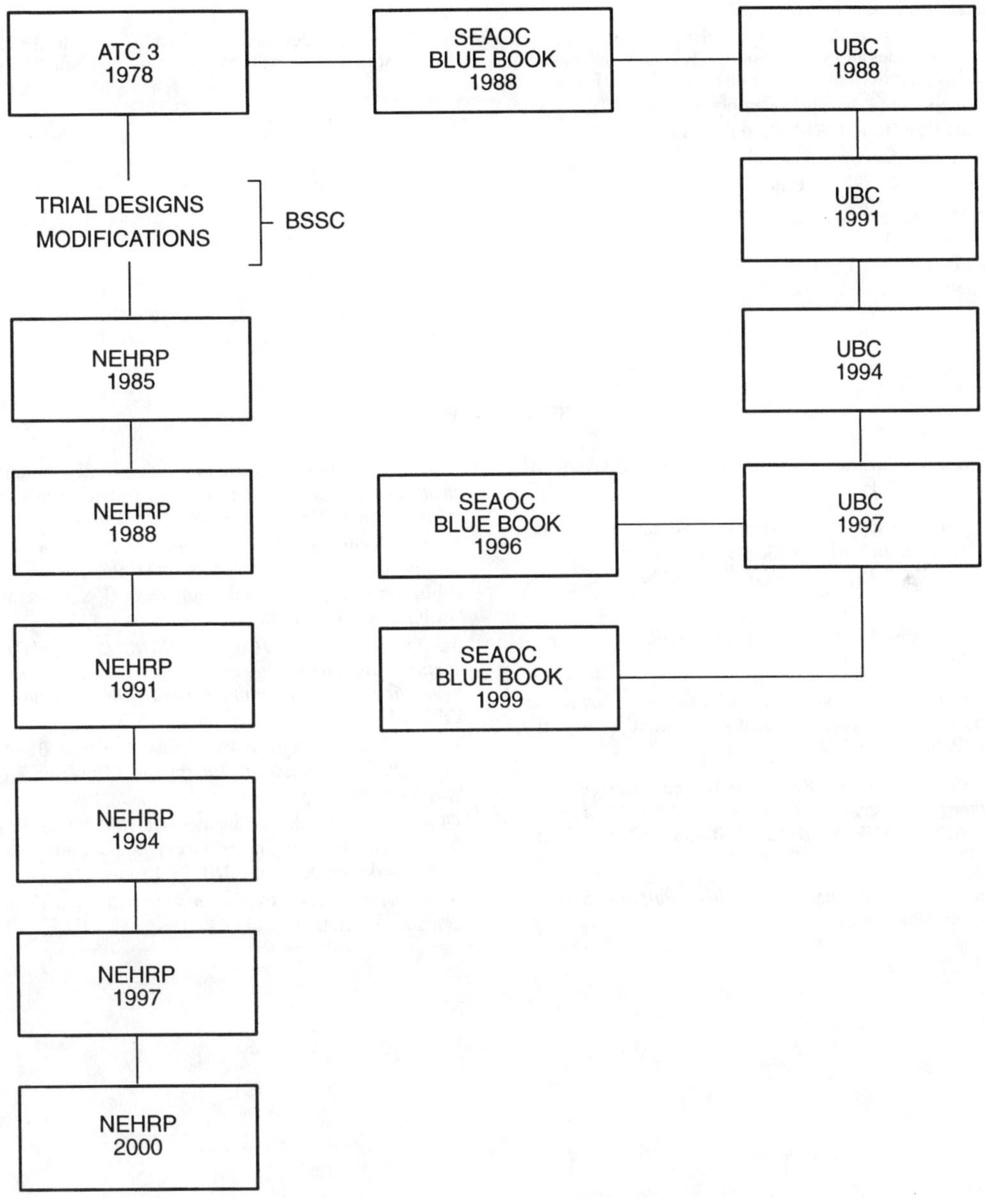

DEVELOPMENT AND SUBSEQUENT ASSIMILATION OF THE NEHRP SEISMIC PROVISIONS IN THE UNIFORM BUILDING CODE

FIGURE 4

TABLE 1. KEY TO SEISMIC DESIGN PROVISIONS OF MODEL CODES

RESOURCE DOCUMENT	EDITION	MODEL CODE	
SEAOC Blue Book[a]	1988	UBC 1994	
	1996, App. C, 1999	UBC 1997	
NEHRP	1991	BOCA/NBC	1993, 1999
			1996
		SBC	1994, 1999
			1997
	1994	See ASCE 7 1995 below	
	1997	IBC 2000	
ASCE 7	1995 (NEHRP 1994 adopted)	BOCA/NBC 1996[b], 1999[b]	
		SBC 1997[b], 1999[b]	

a. Recommended Lateral Force Requirements.

b. The 1991 NEHRP Provisions forms the basis of the seismic design requirements of the 1996 and 1999 editions of the BOCA/NBC and the 1997 and 1999 editions of the SBC. However, both codes allow the use of ASCE 7-95, which has adopted seismic design requirements based on the 1994 NEHRP Provisions. ASCE 7-98 has adopted seismic design provisions based on the 1997 NEHRP Provisions.

BOCA Building Officials and Code Administrators International
NEHRP National Earthquake Hazards Reduction Program
SEAOC Structural Engineers Association of California
ASCE American Society of Civil Engineers
IBC International Building Code
SBC Standard Building Code
NBC National Building Code
UBC Uniform Building Code

REFERENCES

[1] Building Officials & Code Administrators International, *The BOCA National Building Code*, Country Club Hills, IL, 1993, 1996, 1999.

[2] Pacific Coast Building Officials Conference (later the International Conference of Building Officials) Uniform Building Code, Long Beach, CA (later Whittier, CA), 1935,1952, 1967, 1970,1973,1976, 1979, 1982, 1985, 1988, 1991, 1994, 1997.

[3] Southern Building Code Congress International, *Standard Building Code*, Birmingham, AL, 1994, 1997, 1999.

[4] Messersmith Jr., J.J. , Kluver, K.M., and Skalko, S.V., *Concrete Inspection Handbook*, Publication EB 115, Portland Cement Association, Skokie, IL, 1995 (Revised Edition Published in 2000)

[5] American Society of Civil Engineers, *ASCE Standard Minimum Design Loads for Buildings and Other Structures*, ASCE 7-88, ASCE 7-93, ASCE 7-95, ASCE7-98 (also ANSI A58-55, ANSI A58.1-72, ANSI A58.1-82), New York, N.Y. , 1990, 1993, 1995.

[6] Metal Building Manufacturers Association, *Low-Rise Building Systems Manual*, Cleveland, Ohio, 1986.

[7] Seismology Committee, Structural Engineers Association of California, *Recommended Lateral Force Requirements and Commentary*, San Francisco (later Sacramento), CA, 1974, 1988, 1996, 1999.

[8] Applied Technology Council, *Tentative Provisions for the Development of Seismic Regulations for Buildings*, ATC Publication ATC 3-06, NBS Special Publication 510, NSF Publication 78-8, U. S. Government Printing Office, Washington, D.C., 1978.

[9] Building Seismic Safety Council, *NEHRP (National Earthquake Hazards Reduction Program) Recommended Provisions for the Development of Seismic Regulations for New Buildings (and Other Structures)*, Washington, D.C., 1994 (1997).

[10] Ghosh, S.K., "Design of Reinforced Concrete Buildings under the 1997 UBC," *Building Standards*, International Conference of Building Officials, May-June 1998, pp. 20-24.

[11] Ghosh, S.K., "Needed Adjustments in 1997 UBC," Proceedings, 1998 Convention, Structural Engineers Association of California, October 7-10, 1998, Reno-Sparks, Nevada, pp. T9.1-T9.15.

[12] *Strength Design Load Combinations for Concrete Elements*, IS 521, Portland Cement Association, Skokie, IL,1998.

CHAPTER 16
PART 1
STRUCTURAL DESIGN

Scope of Chapter

This chapter explains and provides background on the development of the structural design requirements of Chapter 16 of the 2000 *International Building Code* (IBC). Sources of the provisions are cited whenever practical. As indicated below, many of the provisions are derived from two major sources: ASCE 7-98 and the 1997 NEHRP Provisions. Fortunately, both of these documents come with detailed commentaries. Portions of these commentaries have at times been paraphrased in an attempt to make this handbook reasonably self-contained. In many instances, fairly detailed background to certain provisions has been provided in appendices, so as not to interfere with the flow of the handbook.

Comparisons with the provisions of the three model codes are provided throughout the chapter. All three model code organizations publish useful commentaries to their codes.[1, 2, 3] Commentaries to the seismic design provisions of the UBC are also available in the SEAOC Blue Book.[4] All these are valuable sources of information. Fewer comparisons are explicitly made with the 1999 BOCA *National Building Code* (BOCA/NBC) and the 1999 *Standard Bulding Code* (SBC) seismic design provisions than with the seismic design provisions of the 1997 *Uniform Building Code* (UBC). This is because the seismic design requirements of the BOCA/NBC and the SBC are already based on the NEHRP Provisions (although, as mentioned, an older edition of the document). Numerical examples have been included where they serve to illustrate the design requirements.

SECTION 1601 GENERAL

Chapter 16, Structural Design, governs the structural design of IBC-regulated buildings, nonbuilding structures, and portions thereof. A building is defined in Section 202 as any structure used or intended for supporting or sheltering any use or occupancy.

This chapter provides requirements for the minimum structural loads as well as criteria or methods of load application to be used in the design of buildings and other structures. The various types of structural loads specified by Chapter 16 are either gravity loads or lateral loads. Gravity loads specifically addressed are dead loads, live loads, snow loads and rain loads. Lateral loads specifically dealt with are those due to wind, earthquakes, soil pressure or flood. Loading conditions, such as uniformly distributed and concentrated live loads, impact loads and, most important, the design load combinations are also regulated by the provisions of Chapter 16. Section 1601 presents the scope of Chapter 16. Section 1602 defines terms that are commonly used in the structural design requirements. Section 1603 specifies the minimum information that must be provided on the construction documents. Section 1604 gives general design requirements and specifically addresses strength criteria, serviceability criteria, including deflection limitations, structural analysis, importance factors and load tests. Section 1605 addresses the vital topic of design load combinations. Strength design load combinations, allowable stress design load combinations, as well as special seismic design load combinations are given. Section 1606 specifies design dead loads. Section 1607 specifies the minimum uniformly distributed live loads and minimum concentrated live loads for various types of occupancies. This section also permits a reduction of design live loads under certain conditions. Section 1608 specifies the design snow loads. Section 1609 contains structural design requirements for wind loads. Effects of basic wind speed, terrain features, building occupancy, structural geometry, effective wind area of component and location of component on building are considered. Sections 1610, 1611 and 1612 treat soil lateral loads, rain loads and flood loads, respectively. Sections 1613-1623 are devoted to the seismic design of buildings and other structures. The seismic design provisions are organized as follows:

1613 Earthquake Loads Definitions
1614 Earthquake Loads—General
1615 Earthquake Loads—Site Ground Motion
1616 Earthquake Loads—Criteria Selection
1617 Earthquake Loads—Minimum Design Lateral Force and Related Effects
1618 Dynamic Analysis Procedure for the Seismic Design of Buildings
1619 Earthquake Loads—Soil-Structure Interaction Effects
1620 Earthquake Loads—Design, Detailing Requirements and Structural Component Load Effects
1621 Architectural, Mechanical and Electrical Component Seismic Design Requirements
1622 Nonbuilding Structures Seismic Design Requirements
1623 Seismically Isolated Structures

SECTION 1602 DEFINITIONS

The IBC defines general structural terms in Section 1602.

Two items may be worth commenting on. Up to the First Draft of the IBC, a load bearing wall was defined as "A wall supporting any vertical load in addition to its own weight." Taken literally, this definition would have required a wood-framed partition wall that supported a picture frame or light fixture, or a concrete wall that supported a single run of conduit, to be classified as a load-bearing wall. The definition was overly restrictive when used to apply code requirements for load-bearing walls to walls supporting such insignificant loads. The current definition, based on the 1997 UBC, provides much-needed guidance to the design professionals as to when such loads become of sufficient magnitude to require a wall to be classified as a load-bearing wall.

Next, while some notations are given in Section 1602, symbols and notations are typically defined throughout the IBC following the equation(s) in which they are used. The ICC Structural Subcommittee thought this to be more user-friendly than requiring the reader to refer back to the beginning of a chapter every time an equation appears.

SECTION 1603 CONSTRUCTION DOCUMENTS

This details the items to be shown on construction documents. Most of it is adopted with necessary modifications from the BOCA/NBC.[5]

Construction documents are defined in Section 202. Note that the loads are not required to be on the construction drawings, but must be included within the construction documents in such a way that the design loads are clear for all parts of the structure. Of course, the indicated loads are required to be equal to or greater than the loads required by the code. The information required to be included in the construction documents is useful to the building official in performing plan review and field inspection. It is also typically found to be useful if additions or alterations are made to a structure at a later date. Each of the items indicated in Section 1603.1.3 is an important parameter in the determination of the wind resistance that is required in the structural system of the building.

The exception to Section 1603.1 simplifies the structural design information required for buildings constructed to the conventional light-frame construction provisions of Section 2308. A registered design professional is not required for such buildings. However, the requirements of Sections 1603.1.1 through 1603.1.6 clearly would require the services of such a professional in order to provide the specified design data. The requirements in the exception provide adequate information for the building official to verify the structural design basis of buildings built to these conventional construction provisions.

Sections 1603.1.7 and 1603.2 through 1603.4 go beyond items to be shown on construction documents. To ensure that seismic-resistant systems and components are properly constructed and/or installed, special inspection is required in Section 1707.1. To do this inspection, approved construction documents for these systems and components are required. The 1603.1.7 requirement for construction documents is found in Sections 3.6 and 6.1.7 of the 1997 NEHRP Recommended Provisions. Section 1603.3, Live loads posted, is similar to 1997 UBC Section 1607.3.5. The requirements, however, are somewhat different.

SECTION 1604 GENERAL DESIGN REQUIREMENTS

1604.1 General. This section requiring buildings and other structures and all portions thereof to be designed and constructed in accordance with certain methods is adopted from the 1997 UBC, except that empirical design is not specifically mentioned in the UBC, and conventional construction is mentioned in an exception.

1604.2 Strength. Most of this section is a reproduction of ASCE 7-98[6] Section 1.3.1. The basic requirement is that buildings and structures be sufficient to support the factored loads without exceeding their strength. For structural elements of a building or other structure designed using nominal rather than factored loads, the working stresses are not to exceed the applicable allowable stresses.

1604.3 Serviceability. The basic requirement for serviceability of buildings, nonbuilding structures and all parts thereof is that they be designed and constructed with adequate stiffness so as to limit deflection and lateral drift to an appropriate degree based on the intended use.[1] The general statement is adopted with modification from Section 1.3.2 of ASCE 7-98. The detailed Sections 1604.3.1 through 1604.3.6 are developed from and closely follow the requirements of Section 1604.5 of the 1996 BOCA/NBC. Table 1604.3 was initially developed from the detailed provisions of Sections 1604.5.4 through 1604.5.6 of the BOCA/NBC.

The ASCE 7-98, Section 1.3.2 reads as follows: "Structural systems and members thereof shall be designed to have adequate stiffness to limit deflections, lateral drift, vibration, or any other deformations that adversely affect the intended use and performance of buildings and other structures." The IBC has omitted any reference to vibration or any other deformations that have an adverse impact on intended use and performance of structure because:

1. The code has no objectively defined standard for structural vibration. Acceptable limits are frequently subjective and highly dependent on the specific requirements of occupants of a building. This information is not necessarily available to the building official.
2. It is impossible for the building official to anticipate everything that can "adversely affect the intended use and performance" of a building. Sections 1604.3.1 through 1604.3.6 provide objectively defined deflection limits for structural members. Limits more restrictive than these should properly be a matter of negotiation between the design professional and the client and should not be part of a life-safety building code. For example, there are situations in which sensitive computer, optical, and mechanical equipment require extraordinary measures to provide adequate support for their intended use. These measures are often very complex and well beyond the life-safety requirements of most structures.

1604.4 Analysis. The first two paragraphs are reproduced with minor modifications from Section 1.3.4 of ASCE 7-98. The third paragraph is from the 1997 UBC Section 1605.2, Rationality. The fourth paragraph is from the 1997 UBC Section 1605.2.1, Distribution of horizontal shear. The last paragraph is from UBC Section 1605.2.2, Stability against overturning.

Structural analysis is to be based on fundamental principles of structural mechanics. These principles are equilibrium, stability, geometric compatibility and material properties. While the code in general does not intend to specify the design method used by the engineer, it does intend that the design method be rational and in accordance with well-established principles of mechanics. Departures from this latter requirement can still be made based on the provisions of Section 104.11 when approved by the building official. For example, the structural adequacy of a building may not admit to a rational analysis; a program of full-scale testing may be the only reasonable way to determine its structural behavior. If the testing program shows that a certain building can safely resist the loads required by the code, the building official may approve the construction of the building.[2] The basic requirement for self-straining forces is that those due to moisture, creep, shrinkage, temperature changes and foundation settlement be adequately accounted for. Thus, a structure is to be designed to resist the forces resulting from self-straining, or alternatively, expansion joints must be provided.

The criterion regarding load paths and certain other general criteria for design to resist lateral forces are equally applicable to design for wind and earthquakes.

The requirement for stability against overturning makes reference to specific sections: 1613 for earthquake, 1609.1.3 for wind, 1610 for soil lateral loads.

1604.5 Importance factors. This section and Table 1604.5 make a combined presentation of snow load, wind load and seismic load importance factors.

The snow load importance factors are the same as those in Table 7-4 of ASCE 7-98, if it is remembered that IBC occupancy categories I, II, III and IV correspond to ASCE 7 occupancy categories II, III, IV and I, respectively. The basis of the values is explained in the commentary to ASCE 7-98.

The snow load importance factor attempts to address the need to relate design loads to the consequences of failure. Roofs of most structures having normal occupancies and functions are designed with an importance factor of 1.0, which corresponds to unmodified use of the statistically determined ground snow load for a 2-percent annual probability of being exceeded (50-year mean recurrence interval). Lower and higher risk situations are established using the importance factors for snow loads, which range from 0.8 to 1.2. The factor of 0.8 corresponds to an annual probability of being exceeded of about 4 percent (about a 25-year mean recurrence interval). The factor of 1.2 is nearly that for a 1-percent annual probability of being exceeded (about a 100-year mean recurrence interval).[6]

The wind load importance factors are also the same as those in Table 6-1 of ASCE 7-98, if it is again remembered that IBC occupancy categories I, II, III and IV correspond to ASCE 7 occupancy categories II, III, IV and I, respectively. It may be noted that the last column in ASCE 7 Table 6-1 has been replaced by a footnote to Table 1604.5.

The wind importance factor is used to adjust the level of structural reliability of a building or other structure, depending on its occupancy. The importance factors given in Table 1604.5 adjust the wind velocity pressure to different annual probabilities of being exceeded. Importance factors of 0.87, 1.00 and 1.5 are, for nonhurricane winds, associated with annual probabilities of being exceeded of 0.04, 0.02 and 0.01, respectively (mean recurrence intervals of 25, 50 and 100 years, respectively).

In hurricane-prone regions with basic wind speed V exceeding 100 mph, I_w is changed from 0.87 to 0.77 through footnote b to Table 1604.5. For wind speeds greater than 100 mph, the annual probabilities of exceeding same, implied by the importance factors of 0.77 and 1.15 will vary along the coast; however, the resulting risk levels associated with the use of these importance factors will be approximately consistent with those applied to wind speeds less than 90 mph.[6]

The seismic importance factor is adopted from the 1997 NEHRP Provisions. ATC 3-06,[7] the predecessor document to NEHRP, deliberately decided to drop the importance factor that has long been used in seismic design by the UBC. Instead, ATC 3-06 chose to institute two other requirements to ensure enhanced performance of structures in higher occupancy categories. First, it made drift limits tighter for structures in higher occupancy categories. Second, it made the level of detailing and other restrictions a function not only of the seismic risk at the site of a structure, but also of the occupancy of the structure. With these provisions still in place, the 1997 NEHRP Provisions and the IBC have chosen to bring the importance factor back. The highest value of the importance factor in the IBC is 1.5, whereas the UBC has used a maximum value of 1.25 since 1988.

According to the commentary to the 1997 NEHRP Provisions, the importance factor represents only one of several ways in which control is attempted of the seismic performance capabilities of buildings in different occupancy categories. Specifically, the occupancy importance factor modifies the *R* coefficients used to determine minimum base shear forces. Structures assigned occupancy importance factors exceeding 1.0 are, through this mechanism, designed for larger base shear forces. As a result, they are expected to experience lower ductility demands than structures designed with lower occupancy importance factors and, hence, would be expected to sustain less damage.

Note that the IBC uses the same seismic importance factor, I_E, for structures as well as structural components. It uses an importance factor, I_p, given in Section 1621 but not listed in Table 1604.5, for architectural, electrical, and mechanical components only.

Footnote a to Table 1604.5 indicates that "category" is equivalent to "Seismic Use Group" for the purposes of Section 1616.2. This requires some clarification, because there are three seismic use groups and four occupancy categories. Seismic Use Group I, in fact, includes both Occupancy Categories I and IV.

1604.6 In-situ load tests. This is adapted from Section 1.7 of ASCE 7-98 and is not part of the 1997 UBC. The section is very similar to Section 1604.3 of the 1996 BOCA/NBC. Whenever there is reasonable doubt as to the stability or load-bearing capacity of a completed building, structure or portion thereof for the expected loads, an engineering assessment may be required by the building official. The engineering analysis may involve either a structural analysis or an in-situ load test, or both. See IBC Section 1712 for more details.

1604.7 Preconstruction load tests. This section, almost identical to Section 1604.4 of the BOCA/NBC, is also not a part of the 1997 UBC. In evaluating the physical properties of materials and methods of construction that are not capable of being designed by approved engineering analysis, or which do not comply with applicable material design standards listed in Chapter 35, the structural adequacy must be predetermined based on the load test criteria given in Section 1713.

1604.8 Anchorage. This addresses the anchorage of the various components of a building to resist the uplift and sliding forces that result from the application of the code-prescribed lateral forces. It intends that all members be tied together or anchored to resist the uplift and sliding forces. The section differentiates between the uplift and sliding forces to be resisted in general (Section 1604.8.1) and the lateral support required for concrete and masonry walls (Section 1604.8.2).

Many observed failures of concrete or masonry walls in the 1971 San Fernando and the 1994 Northridge earthquakes were attributable to inadequate anchorage between the walls and the roof system. Although requirements for anchorage to prevent the separation of heavy masonry or concrete walls from floors or roofs have been common (although often insufficient) in highly seismic areas, they have been minimal or nonexistent in most other parts of the country. This section requires that anchorage be provided in any locality to the tune of 200 pounds per linear foot of wall (Figure 1).This requirement alone may not provide complete earthquake-resistant design, but observations of earthquake damage indicate that it can greatly increase the earthquake resistance of buildings and reduce hazards in those localities where earthquakes may occur but are rarely damaging.[8]

Where the spacing between anchors exceeds 4 feet, the bending of a wall between such anchors must be considered in the design of the wall. If the wall being laterally supported is of hollow-unit masonry or a cavity wall, the required anchors must be embedded in a reinforced grouted structural element of the wall.

SECTION 1605
LOAD COMBINATIONS

1605.1 General. This section requires that buildings and other structures and portions thereof be designed to resist the strength design or LRFD load combinations of Section 1605.2 or the ASD load combinations of Section 1605.3, the load combinations specified in Chapters 18 through 23, and the special seismic load combinations of Section 1605.4 where required by Section 1620.1.9 (Elements supporting discontinuous walls or frames) or Section 1620.1.6, Collector elements.

1605.2 Load combinations using strength design or load and resistance factor design. The basic strength design load combinations of the 2000 IBC are adapted from those of the 1997 UBC, which in turn are adapted from the strength design load combinations of ASCE 7-95.[9] The three sets are presented together in Table 1 for convenience of comparison. Between the Final Draft and the 2000 edition of the IBC, the strength design load combinations were made consistent with those of ASCE 7-98, also presented in Table 1.

The 2000 IBC and the 1997 UBC removed all references to F (load due to fluids), H (load due to lateral pressure of soil and water in soil), and T (self-straining force arising from contraction or expansion resulting from temperature changes, shrinkage, moisture change, creep in component materials, movement due to differential settlement, or combinations thereof) from load combination 2. These loads, F, H, T and P (ponding load), which is not specifically addressed in ASCE 7-95, are dealt with under Section 1605.2.2, Other loads. The corresponding 1997 UBC Section 1612.2.2 requires where F, H, P or T are to be considered in design, each applicable load shall be added to applicable load combinations 12-1 through 12-6 as follows: $1.3F$, $1.6H$, $1.2P$ or $1.2T$. Section 1605.2.2 requires that where F, H, P or T are to be considered in design, each applicable load be added to the combinations of 1605.2.1 in accordance with Section 2.3.2 of ASCE 7-98. Interestingly, P is still not addressed in Section 2.3.2 of ASCE 7-98 (see Table 1). Where F_a (flood load) is to be considered in design, the load combinations of Section 2.3.3 of ASCE 7-98 are to be used.

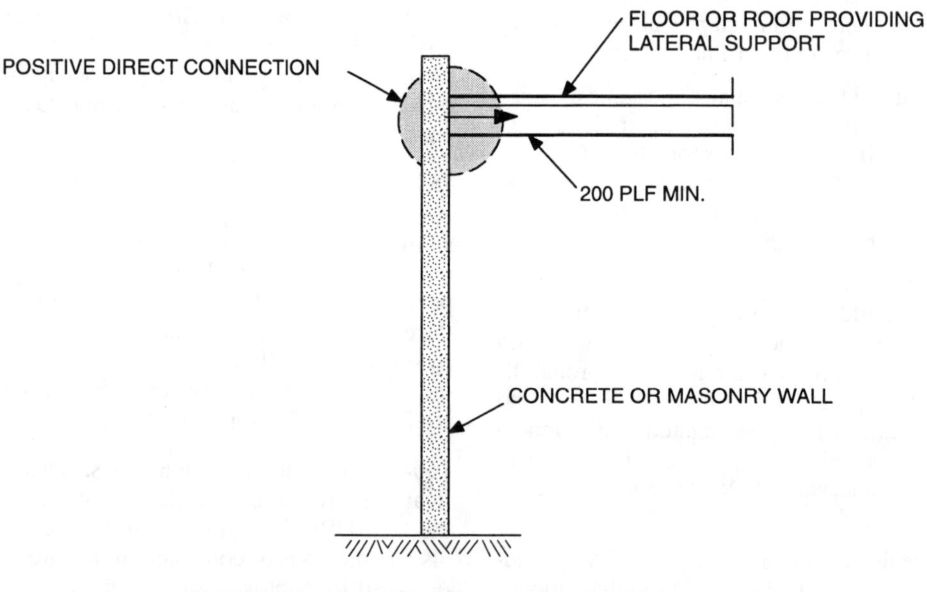

ANCHORAGE OF CONCRETE AND MASONRY WALLS
SEISMIC DESIGN CATEGORY A, NON-SEISMIC (SECTION 1604.8.2)

FIGURE 1

TABLE 1. STRENGTH DESIGN LOAD COMBINATIONS OF THE 2000 IBC, THE 1997 UBC, ASCE 7-95 AND ASCE 7-98

IBC 2000, Section 1605.2.1	
$1.4D$	(Formula 16-1)
$1.2D + 1.6L + 0.5\ (L_r \text{ or } S \text{ or } R)$	(Formula 16-2)
$1.2\ D + 1.6(L_r \text{ or } S \text{ or } R) + (f_1L \text{ or } 0.8W)$	(Formula 16-3)
$1.2D + 1.6W + f_1L + 0.5(L_r \text{ or } S \text{ or } R)$	(Formula 16-4)
$1.2D + 1.0E + f_1L + f_2S$	(Formula 16-5)
$0.9D + (1.0E \text{ or } 1.6W)$	(Formula 16-6)
UBC 1997, Section 1612.2.1	
$1.4D$	(12-1)
$1.2D + 1.6L + 0.5(L_r \text{ or } S)$	(12-2)
$1.2D + 1.6(L_r \text{ or } S) + (f_1L \text{ or } 0.8W)$	(12-3)
$1.2D + 1.3W + f_1L + 0.5(L_r \text{ or } S)$	(12-4)
$1.2D + 1.0E + (f_1L + f_2S)$	(12-5)
$0.9 \pm (1.0E \text{ or } 1.3W)$	(12-6)
ASCE 7-95, Section 2.3.2	
$1.4D$	(1)
$1.2(D + F + T) + 1.6(L + H) + 0.5(L_r \text{ or } S \text{ or } R)$	(2)
$1.2D + 1.6(L_r \text{ or } S \text{ or } R) + (0.5L \text{ or } 0.8W)$	(3)
$1.2D + 1.3W + 0.5L + 0.5(L_r \text{ or } S \text{ or } R)$	(4)
$1.2D + 1.0E + 0.5L + 0.2S$	(5)
$0.9D + (1.3W \text{ or } 1.0E)$	(6)
ASCE 7-98, Section 2.3.2	
$1.4(D + F)$	(1)
$1.2(D + F + T) + 1.6(L + H) + 0.5(L_r \text{ or } S \text{ or } R)$	(2)
$1.2D + 1.6(L_r \text{ or } S \text{ or } R) + (0.5L \text{ or } 0.8W)$	(3)
$1.2D + 1.6W + 0.5L + 0.5(L_r \text{ or } S \text{ or } R)$	(4)
$1.2D + 1.0E + 0.5L + 0.2S$	(5)
$0.9D + 1.6W + 1.6H$	(6)
$0.9D + 1.0E + 1.6H$	(7)

The 1997 UBC, in adopting the basic strength design load combinations of ASCE 7-95, made a cosmetic change to the live load factor and a more substantive change to the snow load factor. The basic strength design load combinations 3 through 5 of ASCE 7-95 use a fixed live load factor of 0.5. However, an exception to ASCE 7-95 Section 2.3.2 requires that the load factor on L in combinations 3 through 5 must equal 1.0 for garages, areas occupied as places of public assembly, and all areas where the live load is greater than 100 psf (4.79 kN/m^2). The 2000 IBC and the 1997 UBC use a variable live load factor, f_1, which equals 1.0 for floors in places of public assembly, for live loads in excess of 100 psf (4.9 kN/m^2), and for garage live load. Factor $f_1 = 0.5$ for other live loads. There is no difference in substance here. Also, ASCE 7-95 uses a fixed snow load factor of 0.2. The 2000 IBC and the 1997 UBC use a variable snow load factor, f_2, which equals 0.7 for roof configurations (such as saw tooth) that do not shed snow off the structure. Factor $f_2 = 0.2$ for other roof configurations. The change in the snow load factor is obviously a substantive change. A flat roof should be conservatively treated as a roof configuration that does not shed snow off the structure.

The 1997 UBC, in adopting the basic strength design load combinations 1 through 6 of ASCE 7-95, dropped all references to rain load, R. The 2000 IBC has retained references to R in load combinations 16-2 and 16-4. The rain load, R, represents one of only two differences between the strength design load combinations of the 2000 IBC and the 1997 UBC.

The other difference is in the wind load factor. In ASCE 7-98, the wind load provisions of which have been adopted into the 2000 IBC, wind directionality is explicitly accounted for in the calculation of the wind loads, while previously it was a component of the wind load factor. A new factor, K_d, has been introduced, which varies depending on the type of structure. It thus became necessary to increase the load factor for wind from 1.3 to 1.6. The strength design load combinations of the 2000 IBC are consistent with those of ASCE 7-98, as shown in Table 1.

Exception 1 to Section 1605.2.1 provides that in the nonseismic design of reinforced concrete structures, the factored load combinations of ACI 318 Section 9.2 continue to be used, rather than the IBC load combinations 16-1 through 16-4. Since W in the ACI 318 load combinations excludes explicit consideration of directionality effects, Exception 1 provides that for concrete structures designed using the design wind forces of ASCE 7-98, W shall be divided by the directionality factor K_d. For concrete structures designed using Section 1609.6 of the IBC, W shall be divided by a directionality factor of 0.85.

There is a hidden difference between the strength design load combinations of the 2000 IBC and those of the 1997 UBC. Section 1908.1.2 requires the use of the strength design load combinations of ASCE 7-98, as adopted into IBC Section 1605.2, rather than the strength design load combinations of ACI 318-99, in the seismic design of reinforced concrete structures. This requirement is the same as in the 1997 UBC. However, the

1997 UBC requires the design loads given by the seismic strength design load combinations of ASCE 7-95 to be amplified by a factor of 1.1. The Working, First and Final Drafts of the IBC contained a corresponding requirement that the reduced strength reduction factors of Appendix C of ACI 318, rather than those of Chapter 9, be used in conjunction with the seismic strength design load combinations of ASCE 7-95. This requirement has been deleted from the 2000 IBC for reasons outlined in References 10 and 11. See Appendix 1 to this publication, Background to Seismic Strength Design Load Combinations.

The use of different strength design load combinations is illustrated in Examples 1 and 2, Part 2 of this chapter, for a structure of material other than concrete and a concrete structure, respectively.

1605.3 Load combinations using allowable stress design. The IBC contains two alternative sets of ASD load combinations adapted from the 1997 UBC. The 1997 UBC in its turn adapted the "basic" ASD load combinations from ASCE 7-95 and the "alternate basic" ASD load combinations from the 1994 UBC. These different sets of ASD load combinations are presented together in Table 2 for convenience of comparison.

The 2000 IBC and the 1997 UBC removed all references to *F* (load due to fluids), *H* (load due to lateral pressure of soil and water in soil) and *T* (self-straining force arising from contraction or expansion resulting from temperature changes, shrinkage, moisture change, creep in component materials, movement due to differential settlement, or combinations thereof) from load combination 2. These loads, *F, H, T* and *P* (ponding load), which is not specifically addressed in ASCE 7-95, are dealt with under Section 1605.3.3.

The corresponding 1997 UBC Section 1612.3.3 requires that where *F, H, P* or *T* is to be considered in design, each applicable load shall be added to the basic ASD load combination or the alternate basic ASD load combination. When using the alternate basic load combination, a one-third increase is permitted in allowable stresses for all combinations including *W* or *E*. Section 1605.3.3 requires that where *F, H, P* or *T* is to be considered in design, the load combinations of Section 2.4.1 of ASCE 7-98 (Table 2) shall be used. Interestingly, *P* is still not addressed in Section 2.4.1 of ASCE 7-98. Where F_a (flood load) is to be considered in design, the load combinations of Section 2.4.2 of ASCE 7-98 are to be used.

Between the Final Draft and the 2000 edition of the IBC, the basic ASD load combinations were made consistent with those of ASCE 7-98, presented in Table 2.

The two sets of ASD load combinations of the 2000 IBC and the 1997 UBC are based on different philosophies and are not specifically intended to be equivalent to each other. The basic set of ASD load combinations adopted from ASCE 7 is based on the premise that the design strength resulting from the allowable stress method should, in general, not be less than that resulting from the basic strength design method. The alternate basic set of ASD load combinations is based on the premise that the designs should be about the same as those resulting from the 1994 UBC.

TABLE 2. ALLOWABLE STRESS DESIGN LOAD COMBINATIONS OF THE 2000 IBC, THE 1997 UBC, ASCE 7-95 AND ASCE 7-98

IBC 2000, Section 1605.3.1*		**IBC 2000, Section 1605.3.2**	
D	(Formula 16-7)		
$D + L$	(Formula 16-8)	$D + L + (L_r$ or S or $R)$	(Formula 16-13)
$D + L + (L_r$ or S or $R)$	(Formula 16-9)	$D + L + \omega W$	(Formula 16-14)
$D + (W$ or $0.7E) + L + (L_r$ or S or $R)$	(Formula 16-10)	$D + L + \omega W + S/2$	(Formula 16-15)
$0.6D + W$	(Formula 16-11)	$D + L + S + \omega W/2$	(Formula 16-16)
$0.6D + 0.7E$	(Formula 16-12)	$D + L + S + E/1.4$	(Formula 16-17)
		$0.9D + E/1.4$	(Formula 16-18)
UBC 1997, Section 1612.3.1		**UBC 1997, Section 1612.3.2**	
D	(12-7)	$D + L + (L_r$ or $S)$	(12-12)
$D + L + (L_T$ or S)	(12-8)	$D + L + (W$ or $E/1.4)$	(12-13)
$D + (W$ or $E/1.4)$	(12-9)	$D + L + W + S/2$	(12-14)
$0.9D \pm E/1.4$	(12-10)	$D + L + S + W/2$	(12-15)
$D + 0.75\ [L + (L_r$ or $S) + (W$ or $E/1.4)]$	(12-11)	$D + L + S + E/1.4$	(12-16)
ASCE 7-95, Section 2.4			
D	(1)		
$D + L + F + H + T + (L_r$ or S or $R)$	(2)		
$D + (W$ or $E)$	(3)		
$D + L + (L_r$ or S or $R) + (W$ or $E)$	(4)		
ASCE 7-98, Section 2.4.2*			
D	(1)		
$D + L + F + H + T + (L_r$ or S or $R)$	(2)		
$D + (W$ or $0.7E) + L + (L_r$ or S or $R)$	(3)		
$0.6D + W + H$	(4)		
$0.6D + 0.7E + H$	(5)		

* It is permitted to multiply the combined effect of two or more transient loads by 0.75 and add to the effect of dead load. The combined load used in design shall not be less than the sum of the effects of dead load and any one of the transient loads. The 0.7 factor on *E* does not apply to this provision.

One very substantive change was made in the basic ASD load combinations of ASCE 7-95 as they were adopted into the 1997 UBC and subsequently into the 2000 IBC. In ASCE-95 load combinations 3 and 4, the strength-level earthquake effect, E, is added directly to the effects of unfactored dead, live, and other loads. The ASCE 7-95 commentary attempts to explain the rationale.

In the 1997 UBC, the strength-level earthquake effect, E, is brought down to service level through division by a factor of 1.4 before it is combined with the effects of unfactored gravity and other loads. The same is true of the alternate basic ASD load combinations of the 1997 UBC and the 2000 IBC. Table 2 shows that the basic ASD load combinations of ASCE 7-98 now correspond with those of the 2000 IBC in this regard.

Load combinations 4 and 5 are new in ASCE 7-98. They address the situation in which the effects of lateral or uplift forces counteract the effect of gravity loads. This eliminates an inconsistency in the treatment of counteracting loads in allowable stress design and strength design, and emphasizes the importance of checking stability. The basic ASD load combinations of the IBC changed rather drastically between the Final Draft and the 2000 edition. ASD load combinations 4 and 5 of ASCE 7-98 have been adopted into the basic ASD load combinations of the 2000 edition of the IBC.

The IBC specifically states that increases in allowable stresses "specified in the appropriate materials section of this code or referenced standard" shall not be used with the basic ASD load combinations, except that a duration of load increase shall be permitted in accordance with Chapter 23. On the other hand, when using the alternate basic load combinations that include wind or seismic loads, allowable stresses are permitted to be increased or load combinations reduced, "where permitted by the material section of this code or referenced standard." The 1997 UBC is very specific in this regard. Section 2316.2 amends Section 2.3.2.3 of the National Design Specification for Wood Construction (NDS), Revised 1991 Edition[12], as follows (refer to Table 2 for corresponding IBC formula numbers).

> 2.3.2.3 When using Section 1612.3.1 basic load combinations, the load Duration Factor, C_D, noted in Table 2.3.2 shall be permitted to be used. When using Section 1612.3.2 alternate load combinations, the one-third increase shall not be used concurrently with the Load Duration Factor, C_D.

The 1997 UBC Section 2316.2 also modifies Table 2.3.2 of the NDS, as shown in Table 3, which reproduces the load duration factor table of NDS-1991[12] together with the amended load duration factor table of the 1997 UBC. Chapter 23 of the 2000 IBC simply adopts NDS-1991 by reference.

The above discussion may be summarized as follows:

ASD and allowable stress "*increases*"

1605.3.1 Basic load combinations. Combined effect of two or more transient loads may be reduced by 0.75, subject to restrictions (see footnote to Table 2). One-third allowable stress increase *not permitted.* See Example 3, Part 2 of this chapter.

For wood, load duration increases are *permitted.*

1605.3.2 Alternate basic load combinations. One-third allowable stress increase *permitted* for all materials other than wood. For wood, load duration increases are *permitted.*

TABLE 3. COMPARISON OF LOAD DURATION FACTORS FOR WOOD OF THE 1997 UBC AND THE 1997 NDS

1997 NDS Table 2.3.2—Frequently Used Load Duration Factors, C_D[1]

Load Duration	C_D	Typical Design Loads
Permanent	0.9	Dead Load
Ten years	1.0	Occupancy Live Load
Two months	1.15	Snow Load
Seven days	1.25	Construction Load
Ten minutes	1.6	Wind/Earthquake Load
Impact[2]	2.0	Impact Load

1. Load duration factors shall not apply to modulus of elasticity, E, nor to compression perpendicular to grain design values, F_{c1}, based on a deformation limit.
2. Load duration factors greater than 1.6 shall not apply to structural members pressure-treated with water-borne preservatives, or fire-retardant chemicals. The impact load duration factor shall not apply to connections.

1997 UBC Table 2.3.2—Load Duration Factors, C_D

DESIGN LOAD	LOAD DURATION	C_D
Dead Load	Permanent	0.9
Floor, Occupancy Live Load	Ten Years	1.0
Snow Load	Two Months	1.15
Roof Live Load	Seven Days	1.25
Earthquake Load[1]	—	1.33
Wind Load[2]	—	1.33
Impact	—	2.0

1. 1.60 may be used for nailed and bolted connections exhibiting Mode III or IV behavior, except that the increases for earthquake are not combined with the increase allowed in Section 1612.3. The 60-percent increase for nailed and bolted connections exhibiting Mode III or IV behavior for earthquake shall not be applicable to joist hangers, framing anchors, and other mechanical fastenings, including straps and hold-down anchors. The 60-percent increase shall not apply to the allowable shear values in . . .
2. 1.60 may be used for members and nailed and bolted connections exhibiting Mode III or IV behavior, except that the increases for wind are not combined with the increase allowed in Section 1612.3. The 60-percent increase shall not apply to the allowable shear values in . . .

The basic ASD load combinations of Section 1605.3.1 are subject to an exception. Flat roof snow loads of 30 psf (1.44 kN/m^2) or less need not be combined with seismic loads. Where flat roof snow loads exceed 30 psf (1.44 kN/m^2), only 20 percent of the flat roof snow load is required to be combined with seismic loads. This is probably an attempt to be consistent with the definition of W, the effective seismic weight of the structure, in Section 1617.4.1.See Example 4, Part 2 of this chapter.

1605.4 Special seismic load combinations. Section 1620.1.6 requires the collector elements of diaphragms and Section 1620.1.9 requires elements supporting discontinuous walls or frames (Figure 2) to be designed by the special seismic load combinations of Section 1605.4. When the definition of maximum earthquake effect, E_m, is incorporated from Section 1617.1.2, Formulas 16-19 and 16-20 become:

$$(1.2 + 0.2\,S_{DS})D + f_1 L + \Omega_o Q_E \qquad (16\text{-}19)$$

and

$$(0.9 - 0.2\,S_{DS})D + \Omega_o Q_E \qquad (16\text{-}20)$$

where Ω_o is the system overstrength factor given in Table 1617.6, and varies between 2 and 3.

Since collector elements of diaphragms and columns supporting discontinued stiff elements are particularly vulnerable

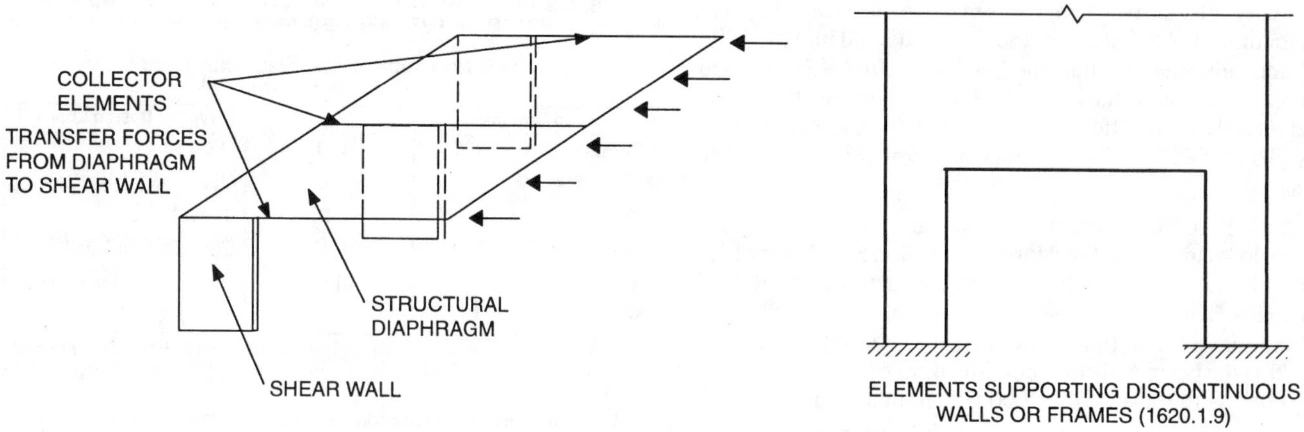

COLLECTOR ELEMENTS OF DIAPHRAGMS (1620.1.6) AND DISCONTINUED SHEAR WALLS (1620.1.9)

FIGURE 2

to earthquake damage, the idea here is to design those for the estimated maximum axial forces that can realistically develop in these elements in an earthquake situation.

The 1997 UBC Section 1630.8.2.1 requires elements supporting discontinuous systems and Section 1633.2.6 requires collector elements of diaphragms to be designed by the special load combinations of Section 1612.4. All of this is in the IBC. The definition of E_m in the 1997 UBC, however, is quite different from that in the IBC. In Section 1630.1.1 of the 1997 UBC, E_m is defined as being equal to $\Omega_o\ E_h$. Thus, the special load combinations of Section 1612.4 become:

$$1.2D + f_1L + \Omega_o\ E_h$$

$$0.9D \pm \Omega_o \qquad (12\text{-}17)$$

The E_h of the 1997 UBC and the Q_E of the 2000 IBC are identical terms. The significant difference between the UBC and the IBC special load combinations is that there is no consideration of vertical earthquake ground motion in the UBC combinations.

1605.5 Heliports and helistops. In this section, the IBC intends that the design of touchdown areas be regulated only when the touchdown area is on a building. The provisions are adopted, with significant modifications, from Section 1611.10 of the 1997 UBC. The criteria in the UBC are essentially the same as those promulgated earlier by the City of Los Angeles. The minimum loading criteria consist of the following:

1. The weight of the helicopter plus the snow load, *S*. The UBC does not include the snow load, *S*.
2. The landing impact effect of the helicopter. This is considered somewhat differently by the IBC and the UBC. Also, the UBC, but not the IBC, recognizes that impact effect will be less when the craft is equipped with hydraulic shock absorbers.
3. A uniform live load of 100 psf. The UBC specifically indicates that the required live load may be reduced, as permitted by that code. The IBC does not.

SECTION 1606 DEAD LOADS

This section is adopted without modification from ASCE 7-98. Sections 1606.1 and 1606.2 are direct reproductions of ASCE 7-98 Sections 3.2 and 3.3, respectively. The definition of dead loads, to be found in ASCE 7-95 Section 3.1, has been placed under Section 1602, Definitions.

According to the ASCE/IBC definition, dead loads consist of the weight of materials of construction incorporated into the building, including but not limited to walls, floors, roofs, ceilings, stairways, built-in partitions, finishes, cladding and other similarly incorporated architectural and structural items, and fixed service equipment, including the weight of cranes.

According to the commentary on ASCE 7-98, to establish uniform practice among designers, it is desirable to present a list of materials generally used in building construction, together with their proper weights. The solution chosen by Committee ASCE 7 has been to present, in the ASCE 7-98 Commentary, an extended list that will be useful to the designer and building official alike. This table, C3-2, is truly a valuable resource. It is conceded that special cases will unavoidably arise. Authority is therefore granted in both ASCE 7-98 and the IBC for the building official to deal with such cases.

Engineers, architects, and building owners are advised in the ASCE 7-98 Commentary to consider factors that result in differences between actual and calculated loads. Conditions have been encountered in the past which, if not considered in design, may reduce the future utility of a building or reduce its margin of safety. The ASCE 7-98 Commentary points out two such conditions:

1. There have been numerous instances in which the actual weights of members and construction materials have exceeded the values used in design. Care is advised in the use of tabular values. Also, allowances should be made for such factors as the influence of formwork and support deflections on the actual thickness of a concrete slab of prescribed nominal thickness.

2. Allowance should be made for the weight of future wearing or protective surfaces where there is a good possibility that such may be applied. Special consideration should be given to the likely types and position of partitions, as insufficient provision for partitioning may reduce the future utility of a building.

The ASCE 7-98 Commentary also directs attention to the possibility of temporary changes in the use of a building, as in the case of clearing a dormitory for a dance or other recreational purposes.

The 2000 IBC Section 1607.5, Partition loads, represents an important difference between the IBC, ASCE 7, and the BOCA/NBC on the one hand, which treat these loads as live loads, and the UBC and the SBC on the other, which treat the same loads as dead loads.

SECTION 1607
LIVE LOADS

Table 4 traces the origin of the IBC provisions concerning live loads. It is obvious that most of the provisions are adopted from ASCE 7-98, with relatively few drawn from the 1996 BOCA/NBC and the 1997 UBC.

1607.1 General. This is the same as ASCE 7-98 Section 4.1, except that the ASCE 7 standard contains the definition of live loads in the section itself, whereas Section 1607.1 refers to Section 1602.1, where the definition of live load has been placed in the IBC. Live loads are defined as those loads produced by the use and occupancy of the building or other structure and do not include construction or environmental loads such as wind load, snow load, rain load, earthquake load, flood load, or dead load.

1607.2 Loads not specified. Essentially identical to Section 4.5 of ASCE 7-98 and also essentially the same as Section 1606.1.1 of the 1996 BOCA/NBC. For occupancies and uses not specifically included in Table 1607.1, the method of determination of the design live load is subject to the approval of the building official. This topic is not specifically addressed in the UBC or the SBC.

Extremely valuable information is provided in the commentary to ASCE 7-98, Tables C4-1 and C4-2, concerning the determination of design live loads for occupancies not listed in Table 1607.1.

1607.3 Uniform live loads. This charges the designer to use the unit live loads set forth in Table 1607.1 and specifies that these loads must be considered minimum live loads. In other words, floors must be designed for the maximum live loads to which they are likely to be subjected during the life of the building based on its intended use, but in no case should the design loads be less than those given in Table 1607.1.

Table 1607.1 is the same as Table 4-1 of ASCE 7-98, but for a few exceptions. The exceptions are detailed in Table 5.

The commentary to ASCE 7-98 advises that in selecting the occupancy and use for the design of a building, the owner should consider the possibility of later changes of occupancy involving loads heavier than originally contemplated. The lighter loading appropriate to the first occupancy should not necessarily be selected.

The commentary to ASCE 7-98 also advises that "The building owner should ensure that a live load greater than that for which a floor or roof is approved by the authority having jurisdiction is not placed, or caused, or permitted to be placed, on any floor or roof of a building or other structure." The UBC, in fact, contains a specific requirement charging the owner of a commercial or an industrial building with posting signs in conspicuous locations. These signs must specify the actual live load for which the floor system was designed. Also, the UBC charges the occupant of the building with the responsibility of maintaining the actual loads at a level below those posted. The intent, of course, is to prevent the overloading of floors.

The commentary to ASCE 7-98 provides background to the development of the design values in Table 4-1 of that standard. To solicit specific informed opinion concerning the design loads in the corresponding table of ANSI A58.1-1972, a panel of 25 distinguished structural engineers was selected. Design values and supporting reasons were requested of each panel member for each occupancy type. The information was summarized and circulated back to the panel members for a second round of responses; those occupancies for which previous design loads were reaffirmed, as well as those for which there was consensus for change, were included.

Many surveys of live loads in buildings, particularly office buildings, have been conducted over the years.[13, 14, 15, 16] Buildings must be designed to resist the maximum live loads they are likely to be subjected to during some reference period, frequently taken as 50 years. Table C4-2 of the ASCE 7-98 Commentary briefly summarizes how load survey data are combined with a theoretical analysis of the load process for some common occupancy types and illustrates how a design load might be selected for an occupancy not specified in ASCE 7-98 Table 4-1.

1607.4 Concentrated loads. Many uses are susceptible to the movement of equipment, files, machinery, etc. Therefore, the code requires that floors for these uses, which are listed in Table 1607.1, be designed for the indicated concentrated load placed on a space $2^1/_2$ feet (750 mm) square whenever this load, on an otherwise unloaded floor, produces stresses greater than those caused by the uniform loads required by the code. As this concentrated load can take many forms in the real world, and as the design structural engineer usually does not know in advance what form the load will take and how it will be applied, the best compromise to cover most situations is to consider the concentrated load to be applied through a rigid base $2^1/_2$ feet (750 mm) square.[2]

Footnote a of Table 1607.1 requires garages and other areas where motor vehicles are stored to be designed for concentrated loads or, alternatively, the uniform loads as specified in Table 1607.1. In the case of garages for storage of private pleasure-type vehicles, the note prescribes a single 2,000-pound (8.9 kN) load over a 20-square-inch (12,500 mm^2) area. For mechanical parking structures without slab or deck for the storage of passenger cars only, 1,500 pounds (6.7 kN) of load per wheel is specified. For sidewalks, vehicular driveways, and yards, subject to trucking, the concentrated wheel load is required to be applied over an area of 20 square inches (12,500 mm^2). On stair treads, a minimum concentrated load of 300 pounds (1.3 kN) is required to be applied over an area of 4 square inches (2500 mm^2).

TABLE 4. SOURCES OF IBC PROVISIONS CONCERNING LIVE LOADS

IBC Section	ASCE 7-95, ASCE 7-98 Section No.	1996, 1999 BOCA/NBC Section No.	1997 UBC Section No.
1607.1 General	4.1		
1607.2 Loads not specified	4.5		
1607.3 Uniform live loads	4.2.1		
1607.4 Concentrated loads	4.3		
1607.5 Partition loads	4.2.2		
1607.6 Truck and bus garages	—	1606.2.1	
1607.6.1 Truck and bus garage live load application	—	1606.2.1.1	
1607.7 Loads on handrails, guards, grab bars and vehicle barriers	4.4	1606.4	
1607.7.1 Handrails and guards	4.4.2A		
1607.7.1.1 Concentrated load	4.4.2A		
1607.7.1.2 Components	4.4.2A		
1607.7.1.3 Stress increase	—		
1607.7.2 Grab bars, shower seats and dressing room bench seats	4.4.2B		
1607.7.3 Vehicle barriers	4.4.2C		
1607.8 Impact loads	4.7		
1607.8.1 Elevators	4.7.1		
1607.8.2 Machinery	4.7.2		
1607.9 Reduction in live loads	4.8.1		
1607.9.1 General	4.8.2		
1607.9.2 Alternate floor live load reduction	—		1607.6
1607.10 Distribution of floor loads	—		1607.3.2
1607.11 Roof loads	—	1607.11	
1607.11.1 Distribution of roof loads	—		1607.4.2
1607.11.2 Minimum roof live loads	—		
1607.11.2.1 Flat, pitched and curved roofs	4.9.1		
1607.11.2.2 Special-purpose roofs	4.9.2		
1607.11.2.3 Landscaped roofs	—	1607.6.1	
1607.11.2.4 Awnings and canopies	—	1607.6.2	
1607.11.2.5 Overhanging eaves	—	1607.4	
1607.12 Crane loads	4.10		
1607.12.1 Maximum wheel load	4.10.1		
1607.12.2 Vertical impact force	4.10.2		
1607.12.3 Lateral force	4.10.3		
1607.12.4 Longitudinal force	4.10.4		
1607.13 Interior walls and partitions		1606.9	

For all the concentrated loads specified in this section, the intent of the code is that each concentrated load shall be placed on the floor in such a position as to create maximum stresses in the structural members. Therefore, the loading condition, either uniform or concentrated, which provides the maximum stresses in the structural members, would be used for the design of the floor system.

1607.5 Partition loads. In those uses where the partitions are subject to change in locations, such as office buildings and flexible-plan school buildings, the code requires that the floor system be designed to support a uniformly distributed live load of 20 psf (0.96 kN/m^2). This requirement is irrespective of whether partitions are shown on the construction documents. The exception is where the specified live load exceeds 80 psf (3.83 kN/m^2). It should be noted that the uniformly distributed load of 20 psf (0.96 kN/m^2) is considered by the code to be a live load. Thus, it should be included with other live loads in factored load combinations.

It has been noted earlier under Section 1606 that the 2000 IBC Section 1607.5 represents an important difference between the IBC, ASCE 7, and the BOCA/NBC on the one hand, which treat these loads as live loads, and the UBC and the SBC on the other, which treat the same loads as dead loads.

1607.6 Truck and bus garages. This is identical to Section 1606.2.1 of the BOCA/NBC. The live load values used in the design of structural floors for garages storing trucks or buses are to conform to the lane load requirements provided in Table 1607.6 or to a uniformly distributed live load of 50 psf (2.40 kN/m^2) of floor area, whichever produces the greater effect.[1] Table 1607.6 reproduces the lane loading requirements in AASHTO's Bridge Specs.[17] The lane loads specified are based on truck trains or the concentrated wheel loads from standard load trucks with gross weight limitations. Truck train loads are uniform loads resulting from a series of closely spaced trucks, one after another.[1] Section 1607.6.1 specifies the application of live loads so as to produce the maximum stresses.

1607.7 Loads on handrails, guards, grab bars and vehicle barriers. The entire section is adopted from ASCE 7-98 Section 4.4, except that Section 1607.7.1.3, Stress increase, is not part of ASCE 7-98. The requirements of this section are intended to provide an adequate degree of structural strength and stability to handrails, guards, grab bars and vehicle barriers.

1607.7.1 Handrails and guards. The IBC adds a second exception that is not in ASCE 7-98. It allows a lesser design load in certain occupancies. These are the same occupancies listed in Section 1003.12.2, which are allowed to have larger openings in the guard.

The commentary to ASCE 7-98 points out that loads that can be expected to occur on handrail and guardrail systems are highly dependent on the use and occupancy of the protected area. It further points out that for cases in which extreme loads can be anticipated, such as long straight runs of guardrail systems against which crowds can surge, appropriate increases in loading need to be considered.

1607.7.2 Grab bars, shower seats and dressing room bench seats. It is noted in the commentary to ASCE 7-98 that when grab bars are provided for use by persons with physical disabilities, the design is governed by ICC/ANSI 117 Accessible and Usable Buildings and Facilities Standard.[18]

1607.8 Impact loads. These provisions are also adopted from ASCE 7-98. Where unusual vibration or impact forces are likely to occur, their effect may be to produce additional stresses and deflections in the structural system. This section requires that the structural design takes these effects into account. Typically, the dynamic effects are approximated through the application of a static load equal in effect to the dynamic loads. In most cases, this is sufficient. However, in certain situations, a dynamic analysis may be necessary to properly consider the natural frequencies of vibration of a structure.[1]

1607.9 Reduction in live loads. The live load reduction provisions of Section 1607.9.1 are based on Section 4.8.1 of ASCE 7-98, while the alternate floor live load reduction provisions of Section 1607.9.2 are those of Section 1607.5 of the 1997 UBC. The alternate floor live load provisions of the 1997 UBC Section 1607.6, on the other hand, are those of Section 4.8.1 of ASCE 7-95.

The alternate floor live load reduction provisions of Section 1607.9.2 or the reduction of live load provisions of Section 1607.5 of the 1997 UBC, based on tributary floor area (Figure 3), represent the "original" live load reduction provisions that used to be in older editions of the ANSI A58.1 standard (predecessor to ASCE 7) and in all three model codes.

The concept of, and method for, determining member live load reductions as a function of a loaded member's influence area, A_I, was first introduced into ANSI A58.1 in 1982 and was the first such change since the concept of live load reduction was introduced over 40 years ago. The revised method was the result of more extensive survey data and theoretical analyses. Figure 4, reproduced from the commentary to ASCE 7-95, illustrates the influence area concept. The influence area-based live load reduction formula of ANSI A58.1-82, ASCE 7-88, ASCE 7-93 and ASCE 7-95 is used in the alternate floor live load reduction provisions of Section 1607.6 of the 1997 UBC.

TABLE 5. COMPARISON BETWEEN IBC TABLE 1607.1 AND ASCE 7-98 TABLE 4-1

IBC			ASCE 7		
Occupancy or Use	**Min. Uniform Load (psf)**	**Min. Conc. Load (lb)**	**Occupancy or Use**	**Min. Uniform Load (psf)**	**Min. Conc. Load (lb)**
4. Assembly areas and theaters			Assembly areas and theaters		
Stages and platforms	125		Platforms (assembly)	100	
Follow spot, projection and control rooms	50		Stage floors	100	
Catwalks	40				
7. Cornices	60		—		
8. Corridors, except as otherwise indicated	100		Corridors		
			First floor	100	
			Other floors, same as occupancy served except as indicated		
15. Garages	Section 1607.6		Garages	**	
Trucks and buses			Trucks and buses		
34. Stairs and exits	100	*	Stairs and exitways	100	
One- and two-family dwellings	40				
All others	100				

* Minimum concentrated load on stair treads (on area of 4 square inches) is 300 pounds.

**Garages accommodating trucks and buses must be designed in accordance with an approved method, which contains provisions for truck and bus loadings.

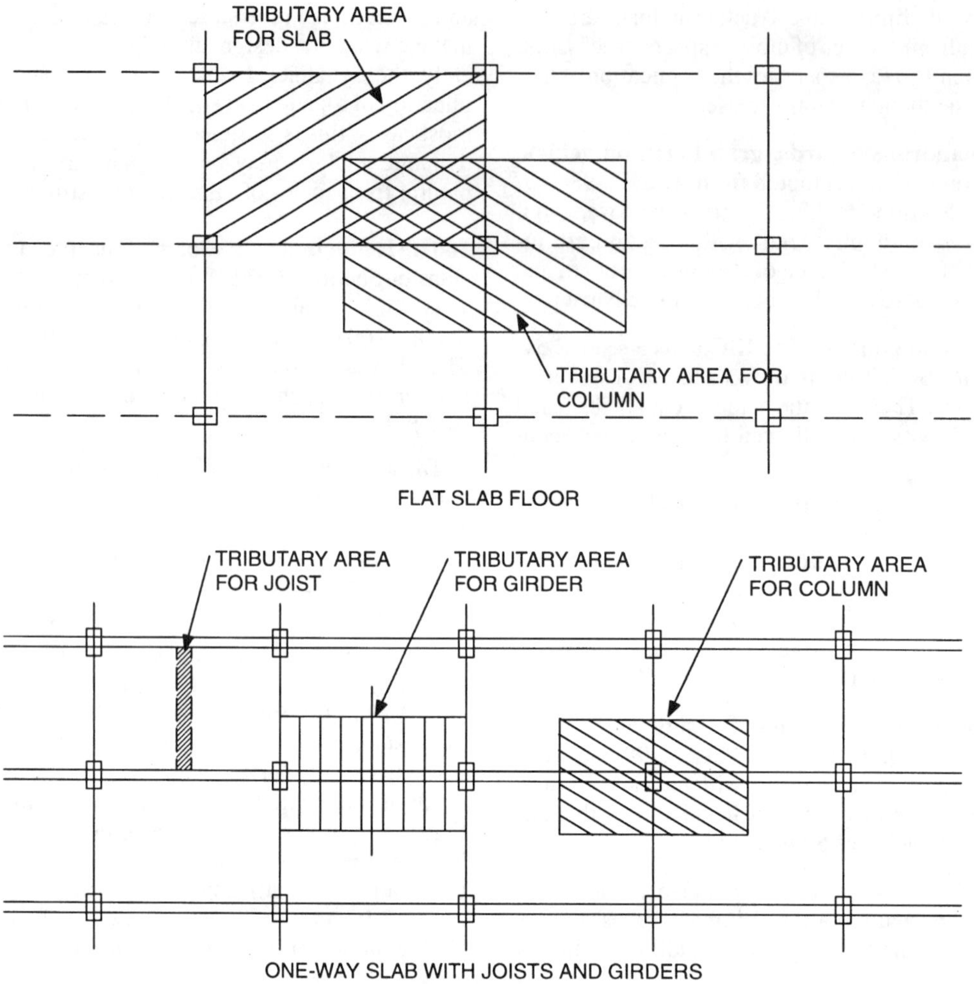

TRIBUTARY AREAS

FIGURE 3

In ASCE 7-98, the influence area has now been defined as a function of the tributary area, A_T. The influence area is defined as that floor area over which the influence surface for structural effects is significantly different from zero. The factor K_{LL} is the ratio of the influence area (A_I) of a member to its tributary area (A_T), i.e.: $K_{LL} = A_I/A_T$ and is used to better define the influence area of a member as a function of its tributary area. Table 1607.9.1 has established K_{LL} values (derived from calculated K_{LL} values) to be used in the formula of Section 1607.9.2 for a variety of structural members and configurations. K_{LL} values vary for column and beam members having adjacent cantilever construction and the Table 1607.9.1 values have been set for these cases to result in live load reductions that are slightly conservative (Figure 5). For unusual shapes, the concept of significant influence effect needs to be applied.

See Example 5, Part 2 of this chapter.

1607.9.1 General. Reductions in the minimum uniformly distributed live load values specified in Table 1607.1 are permitted, based on an influence area of 400 square feet (37.16 m^2) or more. Essentially, the influence area of a structural element is the total floor area surrounding the element from which it derives any of its load. The basis for the permitted reduction is that in the design of structural elements with large influence areas, it is highly unlikely that the floors will be fully loaded over their entire area.

Live load reduction in excess of 50 percent is not permitted for columns or other structural elements (such as bearing walls) that support the loads of a single floor. In essence, this means that the influence area may not exceed 3,600 square feet (334.4 m^2) in calculating the reduced unit floor live load. For columns or other structural elements that support two or more floors, the sum of the reduced live loads from all floors must not be less than 40 percent of the sum of the unreduced live loads.

1607.9.1.1 Heavy live loads. In the case of occupancies involving relatively heavy basic live loads, such as storage buildings, several adjacent floor panels may be fully loaded. However, data obtained in actual buildings indicate that rarely is any story loaded with an average actual live load of more than 80 percent of the average rated live load.[6] ASCE 7 thus concluded that the basic live load should not be reduced for the floor and beam design, but that it may be reduced a flat 20 percent for the design of members supporting more than one floor.

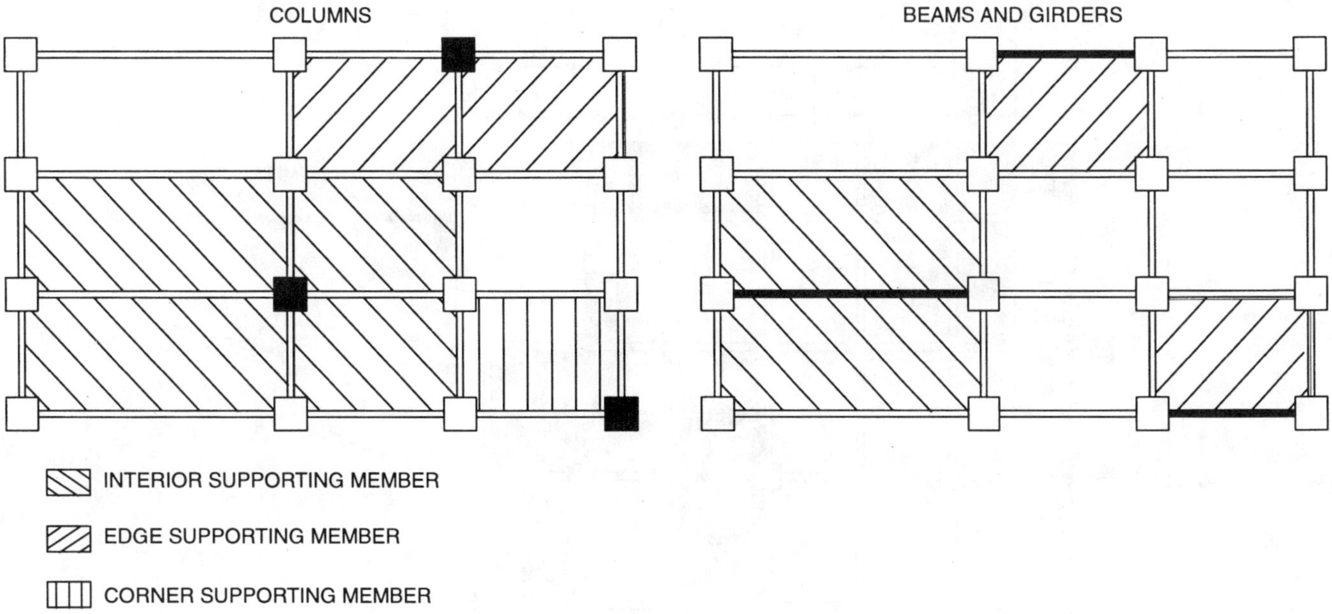

INFLUENCE AREAS

FIGURE 4

1607.9.1.2 Passenger car garages. There are no significant variables in the loads imposed on these facilities, which are often fully loaded. The 20-percent reduction allowed for members supporting two or more floors is based on the reason given above.

1607.9.1.3 Special occupancies. Because of large concentrations of people in these types of facilities, it is possible that two adjacent bays can be fully loaded at one time, resulting in maximum stresses on supporting members.[1]

1607.9.1.4 Special structural elements. The uncertainties of roof loads, including snow loads, preclude live load reductions.[1] The ASCE 7 standard has historically taken a position prohibiting live load reduction for one-way slabs, supposedly because of a lack of redundancy inherent in the design and construction of one-way slabs. According to ASCE 7, "though admittedly conservative, this approach has, over the decades, proved to provide safe structural performance." The 1997 UBC, however, defines *A* as being equal to the product of the span and the full flange width for a precast T-beam, thereby expressly permitting live load reduction for certain one-way slab systems. According to the Final draft of the IBC, for members supporting cantilevered construction, for a one-way slab and a precast T-beam, the influence area is the same as the tributary area. ASCE 7-98 provisions, as adopted into the 2000 IBC, do not allow live load reduction for one-way slabs "except as permitted in Sections 1607.9.1.1." It is important to note that live load reduction for one-way slabs is permitted under the alternate floor live load reduction provisions of Section 1607.9.2.

1607.9.2 Alternate floor live load reduction. This section establishes a minimum tributary area of 150 square feet (13.94 m^2) as the threshold for live load reductions computed from Equation 16-2, which is plotted in Figure 6. No reduction in live load is permitted for assembly areas, because they must be considered to be fully occupied under normal conditions of occupancy. Live loads in excess of 100 psf (4.79 kN/m^2) may not be reduced, except that the design live loads on columns may be reduced 20 percent. The maximum live load reduction permitted is 40 percent for members receiving loads from one level only and 60 percent for other members (such as columns or transfer girders).

Equation 16-13 was derived so that if a structural member supporting a tributary area of sufficient size to qualify for the maximum reduction allowed by the equation were subjected to the full design live load over the entire area, the overstress would not exceed 30 percent.[19]

It may be noted from Equation 16-3 that the maximum live load reduction is proportional to the ratio of dead load to live load. Therefore, for heavy framing systems, the reduction is permitted to be greater than it would be for lighter framing systems. This is in view of the fact that for a given magnitude of overload on a structural system, the system with the heavier dead load is overstressed proportionately less than one with a lighter dead load. For example, if a floor system weighing 30 pounds per square foot (1.44 kN/m^2) and designed for a live load of 40 pounds per square foot (1.92 kN/m^2) were subjected to a 20-pound-per-square-foot (0.96 kN/m^2) overload, the amount by which the structural system would be overstressed is about 30 percent, assuming the system was designed to support just the design live load of 40 pounds per square foot (1.92 kN/m^2). If this floor had a dead load of 60 pounds per square foot (2.88 kN/m^2), the over-stress would be only 20 percent, again assuming that the system were designed to support just the 40-pound-per-square-foot (1.92 kN/m^2) of live load.

1607.10 Distribution of floor loads. Where loads are uniformly distributed on continuous structural members, they shall be arranged so as to create maximum bending moment in any given critical section. This may require a design to consider so-called skip loading or alternate span loading, as shown in Figure 7.

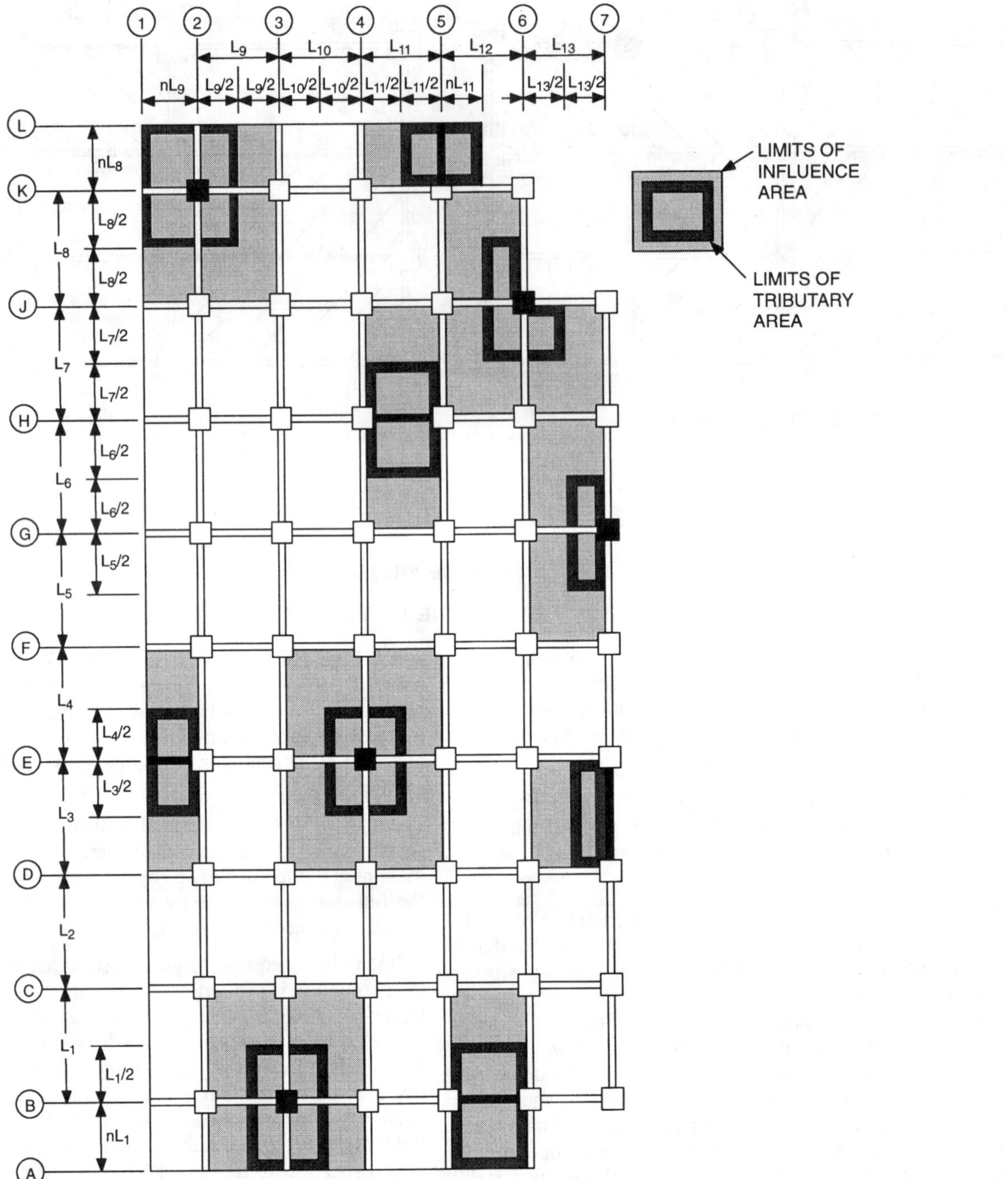

ELEMENT	EXAMPLE MEMBER	ACTUAL K_{LL} FOR MEMBERS w/o CANTILEVERS	ACTUAL K_{LL} FOR MEMBERS w/CANTILEVERS			
			n = 0	n = 0.5	n = 1.0	K_{LL}
Interior columns	E4	4	-	-	-	4
Exterior columns w/o cantilevers	G7, J6	4	-	-	-	4
Edge columns w/ cantilevers	B3	-	4	3	2.67	3
Comer columns w/ cantilevers	K2	-	4	2.25	1.78	2
Edge beams w/o cantilever slabs	D7 - E7	2	-	-	-	2
Interior beams	H4 - H5	2	-	-	-	2
Edge beams w/ cantilever slabs	B5 - B6	-	2	1.5	1.33	1
Cantilever beams w/o cantilever slabs	E1 - E2	2	-	-	-	1
Cantilever beams w/ cantilever slabs	K5 - L5	-	2*	1.5*	1.33*	1

*The value of n for member K5-L5 is used to calculate the distance nL_{11}

TYPICAL TRIBUTARY AND INFLUENCE AREAS

FIGURE 5

1607.11 Roof loads. In addition to dead and live loads (typically during construction), the structural system of a roof is to be designed and constructed to resist environmental loads caused by wind, snow and earthquakes.

1607.11.1 Distribution of roof loads. Nearly identical to Section 1607.10 (see discussion above). Section 1608.5 is referred to for partial snow load.

1607.11.2 Minimum roof live loads. Section 1607.11.2.1 is essentially the same as Section 4.9.1 of ASCE 7-98. The values specified are meant to act vertically upon the projected area and have been selected as minimum roof live loads, even in localities where little or no snowfall occurs. This is because it is considered necessary to provide for occasional loading due to the presence of workers and materials during repair operations.[6] The live load reduction for roofs is a function not only of tributary area but also of the slope of the roof. This is because it becomes less probable that the loads on a roof member will be at maximum levels as the roof slope increases.

Where the design roof snow load exceeds the minium roof live load, the snow load, calculated in accordance with the requirements of Section 1608, is to be used for design of the roof, as specified by the applicable load combination. Only the greater of the roof load value established by the minimum roof live load or the snow load determined as indicated above is required to be applied to the roof.[1]

1607.11.2.2 Special-purpose roofs, 1607.11.2.3 Landscaped roofs, 1607.11.2.4 Awnings and canopies. Designers need to consider any additional dead loads that may be imposed by saturated landscaping materials. Special-purpose or occupancy roof live loads may be reduced in accordance with Section 1607.9.[6]

1607.11.2.5 Overhanging eaves. Eaves, cornices, and other roof projections whose structural supports are not part of the main roof-framing system are required to be designed for a uniformly distributed live load of 60 psf (2.87 kN/m^2). As explained in the BOCA/NBC,[1] because of the cold surfaces of these building elements, snow melt does not occur. The accumulation of layers of snow results in loads heavier than those on the warm roofs of heated buildings. The design of overhanging eaves and other projections formed as a continuation of the roof-framing system is exempt from the 60 psf (2.87 kN/m^2)

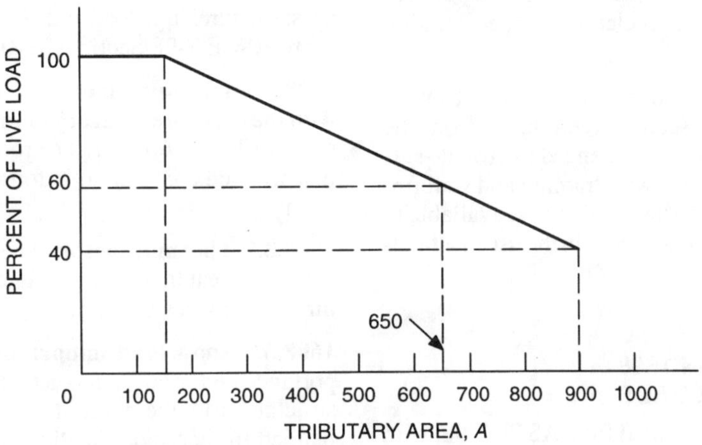

LIVE LOAD REDUCTION EQUATION 16-2

FIGURE 6

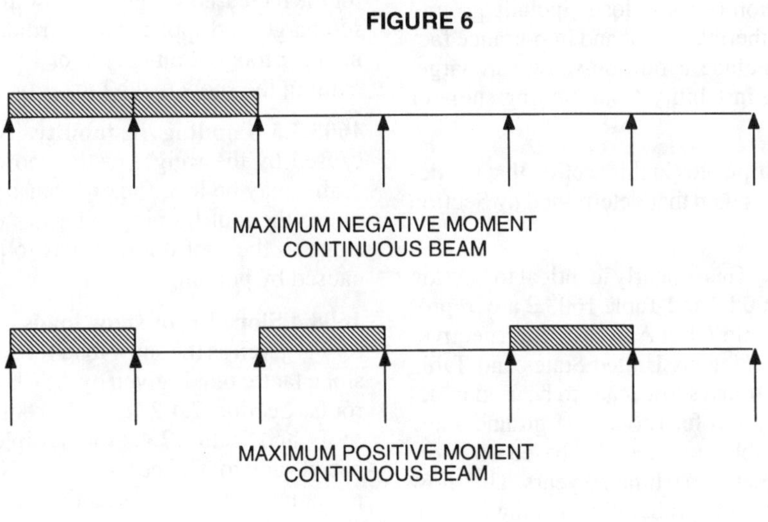

ALTERNATE SPAN LOADING OF CONTINUOUS BEAMS

FIGURE 7

loading requirement because there is redundancy in the framing system. One- and two-family dwellings are also exempt based on a record of satisfactory performance in the past.

1607.12 Crane loads. All craneways and supporting construction must be designed and constructed in compliance with this section, which reproduces the crane load criteria of Section 4.10 of ASCE 7-98. The crane live loads specified by ASCE 7-98 depend on:

- Type of crane (monorail, cab-operated, pendant-operated, hand-geared).
- Rated capacity of crane.
- Maximum wheel loads.

Design lateral, longitudinal, and vertical forces are provided in terms of the above. These live loads are to be applied simultaneously to the structural system of the craneway, including runway beams, connections, support brackets, cross-bracing, columns, and foundations. The vertical impact force accounts for the vibration effect of the crane bridge movement and the movement of the lifted load. The lateral force (perpendicular to the runway girder) results from acceleration or deceleration of the trolley and the lifted load. The longitudinal force (parallel to the runway girder) results from the acceleration or deceleration of the bridge or the lifted load.

1607.13 Interior walls and partitions. According to BOCA/NBC,[1] the requirements of this section, reproduced from the 1999 BOCA/NBC Section 1606.9, are intended to provide sufficient strength and durability of the wall framing and wall finish, so that a minimum level of resistance would be available to nominal impact loads that commonly occur in the use of a facility and to HVAC pressurization.

SECTION 1608
SNOW LOADS

The snow load provisions are adopted from ASCE 7-98, with only a few modifications. Figure 8 has been developed to show the organization of the provisions. The variables that must be determined for the calculation of snow loads include ground snow load, exposure factor, thermal factor and importance factor. Other considerations include a rain-on-snow surcharge, partial loading and ponding instability from melting snow or rain on snow.

1608.1 General. The IBC stipulates in this section that the design roof load shall not be less than that determined by Section 1607, Live Loads.

1608.2 Ground snow loads. This is nearly identical to Section 7.2 of ASCE 7-98. Figure 1608.2 and Table 1608.2 are reproductions of Figure 7-1 and Table 7-1 of ASCE 7-98, respectively. Figure 1608.2 for the contiguous United States and Table 1608.2 for Alaska give the ground snow loads to be used in determining the design snow loads for roofs. The ground snow loads on the map and the table are generally based on snow depths recorded over a period approaching 50 years. The snow loads on the maps have a 2-percent probability of being exceeded (a 50-year mean occurrence interval). The mapped values indicate the ground snow loads in pounds per square foot (psf). In mountainous areas, the map indicates the highest elevation up to which it is appropriate to use a given snow load. For elevations higher than indicated on the map, a site-specific case study is required to determine the appropriate snow load. Some of the mountainous areas of the western United States require site-specific case studies irrespective of elevation. According to BOCA/NBC Commentary,[1] assistance in the determination of an appropriate ground snow load for these areas may be obtained from the U.S. Department of Army Cold Regions Research and Engineering Laboratory in Hanover, New Hampshire.

1608.3 Flat roof snow loads. Refers to Sections 7.3, 7.10 and 7.11 of ASCE 7-98, and reproduces parts of Section 7.3. Table 1608.3.1 for exposure factor and Table 1608.3.2 for thermal factor are reproduced from Tables 7-2 and 7-3 of ASCE 7-98, respectively, except that a line for continuously heated greenhouses has been added to Table 1608.3.2. The snow load importance factors of Table 7-4 of ASCE 7-98 have been made a part of Table 1604.5. Section 1608.3.3 assigns Importance Category IV to greenhouses that are occupied for growing plants on a production or research basis, without public access. ASCE 7 Section 7.3.4 on minimum allowable values of p_f for low-slope roofs is not reproduced in the IBC. Sections 1608.3.4 on rain-on-snow surcharge load and 1608.3.5 on ponding instability refer to ASCE 7-98 Sections 7.10 and 7.11, respectively.

1608.3.1 Exposure factor. The roof exposure factor varies with the exposure category of the site, as described in the footnotes to Table 1608.3.1. The roof snow load is higher for a site in a wooded area than it is for an adjacent site that is flat and open.

1608.3.2 Thermal factor. The thermal factor takes into account the heat that is transmitted from the interior of the structure and reduces the snow depth on the roof.

1608.3.3 Snow load importance factor. The snow load importance factor takes into account the relative importance of a structure from the point of view of life safety. It has been explained further under Section 1604.5.

1608.3.4 Rain-on-snow surcharge load. This load accounts for the increased weight of snow after it rains on the snow. This surcharge load applies only to roofs with a slope of less than $^1/_2$ inch per foot (42 mm per m or 1 in 24), since water tends to remain in the snow much longer on relatively flat roofs.

1608.3.5 Ponding instability. Because of roof deflection caused by the weight of the snow, positive slope to the roof drains may be lost, thereby causing ponding. This section requires the roof framing to be stiff enough to maintain positive slope to the roof drains, so as to prevent potential instability caused by ponding.

1608.4 Sloped roof snow loads. The snow load for a sloped roof is given as the snow load for a flat roof multiplied by a roof slope factor that is given by ASCE 7-98 Section 7.4.1 for warm roofs, Section 7.4.2 for cold roofs, Section 7.4.3 for curved roofs, and Section 7.4.4 for multiple folded plate, sawtooth, and barrel vault roofs. See the BOCA/NBC Commentary[1] for an explanation of the two exceptions to this section.

1608.5 Partial loading. In many situations a reduction in snow load on a portion of a roof by wind scour, melting, or snow removal operations may simply reduce the stresses in the

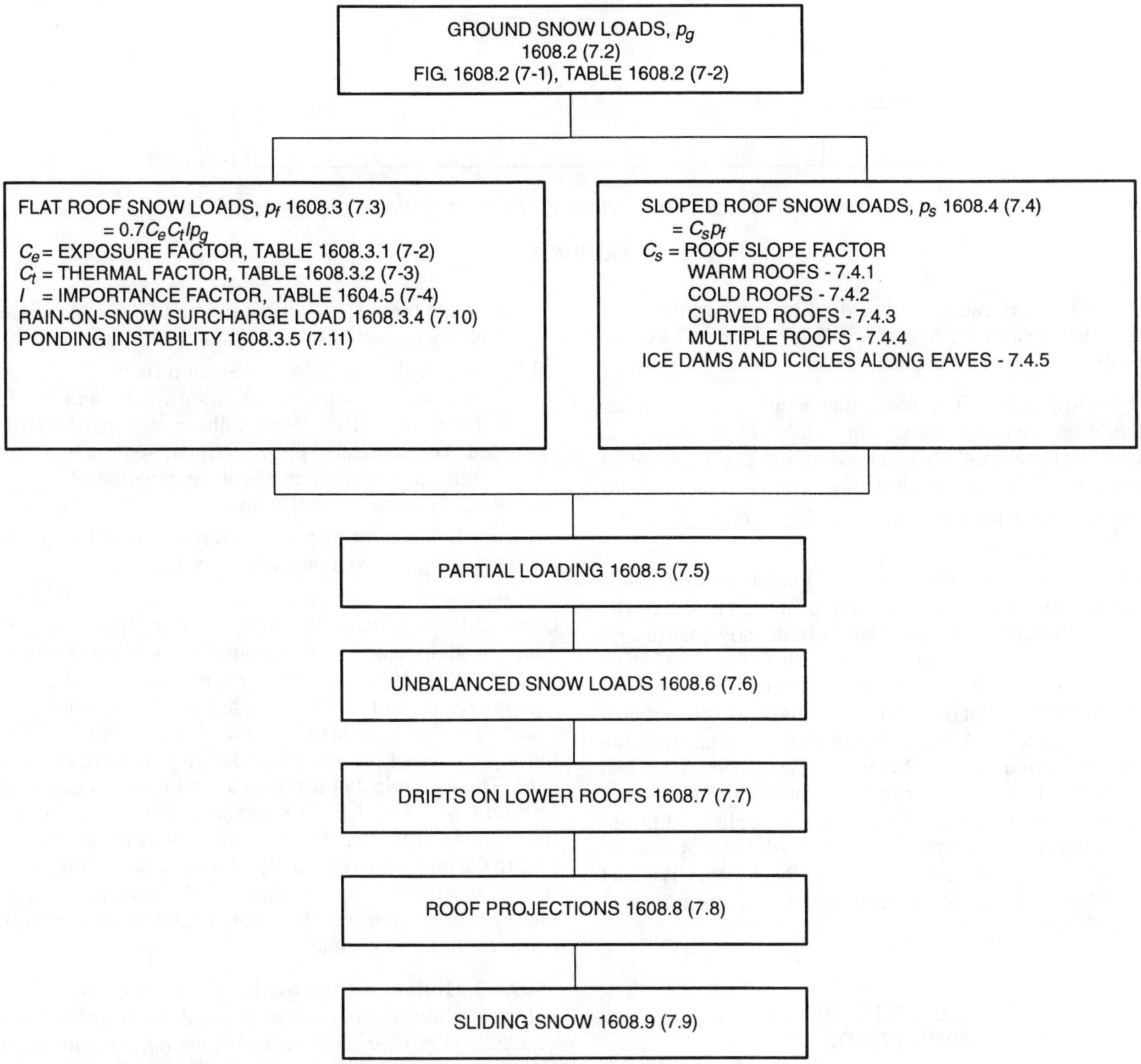

Note: 1608.2 etc. are 2000 IBC section numbers, table numbers, figure numbers
(7.2) etc. are ASCE 7-98 section numbers, table numbers, figure numbers

SNOW LOAD PROVISIONS

FIGURE 8

supporting members. However, in other cases removal of snow from an area may induce heavier stresses in the roof structure than occur when the entire roof is loaded. Cantilevered roof joints are a good example; removing half the snow load from the cantilevered portion increases the bending stress and deflection of the adjacent continuous span. In some situations adverse stress reversals may result.[6] This section requires consideration to be given in design to those adverse situations.

1608.6 Unbalanced snow loads. Snow on the roof of a building rarely accumulates evenly. The code intends that the designer investigate conditions of imbalance by requiring that roof designs consider unbalanced snow loading. One case would be the loading of one slope of a gable roof with snow while the other slope is unloaded (Figure 9). If this creates a less favorable condition in the design of the roof structural members, then it is the loading to be considered. This type of loading covers the case where the snow may have been removed from one side of the roof due to sliding or melting.[2]

1608.7 Drifts on lower roofs. It is extremely important to consider localized drift loads in designing roofs, because drifts onto lower roofs are a common cause of roof failures after a heavy snow (Figure 9). Section 7.7 of ASCE 7-98 separately addresses windward drift that forms on the windward side of a high bay wall area, and leeward drift that forms on the leeward side of a high bay wall area. Equations and design details required to be used for drift loading are given.

1608.8 Roof projections. Solar panels, mechanical equipment, parapet walls, and penthouses are examples of roof

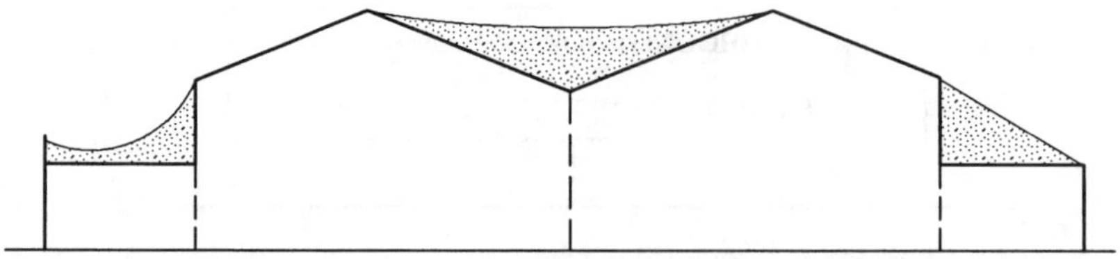

POTENTIAL SNOW ACCUMULATION, GABLE ROOF WITH SIDE SHEDS

FIGURE 9

projections that may cause windward drifts on the roof around them. The drift-load provisions of ASCE 7-98 Section 7.8 cover most of these situations adequately.

1608.9 Sliding snow. The snow that slides from a higher sloped roof imposes loads that are in addition to the snow load already on the lower roof. This section requires consideration of such additional loads in roof design.

Sections 1608.4-1608.9 refer to ASCE 7-98 Sections 7.4 through 7.9, respectively.

The 1997 UBC Section 1614 on snow loads leaves the determination of snow loads to the building official. The 2000 IBC Section 1608 is totally different. The alternate snow load design procedure of Appendix Chapter 16, Division I of the 1997 UBC is much closer to the 2000 IBC Section 1608. The Appendix Chapter 16, Division I of the 1997 UBC is almost a direct reproduction of Chapter 7 of ASCE 7-93, which was the latest edition of the ASCE 7 standard available at the time the 1997 UBC had to be finalized. There were very significant changes in Chapter 7 from ASCE 7-93 to ASCE 7-95 and then a couple of additional, not so substantive changes from ASCE 7-95 to ASCE 7-98. In view of these changes, even Appendix Chapter 16, Division I of the 1997 UBC is significantly different from Section 1608 of the 2000 IBC.

SECTION 1609 WIND LOADS

1609.1 Applications. Two basic requirements are specified. First, wind loads must not be decreased for the effect of shielding by other structures. Second, wind pressures must be assumed to come from any horizontal direction and to act normal to the surfaces considered.

1609.1.1 Determination of wind loads. Section 6 of ASCE 7-98 is to be used, with three exceptions allowed for building structures:

1. The 2000 IBC Section 1609.6 contains a simplified procedure for determining wind loads that is consistent with the provisions of ASCE 7-98. The procedure contains limitations on its own applicability.
2. Subject to the limitations spelled out in Section 1609.1.1.1, the SBCCI SSTD 10-99 *Standard for Hurricane Resistant Residential Construction*[20] is permitted to be used for applicable Group R2 and R3 buildings. SSTD 10 is a standard that was originally developed in 1990 with the intent of providing prescriptive provisions for wind-resistant design and construction of one- and two-story residential buildings of wood-framed construction, and one-, two- and three-story residential buildings of concrete and masonry construction sited in high wind regions.
3. Subject to the limitations of Section 1609.1.1.1, the AFPA *Wood Frame Construction Manual for One and Two Family Dwellings,* High Wind Edition,[21] is permitted to be used. This manual gives prescriptive requirements for the design and construction of one- and two-family dwellings of wood-framed construction.

Figure 10 has been prepared to serve as a road map through the wind design provisions of Section 1609.

A background to the wind load provisions of U.S. model codes and standards has been provided in Appendix 2 of this publication. Included is background on the wind design provisions of ASCE 7-98. The ASCE 7 Commentary on the wind design provisions of the 1998 standard is fairly extensive. Also, Example 6, Part 2, of this chapter has been prepared to illustrate the application of the analytical design procedure of that standard. The example can serve as a road map through much of Section 6 of the ASCE 7-98 standard. The discussion here is thus limited primarily to the modifications made in the 2000 IBC to the provisions of ASCE 7-98 Section 6. Primary among those modifications are the simplified provisions for low-rise buildings of Section 1609.6, which are also illustrated through a complete design example.

1609.1.2 Minimum wind loads. Though somewhat different in format, this section is the same in substance as Section 6.1.4 of ASCE 7-98. The minimum design wind pressure is 10 psf. For components and cladding of buildings, the pressure is required to be considered in either direction acting normal to the surface. For the main wind force-resisting systems of buildings, the minimum design wind load is to be obtained by multiplying the above pressure with an appropriate area, depending on the enclosure of the building. For an enclosed or partially enclosed building or other structure, the area of the building or structure projected onto a vertical plane normal to the assumed wind direction is to be used. For open buildings and other structures, the area A_f is to be used. A_f is area either normal to the wind direction or projected on a plane normal to the wind direction.

1609.1.3 Anchorage against overturning, uplift and sliding. This contains a very basic and general requirement that structural members and systems, and components and cladding in a building or other structure be anchored to resist wind-induced overturning, uplift and sliding, and to provide continuous load paths for those forces to the foundation. ASCE 7-98 Section 6 does not include such an explicit requirement. Section 2.4.4 of ASCE 7-95 did include a fairly explicit requirement concerning overturning and sliding. Buildings and other structures had to be designed so that the overturning moment due to lateral forces

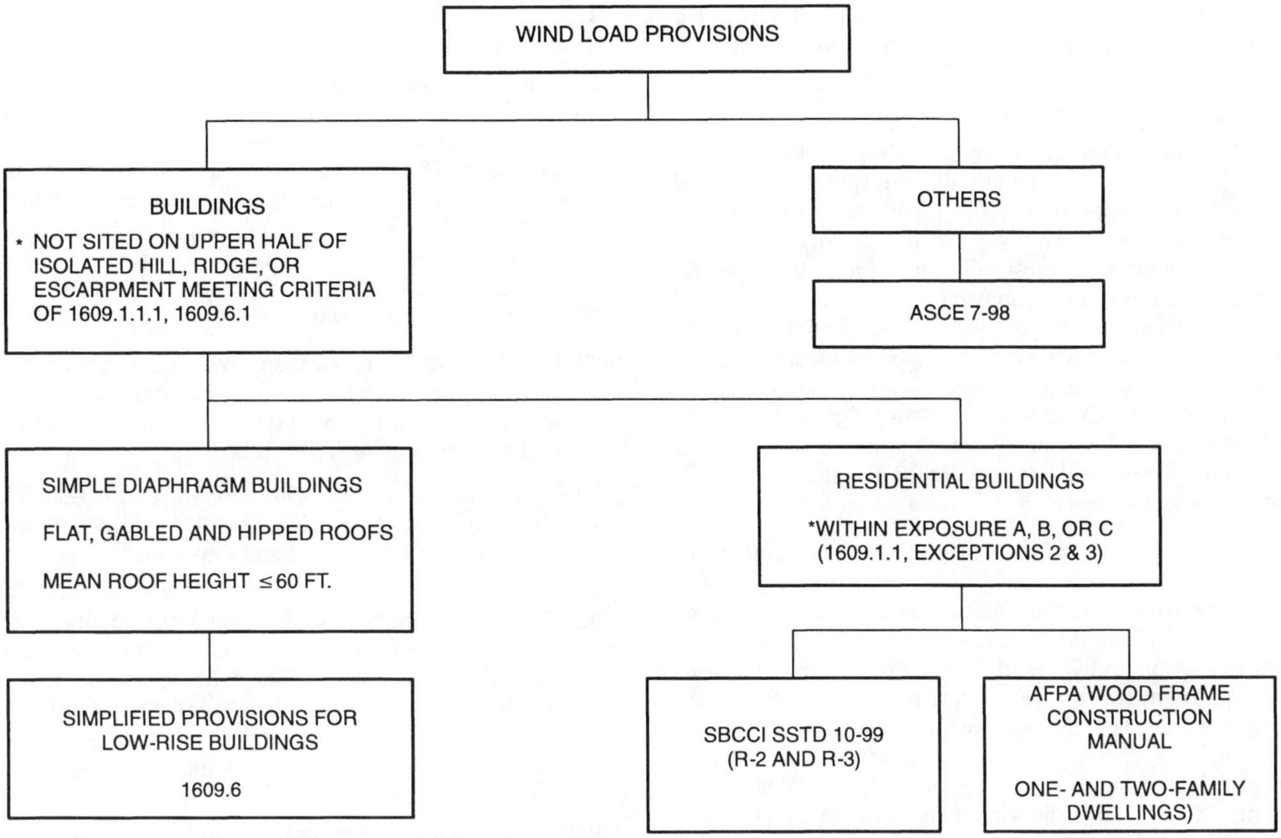

"ROAD MAP" THROUGH IBC WIND LOAD PROVISIONS

FIGURE 10

(wind and flood) acting singly or in combination did not exceed two-thirds of the dead load stabilizing moment unless the building or structure was anchored to resist the excess moment. The base shear due to lateral forces (wind and flood) could not exceed two-thirds of the total resisting force due to friction and adhesion unless the building or structure was anchored to resist the excess sliding force. In the 1998 edition of ASCE 7, the allowable stress design load combinations of Section 2.4 have been modified to incorporate the requirements of ASCE 7-95 Section 2.4.4. The strength design load combinations of ASCE 7-95 presumably already provided adequate protection against overturning and sliding; so no further adjustments to provide added protection against overturning and sliding have been made in ASCE 7-98. This section of the IBC specifically requires, that where a portion of the resistance to overturning, uplift, or sliding is provided by dead load, only two-thirds of the minimum dead load likely to be in place during a design wind event is to be relied upon.

1609.1.4 Protection of openings. This requires that in wind-borne debris regions, glazing in the lower 60 feet (18.3 m) in buildings shall be assumed to be openings unless such glazing is impact-resistant or protected with an impact-resistant covering in compliance with the following: 1) glazed openings located within 30 feet (9.15 m) of grade meet requirements of the Large Missile Test of SSTD 12,[22] and 2) glazed openings located more than 30 feet (9.15 m) above grade meet the provisions of the Small Missile Test of SSTD 12. Since Table 1 of SSTD 12 is based on fastest-mile wind speed, a specific conversion to 3-second gust speed is given.

An exception to the above requirement is provided, which is consistent with an exception currently allowed by the SBC for protection of glazed openings from wind-borne debris in hurricane-prone regions. It would provide the builder and/or owner of one- or two-story buildings with a low-cost alternative to the installation of permanent shutters or laminated glass meeting the requirements of SSTD 12. This exception requires the builder to provide panels precut to fit each glazed opening and further requires that temporary connection hardware be provided that is adequate to withstand the required components and cladding loads of hurricane winds.

1609.2 Definitions. This reproduces a subset of the definitions in Section 6.2 of ASCE 7-98. Under Section 6.4 of ASCE 7-98, Method 1—Simplified Procedure, and more specifically under Section 6.4.1, Scope, a number of qualifications are added to simple diaphragm buildings to which Method 1 of ASCE 7-98 would be applicable. These qualifications have been made a part of the definition of the simple diaphragm building in the 2000 IBC Section 1609.2. No other modification of any substance has been made to any ASCE 7-98 definition.

1609.3 Basic wind speed. The basic wind speed is to be determined from Figure 1609 when using the simplified provisions for low-rise buildings of Section 1609.6, or by ASCE 7-98 Figure 6-1 when using the provisions of ASCE 7-98. Figure 1609 is a direct reproduction of ASCE 7-98 Figure 6-1 and is included to make the Simplified Provisions of Section 1609.6 self-contained.

The wind speed map of ASCE 7-98 Figure 6-1 presents basic wind speeds for the contiguous United States, Alaska, and other selected locations. The wind speeds correspond to 3-second gust speeds at 33 feet (10 m) above ground level for exposure category C. Because the National Weather Service has phased out the measurement of fastest-mile wind speed (see Appendix 2 of this publication), the basic wind speed has been redefined as the peak gust that is recorded and archived for most National Weather Service stations. Given the response characteristics of the instrumentation used, the peak gust is associated with an averaging time of approximately 3 seconds.[6] Because the wind speeds of Figure 6-1 reflect conditions at airports and similar open-country exposures, they account for the effects of significant topographic features.

The map of ASCE 7-98 Figure 6-1 accounts for the more rapid increase of hurricane speeds with return period in comparison to nonhurricane winds. The map is specified so that the loads calculated from the standard, after multiplication by the load factor specified by ASCE 7-98, represent ultimate loads having approximately the same return period as loads for nonhurricane winds. The approach required selection of an ultimate return period, which was chosen as 500 years. A set of design level hurricane wind speed contours were obtained by dividing 500-year hurricane wind speed contours by a factor of 1.225, which is the multiplier that relates nonhurricane wind speeds corresponding to 50-year and 500-year return periods.[6]

Although the wind speed map of ASCE 7-98 Figure 6-1 is valid for most regions of the country, there are special regions in which wind-speed anomalies are known to exist. Some of these special regions are noted in ASCE 7-98 Figure 6-1. Winds blowing over mountain ranges or through gorges or river valleys in these special regions can develop speeds that are substantially higher than the values indicated on the map. When selecting basic wind speeds in these special regions, the IBC requires conformance with ASCE 7-98 Section 6.5.4. ASCE 7 advises use of regional climatic data and consultation with a wind engineer.

Since the basic wind speed of ASCE 7 is now based on 3-second gust speed at 33 feet (10 m) above ground in open country, it is often necessary that regional climatic data based on a different averaging time, for example, hourly mean or fastest mile, be adjusted to reflect peak gust speeds at 33 feet (10 m) above ground in open country. The results of statistical studies of wind speed records, reported by Durst[23] for nonhurricane winds and by Krayer.-Marshall[24] for hurricanes, are given in ASCE 7-95 Figure C6-1, which defines the relation between wind speed averaged over t seconds, v_t, and over 1 hour, v_{3600}.

The basic wind speed map of Figure 1609 does not require use of the Krayer-Marshall curve (for hurricane winds) to convert from 3-second gust wind speeds to fastest mile wind speeds. Using the Durst curve for the conversion of fastest mile wind speeds (see Table 6) indicates that for the range of fastest mile wind speeds examined (70 mph to 150 mph), a constant difference of 20 mph can be conservatively assumed for fastest mile wind speeds of 80 mph or more, and a constant difference of 15 mph for fastest mile wind speeds of 70 and 75 mph.

1609.3.1 Wind speed conversion. When referenced documents are based on fastest mile wind velocities, the 3-second gust wind velocities of Figure 1609 can be converted to fastest mile wind velocities using Table 1609.3.1.

1609.4 Exposure category. This reproduces Section 6.5.6, Exposure Categories, of ASCE 7-98, with modifications made to the definitions of Exposure B and Exposure C.

In the definition of Exposure B, the following sentence from ASCE 7-98 is deleted: "Use of this exposure category shall be limited to those areas for which terrain representative of Exposure B prevails in the upwind direction for a distance of at least 1500 feet (460 m) or 10 times the height of the building or other structure." The following sentence is added: "Exposure B shall be assumed unless the site meets the definition of another type exposure."

In the definition of Exposure C, the following first sentence from ASCE 7-98, "Open terrain with scattered obstructions having heights generally less than 30 feet (9.1 m)," has been expanded to the following two sentences: "Open terrain with scattered obstructions, including surface undulations or other irregularities , having heights generally less than 30 feet (9.1 m)* extending more than 1,500 feet (460 m) from the building site in any quadrant. This exposure shall also apply to any building located within Exposure B type terrain where the building is directly adjacent to open areas of Exposure C type terrain in any quadrant for a distance of more than 600 feet (182.9 m)."

The exposure definitions of ASCE 7-98 were modified in the IBC presumably to improve the enforceability of Section 1609.

1609.5 Importance factor. The wind load importance factors of Section 6.5.5 of ASCE 7-98 are given in Table 6-1 of that standard. Table 1604.5 of the 2000 IBC makes a combined presentation of snow load, wind load, and seismic load importance factors. The wind load importance factors are identical in the ASCE 7-98 Table 6-1 and the 2000 IBC Table 1604.5. However, in making the comparison one has to remember the following equivalence between the IBC and the ASCE 7 occupancy categories.

2000 IBC Occupancy Category	ASCE 7-98 Occupancy Category	General Description
I	II	Standard-occupancy building
II	III	Assembly building
III	IV	Essential or hazardous facility
IV	I	Low-hazard facility

*While the text is reproduced exactly, the metric equivalents may not be exactly as printed in the IBC.

TABLE 6. 3-SECOND GUST VELOCITY VERSUS FASTEST MILE WIND VELOCITY

V_{fm}	sec./hr.	sec./mile	RATIO OF V_{fm}/V_{mh}	V_{mh}	RATIO OF V_{3s}/V_{mh}	V_{3s}
70	3,600	51.4	1.27	55.1	1.53	84.5
80	3,600	45	1.28	62.5	1.53	95.6
90	3,600	40	4.29	69.8	1.53	106.7
100	3,600	36	4.34	76.3	1.53	116.8
120	3,600	32.7	4.32	83.3	1.53	127.5
130	3,600	30	1.33	90.2	1.53	138.0
140	3,600	27.7	1.34	97	1.53	148.4

V_{fm} = Fastest mile velocity
V_{mh} = Mean hourly velocity
V_{3s} = 3-second gust velocity

The wind load importance factor is used to adjust the level of structural reliability of a building or other structure to be consistent with its occupancy or use. Further discussion has been provided under Section 1604.5.

1609.6 Simplified provisions for low rise buildings. The procedure given is based on Method 1, the Simplified Procedure of ASCE 7-98 Section 6.4. It is similar to the simplified procedure in Section 1606.2 of the SBC, 1999 edition, and the 1997 UBC Method 2, both of which procedures are based on projected areas.

The simplified provisions are applicable to simple diaphragm buildings, which must satisfy all the following conditions:

1. Enclosed building.
2. Mean roof height is less than or equal to 60 feet (18.3 m).
3. Mean roof height does not exceed least horizontal dimension.
4. Building has an approximately symmetrical cross section.
5. Building has no expansion joints or structural separations within the building.
6. Wind loads are transmitted through floor and roof diaphragms to the vertical lateral-force-resisting systems.
7. If the building has moment-resisting frames, roof slopes do not exceed 30 degrees.

In addition, the buildings must have flat, gabled or hipped roofs, and must not be sited on the upper half of an isolated hill or escarpment meeting the three conditions listed in Section 1609.6.1.

It may be noted that Method 1 of ASCE 7-98 applies only to essentially flat roof buildings (roof slope less than 10 degrees) and only to buildings not more than 30 feet in height. In contrast, the simplified method of Section 1609.6 has a much broader application . . . gabled or hipped roof buildings apply with a height limitation of 60 feet. The ASCE 7 *Task Committee in Wind Loads* is currently revising Method 1 of ASCE 7 to be more in line with the simplified method of 2000 IBC Section 1609.6, with the intent that the simplified wind load provisions of both documents, the IBC and future editions of ASCE 7, will be identical.

Some examples of simple diaphragm buildings are houses with plywood shear walls, typical CMU (concrete masonry unit) wall buildings, concrete frame buildings, and steel frame buildings with vertically spanning walls and diaphragm floor and roof diaphragms. Metal building frames with horizontally spanning girts are not simple diaphragm buildings.

The method of determining design pressures is quite simple. Pressures for all wind speeds are tabulated directly for Exposure B buildings up to 30 feet (9.1 m) high. Adjustment for buildings with different heights or exposures is accounted for directly by multiplying with a coefficient from a single table. Once the exposure category of the building is established and basic wind speed and wind importance factor are determined from Figure 1609 and Table 1604.5, respectively, only the following tables and figures are needed:

Table 1609.6.2.1(1): Main Wind Force Resisting System Loads For a Building with a Mean Roof Height of 30 feet Located in Exposure B. (Actually gives design pressures in psf, not loads).

Table 1609.6.2.1(2): Component and Cladding Loads for a Building with a Mean Roof Height of 30 feet Located in Exposure B. (Also gives pressures in psf, rather than loads).

Table 1609.6.2.1(3): Roof Overhang Component and Cladding Design Wind Pressures for a Building with a Mean Roof Height of 30 feet Located in Exposure B.

Table 1609.6.2.1(4): Height and Exposure Adjustment Coefficients.

Figure 1609.6(1): Main Wind Force (MWF) Loading Diagram. [Shows end zones needed to use Table 1609.6.2.1(1)].

Figure 1609.6(2): Component and Cladding Loading Diagrams. (Needed to use Tables 1609.6.2.1(2) and 1609.6.2.1(3).

Figure 1609.6(3): Application of Main Wind Force Resisting System (MWFRS) Loads for Simple Diaphragm Buildings. [Goes with Table 1609.6.2.1(1)].

Much of the simplicity of the procedure derives from the fact that internal pressures are not involved in the design pressures for the main wind force-resisting system. Since the wind forces are delivered to the MWFRS via floor slabs and roof diaphragms, and the building, by definition, is enclosed, the internal pressures simply do not come into play (or cancel out).

The mean roof height limitation of 60 feet is much shorter than the mean roof height of 200 feet up to which Method 2 of the 1997 UBC is applicable. Without exception, all buildings with a mean roof height greater than 60 feet must be designed in accordance with ASCE 7, including all of its complexities. This is a significant change for wind design in UBC jurisdictions.

See Example 7, Part 2 of this chapter.

1609.7 Roof systems. The roof system consists of the roof deck and the roof covering. The provisions of this section are largely reproduced from Section 1606.3 of the SBC, 1997 and 1999.[25]

1609.7.1 Roof deck. The roof deck is a structural component of the building. Thus, it is required to be designed to resist the wind pressures determined by the simplified provisions of Section 1609.6, by SBCCI SSTD 10,[20] by the AFPA *Wood Frame Construction Manual for One and Two Family Dwellings* High-wind Edition[21] or by ASCE 7-98. The first three procedures have limits on their applicability, as indicated in Figure 6.

1609.7.2 Roof coverings. If the roof deck is relatively impermeable, the wind pressures will act through the roof deck to the building framing system. If the roof covering is also relatively impermeable and fastened to the roof deck, the two components will be subject to the same wind pressures. If the roof covering is air-permeable, wind pressures are able to develop on both the top of the roof covering and underneath the roof covering. This venting action of the roof negates some of the wind pressures on the roof covering.[3]

1609.7.3 Rigid tile. As explained above, in certain types of installations, the roof covering is not subject to the same wind pressures as the roof deck. Such installations include concrete and clay tile roof coverings. The gaps occurring at the joints allow some equalization of pressure between the inner and outer faces of the tiles, leading to reduced pressures. The equation given in this section has been developed by research for the determination of wind loads (uplift moments) on loose laid and mechanically fastened roof tiles when laid over sheathing with an underlayment.[3] The procedure is based on practical measurements on real tiles to determine the effect of air being able to penetrate the roof covering.

SECTION 1610 SOIL LATERAL LOAD

1610.1 General. This section reproduces part of Chapter 5, Soil and Hydrostatic Pressure and Flood Loads of ASCE 7-98. Table 1610.1 Soil Lateral Load, is a modified version of Table 5-1 of ASCE 7-98. Table 7 compares the soil lateral loads given in ASCE 7-95, 98, the last two editions of the BOCA/NBC, the last two editions of the SBC, and the 2000 IBC. The 1997 UBC does not address soil lateral load except under Section 1611.2, Other Loads. That section simply states in very general terms that "Buildings and other structures and portions thereof shall be designed to resist all loads due to . . . lateral soil pressure, *H*, . . ."

The ASCE 7 Table 5-1 includes high earth pressures, 85 pounds per cubic foot or more, to point out that certain soils are poor back-fill material. The values set forth in the IBC table are closer to, although not exactly the same as the corresponding values used in the BOCA/NBC[5] and the SBC.[3] The issue of variance with the national standard was debated by the ICC Structural Subcommittee who at the final public hearing reaffirmed their decision to use values that have been used in other model codes.

TABLE 7. SOIL LATERAL LOADS IN MODEL CODES AND STANDARDS

Description of Backfill Material[e]	Unified Soil Classification	Design Lateral Soil Load[a], psf per foot of depth			
		ASCE 7-95, 98	BOCA/NBC 1996, 1999	SBC 1997, 1999	IBC 2000
Well-graded clean gravels, gravel-sand mixes	GW	35[c]	30	30	30[c]
Poorly graded clean gravels, gravel-sand mixes	GP	35[c]	30	30	30[c]
Silty gravels, poorly graded gravel-sand mixes	GM	35[c]	41	45	40[c]
Clayey gravels, poorly graded gravel and clay mixes	GC	45[c]	46	45	45[c]
Well-graded clean sands, gravelly sand mixes	SW	35[c]	30	30	30[c]
Poorly graded clean sands, sand-gravel mixes	SP	35[c]	30	30	30[c]
Silty sands, poorly graded sand-silt mixes	SM	45[c]	41	45	45[d]
Sand-silt clay mix with plastic fines	SM-SC	85[d]	44	45	45[d]
Clayey sands, poorly graded sand-clay mixes	SC	85[d]	48	60	60[d]
Inorganic silts and clayey silts	ML	85[d]	45	45	45[d]
Mixture of inorganic silt and clay	ML-CL	85[d]	44	60	60[d]
Inorganic clays of low-to-medium plasticity	CL	100	45	60	60[d]
Organic silts and silt-clays, low plasticity	OL	b	b	b	b
Inorganic clayey silts, elastic silts	MH	b	55	60	b
Inorganic clays of high plasticity	CH	b	b	b	b
Organic clays and silty clays	OH	b	b	b	b

a. ASCE 7, IBC 2000—Design lateral loads are given for moist conditions for the specified soils at their optimum densities. Actual field conditions shall govern. Submerged or saturated soil pressures shall include the weight of the buoyant soil plus the hydrostatic loads.

b. ASCE 7, IBC 2000—Unsuitable as backfill material. BOCA—Soil shall be replaced with controlled backfill. SBC—Compliance with Section 1804.3 (Expansive Soils) is required.

c. ASCE 7, IBC 2000—For relatively rigid walls, as when braced by floors, the design lateral soil load shall be increased for sand- and gravel-type soils to 60 pounds per square foot per foot of depth. Basement walls extending not more than 8 feet below grade and supporting light floor systems are not considered relatively rigid walls.

d. ASCE 7, IBC 2000—For relatively rigid walls, as when braced by floors, the design lateral load shall be increased for silts and clay-type soils to 100 pounds per square foot per foot of depth. Basement walls extending more than 8 feet below grade and supporting light floor systems are not considered relatively rigid walls.

e. IBC 2000—The definition and classification of soil materials shall be in accordance with ASTM D 2487.

In ASCE 7, contrary to what is stated in Footnote a, the soil lateral loads for silts and silt-clay mixtures—unified soil classifications SM-SC, SC, ML and ML-CL—are based on saturated conditions that take hydrostatic pressure into account. Table 8, in addition to showing soil lateral loads from the IBC and the ASCE 7 standard, also shows soil lateral load values using the calculation procedure that formed the basis of the values included in BOCA/NBC. The calculated soil lateral loads are presented for both moist and saturated conditions. Table 8 shows that for gravels and sands, IBC, ASCE and the calculated soil lateral loads for moist conditions agree. Conversely, for silts and silt-clay mixtures, the IBC values agree with the calculated soil lateral loads for moist conditions, whereas ASCE 7 values are closer to the calculated soil lateral loads for saturated conditions. Footnote a to the IBC Table 1610.1 as well as the ASCE 7 Table 5-1, states that the design lateral soil loads are given for moist soil conditions. This appears to be true only in the case of the IBC.

ASCE 7 points out in Footnotes c and d to Table 5-1 that when walls are unyielding, the earth pressure is increased from active pressure toward earth pressure at rest, resulting in 60 pounds per cubic foot for granular soils and 100 pounds per cubic foot for silt and clay-type soils. These footnotes are also used with Table 1610.1 of the 2000 IBC. Examples of light floor systems supported on shallow basement walls, given in the ASCE 7 commentary, are floor systems with wood joists and flooring, and cold-formed steel joists without cast-in-place concrete floors attached.

Expansive soils exist in many parts of the United States and may cause serious damage to basement walls unless special design considerations are provided.[6] Expansive soils should not be used as backfill because they can exert very high pressures against walls. Special soil testing is required to determine the magnitude of these pressures. It is preferable to excavate expansive soils and backfill with nonexpansive freely draining sands and gravels. This topic is covered by Footnote b to Table 1610.1.

1610.2 Retaining walls. This provision is not in ASCE 7-98. The 1997 UBC contains more detailed provisions concerning the design of retaining walls. Retaining walls are required by both codes to be designed to resist sliding by at least 1.5 times the lateral force and overturning by at least 1.5 times the overturning moment, using allowable stress design loads. The subject is not treated in the BOCA/NBC[5] or the SBC.[25]

SECTION 1611 RAIN LOADS

This reproduces Chapter 8, Rain Loads, of ASCE 7-98, except that Section 8.2, Roof Drainage, is not included. Each portion of a roof is required to be designed to sustain the load of rainwater that will accumulate on it if the primary drainage systems for that portion is blocked, plus the uniform load caused by water that rises above the inlet of the secondary drainage system at its design flow. Rain loads are not addressed in the BOCA/NBC, the UBC or the SBC. The IBC requirement to design roofs for rain load represents a change in design practice. It should be obvious from the design load combinations of Sections 1605.2 and 1605.3, however, that the design rain loads would affect design only if they are larger than the design snow loads and the roof live loads.

TABLE 8. SOIL LATERAL LOADS: CALCULATED VERSUS CODE AND STANDARD VALUES

SOIL DESCRIPTION	UNIFIED SOIL CLASSIFICATION	DESIGN LATERAL SOIL LOAD pounds per square foot per foot of depth		CALCULATED LATERAL SOIL LOAD Active Lateral Pressure, pounds per square foot per foot of depth	
		IBC	ASCE 7	Moist	Saturated
Well-graded clean gravels, gravel-sand mixes	GW	30	35	34	81
Poorly graded clean gravel, gravel-sand mixes	GP	30	35	34	80
Silty gravels, poorly graded gravel-sand mixes	GM	40	35	40	84
Clayey gravels, poorly graded gravel-sand-clay mixes	GC	45	45	44	86
Well-graded clean sand, gravelly-sand mixes	SW	30	35	32	80
Poorly graded clean sands, sand-gravel mixes	SP	30	35	32	79
Silty sands, poorly graded sand-silt mixes	SM	45	45	38	82
Sand-silt clay mix with plastic fines	SM-SC	45	85	40	84
Clayey sands, poorly graded sand-clay mixes	SC	60	85	42	85
Inorganic silts and clayey silts	ML	45	85	39	82
Mixture of inorganic silts and clay	ML-CL	60	85	40	83
Inorganic silts and silt-clay, medium plasticity	CL	60	100	46	86
Organic silts and silt-clays, low plasticity	OL	Unsuitable	Unsuitable	—	—
Inorganic clayey silts, elastic silts	MH	Unsuitable	Unsuitable	—	—
Inorganic clays or high plasticity	CH	Unsuitable	Unsuitable	—	—
Organic clays and silty clays	OH	Unsuitable	Unsuitable	—	—

SECTION 1612
FLOOD LOADS

1612.1 General. In the final draft of the IBC, Section 1612.1 simply stated that the design and construction of structural systems and components that resist flood loads must conform to the requirements of Section 5.3 of ASCE 7-98.

Section 5.3 of ASCE 7 presents information on the design of buildings in flood-prone areas. Much of the impetus for flood-resistant design has come from initiatives of flood insurance and flood-damage mitigation sponsored by the federal government.

As indicated in the commentary to ASCE 7-98, the National Flood Insurance Program (NFIP) is based on an agreement between the federal government and participating communities that have been identified as being flood-prone. The Federal Emergency Management Agency (FEMA), through the Federal Insurance Administration, makes flood insurance available to the residents of communities, provided that the community adopts and enforces adequate flood-plain management regulations that meet the minimum requirements. Included in the NFIP requirements, found under Title 44 of the U. S. Code of Federal Regulations, are minimum design and construction standards for buildings located in special flood hazard areas.

Special flood hazard areas are those identified by FEMA's Mitigation Directorate as being subject to inundation during the 100-year flood (flood having a 1-percent chance of being equaled or exceeded in any given year), special flood hazard areas are shown on flood insurance rate maps that are produced for flood-prone communities. Special flood hazard areas are identified on such maps as A Zones (A, AE, Al-30, A99, AR, AO or AK) or V Zones (V, V-E, VO or VI-30). The special flood hazard areas are those in which communities must enforce NFIP-compliant, flood-damage-resistant design and construction practices.

For the 2000 edition of the IBC, the American Society of Civil Engineers (ASCE) and FEMA proposed modifications to the IBC Final Draft for the purpose of ensuring that the provisions of the IBC and the manner in which they are administered is consistent with those of the NFIP. This proposal was accepted. Much of the above is accomplished through adoption by reference of the ASCE 24-98 *Flood Resistant Design and Construction Standard.*[26] The provisions of ASCE 24-98 meet or exceed the building science provisions of the NFIP and present the consensus state-of-the-art approach to flood-resistant construction.

The ASCE Standard for flood-resistant construction (ASCE 24-98) represents the culmination of over 4 years of work by dozens of experts in flood-resistant design and construction from all facets of the land development and regulations community. FEMA was in full support of this effort and provided both financial and technical assistance in this endeavor.

ASCE 24-98 requires that the design of structures within flood hazard areas be governed by the loading provisions of ASCE 7-98. That standard requires that the structural systems of buildings be designed, constructed, connected and anchored to resist flotation, collapse and permanent lateral movement due to the action of wind loads and loads from flooding associated with the design flood. Wind loads and flood loads may act simultaneously at coastlines, particularly during hurricanes and coastal storms. This may also be true in some other situations cited in the ASCE 7-98 commentary Section C5.3.2.1. Flood loads are the loads or pressures on the surfaces of buildings and structures caused by the presence of flood waters. These loads are of two basic types—hydrostatic and hydrodynamic. Impact loads result from objects transported by flood waters striking against structures or parts of structures. Wave loads are considered a special type of hydrodynamic load. Hydrostatic loads, hydrodynamic loads, wave loads, and impact loads are specified in ASCE 24-98. Wave loads may be determined by using an analytical procedure outlined by more advanced numerical modeling procedures, or by laboratory test procedures or physical modeling.

ASCE 24-98 requires that the design and construction of structures located in flood-hazard areas consider all flood-related hazards; including hydrostatic loads, hydrodynamic loads and wave action, debris impacts, alluvial fan flooding, flood-related erosion, iceflows or icejams, or mudslides in accordance with the requirements of that standard if specified or, if not specified in that standard, then in accordance with the requirements approved by the authority having jurisdiction. Design documents must identify, and take into account, flood-related and other concurrent loads that will act on the structure. Design documents must include, but not be limited to, the applicable conditions listed below:

1. Wave action
2. High-velocity flood waters
3. Impacts due to debris in the flood waters
4. Rapid inundation by flood waters
5. Rapid drawdown of flood waters
6. Prolonged inundation by flood waters
7. Wave- and flood-induced erosion and scour
8. Deposition and sedimentation by flood waters

The BOCA/NBC requires that buildings and structures located in flood-hazard zones (A zones) and high-hazard zones (V zones), as defined on the flood-hazard map, be designed, constructed, connected, and anchored to resist flood loads. Flood loads are to be determined in accordance with Section 5.3 of ASCE 7-95. The *SBC* does not address flood loads in Chapter 16. The 1997 UBC has a section on flood-resistant construction. It simply refers the user to Appendix Chapter 31, Division I (UBC Volume 1) for flood-resistant construction requirements where specifically adopted.

1612.2 Definitions. The particular definitions to be noted are Design Flood, Flood-Hazard Area, Flood-Hazard Area Subject to High-Velocity Wave Action, and Special Flood Hazard Area.

1612.3 Establishment of flood-hazard areas. Flood-hazard areas are established by the local jurisdiction through adoption of a flood-hazard map and supporting data. Minimum requirements imposed on the jurisdiction are spelled out.

1612.4 Design and construction. Requires the design and construction of buildings and structures located in flood-hazard areas, including flood-hazard areas subject to high-velocity wave action, to be in accordance with the requirements of ASCE 24.

1612.5 Flood-hazard certificates. This lists a number of certifications that must be furnished to the building official. The requirements are different for construction in flood-hazard areas not subject to high-velocity wave action and for construction in flood-hazard areas subject to high-velocity wave action.

SECTION 1613
EARTHQUAKE LOADS DEFINITIONS

Some terms relating to earthquake regulations have been defined in Section 1602, while others are defined in this section. While Section 1602 includes some notation, this section does not contain any. Also, as mentioned earlier, the 2000 IBC defines symbols and notations as they occur in the text. The ICC Structural Subcommittee thought this to be more user-friendly than requiring the reader to constantly refer back to the beginning of a chapter.

A couple of the definitions listed are worth comments.

Through the final draft of the 2000 IBC, only an active fault was defined. Active fault trace, and the second sentence referring to it, were added to the definition as the result of a code change approved for the 2000 edition. The code change is related to Section 1616.3.1, Site limitation for SDC E and F. Through the final draft, Section 1616.3.1 required that a structure assigned to SDC E or F must not be cited "where there is the potential for an active fault to cause rupture of the ground surface at the structure." It was pointed out that the word "potential" was vague and was likely to result in nonuniform interpretation and enforcement. The text within quotes was changed to "over an identified active fault trace." The revised language embodied the intended level of restriction found in a typical special-study zone. The change in Section 1616.3.1 required that "active fault trace" be defined in Section 1613. The designation of active fault traces has been made subject to identification by a geologic report.

The definitions of design displacement, total design displacement and total maximum displacement relate to Section 1623, Seismically Isolated Structures, and do not have general applicability. The same is true of displacement restraint system, effective damping, and effective stiffness, but in the case of the displacements, some confusion may be created. An identical term, "design displacement," is now defined in Section 21.1 of ACI 318-99. The term, as defined there, is analogous to the design story drift of the IBC as defined in Sections 1617.4.6 or 1617.5.3.

SECTION 1614
EARTHQUAKE LOADS—GENERAL

1614.1 Scope. After stating that every structure and portion thereof must be designed and constructed to resist the effects of earthquake motions and be assigned a seismic design category (Section 1616.3), the IBC proceeds to permit a number of important exemptions. Structures in SDC A need only comply with Section 1616.4. For structures exposed to such low seismic risk, the IBC requires only that a complete lateral-force-resisting system be provided and that all elements of the structure be tied together. A nominal design force of 1 percent of the weight of the structure is used to proportion the lateral-force-resisting system. See discussion on Section 1616.4. The other exemptions are:

1. Detached Group R-3 (one- and two-family) dwellings in SDC A, B, and C when constructed in accordance with the *International Residential Code* (IRC) are totally exempt from all seismic design requirements. Through the final draft of the IBC, the corresponding exemption, adapted from the 1997 NEHRP Provisions, was: "Detached Group R-3 dwellings . . . located where the design spectral response acceleration at short periods, S_{DS}, . . . is less than 0.4 are exempt from requirements of Sections 1613 through 1622." The exemption was modified as the result of an approved change to the final draft. The reason given by the proponent and accepted by the ICC Structural Subcommittee is reproduced below. The term "current" in the following refers to the final draft of the IBC.

   The current IBC exception related to the seismic design of detached Group R-3 dwellings is too conservative and more restrictive than the 1997 UBC requirements. Traditionally, detached one- and two-family dwellings located in Seismic Zones 0, 1 and 2 have been permitted to be built using the design provisions for conventional light-frame construction. Additional, more restrictive requirements were limited to Seismic Zones 3 and 4. However, the current IBC requirements that are based on the 1997 NEHRP Provisions extend these restrictions to include one- and two-family dwellings located in Seismic Zone 2.

   This fact is obscured by using S_{DS}, the design spectral response acceleration at short periods, to define the limits of conventional construction. Comparison of values of S_{DS} to the more traditional seismic zones is not straightforward. It requires adjusting the mapped spectral accelerations for short periods shown in the IBC seismic maps to account for the soil conditions at the building site and then multiplying by two-thirds. For buildings in Seismic Zone 2A with soil profile S_D, the calculated value for S_{DS} is 0.55 (not exempt).

   Builders in lower seismic zones do not typically employ the services of a registered design professional when constructing buildings to the conventional construction provisions. However, calculation of S_{DS} is beyond the capabilities of a typical builder and such services will be required just to determine if conventional construction can be used. The IRC resolves this problem by including a seismic map, based on the IBC, that shows the seismic design categories using the default Site Class D (soil profile S_D). This enables builders to quickly determine if buildings in their area are exempt from the special seismic requirements contained in the IBC. This change allows users of the IBC to do the same.

   The IRC[27] exempts all applicable Group R-3 construction in SDC A, B and C from additional seismic requirements. This change results in a consistent set of requirements that could be more easily applied to both the IBC and IRC.

2. The seismic-force-resisting system of wood-frame buildings that conform to the provisions of Section 2308 (conventional light-frame construction) need not be analyzed as required by Section 1616.1. Although some control is necessary to ensure the integrity of these structures, it is felt that the requirements of Section 2308 are adequate to provide the safety required based on the history of such frame construction—invariably low-rise structures—in earthquakes.
3. Agricultural storage structures intended only for incidental human occupancy are exempt from all seismic design requirements. This is because of the exceptionally low risk to life involved.
4. Structures located where $S_s \leq 0.15g$ [Figures 1615 (1), 1615 (3), 1615 (5), 1615 (7)a and 1615 (8)a], and $S_1 \leq 0.04g$ [Figures 1615(2), 1615(4), 1615(6), 1615(7)b, 1615(8)b], need only comply with Section 1616.4. See commentary following Item 5 below.
5. Structures located where $S_{DS} \leq 0.167g$ and $S_{D1} \leq 0.067g$ need only comply with Section 1616.4. In view of the definitions of seismic design categories in Tables 1616.3(1) and 1616.3(2), this item is a repeat of the SDC A exemption.

Since $S_{DS} = (2/3)\ F_aS_s$ and $S_{D1} = (2/3)F_vS_1$ (Section 1615.1.3), Item 5 can be rewritten as follows:

Structures where $S_s \leq 0.25g/F_a$ and $S_1 \leq 0.1g/F_v$ need only comply with Section 1616.4.

Thus, for F_a and F_v values exceeding 1.67 and 2.50, respectively, Exemption 4 supersedes Exemption 5. Item 5 provides additional exemptions at stiffer soil sites and/or high seismicity areas to those provided by Item 4.

1614.1.1 Additions to existing buildings. The design and construction requirements that apply to a new structure also apply to an addition that is structurally independent from an existing structure.

An addition that is not structurally independent from an existing structure must be designed and constructed so that the entire structure conforms to the seismic-force-resistance requirements for new structures unless two restrictive conditions are met.

While stringent, the IBC restrictions are more relaxed than those of the 1997 NEHRP Provisions on which they are based. An existing structure to which an addition is made is exempted by the NEHRP Provisions from having to conform to the seismic-force-resistance requirements of that document if all the following conditions are satisfied:

1. The addition conforms with the requirements for new structures.
2. The addition does not increase the seismic forces in any structural element of the existing structure by more than 5 percent, unless the capacity of the element subject to the increased forces is still in compliance with the NEHRP Provisions.
3. The addition does not decrease the seismic resistance of any structural element of the existing structure to less than that required for a new structure.

Through the final draft of the 2000 IBC, the second condition above read: ". . . unless the capacity of the element subject to the increased forces is still in compliance with Sections 1613 through 1622." This was changed for the 2000 edition to: ". . . unless the element has the capacity to resist the increased forces determined in accordance with Sections 1613 through 1622." The prior language was confusing because the reference sections do not specify capacities. Capacities are specified in the materials chapters. The revised language clarifies the intent of Condition 2.

Condition 3 was deleted between the final draft and the 2000 edition of the IBC because the language effectively prohibited even minor modifications to many existing elements, even when their force levels were not increased and when they met their original building code requirements both before and after modification. For many elements such as concrete shear walls, it is nearly impossible to retroactively comply with the detailing requirements in the current building code. Condition 3 was also inconsistent with Condition 2, which explicitly permits an increase of up to 5 percent of the mass contributing to seismic forces in any element of the existing structure without bringing the entire structure into compliance with the current code.

1614.2 Change of occupancy. As long as a change of occupancy does not result in a higher seismic use group classification, there are no additional requirements. However, when a structure gets reclassified into a higher seismic use group as the result of a change in occupancy, the structure must conform to the seismic requirements for a new structure.

An important exception to the above requirement is provided. Specific detailing requirements applicable to a new structure need not be met if an equivalent level of performance and seismic safety contemplated for a new structure can be demonstrated. Revised detailing requirements make it impossible in many instances for an existing structure to meet the requirements for a new structure. The intent of this exception is to give guidance to the building official and design professional as to which areas to investigate when alternate methods of complying with new detailing requirements are considered for a change of occupancy to an existing structure.

1614.3 Alterations. Compliance with Sections 1613 through 1622 can be waived for an existing structure being altered only if the four different conditions are met.

Alterations include all significant modifications to existing structures that are not classified as an addition. As in the case of additions, an increase of no greater than 5 percent of the mass contributing to seismic forces is permitted in any structural element of the existing structure without bringing the entire structure into conformance with the current code. Unlike in the case of additions, however, Condition 2 has not been modified from the original NEHRP language; Condition 3 has not been deleted and Condition 4, which is rather vague and unenforceable, has been added.

1614.4 Quality assurance. This section simply provides a cross-reference to the quality assurance plan requirements of Chapter 17.

1614.5 Seismic and wind. The forces that a structure subjected to earthquake motions must resist result directly from the distortions induced by the motion of the ground on which it rests. The response (i.e., the magnitude and distribution of forces and displacements) of a structure resulting from such a base motion is influenced by the properties of both the structure and the foundation, as well as the character of the exciting motion.

A simplified picture of the behavior of a building during an earthquake may be obtained by considering Figure 11. As the ground on which the building rests is displaced, the base of the building moves with it. However, the inertia of the building mass resists this motion and causes the building to suffer a distortion (greatly exaggerated in the figure). This distortion wave travels along the height of the structure in much the same manner as a stress wave in a bar with a free end. The continued shaking of the base causes the building to undergo a complex series of oscillations.

It is important to draw a distinction between forces due to wind and those produced by earthquakes. Occasionally, even engineers tend to think of these forces as belonging to the same category just because codes specify design wind as well as earthquake forces in terms of equivalent static forces. Although both wind and earthquake forces are dynamic in character, a basic difference exists in the manner in which they are induced in a structure. Whereas wind loads are external loads applied and, therefore, proportional to the exposed surface of a structure, earthquake forces are essentially inertial forces. The latter result from the distortion produced by both the earthquake motion and inertial resistance of the structure. Their magnitude is a function of the mass of the structure rather than its exposed surface. Also, in contrast to the structural response to essentially static gravity loading or even to wind loads, which can often be validly treated as static loads, the dynamic character of the response to earthquake excitation can seldom be ignored. Thus, where in designing for static loads one would feel greater assurance about the safety of a structure made up of members of heavy section, in the case of earthquake loading, the stiffer and heavier structure does not necessarily represent the safer design.

When a structure responds elastically to ground motions during a severe earthquake, the maximum response accelerations may be several times the maximum ground acceleration and may depend on the mass and stiffness of the structure and the magnitude of the damping. It is generally uneconomical and also unnecessary to design a structure to respond in the elastic range to the maximum earthquake-induced inertia forces. Thus the design seismic horizontal force recommended by codes, including the 2000 IBC, are generally less than the elastic response inertia forces induced by a major earthquake (in the case of the 2000 IBC, the design earthquake as defined in Section 1613).

Experience has shown that structures designed to the level of seismic horizontal forces recommended by codes can survive major earthquake shaking. This is because of the ability of well-designed structures to dissipate seismic energy by inelastic deformations in certain localized regions of certain members. Decrease in structural stiffness caused by accumulating damage and soil-structure interaction also helps at times. It should be evident that the use of the level of seismic design forces recommended by codes implies that the critical regions of inelastically deforming members should have sufficient inelastic deformability to enable the structure to survive without collapse when subjected to several cycles of loading well into the

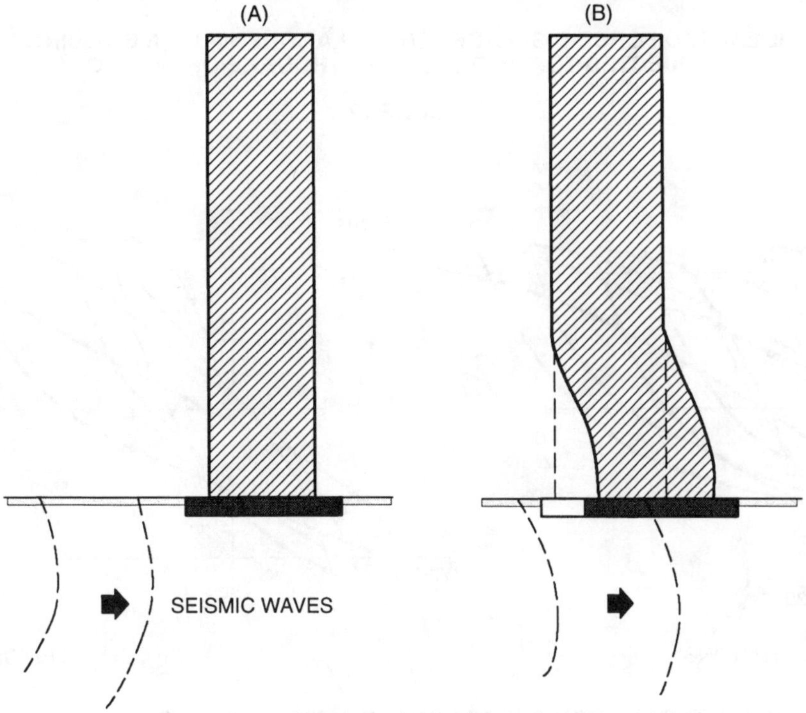

BEHAVIOR OF BUILDINGS DURING AN EARTHQUAKE

FIGURE 11

inelastic range. This means avoiding all forms of brittle failure and achieving adequate inelastic deformability by the yielding of certain localized regions of certain members (or of connections between members) in flexure, shear, or axial action. This is precisely why the materials chapters of codes (Chapters 19, 21, 22 and 23 of the 2000 IBC) contain detailing requirements and other limitations that go hand-in-hand with the code-prescribed seismic forces. The design earthquake forces of the code (Chapter 16 of the IBC) and the detailing requirements and other restrictions of the materials chapters are an integral package.

Figure 12 shows the idealized force-displacement relationship of a particular structure subject to the design earthquake of the 2000 IBC, as defined in Section 1613. On the y-axis are the earthquake-induced forces; along the x-axis are the earthquake-induced displacements. The curve may be thought of as the envelope or the backbone curve of hysteretic force-displacement loops that describe the response of a structure subjected to reversed cyclic displacement histories of the type imposed by earthquake ground motion (see Figure 13.)[28]

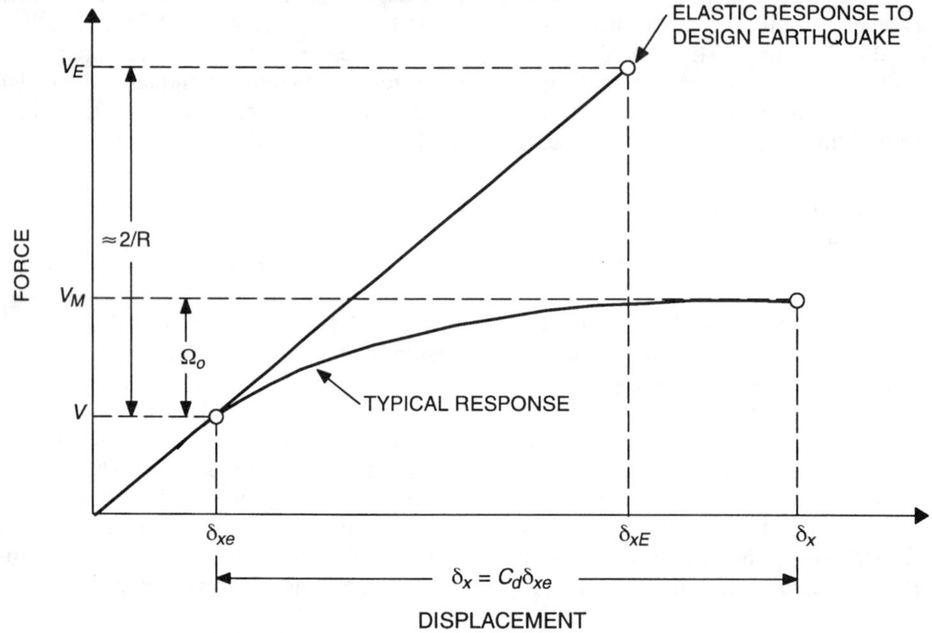

IDEALIZED FORCE-DISPLACEMENT RELATIONSHIP OF A BUILDING SUBJECTED TO THE DESIGN EARTHQUAKE OF THE IBC

FIGURE 12

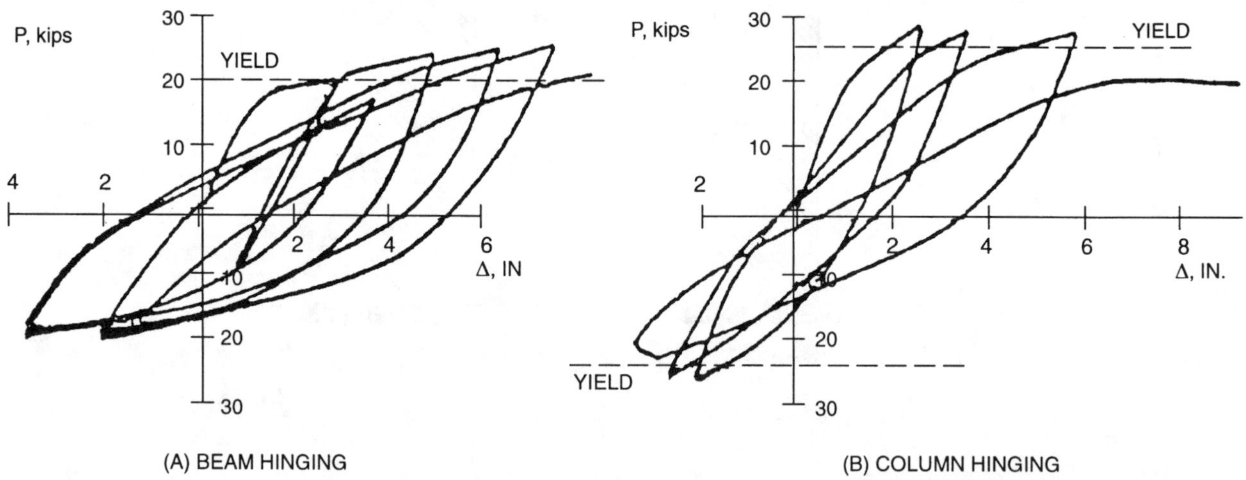

LOAD-DEFLECTION CURVES OF STRUCTURAL SUBASSEMBLIES SUBJECTED TO REVERSED CYCLIC DISPLACEMENTS

FIGURE 13

The quantity, *V*, along the y-axis is the code notation for design base shear, a global force quantity. This *V* is to be distributed along the height of the structure as required by Section 1617.4.3. The distribution results in a series of concentrated lateral forces at the various floor levels. Next, a mathematical model of the structure is to be elastically analyzed under these concentrated lateral forces. The quantity δ_{xe} represents the lateral displacements at various floor levels obtained from this analysis, and Q_E represents the member forces (bending moments, shear forces, axial forces, etc.). As the structure responds inelastically to the design earthquake defined in Section 1613, the lateral displacements at the various floor levels increase from δ_{xe} to $C_d\delta_{xe}$, and the member forces increase from Q_E to $\Omega_o Q_E$. Both the deflection amplification factor, C_d, and the system overstrength coefficient, Ω_o, depend on the structural system used for earthquake resistance, and are given in Table 1617.6. Coefficients V_E and δ_{xE} are the base shear and the lateral displacements at various floor levels corresponding to the hypothetical elastic response of the structure to the design earthquake defined in Section 1613. Figure 12 suggests that an *R*-value of 2 used in design would result in elastic response of a structure to the design earthquake. The basis for this is explained below. The explanation is adapted from the 1999 SEAOC Blue Book, Appendix C.[4]

When a structural system is designed for the seismic force level and details established by its *R* value, there are two behavior properties that allow the structure to perform adequately under the design earthquake ground motion. These are total system resistance and dynamic response modifications. Refer to Figure 14 for the following discussion.

1. **Total system resistance.** Base shear, V_A, is the required design lateral force level for a given system with structural period, T_A, and *R* value for $V_A = V_E'/R$. The path from A to B to E represents the key points on the structure pushover curve.

The actual linear elastic threshold capacity of the structure is the shear, V_B, at point B. This can be larger than the specified strength design value, V_A, due to the actual strength levels of the individual elements that include requirements for the various load combinations; extra system design provisions; contribution from the nonlateral force-resisting system and nonstructural elements; and the as-built sizes and material strengths.

The resistance path from the effective yield at point B to point E represents how the total resistance of the entire system increases as the understressed and redundant members become fully developed with the increasing pushover deformation. The seismic-force amplification factor, Ω_o, provides for an upper-bound load for the design of elements that must resist the maximum demand forces at point E.

2. **Dynamic response modification.** The 5-percent damped multimode base shear demand for the design basis earthquake is $S_{D1}W/T$ along the demand path E' to C. Note that while $S_{D1}W/T$ represents the single-mode response spectrum, the multimode or combined mode response is approximated by the use of the full *W* rather than the effective first mode weight, which would be on the order of 0.7*W*. If the structure were to remain fully linear elastic, without yield at point B, then the resulting base shear demand would have been V_E'. However, since the structure has inelastic behavior from B to E, there are changes in the equivalent dynamic characteristics, that modify the demand response spectrum from path E' - C to E' - E. Along

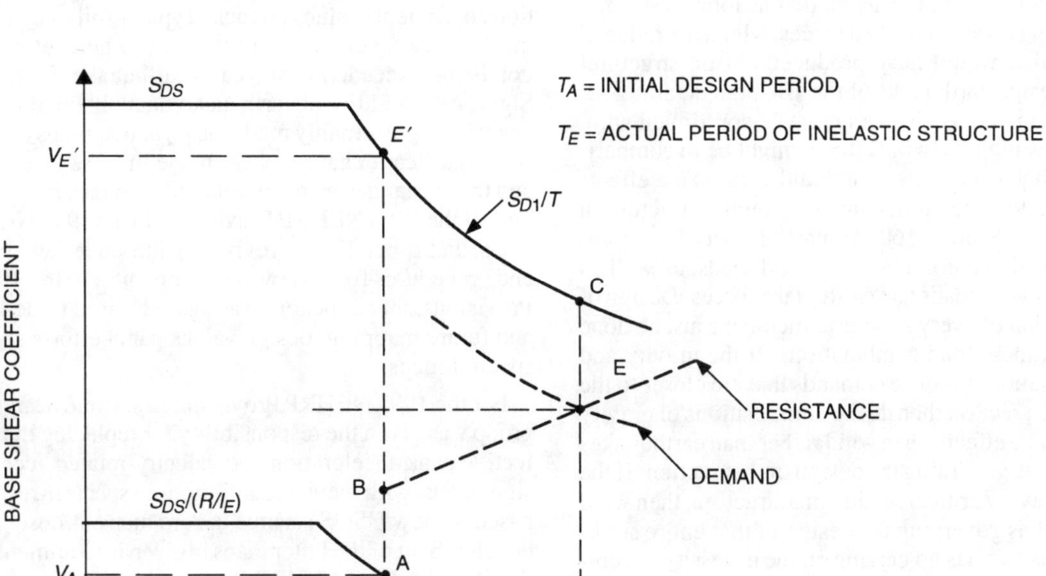

SEISMIC RESISTANCE VERSUS SEISMIC DEMAND

FIGURE 14

the resistance path BE, the period increases from T_A to T_E as the nonlinear softening takes place, and there is a concurrent increase in the equivalent damping. This change in period and damping results in a decrease in demand from V_E' to V_E.

In view of the above, a reduction factor of 2 is appropriate to ensure that the structural system remains essentially elastic for the design earthquake. When the IBC allows a special moment frame system of steel or reinforced concrete to be designed for an R-value of 8, it is allowing that system to be designed for one-quarter of the force level that would have been needed for elastic response to the design earthquake defined in Section 1613. A direct consequence of the relatively low design force level is that a large part of the design earthquake displacement, $C_d\delta_{xe}$, is inelastic [roughly the part equal to $(C_d - 1)\delta_{xe}$]. This part of the displacement has damage associated with it. It is not recovered when the earthquake passes. It is permanent or residual displacement. It is imperative that the inelastic displacements are kept within tolerable limits. For one thing, they should not be so large as to cause collapse of the structure. Also, a structure should preferably be repairable following an earthquake. Both considerations require that the inelastic deformations taking place in the critical regions of inelastically deforming members be kept within their inelastic deformability, as mentioned earlier. The term inelastic deformability, when applied to an entire structure, means the ability of the structure to continue to sustain all or most of its gravity loads while it deforms laterally beyond the onset of inelastic displacements (in a concrete or a masonry structure, this would correspond to yielding of the tension reinforcement in one or more structural members).

It should be obvious from the above that as long as seismic design is done using code-prescribed forces, which are reduced below the level that would have produced elastic structural response to the design earthquake of the IBC, the detailing requirements of the materials chapters must be conformed with, irrespective of how high the wind effects might be in comparison with the earthquake effects. Wind and earthquake effects are not considered to occur simultaneously on the structure in U.S. design practice. Section 1605 contains gravity load combinations, combinations of gravity and wind loads, as well as combinations of gravity loads and earthquake forces. Design of every critical section of every structural member must be done considering all of these load combinations. If the gravity and wind load combinations produce demands that are closer to the design strength of a section than do the combinations of gravity loads and earthquake effects, then wind rather than earthquakes may be thought of as governing the design of that section. If the same happens for every critical section of a structure, then wind may be thought of as governing the design of that entire structure. However, this fact has no bearing on the necessity to comply with the detailing requirements of the materials chapters. Theoretically, it could be argued that if wind effects were larger than unreduced earthquake effects (earthquake effects corresponding to the elastic response of the structure to the design earthquake of the IBC), then the detailing requirements of the code could be dispensed with. However, even that would not be allowed by the IBC. Totally irrespective of the severity of wind effects, the seismic design categories defined in Section 1616 would determine the applicability of the detailing requirements. The seismic design categories are used in the code, irrespective of the severity of wind effects, to determine permissible structural systems, limitations on height and irregularity, those components of the structure that must be designed for seismic resistance, and the type of lateral force analysis that must be performed.

SECTION 1615
EARTHQUAKE LOADS—SITE GROUND MOTION

Two procedures are provided for the determination of ground motion accelerations, represented by response spectra and coefficients derived from these spectra—the general procedure of Section 1615.1 or the site-specific procedure of Section 1615.2. The site-specific procedure is required for use for structures in Site Class F (see Section 1615.1.1).

1615.1 General procedure for determining maximum considered earthquake and design spectral response accelerations. The mapped maximum considered earthquake spectral response acceleration at short periods, S_s and at 1-second period, S_1, for a particular site are to be determined from Figures 1615(1) through 1615(6). Where a site is between contours, straight line interpolation or the value of the higher contour may be used. Figure 1615 is adapted from the Maximum Considered Earthquake Ground Motion Maps 1 through 24 of the 1997 NEHRP Provisions (see Commentary Appendix A to the 1997 NEHRP Provisions).

The Building Seismic Safety Council (BSSC) worked for several years to replace the 1994 NEHRP Provisions Maps 1 through 4, which provided the A_a (effective peak acceleration coefficient) and A_v (effective peak velocity-related acceleration coefficient) values on rock (Type S_1 soil), corresponding to the 474-year average return period (90-percent probability of not being exceeded in 50 years) earthquake, for use in design. Significant additional earthquake data obtained in the past 20 years have presumably made the A_a and A_v maps out-dated. The first significant changes were made in 1982 (see Appendix 3) and these changes were later included in the appendix to Chapter 1 of the 1988 NEHRP Provisions. In the 1991 NEHRP Provisions, that appendix was revised to introduce new spectral maps and procedures for review and comment. For the 1994 NEHRP Provisions, that appendix was again revised to describe recent and future mapping, design values panel efforts and improved spectral maps.

For the 1997 NEHRP Provisions, a seismic design procedure group was given the responsibility for replacing the existing effective peak acceleration and velocity-related acceleration design maps with new ground-motion spectral-response maps based on new USGS seismic hazard maps. A description of the development of the latter maps is given in Commentary Appendix B to the 1997 NEHRP Provisions.

The 1997 NEHRP Provisions include two sets of maps—one for the mapped maximum considered earthquake spectral response accelerations at short periods (S_s) and one at 1-second period (S_1). Each set consists of 12 maps as follows:

- National (Maps 1 and 2)
- California, Nevada (Maps 3 and 4)
- Southern California (Maps 5 and 6)
- San Francisco Bay Area (Maps 7 and 8)

- Pacific Northwest (Maps 9 and 10)
- Intermountain (Maps 11 and 12)
- New Madrid Region (Maps 13 and 14)
- Southeast (Maps 15 and 16)
- Alaska (Maps 17 and 18)
- Hawaii (Maps 19 and 20)
- Puerto Rico, Virgin Islands (Maps 21 and 22)
- Guam, Tutuila (Maps 23 and 24)

Parts 1 through 10 of IBC Figure 1615 correspond to NEHRP Maps 1, 2; 3, 4; 11, 12; 17, 18; 19, 20; 21, 22; and 23, 24, respectively.

Both the USGS probabilistic maps and the 1997 NEHRP/2000 IBC maps for S_S and S_1 are on the USGS web site at *http://geohazards.cr.usgs.gov.eq.* The address *http://geohazards.cr.usgs.gov/eq/html/nehrp/shtml* will take the user directly to the NEHRP maps. Although the maps (in PDF format) can be viewed with various versions of Acrobat Reader, Acrobat 4.0 is recommended. This version eliminates problems such as the elimination of county boundaries encountered with Acrobat 3.0 when printing to some inkjet printers. It also gives greater flexibility in zooming and printing the zoomed areas. In downloading the files, remember that the U.S. map is about 30 inches by 42 inches in size. It may be more convenient to use Acrobat to zoom in to an area of interest and print it. Postscript files are also available. GIS contour files will be added in the future to accommodate those with GIS capability.

Two CDs have also been prepared by USGS in cooperation with BSSC and FEMA.* The first may be called the probabilistic CD and the second, the design CD. The CDs are written to operate on a PC with a Windows 95, 98 and NT operating system. It self-installs and uses the usual mouse and point-and-click approach. The data are interpolated for a specific latitude-longitude or zip code that the user enters. Output for an entry uses the included data base to interpolate for the specific site.

The probabilistic CD includes the national hazard maps in PDF format (a copy of Acrobat Reader 4.0 is also included)—a total of 24 maps. The hazard maps are for peak ground acceleration (PGA) and response spectral ordinates at periods of 0.2 second, 0.3 second and 1.0 second. Each of these maps is for a 10-percent PE (probability of being exceeded) in 50 years, 5-percent PE in 50 years, and 2-percent PE in 50 years. Additionally, the CD includes spectral ordinate data at periods of 0.1 second, 0.5 second, and 2.0 seconds for 10-percent, 5-percent, and 2-percent PE in 50 years. Maps were not prepared for these data. Using this data, uniform hazard response spectra can be prepared at the three different probability levels.

The CD also includes what are called hazard curves for each of the parameters on the CD. These can be used to obtain PGA and the spectral ordinate values at probability levels other than the three standard ones. The data are on a grid of 0.1 degree for the 48 states (0.05 degree in the Southwest). The total number of grid points is over 150,000.

The user may request spectral data for a specific PE or hazard curve data for the site. Tabulated data, which are viewed on-screen, include all of the spectral ordinate values or the hazard curve data for the site, depending on what was requested. These data may be printed in hard copy or saved in an ASCII file. Additionally, the user can request a plot of the spectrum or hazard curve for on-screen viewing. These plots can be printed. The software can also be used to view the various hazard maps by selecting from a list of the maps. Once brought up, the maps can be examined and printed.

The design CD is based on the probabilistic CD, but the data have been modified to incorporate the engineering recommendations of the seismic design procedure group to obtain Maximum Considered Earthquake (MCE) maps. The entire set of maps included with the 1997 NEHRP Provisions, the Rehabilitation Guidelines (FEMA 273),[29] 2000 IBC, and 2000 IRC are included on the CD in PDF format (Acrobat Reader 4.0 is included). Gridded data include the MCE data and the 10 percent in 50-year probabilistic data. Both data sets are required for the Rehabilitation Guidelines.

There are three types of output corresponding to three different design documents—IBC/NEHRP design parameters, Rehabilitation Guidelines design parameters, and IRC design parameters. The same information could be obtained from the maps included on the CD, but it would be much more laborious. Comparison of the map values against the latitude-longitude type of query also provides a good check against input errors such as the wrong latitude-longitude.

The IBC/NEHRP MCE output for a site are the two spectral values required for design. The user can request that site factors be included in the two spectral values. The user can also utilize the program to calculate an MCE response spectrum, with or without site factors. This response spectrum can be viewed on screen and printed. The three types of output are similar to those of the probabilistic CD. Soil factors can be calculated and included in the calculations by simply selecting the site class, the program then calculates the soil factor. In all cases, the user can access the appropriate maps from the software, zoom in for closer examination and print an area.

A lot of effort has gone into these two CDs to make them as user-friendly as possible, give the user the necessary data and still recognize that the application of the numbers in a design procedure is ultimately the responsibility of the designer. The intent of USGS, BSSC and FEMA is to simplify and reduce the time required for at least part of an already complex process.

The design CD is available with the IBC itself from the three model code groups. The probabilistic CD is available from USGS, but not BSSC and/or the code groups because it is not modified for engineering purposes. The CDs are not distributed by FEMA.

1615.1.1 Site class definitions. Appendix 4 of this publication should be referred to for background on consideration of site soil characteristics in seismic design. The 1994 NEHRP Provisions defined six soil profile types as follows:

A. Hard rock with measured shear wave velocity, $\overline{V}_s >$ 5,000 feet/second (1,500 meters/second)

*Information concerning the CDs was provided by E.V. Leyendecker of USGS on the SEAOC list server.

B. Rock with 2,500 feet/second < $\overline{V}_S \le$ 5,000 feet/second (760 meters/second < $\overline{V}_S$ < 1,500 meters/second)

C. Very dense soil and soft rock with 1,200 feet/second < $\overline{V}_S$ < 2,500 feet/second (360 meters/second < $\overline{V}_S$ < 760 meters/second) or with either $\overline{N}$ > 50 or $\overline{S}_u$ > 2,000 psf (1,000 kPa)

D. Stiff soil with 600 feet/second $\le \overline{V}_S$ < 1,200 feet/second (180 meters/second < $\overline{V}_S$ < 360 meters/second) or with either 15 $\le \overline{N} \le$ 50 or 1,000 pounds per square foot $\le \overline{S}_u$ < 2,000 pounds per square foot (50 kPa < $\overline{S}_u$ < 100 kPa)

E. A soil profile with $\overline{V}_S$ < 600 feet/second (180 meters/second) or a profile with more than 10 feet (3 meters) of soft clay defined as soil with PI > 20, $w \ge 40$ percent, and $\overline{S}_u$ < 500 psf (25 kPa).

F. Soils requiring site-specific evaluations:

1. Soils vulnerable to potential failure or collapse under seismic loading such as liquefiable soils, quick and highly sensitive clays, and collapsible weakly cemented soils.
2. Peats and/or highly organic clays [H > 10 feet (3 m) of peat and/or highly organic clay]
3. Very high plasticity clays [H > 25 feet (8 m) with PI > 75]
4. Very thick soft/medium stiff clays [H > 120 feet (36 m)]

In the above,

H = thickness of soil.

$\overline{N}$ = average field standard penetration resistance for the top 100 feet (30 meters) of soil.

PI = plasticity index of soil (ASTM D4318-93).

$\overline{S}_u$ = average undrained shear strength in top 100 feet (30 meters) of soil (ASTM D2166-91 or ASTM D2850-87).

$\overline{V}_S$ = average shear wave velocity in top 100 feet (30 meters) of soil.

w = moisture content of soil in percent (ASTM D 2216-92).

The above classification was adopted and incorporated into Table 16-J of the 1997 UBC. In the process of adoption, one change was made. The above definition of Soil Profile Type E became a footnote to Table 16-J. In the table itself, Soil Profile Type E was defined as a profile with $\overline{V}_S$ < 600 feet/second or $\overline{N}_{CH}$ < 15 or $\overline{S}_u$ < 1,000 pounds per square foot, where $\overline{N}_{CH}$ = average standard penetration resistance for cohesionless soil layers for the top 100 feet (30 m) of soil. Table 1615.1.1 of the IBC is identical to Table 16-J of the 1997 UBC, except that the footnote mentioned above has been incorporated into the table itself.

The 1994 NEHRP Provisions defined a default site class for use in design by requiring that "when the soil properties are not known in sufficient detail to determine the Soil Profile Type, Type D shall be used. Soil Profile Type E or F need not be assumed unless the regulatory agency determines that Type E or F may be present at the site or in the event that Type E or F is established by geotechnical data." This requirement has been retained in the 1997 NEHRP Provisions. The 2000 IBC includes a variation of this requirement in that "when the soil properties are not known in sufficient detail to determine the site class, Site Class D shall be used unless the building official determines that Site Class E or F soil is likely to be present." This is to be compared with the default soil classification in prior design practice, as represented by the 1994 UBC where "in locations where the soil properties are not known in sufficient detail to determine the soil profile type, soil profile S_3 shall be used. Soil profile S_4 need not be used unless the building official determines that soil profile S_4 may be present at the site or in the event that soil profile S_4 is established by geotechnical data, in which case soil profile S_4 will be used."

The default site class of the 2000 IBC is more important than ever, because Table 1615.1.1 requires 100-foot (30 m) borings as the basis of soil classification.

There is no direct correlation between the site classification given by Table 1615.1.1 and the prior S_1 through S_4 soil classifications. An approximate correlation is attempted in Table 9. The table is intended solely to give the reader a rough idea of the correlation between the old and the new classifications. It must not be used for any other purpose.

The soil profile name/generic description column was added to Table 1615.1.1 between the first draft and the final draft of the IBC as the result of a code change submitted by the Structural Engineers Association of Washington (SEAW). These generic descriptions are in the 1997 UBC, but not in the 1997 NEHRP or the 1994 NEHRP Provisions. Where the soil shear wave velocity, $\overline{V}_S$, is not known, Section 1615.1.1 permits site class to be determined from standard penetration resistance, or from soil undrained shear strength, $\overline{S}_u$. SEAW, as a part of their code change, proposed that where the soil shear wave velocity is not known, site class may be determined from the generic description of Table 1615.1.1. The following is quoted from the Reason for Proposal submitted by SEAW:

> As currently written, the determination of site class requires specific geotechnical site investigation and data to a depth of 100 feet for all buildings. In lieu of this site-specific information, the classification defaults to either Site Class D or E, depending on the ruling of the building official. In actual practice, geotechnical investigations are rarely computed to depths of 100 feet. As a result, for most buildings, the building official will be required to deem a site either D or E, and the remaining classes will not be used. The building official may be required to make this determination based on the limited site-specific information specified in Section 1802.
>
> The addition of generic descriptions allows the geotechnical engineer to make a determination of site class based on available site-specific data and professional judgment. This approach removes the burden of site classification from the building official, and has been used successfully in the seismic provisions of building codes for many years.

The SEAW proposal was not approved (although the generic description column was added to Table 1615.1.1). The following language was approved instead for inclusion in Section 1615.1.1: "Where site-specific data are not available to a depth of 100 feet (30 480 mm), appropriate soil properties are permitted to be estimated by the registered design professional preparing the soils report based on known geologic conditions."

1615.1.2 Site coefficients and adjusted maximum considered earthquake spectral response acceleration parameters. Refer to Appendix 4 of this publication. The short- and long-period amplification factors implied by the Loma Prieta strong-motion data and related calculations for the same earthquake by Joyner et al.[30] as well as modeling results at the 0.1g ground acceleration level provided the basis for the consensus values of site coefficients F_a and F_v provided in 1994 NEHRP Tables 1.4.2.3a and 1.4.2.3b, reproduced here as Tables 10 and 11.

Site coefficients F_a and F_v of the 1994 NEHRP are analogous to C_a/Z and C_v/Z, respectively, of the 1997 UBC. The values of C_a/Z and C_v/Z, calculated from the 1997 UBC Tables 16-Q and 16-R, respectively, are given in Tables 12 and 13, respectively. The Seismic Zone 4 values include the near-source factors N_a and N_v that are not part of the 1994 NEHRP, the 1997 NEHRP, or the 2000 IBC. The factors are determined by the closest distance from a site to known seismic sources that are capable of generating large-magnitude earthquakes and the types of those seismic sources. Three types of seismic sources are defined. Seismic Source Type A consists of faults that are capable of producing large-magnitude earthquakes (moment magnitudes $\geq$ 7.0) and that have a high rate of seismic activity (slip rate $\geq$ 5 millimeters/year). Seismic Source Type C consists of faults that are not capable of generating large-magnitude earthquakes (moment magnitude < 6.5) and that have a relatively low seismic activity (slip rate $\leq$ 2 millimeter/year). Seismic Source Type B consists of all faults other than Type A and C. The acceleration-dependent Near-Source Factor, N_a, has values of 1.5, 1.2 and 1.0, respectively, at distances of $\leq$ 2 kilometers, 5 kilometers and $\geq$ 10 kilometers away from a Seismic Source Type A. It has values of 1.3 and 1.0 at distances of $\leq$ 2 kilometers and 5 kilometers away from a Seismic Source Type B. The velocity-dependent Near-Source Factor, N_v, has values of 2.0, 1.6, 1.2 and 1.0 at distances of $\leq$ 2 kilometers, 5 kilometers, 10 kilometers and $\geq$15 kilometers away from Seismic Source Type A. It has values of 1.6, 1.2 and 1.0 at distances of $\leq$ 2 kilometers, 5 kilometers and 10 kilometers away from a Seismic Source Type B. At distances other than those specifically mentioned, N_a and N_v may be established by linear interpolation of the values given.

TABLE 9. SOIL CLASSIFICATIONS OF THE 2000 IBC (AND THE 1997 UBC) VERSUS SOIL CLASSIFICATIONS OF EARLIER CODES

A	Hard rock	S_1 Rock
B	Rock	S_1 Rock
C	Very dense soil or soft rock	S_1, S_2
D	Stiff soil	S_2, S_3
E	Soft soil	S_3, S_4 Soft soil
F	Soils requiring site-specific evaluations	S_4 Soft soil

TABLE 10. VALUES OF F_a AS A FUNCTION OF SITE CLASS AND SHAKING INTENSITY

	SHAKING INTENSITY				
SITE CLASS	$A_a \leq 0.1$	$A_a = 0.2$	$A_a = 0.3$	$A_a = 0.4$	$A_a \geq 0.5$
A	0.8	0.8	0.8	0.8	0.8
B	1.0	1.0	1.0	1.0	1.0
C	1.2	1.2	1.1	1.0	1.0
D	1.6	1.4	1.2	1.1	1.0
E	2.5	1.7	1.2	0.9	a
F	a	a	a	a	a

NOTE: Use straight line interpolation for intermediate values of A_a.
a. Site-specific geotechnical investigation and dynamic site-response analyses required.

TABLE 11. VALUES OF F_V AS A FUNCTION OF SITE CLASS AND SHAKING INTENSITY

	SHAKING INTENSITY				
SITE CLASS	$A_v \leq 0.1$	$A_v = 0.2$	$A_v = 0.3$	$A_v = 0.4$	$A_v \geq 0.5$
A	0.8	0.8	0.8	0.8	0.8
B	1.0	1.0	1.0	1.0	1.0
C	1.7	1.6	1.5	1.4	1.3
D	2.4	2.0	1.8	1.6	1.5
E	3.5	3.2	2.8	2.4	a
F	a	a	a	a	a

NOTE: Use straight line interpolation for intermediate values of A_v.
a. Site-specific geotechnical investigation and dynamic site-response analyses required.

TABLE 12. GROUND MOTION AMPLIFICATION DUE TO SOIL: 1997 UBC SEISMIC COEFFICIENT, C_a/Z

SOIL PROFILE TYPE	SEISMIC ZONE FACTOR-Z				
	$Z = 0.075$	$Z = 0.15$	$Z = 0.2$	$Z = 0.3$	$Z = 0.4$
S_A	0.8	0.8	0.8	0.8	0.8 N_a
S_B	1.0	1.0	1.0	1.0	1.0 N_a
S_C	1.2	1.2	1.2	1.1	1.0 N_a
S_D	1.6	1.5	1.4	1.2	1.1 N_a
S_E	2.5	2.0	1.7	1.2	0.9 N_a
S_F					

TABLE 13. GROUND MOTION AMPLIFICATION DUE TO SOIL: 1997 UBC SEISMIC COEFFICIENT, C_v/Z

SOIL PROFILE TYPE	SEISMIC ZONE FACTOR-Z				
	$Z = 0.075$	$Z = 0.15$	$Z = 0.2$	$Z = 0.3$	$Z = 0.4$
S_A	0.8	0.8	0.8	0.8	0.8 N_V
S_B	1.0	1.0	1.0	1.0	1.0 N_V
S_C	1.7	1.7	1.6	1.5	1.4 N_V
S_D	2.4	2.1	2.0	1.8	1.6 N_V
S_E	3.5	3.3	3.2	2.8	2.4 N_V
S_F					

IBC Table 1615.1.2 (1) is derived directly from 1994 NEHRP Table 1.4.2.3a by converting the ground motion parameter from A_a to S_s, the mapped MCE spectral acceleration at short periods. The conversion is based on $S_s = 2.5\ A_a$. Table 1615.1.2 (2) is likewise derived from 1994 NEHRP Table 1.4.2.3b by converting the ground motion parameter from A_v to S_1, the mapped MCE spectral acceleration at 1-second period. The conversion is based on $S_1 = A_v$. No near-source factors are incorporated into the IBC or the corresponding NEHRP tables because the mapped values of A_a, A_v in 1994 NEHRP and those of S_s and S_1 in the 1997 NEHRP and 2000 IBC are not artificially truncated—these parameters attain high values close to known seismic sources that are capable of generating large-magnitude earthquakes.

It should be noted that the IBC requires site-specific geotechnical investigation and dynamic site response analyses for Soil Profile Type E in areas having $S_s \geq 1.25$g or $S_1 \geq 0.5$g. The 1997 UBC does not require such investigation or analyses for Soil Profile Type E in Seismic Zone 4.

For the 2000 NEHRP Provisions, a number of important modifications have been proposed to the equivalent of Tables 1615.1.2 (1) and 1615.1.2 (2). First, values of site factors for the highest accelerations for Site Class E soils ($F_a = 0.9$, $F_v = 2.4$) are placed in the tables so that site-specific studies are no longer required for Type E soils regardless of level of shaking. The values are considered to be reasonably conservative. Second, the footnote to the equivalent of Table 1615.1.2 (1) is expanded to except liquefiable soils of Site Class F from the requirement to conduct site-specific studies to determine F_a values. Rather, F_a can be taken equal to the value that would be determined for these soils in the absence of liquefaction. (Typically, these soils would be in Site Class D or E.) The reason for this exception is that any amplifying effect of soil liquefaction on ground motion response spectra is expected to be in the long-period range (thus affecting F_v), and short-period response spectra will tend to be deamplified or unchanged by liquefaction. In addition, commentary guidance is provided on how to determine the response of Type F soils for which values of site factors F_a and F_v are not given in Tables 1615.1.2 (1) and 1615.1.2 (2) and for which the note to the tables requires that "site-specific geotechnical investigation and dynamic site response analyses shall be performed." This draft commentary is reproduced, with permission from the Building Seismic Safety Council (BSSC), in Appendix 4 of this publication, for the convenience of the reader. The material has been developed by Technical Subcommittee 3 of the Provisions Update Committee of the BSSC and is being balloted for potential inclusion in the 2000 NEHRP Provisions.

1615.1.3 Design spectral response acceleration parameters. Five-percent damped design spectral response accelerations at short periods, S_{DS}, and at 1-second period, S_{D1}, are equal to two-thirds S_{MS} and two-thirds S_{M1}, respectively. In other words, the design ground motion is 1/1.5 or two-thirds times the soil-modified maximum considered earthquake ground motion. This is in recognition of the inherent margin contained in the NEHRP Provisions that would make collapse unlikely under one and one-half times the design level ground motion (see Appendix 3 of this publication). Table 14 summarizes the derivation of the design quantities S_{DS} and S_{D1}.

TABLE 14. DESIGN GROUND MOTION OF THE 1997 NEHRP AND 2000 IBC

S_S	=	MCE spectral acceleration in the short-period range for Site Class B.
S_1	=	MCE spectral acceleration at 1-second period for Site Class B.
S_{MS}	=	F_aS_S, MCE spectral acceleration in the short-period range adjusted for site class effects.
S_{M1}	=	F_vS_1, MCE spectral acceleration at 1-second period adjusted for site class effects.
S_{DS}	=	$^2/_3\ S_{MS}$, spectral acceleration in the short-period range for the design ground motion.
S_{D1}	=	$^2/_3\ S_{M1}$, spectral acceleration at 1-second period for the design ground motion.

1615.1.4 General procedure response spectrum. This provides a general method for obtaining a 5-percent damped response spectrum from the site design acceleration response parameters S_{DS} and S_{D1}. This spectrum is based on that proposed by Newmark and Hall[31] as a series of three curves representing the short-period range, a region of constant spectral-response acceleration; the long-period range, a region of constant spectral-response velocity; and the very long-period range, a region of constant spectral-response displacement. Response acceleration at any period in the short-period range is equal to the design spectral-response acceleration at short periods, S_{DS}:

$$S_a = S_{DS}$$

The spectral-response acceleration at any point in the constant velocity range can be obtained from the relationship:

$$S_a = \frac{S_{D1}}{T}$$

The constant displacement domain of the response spectrum is not included in the generalized response spectrum because relatively few structures have a period long enough to fall into this range.

The ramp building up to the flat top of the design spectrum is defined by specifying that the spectral-response acceleration at zero period is equal to 40 percent of the spectral-response acceleration corresponding to the flat top, S_{DS}, and that the period T_0 at which the ramp ends is 20 percent of the period, T_s, at which the constant acceleration and the constant velocity portions of the spectra meet. That period,

$$T_s = S_{D1}/S_{DS}$$

is solely a function of the seismicity and the soil characteristics at the site of the structure. It also serves as the dividing line between short- and long-period structures.

1615.1.5 Site classification for seismic design. The definitions of average soil properties of Section 1615.1.5 and the Steps for Classifying a Site of Section 1615.1.5.1 first appeared in the 1994 NEHRP Provisions. The material was adopted virtually unmodified into the 1997 UBC, was retained in the 1997 NEHRP Provisions, and was adopted into the 2000 IBC.

In the 1994 NEHRP, 1997 NEHRP and 2000 IBC, "N_i is the standard penetration resistance (ASTM D 1586-84) not to exceed 100 blows per foot as directly measured in the field without corrections." This definition, unlike the corresponding 1997 UBC definition, is quite specific.

In the 1994 NEHRP, 1997 NEHRP and 2000 IBC, "S_{ui} is the undrained shear strength in pounds per square foot (kPa), not to exceed 5,000 pounds per square foot (240 kPa), ASTM D 2166-91 or D 2850-87." Again, this definition, unlike the corresponding 1997 UBC definition, is quite specific.

It should be noted that Table 1615.1.5 is really a part of Table 1615.1.1, except that Table 1615.1.1 does not include the note below Table 1615.1.5. Table 1615.1.5 was part of the 1994 NEHRP Provisions.

1615.2 Site-specific procedure for determining ground motion accelerations. This specifically enumerates the five significant aspects that must be accounted for in an investigation undertaken to determine site-specific ground motion: 1) regional seismicity and geology; 2) the expected recurrence rates and maximum magnitudes of events on known source zones; 3) the location of the site with respect to these source zones; 4) near source effects, if any; and 5) subsurface site characteristics and conditions.

Section 1615.2.1 defines a probabilistic, site-specific maximum considered earthquake acceleration-response spectrum. Section 1615.2.3 defines a deterministic, site-specific maximum considered earthquake response spectrum. Section 1615.2.2 defines an acceleration-response spectrum that represents a deterministic limit on maximum considered earthquake ground motion. The site-specific maximum considered earthquake ground-motion spectrum is required to be taken as the lesser of the probabilistic maximum considered earthquake ground motion of Section 1615.2.1 or the deterministic maximum considered earthquake ground motion of Section 1615.2.3, subject to a minimum of the deterministic limit ground motion of Section 1615.2.2 (see Exception to Section 1615.2.1 and Figure 15).30

1615.2.1 Probabilistic maximum considered earthquake. This defines the probabilistic maximum considered earthquake acceleration-response spectrum as corresponding to a 2-percent within 50 years. The probabilistic maximum considered earthquake spectral-response acceleration at any time, S_{aM}, is to be taken from this spectrum. It is worthwhile to point out that the same PE over the same period of time is used in the generalized procedure for determining maximum considered earthquake spectral response accelerations.

1615.2.2 Deterministic limit on maximum considered earthquake ground motion. This limit is represented by the acceleration-response spectrum of Figure 1615.2.2, where the coefficients F_a and F_v are as given in Tables 1615.1.2 (1) and 1615.1.2 (2), respectively. For this spectrum, the value of the mapped short-period spectral-response acceleration, S_s, is taken as 1.5g and the value of the mapped spectral response acceleration at 1-second period, S_1, is taken as 0.6g.

1615.2.3 Deterministic maximum considered earthquake ground motion. The median spectral-response accelerations, S_{aM}, at all periods resulting from a characteristic earthquake on any known active fault within the region, amplified by a factor of 1.5, define the deterministic maximum considered earthquake acceleration-response spectrum. The median values are increased by 50 percent to represent maximum considered earthquake ground motion values. The deterministic maximum considered earthquake spectral-response acceleration, S_{aM}, is to be taken from this spectrum.

1615.2.4 Site specific design ground motion. The design spectral-response acceleration, S_a, at any period is to be taken as two-thirds of the maximum considered earthquake response spectral acceleration, S_{aM}, at that period, subject to a minimum of 80 percent of the design spectral-response acceleration, S_a, at the same period determined from the general response spectrum of Figure 1615.1.4. The two-thirds factor is in recognition of the inherent margin contained in the NEHRP Provisions that would make collapse unlikely under 1.5 times the design level ground motion.

1615.2.5 Design spectral response coefficients. The value of S_a, as defined in Section 1615.2.4, at a period of 0.2 second,

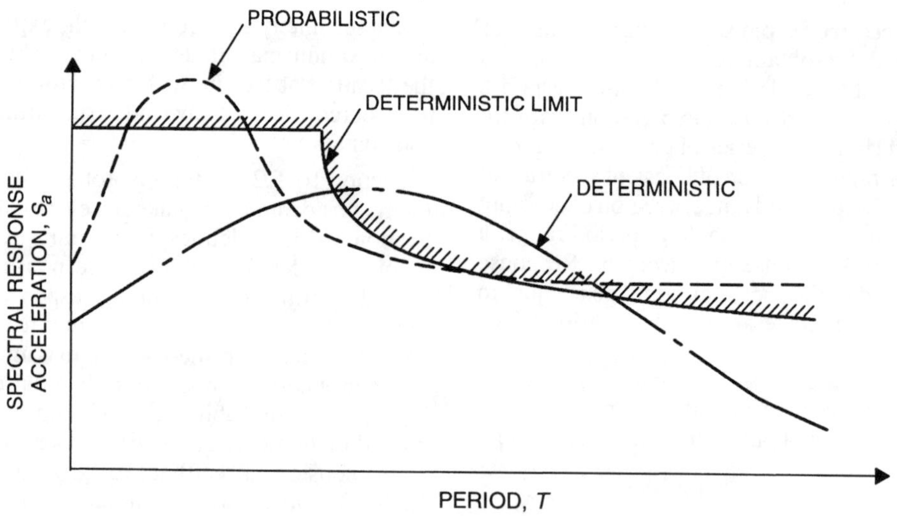

SITE-SPECIFIC MAXIMUM CONSIDERED EARTHQUAKE RESPONSE SPECTRUM

FIGURE 15

divided by g, is to be taken as the design spectral-response acceleration coefficient at short periods, S_{DS}. The value of S_a, as defined in Section 1615.2.4, at a period of 1 second, divided by g, is to be taken as the design spectral-response acceleration coefficient at a period of 1 second, S_{D1}. Neither value is to be taken as less than 80 percent of the corresponding value obtained from Figure 1615.1.4.

SECTION 1616
EARTHQUAKE LOADS—CRITERIA SELECTION

Comparable to 1997 UBC Section 1629, Criteria Selection, This requires each structure to be assigned to a seismic design category, which is not used in the UBC. This item is discussed further under Section 1616.6.3.

1616.1 Structural design criteria. This is comparable to 1997 UBC Section 1629.1, Basis for Design, but the contents are not necessarily the same. IBC criteria include complete lateral- and vertical-force-resisting systems, the assumption that design ground motion can occur along any horizontal direction, and continuous load path. Both sets of criteria address adequate strength, stiffness, and energy dissipation capacity to withstand the design earthquake ground motions within the prescribed deformation limits.

1616.2 Seismic use groups and occupancy importance factors. Seismic Use Group (SUG) is a term adopted into the IBC from the 1997 NEHRP Provisions. In earlier editions of the NEHRP Provisions, the term "Seismic Hazard Exposure Group" was used to describe the categorization of structures by occu-pancy or use. The name "Seismic Use Group" was adopted into the 1997 NEHRP Provisions as being more descriptive of what the categorization is intended to accomplish. Seismic hazard relates to the severity and frequency of ground motion expected to affect a building. Since the buildings contained in the various groups are spread across regions of varying seismicity, from high to low hazard, the groups do not really relate to hazard. Rather, the groups are used to establish design criteria intended to produce the desired levels of performance in design earthquake events, depending on the occupancy or use of a structure. The following paragraph from the commentary to the 1997 NEHRP Provisions is worth reproducing.

> Historically, building code occupancy classifications were based primarily on fire-safety considerations. It was concluded, however, [in the development of the ATC 3-06 document, the predecessor to the NEHRP Provisions] that these traditional classifications would at least in part reflect some considerations contrary to good seismic design. Thus, it was decided that a new approach was needed for defining occupancy exposure to seismic hazards based on a commonality of conditions proposed for the use of a building facility or space. These conditions involve evaluations of parameters consisting of, but not limited to, the number, age, and condition of the persons normally expected to be within or without the immediate environs of the building; the size, height and area of the building; the spacing of the building relative to public rights-of-way over which the designer has no control relative to the future number of persons exposed to risk by the buildings; and the varying degree of built-in or brought-in hazards based on the possible use of the building. Accordingly, early in the development of the preliminary version of the NEHRP Provisions occupancy types were regrouped and expanded to cover the range of factors critical to seismic safety in terms of loss of life. The expanded classification types were derived from the 1973 UBC.

The IBC, instead of directly adopting the seismic use group definitions of the NEHRP Provisions, has chosen to refer to the classification of buildings and other structures of Table 1604.5. Categories I and IV of Table 1604.5 constitute SUG I, while Categories II and III constitute SUGs II and III, respectively.

The classification of buildings and other structures in Table 1604.5 is close to that of Table 1-1 of ASCE 7-98, except that IBC Categories I, II, III and IV correspond to ASCE 7 Categories II, III, IV and I, respectively. ASCE 7, in its 1995 edition, adopted a category numbering that reflects a progression of consequences of failure from lowest hazard to human life (Category I) to highest (Category IV). This system has not been adopted into the IBC.

According to the commentary to ASCE 7-95, "Table 1-1 makes the classification of buildings and other structures according to failure consequences reasonably consistent for all environmental loads." The occupancy classifications given in ASCE 7-95, left unchanged in ASCE 7-98, result from an attempt to reconcile the classification in the previous edition of the standard (ASCE 7-93) and the seismic hazard exposure group classifications from the NEHRP Provisions (1994 edition) upon which the seismic provisions of ASCE 7-95 are based. The intent was to have only one occupancy classification system that would be independent of load.

1616.2.1 Seismic Use Group I. This comprises Categories I and IV of Table 1604.5. Category IV contains buildings and other structures that represent a low hazard to human life in the event of failure either because they have a small number of occupants or because they have a limited period of exposure to extreme environmental loads. Three examples given in the IBC, as in ASCE 7-95 and ASCE 7-98, are agricultural facilities, certain temporary facilities and minor storage facilities. Category I contains all occupancies other than those in Categories II, III and IV and are sometimes referred to as ordinary for the purpose of risk exposure.

1616.2.2 Seismic Use Group II. This use group is the same as Category II of Table 1604.5, except that the building official is permitted to assign a structure to this use group at his discretion. The detailed items listed under this category in Table 1604.5 are the same as those listed under Category III of ASCE 7-95 Table 1-1, with two exceptions:

1. The IBC bullet item, "Any other occupancy with an occupant load greater than 5,000," is not in ASCE 7;
2. The ASCE 7-95 bullet item, "Power-generating stations and other public utility facilities not included in Category IV," is expanded to include "water treatment for potable water, waste water treatment facilities."

The above additions are adopted from the 1997 NEHRP Provisions.

It may be noted that ASCE 7-98 chose to make some important changes in Category III (IBC Category II) items. Buildings and other structures with elementary school, secondary school or day-care facilities with a capacity greater than 150 were placed under Category III (IBC Category II), whereas the corresponding capacity limit in the 2000 IBC and in ASCE 7-95 is 250. Also, ASCE 7-98 chose to furnish the following examples of "Buildings and other structures containing sufficient quantities of toxic, explosive or other hazardous substances to be dangerous to the public if released":

- Petrochemical facilities.
- Fuel-storage facilities.
- Manufacturing or storage facilities for hazardous chemicals.
- Manufacturing or storage facilities for explosives.

Buildings and other structures normally falling into Category III are permitted by ASCE 7-98 to be classified into Category II (IBC Category I) if means (secondary containment) are provided to contain the toxic or explosive substances in the case of a spill or to contain a blast. Buildings and other structures containing toxic or explosive substances could also be classified as Category II (IBC Category I) for hurricane wind loads when mandatory procedures are used to reduce the risk of release of hazardous substances during and immediately after these predictable extreme loadings.

The above ASCE 7-98 modifications may become part of future editions of the IBC.

1616.2.3 Seismic Use Group III. This use group is the same as Category III of Table 1604.5, except that the building official is once again empowered to assign a structure to this use group at his discretion. The detailed items listed under this category in Table 1604.5 are the same as those listed under Category IV of ASCE 7-95 Table 1-1, with the following exceptions:

1. The ASCE 7-95 bullet item, "Communications centers and other facilities required for emergency response," was expanded to "Designated emergency preparedness, communication and operation centers and other facilities required for emergency response."
2. The ASCE 7-95 bullet item, "Power-generating stations and other public utility facilities required in an emergency," was modified to ". . . required as emergency back-up facilities for Category III structures."
3. The following bullet item, not found in ASCE 7-95, has been added, "Structures containing highly toxic materials as defined by Section 307 where the quantity of the material exceeds the exempt amounts of Table 307.7(2)." This is a modification of the 1997 NEHRP item: "Structures containing sufficient quantities of toxic or explosive substances deemed to be hazardous to the public."
4. The following item, not included in ASCE 7-95, has been adopted from the 1997 NEHRP Provisions, "Aviation control towers, air-traffic control centers and emergency aircraft hangars."
5. Another item, not found in ASCE 7-95, has been added from the 1997 Provisions, "Water treatment facilities required to maintain water pressure for fire suppression."

It is left to the discretion of the authority having jurisdiction to determine which structures are required for post-earthquake response and recovery. This is emphasized with the term "designated" before some of the structures listed under Category III.

ASCE 7-98 chose to add Items 4 and 5 above from the 1997 NEHRP Provisions to its list of Category IV (IBC Category III) structures. It also added the following new item: "Ancillary structures (including, but not limited to communication towers, fuel-storage tanks, cooling towers, electrical substation structures, fire water-storage tanks, or other structures housing or supporting water or other fire-suppression materials or equipment) required for operation of Category IV structures during an emergency."

The second paragraph of Section 1616.2.3, adopted from the 1997 NEHRP Provisions, establishes the requirement for access protection for SUG III structures. There is a need for ingress and egress at structures that are essential post-earthquake facilities. This requires consideration in the siting and design of such structures.

1616.2.4 Multiple occupancies. This is adopted directly from the 1997 NEHRP Provisions. For a building with multiple uses, the 1988 edition of the NEHRP Provisions required that the building be assigned the classification of the highest group occupying 15 percent or more of the total building area. This was changed in the 1991 edition to require the building to be assigned to the highest group present. These requirements were further modified subsequently to allow different portions of a structure to be assigned different seismic use groups provided the higher group is not negatively impacted by the lower group.

ASCE 7-95 and ASCE 7-98 have a slightly different approach to multiple occupancies based on structural systems. When a building has multiple uses or occupancies, the relationship between the uses of various parts of the building and the independence of the structural systems for those various parts requires examination. The classification for each independent structural system of a multiple-use building is required to be that of the highest usage group in any part of the building, which is dependent on that basic structural system.

1616.3 Determination of seismic design category. This creates six design categories that are key to establishing the design requirements for any building based on its occupancy or use (seismic use group) and on the level of expected soil-modified seismic ground motion. Once the seismic design category for a building is established, many other requirements such as detailing, quality-assurance plans and height limitations, specialized requirements, and change of use are related to it.

In the UBC, the seismic zone in which a structure is located determines the permissible structural systems, including the level of detailing required for structural members and joints that are part of the lateral-force-resisting system and for the structural components that are not, limitations on height of structure and structural irregularity, the type of lateral load analysis that must be performed as the basis of design, as well as nonstructural component requirements. The 1994 NEHRP provisions and prior editions of the NEHRP Provisions, as well as the predecessor document, ATC 3-06, used a seismic performance category (SPC) for the above purposes. The SPC was a function of occupancy (seismic hazard exposure group) and of the seismic risk at the site of a structure in the form of the peak velocity-related acceleration coefficient, A_v (Table 15). Through this device, a hospital in an area of moderate seismic risk was required to be detailed like, and be subject to the same restrictions as, an office building in an area of high seismic risk.

The 2000 IBC and the 1997 NEHRP Provisions have replaced the SPC with a seismic design category, which plays the same role that the SPC used to play. While the desired performance of a building under the design earthquake was one consideration used to determine which category a building should be assigned to, it was not the only factor. The seismic hazard at the site was, in fact, the prime consideration that affected the categorization of a building. The name was changed to seismic design category (SDC) to better represent the use of these categories, which is to determine the specific design requirements.

The 1997 NEHRP Provisions took the position that the peak velocity-related acceleration coefficient, A_v, used to determine the SPC of a building, does not adequately represent the damage potential of earthquakes on sites with soil conditions other than rock. Consequently, the 1997 NEHRP Provisions have proceeded to make the SDC a function of occupancy (SUG) and of soil-modified seismic risk at the site of the structure in the form of the design spectral-response acceleration at short periods, S_{DS}, and the design spectral-response acceleration of the 1-second period, S_{D1}. For a structure, the seismic design category needs to be determined twice—first as a function of S_{DS} by IBC Table 1616.3 (1) and a second time as a function of S_{D1} by IBC Table 1616.3(1). The more severe category governs.

Seismic Design Category A applies to structures, irrespective of their occupancy or use, in regions where anticipated ground motions are minor, even for very long return periods.

Seismic Design Category B includes SUG I and II structures in regions where moderately destructive ground shaking is anticipated.

Seismic Design Category C includes SUG III structures where moderately destructive ground shaking may occur as well as SUG I and II structures in regions with somewhat more severe ground shaking potential.

Seismic Design Category D includes structures of SUGs I, II and III located in regions expected to experience destructive ground shaking, but not located close to major active faults.

Seismic Design Categories E and F are defined in the footnotes to Tables 1616.3-1 and 1616.3-2. SDC E includes SUG I and II structures in regions located close to major active faults and SDC F includes SUG III structures in those locations.

TABLE 15. SEISMIC PERFORMANCE CATEGORIES PRIOR TO THE 1997 NEHRP PROVISIONS

VALUE OF A_V	SEISMIC HAZARD EXPOSURE GROUP		
	I	II	III
$0.20 \leq A_V$	D	D	E
$0.15 \leq A_V < 0.20$	C	D	D
$0.10 \leq A_V < 0.15$	C	C	C
$0.05 \leq A_V < 0.10$	B	B	C
$A_V < 0.05$	A	A	A

When ATC 3-06 in 1978 made the level of detailing (and other restrictions concerning permissible structural systems, height, irregularity and analysis procedure) a function of occupancy, that was a major departure from prior practice. The departure was continued in all the NEHRP Provisions through the 1994 edition. Now, in the 2000 IBC and the 1997 NEHRP Provisions, the level of detailing and other restrictions have been made a function of the soil characteristics at the site of the structure. This is a further major departure from current practice across the country—a move that is likely to have significant impact on the economic and other aspects of earthquake-resistant design. A preliminary exploration of this impact is presented in Appendix 5 of this publication.

1616.3.1 Site limitation for Seismic Design Category E or F. It is not possible to reliably design a structure to resist the very large forces it may be subjected to if an active fault were to cause rupture of the ground surface at its location. Consequently, this section prohibits the construction of buildings assigned to SDC E and F at sites where such potential exists.

As pointed out in the 1997 NEHRP Commentary, the effects of landsliding, liquefaction, and lateral spreading can also be highly damaging to a building. However, the effects of these site phenomena can more readily be mitigated through the adoption of appropriate measures than can the effects of direct ground-fault rupture. Consequently, construction on sites with these hazards is permitted, if appropriate mitigation measures are undertaken.

Detached one- and two-family dwellings of light-frame construction are exempt from the siting restriction of this section. The risk to this type of construction was judged to be not high enough to justify the restriction.

1616.4 Design requirements for Seismic Design Category A. For structures assigned to SDC A, the IBC requires only that a complete lateral-force-resisting system be provided and that all elements of the structure be tied together. A nominal design force of 1 percent of the weight of the structure is used to proportion the lateral-force-resisting system.

1616.4.1 Minimum lateral force. This requires that a complete load path for lateral forces must first be identified. Then it must be designed for lateral forces produced by 1 percent of g acceleration on the masses at the various floor levels. The background to the requirements of Section 1616.4.1 and 1616.4.2 is provided in the commentary to the 1997 NEHRP Provisions (Section 4.2). The minimum lateral-force requirement is intended to provide a nominal level of structural integrity that will improve the performance of buildings in the event of a possible but rare earthquake and many other types of unanticipated loadings. The 1-percent value has been used in other countries as a minimum value for structural integrity. For many structures, design for the specified wind loads will normally control the lateral-force design when compared to the minimum force specified for structural integrity. However, many low-rise, heavy structures or structures with significant dead loads resulting from heavy equipment may be controlled by the nominal 1-percent acceleration.

The IBC allows orthogonal effects to be neglected in the design of SDC A structures. The design seismic forces may be applied separately in each of the two orthogonal directions.

1616.4.2 Connections. According to the 1997 NEHRP Commentary (Section 5.2.6.1.2), probably the most important single attribute of an earthquake-resisting building is that it is tied together to act as a unit. This is important not only for earthquake resistance but also for resisting high winds, floods, explosion, progressive collapse, and even such ordinary hazards as foundation settlement. The 1997 NEHRP Provisions requires that any smaller portion of a structure (or unit if there are separation joints) be tied to the remainder of the structure with elements having a strength of $S_{DS}/7.5$ times the weight of the smaller portion or 5 percent of the portion's weight, whichever is greater. In the IBC, the minimum strength required of the connection between a smaller portion and the remainder of a structure is a fixed 5 percent of the weight of the smaller portion. It is important to note that this requirement does not apply to the connection between the structure itself and its foundation.

In addition to the above, a positive connection is to be provided to support each beam, girder or truss to resist a horizontal force acting parallel to the member. The connection must have a minimum strength of 5 percent of the vertical dead and live load reaction applied horizontally.

1616.4.3 Anchorage of concrete or masonry walls. This refers to Section 1604.8.2, for which commentary has already been provided.

1616.4.4 Conventional light-frame construction. This exemption is essentially the same as that provided under Exception 2 of Section 1614.

1616.5 Building configuration. Past earthquakes have repeatedly shown that buildings having irregular configurations (in plan or along the height of a structure) suffer greater damage than buildings having regular configuration. This situation prevails even with good design and construction.

The 1997 NEHRP Commentary (Section 5.2.3) has pointed out several reasons for this poor behavior of irregular structures. In a regular structure, inelastic demands produced by strong ground shaking tend to be well distributed throughout the structure, resulting in a dispersion of energy dissipation and damage. However, in irregular structures, inelastic behavior can concentrate in certain localized regions, resulting in rapid deterioration of structural elements in these areas. In addition, some irregularities introduce unanticipated stresses into a structure, which designers frequently overlook when detailing the structural system. Finally, elastic analysis methods typically employed in the design of structures are incapable of accurately predicting the distribution of earthquake demands in an irregular structure, leading to inadequate design in the vicinity of irregular features. For these reasons, the requirements of this section were formulated to encourage that buildings be designed to have regular configurations and to prohibit gross irregularity in buildings located on sites close to major active faults, where strong ground motion and extreme inelastic demands in a structure may be experienced.

1616.5.1 Plan irregularity. This indicates, by reference to Table 1616.5. 1, when a building must be considered to have a plan irregularity for the purposes of the IBC. Structures having plan irregularity, depending upon the type of such irregularity, must comply with the requirements of the applicable sections referenced in Table 1616.5.1.

Torsional irregularity (Plan Irregularity Type 1a) and Extreme torsional irregularity (Plan Irregularity Type 1b). As pointed out in the commentary to the 1997 NEHRP Provisions, a building may have a symmetrical geometric shape without re- entrant corners or wings, but may still have to be classified as irregular in plan because of irregular distribution of mass or of the vertical lateral-force-resisting elements. Torsional effects in earthquakes may and do occur even when the static centers of mass and resistance coincide. Direction of ground motion that is not along one of the principal plan axes of a building may cause torsion. Cracking and yielding in an asymmetrical pattern may also be a source of torsion. These effects may magnify the torsion due to an actual eccentricity between the static centers of mass and resistance. Based on these considerations, buildings having an eccentricity between the static center of mass and the static center of resistance in excess of 10 percent of the building dimension perpendicular to the direction of the seismic force are classified as irregular in plan. The vertical lateral-force-resisting elements may be arranged so that the eccentricity between the static centers of mass and resistance is within the above limitation, but the arrangement may still be asymmetrical so that the prescribed torsional forces would be unequally distributed to the various resisting elements.

In the IBC, as in the 1997 NEHRP Provisions, torsional irregularities have been subdivided into two categories, with a category of extreme torsional irregularity having been created. Extreme torsional irregularity is considered to exist in buildings having an eccentricity between the static center of mass and the static center of resistance in excess of 20 percent of the building dimension perpendicular to the direction of the seismic force. Extreme torsional irregularities are prohibited in structures located close to major active faults and should be avoided, whenever possible, in all structures.

Figures 16A and 16B illustrate the definitions of torsional irregularity and extreme torsional irregularity, respectively, and also enumerate the restrictions that apply when a building is classified in either category. The commentary to the 1997 NEHRP Provisions points out that there is a type of distribution of vertical lateral-force-resisting elements that, while not being classified as irregular, does not produce good structural performance in strong earthquakes. This arrangement produces a core-type building, with the vertical components of the lateral-force-resisting system collected near the center of the building. Better performance is observed when the vertical components are distributed near the perimeter of the building.

Re-entrant corners (Plan Irregularity Type 2). A building having a regular configuration can be square, rectangular or circular. As the commentary to the 1997 NEHRP Provisions points out, a square or rectangular building with minor re-entrant corners would still be considered regular, but large re-entrant corners creating a crucifix form would cause a building to be classified as irregular in plan. The response of the wings of this type of building is generally different from the response of the building as a whole, and this produces higher local forces than would be determined from application of the IBC without modification. Other plan configurations, such as H-shapes, that are geometrically symmetrical would also be classified as irregular because of the response of the wings.

The definition of Plan Irregularity Type 2 is illustrated in Figure 17. The restrictions that become applicable when a building is classified as having Plan Irregularity Type 2 are also clearly indicated in Figure 17.

Diaphragm discontinuity (Plan Irregularity Type 3). Significant differences in stiffness between portions of a diaphragm at a level may cause a change in the distribution of lateral forces to the vertical lateral-force-resisting elements and create torsional forces not accounted for in the distribution considered for a regular building.

Figure 18 illustrates the definition of Plan Irregularity Type 3 and also points out the restrictions that become applicable when a building is classified as having Plan Irregularity Type 3.

Out-of-plane offsets (Plan Irregularity Type 4). Where there are discontinuities in the path of lateral-force resistance, a structure may no longer be considered regular. The most critical of such discontinuities is the out-of-plane offset of vertical elements of the lateral-force-resisting system. Such offsets impose vertical and lateral load effects on horizontal structural elements that are not easy to provide for in design.

The definition of Plan Irregularity Type 4 is illustrated in Figure 19, which also lists the restrictions that apply to a building classified as having Plan Irregularity Type 4.

Nonparallel Systems (Plan Irregularity Type 5). Where vertical elements of the lateral-force-resisting system are not parallel to or symmetric with major orthogonal axes, the static lateral-force procedure of the IBC cannot be applied as given. The structure then must be considered irregular.

Figure 20 illustrates the definition of and shows the restrictions that go with Plan Irregularity Type 5.

1616.5.2 Vertical irregularity. This indicates, by reference to Table 1616.5.2, when a structure must be considered to have a vertical irregularity. Vertical configuration irregularities affect seismic response at various floor levels and induce loads at these levels that depart significantly from the distribution assumed in the equivalent lateral-force procedure. Structures having vertical irregularity, depending upon the type of such irregularity, must comply with the requirements of the applicable sections referenced in Table 1616.5.2.

Stiffness irregularity—soft story (Vertical Irregularity Type 1a), Stiffness irregularity—extreme soft story (Vertical Irregularity Type 1b). A building would be classified in one of these categories if the lateral stiffnesses in adjoining stories differ significantly. This might occur in a moment-resisting frame building if one story were much taller than the adjoining stories and the resulting decrease in stiffness was not, or could not be, compensated for.

In the IBC, as in the 1997 NEHRP Provisions, stiffness irregularities have been subdivided into two categories, with a category of extreme stiffness irregularity having been created.

Figures 21A and 21B illustrate the definitions of stiffness irregularity and extreme stiffness irregularity, respectively, and enumerate the restrictions that apply when a structure is classified in either of these categories.

Weight (Mass) irregularity (Vertical Irregularity Type 2). A building is classified in this category if the masses of

REFER TO SECTION 1616.5.1, TABLE 1616.5.1

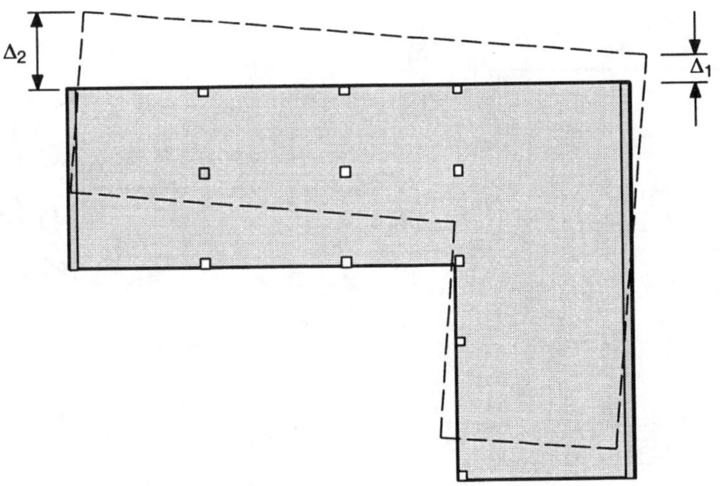

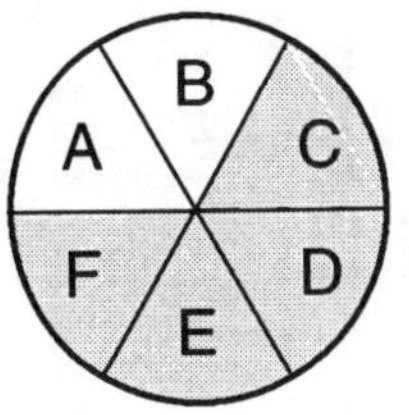

- TORSIONAL IRREGULARITY EXISTS WHEN:

$$\Delta_2 > 1.2\left(\frac{\Delta_1 + \Delta_2}{2}\right)$$

- TORSIONAL IRREGULARITY TO BE CONSIDERED ONLY WHEN DIAPHRAGMS ARE NOT FLEXIBLE (SECTION 1602.1)
- IN SDC D, E AND F, DESIGN FORCES DETERMINED FROM SECTION 1617.4.1 SHALL BE INCREASED 25% FOR CONNECTIONS OF DIAPHRAGMS TO VERTICAL ELEMENTS AND TO COLLECTORS, AND FOR CONNECTIONS OF COLLECTORS TO VERTICAL ELEMENTS (SECTION 1620.3.1)
- IN SDC C, D, E AND F DYNAMIC AMPLIFICATION OF TORSION AS REQUIRED BY SECTION 1617.4.4.5 SHALL BE APPLIED

PLAN IRREGULARITY TYPE 1a, TORSIONAL IRREGULARITY

FIGURE 16A

adjoining stories are significantly different. This might occur when a heavy mass, such as a garden or a swimming pool, is placed at one level.

The definition of Vertical Irregularity Type 2 is illustrated in Figure 22, which also shows the restrictions that apply when a structure is classified as having this type of an irregularity. Note that Exception 1 to Section 1616.5.2 provides a comparative stiffness ratio between stories to exempt structures from being designated as having a vertical irregularity of the type specified. Exception 2 further exempts one-story buildings in any seismic design category and two-story buildings in SDC A through D from being designated as having a vertical irregularity of the type specified.

Vertical geometric irregularity (Vertical Irregularity Type 3). As illustrated in the commentary to the 1997 NEHRP Provisions (Section 5.2.3.3), one type of vertical irregularity is created by asymmetrical geometry with respect to the vertical axis of the building. A building may have a geometry that is symmetrical about the vertical axis and still be classified as irregular because of significant horizontal offsets in the vertical elements of the lateral-force-resisting system at one or more levels. An offset is considered to be significant if the ratio of the larger dimension to the smaller dimension is more than 130 percent. As pointed out in the 1997 NEHRP Commentary, a building would also be considered irregular if the vertical lateral-force-resisting elements having the smaller dimensions supported such elements having the larger dimensions, thus creating an inverted pyramid effect.

Vertical Irregularity Type 3 and the restrictions associated with it are illustrated in Figure 23.

In-plane discontinuity in vertical lateral-force-resisting elements (Vertical Irregularity Type 4). This irregularity is not unlike Vertical Irregularity Type 3. The definition and the applicable restrictions are given in Figure 24.

Discontinuity in capacity—weak story (Vertical Irregularity Type 5). Weak-story irregularities occur whenever the strength of a story to resist lateral demands is significantly less than that of the story above. Buildings with this configuration tend to develop all of their inelastic behavior in the weak story. A significant change in the deformation pattern of the building results with most earthquake-induced displacement occurring within the weak story. This typically results in extensive

REFER TO SECTION 1616.5.1, TABLE 1616.5.1

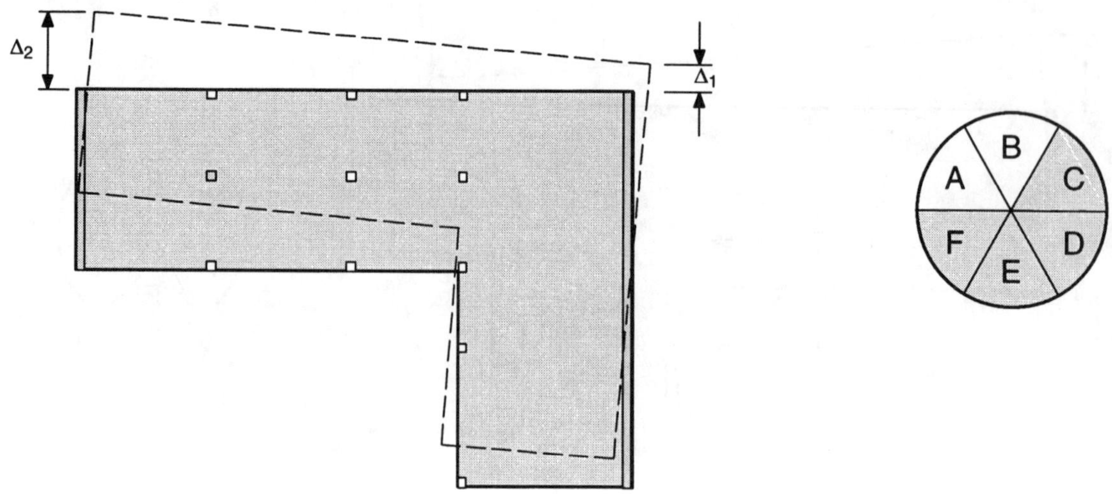

- EXTREME TORSIONAL IRREGULARITY EXISTS WHEN:

$$\Delta_2 > 1.4\left(\frac{\Delta_1 + \Delta_2}{2}\right)$$

- TORSIONAL IRREGULARITY TO BE CONSIDERED ONLY WHEN DIAPHRAGMS ARE NOT FLEXIBLE (SECTION 1602.1)
- SHALL NOT BE PERMITTED IN SDC E AND F (SECTION 1620.4.1)
- IN SDC D, E AND F DESIGN FORCES DETERMINED FROM SECTION 1617.4.1 SHALL BE INCREASED 25% FOR CONNECTIONS OF DIAPHRAGMS TO VERTICAL ELEMENTS AND TO COLLECTORS, AND FOR CONNECTIONS OF COLLECTORS TO VERTICAL ELEMENTS (SECTION 1620.3.1)
- IN SDC C, D, E AND F, DYNAMIC AMPLIFICATION OF TORSION AS REQUIRED BY SECTION 1617.4.4.5 SHALL BE APPLIED

PLAN IRREGULARITY TYPE 1b, EXTREME TORSIONAL IRREGULARITY

FIGURE 16B

damage within the weak story and may even cause instability and collapse.

The definition of Vertical Irregularity Type 5 is illustrated in Figure 25. The restrictions applying to a building classified as having Vertical Irregularity Type 5 are given in the figure. Note that Section 1620.1.3 in effect creates an extreme soft story category that is not allowed to be built more than two stories or 30 feet in height in SDC B, C and D. Also note that an exception is provided for cases where there is considerable overstrength in the "weak" story.

1616.6 Analysis procedures. The design load combinations of Section 1605 involve the terms E (the combined effect of horizontal and vertical earthquake-induced forces) and E_m (the maximum seismic load effect). Both terms are defined in part by Q_E (the effect of horizontal seismic forces), the determination of which requires structural analysis in accordance with the requirements of this section. Such analysis also leads to the determination of the design story drift, Δ, which must be kept within the limits prescribed in Section 1617.3. Structures assigned to SDC A do not require structural analysis in view of the provisions of Section 1616.4. Also, design story drift need not be evaluated per Section 1617.4.6.1 when the Simplified Analysis Procedure of Section 1617.5 is used.

The commentary to the 1997 NEHRP Provisions lists the standard procedures for the analysis of forces and deformations in structures subjected to earthquake ground motion, in the order of expected rigor and accuracy, as follows:

1. Equivalent lateral-force procedure (IBC Section 1617.4),
2. Modal analysis procedure (response spectrum analysis) (IBC Sections 1618.1-1618.9),
3. Inelastic static procedure, involving incremental application of a pattern of lateral forces and adjustment of the structural model to account for progressive yielding under load application (push-over analysis), and
4. Inelastic response history analysis involving step-by-step integration of the coupled equations of motion (IBC Section 1618.10.2).

REFER TO SECTION 1616.5.1, TABLE 1616.5.1

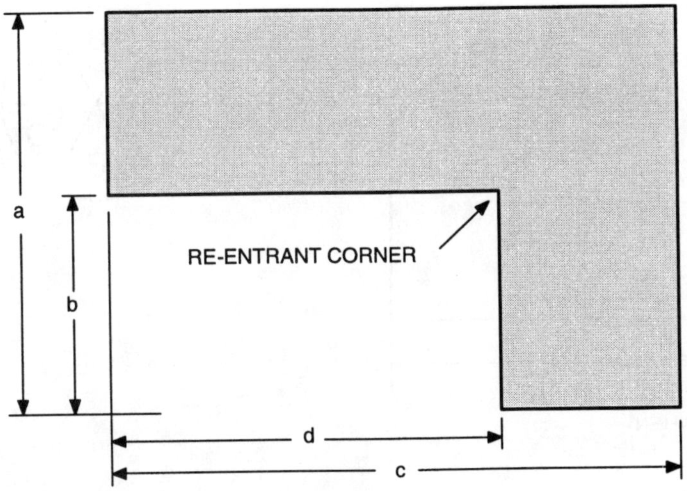

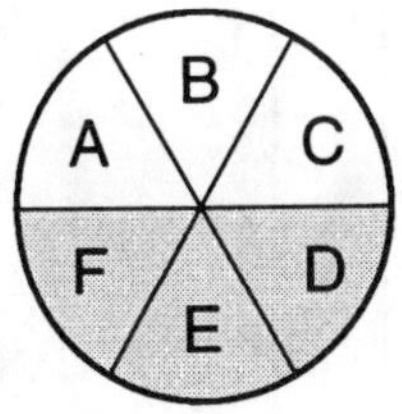

- RE-ENTRANT CORNER EXISTS WHEN:

  PROJECTION b >0.15a, AND

  PROJECTION d >0.15c

- IN SDC D, E and F DESIGN FORCES DETERMINED FROM SECTION 1617.4.1 SHALL BE INCREASED 25% FOR CONNECTIONS OF DIAPHRAGMS TO VERTICAL ELEMENTS AND TO COLLECTORS, AND FOR CONNECTIONS OF COLLECTORS TO VERTICAL ELEMENTS (SECTION 1620.3.1)

PLAN IRREGULARITY TYPE 2, RE-ENTRANT CORNERS

FIGURE 17

The IBC chose to include a simplified analysis procedure (Section 1617.5) that, in the order of expected rigor and accuracy, would precede Item I above. Push-over analysis is not formally recognized in the IBC, although it is high among the recognized analysis procedures in the ATC 33/FEMA 273 *Seismic Rehabilitation Guidelines.*[29]

The IBC also recognizes an elastic or linear time history analysis (Section 1618.10.1.2), that in the order of expected rigor and accuracy, would probably rank the same as Item 2 above. It should be recognized that Items 1 and 3 above and the simplified analysis procedure of Section 1617.5 are static procedures, while the other analysis procedures mentioned are dynamic procedures. The philosophy underlying this section is that dynamic analysis is always acceptable for design. Static procedures are allowed only under certain conditions of regularity, occupancy, and height.

The equivalent lateral-force procedure (Section 1617.4) and the modal analysis procedure (Sections 1618.1 through 1618.9) are both based on the approximation that inelastic seismic structural response can be adequately represented by linear analysis of the lateral-force-resisting system using the design spectrum, which is the elastic acceleration response spectrum amplified by the importance factor, I_E, and reduced by the response modification factor, R. The effects of the horizontal component of ground motion perpendicular to the direction of analysis, the vertical component of ground motion and torsional motions of the structure are all considered in the same approximate manner in both cases, if only two-dimensional analysis is used. The main difference between the two procedures lies in the distribution of the seismic lateral forces over the building. In the modal analysis procedure, the distribution is based on the deformed shapes of the natural modes of vibration, which are determined from the distribution of the masses and the stiffnesses of the structure. In the equivalent lateral-force procedure, the distribution is based on simplified formulas that are appropriate for regular structures (Section 1617.4.3). Otherwise, the two procedures are subject to the same limitations. The total design forces used in the two procedures are also very similar (see Section 1618.7).

According to the 1997 NEHRP Commentary, the equivalent lateral-force procedure and the modal analysis procedure "are all likely to err systematically on the unsafe side if story strengths are distributed irregularly over height. This feature is likely to lead to concentration of ductility demand in a few stories of the building. The inelastic static (or the so-called push-over) procedure is a method to more accurately account for irregular strength distribution. However, it also has limitations and is not particularly applicable to tall structures or structures with relatively long fundamental periods of vibration."

Current professional practice and computational capabilities may lead to the choice of a three-dimensional model for both static and dynamic analyses. Although three-dimensional models are not specifically required for static force procedures, nor for dynamic analysis procedures for regular structures with

REFER TO SECTION 1616.5.1, TABLE 1616.5.1

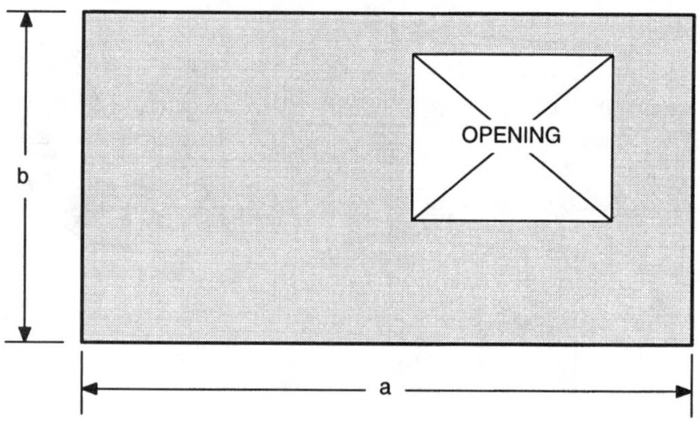

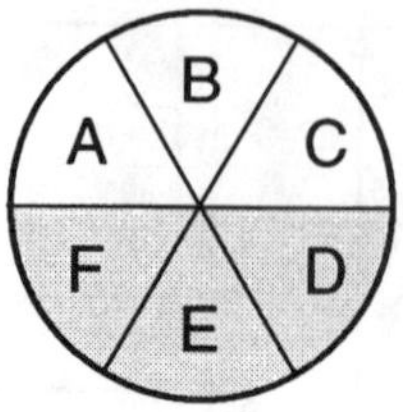

- DIAPHRAGM DISCONTINUITY EXISTS WHEN:

  AREA OF OPENING >0.5 (a) (b) OR

  EFFECTIVE DIAPHRAGM STIFFNESS CHANGES MORE THAN 50% FROM ONE STORY TO THE NEXT

- IN SDC D, E AND F, DESIGN FORCES DETERMINED FROM SECTION 1617.4.1 SHALL BE INCREASED 25% FOR CONNECTIONS OF DIAPHRAGMS TO VERTICAL ELEMENTS AND TO COLLECTORS, AND FOR CONNECTIONS OF COLLECTORS TO VERTICAL ELEMENTS (SECTION 1620.3.1)

PLAN IRREGULARITY TYPE 3, DIAPHRAGM DISCONTINUITY

FIGURE 18

independent orthogonal seismic force-resisting systems, they often have important advantages over two-dimensional models.

A three-dimensional model is appropriate for the analysis of torsional effects (actual plus accidental), diaphragm deformability, and systems having nonrectangular plan configurations. According to the commentary to the 1999 SEAOC Blue Book, when a three-dimensional model is needed for any purpose, "it can also serve for all required loading conditions, including seismic loading in each principal direction, other selected directions and for orthogonal effects."

The actual strength and other properties of the various components of a structure can be explicitly considered only by a nonlinear analysis of dynamic response by direct integration of the coupled equations of motion. If the two translational motions and the torsional motion are expected to be essentially uncoupled, it is sufficient to include only one degree of freedom per floor, in the direction of analysis; otherwise at least three degrees of freedom per floor, two translational and one torsional, need to be included. The 1997 NEHRP Commentary points out, and it cannot be overemphasized, that the results of nonlinear response history analysis of mathematical structural models are only as good as the models chosen to represent the structure vibrating at amplitudes of motion large enough to cause significant yielding at several locations. Proper modeling and proper interpretation of results require background and experience. Also, reliable results can be achieved only by calculating the response to several ground motions—recorded accelerograms and/or simulated motions—and examining the statistics of response.

The least rigorous analytical procedure that may be used in determining the design seismic forces and deformations in a structure depends on the seismic design category and the structural characteristics (in particular, regularity and height). Structural irregularity was discussed under Section 1616.5. Table 16 has been prepared for the convenience of the reader.

1616.6.1 Simplified analysis. The simplified analysis procedure of Section 1617.5 represents slight modifications of a procedure first introduced into the 1997 UBC. It was developed by the SEAOC Seismology Committee in response to a need to provide conservative, simple methods to determine design forces for certain simple buildings. The procedure is limited to buildings of light framed construction not exceeding three stories in height (excluding basements), and to buildings of any construction other than light framed, not exceeding two stories in height. The details of the procedure are discussed later under Section 1617.5.

1616.6.2 Seismic Design Categories B and C. The equivalent lateral-force procedure is the minimum level of analysis, except when the simplified analysis procedure of Section 1617.5 is applicable. A more rigorous analysis is always permitted.

1616.6.3 Seismic Design Categories D, E and F. The least rigorous analysis procedures that may be used are identified in Table 1616.6.3.The same requirements are presented in a different manner in Table 16 and are discussed below with reference to that table.

REFER TO SECTION 1616.5.1, TABLE 1616.5.1

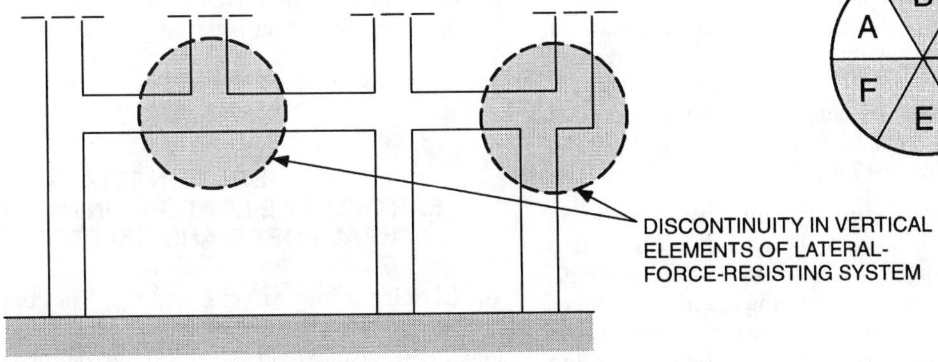

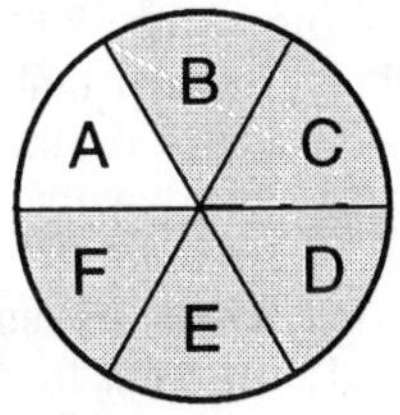

- REQUIRED STRENGTH OF COLUMNS SUPPORTING DISCONTINUOUS VERTICAL ELEMENTS (SECTION 1620.1.9): AS GIVEN BY SECTION 1605.4 - SPECIAL SEISMIC LOAD COMBINATIONS

$1.2D + f_1 L + 1.0E_m$ (Formula 16-19)

$0.9D + 1.0E_m$ (Formula 16-20)

WHERE:

IN FORMULA 16-19

$E_m = \Omega_o Q_E + 0.2\ S_{DS}\ D$ (Eq. 16-30)

AND IN FORMULA 16-20

$E_m = \Omega_o Q_E - 0.2\ S_{DS}\ D$ (Eq. 16-31)

- NOTE SPECIAL DETAILING REQUIREMENTS IN MATERIALS CHAPTERS.
- IN SDC D, E AND F, DESIGN FORCES DETERMINED FROM SECTION 1617.4.1 SHALL BE INCREASED 25% FOR CONNECTIONS OF DIAPHRAGMS TO VERTICAL ELEMENTS AND TO COLLECTORS, AND FOR CONNECTIONS OF COLLECTORS TO VERTICAL ELEMENTS (SECTION 1620.3.1)

PLAN IRREGULARITY TYPE 4, OUT-OF-PLANE OFFSETS

FIGURE 19

REFER TO SECTION 1616.5.1, TABLE 1616.5.1

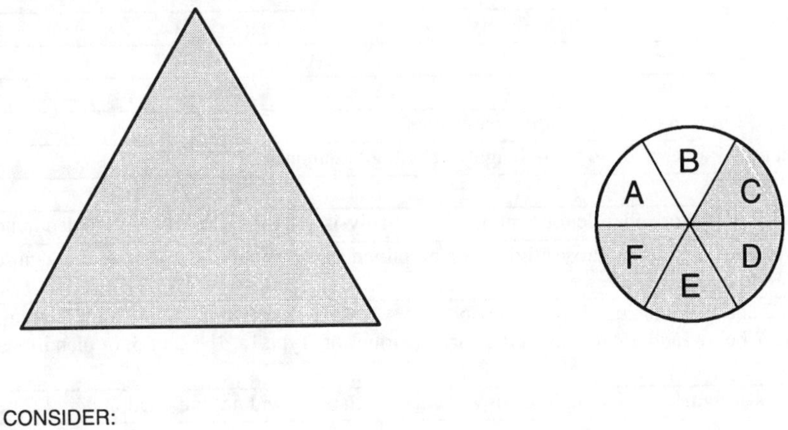

- DESIGN TO CONSIDER:

  EFFECTS OF EARTHQUAKE FORCES ACTING IN A DIRECTION OTHER THAN ALONG PRINCIPAL AXES (SECTION 1620.2.2)

PLAN IRREGULARITY TYPE 5, NONPARALLEL SYSTEMS

FIGURE 20

Item S3. According to the 1999 SEAOC Blue Book Commentary, while short irregular buildings are exempt from the dynamic analysis requirements, the engineer should be aware of the need to evaluate the dynamic characteristics of irregular buildings not more than 65 feet in height where properties and/or characteristics may create dynamic force and deformation patterns significantly different from those resulting from the load distribution of Section 1617.4.3.

Item S4. Special consideration of dynamic characteristics in equivalent static analysis is required for a building assigned to SDC D, E or F, if the building has one or more of the plan irregularities of Type 2, 3, 4, or 5, and the building has one or more of the vertical irregularities of Type 4 or 5. The commentary to the 1997 NEHRP Provisions suggests a procedure for determining whether the modal analysis procedure is needed for a particular structure. This procedure may be useful for structures included in Item S4.

Item D1. Dynamic analysis is required for structures over 240 feet in height in order to determine the possible effects of higher mode response on the force distribution and deformations. In the other cases cited, dynamic analysis is required because the noted irregularities invalidate the assumptions applicable for equivalent static force analysis.

Item D2. A similar requirement was added to the 1988 edition of the UBC in view of experience from the Mexico earthquake of 1985. The requirement has simply been converted to IBC terms. Refer to the 1999 SEAOC Blue Book Commentary for more detailed information on this item.

Section 1616.6.3 allows that for regular structures five stories or less in height, having a period T (Section 1617.4.2) not exceeding 0.5 seconds, S_{DS} need not exceed $(2/3)F_a(1.5g) = F_a g$ and S_{D1} need not exceed $(2/3)F_v(0.6g) = 0.4F_v g$.

Section 1616.6.3 also allows that in the absence of any plan irregularity of Type 2a, 2b or 4 and any vertical irregularity of Type 1a, 1b, 4 or 5, a structure may be considered regular for the purposes of this section. Note that, although the code language is mandatory, the intent is definitely permissive.

SECTION 1617
EARTHQUAKE LOADS—MINIMUM DESIGN LATERAL FORCE AND RELATED EFFECTS

1617.1 Seismic load effect E and E_m. The combined effect of horizontal and vertical earthquake-induced forces, E, and the maximum seismic load effect, E_m, are defined in this section. Both terms are used in the design load combinations of Section 1605.

1617.1.1 Seismic load effect E. In seismic design practice represented by the UBC through its 1994 edition, E was simply the effect of the design base shear, V, (internal forces obtained by elastic analysis of the structure under lateral forces resulting from code-required distribution of V along the height of the structure). ATC 3-06 and the NEHRP Provisions through its 1991 edition included the effect of the vertical earthquake ground motion in the design load combinations. The 1994 NEHRP Provisions modified the definition of E to include the effect of the vertical earthquake ground motion in addition to the effect of V. The 1997 UBC went a step further and defined E as being made of two parts: the effect of the horizontal earthquake ground motion (same as the effect of the design base shear, V) amplified by a redundancy coefficient, ρ, and the effect of the vertical earthquake ground motion. The 1997 NEHRP Provisions adopted the 1997 UBC approach, which in turn has been adopted into the IBC. The redundancy factor is discussed under Section 1617.2. The effect of the vertical earthquake ground motion is discussed here.

TABLE 16. APPLICABILITY OF VARIOUS ANALYSIS PROCEDURES PER 2000 IBC

<u>Exempt</u>
SDC A structures
<u>Simplified Static</u>
Following buildings in SUG I
* Of light frame construction, ≤ 3 stories in height excluding basements
* Of any construction other than light frame, ≤ 2 stories in height excluding basements
<u>Static</u>
S1. All SDC B and C structures other than those eligible for simplified static anlysis and other than those included in item D2 below.
S2. Regular structures in SDC D, E and F, other than those eligible for simplified statistic analysis, and other than those included in item D2 below ≤ 240 ft in height.
S3. Irregular structures in SDC D, E and F, not included in item D2 below, ≤ 5 stories or 65 ft in height. Taller irregular structures in SDC D, E and F, not included in item D2 below, and not having vertical irregularities of Type 1a, 1b, 2, or 3, or plan irregularities of Type 1a or 1b.
S4. Other SDC D, E and F structures designated as having plan or vertical irregularities, and not included in item D2 below.[a]
<u>Dynamic</u>
D1. SDC D, E and F structures having vertical irregularities of Type 1a, 1b, 2 or 3 or plan irregularities of Type 1a or 1b and having a height > 5 stories or 65 ft and all SDC D, E and F structures > 240 ft in height.
D2. Structures: (a) located in areas with S_{D1} > 0.2 g, (b) on Site Class E or F, and (c) with T > 0.7 sec [b]

a. Dynamic characteristics must be included in the analytical model.
b. A Site-specific response spectrum must be used, but the design base shear must not be less than that determined from Section 1617.4 (equivalent lateral-force procedure).

REFER TO SECTION 1616.5.2, TABLE 1616.5.2

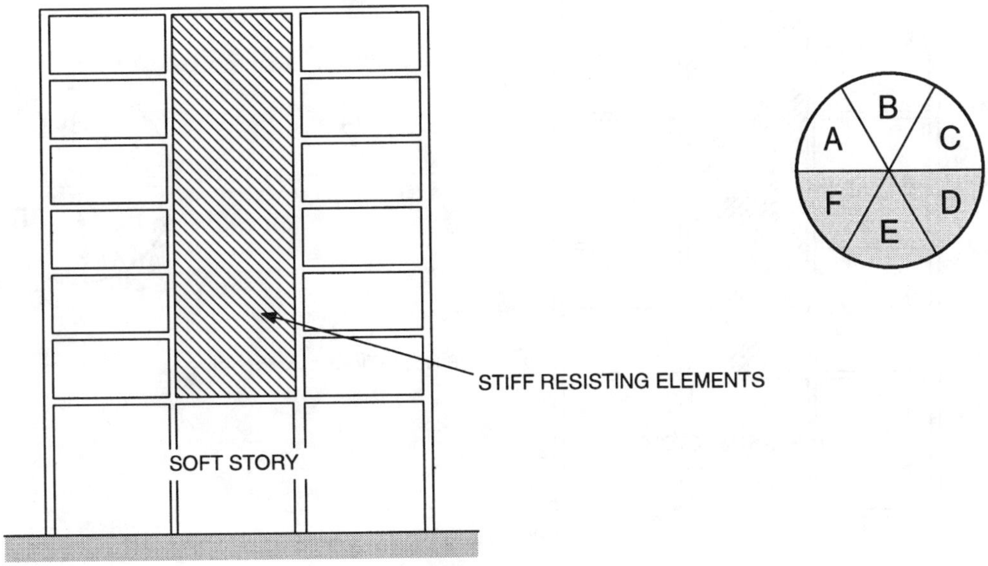

- "SOFT STORY" STIFFNESS <70% STORY STIFFNESS ABOVE OR

  <80% [AVERAGE STIFFNESS OF 3 STORIES ABOVE]

- MODAL ANALYSIS PROCEDURE OF SECTION 1618 OR MORE RIGOROUS ANALYSIS REQUIRED (SECTION 1616.6.3) FOR BUILDINGS IN ALL SUGs ABOVE 5 STORIES OR 65 FEET IN HEIGHT

VERTICAL IRREGULARITY TYPE 1a, SOFT STORY

FIGURE 21A

Table 17 shows that the consideration of vertical earthquake ground motion, as required by Equations 16-28 and 16-29 causes an increase in the dead load factor when gravity and earthquake effects are additive (for instance, gravity causes negative bending moments at a particular support section of a particular beam; earthquake forces also cause a negative bending moment at the same support section of the same beam). A decrease in the dead load factor is caused when gravity counteracts earthquake effects (for instance, gravity causes negative bending moments at a particular support section of a particular beam; earthquake forces cause a positive bending moment at the same support section of the same beam). In other words, when gravity effects add to earthquake effects, the direction of vertical earthquake ground motion is taken in the direction of gravity or vertically downward. When gravity counteracts earthquake effects, the direction of vertical earthquake ground motion is taken in the direction opposite to that of gravity or vertically upward.

The proportioning of shear walls and columns of reinforced concrete as well as masonry is governed by the load combination yielding the minimum axial load in compression or the maximum axial load in tension. This is because designing for lower compressive (or higher tensile) axial loads typically causes an increase in the required flexural reinforcement. The governing load combinations of ATC 3-06, the various editions of the NEHRP Provisions, the 1997 UBC and the 2000 IBC are shown in Table 18. The dead load factor in these load combinations (denoted as DLF in the following discussion), where the effects of factored gravity counteract the effects of strength-level earthquake forces, is of particular importance — the lower the DLF, the more severe the load combination, and the higher the flexural reinforcement requirement.

It is evident from Table 18 that the DLF of ATC 3-06 is a fixed 0.8. In the 1985, 1988 and the 1991 NEHRP Provisions, the DLF is equal to $0.9 - 0.5A_v$, the most severe value of which is 0.7 for an A_v of 0.4. In the 1994 NEHRP Provisions, the 1997 UBC, and the 1997 NEHRP Provisions as well as the 2000 IBC, the DLFs are $0.9 - 0.5C_a$, $0.9 - 0.5C_aI$, and $0.9 - 0.4F_aS_s/3$, respectively. These values are tabulated for different site classes in Tables 19 (a), (b) and (c), respectively. The UBC values are for Seismic Zone 4 only. The NEHRP/IBC values are for regions of varying seismicity. The UBC shows N_a as the acceleration-related near-source factor. It should be apparent that the consideration of vertical earthquake ground motion is more conservative in the 1997 UBC when compared to the other documents. The DLF values of the 2000 IBC are somewhat less and are more consistent with the values used in the NEHRP Provisions through its 1994 edition and in ATC 3-06.

1617.1.2 Maximum seismic load effect, E_m. Section 1620.1.9 requires that elements supporting discontinuous walls or frames in SDC B and higher must have the design strength to resist the special seismic load combinations of Section 1605.4.

REFER TO SECTION 1616.5.2, TABLE 1616.5.2

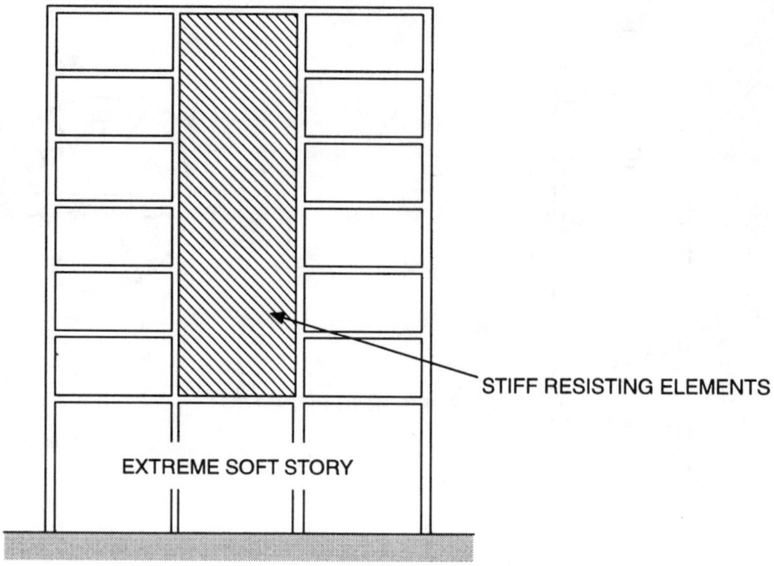

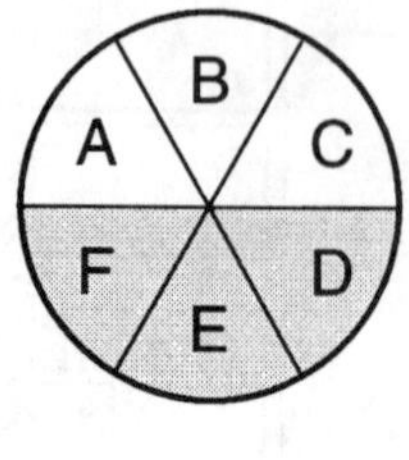

- "EXTREME SOFT STORY" STIFFNESS < 60% STORY STIFFNESS ABOVE, OR < 70% [AVERAGE STIFFNESS OF 3 STORIES ABOVE]
- SHALL NOT BE PERMITTED IN SDC E AND F (SECTION 1620.4.1)
- MODAL ANALYSIS PROCEDURE OF SECTION 1618 OR MORE RIGOROUS ANALYSIS REQUIRED (SECTION 1616.6.3) FOR BUILDINGS IN ALL SUGs ABOVE 5 STORIES OR 65 FEET IN HEIGHT

VERTICAL IRREGULARITY TYPE 1b, EXTREME SOFT STORY

FIGURE 21B

Section 1620.1.6 likewise requires that diaphragm collector elements, splices and their connections to resisting elements have the design strength to resist the special load combinations of Section 1605.4. The term E_m, maximum seismic load effect, involved in the special load combinations of Section 1604.5, is defined in Section 1617.1.2. In the maximum seismic load effect, E_m, given by Equations 16-30 and 16-31, the effect of the horizontal earthquake ground motion, Q_E, which is the same as the effect of the design base shear, V, is amplified by the overstrength factor, Ω_o, of Table 1617.6, which varies between 2 and 3. In the seismic load effect, E, used in the nonspecial load combinations of Section 1605, and as given by Equations 16-28 and 16-29, Q_E, the effect of the design base shear V, is amplified by the redundancy coefficient, ρ, which ranges between 1 and 1.5. This is the sole difference between the two. The consideration of vertical earthquake ground motion is identical in both cases. It may be noted that the consideration of vertical earthquake ground motion is absent in the maximum earthquake effect term, and hence, in the special load combinations of the 1997 UBC. There, E_m is defined simply as equal to $\Omega_o E_h$, E_h of the UBC and Q_E of the IBC being equivalent terms.

1617.2 Redundancy. Redundancy as a concept is simple. It is the concept of the multiple load path — of providing more than one alternate path for every load to travel from its point of application to the ultimate point of resistance. Despite this conceptual simplicity, when the SEAOC Seismology Committee attempted to quantify redundancy for the 1997 UBC, it proved to be a challenging task indeed. The SEAOC formulation, adopted into the 1997 UBC, has now been adopted into the IBC with a few refinements. The formulation will doubtless undergo further refinements in coming editions of the IBC.

For structures assigned to SDC A, B or C, the value of the redundancy coefficient, ρ, is 1.0 (Section 1617.2.1), just as in the 1997 UBC, the value of ρ is 1.0 for structures in Seismic Zones 0,1 and 2. This reflects the belief that providing multiple load paths for the seismic forces is more important in the higher seismic zones and design categories than in lower ones. The redundancy coefficient, ρ, is also equal to 1.0 in drift computations.

TABLE 17. SEISMIC STRENGTH DESIGN LOAD COMBINATIONS OF THE 2000 IBC

Gravity and earthquake effects additive:	
Required strength	
$U = 1.2D + 1.0E + (f_1L + f_2S)$	(Formula 16-5)
$= 1.2D + (\rho Q_E + 0.2S_{DS}D) + (f_1L + f_2S)$	(Formula 16-28)
$= (1.2 + 0.2S_{DS})D + \rho Q_E + (f_1L + f_2S)$	
Gravity and earthquake effects counteractive:	
Required strength	
$U = 0.9D + 1.0E$	(Formula 16-6)
$= 0.9D + (\rho Q_E - 0.2S_{DS}D)$	(Formula 16-29)
$= (0.9 - 0.2S_{DS})D + \rho Q_E$	

REFER TO SECTION 1616.5.2, TABLE 1616.5.2

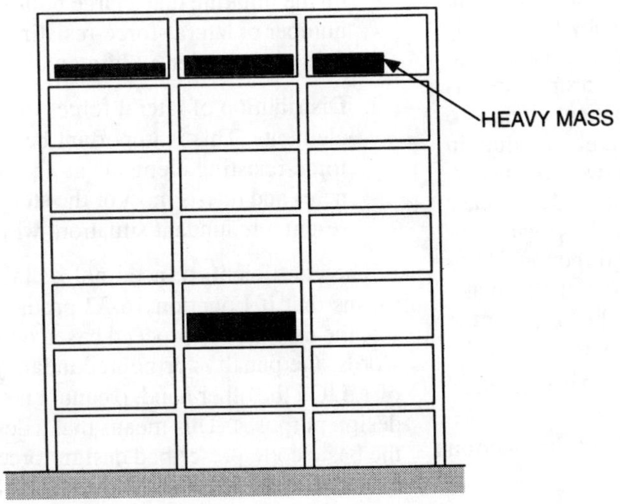

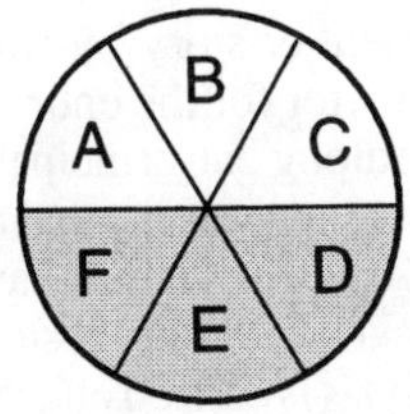

- STORY MASS > 150% ADJACENT STORY MASS
  (A ROOF THAT IS LIGHTER THAN THE FLOOR BELOW NEED NOT BE CONSIDERED)
- MODAL ANALYSIS PROCEDURE OF SECTION 1618 OR MORE RIGOROUS ANALYSIS REQUIRED (SECTION 1616.6.3) FOR BUILDINGS IN ALL SUGs ABOVE 5 STORIES OR 65 FEET IN HEIGHT

VERTICAL IRREGULARITY TYPE 2, WEIGHT (MASS) IRREGULARITY

FIGURE 22

REFER TO SECTION 1616.5.2, TABLE 1616.5.2

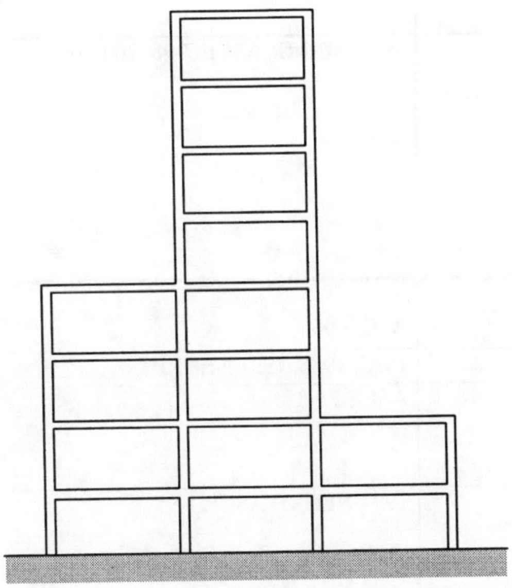

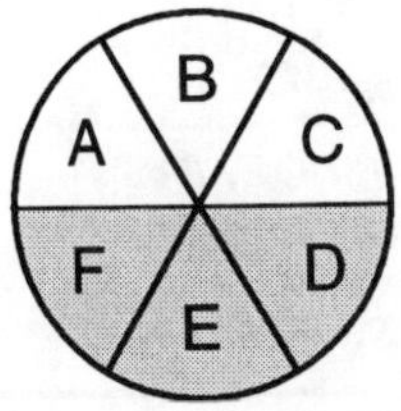

- HORIZONTAL DIMENSION OF LATERAL-FORCE-RESISTING SYSTEM IN STORY > 130% OF THAT IN ADJACENT STORY
- MODAL ANALYSIS PROCEDURE OF SECTION 1618 OR MORE RIGOROUS ANALYSIS REQUIRED (SECTION 1616.6.3) FOR BUILDINGS IN ALL SUGs ABOVE 5 STORIES OR 65 FEET IN HEIGHT

VERTICAL IRREGULARITY TYPE 3, VERTICAL GEOMETRIC IRREGULARITY

FIGURE 23

The redundancy coefficient, ρ, as defined in Section 1617.2.2 for structures assigned to SDC D, E and F, is not an element-by-element or story-by-story redundancy factor. It is the redundancy factor for the entire lateral-force-resisting system of a building along one principal plan axis. If a structure has lateral-force-resisting systems that are not identical along two orthogonal plan axes, then it may have two different ρ-values in the two orthogonal directions. In such cases, if two-dimensional structural analysis is carried out, the effects of the design base shear in the x-direction are to be amplified by the ρ-value for that direction, and similarly for the orthogonal direction. However, if a three-dimensional analysis is carried out, it may make sense to amplify the results of the analysis by the larger of the two ρ-values or by an arithmetic or a statistical average of the two ρ-values. No specific guidance is given as to which of these might be the most appropriate.

The redundancy coefficient, ρ, as defined in Section 1617.2.2, depends on three items:

1. The number of vertical lateral-force-resisting elements. The term "element" is particularized by the code for different lateral-force-resisting systems.
2. Floor areas of the building at different story levels, based on the thinking that a large building would require a larger number of lateral-force-resisting elements to be as redundant as a smaller building with fewer such elements.
3. Distribution of lateral forces to the lateral-force-resisting elements. This is important because if one of the lateral-force-resisting elements at a particular story level dominates and resists most of the story shear, that does not represent a redundant situation, which is to be avoided.

The coefficient, ρ, need not be taken larger than 1.5. This means that if Equation 16-32 produces a ρ-value larger than 1.5, the design may proceed based on a ρ-value of 1.5. In other words, the penalty for nonredundancy is capped at a ρ-value of 1.5. On the other hand, ρ cannot be taken as less than 1.0 for design purposes. This means that a designer may not go below the basic code-prescribed design force level of the code, however redundant the lateral-force-resisting system of a structure might be.

TABLE 18. CONSIDERATION OF VERTICAL SEISMIC GROUND ACCELERATION IN U.S. CODES AND RESOURCE DOCUMENTS

Design Base Shear	
$V = \frac{(1.2A_vS)}{RT^{2/3}}W \le \frac{(2.5A_a)}{R}W$	ATC 3-06, 1985 NEHRP, 1988 NEHRP, 1991 NEHRP, ASCE 7-93
$V = \frac{(1.2C_v)}{RT^{2/3}}W \le \frac{(2.5C_a)}{R}W$	1994 NEHRP, ASCE 7-95
$V = \frac{(C_vI)}{RT}W \le \frac{(2.5C_aI)}{R}W$	1997 UBC
$V = \frac{S_{D1}}{(R/I)T}W \le \frac{S_{DS}}{(R/I)}W$ $\ge 0.044\,S_{DS}IW$ $\ge \frac{0.5S_1}{R/I}W$ (SDC E, F only) $S_{DS} = 2/3\,S_{MS} = 2/3\,F_aS_s$ $S_{D1} = 2/3\,S_{M1} = 2/3\,F_vS_1$	1997 NEHRP, ASCE 7-98, 2000 IBC
Required Strength	
$U = 0.8Q_D \pm 1.0\,Q_E$	ATC 3-06
$U = (0.9 - 0.5A_V)\,Q_D \pm Q_E$	1985, 1988, 1991 NEHRP
$E = \pm\,1.0\,Q_E - 0.5\,A_vD$ $U = 0.9D + 1.0E$ $= (0.9 - 0.5\,A_v)\,D \pm 1.0\,Q_E$	ASCE 7-93
$E = Q_E \pm 0.5C_aD$ $U = 0.9D + 1.0E = (0.9 - 0.5C_a)D + Q_E$	1994 NEHRP, ASCE 7-95
$E = \rho E_h + 0.5C_a\,ID$ $U = 0.9D - 1.0E = (0.9 - 0.5C_a)ID - \rho E_h$	1997 UBC
$E = \rho Q_E - 0.2S_{DS}\,D$ $U = 0.9D + 1.0E = (0.9 - 0.2S_{DS})\,D + \rho Q_E$ $= (0.9 - 0.4F_aS_s/3)\,D + \rho Q_E$	1997 NEHRP, ASCE 7-98, 2000 IBC

Notes:

1. In the 1997 UBC, E_h is the effect of V. In all other documents, the effect of V is Q_E.
2. Special load combinations are not considered in the table.

REFER TO SECTION 1616.5.2, TABLE 1616.5.2

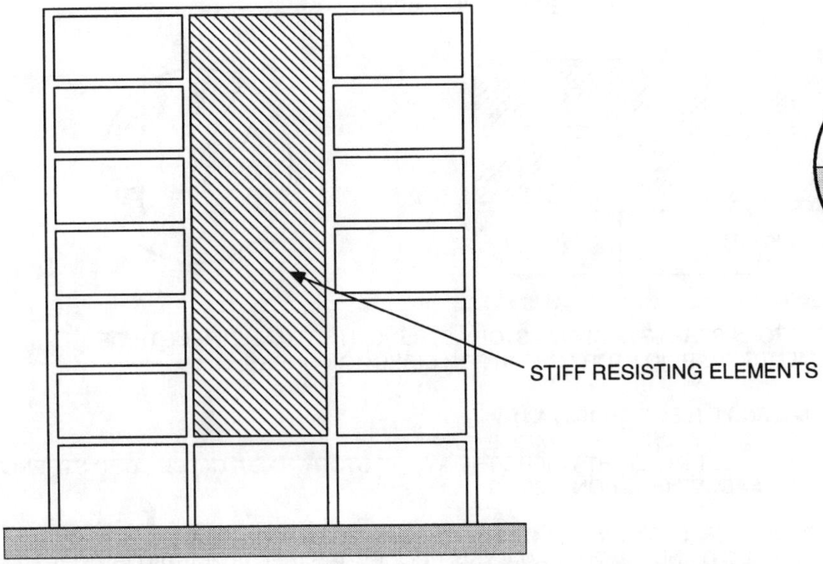

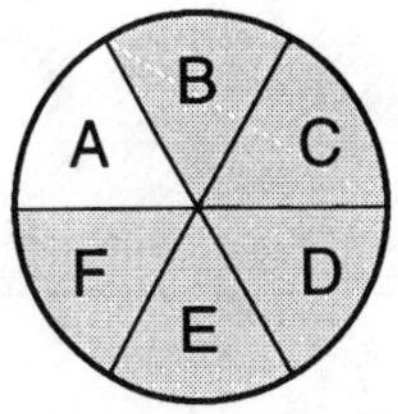

IN-PLANE OFFSET OF LATERAL-FORCE-RESISTING ELEMENTS > LENGTHS OF THOSE ELEMENTS, OR REDUCTION IN STIFFNESS OF RESISTING ELEMENTS IN STORY BELOW

- REQUIRED STRENGTH OF COLUMNS SUPPORTING DISCONTINUOUS SHEAR WALLS (OR BRACED FRAMES) (SECTION 1620.1.9):

  AS GIVEN BY SECTION 1605.4—SPECIAL SEISMIC LOAD COMBINATIONS

  $1.2D + f_1L + 1.0E_m$ (Formula 16-19)

  $0.9D + 1.0E_m$ (Formula 16-20)

WHERE:

IN FORMULA 16-19

$E_m = \Omega_o Q_E + 0.2\ S_{DS}\ D$ (Formula 16-30)

AND IN FORMULA 16-20

$E_m = \Omega_o Q_E - 0.2\ S_{DS}\ D$ (Formula 16-31)

- DESIGN FORCES DETERMINED FROM SECTION 1617.4.1 SHALL BE INCREASED 25% FOR CONNECTIONS OF DIAPHRAGMS TO VERTICAL ELEMENTS AND TO COLLECTORS, AND FOR CONNECTORS OF COLLECTIONS TO VERTICAL ELEMENTS.

- NOTE SPECIAL DETAILING REQUIREMENTS IN MATERIALS CHAPTERS.

VERTICAL IRREGULARITY TYPE 4, IN-PLANE DISCONTINUITY IN VERTICAL LATERAL-FORCE-RESISTING ELEMENTS

FIGURE 24

REFER TO SECTION 1616.5.2, TABLE 1616.5.2

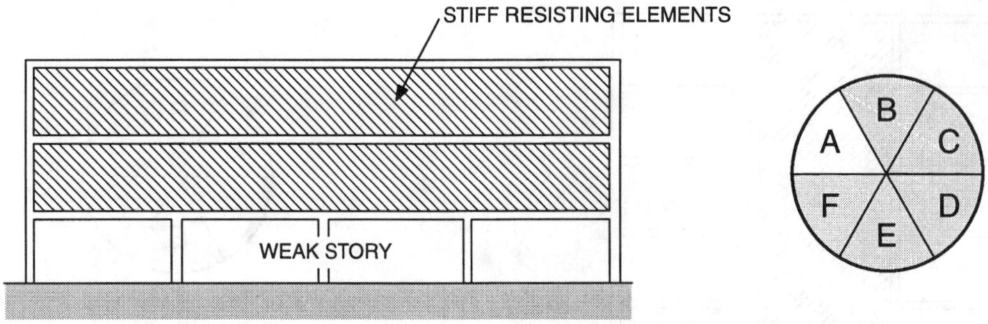

- "WEAK STORY" STRENGTH < 80% STORY STRENGTH ABOVE STORY STRENGTH = TOTAL STRENGTH OF SEISMIC-FORCE-RESISTING ELEMENTS SHARING STORY SHEAR FOR DIRECTION UNDER CONSIDERATION
- SHALL NOT BE PERMITTED IN SDC E AND F (SECTION 1620.4.1)
- SHALL NOT BE OVER 2 STORIES OR 30 FEET IN HEIGHT WHERE THE "WEAK" STORY HAS A CALCULATED STRENGTH OF LESS THAN 65% OF THAT IN STORY ABOVE (SECTION 1620.1.3)
- EQUIVALENT LATERAL FORCE PROCEDURE (SECTION 1617.4) PERMITTED WITH DYNAMIC CHARACTERISTICS INCLUDED IN ANALYTICAL MODEL, IN SDC B AND C MODAL ANALYSIS PROCEDURE (SECTION 1618) OR MORE RIGOROUS ANALYSIS APPEARS TO BE REQUIRED FOR SDC D (SECTION 1616.6.2)

VERTICAL IRREGULARITY TYPE 5, WEAK STORY

FIGURE 25

TABLE 19(a). 1994 NEHRP DEAD LOAD FACTORS, INCLUDING EFFECTS OF VERTICAL GROUND ACCELERATION
DLF = 0.9 – 0.5 C_a

	$A_a \le 0.05$		$A_a = 0.1$		$A_a = 0.2$		$A_a = 0.3$		$A_a > 0.4$	
SITE CLASS	C_a	DLF	C_a	DLF	C_a	DLF	C_a	DLF	C_a	DLF
A	0.04	0.88	0.08	0.86	0.16	0.82	0.24	0.78	0.32	0.74
B	0.05	0.88	0.10	0.85	0.20	0.80	0.30	0.75	0.40	0.70
C	0.06	0.87	0.12	0.84	0.24	0.78	0.33	0.74	0.40	0.70
D	0.08	0.86	0.16	0.82	0.28	0.76	0.36	0.72	0.44	0.68
E	0.13	0.84	0.25	0.78	0.34	0.73	0.36	0.72	0.36	0.72

TABLE 19(b). 1997 UBC DEAD LOAD FACTORS INCLUDING EFFECTS OF VERTICAL GROUND ACCELERATION, FOR SEISMIC ZONE 4
DLF = 0.9 – 0.5 $C_a I$

		$N_a = 1$		$N_a = 1.2$		$N_a = 1.3$		$N_a = 1.5$	
SITE CLASS	C_a	$I = 1.0$	$I = 1.25$	$I = 1.0$	$I = 1.25$	$I = 1.0$	$I = 1.25$	$I = 1.0$	$I = 1.25$
SA	$0.32N_a$	0.74	0.70	0.71	0.66	0.69	0.64	0.66	0.60
SB	$0.40N_a$	0.70	0.65	0.66	0.60	0.64	0.58	0.60	0.53
SC	$0.40N_a$	0.70	0.65	0.66	0.60	0.64	0.58	0.60	0.53
SD	$0.44N_a$	0.68	0.63	0.64	0.57	0.61	0.54	0.57	0.49
SE	$0.36N_a$	0.72	0.68	0.68	0.63	0.67	0.61	0.63	0.56

TABLE 19(c). 1997 NEHRP/ 2000 IBC DEAD LOAD FACTORS, INCLUDING EFFECTS OF VERTICAL GROUND ACCELERATION
DLF = 0.9 – 0.4 $F_a S_s/3$

	$S_s \le 0.25$		$S_s = 0.5$		$S_s = 0.75$		$S_s = 1.00$		$S_s \ge 1.25$	
SITE CLASS	F_a	DLF	F_a	DLF	F_a	DLF	F_a	DLF	F_a	DLF
A	0.8	0.873	0.8	0.847	0.8	0.82	0.8	0.793	0.8	0.767
B	1.0	0.867	1.0	0.833	1.0	0.80	1.0	0.767	1.0	0.733
C	1.2	0.860	1.2	0.820	1.1	0.79	1.0	0.767	1.0	0.733
D	1.6	0.847	1.4	0.807	1.2	0.78	1.1	0.753	1.0	0.733
E	2.5	0.817	1.7	0.787	1.2	0.78	0.9	0.780		

There are two differences between the 1997 UBC formulation and the 2000 IBC formulation of the ρ factor. First, the UBC uses a fixed area, A_B, the ground floor area of the structure, in the equivalent of Equation 16-32. The IBC uses a variable area, A_i, which is the floor area of the diaphragm immediately above story *i*. Second, the UBC defines r_{max} as the largest of the maximum element-to-story shear ratios, $r_{\max_i}$, occurring over the lower two-thirds of the building height. The IBC defines ρ as the largest of the values of ρ_i over the entire height of a structure.

Figure 26A presents the formulation of the redundancy coefficient, ρ, for buildings with their lateral-force-resisting system consisting of shear walls. The $10/\ell_w$ adjustment is noteworthy.

The $10/\ell_w$ adjustment has been the subject of considerable controversy since the publication of the 1997 UBC where it first appeared, because of its adverse impact on wood frame construction. According to one member of the group that formulated the redundancy provisions of the 1997 UBC, "the intent was that each individual wall pier across a horizontal plane cut through the building would be an 'element.' Then someone on the committee noted that if you had a 100-foot by 100-foot tilt-up type structure, with a number of 20-foot-wide panels, this would be considered to have high redundancy (because each 20-foot panel would be an element). However, if you had the same structure with cast-in-place walls, then it would be nonredundant, as the whole side of the structure would be only one element. To solve this problem, for shear walls, we introduced the rule that when a shear wall exceeded 10 feet in length, each 10-foot segment (or part thereof) could be considered an element. The intent was as follows—if you have a wall line with 10-foot by 4-foot piers between windows, each pier would be an element. If you had a wall line with a 40-foot wall, you would have four elements . . . Now each wall segment is multiplied by $10/\ell_w$. This has the desired effect for long walls, but has a penalty effect for short wall segments. This was, in my opinion, never intended." The 1999 edition of the SEAOC Blue Book has, accordingly, imposed an upper limit of 1.0 on the ratio $10/\ell_w$. The same upper limit has been proposed for the 2003 edition of the IBC concerning buildings of light frame construction only.

Figure 26B illustrates applications of the formulation in Figure 26A. All the examples in this section are focused on a particular floor level. The diaphragms in all the examples of Figure 26B are assumed to be flexible. This is strictly out of a desire to keep the examples simple and to avoid complications arising form torsion. However, a direct consequence of this assumption is that the story shears are distributed to the shear walls in proportion to their tributary areas, not stiffnesses. This can have significant effect on the results obtained. For example, the redundancy coefficient does not change from Case 1(a) to 1(b), strictly because of the flexible diaphragm assumption. If the story shears were distributed according to the stiffnesses of the shear walls rather than their tributary areas, there would have been a gain in redundancy from Case 1(a) to Case 1(b). Case 2(b) mainly illustrates the point that $10/\ell_w$ may be larger than 1.0. As long as that is the case, one 10-foot-long shear wall and two 5-foot-long shear walls on each face are equivalent in terms of redundancy. However, if the *1999 SEAOC Blue Book* modification restricting $10/\ell_w$ to be no larger than 1.0 is adopted in the IBC, Case 2(b) will be regarded as more redundant than Case 2(a). Case 2(d) again illustrates the consequences of the flexible diaphragm assumption. Both the short

ρ VARIES DEPENDING ON:

- FLOOR AREA OF BUILDING
- NUMBER OF SHEAR WALLS RESISTING STORY SHEAR
- LENGTHS OF SHEAR WALLS

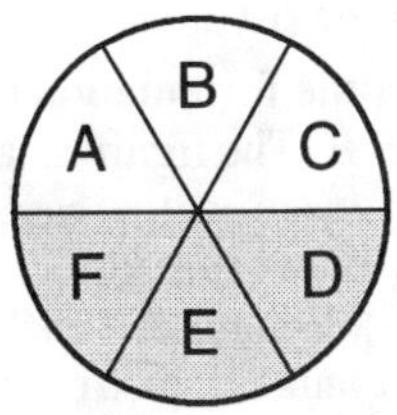

$$\rho_i = 2 - 20/(r_{\max_i}\sqrt{A_i})$$
$$1.0 \le \rho \le 1.5$$

PER STORY

r_{max_i} = (MAXIMUM WALL SHEAR/TOTAL STORY SHEAR) $(10/\ell_W)$

ℓ_W = LENGTH OF WALL OR WALL PIER IN FEET

A_i = FLOOR AREA IN SQUARE FEET OF DIAPHRAGM IMMEDIATELY ABOVE STORY *(i)*

TOTAL BUILDING

ρ = MAXIMUM (ρ_i) OF ANY STORY OVER HEIGHT OF BUILDING

REDUNDANCY (ρ) FOR BUILDINGS WITH LATERAL-FORCE-RESISTING SYSTEM CONSISTING OF SHEAR WALLS (BEARING WALL SYSTEMS, BUILDING FRAME SYSTEMS)—FORMULATION

FIGURE 26A

wall and the long wall carry half the story shear, based on tributary areas. Case 2(e) illustrates the fact that Case 2(c) already represents a fully redundant situation; it cannot be improved upon by increasing either the number of shear walls or the lengths of the shear walls. Case 3 shows that if the diaphragms are flexible, a 5,000-square-foot plan area with two 10-foot-long shear walls on two faces parallel to the direction of earthquake and a 10,000-square-foot plan area with four 10-foot-long shear walls evenly distributed along the long face are equivalent in terms of redundancy.

The formulation of the redundancy coefficient, ρ, for buildings with a lateral-force-resisting system consisting of moment frames is shown in Figure 27A. The columns of the moment frames are now the lateral-force-resisting elements. As noted, for a structure relying solely on special moment frames as the lateral-force-resisting system in a particular direction, ρ in that direction must not exceed 1.25 if the structure is assigned to SDC D, and it must not exceed 1.10 if the structure is assigned to SDC E or F. This restriction means that if Equation 16-32 produces a redundancy coefficient in excess of the above values for a special moment-resisting frame system, the physical configuration of the system must be changed until ρ comes within the target range. This is the only structural system upon which redundancy is literally being forced by the code. For all other structural systems, only a penalty for nonredundancy is imposed. It may be noted that the upper-bound value of ρ for special moment frames in the 1997 UBC is 1.25 in Seismic Zones 3 and 4. Significantly, the restriction on the maximum value of ρ does not apply to ordinary or intermediate moment frames. Ordinary or intermediate frames of concrete are not allowed to be part of the lateral-force-resisting system of buildings assigned to SDC D, E or F. While such systems of steel are allowed as part of the earthquake force-resisting systems of buildings assigned to SDC D, E or F, there is already a penalty in the form of lower *R*-values to be used in design, which may justify the lack of restriction on the ρ-value.

Application of the formulation presented in Figure 27A appears in Figure 27B. The figure is largely self-explanatory. The multiplier of 0.7 used in the cases of three-bay or four-bay moment frames is because the columns carrying the largest shears (interior columns) are each common to two adjacent bays. A moment connection on each face of a column is also important. If, in the case of the three-bay frame, the beam of the center bay were connected to the columns by means of simple connections only, the multiplier of 0.7 would not have been applicable to the interior columns. It should be noted that because of the upper-bound limitation on the value of ρ, anything less than a four-bay moment frame on each face of the example building with a plan area of 22,500 square feet would be an inadmissible design under IBC 2000. If the structure were assigned to SDC E or F, rather than SDC D, even a four-bay moment frame on each face would not have been sufficient.

Figure 28A presents the formulation of the redundancy coefficient, ρ, for buildings with their lateral-force-resisting system consisting of braced frames. The braces are now the lateral-force-resisting elements. Application of the formulation presented in Figure 28A is illustrated in Figure 28B. Because of a lack of an absolute upper-bound restriction, a one-bay braced frame on each face of a building with a plan area of 22,500 square feet is already an admissible solution. There is a penalty in the form of a ρ-value of 1.47, but the code does not prohibit the use of this solution. Also, two bays of braced frames on each face already represent a fully redundant solution. This simply reflects different levels of sophistication in the formulation of the redundancy coefficient for different structural systems. The formulation is less refined in the case of braced frames than in the case of moment frames. This probably has the unintended effect of encouraging the use of braced frames over moment frames. Also, the braced frame formulation is not sophisticated enough to make a distinction between concentrically and eccentrically braced frames or any differentiation among the types of bracing used (K-bracing, X-bracing and so forth).

A dual system consisting of shear walls (or brace frames) and moment frames has two conditions imposed by Section 1617.6.1 of the code. First, the shear walls as well as the moment frames must be designed to carry their share of the design lateral forces, based on an interactive analysis of the combined structural system under those forces. Second, the moment frames must be designed to resist one-quarter of the design lateral forces independent of the shear walls. For a structure satisfying these conditions, ρ is to be calculated on the basis of the proportion of story shears resisted by the shear walls and the moment frame columns at various story levels. The ρ-value calculated on this basis can then be reduced by 20 percent, because there are frames backing up the shear walls as part of the lateral-force-resisting systems. Figure 29A illustrates the application of this code provision. In a building combining shear walls and frames as part of the lateral-force-resisting system, such as the one shown in Figure 29B, most of the story shear is resisted by the shear walls in the lowest portions of the building. The frames pick up more and more of the story shear as one moves up the building from its base. Thus, it can be stated with assurance, without detailed investigation, that the lowest story level will produce the highest value of ρ_i, which then will be the ρ for the entire building in the in-plane direction of the shear walls. For the example of Figure 29, it is assumed that in the up-and-down direction of the building (the direction with one shear wall), the shear wall absorbs 92 percent of the design base shear, with the frames resisting the remaining 8 percent. This is a fairly representative distribution for a building of the type shown. Then r_{max} becomes $0.92 \times 10/20 = 0.46$, because the shear wall in the direction being considered is 20 feet long. This provides a ρ-value of 1.41 based on a floor plan area of 5,400 square feet. However, because the building employs a dual system for lateral resistance, the ρ-value is adjusted to $0.8 \times 1.41 = 1.13$. It should be noted that if the same building had been designed as a building frame system rather than a dual system, the ρ-value would have remained at 1.41; the 0.8 adjustment would not have been applicable.

For structures in which one seismic-force-resisting system occurs in an upper portion and a different system occurs in the lower portion, the redundancy factor for one system does not reflect the redundancy of the other system. The limit on the ratio, R/ρ, is intended to prevent the combinations of the response modification factors and the redundancy coefficients for the upper and lower portions to result in a lower force in the lower portion than occurs in the upper portion.

Examples 8 and 9, Part 2 of this chapter, further illustrate the application of the redundancy coefficient.

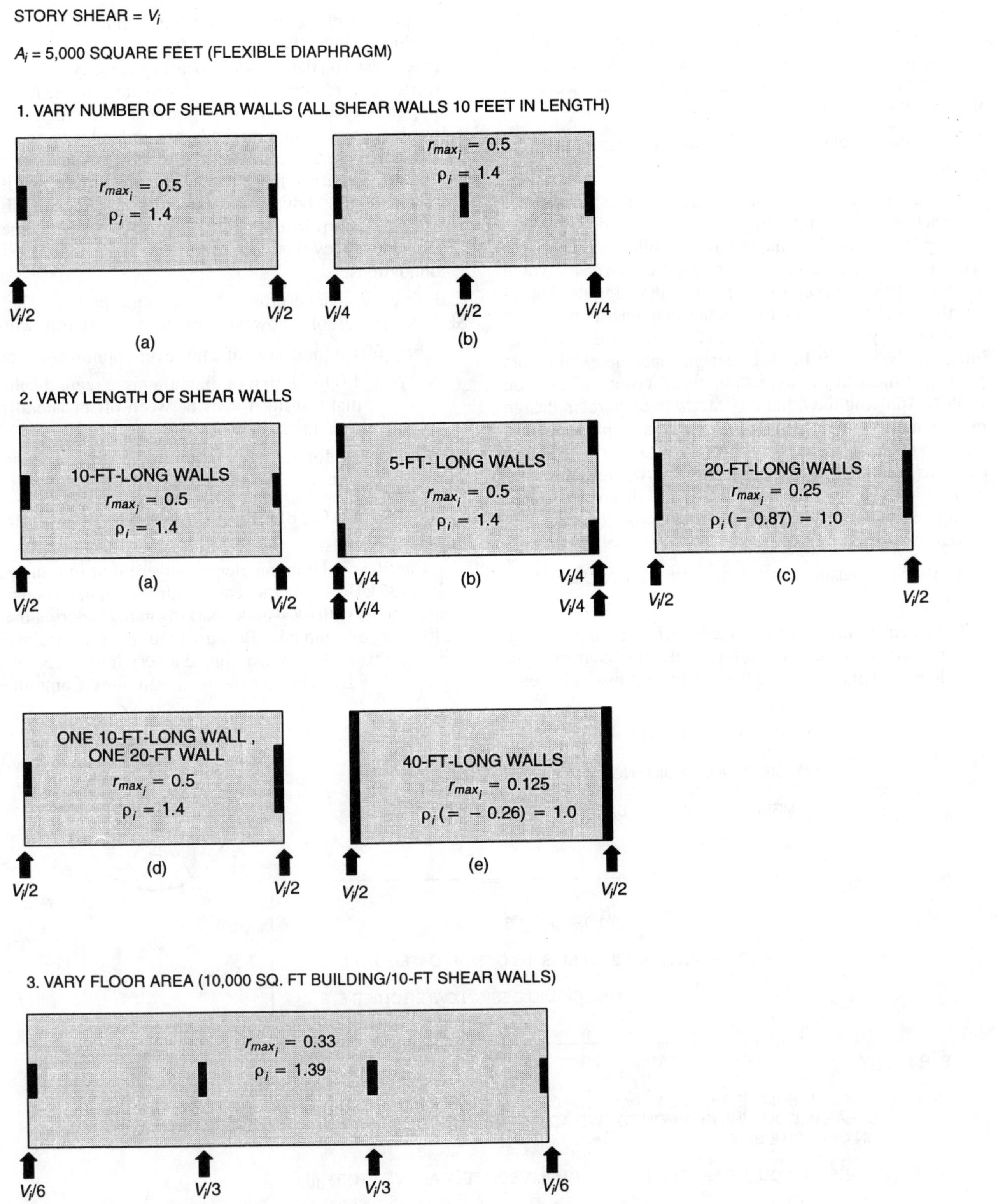

REDUNDANCY (ρ) OF BUILDINGS WITH LATERAL-FORCE-RESISTING SYSTEM CONSISTING OF SHEAR WALLS (BEARING WALL SYSTEMS, BUILDING FRAME SYSTEMS)—EXAMPLE CALCULATIONS

FIGURE 26B

The Structural Engineers Association of Washington submitted changes to the first as well as the final draft of the IBC requesting the following additions to Section 1617.2.2: for design of diaphragms and collectors, a ρ of 1.0 may be used, and a ρ of 1.0 may also be used for design of foundations.

The following reason was submitted to justify the first proposal:

> The reliability is determined by the characteristics of the vertical lateral-force-resisting elements, which do not reflect the characteristics of the diaphragm and collectors. The higher design forces can result in higher construction costs, which are not justified, especially for flexible diaphragms. Applying the reliability factor to flexible diaphragms may also make some systems, such as wood horizontal diaphragms, infeasible because of limits of design capacities. Collectors are still subject to the over-strength provisions of Section 1605.4. Applying the reliability factor to diaphragm design may actually be counterintuitive in that a diaphragm for a highly redundant system may be required to distribute higher forces as redundant vertical elements fail, whereas the force distribution for a nonredundant system will not change as significantly during a larger event because the system is, by definition, nonredundant.

The following reason was submitted to justify the second proposal:

> The intent of the redundancy coefficient is to provide a minimum quantity of lateral-force-resisting elements per unit floor area and to ensure that for low ratios of elements per area, the elements have an additional level of ductility to preclude failure. Footings are typically sized and proportioned based on the allowable bearing capacity of the soil and overturning of the lateral-force-resisting elements(s) they support. Because the size of a footing is determined using allowable stress design methods, the redundancy coefficient does not apply to the sizing of the footing. Additionally, the bearing capacity of the soil is independent of the ductility of the element(s) above and the ductility of element(s) has no effect on the overturning characteristics of the element(s). The redundancy factor, ρ, should not apply to the design of foundations.

Both code change proposals were disapproved. The 1999 SEAOC Blue Book,[4] however, has allowed the following:

- ρ = 1.0 for design of cantilever column elements.
- ρ = 1.0 for design of diaphragms, except diaphragms that transfer forces between offset lateral-force-resisting systems.
- ρ = 1.0 for design of nonbuilding structures and nonstructural elements.

The 1999 SEAOC Blue Book Commentary offers the following explanations:

> Cantilevered column elements were first introduced into the 1996 UBC supplement after failure of many wood framed apartments with tuck-under parking garages during the 1994 Northridge earthquake. Because of its inherent lack of redundancy, this system was assigned a very low force reduction factor, $R = 2.2$. This is why the Seismology Committee felt

ρ VARIES DEPENDING ON:

- FLOOR AREA OF BUILDING
- NUMBER OF FRAME COLUMNS RESISTING STORY SHEAR

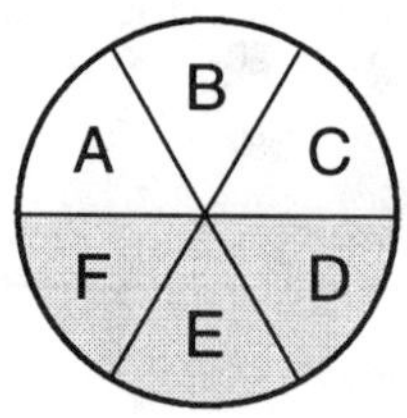

$$\rho_i = 2 - 20/(r_{max_i}\sqrt{A_i})$$

$$1.0 \le \rho \le 1.5$$

FOR SMRF. . . ρ ≤ 1.25 IN SEISMIC DESIGN CATEGORY D

≤ 1.10 IN SEISMIC DESIGN CATEGORIES E, F

PER STORY

r_{max_i} = MAXIMUM SUM OF SHEARS IN TWO ADJACENT COLUMNS/TOTAL STORY SHEAR. CONSIDER 70% OF SHEAR IN COLUMNS COMMON TO TWO ADJACENT BAYS, WITH MOMENT-RESISTING CONNECTIONS ON OPPOSITE SIDES

A_i = FLOOR AREA IN SQUARE FEET OF DIAPHRAGM IMMEDIATELY ABOVE STORY *(i)*

TOTAL BUILDING

ρ = MAXIMUM (ρ_i) OF ANY STORY OVER HEIGHT OF BUILDING

REDUNDANCY (ρ) FOR BUILDINGS WITH LATERAL-FORCE-RESISTING SYSTEM CONSISTING OF MOMENT FRAMES—FORMULATION

FIGURE 27A

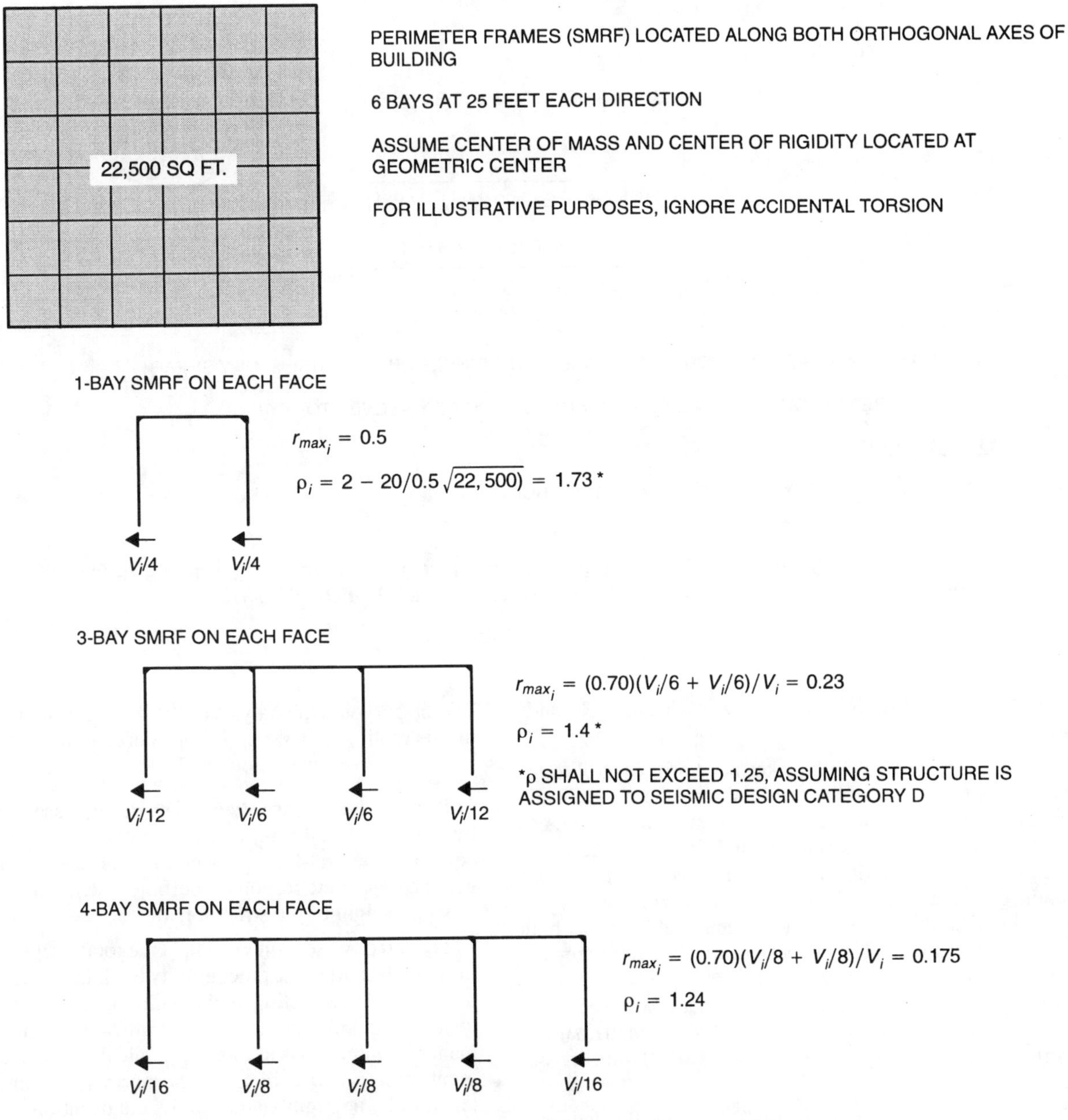

REDUNDANCY (ρ) OF BUILDINGS WITH LATERAL-FORCE-RESISTING SYSTEM CONSISTING OF MOMENT FRAMES—EXAMPLE CALCULATIONS

FIGURE 27B

that a ρ of 1.0 is sufficient and no additional penalty was required.

Drag and collector element design for the special load combination is considered adequate to transfer any amplified shear forces (due to ρ > 1.0) between lateral-force-resisting elements and the diaphragm with no further amplification necessary for diaphragm design. However, application of ρ > 1.0 to the transfer diaphragm design is aimed to envelop the demand between the offset or discontinuous lateral-force-resisting elements and the diaphragm in irregular structures.

1617.3 Deflection and drift limits. The IBC controls "inter-story drift expected to be caused by the design earthquake." This quantity, called the design story drift, is determined as required by Section 1617.4.6 or 1617.5.3, and is discussed under those sections. The commentary to the 1997 NEHRP Provisions gives several reasons for controlling drift.

One reason is "to control member inelastic strain. Although use of drift limitations is an imprecise and highly variable way of controlling strain, this is balanced by the current state of knowledge of what the strain limitations should be."

A stability problem is resolved by limiting the drift on the vertical load-carrying elements and the resulting secondary moments (P-delta effect). Large deformations with heavy vertical loads can lead to significant secondary moments from the

ρ VARIES DEPENDING ON:

- FLOOR AREA OF BUILDING
- NUMBER OF BRACE ELEMENTS RESISTING STORY SHEAR

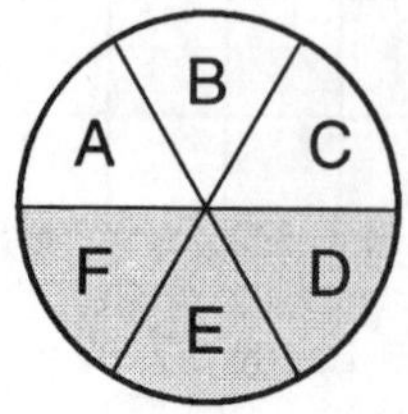

$$\rho_i = 2 - 20/(r_{max_i}\sqrt{A_i})$$

$$1.0 \leq \rho \leq 1.5$$

PER STORY

r_{max_i} = MAXIMUM HORIZONTAL FORCE COMPONENT IN A SINGLE BRACE/TOTAL STORY SHEAR

A_i = FLOOR AREA IN SQUARE FEET OF DIAPHRAGM IMMEDIATELY ABOVE STORY *(i)*

TOTAL BUILDING

ρ = MAXIMUM (ρ_i) OF ANY STORY OVER HEIGHT OF BUILDING

REDUNDANCY (ρ) OF BUILDINGS WITH LATERAL-FORCE-RESISTING SYSTEM CONSISTING OF BRACED FRAMES—FORMULATION

FIGURE 28A

P-delta effects. The drift limits indirectly provide upper bounds on these effects.

Buildings subjected to earthquakes need drift control to restrict damage to partitions, shaft and stair enclosures, glass and other fragile nonstructural elements and, more important, "to minimize differential movement demand on the seismic safety elements. Since general damage control for economic reasons is not the goal ... and since the state of the art is not well developed in this area, the drift limits have been established without regard to considerations such as present worth of future repairs versus additional structural costs to limit drift. These are matters for building owners and designers to examine." To the extent that life safety might be excessively threatened, damage to nonstructural and seismic safety elements is a drift limit consideration.

The design story drift limits of Table 1617.3 reflect consensus judgment taking into account the goals of drift control outlined above. The 2000 IBC limits on story drift depend upon the seismic use group, and generally become more restrictive for the higher use groups, to provide a higher level of performance. The limits also depend on the type of structure. In the 1997 UBC, the drift limits are not dependent on the occupancy of the structure, which is effectively considered because Δ_s is higher for structures in higher occupancy categories with an importance factor, *I*, of 1.25 assigned to them, and because the multiplier of 0.7*R*, which takes the designer from Δ_s to Δ_M is independent of *I*. The UBC drift limits are dependent only on the period of the structure, drift limits being more restrictive for structures having periods greater than or equal to 0.7 second, although some exceptions for this are made.

1617.4 Equivalent lateral-force procedure for seismic design of buildings. The applicability of this procedure was discussed under Section 1616.6, and is summarized in Table 16. For the purposes of analysis under the equivalent lateral forces of this section, a building is considered to be fixed at its base. Base is defined in Section 1613.

1617.4.1 Seismic base shear. The design base shear, as given by Equation 16-34 is the starting point in seismic design by the equivalent lateral-force procedure. The design base shear is given as a seismic response coefficient, C_s, times the effective seismic weight of the structure, *W*.

The effective seismic weight is the total weight of the building and that part of the other gravity loads that might reasonably be expected to be acting on the building at the time of an earthquake. It includes permanent and movable partitions and permanent equipment such as mechanical and electrical equipment, piping and ceilings. "The normal human live load is taken to be negligibly small in its contribution to the seismic lateral forces."[8] Buildings intended for storage or warehouse occupancy must have at least 25 percent of the design floor live load included in the *W*. When it comes to the inclusion of a part of the design snow load in *W*, there is one of the few differences between the requirements of the 1997 NEHRP Provisions and those of the IBC.

According to the 1997 NEHRP Provisions, in areas where the design flat roof snow load does not exceed 30 psf (1.4 kPa), the effective snow load is permitted to be taken as zero. In areas where the design snow load is greater than 30 psf (1.4 kPa) and where siting and load duration considerations warrant and when approved by the authority having jurisdiction, the effective snow load is permitted to be reduced to no less than 20 percent of the design snow load. The 1997 NEHRP Commentary explains that freshly fallen snow would have little effect on the lateral force in an earthquake, but that ice loading would be more or less firmly attached to the roof of the building and would contribute significantly to the inertia force. For this reason, the effective snow load is taken as the full design snow load for those regions where the snow load exceeds 30 psf, with the proviso that the local authority having jurisdiction may allow the snow load to be reduced up to 80 percent. The question of how much snow load should be included in *W* is really a question of how much ice buildup or snow entrapment can be expected for the roof configuration or site topography, and this is a question the 1997 NEHRP Provisions leaves to the discretion of the local authority having jurisdiction. The 1997 UBC also leaves the same matter to the discretion of the building official. The 2000 IBC, however, requires the inclusion of a fixed 20 percent of the flat roof snow load in *W* where the flat roof snow load exceeds 30 psf. When the flat roof snow load is lower, no portion of it needs to be included in *W*.

1617.4.1.1 Calculation of seismic response coefficient. The seismic response coefficient, C_s, as defined by Equations 16-35 and 16-36 describes the design response spectrum of Figure 1615.1.4, with two modifications. First, the "ramp" building up to the "flat-top" of the design spectrum is excluded from consideration under Section 1617.4.1.1. This is because the equivalent lateral-force procedure deals with fundamental mode response. The period of the first mode of a practical building structure is unlikely to be in the very short period range, $T < 0.2T_S$, where the ramp would have been required. In other words, the ramp is excluded from consideration because it is unlikely to be required. Second, the seismic response coefficient defined by Equations 16-35 and 16-36 is the spectral response acceleration of Figure 1615.1.4, amplified by the occupancy importance factor, I_E, and reduced by the response modification factor, *R*.

Equation 16-35 represents the constant acceleration portion of the spectrum of Figure 1615.1.4, while Equation 16-36 represents the constant velocity portion. The design force level defined by Equations 16-34 through 16-36 is based on the

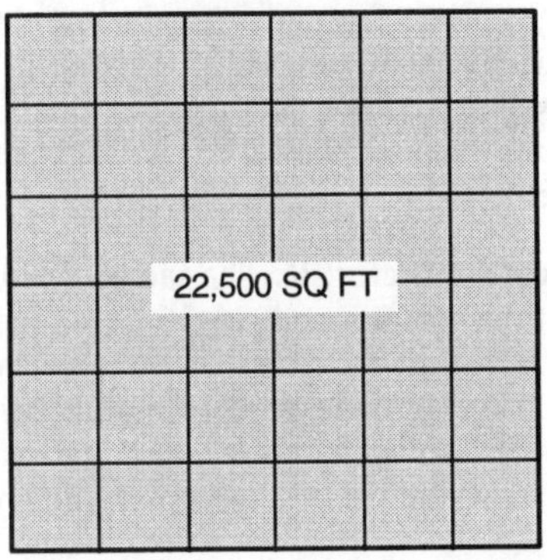

PERIMETER BRACED FRAMES LOCATED ALONG BOTH ORTHOGONAL AXES OF BUILDING

6 BAYS AT 25 FEET EACH DIRECTION

ASSUME CENTER OF MASS AND CENTER OF RIGIDITY LOCATED AT GEOMETRIC CENTER

FOR ILLUSTRATIVE PURPOSES, IGNORE ACCIDENTAL TORSION

ALL BRACED FRAMES IDENTICAL IN CONFIGURATION

1 BRACED FRAME EACH FACE

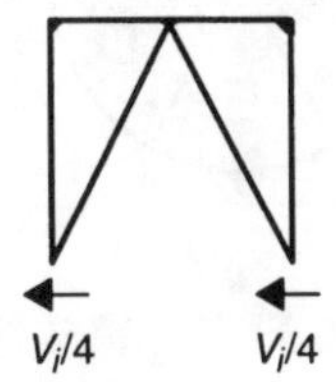

$r_{max_i} = 0.25$

$\rho_i = 2 - 20/(0.25\sqrt{22,500}) = 1.47$

2 BRACED FRAMES EACH FACE

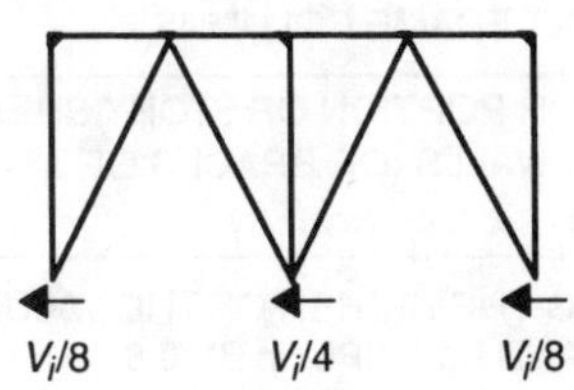

$r_{max_i} = 0.125$

$\rho_i = 2 - 20/(0.125\sqrt{22,500}) = 0.93$

REDUNDANCY (ρ) OF BUILDINGS WITH LATERAL-FORCE-RESISTING SYSTEM CONSISTING OF BRACED FRAMES—EXAMPLE CALCULATIONS

FIGURE 28B

assumption that a structure will undergo several cycles of inelastic deformation during major earthquake ground motion and, therefore, the level is related to the type of structural system and its estimated ability to sustain these deformations and dissipate energy without collapse. The force level defined by Equations 16-34 through 16-36 is used not only for the static lateral- force procedure, but also as the lower bound for the dynamic lateral-force procedure of Section 1618. Thus, it is worthwhile to discuss the physical relationship between the design base shear and the spectral representation of major earthquake ground motion, as well as the idealization of the inelastic behavior of the structure due to this ground motion.

For a given fundamental period, T, the design base shear Equations 16-34 through 16-36 provide values that are equal to the acceleration response spectrum ordinate, S_{DS}, for $T \leq T_S$ and S_{D1}/T for $T > T_S$, as given in Figure 1615.1.4, times the total structure weight, W, multiplied by the importance factor, I, and divided by R. While only the fundamental mode period is employed, the additional response due to higher modes of vibration is represented and approximated by use of the total weight, W. Appendix D to the 1999 SEAOC Blue Book[4] points out that the first or fundamental mode base shear is the effective mass of the first mode times the first mode spectral ordinate, S_a. This effective mass is on the order of 0.7 times the total mass, W/g. Therefore the use of the W in the base shear equations is intended to provide an upper bound value of the combined mode (SRSS or CQC) base shear response.

Descending branch of the design spectrum. The elastic acceleration response spectrum for earthquake ground motion has a descending branch for longer values of T that varies roughly as $1/T$. In the NEHRP Provisions prior to the 1997 edition and in the UBC prior to its 1997 edition, the actual response spectrum that varies in a $1/T$ relationship was replaced with a design spectrum that varied in a $1/T^{2/3}$ relationship. This was intentionally done to provide added conservatism in the design of tall structures. For the 1997 NEHRP Provisions, it was decided that the true shape of the response spectrum, represented by a $1/T$ relationship, was to be maintained in the base shear equations. The 1997 NEHRP Commentary explains: "In order to maintain the added conservatism for tall and high occupancy structures, formerly provided by the design spectra which utilized a $1/T^{2/3}$ relationship, the 1997 Provisions adopted an occupancy importance factor, I, into the base shear equation. This I factor, which has a value of 1.25 for SUG II structures and 1.5 for SUG III structures, has the effect of raising the design spectrum for taller, high-occupancy structures to levels comparable to those for which they were designed in previous editions of the Provisions." This explanation appears to be less than tenable. The 1999 SEAOC Blue Book Commentary offers the right explanation with regard to the 1997 UBC, which has also made the descending branch of the design spectrum a function of $1/T$ rather than $1/T^{2/3}$. To paraphrase the explanation for the IBC, in view of the use of the total weight W (in the design base shear equations), along with appropriate S_{DS} and S_{D1} values, and the long period plateau Equations 16-36 and 16-37, the use of the $1/T$ version of the base shear equation provides reasonable parity with prior requirements that used the $1/T^{2/3}$ relation to represent multi-mode response.

Response modification factor, R. The factor, R, in the denominator of Equations 16-35 and 16-36 is an empirical response reduction factor intended to account for both the damping and the ductility (or inelastic deformability) inherent in a structural system at displacements large enough to surpass initial yield and approach maximum inelastic response

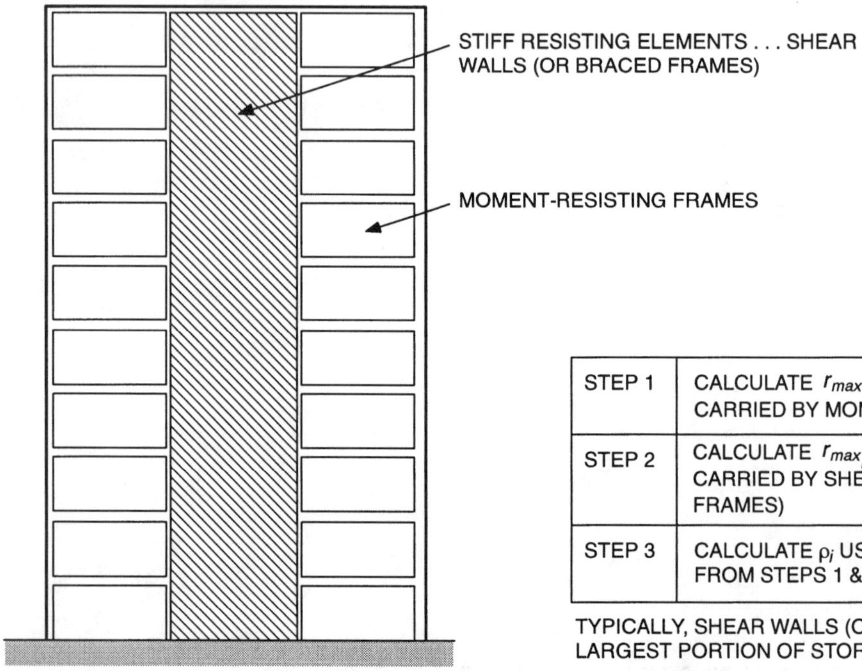

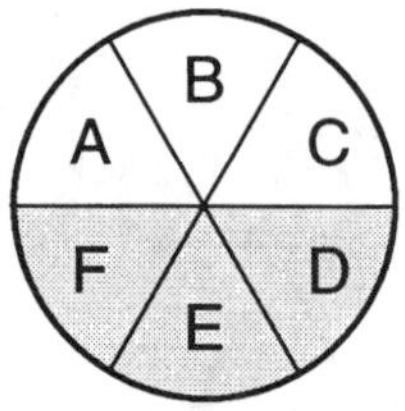

STEP 1	CALCULATE r_{max_i} FOR PORTION OF STORY SHEAR CARRIED BY MOMENT FRAME COLUMNS
STEP 2	CALCULATE r_{max_i} FOR PORTION OF STORY SHEAR CARRIED BY SHEAR WALLS (OR BRACES OF BRACED FRAMES)
STEP 3	CALCULATE ρ_i USING THE HIGHER OF THE VALUES FROM STEPS 1 & 2 AND MULTIPLY ρ BY 0.8

TYPICALLY, SHEAR WALLS (OR BRACED FRAMES) WILL CARRY LARGEST PORTION OF STORY SHEAR AT BASE OF STRUCTURE

REDUNDANCY (ρ) OF DUAL SYSTEMS—FORMULATION

FIGURE 29A

displacements.[8] The factor, R, is also intended to account for overstrength, which is partly material-dependent and partly system-dependent. Since design force levels are based on first yield of the highest stressed elements of a system, the maximum force level that the system can resist after the formation of successive hinges, bracing yield, or shear wall yield or cracking is significantly higher than the initial yield value. Designs are also based on minimum expected yield or strength values, whereas the average strength of a material could be significantly higher. The 1999 SEAOC Blue Book has divided R into two portions: R_o and R_d. While R_o represents the overstrength-dependent part of the R factor, R_d represents the part dependent upon damping and ductility.

As pointed out in the commentary to the 1997 NEHRP Provisions, for a lightly damped building structure of brittle material that would be unable to tolerate any appreciable deformation beyond the elastic range, the factor, R would be close to 1.0 (that is, no reduction from the force level corresponding to linear elastic response would be allowed). At the other extreme, a heavily damped building structure with a very ductile structural system would be able to withstand deformation considerably in excess of initial yield and would, therefore, justify the assignment of a relatively large response modification factor, R. Table 1617.6 stipulates R factors for different types of structural systems using several different construction materials. The coefficient, R, ranges in value from a minimum of 1.5 for a bearing wall system consisting of ordinary plain masonry shear walls to a maximum of 8.0 for a special moment frame system or a dual system consisting of special moment frames. The basis for the R-factor values specified in Table 1617.6 is explained in the 1997 NEHRP Commentary Section 5.2.1.

Modification by importance factor, I_E. The effective value of R used in the base shear equations is adjusted by the occupancy importance factor, I_E. The I_E value, which ranges between 1.0 and 1.5, has the effect of reducing the amount of ductility a structure will be called upon to provide at a given level of ground shaking, thus also reducing the damage inflicted by the same level of ground motion. However, as pointed out in the 1997 NEHRP Commentary, added strength by itself is not sufficient to produce superior seismic performance in buildings with critical occupancies. "Good connections and construction details, quality assurance procedures, and limitations on building deformation are also important to significantly improve the capability for maintenance of function and safety in critical facilities and those with high-density occupancy."[8] Consequently, the reduction in the damage potential of critical facilities is also handled by using more conservative drift controls (Sec. 1617.3) and by providing special design and detailing requirements (Section 1616.3 through 1616.6) and materials limitations (Chapters 19, 21, 22, and 23).

Minimum base shear. Following the Long Beach earthquake of 1933, the Riley Act in California required every building to be designed for a minimum service-level seismic force equal to 3 percent of its weight. This minimum requirement

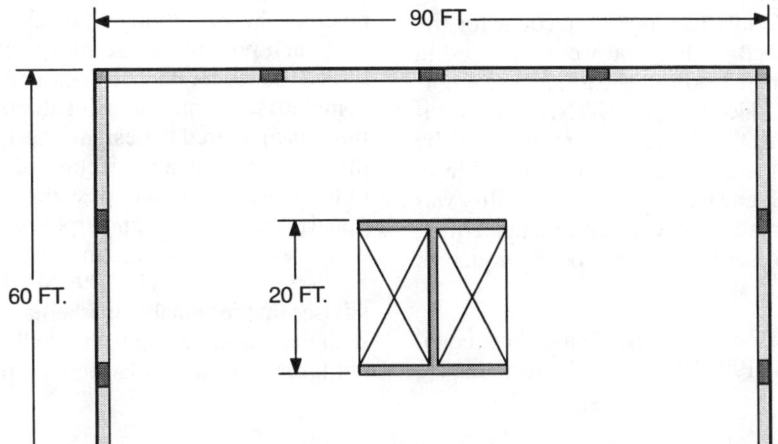

DUAL SHEAR WALL-FRAME BUILDING WITH PERIMETER FRAMES (SMRF) LOCATED ALONG BOTH ORTHOGONAL AXES OF BUILDING AND SHEAR WALL ELEVATOR SHAFT AT CENTER OF FLOOR PLAN

ASSUME AT LOWEST LEVEL, 92% OF STORY SHEAR CARRIED BY SHEAR WALLS, 8% BY MOMENT FRAMES:

$r_{max_1} = (0.92V/V)(10/20) = 0.46$

$\rho = \rho_1 = [2 - 20/\, r_{max_i}\sqrt{A_1}]\ (0.80)$

$\rho = [2 - 20/0.46\ \sqrt{5400}\,]\ (0.80) = 1.41(0.8) = 1.13$

REDUNDANCY (ρ) OF DUAL SYSTEMS—EXAMPLE CALCULATIONS

FIGURE 29B

eventually became seismic zone-dependent in the *Uniform Building Code.* In recent UBC editions prior to 1997, the minimum was 0.075 *ZIW* (service-level) where Z is the Seismic Zone factor (0.4, 0.3, 0.2, 0.15, and 0.075 for Zones 4, 3, 2B, 2A, and 1, respectively), *I* is the importance factor and *W* is the effective seismic weight. In the 1997 UBC, this minimum design base shear was brought up to strength level and was made soil-dependent; it became: 1.4 (0.075) $C_aIW = 0.11C_aIW$ where C_a is a function of *Z* and of the soil characteristics at the site of the structure. The NEHRP Provisions prior to the 1997 edition did not include a lower bound on the design base shear. However, in the 1997 edition, in view of the fact that the descending branch of the design spectrum now varied with $1/T$ rather than $1/T^{2/3}$, a minimum value in terms of the design spectral acceleration at 1-second period, S_{D1}, was added. The minimum design base shear of the 1997 NEHRP Provisions is 0.1 $S_{D1}IW$. In one of a small number of departures from the 1997 NEHRP Provisions, the minimum design base shear of the IBC was changed to 0.044 $S_{DS}I_EW$, making it nearly identical to the minimum value of the 1997 UBC. This minimum value is included in view of the uncertainty and the lack of knowledge of actual structural response of long-period buildings subject to earthquake ground motion. The minimum design base shears given by Equations 16-34 and 16-37 are given in Table 20 for different site classes and for different seismic risks at the site.

Following the Northridge earthquake of 1994, a second lower-bound on the design base shear, applicable in Seismic Zone 4 only, was added to the 1997 UBC. This second minimum is in terms of *Z*, N_v, *I* and *R* where N_v is the velocity-dependent near-source factor, and is specifically intended to account for the large displacement and velocity pulses that were observed in near-fault ground motion in the Northridge earthquake. A corresponding minimum was added to the 1997 NEHRP Provisions, has been adopted into the IBC, and is represented by Equation 16-38. This minimum was originally applicable to structures assigned to SDC E and F only. The applicability was later expanded to all structures located where the mapped MCE spectral response acceleration at 1-second period, S_1, equals or exceeds 0.6g.

Table 21 shows a comparison of the design base shear equations of the 2000 IBC and the 1997 UBC. It can be seen that the two sets of expressions are equivalent if the following conversions are made:

$$S_{D1} = C_v,\ S_{DS} = 2.5C_a$$

There are obvious differences in the applicability of the lower-bound equations that depend on *R*.

1617.4.2 Period determination. In the denominator of Equation 16-36, *T* is the fundamental period of vibration of the building. It is preferable that this be determined "using the structural properties and deformational characteristics of the resisting elements in a properly substantiated analysis." If a mathematical model has been formulated for the dynamic analysis of Section 1618, then the period of the first mode of vibration in a given principal direction can be used for this *T* value.

Unfortunately, the methods of structural mechanics cannot be employed to calculate the period of vibration before a building has been designed. Consequently, this section provides an approximate method that can be used to estimate building period, with minimal information available on the building design. It is based on the use of simple formulas that involve only a general description of the building type (such as steel moment frame, concrete moment frame, etc.) and the overall height or number of stories.

Rationally computed period is a function of modeling assumptions and is dependent in particular on stiffness assumptions. The smaller the assumed stiffness, the longer the rationally computed period, which translates directly into a lower design base shear. Rationally computed period is thus open to possible abuse. Although it would have been preferable to prevent such possible abuse by specifying fairly rigid modeling rules, it has so far not been possible to forge consensus behind a complete set of rules to meet all possible variations and conditions encountered in design. The 1997 NEHRP Provisions and the IBC, just as their predecessor documents and recent editions of the UBC, chose to impose direct control on rationally computed period. For design purposes, it may not be taken any larger than a coefficient, C_u, times the approximate period given in Section 1617.4.2.1. The 1999 SEAOC Blue Book Commentary advises that reasonable mathematical rules should be followed such that the increase in period allowed by the C_u coefficient is not taken advantage of when the structure does not merit it.

TABLE 20. MINIMUM DESIGN BASE SHEARS FROM EQUATIONS 16-34 AND 16-37

SITE CLASS	MAPPED SPECTRAL RESPONSE ACCELERATION AT SHORT PERIODS									
	0.25		0.50		0.75		1.00		1.25	
	S_{DS}	$\frac{V_{min}}{W}$ %	S_{DS}	$\frac{V_{min}}{W}$ %	S_{DS}	$\frac{V_{min}}{W}$ %	S_{DS}	$\frac{V_{min}}{W}$ %	S_{DS}	$\frac{V_{min}}{W}$ %
A	0.133	0.587	0.267	1.173	0.4	1.76	0.533	2.347	0.667	2.933
B	0.167	0.733	0.333	1.467	0.5	2.2	0.667	2.933	0.833	3.667
C	0.2	0.88	0.4	1.76	0.55	2.42	0.667	2.933	0.833	3.667
D	0.267	1.173	0.467	2.053	0.6	2.64	0.733	3.227	0.833	3.667
E	0.417	1.833	0.567	2.493	0.6	2.64	0.6	2.64	*	*

*Site specific geotechnical investigation and dynamic site response analysis required.

TABLE 21. COMPARISON OF DESIGN BASE SHEAR EQUATIONS OF THE 2000 IBC AND THE 1997 UBC

2000 IBC	1997 UBC
$V = \frac{S_{D1}}{(R/I_E)T} W \leq \frac{S_{DS}}{(R/I_E)} W$	$V = \frac{C_v}{(R/I)T} W \leq \frac{2.5C_a}{(R/I)} W$
$\geq 0.044\, S_{DS} I_E W$	$\geq 0.11\, C_a I\, W$
$\geq \frac{0.5S_1}{(R/I_E)} W$ SDC E and F only where $S_1 > 0.6g$	$\geq \frac{0.32N_v}{(R/I)} W$ Seismic Zone 4 only
$S_{DS} = 2/3\ S_{MS} = 2/3\ F_a S_s$ $S_{D1} = 2/3\ S_{M1} = 2/3\ F_v S_1$	

Table 22 expresses the restriction on rationally computed period in terms of design base shear. For example, when T is restricted to be no more than 1.3 times T_a, the design base shear based on T is restricted to be no less than 76.9 percent of the design base shear based on the approximate period of Section 1617.4.2.1. Note, importantly, that Section 1617.4.6.1 on story drift determination specifies that "For purposes of this drift analysis only, the upper bound limitation specified in Section 1617.4.2 on the computed fundamental period, T, in seconds, of the building, shall not apply."

TABLE 22. RESTRICTION ON RATIONALLY COMPUTED PERIOD EXPRESSED IN TERMS OF DESIGN BASE SHEAR

DESIGN SPECTRAL RESPONSE ACCELERATION AT 1-SEC. PERIOD, S_{D1}	COEFFICIENT C_u = MAX. T/T_a	MIN. V/V_a
≥ 0.4	1.2	0.833
0.3	1.3	0.769
0.2	1.4	0.714
0.15	1.5	0.667
≤ 0.1	1.7	0.588

Note: V = Design base shear based on rationally computed period
V_a = Design base shear based on approximate period

It may be noted that larger values of C_u are permitted as the soil-dependent seismic risk of a location decreases. This is because buildings in areas with lower lateral-force requirements are thought likely to be more flexible. Higher values of C_u for lower values of S_{D1} also result in less dramatic changes from prior practice in lower risk areas. As pointed out in the 1997 NEHRP Commentary, it is generally accepted that the equations for T_a are tailored to fit the types of construction common in areas with high lateral-force requirements. It is unlikely that buildings in lower seismic risk areas would be designed to produce as high a drift level as allowed by the 1997 NEHRP Provisions or the IBC, due to stability (P-delta) considerations and wind requirements. For buildings with design "controlled" by wind, the use of a large T will not really result in a lower design force.

1617.4.2.1 Approximate fundamental period. The approximate fundamental period needs to be conservative in the sense that if this period estimate is later not refined through rational period determination, the resulting design should still be safe. Thus, the approximate period needs to be smaller than the true period of a building.

Taking the seismic base shear to vary as 1/T and assuming that the lateral forces are distributed linearly over the height and that deflections are controlled by drift limitations, a simple determination of the vibration period by Rayleigh's method[32] leads to the conclusion that the vibration period of moment resisting frame structures varies roughly with $h_n^{3/4}$ where h_n equals the total height of the building (height above base to the highest level of building). The form of the period Equation 16-39 was therefore adopted into ATC 3-06 where it was originally applicable only to moment-resisting frame systems. Later modifications made it applicable to systems with shear walls and bracing elements. ATC 3-06 originally gave values of C_t equal to 0.035 and 0.025 for steel and concrete frames, respectively. The data upon which the ATC 3-06 values were based were re-examined for concrete frames and the 0.030 value was judged to be more appropriate.

In Figures C5.3.3-1 and C5.3.3-2 of the 1997 NEHRP Commentary, Equation 16-39 is compared with fundamental vibration periods computed from accelerograph records from the upper stories of several steel frame buildings and several concrete frame buildings, respectively, during the 1971 San Fernando earthquake. The figures show that C_t values of 0.035 and 0.030 for steel and concrete moment frames, respectively, produce values of T_a generally lower than the true fundamental period of moment frame buildings.

Subsequent surveys and studies of the particular buildings that provided the period data for the ATC 3-06 equations[33] have shown that these original equations, even with the modified C_t for concrete, provide predictions that are about 80 to 90 percent of the lower bound values of measured periods at deformation values near first yield of the structural elements. The 1999 SEAOC Blue Book Commentary justifies continued use of the 0.035 and 0.030 coefficients for moment frame buildings and makes the following important point:

> It is recognized that the values for C_t provide period estimates that are lower than most measured values in the elastic range, and definitely much lower than nearly all measured values in the cracked section state for concrete buildings and the partially yielded state for steel buildings. However, these estimated period values for each material, when used [in the design base shear equation], provide design values that SEAOC judges to be appropriate and consistent with past design experience. For the usual case of a descending spectrum, the decrease in demand due to the increase in period as the structure deforms into the inelastic range is already included in the R_d value of a given structural system. . . . Therefore, period formulas should provide the period of the structure in its elastic state.

It ought to be noted that for the 0.035 or the 0.030 coefficient to be applicable, 100 percent of the required seismic forces must be resisted by moment frames and such frames must not be enclosed or adjoined by more rigid elements that would keep them from deforming freely under seismic excitation. The second condition is often overlooked. If either condition is violated, a designer must use the 0.02 coefficient for other buildings.

The optional use, $T_a = 0.1N$, in Equation 16-40 is an approximation for low- to moderate-height frames that has long been in use.

1617.4.3 Vertical distribution of seismic forces. It is generally well understood, and it has been succinctly pointed out in the 1997 NEHRP Commentary, that the distribution of lateral forces over the height of a structure is typically quite complex because these forces are the result of superposition of a number of natural modes of vibration. The relative contribution of these vibration modes to the overall distribution of lateral forces over the height of the building depends on a number of factors including the shape of the earthquake response spectrum, the natural period of vibration of the structure, and the characteristic shapes of the natural vibration modes that, in turn, depend on the magnitude and distribution of mass and stiffness over the height of the structure.

ATC 3-06, in 1978, changed the vertical distribution of lateral forces that is still in use in the 1997 UBC. In the UBC, for a structure having fundamental period, T, not exceeding 0.7 second, the entire design base shear, V, is distributed linearly along the height of the structure, with a zero value at the base and the maximum value at the top. This distribution is based on two assumptions: that the structure responds to earthquake ground motion in its fundamental mode, and that the fundamental mode shape is linear. For taller structures (having elastic fundamental period exceeding 0.7 second), an allowance is made to higher-mode response by concentrating a portion of the design base shear, $0.07TV$, at the top level. The remainder of the design base shear, $V - 0.07TV$, is then distributed linearly along the height of the structure, with a zero value at the base and a maximum value at the top.

The IBC, following the 1997 and prior editions of the NEHRP Provisions and ATC 3-06, prescribes a triangular distribution of the entire design base shear for buildings having elastic fundamental period not exceeding 0.5 second. This distribution is in view of the well-known fact that the influence of modes of vibration higher than the fundamental mode is small in the earthquake response of short-period structures and that, in regular structures, the fundamental mode shape departs little from a straight line.

The IBC prescribes a parabolic distribution of the entire design base shear, with a zero value at the base and a maximum value at the top, for structures having elastic fundamental period in excess of 2.5 seconds As pointed out in the 1997 NEHRP Commentary, it has been demonstrated that although the earthquake response of long-period structures is primarily due to the fundamental natural mode of vibration, the influence of higher modes of vibration can be significant and, in regular structures, the fundamental vibration mode lies approximately between a straight line and a parabola with the vertex at the base. The higher mode effects are adequately, indeed conservatively, accounted for when the entire design base shear, rather than only the first mode base shear, is distributed parabolically along the height of a structure.

For structures having periods between 0.5 second and 2.5 seconds a linear interpolation between a linear and a parabolic distribution of the design base shear along the height of a structure is allowed, or the entire design base shear may be distributed parabolically along the height, with a zero value at the base and the maximum value at the top.

1617.4.4 Horizontal shear distribution. Before it branches into subsections, this section essentially defines the term story shear. The story shear in any story is the sum of the lateral forces acting at all levels above the story. Story x is the story immediately below Level x.

1617.4.4.1 Rigid diaphragms. When a diaphragm deformation is less than or equal to twice the associated story drift (see the definition of flexible diaphragm in Section 1602.1), the requirements of this section become applicable. In most cases the diaphragm may be modeled as fully rigid without in-plane deformability. However, as pointed out in the 1999 SEAOC Blue Book Commentary, there are structural configurations—such as vertical resisting elements that have large differences in stiffness or offset between stories, and diaphragms with irregular shapes and/or openings—where the engineer should investigate the effects of diaphragm deformability. The use of the most critical results obtained from the fully rigid and the flexible diaphragm models should generally be acceptable. SEAOC has added a valuable commentary on wood diaphragms in the 1999 Blue Book (Section C805.3),[4] as further discussed in the next section.

1617.4.4.2 Flexible diaphragms. When the diaphragm deformation is more than two times the associated story drift, the diaphragm is considered to be flexible. This definition has been in the UBC since its 1988 edition. The term implies that a diaphragm segment between two vertical lateral-force-resisting elements may be modeled as a simple beam spanning between those elements. This section also allows a designer to ignore an out-of-plane offset in a vertical lateral-force-resisting element, provided the offset does not exceed 5 percent of the plan dimension perpendicular to the direction of lateral load (or parallel to the offset).

The following excerpt from the 1999 SEAOC Blue Book Commentary (Section C805.3) is included here, as being of interest to a large number of potential readers. Only slight modifications of language have been made in a few places.

> Past and present design practice in California and other areas has almost exclusively used flexible diaphragm assumptions for distribution of seismic forces in structures with wood diaphragms. The assumption of flexible behavior of wood diaphragms conforms quite well with the UBC definition of flexible diaphragms for larger buildings with concrete or masonry walls. Lateral-force-resisting systems using wood diaphragms in combination with wood shear walls seldom meet the UBC definition of a flexible diaphragm, suggesting that for many wood shear wall structures the UBC would require that a rigid diaphragm analysis be performed. The adoption of the 1988 UBC did not seem to prompt any significant change in design practice related to the assumption of diaphragm flexibility for wood framed structures. Most designers continued their past practice and most building officials continued to accept this practice. This is one area where a divergence developed between common design practice and a strict interpretation of the code.
>
> In the wood design examples of the Seismic Design Manual,[34] which is in conformance with the 1997 UBC, SEAOC found it necessary to point out that common design practice is not consistent with strict interpretation of the UBC. This has caused consternation among designers of residential structures.

The relative flexibility of cantilevered columns compared to parallel shear walls is thought to have been one factor contributing to the poor performance of buildings with tuck-under parking in the Northridge Earthquake. A rigid diaphragm analysis performed on this type of building should have identified the relative flexibility of the columns, and the resulting redistribution of seismic forces might have been accommodated in the design. Although damage resulting from the relative flexibility of vertical elements should theoretically occur to varying extents in many other types of wood buildings, it has not yet been reported as a major cause of damage. Earthquake damage observed to date suggests that life safety has generally been achieved in structures having a fairly regular configuration and redundancy, with wood structural panel diaphragms that have been designed using flexible diaphragm assumptions.

Consideration of rigid diaphragm behavior is recommended where the diaphragms can be judged by observation to be stiff compared to the vertical lateral-force-resisting elements, and particularly where one or more lines of resistance are substantially less stiff than the rest. Because of many uncertainties that exist in rigid diaphragm analysis for wood structures, use of an envelope considering some combination of rigid and flexible analysis may be appropriate. For small, substantially regular buildings that have a good distribution of lateral resistance and are well tied together, earthquake performance to date suggests that design using flexible diaphragm assumptions is adequate for life-safe performance. It has been suggested that one- and two-family residences be given blanket exemption from consideration of the applicability of rigid diaphragm analysis. Such a blanket exemption does not, however, make sense from an engineering standpoint because many one- and two-family residences have highly irregular configurations with low redundancy and significant discontinuities in the structural system.

1617.4.4.3 Torsion. Actual torsion, resulting from a noncoincidence of the center of mass and the center of rigidity at a particular floor level must be considered in design unless the diaphragm at that level is flexible. Flexible diaphragms, of course, cannot transmit torsion to the vertical lateral-force-resisting elements.

The 1999 SEAOC Blue Book Commentary makes the very important point that torsional shear should be subtracted from the direct load shear when the torsional shear is opposite to the direction of the seismic load. In such cases, the torsional shear must be due to the smaller torsion that is reduced by the accidental torsion requirements. Where the torsional shear is in the same sense and direction as the direct load shear, the more severe loading would be due to the larger torsion that is increased by the accidental torsion requirements and shear added to the direct load. The commentary goes on to explain in detail why the foregoing recommendations are justified and necessary.

1617.4.4.4 Accidental torsion. In addition to the actual torsion, an accidental torsion must also be included in design, provided the diaphragm at a particular floor level is non-flexible. In the fairly recent past, code-required practice used to be to include in design the actual torsion subject to a minimum of the accidental torsion. But now the actual torsion plus the accidental torsion must be included. Where there is no actual torsion, obviously only the accidental torsion need be included.

The location and distribution of all of the weights that have an influence on seismic response cannot be determined with complete certainty. The requirement concerning displacement of the mass at each level was introduced to account for this deficiency.

The following additional reasons for requiring consideration of an accidental torsion in design are important:[4, 8]

1. There may be unforeseeable differences between computed and actual values of stiffnesses, yield strengths, and masses.
2. The real distribution of both the dead and the live loads may be nonuniform.
3. Nonstructural elements such as stairs and interior partitions may introduce eccentricities in the structural stiffness.
4. Differences in the seismic ground motion over the extent of the foundation may impose torsional loading on the structures.

The SEAOC Blue Book Commentary makes the important point that where orthogonal forces are applied simultaneously on a structure, the required 5-percent eccentricity of the center of mass should be applied for only one of the orthogonal forces at a time. Application of the 5-percent displacement for both orthogonal directions concurrently is not consistent with the original intent of the accidental eccentricity provision.

1617.4.4.5 Dynamic amplification of torsion. The provision applies to structures having torsional irregularity or extreme torsional irregularity (Irregularities Type 1a or 1b of Table 1616.5.1) only, and does not apply to any structure assigned to SDC A or B.

The 1999 SEAOC Blue Book Commentary points out that the eccentricity amplification factor, A_x, is intended to represent the increased eccentricity caused by the yielding of perimeter elements. This factor provides a simple yet effective control on systems that might otherwise have excessive torsional yield in a given story. Equation 16-44 is an empirical formula that was developed by the SEAOC Seismology Committee to encourage buildings with good torsional stiffness. The 1999 SEAOC Blue Book Commentary makes the following important points:

1. In calculating A_x by Equation 16-44, the value of δ_{avg} should be found from the displacement resulting from the same torsional moment used to evaluate δ_{max}.
2. Where large eccentricity and low torsional rigidity result in a negative displacement on one side of a given level under static lateral forces, the value of δ_{avg} in Equation 16-44 should be calculated as the algebraic average.
3. For dynamic analysis, the algebraic average needs to be found for each mode and then properly combined to produce the total modal response value for δ_{avg}.
4. Torsional analysis using the amplified accidental torsion need not be repeated beyond the analysis with the initial value of A_x. An iterative process was not intended.

Items 2 and 3 above also apply to the calculation of average story drift for the determination of Plan Irregularities Type 1a and 1b of Table 1616.5.1.

It is important to note that in the 1994 edition of the NEHRP Provisions and the 1997 UBC, the factor, A_x, is used to amplify the accidental torsional moment, M_{ta}, only. In the 1997 NEHRP Provisions and the IBC, the factor, A_x, amplifies the sum of the actual torsional moment, M_t, and the accidental torsional moment, M_{ta}. This is obviously a significantly more severe requirement intended to discourage the design and construction of torsionally irregular buildings.

1617.4.5 Overturning. This section requires that a structure be designed to resist overturning moments statically consistent with the design story shears, except for the reduction factor, τ, in Equation 16-45. At any level, the incremental changes of the design overturning moment are to be distributed to the various resisting elements in the same proportion as the distribution of the horizontal shears to these elements. The 1997 NEHRP Commentary gives the following reasons for reducing the statically computed overturning moments:

1. The distribution of design story shears over height computed from lateral forces of Section 1617.4.3 is intended to provide an envelope, recognizing that the shears in all stories do not attain their maximum values simultaneously. If the shear in a specific story is close to the computed value, the shears in almost all other stories are almost necessarily overestimated. Hence, the overturning moments statically consistent with the design story shears are overestimated.
2. Under the action of overturning moments, one edge of the foundation may lift off the ground for short durations of time. Such behavior leads to substantial reduction in the seismic forces and, consequently, in the overturning moments.

The overturning moments computed statically from the envelope of story shears may be reduced by no more than 20 percent. This value is similar to those obtained from the results of dynamic analysis (not considering Item 2 above). No reduction is permitted in the uppermost 10 stories primarily because Newmark and Rosenblueth[35] have shown that the statically computed overturning moments in these stories may not be on the conservative side. The 1997 NEHRP Commentary points out that there is hardly any benefit anyway in reducing overturning moments in stories near the top of a structure, since the design of vertical elements in these stories is rarely governed by overturning moments. For the eleventh to the twentieth stories from the top, linear variation of τ provides the simplest transition between the minimum and maximum values of 0.8 and 1.0.

Many older building codes and design recommendations used to allow more drastic reduction of overturning moments relative to their value statically consistent with the design story shears. These reductions appeared to be excessive in light of structural damage observed during the 1967 Caracas, Venezuela earthquake where a number of column failures were due primarily to the effect of overturning moments. The 1974 and subsequent editions of the SEAOC Blue Book, and also the 1976 and subsequent editions of the UBC, have not permitted any reduction in overturning moments statically consistent with the story shears. The IBC has chosen to adopt the moderate reduction permitted in Section 5.3.6 of the 1997 NEHRP Provisions.

The above section also includes the following provision: "The foundations of structures, except inverted pendulum-type structures, shall be designed for the foundation overturning design moment, M_f (kip-ft or kN-m), at the foundation-soil interface determined using the equation for the overturning moment at level x, M_x (kip-ft or kN-m), with an overturning moment reduction factor, τ, of 0.75 for all structure heights." The 1997 NEHRP Commentary states that this is appropriate because the slight uplifting of one edge of the foundation during vibration leads to reduction in the overturning moment and because such behavior does not normally cause structural distress. This provision, however, has not been adopted into the 2000 IBC.

1617.4.6 Drift determination and P-delta effects. As pointed out under Section 1617.3, the IBC controls interstory drift expected to be caused by the design earthquake. This quantity, called the design story drift, is determined as required by this section or Section 1617.5.3. The reasons for controlling drift are discussed under Section 1617.3.

1617.4.6.1 Story drift determination. Determination of the design story drift involves the following steps:

1. Determine the lateral deflections at the various floor levels of a building by elastic analysis of a mathematical model of the building under the design base shear of Section 1617.4.1, distributed along the height of the building as required by Section 1617.4.3. While the 2000 IBC, unlike the 1997 UBC, does not prescribe a set of detailed modeling requirements for static analysis, the modeling requirements of Section 1618.1 for dynamic analysis are good to follow. The lateral deflection at floor level x, obtained from this analysis, is δ_{xe}.
2. Amplify δ_{xe} by the deflection amplification factor, C_d, discussed under Section 1614.5. The quantity, $C_d\,\delta_{xe}$, is an estimated design earthquake displacement at floor level x. The IBC requires this quantity to be divided by the importance factor, I_E, because the forces under which the δ_{xe} displacement is computed are already amplified by I_E. Since the IBC drift limits are tighter for buildings in higher occupancy categories, this division by I_E is important. Without it, there would be a two-fold tightening of drift limitations for buildings with seismic importance factors greater than one. The quantity, $C_d\delta_{xe}/I_E$, at floor level x is δ_x, the adjusted design earthquake displacement.
3. Calculate the design story drift, Δ_x, for story x (the story below floor level x) by deducting the adjusted design earthquake displacement at bottom of story x (floor level x-1) from the adjusted design earthquake displacement at the top of story x (floor level x):

$$\Delta_x = \delta_x - \delta_x - 1$$

Figure 30 shows the schematic of story drift determination.

The Δ_x (or simply Δ) values must be kept within tolerable limits as given in Table 1617.3. Three items are worth noting specifically:

1. The design story drift must be computed under the strength-level design earthquake forces of the 2000 IBC, irrespective of whether member design is done using the strength design or the allowable stress design load combinations.

2. The redundancy coefficient, ρ, is equal to 1.0 for computation of the design story drift.
3. For determining compliance with the story drift limitation of Section 1617.3, the deflections, Δ_x, may be calculated as indicated above for the seismic-force-resisting system, using design forces corresponding to the fundamental period of the structure, T, calculated without the limit, $T<C_uT_a$, specified in Section 1617.4.2. The same model of the seismic-force-resisting system used in determining the deflections must be used for determining T. The waiver does not pertain to the calculation of drifts for determining P-delta effects on member forces, overturning moments, etc. If the P-delta effects determined in Section 1617.4.6.2 are significant, the design story drift must be increased by the resulting incremental factor.

1617.4.6.2 P-delta effects. The P-delta effects in a given story are due to the horizontal offset or eccentricity of the gravity load above the story. Referring to Figure 31, if the design story drift due to the lateral forces prescribed in Section 1617.4.3 were Δ, the bending moments in the story would be augmented by an amount equal to Δ times the gravity load above the story. The ratio of the P-delta or secondary moment to the lateral-force story moment (primary moment, equal to story shear times story height) is designated as the stability coefficient as given by Equation 16-47. If the stability coefficient, θ, is less than 0.10 for every story, then the P-delta effects on story shears and moments and member forces may be ignored. If, however, the stability coefficient, θ, exceeds 0.10 for any story, then the P-delta effects on story drifts, shears, member forces, etc., for the whole building must be determined by a rational analysis.

Any of a number of rational analyses may be used. Some published computer programs take P-delta effects into account. A mathematical description of the method employed by several popular programs is given by Wilson and Habibullah.[36]

An acceptable P-delta analysis, when required, may follow the procedure given in older editions of the SEAOC Blue Book Commentary, also reproduced in the 1997 NEHRP Provisions Commentary:

1. Compute the P-delta amplification factor, $a_d = \theta/(1-\theta)$, for each story. In this case, a_d accounts for the multiplier effect due to the initial story drift leading to another increment of drift which would lead to yet another increment, etc. Thus both the effective shear in the story and the computed eccentricity would be augmented by a factor $1 + \theta + \theta^2 + \theta^3 \cdots$, which is $1/(1-\theta)$ or $(1 + a_d)$.
2. Multiply the story shear, V_x, in each story by the factor $(1 + a_d)$ for that story and recompute overturning moments and other seismic force effects corresponding to these augmented story shears.

The columns of moment frames that are designed with P-delta effects included need not be subject to the bending stress amplification factor for steel columns or the moment magnification factor for concrete columns because these factors are intended to account for P-delta effects.

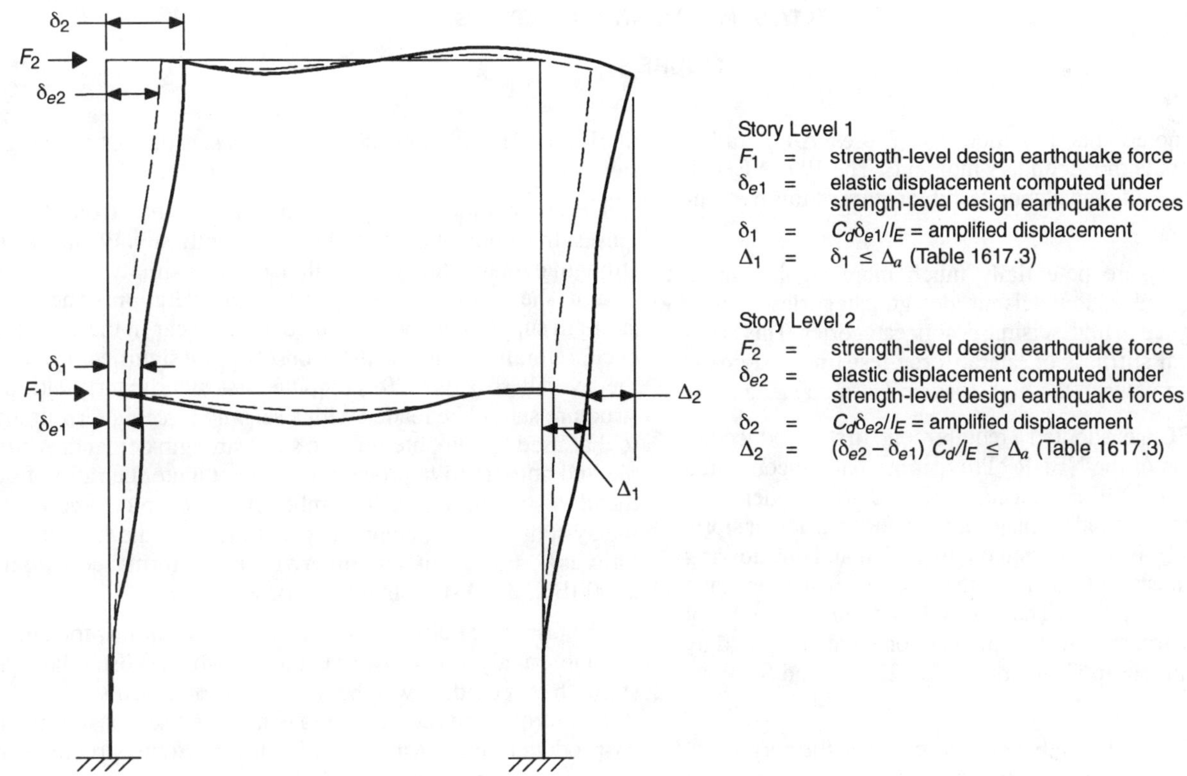

STORY DRIFT DETERMINATION

FIGURE 30

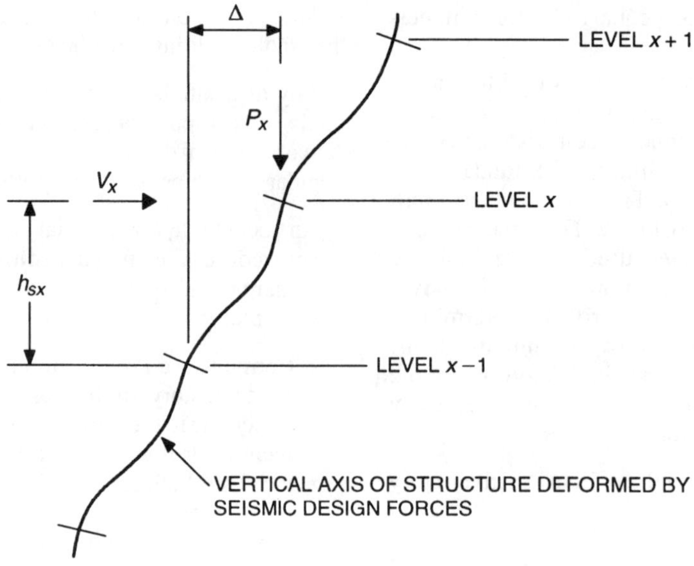

Δ = design story drift

V_x = seismic design shear force acting between level x and level x-1

h_{sx} = story height below level x

$P_x = \sum_{i=x}^{n} (D+L)_i$, total design gravity load at and above level x

Stability Coefficient θ is given by

$$\theta = \frac{P_x \Delta}{V_x h_{sx} C_d}$$

P-DELTA SYMBOLS AND NOTATIONS

FIGURE 31

It may be noted that Equation 16-47 uses Δ/C_d, rather than Δ, to compute the secondary moments. The 1997 NEHRP Commentary provides an elaborate explanation of this particular important aspect.

P-delta effects are potentially much more significant in buildings assigned to low seismic design categories than in buildings assigned to high seismic design categories. This is because the lateral stiffness of lateral-force-resisting systems is required to be greater in the higher seismic design categories.

The 2000 IBC has adopted a requirement, first introduced in the 1991 edition of the NEHRP Provisions, that the computed stability coefficient, θ, not exceed 0.25 or $0.5/\beta C_d$ where β is the ratio of shear demand to shear capacity for a particular story. The factor, βC_d, is an adjusted ductility demand considering that the seismic strength demand may be somewhat less than the code strength supplied. The adjusted ductility demand is not intended to incorporate overstrength beyond that computed by the means available in Chapters 19, 21, 22, 23, and Sections 1622 and 1623.

According to the 1997 NEHRP Commentary, the purpose of this requirement is to protect structures from the possibility of stability failures triggered by post-earthquake residual deformation. The danger of such failures is real and may not be eliminated by apparently available overstrength. This is particularly true of structures assigned to low seismic design categories.

The computation of θ_{max} which, in turn, is based on βC_d, requires the computation of story strength supply and story strength demand. Story strength demand is simply the seismic design shear for the story under consideration. The story strength supply may be computed as the shear in the story that occurs simultaneously with the onset of first significant yield of the overall structure. To compute first significant yield, the structure should be loaded with a seismic force pattern similar to that used to compute seismic story strength demand. A simple and conservative procedure is to compute the ratio of demand to strength for each member of the seismic-force-resisting system in a particular story and then use the largest such ratio as β. For a structure otherwise in conformance with the 2000 IBC, β = 1.0 is obviously conservative.

The principal reason for inclusion of β is to allow for a more equitable analysis of those structures in which substantial extra strength is provided, whether as a result of added stiffness for drift control, from code-required wind resistance, or simply as a by-product of other aspects of the design. Some structures inherently possess more strength than required, but instability is not typically a concern for such structures. For many flexible structures, the proportions of the structural members are controlled by the drift requirements rather than the strength requirements; consequently, β is less than 1.0 because the members provided are larger and stronger than required. This has the effect of reducing the inelastic component of the total seismic drift, so β is placed as a factor on C_d.

Accurate evaluation of β would require consideration of all relevant load combinations to find the maximum value of seismic load effect demand to seismic load effect capacity in each and every member. A conservative simplification is to divide the total demand with seismic effects included by the total capacity; this considers all load combinations in which the effects of dead and live loads add to seismic force effects. If the design of member is controlled by a load combination where the effects of gravity loads counteract earthquake effects, to be correctly computed, the ratio, β, must be based only on the seismic component of demand and capacity, not the total. The vertical load, *P*, in theP-delta computation would be less in such a case and, therefore, θ would be less. The importance of the counteracting load combination does have to be considered, but it rarely controls instability.

1617.5 Simplified analysis procedure for seismic design of buildings. In recent years, engineers and building officials have become increasingly concerned that building codes in general, and the seismic design provisions of those codes in particular, have become increasingly complex, difficult to understand and to implement. The basic driving force behind this increasing complexity is the desire on the part of code writing bodies to provide design guidelines that assure reliable performance of structures. Since the response of buildings to earthquake ground shaking is by nature very complex, realistic accounting for these effects leads to increasingly complex provisions. However, it has also been recognized that for buildings to be reliably constructed to resist earthquakes, it is necessary that designers have sufficient understanding of the design provisions to be able to properly implement them. In recognition of this, the SEAOC Seismology Committee developed a conservative, simple method of determining design forces for certain simple buildings. This procedure, in slightly modified form, was adopted into the 2000 IBC. Limitations on the applicability of the procedure are given in Section 1616.6.1. The IBC specifically states that for the purposes of the simplified analysis procedure of Section 1617.5, a building is to be considered fixed at the base.

There are a number of rather significant differences between the simplified analysis procedures of the 2000 IBC and the 1997 UBC. The UBC requires the use of a default soil profile, S_E, rather than the usual S_D, in the simplified procedure; the IBC does not. The UBC allows the near-source factor, N_a, to be taken as no larger than 1.3 if irregularities of certain types do not exist in a structure; the IBC, of course, does not use near-source factors. The UBC specifically lists certain code sections that are not applicable when the simplified procedure is used (the redundancy factor, ρ, however, is not allowed to be taken equal to unity without computations justifying that value); the IBC does not give such a specific list. Finally, the UBC gives a modified formula for diaphragm design forces when the simplified procedure is used; the IBC does not give a similar modification of the corresponding Equation 16-65.

1617.5.1 Seismic base shear. The seismic base shear of Equation 16-49 is 20 percent higher than the upper-bound design base shear of the equivalent lateral-force procedure (Equations 16-34 and 16-35). The importance factor, I_E, is equal to 1.0, since only structures in SUG I may be designed by this procedure. Also, because only short-period structures may be designed by this procedure, the upper-bound design base shear governs.

1617.5.2 Vertical distribution. The vertical distribution of the design base shear is simpler than that given by Section 1617.4.3. The lateral force at a floor level is proportional to the weight at that floor level. When all the floors in a building support equal weight, the distribution of *V* along the height of the building is uniform.

1617.5.3 Design drift. The design story drift, where needed, is allowed to be taken as 1 percent of the story height.

Application of the simplified design procedure is illustrated in Example 10, Part 2 of this chapter.

1617.6 Seismic force-resisting systems. The following general types of structural systems that may be used to resist earthquake forces are defined in Table 1617.6.

Moment-resisting frame system. This is a structural system with an essentially complete space frame providing support for gravity loads. Moment-resisting frames provide resistance to lateral loads primarily by flexural action of members [Figure 32(a)].

Several aspects of the space frame and the moment-resisting frame require discussion. For a system to qualify as a moment-resisting frame system, it must have a substantially complete vertical load-carrying space frame. The engineer should have the latitude to designate selected portions of the space frame as the moment-resisting frame, as long as these portions satisfy the design and detailing requirements and provide the intended behavior of the selected type of lateral-force-resisting system. This allows the engineer to select the most effective configuration for the lateral-force-resisting system. The need for redundancy should be a primary consideration in this selection process.

For those portions of the space frame that are not part of the designated lateral-force-resisting system, the deformation compatibility requirement of Section 1617.4.3 must be complied with.

Table 1617.6 recognizes moment-resisting frames of concrete, masonry and steel, as well as composite steel-concrete construction. In SDC A and B, the moment-resisting frames can be ordinary moment-resisting frames (OMRF) proportioned to satisfy the requirements of AISC ASD or AISC LRFD for steel systems not detailed for seismic using a response factor $R = 3$ . . . or AISC Seismic[37] using the response factors, *R*, per Table 1617.6. For concrete moment frames in SDC A and B, design can be per ACI 318,[38] exclusive of Chapter 21, with no special seismic detailing required. In SDC C, moment frames of steel can be designed and detailed the same as for SDC A and B. For concrete in SDC C, an intermediate moment-resisting frame (IMRF) is required, proportioned to satisfy the requirements of ACI 318 and the special design and detailing provisions of Sections 21.2.2.3 and 21.10. In SDC D, E and F, moment frames of steel can be OMRF, IMRF, or SMRF, but must be designed and detailed to satisfy the requirements of AISC Seismic, using the response factors, *R*, per Table 1617.6. Note

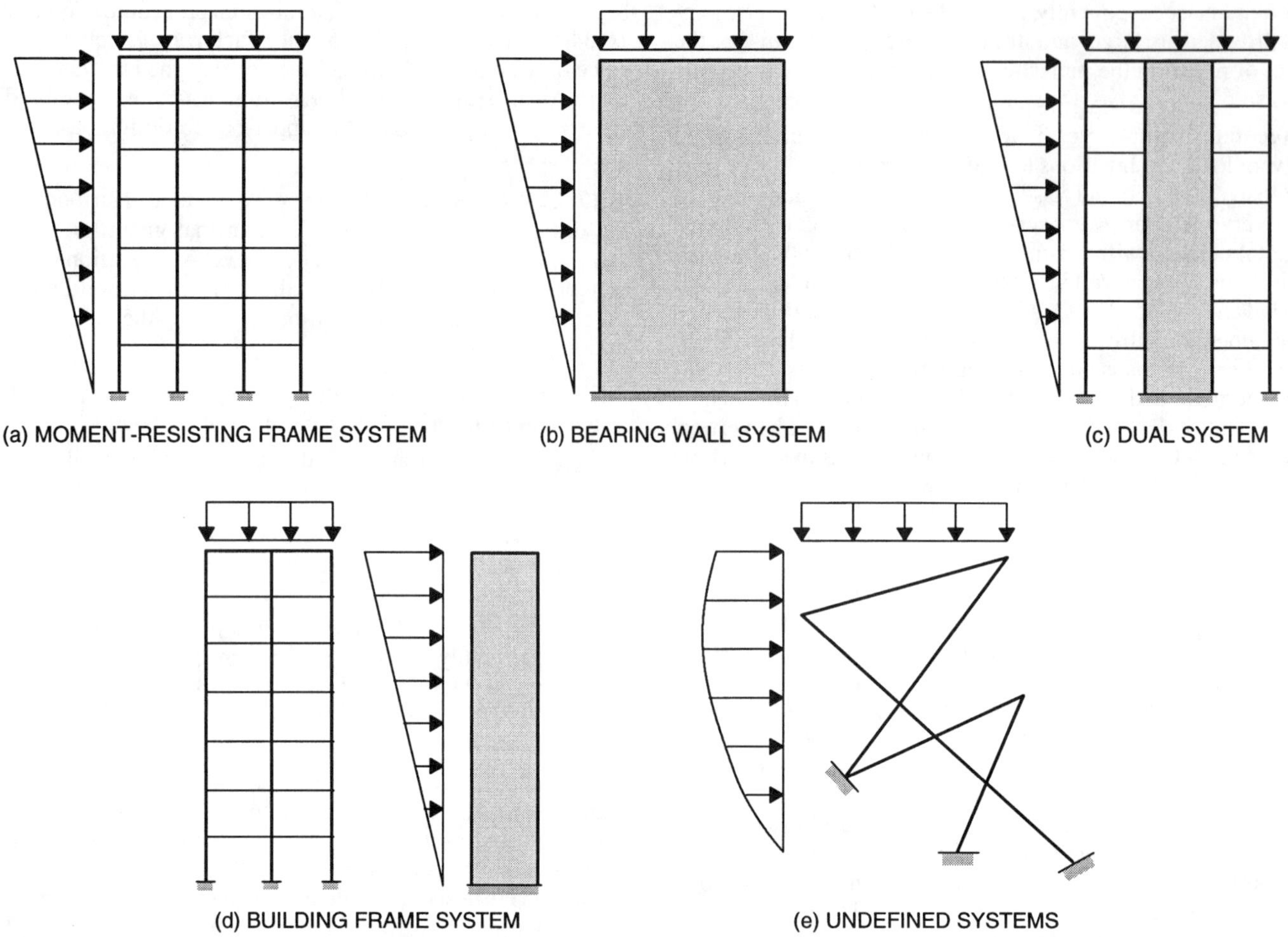

SEISMIC-FORCE-RESISTING STRUCTURAL SYSTEMS

FIGURE 32

the AISC Seismic detailing reference sections listed in Table 1617.6. For concrete, special moment-resisting frames (SMRF) must be used in SDC D, E and F, proportioned to comply with ACI 318 and the special design and detailing requirements of Sections 21.2 through 21.5.

There are two lateral-force-resisting systems listed under moment-resisting frame systems that are somewhat outside of the regular pattern. These are the special steel truss moment frames (AISC Seismic Part I, Section 12), permitted in all seismic design categories other than F, and composite partially restrained moment frames (AISC Seismic Part II, Section 8), permitted in seismic design categories other than E and F.

Research work at the University of Michigan has led to the development of special truss girders that limit inelastic deformations to a special segment of the truss.[39,40] As illustrated in Figure 33, the chords and web members (arranged in an X pattern) of the special segment are designed to withstand large inelastic deformations, while the rest of the structure remains elastic. Special truss moment frames (STMF) have been validated by extensive testing of full-scale subassemblages with story-high columns and full-span special truss girders.

It is desirable to locate the STMF special segment near midspan of the truss girder because shear due to gravity loads is generally lower in that region. The lower limit on special segment length of 10 percent of the truss span length provides a reasonable limit on the ductility demand, while the upper limit of 50 percent of the truss span length represents a more practical limit.

Because it is intended that the special segment yield over its full length, no major structural loads should be applied within the length of the special segment. Accordingly, a restrictive upper limit is placed on the axial force in diagonal web members due to gravity loads applied directly within the special segment.

The ductility demand on diagonal web members in the special segment can be rather large. Flat bars have been suggested in the AISC Seismic Commentary because of their high ductility. Tests[39] have shown that single angles with width-thickness ratios less than $30/\sqrt{F_y}$ also possess adequate ductility for use as web members in an *x* configuration. Chord members in the special segment are required to be compact cross-sections to facilitate the formation of plastic hinges.

Composite partially restrained (PR) moment frames (C-PRMF) consist of structural steel columns and composite beams that are connected with partially restrained (PR) moment connections that meet the requirements in AISC LRFD Specifications.[40] C-PRMF are to be designed so that under earthquake loading yielding occurs in the ductile components of the composite PR beam-to-column moment connections. Limited yielding is permitted at other locations, such as the column base connection. Connection flexibility and composite beam action are to be accounted for in determining the dynamic characteristics, strength and drift of C-PRMF.

Bearing wall system. This is a structural system without an essentially complete space frame providing support for gravity loads. Bearing walls provide support for all or most gravity loads. Resistance to lateral load is provided by the same bearing walls acting as shear walls [Figure 32(b)].

In SDC D, E and F, the lateral-force-resisting shear walls must be special reinforced concrete shear walls or special reinforced masonry shear walls; or they may be ordinary steel braced frames, light frame walls with shear panels made of wood structural panels, or light frame walls with shear panels made of other materials (SDC D only). In SDC C, lateral-force-resisting shear walls may additionally consist of ordinary reinforced concrete shear walls, intermediate reinforced masonry shear walls, and ordinary reinforced masonry shear walls. In SDC A and B, also allowed as lateral-force-resisting shear walls are detailed plain concrete shear walls, ordinary plain concrete shear walls, detailed plain masonry shear walls and ordinary plain masonry shear walls. For each type of shear wall listed in Table 1617.6, an appropriate response factor, *R*, is specified, with increasing values of *R* reflective of the level of potential inelastic deformability. Each shear wall type must comply with the requirements of the respective section number(s) listed in Column 2 of Table 1617.6, dependent on the assigned seismic design category. The special design and detailing requirements for each seismic design category are stated in the material chapters.

Dual system. A dual system [Figure 32(c)] is a structural system with three essential features: 1) An essentially complete space frame provides support for gravity loads, 2) resistance to lateral loads is provided by moment-resisting frames capable of resisting at least 25 percent of the design base shear, and by shear walls or braced frames, 3) The two systems (moment frames and shear walls or braced frames) are designed to resist the design base shear in proportion to their relative rigidities.

In earlier codes including the 1985 edition of theUBC, there was a fourth criterion, in addition to the three enumerated above, that had to be satisfied for a shear wall-frame system or a moment frame-braced frame system to qualify as a dual system. The shear walls or braced frames acting independently of the ductile moment-resisting portions of the space frame had to be able to resist the total required lateral forces. This requirement was at best counterproductive. It took incentive away from the design engineer who preferred to design his shear wall-frame or moment frame-braced frame system as a dual system. If the shear walls or the braced frames had to resist 100 percent of the design lateral forces, what was the benefit of making the moment-resisting frames part of the lateral-force-resisting system? It is true that the design force level went down some when this was done (because of a decrease in the old *K*-value, which is equivalent to an increase in the *R*-value of the IBC). However, the moment-resisting frames then had to be specially detailed. In most cases, the cost of the increased detailing requirements more than outweighed any savings resulting from the reduced design force level. Also, there were many instances where there simply were not sufficient shear walls in a frame-wall building for the shear walls to carry 100 percent of the design lateral forces. The fourth criterion, in addition to being counterproductive, was also not conservative. The unnecessarily

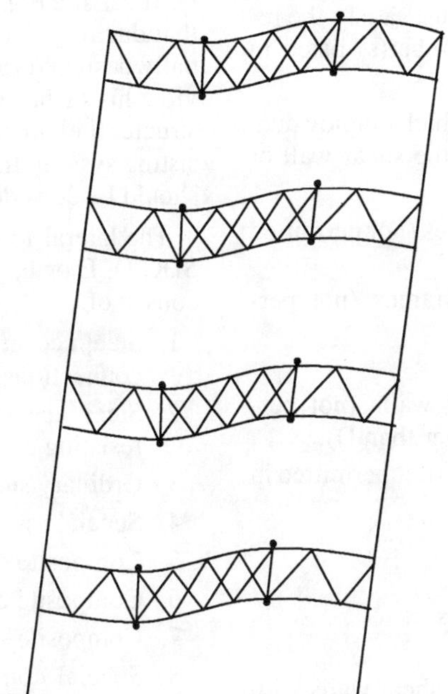

SPECIAL TRUSS MOMENT FRAMES

FIGURE 33

overdesigned shear walls attracted more shear forces to themselves in the event of an actual earthquake, which obviously is not a desirable condition. Fortunately, the undesirable fourth criterion was dropped from the 1988 edition of the UBC, and has not reappeared in recent codes.

The 2000 IBC separately recognizes dual systems in which the moment-resisting frame consists of special moment frames and dual systems in which the moment-resisting frame consists of intermediate moment frames.

In buildings assigned to SDC D, E and F, which employ dual systems with special moment frames, the shear wall or braced frame part may consist of:

1. Steel eccentrically braced frames with moment-resisting connections at columns away from links.
2. Steel eccentrically braced frames with non-moment-resisting connections at columns away from links.
3. Special steel concentrically braced frames.
4. Ordinary steel eccentrically braced frames.
5. Special reinforced concrete shear walls.
6. Composite eccentrically braced frames.
7. Composite concentrically braced frames.
8. Composite steel plate shear walls.
9. Special composite reinforced concrete shear walls with steel elements.
10. Special reinforced masonry shear walls.
11. Intermediate reinforced masonry shear walls (not permitted in seismic design categories higher than D).

In SDC C, additionally allowed are:

12. Ordinary reinforced concrete shear walls.
13. Ordinary composite reinforced concrete shear walls with steel elements.

Each type of shear wall or braced frame must satisfy the requirements of the corresponding section number(s) listed in Column 2 of Table 1617.6.

In buildings assigned to SDC D, E and F, which employ dual systems with intermediate moment frames, the shear wall or braced frame part may consist of:

1. Special steel concentrically braced frames (not permitted in SDC F).
2. Ordinary steel concentrically braced frames (not permitted in SDC F).
3. Special reinforced concrete shear walls.
4. Intermediate reinforced masonry shear walls (not permitted in seismic design categories higher than D).
5. Composite concentrically braced frames (not permitted in SDC F).

Additionally permitted in SDC C are:

6. Ordinary reinforced concrete shear walls.
7. Ordinary reinforced masonry shear walls.
8. Ordinary composite braced frames.
9. Ordinary composite reinforced concrete shear walls with steel elements.

Each of these shear wall or braced frame types must satisfy the requirements of the corresponding section number(s) listed in the second column of Table 1617.6.

SDC A and B are not mentioned above, because the concept of the dual system loses its validity for buildings assigned to SDC A and B, as discussed later.

Building frame system. This is a structural system with an essentially complete space frame providing support for gravity loads. Resistance to lateral loads is provided by shear walls or braced frames [Figure 32(d)].

The seismic safety of the building frame system is totally dependent on good-faith satisfaction of the deformation compatibility requirements (Section 1617.6.4.3). These recognize that when the designated lateral-force-resisting system of a structure deforms laterally under an earthquake of intensity anticipated by the code, the subsystems that have been arbitrarily designated to be outside of the lateral-force-resisting system will have no choice but to deform together, because they are connected at every floor level through the floor systems. If in the course of that earthquake-induced lateral displacement, the subsystems designed for gravity loads only are unable to sustain their gravity load carrying capacity, then life-safety is compromised. It is thus a specific requirement of all seismic codes, including the IBC, that structural elements or subsystems designated not to be part of the lateral-force-resisting system be able to sustain their gravity load carrying capacity at a lateral displacement equal to a multiple times the computed elastic displacement of the lateral-force-resisting system under code-prescribed design seismic forces. The amplified elastic displacement of the lateral-force-resisting system is supposed to provide an estimate of the actual displacement of the entire structure caused by an earthquake of intensity anticipated by the code. If under the estimated earthquake-induced displacements, the gravity loads would cause inelasticity (exceeding the design moment strength or design shear strength) in any structural element initially designed for gravity only, that structural element should also be detailed for inelastic deformability. If satisfaction of deformation compatibility would require that ductility details be provided in structural members originally designed for gravity only, then the engineer ought to review his or her original decision, and consider making such structural elements or subsystems part of the lateral-force-resisting system. In other words, an alternative structural system should be considered for the building.

The lateral-force-resisting system of a building assigned to SDC D, E or F, and utilizing the building frame system may consist of:

1. Steel eccentrically braced frames with moment-resisting connections at columns away from links.
2. Steel eccentrically braced frames with non-moment-resisting connections at columns away from links.
3. Ordinary steel concentrically braced frames.
4. Special reinforced concrete shear walls.
5. Composite eccentrically braced frames.
6. Composite concentrically braced frames.
7. Composite steel plate shear walls.
8. Special composite reinforced concrete shear walls with steel elements.
9. Special reinforced masonry shear walls.
10. Intermediate reinforced masonry shear walls.
11. Light frame walls with shear panels.

In a building utilizing the building frame system and assigned to SDC C, the lateral-force-resisting system may additionally consist of:

12. Ordinary reinforced concrete shear walls.
13. Detailed plain concrete shear walls.
14. Ordinary plain concrete shear walls.
15. Ordinary composite braced frames.
16. Ordinary composite reinforced concrete shear walls with steel elements.
17. Ordinary reinforced masonry shear walls.
18. Detailed plain masonry shear walls.

Each of these shear wall or braced frame types must satisfy the requirements of the corresponding section number(s) listed in column 2 of Table 1617.6.

SDC A and B are not mentioned above, because the concept of the building frame system also loses its validity for buildings assigned to SDC A and B, as discussed later.

Shear wall frame-interactive system. This system was first introduced in the 1997 edition of the UBC, constituting its own category. In the 2000 IBC it has been misplaced under dual systems with intermediate moment frames.

Shear walls or braced frames used in conjunction with moment frames to carry lateral loads in buildings assigned to SDC C, D, E or F must be designed as either building frame systems or as dual systems. Central to the concept of the dual system is the backup frame capable of independently resisting at least 25 percent of the design lateral forces. A buildings frame system, on the other hand, utilizes shear walls or braced frames to resist 100 percent of the design lateral forces. The attraction of this system is that the moment frames, because they are not part of the lateral-force-resisting system, require only ordinary detailing. The concept of the dual system really loses its validity in buildings assigned to SDC A and B, because it is questionable whether the moment frames, which are required to have only ordinary detailing, can act as a backup to the ordinarily detailed shear walls or braced frames, the inelastic deformabilities of both subsystems being comparable. The concept of the building frame system also loses its appeal since there is little to be gained from assigning the entire lateral resistance to the shear wall or braced frame subsystem, in the absence of any special detailing requirements for the beam-column or slab-column frames. In fact, over-designing the shear walls or braced frames to resist 100 percent of the design lateral forces makes them uneconomical. Shear walls with excessive flexural strength are also more likely to fail in a brittle shear-governed mode than in a ductile flexural mode. In areas of low seismicity, it has been usual practice to design the shear walls (or braced frames) and frames in a shear wall-frame (or braced frame-moment frame) structure to resist lateral loads in proportion to their relative rigidities, considering interaction between the two subsystems at all levels. Such a system is now recognized in the 1997 UBC and the 2000 IBC as a shear wall-frame interactive system, and its use is restricted to SDC no higher than B.

Inverted pendulum systems. Inverted pendulum type structures are defined in Section 1613 as structures that have a large portion of their mass concentrated near the top and, thus, have essentially one degree of freedom in horizontal translation. Inverted pendulum structures are singled out in Table 1617.6 for special consideration because of their unique characteristics. These structures have little redundancy and overstrength and concentrate inelastic behavior at their bases. As a result, they have substantially less energy dissipation capacity than other systems. Included under inverted pendulum systems is the cantilevered column system, which was added to the 1997 UBC following the 1994 Northridge earthquake.

Cantilevered column system. This system utilizes cantilevered column elements for resistance to lateral forces. A cantilevered column element is defined in the UBC as a column element in a lateral-force-resisting system that cantilevers from a fixed base and has minimal moment capacity at the top, with lateral forces applied essentially at the top. This type of structural system is common for multi-family residential occupancies over carports, strip shopping center storefronts, and single-family dwellings on oceanside or hillside lots. According to the 1999 SEAOC Blue Book Commentary, inclusion of this class of structures in the table of structural systems of the Blue Book and the UBC does not imply that this is a preferred type of system, but rather recognizes the existence of the cantilevered column system as a separate category with unique characteristics. Typically, this system does not have redundant elements and multiple load paths, nor does the system have added damping, strength, or rotational stiffness developed by the nonstructural elements.

In cantilevered column systems, the column elements acting in cantilever action often provide support for the gravity (vertical) loads in addition to resisting all lateral forces. Hence, there is no independent vertical load-carrying system and the failure of the primary lateral system compromises the ability of the structure to carry gravity loads.

Overstrength in the cantilevered column system is minimal because the ability to form a progression of plastic hinges is limited. Hence, design for higher strength and stiffness (by use of a low R) is necessary to reduce the high ductility demands imposed on the columns. The 1999 SEAOC Blue Book Commentary cautions that this type of system should be used only when the use of more desirable systems is not feasible.

Undefined structural system. Undefined structural systems are those not listed in Table 1617-6. For such systems [Figure 32(e)], the coefficients R, Ω_o and C_d are to be substantiated by approved cyclic test data and analyses. The following items need to be addressed when establishing R, Ω_o and C_d (see 1999 SEAOC Blue Book Section 104.9.2):

1. Dynamic response characteristics.
2. Lateral-force resistance.
3. Overstrength and strain-hardening or -softening.
4. Strength and stiffness degradation.
5. Energy dissipation characteristics.
6. System ductility.
7. Redundancy.

Some of the above terms become clearer in the discussion that follows.

Response modification factor, *R*. The first part of this discussion closely follows the text of the 1997 NEHRP Commentary Section 5.2.

The response modification factor, R, essentially represents the ratio of the forces that would develop under the specified ground motion if the structure had an entirely linear elastic response to the prescribed design forces (Figure 34). The reader would benefit from correlating Figure 34 with Figures 12 and 13. The structure is to be designed so that the level of significant yield exceeds the prescribed design force. The ratio, R, expressed by the equation:

$$R = V_E'/V$$

is always larger than 1.0; thus all structures are designed for forces smaller than those the design ground motion would produce in a completely linear-elastic structure. This reduction is possible for a number of reasons. As the structure begins to yield and deform inelastically, the effective period of response of the structure tends to lengthen, which for many structures results in a reduction in strength demand. Furthermore, the inelastic action results in a significant amount of energy dissipation, also known as hysteretic damping, in addition to the viscous damping. The combined effect, which is also known as ductility reduction, explains why a properly designed structure with a fully yielded strength (V_Y in Figure 34) that is significantly lower than the elastic seismic force demand (V_E' in Figure 34) can be capable of providing satisfactory performance under the design ground motion excitations. A system ductility reduction factor, R_d may be defined as the ratio between V_E' and V_Y.[41]

$$R_d = V_E'/V_Y$$

It is then clear from Figure 34 that the response modification coefficient, R, is the product of the ductility reduction factor and structural overstrength factor:[42]

$$R = R_d\,\Omega_o$$

The energy dissipation resulting from hysteretic behavior can be measured as the area enclosed by the force-displacement curve of the structure as it experiences several cycles of excitation.

The term "significant yield" used above should not be taken as referring to the stage at which first yield occurs in any member. It is defined instead as corresponding to complete plastification of at least the most critical region of the structure (e.g., formation of a first plastic hinge in the structure). A structural steel frame consisting of compact members is assumed to reach this point when a "plastic hinge" develops in the most highly stressed member of the structure. A concrete frame reaches this significant yield when at least one of the sections of its most highly stressed component reaches its design strength as defined in Chapter 19. For other structural materials that do not have their sectional yielding capacities as easily defined, modifiers to working stress values are provided. The IBC requirements contemplate that the design is based on a seismic-force-resisting system with redundant characteristics wherein significant structural overstrength above the level of significant yield can be obtained by plastification at other points in the structure prior to the formation of a complete mechanism. Figure 34 shows the lateral load-deflection curve for a typical structure. Significant yield is the level where plastification occurs at the most heavily loaded element in the structure, shown as the lowest yield hinge on the load-deflection diagram. With increased loading, causing the formation of additional plastic hinges, the capacity increases (following the solid curve) until a maximum is reached. The overstrength capacity obtained by

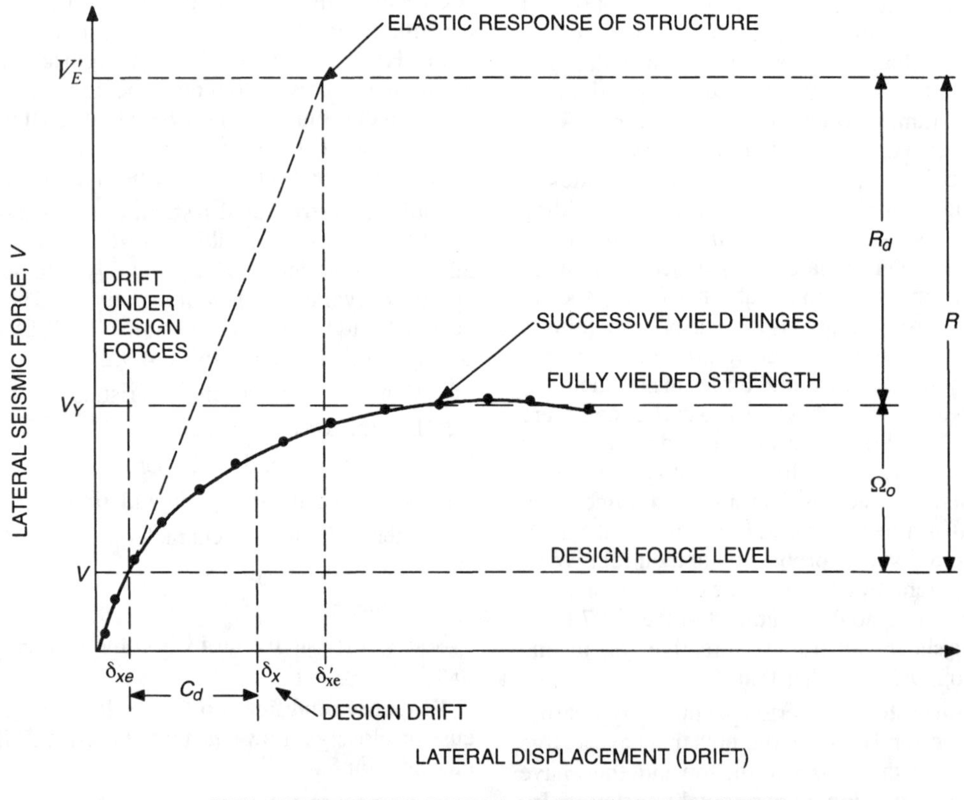

INELASTIC FORCE-DISPLACEMENT RELATIONSHIP

FIGURE 34

this continued inelastic action provides the reserve strength necessary for the structure to resist the extreme motions of the actual seismic forces that may be generated by the design ground motion.

It should be noted that the structural overstrength described above results from the development of sequential plastic hinging in a properly designed, redundant structure. Several other sources will further increase structural overstrength. First, material overstrength (i.e.,actual material strengths higher than the nominal material strengths specified in the design) may increase the structural overstrength significantly. For example, surveys have shown that the mean yield strength of A36 steel is about 30 to 40 percent higher than the minimum specified strength, nominally used in design calculations. The actual yield strength of Grade 60 reinforcing bars is allowed by ACI 318-99 to be 30 percent higher than their specified yield strength. Second, member design strengths usually incorporate a strength reduction (or resistance) factor, ϕ, to ensure a low probability of failure under design loading. Third, designers themselves introduce additional overstrength by selecting sections or specifying reinforcing patterns that exceed those required by the computations. Similar situations occur when minimum code requirements, for example, minimum reinforcement ratios, control the design. Finally, the design of many flexible structural systems, such as moment resisting frames, are often controlled by the drift rather than strength limitations of the governing code, with sections selected to control lateral deformations rather than provide the specified strength. The result is that structures typically have a much higher lateral resistance than specified as a minimum by design codes. According to the 1997 NEHRP Commentary, first actual significant yielding of structures may occur at lateral load levels that are 30 to 100 percent higher than the prescribed design seismic forces. If provided with adequate ductile detailing, redundancy and regularity, full yielding of structures may occur at load levels that are two to four times the prescribed design force levels.

A detailed history of the evolution of *R* factors is presented in the ATC-19 report.[43] The *R* values contained in the 2000 IBC Table 1617.6 are largely based on engineering judgment of the performance of various materials and systems in past earthquakes. The factors and characteristics to be considered in the evaluation of *R* have been determined by SEAOC to include:

1. Observed system performance.
2. Level of inelastic response capability.
3. Possibilities of failure of vertical load-resisting system.
4. Redundancy of lateral-force-resisting system.
5. Multiplicity of lines of defense, such as backup frames.

For ATC 3-06,[7] where the factor, *R* was first introduced, certain agreed-upon reference structures were selected. Two systems having high and low expected levels of performance were chosen to be "a steel ductile frame and a box type masonry or concrete building, respectively." In today's terminology these would be the special moment frame of steel and a bearing wall system consisting of masonry or concrete shear walls, respectively. The *R*-values for these two systems were chosen considering the *K*-values assigned to them by older editions of the UBC. No compelling arguments were offered to change the design basis loads for these systems or to change their interrelationship. The expected performances of other systems were then evaluated relative to these reference systems in order to determine the intermediate *R* values. The same characteristics discussed above were used, and considerations focused on the following issues:[4]

1. The degree to which the system can be allowed to go beyond the elastic range, its degree of energy dissipation in so doing, and the stability of the vertical load-carrying system during inelastic response due to maximum expected ground motion.
2. The consequence of failure or partial failure of vertical elements of the seismic-force-resisting system on the vertical load-carrying capacity and stability of the total building system.
3. The inherent redundancy of the system that would allow some progressive inelastic excursions without overall failure. One localized failure of a part must not lead to failure of the system.
4. When dual systems are employed, important performance characteristics include the ability of the secondary (backup) system to maintain vertical support when the primary system suffers significant damage at the maximum deformation response. The backup system can serve to redistribute lateral loads when the primary system undergoes degradation and should stabilize the building in the event that the primary system is badly damaged.

System overstrength factor, Ω_o, and deflection amplification factor, C_d. These factors, also listed in Table 1617.6, have been explained under Section 1614.5. The system overstrength factor, Ω_o, has also been discussed.

Some contemporary seismic codes, including those adopted in Canada and Europe, have attempted to directly quantify the relative contribution of overstrength and inelastic behavior to the permissible reduction in design strength. SEAOC has incorporated such an approach in their 1999 Blue Book, introducing two *R*-factor components, termed R_o and R_d, to represent the reduction due to structural overstrength and inelastic behavior, respectively. The design forces are then determined by forming a composite *R*, equal to the product of the two components. A similar approach was considered for adoption into the 1997 NEHRP Provisions, but was not adopted for reasons given in the commentary to that document. As a first step in the direction of split *R* values, however, the factor, Ω_o was added to the *R* values table, to replace the previous $2R/5$ factor used for evaluation of brittle structural behavior modes in prior editions of the NEHRP Provisions.

Height limits. In keeping with the practice incorporated into the Uniform Building Code for zones of high seismic risk, the 2000 IBC continues limitations on the use of certain structural systems over 160 feet in height for buildings assigned to SDC D and E (over 100 feet in height for buildings assigned to SDC F). Although, in view of a lack of reliable data on the behavior of SDC F high-risk buildings whose structural systems include shear walls and/or braced frames, it is considered prudent to retain some height limits, the values of 160 and 100 feet chosen for the 1997 NEHRP Provisions and the IBC are arbitrary and must be understood to be such. The height limits of Table 1617.6 are modified by Section 1617.6.4.1.

Structural systems of specific materials. The structural systems of reinforced concrete, steel, masonry and wood that are recognized in Table 1617.6 along with the R, Ω_o, C_d values and height limits for various seismic design categories assigned to them, are listed in Tables 23, 24, 25 and 26, respectively. These are compared with the corresponding structural systems of the same materials recognized by the 1997 UBC and the values of R and Ω_o and the height limits assigned to those systems by the UBC. Comparisons are made with the UBC and not the BOCA/NBC or the SBC because, as mentioned earlier, the IBC, the BOCA/NBC and the SBC are based on the same resource document (the NEHRP Provisions), whereas the UBC is based on a separate resource document (the SEAOC Blue Book). A comparison between the 2000 IBC and the latest editions of the BOCA/NBC and the SBC would really be a comparison between the 1997 and the 1991 editions of the NEHRP Provisions. Readers in UBC jurisdictions may find Tables 23, 24, 25 and 26 particularly useful.

There are some obvious differences between the 2000 IBC Table 1617.6 and the corresponding 1997 UBC Table 16-N:

1. The UBC table does not list C_d values because C_d is not used in the UBC.
2. The IBC table gives height limits by the seismic design category, while the UBC table specifies the limits by the seismic zone.

   For the purposes of Tables 23, 24, 25 and 26, the UBC height limits applicable in Seismic Zone 3 and 4 have been considered applicable to buildings assigned to SDC D, E and F.
3. The IBC table has a column of very useful detailing reference sections, that is not in the UBC.

It should be noted that identical structural systems in the two tables often have slightly different R and C_d values. The item of most importance, however, is the proliferation of structural systems in the IBC table. The reason is a policy decision made with respect to the 1997 NEHRP Provisions that forms the basis of the seismic design requirements of the 2000 IBC. In the 1997 UBC, the bearing wall system with concrete shear walls has been assigned R and Ω_o values of 4.5 and 2.8, respectively. The values do not change from the high to the low seismic zones. In Seismic Zones 3 and 4, the shear walls require special detailing, while in Seismic Zones 1 and 2, ordinary detailing is all that is needed. Thus, in effect, two different seismic-force-resisting systems with different levels of inelastic deformability go under the same name and are assigned the same R and Ω_o values. This situation, it was felt, needed improvement. For the 1997 NEHRP Provisions it was decided that each basic seismic-force-resisting system defined in Table 1617.6 would have its own unique set of detailing requirements and commensurate R and C_d values assigned to it. Thus, four different types of concrete shear walls have been defined: ordinary plain concrete, detailed plain concrete, ordinary reinforced concrete, and special reinforced concrete. This obviously adds to the total number of structural systems defined in the table.

Structural systems for specific seismic design categories. The choice of concrete and masonry structural systems available for buildings assigned to IBC SDC D, E and F, or located in UBC Seismic Zones 3 or 4, is presented in Tables 27 and 28, respectively. There are very few restrictions on steel and wood structural systems that are related to the seismic design category or the seismic zone. With rare exceptions, all steel and wood structural systems listed in Tables 25 and 26 may be used across all seismic zones and in all seismic design categories.

Concrete and masonry structural systems restricted in applicability to seismic design categories no higher than C or seismic zones no higher than 2, are listed in Tables 29 and 30, respectively.

Finally, concrete and masonry structural systems restricted in applicability to seismic design categories no higher than B or seismic zones no higher than 1, are listed in Tables 31 and 32, respectively.

1617.6.1 Dual systems. These were discussed under Section 1617.6.

1617.6.2 Combination along the same axis, 1617.6.3 Combinations of framing systems. There are three basic rules governing combinations of structural systems:

1. Vertical combination: when different structural systems are combined along the height of a building, the rule is that the value of R used in the design of any story must be less than or equal to the value of R used in the given direction for the story above (Figure 35). Also, the value of Ω_o used in the design of any story must be more than or equal to the value of Ω_o used in the given direction for the story above.
2. Combinations along the same axis: For other than dual systems and shear wall-frame interactive systems (which are restricted to seismic design categories no higher than B), where a combination of different structural systems is used to resist lateral forces in the same direction, the value of R used for design in that direction must not be greater than the least value for any of the systems utilized in that same direction (Figure 36).
3. Combinations along different axes: Following observations in the Mexico earthquake of 1985, a rule was added to the 1988 edition of the UBC requiring that in Seismic Zones 3 and 4, where a structure has a bearing wall system in only one direction, the value of R used for design in the orthogonal direction must not be taken greater than that used for the bearing wall system.

   The rule remained unchanged in the 1997 UBC. The IBC has a more generalized requirement. In SDC D, E or F, if a system with $R < 5$ is used as part of the seismic force-resisting system in any direction of a structure, the lower such value must be used in the design of the entire structure (Figure 37).

The IBC waives rules 1 and 3 above for detached one- and two-family dwellings constructed of light framing. Rule 1 need not be applied to supported structural systems with a weight less than or equal to 10 percent of the total weight of the structure. The exception is included to permit the use of such systems as a braced frame penthouse on a moment frame building in which the weight of the penthouse does not represent a significant portion of the total building weight and, thus, would not materially affect the overall building response to earthquake motions. A two-stage analysis procedure, as outlined in Items 3.1 and 3.2 under Exception 3 to Section 1617.6.3.1 is allowed for structures conforming to the requirements in Items 3.3 and 3.4.

The 2000 IBC explicitly states in Section 1617.6.3.2 that the detailing required by the higher R value must be used for structural components common to systems having different R values.

TABLE 23. EARTHQUAKE-FORCE-RESISTING STRUCTURAL SYSTEMS OF CONCRETE—2000 IBC AND 1997 UBC

BASIC SEISMIC-FORCE-RESISTING SYSTEM	DETAILING REF. SEC.	R	Ω_o	C_d	SYSTEM LIMITATIONS AND BUILDING HEIGHT LIMITATIONS (ft) BY SEISMIC DESIGN CATEGORY[1]					1997 UBC	
					A&B	C	D	E	F	R	Ω_o
Bearing Wall System											
Special reinforced concrete shear walls	1910.2.4	5½	2½	5	NL	NL	160	160	100 (160)	4.5	2.8
Ordinary reinforced concrete shear walls	1910.2.3	4½	2½	4	NL	NL	NP	NP	NP	4.5	2.8
Detailed plain concrete shear walls	1910.2.2	2½	2½	2	NL	NL	NP	NP	NP	—	—
Ordinary plain concrete shear walls	1910.2.1	1½	2½	1½	NL	NP	NP	NP	NP	—	—
Concrete braced frames where bracing carries gravity load	—	—	—	—	NL	NL	NP	NP	NP	2.8	2.2
Building Frame Systems											
Special reinforced concrete shear walls	1910.2.4	6	2½	5	NL	NL	160 (240)	160 (240)	100 (240)	5.5	2.8
Ordinary reinforced concrete shear walls	1910.2.3	5	2½	4½	NL	NL	NP	NP	NP	5.5	2.8
Detailed plain concrete shear walls	1910.2.2	3	2½	2½	NL	NL	NP	NP	NP	—	—
Ordinary plain concrete shear walls	1910.2.1	2	2½	2	NL	NP	NP	NP	NP	—	—
Ordinary braced frames of concrete	—	—	—	—	NL	NL	NP	NP	NP	5.6	2.2
Moment-resisting Frame Systems											
Special reinforced concrete moment frames	21.1[6]	8	3	5½	NL	NL	NL	NL	NL	8.5	2.8
Intermediate reinforced concrete moment frames	21.1[6]	5	3	4½	NL	NL	NP[2]	NP[2]	NP[2]	5.5	2.8
Ordinary reinforced concrete moment frames	21.1[6]	3	3	2½	NL[3]	NP	NP	NP	NP	3.5	2.8
Dual System with Special Moment Frames											
Special reinforced concrete shear walls	1910.2.4	8	2½	6½	NL	NL	NL	NL	NL	8.5	2.8
Ordinary reinforced concrete shear walls	1910.2.3	7	2½	6	NL	NL	NP	NP	NP	8.5	2.8
Ordinary braced frames of concrete[4]				—	NL	NL	NP	NP	NP	6.5	2.8
Dual Systems with Intermediate Moment Frames											
Special reinforced concrete shear walls[5]	1910.2.4	6	2½	5	NL	NL	160 (NP)	100 (NP)	100 (NP)	6.5	2.8
Ordinary reinforced concrete shear walls	1910.2.3	5½	2½	4½	NL	NL	NP	NP	NP	6.5	2.8
Ordinary braced frames of concrete[5]				—	NL	NL	NP	NP	NP	4.2	2.8
Dual Systems with Ordinary Moment Frames of Steel											
Special reinforced concrete shear walls				—	NL	NL	160	160	160	4.2	2.8
Ordinary reinforced concrete shear walls	—	—	—	—	NL	NL	NP	NP	NP	4.2	2.8
Shear Wall-Frame Interactive Systems											
Ordinary reinforced concrete moment frames and ordinary reinforced concrete shear walls	21.1[6] 1910.2.3	5½	2½	5	NL	NP	NP	NP	NP	5.5	2.8
Inverted Pendulum Systems											
Special reinforced concrete moment frames	21.1[6]	2½	2	1¼	NL	NL	NL	NL	NL	—	—

[1]Figures within parenthesis are UBC height limits in feet when they are different from corresponding IBC height limits.

[2]IMRF may be used in 1997 UBC Seismic Zones 3 and 4 if 1) the structure is less than 50 ft in height, and 2) the value of R used in reducing calculated member forces and moments does not exceed 2.8

[3]Not permitted for SDC B structures founded on Site Class E or F soils (2000 IBC).

[4]With concrete SMRF, specifically, in UBC 1997.

[5]With concrete IMRF, specifically, in UBC 1997.

[6]ACI 318 Section number.

TABLE 24. EARTHQUAKE-FORCE-RESISTING STRUCTURAL SYSTEMS OF MASONRY—2000 IBC AND 1997 UBC

BASIC SEISMIC-FORCE-RESISTING SYSTEM	DETAILING REF. SEC.	R	Ω_o	C_d	SYSTEM LIMITATIONS AND BUILDING HEIGHT LIMITATIONS (ft) BY SEISMIC DESIGN CATEGORY[1]					1997 UBC	
					A&B	C	D	E	F	R	Ω_o
Bearing Wall System											
Special reinforced masonry shear walls	2106.1.1.5	5	$2\frac{1}{2}$	$3\frac{1}{2}$	NL	NL	160	160	100 (160)	4.5	2.8
Intermediate reinforced masonry shear walls	2106.1.1.4	$3\frac{1}{2}$	$2\frac{1}{2}$	$2\frac{1}{4}$	NL	NL	NP	NP	NP	—	—
Ordinary reinforced masonry shear walls	2106.1.1.2	$2\frac{1}{2}$	$2\frac{1}{2}$	$1\frac{3}{4}$	NL	160 (NL)	NP	NP	NP	4.5	2.8
Detailed plain masonry shear walls	2106.1.1.3	2	$2\frac{1}{2}$	$1\frac{3}{4}$	NL	NP	NP	NP	NP	—	—
Ordinary plain masonry shear walls	2106.1.1.1	$1\frac{1}{2}$	$2\frac{1}{2}$	$1\frac{1}{4}$	NL	NP	NP	NP	NP	—	—
Building Frame Systems											
Special reinforced masonry shear walls	2106.1.1.5	$5\frac{1}{2}$	$2\frac{1}{2}$	4	NL	NL	160	160	100 (160)	5.5	2.8
Intermediate reinforced masonry shear walls	2106.1.1.4	4	$2\frac{1}{2}$	$2\frac{1}{2}$	NL	NL	160	160	100	—	—
Ordinary reinforced masonry shear walls	2106.1.1.2	3	$2\frac{1}{2}$	$2\frac{1}{4}$	NL	160 (NL)	NP	NP	NP	5.5	2.8
Detailed plain masonry shear walls	2106.1.1.3	$2\frac{1}{2}$	$2\frac{1}{2}$	$2\frac{1}{4}$	NL	NP	NP	NP	NP	—	—
Ordinary plain masonry shear walls	2106.1.1.1	$1\frac{1}{2}$	$2\frac{1}{2}$	$1\frac{1}{4}$	NL	NP	NP	NP	NP	—	—
Moment-resisting Frame Systems											
Masonry wall frames	2108.9.6/ 2106.1.1.6	$5\frac{1}{2}$	3	5	NL	NL	160	160	100 (160)	6.5	2.8
Dual Systems with Special Moment Frames											
Special reinforced masonry shear walls	2106.1.1.5	7	3	$6\frac{1}{2}$	NL	NL	NL (160)	NL (160)	NL (160)	5.5	2.8
Intermediate reinforced masonry shear walls	2106.1.1.4	$6\frac{1}{2}$	3	$5\frac{1}{2}$	NL	NL	NL	NP	NP	5.5	2.8
Ordinary reinforced masonry shear walls	2106.1.1.2				NL	NL	NP	NP	NP	5.5	2.8
Dual Systems with Intermediate Moment Frames[2]											
Intermediate reinforced masonry shear walls	2106.1.1.4	5	3	$4\frac{1}{2}$	NL	NL	160	NP	NP	—	—
Ordinary reinforced masonry shear walls	2106.1.1.2	3	3	$2\frac{1}{2}$	NL	160 (NL)	NP	NP	NP	4.2	2.8
Dual Systems with Ordinary Moment Frames of Steel											
Special reinforced masonry shear walls	—	—	—	—	NL	NL	160	160	160	4.2	2.8
Ordinary reinforced masonry shear walls	—	—	—	—	NL	NL	NP	NP	NP	4.2	2.8
Dual Systems with Masonry Wall Frames											
Special reinforced masonry shear walls	—	—	—	—	NL	NL	160	160	160	6.0	2.8
Ordinary reinforced masonry shear walls	—	—	—	—	NL	NL	160	160	160	6.0	2.8

[1]Figures within parentheses are UBC height limits in feet when they are different from corresponding IBC height limits.
[2]Of concrete, specifically, in UBC 1997.

TABLE 25. EARTHQUAKE-FORCE-RESISTING SYSTEMS OF STEEL—2000 IBC AND 1997 UBC

BASIC SEISMIC-FORCE RESISTING SYSTEM	DETAILING REF. SEC.	R	Ω_o	C_d	SYSTEM LIMITATIONS AND BUILDING HEIGHT LIMITATIONS (ft) BY SEISMIC DESIGN CATEGORY[1]					1997 UBC	
					A&B	C	D	E	F	R	Ω_o
Bearing Wall Systems											
Ordinary steel braced frames	Note 9 (14) 2211	4	2	3 1/2	NL	NL	160	160	160	—	—
Light steel-framed bearing walls with tension-only bracing	—	—	—	—	NL	NL	65	65	65	2.8	2.2
Steel braced frames where bracing carries gravity load	—	—	—	—	NL	NL	160	160	160	4.4	2.2
Light frame walls with shear panels—Wood structural panels[2]/sheet steel panels	2306.4.1/ 2211	6	3	4	NL	NL	65	65	65	5.5	2.8
Light frame walls with shear panels—all other materials	2306.4.5	2	2 1/2	2	NL	NL	35 (65)	NP (65)	NP (65)	4.5	2.8
Building Frame System											
Steel eccentrically braced frames, moment-resisting connections at columns away from links	15[8]	8	2	4	NL	NL	160	160	160		
Steel EBF, non-moment-resisting connections at columns away from links	Note 9 (15)	7	2	4	NL	NL	160 (240)	160 (240)	100 (240)	7.0	2.8
Special steel CBF	Note 9 (13)	6	2	5	NL	NL	160 (240)	160 (240)	100 (240)	6.4	2.2
Ordinary steel CBF	Note 9 (14)	5	2	4 1/2	NL	NL	160	100 (160)	100 (160)	5.6	2.2
Light frame walls with shear panels—wood structural panels[2]/sheet steel panels	2306.4.1/ 2211	6 1/2	2 1/2	4 1/2	NL	NL	65	65	65	6.5	2.8
Light frame walls with shear panels—all other materials	2306.4.5	2 1/2	2 1/2	2 1/2	NL	NL	35 (65)	NP (65)	NP (65)	5.0	2.8
Moment-resisting Frame Systems											
Special steel moment frames	Note 9 (9)	8	3	5 1/2	NL	NL	NL	NL	NL	8.5	2.8
Special steel truss moment frames	Note 9 (12)	7	3	5 1/2	NL	NL	160 (240)	100 (240)	NP	6.5	2.8
Intermediate steel moment frames	Note 9 (10)	6	3	5	NL	NL	160	100	NP[4]	—	—
Ordinary steel moment frames	Note 9 (11)	4	3	3 1/2	NL	NL	35[4] (160)	NP[4,5] (160)	NP[4,5] (160)	4.5	2.8
Dual systems with Special Moment Frames											
Steel EBF, moment-resisting connections at columns away from links[3]	Note 9 (15)	8	2 1/2	4	NL	NL	NL	NL	NL	—	—
Steel EBF, non-moment-resisting connections at columns away from links[3]	Note 9 (15)	7	2 1/2	4	NL	NL	NL	NL	NL	8.5	2.8
Special steel CBF	Note 9 (13)	8	2 1/2	6 1/2	NL	NL	NL	NL	NL	7.5	2.8
Ordinary steel CBF	Note 9 (14)	6	2 1/2	5	NL	NL	NL	NL	NL	6.5	2.8
Dual Systems with Intermediate Moment Frames											
Special steel CBF[6]	Note 9 (13)	6	2 1/2	5	NL	NL	160	100	NP	—	—
Ordinary steel CBF[6]	Note 9 (14)	5	2 1/2	4 1/2	NL	NL	160	100	NP	—	—
Dual Systems with Ordinary Moment Frames of Steel											
Special steel CBF	—	—	—	—	NL	NL	160	160	160	4.2	2.8
Ordinary steel CBF	—	—	—	—	NL	NL	160	160	160	4.2	2.8
Inverted Pendulum Systems											
Special steel moment frames	Note 9 (9)	2 1/2	2	2 1/2	NL	NL	NL	NL	NL	—	—
Ordinary steel moment frames	Note 9 (11)	1 1/4	2	2 1/2	NL	NL	NP	NP	NP	—	—
Cantilevered column building systems		2 1/2	2	2 1/2	NL	NL	35[7]	35[7]	35[7]	2.2	2.0
Structural steel systems not specifically detailed for seismic resistance	AISC-ASD AISC-LRFD AISI AISC-HSS	3	3	3	NL	NL	NP	NP	NP	—	—

FOOTNOTES TO TABLE 25

[1]Figures within parentheses are UBC height limits in feet when they are different from corresponding IBC height limits.

[2]For structures three stories or less in height in UBC.

[3]UBC does not distinguish between moment-resisting and non-moment-resisting connections at columns away from links.

[4]Steel ordinary moment frames and intermediate moment frames are permitted in single story buildings up to a height of 60 ft, when the moment joints of field connections are constructed of bolted end plates and the dead load of the roof does not exceed 15 psf. The dead weight of the portion of walls more than 35 ft above the base shall not exceed 15 psf.

[5]Steel ordinary moment frames are permitted in buildings up to height of 35 ft, where the dead load of the walls, floors and roofs does not exceed 15 psf.

[6]Ordinary moment frame is permitted to be used in lieu of intermediate moment frame in SDC B and C.

[7]Total height of the building including cantilevered columns.

[8]AISC Seismic Part I or Part III Section number.

[9]AISC Seismic Part II Section number.

TABLE 26. EARTHQUAKE-FORCE-RESISTING STRUCTURAL SYSTEMS OF WOOD—2000 IBC AND 1997 UBC

BASIC SEISMIC-FORCE RESISTING SYSTEM	DETAILING REF. SEC.	R	Ω_o	C_d	SYSTEM LIMITATIONS AND BUILDING HEIGHT LIMITATIONS (ft) BY SEISMIC DESIGN CATEGORY A&B	C	D	E	F	1997 UBC R	1997 UBC Ω_o
Bearing Wall Systems											
Light frame walls with shear panels—Wood Structural Panels/sheet steel panels	2306.4.1/ 2211	6	3	4	NL	NL	65	65	65		
Light frame walls with shear panels—all other materials	2306.4.5	2	$2\frac{1}{2}$	2	NL	NL	35	NP	NP		
Light-frame walls with shear panels											
Wood structural panel walls for structures three stories or less	—	—	—	—	NL	NL	65	65	65	5.5	2.8
All other light-framed walls	—	—	—	—	NL	NL	65	65	65	4.5	2.8
Heavy timber braced frames where bracing carries gravity load	—	—	—	—	NL	NL	65	65	65	2.8	2.2
Building Frame Systems											
Light framed walls with shear panels											
Wood structural panel walls for structures three stories or less	—	—	—	—	NL	NL	65	65	65	6.5	2.8
All other light-framed walls	—	—	—	—	NL	NL	65	65	65	5.0	2.8
Ordinary heavy timber braced frames	—	—	—	—	NL	NL	65	65	65	5.6	2.2

TABLE 27. CONCRETE STRUCTURAL SYSTEMS FOR IBC SEISMIC DESIGN CATEGORIES D,E,F AND UBC SEISMIC ZONES 3,4

STRUCTURAL SYSTEM	IBC 2000 R	Ω_o	C_d	HEIGHT LIMIT (ft) D	E	F	UBC 1997 R	Ω_o	0.7R	HT. LIMIT (ft)
Bearing Wall Systems										
Special reinforced concrete shear walls	$5\frac{1}{2}$	$2\frac{1}{2}$	5	160	160	100	4.5	2.8	3.2	160
Building Frame Systems										
Special reinforced concrete moment frames	6	$2\frac{1}{2}$	5	160	160	100	5.5	2.8	3.9	240
Moment-resisting Frame Systems										
Special reinforced concrete moment frames	8	3	$5\frac{1}{2}$	NL	NL	NL	8.5	2.8	6.0	NL
Dual Systems with Special Moment Frames										
Special reinforced concrete shear walls	8	$2\frac{1}{2}$	$6\frac{1}{2}$	NL	NL	NL	8.5	2.8	6.0	NL
Dual Systems with Intermediate Moment Frames[1]										
Special reinforced concrete shear walls	6	$2\frac{1}{2}$	5	160	100	100	6.5	2.8	4.6	NP
Dual systems with Ordinary Moment Frames of Steel										
Special reinforced concrete shear walls	—	—	—	—	—	—	4.2	2.8	2.9	160

[1]Of concrete, specifically, in UBC 1997.

TABLE 28. MASONRY STRUCTURAL SYSTEMS FOR IBC SEISMIC DESIGN CATEGORIES D,E,F AND UBC SEISMIC ZONES 3,4

STRUCTURAL SYSTEM	IBC 2000						UBC 1997			
				HEIGHT LIMIT (ft)						
	R	Ω_o	C_d	D	E	F	R	Ω_o	$0.7R$	HT. LIMIT (ft)
Bearing Wall Systems										
Special reinforced masonry shear walls	5	2 1/2	3 1/2	160	160	100	4.5	2.8	3.2	160
Building Frame Systems										
Special reinforced masonry shear walls	5 1/2	2 1/2	4	160	160	100	5.5	2.8	3.9	160
Moment-resisting Frame Systems										
Masonry wall frames	5 1/2	3	5	160	160	100	6.5	2.8	4.6	160
Dual Systems with Special Moment Frames										
Special reinforced masonry shear walls	7	3	6 1/2	NL	NL	NL	5.5	2.8	3.9	160
Dual systems with Ordinary Moment Frames of Steel										
Special reinforced masonry shear walls	—	—	—	—	—	—	4.2	2.8	2.9	160
Dual Systems with Masonry Wall Frames										
Special reinforced masonry shear walls	—	—	—	—	—	—	6.0	2.8	4.2	160

TABLE 29. CONCRETE STRUCTURAL SYSTEMS FOR IBC SEISMIC DESIGN CATEGORY C AND UBC SEISMIC ZONE 2

STRUCTURAL SYSTEM	IBC 2000			UBC 1997		
	R	Ω_o	C_d	R	Ω_o	$0.7R$
Bearing Wall Systems						
Ordinary reinforced concrete shear walls	4 1/2	2 1/2	4	4.5	2.8	3.2
Concrete braced frames where bracing carries gravity load	—	—	—	2.8	2.2	2.0
Building Frame Systems						
Ordinary reinforced concrete shear walls	5	2 1/2	4 1/2	5.5	2.8	3.9
Ordinary braced frames of concrete	—	—	—	5.6	2.2	3.9
Moment-resisting Frame Systems						
Intermediate reinforced concrete moment frames	5	3	4 1/2	5.5	2.8	4.0
Dual System with Special Moment Frames						
Ordinary reinforced concrete shear walls	7	2 1/2	6	8.5	2.8	6.0
Ordinary braced frames of concrete[1]	—	—	—	6.5	2.8	4.6
Dual Systems with Intermediate Moment Frames						
Ordinary reinforced concrete shear walls	5 1/2	2 1/2	4 1/2	6.5	2.8	4.6
Ordinary braced frames of concrete[2]	—	—	—	4.2	2.8	2.9
Dual Systems with Ordinary Moment Frames of Steel						
Ordinary reinforced concrete shear walls	—	—	—	4.2	2.8	2.9

[1]With concrete SMRF, specifically, in UBC 1997.
[2]With concrete IMRF, specifically, in UBC 1997.

TABLE 30. MASONRY STRUCTURAL SYSTEMS FOR IBC SEISMIC DESIGN CATEGORY C AND UBC SEISMIC ZONE 2

STRUCTURAL SYSTEM	IBC 2000				UBC 1997		
	R	Ω_o	C_d	HEIGHT LIMIT (FT)	R	Ω_o	$0.7R$
Bearing Wall Systems							
Intermediate reinforced masonry shear walls	3 1/2	2 1/2	2 1/4	NL	—	—	
Ordinary reinforced masonry shear walls	2 1/2	2 1/2	1 3/4	160	4.5	2.8	3.2
Detailed plain masonry shear walls	2	2 1/2	1 3/4	NP	—	—	—
Building Frame Systems							
Intermediate reinforced masonry shear walls	4	2 1/2	2 1/2	NL	—	—	—
Ordinary reinforced masonry shear walls	3	2 1/2	2 1/4	160	5.5	2.8	3.9
Dual systems with Special Moment Frames							
Intermediate reinforced masonry shear walls	6 1/2	3	5 1/2	NL	—	—	—
Dual Systems with Intermediate Moment Frames[1]							
Intermediate reinforced masonry shear walls	5	3	4 1/2	NL	—	—	—
Ordinary reinforced masonry shear walls	3	3	2 1/2	160	4.2	2.8	2.9

[1]Of concrete, specifically, in UBC 1997

TABLE 31. CONCRETE STRUCTURAL SYSTEMS FOR IBC SEISMIC DESIGN CATEGORIES A, B AND UBC SEISMIC ZONE 1

STRUCTURAL SYSTEM	IBC 2000			UBC 1997		
	R	Ω_o	C_d	R	Ω_o	$0.7R$
Bearing Wall Systems						
Ordinary plain concrete shear walls	$1\frac{1}{2}$	$2\frac{1}{2}$	$1\frac{1}{2}$	—	—	—
Building Frame Systems						
Ordinary plain concrete shear walls	2	$2\frac{1}{2}$	2	—	—	—
Moment-resisting Frame Systems						
Ordinary reinforced concrete moment frames	3	3	$2\frac{1}{2}$	3.5	2.8	2.5
Shear wall—Frame Interactive Systems						
Ordinary reinforced concrete moment frames and ordinary reinforced concrete shear walls	$5\frac{1}{2}$	$2\frac{1}{2}$	5	5.5	2.8	3.9

TABLE 32. MASONRY STRUCTURAL SYSTEMS FOR IBC SEISMIC DESIGN CATEGORIES A, B AND UBC SEISMIC ZONE 1

STRUCTURAL SYSTEM	IBC 2000			UBC 1997		
	R	Ω_o	C_d	R	Ω_o	$0.7R$
Bearing Wall Systems						
Ordinary plain masonry shear walls	$1\frac{1}{2}$	$2\frac{1}{2}$	$1\frac{1}{4}$	—	—	—
Building Frame Systems						
Ordinary plain masonry shear walls	$1\frac{1}{2}$	$2\frac{1}{2}$	$1\frac{1}{4}$	—	—	—

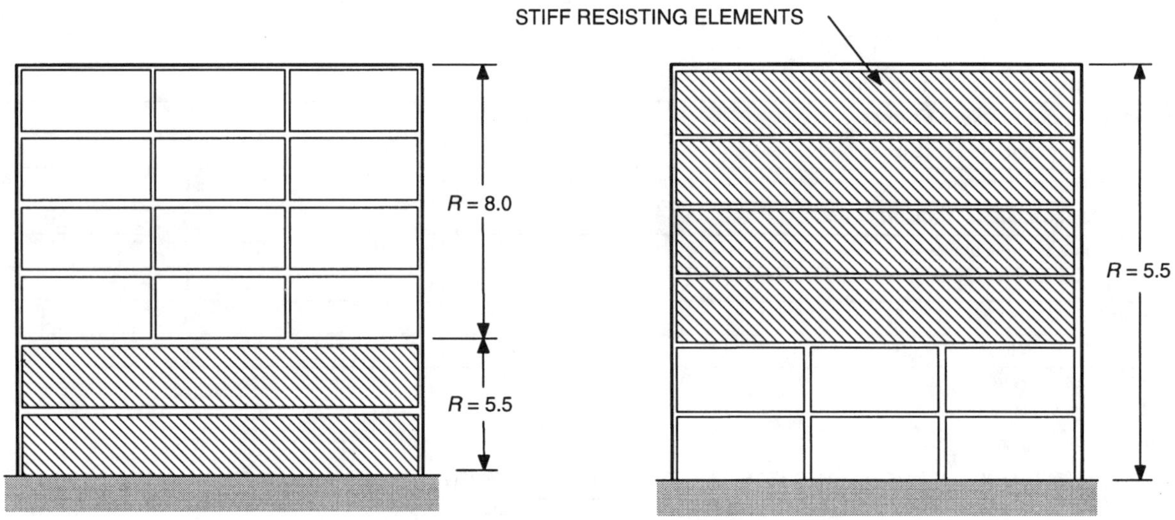

R (ANY STORY) $\leq R$ (STORY ABOVE)

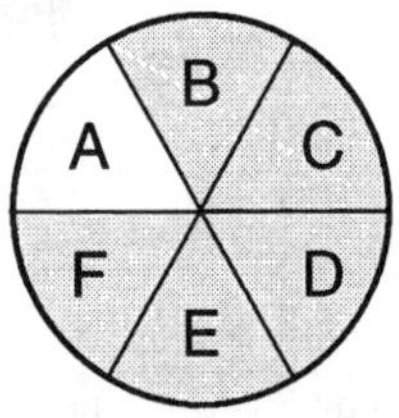

1. DESIGN STRUCTURE FOR LOWEST R FOR STRUCTURAL SYSTEMS USED, OR
2. TWO-STAGE ANALYSIS PERMITTED FOR STRUCTURES WITH FLEXIBLE UPPER PORTION SUPPORTED BY RIGID LOWER PORTION (SECTION 1617.6.3.1 EXCEPTION 3)
3. IN SDC D, E AND F, DYNAMIC ANALYSIS REQUIRED FOR STRUCTURES > 5 STORIES OR 65 FEET IN HEIGHT IF VERTICAL IRREGULARITY OF TYPE 1a, 1b, OR 2 (TABLE 1616.5.2) EXISTS

VERTICAL COMBINATIONS OF STRUCTURAL SYSTEMS (SECTION 1617.6.3.1)

FIGURE 35

1617.6.4 System limitations for Seismic Design Categories D, E and F. It may be noted from Table 1617.6 that buildings in SDC D and E over 160 feet in height and buildings in SDC F over 100 feet in height must have one of the following seismic-force-resisting systems:

1. A moment-resisting frame system with special moment frames capable of resisting the total prescribed seismic forces.
2. A dual system with special moment frames wherein the prescribed forces are resisted by the entire system and the special moment frames are designed to resist at least 25 percent of the prescribed seismic forces.

1617.6.4.1 Limited building height. For buildings assigned to SDC D and E, and having cast-in-place concrete shear walls or steel braced frames, the height limit is allowed to be relaxed from 160 feet to 240 feet, provided that: 1) the braced frames or shear walls in any plane do not resist more than 50 percent of the seismic design force including torsional effects, and 2) the configuration of the lateral-force-resisting system is such that torsional effects result in no more than a 20-percent contribution to the strength demand on the walls or frames. The intent is that each of these shear walls or braced frames shall be in a different plane and that the four or more planes shall be spaced throughout the plan or on the perimeter of the building in such a way that the premature failure of one of the single walls or braced frames will not lead to excessive inelastic torsion.

Although a structural system with lateral-force resistance concentrated in the interior core is allowed by the IBC, it is

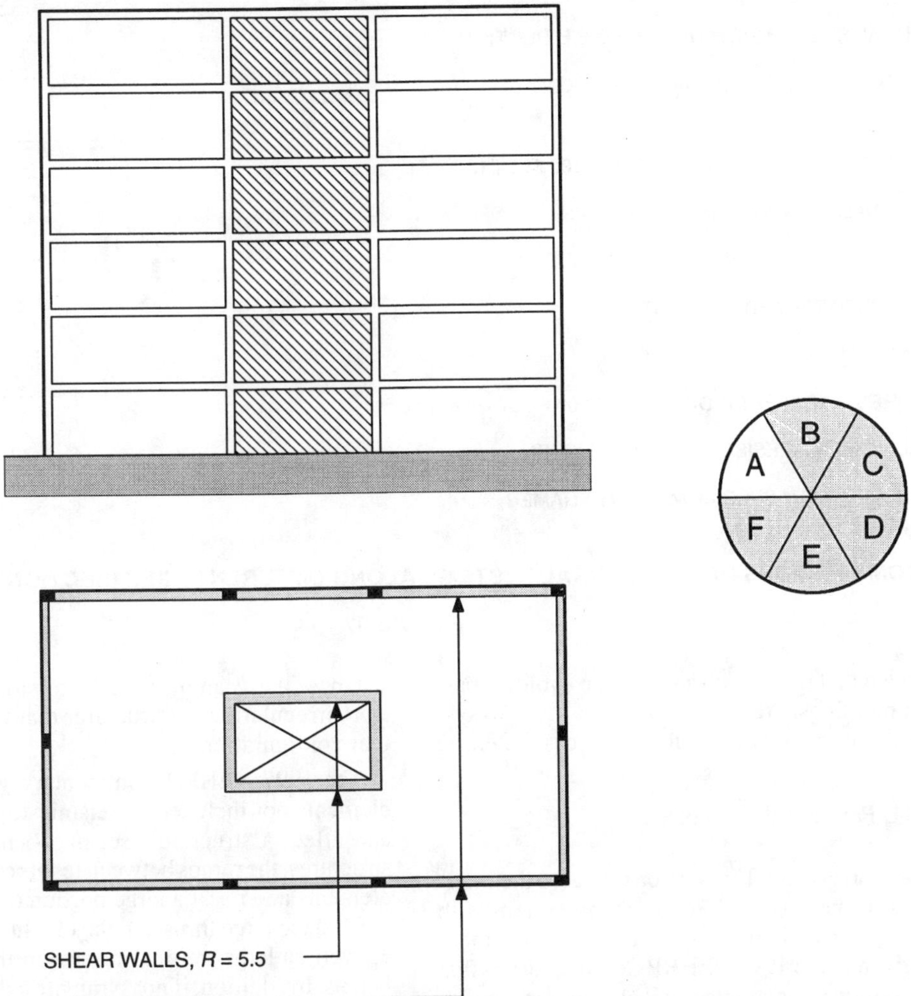

- WITH DIFFERENT STRUCTURAL SYSTEMS IN SAME DIRECTION, VALUE OF *R* IN THAT DIRECTION TO BE TAKEN AS LEAST *R* FOR STRUCTURAL SYSTEMS UTILIZED
- DUAL SYSTEMS. . . AND SHEAR WALL-FRAME INTERACTIVE SYSTEMS ARE EXCLUDED

COMBINATIONS OF STRUCTURAL SYSTEMS ALONG SAME AXES (SECTION 1617.6.2)

FIGURE 36

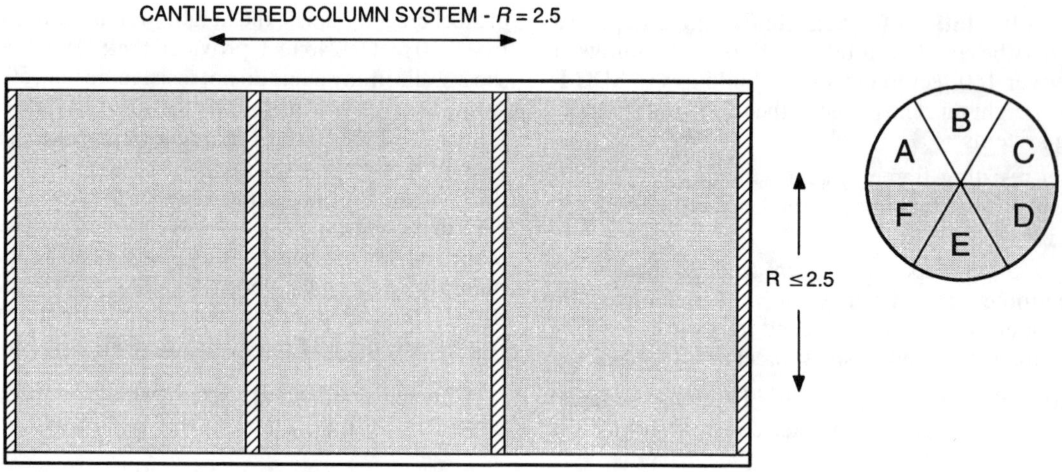

- STRUCTURAL SYSTEM WITH *R* < 5 IN ONE DIRECTION:

  R NO GREATER IN ORTHAGONAL DIRECTION

- STRUCTURES < 160 FEET (SDC D, E) OR 100 FEET (SDC F)

  BEARING WALL SYSTEM

  BUILDING FRAME SYSTEM

  MOMENT-RESISTING FRAME SYSTEM

  DUAL SYSTEM

- STRUCTURES > 160 FEET (SDC D, E) OR 100 FEET (SDC F)

  SPECIAL MOMENT-RESISTING FRAME SYSTEM

  DUAL SYSTEM WITH SPECIAL MOMENT FRAMES

COMBINATIONS OF STRUCTURAL SYSTEMS ALONG DIFFERENT AXES (SECTION 1617.6.3.1)

FIGURE 37

highly recommended that use of such a system be avoided, particularly for taller buildings. Preference should be given to systems with lateral-force resistance distributed across the entire building.

See Example 11, Part 2 of this chapter.

1617.6.4.2 Interaction effects. This section relates to the interaction of elements of the seismic-force-resisting system with elements that are designated not to be part of that system. A classic example given in the 1997 NEHRP Commentary is that of infill masonry walls used as architectural elements in a building provided with a seismic-force-resisting system consisting of moment-resisting frames. Although the masonry walls are not intended to resist seismic forces, at low levels of deformation they are substantially more rigid than the moment-resisting frames and thus participate in lateral-force resistance. Such walls often create shear-critical conditions in the columns of the moment frames by reducing the effective flexural height of these columns to the height of the openings in the walls. If these walls are not uniformly distributed throughout the structure, or not effectively isolated from participation in lateral-force resistance, they can also create torsional irregularities and soft story irregularities in structures that would otherwise have regular configuration.

The 1997 NEHRP Commentary gives another example of elements not included in seismic-force-resisting systems that can affect a structure's seismic behavior. In parking garage structures, the ramps between levels can act as effective bracing elements and resist a large portion of the seismic forces. They can induce large thrusts in the diaphragms where they connect, as well as large vertical forces on the adjacent columns and beams. In addition, if not symmetrically placed in the structure, they can cause torsional irregularities. This section requires consideration of these potential effects.

1617.6.4.3 Deformational compatibility. The concept of deformation compatibility has been introduced and discussed under "Building frame system" above. The deformation compatibility requirement of the UBC was fairly extensively revised in the 1996 Supplement to the UBC in view of observations from the 1994 Northridge earthquake. These revisions, incorporated in the 1997 UBC, require that all structural framing elements and their connections, not required by design to be part of the lateral-force-resisting system, must be designed and/or detailed to be adequate to maintain support of design dead plus live loads when subjected to the expected deformations caused by seismic forces. The following features of the deformation compatibility requirements of the 1997 UBC are important.

1. Expected deformations must be the greater of the Maximum Inelastic Response Displacement, Δ_M, considering P-delta, effects and deformation induced by a story drift of 0.0025 times the story height.
2. When computing expected deformations, stiffening effects of those elements not part of the lateral-force-resisting system must be neglected.
3. Forces induced by expected deformations may be considered factored forces.
4. In computing above forces, restraining effect of adjoining rigid structures and nonstructural elements must be considered . . . rational value of member and restraining stiffness must be used.
5. For concrete elements that are not part of the lateral-force-resisting system, assigned flexural and shear stiffnes properties must not exceed one-half of gross section properties, unless a rational cracked section analysis is performed.
6. Additional deformations that may result from foundation flexibility and diaphragm deflection must be considered.

The deformation compatibility requirements of Section 1617.6.4.3 are essentially the same as those of the 1997 UBC, except that the expected deformation is taken equal to the design story drift, Δ, determined in accordance with Section 1617.3 and 1617.4.6 (see earlier discussion on those sections). When allowable stress design is used, Δ is required to be computed without dividing the specified earthquake forces by 1.4. Item 3 above is specifically mentioned in this IBC section. The other items are not specifically included.

Example 40 of SEAOC Seismic Design Manual Volume 1 presents an approximate, but effective way of determining the moments and shears in components that are not included in the seismic-force-resisting system resulting from the design story drift, Δ, of the lateral-force-resisting system. An adaptation of the approximate SEAOC procedure is presented in Figure 38.

1617.6.4.4 Special moment frames. This specifies that a special moment frame may be discontinued and supported by a stiffer system only as long as it is used, but not required by Table 1617.6. As long as it is required by that table, it may not be discontinued.

SECTION 1618
DYNAMIC ANALYSIS PROCEDURE FOR THE SEISMIC DESIGN OF BUILDINGS

Analysis procedures have been described in detail under Section 1616.6. The code attitude is that dynamic analysis is always acceptable for design. Static procedures are allowed for structures assigned to the higher seismic design categories only under certain conditions of regularity and height.

The IBC formally recognizes three dynamic analysis procedures: modal analysis, elastic time history analysis and inelastic time history analysis. Only modal analysis is treated in the 1997 NEHRP Provisions (Section 5.4). Table 33 shows that the IBC provisions of Sections 1618.1 through 1618.9 closely follow those of Section 5.4 of the NEHRP Provisions. With the help of Table 33, the reader should be readily able to key into the 1997 NEHRP Provisions Commentary. It is largely unnecessary to reproduce much of it here. Section 1618.10 on time-history analysis is adopted from the 1997 UBC. Identical provisions are also to be found in the 1999 SEAOC Blue Book .[4] The following cross-references will help the reader take advantage of the SEAOC Blue Book Commentary:

In view of the ready availability of the commentaries mentioned above, the discussion here is kept very brief.

1618.1 Dynamic analysis procedures. The 1997 edition of the UBC, for the first time, introduced a set of modeling requirements for structural analysis—static as well as dynamic. As pointed out in the 1999 SEAOC Blue Book,[4] certain key assumptions are common to most analysis models: the structure is assumed to be linearly elastic; small deformation theory applies; structural mass is commonly lumped at a few selected joints and nodes; and energy dissipation (damping) is assumed to be viscous or velocity proportional. The 1997 UBC specifically requires that the mathematical model of a physical structure must include:

- all elements of the lateral-force-resisting system,
- stiffnesses and strengths of all elements that are significant to the distribution of forces,
- representation of spatial distribution of mass and stiffness of the structure,

2000 IBC Section No.		1997 UBC Section No.	1999 Blue Book Section No.
1618.10	Time-history analysis	1631.6	106.6
1618.10.1	Time history	1631.6.1	106.6.1
1618.10.2	Elastic time-history analysis	1631.6.2	106.6.2
1618.10.3	Nonlinear time-history analysis	1631.6.3	106.6.3
1618.10.3.1	Nonlinear time history	1631.6.3.1	106.6.3.1
1618.10.3.2	Design review	1631.6.3.2	106.6.3.2

- effects of cracked sections in concrete and masonry structures,
- contribution of panel zone deformations to story drift for steel moment frame structures.

Section 1618.1 specifically includes the last three bullet items. Two-dimensional vs. three-dimensional analysis is addressed. This topic has been discussed under Section 1616.6. Diaphragm flexibility is also addressed.

1618.2 Modes, 1618.3 Modal properties, 1618.4 Modal base shear, 1618.5 Modal forces, deflections and drifts, 1618.6 Modal story shears and moments. Modal analysis is used for calculating the linear response of multi-degree-of-freedom systems and utilizes the fact that the response is the superposition of the responses of individual natural modes of vibration, each mode responding with its own particular deformed shape, its own frequency, and with its own modal damping. The response of the structure can, therefore, be obtained from the responses of a number of single-degree-of-freedom systems with properties chosen to be representative of the modes and the degree to which the modes are excited by the earthquake motion. For certain types of damping, the representation is mathematically exact. Numerous full-scale tests and analyses of earthquake response of structures have shown that the use of modal analysis, with viscously damped single-degree-of-freedom oscillators describing the responses of the structural modes, produces an accurate approximation of linear response.[8]

Modal analysis is useful in design. The Equivalent lateral-force procedure of Section 1617.4 is simply a first mode application of this technique, that assumes all the mass of the structure to be active in the first mode. The purpose of modal analysis is to obtain the maximum response of the structure in each of its important modes, which are then summed in an appropriate manner. Instead of providing further commentary,

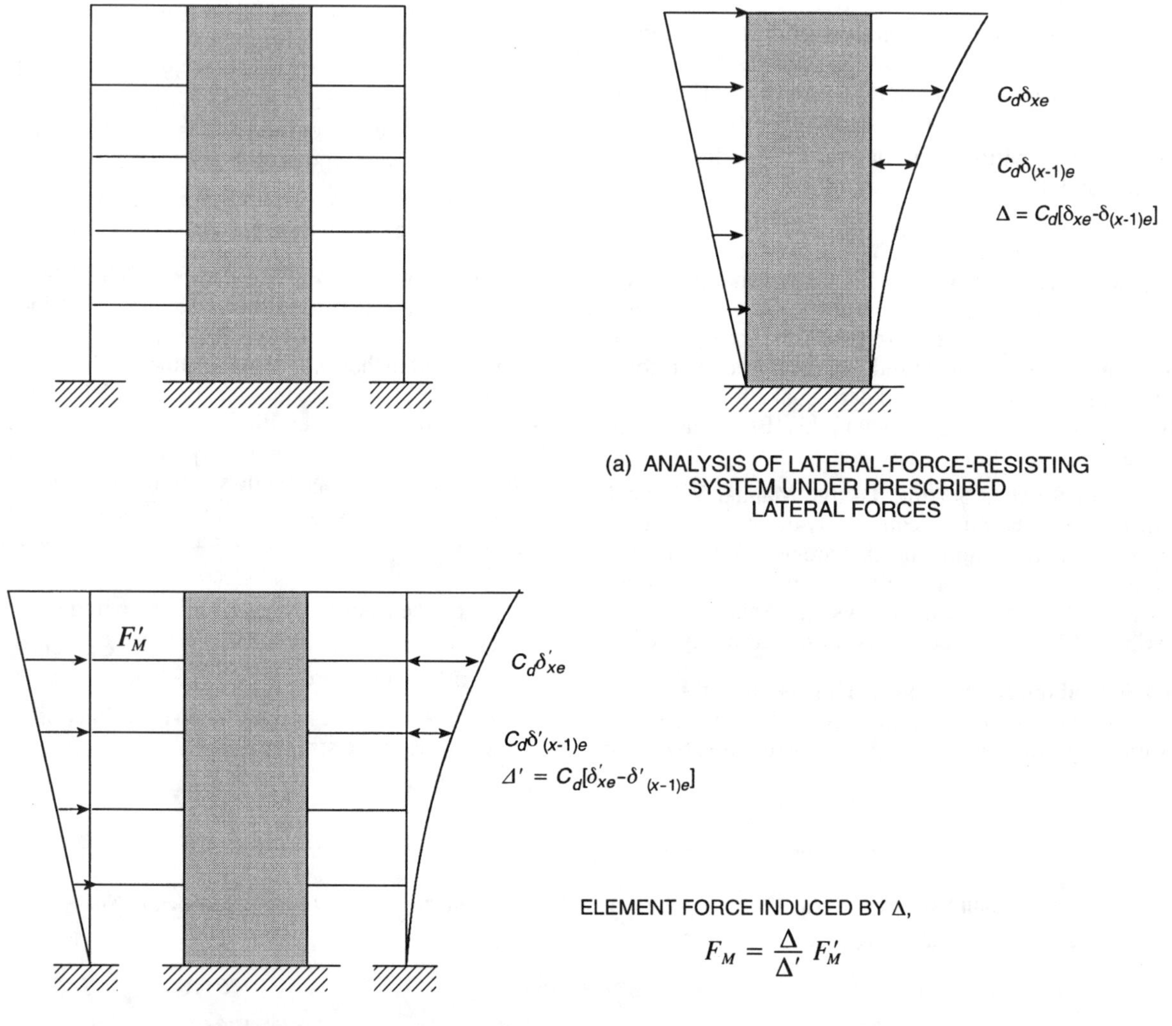

DEFORMATION COMPATIBILITY REQUIREMENT OF SECTION 1617.6.4.3

FIGURE 38

Example 12, Part 2 of this chapter is introduced to illustrate in detail the modal analysis procedure of the IBC. The step-by-step solution is probably the best help that can be provided to the reader, who may want to consult one of the standard references[44, 45] for background, if needed.

1618.7 Design values. The results of spectrum analysis are required to be scaled up to and are permitted to be scaled down to the base shear calculated with the ELF (Equivalent Lateral Force) approach (Table 34) and using a period taken as 1.2 times the upper limit coefficients for period calculation, C_u, times the period calculated using approximate period formulas (Table 35). This scaling is primarily done to ensure that the design forces are not under-estimated through the use of a structural model that is excessively flexible. The rather large period estimate that is permitted when calculating the ELF base shear is an arbitrarily selected approach to providing some incentive for use of dynamic analysis, through limited reductions in base shear.

For buildings with T (rationally determined, subject to a maximum of $C_u T_a$) $\geq$ 0.7 second, located on Site Class E or F sites where $S_{D1} \geq 0.2g$, scaling must be done on the basis of the ELF base shear calculated using the above period.

The scaling provisions are proposed to be changed in the 2000 NEHRP Provisions to require that when the base shear obtained from a dynamic analysis is less than 85 percent of the base shear obtained by the ELF procedure, the dynamic analysis results be scaled to no less than 85 percent of the ELF values (Table 34). However, when the response spectrum analysis produces results that are larger than the ELF values, no scaling would be permitted. The 85-percent rule is felt to be a more direct and less complex way of providing an incentive for performing a dynamic analysis.

The 1997 UBC requires scaling up and permits scaling down of the results of dynamic analysis to 90 percent of the ELF design base shear for regular buildings and 100 percent of the ELF design base shear for irregular buildings (Table 34). This distinction between regular and irregular buildings, always made in the UBC, is not a consideration in the 1997 NEHRP Provisions or the IBC. The distinction was supposed to act as a disincentive against the design of irregular structures. However, it has not been effective in that role.

The scaling rules of the 1994 UBC were somewhat different from those of the 1997 UBC. These are included in Table 34 as being of possible interest to the reader.

The deletion of the scale-down feature in the 2000 NEHRP Provisions is justified by pointing out that the ELF method may result in an underprediction of response for structures with significant higher mode participation. However, with the deletion, there will be no scale-down to static force levels even when a site-specific response spectrum is used in dynamic analysis. This probably places too much confidence in the geotechnical input. The confidence is now felt justified in view of the controls placed on the geotechnical input by the provisions in Section 1615.2.

1618.8 Horizontal shear distribution. This section requires that the design story shears calculated in Section 1618.7 and the torsional moments prescribed in Section 1617.4.4 be distributed to the vertical elements of the lateral-force-resisting system as specified in Section 1617.4.4. See earlier discussion on that section. Also see the 1999 SEAOC Blue Book Commentary Section C106.5.6.

1618.9 P-delta effects. See earlier discussion on Section 1617.4.6.2. Also, to obtain the story drifts when using the modal analysis procedure, the story drift for each mode should be independently determined in each story. The story drift should not be determined from the differential combined lateral structural deflections since this latter procedure will tend to mask the higher mode effects in long-period structures.[8]

1618.10 Time-history analysis. SEAOC Blue Book Commentary Section C106.6[4] should be referred to for a discussion of the provisions. A step-by-step procedure based on the provisions is given in Table 35.

SECTION 1619 EARTHQUAKE LOADS—SOIL-STRUCTURE INTERACTION EFFECTS

This refers to Section 9.2.5 of ASCE 7-98[6] which adopted its requirements from the 1994 NEHRP Provisions. The requirements remain unchanged in Section 5.5 of the 1997 NEHRP Provisions. Detailed background to the requirements is available in the 1997 NEHRP Provisions Part 2—Commentary.[8] A major update of these requirements has been prepared by Technical Subcommittee (TS) 3 of the Provisions Update Committee (PUC) of the Building Seismic Safety Council (BSSC) for possible inclusion in the 2000 NEHRP Provisions.

SECTION 1620 EARTHQUAKE LOADS—DESIGN, DETAILING REQUIREMENTS AND STRUCTURAL COMPONENT LOAD EFFECTS

This presents systematically organized requirements for the design and detailing of the components of the seismic force resisting system. An exception is made for structures assigned to SDC A because they have been exempt from seismic design requirements, as mentioned earlier. Requirements for SDC A structures are given in Section 1616.4 and are discussed under that section. From SDC B onwards, the requirements are "cascading" in the sense that requirements for SDC B also apply to SDC C structures. In the subsection on SDC C, additional requirements for structures assigned to that category are given, which also apply to SDC D, E and F structures.

1620.1 Structural component design and detailing. This concerns requirements applicable to structures assigned to seismic design categories higher than A.

1620.1.1 Second order load effects. This repeats the requirement of Section 1617.4.6.2 that P-delta effects be considered in design when the secondary-to-primary moment ratio, as defined in that section, exceeds 10 percent.

1620.1.2 Openings. This requirement concerning trim reinforcement around openings in plate-type elements repeats in general terms, specific requirements of the concrete and masonry chapters, where they more logically belong.

TABLE 33. COMPARISON OF 2000 IBC TO 1997 NEHRP (DYNAMIC ANALYSIS PROCEDURE)

2000 IBC		1997 NEHRP	
Section	**Provision**	**Section**	**Provision**
1618 DYNAMIC ANALYSIS PROCEDURE FOR THE SEISMIC DESIGN OF BUILDINGS	In addition to Modal Response Spectra Analysis, IBC addresses two other dynamic analysis procedures: 1. Linear Time-history Analysis 2. Non-linear Time-history Analysis	5.4 MODAL ANALYSIS PROCEDURE 5.4.1 General	This chapter provides required standards for the modal analysis procedure of seismic analysis of *structures*. See Sec. 5.2.5 for requirements for use of this procedure. The symbols used in this method of analysis have the same meaning as those for similar terms used in Sec. 5.3, with the subscript *m* denoting quantities in the *m*th mode.
1618.1 Modeling	Identical to NEHRP	5.4.2 Modeling	
1618.2 Modes	Identical to NEHRP	5.4.3 Modes	
1618.3 Modal Properties	Identical to NEHRP	5.4.4 Modal Properties	
1618.4 Modal Base Shear	Identical to NEHRP except that "Exception 2" has been deleted, as being potentially unconservative in some situations.	5.4.5 Modal Base Shear	
1618.5 Modal Forces, Deflections, and Drifts	Identical to NEHRP	5.4.6 Modal Forces, Deflections, and Drifts	
1618.6 Modal Story Shears and Moments	Identical to NEHRP	5.4.7 Modal Story Shears and Moments	
1618.7 Design Values	Identical to NEHRP	5.4.8 Design Values	
1618.8 Horizontal Shear Distribution	Identical to NEHRP	5.4.9 Horizontal Shear Distribution	
	No corresponding provision	5.4.10 Foundation Overturning	
1618.9 P-delta Effects	Identical to NEHRP	5.4.11 P-delta Effects	
1618.10 Time-history Analysis 1618.10.1 Time History 1618.10.2 Elastic time-history analysis 1618.10.3 Nonlinear time-history analysis 1618.10.3.1 Nonlinear time history 1618.10.3.2 Design review	IBC introduces new more advanced approaches for lateral analysis.		

TABLE 34. SCALING OF RESULTS OF DYNAMIC ANALYSIS

Section 1618.7, 2000 IBC **Section 5.4.8, 1997 NEHRP**	**Sec. 5.4.8, 2000 NEHRP**
Regular or Irregular Structures	**Regular or Irregular Structures**
$V_{dyn} \geq V_{static}$ based on $T = 1.2\ C_u\ T_a$ C_u per IBC Table 1617.4.2 T_a per IBC Section 1617.4.2.1	$V_{dyn} \geq 0.85\ V_{static}$ No scale-down
Section 1631.5.4, 1997 UBC **Scaling of Results**	**Sec. 1629.5.3, 1994 UBC** **Scaling of Results**
Regular Structures	**Regular Structures**
$V_{dyn} \geq 0.9\ V_{static}$ Using Figure 16-3 $V_{dyn} \geq 0.8\ V_{static}$ Using site-specific response spectrum	$V_{dyn} \geq 0.8\ V_{static}$ based on T by Method A $V_{dyn} \geq 0.9\ V_{static}$ based on T by Method B
Irregular Structures	**Irregular Structures**
$V_{dyn} \geq V_{static}$	$V_{dyn} \geq V_{static}$
Figure 16-3 is the generalized design spectrum printed as part of the 1997 UBC	Method A—approximate period formulas Method B—rational analysis
Story shears and displacements and other response quantities are to be adjusted proportionately.	

TABLE 35. TIME-HISTORY ANALYSIS (2000 IBC)—STEP-BY-STEP PROCEDURE

Step 1:	• Construct design reponse spectrum (5% damped) as shown in Figure TH1 (similar to Figure 1615.1.4 of the IBC). • Construct deterministic limit on maximum considered earthquake reponse spectrum (5% damped) as shown in Figure TH2 (similar to Figure 1615.2.2 of the IBC). • Draw a spectrum that represents the maximum of two-thirds the values of Figure TH2 and 80% of the values of Figure TH1, as shown in Figure TH3.
Step 2:	Get the ground motion data (a pair of horizontal components for any event).
Step 3:	Construct the Response Spectrum for each pair of horizontal ground motion (e.g., EW + NS) components. Construct the SRSS Spectrum considering both components, as shown in Figure TH4.
Step 4:	Calculate the approximate period, T_a, by using Equation 16-39.
Step 5:	Calculate the fundamental period, T, of the building. The period of 1st mode can be taken as the fundamental period provided it does not exceed $1.2C_u \times T_a$ (C_u from Table 1617.4-2).
Step 6:	Calculate $0.2T$ and $1.5T$.
Step 7:	In this period range ($0.2T - 1.5T$), the average SRSS spectrum (shown in Figure TH4) must be greater than 1.4 times the IBC spectrum (shown in Figure TH3) at every period (Figure TH5). If this is not the case, a scaling factor is applied to the ground motion in Step 2 and the process is repeated.
Step 8:	Each pair of time-histories must be applied simultaneously to the structural model considering torsional effects.
Step 9:	Repeat steps 2 through 8 for other ground motion data (events).
Step 10:	If elastic time-history analysis is used, go to step 11. If nonlinear time-history analysis is used, go to step 12.
Step 11:	Elastic time-history analysis (Section 1618.10.2) — After obtaining the base shear (and other parameters of interest) by using steps 1 through 9, scale the results per Section 1618.7 (i.e., similar to the scaling in the case of modal response spectra analysis). Go to Step 13.
Step 12:	Nonlinear time-history analysis (Section 1618.10.3) — Obtain the results such as base shear and other parameters of interest by using steps 1 through 9. Capacities and characteristics of nonlinear elements must be modeled consistent with test data or substantiated analysis, considering the importance factor. The results must not be scaled as is done for elastic analysis. However, the maximum inelastic response displacement must comply with Table 1617.3.
Step 13:	If three ground motions are used, the design is based on the maximum results from those three ground motions. If three events are not available, use simulated records. However, if seven or more ground motions are available, the average value of the response parameter of interest may be used for design.

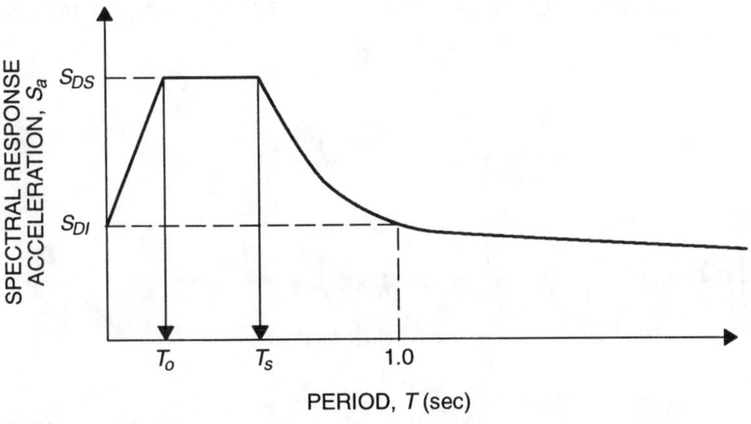

GENERAL DESIGN RESPONSE SPECTRUM

FIGURE TH1

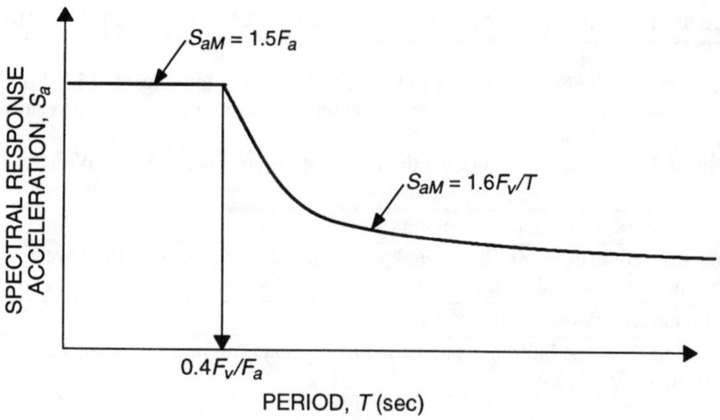

MAXIMUM CONSIDERED EARTHQUAKE RESPONSE SPECTRUM

FIGURE TH2

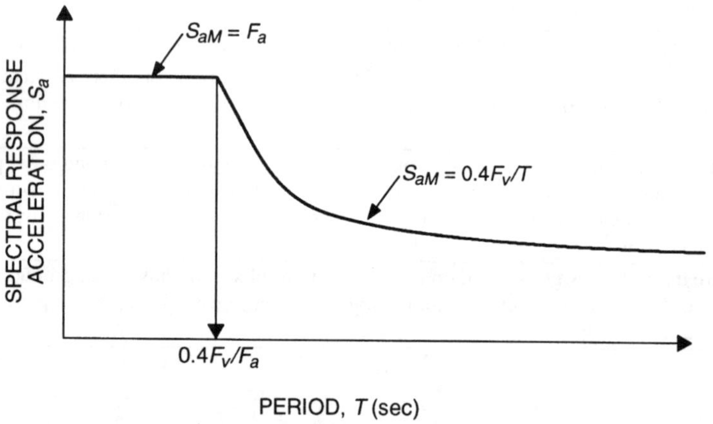

It is assumed that the ordinate at every point of Figure TH3 is greater than 80% of that at corresponding point of Figure TH1

SCALED DESIGN RESPONSE SPECTRUM (FOR TIME-HISTORY ANALYSIS)

FIGURE TH3

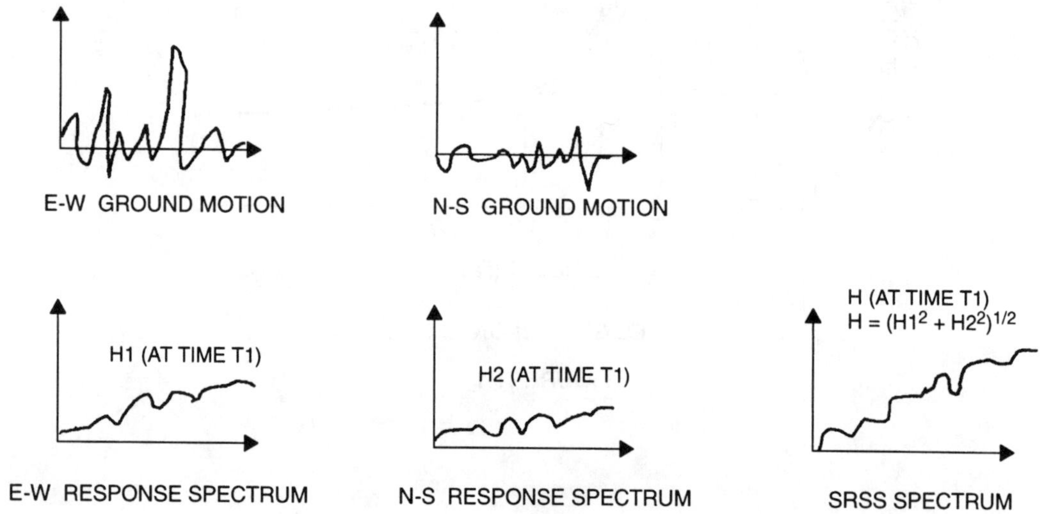

CONSTRUCTION OF SRRS SPECTRUM

FIGURE TH4

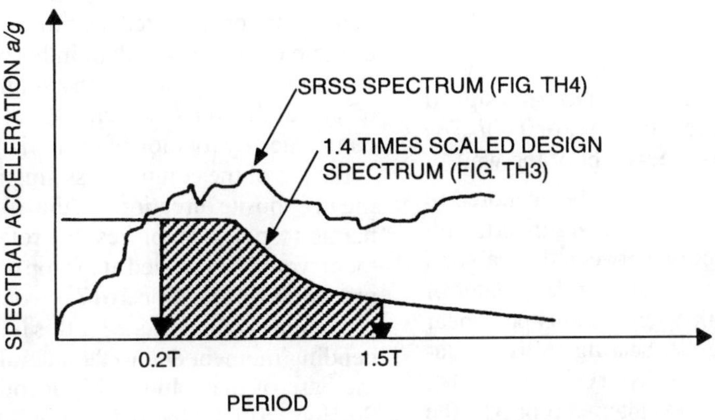

T = ELASTIC FUNDAMENTAL PERIOD OF BUILDING

COMPARISON OF SRSS SPECTRUM WITH DESIGN SPECTRUM

FIGURE TH5

1620.1.3 Discontinuities in vertical system. In Table 1616.5.2, under vertical irregularity Type 5, discontinuity in capacity - weak story, a weak story is defined as one in which the story lateral strength is less than 80 percent of that in the story above. This section restricts the height of a structure with vertical irregularity Type 5 to a maximum of 2 stories or 30 feet when the weak story has a calculated strength of less than 65 percent of the story above. The 1997 UBC has the same requirement. The UBC waives this restriction when the weak story is capable of resisting a total lateral seismic force of Ω_o times the design force prescribed in the static procedure. The 2000 IBC includes a similar exemption, in which the force multiplier used is $0.75C_d$ rather than Ω_o. The UBC multiplier appears to be more logical, because forces, rather than displacements, are being dealt with.

1620.1.4 Connections. This requires all parts of a structure (except at separation joints) to be interconnected and require the connections to be capable of transmitting the seismic force induced by the parts being connected. As a minimum, any smaller portion of the building must be tied to the remainder of the building with elements that are capable of resisting a minimum force equal to a multiplier times the weight of the smaller portion. In this section, the multiplier is the larger of $0.133S_{DS}$ or 0.05. A similar requirement for SDC A structures is given in Section 1616.4. There, the multiplier is a fixed 0.05.

In addition, a positive connection for resisting a horizontal force acting parallel to the member shall be provided for each beam, girder or truss. This force must not be less than 5 percent of the dead plus live load reaction. An identical requirement is included in Section 1616.4 for SDC A structures.

1620.1.5 Diaphragms. The first part of the section addresses permissible deflection in the plane of the diaphragm. The deflections must be minimized in some cases because they could overstress the walls or other elements to which they are connected. The amount of deflection permitted in the diaphragm must be related to the ability of the walls or these other elements to deflect without failure.

The second part of the section requires a floor or roof diaphragm to be designed for a force $F_p = 0.2I_E S_{DS} w_p + V_{px}$ where w_p is the weight of the diaphragm and other elements of the structure attached thereto (see Examples 13-15, Part 2 of this chapter). When the diaphragm is required to transfer design seismic forces from the vertical resisting elements above the diaphragm to the other vertical resisting elements below the diaphragm due to offset in the placement of the elements or to changes in stiffness in the vertical elements, those forces are V_{px}. The 1997 UBC provides diaphragm design forces using a formula equivalent to 2000 IBC Equation 16-65, which is invoked only for structures assigned to SDC D through F. The 1997 UBC specifically adds the force described as V_{px} above to the diaphragm design force given by 2000 IBC Equation 16-65.

The user would benefit greatly from reading the 1999 SEAOC Blue Book Commentary Section C108.2.9, although some of the discussion has relevance only in seismic design categories higher than C.

1620.1.6 Collector elements. This requires collector elements, splices and their connections to resisting elements to have the design strength to resist the special load combinations of Section 1605.4 (see Example 15, which is specifically for a structure assigned to SDC D). The 1997 UBC contains essentially the same requirement and the additional requirement that collector elements, splices, etc. be designed to resist the forces given by the equivalent of 2000 IBC Equation 16-65. As an exception, the IBC allows collector elements, splices and connections to resisting elements to only have the strength to resist the basic strength design or ASD load combinations (basic as well as alternate basic) in structures or portions of structures braced entirely by light frame shear walls. The 1997 UBC includes a similar exception that states that the above items need only be designed to resist forces in accordance with the equivalent of Equation 16-65.

1620.1.7 Bearing walls and shear walls. This requires bearing walls and shear walls and their anchorages to be designed for an out-of-plane force that is the larger of $0.1w_w$ or $0.40I_ES_{DS}$ w_w, whichever is larger, where w_w is the weight of the wall.

Concrete and masonry walls are required to be anchored to the roof and floors and members providing lateral support, with anchorage providing a direct connection between the wall and the supporting construction capable of resisting the greater of the forces: 1) $0.40I_ES_{DS}w_w$ or 2) $400S_{DS}I_E$ pounds per linear foot of wall. A minimum anchorage to bearing walls of diaphragms or other resisting elements is necessary. To ensure that the walls and supporting framing systems interact properly, the interconnection of dependent wall elements and connections to the framing system must have sufficient ductility or rotational capacity, or strength, to stay as a unit. Large shrinkage or settlement cracks can significantly affect the desired interaction. The wall anchorage requirements are illustrated in Figure 39. This figure ought to be compared with Figure 1, which gives comparable requirements for structures assigned to SDC A.Walls must be designed to resist bending between anchors where the anchor spacing exceeds 4 feet.

Parapets are required to be designed as architectural components per Section 1621.2.1. See later discussion on that section.

See Example 16, Part 2 of this chapter, for clarification of the wall anchorage and parapet design provisions, although that example is for a building assigned to SDC D.

1620.1.8 Inverted pendulum-type structures. This design provision for columns or piers supporting inverted pendulum type structures is explained well in the 1997 NEHRP Commentary.[8]

Inverted pendulum-type structures have a large portion of their mass concentrated near the top and, thus, have essentially a single degree of freedom in horizontal translation. Often the structures are T-shaped with a single column supporting a beam or slab at the top. For such a structure, the lateral motion is accompanied by rotation of the horizontal element due to rotation at the top of the column, resulting in vertical accelerations acting in opposite directions on the overhangs of the structure. Dynamic response amplifies this rotation; hence, a bending moment would be induced at the top of the column even though the procedures of Section 1617.4 would not so indicate. A simple provision to compensate for this is specified in this section. The bending moment due to the lateral force is first calculated for the base of the column (M) according to the requirements of Section 1617.4. One-half of the calculated bending moment at the base is applied at the top and the moments along the column are varied from 1.5 M at the base to 0.5 M at the top. The addition of one-half the moment calculated at the base in accordance with Section 1617.4 is based on analyses of inverted pendulums covering a wide range of practical conditions.

Reading the provision of Section 1620.1.8, one might think that the bending moment is supposed to vary from M at the base to 0.5 M at the top. However, the 1997 NEHRP Commentary provides the above clarification.

1620.1.9 Elements supporting discontinuous walls or frames. This section requires that columns or other elements supporting discontinuous walls or frames in structures having in-plane discontinuity of vertical lateral-force-resisting elements or out-of-plane offsets of the vertical elements shall have the design strength to resist the special seismic load combinations of Section 1605.4. Two exceptions to this requirement are provided. The maximum earthquake effect, E_m, need not exceed the maximum force that can be transmitted to the element

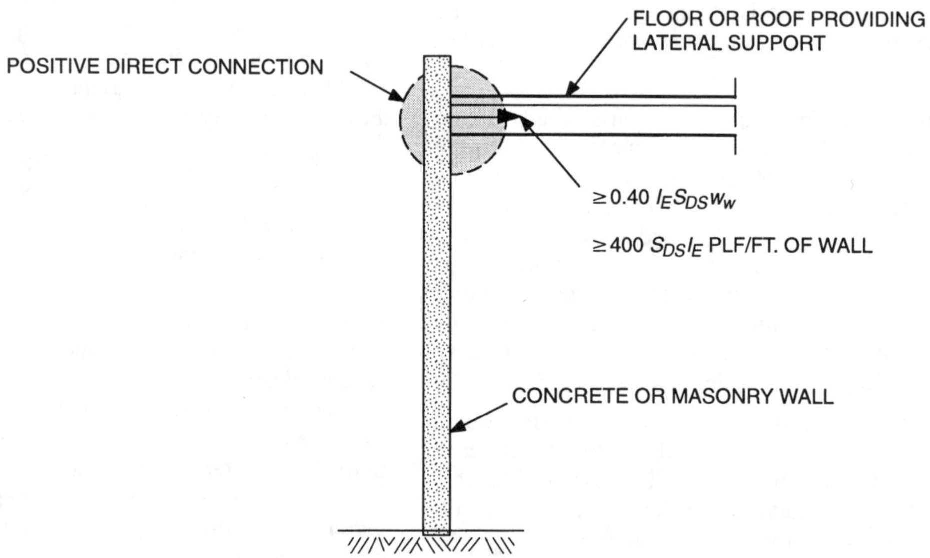

ANCHORAGE OF CONCRETE OR MASONRY WALL —SDC B (SECTION 1620.1.7)

FIGURE 39

by the lateral-force-resisting system. Concrete slabs supporting light-frame walls are exempt from the requirement.

1620.1.10 Direction of seismic load. While it is required that the direction of application of seismic forces be such as to produce the most critical load effect in each component, the requirement is deemed to be satisfied if the design seismic forces are applied separately and independently along each of two principal plan axes.

1620.2 Seismic Design Category C. This section gives additional design requirements for structures assigned to seismic design categories higher than B.

1620.2.1 Anchorage of concrete or masonry walls. The anchorage force that was discussed earlier under Section 1620.1.7, which is applicable in SDC B (Figure 39), is now increased for non-flexible diaphragms to that given by Equation 16-67, subject to a (non-mandatory) maximum given by Equation 16-68 and a (mandatory) minimum given by Equation 16-69 (Figure 40). See later discussion of Section 1621.1.4. For flexible diaphragms, the anchorage force is increased to 1.2 $S_{DS}I_E w_w$ (Figure 40).

The 2000 IBC Section 1620.2.1 also contains detailed requirements concerning: 1) continuous ties or struts between diaphragm chords, 2) wood diaphragms, 3) metal deck diaphragms, and 4) diaphragm to wall anchorage using embedded straps.

The provisions concerning anchorage to a flexible diaphragm have evolved over the years based largely on observation of performance of tilt-up concrete buildings in earthquakes. Tilt-up buildings have at times proved vulnerable to earthquake damage. The first indication of this was in the 1964 Alaska earthquake, which caused several tilt-up buildings to collapse at an Air Force base. The vulnerability was not fully appreciated and understood until the 1971 San Fernando earthquake, which caused the collapse of many tilt-up buildings. The UBC provisions concerning anchorage of concrete and masonry walls to flexible diaphragms have been upgraded in almost every edition since the 1973 edition of the code. The Whittier Narrows earthquake of 1987[46] and the Northridge earthquake of 1994[47] have led to better understanding of the deficiencies in code provisions and to significant changes. The UBC changes, including post-Northridge changes, have been chronicled by Brooks.[48] The post-Northridge changes of the 1997 edition of the UBC are reflected in the IBC provisions of Section 1620.2.1.

1620.2.2 Direction of seismic load. For structures having non-parallel lateral-force-resisting systems (irregularity Type 5, Table 1616.5.1), the requirement that the critical direction of seismic forces (or the so-called orthogonal effects) be considered (Section 1620.1.10) may be satisfied by designing structural elements for 100 percent of the effects of the prescribed design seismic forces in one direction plus 30 percent of the effects of the prescribed design seismic forces in the orthogonal direction. The combination requiring the greater component strength must be used in design. Alternatively, the effects in the two orthogonal directions are permitted to be combined on a square root of the sum-of-the-squares (SRSS) basis.

The foregoing is based on the observation that while earthquake forces act in both principal directions of a building simultaneously, the earthquake effects in the two principal directions are unlikely to reach their maximum values simultaneously. This section provides a reasonable and adequate method of combining the effects.

Orthogonal effects are slight for beams, girders, slabs, and other horizontal elements that are essentially one-dimensional in their behavior. They may be significant in columns or other vertical members that participate in resisting earthquake forces

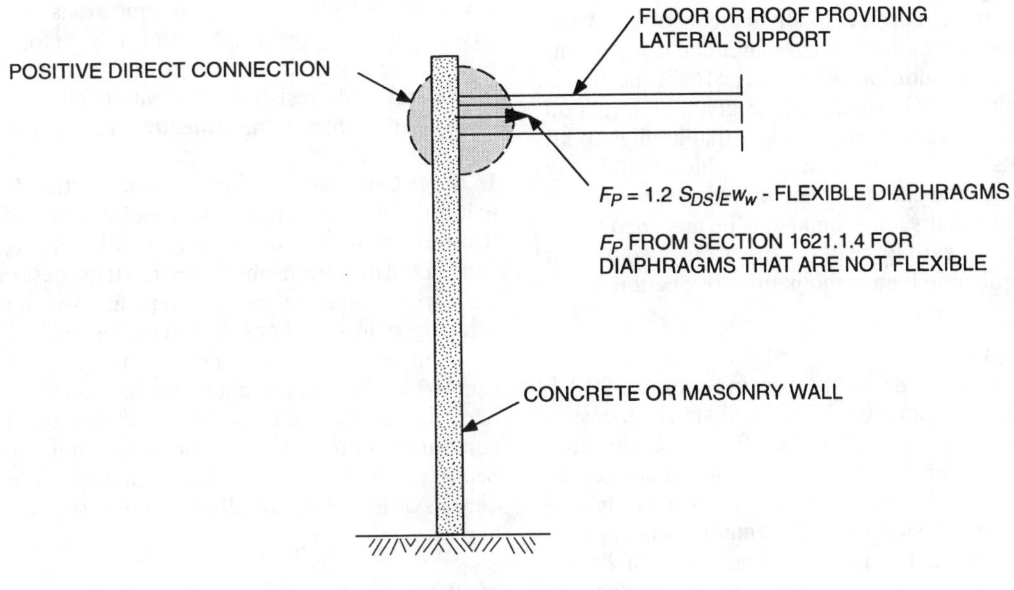

ANCHORAGE OF CONCRETE OR MASONRY WALL — SDC C AND HIGHER (SECTION 1620.2.1)

FIGURE 40

in both principal directions of a building. The 1997 NEHRP Commentary[8] advises that for two-way slabs, orthogonal effects at slab-to-column connections can be neglected, provided the moment transferred in the minor direction does not exceed 30 percent of that transferred in the orthogonal direction and there is adequate reinforcement within lines one and one-half times the slab thickness on either side of the column to transfer all the minor direction moment.

1620.3 Seismic Design Category D. This section gives additional seismic design requirements for structures assigned to seismic design categories higher than C.

1620.3.1 Plan or vertical irregularities. For buildings having torsional irregularity, extreme torsional irregularity, re-entrant corners, diaphragm discontinuity, out-of-plane offsets of the vertical lateral-force-resisting elements (irregularity Type 1a, 1b, 2, 3 or 4, Table 1616.5.1) or in-plane discontinuity in vertical lateral-force-resisting elements (irregularity Type 4, Table 1616.5.2), the design forces determined from the equivalent lateral-force procedure of Section 1617.4.1 must be increased 25 percent for connections of diaphragms to vertical elements and to collectors, and for connections of collectors to the vertical elements. It should be noted that this is in addition to the very severe requirement of Section 1620.3.4, discussed below. This is a 1997 NEHRP Provisions requirement that is not part of the 1997 UBC. It has been recommended for deletion from the 2000 NEHRP Provisions, as being overly conservative.

1620.3.2 Vertical seismic forces. Horizontal cantilever and horizontal prestressed components must be designed to resist the vertical component of earthquake ground motion. This requirement is a carry-over from UBC editions prior to 1994, which only required such components to be designed considering the vertical component of earthquake ground motion. Now, of course, the requirement applies to all elements of the structure. The section states that the above requirement is to be considered satisfied if two conditions are met. The first condition is that E be taken equal to $\rho Q_E - 0.2S_{DS}D$, as given by Equation (16-29). This is also a general requirement that applies to all structural elements. The second condition, which is the only one specific to horizontal cantilever and horizontal prestressed components requires that such components be designed to resist a minimum net upward force of 0.2 times the dead load in addition to the applicable load combinations of Section 1605.

1620.3.3 Diaphragms. This section first gives essentially the same deflection limitations as given earlier in Section 1620.1.5 for SDC C. It then gives Equation 16-65 for diaphragm design forces, which is nearly identical to the 1997 UBC Formula 33-1. It was noted earlier that the UBC formula is applicable across all seismic zones. The IBC formula, however, is applicable only to SDC D, E or F structures. The (non-mandatory) upper-bound and the (mandatory) lower-bound values of Fp are $0.3S_{DS}I_Ew_{px}$ and $0.15S_{DS}I_Ew_{px}$, which are equivalent to $0.75C_aIw_{px}$ and $0.375C_aIw_{px}$, respectively, in UBC terminology, taking $S_{DS} = 2.5C_a$. The upper and lower-bound values in the 1997 UBC are 1.0 C_aIw_{px} and $0.5C_aIw_{px}$, respectively. So both IBC limits are lower.

The V_{px} term of Section 1620.1.5 is to be added to the diaphragm design force given by Equation (16-65), as in the UBC. See Examples 13 and 14 for calculation of diaphragm forces in SDC D and higher.

Diaphragm design has attracted considerable attention in recent times, following the less than satisfactory performance of certain diaphragms in the Northridge earthquake of 1994.[49, 50] There are indications[50] that if elastic diaphragm response in the design earthquake is desired, diaphragm design forces may have to be significantly larger than those given in Section 1620.3.3

It should also be noted that 0.3 $S_{DS}I_Ew_{px}$ is a "need not exceed," rather than a "shall not exceed" upper bound on the diaphragm design forces.

1620.3.4 Collector elements. This requires, as does Section 1620.1.6, applicable to SDC B and higher, that collector elements, splices and their connections to resisting elements have the design strength to resist the special load combinations of Section 1605.4 (see Example 15, Part 2 of this chapter). In addition, collector elements, splices and their connections to resisting elements must be designed to resist the forces given by Equation 16-65 which is equivalent, as has been noted, to the 1997 UBC Formula 33-1. As an exception, the IBC allows collector elements, splices and connections to resisting elements to only have the strength to resist the forces given by Equation 16-65 in structures or portions of structures braced entirely by light frame shear walls.

The collector (or drag strut) is part of the connection between the floor or roof diaphragm and the vertical lateral-force-resisting elements. It is important that these connections be designed to prevent localized slip failure (or rupture), which would in turn prevent inelastic energy dissipation from developing in the lateral-force-resisting system, as assumed.

Collector elements and their connections must be designed to have Ω_o times the specified seismic design forces. The purpose is to ensure that inelastic energy dissipation occurs in the ductile lateral-force-resisting elements (frame members, braces, walls), rather than in the collectors and connections.

1620.3.5 Direction of seismic load. Section 1620.1.10 allows that for SDC B structures, the requirement that the critical direction of seismic forces (or the so-called orthogonal effects) be considered may be deemed satisfied if the design seismic forces are applied separately and independently along each of two principal plan axes. For structures assigned to SDC C and higher and having non-parallel lateral-force-resisting systems, Section 1620.2.2 indicates that this independent orthogonal procedure is not sufficient. As a minimum, the orthogonal combination procedure of that section must be implemented. Section 1620.3.5 mandates the orthogonal combination procedure as a minimum for all structures assigned to SDC D and higher.

1620.3.6 Building separations. This section gives the minimum separation between adjacent buildings on the same property, and minimum setback distance from the property line when a structure adjoins a property line not common to a public way.

The purpose of the separation is to permit adjoining buildings, or portions of buildings, to respond to earthquake ground motion independently without significantly impacting (or pounding) on each other. The effects of pounding have been observed in all recent major and moderate earthquakes.

Seismic separation is critical for the design of new buildings adjacent to existing ones. Since the specific dynamic behavior of the existing building is usually unknown, the engineer needs to be conservative in estimating its motion. Pounding is particularly important in cases where adjacent structures have diaphragms at different levels. Special care must be taken to protect elements of the lateral-force-resisting system from damage due to pounding and to ensure that elements potentially subject to pounding are detailed to retain vertical load-carrying capacity if they are damaged.[4]

The separation distance is the statistical (square root of the sum of the squares) sum of the estimated design earthquake displacements (C_d times the elastically computed displacements under the specified design seismic forces) of the adjoining buildings. In earlier codes, the arithmetic rather than the statistical sum was used. However, the design earthquake displacement used to be underestimated in those codes.

1620.4 Seismic Design Categories E and F. This gives additional seismic design requirements for structures assigned to seismic design categories higher than D.

1620.4.1 Plan or vertical irregularities. Structures having extreme torsional irregularity (Irregularity Type 1b, Table 1616.5.1), stiffness irregularity—extreme soft story or discontinuity in capacity—weak story (Irregularity Type 1b or 5, Table 1616.5.2) are simply not permitted in SDC E and F, both of which include structures located in areas with $S_1 \geq 0.75g$.

SECTION 1621
ARCHITECTURAL, MECHANICAL, AND ELECTRICAL COMPONENT SEISMIC DESIGN REQUIREMENTS

1621.1 Component design. This section is based on and, subject to certain modifications, generally contains the same requirements as Chapter 6 of the 1997 NEHRP Provisions.

A detailed comparison of the 2000 IBC Section 1621 and Chapter 6 of the 1997 NEHRP Provisions is provided in Table 36. The table will help the reader key into the NEHRP Commentary on the various IBC sections.

All architectural, mechanical, electrical, and other nonstructural components in structures must be designed and constructed to resist the equivalent static forces and displacements determined in accordance with Section 1621. The design and evaluation of support structures and attachments of architectural components and equipment must consider their flexibility as well as their strength.

Chapter 6 of the 1997 NEHRP Provisions contains a list of consensus standards that are to be considered part of the Provisions to the extent referred to in Chapter 6. It also includes a second list of "accepted standards," which are standards developed within the industry and which represent acceptable procedures in design and construction. These latter standards are not adopted into Section 1621.

The component design requirements establish minimum design criteria for architectural, mechanical, electrical, and other nonstructural components permanently attached to a structure, and for the attachments and supports of such components. The design criteria establish minimum equivalent static force levels and relative displacement demands for the design of components and their attachments to the structure, recognizing ground motion and structural amplification, component toughness and weight, and performance expectations. Several exemptions are made to the applicability of Section 1621.

The seismic design force for any component is to be applied at the center of gravity of the component and should be assumed to act in any horizontal direction.

This section also establishes minimum seismic design force requirements for nonbuilding structures that are supported by other structures. Seismic design requirements for nonbuilding structures that are supported at grade are given in Section 1622.

Seismic design categories for structures are defined in Section 1616.3. For the purposes of this section, components must be considered to have the same seismic design category as that of the structure they occupy or to which they are attached, unless otherwise noted. In addition, all components are assigned a component importance factor, I_p, given in Section 1621.1.6.

1621.1.3 Component force transfer. Components shall be attached to the building structure so as to be able to transfer the component forces, and all the required attachments shall be fully detailed in the construction documents. These details should take into account the force levels and deformations expected in the structure.

1621.1.4 Seismic forces. The design seismic force is dependent upon the weight of the system or component, the component amplification factor, the component acceleration at point of attachment to the structure, the component importance factor, and the component response modification factor.

The component amplification factor, a_p, represents the dynamic amplification of the component relative to the fundamental period of the structure, T. It is recognized that at the time the components are designed or selected, the structural fundamental period is not always defined or readily available. It is also recognized that the component fundamental period, T_p, is usually only accurately obtained by expensive shake-table or pull-back tests. A listing is provided in Table 1621.2 of a_p values ranging between 1.00 and 2.50, for architectural components and in Table 1621.3 for mechanical and electrical components based on the expectation that the component will usually behave in either a rigid or flexible manner. In general, if the fundamental period of the component is less than 0.06 second, no dynamic amplification is expected. It is not the intention of the IBC to preclude more accurate determination of the component amplification factor when reasonably accurate values of both the structural and component fundamental periods are available (see Table 1621.2, Footnote a).

The component response modification factor, R_p, represents the energy absorption capability of the component's structure and attachments. Conceptually, the R_p value considers both the overstrength and deformability of the component's structure and attachments. The R_p values ranging between 1.0 and 5.0, given in Table 1621.2 for architectural components and Table 1621.3 for mechanical and electrical components, are carefully determined using the collective wisdom and experience of the responsible committee. In general, the following benchmark values were used:

R_p = 1.25 for elements of low deformability

R_p = 2.5 for elements of limited deformability

R_p = 3.5 for elements of high deformability

Equation 16-67 represents a trapezoidal distribution of floor accelerations within the structure, linearly varying from the acceleration at the ground, $0.4S_{DS}$, to the acceleration at the roof, $1.2S_{DS}$. The ground acceleration, $0.4S_{DS}$, is intended to be the same acceleration used as design input for the structure itself, including site effects.

Examination of recorded in-structure acceleration data in response to large California earthquakes reveals that a reasonable maximum value for the roof acceleration is four times the input ground acceleration to the structure. This finding is actually implemented with the 1997 UBC formula corresponding to the IBC Equation 16-67. However, a close examination of recently recorded strong motion data at sites with peak ground accelerations in excess of 0.1g indicates that an amplification factor of 3 is more appropriate. A lower limit for F_p is set to assure a minimal seismic design force. The minimum value for F_p is determined by setting the quantity $(a_p/R_p)(1+2z/h) = 0.7$, which is equivalent to the minimum used in current practice.

To meet the need for a simple formulation, a conservative maximum value of F_p is also set. The maximum value of F_p is determined by setting the quantity $(a_p/R_p)(1+2z/h)$ equal to 4.0.

To clarify the application of vertical seismic design forces in combination with horizontal design forces and service loads, a cross-reference was provided to Section 1617.1. The value for F_p calculated in accordance with Section 1621 should be substituted for the value of Q_E in Section 1617.1.

1621.1.5 Seismic relative displacements. These are needed to support the design of cladding, stairwells, windows, piping systems, sprinkler components, and other components that are connected to the structure(s) at multiple levels or points of connection.

Two equations are given for each situation. Equations 16-70 and 16-72 yield "real" structural displacements as determined by elastic analysis under the code-prescribed seismic forces, with the deflection amplification factor, C_d, applied. Recognizing that elastic displacements are not always defined or available at the time a component is designed or procured, default Equations 16-71 and 16-73 also are provided and allow the use of structural drift limitations. Use of these default equations must balance the need for a timely component design/procurement with the possible conservatism of their use. It is intended that the lesser of the paired equations be acceptable for use.

The effects of seismic relative displacements must be considered in combination with displacements caused by other loads.

1621.1.6 Component importance factor. In this section, all components are assigned a component importance factor, I_p. The default value of I_p is 1.0 for typical components in normal service. Higher values of I_p assigned for components that contain hazardous substances, must have a higher level of assurance of function, or otherwise require additional attention because of their life-safety characteristics. Component importance factors are either 1.0 or 1.5.

1621.1.7 Component anchorage. As pointed out in the 1997 NEHRP Commentary, the requirements of this section reflect the fact that, in general, it is not desirable to rely upon anchors for energy dissipation. Inasmuch as the anchor represents the transfer of load from a relatively deformable material (e.g., steel) to a low-deformability material (e.g., concrete, masonry), the boundary conditions for ensuring deformable, energy-absorbing behavior in the anchor itself are, at best, difficult to achieve. On the other hand, the concept of providing a fuse, or deformable link, in the load path to the anchor is encouraged. This approach allows the designer to provide the necessary level of ductility and overstrength in the connection while at the same time protecting the anchor from overload.

Generally, powder-driven fasteners in concrete tend to exhibit variations in strength that are somewhat larger than those for post-drilled anchors, and do not provide the same levels of reliability. As such, qualification under a simulated seismic test program must be demonstrated prior to use.

1621.1.8 Quality assurance; special inspection and testing. A quality assurance plan must be set up, when required by Section 1705. Special inspection per Section 1704 and testing per Section 1708 are also required.

1621.2 Architectural component design. This section provides for the design of not only architectural components, but also their attachments and supports.

Attachments are means by which components are secured or restrained to the lateral-force-resisting system of a structure. Such attachments and restraints may include anchor bolts, welded connections, and other fasteners.

Component supports are those members or assemblies of members, including braces, frames, struts and attachments, that transmit all loads and forces between the component and the building structure. Component supports also provide structural stability to the component to which they connect.

1621.2.1 Architectural component forces. Requires that architectural components be designed using the forces given in Section 1621.1.4, with a_p and R_p values given in Table 1621.2.

1621.2.2 Architectural component deformation. Architectural components shall be designed for the seismic relative displacement provisions of Section 1621.1.5.

1621.2.3 Exterior wall elements and connections. This is specifically for nonstructural wall panels or elements that are attached to or enclose the structure. Movements of the structure resulting from temperature changes shall be accommodated. Elements addressed in this section must be supported by means of positive and direct supports or mechanical connections and fasteners in accordance with a number of requirements that are given.

1621.2.4 Out-of-plane bending. Most walls are subject to out-of-plane forces when a building is subjected to earthquake ground motion. These forces and the resulting bending must be considered in the design of wall panels, nonstructural walls, and partitions. Conventional limits based on deflections as a proportion of the span may be used with the applied force derived from Section 1621.1.4.

TABLE 36. COMPARISON OF 2000 IBC SECTION 1621 AND 1997 NEHRP CHAPTER 6

IBC Section	NEHRP Section	Comments
1621.1 Component design 1621.1.1 Applicability to components 1621.1.2 Applicability to supported nonbuilding structures	6.1 GENERAL	IBC essentially identical to NEHRP except for the following changes: 1) Exception 5 of NEHRP has been modified to "Mechanical and electrical components in all Seismic Design Categories, where I_p = 1.0 and flexible connections between the components and associated ductwork, piping and conduit are provided, (in NEHRP the underlined words are replaced by: *Seismic Design Categories* D, E, and F) that are mounted at 4 ft (1219 mm) or less above a floor level and weigh 400 lb or less, and are not critical to the continued operation of the structure," and 2) Exception 6 of NEHRP has been modified to "Mechanical and electrical components in *Seismic Design Categories* C, D, E, and F, where *Ip* = 1.0 and flexible connections between the components and associated ductwork, piping and conduit are provided, that weigh 20 lb (89 N) or less".
1621.1.3 Component force transfer	6.1.2 Component Force Transfer	Identical
1621.1.4 Seismic forces	6.1.3 Seismic Forces	Essentially identical. The IBC has added the following to the definition of *z:* For items at or above the roof, *z* is not required to be taken as greater than the roof height h. The IBC has deleted the following sentence from the very end of the section: Similarly when the building code horizontal loads exceed *Fp* for interior partitions, these building code loads shall govern the design.
1621.1.5 Seismic relative displacements	6.1.4 Seismic Relative Displacements	Identical
1621.1.6 Component importance factor	6.1.5 Component Importance Factor	Identical
1621.1.7 Component anchorage	6.1.6 Component Anchorage	IBC identical to NEHRP except for the following modifications: The term "expansion anchors" has been modified to "shallow expansion anchors." 6.1.6.2 (b) has been changed to 1.3 times (2 times in NEHRP) the force in the connected part as given by F_p times R_p
1621.1.8 Quality assurance; special inspection and testing	6.1.7 Construction Documents	IBC has more general requirements, whereas NEHRP requirements are quite specific.
	6.2 ARCHITECTURAL COMPONENT DESIGN	
1621.2 Architectural component design	6.2.1 General	Basically identical
1621.2.1 Architectural component forces and displacements	6.2.2 Architectural Component Forces and Displacements	IBC identical to NEHRP, with the following change in the exception of NEHRP: Components supported by chains or otherwise suspended from the structural system above are not required to meet the lateral seismic force requirements and seismic relative displacement requirements of this section provided that they are capable of moving a minimum of 12 inches (305 mm) or swing 45 degrees off vertical, without damage or contacting an obstruction. (in NEHRP the underlined words are replaced by: cannot be damaged or cannot damage any other *component* when subject to seismic motion and they have ductile or articulating connections to the *structure* at the point of attachment.)
1621.2.2 Architectural component deformation	6.2.3 Architectural Component Deformation	Identical
1621.2.3 Exterior wall elements and connections	6.2.4 Exterior Nonstructural Wall Elements and Connections	Identical
1621.2.4 Out-of-plane bending	6.2.5 Out-of-Plane Bending	Identical
1621.2.5 Suspended ceilings	6.2.6 Suspended Ceilings	IBC identical to NEHRP, with the following exception added: Ceilings in buildings with an I_p equal to 1.0 located in SDC C and less than three stories in height.
1621.2.5.1 Seismic forces	6.2.6.1 Seismic Forces	Identical

(continued)

TABLE 36. COMPARISON OF 2000 IBC SECTION 1621 AND 1997 NEHRP CHAPTER 6—(continued)

IBC Section	NEHRP Section	Comments
1621.2.5.2 Industry standard construction	6.2.6.2 Industry Standard Construction	Identical
1621.2.5.2.1 Seismic Design Category C	6.2.6.2.1 Seismic Design Category C	Identical
1621.2.5.2.2 Seismic Design Categories D, E or F	6.2.6.2.2 Seismic Design Categories D, E and F	IBC identical to NEHRP, with the following changes: The sentence in Item c "the horizontal restraints shall be designed to minimize diaphragm loads." has been replaced in NEHRP by "the tributary areas of the horizontal restraints shall be approximately equal." The sentence in Item d in NEHRP "each area shall be provided with closure angles in accordance with Item b and horizontal restraints or bracing in accordance with Item c" has been dropped in the IBC.
1621.2.5.3 Integral ceiling/sprinkler construction	6.2.6.3 Integral ceiling/sprinkler construction	Identical
1621.2.6 Access floors	6.2.7 Access Floors	Identical
1621.2.6 Access floors	6.2.7.1 General	IBC identical to NEHRP except that the following sentence in Paragraph 2 of NEHRP "The ability of . . . overturning effects of equipment" has been deleted.
1621.2.6.1 Special access floors	6.2.7.2 Special Access Floors	IBC identical to NEHRP except that the underlined words have been added to Item 4 in IBC "Electrical tubing shall not be used <u>for bracing or pedestrals</u>."
1621.2.7 Partitions	6.2.8 Partitions	IBC identical to NEHRP except that the following exception has been added to IBC: Exception: Partitions not taller than 9 feet (2743 mm) when the horizontal seismic load does not exceed the 5 psf (0.24 kN/m^2) required in Section 1607.13.
1621.2.8 Steel storage racks	6.2.9 Steel Storage Racks	IBC identical to NEHRP. The paragraph "Steel storage racks supported above grade shall be designed to meet the general requirements of Sections 1622.1, 1622.2, and the specific requirements of Section 1622.3.4. Steel Storage Racks supported at grade shall be designed in accordance with Section 2210." has been replaced by "Steel *storage racks* shall be designed to meet the force requirements of Chapter 14." in NEHRP.
1621.3 Mechanical and electrical component design	6.3 MECHANICAL AND ELECTRAL COMPONENT DESIGN 6.3.1 General	Identical
1621.3.1 Mechanical and electrical component forces and displacements	6.3.2 Mechanical and Electrical Component Forces and Displacements	IBC identical to NEHRP, with the following changes: Powder-actuated fasteners (shot pins) shall not be used for component anchorage in tension applications in SDC D, E, or F. Components mounted on vibration isolation systems shall have a bumper restraint or snubber in each horizontal direction. The lateral design force for the restraint shall be taken as $2F_p$. In addition, the a_p and R_p factors in Table 1621.3 have been changed from 1.0 and 3.5 for General Electrical distribution systems (bus ducts, conduit, cable tray) to 2.5 and 5.0, respectively.
1621.3.2 Mechanical and electrical component period	6.3.3 Mechanical and Electrical Component Period	Identical
1621.3.3 Mechanical and electrical component attachments	6.3.4 Mechanical and Electrical Component Attachments	Identical
1621.3.4 Component supports	6.3.5 Component Supports	Identical
1621.3.5 Component certification	6.3.6 Component Certification	Essentially identical
1621.3.6 Utility and service lines at structure interfaces	6.3.7 Utility and Service Lines at Structure Interfaces	Identical
1621.3.7 Site-specific considerations	6.3.8 Site-specific Considerations	Basically identical. The following sentence in NEHRP has been dropped in IBC: "Specific attention . . . 0.15."

(continued)

TABLE 36. COMPARISON OF 2000 IBC SECTION 1621 AND 1997 NEHRP CHAPTER 6—(continued)

IBC Section	NEHRP Section	Comments
1621.3.8 Storage tanks	6.3.9 Storage Tanks	Identical
1621.3.9 HVAC ductwork	6.3.10 HVAC Ductwork	Identical
1621.3.10 Piping systems	6.3.11 Piping Systems	Identical
1621.3.10.1 Fire-protection sprinkler systems	6.3.11.1 Fire Protection Sprinkler Systems	Identical
1621.3.10.2 Other piping systems	6.3.11.2 Other Piping Systems	Identical
1621.3.10.2.1 Supports and attachments for other piping	6.3.11.2.1 Supports and Attachments for Other Piping	Identical
1621.3.11 Boilers and pressure vessels	6.3.12 Boilers and Pressure Vessels	Identical
1621.3.11.1 ASME boilers and pressure vessels	6.3.12.1 ASME Boilers and Pressure Vessels	Identical
1621.3.11.2 Other boilers and pressure vessels	6.3.12.2 Other Boilers and Pressure Vessels	Identical
1621.3.11.3 Supports and attachments for boilers and pressure vessels	6.3.12.3 Supports and Attachments for Boilers and Pressure Vessels	Identical
1621.3.12 Mechanical equipment, attachments, and supports	6.3.13 Mechanical Equipment, Attachments, and Supports	Identical
1621.3.12.1 Mechanical equipment	6.3.13.1 Mechanical Equipment	Identical
1621.3.12.2 Attachments and supports for mechanical equipment	6.3.13.2 Attachments and Supports for Mechanical Equipment	Identical
1621.3.12 Electrical equipment attachments and supports	6.13.14 Electrical Equipment, Attachments, and Supports	Identical
1621.3.13.1 Electrical equipment	6.3.14.1 Electrical Equipment	Identical
1621.3.13.2 Attachments and supports for electrical equipment	6.3.14.2 Attachments and Supports for Electrical Equipment	Identical
1621.3.14 Elevator design requirements	6.3.16 Elevator Design Requirements	Identical
1621.3.14.1 Elevators and hoistway structural systems	6.3.16.1 Elevators and Hoistway Structural System	Identical
1621.3.14.2 Elevator machinery and controller supports and attachments	6.3.16.2 Elevator Machinery and Controller Supports and Attachments	Identical
1621.3.14.3 Seismic controls	6.3.16.3 Seismic Controls	IBC identical to NEHRP except that: Item 3 of NEHRP (The individual putting the elevator back in service should ride the elevator from top to bottom and back to top to verify acceptable performance.) has been deleted.
1621.3.14.4 Retainer plates	6.3.16.4 Retainer Plates	Identical

1621.2.5 Suspended ceilings. Suspended ceilings, like all other architectural components, must be designed to meet the force requirements of Section 1621.1.4. In addition, suspended ceilings must be designed to meet the requirements of either Industry Standard Construction as modified in Section 1621.2.5.2 or Integral Construction as set forth in Section 1621.2.5.3.

1621.2.6 Access floors. In addition to meeting the force requirements of Section 1621.1.4, access floors must meet the requirements of this section.

1621.2.7 Partitions. Bracing requirements for partitions are given.

1621.2.8 Steel storage racks. Storage racks are considered nonbuilding structures and are covered in Section 1622.

1621.3 Mechanical and electrical component design. Requirements are given for mechanical and electrical components, their attachments and supports.

1621.3.1 Mechanical and electrical component forces and displacements. The force requirements of Section 1621.1.4, with a_p and R_p values given in Table 1621.3, and the displacement requirements of Section 1621.1.5 must be met.

1621.3.2 Mechanical and electrical component period. Determination of the fundamental period of an item of mechanical or electrical equipment can be by Equation (16-74), if the component and attachment can be reasonably represented analytically by a simple spring and mass single-degree-of-freedom system. Otherwise, period must be determined from experimental test data or by analysis.

1621.3.3 Mechanical and electrical component attachments. The attachment stiffness must be so chosen as to enable the load path for the component to perform its intended function.

1621.3.4 Component supports. Component supports are differentiated here from component attachments to emphasize that the supports themselves—"the structural members, braces, frames, skirts, legs, saddles, pedestals, cables, guys, stays, snubbers, and tethers[8]—even if fabricated by the mechanical or electrical component manufacturers, must be designed for seismic forces and displacements.

1621.3.5 Component certification. Submission (to the building official) of the manufacturer's certificate of compliance with the IBC force requirements is made mandatory in this section, whereas, according to the 1997 NEHRP Provisions, the submission is to be made "when required by the contract documents or when required by the authority having jurisdiction."

1621.3.6 Utility and service lines at structure interfaces. Adequate flexibility shall be provided for utilities at the interface of adjacent and independent structures to accommodate anticipated differential displacement.

1621.3.7 Site-specific considerations. The possible interruption of utility services must be considered while ensuring continued functioning of designated seismic systems in essential facilities.

1621.3.8 Storage tanks. Storage tanks are considered nonbuilding structures and are covered in Section 1622.

1621.3.9 HVAC ductwork. Attachments and supports of HVAC ductwork, in addition to meeting the force and displacement requirements of Sections 1621.1.4 and 1621.1.5, respectively, must meet the additional requirements in this section.

1621.3.10 Piping systems. Attachments and supports for piping systems, in addition to meeting the force and displacement requirements of Sections 1621.1.4 and 1621.1.5, respectively, must meet the additional requirements of this section.

1621.3.11 Boilers and pressure vessels. Attachments and supports for boilers and pressure vessels, in addition to meeting the force and displacement requirements of Sections 1621.1.4 and 1621.1.5, respectively, must be designed to meet the additional requirements of this section.

1621.3.12 Mechanical equipment attachments and supports. Additional requirements are given for attachments and supports of mechanical equipment not covered in the other subsections of Section 1621.3; such attachments and supports must also satisfy the force and displacement requirements of Sections 1621.1.4 and 1621.1.5, respectively.

1621.3.13 Elevator design requirements. The ASME Safety Code for Elevators and Escalators[51] has adopted many requirements to improve the seismic response of elevators; however, they do not apply to some items covered by this chapter. The requirements of Section 1621.3.14.1 through 1621.3.1.3 extend the force requirements for elevators, to be consistent with the rest of Section 1621.

Differences between IBC Section 1621 and 1997 NEHRP Chapter 6

Reference should be made to Table 36.

1621.1.1 Exceptions 5, 6—Equipment that contains hazardous substances, $I_p = 1.5$, would not have been required to be anchored in the absence of this modification. The 1997 NEHRP Commentary Section 6.1 notes that exemptions to anchorage are allowed, but only for $I_p = 1.0$, so that a higher level of reliability is achieved with those elements that contain hazardous materials. Flexible connections are required because, otherwise, the pipes, ducts or conduit could in effect become a restraint for the component.

1621.1.4—The addition to the definition of z has been made to clarify that the ratio z/h need not exceed 1.0.

The deletion is made because Section 1607.13 adequately covers this subject.

1621.1.7—The meaning of the text deleted in Section 1621.1.7 Item 1 was unclear. If the anchor is weak, it will fail before high forces can develop in the connected parts.

The change in Section 1621.1.7 Item 2.2 harmonizes the approach contained in that section with Table 1621.2 and eliminates the arbitrary overstrength factor of 2.

1621.2.1—The IBC language is much less prescriptive (eliminates talk of links, etc.) and is similar to the current California Administrative Code Title 24 Table 16-0, Footnote 18, which works quite well.

1621.2.5.1—Suspended ceiling systems in areas of lower seismic activity are more prone to serious damage and more likely to pose a life-safety threat in buildings three stories high or higher, because such buildings tend to amplify ground motion from distant earthquakes more than short buildings. Therefore, it is reasonable to exempt suspended ceilings in short buildings that fall under SDC C. This will result in significant cost savings with only a very marginal increase in life-safety risk.

SECTION 1622 NONBUILDING STRUCTURES SEISMIC DESIGN REQUIREMENTS

The 2000 IBC Section 1622 is essentially identical to Chapter 14 of the 1997 NEHRP Provisions. That chapter, did not exist previously as a separate chapter. It represents a major expansion of Section 2.7 of the 1994 NEHRP Provisions, the requirements of which were also modified to reflect the new design procedures of the 1997 NEHRP Provisions.

A detailed comparison of the 2000 IBC Section 1622 and Chapter 14 of the 1997 NEHRP Provisions is presented in

Table 37. The table will serve to guide the reader to the NEHRP Provisions Commentary on the various IBC sections. Therefore, the discussion below is kept to a bare minimum and is includes a discussion of the modifications made in IBC Section 1622 to the provisions of the 1997 NEHRP Provisions Chapter 14.

Building codes traditionally have been perceived as minimum standards of care for the design of nonbuilding structures and building code compliance of these structures in required by building officials in many jurisdictions. However, requirements in the industry standards are often at odds with building code requirements. In some cases, the industry standards need to be altered, while in other cases the building codes need to be modified. Design professionals are not always aware of the numerous accepted standards within an industry or if the accepted standards are adequate. The requirements of the 1997 NEHRP Provisions for nonbuilding structures attempt to bridge the gap between building codes and existing industry standards.

One of the goals of Chapter 14 of the 1997 NEHRP Provisions was to review and list appropriate industry standards to serve as a resource. Such a list is included in an appendix to Chapter 14 of the 1997 NEHRP Provisions. The appendix, however, has not been adopted by the 2000 IBC.

The scope of the nonbuilding structure requirements is limited to self-supporting structures, carrying gravity loads, that are not building structures, vehicular and railroad bridges, nuclear power plants, and dams. The excluded structures are covered either by other sections of the IBC or by other well-established design criteria as embodied in specific industry standards approved by the building official. In the latter case, the approved standards will apply within limitations imposed by this section.

In its 1988 edition, the UBC added a section on nonbuilding structures for the first time. This section, which remained essentially unchanged in the 1994 and 1997 editions of the UBC, formed the basis of Section 2.7 of the 1994 Provisions.

TABLE 37. COMPARISON OF 2000 IBC SECTION 1622 AND 1997 NEHRP CHAPTER 14

IBC Section	NEHRP Section	Comments
1622.1 Nonbuilding structures	14.1 GENERAL 14.1.1 Scope	Essentially identical
1622.1.1 Nonbuilding structures supported by other structures	14.1.2 Nonbuilding Structures Supported by Other Structures	Identical
1622.1.2 Architectural, mechanical, and electrical components	14.1.3 Architectural, Mechanical, and Electrical Components	Identical
1622.2 Seismic design requirements		
1622.2.1 Weight	14.1.4 Loads	Identical
1622.2.2 Fundamental period	14.1.5 Fundamental Period	Identical
1622.2.3 Drift limitations	14.1.6 Drift Limitations	Identical
1622.2.4 Seismic requirements of materials	14.1.7 Materials Requirements	Identical
1622.2.5 Minimum seismic forces	14.2 STRUCTURAL DESIGN REQUIREMENTS 14.2.1 Design Basis	IBC identical to NEHRP, with the following additions: 1) For nonbuilding systems with response modification coefficients, *R*, provided in Table 1622.2.5 (1), the minimum value specified in Equation 16-37 shall be replaced by the following: $C_s = 0.14\, S_{DS}\, I/R$ (Eq. 16-75) and the minimum value specified in Equation 16-38 shall be replaced by the following: $C_s = 0.8\, S_1\, I_E/R$ (Eq. 16-16) 2) Another clause has been added to Item 7 of NEHRP as given below: Where seismic force is determined in accordance with an approved national standard, it shall not be taken as less than 80 percent of that in Section 1622.2.5.
Table 1622.2.5 (1) Table 1622.2.5 (2)	14.2.1.1 Seismic Factors 14.2.1.2 Importance Factors and Seismic Use Group Classifications	Identical
1622.2.6 Rigid nonbuilding structures	14.2.2 Rigid Nonbuilding Structures	Identical
1622.2.7 Deflection limits and structure separation	14.2.3 Deflection Limits and Structure Separation	Identical
1622.3 Nonbuilding structures similar to buildings 1622.3.1 Design basis 1622.3.2 Determination of seismic effect E	14.3 NONBUILDING STRUCTURES SIMILAR TO BUILDINGS 14.3.1 General	Essentially identical
1622.3.3 Pipe racks	14.3.2 Pipe Racks 14.3.2.1 Design Basis	Identical

(continued)

TABLE 37. COMPARISON OF 2000 IBC SECTION 1622 AND 1997 NEHRP CHAPTER 14—(continued)

IBC Section	NEHRP Section	Comments
1622.3.4 Steel storage racks	14.3.3 Steel Storage Racks	IBC provides more detailed and specific guidance compared to NEHRP.
1622.3.4.1 General	14.3.3.1 General Requirements	Essentially identical
1622.3.4.2 Operating weight	14.3.3.2 Operating Weight	Identical
1622.3.4.3 Vertical distribution of seismic forces	14.3.3.3 Vertical Distribution of Seismic Forces	Identical
1622.3.4.4 Seismic displacements	14.3.3.4 Seismic Displacements	Essentially identical
1622.3.5 Electrical power-generating facilities	14.3.4 Electrical Power Generating Facilities 14.3.4.1 General 14.3.4.2 Design Basis	Identical
1622.3.6 Structural towers for tanks and vessels	14.3.5 Structural Towers for Tanks and Vessels 14.3.5.1 General	IBC identical to NEHRP, with the following addition: When the sloshing period of the stored liquid is within 70% to 150% of the fundamental period of the supporting structure, the effects of sloshing shall be included in the design of the tank and supporting structure.
1622.3.7 Piers and wharves	14.3.6 Piers and Wharves 14.3.6.1 General 14.3.6.2 Design Basis	Identical
1622.4 Nonbuilding structures not similar to buildings 1622.4.1 Determination of seismic effect E	14.4 NONBUILDING STRUCTURES NOT SIMILAR TO BUILDINGS 14.4.1 General	Essentially identical
1622.4.2 Earth-retaining structures	14.4.2 Earth Retaining Structures 14.4.2.1 General	IBC provides more detailed and specific guidance compared to NEHRP.
1622.4.3 Tanks and vessels	14.4.3 Tanks and Vessels 14.4.3.1 General 14.4.3.2 Design Basis	IBC provides more detailed and specific guidance compared to NEHRP.
1622.4.3.1 Above-grade storage tanks		
1622.4.3.2 At-grade storage tanks	14.4.3.3 Additional Requirements	Identical
1622.4.4 Telecommunication towers	14.4.5 Telecommunication Towers 14.4.5.1 General 14.4.5.2 Design Basis	Identical
1622.4.5 Stacks and chimneys	14.4.6 Stacks and Chimneys 14.4.6.1 General 14.4.6.2 Design Basis	Essentially identical
1622.4.6 Amusement structures	14.4.7 Amusement Structures 14.4.7.1 General 14.4.7.2 Design Basis	Essentially identical
1622.4.7 Special hydraulic structures	14.4.8 Special Hydraulic Structures 14.4.8.1 General 14.4.8.2 Design Basis	Identical
1622.4.8 Buried structures	14.4.9 Buried Structures 14.4.9.1 General 14.4.9.2 Design Basis	Identical
1622.4.9 Inverted pendulums	14.4.10 Inverted Pendulums	Essentially identical

1622.1 Nonbuilding structures. The design of nonbuilding structures must provide sufficient strength, stiffness, and ductility, consistent with the requirements specified for buildings, to resist the effects of seismic ground motions as represented by the following:

1. Applicable strength and other design criteria must be obtained from other sections of the IBC or its referenced codes and standards.

2. When applicable strength and other design criteria are not contained in or referenced by the IBC, such criteria are to be obtained from approved standards. When approved standards define acceptance criteria in terms of allowable stresses as opposed to strength, the design seismic forces are to be obtained from the IBC and reduced by a factor of 1.4 for use with allowable stresses. Allowable stress increases used in approved standards are permitted. Detailing must be in accordance with the approved standards.

1622.1.1 Nonbuilding structures supported by other structures. Figure 41 explains the provisions.

1622.1.2 Architectural, mechanical, and electrical components. Section 1621 governs the design of architectural, mechanical, and electrical components supported by nonbuilding structures.

1622.2 Seismic design requirements. The provisions of this section govern the seismic design of nonbuilding structures included in the scope of Section 1622.

1622.2.1 Weight. Normal operating contents of items such as tanks, vessels and bins, and the contents of piping must be included in the weight, *W*, for the purpose of calculating the design seismic forces. Snow and ice loads are to be included when they constitute 25 percent or more of *W*.

1622.2.2 Fundamental period. The rational methods for period determination contained in Section 1617.4 were developed for building structures. If a nonbuilding structure has dynamic

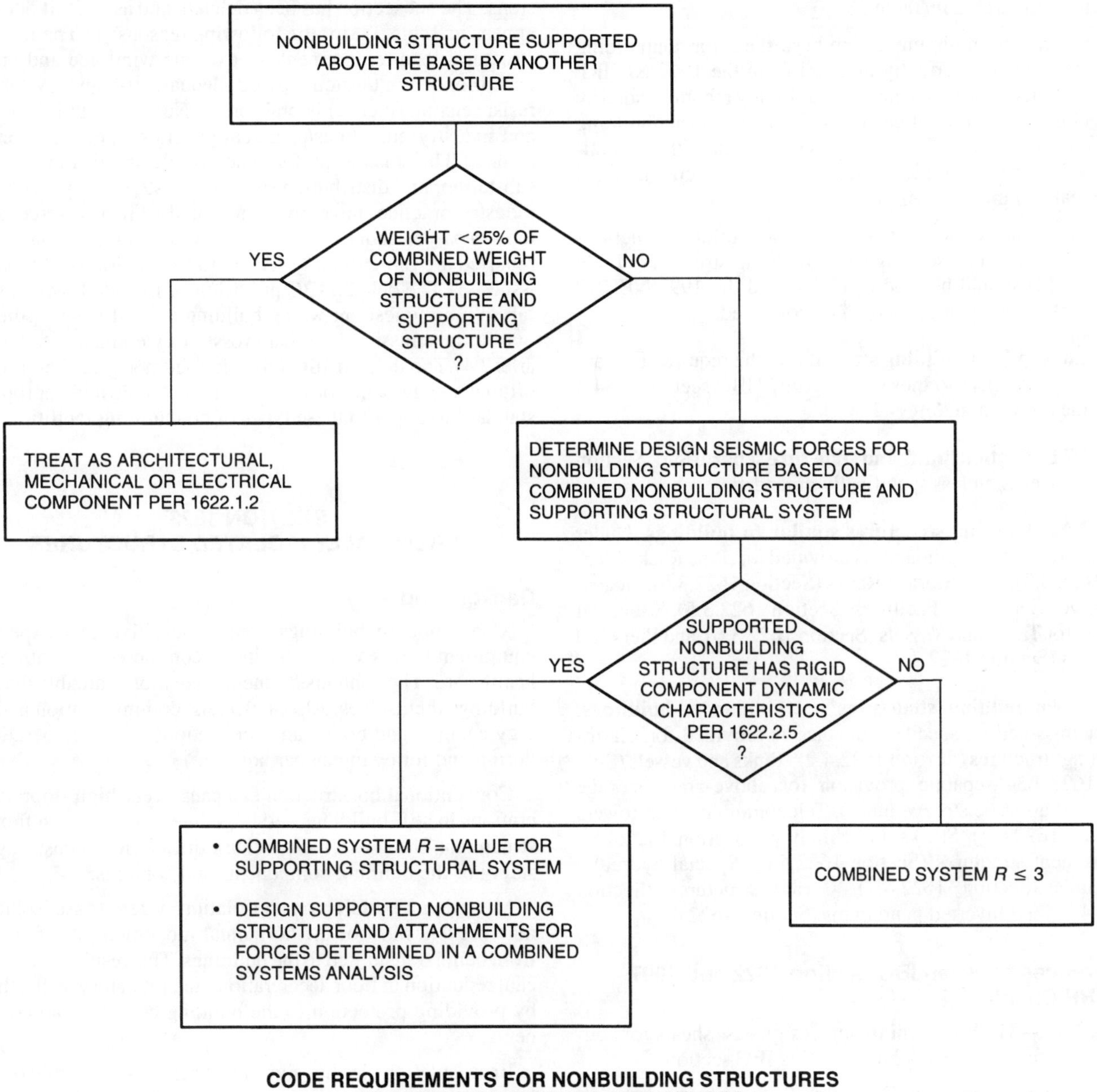

CODE REQUIREMENTS FOR NONBUILDING STRUCTURES SUPPORTED BY OTHER STRUCTURES

FIGURE 41

characteristics similar to those of a building, the methods are directly applicable. If that is not the case, other techniques for period calculation may be required. Some of the references In the Appendix to Chapter 14 of the 1997 NEHRP Provisions contain more accurate methods for period determination.

1622.2.3 Drift limits. The drift limits of Section 1617.3 are allowed to be exceeded when it can be shown by rational analysis, including consideration of P-delta effects, that they may be exceeded without adversely affecting structural stability.

1622.2.4 Seismic requirements of materials. The seismic requirements of Chapters 19-23 remain applicable, unless specifically exempted in Section 1622.

1622.2.5 Minimum seismic forces. The provisions of this section are summarized in Table 38.

The increased minimum design base shear for nonbuilding structures was inadvertently dropped from the 1997 NEHRP Provisions; its insertion in the IBC was highly recommended by the technical subcommittee responsible for the nonbuilding structures provisions. This change is consistent with the minimum values recommended in the 1997 ASCE Petrochemical Technical Committee Task Report.

The importance factors assigned to nonbuilding structures are different from those assigned to building structures. Table 1622.2.5 (2) should be read carefully, and the 1997 NEHRP Commentary on the topic should be consulted.

1622.2.6 Rigid nonbuilding structures. the requirements are essentially identical to those of the 1997 UBC section 1634.3 (with the conversion, $S_{DS} = 2.5C_a$).

1622.2.7 Deflection limits and structure separation. Section 1617.3 governs, unless specifically amended.

1622.3 Nonbuilding structures similar to buildings. Under this section, specific guidance is provided for: Pipe Racks (Section 1622.3.3), Steel Storage Racks (Section 1622.3.5), electrical Power Generating Facilities (Section 1622.3.5), Structural Towers for Tanks and Vessels (Section 1622.3.6), and Piers and Wharves (Section 1622.3.7).

1622.4 Nonbuilding structures not similar to buildings. Under this section, specific guidance is provided for: Earth-retaining structures (Section 1622.4.2), Tanks and vessels (Section 1622.4.3—separate provision for above-grade storage tanks and at-grade storage tanks), Telecommunication towers (Section 1622.4.4), Stacks and chimneys (Section 1622.4.5), Amusement structures (Section 1622.4.6), Special hydraulic structures (Section 1622.4.7), Buried structures (Section 1622.4.8), and Inverted pendulums (Section 1622.4.9).

Differences between IBC Section 1622 and 1997 NEHRP Chapter 14

1622.2.5—The higher minimum design base shears for nonbuilding structures are explained in this IBC section.

The new item added to Exception 2 sets minimum design seismic forces for nonbuilding structures that are designed using a nationally approved standard that is typically based on specific knowledge of the performance and behavior of the particular type of nonbuilding structure it addresses.

1622.3.6—The reason for the addition is the possibility of resonance between the sloshing of stored liquid in a tank or vessel, and the seismic vibration of the supporting structure.

1622.3 Nonbuilding structures similar to buildings. Under this section, specific guidance is provided for: Pipe racks (Section 1622.3.3), Steel storage racks (Section 1622.3.5), Electrical power generating facilities (Section 1622.3.5), Structural towers for tanks and vessels (Section 1622.3.6), and Piers and wharves (Section 1622.3.7).

1622.4—This section originally contained provisions for Electrical transmission, substation, and distribution structures, reproduced from Section 14.4.4 of the 1997 NEHRP Provisions. The subsection has been deleted, and as a result does not appear in Table 37, for the following reasons: 1) The industry structural load requirements of extreme wind, ice and unbalanced conductor tension provide adequate structural systems to resist seismic (inertia) lateral forces. Numerous utility studies and industry guidelines/technical papers support this conclusion. 2) The seismic performance of electrical transmission, substation, and distribution structural systems, as provided by industry practice, have not contributed to inertia force problems in past earthquakes. The very few problems that have been reported are more directly related to foundation/facility siting issues. 3) The deleted IBC provision, if included, would have raised a big question: which building official has jurisdiction over a transmission line that crosses city/county/state boundaries? 4) The deleted IBC provision did not give the building official any guidance on what is an acceptable and appropriate standard to apply to these types of nonbuilding facilities.

SECTION 1623
SEISMICALLY ISOLATED STRUCTURES

Background

Many modern buildings contain sensitive and expensive equipment that is vital in business, commerce, education and health care. The contents frequently are more valuable than the buildings themselves. Also, hospitals, communication and energy centers, and police and fire stations must be operational during and following an earthquake.

Conventional construction can cause very high floor accelerations in stiff buildings and large interstory drifts in flexible structures. These two factors cause difficulties in ensuring the safety of the building components and contents.

Mounting a building on an isolation system (base isolation) may prevent most of the horizontal movement of the ground from being transmitted to the buildings. This results in a significant reduction in floor accelerations and interstory drifts, thereby providing protection to the building contents and components.[52]

Base isolation also has significant benefits in seismic retrofit where, because of a desire to preserve the historical character of a building or to avoid disruption, conventional seismic strengthening may not be practical.

TABLE 38. MINIMUM SEISMIC DESIGN FORCES FOR NONBUILDING STRUCTURES

$V = C_s W$	(Eq. 16-34)
$= \frac{S_{D1} I_E W}{TR} \le \frac{S_{DS} I_E}{R}$	(Eq. 16-35 and Eq. 16-36)
$\ge 0.14 S_{DS} I_E$ (instead of $0.044\, S_{DS} I_E$)	(Eq. 16-75)
$\ge \frac{0.8 S_1 I_E}{R}$ (instead of $\frac{0.5 S_1 I_E}{R}$)	(Eq. 16-76)
where: R = lesser value given by Tables 1622.2.5 (1) and 1617.6 I_E = value given in Table 1622.2.5 (2)	
Important Points: 1. Distribute seismic lateral forces vertically per 1617.4.3 or 1618 2. Where required, use Ω_o as given in Table 1622.2.5 (1) 3. Apply height limitations of Table 1622.2.5 (1) 4. Note exceptions	

The concept of base isolation was implemented in Japan and New Zealand before it was first used in the United States to isolate buildings from earthquake ground motions in 1986. Base-isolated structures have by now been built in at least 17 countries throughout the world. The total number of base-isolated structures built or under construction as of 1994 was in excess of 300.[53] Most of these were in Japan, New Zealand, and the United States. Kelly[54] has provided an excellent history, and Buckle[55] an excellent world overview. Excellent state-of-the-art information is available in Reference 52. The EERI has devoted an entire issue of Earthquake Spectra to the theme of "Seismic Isolation: From Idea to Reality."[56] Perhaps the most lucid presentation of the concept has been provided by Bachman.[53] The material presented here is drawn largely from References 52 and 53.

Base isolation is founded on fundamental principles of earthquake engineering and accepted assumptions regarding earthquake ground motions. Most lower-rise structures (less than 10 stories in height) have a fixed-base fundamental period of 1 second or less. It has been observed in past earthquakes that these structures typically respond to earthquake motions by amplifying their acceleration response by two to four times. However, for structural systems with periods of 2 to 3 seconds, the acceleration responses are no longer amplified and are in fact generally reduced. Base isolation takes advantage of this characteristic of structural response to earthquake ground motion.

In Figure 42, a comparison of the response of a conventional fixed-base structure and a base-isolated structure is illustrated. In a base-isolated structure, the columns of the structure are typically supported on individual base isolation bearings. These bearings usually have relatively low horizontal stiffness and relatively high vertical stiffness. The relatively low horizontal stiffness shifts the response characteristics of a typical lower-rise building system from maximum roof accelerations of 1.0g to 1.5g to maximum roof accelerations of 0.2g to 0.3g. This reduction is further enhanced if the bearings have inherent increased damping (Figure 43).

Typically, bearings behave non-linearly with equivalent viscous damping of 10 to 20 percent of critical or more. This compares with approximately 5 percent for conventional

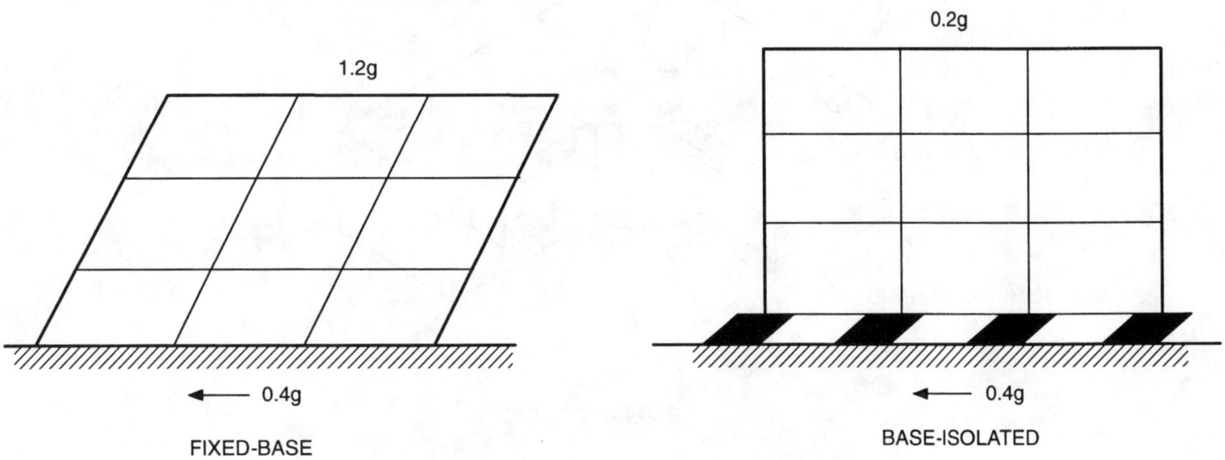

PERFORMANCE COMPARISON OF RESPONSES OF FIXED-BASE AND BASE-ISOLATED BUILDING

FIGURE 42

construction. It should be noted that, as the period shifts to larger values, the earthquake response displacements increase. This increase can also be tempered by an increase in damping (Figure 43). Since with base isolation the greatest portion of the response occurs across the base isolation bearings, almost all of the response displacement occurs between the base of the structure and the ground. This means that, in high earthquake zones, relative displacements of 6 to 24 inches must be accommodated across the isolator interface by utility lines and entrance ways during maximum design earthquake ground motions. The vertical stiffness of bearings is typically 50 to 1000 times the horizontal stiffness so that rocking and vertical amplifications of response are minimized.

Types of Bearings

The four types of bearings commonly available include: laminated, high-damping rubber bearings; laminated rubber bearings with lead core; steel sliding bearings using dished surfaces; and coil spring systems. Laminated rubber bearings (high-damping and lead core) are most often used. They consist of layered sheets of alternating rubber and steel plates vulcanized together. Typically square or round in plan, these bearings range in width from 14 to 45 inches and some contain a lead core to provide additional damping (Figure 44).

Basic Elements of Seismic Isolation Systems

There are three basic elements in any practical seismic isolation system. These are:

1. A flexible mounting so that the period of vibration of the total system is lengthened sufficiently to reduce the force response.
2. A damper or energy dissipator so that the relative deflections between building and ground can be controlled to a practical design level.
3. A means of providing rigidity under low (service) levels of excitation such as caused by wind and minor earthquakes.

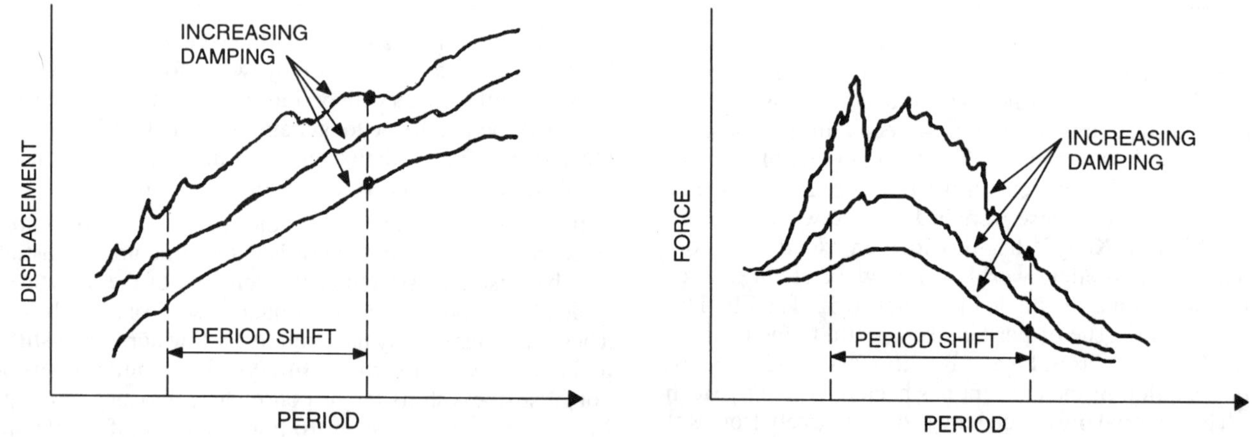

EFFECTS OF PERIOD SHIFT AND INCREASED DAMPING

FIGURE 43

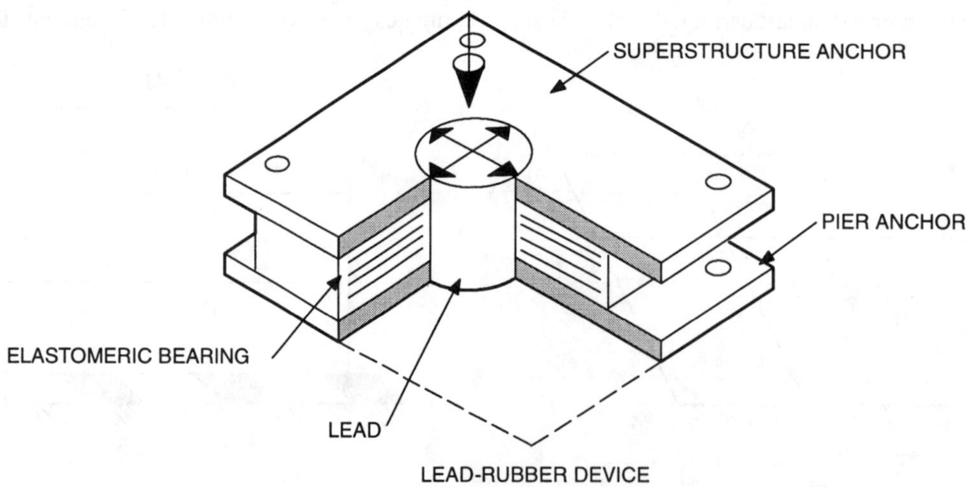

A MECHANICAL ENERGY DISSIPATOR

FIGURE 44

While lateral flexibility is highly desirable for high seismic loads, it is clearly undesirable to have a structural system that will vibrate perceptibly under frequently occurring excitations such as those caused by minor earthquakes or wind. Lead-rubber bearings (and other mechanical energy dissipators) provide the desired initial rigidity by virtue of their high elastic stiffness. Some other seismic isolation systems require a wind-restraint device for this purpose—typically a rigid component designed to fail under a given level of lateral load. This can result in a shock loading being transferred to the structure because of the sudden loss of load in the restraint. Nonsymmetrical failure of such devices can also introduce undesirable torsional effects in a building. Further, such devices need to be replaced after each failure.

Practicability

As pointed out by Mayes,[52] five developments over the last two decades are together responsible for the ever-increasing application of the seismic isolation concept:

1. The design and manufacture of high-quality elastomeric (rubber) pads, frequently called bearings, that are used to support the weight of the structure but at the same time protect it from earthquake-induced forces.
2. The design and manufacture of mechanical-energy dissipators (absorbers) and high-damping elastomers that are used to reduce the movement across the bearings to practical and acceptable levels and to resist wind loads.
3. The development and acceptance of computer software for the analysis of seismically isolated structures, which includes nonlinear material properties and the time-varying nature of the earthquake loads.
4. The ability to perform shaking-table tests using real recorded earthquake ground motions to evaluate the performance of structures and provide results to validate computer modeling techniques.
5. The development and acceptance of procedures for estimating site-specific earthquake ground motions for different return periods.

Seismic Isolation Design Principles[52]

The design principles for seismic isolation are illustrated in Figure 45. The top curve on this figure shows the realistic elastic forces based on a 5-percent damped-response spectrum that will be imposed on a nonisolated structure designed by recent codes, including the 2000 IBC. The spectrum shown is for a soft rock (Site Class B) site if the structure has sufficient elastic strength to resist this level of load. The lowest curve shows the forces that the IBC requires a structure to be designed for, and the second-lowest curve shows the probable strength assuming the structure is designed for the IBC forces. The probable strength is at least two times the design strength because of the design load factors, actual material strengths that are greater in practice than those assumed for design, conservatism in structural design, and other factors. The difference between the maximum elastic force and the probable yield strength is an approximate indication of the energy that must be absorbed by ductility in the structural elements.

When a building is isolated, the maximum elastic forces are reduced considerably because of period shift and energy

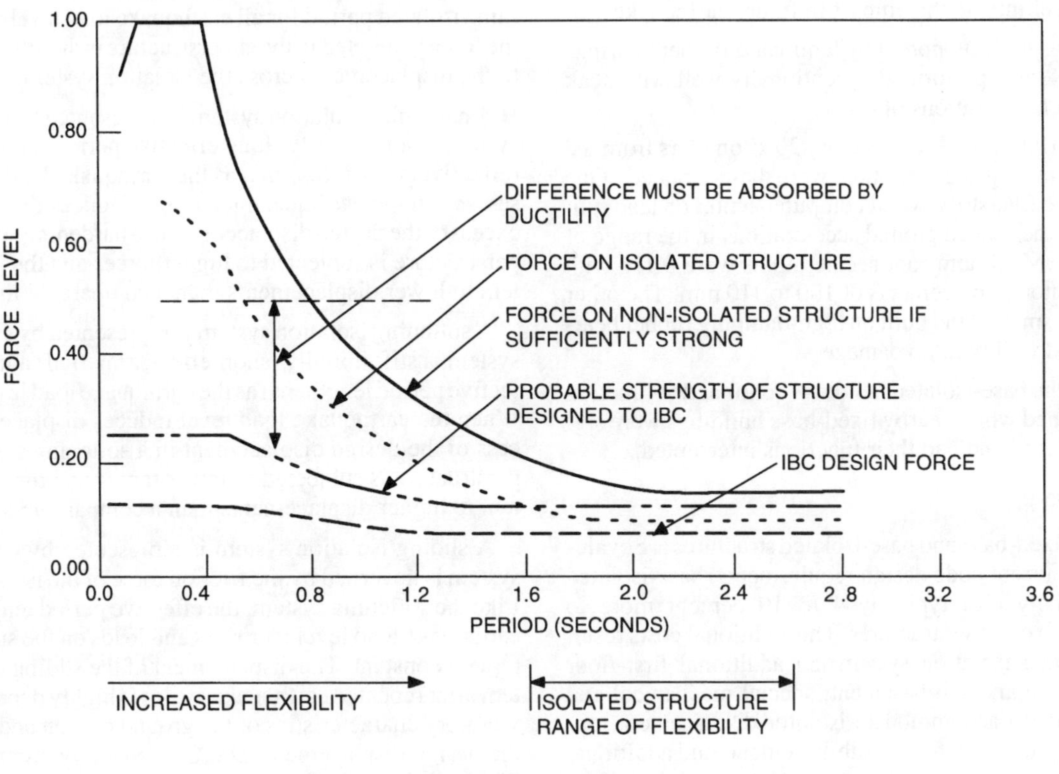

DESIGN PRINCIPLES OF SEISMIC ISOLATION

FIGURE 45

dissipation, as shown in Figure 44.[46] The elastic forces on a seismically isolated structure are shown by the dashed curve in Figure 45. This curve corresponds to a system with approximately 30 percent equivalent viscous damping.

If a stiff building, with a fixed-base fundamental period of 1.0 second or less, is isolated, then its fundamental period will be increased into the 1.5- to 2.5-second range (Figure 45). This results in a reduced design force but, more important, in the 1.5- to 2.5-second range, the probable yield strength of the isolated building is approximately the same as the maximum forces to which it will be subjected. Therefore, there will be little or no ductility demand on the structural system, and the lateral design forces are reduced by approximately 50 percent.

Performance In Earthquakes[53]

During the Northridge and Hyogo-Ken Nanbu (Kobe) Earthquakes, base-isolated buildings were for the first time subjected to strong ground motion associated with Richter Magnitude 6+ earthquakes. During the Northridge Earthquake, the Los Angeles County Fire Command and Control Facility and the University of Southern California (USC) Hospital experienced ground accelerations of 0.32g and 0.49g, respectively. The Los Angeles County Fire Command and Control Facility, supported by laminated high-damping rubber bearings, performed well and continued to function fully during and following the earthquake. Some intentionally sacrificial architectural tile was damaged at a seismic joint, at the main entrance as planned. However, the tile grout across the joint was thicker and stronger than anticipated and caused some localized "spike" type accelerations in one direction because of impact at the building entrance. This detail has since been replaced with a "pop-out" tile detail that will eliminate this impact in future earthquakes.

The USC Hospital, supported by laminated rubber bearings with lead cores, also performed exceptionally well with peak horizontal roof accelerations of 0.21g.

In Kobe, two buildings located about 20 kilometers from the zone of maximum ground motion were base-isolated. One building, a large five-story postal computer center on lead rubber bearings, experienced ground accelerations in the range of 0.25g to 0.30g. Maximum roof accelerations were 0.11g with maximum isolator displacements of 100 to 110 mm. The other Kobe building, smaller and built on high-damping rubber bearings, performed well with no damage.

In all cases, the base-isolated buildings continued to function exactly as planned while nearby fixed-base buildings were significantly damaged and had their functions interrupted.

Cost Issues[53]

When both fixed-base and base-isolated structures are evaluated based on current code design requirements, base-isolated structures initially cost typically 4 to 10 percent more to construct than fixed-base structures. The additional costs result from: the seismic isolation system, an additional first-floor beam-slab system and sub-basement, special mechanical and electrical details to accommodate isolator displacement, optional weather protection for the sub-basement, and additional engineering costs. There may be some off-setting cost reduction of the base-isolated structural system due to the reduced structural system design forces.

If a fixed-base building and its contents are designed, strengthened, and tested to have the same expected fully functional performance as a base-isolated building during design earthquake-level ground motions, the base-isolated building has been shown to be less expensive. In the case of the Los Angeles County Fire Command and Control Facility, the savings were estimated as approximately 6 percent.

Force-Deflection Characteristics of Isolation Systems

As pointed out in the commentary to Chapter 13 of the 1997 NEHRP Provisions,[8] a general concern has long existed regarding the applicability of different types of isolation systems. Rather than addressing a specific method of base isolation, the 2000 IBC provides general design requirements applicable to a wide range of possible seismic isolation systems. Although remaining general, the design requirements rely on mandatory testing of isolation-system hardware to confirm the engineering parameters used in the design and to verify the overall adequacy of the isolation system. Some systems may not be capable of demonstrating acceptability by test and, consequently, would not be permitted. In general, acceptable systems will: 1) remain stable for required design displacements, 2) provide increasing resistance with increasing displacement, 3) not degrade under repeated cyclic load, and 4) have quantifiable engineering parameters (e.g., force-deflection characteristics and damping).

Conceptually, there are four basic types of isolation system force-deflection relationships.[8, 52] These idealized relationships are shown in Figure 46 with each idealized curve having the same design displacement, D_D, for the design earthquake. A linear isolation system is represented by Curve A and has the same isolated period for all earthquake load levels. In addition, the force generated in the superstructure is directly proportional to the displacement across the isolation system.

A hardening isolation system is represented by Curve B. This system is soft initially (long effective period) and then stiffens (effective period shortens) as the earthquake load level increases. When the earthquake load level induces displacements in excess of the design displacement in a hardening system, the superstructure is subjected to higher forces and the isolation system to lower displacements than a comparable linear system.

A softening isolation system is represented by Curve C. This system is stiff initially (short effective period) and softens (effective period lengthens) as the earthquake load level increases. When the earthquake load level induces displacements in excess of the design displacement in a softening system, the superstructure is subjected to lower forces and the isolation system to higher displacements than a comparable linear system.

A sliding isolation system is represented by Curve D. This system is governed by the friction force of the isolation system. Like the softening system, the effective period lengthens as the earthquake load level increases and loads on the superstructure remain constant. The displacement of the sliding isolation system after repeated earthquake cycles is highly dependent on the vibratory characteristics of the ground motion and may exceed the design displacement, D_D. Consequently, minimum design requirements do not adequately define peak seismic displacement for seismic isolation systems governed solely by friction forces.

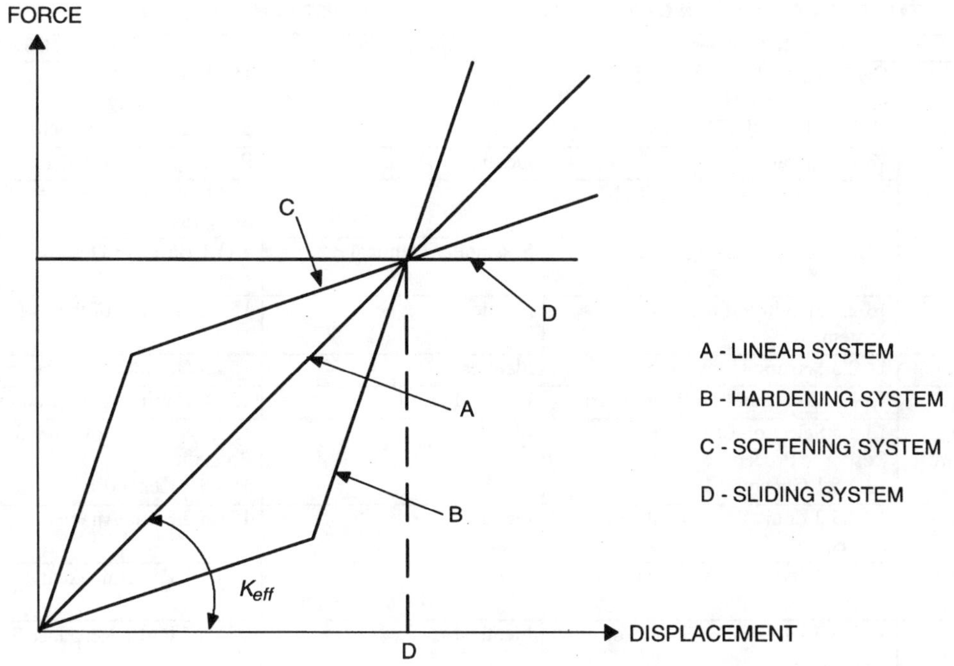

IDEALIZED FORCE-DISPLACEMENT RELATIONSHIPS FOR ISOLATION SYSTEMS

FIGURE 46

Code Provisions for Base Isolation

In the late 1980s, the leadership of the Structural Engineers Association of California realized the significant benefits of base isolation in seismic design. They also recognized that base isolation would only be widely accepted if code requirements existed for its design and implementation. Accordingly, in late 1989, the SEAOC Seismology Committee adopted an "Appendix to Chapter 2" of the SEAOC Blue Book[4] entitled, "General Requirements for the Design and Construction of Seismic-Isolated Structures." These requirements were adopted as an appendix to the 1991 UBC. The isolation appendix of the UBC has been updated on an annual basis since that time and the most current version of these regulations may be found in the 1997 UBC Appendix Chapter 16, Division IV.

During development of the 1994 NEHRP Provisions, it was decided to use the then-latest version (1993 approved changes) of the SEAOC/UBC provisions as a basis for the development of the requirements included in the Provisions. The only significant changes involved an appropriate conversion to strength design and making the requirements applicable on a national basis. For the 1997 NEHRP Provisions, it was decided to incorporate the 1997 UBC provisions. Since the 1997 UBC is based on strength design, Appendix Chapter 16, Division IV of the 1997 UBC and Chapter 13 of the 1997 NEHRP Provisions are almost identical, except for seismic criteria. The seismic criteria of the 1997 NEHRP Provisions are based on the new national earthquake maps and the associated ground motion parameters.

The 2000 IBC Section 1623 is equivalent to the 1997 NEHRP Provisions Chapter 13, except for one minor item, as can be seen from the detailed comparison given in Table 39. The IBC is slightly less stringent in its requirement concerning sequences and cycles for required tests of isolation systems. Table 39 also lists against each provision of Section 1623 of the 2000 IBC, the corresponding 1999 Blue Book[4] provisions, because the Blue Book provides commentary on the 1997 UBC provisions for seismic-isolated structures. With the help of Table 39, the reader should be able to readily key into two sources of commentary on the base-isolation provisions of the 2000 IBC. The discussion here is, therefore, kept to a minimum.

1623.1 Determination of seismic characteristics and selection of design criteria. The procedures and limitations for the design of seismically isolated structures are to be determined considering seismic ground motion, site characteristics, vertical acceleration, cracked section properties for concrete and masonry members, seismic use group, configuration, structural system, and height in accordance with Sections 1614 through 1616, except as noted in Section 1623.1.

It is necessary to check the stability of the vertical load-carrying elements of the isolation systems by analysis and test, as required, for lateral seismic displacements equal to the total maximum displacement (see Figure 47 for terminology).

1623.1.1 Seismic use group. SUG is assigned per Section 1616.5.

1623.1.2 Configuration. The structural configuration of a building above the base determines its irregularity or lack thereof.

TABLE 39. COMPARISON OF 2000 IBC SECTION 1623 AND 1997 NEHRP CHAPTER 13

IBC Section	NEHRP Section	Comments	Blue Book Section
1623 SEISMICALLY ISOLATED STRUCTURES	CHAPTER 13 SEISMICALLY ISOLATED STRUCTURES DESIGN REQUIREMENTS		150 Division IV Earthquake Regulations for Seismic-Isolated Structures
1623.1 Paragraphs 1 and 2	13.1 General	Identical	Paragraph 1 and Part 1
	13.2 CRITERIA SELECTION		153 Criteria Selection for Seismic-Isolated Structures
1623.1 Design requirements	13.2.1 Basis for Design	Essentially identical	153.1 Basis for Design
1623.1 Paragraph 3	13.2.2 Stability of the Isolation System	Identical	153.2 Stability of the Isolated System
1623.1.1 Seismic use group	13.2.3 Seismic Use Group	Identical	153.3 Occupancy Categories
1623.1.2 Configuration	13.2.4 Configuration Requirements	Identical	153.4 Configuration Requirements
1623.1.3 Selection of lateral response procedure	13.2.5 Selection of Lateral Response Procedure 13.2.5.1 General	Identical	153.5 Selection of Lateral Response Procedure 153.5.1 General
1623.1.3.1 Equivalent lateral-force procedure	13.2.5.2 Equivalent lateral-force Procedure	Identical	153.5.2 Static Analysis
1623.1.3.2 Dynamic lateral response procedure	13.2.5.3 Dynamic Analysis	Identical	153.5.3 Dynamic Analysis
1623.1.3.3 Response-spectrum analysis	13.2.5.3.1 Response-Spectrum Analysis	Identical	153.5.3 Part 1 Response Spectrum Analysis
1623.1.3.4 Time-history analysis	13.2.5.3.2 Time-History Analysis	Identical	153.5.3 Part 2 Time-History Analysis
1623.1.3.5 Site-specific design spectra	13.2.5.3.3 Site-Specific Design Spectra	Identical	153.5.3 Part 3 Site-Specific Design Spectra
1623.2 Equivalent lateral response procedure	13.3 EQUIVALENT LATERAL-FORCE PROCEDURE 13.3.1 General	Identical	154 Static Lateral Response Procedure for Seismic-Isolated Structures 154.1 General
1623.2.1 Deformation characteristics of the isolation system	13.3.2 Deformation Characteristics of the Isolation System	Identical	154.2 Deformation Characteristics of the Isolation System
1623.2.2 Minimum lateral displacements	13.3.3 Minimum Lateral Displacements		154.3 Minimum Lateral Displacements
1623.2.2.1 Design displacement	13.3.3.1 Design Displacement	Identical	154.3.1 Design Displacement
1623.2.2.2 Effective period at design displacement	13.3.3.2 Effective Period	Identical	154.3.2 Effective Period at Design Displacement
1623.2.3 Maximum lateral displacement	13.3.3.3 Maximum Displacement	Identical	154.3.3 Maximum Displacement
1623.2.3.1 Effective period at maximum displacement	13.3.3.4 Effective Period at Maximum Displacement	Identical	154.3.4 Effective Period at Maximum Displacement
1623.2.4 Total lateral displacement	13.3.3.5 Total Displacement	Identical	154.3.5 Total Displacement
1623.2.5 Minimum lateral forces	13.3.4 Minimum Lateral Forces		154.4 Minimum Lateral Forces
1623.2.5.1 Isolation system and structural elements at or below the isolation system	13.3.4.1 Isolation System and Structural Elements At or Below the Isolation System	Identical	154.4.1 Isolation System and Structural Elements at or Below the Isolation Interface
1623.2.5.2 Structural elements above the isolation system	13.3.4.2 Structural Elements Above the Isolation System	Identical	154.4.2 Structural Elements Above the Isolation System
1623.2.5.3 Limits on V_s	13.3.4.3 Limits on V_s	Identical	154.4.3 Limits on V_s
1623.2.6 Vertical distribution of force	13.3.5 Vertical Distribution of Force	Identical	154.5 Vertical Distribution of Force
1623.2.7 Drift limits	13.3.6 Drift Limits	Identical	154.6 Drift Limits
1623.3 Dynamic lateral response procedure	13.4 DYNAMIC LATERAL RESPONSE PROCEDURE 13.4.1 General	Identical	155 Dynamic Lateral Response Procedure for Seismic-Isolated Structures 155.1 General

(continued)

TABLE 39. COMPARISON OF 2000 IBC SECTION 1623 AND 1997 NEHRP CHAPTER 13—(continued)

IBC Section	NEHRP Section	Comments	Blue Book Section
1623.3.1 Isolation system and structural elements below the isolation system	13.4.2 Isolation System and Structural Elements Below the Isolation System	Identical	155.2 Isolation System and Structural Elements at or Below the Isolation Interface 155.2.1, 155.2.2, 155.2.3, 155.2.4
1623.3.2 Structural elements above the isolation system	13.4.3 Structural Elements Above the Isolation System	Identical	155.3 Structural Elements Above the Isolation System
1623.3.3 Ground motion	13.4.4 Ground Motion		155.4 Ground Motion
1623.3.3.1 Design spectra	13.4.4.1 Design Spectra	Essentially identical	155.4.1 Design Spectra
1623.3.3.2 Time histories	13.4.4.2 Time Histories	Identical	155.4.2 Time Histories
1623.3.4 Mathematical model	13.4.5 Mathematical Model 13.4.5.1 General	Identical	155.5 Mathematical Model for Seismic-Isolated Structures 155.5.1 General
1623.3.4.1 Isolation system	13.4.5.2 Isolation System	Identical	155.5.2 Isolation System
1623.3.4.2 Isolated structure	13.4.5.3 Isolated Building		155.5.3 Isolated Structure
1623.3.4.2.1 Displacement	13.4.5.3.1 Displacement	Identical	155.5.3.1 Displacement
1623.3.4.2.2 Forces and displacements in elements of the lateral-force-resisting system	13.4.5.3.2 Forces and Displacements in Elements of the Lateral-Force-Resisting System	Identical	155.5.3.2 Forces and Displacements in Key Elements
1623.3.5 Response-spectrum and time-history analysis procedure	13.4.6 Description of Analysis Procedures 13.4.6.1 General	Identical	155.6 Description of Analysis Procedures 155.6.1 General
1623.3.5.1 Input earthquake	13.4.6.2 Input Earthquake	Identical	155.6.2 Input Earthquake
1623.3.5.2 Response-spectrum analysis	13.4.6.3 Response-Spectrum Analysis	Identical	155.6.3 Response Spectrum Analysis
1623.3.5.3 Time-history analysis	13.4.6.4 Time-History Analysis	Identical	155.6.4 Time-History Analysis
1623.3.6 Design lateral force	13.4.7 Design Lateral Force	Identical	155.7 Design Lateral Force
1623.3.6.1 Isolation system	13.4.7.1 Isolation System and Structural Elements At or Below the Isolation System	Identical	155.7.1 Isolation System and Structural Elements at or Below the Isolation System
1623.3.6.2 Structural elements above the isolation system	13.4.7.2 Structural Elements Above the Isolation System	Identical	155.7.2 Structural Elements Above the Isolation System
1623.3.6.3 Scaling of results	13.4.7.3 Scaling of Results	Identical	155.7.3 Scaling of Results
1623.3.6.4 Drift limits	13.4.7.4 Drift Limits	Identical	155.8 Drift Limits
1623.4 Lateral load on elements of structures and nonstructural components supported by buildings	13.5 LATERAL LOAD ON ELEMENTS OF STRUCTURES AND NONSTRUCTURAL COMPONENTS SUPPORTED BY BUILDINGS 13.5.1 General	Identical	156 Lateral Load On Elements Of Structures and Nonstructural Components Supported by Seismic-Isolated Structures 156.1 General
1623.4.1 Forces and displacements	13.5.2 Forces and Displacements		156.2 Forces and Displacements
1623.4.1.1 Components at or above the isolation interface	13.5.2.1 Components At or Above the Isolation Interface	Identical	156.2.1 Components at or Above the Isolation Interface
1623.4.1.2 Components crossing the isolation interface	13.5.2.2 Components Crossing the Isolation Interface	Identical	156.2.2 Components That Cross the Isolation Interface
1623.4.1.3 Components below the isolation interface	13.5.2.3 Components Below the Isolation Interface	Identical	156.2.3 Components Below the Isolation Interface

(continued)

TABLE 39. COMPARISON OF 2000 IBC SECTION 1623 AND 1997 NEHRP CHAPTER 13—(continued)

IBC Section	NEHRP Section	Comments	Blue Book Section
1623.5 Detailed system requirements	13.6 DETAILED SYSTEM REQUIREMENTS 13.6.1 General	Identical	157 Detailed System Requirements for Seismic-Isolated Structures 157.1 General
1623.5.1 Isolation system	13.6.2 Isolation System		157.2 Isolation System
1623.5.1.1 Environmental conditions	13.6.2.1 Environmental Conditions	Identical	157.2.1 Environmental Conditions
1623.5.1.2 Wind forces	13.6.2.2 Wind Forces	Identical	157.2.2 Wind Forces
1623.5.1.3 Fire resistance	13.6.2.3 Fire Resistance	Identical	157.2.3 Fire Resistance
1623.5.1.4 Lateral-restoring force	13.6.2.4 Lateral-Restoring Force	Identical	157.2.4 Lateral Restoring Force
1623.5.1.5 Displacement restraint	13.6.2.5 Displacement Restraint	Identical	157.2.5 Displacement Restraint
1623.5.1.6 Vertical-load stability	13.6.2.6 Vertical-Load Stability	Identical	157.2.6 Vertical-Load Stability
1623.5.1.7 Overturning	13.6.2.7 Overturning	Identical	157.2.7 Overturning
1623.5.1.8 Inspection and replacement	13.6.2.8 Inspection and Replacement	Identical	157.2.8 Inspection and Replacement
1623.5.1.9 Quality control	13.6.2.9 Quality Control	Identical	157.2.9 Quality Control
1623.5.2 Structural system	13.6.3 Structural System		157.3 Structural System
1623.5.2.1 Horizontal distribution of force	13.6.3.1 Horizontal Distribution of Force	Identical	157.3.1 Horizontal Distribution of Force
1623.5.2.2 Building separations	13.6.3.2 Building Separations	Identical	157.3.2 Building Separations
1623.5.2.3 Nonbuilding structures	13.6.3.3 Nonbuilding Structures	Identical	158 Nonbuilding Seismic-Isolated Structures
1623.6 Foundations	13.7 FOUNDATIONS	Identical	159 Foundations of Seismic-Isolated Structures
1623.7 Design and construction review	13.8 DESIGN AND CONSTRUCTION REVIEW 13.8.1 General 13.8.2 Isolation System	Identical	160 Design and Construction Review for Seismic-Isolated Structures 160.1 General 160.2 Isolation System
1623.8 Required tests of the isolation system	13.9 REQUIRED TESTS OF THE ISOLATION SYSTEM 13.9.1 General	Identical	161 Required Tests of the Isolation System for Seismic-Isolated Structures 161.1 General
1623.8.1 Prototype tests	13.9.2 Prototype Tests 13.9.2.1 General	Identical	161.2 Prototype Tests 161.2.1 General
1623.8.1.1 Record	13.9.2.2 Record	Identical	161.2.2 Record
1623.8.1.2 Sequences and cycles	13.9.2.3 Sequence and Cycles:	IBC identical to NEHRP except for the following change: Item 4 of NEHRP was changed from $30S_{D1}B_D/S_{DS}$ to $15S_{D1}B_D/S_{DS}$	161.2.3 Sequence and Cycles
1623.8.1.3 Units dependent on loading rates	13.9.2.4 Units Dependent on Loading Rates	Identical	161.2.4 Units Dependent on Loading Rates
1623.8.1.4 Units dependent on bilateral load	13.9.2.5 Units Dependent on Bilateral Load	Identical	161.2.5 Units Dependent on Bilateral Load
1623.8.1.5 Maximum and minimum vertical load	13.9.2.6 Maximum and Minimum Vertical Load	Identical	161.2.6 Maximum and Minimum Vertical Load
1623.8.1.6 Sacrificial wind-restraint systems	13.9.2.7 Sacrificial-Wind-Restraint Systems	Identical	161.2.7 Sacrificial Wind-Restraint Systems
1623.8.1.7 Testing similar units	13.9.2.8 Testing Similar Units	Identical	161.2.8 Testing Similar Units
1623.8.2 Determination of force-deflection characteristics	13.9.3 Determination of Force-Deflection Characteristics	Identical	161.3 Determination of Force-Deflection Characteristics

(continued)

TABLE 39. COMPARISON OF 2000 IBC SECTION 1623 AND 1997 NEHRP CHAPTER 13—(continued)

IBC Section	NEHRP Section	Comments	Blue Book Section
1623.8.3 Test specimen adequacy	13.9.4 Test Specimen Adequacy	IBC identical to NEHRP except for the following change: In items 2 and 3 of NEHRP, the term $30S_{D1}B_D/S_{DS}$ was modified to $15S_{D1}B_D/S_{DS}$	161.4 System Adequacy
1623.8.4 Design properties of the isolation system	13.9.5 Design Properties of the Isolation System		161.5 Design Properties of the Isolation System
1623.8.4.1 Maximum and minimum effective stiffness	13.9.5.1 Maximum and Minimum Effective Stiffness	Identical	161.5.1 Maximum and Minimum Effective Stiffness
1623.8.4.2 Effective damping	13.9.5.2 Effective Damping	Identical	161.5.2 Effective Damping

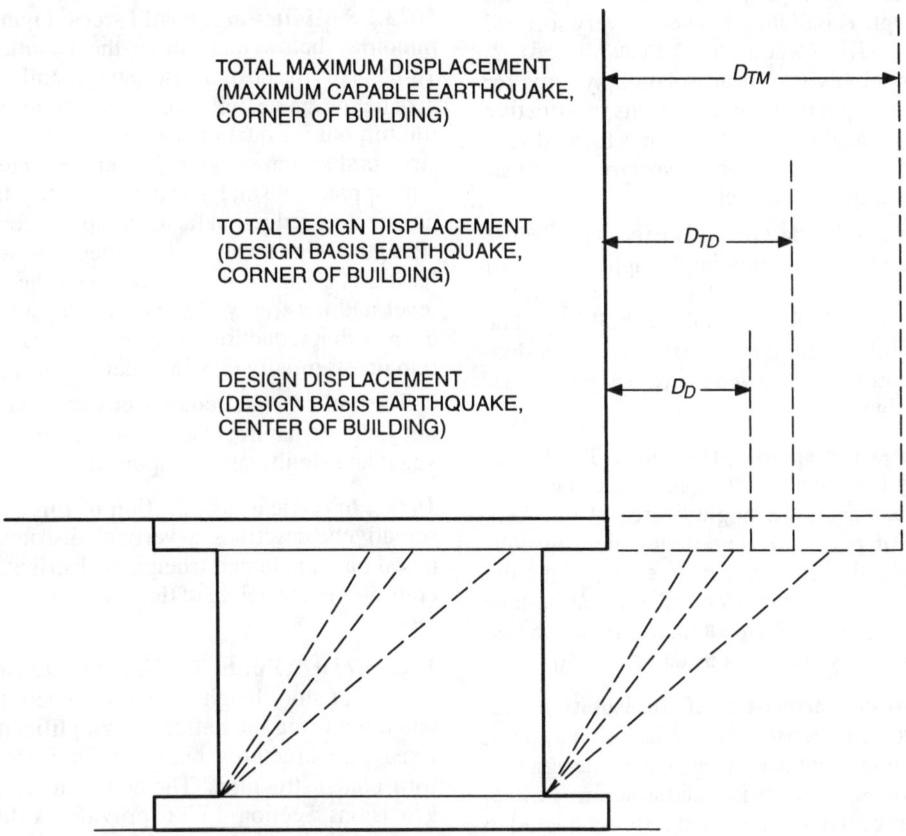

DISPLACEMENT TERMINOLOGY USED IN THE IBC

FIGURE 47

1623.1.3 Selection of lateral response procedure. Three procedures are included in the IBC: equivalent lateral response or static analysis procedure, response spectrum analysis, and time-history analysis.

Rather severe limitations are placed on the applicability of the simplified lateral-force design procedure at this time. The limitations cover the site location with respect to active faults; soil characteristics at the site, the height, regularity and stiffness characteristics of the building; and the characteristics of the isolation system.

The static procedure is based on a spectral shape that varies with the inverse of the elastic fundamental period, $1/T$, consistent with the constant velocity domain. The static procedure may not be used when the spectral demands may not be adequately characterized using the assumed shape, namely, for:[4]

1. Isolated buildings located in the near-field.
2. Isolated buildings on soft soil sites.
3. Long-period isolated buildings (beyond the constant velocity domain).

Further, the static procedure may not be used for other than regular superstructures or for highly nonlinear isolation systems. The restrictions placed on the use of equivalent lateral response design procedures effectively require dynamic analysis for virtually all isolated structures. However, lower-bound limits on isolation system design displacements and structural design forces are specified by the 2000 IBC in Section 1623.3 as a percentage of the values obtained from the equivalent lateral response design formulas, even when dynamic analysis is used as the basis for design. These lower-bound limits on key design parameters ensure consistency in the design of isolated structures and serve as a safety net against gross under-design[8]. Table C13.2 of the 1997 NEHRP Commentary provides a nice summary of the lower-bound limits on parameters obtained from dynamic analysis.

Response spectrum analysis is permitted for the design of all isolated buildings except: 1) buildings located on very soft soil sites (for which site-specific spectra must be established), 2) buildings supported by highly nonlinear isolation systems for which the assumptions implicit in the definitions of effective stiffness and damping break down, or 3) buildings located very close to major active faults where response spectrum analysis may not capture pulse effects adequately.[4]

Time-history analysis is the "last resort" analysis procedure that must be used when the conditions for the applicability of the static and the response spectrum analysis cannot be met. It may be used for the analysis of any isolated building. The SEAOC Blue Book rightly cautions that the results of time-history analysis must be carefully reviewed to avoid any gross design errors or over-design.

1623.2 Equivalent lateral response procedure. The lateral displacement given by Equation 16-79 approximates peak design earthquake displacement of a single-degree-of-freedom, linear elastic system of period, T_D, and equivalent viscous damping, β_D. The lateral displacement given by Equation 16-81 approximates peak maximum considered earthquake displacement of a single-degree-of-freedom, linear elastic system of period, T_M, and equivalent viscous damping, β_M.

1623.2.1 Deformation characteristics of the isolation system. The deformation characteristics of the isolation system, used to determine the minimum lateral earthquake design displacements and forces on seismically isolated structures, are required to be based on properly substantiated tests conducted in accordance with Section 1623.8.

1623.2.2 Minimum lateral displacements. Equation 16-79 gives an estimate of peak displacement expected in the isolation system in the design earthquake. In this equation, the spectral acceleration, S_{D1}, is the same as that required for the design of a conventional fixed-base structure of period, T_D, as given by Equation (16-80). A damping term, B_D, is used to increase or decrease the computed displacement when the equivalent damping coefficient of the isolation system is smaller or larger, respectively, than 5 percent of critical damping. Values of the coefficient, B_D, are given in Table 1623.2.2.1 for different values of isolation system damping, β_D.

1623.2.3 Maximum lateral displacement. Equation 16-81 gives an estimate of peak displacement expected in the isolation system in the maximum considered earthquake. In this equation, the spectral acceleration, S_{M1}, is the same as that required for the design of a conventional fixed-base structure of period, T_M, as given by Equation 16-82. The damping term, B_M, increases or decreases the computed displacement when the equivalent damping coefficient of the isolation system is smaller or larger, respectively, than 5 percent of critical damping. Values of the coefficient, B_M, are given in Table 1623.2.2.1 for different values of isolation system damping, β_M.

1623.2.4 Total lateral displacement. As in the case of conventional structures, accidental eccentricity in both horizontal directions must be considered. Figure 47 defines the displacement terminology used in the IBC. Equation 16-83 (or Equation 16-84 for the maximum considered earthquake) provides a simplified formula for estimating the response including the effects of torsion in the absence of more refined analysis.

1623.2.5 Minimum lateral forces. Figure 48 defines the terminology below and above the isolation system. Equation 16-85 gives the design base shear for all structural components at or below the seismic interface, without any reduction for ductile response. Equation 16-86 gives the design base shear for structural systems above the seismic interface. For structures with appreciable inelastic deformability, this equation includes an effective reduction factor of up to 2 for response beyond the strength design level. As explained in Reference 8, a factor of at least 2 is assumed to exist between the strength-design force level and the true yield level of the structural system. Thus, even with a reduction factor of 2, the structure is expected to remain essentially elastic under the design earthquake.

The limits on V_s attempt to ensure that the superstructure will not yield prematurely before the isolation system has been activated and significantly displaced.

1623.2.6 Vertical distribution of force. Equation 16-87 conservatively describes a vertical distribution of lateral force based on an assumed triangular distribution of seismic acceleration over the height of the structure above the isolation interface.

1623.2.7 Drift limits. The limit on interstory drift is a fixed 1.5 percent of story height. However, the interstory drift is computed not using the deflection amplification factor, C_d, as for fixed-base structures, but using the force reduction factor, R_I, for isolated structures. The commentary on the 1997 NEHRP Provisions Section 13.3.6 provides a direct comparison between drift limits for fixed-base structures and base-isolated structures. It is noted that drift limits for isolated structures are generally more conservative than those for conventional fixed-base structures, even when fixed-based structures are designed as Seismic Use Group III buildings.

1623.3 Dynamic lateral response procedure. As pointed out earlier, the restrictions placed on the use of the static lateral response procedure effectively require dynamic analysis for most isolated structures. Earlier discussion under Section 1623.1.3 has pointed out situations where the dynamic rather than the static lateral response procedure must be used. It has also pointed out situations where time-history analysis, rather than response spectrum analysis, must be used. Lower-bound limits on design displacements and design forces are specified in Section 1623.3 as a percentage of the values prescribed by the static procedure. As already pointed out, the lower-bound limits on key design parameters ensure consistency in the design of isolated structures and serve as a safety net against gross underdesign. The lower bound limits have been summarized in the 1997 NEHRP Provisions Commentary Table C13.2.

When time-history analysis is used as the basis for design, at least three separate analyses must be carried out, each using a different pair of horizontal time histories. Each pair of horizontal time histories must be consistent with the magnitudes, fault distances, and source mechanisms that control the design earthquake (or maximum considered earthquake). Additionally, the square root of the sum of the squares combination of the spectral ordinates for the two horizontal components in each pair must equal or exceed 1.3 times the spectral ordinate of the target spectrum at each period between $0.5T_D$ and $1.25T_M$.

1623.4 Lateral load on elements of structures and nonstructural components supported by buildings. This section applies to parts and portions of an isolated structure, permanent nonstructural components and the attachments to them, and the attachments for permanent equipment supported by a structure (collectively referred to here as components). For components at or above the isolation interface, the exception to Section 1623.4.1.1 provides a straightforward and usually conservative design procedure. However, according to the SEAOC Blue Book Commentary,[4] to obtain the full benefits of a seismically isolated building, it is necessary to base the design of these components on the dynamic response of the isolated structure, through the generation of floor spectra for the building. For critical buildings being designed to remain operational after an earthquake, this approach to the design of nonstructural components and equipment may be necessary. Section 1623.4.1.2 addresses components crossing the isolation interface. To accommodate the differential movement between the isolated building and the ground, provisions for flexible utility connections must be made. In addition, rigid components crossing the interface (stairs, elevator shafts, and walls) must have details to accommodate the differential movement at the isolator level without sustaining damage of such magnitude as may endanger life safety. Components below the isolation interface must be designed to ensure complete load path, per Section 1616.1.

1623.5 Detailed system requirements. This section gives a number of detailed requirements with which the isolation system and the structural system must comply.

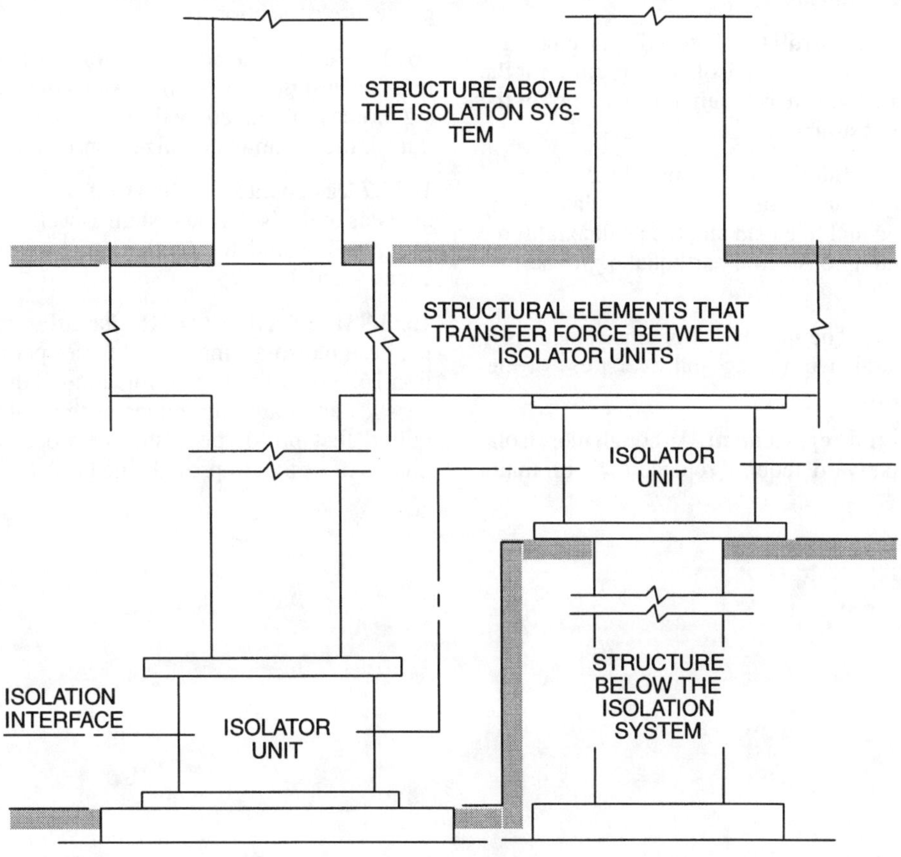

ISOLATION SYSTEM TERMINOLOGY

FIGURE 48

1623.5.1 Isolation system. The requirements of this section apply to the isolation system.

1623.5.1.1 Environmental conditions. In addition to the requirements of gravity and lateral loads due to wind and earthquakes, other environmental conditions that must be considered in the design of the isolation system include: aging effects, creep, fatigue, operating temperature, and exposure to moisture or damaging substances.

1623.5.1.2 Wind forces. Lateral displacement in the isolation system is required to be limited to a value similar to that required for other story heights.

1623.5.1.3 Fire resistance. If a base-isolated building is exposed to fire, the isolation system should be capable of supporting the weight of the building, as required for other vertical-load-carrying elements of the structure, but may end up having diminished resistance to lateral loads.[8]

1623.5.1.4 Lateral-restoring force. The isolation system must be configured so as to develop a restoring force sufficient to avoid significant residual displacement in an earthquake. This is necessary to ensure that the isolated structure will not have a stability problem and that it will be in a condition to withstand aftershocks and future earthquakes.

1623.5.1.5 Displacement restraint. Where a displacement restraint is used, explicit analysis of the isolated structure for the maximum considered earthquake is required to account for the effects of engaging the restraint.

1623.5.1.6 Vertical-load stability. The vertical load to be used in checking the stability of an isolator must be calculated using the maximum dead load and live load and the peak axial force induced by the maximum considered earthquake ground motion.

1623.5.1.7 Overturning. The intent of this requirement is to prevent global, structural overturning and overstress of elements due to local uplift.

1623.5.1.8 Inspection and replacement. Although most isolation systems are unlikely to require replacement of major components following an earthquake, this section provides for access for inspection and replacement as well as for certain specific inspections, including a periodic monitoring, inspection and maintenance program for the isolator system.

1623.5.1.9 Quality control. A test and inspection program is necessary for both fabrication and installation of the isolator system.

1623.5.2 Structural system. The requirements of this section apply to the structural system above the isolation interface.

1623.5.2.1Horizontal distribution of force. This section emphasizes the need to provide for transfer of lateral forces from the isolation system across the isolation interface to the structural system above.

1623.5.2.2 Building separations. A minimum separation between an isolated structure and a rigid obstruction is required to be provided. This minimum separation must be no smaller than the maximum total displacement defined in Section 1613.

1623.5.2.3 Nonbuilding structures. Base-isolated nonbuilding structures must be designed by Section 1622, using the design forces and design displacements calculated by the equivalent lateral response procedure or the dynamic lateral response procedure of Section 1623.

1623.6 Foundations. Foundations of base-isolated structures must be designed by the provisions of Chapter 18 using the design forces calculated by the equivalent lateral response procedure or the dynamic lateral response procedure of Section 1623.

1623.7 Design and construction review. Review of design and analysis of the isolation system as well as of the isolator testing program is mandated by the IBC for reasons given in References 4 and 7.

1623.8 Required tests of the isolation system. Calculation of the design displacements and forces per the provisions of Section 1623 require the determination of the deformation characteristics and damping values of the isolation system. It is required that prototype systems be designed during the early phases of design to provide the basis for such determination.

CHAPTER 16—PART 2

EXAMPLE 1. DESIGN AXIAL FORCE, SHEAR FORCE AND BENDING MOMENT FOR SHEAR WALL DUE TO LATERAL AND GRAVITY LOADS (STRENGTH DESIGN)

Load Effect	Symbol	Axial Force (kips)	Shear Force (kips)	Bending Moment (ft-kips)
Dead Load Effect	D	5381	0	0
Live Load Effect	L	837	0	0
Wind Load Effect	W	0	289	18,711
Effect of (Horizontal) Design Earthquake Forces	Q_E	0	1571	118,596

Code Formula	Combination	Axial Force (kips)	Shear Force (kips)	Bending Moment (ft-kips)
(16-1)	$1.4D$	7533	0	0
(16-2)	$1.2D+1.6L$ (1)	7796	0	0
(16-4)	$1.2D+1.6W+0.5L$ (2)	6876	462	29,938
(16-5)	$1.2D+(\rho Q_E+0.2S_{DS}D)+0.5L$ (3)	7952	1571	118,596
(16-6)	$0.9D + 1.6W$	4843	-462	-29,938
(16-6)	$0.9D + (\rho Q_E + 0.2S_{DS}D)$	3767	-1571	-118,596

Note: (1) The effect of roof live load, snow load or rain load not considered here.
Note: (2) The live load was assumed to be less than 100 psf.
Note: (3) $\rho = 1.0$ and $S_{DS} = 1.0$

EXAMPLE 2. DESIGN AXIAL FORCE, SHEAR FORCE AND BENDING MOMENT FOR SHEAR WALL DUE TO LATERAL AND GRAVITY LOADS (STRENGTH DESIGN FOR CONCRETE STRUCTURES)

Load Effect	Symbol	Axial Force (kips)	Shear Force (kips)	Bending Moment (ft-kips)
Dead Load Effect	D	5381	0	0
Live Load Effect	L	837	0	0
Wind Load Effect	W	0	289	18,711
Effect of (Horizontal) Design Earthquake Forces	Q_E	0	1571	118,596

Code Eqn.	Combination	Axial Force (kips)	Shear Force (kips)	Bending Moment (ft-kips)
ACI318: (9-1)	$1.4D+1.7L$ (1)	8956	0	0
ACI318: (9-2)	$0.75(1.4D+1.7W/K_d+1.7L)$ (2)	6721	434	28,067
(16-5)	$1.2D+(\rho Q_E+0.2S_{DS}D)+0.5L$ (3)	7952	1571	118,596
ACI318: (9-3)	$0.9D + 1.3W/K_d$ (4)	4843	-442	-28,628
(16-6)	$0.9D + (\rho Q_E+0.2S_{DS}D)$	3767	-1571	-118,596

Note: (1) The effect of roof live load, snow load or rain load not considered here.
Note: (2) The live load was assumed to be less than 100 psf.
Note: (3) $\rho = 1.0$ and $S_{DS} = 1.0$
Note: (4) Wind directionality factor, K_d was taken to be 0.85

EXAMPLE 3. DESIGN AXIAL FORCE, SHEAR FORCE AND BENDING MOMENT FOR SHEAR WALL DUE TO LATERAL AND GRAVITY LOADS (ALLOWABLE STRESS DESIGN USING BASIC LOAD COMBINATIONS)

Load Effects	Symbol	Axial Force (kips)	Shear Force (kips)	Bending Moment (ft-kips)
Dead Load Effect	D	5381	0	0
Live Load Effect	L	837	0	0
Wind Load Effect	W	0	289	18,711
Effect of Horizontal Design Earthquake Forces	Q_E	0	1571	118,596

Code Formula	Combination	Axial Force (kips)	Shear Force (kips)	Bending Moment (ft-kips)
(16-7)	D	5381	0	0
(16-8)	$D+L$	6218	0	0
(16-10)	$D+W+L$ (1)	6218	289	18,711
(16-10)	$D+0.7(\rho Q_E+0.2S_{DS}D)+L$ (2)	6971	1100	83,017
(16-11)	$0.6D+W$	3229	-289	-18,711
(16-12)	$0.6D+0.7(\rho Q_E+0.2S_{DS}D)$	2475	-1100	-83,017
Section 1605.3.1.1	$D+0.75(W+L)$	6009	217	14,033
Section 1605.3.1.1	$D+0.75(\rho Q_E+0.2S_{DS}D)+0.75L$	6816	1178	88,947

Note: (1) The effect of roof live load, snow load or rain load not considered here.
Note: (2) $\rho = 1.0$ and $S_{DS} = 1.0$

EXAMPLE 4. DESIGN AXIAL FORCE, SHEAR FORCE AND BENDING MOMENT FOR SHEAR WALL DUE TO LATERAL AND GRAVITY LOADS (ALLOWABLE STRESS DESIGN USING ALTERNATE BASIC)

Load Effects	Symbol	Axial Force (kips)	Shear Force (kips)	Bending Moment (ft-kips)
Dead Load Effect	D	5381	0	0
Live Load Effect	L	837	0	0
Wind Load Effect	W	0	289	18,711
Effect of Design Horizontal Earthquake Forces	Q_E	0	1571	118,596

Code Formula	Combination	Axial Force (kips)	Shear Force (kips)	Bending Moment (ft-kips)
(16-13)	$D+L$ (1)	6218	0	0
(16-14)	$D+L+\omega W$ (2)	6218	376	24,324
(16-16)	$D+L+\omega W/2$	6218	188	12,162
(16-17)	$D+L+(\rho Q_E+0.2S_{DS}D)/1.4$ (3)	6987	1122	84,678
(16-18)	$0.9D+(\rho Q_E+0.2S_{DS}D)/1.4$	4073	-1122	-84,678

Note: (1) The effect of roof live load, snow load or rain load not considered here.
Note: (2) $\omega = 1.3$ as wind forces are calculated per ASCE 7
Note: (3) $\rho = 1.0$ and $S_{DS} = 1.0$

EXAMPLE 5. CALCULATION OF LIVE LOAD REDUCTION

The computation of live load reduction for roof and floor per Sections 1607.9 and 1607.11 is illustrated in the following example.

Given: Plan dimensions: (as shown)
Story height = 12 ft
Live load: Floors = 50 psf (for a typical office building, see Table 1607.1)
Roof = 20 psf (assumed)
Dead load: Floors = 120 psf (assumed)
Roof = 90 psf (assumed)

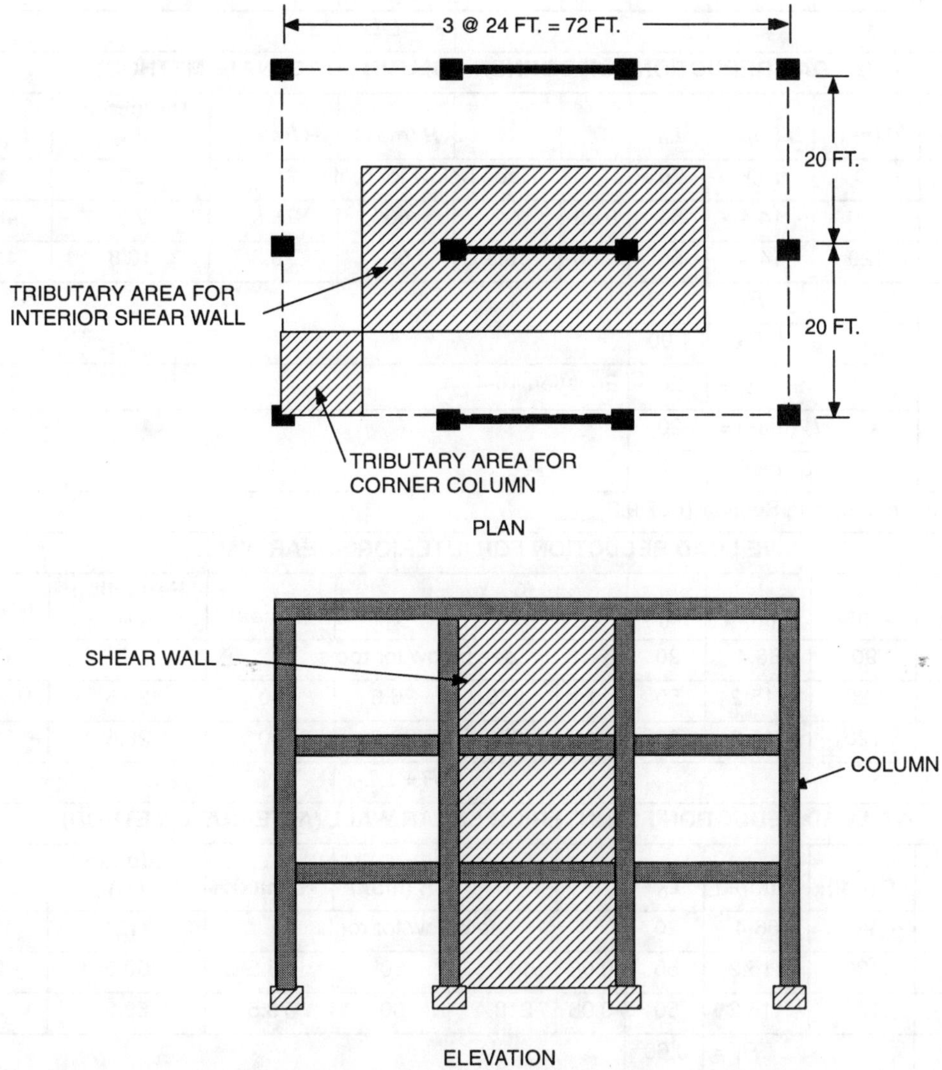

Plan and Elevation of the Example Building Studied

EXAMPLE 5—(continued)

LIVE LOAD REDUCTION FOR CORNER COLUMN											
Level	A_T (sq.ft.)	D (psf)	D (kips)	L_0	K_{LL}	K_{LL} x A_T	R	R (max)	Reduction (%)	L (psf)	L (kips)
3	120	90	10.8	20	see below for roofs				20	16	1.9
2	120	120	14.4	50	1	120	0.00	40	0.00	50	6.0
1	120	120	14.4	50	1	120	0.00	40	0.00	50	6.0
							$R = L/L_0$				

LIVE LOAD REDUCTION FOR CORNER COLUMN (ALTERNATE METHOD)											
Level	A_T (sq.ft.)	D (psf)	D (kips)	L_0	r	R	R (max)	R (max)*	Reduction (%)	L (psf)	L (kips)
3	120	90	10.8	20	see below for roofs				20	16	1.9
2	240	120	14.4	50	0.08	7.2	60	78.5	7.2	46.4	5.6
1	360	120	14.4	50	0.08	16.8	60	78.5	16.8	41.6	5.0
Roof			R_1 =	1.00							
			R_2 =	1.00							
			L_r =	20	Equation 16-4						
			L_r (max) =	20							
			L_r (min) =	12							
* as given by the second equation in Section 1607.9.2											

LIVE LOAD REDUCTION FOR INTERIOR SHEAR WALL											
Level	A_T (sq.ft.)	D (psf)	D (kips)	L_0	K_{LL}	K_{LL} x A_T	R	R (max)	Reduction (%)	L (psf)	L (kips)
3	960	90	86.4	20	see below for roofs				12	17.6	16.9
2	960	120	115.2	50	1	960	26.6	40	26.6	36.7	35.2
1	960	120	115.2	50	1	960	26.6	40	26.6	36.7	35.2
							$R = L/L_0$				

LIVE LOAD REDUCTION FOR INTERIOR SHEAR WALL (ALTERNATE METHOD)											
Level	A (sq.ft.)	D (psf)	D (kips)	L_0	r	R	R (max)	R (max)*	Reduction (%)	L (psf)	L (kips)
3	960	90	86.4	20	see below for roofs				12	17.6	16.9
2	1920	120	115.2	50	0.08	141.6	60	78.5	60.0	20	19.2
1	2880	120	115.2	50	0.08	218.4	60	78.5	60.0	20	19.2
Roof			R_1 =	0.60							
			R_2 =	1.00							
			L_r =	12	Equation 16-4						
			L_r (max) =	20							
			L_r (min) =	12							

EXAMPLE 6. DESIGN OF A 20-STORY REINFORCED CONCRETE BUILDING FOR WIND FORCES

General

The main wind force-resisting system of a 20-story reinforced concrete office building is designed following the requirements of the 2000 IBC concerning wind forces.

According to Section 1609.1.1 (Determination of wind loads), wind loads on every building or other structure must be determined by the provisions of Section 6 of ASCE 7-98 (Minimum Design Loads for Buildings and Other Structures). The 20-story example building does not fall under any of the four exceptions provided in that section.

Design Criteria

Wind Design Data:

Location of building:	Los Angeles, California
Plan dimensions of the building:	130 ft × 130 ft
Height of the building:	258 ft = (255 ft + 3-ft parapet)

Building is partially enclosed per definition under Sec. 1609.2
Building is regular in shape (as shown in Fig. E6.1)
Assume Exposure B (per Sec. 1609.4)
Wind importance factor for the building; $I_w = 1.0$ (Category I, Table 1604.5)

Calculation of Flexibility of Structure

A structure is considered flexible per definition under Sec. 1609.2 if it has a fundamental natural frequency of less than 1 Hz (i.e., a fundamental period $T > 1$ sec). Using the approximate period formula of Sec. 1617.4.2.1 (Formula 16-40), the period $T = 0.1\ N$ (number of stories) $= 0.1 \times 20 = 2.0$ sec. The corresponding fundamental frequency is $^1/_2$ or 0.5 Hz, which indicates that the building is flexible.

Allowed Procedures

The design for wind loads of buildings and other structures, including the main wind force-resisting system (MWFRS) and components and cladding elements thereof, needs to be based on one of the following procedures:

(1) Method 1—The Simplified Procedure of ASCE 7-98 Sec. 6.4, applicable to buildings meeting the requirements specified in that section. This method is not applicable to the example building, since all the conditions under Sec. 6.4.1 are not met (for example, the height of the building is not less than 30 ft).

(2) Method 2—The Analytical Procedure of ASCE 7-98 Sec. 6.5 for buildings meeting the requirements specified in that section. This method is applicable to the example building as it satisfies the two conditions set forth in Sec. 6.5.1 (given below):

1. The building is regular in shape as defined in ASCE 7-98 Sec. 6.2.
2. The building does not have response characteristics making it subject to across wind loading, vortex shedding, instability due to galloping or flutter; or does not have a site location for which channeling effects or buffeting in the wake of upwind obstructions warrant special consideration.

(3) Method 3—The Wind Tunnel Procedure of ASCE 7-98 Sec. 6.6. This method is not necessary for the example building.

Design Procedure

The design load due to wind can be calculated after determining the following quantities (ASCE 7-98 Sec. 6.5.3, as modified by Sec. 1609):

1. The basic wind speed, V, and wind directionality factor, K_d, per ASCE 7-98 Sec. 6.5.4.
2. An importance factor, I_w, per Sec. 1609.5.
3. An exposure category per Sec. 1609.4 and velocity pressure exposure coefficient, K_z or K_h, as applicable, per ASCE 7-98 Sec. 6.5.6.
4. A topographic factor, K_{zt}, per ASCE 7-98 Sec. 6.5.7.
5. A gust effect factor, G or G_f, as applicable, per ASCE 7-98 Sec. 6.5.8.
6. An enclosure classification per ASCE 7-98 Sec. 6.5.9 (or Sec. 1609.2).
7. Internal pressure coefficient, GC_{pi}, per ASCE 7-98 Sec. 6.5.11.1.
8. External pressure coefficients, C_p or GC_{pf}, or force coefficients, C_f, as applicable, per ASCE 7-98 Sec. 6.5.11.2 or 6.5.11.3.
9. Velocity pressure, q_z or q_h, as applicable, per ASCE 7-98 Sec. 6.5.10.
10. Design wind pressure, p, or load, F, per ASCE 7-98 Sec. 6.5.12 and 6.5.13, as applicable.

EXAMPLE 6—(continued)

Basic Wind Speed (IBC Section 1609.3, ASCE 7-98 Section 6.5.4)

The basic wind speed, *V*, used in the determination of design wind loads on buildings and other structures is as given in ASCE 7-98 Figure 6-1, except as provided in ASCE 7-98 Sec. 6.5.4.1 and 6.5.4.2. The wind must be assumed to come from any direction. According to ASCE 7-98 Sec. 6.5.4.4, the wind directionality factor, K_d, must be determined from ASCE 7-98 Table 6-6. This factor is to be applied in conjunction with the design load combinations of Sec. 1605.2.1 (see Exception 1).

V = 85 mph (for Los Angeles from ASCE 7-98 Fig. 6-1)

K_d = 0.85 (from ASCE 7-98 Table 6-6 for main wind force-resisting system)

Importance Factor (IBC Section 1609.5)

An importance factor, I_w, for the building needs to be determined from IBC Table 1604.5, based on the building and structure categories listed in that table.

The example office building can be placed under Category I.

Importance factor I_w = 1.00 (IBC Table 1604.5 for Category I)

Exposure Categories (IBC Section 1609.4)

For each wind direction considered, an exposure category that adequately reflects the characteristics of ground surface irregularities needs to be determined for the site at which the building is to be constructed. Sec. 1609.4 states that an Exposure B shall be assumed unless the site meets the definition of another type exposure.

Assume Exposure Category B for the example building in both orthogonal directions.

Based on the exposure category, a velocity pressure exposure coefficient, K_z or K_h, as applicable, needs to be determined from ASCE 7-98 Table 6-5.

For MWFRS of building, Case 2 of ASCE 7-98 Table 6-5 is applicable.

$K_z = 2.01\,(z/z_g)^{2/\alpha}$ for $15 \text{ ft} \le z \le z_g$

where: z = height above ground level, ft

α = 3-second gust speed power law exponent from ASCE 7-98 Table 6-4

z_g = nominal height of the atmospheric boundary layer, ft (ASCE 7-98 Table 6-4)

From ASCE 7-98 Table 6-4 (for Exposure B), α = 7.0

z_g = 1200 ft

The values of K_z at different height levels and K_h are shown in Table E6.1.

Topographic Effects (ASCE 7-98 Section 6.5.7)

Wind speed-up effects at isolated hills, ridges, and escarpments, constituting abrupt changes in the general topography, located in any exposure category, need to be included in the design when the conditions set forth in ASCE 7-98 Sec. 6.5.7.1 are met. This effect is given by a factor K_{zt}:

$K_{zt} = (1 + K_1 K_2 K_3)^2$ (ASCE 7-98 Eq. 6-1)

where: K_1, K_2, and K_3 are given in ASCE 7-98 Fig. 6-2. For the example building, assuming it to be situated on level ground (i.e., with *H*, as shown in ASCE 7-98 Fig. 6-2, equal to zero), the K_{zt} factor may be taken equal to 1.

Gust Effect Factor (ASCE 7-98 Section 6.5.8)

The structure is flexible as defined in ASCE 7-98 Sec. 6.2. So the gust factor must be calculated by (ASCE 7-98 Sec. 6.5.8.2):

$$G_f = 0.925\left(\frac{1 + 1.7 I_{\bar{z}} \sqrt{g_Q^2 Q^2 + g_R^2 R^2}}{1 + 1.7 g_v I_{\bar{z}}}\right) \quad \text{(ASCE 7-98 Eq. 6-6)}$$

where: g_Q = 3.4

g_v = 3.4

$I_{\bar{z}} = c\,(33\,\bar{z}\quad)^{1/6}$ (ASCE 7-98 Eq. 6-3)

$Q = 1/\sqrt{[1 + 0.63\{(B + h)/\,L_{\bar{z}}\}^{0.63}]}$ (ASCE 7-98 Eq. 6-4)

$L_{\bar{z}} = \ell\,(\bar{z}/33)^{\bar{\varepsilon}}$ (ASCE 7-98 Eq. 6-5)

From Table 6.4 (Exposure B): $\alpha 1$ = 0.25

$b1$ = 0.45

c = 0.3

$\bar{\varepsilon}$ = 0.33

ℓ = 320 ft

z_{min} = 30 ft

EXAMPLE 6—(continued)

So:

$\bar{z} = 0.6h = 0.6 \times 258 = 155$ ft

$\geq z_{min} = 30$ ft Use $\bar{z} = 155$ ft

$B = 130$ ft (plan dimension of building normal to wind direction)

$L = 130$ ft (plan dimension of building parallel to wind direction)

$I_{\bar{z}} = 0.3\,(33/155)^{1/6} = 0.231$

$L_{\bar{z}} = 320\,(155/33)^{0.33} = 533$ ft

$$Q = 1/\sqrt{[1 + 0.63\{(130 + 258)/533\}^{0.63}]} = 0.812$$

$$g_R = \sqrt{\{2\ell n\,(3600 n_1)\}} + 0.577/\sqrt{\{2\ell n\,(3600 n_1\}} \quad \text{(ASCE 7-98 Eq. 6-7)}$$

$n_1 = 0.5$ *Hz* (building natural frequency)

$g_R = 4.021$

$$R = \sqrt{\{(1/\beta)\,R_n\,R_h\,R_B\,(0.53 + 0.47\,R_L)\}} \quad \text{(ASCE 7-98 Eq. 6-8)}$$

$\beta = 0.01$ (assumed) (damping ratio)

$R_n = 7.47\,N_1/(1+10.3\,N_1)^{5/3}$ (ASCE 7-98 Eq. 6-9)

$N_1 = n_1\,L_{\bar{z}}/\overline{V}_{\bar{z}}$ (ASCE 7-98 Eq. 6-10)

$R_\ell = 1/\eta - (1 - e^{-2\eta})/2\eta^2$ for $\eta > 0$ (ASCE 7-98 Eq. 6-11a)

$R_\ell = 1$ for $\eta = 0$ (ASCE 7-98 Eq. 6-11b)

where the subscript ℓ in ASCE 7-98 Eq. 6-11 shall be taken as *h, B,* and *L*, respectively.

$R_\ell = R_h$ setting $\eta = 4.6 n_1\,h / \overline{V}_{\bar{z}}$

$R_\ell = R_B$ setting $\eta = 4.6 n_1\,B / \overline{V}_{\bar{z}}$

$R_\ell = R_L$ setting $\eta = 15.4 n_1\,L / \overline{V}_{\bar{z}}$

$\overline{V}_{\bar{z}} = \bar{b}\,(\bar{z}/33)^{\bar{\alpha}}\;V\,(88/60)$ (ASCE 7-98 Eq. 6-12)

The above quantities can be computed as follows:

$\overline{V}_{\bar{z}} = 0.45\,(155/33)^{0.25}\,85\,(88/60) = 82.6$ ft/s

$\eta_h = 4.6 \times 0.5 \times 258 / 82.6 = 7.184$

corresponding R or $R_h = 1/7.184 - (1 - e^{-2 \times 7.184})/2 \times 7.184^2 = 0.130$

$\eta_B = 4.6 \times 0.5 \times 130 / 82.6 = 3.62$

corresponding R or $R_B = 1/3.62 - (1 - e^{-2 \times 3.62})/2 \times 3.62^2 = 0.238$

$\eta_L = 15.4 \times 0.5 \times 130 / 82.6 = 12.12$

corresponding R or $R_L = 1/12.12 - (1 - e^{-2 \times 12.12})/2 \times 12.12^2 = 0.079$

$N_1 = 0.5 \times 533 / 82.6 = 3.226$

$R_n = 7.47 \times 3.226 / (1+10.3 \times 3.226)^{5/3} = 0.067$

$$R = \sqrt{\{(1/0.01) \times 0.067 \times 0.130 \times 0.238(0.53 + 0.47 \times 0.079)\}} = 0.343$$

$$G_f = 0.925\left\{1 + 1.7 \times 0.231\sqrt{3.4^2 \times 0.812^2 + 4.021^2 \times 0.343^2}\right\}/\{1+1.7 \times 3.4 \times 0.231 = 0.876$$

Enclosure Classifications (ASCE 7-98 Section 6.5.9 or Section 1609.2)

For the purpose of determining internal pressure coefficients, all buildings shall be classified as enclosed, partially enclosed, or open as defined in Sec. 6.2 of ASCE 7-98 or IBC Sec. 1609.2.

Based on the conditions set forth in ASCE 7-98 Sec. 6.2 or IBC Sec. 1609.2, the building is assumed to be partially enclosed.

Internal Pressure Coefficients (ASCE 7-98 Section 6.5.11.1)

Internal pressure coefficients, GC_{pi}, shall be determined from ASCE 7-98 Table 6-7 based on building enclosure classifications determined from ASCE 7-98 Section 6.5.9.

$GC_{pi} = +0.55$ (ASCE 7-98 Table 6-7)

-0.55

The reduction factor for large volume buildings is not applicable for the example building, assuming proper partitioning of each floor area.

EXAMPLE 6—(continued)

External Pressure Coefficients (ASCE 7-98 Section 6.5.11.2)

For MWFRS, C_p coefficients are given in ASCE 7-98 Figure 6-3 and Table 6-8.

Wall: L/B = 130/130 = 1

Windward C_p = 0.8 To be used with q_z

Leeward C_p = −0.5 To be used with q_h

Side: C_p = −0.7 To be used with q_h

Roof: h/L = 258/130 = 1.98 $\geq$ 1.0

θ = 0 < 10° (assuming a flat roof)

Horizontal distance from windward edge

0 to $h/2$: C_p = −1.3 To be used with q_h

> $h/2$: C_p = −0.7

The above values for roof can be reduced depending on the area

Roof Area = 130 × 130 = 16,900 sq ft $\geq$ 1000 sq ft

Reduction factor = 0.8 (Fig. 6-3 of ASCE 7-98)

Velocity Pressure (ASCE 7-98 Section 6.5.10)

Velocity pressure, q_z, evaluated at height z shall be calculated by the following equation:

$q_z = 0.00256\ K_z\ K_{zt}\ K_d$ (Velocity) $V^2 I$ (psf) (ASCE 7-98 Eq. 6-13)

q_h is the velocity pressure calculated using ASCE 7-98 Eq. 6-13 at mean roof height h.

Table E6.1 shows the computation of velocity pressure using the above expression, with $I = I_w$, as given by Table 1604.5.

Design Wind Force p (ASCE 7-98 Section 6.5.12)

ASCE 7-98 Sec. 6.5.12 is applicable here because the building is considered partially enclosed. In particular, Sec. 6.5.12.2.3 is applicable, because the building is flexible and, because the design force is being computed for the main wind force-resisting system. The design wind pressure shall be determined from the following equation:

$p = q\,G_f C_p - q_i\,(GC_{pi})$ (ASCE 7-98 Eq. 6-17)

Where: q = q_z for windward walls evaluated at height z from the ground

= q_h for leeward walls, side walls, and roofs, evaluated at height h

q_i = q_h for negative internal pressure evaluation in partially enclosed buildings

= q_z for positive internal pressure evaluation in partially enclosed buildings. For positive internal pressure evaluation, q_i may conservatively be taken equal to q_h, which was done in this example.

The distribution of the design wind pressures and loads along the height of the building is shown in Tables E6.2 and E6.3.

Lateral Analysis

A three-dimensional elastic analysis of the structure was performed under the lateral forces shown in Table E6.3 using the SAP 2000 computer program. In the model, rigid diaphragms were assigned at each level, and rigid-end offsets were defined at the ends of each member so that results were automatically obtained at the faces of each support. The mathematical model must consider cracked section properties.

The stiffnesses of members used in the analyses were as follows:

For columns and shear walls $I_{eff} = I_g$

For beams $I_{eff} = 0.5I_g$ (considering slab contribution)

P-delta effects were considered in the lateral analysis.

Results of Analysis

The maximum shear force and bending moment at the base of the shear wall were found to be 289 kips, and 18,711 ft-kips, respectively. Because of the location of the shear walls within the plan of the building, the wind-induced axial force in each shear wall is equal to zero.

EXAMPLE 6—(continued)

TABLE E6.1. COMPUTATION OF K_Z, K_h AND q_z FOR THE EXAMPLE BUILDING

Height, *z*, ft	K_z	K_{zt}	K_d	*V* mph	I_w	q_z psf
0	0.575	1	0.85	85	1	9.04
15	0.575	1	0.85	85	1	9.04
17.5	0.601	1	0.85	85	1	9.44
30	0.701	1	0.85	85	1	11.01
42.5	0.774	1	0.85	85	1	12.17
55	0.833	1	0.85	85	1	13.10
67.5	0.883	1	0.85	85	1	13.89
80	0.927	1	0.85	85	1	14.58
92.5	0.966	1	0.85	85	1	15.19
105	1.002	1	0.85	85	1	15.75
117.5	1.035	1	0.85	85	1	16.27
130	1.065	1	0.85	85	1	16.75
142.5	1.093	1	0.85	85	1	17.19
155	1.120	1	0.85	85	1	17.61
167.5	1.145	1	0.85	85	1	18.00
180	1.169	1	0.85	85	1	18.38
192.5	1.192	1	0.85	85	1	18.73
205	1.213	1	0.85	85	1	19.07
217.5	1.234	1	0.85	85	1	19.40
230	1.254	1	0.85	85	1	19.71
242.5	1.273	1	0.85	85	1	20.01
255	1.291	1	0.85	85	1	20.30
258	1.296	1	0.85	85	1	20.37

$\alpha = 7$
$z_t = 1200$
$K_h = 1.296$ i.e., K_z at height of 258 ft
$q_h = 20.37$ psf i.e., q_z at height of 258 ft

EXAMPLE 6—(continued)

TABLE E6.2. CALCULATION OF DESIGN WIND PRESSURE FOR THE EXAMPLE BUILDING

Location	Height	External Pressure				Internal Pressure			Combined Pressure	
	z ft	q_z psf	C_p	G_f	$q_zG_fC_p$ psf	q_i	GC_{pi}	q_iGC_{pi} psf (+)	$q_zG_fC_p + q_iGC_{pi}$ (psf)	$q_zG_fC_p - q_iGC_{pi}$ (psf)
Windward Side	0	9.04	0.8	0.876	6.33	20.37	0.55	11.20	17.53	-4.87
	15	9.04	0.8	0.876	6.33	20.37	0.55	11.20	17.53	-4.87
	17.5	9.44	0.8	0.876	6.62	20.37	0.55	11.20	17.82	-4.59
	30	11.01	0.8	0.876	7.72	20.37	0.55	11.20	18.92	-3.48
	42.5	12.17	0.8	0.876	8.53	20.37	0.55	11.20	19.73	-2.68
	55	13.10	0.8	0.876	9.18	20.37	0.55	11.20	20.38	-2.02
	67.5	13.89	0.8	0.876	9.73	20.37	0.55	11.20	20.93	-1.47
	80	14.58	0.8	0.876	10.22	20.37	0.55	11.20	21.42	-0.99
	92.5	15.19	0.8	0.876	10.65	20.37	0.55	11.20	21.85	-0.55
	105	15.75	0.8	0.876	11.04	20.37	0.55	11.20	22.24	-0.16
	117.5	16.27	0.8	0.876	11.40	20.37	0.55	11.20	22.60	0.20
	130	16.75	0.8	0.876	11.74	20.37	0.55	11.20	22.94	0.53
	142.5	17.19	0.8	0.876	12.05	20.37	0.55	11.20	23.25	0.84
	155	17.61	0.8	0.876	12.34	20.37	0.55	11.20	23.54	1.14
	167.5	18.00	0.8	0.876	12.62	20.37	0.55	11.20	23.82	1.41
	180	18.38	0.8	0.876	12.88	20.37	0.55	11.20	24.08	1.68
	192.5	18.73	0.8	0.876	13.13	20.37	0.55	11.20	24.33	1.93
	205	19.07	0.8	0.876	13.37	20.37	0.55	11.20	24.57	2.16
	217.5	19.40	0.8	0.876	13.59	20.37	0.55	11.20	24.80	2.39
	230	19.71	0.8	0.876	13.81	20.37	0.55	11.20	25.02	2.61
	242.5	20.01	0.8	0.876	14.02	20.37	0.55	11.20	25.23	2.82
	255	20.30	0.8	0.876	14.23	20.37	0.55	11.20	25.43	3.02
	258	20.37	0.8	0.876	14.27	20.37	0.55	11.20	25.48	3.07
Leeward	ALL	20.37	-0.5	0.876	-8.92	20.37	0.55	11.20	2.28	-20.12
Side Walls	ALL	20.37	-0.7	0.876	-12.49	20.37	0.55	11.20	-1.29	-23.69
Roof	ALL	20.37	-1.04	0.876	-18.56	20.37	0.55	11.20	-7.35	-29.76

Note that the internal pressures do not come into play in the overall design of the building. One can go from this table to Table E6.3 by using just the external pressures on the windward and leeward faces.

EXAMPLE 6—(continued)

TABLE E6.3. CALCULATION OF DESIGN WIND LOADS FOR LATERAL ANALYSIS

		Windward Face		Leeward Face		
Height z ft	Tributary Height ft	Design Wind Pressure psf	Design Wind Load plf	Design Wind Pressure psf	Design Wind Load plf	Combined Design Wind Load plf
0		17.53		2.28		
15		17.53		2.28		
17.5	15	17.82	267	2.28	34	**233**
30	12.5	18.92	237	2.28	29	**208**
42.5	12.5	19.73	247	2.28	29	**218**
55	12.5	20.38	255	2.28	29	**226**
67.5	12.5	20.93	262	2.28	29	**233**
80	12.5	21.42	268	2.28	29	**239**
92.5	12.5	21.85	273	2.28	29	**245**
105	12.5	22.24	278	2.28	29	**250**
117.5	12.5	22.60	283	2.28	29	**254**
130	12.5	22.94	287	2.28	29	**258**
142.5	12.5	23.25	291	2.28	29	**262**
155	12.5	23.54	294	2.28	29	**266**
167.5	12.5	23.82	298	2.28	29	**269**
180	12.5	24.08	301	2.28	29	**273**
192.5	12.5	24.33	304	2.28	29	**276**
205	12.5	24.57	307	2.28	29	**279**
217.5	12.5	24.80	310	2.28	29	**281**
230	12.5	25.02	313	2.28	29	**284**
242.5	12.5	25.23	315	2.28	29	**287**
255	9.25	25.43	235	2.28	21	**214**
258		25.48		2.28		

EXAMPLE 6—(continued)

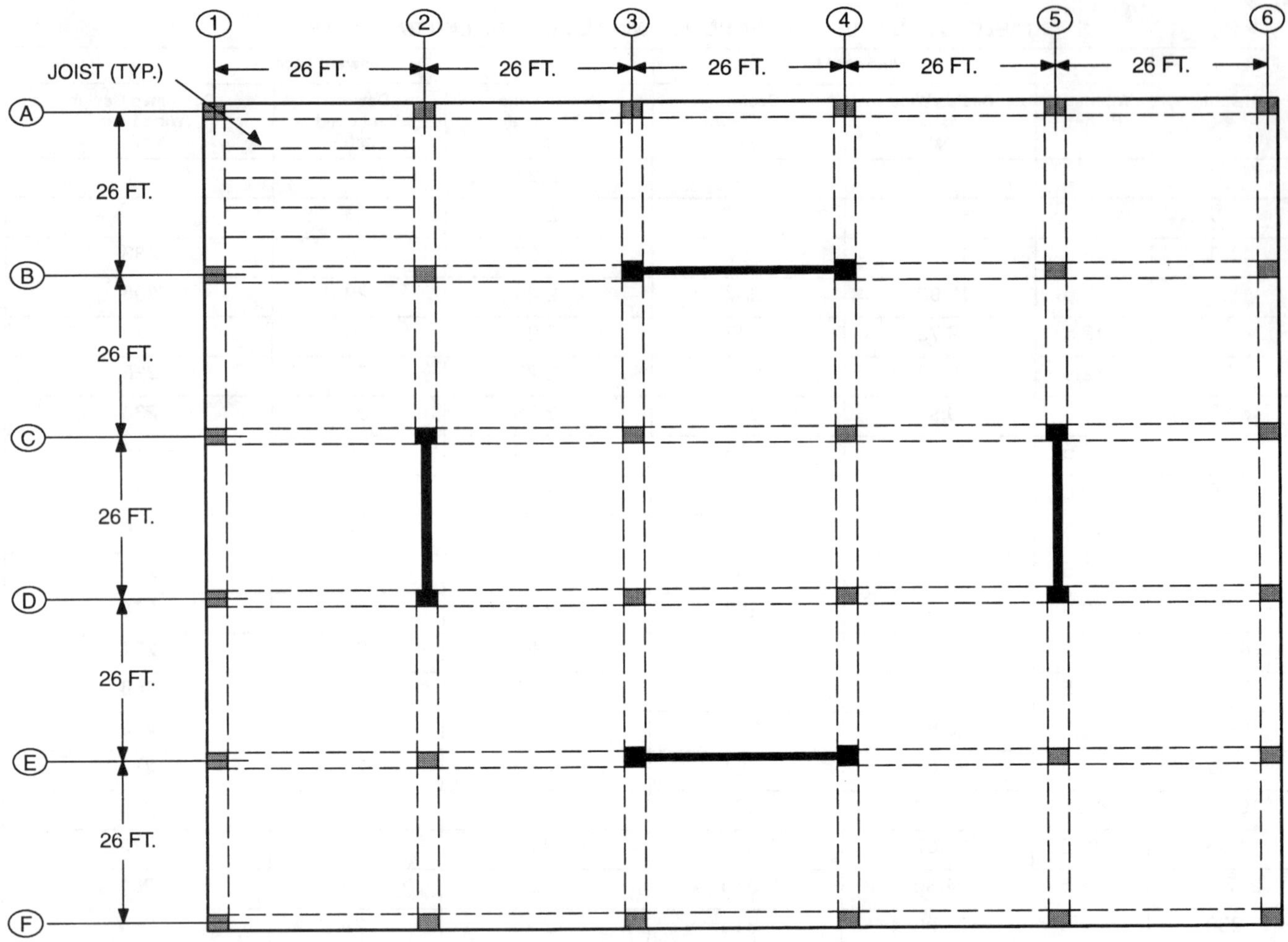

Figure E6.1. Plan of Example Building Considered

EXAMPLE 6—(continued)

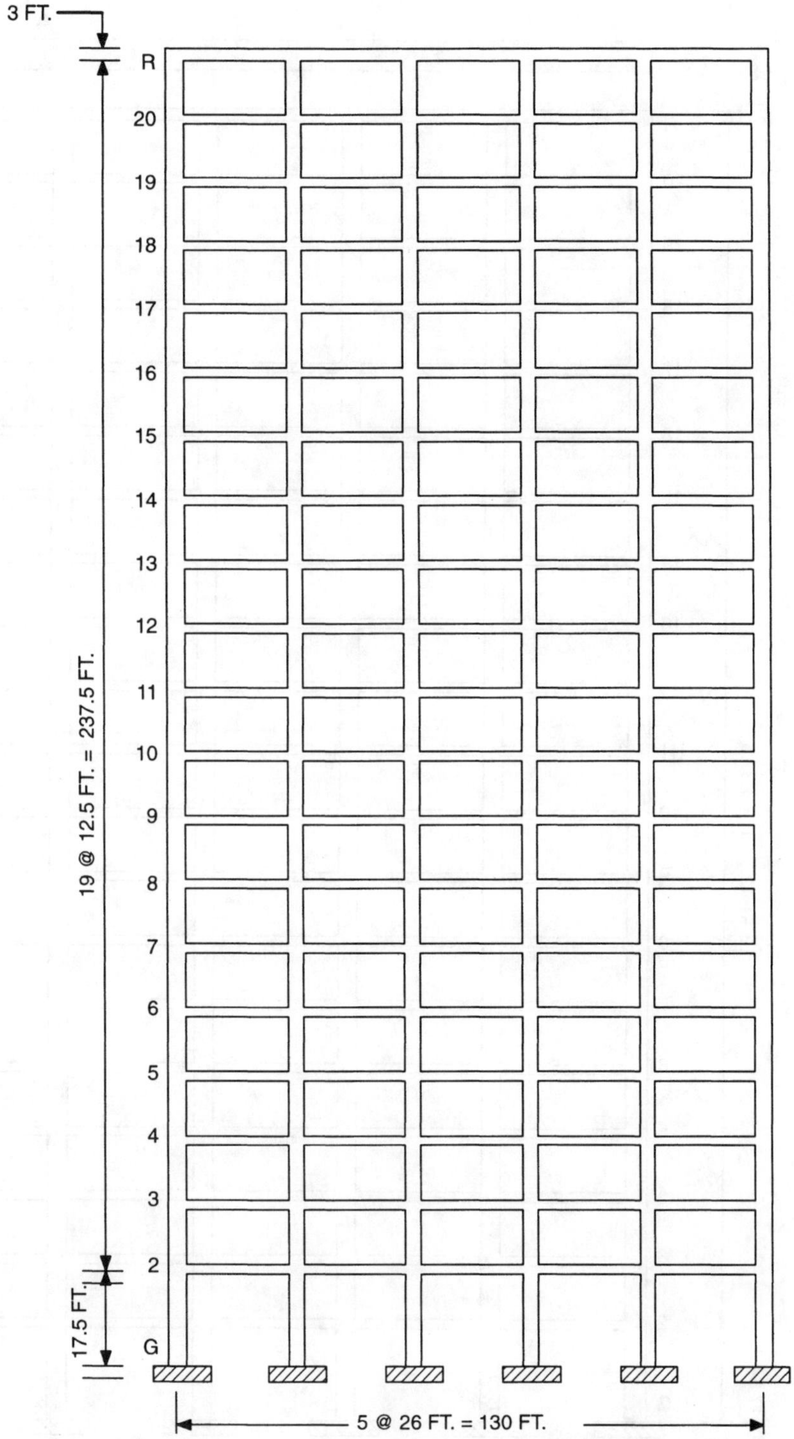

Figure E6.2. Elevation of Example Building Considered

EXAMPLE 6—(continued)

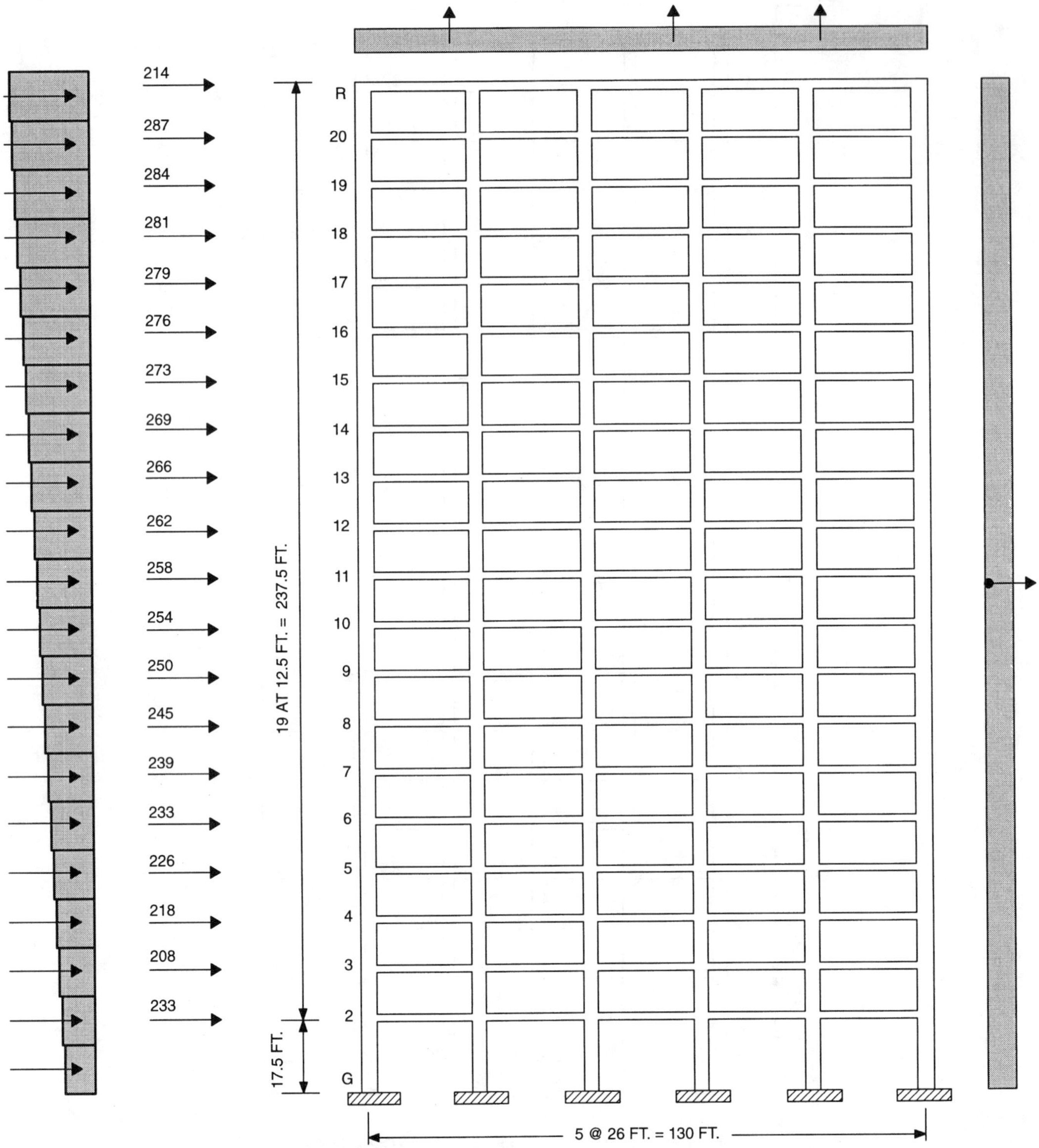

Figure E6.3: Lateral Forces on MWFRS for Wind Normal to the 258-foot-tall Face

EXAMPLE 7. CALCULATION OF WIND PRESSURES FOR A LOW-RISE BUILDING

General

This example illustrates the use of the new low-rise building provisions of IBC 2000 to determine design pressures for the MWFRS (Main Wind Force Resisting System). The building data are as follows:

Location:	Memphis, Tennessee
Terrain:	Flat farmland
Dimensions:	200 ft × 250 ft in plan (Fig. E7.1)
	Eave height of 20 ft
	Roof Slope 4:12 (18.4 degrees)
Framing:	Moment frame spans the 200-ft direction
	Moment frame spacing is 25 ft
	Cross bracing in 250-ft direction
	Openings uniformly distributed

Low-Rise Building

Per Sec. 1609.6, the simplified provisions for low-rise buildings are applicable (with few exceptions) to simple diaphragm buildings with flat, gabled and hipped roofs if the following condition is met:

"The mean roof height is equal to or less than the least horizontal dimension or 60 feet, whichever is less." This condition, in fact, is included in the definition of a simple diaphragm building.

The example building meets all the criteria given under the definition of a simple diaphragm building in Sec. 1609.2.

Also, the mean roof height	= 20 + 100 × 4/(12 × 2)	= 36.7 ft
Least horizontal dimension	= 200 ft > 60 ft	60 ft governs
Mean roof height, *h*	= 36.7 ft < 60 ft	Provisions of Sec. 1609.6 can be used.

Exposure, Building Classification and Basic Wind Speed

The building is in a flat farmland; therefore, use Exposure C (Sec. 1609.4)

Building Category is I, per definitions of Table 1604.5 — Wind importance factor $I_w = 1.0$

The basic wind speed can be taken as 90 mph (Fig. 1609).

Per Section 1609.6.2.1, "Structural members, cladding, fasteners, and systems providing for the structural integrity of the building shall be designed for the loads from Tables 1609.6.2.1(1), 1609.6.2.1(2) and 1609.6.2.1(3) using Figure 1609, multiplied by the appropriate height and exposure coefficient from Table 1609.6.2.1(4) and importance factor from Table 1604.5."

Main Wind Force Resisting System (MWFRS)

According to Section 1609.6.4, "All elements and connections of the MWFRS shall be designed for vertical and horizontal loads based on the combined leeward and windward wall pressures and roof pressures determined from Table 1609.6.2.1(1). Pressures shall be applied in accordance with the loading diagrams shown in Figure 1609.6(3) to the end zone and interior zone as shown in Figure 1609.6(1). The building shall be designed for all wind directions. For buildings having flat roofs, a ridge line normal to the wind direction shall be assumed at the mid-length dimension of the roof for all directions considered. Each corner shall be considered in turn as the windward corner."

Edge strip width:	≤	0.1 B= 0.1 × 200	= 20 ft		
	≤	0.4 × eave ht	= 0.4 × 20	= 8 ft	
	≥	0.04 B	= 0.04 × 200	= 8 ft	governs
	≥	3 ft			

End Zone: 2 times the edge strip width = 2 × 8 = 16 ft

Table E7.1 shows the detailed calculation of the wind pressures on different zones (surface locations). Figures E7.2 through E7.4 show the direction of wind pressure on different surface locations of the low-rise building.

REFERENCE:

E7.1. Mehta, K.C., and Marshall, R.D., *Guide to the Use of Wind Load Provisions of ASCE 7-95,* American Society of Civil Engineers, New York, N.Y., 1998.

EXAMPLE 7—(continued)

TABLE E7.1. CALCULATION OF WIND PRESSURE

Basic Wind Pressure

			HORIZONTAL LOADS				VERTICAL LOADS					
			End Zone		Interior Zone		End Zone		Interior Zone		Windward Overhang	
	Load Direction	Roof Angle	Wall	Roof	Wall	Roof	Windward Roof	Leeward Roof	Windward Roof	Leeward Roof	End Zone	Interior Zone
Table 1609A	Transverse	5	12.8	-6.7	8.5	-4	-15.4	-8.8	-10.7	-6.8	-21.6	-16.9
		20	17.8	-4.7	11.9	-2.6	-15.4	-10.7	-10.7	-8.1	-21.6	-16.9
Transverse*		18.4	17.3	-4.9	11.5	-2.7	-15.4	-10.5	-10.7	-8.0	-21.6	-16.9
Longitudinal		all	12.8	-6.7	8.5	-4	-15.4	-8.8	-10.7	-6 .8	-21.6	-16.9

Revised for Exposure and Height

Loading in Transverse Direction (Fig. E7.2)										
Wind Pressure	25.2	-7.2	16.8	-4.0	-22.5	-15.3	-15.6	-11.6	-31.5	-24.7
Building Surface Location	1E**	2E	1***	2	2E	3E	2	3	NA	NA

Loading in Longitudinal Direction (Fig. E7.3)										
Wind Pressure	18.7	-9.8	12.4	-5.8	-22.5	-12.8	-15.6	-9.9	-31.5	-24.7
Building Surface Location	1E**	NA	1***	NA	2E	3E	2	3	NA	NA

Modification factor for Height and Exposure = 1.46 [Table 1609.6.2.1 (4)]

Notes:
1. Pressures are applied in accordance with the loading diagrams shown in Fig. 1609.6(3), as shown in Fig. E7.4
2. The basic wind pressures are obtained from Table 1609.6.2.1(1) (for wind speed of 90 mph and roof angle of 18.4 degrees). The mean roof height and exposure for this table are assumed to be 30 ft and B, respectively. These wind pressures are modified for mean roof height of 36.7 ft and Exposure C, as shown.
3. Each corner should be considered in turn as the windward corner.
4. If roof pressure under horizontal loads is less than zero, use zero.

* Interpolated for appropriate roof angle.

** Includes 4E.

***Includes 4.

EXAMPLE 7—(continued)

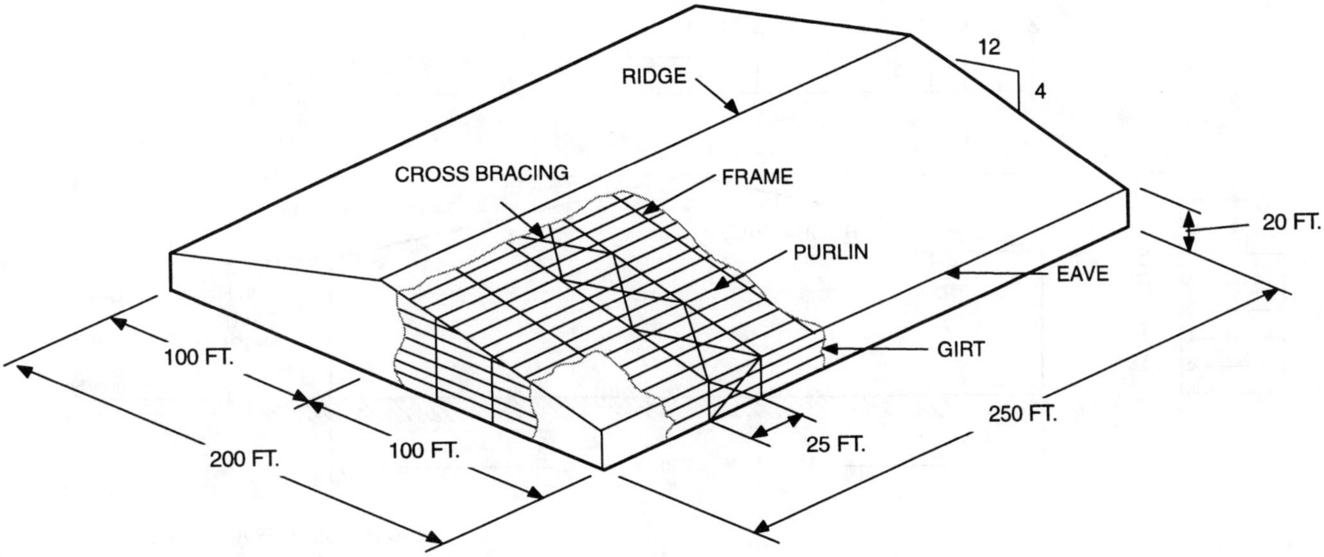

Figure E7.1. Dimensions and Framing of a Low-Rise Building

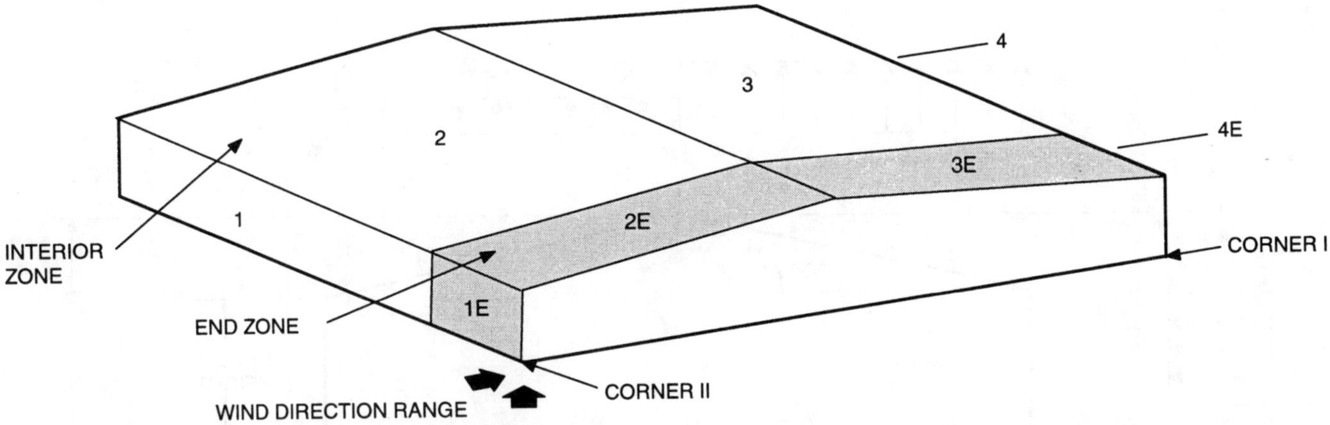

Figure E7.2. MWF Loading Diagram (Loading in Transverse Direction only)

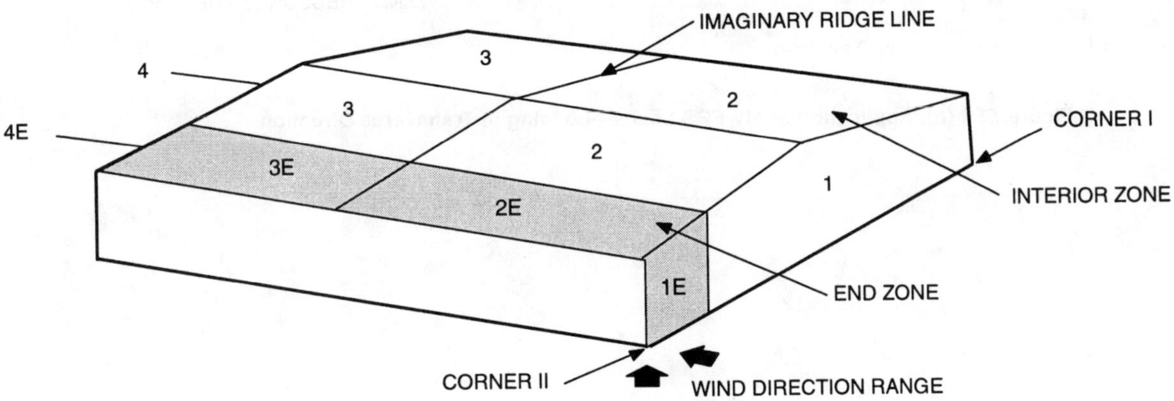

Figure E7.3. MWF Loading Diagram (Loading in Longitudinal Direction only)

EXAMPLE 7—(continued)

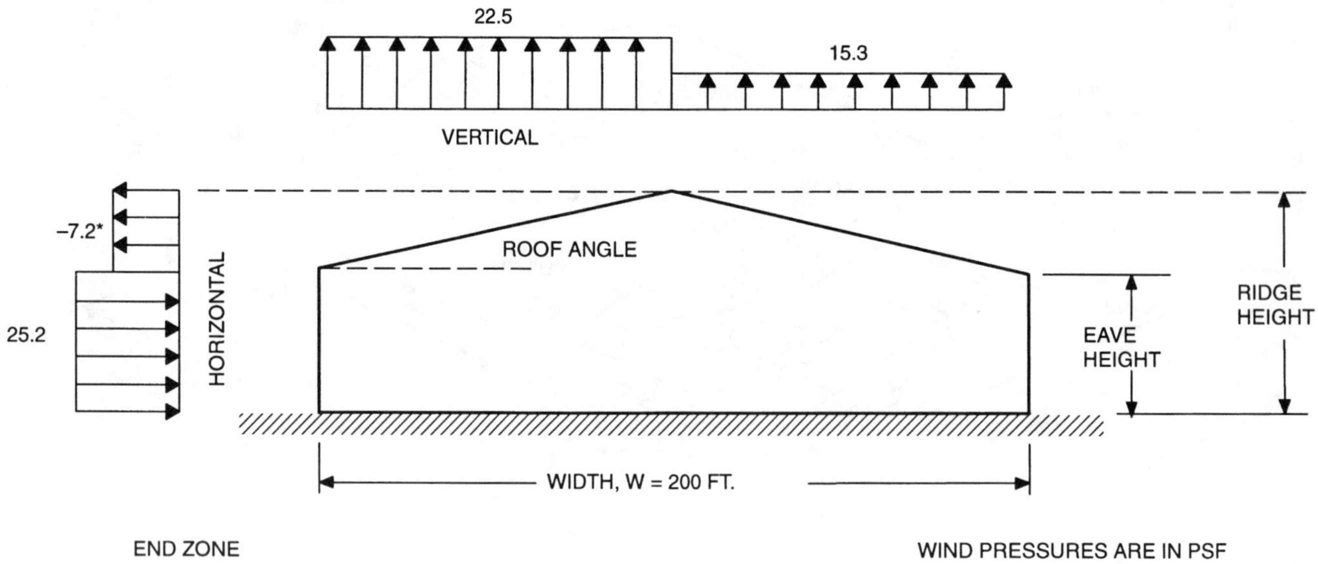

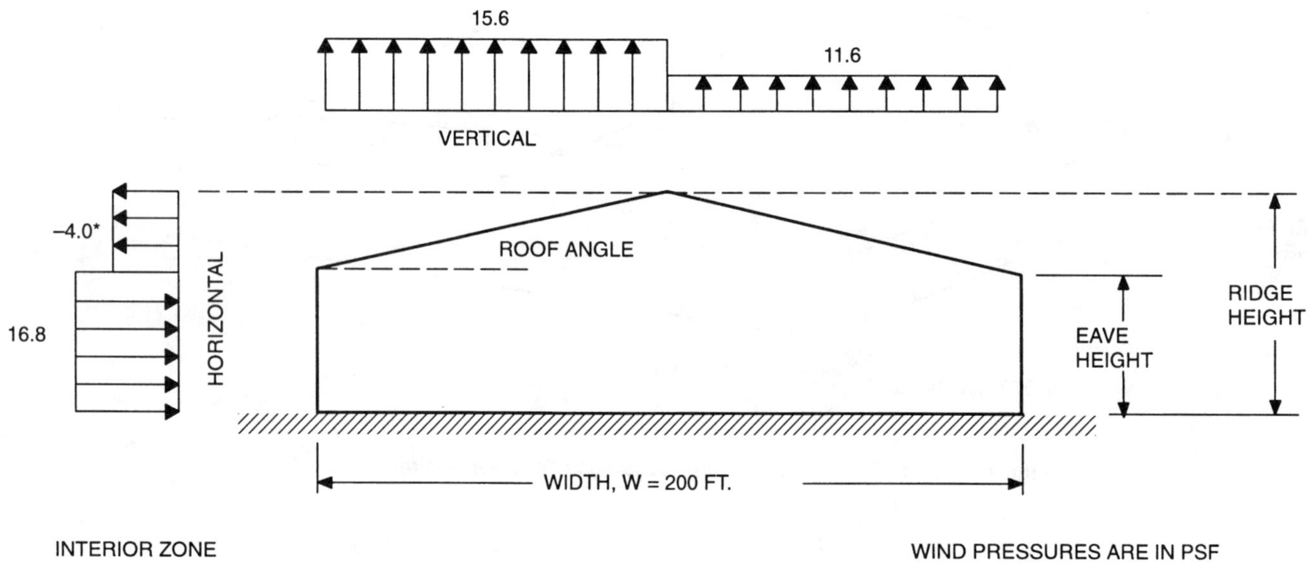

*Since wind presence is less than zero (0), use 0 for design.

Figure E7.4 (a). Application of MWFRS Loads—Loading in Transverse Direction

EXAMPLE 7—(continued)

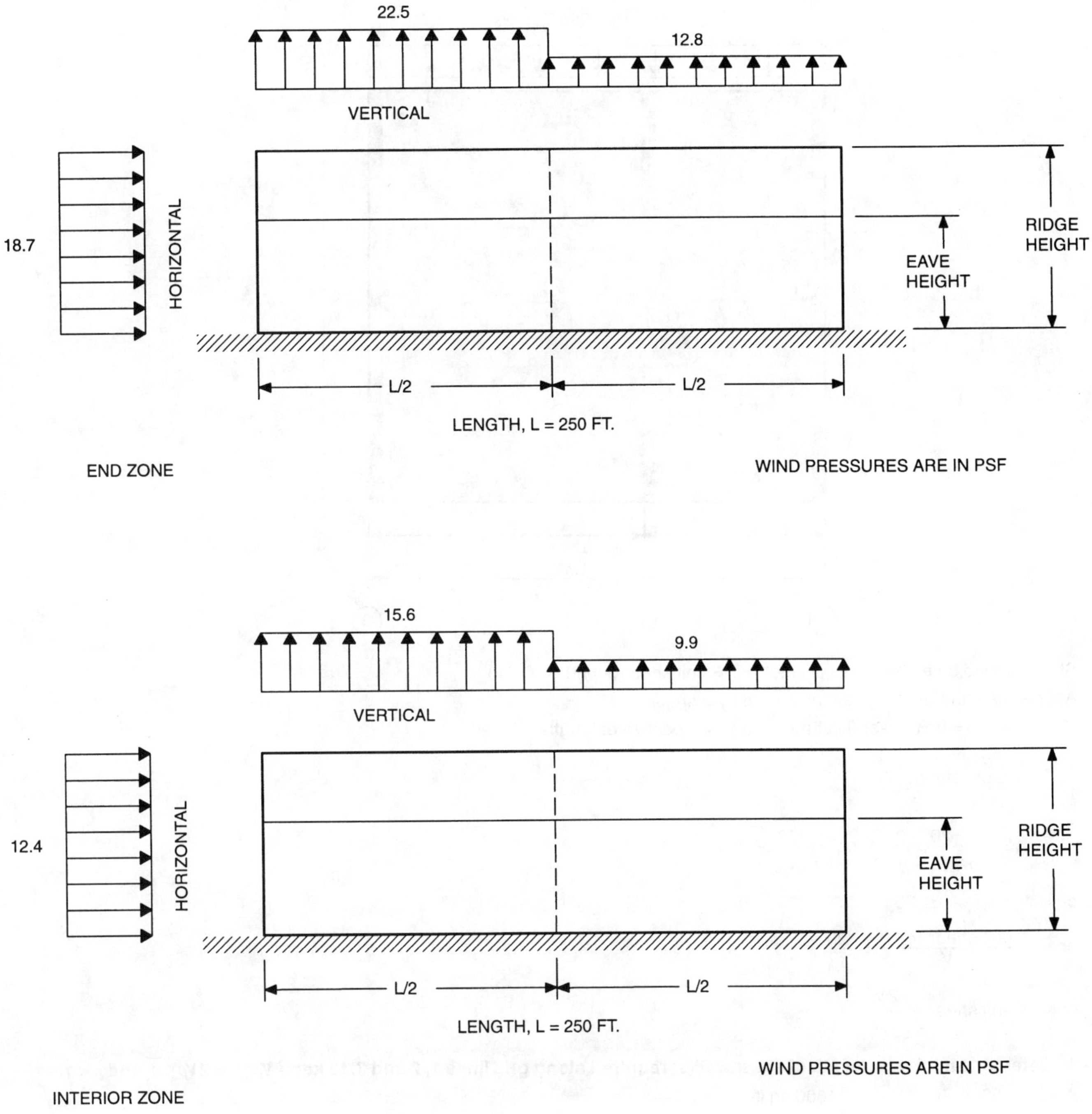

Figure E7.4 (b). Application of MWFRS Loads—Loading in Longitudinal Direction

EXAMPLE 8. REDUNDANCY (ρ) AND WOOD SHEAR WALLS

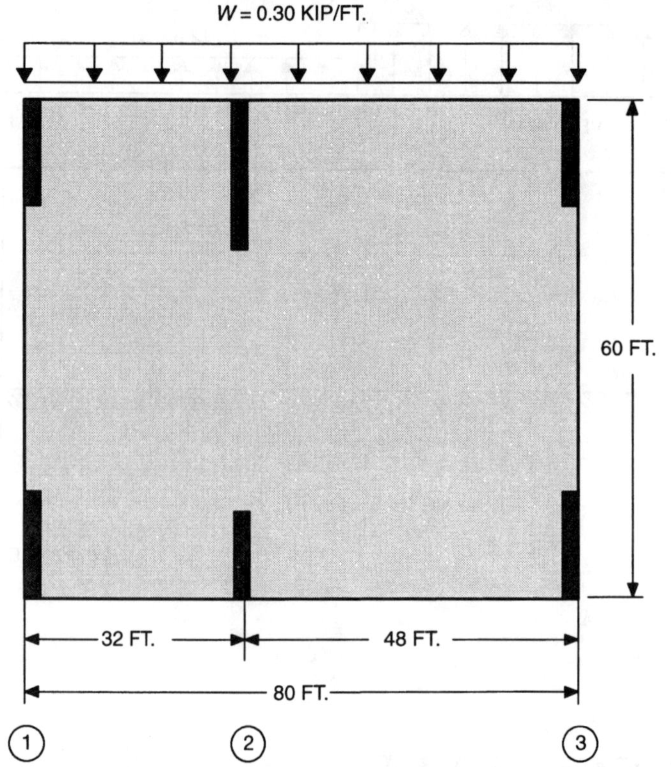

Shear carried by a shear wall of length ℓ_w = unit shear (kip/ft) × ℓ_w (ft)

After adjustment by $10/\ell_w$, shear carried by a shear wall

= unit shear (kip/ft) × 10 (ft), irrespective of length

$$r_{max_i} = \frac{\text{unit shear} \times 10}{\text{story shear, } V_i}$$

For $\rho_i < 1$

$$2 - \frac{20}{r_{max_i}\sqrt{A_i}} \leq 1 \text{ or, } \frac{20}{r_{max_i}\sqrt{A_i}} \geq 1$$

or $r_{max_i}\sqrt{A_i} \leq 20$

or $$\frac{\text{unit shear} \times 10}{V_i} \leq \frac{20}{\sqrt{A_i}}$$

or $$\text{unit shear} \leq \frac{2V_i}{\sqrt{A_i}}$$

1. Determine minimum length of shear wall(s) required along grid lines 1, 2 and 3, to keep $V_{max} < 2V_i/\sqrt{A_i}$ and $\rho < 1.0$

A_i = 60 × 80 = 4800 sq ft

V_i = 0.30 × 80 = 24.0 kips

V_{max} = $2(24)/\sqrt{4800}$ = 0.693 kip/ft

At grid 1

V_1 = 0.30 × 16 = 4.80 kips

ℓ_{min} = 4.80/0.693 = 6.9 ft

At least 6.9 ft of shear wall(s) required along grid line 1

At grid 2

V_2 = 0.30 × (16+24) = 12.0 kips

ℓ_{min} = 12.0/0.693 = 17.3 ft

At least 17.3 ft of shear wall(s) required along grid line 2

EXAMPLE 8—(continued)

At grid 3

$V_3 = 0.30 \times 24 = 7.20$ kips

$\ell_{min} = 7.20/0.693 = 10.4$ ft

At least 10.4 ft of shear wall(s) required along grid line 3

2. Check (ρ) for shear wall plan layout shown below

All walls have 0.693 kip/ft shear.

$V_{max} = 9.3 \times 0.693 = 6.45$ kips

$r_{max_i} = (V_{max}/V_i)(10/\ell_w) = (6.45/24.0)(10/9.3) = 0.289$

$\rho_i = 2 - 20/(0.289\sqrt{4800}) = 1.0$

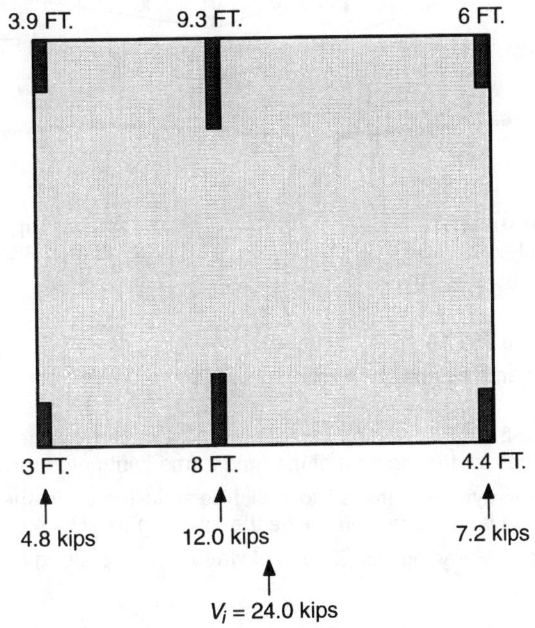

Note that the above example will change significantly if the $10/\ell_w < 1$ limitation is adopted.

EXAMPLE 9. REDUNDANCY, ρ, OF PRE-ENGINEERED FRAME BUILDING

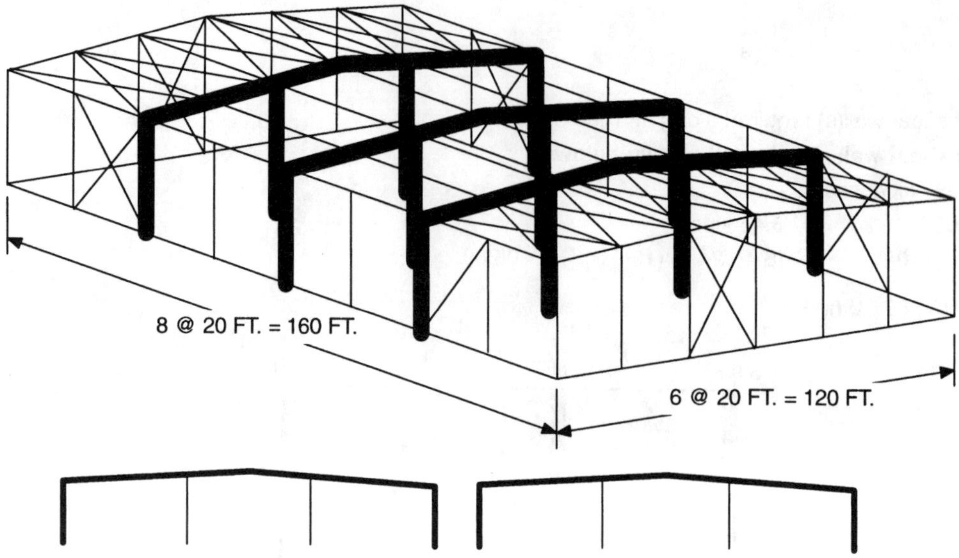

1. Determine structural system per Table 1617.6

The basic structural system is a "building frame system" consisting of ordinary moment-resisting frames (OMRF) and ordinary braced frames (X-bracing).

Laterally, building has three OMRFs on 40-ft centers with a braced frame (X-bracing) at each end. There is no roof diaphragm to redistribute any lateral forces. Two possibilities for the location of the rigid frame joints are indicated.

With the combination of different structural systems utilized to resist seismic forces in the same direction (OMRF: R = 4.0 and X-bracing: R = 5.0), R used for design in the lateral direction will be the lower value (R = 4.0). See Sec. 1617.6.

Longitudinally, building has two bays of roof X-bracing with 2 bays of wall X-bracing along each side (R = 5.0).

2. Determine building redundancy, ρ

Distribute lateral forces as for flexible diaphragm.

Lateral direction

Main frame with outer columns rigid

A_i = 160 × 120 = 19,200 sq ft

$\rho_i = 2 - 20 / r_{max_i} \sqrt{A_i}$

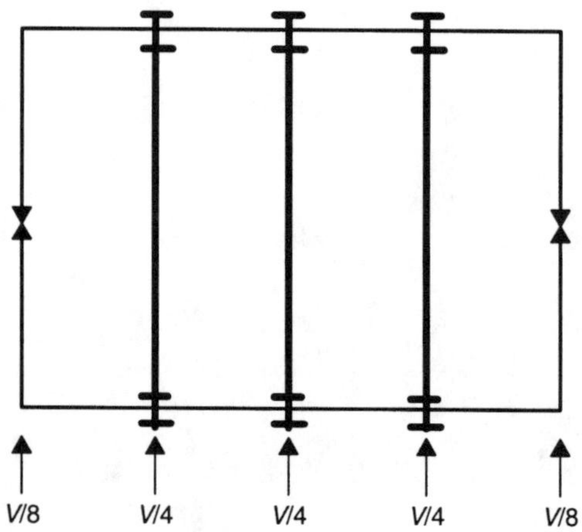

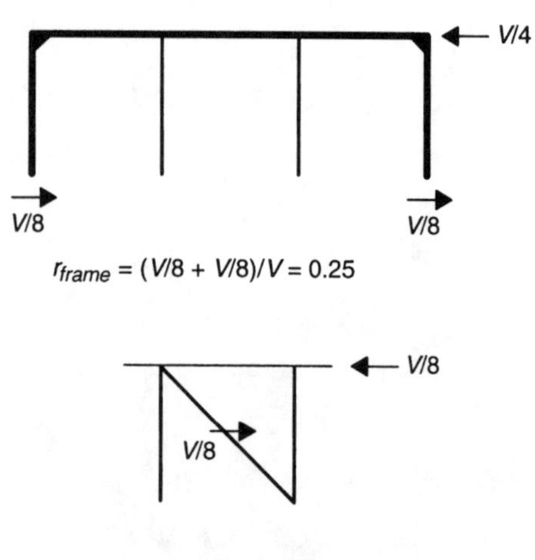

$r_{frame} = (V/8 + V/8)/V = 0.25$

$r_{brace} = (V/8)/V = 0.125$

EXAMPLE 9—(continued)

$r_{max_i} = 0.25$

$\rho = 2 - 20/0.25\sqrt{19,200} = 1.42$

Recalculate ρ for main frame with all columns rigid.

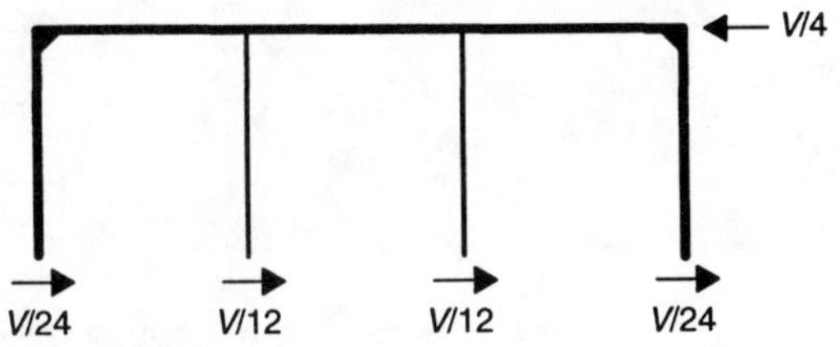

$r_{frame} = [V/24 + 0.7(V/12)]/V = 0.10$

$r_{frame} = [0.7(V/12 + V/12)]/V = 0.117$

$r_{brace} = 0.125$

$r_{max_i} = 0.125$

$\rho = 2 - 20/0.25\sqrt{19,200} = 0.845 < 1.0 \ldots$ Use $\rho = 1.0$

Longitudinal direction

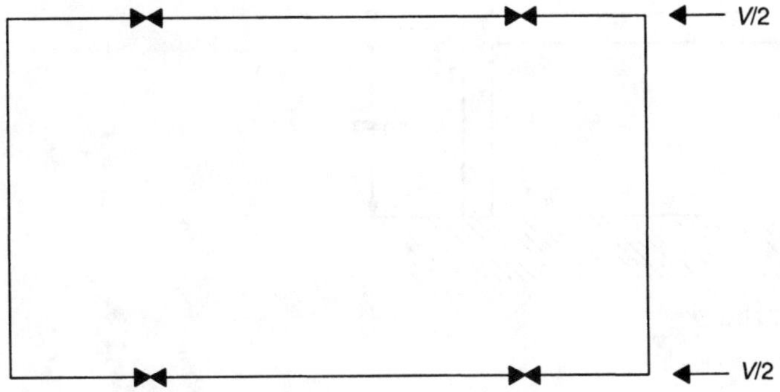

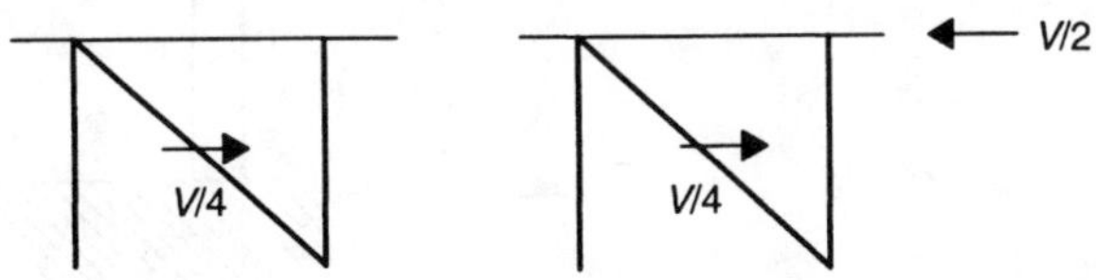

$r_{max_i} = (V/4)/V = 0.25$

$\rho = 2 - 20/0.25\sqrt{19,200} = 1.42$

Add one additional braced frame per side . . .

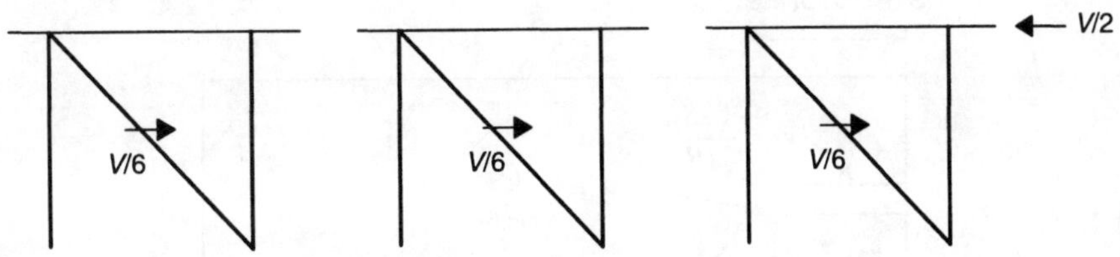

$r_{max_i} = (V/6)/V = 0.167$

$\rho = 2 - 20/0.167\sqrt{19,200} = 1.14$

EXAMPLE 10. SIMPLIFIED DESIGN PROCEDURE

A two-story reinforced concrete MRF building is considered for the example. The following parameters are assumed for the building:

Weight at each floor, w_x = 390 kips

Response modification factor, R = 8

Design spectral response acceleration at short periods, S_{DS} = 1.0

1. **Determine seismic base shear (Sec. 1617.5.1)**

The effective seismic weight, $W = 2 \times 390 = 780$ kips

$$V = \frac{1.2S_{DS}}{R} W$$

$$= 1.2 \times 1.0 \times 780 / 8 = 117 \text{ kips}$$

2. **Determine vertical distribution (Sec. 1617.5.2)**

$$F_x = \frac{1.2S_{DS}}{R} w_x$$

$$= 1.2 \times 1.0 \times 390 / 8 = 58.5 \text{ kips at each level}$$

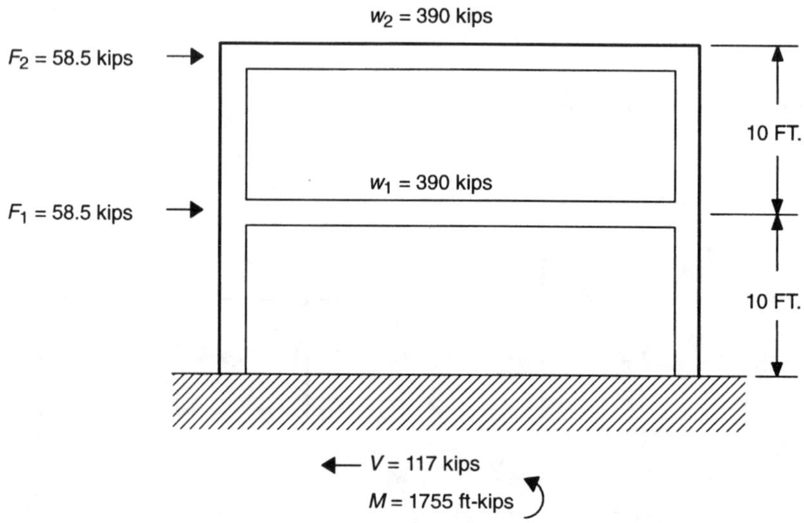

Distribution of Lateral Force by Simplified Method

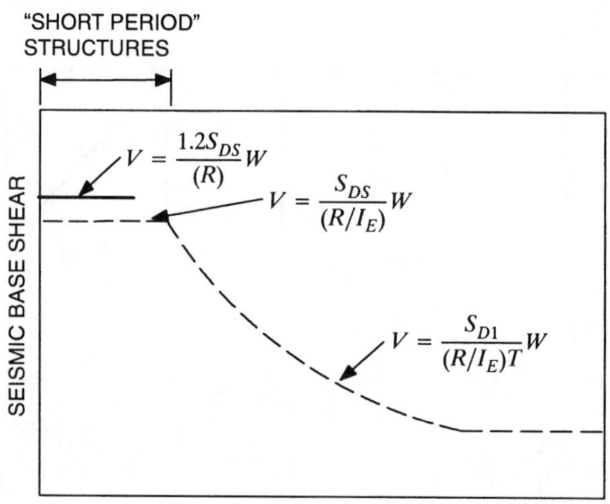

Simplified vs. Equivalent Lateral-Force Procedure

EXAMPLE 10—(continued)

3. For comparison with equivalent lateral-force procedure seismic base shear (Sec. 1617.4)

By the equivalent lateral-force procedure,

$$V = \frac{S_{DS}}{(R/I_e)} W$$

$$= 1.0 \times 1.0 \times 780 / 8 = 97.5 \text{ kips}$$

Vertical distribution (1617.4.3)

$$F_x = \frac{w_x h_x}{\sum_{1}^{2} w_i h_i} V$$

$$F_1 = \frac{390 \times 10}{390 \times 10 + 390 \times 20} \times 97.5 = 32.5 \text{ kips}$$

$$F_2 = \frac{390 \times 20}{390 \times 10 + 390 \times 20} \times 97.5 = 65.0 \text{ kips}$$

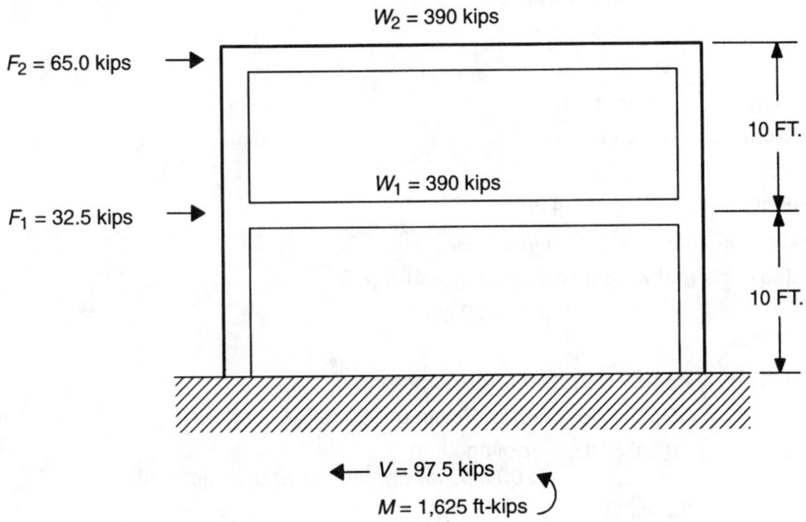

Distribution of Lateral Force by Equivalent Lateral-Force Procedure

EXAMPLE 11. DESIGN OF MULTISTORY REINFORCED CONCRETE BUILDING SUBJECTED TO EARTHQUAKE FORCES

General

A 20-story reinforced concrete building is designed following the requirements of the 2000 IBC. Design wind forces for the same building were calculated in Example 6. The building is located in Los Angeles (on Site Class D). The static lateral-force procedure is used as the basis of design.

The building is symmetrical about both principal plan axes. Along each axis a dual shear wall-frame interactive system is utilized for resistance to lateral forces.

A dual system is defined as a structural system with the following features (1617.6.1):

1. The moment frames must be capable of resisting at least 25 percent of the design forces.
2. The total seismic-force resistance is to be provided by the combination of the moment frames and the shear walls or braced frames in proportion to their stiffnesses.

Design Criteria

A typical plan and elevation of the building are shown in Figures E11.1 and E11.2, respectively. The member sizes for the structure are chosen as follows:

Spandrel beams (width = 34 in.)	34 × 24 in.
Interior beams	34 × 24 in.
Columns	34 × 34 in.
Shear walls:	
Grade to 9th floor	16 in. thick
10th floor to 16th floor	14 in. thick
17th floor to roof	12 in. thick
Shear wall boundary elements	34 × 34 in.

Material properties: Concrete (all members): $f_c' = 4000$ psi

All members are constructed of normal weight concrete ($w_c = 145$ pcf)

Reinforcement: $f_y = 60{,}000$ psi

Service loads:

Superimposed dead load (SDL):	20 psf – partition and equipment	
Live load (LL):	80 psf – per practice, minimum 50 psf	(Table 1607.1)
Loads on Roof:	10 psf SDL – roofing + 200 kips for penthouse and equipment	
	20 psf LL	(Section 1607.11.2.1)
Joists and Topping:	86 psf	
Cladding:	8 psf	

Seismic Design Data:

The maximum considered earthquake spectral response acceleration at short period, $S_S = 1.5$, and that at 1.0 sec period, $S_1 = 0.6$.

Assume standard occupancy or Seismic Use Group = *I*, which gives seismic importance factor, $I_E = 1.0$ (Table 1604.5)

Use default soil type = S_D

Site coefficient $F_a = 1.0$ (Table 1615.1.2 (1))

Site coefficient $F_v = 1.5$ (Table 1615.1.2 (2))

Adjusted $S_s = S_{MS} = F_a S_s = 1.0 \times 1.5 = 1.5$ (Eq. 16-16)

Adjusted $S_1 = S_{M1} = F_v S_1 = 1.5 \times 0.6 = 0.9$ (Eq. 16-17)

Design Spectral Response Acceleration Parameters (at 5% damping):

At short periods: $S_{DS} = 2/3\ S_{MS} = 2/3 \times 1.5 = 1.0$ (Eq. 16-18)

At 1.0 sec. period: $S_{D1} = 2/3\ S_{M1} = 2/3 \times 0.9 = 0.6$ (Eq. 16-19)

Dual system (RC shear walls with SMRF) indicates $R = 8$; $C_d = 6.5$ (Table 1617.6)

where: R and C_d are the response modification factor and the deflection amplification factor, respectively.

EXAMPLE 11—(continued)

Seismic Design Category: based on both S_{DS} (Table 1616.3-1) and S_{D1} (Table 1616.3-2), the seismic design category for the example building is D.

Design Basis

Calculation of the design base shear and distribution of that shear along the height of the building using the equivalent lateral-force procedure (which is used in a majority of designs) is not appropriate and is not allowed by the IBC for buildings exceeding 240 feet in height in SDC D (Table 1616.6.3, Item 3). However, only the equivalent lateral-force procedure (Section 1617.4) is illustrated here. These calculations are required even when design is based on dynamic analysis.

Weights at Each Floor Level

Table E11.1 shows the weights (self weight + SDL) at each floor level. The weights are calculated as follows:

Total weight of the building: $W = \sum_{i=1}^{20} W_i = 67{,}246$ kips

EQUIVALENT LATERAL-FORCE PROCEDURE (1617.4)

Design Base Shear (1617.4.1)

$$V = C_S W \quad \text{(Eq. 16-34)}$$

where:

$$C_S = \frac{S_{D1} I_E}{RT} \quad \text{(Eq. 16-35)}$$

$$\leq \frac{S_{DS} I_E}{R} \quad \text{(Eq. 16-36)}$$

$$\geq 0.44\, S_{DS} I_E \quad \text{(Eq. 16-37)}$$

$$\geq 0.5 \frac{S_1 I_E}{R} \quad \text{(Eq. 16-38) \{for SDC E and F only or where } S_1 > 0.6g\}$$

For the example building considered

S_{DS} = 1.0

S_{D1} = 0.6

S_1 = 0.6

R = 8

I_E = 1.0

Approximate fundamental period T (1617.4.2.1)

$$T = C_T (h_n)^{3/4} \quad \text{(Eq. 16-39)}$$

C_T = 0.02 for a dual system

h_n = total height = 255 feet

$T = 0.02 \times (255)^{3/4} = 1.28$ sec

$$\frac{S_{D1} I_E}{RT} W = \frac{0.6 \times 67{,}246}{8 \times 1.28} = 3940 \text{ kips} \ldots \text{governs}$$

$$\frac{S_{DS} I_E}{R} W = \frac{1.0 \times 67{,}246}{8} = 8406 \text{ kips}$$

$0.044\, S_{DS} I_E\, W = 0.044 \times 67{,}246 = 2959$ kips

Equation 16-38 is not applicable for the example building in SDC D

Use $V = 3940$ kips

Vertical Distribution of Base Shear (1617.4.3)

Distribute the base shear as follows:

$$F_x = C_{vx} V \quad \text{(Eq. 16-41)}$$

$$C_{vx} = \frac{w_x h_x}{\sum w_i h_i^k} \ (i = 1 \text{ to } 20) \quad \text{(Eq. 16-42)}$$

T = 1.28 sec.

$k = 1 + 0.5\,(T - 0.5) \leq 2 = 1.39$ (1617.4.3)

The distribution of the design base shear along the height of the building is shown in Table E11.1.

Lateral Analysis

Three-dimensional analysis of the structure was performed under the lateral forces shown in Table E11.1 using the SAP 2000 computer program. To account for accidental torsion, the mass at each level was assumed to be displaced from the center of mass by a distance equal to 5% of the building dimension perpendicular to the direction of force (1617.4.4.4). In the model, rigid diaphragms were assigned at each level, and rigid-end offsets were defined at the ends of each member so that results were automatically obtained at the faces of each support.

EXAMPLE 11—(continued)

The stiffnesses of members used in the analyses were as follows:

For columns and shear walls $I_{eff} = I_g$

For beams $I_{eff} = 0.5 I_g$ (considering slab contribution)

P-Δ effects were considered in the lateral analysis. It may be noted that this effect is allowed to be neglected in many situations as explained later (1617.4.6.2).

The lateral displacements of the example building, computed elastically under the distributed lateral forces of Table E11.1 are shown in Table E11.2.

Modification of Approximate Period

Often the use of period by the approximate method (1617.4.2.1) results in a conservative design. It is appropriate to use a more rational method for computation of period to reduce the design forces. However, the modified period must not exceed the approximate period by a factor (referred to as coefficient C_u) shown in Table 1617.4.2. The following expression is used for a rational method:

$$T = 2\pi \sqrt{(\Sigma w_i \delta_i^2 / g\Sigma F_i \delta_i)}$$

where: the values of F_i represent any lateral force distributed approximately; the elastic deflections, δ_i, must be calculated using the applied lateral forces, F_i.

Table E11.2 shows the F_i and corresponding δ_i based on approximate period. The modified period can be found as follows:

$$T = 2\pi \sqrt{(\Sigma w_i \delta_i^2 / g\Sigma F_i \delta_i)}$$

$$= 2\pi \sqrt{2,378,842/(386 \times 28,202)} \quad \text{(Table E11.2)}$$

$$= 2.94 \text{ sec}$$

$$\leq 1.2 \times T \text{ from Approximate Method (Table 1617.4.2 for } S_{D1} > 0.4)$$

$$\leq 1.2 \times 1.28 = 1.54 \text{ sec} \ldots \text{governs}$$

Revised Design Base Shear

Using the modified period of $T = 1.54$ sec., the design base shear is recalculated:

$$\frac{S_{D1} I_E}{RT} W = \frac{0.6 \times 67,246}{8 \times 1.54} = 3,284 \text{ kips} \ldots \text{governs}$$

$$\leq \frac{S_{DS} I_E}{R} W = \frac{1.0 \times 67,246}{8} = 8,406 \text{ kips}$$

$$\geq 0.044 S_{DS} I_E W = 0.044 \times 1.0 \times 67,246 = 2,959 \text{ kips}$$

Use $V = 3,284$ kips

Figure E11.3 shows the graphical representation of the above three expressions in nondimensionalized form.

Distribute the base shear as follows:

$$F_x = C_{vx} V \quad \text{(Eq. 16-41)}$$

$$C_{vx} = \frac{w_x h_x}{\Sigma w_i h_i^k} \; (i = 1 \text{ to } 20) \quad \text{(Eq. 16-42)}$$

$$T = 1.54 \text{ sec}$$

$$k = 1 + 0.5 (T - 0.5) \leq 2 = 1.52 \quad \text{(Sec. 1617.4.3)}$$

The distribution of the design base shear along the height of the building is shown in Table E11.3.

Results of Analysis

The maximum shear force and bending moment at the base of the shear wall were found to be 1571 kips and 118,596 ft-kips, respectively. Because of the location of the shear walls within the plan of the building, the earthquake-induced axial force in each shear wall is equal to zero.

The lateral displacement at every floor level (δ_{xe}) are shown in Table E11.4. The maximum inelastic response displacements (δ_x) and story drifts are computed and shown in Table E11.4.

δ_x is calculated per 1617.4.6.1:

$$\delta_x = \frac{C_d \delta_{xe}}{I_E} \quad \text{(Eq. 16-46)}$$

Story Drift Limitation

According to Section 1617.3, the calculated story drift, Δ, as shown in Table E11.4, shall not exceed 0.020 times the story height (Table 1617.3 for all other buildings under SUG I category).

EXAMPLE 11—(continued)

Floor	Maximum allowable drift	Largest drift: (Table E11.4)	
1st	0.02 × 17.5 ft = 4.2 inches	> 0.85 in.	O.K.
Others	0.02 × 12.5 ft = 3.0 inches	> 2.60 in.	O.K.

P-Δ Effects

According to 1617.4.6.2, P-Δ effects on story shears and moments, the resulting member forces and moments, and story drifts induced by these effects need not be considered when the stability coefficient, θ, as detemined by the following formula, is equal to or less than 0.1:

$$\theta = \frac{P_x \Delta}{V_x h_{sx} C_d} \qquad \text{(Eq. 16-47)}$$

where:
- P_x = the total unfactored vertical force
- Δ = the design story drift
- V_x = the seismic shear force acting between level x and x-1
- h_{sx} = the story height below level x
- C_d = the deflection amplification factor

In the lateral analysis performed using SAP 2000, the P-Δ effects were included. However, for illustration purposes, the stability coefficient is calculated as shown in Table E11.5. As the maximum stability coefficient θ (= 0.044) is less than 0.1, the P-Δ effect need not be considered.

Redundancy factor, ρ

$$1 \le \rho = 2 - \frac{20}{r_{max}\sqrt{A_i}} \le 1.5 \qquad \text{(Eq. 16-32)}$$

where:
- A_i = floor area of the diaphragm level immediately above the story, ft²

$$r_{max} = \frac{\text{maximum design shear in wall at base}}{\text{total design base shear}} \times 10/l_w$$

$$= \frac{1571}{3284} \times \frac{10}{28.83} = 0.166$$

$$A_i = 132.83 \times 132.83 \text{ ft}^2$$

$$\rho = 2 - \frac{20}{0.166 \times 132.83^2} = 1.09$$

For dual systems, the value of ρ need not exceed 80 percent of the value calculated above (1617.2.2).

80% of above = 0.8 × 1.09 = 0.87 < 1

Use ρ = 1

EXAMPLE 11—(continued)

Table E11.1. Lateral Forces by Equivalent Lateral-Force Procedure Using Approximate Period

V = 3940 kips, T = 1.28 sec. k = 1.390					
Floor Level x	Weight w_x, kips	Height h_x, ft	$w_x h_x^k$, ft-kips	Lateral Force F_x, kips	Story Shear V_x, kips
1	2	3	4	5	6
21	2987	255.0	6,611,897	392	392
20	3338	242.5	6,890,261	409	801
19	3338	230.0	6,401,592	380	1181
18	3338	217.5	5,923,177	351	1532
17	3352	205.0	5,478,250	325	1857
16	3366	192.5	5,040,491	299	2157
15	3366	180.0	4,591,376	272	2429
14	3366	167.5	4,154,270	246	2675
13	3366	155.0	3,729,711	221	2897
12	3366	142.5	3,318,309	197	3094
11	3366	130.0	2,920,757	173	3267
10	3380	117.5	2,548,410	151	3418
9	3394	105.0	2,188,593	130	3548
8	3394	92.5	1,835,054	109	3657
7	3394	80.0	1,499,709	89	3746
6	3394	67.5	1,184,252	70	3816
5	3394	55.0	890,873	53	3869
4	3394	42.5	622,547	37	3906
3	3394	30.0	383,628	23	3929
2	3559	17.5	190,174	11	3940
Σ	67,246	Σ	66,403,331	3940	

EXAMPLE 11—(continued)

Table E11.2. Calculation of Period by Rational Method (Equivalent Lateral Procedure)

Floor Level x	Weight w_x, kips	Lateral Force F_x, kips	Displacement δ_x, in	$w_x\delta_x^2$,kip-in^2	$F_x\delta_x$, kip-in.
1	2	3	4	5	6
21	2987	392	10.20	310,601	4001
20	3338	409	9.75	317,097	3985
19	3338	380	9.27	286,794	3521
18	3338	351	8.77	256,932	3083
17	3352	325	8.26	228,441	2683
16	3366	299	7.72	200,388	2308
15	3366	272	7.16	172,326	1949
14	3366	246	6.58	145,520	1621
13	3366	221	5.98	120,307	1323
12	3366	197	5.37	97,028	1057
11	3366	173	4.75	75,993	823
10	3380	151	4.13	57,715	625
9	3394	130	3.52	42,055	457
8	3394	109	2.92	28,955	318
7	3394	89	2.34	18,636	209
6	3394	70	1.80	10,969	126
5	3394	53	1.30	5701	69
4	3394	37	0.85	2462	31
3	3394	23	0.48	782	11
2	3559	11	0.20	140	2
Σ	67,246		Σ	2,378,842	28,202

EXAMPLE 11—(continued)

Table E11.3. Lateral Forces by Equivalent Lateral-Force Procedure Using Period from Rational Analysis

V = 3284 kips, T = 1.54 (sec.) k = 1.52					
Floor Level x	Weight w_x, kips	Height h_x, ft	$w_x h_x^k$, ft-kips	Lateral Force F_x, kips	Story Shear V_x, kips
1	2	3	4	5	6
21	2987	255.0	13,438,884	344	344
20	3338	242.5	13,914,857	356	700
19	3338	230.0	12,840,714	328	1028
18	3338	217.5	11,796,400	302	1330
17	3352	205.0	10,827,953	277	1607
16	3366	192.5	9,882,799	253	1859
15	3366	180.0	8,925,196	228	2088
14	3366	167.5	8,001,448	205	2292
13	3366	155.0	7,112,751	182	2474
12	3366	142.5	6,260,443	160	2634
11	3366	130.0	5,446,031	139	2774
10	3380	117.5	4,690,662	120	2894
9	3394	105.0	3,970,793	102	2995
8	3394	92.5	3,275,782	84	3079
7	3394	80.0	2,627,861	67	3146
6	3394	67.5	2,030,462	52	3198
5	3394	55.0	1,487,930	38	3236
4	3394	42.5	1,006,019	26	3262
3	3394	30.0	592,901	15	3277
2	3559	17.5	274,321	7	3284
Σ	67,246	Σ	128,404,210	3284	

EXAMPLE 11—(continued)

Table E11.4. Lateral Displacements and Drifts of Example Building by Equivalent Lateral-Force Procedure (in.) (along outer frame line F)

Floor Level	δ_{xe}	C_d	δ_x	Drift
1	2	3	4	5
21	6.47	6.50	42.06	1.76
20	6.20	6.50	40.30	1.89
19	5.91	6.50	38.42	1.95
18	5.61	6.50	36.47	2.15
17	5.28	6.50	34.32	2.21
16	4.94	6.50	32.11	2.28
15	4.59	6.50	29.84	2.41
14	4.22	6.50	27.43	2.47
13	3.84	6.50	24.96	2.54
12	3.45	6.50	22.43	2.60
11	3.05	6.50	19.83	2.60
10	2.65	6.50	17.23	2.60
9	2.25	6.50	14.63	2.47
8	1.87	6.50	12.16	2.41
7	1.50	6.50	9.75	2.28
6	1.15	6.50	7.48	2.15
5	0.82	6.50	5.33	1.82
4	0.54	6.50	3.51	1.56
3	0.30	6.50	1.95	1.11
2	0.13	6.50	0.85	0.85
1	0.00	0.00	0.00	0.00

Table E11.5. Calculation of Stability Coefficient

Story Level	*DL* psf	*LL* psf	Area sq ft	P_x kips	V_x kips	h_{sx} ft	Drift, Δ in.	θ
1	2	3	4	5	6	7	8	9
21	177	12	16,900	3194	344	12.5	1.76	0.017
20	198	32	33,800	7774	700	12.5	1.89	0.021
19	198	32	50,700	11,661	1028	12.5	1.95	0.023
18	198	32	67,600	15,548	1330	12.5	2.15	0.026
17	198	32	84,500	19,435	1607	12.5	2.21	0.027
16	199	32	101,400	23,423	1859	12.5	2.28	0.029
15	199	32	118,300	27,327	2088	12.5	2.41	0.032
14	199	32	135,200	31,231	2292	12.5	2.47	0.035
13	199	32	152,100	35,135	2474	12.5	2.54	0.037
12	199	32	169,000	39,039	2634	12.5	2.60	0.040
11	199	32	185,900	42,943	2774	12.5	2.60	0.041
10	200	32	202,800	47,050	2894	12.5	2.60	0.043
9	201	32	219,700	51,190	2995	12.5	2.47	0.043
8	201	32	236,600	55,128	3079	12.5	2.41	0.044
7	201	32	253,500	59,066	3146	12.5	2.28	0.044
6	201	32	270,400	63,003	3198	12.5	2.15	0.043
5	201	32	287,300	66,941	3236	12.5	1.82	0.039
4	201	32	304,200	70,879	3262	12.5	1.56	0.035
3	201	32	321,100	74,816	3277	12.5	1.11	0.026
2	210	32	354,900	85,886	3284	17.5	0.85	0.016

EXAMPLE 11—(continued)

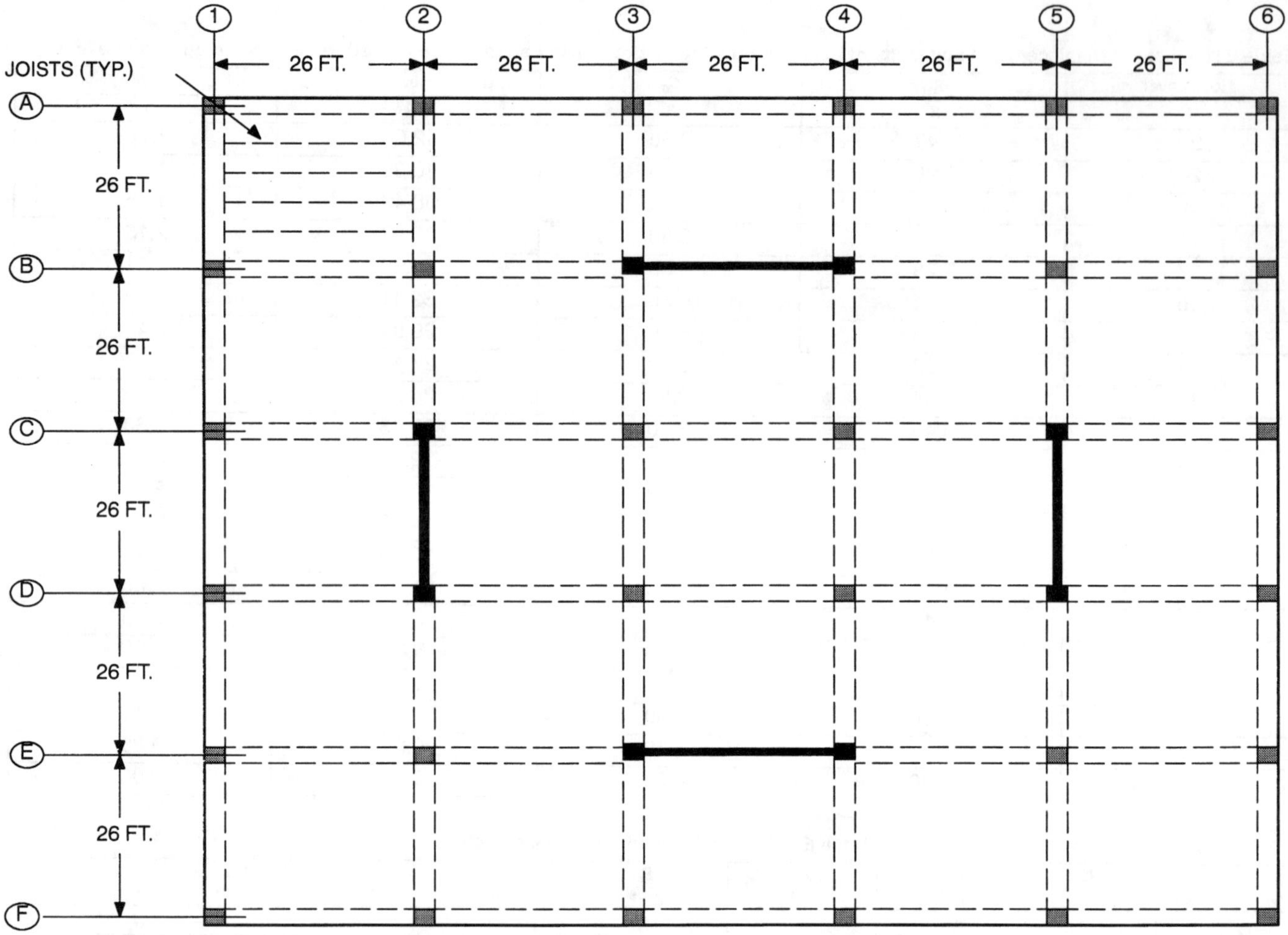

Figure E11.1. Plan of Example Office Building

EXAMPLE 11—(continued)

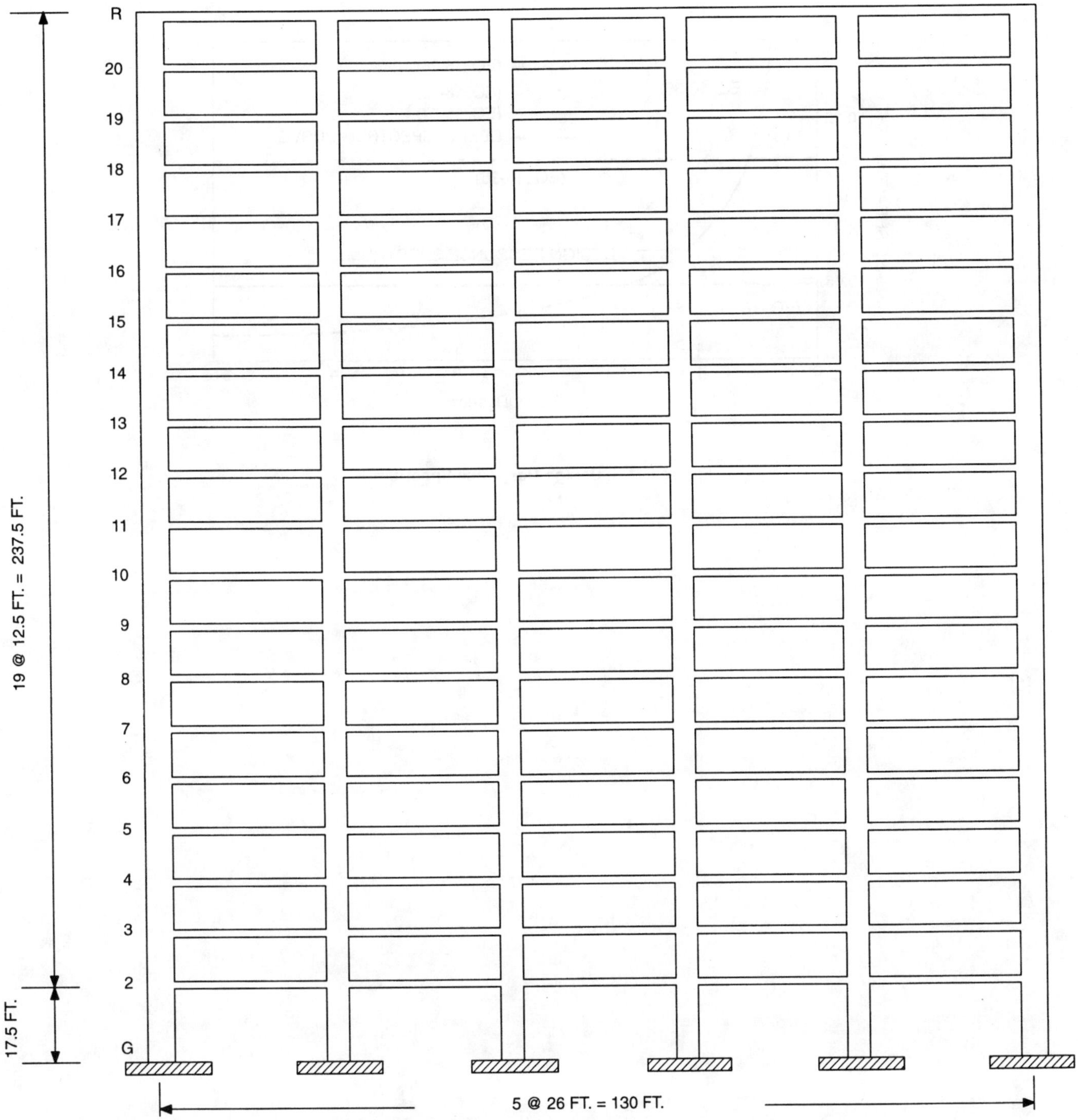

Figure E11.2. Elevation of Example Office Building

EXAMPLE 11—(continued)

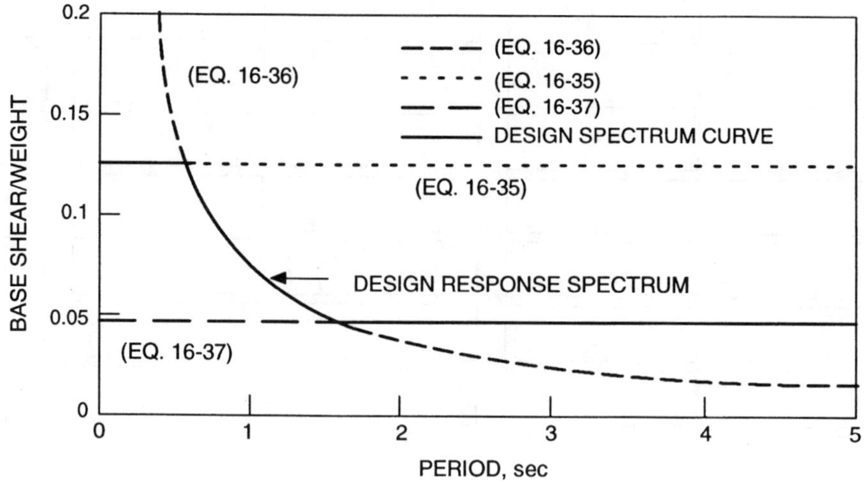

Figure E11.3. Design Response Spectrum

EXAMPLE 12. DYNAMIC ANALYSIS PROCEDURE (RESPONSE SPECTRUM ANALYSIS)

General

A three-story reinforced concrete building is designed following the requirements of the 2000 IBC. The building is located in Los Angeles (on Site Class D). The dynamic analysis procedure is used as the basis of design.

Design Criteria

A typical elevation of the building is shown below. The member sizes for the structure are chosen as follows:

Beams 16.67 × 12 in.

Columns 16.67 × 16.67 in.

Material properties:

Concrete (all members): $f'_c = 4{,}000$ psi

All members are constructed of normal weight concrete ($w_c = 145$ pcf)

Reinforcement: $f_y = 60{,}000$ psi

Service Loads:

Assumed floor load = 390 kips/floor

Total weight W = 390 × 3 = 1170 kips

Seismic Design Data:

The maximum considered earthquake spectral response acceleration at short period, $S_S = 1.5$, and that at 1-sec period, $S_1 = 0.6$.

Assume standard occupancy or Seismic Use Group = I and seismic importance factor, $I_E = 1.0$ (Table 1604.5)

Use default soil type $= S_D$

Site coefficient $F_a = 1.0$ [Table 1615.1.2 (1)]

Site coefficient $F_v = 1.5$ [Table 1615.1.2 (2)]

Adjusted S_s $= S_{MS} = F_a S_s$ (Eq. 16-16)

$= 1.0 \times 1.5 = 1.5$

Adjusted S_1 $= S_{M1} = F_v S_1$ (Eq. 16-17)

$= 1.5 \times 0.6 = 0.9$

Design Spectral Response Acceleration Parameters (at 5% damping):

At short periods: $S_{DS} = 2/3\ S_{MS}$ (Eq. 16-18)

$= 2/3 \times 1.5 = 1.0$

At 1 sec. period: $S_{D1} = 2/3\ S_{M1}$ (Eq. 16-19)

$= 2/3 \times 0.9 = 0.6$

SMRF system gives $R = 8$; $C_d = 6.5$ (Table 1617.6)

where: R and C_d are the response modification factor and the deflection amplification factor, respectively.

Seismic Design Category: based on both S_{DS} [Table 1616.3 (1)] and S_{D1} [Table 1616.3 (2)], the seismic design category for the example building is *D*.

Design Basis

Calculation of the design base shear and distribution of that shear along the height of the building using the equivalent lateral-force procedure (which is used in a majority of designs) is not appropriate and is not allowed by the *International Building Code* for buildings exceeding 240 feet in height in SDC D (Table 1616.6.3 Item 3). In these cases, the dynamic lateral-force procedure (Section 1617.4) must be used. For this example, the equivalent lateral-force procedure used as the height of the building is 30 ft in SDC D (less than 240 ft). However, for illustration purposes, the dynamic analysis procedure (Section 1618) has been used.

EXAMPLE 12—(continued)

- **Given:**

h_s = 10 feet
w = 390 kips/floor
E = 4,000 ksi
I_{col} = 4,500 inches^4 each column (taken equal to 0.7 I_g)

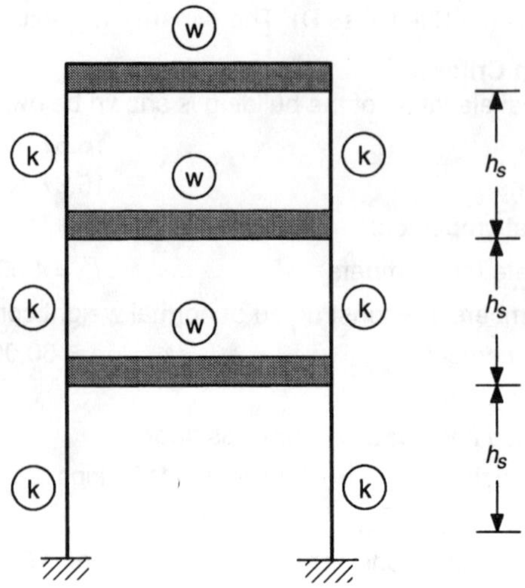

- **Determine mass matrix**

$m = w/g = 390/386.4$
$= 1.0$ kip-sec^2/in.

$$[m] = \begin{bmatrix} 1 & 0 & 0 \\ 0 & 1 & 0 \\ 0 & 0 & 1 \end{bmatrix}$$

- **Determine stiffness matrix**

$12EI/h_s^3 = 12 \times 4000 \times 9000/(12 \times 10)^3 = 250$ kips/in

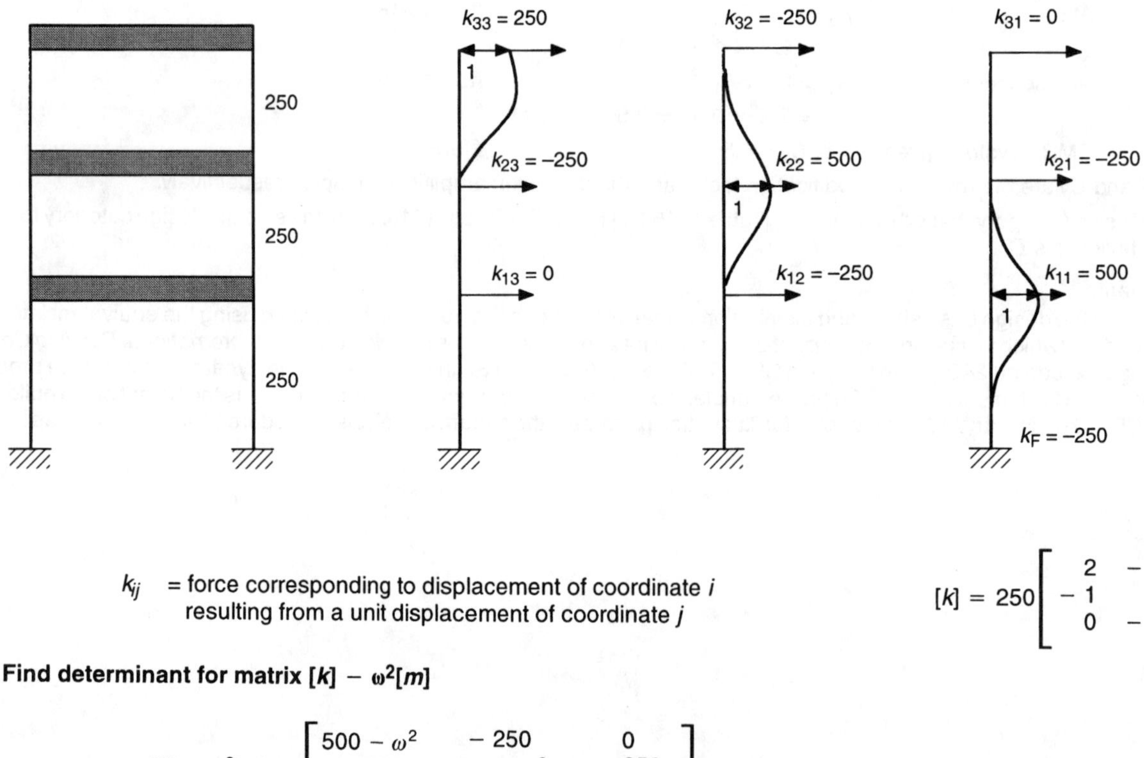

k_{ij} = force corresponding to displacement of coordinate i resulting from a unit displacement of coordinate j

$$[k] = 250 \begin{bmatrix} 2 & -1 & 0 \\ -1 & 2 & -1 \\ 0 & -1 & 1 \end{bmatrix}$$

- **Find determinant for matrix $[k] - \omega^2[m]$**

$$[k] - \omega^2[m] = \begin{bmatrix} 500 - \omega^2 & -250 & 0 \\ -250 & 500 - \omega^2 & -250 \\ 0 & -250 & 250 - \omega^2 \end{bmatrix}$$

EXAMPLE 12—(continued)

Setting the determinant of the above matrix equal to zero yields the following frequencies:

ω_1 = 7.036 radians/sec

ω_2 = 19.685 radians/sec

ω_3 = 28.491 radians/sec

The period is equal to $2\pi/\omega$:

T_1 = 0.893 sec

T_2 = 0.319 sec

T_3 = 0.221 sec

- **Find modal shapes**

First mode:

$$\begin{bmatrix} 500-(7.036)^2 & -250 & 0 \\ -250 & 500-(7.036)^2 & -250 \\ 0 & -250 & 250-(7.036)^2 \end{bmatrix} \begin{bmatrix} \phi_{31} \\ \phi_{21} \\ \phi_{11} \end{bmatrix} = \begin{bmatrix} 0 \\ 0 \\ 0 \end{bmatrix}$$

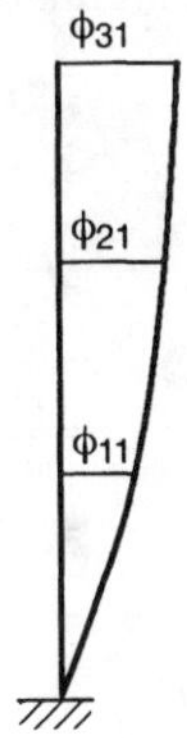

$\phi_{31} = 1.0, \quad \phi_{21} = 0.802, \quad \phi_{11} = 0.445$

Second mode:

$$\begin{bmatrix} 500-(19.685)^2 & -250 & 0 \\ -250 & 500-(19.685)^2 & -250 \\ 0 & -250 & 250-(19.685)^2 \end{bmatrix} \begin{bmatrix} \phi_{32} \\ \phi_{22} \\ \phi_{12} \end{bmatrix} = \begin{bmatrix} 0 \\ 0 \\ 0 \end{bmatrix}$$

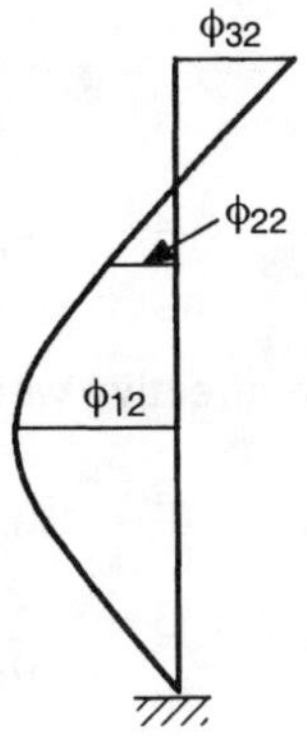

$\phi_{32} = 1.0, \quad \phi_{22} = -0.55, \quad \phi_{12} = -1.22$

Third mode:

$$\begin{bmatrix} 500-(28.491)^2 & -250 & 0 \\ -250 & 500-(28.491)^2 & -250 \\ 0 & -250 & 250-(28.491)^2 \end{bmatrix} \begin{bmatrix} \phi_{33} \\ \phi_{23} \\ \phi_{13} \end{bmatrix} = \begin{bmatrix} 0 \\ 0 \\ 0 \end{bmatrix}$$

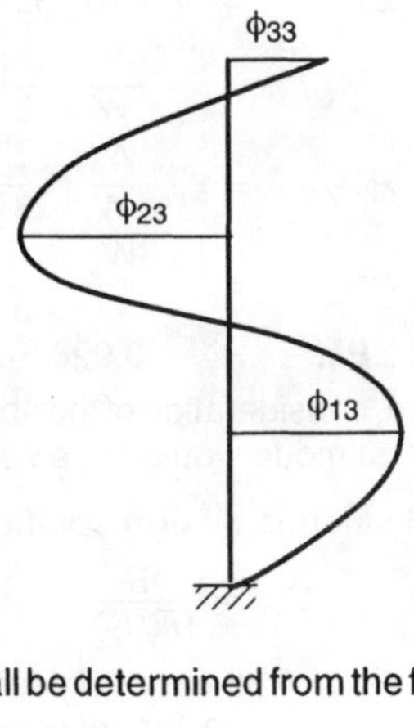

$\phi_{33} = 1.0, \quad \phi_{23} = -2.25, \quad \phi_{13} = 1.802$

According to Section 1618.4, the portion of base shear contributed by the mth mode, V_m, shall be determined from the following formulas:

$V_m = C_{sm}\overline{W}_m$ (Eq. 16-51)

$\overline{W}_m = L_m^2/M_m$ (Eq. 16-52)

EXAMPLE 12—(continued)

$$L_m = \sum_{i=1}^{n} w_i \phi_{im}$$

$$M_m = \sum_{i=1}^{n} w_i \phi_{im}^2$$

where: C_{sm} = the modal seismic response coefficient determined in Equation 16-53

$\overline{W}_m$ = the effective modal gravity load

w_i = the portion of total gravity load, W, of the building at Level i

ϕ_{im} = the displacement amplitude at the ith level of the building when vibrating in its mth mode.

- **Determine modal mass and participation factors for each mode**

$L_1 = \sum_{i=1}^{3} \frac{w_i \phi_{i1}}{g} = 1.0 \text{ kip-sec}^2\text{/in.} (\phi_{11} + \phi_{21} + \phi_{31})$

$= 1.0\,(0.445 + 0.802 + 1.0) = 2.247 \text{ kip-sec}^2\text{/in.}$

$M_1 = \sum_{i=1}^{3} = 1.0 \text{ kip-sec}^2\text{/in.} (\phi_{11}^2 + \phi_{21}^2 + \phi_{31}^2)$

$= 1.0\,(0.445^2 + 0.802^2 + 1.0^2 = 1.0\,(0.198 + 0.643 + 1)$

$= 1.841 \text{ kip-sec}^2\text{/in.}$

$L_2 = \sum_{i=1}^{3} \frac{w_i \phi_{i2}}{g} = 1.0 \text{ kip-sec}^2\text{/in.} (\phi_{12} + \phi_{22} + \phi_{32})$

$= 1.0\,(-1.22 - 0.55 + 1.0) = -0.77 \text{ kip-sec}^2\text{/in.}$

$M_2 = \sum_{i=1}^{3} \frac{w_i \phi_{i2}^2}{g} = 1.0 \text{ kip-sec}^2\text{/in.} (\phi_{12}^2 + \phi_{22}^2 + \phi_{32}^2)$

$= 1.0\,(1.488 + 0.303 + 1) = 2.791 \text{ kip-sec}^2\text{/in.}$

$L_3 = \sum_{i=1}^{3} \frac{w_i \phi_{i3}}{g} = 1.0 \text{ kip-sec}^2\text{/in.} (\phi_{13} + \phi_{23} + \phi_{33})$

$= 1.0\,(1.802 - 2.25 + 1.0) = 0.552 \text{ kip-sec}^2\text{/in.}$

$M_3 = \sum_{i=1}^{3} \frac{w_i \phi_{i3}^2}{g} = 1.0 \text{ kip-sec}^2\text{/in.} (\phi_{13}^2 + \phi_{23}^2 + \phi_{33}^2)$

$= 1.0\,(3.247 + 5.063 + 1) = 9.310 \text{ kip-sec}^2\text{/in.}$

- **Determine effective weight and participating mass (pm) for each mode**

$W_1 = \frac{L_1^2}{M_1} g = \frac{2.247^2}{1.841} \times 386.4 \frac{\text{kip-sec}^2}{\text{in.}} \times \frac{\text{in.}}{\text{sec}^2} = 1059.58 \text{ kips}$

$W_2 = \frac{L_2^2}{M_2} g = \frac{(-0.77)^2}{2.791} \times 386.4 = 82.09 \text{ kips}$

$W_3 = \frac{L_3^2}{M_3} g = \frac{(0.552)^2}{9.310} \times 386.4 = 12.65 \text{ kips}$

$\Sigma W_i = 1154.32 \text{ kips}$

$PM_1 = \frac{W_1}{W} = \frac{1059.58}{3 \times 386.4} = 0.914$

$PM_2 = \frac{W_2}{W} = \frac{82.09}{3 \times 386.4} = 0.071$

$PM_3 = \frac{W_3}{W} = \frac{12.65}{3 \times 386.4} = 0.011$

$\Sigma PM = 0.996 \simeq 1.0$

Therefore, consideration of the above three modes (modes 1,2,3) is sufficient per Section 1618.2. Indeed, the consideration of just the first mode would have been sufficient (as $PM_1 \geq 0.90$.

- **Modal seismic design coefficients, C_{sm}**

$$C_{sm} = \frac{S_{am}}{(R/I_E)} \qquad \text{(Eq. 16-53)}$$

where: S_{am} = the modal design spectral response acceleration at period T_m determined from either the general design response spectrum of Section 1615.1 or a site-specific response spectrum per Section 1615.2.

In the example considered here, the general procedure of Section 1615.1 will be followed. Under this procedure, the spectral response acceleration, S_a, can be expressed by the following equations (Figure 1615.1.4):

EXAMPLE 12—(continued)

For $T \geq T_s \quad S_a = \frac{S_{DI}}{T}$

$T_o < T < T_s \quad S_a = S_{DS}$

$T \leq T_o \quad S_a = 0.6 S_{DS} \frac{T}{T_o} + 0.4\ S_{DS}$

where: $T_S = S_{D1}/S_{DS}$, and $T_o = 0.2\ T_S$

For the example building, $T_S = 0.6/1.0 = 0.60$ sec

$T_o = (0.2)\ (0.60) = 0.12$ sec

Mode 1: T_1 = 0.893 sec > 0.60 sec $\quad C_{s1} = \frac{S_{D1}}{0.893 \times (8/1)} = 0.0840g$

Mode 2: T_2 = 0.319 sec > 0.12 sec < 0.60 sec $\quad C_{s2} = \frac{S_{DS}}{(8/1)} = 0.1250g$

Mode 3: T_3 = 0.221 sec > 0.12 sec < 0.60 sec $\quad C_{s3} = \frac{S_{DS}}{(8/1)} = 0.1250g$

- **Base Shear Using Modal Analysis**

$$V_m = C_{sm}\ \overline{W}_m = \frac{L_m^2}{M_m} C_{sm}$$

Mode 1: $V_1 = 0.0843 \times 1059.58 = 89.3$ kips

Mode 2: $V_2 = 0.1250 \times 82.09 = 10.3$ kips

Mode 3: $V_3 = 0.1250 \times 12.65 = 1.6$ kips

The modal base shears are combined by the SRSS method to give the resultant base shear (1618.7)

$V_d = [89.3^2 + 10.3^2 + 1.6^2]^{1/2} = 90$ kips

- **Design Base Shear Using Equivalent Lateral-Force Procedure (1617.4)**

Design Base Shear (1617.4.1)

$V = C_s W$ (Eq. 16-34)

where: $C_s = \frac{S_{D1} I_E}{RT}$ (Eq. 16-36)

$\leq \frac{S_{DS} I_E}{R}$ (Eq. 16-35)

$\geq 0.044\ S_{DS} I_E$ (Eq. 16-37)

$\geq 0.5 \frac{S_1 I_E}{R}$ (Eq. 16-38) {for SDC E and F, or where $S_1 > 0.6g$}

For the example building considered

S_{DS} = 1.0

S_{D1} = 0.6

S_1 = 0.6

R = 8

I_E = 1.0

Approximate fundamental period T (1617.4.2.1)

$T_a = C_T (h_n)^{3/4}$ (Eq. 16-39)

C_T = 0.03 for a MRF system

h_n = total height = 30 ft

$T_a = 0.03 \times (30)^{3/4} = 0.385$ sec

T from rational analysis = 0.893 sec, which should not exceed the approximate period by more than a factor of C_u (obtained from Table 1617.4.2.1).

EXAMPLE 12—(continued)

C_u	$= 1.2$	
T	$= \text{min. of } (0.893, 1.2 \times 0.385 = 0.462)$	$= 0.462$ sec
$\frac{S_{D1} I_E}{RT} W$	$= \frac{0.6 \times 1 \times 1170}{8 \times 0.462}$	$= 190$ kips
$\frac{S_{DS} I_E}{R} W$	$= \frac{1.0 \times 1 \times 1170}{8}$	$= 146$ kips . . . governs
$0.044\, S_{DS} I_E W$	$= 0.044 \times 1.0 \times 1170$	$= 51.5$ kips
$0.5 \frac{S_1 I_E}{R} W$	$= \frac{0.5 \times 0.6 \times 1 \times 1170}{8}$	$= 43.9$ kips

Use $V = 146$ kips

- **Scaling of Elastic Response Parameters for Design**

Section 1618.7 stipulates that the base shear using modal analysis should be scaled up when the base shear calculated using equivalent lateral-force procedure is greater. However, it is permissible to use a fundamental period of $T = 1.2\, C_u T_a$ instead of $C_u T_a$ in the calculation of base shear by equivalent lateral-force procedure.

Based on the new period $T = 1.2 \times 0.462 = 0.554$ sec, the design base shear is recalculated as follows:

$\frac{S_{D1} I_E}{RT} W$	$= \frac{0.6 \times 1 \times 1170}{8 \times 1.832}$	$= 158$ kips
$\leq \frac{S_{DS} I_E}{R} W$	$= \frac{1.0 \times 1 \times 1170}{8}$	$= 146$ kips . . . governs
$\geq 0.044\, S_{DS} I_E W$	$= 51.5$ kips	
$\geq 0.5 \frac{S_1 I_E}{R} W$	$= 43.9$ kips	

Use $V = 146$ kips

146 kips (equivalent lateral force base shear) > 90 kips (modal base shear)

So the modal forces must be scaled up.

Scale factor = 146/90 = 1.622

The modified modal base shears are as follows:

$V_1 = 1.622 \times 89.3 = 144.8$ kips

$V_2 = 1.622 \times 10.3 = 16.7$ kips

$V_3 = 1.622 \times 1.6 = 2.6$ kips

$V = [144.8^2 + 16.7^2 + 2.6^2]^{1/2} = 146$ kips

- **Distribution of Base Shear**

Lateral force at Level x (1 to 3) for mode m (1 to 3), is to be calculated as:

$$F_{xm} = C_{vxm} V_m \qquad \text{(Eq. 16-55)}$$

$$C_{vxm} = \frac{w_x \phi_{xm}}{\sum_{i=1}^{n} w_i \phi_{im}} \qquad \text{(Eq. 16-56)}$$

where:

C_{vxm} = The vertical distribution factor in the mth mode,

V_m = The total design lateral force or shear at the base in the mth mode.

w_i, w_x = The portion of the total gravity load of the building, W, located or assigned to Level i or x.

ϕ_{im} = The displacement amplitude at the ith level of the building when vibrating in its mth mode.

ϕ_{xm} = The displacement amplitude at the xth level of the building when vibrating in its mth mode.

The distribution of the modal base shear for each mode is shown in table below and also in figure below.

EXAMPLE 12—(continued)

Mode = 1 V_m = 144.8 kips

Level, i	Weight, w_i	ϕ_{i1}	$w_i\,\phi_{i1}$	F_{i1}
3	390	1	390.0	64.4
2	390	0.802	312.8	51.7
1	390	0.445	173.6	28.7
		Σ =	876.3	144.8

Mode = 2 V_m = 16.7 kips

Level, i	Weight, w_i	ϕ_{i2}	$w_i\,\phi_{i2}$	F_{i2}
3	390	1	390.0	-21.7
2	390	-0.55	-214.5	11.9
1	390	-1.22	-475.8	26.5
		Σ =	-300.3	16.7

Mode = 3 V_m = 16.7 kips

Level, i	Weight, w_i	ϕ_{i3}	$w_i\,\phi_{i3}$	F_{i3}
3	390	1	390.0	4.7
2	390	-2.25	-877.5	-10.6
1	390	1.802	702.8	8.5
		Σ =	215.3	2.6

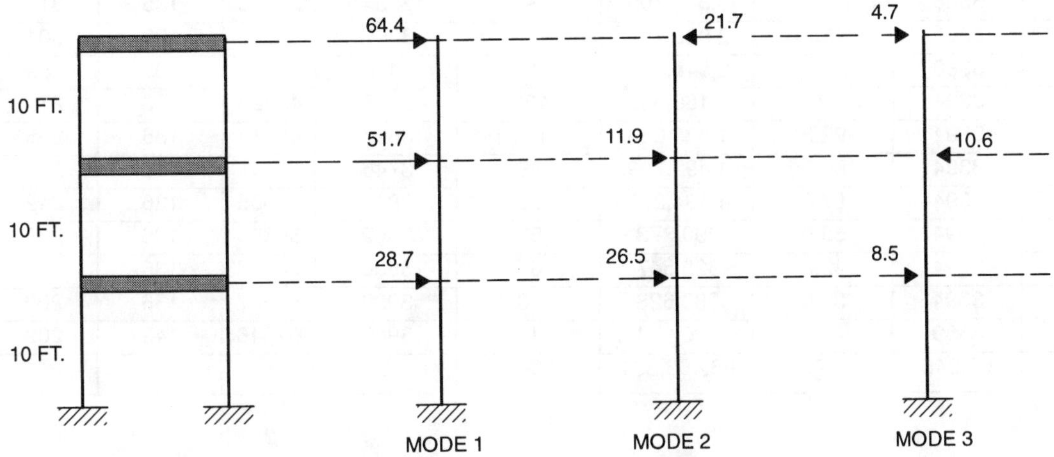

- **Lateral Analysis**

The stiffnesses of members used in the analyses were as follows:

For columns $I_{eff} = 0.7I_g$

For beams $I_{eff} = 0.5I_g$

The bending moments and shear forces at beam ends at various levels for different modes are obtained from lateral analysis and are shown in table below:

Design Negative Bending Moments at Beam Ends (ft-kips)				
Level, i	**Mode 1**	**Mode 2**	**Mode 3**	**Resultant, M**
3	254	-49	5.6	259
2	335	-45	0.2	338
1	316	-10	-2.5	316
Design Shear Forces at Beam Ends (kips)				
Level, i	**Mode 1**	**Mode 2**	**Mode 3**	**Resultant, F**
3	28	-5.5	0.6	28.5
2	37	-5	0	37.3
1	35	-1.1	-0.3	35.0

EXAMPLE 13. CALCULATION OF DIAPHRAGM DESIGN FORCES

Diaphragm design forces are calculated for the multistory building of Example 11.

The last column gives the diaphragm design forces calculated by Equation 16-65, assuming the building is assigned to SDC D or higher. Column 8 gives the diaphragm design forces calculated by Equation 16-62, assuming:

1) the building is assigned to SDC B or C
2) S_{DS} = 0.2
3) I_E = 1.0
4) V_{px} = 0

V = 3940 kips, T = 1.28 (sec.) k = 1.390								
Floor Level x	Weight w_x, kips	Height h_x, ft	$w_x h_x^k$, ft-kips	Lateral Force F_x, kips	$\sum_{i=x}^{n} F_i$	$\sum_{i=x}^{n} w_i$	F_{px} in SDC B, C	F_{px} in SDC D
1	2	3	4	5	6	7	8	9
21	2987	255.0	6,611,897	392	392	2987	119	392
20	3338	242.5	6,890,261	409	801	6325	134	423
19	3338	230.0	6,401,592	380	1181	9663	134	408
18	3338	217.5	5,923,177	351	1532	13001	134	393
17	3352	205.0	5,478,250	325	1857	16353	134	381
16	3366	192.5	5,040,491	299	2157	19719	135	368
15	3366	180.0	4,591,376	272	2429	23085	135	354
14	3366	167.5	4,154,270	246	2675	26451	135	340
13	3366	155.0	3,729,711	221	2897	29817	135	327
12	3366	142.5	3,318,309	197	3094	33183	135	314
11	3366	130.0	2,920,757	173	3267	36549	135	301
10	3380	117.5	2,548,410	151	3418	39929	135	289
9	3394	105.0	2,188,593	130	3548	43323	136	278
8	3394	92.5	1,835,054	109	3657	46717	136	266
7	3394	80.0	1,499,709	89	3746	50111	136	254
6	3394	67.5	1,184,252	70	3816	53505	136	242
5	3394	55.0	890,873	53	3869	56899	136	231
4	3394	42.5	622,547	37	3906	60293	136	220
3	3394	30.0	383,628	23	3929	63687	136	209
2	3559	17.5	190,174	11	3940	67246	142	209
Σ	67,246	Σ	66,403,331	3940				

EXAMPLE 14. CALCULATION OF DIAPHRAGM FORCES

This example illustrates the design of the roof diaphragm of the three-story building shown in Figure E14.1. The same building was analyzed in Example 12. The lateral forces shown are those obtained from the Mode 1 analysis in that example.

w_x = 390 kips at roof and each floor

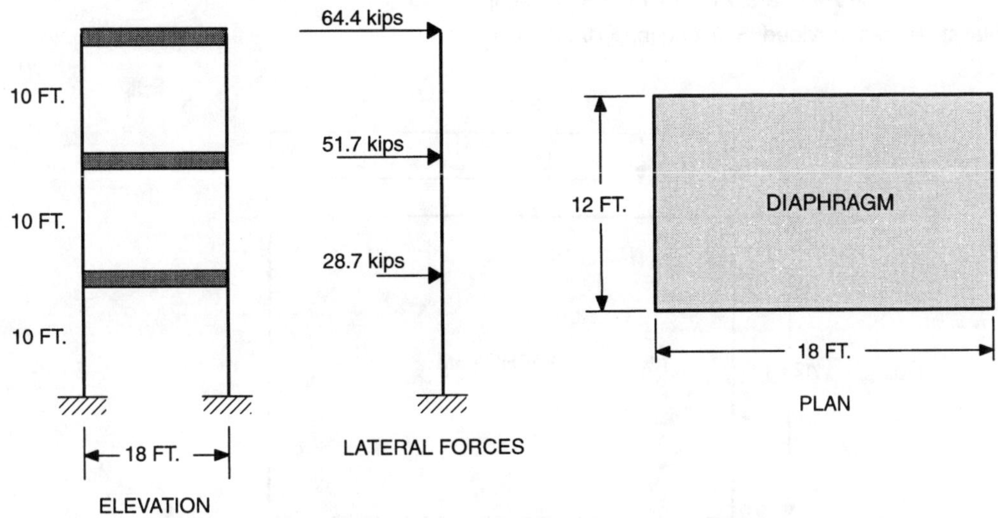

Figure E14.1. Plan and Elevation of Example Building Studied

Calculation of Diaphragm Forces for Structures in Seismic Design Category D (based on Formula 16-65)

Level, i	F_i	ΣF_i ($i = x$ to n)	w_{px}	Σw_i ($i = x$ to n)	F_{px}	Maximum	Minimum	Design
						$0.3 S_{DS} I_E w_{px}$	$0.15 S_{DS} I_E w_{px}$	F_{px}
roof	64.4	64.4	390	390	64.4	117	58.5	64.4
2	51.7	116.1	390	780	58.1	117	58.5	58.5
1	28.7	144.8	390	1170	48.3	117	58.5	58.5

All values are in kips

Number of levels, n = 3 Importance Factor, I_E = 1.0
S_{DS} = 1.0 SDC (based on S_{DS}) = D Table 1616.3 (1)
S_{D1} = 0.6 SDC (based on S_{D1}) = D Table 1616.3 (2)

Input:
Diaphragm force, F_{px} = 64.4 kips (at roof level)
Span length, L = 18 ft
Span width, B = 12 ft
Approx. uniformly distributed load, $w = F_{px}/L$ = 3.58 klf

EXAMPLE 14—(continued)

Design of Chord Steel along Exterior:

Max. bending moment, M = $w L^2/8$ = 145 ft-kips (conservatively)

Chord Tension, $T_c = M/B$ = 12 kips

Area of steel required, A_s = $T_c/(\phi f_y)$ = 0.22 sq in. (using Gr. 60 steel & $\phi = 0.9$)

Use **2 #4** bars; Area of 1 bar = 0.2 sq in.

Total steel area provided = 0.4 sq in. > 0.22 sq in.

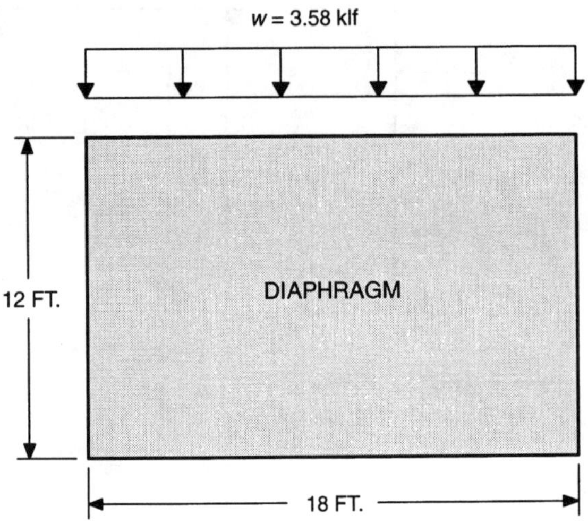

EXAMPLE 15. CALCULATION OF COLLECTOR STRENGTH

(Adapted from Example 45 of SEAOC Seismic Design Manual Vol. 1*)

In this example, the collector strength is calculated in SDC B per IBC Section 1620.1.5

Given: A tilt-up building with a panelized wood roof has a partial shear wall along the collector element line (as shown below)

S_{DS} = 0.24

S_{D1} = 0.13

Importance factor, I_E = 1.0

Roof dead load = 20 psf

Wall weight = 100 psf

Calculate the roof diaphragm forces, collector design force at tie to wall, and required collector strength

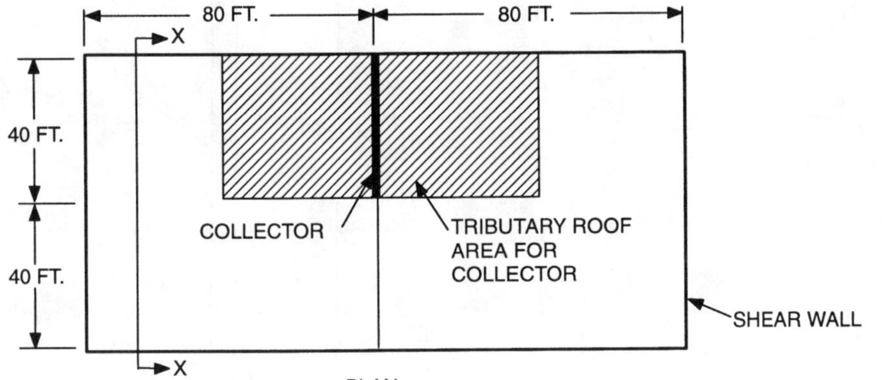

PLAN

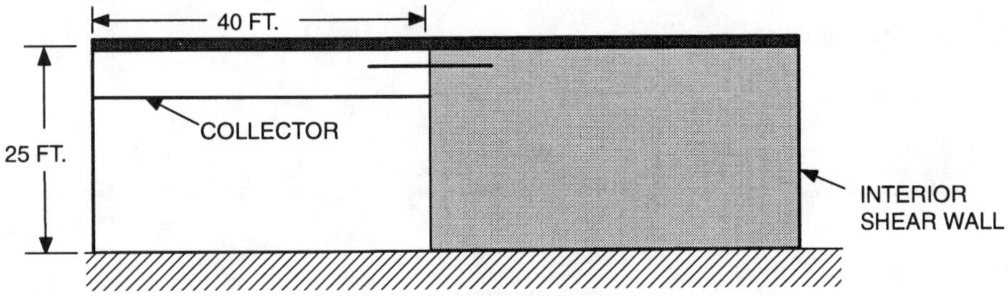

ELEVATION AT SECTION X-X

SDC (based on S_{DS}) = B [Table 1616.3 (1)]

SDC (based on S_{D1}) = B [Table 1616.3 (2)]

Use Equation 16-62 for diaphragm forces in SDC B

Weight of the diaphragm and other elements of the structure attached to it

w_p = $20 \times 160 \times 80 + 100 \times (25/2) \times (2 \times 80 + 2 \times 160 + 40) = 906$ kips

V_{px} = 0.0, as no offsets or changes in stiffness of vertical components above or below the diaphragm exist

Diaphragm design force = $0.2 \times 1 \times 0.24 \times 906 = 43.5$ kips

In designing the collector element, it is necessary to modify the weight, w_p, calculated above.

The tributary roof weight and out-of-plane wall weight is

w_p = $20 \times 80 \times 40 + 100 \times (25/2) \times (80) = 164$ kips

Collector design force = $0.2 \times 1 \times 0.24 \times 164 = 7.9$ kips

Collectors must resist special seismic load specified in 1605.4, i.e., $E_m = \Omega_o Q_E$

Overstrength factor, Ω_o = 2.5 (for building frames — light frame walls with shear panels in Table 1617.6)

Required collector strength = 2.5×7.9 = 19.75 kips

*Structural Engineers Association of California, *Seismic Design Manual, Vol. 1,* Sacramento, CA, 1999, 163 pp.

EXAMPLE 16. LATERAL FORCE ON ELEMENTS OF STRUCTURES

Determine lateral seismic forces for design of concrete tilt-up wall panel shown below. Embedded plates to be provided at 5-ft centers to match joist spacing, with ledger angle welded to each embed plate at each joist bearing. Wall to be designed as structural component according to Section 1620.

Design Data:

Seismic Design Category D

S_{DS} = 1.30 (based on geotechnical report)

Component Importance Factor, I_p = 1.0 (Sec. 1621.1.6)

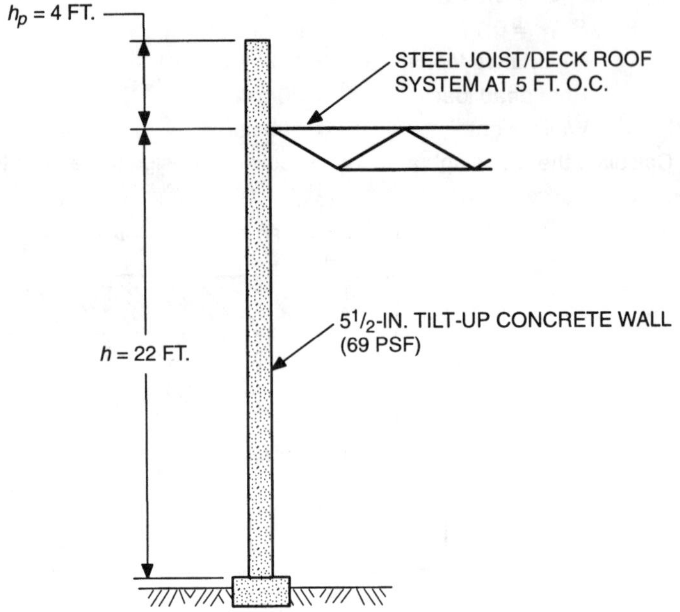

Seismic lateral forces for wall design

$$F_p = \frac{0.4 a_p S_{DS} I_p}{R_p}\left[1 + \frac{2z}{h}\right] W_p \qquad \text{(Eq. 16-67)}$$

but need not be more than . . . $1.6 S_{DS} I_p W_p$ (Eq. 16-68)

but not less than . . . $0.3 S_{DS} I_p W_p$ (Eq. 16-69)

PARAPET PORTION . . .

a_p = 2.5 Table 1621.2

R_p = 2.5

S_{DS} = 1.30

z = h = 22 ft

F_p = [0.4(2.5)(1.30)(1.0)/2.5] (1 + 2 × 22/22)W_p ≥ 0.3(1.30)(1.0)W_p

F_p = 1.56W_p ≥ 0.39W_p

F_p ≤ 1.6(1.30)(1.0)W_p = 2.08W_p

F_p = 1.56(69) = 107.6 psf (plf/ft width of wall)

EXAMPLE 16—(continued)

WALL PORTION (SECTION 1620.1.7) . . .

$F_P = 0.40\ I_E S_{DS}\ w_w \geq 0.10\ w_w$

$F_P = [0.40\ (1.0)(1.30)]\ w_w \geq 0.10\ w_w$

$F_P = 0.52\ w_w \geq 0.10\ w_w$

$F_P = 0.52\ (69) = 35.9$ psf (plf/ft width of wall)

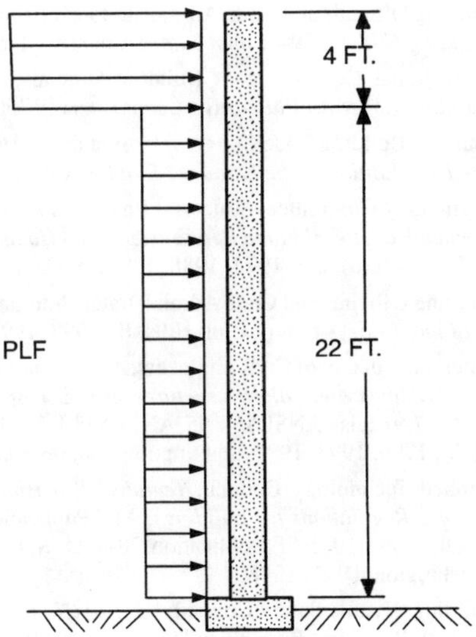

Seismic Forces for Wall Design
(per ft width)

Seismic force for wall anchorage at roof joists

In SDC C and above, wall anchorage to diaphragms is governed by the provisions of Section 1620.2.1.

Elements of wall anchorage system must be designed for forces specified in Equation 16-64 if the diaphragm is flexible as defined in Section 1602.1.

$F_p = 1.2 S_{DS} I_E w_w$ (Eq. 16-64)

$F_p = [1.2(1.30)(1.0)](69) = 107.6$ psf

In SDC B and above, F_p used for design of the elements of the wall anchorage system must not be less than $(400 S_{DS} I_E)$ plf of wall. Using a joist spacing of 5 ft

5(107.6) = 538 plf

Wall anchorage force . . .

$538 \times 26^2/2 = 22R$

$R = 8.27$ kips $> 400(13)(1.0) \times 5 = 2.60$ kips

All steel elements of wall anchorage system (plates/angles/welds) must be designed for a strength-level force of 8.27 kips

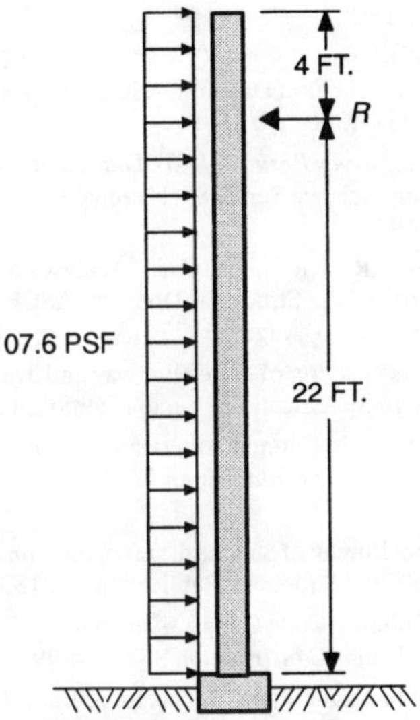

Seismic Forces For Wall Anchorage Design

REFERENCES

[1]Building Officials and Code Administrators International, *The BOCA National Building Code/1999—Commentary,* Country Club Hills, IL, 1999.

[2]International Conference of Building Officials, *Handbook to the Uniform Building Code: An Illustrative Commentary,* Whittier, CA, 1998.

[3]Southern Building Code Congress International, *An Illustrated Commentary to the 1999 Edition of the Standard Building Code,* Birmingham, AL, 1999.

[4]Seismology Committee, Structural Engineers Association of California, *Recommended Lateral Force Requirements and Commentary,* San Francisco (later Sacramento), CA, 1974, 1988, 1996, 1999.

[5]Building Officials and Code Administrators International, *The BOCA National Building Code,* Country Club Hills, IL, 1993, 1996, 1999.

[6]American Society of Civil Engineers, *ASCE Standard Minimum Design Loads for Buildings and Other Structures,* ASCE 7-88, ASCE 7-93, ASCE 7-95, ASCE 7-98 (also ANSI A58-55, ANSI A58.1-72, ANSI A58.1-82), New York, N. Y., 1990, 1993, 1995, and unpublished, respectively.

[7]Applied Technology Council, *Tentative Provisions for the Development of Seismic Regulations for Buildings,* ATC Publication ATC 3-06, NBS Special Publication 510, NSF Publication 78-8, U. S. Government Printing Office, Washington, D. C., 1978.

[8]Building Seismic Safety Council, *NEHRP (National Earthquake Hazards Reduction Program) Recommended Provisions for the Development of Seismic Regulations for New Buildings (and Other Structures),* Washington, D. C., 1994 (1997).

[9]Messersmith Jr., J. J., Kluver, K.M., and Skalko, S.V., *Concrete Inspection Handbook,* Publication EB115, Portland Cement Association, Skokie, IL, 1995 (Revised Edition to be Published in 2000).

[10]Ghosh, S. K., "Design of Reinforced Concrete Buildings under the 1997 UBC," *Building Standards,* International Conference of Building Officials, May-June 1998, pp. 20-24.

[11]Ghosh, S. K., "Needed Adjustments in 1997 UBC," Proceedings, 1998 Convention, Structural Engineers Assocation of California, October 7-10, 1998, Reno-Sparks, Nevada, pp. T9.1-T9.15.

[12]American Forest & Paper Association (formerly National Forest Products Association) and American Wood Council,*National Design Specification for Wood Construction,* ANSI/NfoPA NDS-1991, ANSI/AF&PA NDS-1997, Washington, D.C., 1991,1997.

[13]Peir, J.C., and Cornell, C.A., "Spatial and Temporal Variability of Live Loads," Journal of the Structural Division, ASCE, *Proceedings* Vol. 99, No. ST5, May 1973, pp. 903-922.

[14]McGuire, R.K., and Cornell, C.A., "Live Load Effects in Office Buildings," Journal of the Structural Division, ASCE, *Proceedings* Vol. 100, No. ST7, July 1974, pp. 1351-1366.

[15]Culver, C.G., *Survey Results of Fire Loads and Live Loads in Office Buildings,* NBS Building Science Series 85, National Bureau of Standards, Washington, D.C., May 1976.

[16]Ellingwood, B.R., and Culver, C.G., "Analyses of Live Loads in Office Buildings," Journal of the Structural Division, ASCE, *Proceedings* Vol. 103, No. ST8, pp. 1551-1560, August 1977.

[17]American Association of State Highway and Transportation Officials, LRFD Bridge Design Specifications, Second edition, 1998.

[18]International Code Council/American National Standards Institute, Inc., *Accessible and Usable Buildings and Facilities,* A117.1-98, Falls Church, VA, 1998.

[19]The National Bureau of Standards, *Live Loads on Floors and Buildings,* Building Materials and Structures Publication No. 133, Washington, D.C., 1952.

[20]Southern Building Code Congress International, *Standard for Hurricane Resistant Residential Construction,* SSTD 10-99, Birmingham, AL, 1999.

[21]American Forest and Paper Association, *Wood Frame Construction Manual for One and Two Family Dwellings,* High-Wind Edition, WFCM-95, 1996.

[22]Southern Building Code Congress International, *SBCCI Test Standard for Determining Impact Resistance from Windborne Debris,* SSTD 12-97, Birmingham, AL, 1997.

[23]Durst, C.S., "Wind Speeds over Short Periods of Time," *Meteorological Magazine,* Vol. 89, 1960, pp. 181-187.

[24]Krayer, W.R., and Marshall, R.D., "Gust Factors Applied to Hurricane Winds," *Bulletin of the American Meteorological Society,* Vol. 73, 1992, pp. 613-617.

[25]Southern Building Code Congress International, *Standard Building Code,* Birmingham, AL, 1994, 1997, 2000.

[26]American Society of Civil Engineers, *Flood Resistant Design and Construction Standard,* Reston, VA, 1998.

[27]International Code Council, *International Residential Code for One- and Two-Family Dwellings,* Final Draft, Falls Church, VA, September 1998.

[28]Jirsa, J.O., "Behavior of Elements and Subassemblages—R.C. Frames," *Proceedings* of a Workshop on Earthquake—Resistant Reinforced Concrete Building Construction, Berkeley, July 1977, Vol. III, pp. 1196-1214.

[29]Federal Emergency Management Agency, *NEHRP Guidelines for the Seismic Rehabilitation of Buildings,* Washington, D.C., October 1997.

[30]Joyner, W.B., Fumal, T.E., and Glassmoyer, G., "Empirical Spectral Response Ratios for Strong Motion Data from the 1989 Loma Prieta, California Earthquake," Proceedings of the NCEER/SEAOC/BSSC Workshop on Site Response during Earthquakes and Seismic Code Provisions, November 18-20, 1992, University of Southern California, Los Angeles, Martin, G.M., Ed., 1994.

[31]Newmark, N.M., and Hall, W.J., "Seismic Design Criteria for Nuclear Reactor Facilities," Proceedings, Fourth World Conference on Earthquake Engineering, Santiago, Chile, 1969, Vol. 2, pp. B-4 39-50.

[32]Pacific Coast Building Officials Conference (later the International Conference of Building Officials), *Uniform Building Code,* Long Beach, CA (later Whittier, CA), 1935, 1952, 1967, 1970, 1973, 1976, 1979, 1982, 1985, 1988, 1991, 1994, 1997.

[33]Bertero, V.V., Bendimerad, M.F., and Shah, H.C., *Fundamental Period of Reinforced Concrete Moment Resisting Frame Structures,* The John A. Blume Earthquake Engineering Center Report No. 87, Stanford University, Stanford, CA, 1988.

[34]Structural Engineers Association of California, *Seismic Design Manual, Volume I, Code Application Examples,* Sacramento, CA, April 1999.

[35]Newmark, N.M., and Rosenblueth, E., *Fundamentals of Earthquake Engineering,* Prentice-Hall, New York, 1971.

[36]Wilson, E.L., and Habibullah, A., "A Static and Dynamic Analysis of Multistory Buildings Including P-delta Effects," *Earthquake Spectra,* Earthquake Engineering Research Institute, Oakland, CA, Vol. 3, No. 2, 1987.

[37]American Institute of Steel Construction, *Seismic Provisions for Structural Steel Buildings,* Chicago, IL, April 1997.

[38]American Concrete Institute, *Building Code Requirements for Structural Concrete,* ACI 318-99, Detroit, MI, 1999.

[39]Hani, A., and Goel, S.C., *Earthquake Resistant Design of Open Web Framing Systems,* Research Report No. UMCE 91-21, University of Michigan, Ann Arbor, MI, 1991.

[40]American Institute of Steel Construction, *Manual of Steel Construction: Load & Resistance Factor Design,* Volume 1, Chicago, IL, 1994.

[41]Newmark, N.M., and Hall, W., *Earthquake Spectra and Design,* Monograph, Earthquake Engineering Research Institute, Oakland, CA, 1982, 103 pp.

[42]Uang, C.M., "Establishing R (or R_N) and C_d Factors for Building Seismic Provisions," *Journal of Structural Engineering,* ASCE, Vo. 117, No. 1, 1991, pp. 19-28.

[43]Applied Technology Council, *Structural Response Modification Factors,* ATC 19, Redwood City, CA, 1995, 64 pp.

[44]Clough, R.W., and Penzien, J., *Dynamics of Structures,* 2nd Edition, McGraw-Hill, Inc., New York, 1993.

[45]Chopra, A.K., *Dynamics of Structures,* Prentice Hall, Englewood Cliffs, NJ, 1995.

[46]Hamburger, R.O., McCormick, D.L., and Holm, S., "The Whittier Narrows, California Earthquake of October 1, 1987 - Performance of Tilt-up Buildings," *Earthquake Spectra,* Vol. 4, No. 2, 1988, pp. 219-253.

[47]Hamburger, R.O., and McCormick, D.L., "Implications of the January 17, 1994 Northridge Earthquake on Tiltup and Masonry Buildings with Wood Roofs," Draft Report, 1994.

[48]Brooks, H., "Building Code Provisions Affecting Tilt-Up Including Proposed Post-Northridge Code Changes," *Proceedings* of the Third National Concrete & Masonry Engineering Conference, San Francisco, CA, June 1995, pp. 173-191.

[49]Iverson, J.K., and Hawkins, N.M., "Performance of Precast/Prestressed Concrete Building Structures during the Northridge Earthquake," *PCI Journal,* Vol. 39, No. 2, March-April 1994, pp. 38-55.

[50]Fleischman, R.B., Sause, R., Pessiki, S., and Rhodes, A.B., "Seismic Behavior of Precast Parking Structure Diaphragms," *PCI Journal*, Vol. 43, No. 1, January-February 1998, pp. 38-53.

[51]American Society of Mechanical Engineers, *Safety Code for Elevators and Escalators,* ASME A17.1, New York, N.Y., 1996.

[52]Mayes, R.L. "Design of Structures with Seismic Isolation," Chapter 13, *The Seismic Design Handbook*, F. Naeim ed., Van Nostrand Reinhold, New York, 1989, pp. 413-438.

[53]Bachman, R.E. "Base Isolation: A New Concept for Earthquake Resistant Design," *Structure*, National Council for Structural Engineering Associations, Spring 1995.

[54]Kelly, J.M. "Aseismic Base Isolation: Its History and Prospects," *Joint Sealing and Bearing Systems for Concrete*, Publication SP-70, American Concrete Institute, Detroit, 1982.

[55]Buckle, I.G. "Development and Application of Base Isolation and Passive Energy Diissipation: A World Overview," Publication ATC 17, Applied Technology Council, Palo Alto, CA, March 1986.

[56]Theme Issue—Seismic Isolation: From Idea to Reality, *Earthquake Spectra*, Earthquake Engineering Research Institute, Vol. 6, No. 2, May 1990.

BIBLIOGRAPHY

Metal Building Manufacturers Association, *Low-Rise Building Systems Manual,* Cleveland, Ohio, 1986.

Strength Design Load Combinations for Concrete Elements, IS 521, Portland Cement Association, Skokie, IL, 1998.

Goel, S.C., and Hani, A., "Seismic Resistant Special Truss Moment Frames," *Journal of Structural Engineering*, ASCE, Vol. 120, No. 6, June 1994, pp. 1781-1797.

Basha, H.S., and Goel, S.C., *Seismic Resistant Truss Moment Frames with Ductile Vierendeel Segment*, Research Report No. UMCEE 94-29, University of Michigan, Ann Arbor, MI, 1994.

CHAPTER 17
STRUCTURAL TESTS AND SPECIAL INSPECTIONS

This chapter sets forth provisions for quality of materials, workmanship, testing, and labeling of materials incorporated into the construction of buildings or structures regulated by the code. Generally, all materials used must conform to the applicable standards listed in the code. Specific tests and standards are referenced in other parts of the code; e.g., Chapter 35 has reference standards for material requirements.

This chapter also provides the requirements for special inspection of the construction at various stages, structural observation by the registered design professional, and alternative methods to establish test procedures for products that do not have applicable standards.

SECTION 1701
GENERAL

This section sets forth the scope for Chapter 17 and the general requirements for both new and used materials.

1701.2 New materials. Testing is required for all materials that are not specifically provided for in the code. For example, a composite wood material that is not listed in Chapter 23 would be required to follow the procedures set forth in this chapter. A similar provision for acceptance of alternative materials, systems or methods for which the standards are not adopted in the code is set forth in Section 104.11. This section restates that alternative or new materials and methods may be used if it can be established by tests or other means that the performance of the new material or method will equal that required by the code for the replaced product.

1701.3 Used materials. Materials may be reused, provided that they meet *all* the code requirements for new materials. Note, however, that Section 104.9.1 specifically restricts the use of used equipment and devices unless specifically approved by the building official. One should exercise caution in approving reuse of materials. The applicable material or design standards must be consulted to determine if reuse of materials is allowed or prohibited. For example, reuse of high strength structural A490 bolts is prohibited by the AISC specifications. Even a piece of used structural steel would need to be carefully checked for conformance to the design and code requirements.

SECTION 1702
DEFINITIONS

1702.1 General. Definitions of various terms help in the understanding and application of code requirements. The definitions are provided in this chapter so that the reader does not constantly have to refer back to Chapter 2. These definitions are also cross referenced in Chapter 2.

APPROVED AGENCY. The definition of this term is needed in order to effect the requirements of Section 1703.1. The word "approved" means "acceptable to the building official or authority having jurisdiction" (see the definition of *approved* in IBC Section 202.1). The basis for approval of an agency for a particular activity by the building official includes the capacity or technical capability to perform the work in accordance with Section 1703.

CERTIFICATE OF COMPLIANCE. An "approved" fabricator is required to submit a Certificate of Compliance for work performed without special inspection. See Section 1704.2.2.

FABRICATED ITEM. Fabricated items are materials assembled prior to installation in a building and are referred to in Section 1704.2. The definition is provided to clarify the intent of the code as the term "fabricated items" could easily be interpreted to mean items for which special inspection is not intended per code. An example of a "fabricated item" for which special inspection is required is a roof truss.

INSPECTION CERTIFICATE. An inspection certificate is an identification applied to a product indicating that the individual product has been inspected by an approved agency. The inspection certificate is obligatory for components subject to special inspection requirements for seismic resistance (see Section 1707). Note that the requirements for an inspection certificate differ from the requirements for a label. An inspection certificate is issued for the specific piece of a product when it is inspected and is an ongoing process, whereas a label requires only that a representative sample of a product be periodically tested.

LABEL. A label is an identification for a product as set forth in Section 1703.5. A label identifies the manufacturer, the function of the product, and the quality control agency that allows the use of its label based on periodic audits and inspections of the manufacturer's facilities.

MANUFACTURER'S DESIGNATION. The manufacturer's self certification that a product complies with a given standard. There is no independent certification.

MARK. A manufacturer's identification of a product stating who made the product and the intended function. There is no certification that the product meets any given standard and no third party verification.

SPECIAL INSPECTION. That category of inspection for which special knowledge, special attention, or both is required. For example, inspection of complete penetration welds requires both special knowledge and special attention to ensure that the requirements of the code are met.

SPECIAL INSPECTION, CONTINUOUS. Continuous full-time inspection is required where compliance of the work or product cannot be determined after incorporation into the building or structure. For example, one cannot determine whether a multi-pass fillet weld is in compliance with the code requirements unless each pass of the weld is inspected.

SPECIAL INSPECTION, PERIODIC. Intermittent or part-time inspection, which may be allowed when the compliance of the work or product can be determined after being incorporated into the structure. For example, compliance with the design nailing requirements of a wood shear wall can be determined after completion of the wall (but before closure); hence, verification by periodic special inspection is adequate.

STRUCTURAL OBSERVATION. Note that structural observation by the registered design professional does not replace any of the requisite special inspections or inspections required by Section 109. Structural observation is for determining general conformance with the design intent, and not for specific conformance with the design documents and the code.

SECTION 1703 APPROVALS

1703.1 Approved Agency. The word "approved" means "acceptable to the building official or the authority having jurisdiction" (see the definition of *approved* in IBC Section 202.1). The basis for approval of an agency for a particular activity by the code or building official may include the capacity or technical capability to perform the work in accordance with Section 1703. For example, if an agency wishes to be approved for the special inspection of structural welds, the agency should submit evidence that its welding inspector is certified in accordance with applicable American Welding Society (AWS) or American Society of Nondestructive Testing (ASNT) requirements.

1703.1.1 Independent. The agency should have objectivity as well as competence. Objectivity can be measured by the agency's financial and fiduciary independence. The agency should have no financial ties to the organization it inspects. For example, a testing laboratory checking concrete strength should have no financial ties to either the contractor, its subcontractors, or the concrete supplier.

1703.1.2 Equipment. The building official should evaluate any testing laboratory for compliance with the requirements of applicable standards. To be approved, the laboratory should have its equipment calibrated at least annually. The laboratory must have the necessary calibrated equipment. For example, the laboratory must have the requisite temperature and humidity controlled storage for concrete cylinders in order to certify concrete cylinder strength.

1703.1.3 Personnel. The building official should evaluate both the experience and qualifications of the personnel. An agency may have personnel with the appropriate certifications, but not the necessary experience. Supervisory and inspection personnel should have certifications as well as the requisite experience and or education. For example, a concrete technician may be certified in accordance with the ACI technician program.

If the services being provided by an inspection or testing agency come under the purview of the professional registration laws of the state of jurisdiction, the building official should request evidence that the personnel are qualified to perform the work in accordance with the requisite professional registration.

1703.2 Written approval. A written approval by the building official is required for all material, appliance, equipment, or system incorporated into the work in order to have a documented record of approval and the basis for approval.

1703.3 Approved record. Records must be kept for all approvals, including conditions and limitations of approval. The approvals must be kept on file and available for public inspection. The records must demonstrate compliance with the code requirements of any material, appliance, equipment, or system incorporated into the structure.

1703.4 Performance. When conformance with the code is predicated on the performance and quality of materials or products, the building official must require the submission of test reports from an approved agency establishing this conformance. In the absence of such reports, the building official should require specific data that show compliance with the intent of the applicable code requirements in accordance with Chapter 16 (see IBC Sections 1604.6 and 1604.7). For example, core tests of in-situ concrete could be used to determine compliance with design strength if the sample cylinders required in Section 1905.6 were destroyed.

Materials and products must be subjected to various levels of quality control and identification in order to determine that the material complies with the requirements of the code. The degree of quality control and identification to which a material must be subjected is based on its relative importance to the structure's performance and function. By use of the terms *mark*, *manufacturer's designation*, *label*, and *inspection certificate*, the code establishes a hierarchy of quality control and identification as follows:

Level 1: Manufacturer identifies the material or product with the name of the material or product, the manufacturer's name, and the intended usage (see *Mark*).

Level 2: Manufacturer identifies the material or product as in Level 1 and also certifies compliance with a given standard or set of rules (see *Manufacturer's designation*).

Level 3: Manufacturer identifies the material or product as in Level 1. An approved quality control agency performs periodic audits of the manufacturer's facilities and QA/QC procedures.

Level 4: Each batch of material or individual product is inspected by an approved quality control agency (see *Inspection Certificate*).

1703.4.1 Research and investigation. This section is intended to implement the requirements of Section 104.11 for use of innovative or alternative materials, design, and methods of construction. For example, an innovative prestressed concrete system that did not emulate the performance of cast-in-place concrete could be evaluated per this section.

1703.4.2 Research reports. Evaluation reports prepared by approved agencies, such as those published by the organizations affiliated with the model code groups, such as ICBO Evaluation Service, may be accepted as part of the data needed by the building official to form the basis of approval of a material or product. Such reports supplement the resources of the building official and eliminate the need for the official to conduct detailed analysis on every new product. The building official is not mandated to approve the evaluation reports issued by the model code affiliated organizations, as these reports are advisory only and are intended for technical reference.

1703.5 Labeling. When materials or assemblies are required to be labeled by the code, such as plywood, fire doors, etc., the labeling must be in accordance with the procedures outlined in this section and its sub-sections. Labeling of materials or assemblies is an indication that the materials or assemblies have been subjected to testing, inspection, and/or other operations by the labeling agency. The presence of a label does not necessarily indicate compliance with code requirements. For example, use of plywood sheathing rated C-C, although labeled, would not comply with the code if Structural I sheathing was required to resist the design lateral forces.

The installation of labeled products must comply with the specific requirements and limitations of the labeled product. For example, a fire rated door is labeled with the hardware requirements specified on the label. The building inspector must ensure that the hardware used in the installation of the door meets the labeling requirements to ensure that the door complies with the code.

1703.5.1 Testing. For a material or product to be labeled, the labeling agency is required to perform testing on representative samples of the material or product in accordance with standards referenced by the code. An example is factory built fireplace assemblies that must be tested in accordance with UL 127 (see Chapter 35).

1703.5.2 Inspection and identification. The approved agency whose label is applied to a material or product must perform periodic inspections of the manufacture of the material or product to determine that the manufacturer is indeed producing the same material or product as tested and labeled. For example, if the labeling agency had tested $^{1}/_{2}$-inch C-C plywood sheathing made with five plies but the manufacturer was now making the plywood with only three plies, the agency would need to withdraw the use of its label and listing.

1703.5.3 Label information. This specifies the minimum information necessary on a label for the building inspector to determine that the installed material conforms with the approved plans. See Figure 1 as an example of typical lumber grade labels.

1. Panel Grade
2. Span Rating
3. Thickness
4. Exposure Durability Classification
5. Mill Number
6. Species Group Number
7. Product Standard PS 1-83
8. Product Standard PS 1 Grade Conformance Where Applicable
9. Tongue and Groove
10. Evaluation Service Report Number
11. FHA Use of Material Bulletin Number

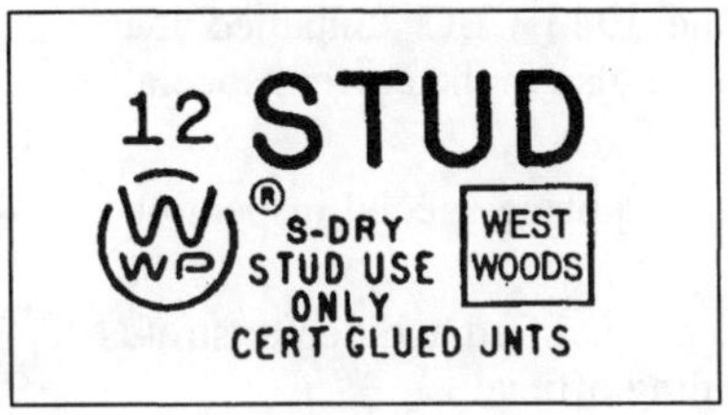

THE AWPB QUALITY MARK

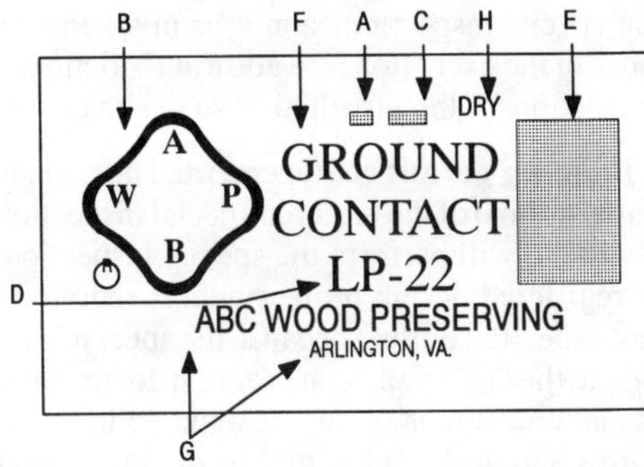

A. Year of treatment
B. American Wood Preservers Bureau Trademark
C. The preservative use for treatment
D. The applicable American Wood Preservers Bureau quality standard
E. Trademark of the agency supervising the treating plant
F. Proper exposure conditions
G. Treating company and plant location
H. Dry or KDAT if applicable

EXAMPLES OF LUMBER GRADE LABELS

FIGURE 1

1703.6 Heretofore approved materials. If a material was approved under a previous edition of the code, it can continue to be used as long as the use is not detrimental to the health and safety of the building occupants or the general public. The code is not retroactive.

1703.7 Evaluation and follow-up inspections. This applies where the structural component cannot be inspected after completion of a prefabricated assembly. An example might be a prefabricated shear wall consisting of plywood over a welded steel frame; the welding must be inspected prior to the installation of the plywood and the entire assembly inspected after application of the plywood. The testing and inspection should follow the concepts set forth above for Section 1703.

SECTION 1704 SPECIAL INSPECTIONS

The oldest mechanism for providing quality assurance in the construction is the process known as special inspection. The purpose of special inspection is to ensure proper fabrication, installation, and placement of components or materials that require special knowledge or expertise such as welding of structural steel or placement of grouted masonry. The knowledge and duties of a special inspector differs from that of the jurisdiction building inspector in that the special inspector's expertise is more narrow in scope yet very specialized, such as a structural steel welding inspector.

The concept of special inspection dates back to the 1927 edition of the *Uniform Building Code* (UBC) where it existed under the designation of Special Engineering Supervision. The first special inspection provisions similar to those presently used appeared in the 1943 UBC under the designation of Registered Inspectors. The requirements in the 1943 UBC contained the following essential elements that are also in the current special inspection provisions:

1. The particular types of work requiring special inspection were specified.
2. The special inspector had to be qualified and demonstrate his qualifications to the building official.
3. The requisite special inspections were in addition to those performed by the jurisdiction building inspector.
4. The special inspector was to be employed by the owner or design professional, not the contractor, so as to avoid any conflict of interest.

The special inspection provisions in the 1997 UBC continue with the same elements. Although similar, the special inspection provisions in this IBC section are more extensive than those in the 1997 UBC.

The special inspection requirements in the IBC address three areas:

1. Adequacy or quality of materials, such as concrete strength.
2. Adequacy of fabrication, such as a fillet weld on a steel fabrication.
3. Adequacy of construction techniques, such as tensioning of high-strength bolts.

Special inspection is that category of inspection requiring special knowledge, special attention, or both. The knowledge required is generally more specialized than that required by a general inspector. An individual with a high degree of specialized knowledge is usually required; hence, the term special inspection.

Most building departments do not have the staff necessary to do detailed inspections on large or complex structures, nor do the permit fees allow the level of inspection necessary for the types of construction where extra care in quality control must be exercised to assure compliance with the code. Hence the need for special inspection.

A good example of a checklist document for special inspection is *Guidelines for Special Inspection in Construction* by the California Council of Testing and Inspection Agencies.[1] Copies of this document are also available from any of the member organizations of the council which include most of the major testing laboratories in California.

Note that there are additional special inspection requirements in Section 1707 for seismic resistance.

1704.1 General. The owner is responsible for the employment of special inspectors meeting the approval of the building official. The owner is also responsible for all costs associated with the employment of special inspectors. Note that the special inspectors must be employed by the owner, or the responsible registered design professional acting as the owner's agent, not by the contractor or builder. This ensures independence of the special inspector and avoids any conflict of interest that could occur if the special inspector were employed by the contractor or builder. Note also that the special inspections required are in addition to the inspections required by Section 109.

Exceptions to the requirement for special inspections are only for minor work or work not required to be designed or sealed by a registered design professional. The exception for R-3 occupancies and U occupancies accessory to a residential occupancy are for those structures typically not required to be designed by a registered design professional or those designed and constructed in accordance with the *International Residential Code.* Exception 1 does not mean that the inspections listed are not required, but that they are not required to be made by a special inspector. Also, Exception 1 refers to "conditions in the jurisdiction" as a possible exception. The primary "condition" envisioned by the code writers is that the jurisdiction has the resources and skill level necessary to perform the requisite special inspection tasks, thus obviating the need for a special inspector. Note that this exception for special inspection cannot be invoked by the owner. One purpose of the exception is to allow jurisdictions to perform special inspections if the jurisdiction so desires.

1704.1.1 Building permit requirement. The owner must submit a detailed outline of the required special inspections and designate those who will perform the special inspections. The responsible registered design professional is required to prepare the special inspection outline because the special inspections relate directly to the design and construction documents. The qualifications and credentials of any designated individuals, agencies, or firms should be submitted to the building official for approval.

1704.1.2 Report requirement. Records of each inspection must be kept and submitted to the building official so as to document compliance with the code. The records must include all inspections made and compliance with the code requirements as well as all violations and discrepancies. A final report must show that all required special inspections have been made and that discrepancies have been resolved before a certificate of occupancy can be issued. It is the responsibility of the special inspector to document and submit inspection records to the building official and to the registered design professional in responsible charge.

1704.2 Inspection of fabricators. This section should be used in conjunction with Section 1703.7 relating to evaluation and follow up reports. The use of a special inspector does not relieve the fabricator from the requirements to have his own quality control procedures and personnel.

1704.2.1 Fabrication and implementation procedures. The special inspector acts in the quality assurance role in this instance by verifying that the quality control procedures that the fabricator has in place will ensure compliance and that the fabricator follows the requisite quality control procedures. For example, welding of structural steel is to be done in accordance with the requirements of AWS D1.1.[2] AWS D1.1 requires that the fabricator have its own quality control procedures and personnel. The fabricator's QC personnel are responsible for determining conformance of the welds with the requirements of AWS D1.1 by applicable visual and nondestructive testing (NDT) methods. Note that NDT is supplementary to, not in place of, visual inspection. The special inspector acts as the owner's agent for verification by auditing the fabricator's QC program. The fabricator's welding inspector is responsible for: 1) making sure that all welders are qualified in accordance with D1.1, 2) making sure that weld procedure specifications (WPS) are in place for all welds (both pre-qualified and unqualified welds), 3) visually inspecting fit-up of the weld, 4) verifying that the machine settings, electrodes, and other parameters match those set forth in the WPS, 5) observing the welding operation, 6) performing any required NDT, and 7) keeping documentation for each weld made in the fabrication shop. The special inspector, on the other hand, is responsible for reviewing the qualification records of the welders, for determining that the WPS were suitable for the specified weld and were properly qualified, for reviewing NDT procedures and records, and for observing a representative number of welds in order to ensure that the fabricator's QC program is adequate and being followed.

1704.2.2 Fabricator approval. Special inspection is not required where a fabricator has been specifically preapproved by the building official. This preapproval is based on a review of the fabricator's written procedures and quality assurance/quality control program. The fabricator should be periodically audited by an independent, approved special inspection agency. This section is intended to apply to programs such as the Quality Certification Program for steel fabricators by AISC, the Plant Certification Program for steel joists by the Steel Joist Institute, or the Plant Certification Program for precast concrete products by the Precast/Prestressed Concrete Institute.[3]

1704.3 Steel construction. This section sets forth the special inspection requirements for the fabrication and erection of structural steel elements. Detailed requirements are in Table 1704.3 and the subsections of 1704.3. Table 1704.3 sets forth the verification and inspection requirements, whether the frequency of inspection is to be continuous or periodic, the appropriate reference standard, and the applicable IBC code section.

Exception 1 eliminates the need for special inspection in certain cases. Special inspection is not required if the fabricator does not alter the properties of the parent material by welding, thermal cutting, or heating operations. For example, if the members being fabricated were cut by mechanical means, such as a band saw, and punched or drilled for bolt holes, with no application of heat, special inspection would not be required. But if the same members were cut with an oxy-acetylene torch, special inspection would be required. Even if special inspection is not required, the fabricator must provide evidence that his tracking procedures are adequate to verify that the material used in any member meets the required specification, is of the proper grade, and has an associated mill test report.

Exception 2 does not exempt the work from special inspection. The exception relaxes the amount of special inspection for welding from continuous to periodic when the quality of the weld can be readily determined after completion of the weld. For example, welded studs can be given the "hammer" test and small, single pass fillet welds can be readily inspected by visual inspection and dye penetrant methods for conformance with the AWS D1.1 requirements after the weld is completed.

1704.3.1 Welding. Welding inspection must be in accordance with AWS D1.1. The weld inspector should be (but is not required to be) a AWS Certified Weld Inspector. Any nondestructive testing such as dye penetrant or ultrasonic testing should be performed by an inspector qualified under the American Society for Nondestructive Testing (ASNT) and should be certified as a ASNT Level II NDT inspector for that process.

Welding inspection relies on *visual inspection* as the primary method used to evaluate conformance of welds with the applicable quality requirements. *Visual inspection* is *supplemented* by various nondestructive test methods such as ultrasonic and dye penetrant methods. *Visual inspection* means that inspection is performed *prior to, during*, and *after* welding, not just after welding as is often practiced. A Welding Procedure Specification should be prepared and approved for each weld prior to welding (including prequalified welds). Weld metal and shielding gases should be checked for conformance with the WPS. Joints should be examined prior to welding to ensure that fit-up, bevel preparation requirements, alignment, preheat and other variables match the WPS requirements. Prior to and during welding, the welding equipment settings should be verified to be within the correct amperage and voltage range per the WPS. The welding techniques of the welder should be observed during welding, particularly observation of the weld pool and electrode travel rates. After each pass of weld is completed, visual inspection should verify that the width, depth, convexity, undercut, and other requirements of D1.1 are met. Use of ultrasonic testing alone after completion of the weld without *visual inspection* as noted above, does *not* meet the requirements of AWS D1.1.

1704.3.2 Details. The special inspector must verify that the fabricated elements match the requirements of the approved construction documents, such as the beam-column joint has the correct geometry, the correct number and type of fasteners, etc.

1704.3.3 High-strength bolts. This section references the AISC specification for high-strength bolts. However, the AISC ASD specification[4] or AISC LRFD specification[5] in turn references the applicable Research Council on Structural Connections (RCSC) *Specification for Structural Joints Using A325 or A490 Bolts*.[6] Hence, the special inspection is to be done in accordance with the applicable RCSC requirements. Note that Section 1704.3.3.3 requires continuous inspection for pretensioning bolts by calibrated wrench or turn-of-nut.

1704.3.3.1 General. High-strength bolts are used in two types of connections: 1) friction connections where the clamping force provided by pretensioning of the bolts is necessary for proper performance of the connection, and 2) bearing connections where friction, and hence pretensioning, is not critical to the performance of the connection. Bearing connections require only snug-tight bolts that bring the layers of steel into contact, whereas friction connections require that the clamping force is obtained fully by pretensioning the bolts to a specified minimum tensile force.

There are three types of high-strength bolts, and the type specified depends on the usage. Matching nuts and washers must be used with high-strength bolts. Consult the appropriate RCSC *Specification* for correct type of bolt, matching nuts, and washer requirements. Note that all A325 and A490 bolts are quenched and tempered (Q and T). Welding, thermal cutting, or sustained high temperatures will change the metallurgy and strength of the bolt and must be avoided.

The *Structural Bolting Handbook*,[7] published by Steel Structures Technology Center, Inc., is a good resource on installation, tightening, and inspection of high strength bolts.

1704.3.3.2 Periodic monitoring. Periodic monitoring is permitted in two cases: 1) in a friction connection when it can be determined after tensioning that the required tension has been induced in the bolt, as with a calibrated direct tension indicator, or 2) in a bearing connection using snug-tight bolts.

1704.3.3.3 Continuous monitoring. Continuous monitoring is required when it is necessary to observe the tightening of the bolt in order to determine that the minimum pretensioning force is induced in the bolt. Use of a calibrated torque wrench or turn-of-nut method without match marking both require continuous monitoring.

Table 1704.3 Required Verification and Inspection of Steel Construction. This presents the requirements for special inspection in a concise format along with the inspection frequency, reference standard and applicable code section. Some of the items in the table are also required in the preceding code text. For Item 2, inspection of high strength bolting, see the discussion in Section 1704.3.3. Items 1, 3, and 4 are verification that the correct material and grade are being used. Item 5, inspection of welding, only summarizes the welding inspection requirements and the required frequency. Refer to documents AWS D1.1, D1.3, and D1.4 for more complete inspection requirements. Note that the requirements for welding of reinforcing steel are in this table rather than in the concrete or masonry section. These requirements are placed in this table because the inspection requirements are similar to structural steel welding and the personnel and equipment involved are often the same as those inspecting structural steel welding. See analysis of Section 1704.3.1 for a discussion of the term visual inspection for welding. See also the commentary in AWS D1.1, D1.3, and D1.4.

1704.4 Concrete construction. This sets forth the special inspection requirements for the construction of concrete foundations, structures or elements. Detailed requirements are covered in Table 1704.4, which sets forth the verification and inspection requirements, whether the frequency of inspection is to be continuous or periodic, the reference standard, and the IBC code section. Exceptions for special inspection are concrete elements that are nonstructural such as sidewalks, lightly loaded elements such as slabs on grade, concrete foundations that are not heavily loaded, or plain concrete basement walls.

1704.4.1 Materials. Constituent materials for concrete such as aggregate, cement, admixtures, and water must conform to the requirements set forth in Section 1903 and the standards of Chapter 3 of ACI 318. When sufficient documentation is not available to verify that constituent materials conform to these requirements, the building official should require testing of the materials.

Table 1704.4. Required Verification and Inspection of Concrete Construction. This presents the requirements for special inspection of concrete in a concise format along with the inspection frequency and reference standard. The table summarizes the required inspections and test samples necessary to verify that the in-place concrete meets the code requirements. Refer to ACI 318[8] and the applicable ASTM standards for more details of the constituent material tests, sampling of fresh concrete, testing of slump or air content, casting of test specimens, and other test requirements.

Item 1: Inspections per Item 1 should check that the reinforcement is of the correct size and grade, as required by the approved drawings and specifications, and is properly placed prior to placement of concrete. Proper placement of reinforcement has a significant impact on the integrity and strength of reinforced concrete. The reinforcement should be placed within the tolerances set forth in ACI 318 Section 7.5 and ACI 117, *Standard Tolerances for Concrete Construction and Materials*. Additional requirements of ACI 318 such as surface conditions of reinforcement (Section 7.4), spacing limitations (Section 7.6), and concrete protection for reinforcement or cover (Section 7.7), must also be checked.

Item 2: Note that Item 2, inspection of reinforcing steel welding, is referred to Table 1704.3 for steel.

Item 3: Item 3 comes into effect when anchor bolts are designed for the higher load allowed by special inspection (see Section 1912.5). Most jobs that require special inspection for concrete will be designed to take advantage of the higher allowable bolt loads with special inspection. Hence, if special inspection is required for the concrete, most likely it will also be required for the anchor bolts. Proper placement and embedment of anchor bolts is of extreme importance. If an anchor bolt is set too low for proper thread engagement, there are few satisfactory methods to remedy the situation. The common practice of placing a puddle weld in the nut is of questionable value, as neither the bolt nor the nut may be weldable material. The chemistry of nuts is not controlled by the ASTM requirements, and the chemistry allowed for an A307 bolt is such that it may or may not be weldable. In either case, the weld is not a prequalfied weld in accordance with AWS D1.1 and a Procedure Qualification Record must be developed to qualify the welding procedure. Note also that if the anchor bolt is a high strength bolt such as an ASTM A 325 or

ASTM A 449, the bolt is quenched and tempered and application of heat by welding will destroy the strength of the bolt and make the bolt brittle.

Item 4: Item 4 is a particularly important verification on larger jobs that may have many required mix designs with differing strengths and aggregate sizes.

Item 5: Sampling of fresh concrete for making specimens for strength tests is extremely important for quality control. Properly sampled and prepared specimens are necessary to determine that the concrete will meet or exceed the design strength. The frequency of sampling should be in accordance with IBC Section 1905.6.2.1—one set of specimens for each class of concrete not less than once per day, once per 150 cubic yards, or once per 5,000 square feet of slab or wall. Sampling should be done in accordance with ASTM C172 to ensure representative samples for determining compressive strength. The tests specified in Item 5 may be supplemented by other tests such as unit weight or air content.

Item 6: Observation of the actual placement is important to determine that the fresh concrete is properly handled so that it does not segregate during placement and that the concrete is properly consolidated by vibration. The mixing requirements (see IBC Section 1905.8), conveying requirements (see IBC Section 1905.9), and depositing requirements (see IBC Section 1905.10) should be strictly enforced to ensure proper placement with adequate consolidation and without segregation. Concrete "rock pockets" adversely affect design strength and are unattractive.

Item 7: Maintenance of proper cure is essential to obtaining quality concrete that will reach the design strength. Concrete that is not properly cured often will be below design strength and may suffer degradation at the surface from use or from environmental effects much earlier than properly cured concrete.

Item 8: The inspections required by Item 8 are of extreme importance as the strength of a prestressed member is highly dependent on proper prestressing. When checking the application of prestressing force, both the force applied to the tendon and the tendon elongation should be checked simultaneously to ensure that the tendon has not hung up in the tendon sheath.

Item 9: Criteria for the erection procedures of precast concrete must be provided on the design drawing by the design engineer. The special inspector should ensure that the erection complies with the approved procedures.

1704.5 Masonry construction. This section sets forth the special inspection requirements for the construction of masonry foundations, structures or elements. Detailed requirements are in Tables 1704.5.1 and 1704.5.3. These tables set forth the verification and inspection requirements, whether the frequency of inspection is to be continuous or periodic, the reference standard, and the applicable IBC code section. Table 1704.5.1, Level 1 Special Inspection, is required for engineered masonry in structures that are not classified essential, whereas Table 1704.5.3, Level 2 Special Inspection, with its higher requirements is required for engineered masonry in essential facilities. Excepted from special inspection are masonry elements that are nonstructural such as glass unit masonry and masonry veneers when used in nonessential structures; empirically designed masonry that is generally lightly loaded; and plain masonry foundation walls constructed in accordance with the empirical requirements of IBC Chapter 18, Tables 1805.5 (1) through 1805.5 (4).

Note that in the IBC, masonry elements using working stress design are developed using the requirements of the Masonry Standards Joint Committee documents ACI 530/ASCE 5/TMS 402[9] and ACI 530.1/ASCE 6/TMS 602,[10] whereas masonry elements using strength design follow the provisions of IBC Chapter 21. See also the testing requirements for seismic resistance in the analysis of Section 1708.

1704.5.1 Empirically designed masonry, glass unit masonry and masonry veneer in essential facilities. Masonry elements of this type of construction in essential facilities must be inspected to Level 1 requirements, which are periodic inspections except for grouting and welding of reinforcing steel.

1704.5.2 Engineered masonry in nonessential facilities. Engineered masonry elements designed using either working stress or strength design in nonessential facilities must be inspected to Level 1 requirements, which are periodic inspections except for grouting, preparation of grout or mortar specimens, and welding of reinforcing steel, which are continuous inspections.

1704.5.3 Engineered masonry in essential facilities. Engineered masonry elements designed using either working stress or strength design in essential facilities must be inspected to Level 2 requirements. Level 2 inspection requires continuous inspection for grout space prior to grouting, placement of grout, placement of anchors, preparation of grout or mortar specimens, and welding of reinforcing steel.

Table 1704.5.1. Level 1 Special Inspection. This presents the requirements for Level 1special inspection of masonry in a concise format along with the inspection frequency and reference standard. Level 1 special inspection is used for engineered masonry in nonessential facilities and empirically designed masonry, glass unit masonry and masonry veneer in essential facilities. Note that all inspections are periodic except for welding of reinforcing bars, placement of grout, and preparation of specimens, which are continuous. The table summarizes the required inspections and test samples necessary to verify that the in-place masonry meets the code requirements. Refer to ACI 530/ASCE 5/TMS 402 and ACI 530.1/ASCE 6/TMS 602 and the applicable ASTM standards for additional details of the constituent material tests, sampling of mortar or grout, preparation of prisms, and other test requirements.

Item 1: Inspection per Item 1 should check that the mortar is being properly batched and mixed. The influence of the mortar on the strength of the finished masonry is directly related to the degree of grouting. The mortar has little influence on the strength of a fully grouted wall, but a significant influence on a plain masonry wall. If the mortar deviates too much from the specifications, often the mason will reject the mortar because it has poor workability; e.g., it is too wet or too harsh (oversanded). The inspector should also look for fully mortared head and bed joints, particularly in plain masonry walls. In addition, the reinforcing steel must be of the correct size , type and grade, and placed and held in the correct position. Proper placement of reinforcement has a significant impact on the integrity and strength of reinforced masonry. The reinforcement should be placed within the tolerances set forth in ACI 530.1/ASCE 6/TMS 602, Section 3.4.

Item 2: Most of the inspections for Item 2 are verifications that materials of the correct type and grade are located in accordance with the approved plans. Although welding of reinforcing bars is not referred back to Table 1704.3, Steel, ACI 530/ASCE 5/TMS 402 requires use of AWS D1.4.

Item 3: In grouted masonry, cleanliness of the cells prior to grouting is next to godliness. Cells to be grouted should be clean and free from debris and mortar projections greater than $^1/_2$ inch.

Item 4: Grouting should be in accordance with ACI 530/ASCE 5/TMS 402, Section 3.5. Grout should be initially consolidated by vibration and reconsolidated after initial water loss and settlement while the grout is still plastic.

Item 5: Sampling of fresh grout or mortar for the making of specimens for strength tests is extremely important for quality control. Properly sampled and prepared specimens are necessary to determine that the grout or mortar will meet or exceed the minimum design strength. The frequency of sampling should be not less than one set of specimens for each 5,000 square feet of wall. Sampling and testing for grout should be done per ASTM C 1019, for mortar per ASTM C 270, and for prisms per ASTM C 1314.

Table 1704.5.3. Special Inspection of Masonry Construction—Level 2. This table presents the requirements for Level 2 special inspection of masonry in a concise format along with the inspection frequency and reference standards. Level 2 special inspection is used for engineered masonry in essential facilities. Note that some inspections are periodic but inspections for welding of reinforcing bars, placement of grout, inspection of grout space prior to grouting, and preparation of specimens must be continuous. The table summarizes the required inspections and test samples necessary to verify that the in-place masonry meets the code requirements. Refer to ACI 530/ASCE 5/TMS 402 and ACI 530.1/ASCE 6/TMS 602 and the applicable ASTM standards for additional details of the constituent material tests, sampling of mortar or grout, preparation of prisms, and other test requirements.

Item 1: Inspection per Item 1 should check that the mortar is being properly batched and mixed. The influence of the mortar on the strength of the finished masonry is directly related to the degree of grouting. The mortar has little influence on the strength of a fully grouted wall, but a significant influence on a plain masonry wall. If the mortar deviates from the specifications, often the mason will reject the mortar because it has poor workability; e.g., it is too wet or too harsh (oversanded). The inspector should also look for fully mortared head and bed joints, particularly in plain masonry walls. In addition to the reinforcing steel being the correct size, type and grade, proper placement of reinforcement has a significant impact on the integrity and strength of reinforced masonry. The reinforcement should be placed within the tolerances set forth in ACI 530.1/ASCE 6/TMS 602, Section 3.4. Cleanliness is next to godliness in grouted masonry. Cells to be grouted should be clean and free from debris and mortar projections greater than $^1/_2$ inch. Grouting should be in accordance with ACI 530/ASCE 5/TMS 402, Section 3.5. Grout should be initially consolidated by vibration and reconsolidated after initial water loss and settlement while the grout is still plastic.

Item 2: Most of the inspections for Item 2 are verification that materials of the correct type and grade are in the location shown in the approved plans. Although welding of reinforcing bars is not referred back to Table 1704.3, Steel, ACI 530/ASCE 5/TMS 402 requires use of AWS D1.4.

Item 3: Sampling of fresh grout or mortar for the making of specimens for strength tests is extremely important for quality control. Properly sampled and prepared specimens are necessary to determine that the grout or mortar will meet or exceed the minimum design strength. The frequency of sampling should be not less than one set of specimens for each 5,000 square feet of wall. Sampling and testing for grout should be done per ASTM C1019; for mortar per ASTM C270; and for prisms per ASTM C1314.

1704.6 Wood construction. This section sets forth the special inspection requirements for the wood construction. The requirement is for inspection of prefabricated elements such as wood trusses. (See IBC Section 1704.2). For portions of wood structures designated as the seismic lateral force resisting system, see also the special inspection requirements in the analysis of Section 1707.

1704.7 Soils. This names the special inspection requirements for site preparation and engineered fills. The loadbearing capacity of the site and any fill has a significant impact on the structural integrity of a building supported by the fill. For example, settlements in an improperly compacted fill can cause significant structural distress. Differential settlements of $^1/_4$ inch in a 20-foot grade beam can induce stresses that exceed the yield limits. Hence, fills should be engineered and compaction carefully controlled. Inspection shall verify compliance with the approved foundation and soils report required by Section 1802.2. No special inspection is required for placement of fills less than 12 inches deep.

1704.7.1 Site preparation. The first important step for engineered fill is preparation of the site in accordance with the requirements in the approved soils report, such as stripping, scarification and precompaction.

1704.7.2 During fill placement. Inspection should observe that the maximum lift thickness is not exceeded and that the compaction method conforms to the soils report.

1704.7.3 Evaluation of in-place density. The loadbearing capacity of the fill is directly related to the in-place density. The evaluation is necessary to ensure that the methods used to achieve compaction during fill placement result in the required in-place density.

1704.8 Pile foundations. Special inspection for piles and pile tests must be continuous. Inspection should include: 1) inspection of the pile driving or drilling equipment; 2) inspection and acceptance of all piles (driven) or pile construction materials (drilled) for conformance with specification; 3) verification that pile location stakes are in the correct location per the approved drawings; and 4) observation and recording of all pertinent data relating to the installation of the pile foundation.

For driven piles, records should, at a minimum, contain for each pile a driving log showing the number of hammer blows for each foot (and the energy) and the resistance at final penetration in blows per inch or blows per foot as applicable. The inspector should verify that the hammer throttle is set correctly to give the desired energy. The driving log should also give information on the duration and cause of any delays, the depth of any pre-excavation, and the elevation of the tip and the cutoff. Any known or suspected pile damage, as well as any observation of pile drift or heave, should be noted.

For drilled piles, data should include for each pile, a drilling log showing the types of soils encountered for each foot and the material stratum at the required tip elevation. The inspector should verify that the soil at required tip elevation is the correct soil. The drilling log should also give information on the duration and cause of any delays, data on the rebar cage and concreting procedures, casing or other procedures necessary to prevent intrusion of ground water, as well as the results of any concrete strength tests.

1704.9 Pier foundations. The requirements for special inspection of drilled piers are the same as for drilled piles. Pier foundations in Seismic Design Category (SDC) C, D, E or F require special inspection. The exceptions outlined in Section 1704.4 do not apply to pier foundations.

1704.10 Wall panels and veneers. Special inspection is necessary to ensure that wall panels and veneers in high seismic risk areas, such as SDC E and F, perform in a satisfactory manner. Falling veneers or panel are a significant safety hazard.

1704.11 Sprayed fire-resistant materials. This presents the requirements for the special inspection of spray applied fire-resistant materials (SFRM). For an SFRM to perform as intended, its application must be within the proper range for certain parameters as determined by the system manufacturer. These include temperature at time of application, substrate conditions, thickness, bond strength and density. These parameters must be checked prior to and during installation of the SFRM.

1704.11.1 Structural member surface conditions. The integrity of an SFRM system primarily depends on the condition of the surface of the steel member to which it is applied. The system must be fully adhered to the surface for proper performance.

1704.11.2 Application. During the application and curing of SFRMs, several parameters must be controlled including ambient temperature, temperature of the substrate, and the temperature of the applied SFRM. Control of these temperatures is necessary so that the chemical reactions needed to make the SFRM bond to the steel substrate properly occur. The minimum or maximum temperatures needed for proper bond and cure depend on the particular system.

1704.11.3 Thickness. The SFRM must be applied at the correct thickness for the system to provide the required fire resistance. The sampling and thickness determinations are based on ASTM E605. This standard also provides testing methods commonly used by industry. See Reference 11 for additional information on inspection of SFRM.

1704.11.3.1 Floor, roof and wall assemblies. The frequency of thickness measurements for membrane assemblies; i.e., walls, floors and roofs, is based on square footage.

1704.11.3.2 Structural framing members. The frequency of thickness measurements for structural framing members such as columns is based on the number of members with a minimum of 25 percent of the structural members on each floor.

1704.11.4 Density. The SFRM must be applied at the correct density in order for the system to provide the required fire resistance. The sampling and density determinations are based on ASTM E 605.

1704.11.5 Bond strength. The bond of the SFRM to the steel substrate is essential for the SFRM to provide the required fire resistance. The sampling and bond strength determinations are based on ASTM E 736. The minimum cohesive/adhesive bond strength of 150 pounds per square foot is based on the American Institute of Architects (AIA) Master Specifications. The sampling rates for bond strength, as set forth in IBC Sections 1704.11.5.1 and 1704.11.5.2, are lower than those for thickness and density, as the determinations for thickness and density give an indirect indication of bond.

1704.12 Exterior insulation and finish systems (EIFS). Special inspection for EIFS systems should be based on the manufacturer's installation instructions. Critical areas necessary for adequate EIFS performance are proper installation of the waterproofing membrane and installation of flashings at windows, doors, joints, eaves, corners, and penetrations.

1704.13 Special cases. This section requires special inspections for proposed work that is unique or unusual and not specifically addressed in the code or in standards referenced by the code.

1704.14 Special inspection for smoke control. This section, although related to mechanical systems rather than structural or architectural systems, is in this code because the mechanical ductwork and signaling devices are likely to be concealed during the building construction and the ductwork needs to be leakage tested prior to concealment.

SECTION 1705 QUALITY ASSURANCE FOR SEISMIC RESISTANCE

1705.1 Scope. A building may have meticulous design but still perform poorly when subjected to seismic ground shaking if the building was not constructed in accordance with the design requirements. Post-earthquake studies indicate that a substantial number of earthquake related structural and nonstructural failures can be attributed to poor quality control during construction. Hence, it is necessary to have extensive quality assurance/quality control (QA/QC) to ensure adequate seismic resistance. The lateral-force-resisting systems for structures in higher seismic design categories are complex and can be difficult to construct. Hence, these structures rely on good quality control for performance. For example, the welded joints in steel moment frames are critical to performance that meets the safety requirements of the code. QA/QC programs and special inspection are necessary to ensure that the welds meet the code requirements.

Additionally, experience in high seismic risk regions has shown that nonstructural components and systems are vulnerable to damage if not properly installed or anchored. Ductwork and piping can be damaged by swaying if not restrained. Similarly, suspended ceiling systems are particularly vulnerable if not properly installed and create a falling hazard. Note that several of the hospitals were not operable after the 1994 Northridge earthquake because of damage to mechanical and electrical systems, not the structural systems themselves.

The quality assurance plan outlined in this section, which only applies to seismic requirements, did not originate from the model codes but was developed from the 1997 NEHRP provisions.[12] The quality assurance plan applies to the seismic lateral-force-resisting system, the designated seismic systems, and certain mechanical and electrical equipment depending on the seismic design category assigned to the structure. The designated seismic systems are those architectural, mechanical, and electrical systems that have a component importance factor, I_P, greater than 1. (See IBC Section 1613 for definition of the above terms and Section 1621.1.6 for values of I_P.)

There are several specific exceptions in which a quality assurance plan is not required:

1. When the structure is designed and constructed in accordance with the light frame wood conventional construction provisions of Section 2308.
2. When the structure is constructed of light frame wood or cold-formed light gauge steel, and S_{DS} does not exceed 0.5g, and the height of the structure does not exceed 35 feet, and the structure is classified as Seismic Use Group I per Section 1616.2, and the structure has none of the listed plan or vertical irregularities.
3. When the structure has a reinforced concrete or reinforced masonry structural system, and S_{DS} does not exceed 0.5 g, and the height of the structure does not exceed 25 feet, and the structure is classified as Seismic Use Group I, and the structure has none of the listed plan or vertical irregularities.
4. When the structure is a detached one- or two-family dwelling not exceeding two stories in height, and the structure is classified as Seismic Use Group I, and the structure has none of the listed plan or vertical irregularities.

Note that under Exception 2, Item 2.1 or 2.2 or 2.3 must be complied with, as well as both 2.3.1 and 2.3.2.

1705.2 Quality assurance plan preparation. The quality assurance plan should be prepared by a registered design professional and in cooperation with the registered design professional responsible for the structure design.

1705.3 Contractor responsibility. Each contractor who is responsible for the construction of any of the systems designated in Section 1705.1 must acknowledge the requirements of the quality assurance plan and submit a quality control plan detailing his or her QC plan requirements and personnel.

SECTION 1706
QUALITY ASSURANCE FOR WIND REQUIREMENTS

1706.1 Scope. A building may have meticulous design but still perform poorly when subjected to high wind speeds if the building was not properly constructed in accordance with the design requirements. Post hurricane studies indicate that a substantial number of wind-related structural and nonstructural failures can be attributed to poor quality control during construction. Hence, it is necessary to have QA/QC plans to ensure wind resistance. The wind quality assurance requirements are aimed at having a complete load path for the wind loads from the cladding through the main wind-force-resisting structural system to the foundation.

The quality assurance plan for wind requirements applies to buildings in Wind Exposure Categories A and B where the 3-second-gust basic wind speed is 120 mph or greater, and Wind Exposure Categories C and D where the 3-second-gust basic wind speed is 110 mph or greater.

There is one specific exception in which a quality assurance plan is not required: when the structure is designed and constructed in accordance with the wood conventional construction provisions of Section 2308 or the *International Residential Code* and the applicable items listed in Section 1706.1.2 are inspected. These inspections are required even though the quality assurance plan is not.

1706.2 Quality assurance plan preparation. The quality assurance plan should be prepared by a registered design professional in cooperation with the registered design professional responsible for the structure design.

1706.3 Contractor responsibility. Each contractor who is responsible for the construction of any of the systems designated in the QA plan must acknowledge the requirements of the quality assurance plan and submit a quality control plan detailing his or her QC plan requirements and personnel.

SECTION 1707
SPECIAL INSPECTIONS FOR SEISMIC RESISTANCE

Section 1707 sets forth the specific requirements for special inspection for seismic resistance, whereas Section 1704 sets forth the special inspection requirements in general. The special inspections required in this section are in addition to those required in Section 1704.

1707.1 Special inspection for seismic resistance. Special inspection for seismic resistance is only required for structures in SDC C, D, E or F and only when required by Section 1704. Special inspection for designated systems is a function of the Component Importance Factor, I_P, as given in Section 1621.1.6. See analysis of Section 1707.7.

1707.2 Steel. The requirements are the same as those set forth in Table 1704.3, Item 5, continuous inspection of welding in accordance with AWS D1.1.

1707.3 Structural wood. The inspections are to ensure continuity of load path within the seismic lateral-force-resisting system. The walls will transfer their inertial loads to the diaphragms which will in turn transmit the inertial loads to the lateral-force-resisting system and thence to the foundation. Particular care should be given to the nailing of diaphragms and shear walls. Common nails are often specified in the design, but smaller diameter sinkers or power driven (gun) nails are often substituted— the smaller diameter nails have a lower lateral resistance. For example, the lateral resistance of a 0.131-inch diameter power driven nail used as a replacement for a 10d common nail in Douglas Fir-Larch is only 76 pounds, whereas the value for the 10d common nail is 90 pounds. Also of particular importance is the connection of drag struts or collectors to the shear walls and the proper installation and tightening of hold-down bolts in shear walls.

1707.4 Cold-formed steel framing. The inspections are to ensure continuity of load path within the seismic lateral-force-resisting system; i.e., the walls will transfer their inertial loads to the diaphragms, which will in turn transmit the inertial loads to the lateral-force-resisting system and thence to the foundation. Particular care should be given to connections of braces and hold-downs.

1707.5 Storage racks and access floors. Proper anchorage is critical to keep racks from overturning.

1707.6 Architectural components. Exterior cladding and veneers can be lethal if detached from the structure during seismic shaking as well as potentially blocking exit paths.

1707.7 Mechanical and electrical components. Inspection is necessary for components that must function in post earthquake conditions such as emergency electrical systems or for anchorage of mechanical equipment, piping and ducting using or carrying flammable or hazardous materials.

1707.7.1 Component inspection. The special inspection required for installation of the components listed in Section 1707.7.1 should include a quality control program.

1707.7.2 Component and attachment testing. The component manufacturer is required to test the components and their mounting and anchorage system to sustain the design forces of Chapter 16.

1707.7.3 Component manufacturer certification. The manufacturer of equipment located in buildings assigned to SDC E or F must maintain an approved quality control program.

1707.8 Seismic isolation system. The performance of seismic isolators is critical to the performance of isolation systems. See analysis of Section 1623.5 for the inspection requirements.

SECTION 1708
STRUCTURAL TESTING FOR SEISMIC RESISTANCE

Section 1708 sets forth the required structural testing for seismic resistance. The trigger mechanisms for the required tests parallel those for special inspection for masonry structures in Section 1704.5 and parallel those for special inspection for seismic resistance for all other structures in SDC C, D, E and F in Section 1707.1.

1708.1 Masonry. Certificates of compliance for materials used is required for all categories. Testing is required only as set forth below. In actuality, the testing is for verification that actual compressive strength, f'_m, using the proposed constituent masonry, mortar, and grout, meets or exceeds that specified prior to construction. Compressive strength, f'_m, can be determined by testing the strength of the constituent materials or the strength of masonry prisms.

1708.1.1 Empirically designed masonry and glass unit masonry in nonessential facilities. Certificates of compliance for the materials used are required in accordance with Table 1708.1.1.

1708.1.2 Empirically designed masonry and glass unit masonry in essential facilities. Certificates of compliance for the materials used are required, and verification of compressive strength, f'_m, prior to construction is required in accordance with Table 1708.1.2.

1708.1.3 Engineered masonry in nonessential facilities. Certificates of compliance for the materials used are required, and verification of compressive strength, f'_m, prior to construction is required in accordance with Table 1708.1.2.

1708.1.4 Engineered masonry in essential facilities. Certificates of compliance for the materials used are required, and verification of compressive strength, f'_m, prior to construction is required. In addition, verification of the proportions in the mortar and grout as delivered. See Table 1708.1.4.

1708.2 Testing for seismic resistance. Structural testing for seismic resistance is required only for structures in SDC C, D, E or F, and when required by Section 1704. Structural testing for designated systems is a function of the Component Importance Factor, I_P, as given in Section 1621.1.6. See also analysis of Section 1707.7.

1708.3 Reinforcing and prestressing steel. Certified mill reports are used in lieu of testing to establish conformance to code requirements except that when reinforcing steel conforming to ASTM A615 is used in special moment-resisting frames or in the boundary elements of shear walls in SDC D, E or F, the steel yield and ultimate strengths must be specifically tested.

Additionally, if A615 reinforcing steel is to be welded, the chemical composition must be determined. The weldability of the steel is determined by its chemical content. AWS D1.4, *Structural Welding Code—Reinforcing Steel,* bases the welding requirements, including preheat and interpass temperature, on the carbon equivalent, which is based on the steel chemistry and the bar size. See analysis of Section 1704.3.1 concerning requirements for welding procedures.

1708.4 Structural Steel. The required testing is set forth in the AISC LRFD Specification, Section M2,[5] supplemented by the following requirements:

1. All complete joint penetration and partial joint penetration groove welds subject to net tension forces must be tested by nondestructive methods.
2. The acceptance criteria for nondestructive testing are either those for static loading or dynamic loading as designated by the registered design professional.
3. Base metal thicker than $1^1/_2$ inches subject to through thickness weld shrinkage strains. For example, a T-joint or the column flange in a typical beam-column connection, must be tested for discontinuities, such as lamellar tearing, after testing. See Figure 2 for an example of a weld susceptible to weld shrinkage strains.

1708.5 Mechanical and electrical equipment. This requirement applies to designated seismic system components as outlined in Section 1707.1 and 1707.7. The mechanical and electrical components must be seismically qualified to resist the forces set forth in Chapter 16. Qualification may be by shake table testing, shock testing, analysis where appropriate, or by historical data showing acceptable seismic performance. See the commentary in the 1996 SEAOC *Recommended Lateral Force Requirements*[13] for an excellent discussion of equipment that has a historical record of good seismic performance.

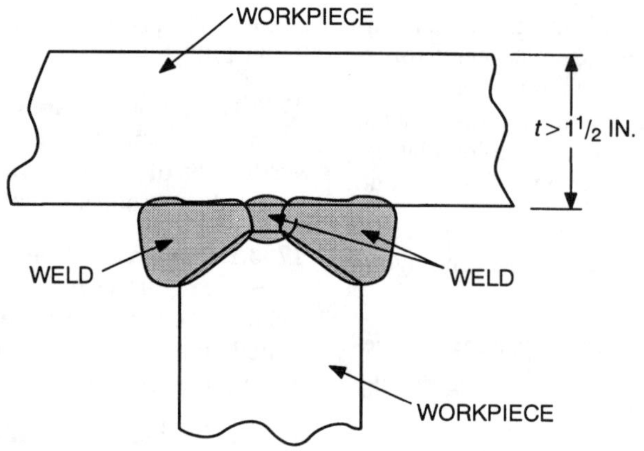

WELD SUSCEPTIBLE TO SHRINKAGE STRESSES

FIGURE 2

1708.6 Seismically isolated structures. See analysis of Section 1623.8.

SECTION 1709 STRUCTURAL OBSERVATIONS

1709.1 Structural observation. Structural observation requirements first appeared in the 1988 UBC. The requirements were applicable for buildings in high seismic risk areas. The purpose of structural observation is to ensure that the lateral-force-resisting system is constructed in general conformance with the approved structure drawings and specifications. Since the registered design professional is most familiar with the design concept of the lateral-force-resisting system, he or she is the most appropriate person to execute the requisite observation. Note that structural observation is in addition to, not in place of, special inspection.

Structural observation is required for the lateral-force-resisting system for both wind and seismic, but the requirements for seismic are limited to structures in high seismic risk areas (SDC D, E and F) that are either essential structures, structures that represent a substantial hazard to human life in the event of a failure, structures that exceed 75 feet in height or ordinary structures in SDC E exceeding two stories in height. Similarly, the requirements for wind are limited to areas where wind speeds exceed 110 mph (3-second gust) and the structures are either essential structures, structures that represent a substantial hazard to human life in the event of a failure or structures that exceed 75 feet in height.

SECTION 1710 DESIGN STRENGTHS OF MATERIALS

This section requires structural materials to conform to design standards or accepted engineering practices.

1710.1 Conformance to standards. Structural materials must conform to design standards, approved rules or accepted engineering practices.

1710.2 New materials. Materials not explicitly covered by the code are allowed subject to testing that demonstrates adequate performance (see Section 1711).

SECTION 1711 ALTERNATIVE TEST PROCEDURES

Test reports from approved agencies may be used as the basis for approval of materials not covered by the code or any approved rules. New materials are mentioned in Section 1701.2. Note that this section references the use of new, innovative, or alternative materials from Section 104.11. The building official has the authority to accept such materials based on reports from an approved agency that is independent from the material supplier.

SECTION 1712 TEST SAFE LOAD

Testing to determine a safe load is required when a structure or component cannot be designed or analyzed in accordance with accepted engineering principles and practices, or where the construction design method does not fully comply with the respective material design standards found in Chapter 35.

SECTION 1713 IN-SITU LOAD TESTS

This section covers load testing for existing structures or portions thereof, where the load-bearing capacity or stability is in doubt. The requirements should not be confused with the test procedures set forth in Section 1714 for materials, components and assemblies prior to construction.

1713.1 General. When there is doubt as to the structural integrity, load-carrying capacity, or stability of an existing structure or portion thereof, the building official has the option of requiring a structural analysis or a load test or both. If the structural analysis shows that the structure is not capable of safely carrying the code-design loads, the structure must be load-tested.

1713.2 Test standards. When load test procedures are given in a referenced standard, those procedures should be followed. An example would be the test procedures in the SJI standard specification.[14] When the referenced standard lacks a load test procedure or there is no reference standard for the structure or portions thereof, a registered design professional should develop a test procedure and test protocol that simulate the actual loading conditions, both loads and displacements, that the structure is expected to experience.

1713.3 In-situ load tests. In-situ tests fall into two categories: procedures specified and procedures not specified (see below). The test must be performed under the supervision of the registered design professional.

1713.3.1 Load test procedure specified. When the applicable standard has a test procedure and acceptance criteria specified, the standard shall apply.

1713.3.2 Load test procedures not specified. When there is no applicable load test procedure in a referenced standard, the structure or portion thereof should be tested with a loading protocol that simulates the actual loads and deformations, both lateral and vertical, that the structure is expected to receive. For the gravity system, the vertical loads shall be twice the unfactored design loads. Dead loads should include expected partition loads.

SECTION 1714
PRECONSTRUCTION LOAD TESTS

1714.1 General. When the load carrying capacity and the physical properties of materials or methods of construction are not amenable to analysis by accepted engineering methods or the material or method does not comply with applicable standards, the structural load capacity and physical properties must be determined by tests. This section is applicable to components, assemblies, and elements of structures; e.g., windows. This section is not applicable to load testing of existing structures (see analysis of Section 1713).

1714.2 Load test procedures specified. When an applicable standard has a test procedure and acceptance criteria, the standard shall apply.

1714.3 Load test procedures not specified. When there is no applicable load test procedure in a referenced standard, the structure or portion thereof should be tested with a loading protocol that simulates the actual loads and deformations, both lateral and vertical, that the structure is expected to receive. For components, assemblies and elements that are not part of the lateral force resisting system, the loading and acceptance criteria are set forth in Section 1714.3.1.

1714.3.1 Test procedure. The loading procedure and acceptance criteria use commonly accepted engineering practices to test the adequacy of the component or assembly to resist structural failure at the design loads. This procedure should be used only for loads for which the upper bounds can be established with a reasonable degree of accuracy such as dead and live loads. This procedure should not be used for earthquake loads and should be used with care for wind loads.

1714.3.2 Deflection. Deflection under design load is limited to those set forth in Section 1604.3

1714.4 Wall and partition assemblies. The assembly must be tested for simultaneous vertical and lateral loads, both with and without window framing.

1714.5 Exterior window and door assemblies. Doors and window assemblies are generally qualified by tests. The allowable wind pressures for smaller units made of identical components, including glass thickness, may be higher as determined by analysis, provided that an additional test be made on the assembly with the highest pressure to validate the analysis.

1714.5.1 Aluminum, vinyl, and wood exterior windows and glass doors. These window and door assemblies must be tested and labeled to the cited standard, which is a performance-based specification (see Sections 1702 and 1703.5). The glass in these tested and labeled assemblies is not subject to the deflection limits of Section 2403. The test load is equal to 1.5 times the design pressure, as determined by IBC Chapter 16, applied for 10 seconds.

1714.5.2 Exterior windows and door assemblies not provided for in Section 1714.5. Test per ASTM E 330. The test load is equal to 1.5 times the design pressure, as determined per Chapter 16, applied for 10 seconds.

1714.6 Test specimens. Test specimens should be representative. Tests must be conducted or witnessed by an independent approved agency.

SECTION 1715
MATERIAL AND TEST STANDARDS

This section sets forth the test standards and acceptance criteria for joist hangers and concrete and clay roof tiles.

1715.1 Test standards for joist hangers and connectors.

1715.1.1 Test standards for joist hangers. Testing is typically performed using specimens of Douglas Fir-Larch (specific gravity 0.50) or Southern Pine (specific gravity 0.55) per ASTM D 1761.

1715.1.2 Vertical load capacity for joist hangers. This section sets forth the test and acceptance criteria. Note that items 1 and 2 are the strength limit states of the hangar, item 3 is a deflection limit state, and items 4 and 5 are design load limit states for the fasteners and wood respectively.

1715.1.3 Torsional moment capacity for joist hangers. The allowable load is based on a deflection limit.

1715.1.4 Design value modifications for joist hangers. Only the design value based on the design load limit states for the fasteners or wood member (items 4 or 5 in Section 1715.1.2) are allowed to be increased for duration of load per the NDS. No increase is allowed for loads limited by steel strength or deflection.

REFERENCES

[1] CCTIA, *Guidelines for Special Inspection in Construction*, California Council of Testing and Inspection Agencies, c/o Testing Engineers, 2811 Adeline Street, Oakland, CA 94608, 1996.

[2] AWS D1.1-98, *Structural Welding Code—Steel*, American Welding Society, Miami, FL, 1998.

[3] PCI MNL 116-85, *Manual for Quality Control for Plants and Production of Precast Concrete Products*, Prestressed/Precast Concrete Institute, Chicago, IL, 1987.

[4] AISC ASD-89, *Specification for Structural Steel Buildings—Allowable Stress Design*, American Institute for Steel Construction, Inc., Chicago, IL, 1989.

[5] AISC LRFD-93, *Load and Resistance Factor Design Specification for Structural Steel Buildings*, American Institute for Steel Construction, Inc., Chicago, IL, 1998.

[6] RCSC-85, *Specification for Structural Joints Using A325 or A490 Bolts* (with 1988 Revisions), Research Council on Structural Connections, Chicago, IL, 1988.

[7] SSTC, *Structural Bolting Handbook*, Steel Structures Technology Center, Inc., Novi, MI, 1999.

[8] ACI 318-99, *Building Code Requirements for Structural Concrete*, American Concrete Institute, Farmington Hills, MI, 1999.

[9] ACI 530/ASCE 5/TMS 402, *Building Code Requirements for Masonry Structures*, American Concrete Institute, Farmington Hills, MI, 1995.

[10] ACI 530.1/ASCE 6/TMS 602, *Specification for Masonry Structures*, American Concrete Institute, Farmington Hills, MI, 1995.

[11] AWCI, Technical Manual 12-A, Standard Practice for the Testing and Inspection of Field Applied Sprayed Fire-Resistive Materials; An Annotative Guide, The Association of the Wall and Ceiling Industries—International, Falls Church, VA, 1997.

[12] NEHRP, *NEHRP (National Earthquake Hazard Reduction Program) Recommended Provisions for the Development of Seismic Regulations for New Buildings (and Other Structures)*, Building Seismic Safety Council, Washington, D.C., 1994 (1997).

[13] SEAOC, *Recommended Lateral Force Requirements and Commentary*, Structural Engineers Association of California, Sacramento, CA, 1996.

[14] SCI-1994, *Standard Specification, Load Tables, and weight Tables for Steel Joists and Joist Girders*, Steel Joist Institute, Myrtle Beach, SC, 1994.

BIBLIOGRAPHY

AISC Seismic-97, *Seismic Provisions for Structural Steel Buildings* (including Supplement No. 1, February 1999), American Institute for Steel Construction, Inc., Chicago, IL, April 1997.

AWS D1.4-98, *Structural Welding Code—Reinforcing Steel*, American Welding Society, Miami, FL, 1998.

BOCA, *The BOCA National Building Code—Commentary Volume 2*, Building Officials & Code Administrators International, Inc., Country Club Hills, IL, 1999.

ICBO, *Handbook to the Uniform Building Code: An illustrative commentary*, International Conference of Building Officials, Inc., Whittier, CA, 1998.

ICC, *Proposed Changes to the Final Draft of the International Building Code*, International Code Council, January 1999.

ICC, *1998 Proposed Changes to the First Draft of the International Building Code*, International Code Council, April 1998.

UBC-IBC Structural Comparison & Cross Reference, International Conference of Building Officials, Inc., Whittier, CA, 2000.

CHAPTER 18
SOILS AND FOUNDATIONS

The satisfactory performance of foundations is critical to the satisfactory performance of structures. Most building structures are designed assuming a fixed unyielding base that is not subjected to large total or differential settlements or displacements. Shallow foundations on firm soils will generally perform satisfactorily if the requirements of these provisions are followed.

Foundation design, however, becomes a significant factor for large structures, embedded structures, such as a tall building constructed over a multi-level basement garage, structures on soft soils, structures supporting rotating or reciprocating equipment, and structures sensitive to differential displacements. It is important to have a good knowledge of the behavior of the various foundation types, including their limitations. In addition, for structures subject to high wind forces or seismic ground shaking, special consideration must be given to the lateral load path, and, in the case of deep foundation pile-supported structures, the ability of the deep foundation to survive the displacements and curvatures imposed on the pile by seismic ground motion.

Sufficient understanding of the behavior and limitations of the various deep and shallow foundations is necessary to determine that the foundation and the supported structure will provide the intended serviceability. It is important to determine whether the estimated total and differential settlements of the foundation are compatible with the selected structure type. For example, a stiff bearing wall structure with openings may be more sensitive to differential settlements than a more flexible light frame structure. When considering seismic ground shaking, sufficient knowledge of ground shaking effects on the foundation is important, particularly in soft soils.

SECTION 1801
GENERAL

1801.1 Scope. The provisions apply to foundations not subject to scour or water pressure by wind or wave action. For example, these provisions would not be applicable to a beach-front structure that would be subjected to wave runup and inundation during hurricanes. See Section 1612 for flood loads.

1801.2 Design. Note that bearing pressures, stresses, and lateral pressures used in this chapter are allowable pressures or stresses, not strength level values. These allowable pressures are to be used with the allowable stress design load combinations set forth in Section 1605.3 unless noted otherwise.

1801.2.1 Foundation design for seismic overturning. This section was added to clarify that when strength design loads are used to proportion the foundations, the seismic overturning moment need not exceed 75 percent of the moment determined in accordance with Section 1617 or 1618. This maximum recognizes that the seismic forces determined in those sections are based on strength design, not allowable stress design (ASD). The strength design seismic loads set forth in Chapter 16 are approximately 1.4 times the previous ASD seismic loads. Hence, $0.75 \approx 1/1.4$. Foundations proportioned in accordance with ASD procedures have historically performed satisfactorily.

SECTION 1802
FOUNDATION AND SOILS INVESTIGATIONS

The reorganization of this section consolidates all the conditions for which a soils investigation and report is necessary into Section 1802.2 and, the information necessary to be included in a soils report is in Section 1802.6.

1802.1 General. A foundation and soils investigation must be conducted when required by the building official. In general, the investigation should be required unless the foundation is designed and constructed in accordance with the presumptive allowable foundation pressures and lateral bearing pressures set forth in Section 1804.2. Some minimal knowledge of soil classification at the bearing elevation of the foundation is required by Section 1804.2 A registered design professional should be used as required by the professional practice laws of the state in which the jurisdiction lies. The practice of geotechnical or soils engineering is a branch of civil engineering and the practice of geotechnical or soils engineering is generally regulated by the various states.

1802.2 Where required. A foundation and soils investigation is required for any of the adverse subsurface conditions listed in Sections 1802.2.1 through 1802.2.7.

The exception allows the building official some flexibility in requiring a foundation and soils investigation when the soil conditions of the site are already known from other soils reports. For example, if the site is located in an area where there are reasonably uniform and horizontal soil strata and a soils report is available for the adjacent parcels, then a new soils report should not be necessary.

1802.2.1 Questionable soil. Two cases trigger a foundation and soils investigation:

1. Where the design load bearing value is greater than the presumptive allowable foundation pressures and lateral bearing pressures set forth in Section 1804.2.
2. Where the bearing capacity of the soil is questionable such as in areas subject to liquefaction from strong ground shaking, in areas containing soft or sensitive clays such as bay muds, or in areas with unconsolidated or improperly consolidated fills.

Generally, the first case will be triggered for buildings other than light frame construction, whereas the second case will be triggered for all buildings.

1802.2.2 Expansive soils. Expansive soils are those that shrink and swell appreciably because of changes in soil moisture content. See Section 1802.3.2 for classification of expansive soils, and Section 1805.8 for mitigation methods for expansive soils. Frost heave is not considered in this section.

1802.2.3 Groundwater table. This section may cause significant changes to the conventional approach to foundation design and construction for light-framed buildings with subsurface floors, either a basement or a hillside building with a floor cut into the hillside. A foundation and soils investigation is required to show that the ground-water table is at least five feet below the elevation of the lowest floor level unless waterproofing is provided in accordance with Section 1806.

1802.2.4 Pile and pier foundations. It is generally not economical or feasible to use pier or pile foundations without a soils investigation and report.

1802.2.5 Rock strata. If a rock stratum is being used for bearing, the characteristics of the layer must be known in sufficient detail to classify the rock per Section 1802.3.

1802.2.6 Seismic Design Category C. For all structures, a foundation and soils investigation is required to evaluate liquefaction, slope stability, and surface rupture caused by faulting or lateral spreading. Significant ground motion can occur even in areas with moderate seismic risk. Liquefaction typically occurs at sites with loose sands and high water tables. Surface rupture generally occurs with large magnitude earthquake events. Lateral spreading generally occurs adjacent to waterways where a saturated soil has a free edge.

1802.2.7 Seismic Design Categories D, E, and F. In addition to the investigation required for Seismic Design Category (SDC) C by Section 1802.2.6, the investigation must evaluate the additional lateral pressures on basement or retaining walls from ground shaking, the detrimental effects of liquefaction or soil strength loss, and mitigation methods. The potential for liquefaction and soil strength loss must be evaluated using the peak acceleration based on a site specific study and including the effects of soil amplification.

Liquefaction causes loss of bearing capacity with resulting large differential or total settlements. Structures with high height to width ratios that have liquefaction occur under a portion of the structure are subject to overturning. Many of the structures damaged in various Japanese earthquakes suffered the consequences of liquefaction and overturned.

Soil strength loss is associated with "sensitive" or "quick" clays that are sensitive to remolding effects. These soft clays typically occur in marine (or former marine) environments and are often called "bay muds." These clays lose significant strength when remolded. Remolding and subsequent strength loss occurs when a pile foundation through these clays is subjected to strong ground shaking. As a consequence, lateral support for the pile is lost.

Mitigation methods for liquefaction include:

1. In-situ densification of the loose sands subject to liquefaction.
2. Use of pile foundations penetrating through the liquefying layers. The pile capacity must be developed through bearing or skin friction in the soils below the liquefying layers.
3. Use of rigid raft foundations that can minimize the effects of settlement caused by loss of bearing capacity.

Mitigation methods for soils susceptible to strength loss such as "sensitive" or "quick" clays include:

1. Replacement of the soft clay.
2. In-situ consolidation of the soft clays by preloading or water removal.
3. Use of pile foundations penetrating through the soft clay layers. The pile capacity must be developed through bearing or skin friction in the soils below the soft clay layers.

If using pile foundations, the effects of the layers of liquefaction or soils susceptible to strength loss on the curvature (and hence, moment) demands on the pile must be investigated. Often these soil induced curvatures place a much higher moment demand on the piles than would be determined from conventional lateral force P-y analyses. The curvatures are significantly increased at the interface between the soft soils and stiffer soils. The curvature demands increase as the ratio of stiffness of the stiff layer to the soft layer increases.

1802.3 Soil classification.

1802.3.1 General. Soils are classified in accordance with the Unified Soil Classification System as set forth in ASTM D 2487.

1802.3.2 Expansive soils. Expansive soils are those that shrink and swell appreciably in accordance with changes in soil moisture content. Expansive soils are present or prevalent in all 50 states. Soils must meet all four of the criteria to be classified expansive, not just a high Plasticity or Expansion Index. See Section 1805.8 for mitigation methods for expansive soils.

1802.4 Investigation. The investigation must consider all the evaluations set forth in this section as applicable. Slope stability is a new variable.

1802.4.1 Exploratory boring. The investigation must be under the supervision of a registered design professional experienced in soils exploration.

1802.5 Soil boring and sampling. Whenever the allowable bearing capacity is in doubt or a foundation and soils investigation is necessary, exploratory borings, conducted in accordance with generally accepted practices, are necessary to determine the soil characteristics and determine the load bearing capacity. All borings and sampling should be done under the supervision of the registered design professional.

1802.6 Reports. The objective of a foundation and soils investigation is to produce all the necessary information for design and construction of the structure foundations. To ensure that the report of the foundation and soils investigation meets this objective and provides enough data to ensure compliance with the code and a safe foundation, the report must contain at a minimum the enumerated items. See also report requirements for compacted fill in Section 1803.4. Other data such as results of consolidation tests, compaction curves, sieve analyses, Attaberg Limits tests, Plasticity and Expansion Index tests, etc., should be included in the report where available.

SECTION 1803
EXCAVATION, GRADING, AND FILL

Some of the requirements relating to excavation, grading, and placement of fill were taken from the 1997 UBC, Chapter 33. See also the special inspection requirements in the analysis of Section 1704.7.

1803.1 Excavations near footings or foundations. The intent of this section is clear—do not remove lateral and subjacent support. For example, the area shown in Figure 1 should not be excavated without providing support for the foundation.

1803.2 Placement of backfill. Backfill should be performed in accordance with an approved soils report. If no soils report is needed, the backfill should be placed in maximum 6-inch layers free from any rocks or cobbles larger than 4 inches and compacted to a minimum 90-percent relative density (Modified Proctor per ASTM D 1557) using the appropriate compaction equipment.

1803.3 Site grading. Surface water must drain away from foundations. Minimum slope is 5 percent for a distance of 10 feet.

1803.4 Compacted fill material. When compacted fill is used for foundation support, the foundation and soils investigation report required in Section 1802.6 must also contain the items listed in this section. See also the special inspection requirements in analysis of Section 1704.7.

SECTION 1804
ALLOWABLE LOAD BEARING VALUES OF SOILS

1804.1 Design. The presumptive bearing values are allowable stress values, not strength level values.

1804.2 Presumptive load-bearing values. The presumptive allowable bearing and lateral pressures must be used unless a foundation and soils investigation substantiates higher values. The term "unprepared fill" means fill that was not placed and compacted in accordance with an approved soils report.

The format of IBC Table 1804.2 comes from the 1997 UBC. However, some of the unwieldy footnotes from the UBC version have been moved into the text of the code. Each of the model codes used a different approach to generate their allowable values. Hence, there was a disparity between the values shown in the model codes. The tabular values for allowable foundation pressure cannot be increased for width or depth as was allowed by the UBC. Jurisdictions that used the UBC will see larger footings under the IBC 2000 provisions. Note, however, that the allowable foundation pressures are permitted to be increased by one third for combinations including wind or earthquake to be consistent with previous editions of the model codes.

The classifications in Table 1804.2 are from the Unified Soil Classification System. Most foundation-bearing strata can be classified into one of the classifications in the table. The allowable bearing pressures and lateral bearing values are based on long experience with the behavior of these materials. However, the presumptive value for CL and CH may not be conservative for "soft" clays depending on the degree of consolidation of the clay. The selection of an allowable bearing pressure should take into account the strength of weaker underlying soil strata so that the pressure in any weaker stratum does not exceed the allowable pressure, particularly in clay soils. Because of this, it is important to know the soil profile and classifications of the different strata.

1804.3 Lateral sliding resistance. The classifications for lateral bearing in Table 1804.2 are from the Unified Soil Classification System. The lateral bearing values are based on long experience with the behavior of these materials. The limitation on frictional resistance for silts and clays in intended to provide structural stability and improve serviceability.

1804.3.1 Increases in allowable lateral sliding resistance. The formulae for lateral bearings (found in IBC Section 1805.7) were originally for outdoor advertising structures. For these

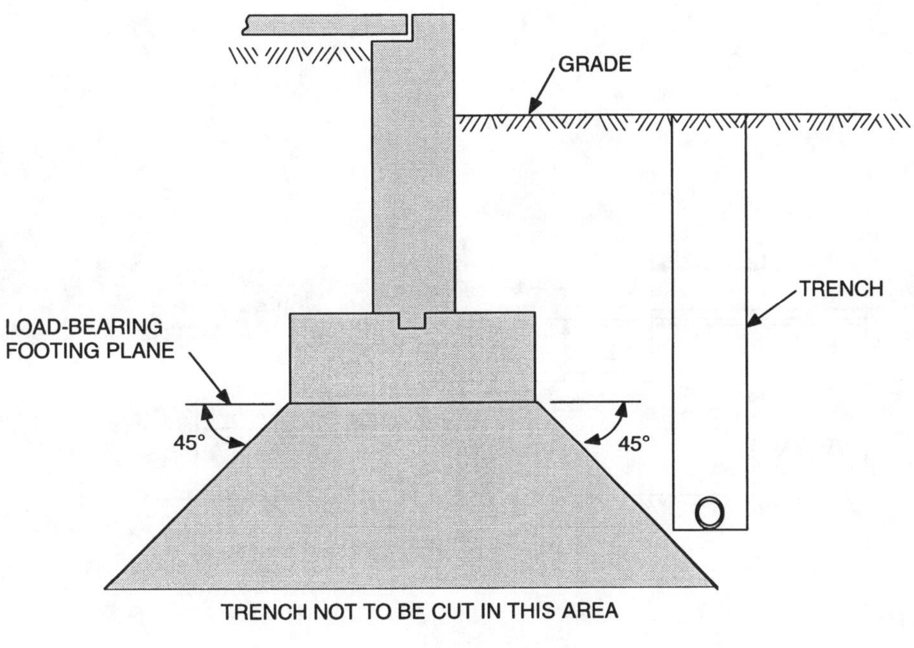

LATERAL SUPPORT

FIGURE 1

structures, deflections of $^1/_2$ inch at the surface do not affect serviceability. Thus, the allowance of two times the tabular value for these structures.

SECTION 1805 FOOTINGS AND FOUNDATIONS

This section contains design requirements for footings and foundations, including minimum footing size and depth, distance of footings from slopes, prescriptive foundation (basement) wall designs, foundations employing lateral bearing (pole foundations), and design procedures for expansive soils.

1805.1 General. Footings are required to be stepped when the slope of the bearing surface exceeds 1 in 10, but provides no recommendations or restrictions. Figure 2 schematically represents a satisfactory stepped foundation. The figure shows a recommended horizontal overlap of the top of the foundation wall beyond the step in the foundation to be larger than the vertical step in the foundation wall at that point. This is recommended to keep any crack propagation approximately at a 45-degree angle. To keep this cracking to a minimum, it is also recommended that the height of each step not exceed 1 to 2 feet. Other measures to protect against cracking such as special reinforcing details may also be needed.

1805.2 Depth of footings. Footings should always be placed on either firm undisturbed earth or properly compacted fill.

1805.2.1 Frost protection. To prevent frost heave during winter and subsequent settlement upon thawing, footings should be placed on a stratum with adequate load-bearing resistance that is below the frost line. Frost heave occurs because of the increased soil volume from the freezing of pore water in the soil. Clay soils, particularly saturated clays, are most susceptible to frost heave. Well-drained sands and gravels will not be susceptible to significant movement. If the foundations are built on soils that can freeze, the resulting frost heave, which is rarely uniform, can cause serious damage from differential settlements.

The frost line is defined as the lowest depth below the ground surface to which a temperature of 32°F extends. The factors governing the depth of the frost line are air temperature, the length of time the air temperature is below freezing (32°F), and the soil's thermal conductivity. Frost lines vary significantly throughout the country from no penetration in southern Florida to 100 inches in the northern regions of Michigan and Maine. Data on frost penetration is available from the U. S. Department of Commerce Weather Bureau. See Figure 3.

1805.2.2 Isolated footings. This restriction is intended to minimize the influence of vertical and lateral loads from footings at a higher elevation on footings at a lower elevation. See Figure 4.

1805.2.3 Shifting or moving soils. For example, loose sands.

1805.3 Footings on or adjacent to slopes. The provisions of this section apply only to buildings placed on or adjacent to slopes steeper than 1 vertical to 3 horizontal.

1805.3.1 Building clearance from ascending slopes. This setback requirement is intended to provide protection to the structure from shallow slope failure (sloughing) and protection for erosion and slope drainage. The setback space also provides access around the structure and helps to create a light and open environment. IBC Figure 1805.3.1 depicts the criterion for the setback or clearance. Figure 5 also depicts the criteria set forth in this item for determination of the toe of the slope when the slope exceeds 1:1.

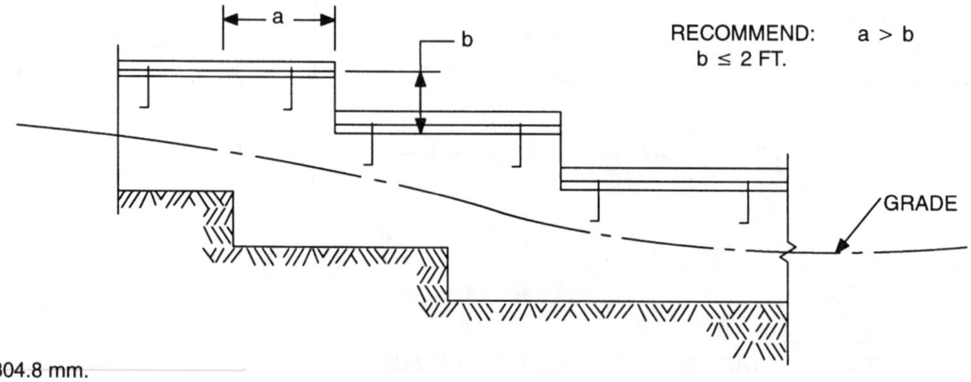

For SI: 1 foot = 304.8 mm.

STEPPED FOUNDATIONS

FIGURE 2

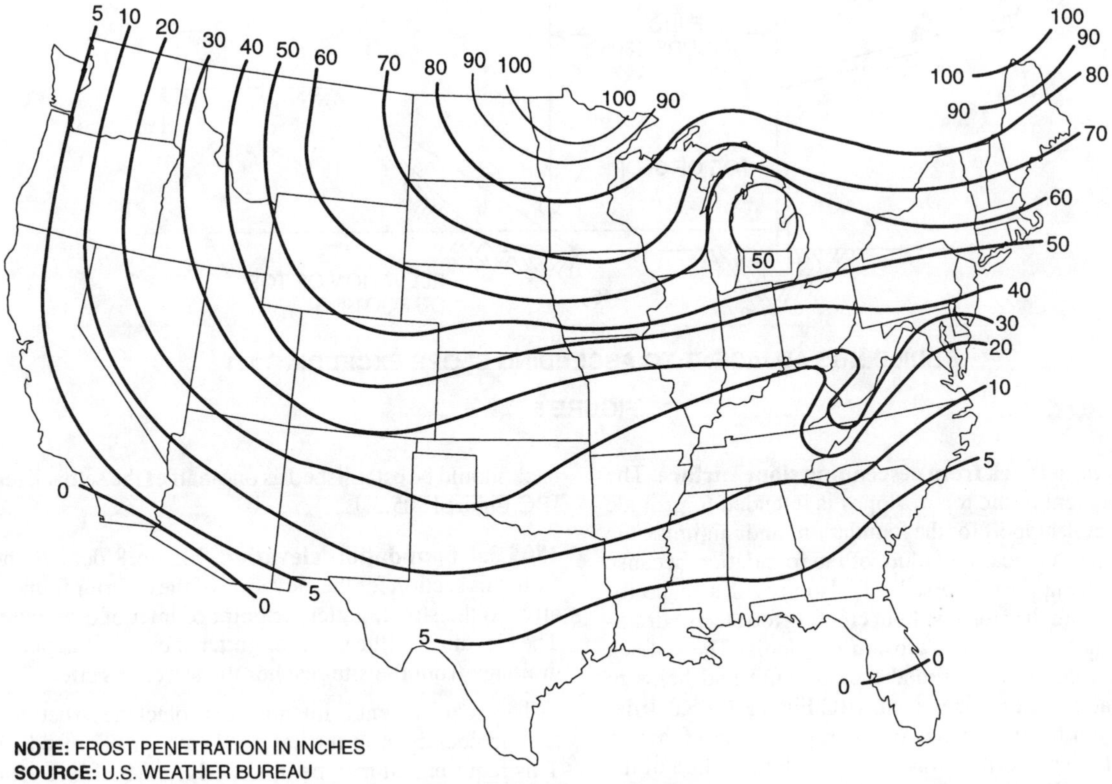

FROST PENETRATION DEPTHS

FIGURE 3

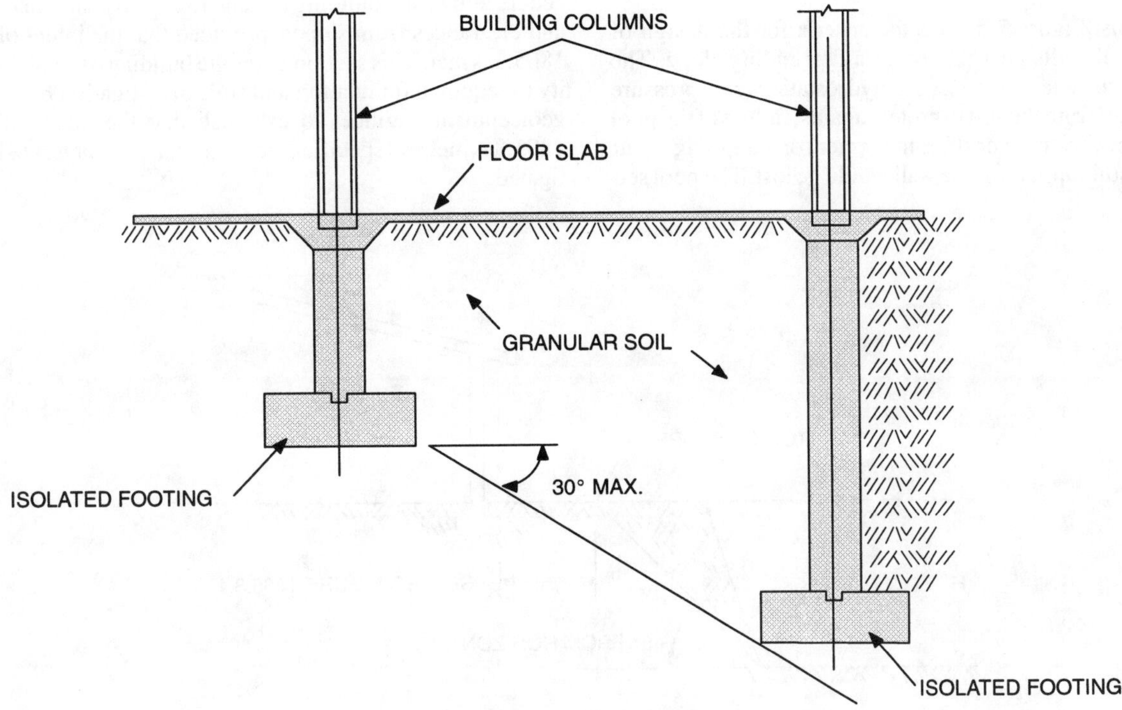

ISOLATED FOUNDATIONS

FIGURE 4

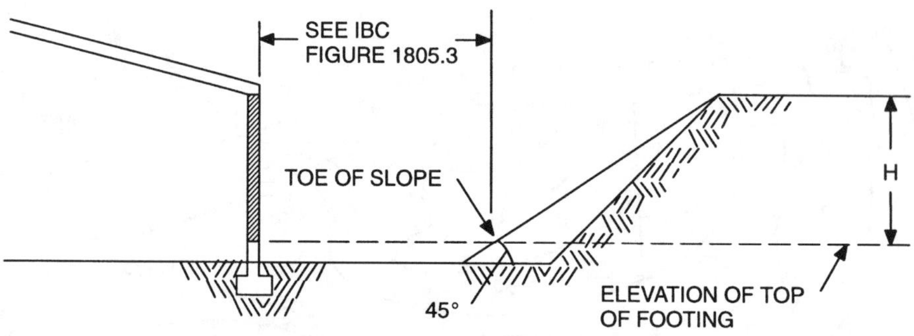

BUILDINGS ADJACENT TO ASCENDING SLOPE EXCEEDING 1:1

FIGURE 5

1805.3.2 Footing setback from descending slope surface. The setback requirement at the top of slopes is intended to provide vertical and lateral support for the foundations and minimize the possibility of shallow bearing failure of the foundation because of lack of lateral support. The setback also provides space for drainage away from the slope without creating too steep a drainage profile, which could cause erosion problems. The setback space also provides access around the structure and helps to create a light and open environment. IBC Figure 1805.3.1 depicts the criterion for the setback or clearance. Figure 6 herein depicts the criteria set forth in this item for determination of the toe of the slope when the slope exceeds 1:1.

It is possible to locate a structure closer to the slope than indicated in IBC Figure 1805.3.1. The footing of the structure may be located on the slope itself, provided that the depth of embedment of the footing is such that the face of the footing at the bearing plane is set back from the edge of the slope at least H/3.

1805.3.3 Pools. Figure 7 depicts the criteria for the design of swimming pool walls near the top of a descending slope. The wall must be sufficient to resist the hydrostatic water pressure without support from the soil to protect against failure of the pool wall should localized minor slope movement or sloughing occur such that the soil support for the wall would be lost. The pool setback should be established as one-half of the setback required by IBC Figure1805.3.1.

1805.3.4 Foundation elevation. Figure 8 depicts the criteria from this section for the elevation of the exterior foundations relative to the street, gutter, or point of inlet of a drainage device. The elevation of the street or gutter shown is that point at which drainage from the site reaches the street or gutter.

This requirement is intended to protect the structure from water encroachment in the case of heavy or unprecedented rains. This requirement may be modified if the building official finds that positive drainage slopes are provided to drain water away from the building and that the drainage pattern is not subject to temporary flooding from clogged drains, landscaping, or other impediments.

1805.3.5 Alternate setback and clearance. This alternate procedure allows the building official to approve alternate setbacks and clearances from slopes, provided that the intent of Section 1805.3 is met. This section gives the building official the authority to require a foundation and soils investigation by a qualified geotechnical engineer to establish that the intent of Section 1805.3 is met and specifies the minimum parameters to be investigated.

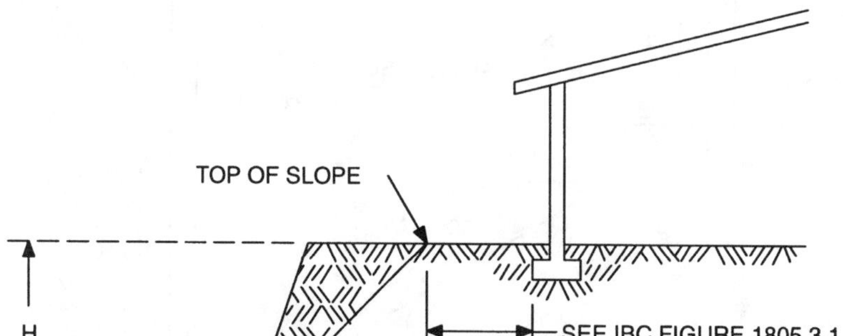

BUILDINGS ADJACENT TO DESCENDING SLOPE EXCEEDING 1:1

FIGURE 6

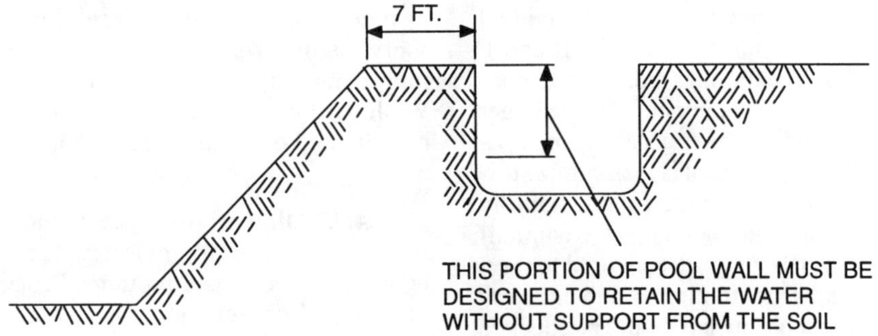

For SI: 1 foot = 304.8 mm.

SWIMMING POOL ADJACENT TO DESCENDING SLOPE

FIGURE 7

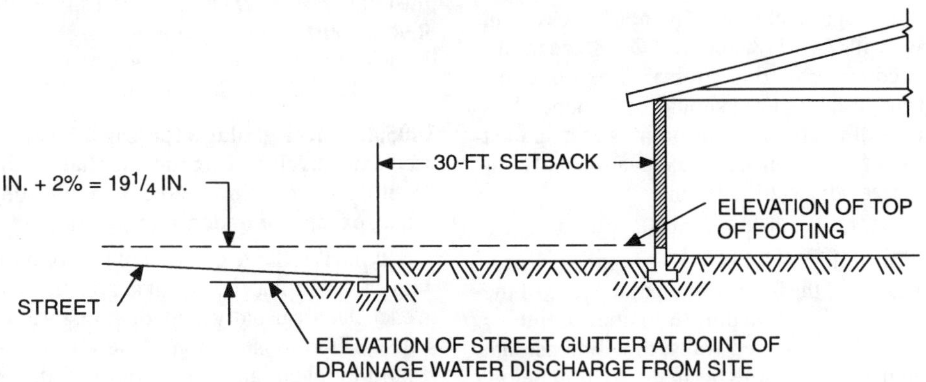

For SI: 1 inch = 25.4 mm, 1 foot = 304.8 mm.

FOOTING ELEVATION ON GRADED SITES

FIGURE 8

1805.4 Footings. This section contains the design requirements for footings and foundations, including minimum footing size and depth.

1805.4.1 Design. Footings should be designed for approximately equal settlements to minimize differential settlements. For footings on sands, this may require unequal footing pressures to effect equal settlements. For example see Terzaghi.[1]

1805.4.1.1 Design loads. Footings are to be designed using full dead load (including overlying fill materials), floor and roof live loads, snow load, wind or seismic forces, and any other loads required by Section 1613 that will produce the most severe loading. Live loads may be reduced based on the reduced probability of simultaneous occurrence of maximum live loads. The topic of reduction of live loads for footing design has not been previously addressed in some model codes.

1805.4.1.2 Vibratory loads. Footings supporting equipment should be designed to minimize the transmission of vibratory loads to the soils. The dynamic interaction of the footing, equipment, and soil mass should be analyzed, and the footing "tuned" to minimize the transmission. As a rough rule of thumb, footings for rotating or reciprocating equipment should have a mass that is at least four times the mass of the equipment.

Vibratory loads from equipment foundations that are transmitted to the soil can cause significant and damaging settlements. The transmitted vibration will cause densification of granular materials, particularly loose or medium dense sands. The reduction in volume can cause large settlements depending on the initial density of the sands. In saturated granular materials, such as loose or medium dense sands with a high water table, the transmitted vibrations can cause a buildup or pore pressure and liquefaction of the sands, with resulting loss of bearing capacity and settlements. In saturated clays, the vibrations can enhance the drainage of water from the pores and increase long term settlements.

1805.4.2 Concrete footings. Footings may be designed or the requirements of Table 1805.4.2 may be used for structures with light framed walls of conventional construction, where frost heave or expansive soils are not a problem. Table 1805.4.2, which was excerpted from the UBC, is based on anticipated dead and live loads from the floors and roof and an assumed soil classification of ML, MH, CL, or CH.

1805.4.2.1 Concrete strength. The minimum concrete strength is set to provide a material of adequate strength and durability. Concrete of lower strength may not have adequate durability, particularly in freeze-thaw areas.

1805.4.2.2 Footing seismic ties. Interconnection of individual spread footings is required for structures in SDC D, E and F sited on soils in Site Class E or F. The footings must be interconnected with ties capable of transmitting a force equal to the larger footing load times the short period response acceleration, S_{DS}, divided by 10. The intent of this requirement is to minimize differential movement or spreading between the footings during ground shaking, and have the individual footings act as a unit. If slabs on grade, or beams within slabs on grade, are used to meet the tie requirement, the load path from footing to slab or beam/slab and across joints in the slab or beam/slab should be checked for continuity. The slab or beam must be reinforced for the design tension load. In addition, the slab should be checked for buckling under the required compression load using an assumed slab width of no more than six times the slab thickness.

1805.4.2.3 Plain concrete footings. In compliance with ACI 318, Section 22.7.4, the edge thickness must not be less than 8 inches. In accordance with ACI 318, Section 22.4.8, the thickness or depth used to compute footing stresses (flexure, combined axial load and flexure, or shear) should be 2 inches less than the actual thickness of the footing for footings cast against soil. This is done to allow for unevenness of excavation and contamination of the concrete adjacent to the soil.

The edge thickness can be reduced to 6 inches for one story light frame buildings or buildings with R-3 occupancies, provided that the edge distance of the footing beyond the face of the stem wall does not exceed the depth (6 inches depth = 6 inches extension). For lightly loaded walls, this dimensional limitation should keep the flexural stresses in the footing below the limit of $5\phi\sqrt{f'_c}$ and the shear stresses below $2\phi\sqrt{f'_c}$. These stresses should be checked for heavily loaded walls.

1805.4.2.4 Placement of concrete. Placement of concrete through water should be avoided because of the increased risk of segregation and dilution of the concrete paste. When concrete is placed under water, by tremie or other approved method, the mix must be different from the standard mix used for ordinary concrete foundations. The mix must be proportioned so that it is plastic with high workability and will flow without segregation. The desired consistency can be obtained by using rounded aggregates, high sand contents, entrained air, and superplasticizers. Higher cement contents are necessary to compensate for the increase in the water/cementitious materials ratio caused by dilution from placement through water. Minimum cement content should be 600 pounds per yard.

1805.4.2.5 Protection of concrete. Concrete footings should not be placed during rain, sleet, snow or freezing weather without protection against freezing or without protection against increase in water content at the surface from rain while plastic. See ACI 306R and ACI 306.1 for cold weather concrete operations.

1805.4.2.6 Forming of concrete. The soil should have sufficient strength and cohesion that the shape, dimensions, and vertical sides of the excavation can be maintained without sloughing prior to and during the concreting operations. Excavations in loose granular materials must be formed.

1805.4.3 Masonry unit footing. Masonry footings were widely used until the middle of the last century when they were replaced by steel or wood grillage footings, which in turn were replaced by more economical plain or reinforced concrete footings. Masonry footings were often built of stone cut to a specific size or rubble masonry of random size stones bonded with mortar. While seldom used, masonry footings may be constructed of hard-burned brick set in cement mortar to support lightweight buildings.

1805.4.3.1 Dimensions. Type M mortar is suitable for unreinforced masonry below grade or with earth contact. Type S should be used for reinforced footings. Projections of the footing beyond a wall or pier should not exceed one half of the footing depth to keep the shear and flexural stresses in the footing within safe limits. For example, a footing with a 12-inch depth should project no more than 6 inches beyond the face of the wall.

1805.4.3.2 Offsets. The stepping back, or racking, of successive courses of the foundation wall supported by a masonry footing must not exceed $1^1/_2$ inches for a single course or 3 inches for a double course. Where wide footings are necessary for bearing, the wall must be stepped back to keep the footing projection within the limits of Section1805.4.3.1. See Figure 9.

1805.4.4 Steel grillage footings. Steel grillage footings were used extensively during the later half of the last century, but the development of reinforced concrete made grillage footings obsolete, except for underpining work.

A typical grillage consists of two or more tiers of steel beams with each tier placed at right angles to the tier below. The beams in each tier are usually held together by a system of bolts and pipe spacers. For construction of new grillage footings, the beams should be clean and unpainted and the entire grillage system filled with and encased in concrete with at least three inches of cover. The grillage should be placed on a concrete pad at least 6 inches thick to distribute the load evenly to the soil.

1805.4.5 Timber footings. Use of timber footings is allowed only for Type V structures. Timber must be pressure treated to American Wood Preservers Association (AWPA) C2 or C3 standards, except for foundations permanently below the groundwater table. The pressure preservative treatment protects the timber from decay, fungi, and harmful insects. Stronger preservatives than specified in AWPA C22 (ammoniacal copper arsenate, ACA, or chromated copper arsenate, CCA) are necessary to prevent marine borers when timber foundations are used in coastal brackish or marine environments.

Preservative treatment by the pressure process within the limitations of the AWPA C2 or C3 should not significantly affect the strength of the wood. Part of the process, however, involves the conditioning of the wood prior to treatment by steaming or boiling under vacuum. This conditioning can cause significant reductions in strength. This strength loss is recognized in the AFPA *National Design Specification for Wood Construction* by use of the Untreated Factor, C_u.

Untreated timber may be used when the footings are completely embedded in soil below the ground-water table. Long experience has shown that timber permanently confined in water will stay sound and durable indefinitely. Wood submerged in fresh water cannot decay because the necessary air is excluded. Because ground-water levels can sometimes change appreciably, untreated timber should only be used at depths sufficiently below the water table that small drops in the water level will not expose the timbers to air.

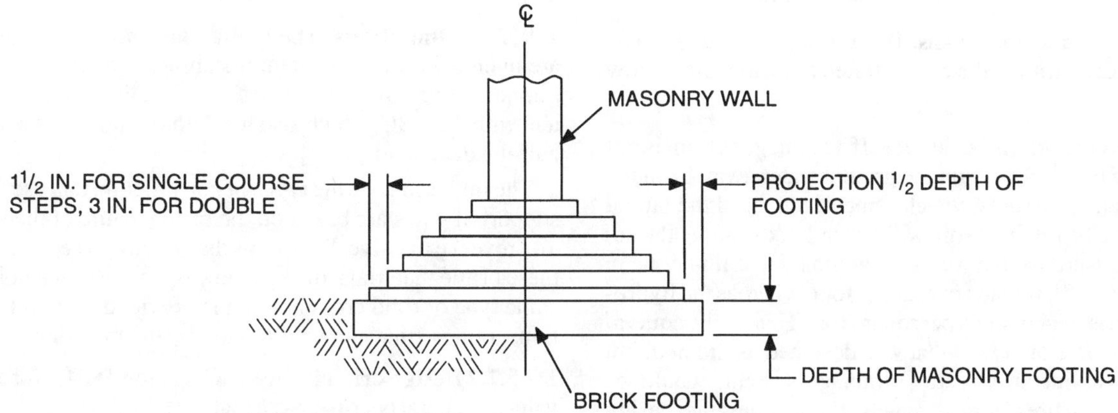

BRICK FOOTING WALL OFFSETS

FIGURE 9

1805.4.6 Wood foundations. The requirements set forth in AFPA Technical Report No. 7 must be rigidly followed. The wood foundation system is an assembly similar to a fire assembly—no substitution of materials or methods is allowed. All lumber and plywood must be treated with ACA or CCA per AWPA C22 and must be identified and labeled in accordance with Section 2303.1.8.1. All hardware and fasteners must be corrosion resistant. Metals in contact with the preservative salts will corrode at a much faster rate that normal because of the influence of the salts. Hence, only corrosion-resistant fasteners made of silicon bronze, copper, or Type 304 or 316 stainless steel may be used, except that hot-dipped galvanized nails may be used when installed under the specific conditions set forth in the technical report for surface treatment of the nails and moisture protection of the foundation.

1805.5 Foundation walls. Foundation walls must be designed with the applicable portions of IBC Chapters 19 and 21. However, if the foundation wall is laterally supported top and bottom, such as a basement wall laterally supported by a floor diaphragm at the top and a basement floor slab at the base, the wall may be constructed in accordance with the prescriptive provisions of Tables 1805.5 (1) through 1805.5 (4). These tables allow the use of unreinforced and plain (lightly reinforced) concrete or masonry walls that have been used in low or very low seismic risk area. Walls in moderate to high seismic risk areas will be subjected to ground shaking and ground displacements of unknown magnitudes and the walls will have an additional lateral load caused by the ground shaking. The tables do not take into consideration these additional lateral seismic soil pressures or the additional lateral inertial loads from the floor diaphragm and superstructure. Hence, these prescriptive provisions should not be used in structures classified as SDC C, D, E and F. Additionally, if the prescriptive provisions are used, sufficient soil investigation should be done to classify the retained soils in accordance with the Unified Soil Classification Method (see IBC Section 1802.3) and the construction materials must comply with IBC Section 1805.5.2 as a minimum.

1805.5.1 Foundation wall thickness.

1805.5.1.1 Thickness based on walls supported. These minimum thickness provisions are to facilitate support of the wall above. These thickness provisions are empirical and have been used successfully in low or very low seismic risk area. However, these prescriptive provisions should not be used in structures classified as SDC C, D, E and F. See Section 2104.2 if corbeling is necessary or desired to match the width of a masonry cavity wall above the foundation wall.

1805.5.1.2 Thickness based on soil loads, unbalanced backfill height and wall height. Wall thickness must comply with the requirements of Tables 1805.5 (1) through 1805.5 (4). Note the requirement for Type M or S mortar, and the definition of unbalanced fill.

1805.5.1.3 Rubble stone. Because rubble masonry uses rough stones of irregular shape and size, a larger thickness, as compared to hollow unit masonry or concrete, is required for adequate bonding of the stone and mortar. Rubble stone foundation walls are not permitted in SDC C, D, E or F.

1805.5.2 Foundation wall materials. This specifies the material requirements for walls constructed in accordance with the prescriptive tables. Note the effective depth, "d," in the title of the table. Placement of reinforcing at the prescribed "d" is critical to develop adequate flexural strength necessary to resist the combined vertical and lateral loads.

1805.5.3 Alternative foundation wall reinforcement. A critical consideration for basement walls is crack control. If the reinforcing is spaced too widely, crack widths will be larger than if the reinforcing is closely spaced. See ACI 318, Section 10.6 for a discussion of reinforcing spacing for crack control for one-way slabs. If alternative reinforcement is used, the alternative should be to reduce bar size and reduce spacing. There is the additional consideration of development of the reinforcing. The bar size must be small enough that the reinforcing, and any splices, can be developed. A rule of thumb to prevent splitting of concrete masonry is that the bar size number should not exceed the (t-1) where "t" is the nominal thickness of the wall in inches.

1805.5.4 Hollow masonry walls. The masonry is required to be solid in order to distribute the concentrated force into the hollow unit masonry.

1805.5.5 Foundation wall drainage. If a drainage system is not placed behind the wall to drain the ground water away from the wall, hydrostatic pressures, which can easily exceed the lateral pressures from the retained soil, will occur. For example, the active lateral pressure from a well graded granular soil may be in the range of 30 to 35 pounds per square foot, whereas the hydrostatic pressure is 62.4 pounds per square foot. Hence, the equivalent fluid pressures on a wall that was designed as drained, but constructed without an effective drainage system, would be subjected to pressures approximately three times the design pressure.

1805.5.6 Pier and curtain wall foundations. Pier foundations may not be used to support structures assigned to SDC E and F.

1805.6 Foundation plate or sill bolting. The requirements for the bolting of foundation sill plates were moved to Chapter 23, Wood. This was done to clarify that the prescriptive anchor bolt provisions are applicable only to structures constructed using wood conventional construction provisions (see IBC Section 2308). Anchor bolt designs must be engineered when the conventional construction provisions are not used.

1805.7 Designs employing lateral bearing. The design criteria for the use of poles embedded in the ground or in concrete footings in the ground and unconstrained at the ground surface were developed for the Outdoor Advertising Association of America, Inc. The research was conducted at Purdue University from 1938 to 1940, and continued in 1947 at the University of Notre Dame. The results of this research were used by the association for the design of outdoor advertising structures, which had previously used trussed A-frame supporting systems. Charts and a nomograph were developed, which the association used for the design of poles as cantilever uprights for support of its outdoor advertising structures. These data were subsequently submitted through the ICBO code change process and were incorporated into the 1964 edition of the UBC.

The criteria relate to lateral bearing and apply to a vertical pole considered as a column embedded in either earth or in a concrete footing in the earth and used to resist lateral loads. In order for the pole to meet the conditions of research which resulted in the code formula, the code requires that the backfill in the annular space around a column which is not embedded in a concrete footing be either of 2,000 psi (13.78 Mpa) concrete or of clean sand thoroughly compacted by tamping in layers not more than 8 inches in depth.

The original design criteria established for the Outdoor Advertising Association of America, Inc., resulted in a $^1/_2$-inch lateral pole deformation at the surface of the ground. These criteria were also based on field tests conducted in a range of sandy and gravelly soils and of silts and clays.

The IBC employs allowable lateral bearing stresses in IBC Table 1804.2, which are considerably lower than those developed for the Outdoor Advertising Association of America. Consequently, Section 1804.3.1 permits a doubling of the lateral bearing values for isolated poles and poles supporting structures that can tolerate the $^1/_2$-inch movement at the ground surface.

1805.7.1 Limitations. The limitations imposed by this section are intended for both structural stability and serviceability. The limitation of the frictional resistance for silts and clays is consistent with the UBC, which also limits the sliding resistance to one-half the dead load.

The limitations on the types of construction that use the lateral support of poles are based on the brittle nature of the materials. To prevent excessive distortions that would cause the cracking of these brittle materials, the code limits the use of the poles unless some type of rigid cross bracing is provided to limit the deflections to those that can be tolerated by the materials.

1805.7.2 Design criteria. See IBC Section 1804.3 for allowable values of lateral bearing. Note that the two-time increase allowed per Section 1804.3.1 may only be used for structures where deflection of $^1/_2$ inch at the surface is tolerable such as signs, flagpoles, and light poles.

1805.7.2.1 Nonconstrained. See Section 1805.7 for the empirical basis of the formula. This formula should be used only for minor foundations of moderate size, which will fit within the constraints of the data from which the formula was developed. For large size piers, i.e., more than 2 feet in diameter, a more appropriate method should be used. See Winterkorn, et al.[2]

1805.7.2.2 Constrained. The term pavement means a rigid pavement such as reinforced concrete that will form a fulcrum for the column. Columns in flexible pavements such as asphalt concrete must use the formula in Section 1805.7.2.1 for unconstrained conditions.

1805.7.2.3 Vertical load. There is no requirement to consider a combined lateral and vertical load. The vertical loads for which the formulae were derived were less than 0.1 $F_c\, A_g$. If there are vertical loads greater than 0.1 $F_c\, A_g$, these formulae should not be used.

1805.7.3 Backfill. Backfill in accordance with the requirements is necessary to achieve the strength predicted by the formulae. The required backfill was used as part of the research conducted to develop the formulae. Note that the sand should be compacted to a relative density of at least 85 percent.

1805.8 Design for expansive soils. The requirements to mitigate the effects of expansive soils are set forth. In addition to mitigation by foundation design, the effects of expansive soils may also be mitigated by removal of the expansive soils or stabilization by chemical means, presaturation, or dewatering . Expansive soils are cohesive soils, typically high plasticity clays, with a high Plasticity Index and a high Swell Index.

1805.8.1 Foundations. The large volume changes in expansive soils caused by changes in the soils' water content can cause large differential deflections in a building if not uniform. In a typical building on expansive soils, the soils at the perimeter of the building will have seasonal moisture changes whereas the soils at the interior of the building will remain at a fairly constant moisture content. The perimeter foundations will rise and fall with the seasonal volume changes in moisture content, while the soil at the interior footings or slab will not have any volume changes because of a constant moisture content. The resulting differential displacements between the interior and exterior footings can cause significant structural distress. Hence, the requirements that the foundation be designed to resist the differential volume changes and minimize racking or differential displacements in the structure.

1805.8.2 Slab-on-ground foundations. The slab-on-ground or raft foundation design methods cited herein result in a raft that has sufficient stiffness to bridge the differential displacements caused by the volume changes.

1805.8.3 Removal of expansive soil. Removal of the expansive soil is a suitable mitigation method and is the preferred method if the stratum of expansive soil is near the surface and reasonably thin. This method may also be the least expensive method if the expansive soil is at the surface.

1805.8.4 Stabilization. Expansive soils may be stabilized so that the moisture content does not change; hence, there will be no volume changes to cause differential displacements. Stabilization can be by chemical methods, by presaturating the soils to a maximum swell and capping the expansive layer to keep the moisture content constant, or by dewatering to a minimum shrinkage and providing drainage to keep the moisture content constant.

1805.9 Seismic requirements. The requirements for minimum reinforcement for foundations for SDC C through F structures have been moved to IBC Section 1910.4, which contains the requirements for plain concrete. Plain concrete is unreinforced or lightly reinforced concrete that contains less reinforcing than required to meet the minimum reinforcement requirements set forth in ACI 318, Section 10.5.

SECTION 1806 DAMPPROOFING AND WATERPROOFING

This covers the requirements for waterproofing and dampproofing those parts of substructure construction that need to be provided with moisture protection. Sections 1806.1 through 1806.4 identify the locations where moisture barriers are required and specify the materials to be used and the methods of application. The provisions also deal with subsurface water conditions, drainage systems and other protection requirements.

Dampproofing requirements are outlined in Section 1806.2, and waterproofing requirements are covered in Section 1806.3. Although both terms are intended to apply to the installation and the use of moisture barriers, dampproofing does not furnish the same degree of moisture protection as does waterproofing.

Dampproofing generally refers to the application of one or more coatings of a compound or other materials that are impervious to water, which are used to prevent the passage of water vapor through walls or other building components, and which restrict the flow of water under slight hydrostatic pressure. Waterproofing, on the other hand, refers to the application of coatings and sealing materials to walls or other building components to prevent moisture from penetrating in either a vapor or liquid form, even under conditions of significant hydrostatic pressure. Hydrostatic pressure is created by the presence of water under pressure. This pressure can occur when the groundwater table rises above the bottom of the foundation wall, or the soil next to the foundation wall becomes saturated with water caused by uncontrolled storm water runoff.

1806.1 Where required. This section is an overall requirement specifying that waterproofing and dampproofing applications are to be made to horizontal and vertical surfaces of those below-ground spaces where the occupancy would normally be adversely affected by the intrusion of water or moisture. Moisture or water in a floor below grade can cause damage to structural members such as columns, posts or load-bearing walls, as well as pose a health hazard by promoting growth of bacteria or fungi and adversely affect any mechanical and electrical appliances that may be located at that level. It can also cause a great deal of damage to goods that may be located or stored in that lower level. These vertical and horizontal surfaces include foundation walls, retaining walls, underfloor spaces and floor slabs. Waterproofing and dampproofing are not required in locations other than residential and institutional occupancies where the omission of moisture barriers would not adversely affect the use of the spaces. An example of a location where waterproofing or dampproofing would not be required is in an open parking structure as long as the structural components are individually protected against the effects of water. Waterproofing and dampproofing are not permitted to be omitted from residential and institutional occupancies where people may be sleeping or services are provided on the floor below grade. A person waking in a flooded basement may find themselves in a very hazardous situation, particularly if there exists the possibility of an electrical charge in the water caused by electrical service at that level.

Section 1806.1.1 addresses the type of problem faced when a portion of a story is above grade, while Section 1806.1.2 limits any infiltration of water into crawl spaces so as to protect this area from potential water damage and prevent ponding of water in the crawl space. These sections reference other applicable sections of Chapter 18.

1806.1.1 Story above grade. The provisions of this section require that where a basement is deemed to be a "story above grade," the section of the basement floor that occurs below the exterior ground level and the walls that bound that part of the floor are to be dampproofed in accordance with the requirements of Section 1806.2.

The use of dampproofing, rather than waterproofing, is permitted here because high hydrostatic pressure will not tend to develop against the walls if the basement is a story above grade and the ground level adjacent to the basement wall is below the basement floor elevation for not less than 25 percent of the basement perimeter.

Any water pressure that may occur against the walls below ground or under the basement floor would be relieved by the water drainage system required in this section. The drainage system would be installed at the base of the wall construction in accordance with Section 1806.4.2 for a minimum distance along those portions of the wall perimeter where the basement floor is below ground level.

Because of the relationship of grade to the basement floor and the inclusion of foundations drains, the potential for hydrostatic pressure buildup is not significant. Therefore, a ground-water table investigation, waterproofing and the basement floor gravel base course is not required.

The objective of this section is to prevent moisture migration in basement spaces. In story-above-grade construction that meets the requirements of this section, the basement floor would be only partly below ground level (sometimes a small part) and the need for section-required moisture protection is unnecessary. Dampproofing of the floor slab would be required, however, in accordance with Section 1806.2.1.

1806.1.2 Underfloor space. Essentially, the requirements of this section are designed to prevent any ponding of water in underfloor areas, such as crawl spaces. Crawl spaces are particularly susceptible to ponding of water since they are usually uninhabitable spaces that are infrequently observed. Water can build up in these spaces and remain for an extended period of time without being noticed by the building occupants. Stagnant water collected under a building can result in a serious health concern. Water buildup in a crawl space can also damage the structural integrity of the building. Wood exposed to water can deteriorate and rot, while concrete and masonry exposed to water can deteriorate with a loss of strength.

Steel exposed to water or high humidity can eventually rust to the extent that effective structural capability is jeopardized. Water buildup in a crawl space can also damage mechanical or electrical appliances located in the space by causing corrosion of electrical parts or metal skins and deterioration to insulation used to protect heating elements.

Where it is known that the water table can rise to within 6 inches of the outside ground level, or where there is evidence that surface water cannot readily drain from the site, then the finished ground surface in underfloor spaces is to be set at an elevation equal to the outside ground level around the perimeter of the building unless an approved drainage system is provided. For the drainage system to be approved, it must be demonstrated that the system will be adequate to prevent the infiltration of water into the underfloor space. This is done by determining the maximum possible flow of water near the foundation wall and footing and designing the drainage system to remove that flow of water as it occurs, preventing the buildup of water at the foundation wall.

To prevent the ponding of water in the underfloor space from a rise in the ground-water table, or from storm water runoff, the finished ground level of an underfloor space is not to be located below the bottom of the foundation footings.

Dampproofing, waterproofing or providing subsoil drainage is not necessary if the ground level of the underfloor space is as high as the ground level at the outside of the building perimeter, since the foundation walls do not enclose an interior space below grade. Compliance with Sections 1806.2, 1806.3 and 1806.4 would be required where the finished ground surface of the underfloor space is below the outside ground level.

1806.1.2.1 Flood hazard areas. The requirement is to prevent water from ponding under the structure if it is flooded.

1806.1.3 Ground-water control. After completion of building construction, it is necessary to maintain the water table at a level that is at least 6 inches below the bottom of the lower floor to prevent the flow or seepage of water into the basement. Where the site consists of well-draining soil and the highest point of the water table occurs naturally at or lower than the required level stated above, then there is no need to provide any kind of a site drainage system specifically designated to control the ground-water level. Where the soil characteristics and the site topography are such that the water table can rise to a level that will produce a hydrostatic pressure against the basement structure, a site drainage system may be installed to reduce the water level. When ground-water control in accordance with this section is provided, waterproofing in accordance with Section 1806.3 is not required.

There are many types of site drainage systems that can be employed to control ground-water levels. The most commonly used systems may involve the installation of drainage ditches or trenches filled with pervious materials, sump pits and discharge pumps, well point systems, drainage wells with deep-well pumps, sand-drain installations, etc. This section requires that all such systems be designed and constructed using accepted engineering principles and practices based on considerations that include the permeability of the soil, amount and rate at which water enters the system, pump capacity, capacity of the disposal area and other such factors that are necessary for the complete design of an effective drainage system.

1806.2 Dampproofing required. Where a ground-water table investigation has established that the high water table will occur at such a level that the building substructure will not be subjected to significant hydrostatic pressure, then dampproofing in accordance with this section and a subsoil drain in accordance with Section 1806.4 are sufficient to control moisture in the floor below grade. Because the wall will not be subject to high hydrostatic pressure, the more restrictive provisions of waterproofing, as provided for in Section 1806.3, are not required. Wood foundation systems specified in Section 1805.4.6 are to be dampproofed as required by AFPA TR7.

1806.2.1 Floors. Floors requiring dampproofing in accordance with Section 1806.2 are to employ materials specified in Section 1806.2.1. The dampproofing materials must be placed between the floor construction and the supporting gravel or stone base as shown in Figure 10. Even if a floor base is not required, dampproofing should be placed under the slab.

The installation is intended to provide a moisture barrier against the passage of water vapor or seepage into below-ground spaces.

The dampproofing material most commonly used for underslab installations consists of a polyethylene film not less than 6 mil in thickness, which is applied over the gravel or stone base required in Section 1806.4.1. Care must be used in the installation of the material over the rough surface of the base and during the concreting operation so as not to puncture the polyethylene. Joints must be lapped at least 6 inches.

Dampproofing materials can also be applied on top of the base concrete slab if a separate floor is provided above the base slab, since the dampproofing is provided to prevent moisture infiltration of the interior space, and not the concrete slab.

Materials commonly used for dampproofing floors are listed in Table 1.

1806.2.2 Walls. Walls requiring dampproofing in accordance with Section 1806.2 are first to be prepared as required in Section 1806.2.2.1 then coated with any of the bituminous materials listed in Table 1 or by other approved materials and methods of application. Approved materials are those that will prevent moisture from penetrating the foundation wall.

Coatings are applied to cover prepared exterior wall surfaces extending from the top of the wall footings to slightly above ground level so that the entire wall that contacts the ground is

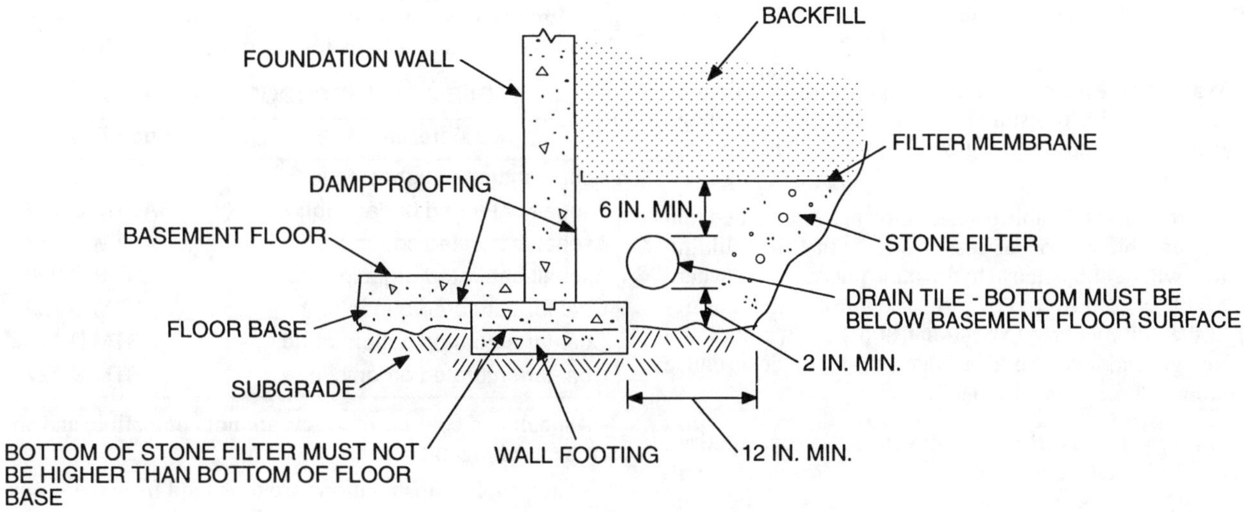

A FOUNDATION DRAINAGE SYSTEM

FIGURE 10

protected. Surfaces are usually primed to provide a bond coat and then dampproofed with a protection coat of asphalt or tar pitch.

Dampproofing materials for walls may be any of the materials specified in Section 1806.3.2 for waterproofing. Table 1 gives a list of bituminous materials that can be used, including the applicable standards that may be used as the basis of acceptance of such materials. Included in Table 1 is ASTM D 1668 for glass fabric that is treated with asphalt (Type I), coal-tar pitch (Type II) or organic resin (Type III).

Surface-bonding mortar complying with ASTM C 887 may be utilized. This specification covers the materials, properties, and packaging of dry, combined materials for use as surface-bonding mortar with concrete masonry units that have not been prefaced, coated or painted. Since this specification does not address design or application, manufacturer's recommendations should be followed. This standard covers proportioning, physical requirements, sampling and testing. The minimum thickness of the coating is $^1/_8$ inch.

Acrylic-modified cement coatings may be utilized at the rate of 3 pounds per square foot. These types of materials have been used successfully as dampproofing materials for foundation walls. Surface-bonding mortar and acrylic-modified cement are limited in use to dampproofing. The ability of these two types of products to bridge nonstructural cracks, as required in Section 1806.3.2 for waterproofing materials, is not known. Therefore, their use is limited to dampproofing and they are not permitted to be used as waterproofing. Dampproofing may also include other materials and methods of installation acceptable to the building official.

TABLE 1. DAMPPROOFING MATERIALS

Material	Specification
Aphalt	ASTM D 449
Asphalt primer	ASTM D 41
Coal-tar	ASTM D 450
Concrete and masonry oil primer (for coal-tar applications only)	ASTM D 43
Treated glass fabric	ASTM D 1668

1806.2.2.1 Surface preparation of walls. Before applying dampproofing materials, the concrete must be free of any holes or recesses that could affect the proper sealing of the wall surfaces. Air trapped beneath the dampproofing coating or membranes can cause blistering, while rocks and other sharp objects can puncture membranes. Irregular surfaces can also create uneven layering of coatings, which can result in vulnerable areas of dampproofing. Surface irregularities commonly associated with concrete wall construction can be sealed with bituminous materials or filled with portland cement grout or other approved materials.

Unit masonry walls are usually parged (plastered) with a $^1/_2$-inch-thick layer of portland cement and sand mix (1:2 $^1/_2$ by volume) or with a Type M mortar proportioned in accordance with the requirements of ASTM C 270, and applied in two $^1/_4$-inch-thick layers. In no case is parging to result in a final thickness of less than $^3/_8$ inch. The parging is to be coved at the joint formed by the base of the wall and the top of the wall footing to prevent the accumulation of water at that location.

The moisture protection of unit masonry walls provided by the parging method may not be required where approved damp-proofing materials, such as grout coatings, cement-based paints or bituminous coatings, can be applied directly to the masonry surfaces.

1806.3. Waterproofing required. Waterproofing installations are intended to provide moisture barriers against water seepage that may be forced into below-ground spaces by hydrostatic pressure.

Where a ground-water table investigation has established that the high-water table will occur at such a level that the building substructure will be subjected to hydrostatic pressure, and where the water table is not lowered by a water control system, as described in the commentary to Section 1806.4.2, all floors and walls below ground level are to be waterproofed in accordance with Sections 1806.3.1 and 1806.3.2.

1806.3.1 Floors. Because floors required to be waterproofed are subjected to hydrostatic uplift pressures, such floors must, for all practical purposes, be made of concrete and designed and constructed to resist the maximum hydrostatic pressures possible. It is particularly important that the floor slab be properly designed, since severe cracking or movement of the concrete would allow water seepage into below-ground spaces. The ability of the waterproofing materials to bridge cracks is limited. Concrete floor construction is to comply with the applicable provisions of Chapter 19.

Materials used for waterproofing below-ground floors are to conform to the requirements of Section 1806.3.1.

Below-ground floors subjected to hydrostatic uplift pressures are to be waterproofed with membrane materials placed as underslab or split-slab installations, including such materials as rubberized asphalt, butyl rubber and neoprene or with polyvinyl chloride or polybutylene films not less than 6 mil in thickness, lapped at least 6 inches. There are many proprietary membrane products available that are specifically made for waterproofing floors and walls (i.e., polyethylene sheets sandwiched between layers of asphalt), which may be used when approved by the building official.

All membrane joints are to be lapped and sealed in accordance with the manufacturer's instructions to form a continuous, impermeable waterproof barrier.

1806.3.2 Walls. Walls that are required to be waterproofed in accordance with Section 1806.3 must first be prepared as required in this section and then waterproofed with the required membrane-type installations.

The walls must be designed to resist the hydrostatic pressure anticipated at the site, as well as any other lateral loads to which the wall will be subjected, such as soil pressures or seismic loads. As with the floors required to be waterproofed, it is particularly important that the walls required to be waterproofed be properly designed to resist all anticipated loads, since cracking and other damages would allow water seepage into below-ground spaces. Water seepage can lead to the deterioration of the foundation as wood rots, concrete and masonry erode and steel rusts. Such deterioration can cause structural failure of the foundation. More important, failure of the foundation wall can lead to structural failure of the building since the foundation supports the building structure. Masonry or concrete construction must comply with the applicable provisions of Chapters 21 and 19, respectively.

Table 2 lists materials commonly used for the installation of moisture barriers in wall construction and the related standards that may be used as a basis for acceptance of such materials.

TABLE 2. WATERPROOFING MATERIALS

Material	Specification
Aphalt-saturated asbestos felt	ASTM D 250
Asphalt-saturated burlap fabric	ASTM D 1327
Asphalt-saturated cotton fabric	ASTM D 173
Asphalt-saturated organic felt	ASTM D 226
Coal-tar-saturated burlap fabric	ASTM D 1327
Coal-tar-saturated cotton fabric	ASTM D 173
Coal-tar-saturated organic felt	ASTM D 227

Asphalt and coal-tar products are not compatible and should not be used together.

Waterproofing installations are to extend from the bottom of the wall to a height not less than 12 inches above the maximum elevation of the ground-water table. The remainder of the wall below ground level (if the height is small) may be either waterproofed as a continuation of the installation or must be damp-proofed in accordance with the requirements of Section 1806.2.

This section requires that waterproofing must consist of two-ply hot-mopped felts. The practice of the waterproofing industry is to select the number of plies of membrane material based on the hydrostatic head (height of water pressure against the wall). As a general practice, if the head of water is between 1 and 3 feet, two plies of felt or fabric membrane are used; between 4 and 10 feet, three-ply construction is needed; and between 11 and 25 feet, four-ply construction is necessary.

Waterproofing installations may also use polyvinyl chloride materials of not less than 6 mil thick, 40 mil polymer-modified asphalt, or 6 mil polyethylene. These materials have been widely recognized for their effectiveness in bridging nonstructural cracks. Other approved materials and methods may be used provided that the same performance standards are met. All membrane joints must be lapped and sealed in accordance with the manufacturer's instructions.

1806.3.2.1 Surface preparation of walls. Before applying waterproofing materials to concrete or masonry walls, the wall surfaces must be prepared in accordance with the requirements of Section 1806.2.2.1, which requires the sealing of all holes and recesses. Surfaces to be waterproofed must also be free of any projections that might puncture or tear membrane materials that are applied over the surfaces.

1806.3.3 Joints and penetrations. This section requires that all joints occurring in floors and walls and at locations where floors and walls meet, as well as all penetrations in floors and walls, be made watertight by approved methods. Sealing the joints and penetrations in the waterproofing is of primary importance to ensure the effectiveness of the waterproofing. If the joints or penetrations are not sealed properly, they can develop leaks, which become a passageway for water to enter the building. Since the remainder of the foundation is wrapped in waterproofing, moisture can actually become trapped in the foundation walls or floor slab, and serious damage to these structural components can occur. Such methods may involve the use of construction keys between the base of the wall and the top of the footing, or, if there is a hydrostatic pressure, then floor and wall joints may require the use of manufactured waterstops made of metal, rubber, plastic, or mastic materials. Floor edges along the walls and floor expansion joints may employ any of a number of preformed expansion joint materials, such as asphalt, polyurethane, sponge rubber, self-expanding cork, cellular fibers bonded with bituminous materials, etc., which all comply with applicable ASTM standards or other approved specifications. A variety of sealants may be used together with the preformed joint materials. Gaskets made of neoprene and other materials are also available for use in concrete and masonry joints. The National Roofing Contractor's NRCA Roofing and Waterproofing Manual provides details for the reinforcement of membrane terminations, corners, intersections of slabs and walls, through-wall and slab penetrations and other locations.

Penetrations in walls and floors may be made watertight with grout or manufactured fill materials and sealants made for the purpose.

1806.4 Subsoil drainage system. Subsoil drainage systems are required to drain the area adjacent to basement walls to eliminate hydrostatic loads.

This section covers subsoil drainage systems in conjunction with dampproofing (see Section 1806.2) to protect below-ground spaces from water seepage. Such systems are not used where basements or other below-ground spaces are subject to hydrostatic pressure because they would not be effective in disposing of the amount of water anticipated if hydrostatic pressure conditions exist. Ground-water tables may be reduced to acceptable levels by methods described in the commentary to Section 1806.1.3.

The details of subsoil drainage systems are covered in the requirements of Sections 1806.4.2 through 1806.4.3.

1806.4.1 Floor base course. This section requires that floors of basements, except for story-above-grade construction, must be placed on a gravel or stone base not less than 4 inches thick. Not more than 10 percent of the material is to pass a No. 4 sieve to provide a porous installation and provide a capillary break. Material that passes a No. 4 sieve would be silt or clay that does not permit the free movement of water through the floor base, but allows for upward migration by capillary action.

This requirement serves three purposes. The first is to provide an adjustment to the irregularities of a compacted subgrade so as to produce a level surface upon which to cast a concrete slab. The second purpose is to provide a capillary break so that moisture from the soil below will not rise to the underside of the floor. Finally, where required, the porous base can act as a drainage system to expel underslab water by means of gravity, or the use of a sump pump or other approved methods.

The exception allows for the omission of the floor base when the natural soils beneath the floor slab consist of well-draining granular materials such as sand, stone or mixtures of these materials. Some caution, however, is justified in the use of this exception. If the granular soils contain an excessive percentage of fine materials, the porosity and the ability of the soil to provide a capillary break may be considerably diminished. The exception should be applied only if the natural base is equivalent to the floor base otherwise required by this section.

1806.4.2 Foundation drain. This describes in considerable detail the materials and features of construction required for the installation of foundation drain systems.

This type of drain system is suitable where the water table occurs at such elevation that there is minimal hydrostatic pressure exerted against the basement floor and walls and where the amount of seepage from the surrounding soil is so small that the water can be readily discharged by gravity or by mechanical means into sewers or ditches. The objective is to combine the protection afforded by the dampproofing of walls and floors (see Section 1806.2) and that given by the perimeter drains to maintain below-ground spaces in a dry condition.

A foundation drain system usually consists of the installation of drain tiles made of clay or concrete or of drain pipes of corrugated metal or nonmetallic pipes surrounded by crushed stone or gravel and a filter membrane material (filter fabric). The foundation drain is set adjacent to the wall footing and extends around the perimeter of the building. Drain tiles are placed end to end with open joints to permit water to enter the system. Metallic and nonmetallic drains are made with perforations at the invert (bottom) section of the pipe and are installed with connected ends. Where drain tile or perforated drain pipe is used, the invert must not be set higher than the basement floor line so that water conveyed by the drain does not seep into the filter material and then create a hydrostatic pressure condition against the foundation wall and footing. The inverts should not be placed below the bottom of the adjacent wall footings to avoid carrying away fine soil particles whose loss, in time, could possibly undermine the footing and cause settlement of the foundation walls.

Tile joints or pipe perforations should be covered with an approved filter membrane material to prevent them from becoming clogged, and preventing fine particles that may be contained in the surrounding soil from entering the system and being carried away by water.

The filter material around the drain tiles or pipes (not to be confused with filter membrane material) should consist of selected gravel and crushed stone containing not more than 10 percent of material that passes a No. 4 sieve. The filter materials should be selected to prevent the movement of particles from the protected soil surrounding the drain installation into the drain. Filter material is to be placed in the excavation so that it will extend out from the edge of the wall footing a distance of at least 12 inches, with the bottom of the fill being no higher than the bottom of the base under the floor (see Section 1806.4.1) and the top of the footing.

Requiring the bottom of the foundation drain to be no higher than the bottom of the floor base is necessary so that if the water table rises into the floor base, it will also be able to rise unobstructed into the foundation drain. The foundation drain will then drain the water away from the building, as required by Section 1806.4.3. The top of the filter fill material must be covered with an approved filter membrane to allow water to pass through to the perimeter drain tile or pipes without allowing fine soil materials to enter the drainage system.

Drain tiles or pipes are to be installed in the filter bed and should be seated on at least 2 inches of filter material and covered with at least 6 inches of filter material to maintain good water flow into the drain tile of pipe.

1806.4.3 Drainage discharge. This section references the *International Plumbing Code* (IPC) for requirements for installing piping systems for the disposal of water from the floor base and the foundation drains. Chapter 11 of the IBC considers the piping materials, applicable standards and methods of installation of subsurface storm drains to facilitate water discharge either by gravity or mechanical means.

Where the soil at the site consists of well-drained granular materials, such as gravel or sand-gravel mixtures, to prevent the occurrence of hydrostatic pressure against the foundation walls and under the floor slab, the use of a dedicated drainage system as prescribed in the IPC is not required, because the site soils would permit natural drainage.

SECTION 1807 PIER AND PILE FOUNDATIONS

These sections cover the requirements for deep foundation systems (piles and piers). New definitions have been added to clarify the terms used in Section 1807, which also contains the requirements that are common for all types of piles and piers. Sections 1808, 1809, and 1810 cover the more specific requirements for driven piles, cast-in-place piles, and composite piles, respectively. Section 1811 covers the requirements that are specific to pier foundations. For the most part, the requirements in these sections are based on the Board for Coordination of the Model Codes (BCMC) report on Pile Foundation Systems published in July, 1979, as adopted by the other model codes. The exception is the seismic requirements, which are based on the 1997 NEHRP provisions. The provisions in the 2000 IBC cover more deep foundation types and are more detailed than the requirements in the UBC. Required material properties (e.g., allowable concrete or steel stresses) were also added to types of piles where none were specified in any of the model codes, and some requirements were modified as compared to the other model codes. The intent was to coordinate all the material property requirements, not just the new ones, to eliminate conflicts or inconsistencies among the model codes.

1807.1 Definitions. One major change was to add new definitions for piles and piers, and to standardize the definitions of other terms that are used inconsistently in the design, enforcement, and scientific communities. As defined in the 2000 IBC, piles are relatively slender (long in comparison to their cross-sectional dimension), whereas piers are relatively stocky (short in comparison to their cross-sectional dimension). The definitions were arrived at by balancing the definitions found in various foundation engineering references[1,2,3,4,5,6] with the code language already in use.

Piles and piers are defined based on the ratio of the length to least dimension. A more accurate method to classify piers and piles is by considering the stiffness of the member relative to the surrounding soil similar to the relative stiffness parameter, β, for the beam-on-an-elastic foundation problem. Piles tend to be flexible relative to soil stiffness whereas piers are stiff relative to the soil stiffness. See, for example, Winterkorn, et al.[2]

1807.2 Piers and piles—general requirements.

1807.2.1 General. The purpose of a foundation investigation is to define the general subsurface stratifications of soil and rock materials, determine the soil and rock profiles and locate the ground-water table. Such information will help in selecting the type of pile foundation and in estimating pile lengths. Furthermore, a foundation investigation is often required to render data on specific soil properties, such as shear strength, relative density, compressibility of the soil and other such findings that will help in analyzing subsurface conditions for determining design loads, type of pile foundations, driving criteria, suitable bearing strata, probable durability of pile materials relative to the particular soil conditions found at the construction site, etc.

Subsurface information is normally obtained by means of test borings that yield suitable samples of soils and rock and give the depths from which they are obtained. Sometimes, certain in-situ tests are also conducted, but these should not be made without first making test borings.

This section outlines the kinds of information to be derived from a foundation investigation and report. In addition to the items listed in the code provision, the investigation could include other valuable and applicable data that would help in the evaluation, such as:

- Information on existing construction at the site or at adjacent sites, including the type and condition of these structures, age, types of foundations used, performance data, etc.
- Information on the existence of deleterious substances in the soils or other conditions that could seriously affect the durability and structural performance of the piles.
- Information on the geologic conditions at the site, which could include such items as the existence of mines, earth cavities, underground streams or other adverse water conditions, history of seismic activity, etc.

1807.2.2 Special types of piles. Pile types are basically classified in accordance with the structural material used, such as concrete, steel or wood. They can also be categorized in accordance with the method of construction or installation. There are many variations of pile types used in the construction of deep foundations, including some special or proprietary types beyond the scope of the code. This section, as well as other sections of Chapter 18 that deal with pile foundations, generally include only those basic pile types commonly used today.

Special pile types that are not specifically included in the provisions of the code are not precluded from use, provided that adequate information covering test data, calculations, structural properties, load capacity and installation procedures is submitted and accepted by the building official.

1807.2.3 Pile caps. Pile caps are to be of reinforced concrete and designed in accordance with the requirements of ACI 318. For footings (pile caps) on piles, computations for moments and shears may be based on the assumption that the load reaction from any pile is concentrated at the pile center. See ACI 318 for loads and reactions of footings on piles.

The soil immediately under the pile cap is not considered to provide any support for vertical loads. For a more detailed explanation of this requirement, see the commentary to Section1807.2.9.3.

The heads of all piles are to be embedded not less than 3 inches into pile caps and the edges of the pile caps are to extend at least 4 inches beyond the closest sides of all piles. The degree of fixity between a pile head and the concrete cap depends on the method of connection required to satisfy design considerations.

1807.2.4 Stability. A group of piles designed to support a common load or to resist horizontal forces, must be braced or rigidly tied together to act as a single structural unit that will provide lateral stability in all directions. Piles connected by a rigid, reinforced concrete pile cap are deemed to be sufficiently braced to meet the intent of this provision.

Three or more piles are generally used to support a building column load or other isolated, concentrated load. In a three-pile group, lateral stability is assured by requiring that the piles are located such that they will not be less than 120 degrees apart as measured from the centroid of the group in a radial direction.

For stability of a pile group supporting a wall structure, the piles are braced by a continuous, rigid footing and are alternately staggered in two lines at least 1 foot apart and symmetrically located on each side of the center of gravity of the wall. Other approved pile arrangements may be used to support walls, provided the piles are adequately braced and lateral stability of the foundation construction is assured.

This section clarifies that for pile or pier groups to be considered to provide lateral stability, they must meet the radial spacing requirements defined herein. With the exception of smaller one- and two-family dwellings, foundation walls are required to be supported by two lines of piles or piers. For lightweight construction, such as R-3 buildings not exceeding two stories or 35 feet in height, a single row of piles located within the width of the wall is permitted. These specifications should provide the building official with better guidelines as to what is acceptable.

1807.2.5 Structural integrity. Piles are generally installed by either driving, vibration, jacking, jetting, direct weight or a combination of such methods. While most types of piles are exposed to some degree of damage during placement, with the knowledge of the soil conditions and the proper selection of equipment, installation methods and techniques, damage may be entirely prevented or minimized.

Due care must be exercised during pile installation to avoid interference with adjacent piles or other structures so as to leave their strength and load capacity unimpaired. If any pile is damaged during installation so as to affect its structural integrity, the damage must be satisfactorily repaired or the pile rejected.

Many of the code provisions within Section 1807 are to ensure pile structural integrity by adhering to proper installation procedures. The code cannot cover all possibilities, however, thus establishing the need for this general nature of the section.

1807.2.6 Spacing. The determination of the proper spacings of a pile group in relation to the type of pile foundation employed and the soil conditions encountered is a matter of design. The spacing of piles must be such that the loads transferred to the load-bearing strata do not exceed the safe load-bearing values of the supporting strata as determined by test borings, field load tests or other approved methods.

1807.2.7 Splices. This section specifies the requirements for splicing of piles. One provision that raised questions during the drafting process is the second sentence of the section, which requires that splices shall develop not less than 50 percent of the least capacity of the pier or pile in bending. While this may appear to be allowing the pile or pier to be underdesigned in bending, the preceding sentence does require the splice to be able to transmit the driving and service loads acting on the pile or pier at that location. The 50 percent requirement actually provides more strength where the bending moments are low, since it is based on the capacity of the pile or pier, not the design loads.

While it is physically and economically better to drive piles in one piece, site conditions sometimes necessitate that piles be driven in spliced sections. For example, when the soil or rock-bearing stratum is located so deep below the ground that the leads on the driving equipment will not receive full-length piles, it becomes necessary to install the piles sectionally or, where possible, to take up the extra length by setting the tip in a preexcavated hole (see commentary, Section 1807.2.13). When piles are installed in areas such as existing buildings with restricted headroom, they are also required to be placed in spliced sections. There are a number of other reasons for field-splicing piles, such as restrictions on shipping lengths or the use of composite piles.

This provision requires that splices be constructed to provide and maintain true alignment and position of the pile sections during installation. Splices must be of sufficient strength to transmit the vertical and lateral loads on the piles, as well as to resist the bending stresses that may occur at splice locations during the driving operations and under long-term service loads. Splices are to develop at least 50 percent of the value of the pile in bending. Consideration should be given to the design of splices at locations where the piles may be subject to tension. Splices that occur in the upper 10 feet of pile embedment are to be designed to resist the bending moments and shears at the allowable stress levels of the pile material, based on an assumed pile load eccentricity of 3 inches, unless the pile is properly braced. Proper bracing of a spliced pile is deemed to exist if stability of the pile group is furnished in accordance with the provisions of Section 1807.2.4, provided that other piles in the group do not have splices in the upper 10 feet of their embedded length.

There are different methods employed in splicing piles depending upon the materials used in pile construction. For example, timber piles are spliced by one of two commonly used methods. The first method uses a pipe sleeve with a length of about four to five times the diameter of the pile. The butting ends of the pile are sawn square for full contact of the two pile sections, and the spliced portions of the timber pile are trimmed smoothly around their periphery to fit tightly into the pipe sleeve. The second splicing method involves the use of steel straps and bolts. The butting ends of the pile sections are sawn square for full contact and proper alignment and the four sides are planed flat to receive the splicing straps. This type of splicing can resist some uplift forces.

Splicing of precast concrete piles usually occurs at the head portions of the piles. After the piles are driven to their required depth, pile heads are cut off or spliced to the desired elevation for proper embedment in the concrete pile caps. Any portion of the pile that is cracked or shattered by the driving operations or cutting off of pile heads should be removed and spliced with fresh concrete. To cut off a precast concrete pile section, a deep groove is chiseled around the pile exposing the reinforcing bars, which are then cut off (by torch) to desired heights or extensions. The pile section above the groove is snapped off (by crane) and a new pile section is freshly cast to tie in with the precast pile.

Steel H-piles are spliced in the same manner as steel columns, usually by welding the sections together. Welded splices may be welded-plate or bar splices, butt-welded splices, special welded splice fittings or a combination of these. Spliced materials should be kept on the inner faces of the H-pile sections to avoid forcing a hole in the ground larger than the pile, causing at least a temporary loss in frictional value and lateral support that might result in excessive bending stresses.

Steel pipe piles may be spliced by butt welding, sometimes using straps to guide the sections and to provide more strength to the welded joint. Another method is to use inside sleeves having a driving fit, with a flange extending between the pipe sections. By applying bituminous cement or compound on the outside of the ring before driving, a water-tight joint is obtained.

1807.2.8 Allowable pier or pile loads.

1807.2.8.1 Determination of allowable loads. The International Code specifies that the determination of allowable loads shall be based on three methods:

1. An approved driving formula.
2. Load tests.
3. Foundation analysis.

In most cases, the allowable loads will be determined by a combination of Items 2 and 3. However, there may be circumstances where the soil conditions, such as granular soils, and the types of piles selected are such that the use of an approved dynamic pile-driving formula can be an aid to a qualified practitioner in establishing reasonable but safe allowable loads for the foundation system. Nevertheless, some literature indicates that "The use of a complicated formula is not recommended since such formulas have no greater claim to accuracy than the more simple ones."[7]

The dynamic pile-driving formula included in the 1970 and earlier editions of the UBC was dropped from the code because of its unreliability for cohesive soils. It is interesting to note that the earliest editions of the UBC utilized the so-called Engineering News formula, $R = 12WH/S{+}c$, which is the most simple of the dynamic pile-driving formulas. In 1937, the Pacific Coast formula was adopted into the UBC until its deletion prior to the 1973 edition of the code. This was one of the more complex dynamic pile-driving formulas and was based on a dynamic pile-driving formula developed by Terzaghi. However, as stated previously, in the hand of a qualified practitioner, a dynamic pile-driving formula does have some utility even though the UBC no longer provides such a formula.

There are two general considerations for determining pile capacity as required for the design and installation of pile foundations. The first consideration involves the determination of the underlying soil or rock characteristics. The second is the application of approved driving formulas, load tests or accepted methods of analysis to determine the pile capacities required to resist the applied axial and lateral loads, as well as to provide the basis for the proper selection of pile-driving equipment.

1807.2.8.2 Driving criteria. For many decades, it has been the practice to try to predict the capacity of a pile from its resistance to driving. The usual procedure has been to make such determinations by the application of pile-driving formulas, none of which have been completely dependable. The singular premise used in the development of these formulas is simple, and is best expressed by R.B. Peck as follows: The greater the resistance of a pile to driving, the greater is the pile's capacity to support load. With complex engineering problems, however, occasionally there are special circumstances under which there will be exceptions to general statements of this kind.

There are many pile-driving formulas. The simplest and most widely used formula in the United States is the Engineering News formula. This particular expression, and other formulas in common use today, have all generally shown poor correlations with load test results. Such comparisons are considerably better, however, when they are applied to the determination of pile capacity in soils consisting of free-draining, coarse-grained materials, such as sand and gravel. In soils such as silt, clay and fine sand the water cannot escape fast enough during driving operations to not have an adverse influence on the frictional resistance of the piles and, as a consequence, render unreliable information.

This section limits the allowable compression load on a pile as established by an approved driving formula to a maximum of 40 tons. Generally, the use of pile-driving formulas to determine pile capacity should be avoided except, perhaps, in cases involving small jobs where the piles are to be driven in well-drained granular soils and load testing cannot be economically justified.

1807.2.8.3 Load tests. This section specifies the standards to be used to load test piles or piers, where higher compressive loads than allowed in other sections of the code are exceeded. Questions were raised at the public hearings as to whether or not ASTM D 4945, which is a dynamic test, is sufficient by itself to verify the pile capacity. Many standards, including ASTM D 4945 indicate that a dynamic test may not be sufficient without a static test (ASTM D 1143) to calibrate the results, but leave it up to the registered design professional to decide if the dynamic test is sufficient. Other standards require a static load test to calibrate the dynamic test.

The safest method for determining pile capacity is by load test. A load test should be conducted wherever feasible and used where the pile capacity is intended to exceed 40 tons per pile (see Section 1807.2.8.3). Test piles are to be of the same type and size as intended for use in the permanent foundation and installed with the same equipment, by the same procedure, and in the same soils intended or specified for the work.

Load tests are to be conducted in accordance with the requirements of ASTM D 1143, which covers procedures for testing vertical or batter foundation piles, individually or in groups, to determine the ultimate pile load (pile capacity) and whether the pile or pile group is capable of supporting the loads without excessive or continuous settlement. Recognition, however, must be given to the fact that load-settlement characteristics and pile capacity determinations are based on data derived at the time and under conditions of the test. The long-term performance of a pile or group of piles supporting actual loads may produce behaviors that are different than those indicated by load test results. Judgement based on experience must be used to predict pile capacity and expected behavior.

The load-bearing capacity of all piles, except those seated on rock, does not reach the ultimate load until after a period of rest.

The results of load tests cannot be deemed accurate or reliable unless there is an allowance for a period of adjustment. For piles driven in permeable soils, such as coarse-grained sand and gravel, the waiting period may be as little as 2 or 3 days. For test piles driven in silt, clay or fine sand, the waiting period may be 30 days or longer. The waiting period may be determined by testing (i.e., by redriving piles) or from previous experience.

This section also requires that at least one pile be tested in each area of uniform subsoil conditions. The statement should not be misconstrued to mean that the area of test is to have only one uniform stratum of subsurface material, but rather that the soil profile, which may consist of several layers (strata) of different materials, must represent a substantially unchanging cross section in each area to be tested.

The allowable pile load to be used for design purposes is not to be more than one-half of the ultimate pile capacity, as determined by the load test in which the net settlement of the test pile is not to exceed 0.01 inch per ton, nor more than a total of $^3/_4$ inch. The rate of penetration of permanent foundation piles must be equal to or less than that of the test pile(s).

All production piles should be of the same type, size and approximate length as the prototype test pile, as well as installed with the same or comparable equipment and methods. They should also be installed in soils similar to those for the test pile.

1807.2.8.4 Allowable frictional resistance. Skin friction is limited to a maximum of 500 psf.

1807.2.8.5 Uplift capacity. This section gives both designer and building official needed guidance on criteria to use for design of piles or piers for uplift. The 1997 UBC was silent on the requirements, but the 2000 IBC now requires a test or approved method of analysis, with a safety factor of 3. The capacity of pile or pier groups is also limited to two-thirds of the weight of the group and the soil contained in the group. This is consistent with requirements in other sections in the code on uplift and overturning, where the dead load resistance is limited to two-thirds of the weight.

When piles are designed to withstand uplift forces, they act in tension and are actually friction piles. The amount of tension that can be developed not only depends on the strength properties of the pile, but also on the frictional or cohesive properties of the soil. The uplift or tensile resistance of a pile is not necessarily a function of its load-bearing capacity under compressive load. For example, the tensile resistance of a friction pile in clay will usually be about the same value as its load-bearing capacity, since the skin friction developed in such soils is very large. In contrast, a friction pile in sand or in other granular materials will develop a tensile resistance considerably less than its load-bearing capacity.

Where the properties of the soil are known, the ultimate uplift resistance value of a pile can be determined by approved analytical methods. This section requires that where the ultimate tensile value is determined by analysis, a safety factor of 3 must be applied to establish the allowable uplift load of the pile.

The best way to determine the response of a vertical or batter pile to a static tensile load (uplift force) applied axially to the pile is by applying an extraction test in accordance with the requirements of ASTM D 3689. The maximum allowable uplift load is not to be more than one-half of the total test load. This section of the code gives a limitation on the upward movement of the pile in compliance with the provisions of the ASTM D 3689 test method. The measurements of pile movement in the standard test procedure, however, are time-dependent incremental measurements and should be adhered to in determining allowable pile load.

The allowable uplift load on a group of piles is to be reduced from the value obtained on a single pile as briefly described in this section of the code and in compliance with comprehensive analytical methods.

To be effective in resisting uplift forces as tension members of a foundation system, piles must be well-anchored into the pile cap by adequate connection devices. In turn, the cap must be designed for the uplift stresses. Piles must also be designed to take the tensile stresses imposed by the uplift forces. For example, concrete piles must be reinforced with longitudinal steel to take the full net uplift. Special consideration needs to be given in the design of pile splices that are intended to act in tension.

1807.2.8.6 Load-bearing capacity. The load-bearing capacity of a pile foundation is determined as a pile-soil system. For example, the load-bearing capacity of a single pile is the function of either the structural strength of the pile or the supporting strength of the soil. The load-bearing capacity of the pile is controlled by the smaller value obtained in the two considerations. The load-bearing capacity of a pile group may be greater than, equal to or less than the capacity of a single pile multiplied by the number of piles in the group, depending on pile spacing and soil conditions.

Since the supporting strength of the soil generally controls the load-bearing capacity of a pile foundation, this section requires that the load-bearing capacity of an individual pile or a group of piles be not more than one-half of the ultimate load capacities of the piles in terms of the supporting load-bearing strata.

Sometimes, weaker layers of soil underlie the soil load-bearing strata supporting a pile foundation and may cause damaging settlements. Under such subsurface conditions, it must be determined by an approved method of analysis that the safety factor has not been reduced to a figure less than 2. Otherwise the piles are to be driven to deeper load-bearing soils to obtain adequate and safe support, or the design capacity is to be reduced and the number of piles increased.

1807.2.8.7 Bent piers or piles. Piles that are discovered to have sharp or sweeping bends because of obstructions encountered during the driving operations or for any other cause are to be analyzed by an approved method, or a representative pile is to be load tested to determine its load-carrying capacity. Otherwise, the piles could be used at some reduced capacity as determined by test or analysis or, if necessary, the piles can be abandoned and replaced.

1807.2.8.8 Overloads on piers or piles. Because of subsurface obstructions or other reasons, it is sometimes necessary to offset piles a small distance from their intended locations or else they may become driven out of position. In such cases, the load distribution in a group of piles may be changed from the design requirements and cause some of the piles to be overloaded. This section requires that the maximum compressive load on any pile caused by mislocation not exceed 110 percent of the allowable design load. Piles exceeding this limitation must be extracted and redriven in the proper location or other approved remedies applied, such as installing additional piles to balance the group.

1807.2.9 Lateral support. This section provides needed guidance to the designer and building official on what constitutes adequate lateral support for piles and piers. Section 1807.2.9.1 specifies that any soil other than fluid soil is allowed to be considered to provide lateral support to prevent buckling of piles or piers, and Section 1807.2.9.3 establishes the acceptance criteria for tests that establish the allowable lateral load.

1807.2.9.1 General. Liquefaction causes loss of lateral bearing capacity with resulting loss of support for piles. Loss of lateral support can also occur from the soil strength loss associated with "sensitive" or "quick" clays that are sensitive to remolding effects. These soft clays typically occur in marine or former marine environments and are often called "bay muds." These clays lose significant strength when remolded as might occur when a pile foundation is moved through muds by seismic induced displacements.

1807.2.9.2 Unbraced piles. (Column Action.) The code requires that piles standing unbraced in air, water, or material not capable of providing adequate lateral support shall be designed in accordance with the column formulas of the code. Obviously, water and air do not provide lateral support. On the other hand, most soils do provide lateral support, although exceptionally loose and unconsolidated fills, liquified sands, and remolded clays, are inadequate to provide lateral support.

1807.2.9.3 Allowable lateral load. Because of wind loads, unbalanced building loads, earth pressures and seismic loads, it is inevitable that individual piles or groups of vertical piles supporting buildings or other structures will be subjected to lateral forces. The distribution of these lateral forces to the piles largely depends on how the loads are carried down through the structural framing system and transferred through the supporting foundation to the piles. The amount of lateral load that can be taken by the pile foundation is a function of 1) the type of pile used; 2) the soil characteristics, particularly in the upper 10 to 30 feet of the piles; 3) the embedment of the pile head (fixity); 4) the magnitude of the axial compressive load on the piles; 5) the nature of the lateral forces; and 6) the amount o f horizontal pile movement deemed acceptable.

The degree of fixity of the pile head is an important design consideration under very high lateral loading unless some other method, such as the use of batter piles, is employed to resist lateral loads. The fixing of the pile head against rotation reduces the lateral deflection. In general, pile butts are embedded 3 to 4 inches into the pile cap (see Section 1807.2.3) with no ties to the cap. These pile heads are neither fixed nor free, but somewhere in between. Such construction is satisfactory for many loading conditions, but not for high seismic loads.

The magnitude of friction developed between the surfaces of two structural elements in contact with each other is a function of the weight or load applied. The larger the weight, the greater the frictional resistance developed. In the design of pile foundations, frictional resistance between the soil and the bottom of the pile caps (footings) should not be relied on to provide lateral restraint because the vertical loads are transmitted through the piles to the supporting soil below and to the ground immediately under the pile caps. Only the weights of the pile caps can supply some frictional resistance because such footings are constructed by placing fresh concrete on the soil, thus providing a positive contact. The weights of the pile caps in comparison to the magnitude of loads and lateral forces transmitted to the piles is nominal, and not significant from a structural design standpoint. Also, in rare occurrences, soils has been known to settle under pile caps, leaving open spaces and thus eliminating the development of any frictional restraint.

Where vertical piles are subjected to lateral forces exceeding acceptable limitations, the use of batter piles may be required. Lateral forces on many structures are also resisted by the embedded foundation walls and the sides of the pile caps.

The allowable lateral-load capacity of a single pile or group of piles is to be determined either by approved analytical methods or load tests. Load tests are to be conducted to produce lateral forces that are twice the proposed design load; however, in no case is the allowable pile load to exceed one-half of the test load, which produces a gross lateral pile movement of 1 inch as measured at the ground surface.

1807.2.10 Use of higher allowable pier or pile stresses. In those sections of Chapter 18 that specifically deal with the several types of piles most commonly used in the construction of pile foundations, there are limitations placed on the stresses that can be used in the pile design. In most cases the allowable stresses are stated as a percentage of some limiting strength property of the pile material. For example, in the case of piles made of steel materials, the allowable stresses are prescribed as a percentage of the yield strengths of the several grades of steel that can be used for pile construction. For concrete, the allowable stress is stated as a percentage of the 28-day specified compressive strength of the material. The allowable stresses for timber piles are based on tabulations of already reduced stresses. The reduced stresses are based on the strength values of different species of wood and reductions in strength caused by preservative treatment.

The allowable design stresses designated in Chapter 18 for each of the different types of piles are intended to provide a factor of safety against the dynamic forces of pile driving that may cause damage to the pile, and to avoid overstresses in the pile under the design loads and other loads that may be induced by subsoil conditions.

This section allows the use of higher allowable stresses when evidence supporting the values is submitted and approved by the building official. The data submitted to the building official should include analytical evaluations and findings from a foundation investigation as specified in Section 1807.2.1, and the results of load tests performed in accordance with the requirements of Section 1807.2.8.3. The technical data and the recommendation for the use of higher stress values must come from a registered design professional who is knowledgeable in soil mechanics and experienced in the design of pile foundations. This registered design professional must supervise the pile design work and witness the installation of the pile foundation so as to certify to the building official that the construction satisfies the design criteria. In any case, the use of greater design stresses should not result in design loads that are larger than one-half of the test loads (see Section 1807.2.8.3).

1807.2.11 Piles in subsiding areas. Where piles are driven through subsiding soils and derive their support from underlying firmer materials, the subsiding soils cause an additional load to the piles through so-called negative friction. This negative friction is actually a downward friction force on the piles, which increases the axial load on the piles. The code permits an increase in the allowable stress on the piles if an analysis of the foundation investigation indicates that the increase is justified.

1807.2.12 Settlement analysis. The purpose of a settlement analysis is to provide the data needed to design a pile foundation system that will maintain the stability and structural integrity of the supported building or structure.

The load-bearing stratum of every soil must support the loads transferred through the pile system, as well as the weight of all soil above. The capability of the strata underlying the pile tips to support additional loads without detrimental settlement can often be determined by analytical procedures. Serious settlements in a pile foundation system, particularly differential settlements, can cause great structural damage to the supported structure and the foundation itself.

While the settlement analysis of an individual pile is complex, the analysis of a group of piles is significantly more complicated because of the overlapping soil stresses caused by closely spaced piles. Analytical procedures vary with the type of piles and especially with the soil conditions. Settlement analysis would generally include cases involving point-bearing piles on rock, and in granular soils and hard clay. It would also involve friction piles in sand and gravel soils, and in clay materials.

Load tests are often used to aid in the analysis. In the case of pile foundations in clay soils, however, there are no practical ways to determine long-term settlement from load tests, and therefore, only approximations of settlement may be derived from laboratory tests.

1807.2.13 Pre-excavation. There are several important reasons for the use of pre-excavation to facilitate the installation of foundation piles. Some of these purposes are:

- To install piles through upper strata of hard soil.
- To penetrate through subsurface obstructions, such as timbers, boulders, rip rap, thin stone strata and the like.
- To reduce or eliminate the possibility of ground heave that could lift adjacent structures or piles already driven.
- To reduce ground pressures resulting from soil displacement during driving and to prevent the lateral movement of adjacent piles or structures.
- To reduce the amount of driving required to seat the piles in their proper load bearing strata.
- To reduce the possibility of damaging vibrations or jarring of adjacent structures, as well as reduce the amount of noise, all of which are associated with pile driving operations.
- To accommodate the placement of piles that may be somewhat longer than the leads of the pile driving equipment.

The two most common methods employed in pre-excavation in operations are prejetting and predrilling. Jetting is usually effective in most types of soils, except very coarse and loose gravel and highly cohesive soils. Jetting is most effective in granular materials. Generally, jetting in cohesive soils is not very practical or especially useful and should be avoided in soils containing very coarse gravel, cobbles or small boulders. These stones cannot be removed by the jet and tend to collect at the bottom of the hole, preventing pile penetration below that depth.

Jetting operations must be carefully controlled to avoid excessive loss of soil, which could affect the load-bearing capacity of piles already installed or the stability of adjacent structures.

Piles should be driven below the depth of the jetted hole until the required resistance or penetration is obtained. Before this pre-excavation method is used, consideration should be given to the possibility that jetting, unless strictly controlled, can adversely affect load transfer, particularly as it involves the placement of nontapered piles.

Predrilling or coring before driving is effective in most types of soils and is a more controllable method of pre-excavation than jetting. The risk of adversely affecting the structural integrity of adjacent piles or structures or the frictional capacity of piles is considerably less than jetting.

Predrilling can be performed as a dry operation or as a wet rotary process. Dry drilling can be done by using a continuous-flight auger or a short-flight auger attached to the end of a drill stem or kelly bar. Wet drilling requires a hollow-stem continuous-flight auger or a hollow drill stem employing the use of spade bits. When the wet rotary process of predrilling is used, bentonite slurry or plain water is circulated to keep the hole open. As in the case of jetting, piles should be driven with tips below the predrilled hole. This is necessary to prevent any voids or very loose or soft soils from occurring below the pile tip.

There are other methods used for pre-excavation purposes, such as the dry tube method and spudding, but such procedures are seldom used. In any case, the methods to be employed for pre-excavation are subject to the approval of the building official.

1807.2.14 Installation sequence. As displacement piles are driven within a group, progressive compaction of the surrounding soil occurs, particularly where it involves closely spaced piles. This can cause piles to be deflected off-line because of the buildup of unequal soil pressures around the piles. Soil compaction during driving operations can cause extreme variations in pile lengths within a group, with some piles failing to reach specified load-bearing material. Ground heave is another effect of soil compaction (see commentary, Section 1807.2.19).

To prevent or reduce significantly the problems associated with soil compaction, the driving sequence of pile installations becomes an important consideration. For example, if the outer piles of a group are driven first so that the inner piles, because of soil compaction, fetch up to specified sets (hammer blows) at much higher elevations than the outer piles, the total load-bearing value of the group will be adversely affected. As another example, starting pile driving at the edge of a group makes the piles progressively more difficult to drive and results in a one-sided bearing group. The general driving practice is to work from the center of a group outward. For large groups consisting of rows of widely spaced piles, driving can be done progressively from one side to the other.

1807.2.15 Use of vibratory drivers. The use of vibratory drivers for the installation of piles is not applicable to all types of soil conditions. They are effective in granular soils with the use of nondisplacement piles, such as steel H-piles and pipe piles driven open ended. Vibratory drivers are also used for extracting piles or temporary casings employed in the construction of cast-in-place concrete piles.

Vibratory drivers, either low or high frequency, cause the pile to penetrate the soil by longitudinal vibrations. While this type of pile driver can produce good results in the installation of nondisplacement piles under favorable soil conditions, the greatest difficulty is the lack of a reliable method of estimating the load-bearing capacity. After the pile has been installed with a vibratory driver, pile capacity can be determined by using an impact-type hammer to set the pile in its final position.

One method to determine pile capacity is to calibrate the power consumption in relation to the rate of penetration. Nonetheless, the use of a vibratory driver is only permitted where the pile load capacity is established by load tests in accordance with the requirements of Section 1807.2.8.3.

1807.2.16 Pile driveability. Piles must be of a size, strength and stiffness capable of resisting without damage:

- Crushing caused by impact forces during driving.
- Bending stresses during handling.
- Tension from uplift forces or from rebound during driving.
- Bending stresses caused by horizontal forces during driving.
- Bending stresses caused by pile curvatures.

Additionally, the pile must be capable of transmitting dynamic driving forces to mobilize the required ultimate pile capacity within the soil without severe elastic energy losses. Pile driveability depends on the pile stiffness, which is a function of pile length, cross-sectional area, and modulus of elasticity. Yield strength does not affect stiffness. Thus, caution should be observed in the use of high-yield-strength steels for high loads on smaller cross sections requiring high dynamic driving energy. A wave equation analysis would reflect pile stiffness or driveability. The selection of pile types and dimensional requirements for driveability is a function of soil characteristics.

1807.2.17 Protection of pile materials. Unless properly protected, piles may deteriorate because of biological, chemical or physical actions caused by particular conditions that exist or that may later develop at the site. The durability of piles will be long lasting if care is taken in the selection and protection of pile materials.

Some of the problems associated with pile durability are as follows:

- Untreated timber piles may be successfully used if they are entirely embedded in earth and their butts (cutoffs) are below the lowest ground-water level or are submerged in fresh water. The risk, however, is in situations where unexpected lowering of the water table occurs and exposes the upper parts of piles to decay and insect attack. Such conditions may especially occur in urban areas where the water table may be significantly lowered by pumping or deep drainage. There is also the remote possibility that wood piles will be damaged by the percolation of ground water heavily charged with alkali or acids.
- Wood piles extending above the water table or exposed to air or saltwater are subject to decay, attack by insects and marine borers, and need to be pressure treated with preservatives conforming to the requirements of AWPA C1 and C2.
- Steel piles that are driven and embedded entirely in undisturbed soil are generally not significantly affected by corrosion caused by oxidation, regardless of soil types or soil properties. The reason for this is that undisturbed soil is so deficient in oxygen at levels only a few feet below the ground line or below the water table that progressive corrosion is inhibited. Where upper portions of steel piles protrude above ground into the air, where piles are placed in corrosive soils, or where ground water contains deleterious substances from sources such as coal piles, alkali soils, active cinder fills, chemical wastes from manufacturing operations or other sources of pollutants, however, the steel may be subject to corrosive action. Under such conditions, steel piles may be protected by a concrete encasement or a suitable coating, extending from a level slightly above ground to a depth below the layer of disturbed earth. For piles above ground level that are exposed to air and subject to rusting, the steel should be protected by painting it as any other type of structural steel construction would be protected.
- Steel piles installed in saltwater or exposed to a saltwater environment are subject to corrosion and, therefore, should be protected with approved coatings or encased in concrete.
- Concrete piles, plain or reinforced, that are entirely embedded in undisturbed earth are generally considered permanent installations. The level of the water table does not normally affect the durability of concrete piles. Ground water that readily flows through granular materials or through disturbed soil and contains deleterious substances can have deteriorating effects. Concrete piles embedded in impervious clay materials will not generally suffer from ground water containing harmful substances. The primary deleterious substances that attack concrete are acids and sulphates. In the case of acids, it is best to use an alternative pile material if the acid attack is potentially destructive as coating piles may be ineffective due to soil abrasion during driving. Concrete can be attacked, however, by exposure to soils with high sulfate content. In the case of high alkaline soils with sulphate salts, Type V portland cement may be used. Where the exposures are only moderate, a Type II portland cement will usually be adequate. If the piles are in a marine environment, Type V or Type II portland cement is also indicated to provide the necessary sulphate resistance.

The conditions of the underground environment should be ascertained so as to protect piles against possible corrosion of either the concrete or exposed load-bearing steel. For example, corrosion can be caused by chemical attack from the corrosive soil, industrial wastes, organic fills, oxidation or even by electrolytic action. Corrosion by oxidation is generally very minor and often disregarded. Corrosion caused by electrolytic action or by destructive chemicals on load-bearing steel can be protected by suitable coating, concrete encasement and cathodic protection. This also applies to bare steel piles previously discussed. Concrete can be protected from chemical attack by the use of special cements, dense concrete mixtures and special coatings.

Piles installed in saltwater, such as for buildings or other structures in waterfront construction, are subject to chemical action on concrete materials coming from polluted waters, frost action on porous concrete, spalling of concrete, and rusting of steel reinforcement. Spalling may become particularly serious under tidal conditions where alternate wetting and drying occurs coupled with cycles of freezing and thawing. Spalling can be minimized or prevented by providing additional cover over the reinforcement, by the use of rich, dense concrete; air entrainment and suitable concrete admixtures; and, in the case of precast piles, by careful handling to minimize stresses and avoid cracking during placement. See analysis of Chapter 19 for more detailed information on concrete quality and concrete materials.

1807.2.18 Use of existing piers or piles. This section allows the reuse of existing piles or piers where sufficient information is submitted to the building official to demonstrate they are adequate. This introduces flexibility for both the building designer and the building owner to make use of existing materials where it makes sense to do so.

Piles remaining after structures are demolished should not be used for the support of new loads, unless evidence shows them to be adequate. This is because of the lack of soil data or detailed information on the piling material, and to the unavailability of the pile driving records made during the construction of these older buildings or structures. As such, the true condition of the piles is unknown and, over time, the piles may have deteriorated or their load capacity may have been reduced. Such piles may be used, however, if they are load tested or retracted and redriven to verify their capacities. Only the lowest allowable load capacity as determined by test data or redriving information should be used in the design.

1807.2.19 Heaved piles. Piles that are driven into saturated plastic clay materials can often displace a volume of soil equal to that of the piles themselves. When this happens, the soil displacement sometimes occurs as ground heave and may lift adjacent piles already driven. Under such conditions, heaved piles may no longer be properly seated and a loss of pile capacity occurs. Heaved piles must be redriven to firm bearing to again develop the required capacity and penetration. If heaved piles are not redriven, their capacity must be verified by load tests made in accordance with the requirements of Section 1807.2.8.3.

This section applies only to piles that can be safely redriven after installation. Heaved uncased cast-in-place concrete piles or sectional piles with joints that cannot take tension should be abandoned and replaced. When redriving heaved piles, a comparable driving system or the same as that of the initial driving should be employed. It should be noted that in redriving concrete-filled pipe piles, the driving characteristics of the pile have been altered and the pile is substantially stiffer than when the empty pipe was initially driven. In such cases, the required driving resistance would be less than originally required.

One method used to prevent or reduce objectionable soil displacement is to remove some of the soil in the spaces to be occupied by the piles. This is done by predrilling the pile holes (see commentary, Section 1807.2.13).

1807.2.20 Identification. All pile materials must be identified for conformity to the code requirements and construction specifications. Information such as strength (species and grade for timber piles), dimensions, and other pertinent information as may be required. Such identifications must be provided for all piles, whether they are taken from manufacturer's stock or made for a particular project. Identifications are to be maintained from the point of manufacture on through to the shipment, on-site handling, storage, and the installation of the piles. Manufacturers, upon request, usually furnish certificates of compliance with construction specifications. In the absence of adequate data, piles must to be tested to demonstrate conformity to the specified grade.

In addition to mill certificates (steel piles), identification is made through plant manufacturing or inspection reports (precast concrete and timber piles) and delivery tickets (concrete). Timber piles are stamped (labeled) with information such as producer, species, treatment, and length.

Identification is essential when high-yield-strength steel is specified. Frequently, pile cutoff lengths are reused and pile material may come from a jobber, a contractor's yard or a material supplier. In such cases, mill certificates are not available and the steel should be tested to see if it complies with the code requirements and the project specifications.

1807.2.21 Pier or pile location plan. A plan clearly showing the designation of all piles on a project by an identification system is to be filed with the building official before the installation of piling is started. The pile inspector (see analysis of Section 1807.2.22) must keep piling logs and other records and submit written reports based on this identification system. The use of such a system becomes particularly important at sites where the variations in soil profiles are so extensive that it becomes necessary to manufacture piles of different lengths to satisfy bearing conditions.

The building official should also be furnished copies of all modifications to the original pile location plan that may be necessary as the work proceeds (as-built drawings). This would show piles added, deleted or relocated. Such records would facilitate the use of existing piles in the future (see Section 1807.2.18) if the structure is altered or another structure is built on the site.

1807.2.22 Special inspection. See analysis of Sections 1704.8 and 1704.9.

1807.2.23 Seismic design of piers or piles. This section specifies the requirements for pile or pier designs in SDC C through F. Requirements for interconnection of pile caps, anchorage of the piles to pile caps, transverse reinforcement in the pile, strength of pile splices, consideration of group effects, and a consideration of nonlinear interaction of the pile and the soil begin in SDC C. This reflects the CRDC's concern that significant ground motions can occur in SDC C, despite the approximate correspondence to Zone 2 in the 1997 UBC. Additional requirements are imposed on piles and piers in SDC D through F, including a requirement that the upper portion of piles be detailed as special moment-resisting-frame columns, to prevent failure of the piles under severe ground motions.

The purpose of this section is to include the pile bending and curvatures resulting from horizontal ground movement during an earthquake in the structural design. The reinforcement in the pile, required to resist the pile curvature effect, increases ductility of the foundation such that bending or shear failure is precluded.

1807.2.23.1 Seismic Design Category C. Interconnection of piles and caissons is necessary to prevent differential movement of the components of the foundation during an earthquake. It is well known that a building must be thoroughly tied together if it is to successfully resist earthquake ground motion.

Individual piles, piers, or pile caps required for structures in SDC C must be interconnected with ties capable of transmitting a force equal to the larger pile cap or column load times the short period response acceleration, S_{DS}, divided by 10. The intent of this requirement is to minimize differential movement or spreading between the footings during ground shaking. If slabs on grade, or beams within slabs on grade, are used to meet the tie requirement, the load path from footing to slab or beam/slab and across joints in the slab or beam/slab should be checked for continuity. The slab or beam must be reinforced for the design tension load. In addition, the slab should be checked for buckling under the required compression load using an assumed slab with of no more than six times the slab thickness.

Piles in structures subject to seismic ground shaking are likely to be subjected to uplift (tension) forces, either by design or because of insufficient resistance to overturning forces by gravity loads. Hence, concrete piles and concrete-filled steel pipe piles must be able to develop the strength of the pile (in tension) in the connection to the cap. This is accomplished by the requirement that the pile be embedded in the cap by a distance equal to the development length. The development length *may not be reduced* by the ratio $A_{required} / A_{supplied}$. Alternative means, such as increasing concrete confinement, may be used to reduce the development length.

Similarly, the various types of steel piles are required to develop the strength in tension and to transmit this strength to the cap by positive means other than bond to the bare steel, e.g., welded studs or welded reinforcement must be used.

Splices must develop the full strength of the pile, both tension and compression, for all pile types.

Moments, shears, and deflections must be based on non-linear soil-pile interaction. If using pile foundations in soils with lenses of soft clays, lenses subject to liquefaction, or soils susceptible to strength loss from remolding, the effects of the these layers on the curvature and, hence, moment demands on the pile should be investigated. Often these soil-induced curvatures place a much higher moment demand on the piles than would be determined from conventional lateral force P-y analyses.

Note that the sixth paragraph states when a "pile may be assumed to be rigid". An element with l/D < 12 is defined as a pier. See Winterkorn, et al.[2] for methods of analysis of rigid piers.

1807.2.23.2 Seismic Design Category D, E or F. In addition to the requirements for SDC C, moments, shears, and deflections must be based on non-linear soil-pile interaction. If using pile foundations in soils with layers of soft to medium stiff clays, layers subject to liquefaction, or soils susceptible to strength loss from remolding (see Site Class E and F), the effects of the these layers on the curvature and, hence, moment demands on the pile, must be investigated. Often these soil induced curvatures place a much higher moment demand on the piles than would be determined from conventional lateral force P-y analyses. In addition, at the interfaces of the layers described above and stiffer layers, plastic hinging may occur. Hence, confinement reinforcement per the concrete special-moment frame provisions must be provided at these interfaces and at the pile-to-cap connection for concrete piers and piles. See IBC Section 1617.6.

Grade beams must be designed as ductile unless the beam is strong enough to resist the anticipated maximum earthquake force as set forth in the load combination of IBC Section 1605.4 and 1617.1.2. That is, grade beams must be either strong or ductile.

Anchorage of piles or piers into pile caps must consider the combined effects of uplift and pile fixity. For piles not subject to uplift by design or not required to provide rotational restrain, the anchorage must develop at least 25 percent of the strength of the pile in tension. For piles subject to uplift or required to provide rotational restraint, the anchorage must develop the lesser of the tensile capacity of the pile or 1.3 times the uplift capacity based on the soil strength. Because of the large variability in soils, it would be prudent to design these piles for the full tensile capacity rather than 1.3 times the uplift capacity.

Batter piles have performed poorly in past earthquakes. This is because the batter piles are laterally stiff relative to vertical piles and resist most of the seismic induced inertial forces. The piles are not usually designed to resist the actual forces, but are designed to resist an inertial force reduced by an assumed ductility. However, the batter piles are axially stiff and generally not detailed for ductility; hence the failures. To preclude this type of failure in batter piles, the piles and their connections must be designed to resist the anticipated maximum earthquake forces from the load combinations of IBC Section 1605.4.

SECTION 1808
DRIVEN PILE FOUNDATIONS

Except for steel H-piles, driven piles covered in this section are the displacement type. That is, as the pile is driven, a volume of soil is displaced by the pile volume resulting in compaction of the surrounding soils.

1808.1 Timber piles. Timber piles, while not having the high load capacities of steel or concrete piles, are the most commonly used type of pile, mainly because of their availability and ease of handling. Timber piles are shaped from tree trunks and are tapered because of the natural taper of the trunk. Round timber piles are generally made from Southern Pine in lengths up to about 80 feet or Pacific Coast Douglas Fir in lengths up to approximately 120 feet. Other species that are used are red oak and red pine in lengths up to 60 feet.

Untreated timber piles that are embedded permanently below the ground-water level (fresh water only, not brackish or marine conditions) may last indefinitely. If embedded above the water table, the piles are subject to decay, and if above ground are also subject to insect attack. Hence, piles should be preservative treated.

1808.1.1 Materials. Timber piles may be either end-bearing or friction piles. ASTM D 25 sets forth the minimum circumference at the butt and the tip based on pile taper, as well as quality of the wood and tolerances on straightness, knots, twist of grain, and other requirements.

1808.1.2 Preservative treatment. Piles must be pressure treated to prevent decay and insect attack. See discussion in Section 1805.4.5.

1808.1.3 End-supported piles. Damage to the pile, including breakage, should be suspected when there is a sudden drop in penetration resistance while driving that cannot be explained by the soil profile. A pile can be withdrawn for examination. If penetration resistance should suddenly increase, driving should be stopped to avoid possible damage. A significant problem encountered during installation of timber piles is damage while overdriving. Overdriving can cause failure by bending, brooming of the tip, crushing, brooming at the butt end, or splitting or breaking along the pile section. See Figure 11.

1808.2 Precast concrete piles.

1808.2.1 General. Precast concrete piles are manufactured as conventionally reinforced concrete or as prestressed concrete. Both types can be formed by bed casting, centrifugal casting, slipforming, or extrusion methods. Piles are usually square, octagonal or round, and either solid or hollow. Precast piles, which may be either friction or end-bearing piles, are of the displacement type and are driven into place.

1808.2.1.1 Design and manufacture. Piles must be designed to resist driving and handling stresses in addition to anticipated service loads. In long piles, tensile stresses resulting from driving may govern the design. In shorter piles, the handling loads may dominate.

1808.2.1.2 Minimum dimension. This is the minimum practical dimension to accommodate reinforcement.

1808.2.1.3 Reinforcement. The closely spaced spirals or ties at the ends are to accommodate radial tensile principle stresses from driving.

1808.2.1.4 Installation. Care must be used during installation to prevent damage during handling and driving. The proper cushion must be used at the driving end. Recommendations for design, manufacture, and installation are given in ACI 543R. Damage to piles can be classified into four types:

1. Spalling at the butt or head (driving end) caused by high or irregular compressive stress concentrations. The spalling may be caused by insufficient cushioning, pile butt not square with the pile longitudinal axis, hammer and pile not aligned, reinforcing steel not flush or below the top of the pile allowing the hammer force to be transmitted through the steel, or insufficient transverse reinforcement.
2. Spalling at the tip, which is usually caused by an extremely high driving resistance such as when the tip is bearing on a rock.
3. Breaking or transverse cracking. This is caused by the rarefaction wave reflected from the tip. When the hammer strikes the cushion or head, a compression wave is produced that travels down the pile. The wave can be reflected from the tip as a rarefaction (tension) wave or a compression wave depending on the soil stiffness. Rarefaction waves usually occur when the soil at the tip is soft with very little resistance to penetration, causing tension waves that can cause significant tensile damage. This phenomenon usually occurs only in long piles exceeding 50 feet. Prestressed piles have more resistance to rarefaction damage than do conventionally reinforced piles. The hammer energy should be reduced when driving long piles through soft soils.

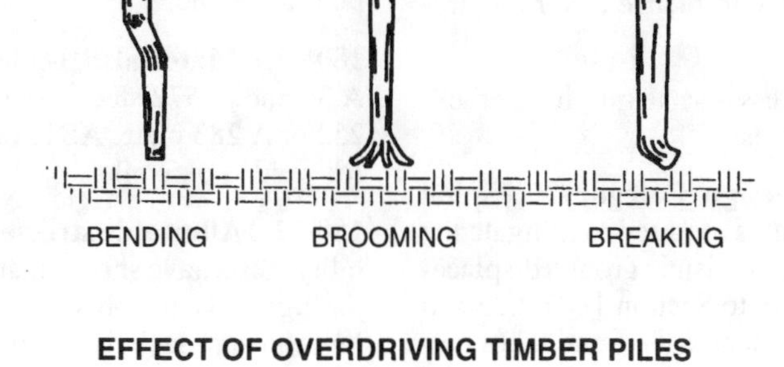

EFFECT OF OVERDRIVING TIMBER PILES

FIGURE 1808-1

4. Spiral or transverse cracking may be caused by a combination of torsional stress and rarefaction stress. Torsion is usually caused by excessive restraint in the leads.

1808.2.2 Precast nonprestressed piles.

1808.2.2.1 Materials. Although piles are excluded from ACI 318, the material, quality, and mixing requirements of ACI 318 apply to the concrete mix. Concrete is required to have a minimum specified compressive strength of not less than 3,000 psi.

1808.2.2.2 Minimum reinforcement. Four bars are the practical minimum for placement.

1808.2.2.2.1 Seismic reinforcement in Seismic Design Category C. Minimum longitudinal steel and ties or spirals for confinement are required to provide some ductility.

1808.2.2.2.2 Seismic reinforcement in Seismic Design Category D, E or F. Spirals or ties are spaced closer to provide for the higher ductility requirements in SDC D and higher. The last sentence requiring ties over the top half of the pile is in addition to that of Section 1808.2.2.2.1, which requires longitudinal reinforcing and ties or spirals over the full length of the pile.

1808.2.2.3 Allowable stresses. The allowable stress limits are set to provide an adequate margin of safety.

1808.2.2.4 Installation. Handling and driving forces will likely govern pile strength requirements. Through the use of steam cure and Type III cements, 75 percent of specified strength can be achieved relatively quickly.

1808.2.2.5 Concrete cover. Cover requirements are set to provide protection and minimize steel corrosion.

1808.2.3 Precast prestressed piles. The purpose of prestressing piles is to place the concrete under a compressive stress so that hairline cracks caused by any subsequent tensile stress that may occur from handling, driving, superimposed loads, or seismic imposed curvatures, and which are larger than the prestressed compression stress, will close when the tensile stresses are removed. This is easily achievable for handling and driving loads, but may not be feasible for seismic imposed curvatures.

Prestressed piles can be either pretensioned or post-tensioned. Pretensioned piles are generally cast full length in a casting bed at a manufacturing plant and often contain only prestressing steel reinforcement. Post-tensioned piles may be plant cast or site cast and generally contain mild steel reinforcing to resist handling stresses.

1808.2.3.1 Materials. Higher strength concrete is used in piles to reduce the volume changes, which reduces prestress losses, and to provide a more dense concrete to reduce cover requirements.

1808.2.3.2 Design. Minimum prestress is set to minimize cracking from handling and driving stresses.

1808.2.3.2.1 Design in Seismic Design Category C. Spiral transverse (confining) reinforcement is required to mitigate the effects of soil induced curvatures from seismic ground displacements. See discussion in commentary to Section 1807.2.23 and subsections. The volumetric requirement is the same as for columns in ductile frames. (See ACI 318, Section 21.4.2.) When using prestressing strand to anchor the pile in the cap, the development length should be sufficient to develop the strength of the strand.

1808.2.3.2.2 Design in Seismic Design Category D, E or F. These transverse reinforcing requirements are based on testing of prestressed piles in New Zealand and the subsequent recommendations by the Prestressed Concrete Institute (PCI). The requirements result in prestressed piles with good ductility without creating construction problems from reinforcement congestion. In Item 2, the "distance from the underside of the pile cap to the point of zero curvature" is determined as in Section 1809.1.2.1 below. See Sheppard[8] and Joen, et al.[9]

1808.2.3.3 Allowable stresses. The term $0.33f'_c$ is the same as conventionally reinforced piles. Since prestressing places additional compressive stresses on the pile, this stress must be subtracted from the allowable compressive stress; hence, the subtractive term $-0.27f_{pc}$. The term f_{pc} is the effective prestress on the gross area, which is the prestressing force remaining after losses have occurred.

1808.2.3.4 Installation. Because of the precompression, less care is needed in the handling and driving than for conventionally reinforced piles, and prestressed piles are, in general, more durable than conventionally reinforced precast concrete piles.

1808.2.3.5 Concrete cover. Cover requirements are set to minimize steel corrosion.

1808.3 Structural steel piles. Structural steel piles are characterized by axial high load capacity. Piles may be H-piles or steel pipe piles.

H-piles are usually used as deep end-bearing piles because they are essentially nondisplacement that can readily penetrate solid strata to reach rock or other suitable hard bearing strata such as dense gravels. Ideally, steel H-piles are driven to hard or medium hard rock.

Driven pipe piles are displacement type piles if driven closed; nondisplacement if driven open. Pipe piles are made of seamless or welded pipes and are frequently filled with concrete after driving. Pipe piles conforming to ASTM A 252 are used in both friction and end-bearing applications. Pipe piles may be driven open ended or closed ended. Open ended pipe piles are generally used when the soils investigation shows rock or a suitable end bearing stratum close to the ground surface, especially if the loads to be supported are large. The pipe is driven to bearing, the soils forced into the pipe during driving are cleaned out, and the pipe filled with concrete. Closed end piles are generally used as friction piles when a suitable bearing stratum is not available at suitable depths. There are several proprietary closed end pipe piles available.

1808.3.1 Materials. H-piles are typically available in ASTM A 36 and A 572 steel. Pipe piles are fabricated from ASTM A 252 or A 283 plate. ASTM A 252 is a specification specifically for welded pipe piles.

1808.3.2 Allowable stresses. The stresses allowed consider stability. Tests have shown that for H-piles driven to refusal in rock through soils that provide full lateral support, the stresses at failure can approach the yield stress of the material. Hence, higher stresses are allowed if a soils investigation and load tests are performed.

1808.3.3 Dimensions of H-piles. H-piles are proportioned to withstand the impact stresses from hard driving. The flange and web thicknesses are usually equal. The flange widths are proportioned such that the section modulus, S_y, in the weak axis is approximately one third of S_x.

1808.3.4 Dimensions of steel pipe piles. This requirement differs from previous model code requirements in that it replaces an empirical requirement for a minimum thickness of $^1/_4$ inch with a more rational requirement that relates the minimum thickness to diameter and hammer energy by requiring a minimum area per kip-foot of energy. This requirement equates to a wall thickness of 0.27 inch for a 10-inch pipe driven with a hammer energy of 25 kip-feet. Note that if the wall thickness is less than $^3/_{16}$-inch, a driving shoe is required to prevent local buckling at the tip from hard driving regardless of diameter or hammer energy.

1808.3.5 Design in Seismic Design Category D, E or F. The unsupported flange width-thickness ratios or diameter-thickness ratios were established to minimize failure from local buckling caused by curvatures induced on piles by soils subjected to strong ground motions. Curvatures demands and, hence, moments on piles can be severe on layered sites with soft or liquifiable soils or sensitive clays overlain and underlain by stiffer layers that are subjected to strong ground shaking. This requirement is consistent with the requirements for compression members in IBC Section 2213.

SECTION 1809 CAST-IN-PLACE CONCRETE PILE FOUNDATIONS

1809.1 General. Cast-in-place (CIP) concrete piles are installed by placing concrete into holes preformed by drilling or by driving a temporary or permanent casing to the required bearing depth. Drilled or augered piles are also known as cast-in-drill-hole or CIDH piles. CIP piles may be either cased or uncased. Uncased piles are difficult to construct when below the groundwater table. Except for enlarged base piles, the concrete in CIP piles is not subjected to driving forces, only the forces imposed by the service loads and downdrag from settlement. One advantage of drilled CIP piles is that the tip elevation can easily be adjusted to have the tip on the correct bearing stratum. Reinforcement is installed during the concreting operation. CIP drilled piles are of the nondisplacement type, i.e., the soil is not displaced or compacted by the drilling operation. CIP piles constructed by first driving a closed end shell are displacement piles where the soil surrounding the shell is displaced and compacted during the driving operation. CIP piles constructed by driving an open-ended casing without a mandrel or temporary tip closure are nominally a nondisplacement pile, although some compaction around the shell may occur in cohesive soils and densification may occur from driving in granular soils.

1809.1.1 Materials. The slump requirements stated are for cased piles. Slump requirements must be adjusted for other conditions. For example, concrete placed in uncased drilled holes needs to be in the 6-8 inch range so that the concrete flows readily into the irregularities in the drilled hole. Use of superplasticizers will provide the desired slump while keeping the water/cementitious material ratio low.

1809.1.2 Reinforcement. With two exceptions, reinforcing steel must be assembled into a cage and placed in the hole or casing prior to concreting, not stabbed after concreting. One exception is dowels less than 5 feet in length, and the other exception is for auger injected piles, which are placed by injecting the concrete through a hollow stem auger. The last sentence referencing "augered uncased cast-in-place piles" applies only to these auger injected piles.

1809.1.2.1 Reinforcement in Seismic Design Category C. Minimum steel requirements are established to provide some ductility. The minimum reinforcement must be continued throughout the "flexural length" of the pile. The term "flexural length" is not defined in the IBC. However, the term is defined in the 1997 UBC (from which the requirements were derived) as the "length of the pile from the first point of zero lateral deflection to the underside of the pile cap or grade beam." The point of zero lateral deflection can be determined from the P-y analysis.

1809.1.2.2 Reinforcement in Seismic Design Category D, E or F. In addition to the requirements for SDC C, the minimum reinforcement ratio is higher and extends over a longer length to improve ductility. In addition, closed ties or spirals are required to provide confinement in regions of plastic hinging, i.e., at the pile-cap interface, at the interface of soft to stiff layers, and in liquefaction zones. Confinement reinforcing should also be used for bay muds and sensitive clays. See also Section 1802.2.7.

1809.1.3 Concrete placement. Holes should be free from debris, loose soils, or water. Water should be baled from the hole prior to concreting because excess water will cause segregation and dilution of the cement paste. If the water cannot be removed, the concrete should be placed by tremie methods and the concrete mix enriched and adjusted accordingly. When not placed by tremie, concrete should always be placed through an "elephant trunk" (funnel hopper) to avoid segregation

1809.2 Enlarged base piles. Enlarged base piles are intended to be end-bearing type piles that spread the bearing load over a larger area than a prismatic pile, thereby increasing capacity. Enlarged based piles may be either cased or uncased. Enlarged base piles are used only in granular soils which, because of the voids between soil particles, allow densification of the soils around the pile tip without creating excessive pressures. One type is the compacted base type, which consists of a bulb-shaped footing formed after driving the shaft casing to its final depth. See Section 1809.2.3 for a discussion of forming the bulb. Another type is the concrete-pedestal type, in which a truncated cone or pyramid shaped precast concrete tip larger than the steel casing diameter is driven into the soil with the casing. See Figure 12.

1809.2.1 Materials. Concrete used for the bulb type of pile must have a zero slump to be stiff enough to be compacted by the drop weight.

1809.2.2 Allowable stresses. Pile capacity must be based on concrete strength alone without consideration of soil capacity, and the area of the internal cross section of the pile, i.e., casing inside diameter.

1809.2.3 Installation. Installation must employ the same methods used to install the load test piles. The compacted base pile is usually installed by driving a steel casing. A zero slump concrete plug is placed at the tip of the casing and impacted with a heavy

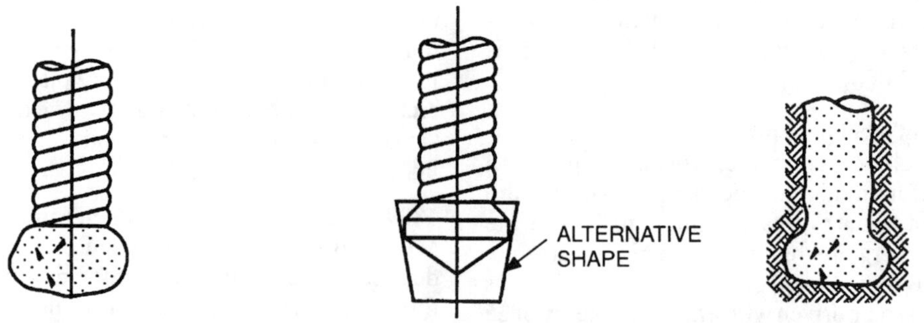

ENLARGED BASE PILES—CASED OR UNCASED SHAFTS

FIGURE 12

drop weight thereby driving the casing and plug. Sometimes a gravel plug is used rather than zero slump concrete. When the casing and plug have been driven to the required depth, the plug is driven out and the bulb is formed by progressively compacting additional layers of zero slump concrete. A welded reinforcing steel cage is added where required. If the pile is to be uncased, the shaft is formed by compacting zero slump concrete in small lifts as the casing is withdrawn. If the pile is to be cased, as would be required for piles through peats or other organic soils, the shaft is formed by inserting a steel shell inside the drive casing after forming the bulb, withdrawing the drive casing, and filling the shell with conventional concrete. The precast base type pile is installed with the precast base placed at the tip of a mandrel driven steel shell.

A problem that occurs with the precast base type and the cased bulb type piles is that an annular space between the casing and the soil remains. Either the pile must be designed as a slender reinforced concrete column governed by buckling or the annular space must be filled to provide the requisite lateral support. The ususal practice is to fill the annular space by pumping grout.

1809.2.4 Load-bearing capacity. The load-bearing capacity of enlarged base piles must be determined from load tests.

1809.2.5 Concrete cover. Concrete cover requirements are to provide protection and minimize corrosion of the steel in uncased piles.

1809.3 Drilled or augered uncased piles. This type of nondisplacement pile is installed by drilling or augering a hole and filling the uncased hole with concrete, either during or after withdrawing the auger.

1809.3.1 Allowable stresses. The allowable stresses for drilled uncased piles are the same as for cast-in-place piles for which holes are formed by machine drilling with auger or bucket type drills, with or without temporary casing. Concrete is placed by conventional methods including tremies or funnel hoppers. The allowable stresses for augered piles are lower because of the problems of installation of augered piles. In this type of pile, the holes are formed by a hollow stem auger and concrete is injected through the hollow stem auger as the auger is withdrawn. Reinforcement, if placed without lateral ties, is also placed through ducts in the hollow stem auger.

1809.3.2 Dimensions. The minimum 12-inch diameter is for inspection purposes. The length-to-diameter ratio is based on construction and stability considerations.

1809.3.3 Installation. These requirements are intended to result in a satisfactory pile. The construction of drilled piles is fraught with problems; caving, ground water, etc. See BOCA[10] Section 1820.3 for a discussion of problems.

1809.3.4 Reinforcement. The concrete must be quite fluid to allow for placement into the concrete. The concrete slump must exceed the limits of Section1809.1.1.

1809.3.5 Reinforcement in Seismic Design Category D, E or F. The reinforcement must meet minimum longitudinal reinforcement ratios and transverse reinforcement spacing to provide ductility.

1809.4 Driven uncased piles. This type of displacement pile is constructed by driving a temporary casing, removing the soils from the casing, and placing concrete in the hole as the casing is removed. The casing is driven with a closed end thereby displacing and compacting adjacent soil during driving. The casing is kept closed either by a detachable tip, which is left in place when the casing is withdrawn, or by a mandrel that closes off the casing tip during driving. This type of pile will appear new to users of the 1997 UBC.

1809.4.1 Allowable stresses. The area of the actual pile hole cannot be established with any certainty because of dimensional irregularities of the hole after removal of the casing. Hence, the allowable load is based on the inside diameter of the casing used during construction.

1809.4.2 Dimensions. The minimum 12-inch diameter is primarily for inspection purposes. The length-to-diameter ratio is based on construction and stability considerations. The requirements are the same as for drilled or augered uncased piles.

1809.4.3 Installation. The requirements are intended to prevent damage to uncured concrete in adjacent piles from the soil displacements caused by driving adjacent casings. The spacing requirements should not be construed to mean that the center-to-center spacing must not be closer than one half the pile depth; just that casing cannot be driven at that spacing within 48 hours of placement of concrete.

1809.4.4 Concrete cover. Concrete cover requirements are to provide protection and minimize corrosion of the steel.

1809.5 Steel-cased piles. The steel-cased pile is the most widely used type of cast-in-place concrete pile. This pile type is characterized by a thin steel shell and is a displacement pile. This pile type consists of a closed-end light-gage steel shell or a thin-walled pipe driven into the soil and left permanently in place, reinforced when required for uplift, lateral bending, or seismic induced curvatures, and filled with concrete. The shell or pipe is usually driven with a removable mandrel. The shell is either a constant section or a tapered shape. Steel encased piles are generally friction piles.

1809.5.1 Materials. The steel shell must have sufficient strength to remain watertight and not collapse from ground pressure when the mandrel is removed.

1809.5.2 Allowable stresses. The allowable stress is $0.33f'_c$ as for other concrete piles. The steel shell is too thin to act as a composite pile but does act as confinement reinforcement. The allowable stress can be increased to $0.40f'_c$ if the shell meets the confinement conditions in Section 1809.5.2.1 through 1809.5.2.4, in regard to thickness, strength, and diameter.

1809.5.2.1 Shell thickness. The shell thickness is not considered load carrying.

1809.5.2.2 Shell type. The shell must be seamless or spirally welded.

1809.5.2.3 Strength. The yield strength of steel normally used for the casings is 30 ksi.

1809.5.2.4 Diameter. The maximum diameter is set so that the volumetric ratio of shell to concrete is sufficient to provide confinement for the concrete.

1809.5.3 Installation. The restrictions on driving are primarily to avoid damage to uncured concrete in adjacent piles.

1809.5.4 Reinforcement. Reinforcing is required when bending or tensile stresses are induced in the piles by imposed loads.

1809.5.4.1 Seismic reinforcement. Reinforcement is required where seismic induced displacements cause bending in the pile.

1809.6 Concrete-filled steel pipe and tube piles. Concrete-filled steel piles are either seamless or welded pipe, or closed end tubular piles with either straight or tapered sections that are driven into the soil. The piles may be installed as either friction or end-bearing piles. This pile type is characterized by a steel shell that is thicker than the thin shell used in a steel-cased pile of section1809.5. Hence, both the concrete and steel shell are assumed to carry load compositely. If driven open ended, the earth core is removed from the shell prior to concreting. The shell may be driven with an internal mandrel.

1809.6.1 Materials. The steel shell must be seamless or welded.

1809.6.2 Allowable stresses. The allowable stress on the concrete is $0.33f'_c$, as it is for other concrete piles. The steel shell acts compositely with the concrete. For mandrel driven pipe piles the walls are usually so thin that the strength of the shell is disregarded.

1809.6.3 Minimum dimensions. The minimum diameter is primarily for inspection purposes.

1809.6.4 Reinforcement. Reinforcing is required when bending or tensile stresses are induced in the piles by imposed loads.

1809.6.4.1 Seismic reinforcement. For piles used in a structure assigned to SDC C, D, E or F, the minimum wall thickness is necessary to provide a minimum degree of concrete confinement, which is necessary for ductile concrete. Seismic induced displacements cause bending in the pile, thus requiring minimum reinforcement.

1809.7 Caisson piles. The caisson pile, commonly known as a drilled-in caisson, is installed as a special type of high load-capacity pile. Caissons are characterized by a structural steel core, an upper cased section extending to bedrock, and a lower uncased tip that is socketed into rock.

1809.7.1 Construction. The caisson pile is a cased cast-in-place concrete pile that is formed by 1) driving a heavy-wall open-ended pipe down to bedrock, 2) cleaning out the soil materials within the pipe, 3) drilling an uncased socket into the bedrock, 4) inserting a structural steel core into the pipe, and 5) filling the entire pipe and drilled socket with concrete.

The core material is usually made of hot-rolled structural steel wide flange or I-beam sections, or steel rails. This section specifies that the steel core is to extend full length from the base of the drilled socket to the top of the steel pipe or, as an alternative and depending on design requirements, the steel core may extend halfway up the pipe, or as a stub core to a distance in the pipe at least equal to the depth of the socket.

1809.7.2 Materials. The pipe is a welded or seamless pipe conforming to ASTM A252 with a minimum thickness of $^3/_8$ inch.

1809.7.3 Design. The strength of the cassion is developed in combined friction and end-bearing of the rock socket.

1809.7.4 Structural core. The core material is usually made of hot-rolled structural steel wide flange or I-beam sections, or steel rails. This section specifies that the steel core is to extend full length from the base of the drilled socket to the top of the steel pipe or, as an alternative and depending on design requirements, the steel core may extend halfway up the pipe, or as a stub core to a distance in the pipe at least equal to the depth of the socket.

1809.7.5 Allowable stresses. The concrete and heavy walled shell are designed to act compositely.

SECTION 1810
COMPOSITE PILES

Composite piles, as used herein, refers to piles placed in series, such as a cast-in-place concrete pile placed over a submerged wood pile. The maximum load is limited by the capacity of the weakest section.

SECTION 1811
PIER FOUNDATIONS

Pier foundations are isolated masonry or cast-in-place concrete structural elements extending into firm materials. Piers are relatively short relative to their width, with lengths less than or equal to twelve times the least dimension of the pier. Hence piers are rigid or semi-rigid. See Winterkorn, et al[2] for methods of analysis of rigid piers. The provisions for piers in this section are primarily exceptions to the requirements of Section 1807.2 when used for one- or two-family residential structures and appurtenant U occupancies not exceeding two stories built with light-frame construction.

1811.1 General. The piers must meet all applicable provisions of Section1807.2.

1811.2 Lateral dimensions and height. The length must be less than or equal to twelve times the least dimension of the pier.

1811.3 Materials. Concrete with $f'_c = 2{,}500$ psi is allowed.

1811.4 Reinforcement. Minimum reinforcement is 0.25 percent in the top one third of the pier, but not less than 10 feet.

1811.7 Masonry. Masonry may be used subject to dimensional limitations.

1811.8 Concrete. Plain (unreinforced) concrete may be used subject to dimensional limitations; otherwise, the pier must be reinforced per the column provisions of ACI 318.

REFERENCES

[1] Terzaghi, Karl and Peck, Ralph B., *Soil Mechanics in Engineering Practice*, John Wiley and Sons, 1967

[2] Winterkorn, Hans. F, and Fang, Hsai-Yang, *Foundation Engineering Handbook*, Van Nostrand Reinhold Company, Inc., New York, NY, 1975

[3] Bowles, J. E., *Foundation Analysis and Design*, 5th Edition, McGraw Hill, Inc., 1996

[4] Johnson, S. M. and Kavanagh, T. C., *The Design of Foundations for Buildings*, McGraw Hill, Inc.

[5] Liu, C. and Evett, J. B., *Soils and Foundations*, 2nd Edition, Prentice-Hall, Inc.

[6] Sowers, G. B., and Sowers, G. F., *Introductory Soil Mechanics in Engineering Practice*, Macmillian Publishing Co.

[7] Committee on the Bearing Value of Pile Driving Foundations, *Pile-driving Formulas—Progress Report*, Proceedings, May, American Society of Civil Engineers, New York, NY, 1941

[8] Sheppard, David A., *Seismic Design of Prestressed concrete Piling*, PCI Journal, March-April, 1993

[9] Joen, Pam Hoat, and Park, Robert, *Simulated Seismic Load Tests on Prestressed Concrete Piles and Pile-Cap Connections*, PCI Journal, November-December 1990

[10] BOCA, *The BOCA National Building Code—Commentary Volume 2*, Building Officials & Code Administrators International, Inc. Country Club Hills, IL, 1999

BIBLIOGRAPHY

ACI 318-95, *Building Code Requirements for Structural Concrete*, American Concrete Institute, Farmington Hills, MI, 1995

ACI 530/ASCE 5/TMS 402, *Building Code Requirements for Masonry Structures*, American Concrete Institute, Farmington Hills, MI, 1995

ACI 530.1/ASCE 6/TMS 602, *Specification for Masonry Structures*, American Concrete Institute, Farmington Hills, MI, 1995

ICBO, *Handbook to the Uniform Building Code: An illustrative commentary*, International Conference of Building Officials, Inc., Whittier, CA, 1998

ICC, *Proposed Changes to the Final Draft of the International Building Code*, International Code Council, January 1999

ICC, *1998 Proposed Changes to the First Draft of the International Building Code*, International Code Council, April 1998

NEHRP, *NEHRP (National Earthquake Hazard Reduction Program) Recommended Provisions for the Development of Seismic Regulations for New Buildings (and Other Structures)*, Building Seismic Safety Council, Washington, D.C., 1994 (1997)

SEAOC, *Recommended Lateral Force Requirements and Commentary*, Structural Engineers Association of California, Sacramento, CA, 1996

UBC-IBC Structural Comparison & Cross Reference, International Conference of Building Officials, Whittier, CA

Zeevaert, L., *Foundation Engineering for Difficult Soil Conditions*, 2nd Edition, Van Nostrand Reinhold Company, Inc., New York, NY

CHAPTER 19
PART 1
CONCRETE

INTRODUCTION

Of the three existing model codes, the *Uniform Building Code*™ (UBC)[1] adopts standards by transcription, while the BOCA *National Building Code* (BOCA/NBC)[2] and the *Standard Building Code* (SBC)[3] adopt standards by reference. The last edition of the UBC, dated 1997, transcribes the text of the 1995 edition of ACI 318 *Building Code Requirements for Structural Concrete* (ACI 318-95)[4] with amendments, which are printed in italics. The last editions of the BOCA/NBC and the SBC, dated 1999, adopt ACI 318–95 by reference, with Chapters 2 through 7 of that standard reproduced for the convenience of building inspectors and other building department personnel.

Chapter 19 of the 2000 *International Building Code*® (IBC) is based on the 1999 edition of the ACI 318 Standard (ACI 318–99)[4]. At the working draft stage of development of the 2000 IBC, the drafting committee decided that the only portions of ACI 318 requiring reproduction in the IBC were the inspection-related provisions. Thus, only portions of Chapters 2 through 7 of ACI 318–99 are reproduced in the 2000 IBC, with a small number of amendments printed in italics. Appropriate changes in format have been made to conform to the IBC style. The remainder of ACI 318–99 is adopted by reference, subject to 11 amendments listed in Section 1908. This is in keeping with the Building Officials and Code Administrators International and Southern Building Code Congress International practice of adopting standards by reference. The reproduction of much of Chapters 2 through 7 is for the convenience of the building inspector who, particularly in smaller jurisdictions, may not have ready access to the ACI 318 Standard. The engineering provisions of ACI 318 (Chapter 8 and subsequent chapters) are not reproduced because it is assumed that access to the ACI 318 Standard will be readily available to design professionals and structural plan reviewers. It is also desirable that the design professionals have access to the official ACI 318 Commentary (ACI 318R–99), which is published side-by-side with the ACI 318 Standard under the same cover.

Through the working draft, the first draft and the final draft of the 2000 IBC, the reference standard for concrete design and construction was ACI 318–95. The adoption of ACI 318–95 was subject to many significant amendments. Many of these modifications reflected changes made to the ACI 318–95 provisions by the 1997 UBC. The majority of these modifications were to the provisions of Chapter 21 (Special Provisions for Seismic Design) of ACI 318–95. Faced with the large number of significant modifications, ACI Committee 318 carefully considered them and adopted many (some with significant further modifications) into ACI 318–99. The ACI code change cycle was permanently altered to allow this to happen. What in the normal course would have been the revised 1998 edition of ACI 318–95 became ACI 318–99 instead. In view of all this, at the Final IBC Public Hearings held in Costa Mesa, California in March 1999, ACI 318–99 was approved for adoption into the first edition of the IBC, subject to a relatively small number of amendments, as mentioned above.

For reader information, an explanation of the significant changes from ACI 318-95 to ACI 318-99 are addressed in an appendix to this chapter.

Chapter 19 of the 2000 IBC includes substantive provisions additional to those of the ACI 318 Standard. This added material is contained in Sections 1911: Minimum Slab Provisions; 1912: Anchorage to Concrete—Allowable Stress Design; 1913: Anchorage to Concrete—Strength Design; 1914: Shotcrete; 1915: Reinforced Gypsum Concrete; and 1916: Concrete-Filled Pipe Columns. All these sections (except 1913) are from one or more of the existing model codes. Therefore, Section 1913, requires some explanation.

It had been anticipated that ACI 318–99 would contain a new Appendix D, Fastening to Concrete. The appendix was to have been applicable to the strength design of anchors cast in concrete as well as to post-installed anchors (i.e., anchors installed in hardened concrete). The provisions for post-installed anchors were dependent upon the completion of a standard test method (ACI 355.1) for evaluating the strengths of such anchors; however, the development of that standard ran into difficulties and it was not completed in time to be referenced in ACI 318–99. Next, consideration was given within ACI to modifying Appendix D to address only cast-in-place anchors, to the total exclusion of drilled-in anchors. However, this move failed to garner sufficient support within ACI. Therefore, ACI 318–99 has been issued without any provisions for fastening to concrete.

The concrete industry then asked ACI for permission to submit the provisions of the proposed Appendix D on cast-in anchors to the IBC as a replacement for the strength design provisions of IBC Section 1912. ACI agreed to permit the submission of this copyright-protected material for inclusion in the IBC, provided it was understood that ACI retained exclusive copyright to the material. In addition, when provisions for fastening to concrete are included in a future edition of ACI 318, a code change will be submitted to remove the IBC provisions and reference the new provisions of the standard. It is also to be understood that the material included in the IBC does not have official ACI approval; it continues to be processed by ACI Committee 318 through its consensus standards development process.

SECTION 1901
GENERAL

1901.1 Scope. This chapter provides minimum requirements governing the materials, quality control, design and construction of structural concrete elements of any structure erected under the requirements of the 2000 IBC.

1901.2 Plain and reinforced concrete. This section requires that structural concrete be designed and constructed in accordance with the requirements of Chapter 19 and ACI 318 as amended in Section 1908 of the 2000 IBC. Chapter 35 specifies that ACI 318–99 in particular must be used. This section states that Chapter 19 does not govern the design and construction of soil-supported slabs, unless the slab transmits vertical loads or lateral forces from other portions of the structure to the soil, although Sections 1904, Durability Requirements, and 1911, Minimum Slab Provisions, do apply. A similar statement is to be found in Section 1.1.6 of ACI 318–99, although that statement does not make ACI 318 Chapter 4, Durability Requirements, applicable to slabs on grade. As mentioned, the equivalent of Section 1911 does not exist in ACI 318–99. Section 1.1.6 of ACI 318–95 mentions gravity loads only; reference to lateral forces was added in the 1999 edition of that standard.

1901.3 Source and applicability. Sections 1902 through 1907 are largely reproductions, with occasional amendments shown in italics, of Chapters 2 through 7 of ACI 318–99. Where sections within Chapters 2 through 7 of ACI 318–99 are referenced in other chapters and appendices of ACI 318, any IBC modifications made in Sections 1902 through 1907 will remain applicable. For instance, any time the term "cement" is used, it will include blended cement complying with ASTM C 1157, per the IBC modification made to the definition of cement in Section 1903.2.

1901.4 Construction documents. This section reproduces from ACI 318–99, Section 1.2.1, the list of items to be shown on design drawings and specifications. Two items on the ACI list are omitted from the IBC. These are the name and date of issue of the code and supplement to which the design conforms; and live load and other loads used in design. It may be noted that Items 9 through 11 are new in ACI 318–99 and were not included in the corresponding list of ACI 318–95. See Section 1603 for additional items.

1901.5 Special inspection. Section 1704 of the 2000 IBC contains special inspection requirements for structural concrete. ACI 318–99, in general, does not contain provisions for special inspection of structural concrete, except that Section 1.3.5 requires continuous inspection of the placement of the reinforcement and concrete in special moment frames resisting seismic forces in regions of high seismic risk. Section 1901.5 provides a cross-reference to the inspection requirements of IBC Chapter 17.

SECTION 1902 DEFINITIONS

This reproduces some of the definitions in Chapter 2 of ACI 318–99. The definitions that are not used in the transcribed sections of ACI 318–99 are not reproduced.

SECTION 1903 SPECIFICATIONS FOR TESTS AND MATERIALS

1903.1 General. This section specifies that materials required to produce concrete and the testing of such materials must be in compliance with the provisions of this section (which is largely a reproduction of Chapter 3 of ACI 318–99) and with the applicable standards listed in Section 3.8 of ACI 318–99.

Chapter 17 of the 2000 IBC contains special inspection requirements that are not included in ACI 318–99, except that Section 1.3.5 does require continuous inspection of special moment frames. Chapter 17 also contains test requirements that are not included in ACI 318–99. Section 1903.1 makes these IBC Chapter 17 requirements applicable whenever required by the provisions of that chapter.

1903.2 Cement. This requires cements used for making concrete to comply with ACI 318–99 Section 3.2. Additionally, it permits the use of blended cements that are in compliance with ASTM Standard C 1157. This is one of the few modifications made to the provisions of ACI 318–99. That standard requires cements to conform to ASTM C 150, Specification for Portland Cement; ASTM C 595, Specification for Blended Hydraulic Cements (excluding Types S and SA, which are not intended as principal cementing constituents of structural concrete); and ASTM C 845, Specification for Expanded Hydraulic Cement. ACI 318–99 Section 3.2.2 requires that "cement used in the work shall correspond to that on which selection of concrete proportions was based." Refer to ACI 318–99 Commentary Section R3.2.2 for explanation of this requirement.

1903.3 Aggregates. This requires aggregates used for making concrete to comply with the requirements of ACI 318–99, Section 3.3. ACI 318–99 requires concrete aggregates to conform to either ASTM C 33, Specification for Concrete Aggregates, or ASTM 330, Specification for Lightweight Aggregates for Structural Concrete. However, aggregates conforming to these ASTM specifications are not always economically available and, in many instances, noncomplying materials have a long history of satisfactory performance. Such nonconforming materials are permitted with the approval of the building official when acceptable evidence of satisfactory performance is provided.

ACI 318–99, Section 3.2.2 specifies size limitations on aggregates to ensure the proper encasement of reinforcement and to minimize honeycombing. These requirements are waived if, in the judgment of the engineer, workability, and methods of construction are such that concrete can be placed without honeycombs or voids.

1903.4 Water. This reproduces Section 3.4.1 of ACI 318–99 concerning impurities in mixing water and requires compliance with the rest of Section 3.4.

Almost any water that is drinkable and has no pronounced taste or odor can be used as mixing water for making concrete. However, some waters that are not fit for drinking may still be suitable for mixing concrete.

Excessive impurities in mixing water may not only affect setting time and concrete strength but may also cause efflorescence, staining, corrosion of reinforcement, volume instability, and reduced durability. Reference 5 advises that certain optional limits may be set on chlorides, sulfates, alkalis, and solids in the mixing water, or that appropriate tests can be performed to determine the effect that the impurities have on various properties. Some impurities may have little effect on strength and setting time, yet they can adversely affect durability and other properties.

According to Reference 5, water containing no more than 2,000 parts per million (ppm) of total dissolved solids can generally be used satisfactorily for making concrete. Water containing more than 2,000 ppm of dissolved solids should be tested for its effect on strength and time of set.

Concern over high chloride content in mixing water is chiefly due to the possible adverse effect of chloride ions on the corrosion of reinforcing steel or prestressing strand. In fact, prestressing strand and aluminum embedments are singled out as areas of concern in ACI 318–99, Section 3.4.2. Chloride ions attack the protective oxide film formed on the steel or aluminum by the highly alkaline (pH > 12.5) chemical environment present in concrete. Chlorides can be introduced into concrete with the separate mix ingredients—admixtures, aggregates, cement and mixing water—or through exposure to deicing salts, seawater or salt-laden air in coastal environments. Placing an acceptable limit on chloride content for any one ingredient, such as mixing water, is difficult considering the several possible sources of chloride ions in concrete. An acceptable limit depends primarily upon the type of structure and the environment to which it is exposed during its service life.[5] ACI 318-99, Section 4.4.1 is devoted to this topic.

Water of questionable suitability can be used for making concrete if mortar cubes (ASTM C 109) made with it have 7-day and 28-day strengths equal to at least 90 percent of the corresponding strengths of companion specimens made with drinkable or distilled water. Reference 5 advises that ASTM C 191 tests should additionally be made to ensure that impurities in the mixing water do not adversely shorten or extend the setting time of the cement. Acceptable criteria for water to be used in concrete are given in ASTM C 94 and the American Association of State Highway and Transportation Officials (AASHTO) T 26.[6]

1903.5 Steel reinforcement. This regulates reinforcement as well as welding of reinforcement to be placed in concrete.

1903.5.1 Reinforcement type. This section specifies materials permitted for use as reinforcement by reproducing Section 3.5.1 of ACI 318–99, and also requires reinforcement to comply with Section 3.5 of ACI 318–99. Reinforcement is required to be deformed reinforcement, except that plain reinforcement is allowed for spirals or tendons. Reinforcement consisting of structural steel, steel pipe or steel tubing is permitted as specified in ACI 318. Other metal elements such as inserts, anchor bolts, or plain bars for dowels at isolation or contraction joints, are not normally considered to be reinforcement under the provisions of ACI 318.

1903.5.2 Welding. Welding of reinforcing bars is required to conform to "Structural Welding Code—Reinforcing Steel," AWS D1.4 of the American Welding Society.[7] This document covers aspects of welding reinforcing bars, including criteria to qualify welding procedures.

The type and location of welded splices and other required welding of reinforcing bars must be indicated on the design drawings or in the project specifications. Much of this is also required under Section 1.2.1 of ACI 318–99.

Weldability of steel is based on its chemical composition or carbon equivalent. The AWS D1.4 Welding Code establishes preheat and interpass temperatures for a range of carbon equivalents and reinforcing bar sizes. Carbon equivalent is calculated from the chemical composition of the reinforcing bars. For bars other than ASTM A 706, the chemical analysis required to calculate the carbon equivalent is not routinely provided by the producer of the reinforcing bars. For welding reinforcing bars other than ASTM A 706 bars, the design drawings or project specifications need to specifically require that results of the chemical analysis be furnished.

The ASTM A 706 specification covers low-alloy steel reinforcing bars intended for applications requiring controlled tensile properties or welding. Weldability is accomplished in the ASTM A 706 specification by limits or controls on chemical composition or carbon equivalent. The producer is required by the ASTM A 706 specification to report the chemical composition and carbon equivalent.

The AWS D1.4 Welding Code requires the contractor to prepare written welding procedure specifications conforming to the requirements of the Welding Code. Appendix A of the Welding Code contains a suggested form that shows the information required for such a specification.

It is often necessary to weld to existing reinforcing bars in a structure when no mill test report of the existing reinforcement is available. This condition is particularly common in alterations or additions to existing buildings. The AWS D1.4 Welding Code provides guidance concerning this situation.

Welding of wire to wire, and of wire or welded wire fabric to reinforcing bars or structural steel elements is not covered by AWS D1.4. Some guidance on this subject is available in the ACI 318–99 Commentary, Section R3.5.2.

The different types of reinforcement recognized by ACI 318–99 for use in concrete are listed in Tables 1, 2 and 3.

1903.6 Admixtures. This section, like ACI 318–99 Section 3.6.1, requires admixtures used in concrete to be subject to prior approval by the registered design professional. It further requires such admixtures to comply with ACI 318, Section 3.6.

The admixtures recognized for use in concrete in Section 3.6 of ACI 318–99 are listed in Table 4.

1903.7 Storage of materials. This is a reproduction, in a slightly different format, of Section 3.7 of ACI 318–99.

TABLE 1. DEFORMED REINFORCEMENT RECOGNIZED IN ACI 318-99

PRODUCT	ASTM SPECIFICATIONS	GRADE OR TYPE	MINIMUM YIELD STRENGTH ksi	MINIMUM TENSILE STRENGTH ksi
Reinforcing bars	A 615	40* 60 75*	40 60 75	70 90 100
	A 616	50 60	50 60	80 90
	A 617	40 60	40 60	70 90
	A 706	60	60 (78 max.)	80
Bar mats[a]	A 184	—	—	—
Wire, deformed	A 496	—	75	85
Welded wire fabric, plain deformed	A 185 A 497	—	65 70	75 80
Galvanized reinforcing bars	A 767	—	—	—
Epoxy-coated reinforcing bars[a]	A 775 A 934	—	—	—
Epoxy-coated wires[b] and welded wire fabric[c]	A 884	—	—	—

* Grade 40 bars are furnished only in sizes 3 through 6. Grade 75 bars are furnished only in sizes 6 through 18.

a. Same as reinforcing bars

b. Same as wires

c. Same as welded wire fabric

TABLE 2. PLAIN REINFORCEMENT AND PRESTRESSING TENDONS RECOGNIZED IN ACI 318–99

PRODUCT	ASTM SPECIFICATIONS	GRADE OR TYPE	MINIMUM YIELD STRENGTH ksi	MINIMUM TENSILE STRENGTH ksi
Reinforcing bars	A 615	40	40	70
		60	60	90
		75	75	100
	A 616	50	50	80
		60	60	90
	A 617	40	40	70
		60	60	90
Reinforcing bars	A 706	60	60	80
Wire, plain	A 82	—	70	80
Prestressing wire	A 421	—	188-200	235-250
Prestressing wire, low-relaxation	A 421+ Supplement	—	188-200	235-250
Prestressing strand	A 416	250	212.5	250
		270	229.5	270
Prestressing bar	A 722	Type I	127.5	150
		Type II	120	150

TABLE 3. STRUCTURAL STEEL, STEEL PIPE OR TUBING RECOGNIZED BY ACI 318-99 FOR USE IN COMPOSITE COMPRESSION MEMBERS

PRODUCT	ASTM SPECIFICATION
Structural steel used with reinforcing bars in composite compression members meeting requirements of Sec. 10.16.7 or 10.16.8	
Carbon structural steel	A 36
High-strength low-alloy structural steel	A 242
High-strength low-alloy columbium-vanadium structural steel	A 572
High-strength low-alloy structural steel with 50 ksi minimum yield strength up to 4 in. thick	A 588
Steel pipe or tubing for composite compression members composed of steel encased concrete core meeting requirements of Sec. 10.16.6	
Seamless and welded black and hot-dipped galvanized steel pipe	A 53 Grade B
Cold-formed welded and seamless carbon steel structural tubing in rounds and shapes	A 500
Hot-formed welded and seamless carbon steel structural tubing	A 501

TABLE 4. CONCRETE ADMIXTURES RECOGNIZED BY ACI 318–99

PRODUCT	ASTM SPECIFICATION	DESIRED EFFECT
Accelerators	C 494, Type C	Accelerate setting and develop early strength
Air-entraining admixtures	C 260	Improve durability in environments of freeze-thaw, de-icers, sulfate, and alkali reactivity Improve workability
Fly ash or other pozzolans	C 618	Pozzolanic activity Improve workability, plasticity, sulfate resistance; reduce alkali reactivity, permeability, heat of hydration Partial cement replacement Filler
Ground granulated blast furnace slag	C 989	Same as above
Retarders	C 494, Type B	Retard setting time
Silica fume	C 1240	Same as fly ash or other pozzolans
Superplasticizers	C 1017, Type 1	Reduce water-cement ratio Produce flowing concrete
Superplasticizer and retarder	C 1017, Type 2	Produce flowing concrete with retarded set Reduce water
Water reducer	C 494, Type A	Reduce water demand by at least 5%
Water reducer and accelerator	C 494, Type E	Reduce water (minimum 5%) and accelerate set
Water reducer and retarder	C 494, Type D	Reduce water (minimum 5%) and retard set
Water reducer—high range	C 494, Type F	Reduce water demand (minimum 12%)
Water reducer—high range and retarder	C 494, Type G	Reduce water demand (minimum 12%) and retard set

SECTION 1904 DURABILITY REQUIREMENTS

This is a reproduction of Chapter 4 of ACI 318–99, with certain exceptions. The provisions of that chapter emphasize the importance of considering durability requirements before the designer selects f'_c and cover over reinforcing steel.

As pointed out in the commentary to Chapter 4 of ACI 318–99, maximum water-cementitious materials ratios of 0.40 to 0.50 that may be required for concrete exposed to freezing and thawing, sulfate soils or waters, or for preventing corrosion of reinforcement, will typically be equivalent to requiring an f'_c of 5,000 to 4,000 pounds per square inch (psi), respectively. Generally, the required average concrete strengths, f'_{cr}, will be 500 to 700 psi higher than the specified compressive strength, f'_c. Since it is difficult to accurately determine the water-cementitious materials ratio of concrete during production, the f'_c specified should be reasonably consistent with the water-cementitious materials ratio required for durability. This will help ensure that the required water-cementitious materials ratio is actually obtained in the field. Because the usual emphasis in inspection is on strength, test results substantially higher than the specified strength may lead to a lack of concern for quality and production of concrete that exceeds the maximum water-cementitious materials ratio. Thus an f'_c of 3,000 psi and a maximum water cementitious materials ratio of 0.45 should not be specified for a parking structure, if the structure will be exposed to de-icing salts.

The commentary to Chapter 4 of ACI 318–99 also points out that the chapter does not include provisions for especially severe exposures, such as acids or high temperatures, and is not concerned with aesthetic considerations such as surface finishes. These items should be covered in project specifications.

1904.1 Water-cementitious materials ratio. This section is the same as ACI 318–99, Section 1904.1, except that it permits blended cements conforming to ASTM C 1157 to be included in the calculation of water-cementitious materials ratio.

1904.2 Freezing and thawing exposures. This section is based on the ACI 318–99 Section 4.2. Section 1904.2.1 requires normal-weight as well as light-weight concrete exposed to freezing and thawing or de-icing chemicals to be entrained with air in amounts specified in Table 1904.2.1, subject to a tolerance of ±1.5 percent. Section 1904.2.2 requires that concrete subject to the exposures listed in Table 1904.2.2(1) must not exceed the maximum water-cementitious materials ratios given in that table, and must not fall below the minimum specified compressive strength requirements of that table. While the minimum strength requirements are given for normal-weight as well as for light-weight concrete, the maximum water-cementitious materials ratio requirements are given only for normal-weight concrete. This is because determination of absorption of light-weight aggregates is uncertain, making calculation of the water-cementitious materials ratio uncertain. Section 1904.2.3 introduces Table 1904.2.3, which establishes limitations on the amount of fly ash, other pozzolans, silica fume and slag that can be included in concrete exposed to de-icing chemicals.

The IBC Table 1904.2.1 has an additional Footnote b, taken largely from the ACI 318 Commentary, Section R4.2.1, that is not part of ACI 318–99 Table 4.2.1. The footnote seeks to define severe and moderate exposures, and gives examples of each.

The IBC Section 1904.2.2 has added an exception requiring that in buildings less than four stories in height, that house Group R (residential) Occupancies, normal-weight concrete subject to weathering (freezing and thawing), as determined from Figure 1904.2.2, or deicer chemicals, must comply with the requirements of Table 1904.2.2(2). Neither Figure 1904.2.2 nor Table 1904.2.2(2) is part of ACI 318–99. The exception, the table and the figure are adopted into the IBC from the *International Residential Code*™ (formerly the *CABO One- and Two-Family Dwelling Code*).[8] Table 1904.2.2(2) mandates a minimum specified compressive strength as a function of the concrete element and exposure, but no maximum water-cementitious materials ratio. Figure 1904.2.2 shows the geographic regions within the U.S. mainland that are classified as having negligible, moderate and severe weather exposures for the purposes of Table 1904.2.2(2). It is clearly indicated in a note to the figure that the boundary lines defining the weather regions are only approximate. Building officials in communities near a boundary line must establish applicable exposure classifications.

1904.3 Sulfate exposures. This is largely a reproduction of Section 4.3 of ACI 318–99. Section 1904.3.1 requires concrete exposed to injurious concentrations of sulfates from soil and water to be made with a sulfate-resisting cement. Table 1904.3 lists the appropriate types of cement and the maximum water-cementitious materials ratios and minimum strengths for various exposure conditions. Section 1904.3.2 prohibits the use of calcium chloride as an admixture in concrete that is to be exposed to severe and very severe sulfate-containing solutions, as defined in Table 1904.3. Such use, because of the calcium content of the admixture, would adversely affect the performance of cement in resisting sulfate attack.

1904.4 Corrosion protection of reinforcement. This section reproduces Section 4.4 of ACI 318–99. The maximum concentration of water soluble chloride ion permitted in hardened concrete from all sources is given in Table 1904.4.1, Section 1904.4.1. The soluble chlorides induce corrosion, while chlorides that are chemically combined with other ingredients have little or no corrosive effect. Additional information on the effects of chlorides on the corrosion of reinforcing steel is given in the *Guide to Durable Concrete* reported by ACI Committee 201[9] and the *Corrosion of Metals in Concrete* reported by ACI Committee 222.[10] To provide the properties of concrete that will resist the harmful effects of exposure to chlorides from de-icing chemicals, salts, seawater or brackish water, Section 1904.4.2 requires concrete mixtures to conform to the maximum water-cementitious materials ratio (in the case of normal-weight aggregate concrete only) and the minimum specified compressive strength requirements of Table 1904.2.2(1).

Minimum concrete cover requirements for the protection of reinforcement are given in Section 1907.7. Section 1907.7.5 mandates that such requirements be suitably increased in corrosive environments or under other severe exposure conditions. Section 18.16 of ACI 318–99 contains provisions for corrosion protection of unbonded prestressing tendons.

SECTION 1905
CONCRETE QUALITY, MIXING AND PLACING

As pointed out in the commentary to Chapter 5 of ACI 318–99, of which Section 1905 is largely a reproduction, the requirements for proportioning concrete mixes are based on the premise that concrete should provide both adequate durability (Section 1904) and strength. The criteria for acceptance of concrete are intended primarily to protect the safety of the public. Section 1905 describes procedures by which concrete of adequate strength can be obtained, and provides procedures for checking the quality of the concrete during and after its placement.

The provisions of Sections 1905.2, 1905.3 and 1905.4, together with Section 1904, establish required mix proportions. The basis for determining the adequacy of concrete strength is in Section 1905.6.

Section 1905 also provides minimum criteria for preparation of equipment and place of deposit (Section 1905.7), mixing (Section 1905.8), conveying (Section 1905.9), placing (Section 1905.10), and curing (Section 1905.11) of concrete. Requirements for cold weather concreting and hot weather concreting (Sections 1905.11 and 1905.12, respectively) are also given.

1905.1 General. Sections 1905.1.1 through 1905.1.5 are largely reproductions of Sections 5.1.1 through 5.1.5 of ACI 318-99, with one modification noted below.

The basic premises governing the designation and evaluation of concrete strength are presented in Section 1905.1.1 through 1905.1.3. It is emphasized that the average strength of concrete produced should always exceed the specified value of f'_c used in the structural design calculations. This is based on probabilistic concepts and is intended to ensure that adequate concrete strength will be developed in the structure. Additionally, the durability requirements of Section 1904 are to be satisfied.

In a rare modification (in this case addition) to ACI 318 requirements, the minimum specified compressive strength of concrete is required to be 2,500 psi for concrete designed and constructed in accordance with the IBC Chapter 19.

Tests for splitting tensile strength of light-weight aggregate concrete (as required by Section 1905.1.5) are not intended for control or acceptance of such concrete in the field. Indirect control is maintained through the normal compressive strength test requirements provided by Section 1905.6.

1905.2 Selection of concrete proportions. Sections 1905.2.1 through 1905.2.3 are reproduced from Sections 5.2.1 through 5.2.3 of ACI 318-99.

Recommendations for selecting proportions for concrete are given in detail in *Standard Practice for Selecting Proportions for Normal, Heavyweight, and Mass Concrete*[11] reported by ACI Committee 211. It provides two methods for selecting and adjusting proportions for normal-weight concrete: the estimated weight and absolute volume methods. Example calculations are shown for both methods. Proportioning by the absolute volume method is also illustrated in Reference 5. Recommendations for light-weight concrete are given in *Standard Practice for Selecting Proportions for Structural Lightweight Concrete*[12] also reported by ACI Committee 211.

Section 1905.2.1 requires that the selected water-cementitious materials ratio be low enough, or in the case of light-weight concrete, the compressive strength high enough to satisfy both the strength criteria (Section 1905.3 or 1905.4) and the special exposure requirements (Section 1904). At the same time, workability needed for proper placement must be provided.

The use of field experience or laboratory trial mixtures (Section 1905.3) is emphasized as the preferred method for selecting concrete mixture proportions. When no prior experience or trial mixture data are available, estimation of the water-cementitious materials ratio as prescribed in ACI 318-99 Section 5.4 is permitted, subject to approval by the registered design professional.

1905.3 Proportioning on the basis of field experience and/or trial mixtures. This refers to ACI 318-99 Section 5.3.

Proportioning from field data. A previously used concrete mix design may be used for a new project if strength test data and standard deviations (ACI 318–99 Commentary Section R5.3.1) show that the mixture is acceptable. Durability requirements must also be met. The statistical data must essentially represent the same materials, proportions, and concreting conditions to be used on the new project. The data used for proportioning must be from a concrete with an f'_c within 1,000 psi of the strength required for the proposed work. Also, the data must represent at least 30 consecutive tests or two groups of consecutive tests totaling at least 30 tests (one test requires the average strength of two cylinders from the same sample). If only 15 to 29 consecutive tests are available, an adjusted standard deviation can be obtained by multiplying the standard deviation *(S)* for the 15 to 29 tests and a modification factor from ACI 318–99 Table 5.3.1.2. The data must represent 45 or more days of tests.

The modified standard deviation is then used in ACI 318–99 Equations 5-1 and 5-2. The average compressive strength from the test record must equal or exceed the ACI 318 required average compressive strength, f'_{cr}, in order for the concrete proportions to be acceptable. The f'_{cr} for the selected mix proportions is equal to the larger of:

$$f'_{cr} = f'_c + 1.34S \qquad \text{ACI 318-99 Equation 5-1}$$

$$f'_{cr} = f'_c + 2.33S - 500 \qquad \text{ACI 318-99 Equation 5-2}$$

where:

f'_{cr} = required average compressive strength of concrete used as the basis for selection of concrete proportions, psi

f'_c = specified compressive strength of concrete, psi

S = standard deviation, psi

When field strength test records do not meet the previously discussed requirements, f'_{cr} can be obtained from ACI 318-99 Table 5.3.2.2. A field strength test record, several strength test records, or tests from trial mixtures must be used for documentation showing that the average strength of the mixture is equal to or greater than f'_{cr}.

If fewer than 30 but not fewer than 10 tests are available, the tests may be used for average strength documentation if the time period is not less than 45 days. Mix proportions may also be established by interpolating between two or more test records if each meets the above and project requirements. If a significant difference exists between the mixes used in the interpolation, a trial mix should be considered to check strength gain. If the test records meet the above requirements and limitations of ACI 318, the proportions for the mix may then be considered acceptable for the proposed work.

Proportioning by trial mixtures. When field test records are not available or are insufficient for proportioning by field experience methods, the selection of concrete proportions may be based on trial mixes. The trial mixes must use the same materials proposed for the work. At least three mixes with three different water-cementitious materials ratios or cement contents must be made to produce a range of strengths that encompass f'_{cr}. The trial mixes must have slump and air content within ± 0.75 inch and ± 0.5 percent, respectively, of the maximum permitted. At least three cylinders per water-cementitious materials ratio must be made and cured according to ASTM C192. At 28 days or the designated test age, the compressive strength of the concrete must be determined by testing the cylinders in compression. A water-cementitious materials ratio versus strength curve (for example, see Figure 1) can then be plotted and the proportions interpolated from the data. It is also good practice to test the properties of the newly proportioned mix in a trial batch.

1905.4 Proportioning without field experience or trial mixtures. This section refers to ACI 318–99 Section 5.4, which makes special provisions for mix proportioning based on other experience where test data are not available and it is impractical to make trial batches. Permission of the registered design professional is a requirement of Section 5.4. Because combinations of different ingredients may vary considerably in strength level, this procedure is not permitted for f'_c greater than 4,000 psi, and the required average strength must exceed f'_c by 1,200 psi. The purpose of this provision is to allow work to continue when there is an unexpected interruption in concrete supply and there is not sufficient time for tests and evaluation, or in small structures where the cost of trial mix data is not justified.

1905.5 Average strength reduction. This reproduces Section 5.6.1 through 5.6.5 of ACI 318–99.

1905.6.1 Qualified technicians. This section specifically requires field testing of concrete to be done by qualified field testing technicians and laboratory testing of concrete to be done by

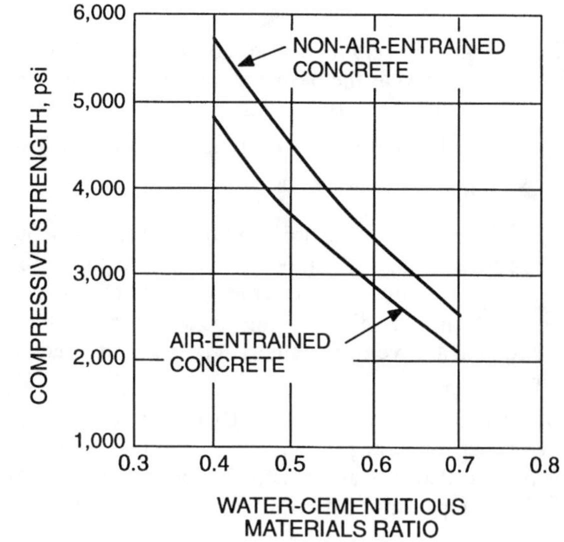

TYPICAL TRIAL MIXTURE OR FIELD DATA STRENGTH CURVES

FIGURE 1

qualified laboratory testing technicians. According to ACI 318–99 Commentary Section R5.6.1, a qualified field testing technician should be certified in accordance with the requirements of ACI Concrete Field Testing Technician—Grade I Certification Program, or the requirements of ASTM C1077, or an equivalent program. A qualified laboratory testing technician should be certified in accordance with the requirements of ACI Concrete Laboratory Testing Technician, Concrete Strength Testing Technician, or the requirements of ASTM C1077.

1905.6.2 Frequency of testing. This specifies that strength tests for each class of concrete placed each day should be taken not less than once a day, nor less than once for each 150 cubic yards of concrete, nor less than once for each 5,000 square feet of surface area for slabs or walls. The average strength of two cylinders is required for each test. Additional specimens may be required when high-strength concrete is involved or where structural requirements are critical. The specimens should be laboratory-cured. Specifications may require that additional specimens be made and field-cured as nearly as practical in the same manner as the concrete in the structure. A 7-day test cylinder, along with the two 28-day test cylinders, is often made and tested to provide an early indication of strength development. As a rule of thumb, the 7-day strength is about 60 percent to 75 percent of the 28-day strength, depending upon the type and amount of cement, water-cementitious materials ratio, curing temperature and other variables.

1905.6.3 Laboratory-cured specimens. This section specifies sampling and testing requirements for laboratory-cured specimens and also gives criteria for acceptance of test results. Samples must be taken in accordance with ASTM C1072, Standard Practice for Sampling Freshly Mixed Concrete.

Premolded specimens for strength testing must be made and cured in accordance with ASTM C31, Standard Practice for Making and Curing Concrete Test Specimens in the Field.

The standard test specimen for compressive strength of concrete with a maximum aggregate size of 2 inches or smaller is a cylinder 6 inches in diameter by 12 inches high. For larger aggregates, the diameter of the cylinder should be at least three times the maximum-size aggregate, and the height should be twice the diameter. While rigid metal molds are preferred, paraffined cardboard, plastic, or other types of disposable molds conforming to ASTM C470 may be used. They should be placed on a smooth, level surface and filled carefully to avoid distortion of their shape. Unless required by the project specification, cylinders smaller than 6 inches by 12 inches must not be made in the field.

The cylinders, cured under standard laboratory conditions, must be tested in compression at a specified rate of loading at 28 days of age or at the designated test age, in accordance with the requirements of ASTM C39.

The concrete strength is considered to be satisfactory as long as averages of any three consecutive strength tests remain above the specified f'_c, and no individual strength test falls below the specified f'_c by more than 500 psi. When concrete fails to meet either of the criteria, steps must be taken to increase the average of the subsequent concrete test results. See ACI 318–99 Section 5.6.5 for investigation of low strength test results.

1905.6.4 Field-cured specimens. Strength tests of cylinders cured under field conditions (in conformance with the requirements of ASTM C31) may be required to check the adequacy of curing and protection of concrete in the structure. Procedures for protecting and curing concrete are required to be improved when strength of field-cured cylinders at test age designated for determination of f'_c is less than 85 percent of that of companion laboratory-cured cylinders. However, results for the job-cured cylinders are considered satisfactory if the job-cured cylinders exceed the specified f'_c by more than 500 psi, even though they fail to reach 85 percent of the strength of the companion laboratory-cured cylinders.

1905.6.5 Low-strength test results. Instructions are provided concerning the procedure to be followed when strength tests have failed to meet the specified acceptance criteria. If, after properly assessing the significance of low test results and determining whether they indicate need for concern, further investigation is deemed necessary, such investigation may include nondestructive tests, or in extreme cases, strength tests of cores taken from the structure.

For cores, if required, conservatively safe acceptance criteria are provided that should ensure structural adequacy of virtually any type of construction. Core tests yielding an average of 85 percent of the specified strength is entirely realistic. To expect core tests to yield 100 percent of f'_c is not realistic, since differences in the size of specimens, conditions of obtaining samples, and procedures of curing do not permit equal values to be obtained. When the core tests fail to provide assurance of structural adequacy, it may be practical, particularly in the case of floor or roof systems, for the building official to require a load test (Chapter 20 of ACI 318–99).

1905.7 Preparation of equipment and place of deposit. This reproduces Section 5.7 of ACI 318–99. Detailed recommendations for mixing, handling and transporting, and placing concrete are given in *Guide for Measuring, Mixing, Transporting and Placing Concrete* reported by ACI Committee 304.[5,13]

This section mandates the use of clean equipment and the cleaning of forms and reinforcement thoroughly before beginning to deposit concrete. In particular, sawdust, nails, wood pieces, and other debris that may collect inside the forms must be removed. Reinforcement must be thoroughly cleaned of ice, dirt, loose rust, mill scale or other coatings. Water must be removed from the forms.

1905.8 Mixing. Sections 1905.8.1 and 1905.8.2 are reproductions of ACI 318-99 Sections 5.8.1 and 5.8.2, respectively. Section 1905.8.3 refers to ACI 318-99 Section 5.8.3.

All concrete must be mixed thoroughly until it is uniform in appearance, with all ingredients evenly distributed. Reference 5 points out that mixers should not be loaded above their rated capacities and must be operated at approximately the speeds for which they were designed. Increased output should be obtained by using a larger mixer or additional mixers, rather than by speeding up or overloading the equipment on hand. If the blades of the mixer become worn or coated with hardened concrete, the mixing action is going to be less efficient. Badly worn blades should be replaced and hardened concrete should be removed periodically.

If concrete has been adequately mixed, samples taken from different portions of a batch will have essentially the same unit weight, air content, slump, and coarse aggregate content. Maximum allowable differences in test results within a batch of ready-mixed concrete are given in ASTM C94.

The necessary time of mixing will depend on many factors, including batch size, stiffness of the batch, size and grading of the aggregate, and the efficiency of the mixer. Excessively long mixing times need to be avoided to guard against grinding of the aggregates.

1905.9 Conveying. This reproduces Sections 5.9.1 and 5.9.2 of ACI 318–99.

It is important and necessary to control each step in the handling and transporting of concrete to maintain uniformity within a batch and from batch to batch. Segregation of the coarse aggregate from the mortar or of water from the other ingredients must be avoided.

The equipment for handling and transporting concrete is required to be capable of supplying concrete to the place of deposit continuously and reliably under all conditions and for all methods of placement. Placing equipment commonly utilized are pumps, belt conveyors, pneumatic systems, wheelbarrows, buggies, crane buckets and tremies.

As pointed out in the ACI 318 Commentary Section R5.9, serious loss in strength can result when concrete is pumped through pipe made of aluminum or aluminum alloy, because of hydrogen generated by the reaction between the cement alkalies and the aluminum. It is, therefore, important not to use equipment made of aluminum or aluminum alloys for pump lines, tremies or chutes other than short ones.

1905.10 Depositing. This section reproduces Sections 5.10.1 through 5.10.8 of ACI 318–99.

Concrete must be deposited continuously as near as possible to its final position. To avoid segregation, concrete should not be moved horizontally over too long a distance as it is being placed in forms or slabs.

In general, concrete should be placed in horizontal layers of uniform thickness, each layer having been thoroughly consolidated before the next is placed. The rate of placement should be rapid enough so that a layer of concrete has not yet set when a new layer is placed upon it. This avoids flow lines, seams and planes of weakness (cold joints) that result when freshly mixed concrete is placed on hardened concrete. It is recommended in Reference 5 that layers be about 6 inches to 20 inches thick for reinforced members, and 15 inches to 20 inches thick for mass concrete, the thickness depending on the width between forms and the amount of reinforcement.

Rehandling concrete can cause segregation of the materials. Hence caution is sounded against this practice.

Consolidation is the process of compacting fresh concrete to mold it within the forms and around embedded items and reinforcement and to eliminate stone pockets, honeycomb and entrapped air. It should not remove significant amounts of intentionally entrained air from air-entrained concrete. Proper mechanical consolidation makes possible the placement of stiff mixtures with the low water-cementitious materials ratios and high coarse aggregate contents associated with high-quality concrete, even in highly reinforced elements. Vibration, either internal or external, is the most widely used method for consolidation of concrete. Detailed recommendations for consolidation of concrete are given in *Guide to Consolidation of Concrete* reported by ACI Committee 309.[14]

The ACI 318–99 Commentary Section R5.10 provides a recommended practice "when conditions make consolidation difficult, or where reinforcement is congested . . ."

Where construction joints are required, they must be in accordance with Section 1906.4.

1905.11 Curing. This section essentially reproduces ACI 318–99 Sections 5.11.1 and 5.11.2, and refers to ACI 318–99 Section 5.11.3 for accelerated curing.

Curing is the maintenance of satisfactory moisture content and temperature in concrete during some definite period immediately following placement and finishing, so that the desired properties may develop. The need for adequate curing of concrete cannot be overemphasized. Curing has a strong influence on such properties of hardened concrete as durability, strength, water tightness, abrasion resistance, volume stability, and resistance to freezing and thawing and de-icer salts.[5] Recommendations for curing concrete are given in detail in *Standard Practice for Curing Concrete* reported by ACI Committee 308.[15]

Accelerated curing procedures require careful attention to obtain uniform and satisfactory results. Preventing moisture loss during the curing is essential. Guidance is available in *Accelerated Curing of Concrete at Atmospheric Pressure—State of the Art* reported by ACI Committee 517.[16]

While accelerated curing produces early strength gain, the compressive strength of steam-cured concrete is not as high as that of similar concrete continuously cured under moist conditions at moderate temperatures. Also, the modulus of elasticity of steam-cured specimens may vary from that of specimens moist-cured at normal temperatures.

The ACI 318–99 Commentary Section R11.5.3 suggests that when steam curing is used, it is advisable to base the concrete mix proportions on steam-cured test cylinders.

1905.12 Cold weather requirements. This section is essentially a reproduction of ACI 318–99 Section 5.12. Detailed recommendations concerning cold weather concreting are given in *Cold Weather Concreting* reported by ACI Committee 306.[5,17]

1905.13 Hot weather requirements. ACI 318–99 Section 5.13 is essentially reproduced here. Detailed recommendations concerning hot weather concreting are given in *Hot Weather Concreting* reported by ACI Committee 305.[5,18]

SECTION 1906 FORMWORK, EMBEDDED PIPES AND CONSTRUCTION JOINTS

1906.1 Formwork. This reproduces Section 6.1, Design of formwork, from ACI 318–99.

As pointed out in ACI 318–99 Commentary Section R6.1, only minimum performance requirements for formwork, necessary to provide for public health and safety, are prescribed. Detailed information on formwork for concrete is given in *Guide to Formwork for Concrete* reported by ACI Committee 347[19] and in *Formwork for Concrete* prepared under the direction of ACI Committee 347.[20] The former provides recommended practice for design and construction of formwork, including recommendations for loads and pressures. The latter is a manual that extensively describes systems and provides design procedures, design aids and examples. Valuable information on formwork is also contained in Reference 21.

1906.2 Removal of forms, shores, and reshores. The removal of formwork for multistory construction must be part of a planned procedure considering the temporary support of the whole structure as well as that of each individual member. Such a procedure must be worked out prior to construction and, according to ACI 318–99 Commentary Section R6.2, should be based on structural analyses taking into account the following items, as a minimum:

1. The structural system that exists at the various stages of construction and the construction loads corresponding to those stages. The construction loads are frequently at least as large as the specified live loads.
2. The strength of the concrete at the various ages during construction.
3. The influence of deformations of the structure and shoring system on the distribution of dead loads and construction loads during the various stages of construction. The deformations themselves are of interest and must be limited. At early ages, a structure may be adequate to support the applied loads, but may deflect sufficiently to cause permanent damage.
4. The strength and spacing of shores or shoring systems used, as well as the method of shoring, bracing, shore removal, and reshoring, including the minimum time intervals between the various operations.
5. Any other loading or condition that affects the safety or serviceability of the structure during construction.

Further information on many of the above aspects may be found in Reference 22.

For multistory construction, the strength of the concrete in beams and slabs during the various stages of construction must be substantiated by tests of field-cured specimens or other methods approved by the building official.

1906.3 Conduits and pipes embedded in concrete. This adopts Section 6.3 of ACI 318–99 by reference.

Conduits, pipes and sleeves made of any material that is not harmful to concrete is allowed to be embedded in the concrete, subject to the approval of the registered design professional, provided such embedment does not have an adverse impact on the strength of the structure. The contractor must not be permitted to install conduits, pipes, ducts, or sleeves that are not shown on the plans or not approved by the registered design professional.

The use of aluminum in structural concrete is prohibited, unless it is effectively coated or covered. Aluminum reacts with concrete and, in the presence of chloride ions, may also react electrolytically with steel, causing cracking and/or spalling of the concrete. Aluminum electrical conduits present a special problem because stray electric current accelerates the adverse reaction.

1906.4 Construction joints. This reproduces Section 6.4 of ACI 318–99.

Construction joints occur where concrete work is concluded for the day; they separate areas of concrete placed at different times. The ACI 318–99 Commentary Section R6.4 points out that, for the integrity of the structure, it is important for all construction joints to be defined in construction documents and constructed as required. Any deviations should be approved by the registered design professional.

When freshly mixed concrete is placed on or against recently hardened concrete, certain precautions need to be taken to secure a well-bonded, watertight joint. The hardened concrete must be clean, sound, fairly level, and reasonably rough with some coarse aggregate particles exposed. Any laitance, soft mortar, dirt, wood chips, form oil, or other foreign materials should be removed because they would interfere with proper bonding of the subsequent placement. All construction joints are required to be wetted immediately before new concrete placement, and all standing water removed.

Construction joints are to be located where they cause the least weakness in the structure. Where shear due to gravity load is not significant, as is usually the case in the middle of the span of flexural members, a simple vertical joint may be adequate. The necessity to transfer the effects of lateral forces may require special design treatment of construction joints. Shear keys, intermittent shear keys, diagonal dowels or shear friction (ACI 318–99 Section 11.7) may be used whenever a force transfer is required.

The casting of beams, girders, or slabs supported by columns or walls is required to be delayed until concrete in the vertical support members is no longer plastic. This is necessary to prevent cracking at the interface of the slab and supporting member caused by bleeding and settlement of plastic concrete in the supporting member.

Separate placement of slabs and beams, haunches, and similar elements is permitted only when shown in design drawings or specifications and where provisions have been made for all necessary transfer of forces.

SECTION 1907
DETAILS OF REINFORCEMENT

This section is based on Chapter 7 of ACI 318–99.

Good reinforcing details are vital to satisfactory performance of reinforced concrete structures. Standard practice for reinforcing details has evolved gradually. The ACI Detailing Manual[23] provides recommended methods and standards for preparing design drawings, typical details, and drawings for fabrication and placing of reinforcing steel in reinforced concrete structures. As an aid to designers, Recommended Industry Practice for Estimating, Detailing, Fabrication, and Field Erection of Reinforcing Materials are included in the CRSI Manual of Standard Practice,[24] for direct reference in project drawings and specifications. The WRI Structural Welded Wire Fabric Detailing Manual[25] provides information on detailing welded wire fabric reinforcement systems. Chapter 3 of Reference 26 effectively summarizes much available information on reinforcement detailing.

1907.1 Hooks. This refers to Section 7.1, standard hooks, of ACI 318–99.

The standard hooks defined in Section 7.1 of ACI 318–99 are illustrated in Figure 2.

1907.2 Minimum bend diameters. This section refers to ACI 318–99 Section 7.2.

Standard bends in reinforcing bars are described in terms of the inside diameter of bend since this is easier to measure than the bend radius. The primary factors affecting the minimum bend diameter are the practicality of bending without breakage and the avoidance of crushing of concrete inside the bend.

The minimum bend diameters for bars used as primary reinforcement and as stirrup or tie reinforcement are shown in Figure 2. The minimum diameters of bend in welded wire fabric (plain or deformed) used for stirrups and ties are shown in Table 5.

STANDARD HOOKS FOR PRIMARY REINFORCEMENT

BAR SIZE	MINIMUM FINISHED BEND DIAMETER*
#3 through #8	$6d_b$
#9, #10, #11	$8d_b$
#14 and #18	$10d_b$

*measured on inside of bar

STANDARD HOOKS FOR STIRRUPS AND TIE REINFORCEMENT

BAR SIZE	MINIMUM FINISHED BEND DIAMETER*
#3 through #5	$4d_b$
#6 through #8	$6d_b$

*measured on inside of bar

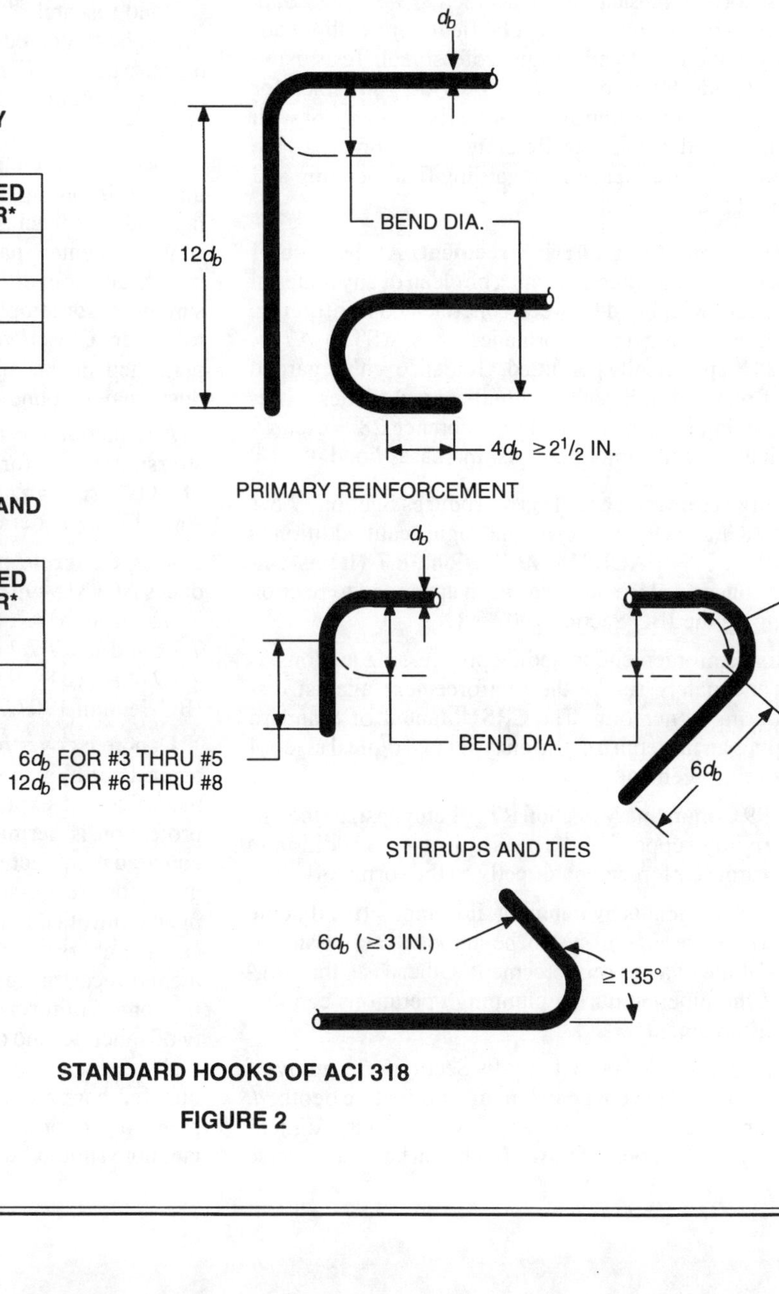

STANDARD HOOKS OF ACI 318

FIGURE 2

TABLE 5. MINIMUM DIAMETERS OF BEND IN WELDED WIRE FABRIC

WIRE SIZE	MINIMUM BEND DIAMETER
D6 and smaller	$2d_b$
All other	$4d_b$

Note: Bends with inside diameter of less than $8d_b$ must not be closer than $4d_b$ to nearest welded intersection.

1907.3 Bending. This section essentially reproduces Section 7.3 of ACI 318–99.

All reinforcement must be bent cold unless otherwise permitted by the registered design professional. For unusual bends, special fabrication including heating may be required and the registered design professional must give approval to the techniques used.

Reinforcing bars partly embedded in concrete are frequently subjected to bending and straightening in the field. Protruding bars often must be bent to provide clearance for construction operations. Field bending and straightening may also be required because of incorrect fabrication or accidental bending. Bars partly embedded in concrete must not be field-bent without authorization from the registered design professional. Tests using ASTM A615 Grade 60 deformed bars provide guidelines for field bending and straightening, and heating if necessary, of such bars partly embedded in concrete. Reference 26 summarizes the recommendations of Reference 27 regarding field bending and straightening of rebars.

1907.4 Surface conditions of reinforcement. At the time of concrete placement, reinforcement must be clean of any material that may interfere with bond between concrete and reinforcing, although epoxy coating in conformance with ASTM A775, A934 or A884 is specifically permitted. Guidance with regard to the effects of rust and mill scale on bond characteristics of deformed reinforcing bars is provided in Reference 28. Research has shown that a normal amount of rust increases bond.

1907.5 Placing reinforcement. This reproduces Sections 7.5.1 and 7.5.2 of ACI 318–99; however, one significant addition is made to Section 7.5.1. ACI 318–99 Section 16.7 (Items embedded after concrete placement) has been appended to Section 7.5.1, making up the IBC Section 1907.5.1.

Support for reinforcement, including prestressing tendons, is required to adequately secure the reinforcement against displacement during concreting. The CRSI Manual of Standard Practice[24] gives an in-depth treatise on types and typical sizes of supports for reinforcement.

ACI 318–99 Commentary Section R7.5.1 emphasizes the importance of rigidly supporting the beam stirrups, in addition to the main flexural reinforcement, directly to the formwork.

If concrete placement is by pumping, it is imperative that the pipelines and pipeline support system be supported above and independently of the chaired reinforcement. Otherwise, the surging action of the pipeline during pumping operations can dislodge the reinforcement.

The tolerances provided in ACI 318–99 Section 7.5.2 apply simultaneously to concrete cover and member effective depth, d. The dimension d is critical because any deviation in this dimension, especially for members of lesser depth, can have an adverse effect on the strength provided in the completed construction. The permitted variation in d takes this strength reduction into account. The critical dimensional tolerances for locating the longitudinal reinforcement are illustrated in Figure 3, adapted from Reference 26.

For ends of bars and longitudinal location of bends, the tolerance is ± 2 inches, except at discontinuous ends of members where the tolerance is $\pm ^1/_2$ inch. These tolerances are also illustrated in Figure 3.

Note that welding of crossing bars (tack welding) for assembly of reinforcement is prohibited except as specifically authorized by the registered design professional.

1907.6 Spacing limits for reinforcement. This section refers to ACI 318–99 Section 7.6.

The minimum spacing limitations of Sections 7.6.1 through 7.6.3 are illustrated in Figure 4, adapted from Reference 26.

In walls and slabs other than concrete joists, the spacing of primary flexural reinforcement must not exceed the wall or slab thickness or 18 inches.

Bond research[29] has shown that bar cutoffs within bundles should be staggered. Bundled bars, limited to no more than four bars to a bundle (Figure 5), must be tied, wired, or otherwise fastened together to ensure remaining in position, whether vertical or horizontal.

Spacing of pretensioning tendons is handled separately from that of reinforcing bars. Center-to-center spacing of pretensioning tendons at each end of a member is specified. This is because center-to-center spacing is what was used in the referenced research, and converting to clear spacing is unnecessary; and measurements for templates used in manufacture are always center-to-center. Closer vertical spacing or bundling of tendons is permitted in the middle portion of the span. Post-tensioning ducts may be bundled subject to certain preconditions.

A reduction has been made in the allowable spacing of prestressing strands for concrete strengths at the transfer of prestress of 4,000 psi or greater, based on several research projects sponsored by the Federal Highway Administration.[30,31]

1907.7 Concrete protection for reinforcement. This reproduces ACI 318–99 Section 7.7.1, refers to ACI 318–99 Sections 7.7.2 through 7.7.4, reproduces ACI 318–99 Sections 7.7.5, 7.7.6 and also 7.7.7 in a slightly modified form. Whereas Section 7.7.7 of ACI 318–99 refers to the general building code, the 2000 IBC Section 1907.7.7 refers to the IBC itself.

Concrete cover requirements are specified for members cast against earth, in contact with earth or weather, and for interior members not exposed to weather. Slightly reduced cover or protection is permitted under the same conditions for precast concrete manufactured under plant control, and other values are given for prestressed concrete. The term "manufactured under plant controlled condition" does not necessarily mean that precast members must be manufactured in a plant. Structural elements precast at the job site will also qualify for the lesser cover if the control of form dimensions, placing of reinforcement, quality of concrete, and curing procedure are equivalent to those normally expected in a plant operation. Larger diameter bars and bundled bars require slightly larger cover. Corrosive environments or fire protection may also warrant increased cover. Special note should be taken of the commentary recommendations

CRITICAL DIMENSIONAL TOLERANCES FOR PLACING REINFORCEMENT

EFFECTIVE DEPTH *d*	TOLERANCE ON *d*	TOLERANCE ON MIN. COVER
$d \leq 8$ in.	$\pm ^3/_8$ in.	$-^3/_8$ in.
$d > 8$ in.	$\pm ^1/_2$ in.	$-^1/_2$ in.

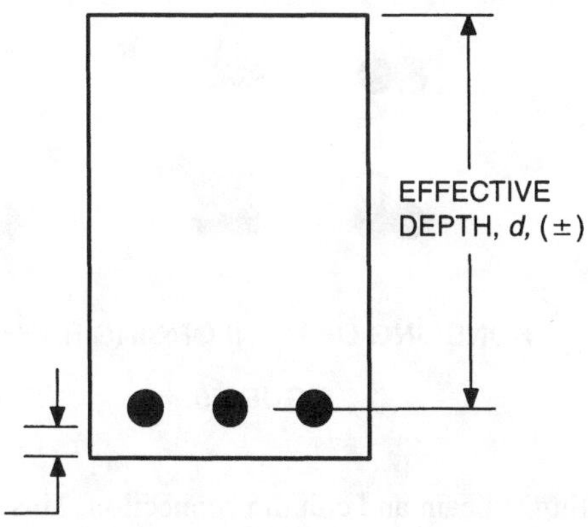

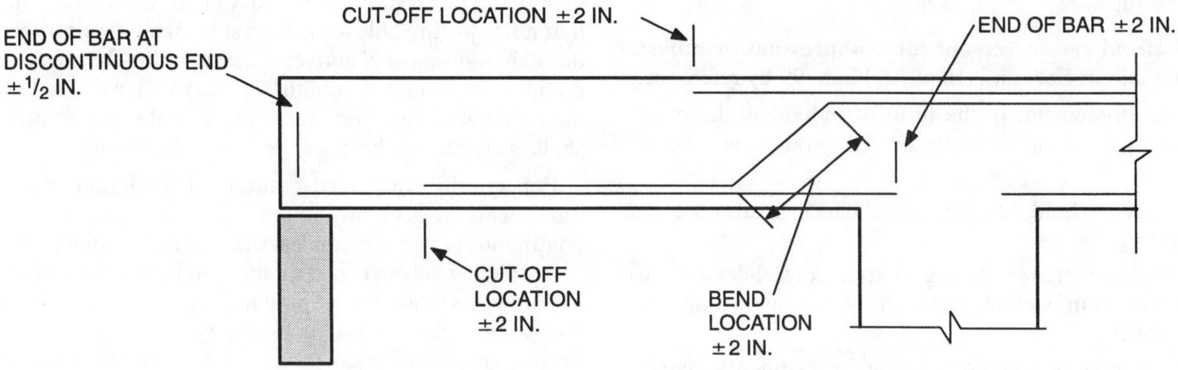

DIMENSIONAL TOLERANCES FOR PLACING REINFORCEMENT

FIGURE 3

CLEAR DISTANCE BETWEEN BARS OR BAR BUNDLES

REINFORCEMENT TYPE	MEMBER TYPE	CLEAR DISTANCE
Deformed bars	Flexural members	$d_b \geq 1$ in.
	Compression members, tied or spirally reinforced	1.5 d_b $\geq 1^1/_2$ in.

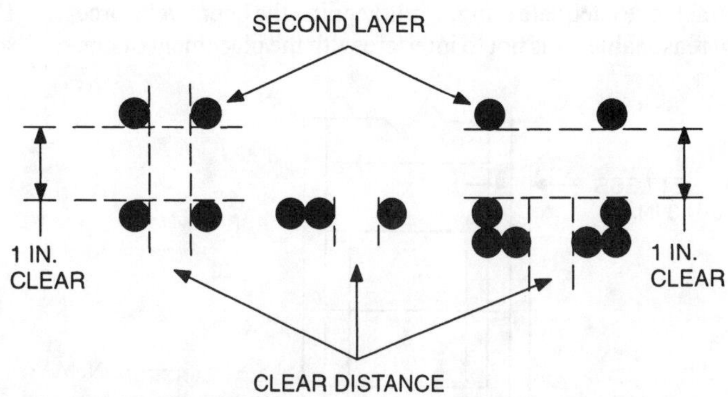

CLEAR DISTANCES BETWEEN BARS OR BAR BUNDLES

FIGURE 4

(ACI 318–99 Commentary Section R7.7.5) for increased cover when concrete will be exposed to external sources of chlorides in service, such as de-icing salts and seawater. As noted in ACI 318–99 Commentary Section R7.7, alternative methods of protecting the reinforcement from weather may be used if they provide protection equivalent to the additional concrete cover required in IBC Table 1907.7.1, Item 2, and ACI 318 Sections 7.7.2(a) and 7.7.3.1(b), as compared to IBC Table 1907.7.1, Item 3, and ACI 318 Sections 7.7.2 (b) and 7.7.3.1(c), respectively.

1907.8 Special reinforcement details for columns. This section adopts by reference Section 7.8 of ACI 318–99, which provides special detailing requirements for offset bent bars in columns (Figure 6) and requirements governing load transfer in structural steel cores of composite compression members.

1907.9 Connections. This refers to Section 7.9 of ACI 318-99, which requires enclosures to be provided for splices of continuing reinforcement, and for end anchorage of reinforcement

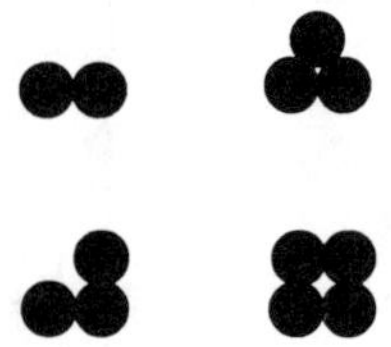

BUNDLING OF REINFORCING BARS

FIGURE 5

terminating at beam and column connection. This confinement may be provided by surrounding concrete or internal closed ties, spirals or stirrups.

1907.10 Lateral reinforcement for compression members. This section adopts Section 7.10 of ACI 318–99 by reference.

Lateral reinforcement, in the form of individual discretely spaced ties or a continuous closely spaced spiral, serves several functions.

1. It is needed to hold the longitudinal bars in position during concreting.
2. It is needed to prevent the highly stressed, slender longitudinal bars from buckling outward by busting the thin concrete cover.
3. It can serve as shear and/or torsion reinforcement where required.
4. It confines the concrete in compression, thereby slightly increasing strength but more important, enhancing its ability to sustain high compressive stresses over a significant range of deformations.

To achieve adequate tying, while keeping the lateral reinforcement reasonable so as not to interfere with the placement of concrete, Section 7.10.5 gives a number of rules for tie arrangement. All bars of tied columns shall be enclosed by lateral ties, at least No. 3 in size for longitudinal bars up to No. 10, and at least No. 4 in size for Nos. 11, 14 and 18 and bundled longitudinal bars. The spacing of the ties shall not exceed 16 diameters of longitudinal bars, 48 diameters of tie bars, nor the least dimension of the column. The ties shall be so arranged that every corner and alternate longitudinal bar shall have lateral support provided by the corner of a tie having an included angle of not more than 135 degrees, and no bar shall be farther than 6 inches clear on either side from such a laterally supported bar (Figure 7). Deformed wire or welded wire fabric of equivalent area may be used instead of ties. Where the bars are located around the periphery of a circle, complete circular ties may be used. Ties must be located at no more than half a tie spacing above floor or footing and no more than half a tie spacing below the lowest horizontal reinforcement in the slab or drop panel above. If beams or brackets from four directions frame into a column, ties may be terminated not more than 3 inches below the lowest horizontal reinforcement in the shallowest of such beams or brackets (Figure 8).

For spirally reinforced columns, lateral reinforcement requirements are given in Section 7.10.4. Spirals must consist of a continuous bar or wire not less than $^3/_8$ inch in diameter, and the clear spacing between turns of the spiral must not exceed 3 inches nor be less than 1 inch. Spiral reinforcement must extend from the top of footing or slab in any story to the level of the lowest horizontal reinforcement in slabs, drop panels or beams above. If beams or brackets do not frame into all sides of the column, ties must extend above the top of the spiral to the bottom of the slab or drop panel (Figure 9). In addition, a minimum ratio of spiral steel is imposed (Section 10.9.3) such that the structural performance of the column is significantly improved.

1907.11 Lateral reinforcement for flexural members. This section refers to section 7.11 of ACI 318–99.

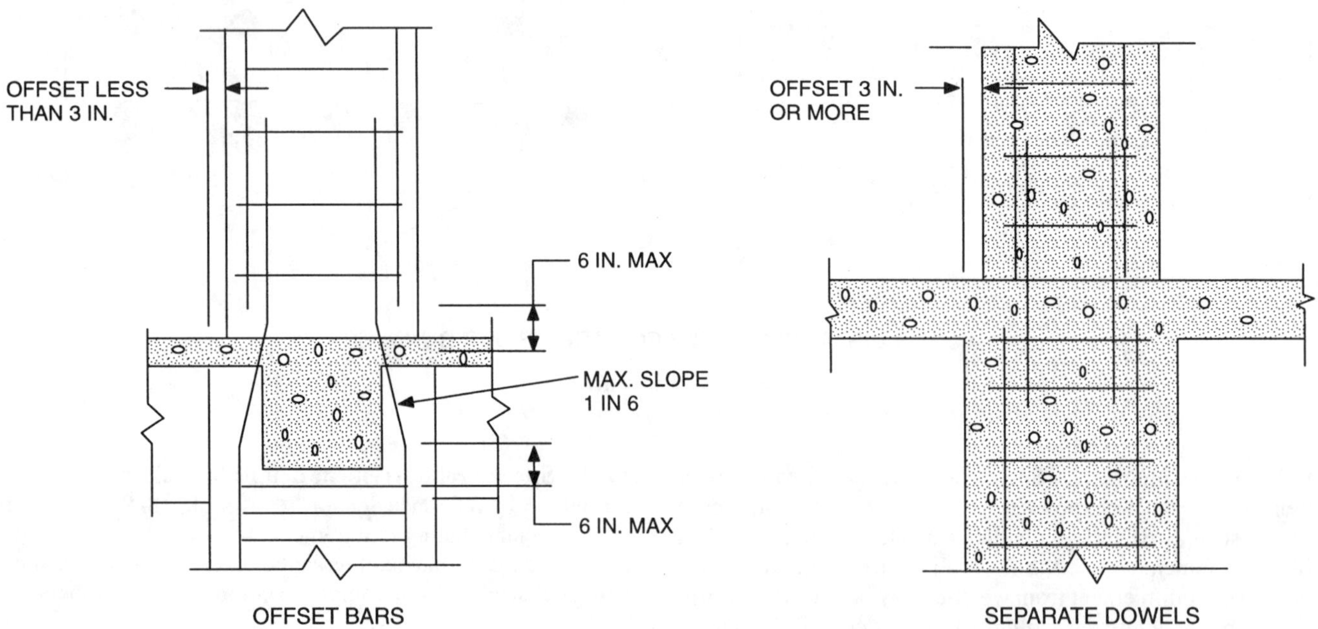

SPECIAL COLUMN DETAILS

FIGURE 6

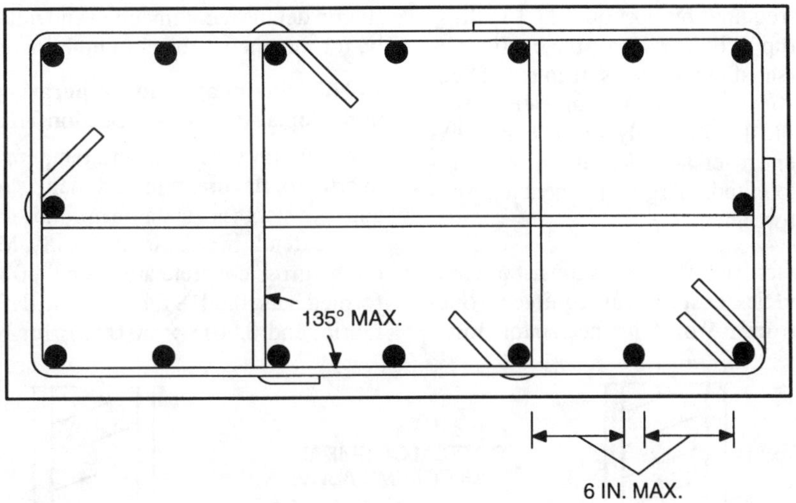

LATERAL SUPPORT OF COLUMN BARS BY HOOPS AND CROSS-TIES

FIGURE 7

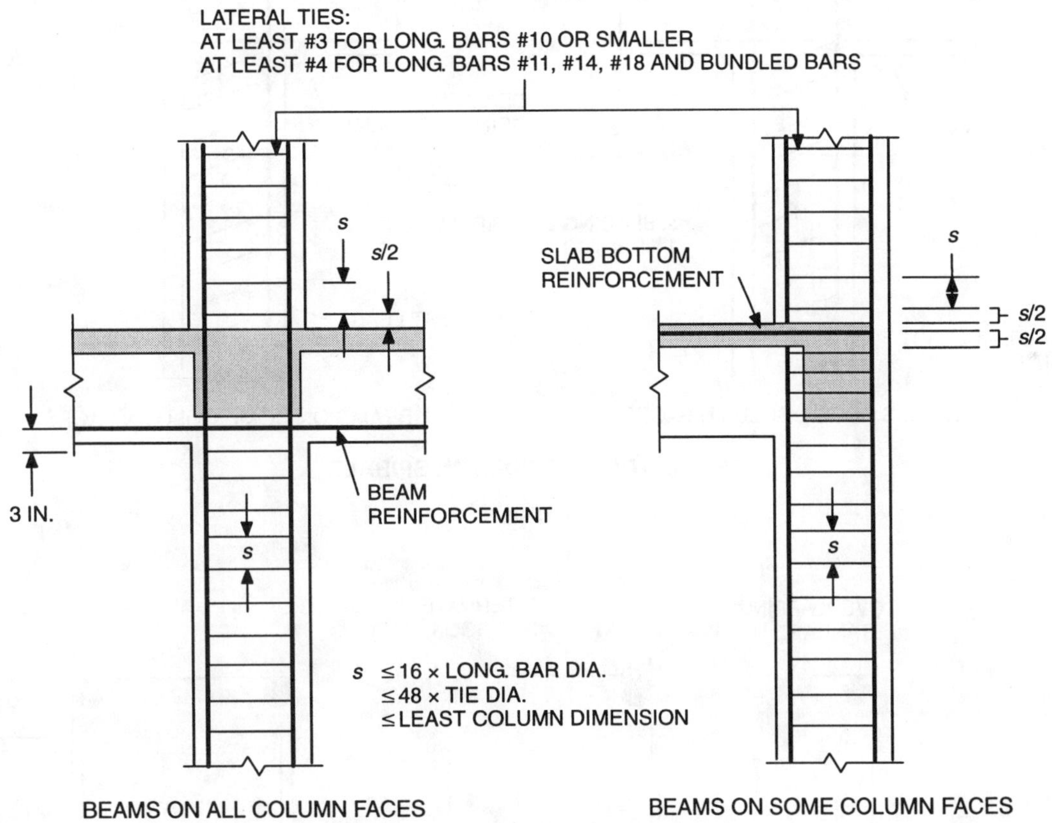

TERMINATION OF COLUMN TIES

FIGURE 8

Where compression reinforcement is used to increase the flexural strength of a member, or to control long-term deflection, Section 7.11.1 requires that such reinforcement be enclosed by ties or stirrups. Requirements for size and spacing of the ties or stirrups are the same as for ties in tied columns. Welded wire fabric of equivalent area may be used. The ties or stirrups must extend throughout the distance where the compression reinforcement is required for flexural strength or deflection control. Section 7.11.1 is interpreted not to apply to reinforcement located in a compression zone to help assemble the reinforcing cage and hold the web reinforcement in place during concrete placement.

Enclosing reinforcement required by Section 7.11.1 is illustrated by the U-shaped stirrup in Figure 10(a); the continuous bottom portion of the stirrup satisfies the enclosure intent of Section 7.11.1 for the two bottom bars shown. A completely closed stirrup [Figures 10(b) and 10(c)] is ordinarily not necessary, except in cases of high moment reversal, where the reversal requires both top and bottom longitudinal reinforcement to be designed as compression reinforcement.

Torsion reinforcement, where required, must consist of completely closed stirrups, closed ties, or spirals, as required by Section 11.6.4. See Figures 3-10 and 3-9 of Reference 26 for closed stirrup details recommended and not recommended, respectively, for members subject to high torsion.

1907.12 Shrinkage and temperature reinforcement. This section adopts ACI 318–99 Section 7.12 by reference.

Minimum shrinkage and temperature reinforcement normal to primary flexural reinforcement is required for structural floor and roof slabs (not slabs on ground) where the flexural reinforcement extends in one direction only. Minimum steel ratios, based on the gross concrete area, are 0.0020 for Grade 40 and 50 deformed bars; 0.0018 for Grade 60 deformed bars or welded wire fabric; and $0.0018 \times 60{,}000/f_y$ for reinforcement with a yield

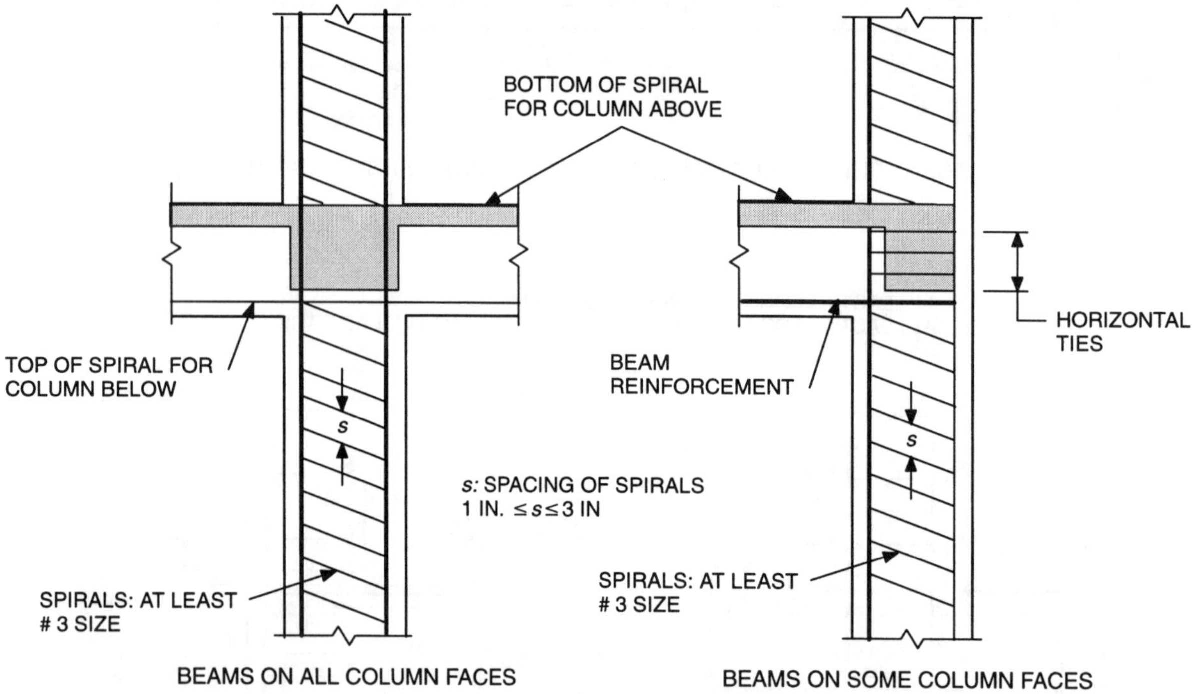

TERMINATION OF COLUMN SPIRALS

FIGURE 9

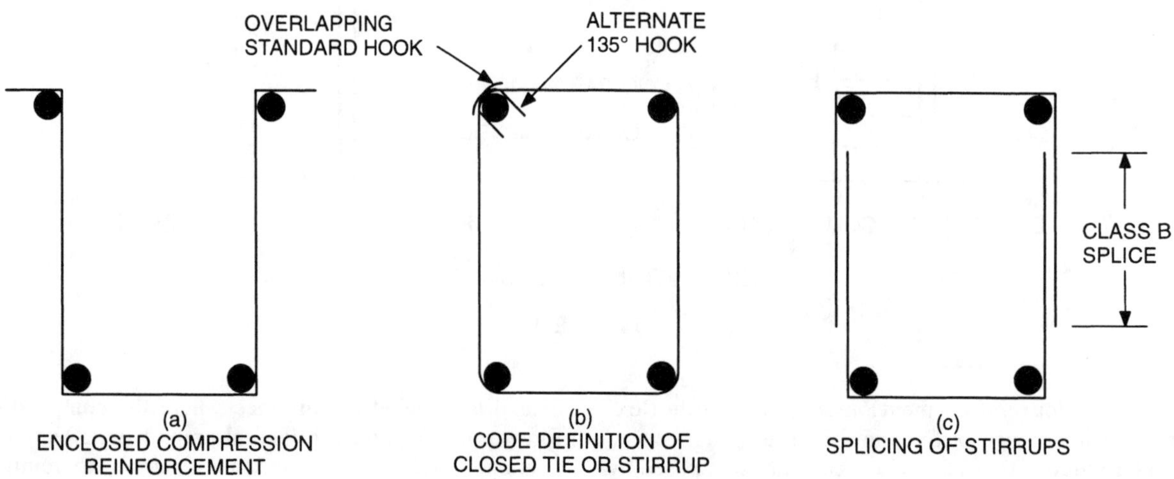

CLOSED TIE OR STIRRUP

FIGURE 10

strength greater than 60,000 psi, but not less than 0.0014. Spacing of shrinkage and temperature reinforcement must not exceed 5 times the slab thickness or 18 inches. Splices and end anchorages of such reinforcement must be designed for the full specified yield strength.

Bonded or unbonded prestressing tendons may be used for shrinkage and temperature reinforcement in structural slabs (Section 7.12.3). The tendons must provide a minimum average compressive stress of 100 psi on the gross concrete area, based on effective prestress after losses. Spacing of tendons must not exceed 6 feet. When the spacing is greater than 54 inches, additional bonded reinforcement must be provided at slab edges.

1907.13 Requirements for structural integrity. ACI 318–99 Section 7.13 is adopted by reference in this section.

Experience has shown that the overall integrity of a structure can be substantially enhanced by minor changes in detailing of reinforcement. It is the intent of ACI 318-99 Section 7.13 to improve the redundancy and ductility in structures so that in the event of damage to a major supporting element or an abnormal loading, the damage may be confined to a relatively small area and the structure may have a better chance to maintain overall stability. The requirements of Section 7.13 are summarized in Figure 11.

SECTION 1908
MODIFICATIONS TO ACI 318

1908.1 General. A number of modifications to the provisions of ACI 318-99 are made in this section.

1908.1.1. As an alternative to the strength design of Chapter 9 of ACI 318–99, the design provisions of Appendix A are allowed by ACI 318 to be used to proportion nonprestressed reinforced concrete members. In the alternate method, a flexural member is designed to keep the stresses resulting from the action of service loads (without load factors), and computed by the straight-line theory for flexure, within permissible service load stresses. Service load is the load, such as dead, live, or wind, which is assumed actually to occur when the structure is in service. The required service loads to be used in design are expected to be those prescribed in the general building code. The stresses computed under the action of service loads are limited to values well within the elastic range of the materials so that the straight-line relationship between stress and strain may be used.

The alternate method is similar to the working stress design method of the 1963 edition of the ACI *Building Code* (ACI 318–63). For members subject to flexure without axial load, the method is identical. Major differences in procedure occur in design of compression members with or without flexure and in considering bond stress and development of reinforcement. For shear, the shear strengths provided by concrete for the strength design method are divided by a factor of safety and the resulting permissible service load stresses restated in Appendix A.

In view of the simplifications permitted, the alternate design method of Appendix A generally results in more conservative designs than designs obtained using the strength design method of Chapter 9.

In the working stress method, no individual load factors are used; i.e., all types of loads are treated the same no matter how different their individual variability and uncertainty. Also, stresses are calculated on an elastic basis, while in reality the strength of a member depends on the inelastic stress-strain behavior near and at the strain at which that strength is attained. Hence, the allowable stress method does not permit an explicit evaluation of the margin of safety. In contrast, in the strength design method, individual load factors are adjusted to represent different degrees of uncertainty for the various types of loads, strength reduction factors are likewise adjusted to the precision with which various types of nominal strength (bending, shear, torsion, etc.) can be calculated, and the nominal strength itself is calculated with due explicit regard for inelastic action.

Because of these differences in realism and reliability, over the past decade or two, the strength design method has rapidly displaced the older service load stress approach.

The basis of seismic design was changed in ATC 3-06,[32] the predecessor document to the NEHRP Provisions, from prior codes wherein the prescribed earthquake forces and sizing of members were at service or working stress levels. In ATC 3 and the NEHRP Provisions, the design of the structure (sizing of individual members, connections, and supports) is based on the internal forces resulting from a linear elastic analysis using the prescribed seismic forces, and assumes that the structure as a whole under these prescribed forces should not deform beyond a point of significant yield. The term "significant yield" specifically is not the point where first yield occurs in any member but is defined as that level causing complete plastification of at least the most critical region of the structure, such as formation of the first plastic hinge in the structure. A structural steel frame of compact members is assumed to reach this point when a plastic hinge develops in the most critical member of the structure. A concrete frame reaches this significant yield in its response to the prescribed forces when at least one of the sections of its most critical component reaches its design strength as set forth in ACI 318. For other structural materials that do not have their sectional yielding capacities as easily defined, modifiers to working stress values are provided in the materials chapters of ATC- and NEHRP-based codes.

Strength-level, rather than service-level seismic design forces, first introduced in ATC 3-06, became a feature of the BOCA/*National Building Code* starting with its 1993 edition, the *Uniform Building Code* starting with its 1997 edition and the *Standard Building Code* starting with its 1994 edition (Table 6). It is also a feature of the 2000 IBC.

Attempting to size members using working stresses with the strength-level earthquake design forces of the modern codes requires adjustments to bring the earthquake forces back to the service level; it entails an exercise that is not necessary, meaningful or beneficial, at least for concrete, a material with a well established strength design tradition by now. Section 1908.1.1 thus prohibits the use of the Alternate Design Method of ACI 318–99 Appendix A in the seismic design of reinforced concrete structures.

1908.1.2. This modification requires that the IBC seismic strength design load combinations (Formula 16-5 and Formula 16-6) must be used in the seismic design of concrete structures, rather than the seismic strength design load combinations of Chapter 9 of ACI 318. Some background to this requirement may be of interest.

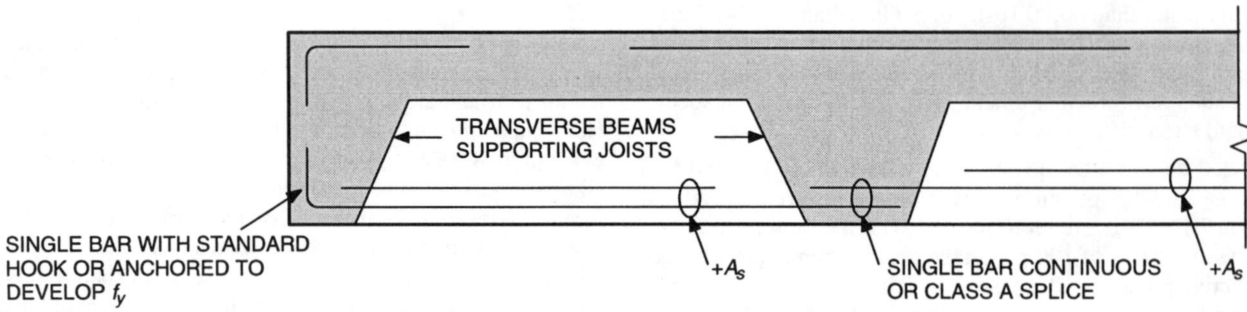

(a) Continuity reinforcement for joist construction

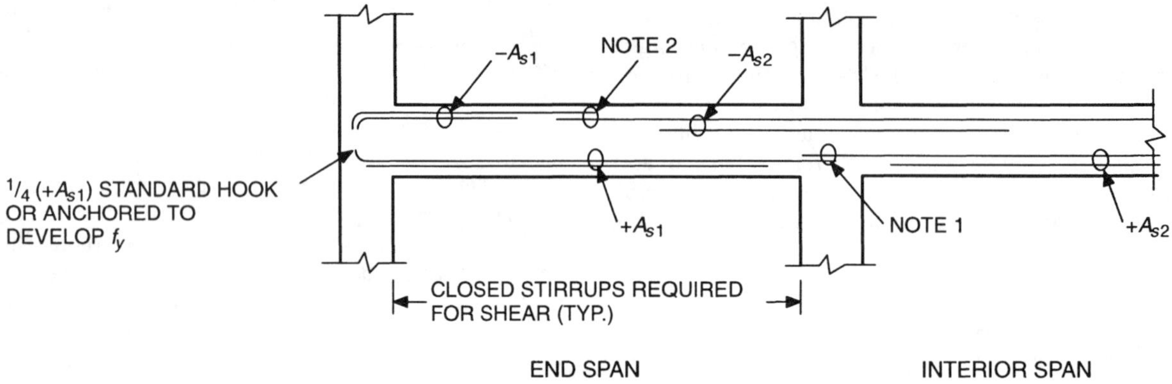

NOTE: (1) Larger of $^1/_4\ (+A_{s1})$ or $^1/_4\ (+A_{s2})$ continuous or spliced with Class A splices
(2) Larger of $^1/_6\ (-A_{s1})$ or $^1/_6\ (-A_{s2})$ continuous or spliced with Class A splices

(b) Continuity reinforcement for perimeter beams

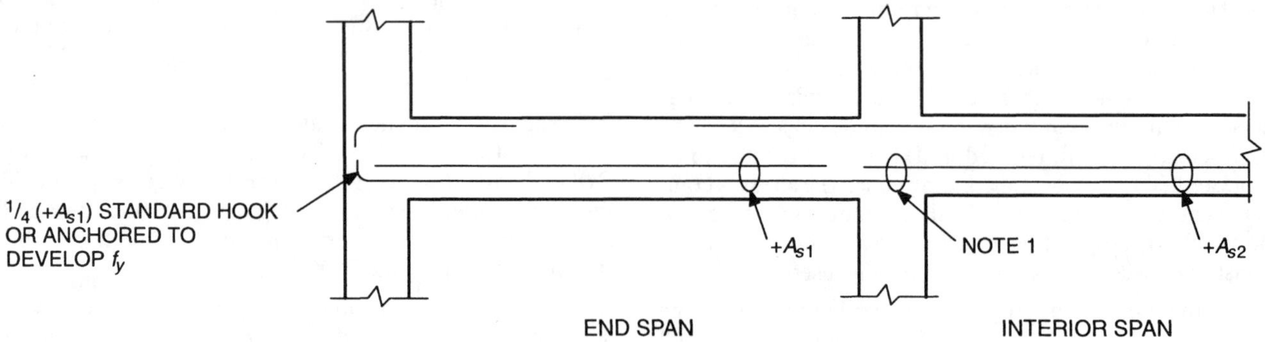

NOTE: (1) Larger of $^1/_4\ (+A_{s1})$ or $^1/_4\ (+A_{s2})$ continuous or spliced with Class A splices

(c) Continuity reinforcement for other than perimeter beams without closed stirrups

REQUIREMENTS FOR STRUCTURAL INTEGRITY

FIGURE 11

TABLE 6. SEISMIC DESIGN FORCES IN VARIOUS CODES, STANDARDS, AND RESOURCE DOCUMENTS

	SERVICE-LEVEL SEISMIC DESIGN FORCES	STRENGTH-LEVEL SEISMIC DESIGN FORCES
CODES	**Editions**	**Editions**
BOCA/NBC	1990 and prior	1993, 1996, 1999
UBC	1994 and prior	1997
SBC	1991 and prior	1994, 1997, 1999
IBC		2000
STANDARDS		
ASCE 7/ANSI A58.1	1988 and prior	1993, 1995, 1998
RESOURCE DOCUMENTS		
ATC 3		1978
NEHRP Provisions		1985, 1988, 1991, 1994, 1997, 2000
SEAOC Blue Book	1996[a] and prior	1999

a. Appendix C included strength-level seismic design forces [33]

ATC 3-06, while introducing strength-level seismic design forces, also introduced its own seismic strength design load combinations:

$1.2Q_D + 1.0Q_L + 1.0Q_S \pm 1.0Q_E$

$0.8Q_D \pm 1.0Q_E$

where Q_D, Q_L, Q_S, and Q_E are the effects of dead load, live load, snow load and earthquake forces respectively. A factor differing by ±20 percent was placed on the dead load to account for the effects of vertical acceleration due to earthquake ground motion.

The above were modified in the 1985 and the 1988 editions of the NEHRP Provisions to:

$(1.1 + 0.5A_V)Q_D + 1.0Q_L + 1.0Q_S \pm 1.0Q_E$

$(0.9 - 0.5A_V)Q_D \pm 1.0Q_E$

Consideration of the effect of vertical earthquake ground acceleration is explicit in the above, and is in terms of A_V, the effective peak velocity-related acceleration coefficient. The first combination was slightly changed in the 1991 NEHRP Provisions to:

$(1.1 + 0.5A_V)Q_D \pm 1.0Q_E + (1.0Q_L + 0.7Q_S)$

The only change, obviously, was in the snow load factor.

ASCE 7-93 was the first edition of the national loading standard to switch from service-level to strength-level earthquake design forces. The seismic strength design load combinations were:

$1.2D + 1.0E + 0.5L + 0.2S$

$0.9D + 1.0E$

where E can be positive or negative. D, L, S and E are the same as Q_D, Q_L, Q_S, and Q_E, respectively. The above remained unchanged in ASCE 7-95. In ASCE 7-98, the second load combination has been changed to:

$0.9D + 1.0E + 1.6H$

where H is effect of load due to lateral pressure of soil and water in soil. The first load combination governs when the effects of gravity and earthquake forces are additive and may be referred to as the additive load combination. The second load combination governs when the effects of gravity and earthquake forces are counteractive. It may be referred to as the counteractive load combination.

The 1994 NEHRP Provisions adopted the seismic strength design load combinations of ASCE 7-93, but modified the earthquake effect term E to:

$E = Q_E + 0.5C_aD$ for the additive load combination and $E = Q_E - 0.5C_aD$ for the counteractive load combination

C_a is the effective peak acceleration coefficient A_a modified by a short-period or acceleration-related site coefficient F_a.

The 1997 UBC adopted the seismic strength design load combinations of ASCE 7–95 with minor modifications:

$1.2D + 1.0E + (f_1L + f_2S)$

$0.9D \pm 1.0E$

where $f_1 = 0.5$, except that it equals 1.0 for floors in places of public assembly, for live loads in excess of 100 psf, and for garage live loads. The higher values of the live load factor are also required in ASCE 7–93, –95 and –98, in the three cases cited. The factor $f_2 = 0.2$, except that it is 0.7 for roof configurations that cannot shed snow off the structure. E is modified in the 1997 UBC as follows:

$E = \rho E_h + E_v$

$= \rho E_h + 0.5C_aID$

where C_a is a soil-modified short-period ground motion parameter (virtually identical with the C_a of the 1994 NEHRP Provisions), I is an occupancy importance factor, and E_h is analogous to Q_E, the elastically computed effect of the code-prescribed seismic forces. Here, ρ is a redundancy factor, first introduced in the 1997 UBC (see discussion of Section 1617.2).

The 1997 NEHRP Provisions adopted the seismic strength design load combinations of ASCE 7–95 and modified the earthquake effect E to:

$E = \rho Q_E + 0.2S_{DS}D$ for the additive load combination

$E = \rho Q_E - 0.2S_{DS}D$ for the counteractive load combination

Where S_{DS} is the design spectral response acceleration at short periods.

The 2000 IBC has adopted the above modifications to the earthquake effect, E, along with the seismic strength design load combinations of ASCE 7–98.

All the documents mentioned above have required the design of concrete structures to be done by the seismic strength design load combinations of the respective documents, because the strength design load combinations of ACI 318 consider service-level earthquake forces. Strength-level earthquake forces simply cannot be used directly in these combinations. The requirement of Section 1908.1.2 is exactly the same.

For the very first time, ACI 318–95 permitted the proportioning of concrete structural elements by the ASCE 7 load combinations (seismic as well as non-seismic) "if the structural framing includes primary members of other material." Thus, a designer faced with the design of a building with a reinforced concrete shear wall core and steel framing outside of the core could choose to design the shear walls using the ASCE 7 rather than the ACI 318 load combinations. The ASCE 7 gravity design load combinations provide lower design loads than the ACI 318 gravity design load combinations. While it is unclear how the design loads compare when it comes to gravity plus lateral load (wind or earthquake) combinations, a desire to preserve the margin of safety in going from the ACI 318 to the ASCE 7 load combinations led to the development of a set of strength reduction factors with slightly lower values than the Chapter 9 ϕ-factors. This set of factors was listed in Appendix C of ACI 318–95. If the ASCE 7 load combinations are chosen, they must be used with the strength reduction factors of Appendix C.

The Supplementary Provisions for Reinforced Concrete of ASCE 7–93 required that the design loads given by the seismic strength design load combinations of that document be multiplied by a factor of 1.1, to account for "an incompatibility between the ϕ-factors of [ACI 318] and the load factors of this document." The same requirement has been in ASCE 7–95, ASCE 7–98 and also in the 1997 UBC. As a load standard, ASCE 7 was not the proper place for modification of strength reduction factors. The multiplier of 1.1 was intended to provide the same level of safety as that produced by the reduced ϕ-factors of Appendix C to ACI 318–95.

Instead of adopting a multiplier of 1.1 on the design load, the 1997 NEHRP Provisions require that: "For load combinations that include earthquake loads, the design strength shall be computed using the strength reduction factors, ϕ, listed in Appendix C [of ACI 318–95]." This requirement has been deleted from the 2000 IBC for reasons outlined in References 34 and 35.

Further information on strength design load combinations for concrete elements may be found in Reference 36.

1908.1.3. ACI 318–99 Section 18.9.3, which relaxes the minimum bonded reinforcement requirements of Section 18.9.2, applies only to flat plates and not to other two-way slab systems. The ACI Commentary to this section states that while recognizing that the behavior of other two-way slab systems is similar to that of the two-way flat plate, a conservative limitation is placed in the code requiring two-way slabs to have minimum reinforcement similar to that in a one-way system "until more complete information is available." This section of the code has been one of the most widely ignored sections in design and practice. Generally, unbonded post-tensioned two-way slab systems (not just two-way flat plates) have been designed according to this section for the past thirty years. The successful performance in practice of these unbonded two-way slab systems has demonstrated clearly that the present practice under ACI 318 Section 18.9.3, and not 18.9.2, provides safe and desirable structures.

1908.1.4, 1908.1.5, 1908.1.6, 1908.1.7, and 1908.1.9. These modifications add specific design requirements for precast structures assigned to Seismic Design Categories D, E, and F, which are not part of ACI 318-99. Until recently, a precast concrete structure could only be built in UBC Seismic Zones 3 and 4 under an ACI 318 provision adopted into the UBC, which required it to be "demonstrated by experimental evidence and analysis that the proposed system will have strength and toughness equal to or exceeding those provided by a comparable monolithic reinforced concrete structure . . ." The interpretation, implementation and enforcement of this vague, qualitative requirement was, for obvious reasons, quite nonuniform. The very first set of specific design provisions ever developed in this country for precast concrete structures exposed to high seismic risk appeared in the 1994 edition of the NEHRP Provisions. These provisions, with significant modifications and additions, were adopted into the 1997 UBC. The 1997 UBC provisions, applicable in Seismic Zones 3 and 4, have been adopted without any further modification in the 2000 IBC, and have been made applicable to structures in Seismic Design Categories D, E, and F.

Precast Concrete Lateral-Force-Resisting System

The 1994 NEHRP Provisions presented two alternatives for the design of precast concrete lateral-force-resisting systems (Figure 12). One choice is emulation of monolithic reinforced concrete construction. The other alternative is the use of the unique properties of precast concrete elements interconnected predominantly by dry connections (jointed precast). A "wet" connection uses any of the splicing methods permitted by ACI 318, to connect precast or precast and cast-in-place members, and uses cast-in-place concrete or grout to fill the splicing closure. A "dry" connection is a connection between precast or precast and cast-in-place members that does not qualify as a wet connection.

Design procedures for the second alternative (jointed precast) were included in an appendix to the chapter on concrete in the 1994 NEHRP Provisions. These procedures were intended for information and trial design only.

The 1994 NEHRP requirements for precast concrete lateral-force-resisting systems were used as a starting point for the 1997 UBC provisions. However, it was decided to limit the scope to frames only (excluding panel systems) and to the monolithic emulation option only. Jointed precast concrete is allowed only under the "undefined structural systems" provisions of the 1997 UBC. The intent of this restriction is not to limit the development of alternative systems but to continue to rely on experimental evidence and analysis, which demonstrate that a unique system will satisfy the intent of the code.

For emulation of the behavior of monolithic reinforced concrete construction, two alternatives are provided (Figure 12): structural systems with "wet" connections and those with "strong" connections.

Precast structural systems with wet connections must comply with all requirements applicable to monolithic reinforced concrete construction resisting seismic forces. Prescriptive requirements are given for precast frame systems with strong connections. Such requirements for precast wall systems with strong connections are yet to be developed.

A joint is defined as the geometric volume common to intersecting members. A "connection" is defined as an element that

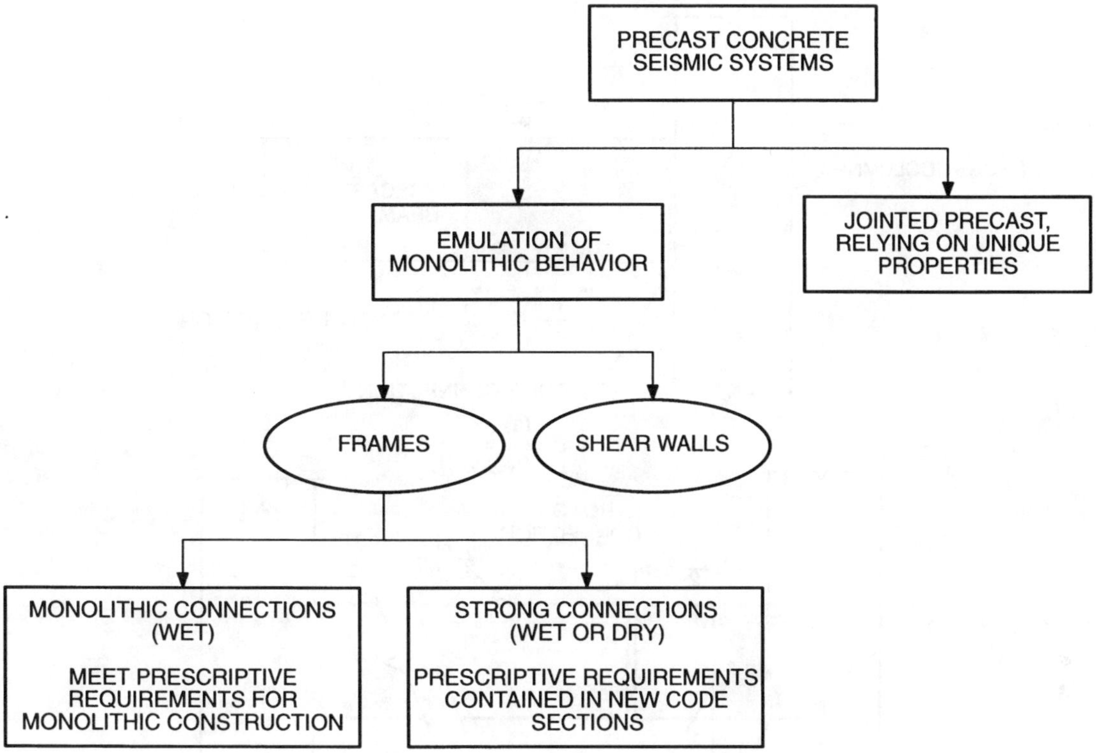

EMULATION OF MONOLITHIC BEHAVIOR—OPTIONS

FIGURE 12

joins two precast members or a precast member and a cast-in-place member. A "strong" connection is a connection that remains elastic while the designated nonlinear action regions undergo inelastic response under the "Design Basis Ground Motion" (Figure 13).

The 1994 NEHRP Provisions also addressed emulation of monolithic construction using ductile connections, covering both frame and panel systems, where the connections have adequate nonlinear response characteristics and it is not necessary to ensure plastic hinges remote from the connections. Usually, experimental verification is required to ensure that a connection has the necessary nonlinear response characteristics. The designer is required to consider the likely deformations of any proposed precast structure, compared to those of the same structure in monolithic reinforced concrete, before claiming that the precast form emulates monolithic construction. The 1997 UBC does not directly address ductile connections.

For frame systems that use strong connections, considerable freedom is given to locating the nonlinear action zones (plastic hinges) along the length of a precast member. However, the nonlinear action location or the center of the region of yielding in flexure must be separated from the connection by a distance equal to at least one-half the member depth (Figure 13). The $h/2$ distance was selected with h taken as the estimated plastic hinge length. The nonlinear action locations must also provide for a strong column-weak beam deformation mechanism.

The strength required for a strong connection depends on the distance the hinges are separated from the connection, the strength of the hinges, and the nonlinear deformation mechanism envisioned. Because the strong connection must not yield or slip, its design strengths in both flexure and shear must be greater than the bending moment and the shear force, respectively, corresponding to the development of probable flexural or shear strengths at the nonlinear action locations.

A strong connection may be wet or dry. However, any strong connection located outside the middle half of a beam span is required to be a wet connection "unless a dry connection can be substantiated by approved cyclic test results." Any mechanical connector located within such a column-face strong connection is required to be a Type 2 mechanical splice.

For columns above the ground floor, moments at a joint may be limited by the flexural strengths of the beams framing into that joint. However, for a strong column-weak beam deformation mechanism, dynamic inelastic analysis and studies of strong motion measurements have shown that beam end moments are not equally divided between top and bottom columns, even where those columns have equal stiffness. Accordingly, a dynamic amplification factor of $\psi = 1.4$ is used for column-to-column connection design (Figure 14). In addition, special transverse reinforcement, which is typically required only over the regions of potential plastic hinging at column ends, is required to be provided over the full column height if the axial compressive force including seismic effects exceeds $A_g f'_c/10$.

The above requirements do not apply to column-to-column connections located within the middle third of the clear column height. However, two other restrictions then apply: 1) the design

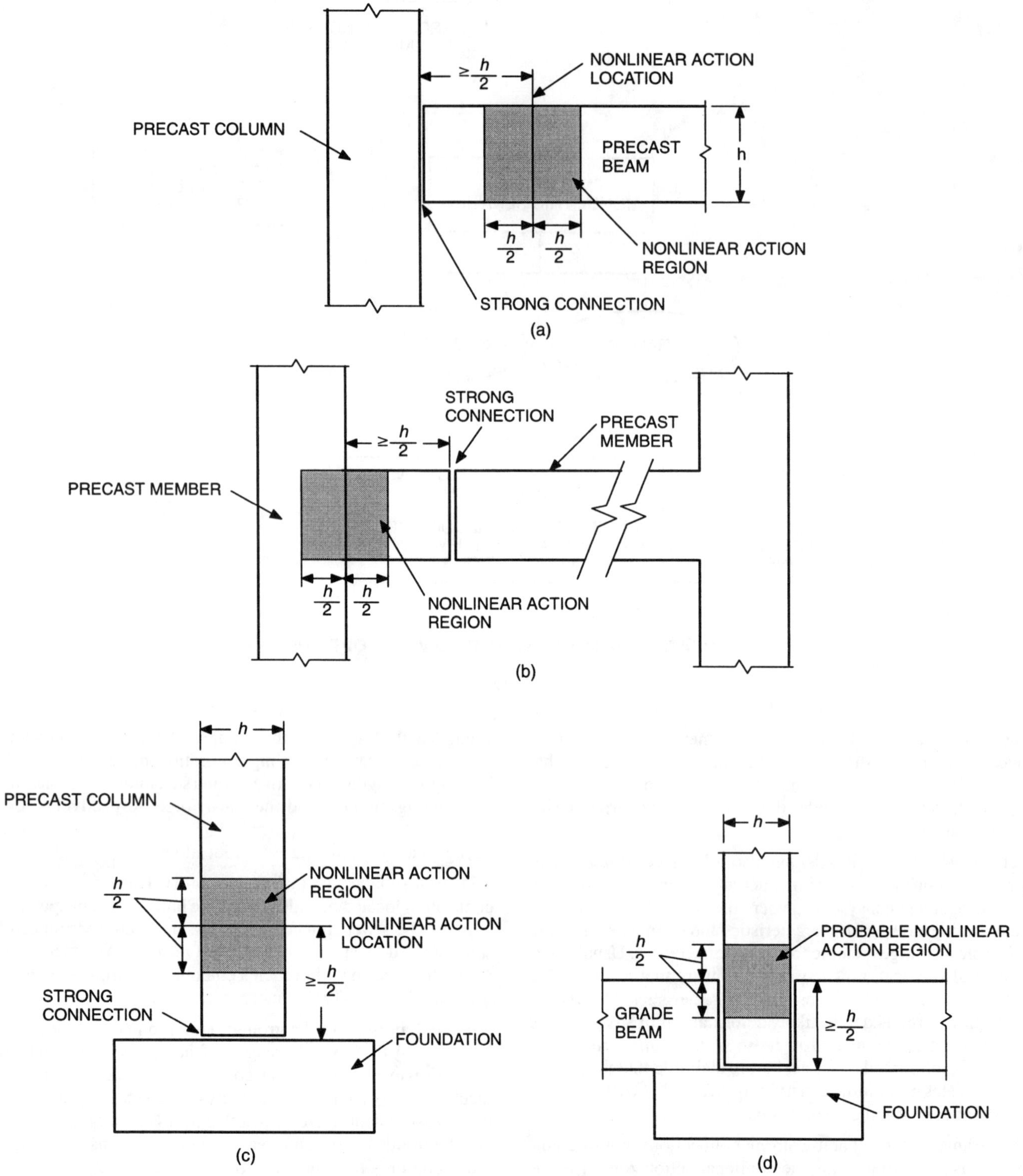

NONLINEAR ACTION REGION AND LOCATION—EXAMPLES

FIGURE 13

moment strength, ϕM_n, of the connection must not be less than 0.4 times the maximum M_{pr} (probable flexural strength) for the column within the story height (Figure 14); 2) The design shear strength, ϕV_n, of the connection must not be less than the shear corresponding to moments equal to probable flexural strengths acting at the two ends of the column, unless the beams framing in are not strong enough to develop M_{pr} at a column end. In the latter case, the largest moment that can develop at that column end must be used in computing shear.

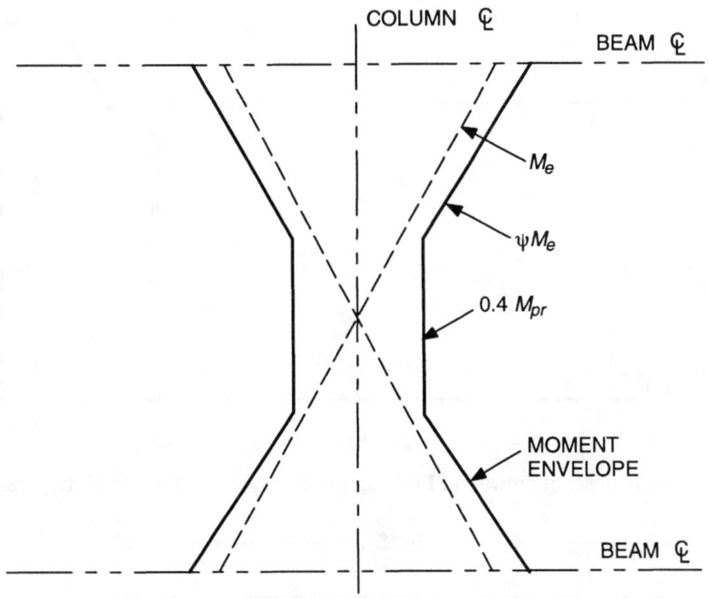

COLUMN-TO-COLUMN CONNECTION—MOMENT ENVELOPE

FIGURE 14

Reinforcement in the nonlinear action (plastic hinge) regions must be fully developed outside both the strong connection region and the nonlinear action region. Noncontinuous anchorage reinforcement of a strong connection must be fully developed between the connection and the beginning of the nonlinear action region.

See Example 1 in Part 3 of this chapter.

Precast Gravity System

Where the gravity system (consisting of structural members that are not part of the lateral-force-resisting system) of a structure is precast rather than cast-in-place, overall structural performance equivalent or at least similar to that provided by monolithic gravity systems is sought to be ensured by two alternative provisions.

The first seeks to provide backup frame action, which is expected from monolithic gravity frames, by increasing the redundancy of the lateral-force-resisting system, specifically by requiring well distributed lateral-force-resisting elements. A limitation on the aspect ratios of horizontal diaphragms (span-to-depth ratio of diaphragm or diaphragm segment ≤ 3) is imposed, thus requiring multiple lines of resistance as well as minimizing excessive diaphragm deformations under the Design Basis Ground Motion (Figure 15). In addition, along each line of resistance, if moment frames are utilized to carry the seismic forces, at least $[(N_b/4) + 1]$ of the bays (rounded up to the nearest integer) along any frame line at any story must be part of the lateral-force-resisting system, where N_b is the total number of bays along that line at that story (Figure 15). This requirement applies to only the lower two-thirds of the stories of buildings three stories or more in height.

Although using interior lines of resistance is very desirable, a second alternative may be considered when the diaphragm aspect ratio limitations cannot be economically met. In that case, steps are taken to ensure that the integrity of precast lateral-force-resisting frames or shear walls combined with precast gravity frames is maintained during severe seismic excitations. All precast gravity frame beam-to-column connections are required to be partially restrained.[36]

In addition, complete calculations for the deformation compatibility of the gravity-load-carrying system must be made using cracked section stiffnesses of the lateral-force-resisting elements and considering the effects of possible diaphragm flexibility.

For gravity columns that are not laterally supported on all sides, such as those located at floor openings or at exterior slab boundaries, a positive connection along each unsupported direction parallel to a principal plan axis of the structure is required. The connection is required to be designed for a horizontal force equal to 4 percent of the axial load strength, P_o, of the column. This is to prevent any inadvertent increase in unsupported column height during strong ground motion. The above horizontal force will stabilize a column subject to a 4-percent story drift. The required detail provides a load path for the additional shears generated by a 4-percent story drift.

Bearing length is required to be 2 inches more than that needed for bearing strength. This is to prevent slippage of the horizontal members off their supports during a severe seismic event. The increase was based on an average girder depth of 50 inches, when the member is presumably displaced through a 4-percent angular rotation, as the frame drifts laterally.

1908.1.8. Section 21.2.5 of ACI 318–99 requires "reinforcement resisting earthquake-induced flexural and axial forces in frame members and in structural wall boundary elements" to comply with ASTM A706. ASTM A615 Grade 40 and 60 reinforcement is permitted subject to two supplementary requirements. This obviously precludes the use of prestressing tendons to resist earthquake-induced flexural and axial forces in frame members and in shear wall boundary elements. This modification permits such usage, provided two different conditions are satisfied.

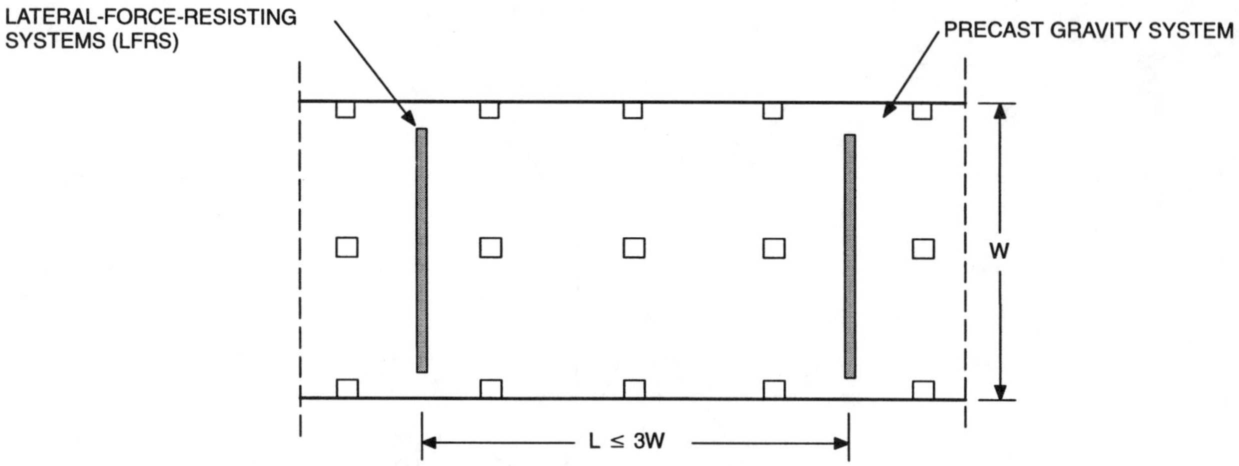

(a) Span of diaphragm between LFRS not more than 3 times width of diaphragm

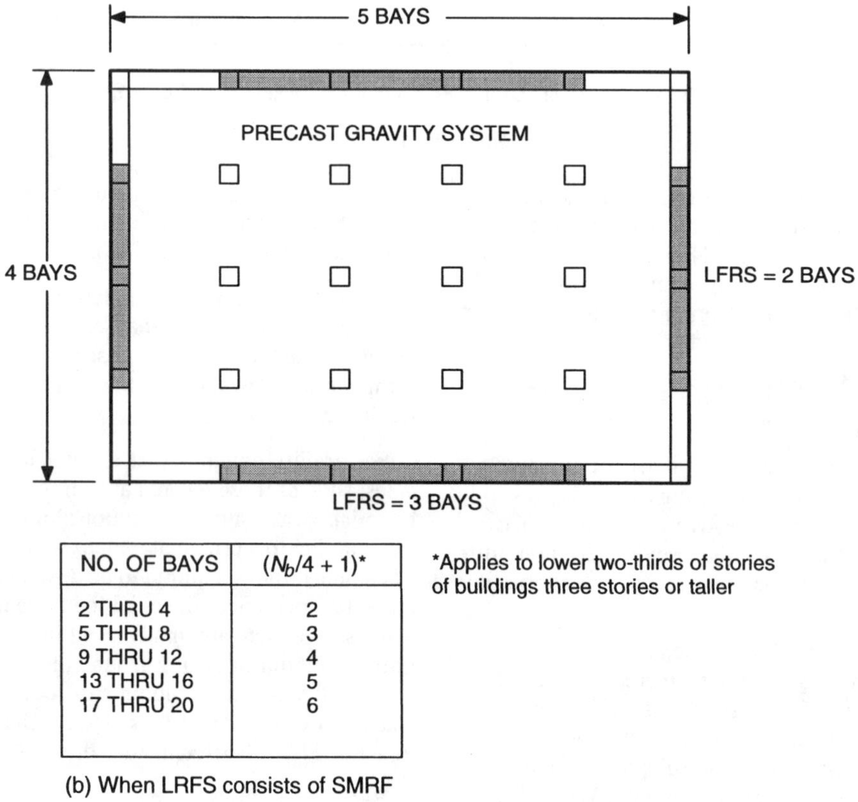

NO. OF BAYS	$(N_b/4 + 1)$*
2 THRU 4	2
5 THRU 8	3
9 THRU 12	4
13 THRU 16	5
17 THRU 20	6

*Applies to lower two-thirds of stories of buildings three stories or taller

(b) When LRFS consists of SMRF

DISTRIBUTION OF LATERAL-FORCE-RESISTING SYSTEMS IN STRUCTURES HAVING PRECAST GRAVITY SYSTEMS

FIGURE 15

The use of prestressing tendons, in conjunction with deformed reinforcing bars, in frames resisting earthquake forces was first allowed in the 1994 NEHRP Provisions, based on research by Ishizuka and Hawkins.[37] The prestress f_{pc} calculated for an area equal to the member's shortest cross-sectional dimension multiplied by the perpendicular dimension (worded this way to specifically address T-beams, L-beams and other such shapes) was restricted in the 1994 NEHRP Provisions to the greater of 350 psi or $f'_c/12$. This restriction and the condition set forth in the added Section 21.2.5.2 came directly from the research reported in Reference 37. When the 1997 UBC adopted the same provision, the limit on f_{pc} was changed to the lesser of 350 psi or $f'_c/12$. The requirement to demonstrate the satisfactory seismic performance of anchorages for tendons was dropped, perhaps inadvertently. A third condition was added requiring that shear strength provided by prestressing tendons not be considered in design. In the 1997 NEHRP Provisions, the limit has been increased to the lesser of 700 psi or $f'_c/6$, based on newer research.[38] The second condition remained unchanged from the 1994 NEHRP Provisions, including the requirement to demonstrate the satisfactory seismic performance of tendon anchorages. The third condition added by the 1997 UBC was not adopted. The 2000 IBC has the same provision that is in the 1997 NEHRP Provisions.

1908.1.10. This section represents one of the modifications made by the 1997 UBC to the ACI 318 requirements, that is not part of ACI 318-99. The section specifies transverse reinforcement requirements for wall piers, defined in Section 1908.1.5 (Figure 16), when they are not designed as part of a special moment frame. The requirements were added to the 1988 edition of the UBC out of concern that thin column-like elements between openings in shear walls were being designed without proper transverse reinforcement. There are two important exemptions to the requirements of Section 1908.1.10. A wall pier satisfying the requirement of deformation compatibility with the lateral-force-resisting system need not be detailed by Section 21.6.10.2. Wall piers laterally supported by much stiffer shear walls along the same line within a story also need not be detailed by Section 21.6.10.2.

1908.1.11. This introduces an important amendment to ACI 318–99 Section 21.7.2.2. The difference between ACI 318 and this IBC amendment to ACI 318 is that ACI 318 as well as the 1997 UBC requires that lap splices be located within the middle half of the column height in columns not proportioned to resist earthquake effects, whereas the amendment allows the lap splices to be located anywhere, including the column ends, taking designers back to ACI 318 editions prior to 1995. This amendment is justified because gravity columns are required to sustain only their gravity-load-carrying capacity under the design displacement, whereas columns forming part of the lateral-force-resisting system are required to sustain full gravity as well as lateral loads under the same displacement. Also, ACI 318–99 requires gravity columns to be reinforced throughout their height with ties at a spacing not to exceed 1) 6 diameters of the smallest longitudinal bar enclosed, 2) 16 tie-bar diameters, 3) one-half the least cross-sectional dimension of the column, and 4) 6 inches (150 mm). This close tie spacing makes it unnecessary to restrict the lap splice locations.

SECTION 1909
STRUCTURAL PLAIN CONCRETE

This section reproduces parts of Chapter 22 of ACI 318–99, refers to the rest of it, reformats and rearranges the reproduced text (Table 7), but otherwise makes only two deviations from ACI 318–99.

TABLE 7. CORRELATION BETWEEN SECTION 1909 (STRUCTURAL PLAIN CONCRETE) OF THE 2000 IBC AND CHAPTER 22 OF ACI 318–99

2000 IBC SECTION NOS.	ACI 318-99 SECTION NOS.
1909.1 1909.1.1	22.1.2
1909.2	22.2.2 22.7.3
1909.3	22.3
1909.4	Refers to 22.4-22.8
1909.5	Refers to 22.9
1909.6 1909.6.1	22.6.6.3 22.1.1.1
1909.6.2 1909.6.3	22.6.6.2 22.6.6.5

First, under Section 1909.2, Limitations, the IBC directs the user to Section 1910 (Seismic Design Provisions) for additional limitations on the use of structural plain concrete.

Second, an exception is added under Section 1909.4, Design. For detached one- and two-family dwellings and other occupancies less than two stories in height of light frame construction, the required edge thickness of ACI 318 (8 inches) is permitted to be reduced to 6 inches, provided the footing does not extend more than 4 inches on either side of the supported wall.

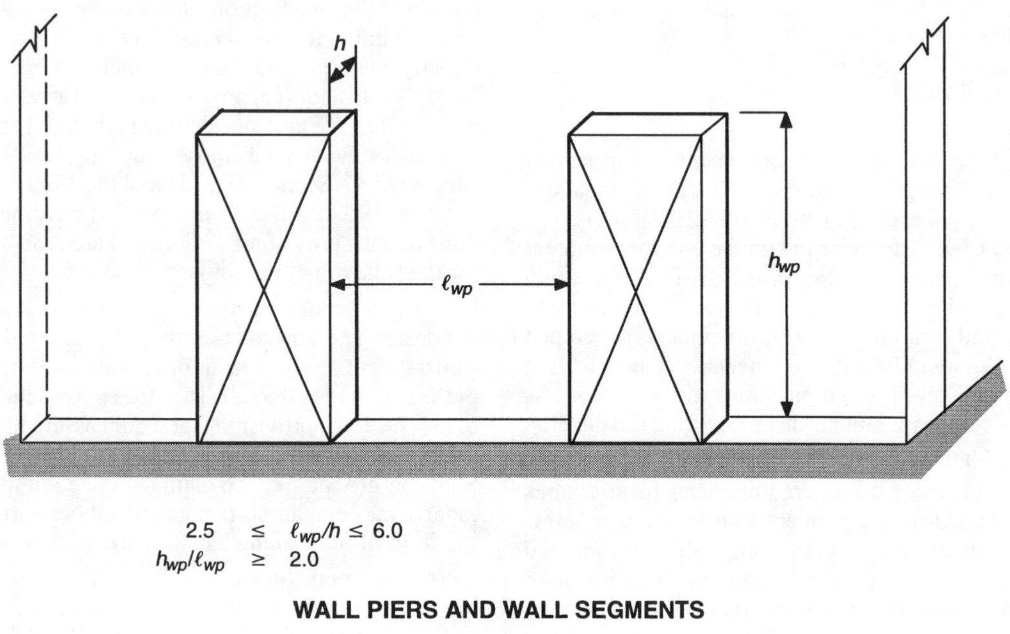

$2.5 \leq \ell_{wp}/h \leq 6.0$

$h_{wp}/\ell_{wp} \geq 2.0$

WALL PIERS AND WALL SEGMENTS

FIGURE 16

SECTION 1910
SEISMIC DESIGN PROVISIONS

This section first provides a classification of seismic-force-resisting components, in the same manner as the 1997 NEHRP Provisions Section 9.3. Classification of moment frames has been dropped from this section of the IBC because ACI 318–99 has revised its terminology for moment frames to make it consistent with the IBC. In Section 1910.2, structural concrete shear walls are classified into four categories: plain concrete shear walls, detailed plain concrete shear walls,ordinary reinforced concrete shear walls, and special reinforced concrete shear walls. For each seismic-force-resisting component, the applicable provisions of ACI 318–99 Chapter 21 are indicated, thereby providing much needed coordination with that chapter. Plain concrete shear walls are specifically required to conform to ACI 318–99 Chapter 22. Detailed plain concrete shear walls are additionally required to contain a specified minimal amount of reinforcement. It may be noted that detailed plain concrete shear walls are not recognized in ACI 318–99. Table 8 gives an overview of the seismic-force-resisting structural systems recognized in Section 1910.

TABLE 8. EARTHQUAKE-RESISTING STRUCTURAL SYSTEMS OF CONCRETE

SEISMIC-FORCE-RESISTING STRUCTURAL SYSTEMS	APPLICABLE ACI 318 PROVISIONS	RESTRICTIONS
Ordinary moment frames	Ch. 1-18[a]	SDC B or lower
Intermediate moment frames	Ch 1-18 + 21.10	SDC C or lower
Special Moment frames	Ch. 1-17 + 21.2-21.5	None
Ordinary Plain concrete shear walls	Ch. 22	SDC B or lower
Detailed plain concrete shear walls	Ch. 22 + IBC Sec. 1910.2.2	SDC B or lower
Ordinary reinforced concrete shear walls	Ch. 1-18	SDC C or lower
Special reinforced concrete shear walls	Ch. 1-18 + 21.2, 21.6	None

a. Plus IBC Sec. 1910.3.1 for SDC B

Section 1910.3 provides specific requirements for structures assigned to Seismic Design Category (SDC) B. Additional detailing requirements, to be found in the 1997 NEHRP Provisions, but not in the 1997 UBC, are imposed on the ordinary moment frame of reinforced concrete assigned to SDC B. At least two longitudinal reinforcing bars must be provided continuously through the top and bottom of flexural members, developed within exterior columns or boundary elements. A column having a clear height to maximum plan dimension ratio of five or less must be designed for the maximum shear force that can develop in the column, computed per ACI 318 Section 21.10.3.

Section 1910.4 provides specific requirements for structures assigned to SDC C. Ordinary moment frames, plain concrete shear walls and detailed plain concrete shear walls are prohibited from use in SDC C. Specific detailing requirements are given for columns supporting reactions from discontinuous stiff members such as walls, and for anchor bolts set into column tops. These anchor bolt requirements are from the 1997 UBC where they were not placed in the proper sections, considering their applicability. The UBC requirements have been collected and properly located in the IBC. Also, provisions are included for structural plain concrete members in structures assigned to SDC C. The exception to Section 1910.4.4.1 gives specific requirements for basement walls, foundation walls or other walls below the base as well as for walls above the base. Section 1910.4.4.2 gives specific requirements for footings. Section 1910.4.4.3 prohibits the use of plain concrete pedestals in SDC C and above.

Section 1910.4.4.2 contains the provisions for plain concrete footings that were found in Section 1904 of the 1996 BOCA/NBC and Section 1912 of the 1997 SBC. The amount of reinforcing required is essentially the same between the IBC and the other two codes, as is the required placement. However, the 2000 IBC adds exceptions to allow plain concrete footings without longitudinal reinforcement for detached one- and two-family dwellings of light-frame construction, three stories or less in height, regardless of the seismic design category. Also, where a slab-on-grade is cast monolithically with the footing, one No. 5 bar may be located in either the top or bottom of the footing. In another exception, in detached one- and two-family dwellings three stories or less in height, the projection of the footing beyond the face of the supported member may exceed the footing thickness.

Section 1910.5 gives specific requirements for structures assigned to SDCs D, E, and F. The only reinforced concrete structural systems allowed are the special moment frame or the special shear wall. Frame members not proportioned to resist forces induced by earthquake motions are required to conform to Section 21.9 of ACI 318–99. Structural plain concrete members are prohibited other than in applications listed under Section 2210.1 of ACI 318–99.

SECTION 1911
MINIMUM SLAB PROVISIONS

Section 1905.0 of the 1999 BOCA/NBC, Section 1900.4.4 of the 1997 UBC and Section 1909.1 of the 1999 SBC contain identical minimum thickness requirements for floor slabs supported directly on the ground. These are included in Section 1911 of the 2000 IBC. In addition, provisions aimed at retarding vapor transmission through the floor slab are included. These provisions are essentially the same as those found in the 1999 edition of the BOCA/NBC (Section 1905.1) and the 1999 edition of the SBC (Section 1909.2). BOCA and SBCCI have published explanations of their provisions,[39,40] which are used as source material for the following discussion.

It is specifically stated in ACI 318–99 that it does not govern the design and construction of soil-supported slabs, unless the slab transmits vertical loads or lateral forces from other portions of the structure to the soil. This does not preclude the application of any ACI 318 provision that would assure the proper strength, durability, and abrasion resistance of concrete slabs on ground. Slabs on ground may be plain concrete without any reinforcement or may contain shrinkage and temperature reinforcement in the form of reinforcing bars or wire mesh.

The minimum thickness of $3^1/_2$ inches is based on the fact that the largest aggregate size typically used in the construction of slabs on grade is 1 inch. ASTM C33 allows 5 percent of 1-inch graded material to be larger than 1 inch in size, but smaller than

$1^1/_2$ inches. Therefore, in accordance with the requirement of ACI 318 Section 3.3.2 that the nominal size of coarse aggregate must be no larger than one-third the depth of a slab, the minimum depth becomes $3^1/_2$ (3 times 1 inch plus a $^1/_2$-inch allowance for larger stones).

While good quality concrete is practically impermeable to the passage of water (that is not under significant pressure), concrete is not impervious to the passage of water vapors. If the surface of the slab is not sealed, water vapor will pass through the slab. If a floor finish such as linoleum, vinyl tile, wood flooring, or any type of covering is placed on top of the slab, the moisture is trapped in the slab. Any floor finish adhering to the concrete may eventually loosen or buckle or blister.

Many of the moisture problems associated with enclosed slabs on ground can be prevented or minimized by installing vapor retarders, such as polyethylene sheeting or other approved materials, between the slab and the ground. Such retarders are needed under slabs in habitable spaces. Where garages, utility areas, and similar spaces are not to be heated or occupied, the use of vapor barriers is generally not necessary. If moisture migration is not expected to be a problem based on the occupancy of a building, Exception 3 permits the vapor retarder to be omitted. The vapor retarder provisions of Section 1911 should not change current practice in UBC territory because typically the soil investigation report already required such vapor retarders.

SECTION 1912 ANCHORAGE TO CONCRETE— ALLOWABLE STRESS DESIGN

The 2000 IBC provides two distinct methods for designing anchorage to concrete. Section 1912 presents an allowable stress design (ASD) method of limited applicability. Section 1913 presents a strength design method of broader applicability.

1912.1 General. The ASD provisions of this section are adapted from the 1997 edition of the *Uniform Building Code*. They are based on limited test data on headed bolts cast in normal-weight concrete subjected to static loading. It is, therefore, not applicable to hooked (J- or L-) bolts, lightweight aggregate concrete, post-installed anchors (meaning anchors installed in hardened concrete), or when load combinations include earthquake effects.

1912.2 Allowable Service Load. Table 1912.2 provides allowable service loads for headed bolts or stud anchors cast in normal-weight concrete, that are subject to tension only or shear only. The table values are for a particular range of bolt sizes ($^1/_4$ to $1^1/_4$ inches) and concrete strengths (2500, 3000, and 4000 psi). When using the tabulated values, minimum edge distances and spacing between bolts, specified in the table, must be carefully maintained. Edge distances are measured from the face of the bolt to the sides and ends of concrete members. Section 1912.3 provides for decreases up to 50 percent in edge distances and/or spacing.

For a headed bolt and stud anchor subjected to combined tension and shear loading, Section 1912.2 requires that the applied service-level load in tension and the applied service-level load in shear satisfy the interaction formula given in that section, which involves the allowable values given by Table 1912.2.

1912.3 Required edge distance and spacing. The purpose of this section is to expand the applicability of Table 1912.2 by providing for situations where bolt locations cannot meet the required minimum edge distances and/or the spacing requirements of the table. Both the minimum edge distance and the minimum spacing requirements of the table may be reduced up to 50 percent for a corresponding 50-percent reduction in the allowable service loads. Where reduction in edge distance and spacing is less than 50 percent, the allowable service loads may be determined by linear interpolation.

1912.4 Increase in allowable load. This section allows one-third increase in the tabulated values of allowable service loads of Table 1912.2 when service loads include those due to wind, in addition to dead loads, live loads, and other loads such as snow. Wind loads are transitory in nature. It is considered highly unlikely that two or more variable loads such as wind and live loads will attain their design values simultaneously. This is the rationale behind the one-third increase in allowable stresses permitted when the alternate basic load combinations of Section 1605.3.2 are used in design and load combinations include the effects of wind or seismic loads.

1912.5 Increase for special inspection. The provisions of this section have been taken from footnotes 5 and 6 to Table 19-D (Allowable Service Load on Embedded Bolts) of the 1997 UBC, which is essentially identical to Table 1912.2 of the 2000 IBC. These footnotes first appeared in the 1976 edition of the UBC. Footnote 5 applies to allowable service loads in tension, and states that the values shown are for work without special inspection; where special inspection is provided, values may be increased 100 percent. Footnote 6 applies to allowable service loads in shear, and states that the values shown are for work with or without special inspection.

See Example 2 in Part 3 of this chapter.

SECTION 1913 ANCHORAGE TO CONCRETE—STRENGTH DESIGN

IBC Section 1913 was approved by the IBC Structural Subcommittee with the knowledge that it is based on work-in-progress for eventual incorporation into Appendix D of ACI 318 (see the Introduction section). Ideally this work would have been completed prior to the publication of the 2000 IBC; however, these provisions are still being considered through the ACI consensus process. It is expected that Section 1913 will not appear in the 2003 IBC, but rather the provisions of Appendix D of ACI 318–02 will be adopted by reference.

Fortunately, these anchorage strength design provisions and their accompanying commentary, as they were proposed through the ACI 318 process, have been reprinted in a Portland Cement Association (PCA) publication entitled *Strength Design of Anchorage to Concrete*.[41] This publication contains valuable information for anyone applying the provisions of IBC Section 1913. In addition to an historical background discussion, the provisions and the commentary, this document of over 75 pages includes the following six design examples:

Single Tension Fastener Away from Edges
Group of Tension Fasteners Near an Edge
Single Fastener in Shear Near an Edge
Single Fastener in Tension and Shear Near an Edge

Group of Tension and Shear Fasteners Near Two Edges

Group of Tension Fasteners Near an Edge with Eccentricity

It is expected that when Appendix D to ACI 318 completes the consensus process, it will include design provisions for not only cast-in-place anchors but also for post-installed anchors. At this time, Section 1913 provides strength design provisions for the following type of anchors:

CAST-IN-PLACE ANCHORS

Headed Studs
Headed Bolts
Hooked Bolts (J and L)

Hooked bolts are anchored mainly by mechanical interlock from the 90-degree bend (L-bolt) or 180-degree bend (J-bolt) at the embedded end.

The code does not include design provisions for anchors installed in hardened concrete (post-installed anchors); acceptance of evaluation reports is typically relied upon for the use of these types of anchors.

1913.1 Scope. In addition to listing the types of anchors that can be designed using this section, the scope also sets forth requirements for acceptable geometry of anchor heads. According to Reference 41, headed studs and bolts with geometries consistent with ANSI/ASME B1.1 [Unified Inch Screw Threads (UN and UNR Thread Form)], B18.2.1 (Square and Hex Bolts and Screws, Inch Series) and B18.2.6 (Fasteners for Use in Structural Applications) are geometrically compliant.

1913.2 Notations and Definitions. The designer and plan reviewer should refer to this section for clarification of seldom used terms such as "attachment," "brittle steel element" and "ductile steel element."

1913.3 General Requirements. This section outlines the acceptable types of analysis and sets forth the required load combinations. In the case of seismic design load determination, Section 1621.1.7 may apply depending upon the applicability provisions of Section 1621.1.1.

Next are provisions that only apply in SDC C and higher. For these more seismically vulnerable structures, the design strength of anchors must be reduced by 25 percent as compared to the design strength of anchors used in structures that fall under SDC A or B. In addition, the assurance of a ductile failure is addressed by requiring that either, 1) the design of the "anchor" be governed by the tensile or shear strength of a "ductile steel element" as defined in Section 1913.2.2, or 2) the "attachment" as defined in Section 1913.2.2 be designed so that it will undergo ductile yielding at a load level no greater than 75 percent of the minimum anchor design strength.

The section concludes with reduced design values if lightweight concrete is used and sets the maximum concrete strength for use with these design provisions at 10,000 psi.

1913.4 General Requirements for Strength of Anchors. This provides a global overview of the considerations that must be made when designing anchors. The first half of the section addresses the different failure modes (related to steel strength as well as to the strength of the embedment) that need to be checked. These can be summarized as in Table 9:

Subsequent sections set forth formulas to determine the strengths for the above described failure modes. Note that the concrete breakout strength provisions of Sections 1913.5.2 and 1913.6.2 are applicable only for anchors with diameters not exceeding 2 inches and tensile embedments not exceeding 25 inches in depth. These limitations exist because no significant experimental results are available beyond this range. The designer is obligated to determine the lowest design strength in shear and tension, and ensure compliance with the following formulas:

$$\phi V_n \geq V_u$$

$$\phi N_n \geq N_u$$

Section 1913.4.2 contains some interesting performance-based language. Initially upon reading this section, one would assume tests are required to determine nominal strengths. However, upon further review of Sections 1913. 5 and 1913.6, the reader is relieved to learn that nominal strengths may also be calculated. Section 1913.4.2 allows "design models that result in substantial agreement with results of comprehensive tests" to be used. This generalized wording allows current procedures such as those in ACI 349 Appendix B[42] or the PCI Design Handbook[43] to be used in applicable ranges if desired. The section also allows the use of test results "for design by test" as long as they are interpreted to give the 5-percent fractile values (defined in Section 1913.2) and not the mean. A rectangular prism model for both single anchors and anchor groups is provided as a "deemed to comply" method.[44,45] The provisions consider anchors in both cracked and uncracked concrete.

TABLE 9. DIFFERENT FAILURE MODES AND CORRESPONDING STRENGTHS

TENSILE FAILURE MODE	CORRESPONDING STRENGTH	IBC SECTION NO.	SHEAR FAILURE MODE	CORRESPONDING STRENGTH	IBC SECTION NO.
Tensile failure of fastener steel	Ns	1913.5.1	Shear failure of fastener steel	V_s	1913.6.1
Anchor pullout	N_p	1913.4.2 1913.5.3	Concrete pryout	V_{cp}	1913.4.2 1913.6.3
Concrete side face blowout	N_{sb}	1913.4.2 1913.5.4	Concrete breakout	V_{cb}	1913.4.2 1913.6.2
Concrete breakout	N_{cb}	1913.4.2 1913.5.2			
Splitting failure	Note a				

a. Precluded by requiring minimum edge distances, spacings, and thicknesses (1913.4.2, 1913.8)

The second half of Section 1913.4 sets forth the strength reduction factors, ϕ, depending upon the failure mode governing strength. It is assumed that the code user will typically be using the ACI 318 load combinations of Section 9.2 unless seismic loads are included, in which case the load combinations of Section 1605.2 are required to be used by Section 1913.3.2. Nominal values of the strengths listed in Table 9 must be modified to include the appropriate ϕ factors listed in Table 10:

The reduction factors listed in the last subsection (1913.4.5) apply when the structural framing includes primary members of materials other than concrete, and the designer opts to use the load combinations set forth in Appendix C of ACI 318.

1913.5 Design Requirements for Tensile Loading and 1913.6 Design Requirements for Shear Loading. These sections include numerous formulas that are needed for the determination of the nominal strength of an anchor or a group of anchors for a given failure mode. These nominal strengths are based on a plethora of factors including:

1. Embedment in cracked or uncracked concrete
2. Single anchor or group of anchors
3. Embedment depth
4. Presence of plate or washer
5. Edge distances
6. Center-to-center spacing of anchors
7. Eccentric loading
8. Thickness of concrete element

For a complete discussion, explanation and application of these formulas, Reference 41 should be consulted.

1913.7 Interaction of Tensile and Shear Forces. This section addresses how to check anchors that are subject simultaneously to both shear and tensile loads.

1913.8 Required Edge Distances, and Spacings to Preclude Splitting Failure. Despite the title, this section only addresses required edge distances. In the case of untorqued headed anchors, simply the minimum concrete cover protection for reinforcement applies (Section 7.7 of ACI 318–99). If the headed anchor will be torqued (as is done during the connection of attachments to cast-in-place anchors), the minimum edge distance is increased to 6 times the anchor shaft diameter.

SECTION 1914
SHOTCRETE

This section contains provisions very similar to those in Section 1911 of the BOCA/NBC, Section 1924 of the UBC and Section 1915 of the SBC (latest editions). BOCA and SBCCI have published commentaries on their shotcrete provisions,[39,40] from which the material here is largely drawn.

1914.1 General. Shotcrete is pneumatically projected concrete or mortar. Other terms such as spraycrete, sprayed concrete and gunite are also associated with shotcrete construction. Shotcrete needs to conform to Chapter 19 requirements for plain or reinforced concrete, unless specifically exempted by Section 1914.

1914.2 Proportions and materials. Proportions of shotcrete mixtures should be determined prior to the beginning of construction by trial applications on test specimens. The test specimens should be representative of the in-place application (flat, vertical, overhead) and the shotcrete should be applied using the same materials and equipment that will be used for construction.

1914.3 Aggregate. For construction applications in which the shotcrete will be several inches thick, coarse aggregate may be used in the mixture. In those cases, the aggregate size is limited to $^3/_4$ inch, to minimize the effects of rebounding during placement and the creation of voids in the shotcrete. Rebound refers to shotcrete that ricochets off the receiving surface. See Section 1914.6.

1914.4 Reinforcement. The size and the spacing of the reinforcement are required to be such as to minimize interference with the high-velocity placement of the shotcrete and to ensure that the reinforcement is completely covered. The clearance between the form and the reinforcement may vary depending on whether concrete or mortar is used for the shotcrete. The use of reinforcing bars or welded wire fabric can also affect the minimum clearance from the form. The exception allowing reduction of required clearances, subject to approval of the building official and preconstruction testing, should be noted.

TABLE 10. REDUCTION FACTORS FOR STRENGTHS GOVERNED BY DIFFERENT FAILURE MODES

TENSILE FAILURE MODE	ϕ	SHEAR FAILURE MODE	ϕ
Tensile failure of fastener steel	Ductile steel element – 0.90 Brittle steel element – 0.75	Shear failure of fastener steel	Ductile steel element -0.90 Brittle steel element - 0.75
Anchor pullout	With supplementary reinforcement – 0.85 Without supplementary reinforcement – 0.75	Concrete pryout	With supplementary reinforcement – 0.85 Without supplementary reinforcement – 0.75
Side Face Blowout	With supplementary reinforcement – 0.85 Without supplementary reinforcement – 0.75	Concrete breakout	With supplementary reinforcement – 0.85 Without supplementary reinforcement – 0.75
Concrete Breakout	With supplementary reinforcement – 0.85 Without supplementary reinforcement – 0.75		

Non-contact lap splices are preferred, to minimize the creation of weak sections in the shotcrete. Where possible, at least 2 inches should separate lapped bars. Welded wire fabric should be lapped by one square in all directions.[39] When adequate encasement can be shown, contact lap splices are permitted with the approval of the building official.

1914.5 Preconstruction tests. The preconstruction tests provided for in this section are at the discretion of the building officials. It is part of the UBC provisions, but not part of the BOCA/NBC or the SBC provisions. The requirements are quite explicit and self-explanatory.

1914.6 Rebound. As mentioned earlier, rebound is shotcrete that ricochets off the receiving surface. The position of the work (flat, vertical or overhead), layer thickness, discharge pressure, cement content, water content, size and gradation of aggregate, and type and amount of reinforcement can affect the amount of rebounding that occurs.[39] Rebounded material may not be reused or worked back into the construction, and must be removed from the surface prior to placement of additional layers of shotcrete.

1914.7 Joints. Construction joints are generally tapered to a thin edge over a width of approximately 12 inches. Square construction joints should be avoided, except as specifically permitted by this section.

1914.8 Damage. After placement, any shotcrete that lacks uniformity or that exhibits segregation, honeycombing or delamination, or which contains dry patches, slugs, voids, or sand pockets (porous areas low in cement content), or that sags or sloughs must be removed and replaced.

1914.9 Curing. As in most construction involving cementitious materials, proper curing practices need to be followed from the time of completion of the shotcrete application, as outlined in this section.

1914.10 Strength tests. The BOCA/NBC and the SBC require strength tests of shotcrete to be made in accordance with the quality assurance provisions of ACI 506.2.[46] Test specimens are obtained from the in-place shotcrete or from a test panel that is representative of the work, and tested in accordance with ASTM C42, Test Method for Obtaining and Testing Drilled Cores and Sawed Beams of Concrete. The IBC, like the UBC, spells out strength test provisions, including sampling requirements and acceptance criteria.

SECTION 1915 REINFORCED GYPSUM CONCRETE

Provisions on reinforced gypsum concrete are included in Section 1925 of the 1997 UBC and Section 1914 of the 1999 SBC.

The specifications of Section 1915 cover poured-in-place reinforced gypsum concrete over permanent formboard. Gypsum concrete is used as a structural material in the construction of roof decks or slabs and as a nonstructural material in floor topping.

Gypsum concrete is required to conform to the specifications of ASTM C317 (Gypsum Concrete). The design and application of reinforced gypsum concrete must be in accordance with the requirements of ASTM C956 (Installation of Cast-in-Place Reinforced Gypsum Concrete).

The minimum thickness of reinforced gypsum concrete is required to be 2 inches, except that this may be reduced to no less than $1^1/_2$ inches if certain conditions given in Section 1915.2 are met.

SECTION 1916 CONCRETE-FILLED PIPE COLUMNS

These provisions are largely the same as those of Section 1912 of the 1999 edition of the BOCA/NBC. The BOCA Commentary[39] is used as a source for this discussion.

1916.1 General. According to Reference 39, steel pipe should be manufactured to the requirements of ASTM A501 for hot-formed welded and seamless carbon steel of round, square or rectangular shape for general structural purposes. The steel must have a minimum tensile strength of 58,000 psi and a minimum yield strength of 36,000 psi.

Cold-formed welded and seamless carbon steel of square or rectangular shape conforming to the Grade B requirements of ASTM A500, having a minimum tensile strength of 58,000 psi and a minimum yield strength of 36,000 psi, may also be used for concrete-filled pipe columns.

1916.2 Design. The load-carrying capacity of concrete-filled pipe columns may be computed in accordance with approved rules such as those in Section 10.16 of ACI 318–99, or may be determined by load tests.

1916.3 Connections. Conditions for making structural connections to concrete-filled pipe columns are prescribed. If connections require welding to the steel shell, it must be done before the core is filled with concrete, unless it is possible to demonstrate that the concrete will not be damaged from the heat of welding.

1916.4 Reinforcement. Reinforcement must comply with the requirements of this section as well as with the applicable provisions of ACI 318. A minimum clearance of 1 inch between any such reinforcement and the outer shell must be provided. This is to permit the concrete to flow around the reinforcement and bond to it, which is necessary for composite action.

1916.5 Fire-resistance-rating protection. Concrete-filled pipe columns are required to be fire-resistance rated in accordance with IBC Table 601. Irrespective of whether the protective cover is of concrete, concrete with a metal encasement, or a metal cover that encases other fire-insulating materials, it must not be considered to contribute to the load-carrying capacity of the column.

1916.6 Approvals. Concrete-filled pipe columns, including their connection details and splices, which are shop-fabricated as pre-engineered items, are subject to certain inspection and approval requirements spelled out in this section.

CHAPTER 19—PART 2

APPENDIX TO CHAPTER 19
SIGNIFICANT CHANGES FROM ACI 318-95 TO ACI 318-99

Many significant changes from ACI 318-95, the reference document for the last editions of the BOCA/NBC, the SBC, and the UBC, to ACI 318-99, the reference document for the 2000 IBC, are described below.

CHAPTER 1

1.1.5. This section of ACI 318–95 states that ACI 318 does not govern the design and installation of concrete piles and drilled piers embedded in the ground. The section in ACI 318–99 states that ACI 318 does not govern the design and installation of portions of concrete piles, drilled piers and caissons embedded in the ground except for structures in regions of high seismic risk or assigned to high seismic performance or design categories. Cross-reference is made to Section 21.8.4 for requirements for concrete piles, drilled piers and caissons supporting structures in regions of high seismic risk or assigned to high seismic performance or design categories. This is in view of the addition of the new Section 21.8, Foundations, in ACI 318–99. Commentary Section R1.1.5 of ACI 318–99 has new text pointing out that detailed recommendations for precast, prestressed concrete piles are given in "Recommended Practice for Design, Manufacture and Installation of Prestressed Concrete Piling" prepared by the PCI Committee on Prestressed Concrete Piling.[47] This reference is currently the most authoritative available on precast, prestressed concrete piles that are used for one of the most common types of concrete pile foundations.

1.1.6. This section of ACI 318–95 makes ACI 318 applicable to soil-supported slabs transmitting vertical loads from other portions of the structure to the soil. In ACI 318–99, "vertical loads" has been modified to "vertical loads or lateral forces."

1.1.8.1. This section of ACI 318–95 indicates that Chapter 21 is not applicable in regions of low seismic risk. The non-applicability is now for buildings located in regions of low seismic risk, or for structures assigned to low seismic performance or design categories. Low seismic performance categories are Seismic Performance Categories A and B of BOCA/NBC (1993, 1996 and 1999), SBC (1994, 1997 and 1999), NEHRP Provisions prior to the 1997 edition,[48] ASCE 7–93 and ASCE 7–95.[49] Low seismic design categories are SDC A and B of the 2000 IBC, 1997 NEHRP Provisions, and ASCE 7–98. This change and the following are in recognition of the fact that seismic detailing requirements are no longer governed only by seismic risk at the site of the structure. In the NEHRP Provisions prior to the 1997 edition, and in codes and standards based on those documents, detailing requirements were governed by the seismic performance category, which combines the occupancy of a structure with the seismic risk at the site of the structure. In the 1997 NEHRP Provisions and in the 2000 IBC (and ASCE 7–98) based on it, the detailing requirements are governed by the seismic design category, which combines the occupancy of a structure with the soil-modified seismic risk at the site of the structure.

1.1.8.2. This section of ACI 318–95 indicates that Chapter 21 is applicable in regions of moderate or high seismic risk. The applicability is now in regions of moderate or high seismic risk, or for structures assigned to intermediate or high seismic performance or design categories. The intermediate seismic performance category is Seismic Performance Category C of the BOCA/NBC (1993, 1996 and 1999), the SBC (1994, 1997 and 1999), the NEHRP Provisions prior to the 1997 edition and ASCE 7–93 and ASCE 7–95. High seismic performance categories are Seismic Performance Categories D and E of these documents. The intermediate seismic design category is SDC C of the 2000 IBC, 1997 NEHRP Provisions and ASCE 7–98. High seismic design categories are SDCs D, E and F of these documents.

1.1.8.3. In a change analogous to the above, this section of ACI 318–99 states that the seismic risk level of a region, or seismic performance or design category, is to be regulated by the legally adopted general building code.

1.2.1. In the list of items to be shown on the design drawings and specifications, "welded splices and mechanical connections" of ACI 318–95 has been revised to "mechanical and welded splices." This change addressed inconsistencies in the use of the terms "mechanical connections" and "mechanical connectors." The terms have been replaced with "mechanical splices" when the joinery of reinforcing bars is involved. In addition, editorial revisions have been made to position "mechanical splices" before "welded splices" whenever they appear in the same heading, in the same sentence or in consecutive sections.

Items k, l, and m are new in ACI 318–99 and represent additions to the ACI 318–95 list.

1.3.1. Concrete construction must be inspected as required by the legally adopted general building code. In the absence of such requirements, concrete construction is required in ACI 318–95 to be inspected throughout the various work stages "by an engineer or architect, or by a competent representative responsible to that engineer or architect." Such inspection, in ACI 318–99, is required to be "by or under the supervision of a licensed design professional or by a qualified inspector." This change clarifies the intent of the code, which is to ensure quality construction by having inspection performed by a qualified inspector when inspection is not provided by the building department. It also provides for engineers responsible for the design to be involved with the construction inspection process. Inspection needs to be done by a competent individual. Therefore, Section R1.3.1 now has added text recommending that qualified inspectors should establish their qualification by becoming certified to inspect and record the results of inspection of concrete construction, including preplacement, placement, and postplacement operations through the Reinforced Concrete Special Inspector programs sponsored by ACI, ICBO, BOCA, SBCCI, or an equivalent program.

1.3.5. Continuous inspection of the placement of the reinforcement and concrete in special moment frames can now be under the supervision of "an engineer with demonstrated capability for supervising inspection of special moment frames resisting seismic loads in regions of high seismic risk." Previously, such inspection had to be done under the supervision of the engineer responsible for the structural design.

CHAPTER 2

2.1. Seven new definitions have been added to this section:

1. Anchorage Device
2. Anchorage Zone
3. Basic Monostrand Anchorage Device
4. Basic Multi-Strand Anchorage Device
5. Sheathing
6. Special Anchorage Device
7. Unbonded Tendon

These are all related to the new provisions for post-tensioned tendon anchorage zones added to Chapter 18. With the new addition, the definition of "anchorage" that was in ACI 318–95 has been deleted.

The definition of "pedestal" has been modified to include compression members with a ratio of unsupported height to average least lateral dimension equal to three.

CHAPTER 3

3.1.3. Whereas ACI 318–95 required that a complete record of tests of materials and of concrete "shall be preserved by inspecting engineer or architect" (for 2 years after completion of project), ACI 318–99 now requires that such records be retained "by the inspector." This change was made necessary by the change in Section 1.3.1, which now allows inspection by a qualified inspector.

3.8.1. The reference ASTM standards are updated to the latest editions available at the time ACI 318–99 was finalized.

3.8.2. The Structural Welding Code, AWS D1.4, which is declared to be part of ACI 318–99, is updated to the 1998 edition.

3.8.3. Section 2.3 (Strength design load combinations) of ASCE 7–95, rather than ASCE 7–88, is declared to be part of ACI 318–99 for the purpose cited in Section 9.3.1.1 and Appendix C.

3.8.5. Articles 9.21.7.2 and 9.21.7.3 of Division I and Article 10.3.2.3 of Divisions II of AASHTO Standard Specifications for Highway Bridges, 16th Edition, 1996,[50] are declared to be part of ACI 318–99. This adoption is new and necessitated by the addition of post-tensioning anchorage provisions in Chapter 18.

CHAPTER 5

5.6.1. This section concerning testing of concrete by quaified personnel is new in ACI 318-99.

CHAPTER 7

7.1.4. Seismic hooks as defined in ACI 318–99 Section 21.1 are now added to the list of standard hooks. This item was previously covered in a footnote to Section 7.1.3.

R7.4.3. A new Reference 7.5 has been added to the list of references, which may be consulted for guidance on evaluating the degree of rusting on strand.

7.6.7.1 Two changes have been made.

Center-to-center spacing of pretensioning tendons at each end of a member, rather than clear distance between pretensioning tendons as in ACI 318–95, is now specified. This is because center-to-center spacing is what was used in the referenced research, and converting to clear spacing is unnecessary; and measurements for templates used in manufacture are always center-to-center.

A reduction has been made in the allowable spacing of prestressing strands for concrete strengths at the transfer of prestress of 4,000 psi or greater, based on several research projects sponsored by the Federal Highway Administration[30,31].

7.10.4.5. Splice requirements have changed for epoxy-coated and plain spirals. Lap splice lengths have been modified; full mechanical splices are now allowed.

CHAPTERS 8 - 20, CHAPTER 22 AND APPENDICES

10.6.4. Provisions concerning distribution of flexural reinforcement for crack control have been totally rewritten. The *z* factor requirements of the 1995 and prior code editions have been replaced. The maximum bar spacing is now specified directly.

As pointed out in Reference 26, there are three reasons for limiting crack widths in concrete. These are appearance, corrosion protection and water tightness. The three seldom apply simultaneously in a particular structure. Appearance is important for concrete exposed to view. Corrosion is important for concrete exposed to aggressive environments. Water tightness may be required for marine/sanitary structures. Appearance requires limiting of crack widths on the surface. This can be ensured by locating the reinforcement as close as possible to the surface (using small cover) to prevent cracks from widening. Corrosion control, on the other hand, is obtained by using better quality concrete and by increasing the thickness of concrete cover. Water tightness requires severe limits on crack widths, applicable only to specialty structures. Thus it should be recognized that a single provision, such as Equation 10-5 of ACI 318–99, may not be sufficient to address the control of cracking for all three reasons.

There is a strong correlation between surface crack width and cover, d_c, (see Figure A-1). For a particular magnitude of strain in the steel, the larger the cover, the larger is the surface crack width affecting the appearance. From 1971 through 1995, the ACI 318 restrictions concerning distribution of tension reinforcement were based on the concept that the width of surface cracks needs to be limited.

ACI 318 required that when the yield strength of the reinforcement exceeds 40,000 psi, detailing of the flexural tension reinforcement must be such that the following equation is satisfied:

$$z = f_s\sqrt[3]{d_cA} \leq 175 \text{ kips/in for interior exposures}$$

$$\leq 145 \text{ kips/in for exterior exposures}$$

where:

f_s = calculated stress in the reinforcement at service loads (ksi), which may be taken as $0.6f_y$.

d_c = thickness of the concrete cover measured from the extreme tension fiber to the center of the bar or wire located closest to it (inches)

A = effective tension area of concrete surrounding the flexural tension reinforcement and having the same centroid as that reinforcement, divided by the number of bars or wires (square inches)

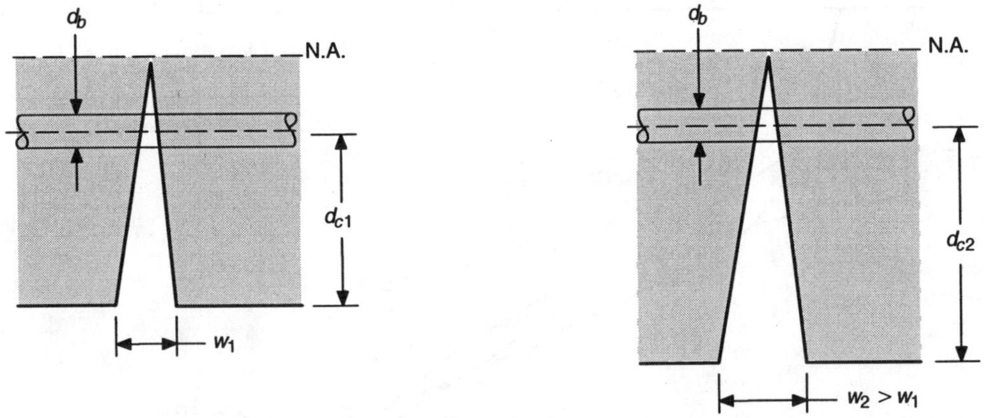

CRACK WIDTH FOR DIFFERENT COVER THICKNESSES

FIGURE A-1

When the flexural reinforcement consists of different bar or wire sizes, the number of bars or wires is computed as the total area of reinforcement divided by the area of the largest bar or wire used (see Figure A-2). The above equation was derived from the Gergely-Lutz[51] expression $w/0.076\beta = f_s\sqrt[3]{d_cA}$, where w is the crack width in units of 0.001 inch, and β is the ratio of the distances to the neutral axis from the extreme tension fiber and from the centroid of the reinforcement. To simplify practical design of beams, an approximate value of 1.2 for β was used in the above equation. The numerical limitations of $z = 175$ and 145 kips/inches for interior and exterior exposure, respectively, correspond to limiting crack widths of 0.016 inch and 0.013 inch. Since the derivation of the original expression, additional tests indicated that the crack width expression is also applicable to one-way slabs, with a value of β of about 1.35. Accordingly, ACI 318–95 Commentary Section R10.6.4 suggested that the maximum value of z for one-way slabs be reduced by the ratio of 1.2/1.35, which yields $z = 156$ kips/inch for interior exposures and 129 kips/inch for exterior exposures. It was assumed that by limiting the crack width to these values, one would achieve corrosion protection. But, to comply with the specified z-value limits, the method essentially encouraged reduction of the reinforcement cover, which could be detrimental to corrosion protection. Furthermore, the method severely penalized structures with covers of more than 2 inches by either reducing the spacing (Figure A-3) or the service load stress of the reinforcement.

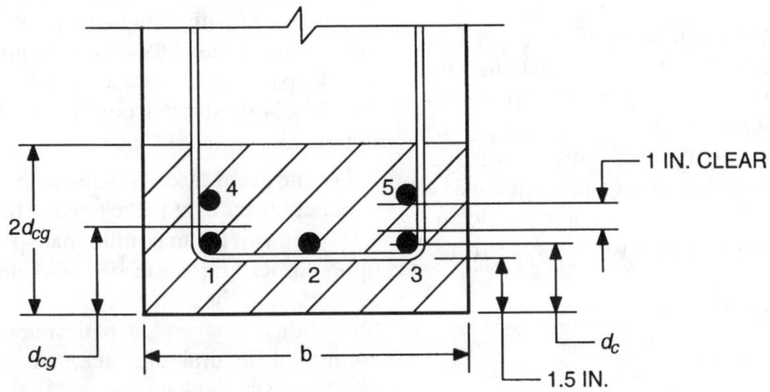

Examples for determining A

1. Bars 1, 2 and 3 are #9 (area = 1.00 in^2)
   Bar 4 and 5 are #8 (area = 0.79 in^2)
   Equivalent no. of #9 bars = (3 × 1.00 + 2 × 0.79)/1.00 = 4.58
   $A = 2d_{cg} \times b/4.58$
   d_{cg} = distance from extreme tension fiber to center of gravity of steel

2. Bars 1, 3, 4 and 5 are #8 (area = 0.79 in^2)
   Bar 2 is #9 (area = 1.00 in^2)
   Equivalent no. of #9 bars = (4 × 0.79 + 1 × 1.00)/1.00 = 4.16
   $A = 2d_{cg} \times b/4.16$
   d_{cg} = distance from extreme tension fiber to center of gravity of steel

EFFECTIVE TENSION AREA

FIGURE A-2

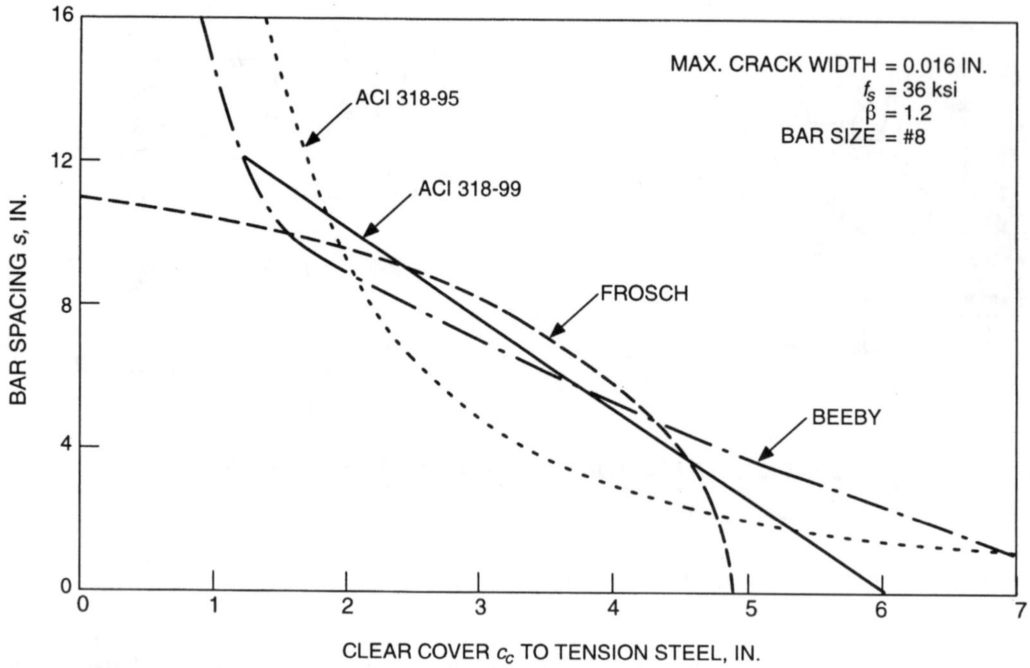

COMPARISON OF MAXIMUM REINFORCEMENT SPACING FOR CRACK CONTROL

FIGURE A-3

The role of cracks in the corrosion of reinforcement has been found to be controversial. Research[52, 53] has shown that corrosion is not clearly correlated with surface crack widths in the range of reinforcement stresses normally found at service load levels. In fact, it is weakly related to the surface crack width limits of 0.013 to 0.016 in. Further, it is a fact that actual crack widths in structures are highly variable. A scatter of the order of ± 50 percent is observed.

Addressing some of the limitations of the previous approach, an equation has been adopted into ACI 318-99, which directly limits the maximum reinforcement spacing. The new approach is intended to control surface cracks to a width that is generally acceptable in practice but may vary widely in a given structure. For this reason, crack widths in the field cannot be predicted using the new ACI 318-99 Equation 10-5. According to the new approach, the spacing of reinforcement closest to a tension surface shall not exceed:

$$s = (540 / f_s) - 2.5c_c$$
$$\leq 12\,(36 / f_s)$$

where:

s = center-to-center spacing of flexural reinforcement nearest to the extreme tension face, inches (where there is only one bar or wire nearest to the extreme tension face, s is the width of the extreme tension face).

f_s = calculated stress in reinforcement at service load computed as the unfactored moment divided by the product of steel area and internal moment arm, which may be taken equal to 60 percent of the specified yield strength of nonprestressed reinforcement, ksi.

c_c = clear cover from the nearest surface in tension to the surface of flexural tension reinforcement, inches.

Figure A-3 compares maximum reinforcement spacing according to the 1999 edition of the code with that of the 1995 edition for slabs with a single layer of reinforcement. Note that the provisions of the 1999 edition (Equation 10-5) significantly relax the spacing requirement for large cover, between 2 inches and 4 inches. Note also that contrary to the 1995 provision, this spacing is independent of the exposure condition.

For the usual case of beams with Grade 60 reinforcement with 2 inches clear cover to the tension face and assuming that $f_s = 0.6 \times 60 = 36$ ksi, the maximum bar spacing is 10 inches. Using the upper limit of Equation 10-5, the maximum spacing allowed, irrespective of the cover, is 12 inches for $f_s = 36$ ksi. The spacing limitation is independent of the bar size used. Thus, for a required amount of flexural reinforcement, this approach would encourage use of smaller bar sizes to satisfy the spacing criteria of Equation 10-5.

Figure A-3 compares the crack control requirements of ACI 318–95 and ACI 318-99, and requirements suggested by Beeby[54] and Frosch.[55] It is clear that the ACI 318–99 approach compares more favorably with other suggested approaches.

11.0. The definition of effective depth, d, has been modified such that d for circular sections is now allowed to be taken no less than 80 percent of the total depth, h. This option was previously allowed only for prestressed concrete sections.

11.1.3. The computation of maximum factored shear force at a critical section away from the support face, as defined in Section 11.1.3.1 for nonprestressed members and Section 11.1.3.2 for prestressed members, is now subject to an additional condition: loads must be applied at or near the top of the member. In Figure A-4, loads are shown acting near the bottom of a beam. The shear force acting on the critical section must include all loads applied below the potential inclined crack. In this case, the critical section must be taken at the face of the support.

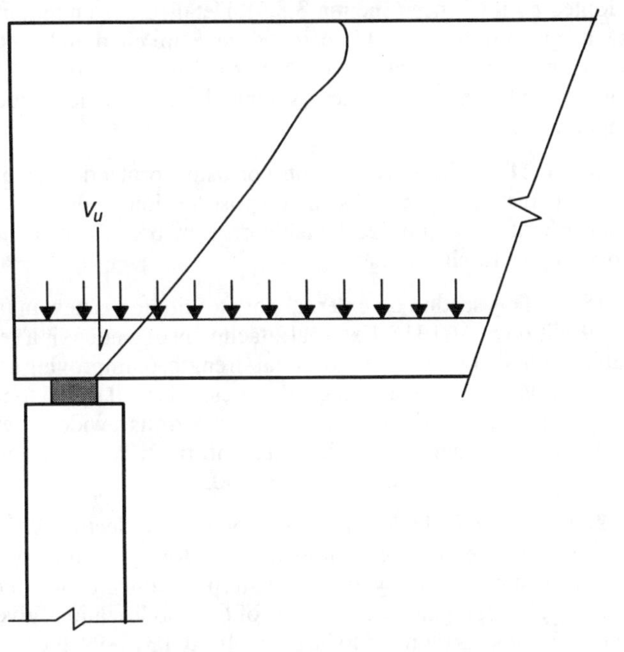

LOCATION OF CRITICAL SECTION FOR SHEAR IN MEMBER LOADED NEAR BOTTOM

FIGURE A-4

11.2.1. In the 1995 edition of ACI 318, reference to torsion was omitted for cases where lightweight concrete affects design values. This has been rectified in ACI 318–99. When lightweight aggregate concrete is used, the required modification to $\sqrt{f'_c}$ of Section 11.2.1.1 or Section 11.2.1.2 has now been made applicable to torsion as well as shear strength.

11.3.3 and 11.5.6.3. ACI 318–95 had no specific provisions for shear strength of circular columns, whereas the 1997 UBC Section 1911.5.6.2 does contain a specific provision. The newly added Section 11.3.3 of ACI 318–99 specifies the computation of the contribution of concrete to the shear strength of a circular member. The newly added Section 11.5.6.3 specifies how to compute the contribution of shear reinforcement to shear strength when circular hoops, ties or spirals are used. The ACI 318–99 provision is somewhat different from the existing 1997 UBC provision.

11.5.1. "Spirals, circular ties, or hoops" has now been added to Section 11.5.1.1 (which reads: "Shear reinforcement consisting of the following shall be permitted:"). "Spirals" has now been deleted from Section 11.5.1.2 (which reads: "For nonprestressed members, shear reinforcement shall be permitted to also consist of:").

13.3.6.4. In slabs with beams between supports, special top and bottom slab reinforcement is required to be provided at exterior corners. ACI 318–95 allowed the special reinforcement to be placed in two layers parallel to the sides of the slab "in either the top or bottom of the slab." ACI 318–99 has switched to "both the top and bottom of the slab" to reflect the intent of ACI 318 editions prior to 1995.

13.3.8.6. In slabs with shearheads and in lift-slab construction, in some instances, there is sufficient clearance so that the bonded bottom bars required for structural integrity can pass under shearheads and through the column. In such a situation, this section now requires these bars to pass through the column. Only where clearance under the shearhead is inadequate, the bottom bars may pass through holes in the shearhead arms or within the perimeter of the lifting collar, but must remain as close to the column as practicable.

13.5.1.2. This section requires that, for lateral loads, analysis of frames must take into account effects of cracking and reinforcement on stiffness of frame members. The word "unbraced" before "frames" that used to exist in prior editions of the code has been removed to clarify that slab stiffness reduction associated with cracking is not limited to sway frames. Important changes have been made in the commentary to this section. Prior text indicating that Equation 9-7, giving effective stiffness, can be used in lateral load analysis has been removed. It is a fact that even in the best of environments, Equation 9-7 is not likely to provide an accurate assessment of stiffness. An addition has been made to note that plate-bending finite element models, effective beam width models, and equivalent frame models can be used to model lateral load stiffness. The difference between stiffnesses of post-tensioned and non-post-tensioned slabs has been noted. Clarification has been provided to indicate that lower bound stiffnesses are to be used for estimating lateral drift and P-delta effects, and that a range of stiffnesses should be investigated where the slab-column frame interacts with other elements.

R13.5.3.3. A new sentence has been added, that reads: "Interior, exterior, and corner supports refer to slab-column connections for which the critical perimeter for rectangular columns has four, three or two sides, respectively." This has been done to define an exterior column with a cantilevered slab as either an interior or edge support, depending on whether the critical section has three or four sides. ACI 318-99 Section 11.12.5 appears to indicate that a cantilever must extend at least 10 times the slab thickness from the column face for it to be counted as a cantilever.

14.8. An alternative to the requirements of ACI 318–99 Section 10.10 is presented. The UBC, since its 1988 edition, has had a section on alternate design of slender walls, based on experimental research reported in Reference 56 that was not contained in ACI 318 until its 1999 edition. The new Section 14.8 is based on the 1997 UBC Section 1914.8. The following modifications have been included:

Changes have been made in nomenclature and wording to comply with the ACI 318 style.

The whole procedure has been limited to out-of-plane flexural effects on simply supported wall panels with maximum moments and deflections occurring at midspan.

The procedure has been converted from one based on working stresses to one based on factored loads.

The procedure has been made as compatible as possible with the procedure for obtaining the cracking moment and the effective moment of inertia in Section 9.5.2.3 of ACI 318.

The alternate design of slender walls in Section 14.8 is subject to the many limitations given in Section 14.8.2. The reader is referred to Chapter 23 of Reference 26 for a description and discussion of this alternate method. Example 23.4 of Reference 26 illustrates the design of a nonprestressed precast wall panel by the alternate design method.

18.8.3. The joint ACI-ASCE Committee 423 on prestressed concrete has long recommended the waiving of the ACI 318 requirement for a total amount of prestressed and nonprestressed reinforcement sufficient to develop 1.2 times the cracking load for two-way slab systems with unbonded tendons.[57] ACI 318-99 Section 18.8.3 now permits the waiving of this requirement for two-way, unbonded post-tensioned slabs.

18.9.3.3. ACI 318–95 requirements for minimum bonded reinforcement in negative moment areas of two-way flat plates with unbonded tendons result in less reinforcement than recommended by research at interior columns supporting rectangular panels. Section 18.9.3.3 has been revised (Figure A-5) to increase the minimum reinforcement requirement over interior columns for rectangular panels in one direction. For square panels, the revision doubles the minimum reinforcement requirement over exterior columns normal to the slab edge.

18.13, 18.14, 18.15. Section 18.13 of ACI 318–95 has been modernized and expanded into three sections. They apply to post-tensioned anchorages. There have not been many serious problems with monostrand tendons meeting the PTI Specifications,[58] so the requirements of that specification are included by reference in Section 18.14.

Much of the new provision is now directed at the proper anchorage of large multistrand post-tensioning tendons using the very compact proprietary anchorage systems now in widespread use. Such tendons have been widely used in bridge systems. A comprehensive study was summarized in NCHRP (National Cooperative Highway Research Program) Report 356,[59] and design and construction provisions were adopted in the 1994 AASHTO Standard Specifications for Highway Bridges.[50] Previous AASHTO Specifications and ACI Building Codes gave little guidance to control of bearing, bursting and spalling stresses in the tendon anchorage areas. Most of the modern compact tendon anchorage devices for multiple strands require substantial confining reinforcement immediately around the anchor device and many require supplemental face steel in the anchorage region to fully develop strength and control cracking.

The growing usage of multistrand tendons in building-type structures and the experience of AASHTO made it timely to expand ACI 318 coverage in this area. It was decided by Committee 318 not to utilize the full AASHTO provisions but to condense them for building-type applications. The AASHTO acceptance test procedures for special anchorage devices are adopted by reference (Section 3.8.5). Detailed design requirements given in AASHTO Specifications[56] are cited in the ACI 318 Commentary for guidance. This expansion of Section 18.13 should result in more consistent, safer and better detailed tendon anchorage zones.

18.16, 18.17. The sections on corrosion protection of unbonded prestressing tendons and on post-tensioning ducts have been rewritten to provide better corrosion protection of unbonded prestressing strands.

18.22. This section on external post-tensioning is new in the 1999 edition of ACI 318. External attachment of tendons is a versatile method of providing additional strength, or improving serviceability, or both, in existing structures. It is well suited to repair or upgrade of existing structures and permits a wide variety of tendon arrangements. Additional information on external post-tensioning is given in Reference 60.

22.5.6. In ACI 318-95, there is a footnote to Section 22.5.1 stating that the equations in those sections for nominal flexural and shear strengths apply to normal-strength concrete only. For lightweight aggregate concrete, one of two modifications given in that footnote is required to be made. In ACI 318–99, the footnote has been deleted, and the substance of the footnote has been moved to the new Section 22.5.6.

22.10. This new section, for the first time in the ACI 318 standard, addresses the use of plain concrete elements in structures located in regions of high seismic risk or assigned to high seismic design categories. The new requirements, based on similar provisions in the *National Building Code* and the *Standard Building Code*, prohibits such use, except in three specific cases cited. The exceptions are:

1. In detached one- and two-family dwellings not exceeding three stories in height and constructed with wood or steel stud bearing walls, the following are permitted:
   a. plain concrete footings supporting walls, columns or pedestals; and

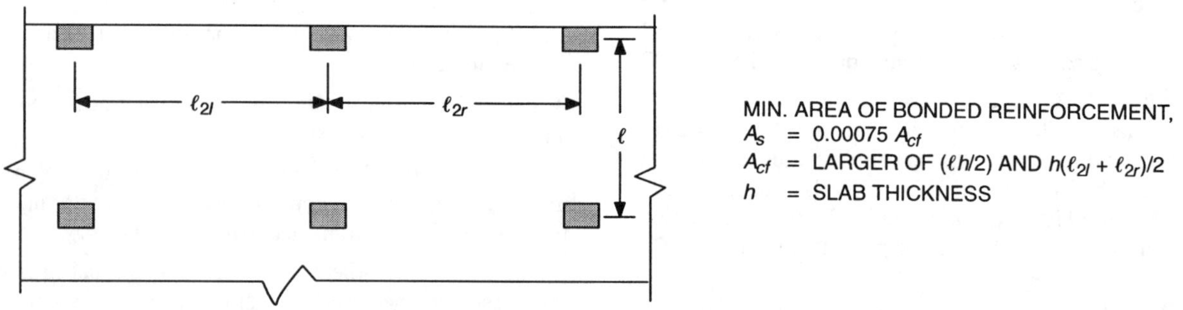

BONDED REINFORCEMENT AT POST-TENSIONED FLAT PLATE—COLUMN JOINTS

FIGURE A-5

b. plain concrete foundation or basement walls, provided the wall is not less than $7^1/_2$ inches thick, and it retains no more than 4 feet of unbalanced fill.

2. In structures other than those covered by exception 1 above, plain concrete footings supporting walls are permitted, provided the footing has at least two continuous No. 4 longitudinal reinforcing bars that provide an area of steel of not less than 0.002 times the gross transverse cross-sectional area of the footing. Continuity of reinforcement must be provided at corners and intersections.

B.9.2. The only factored load combination specifically mentioned in ACI 318–95 Section B.9.2 is the gravity load combination 1.4D + 1.7L. This section has been deleted because it was never the intention to have Appendix B apply only to the gravity load case.

C.1.1.3(c) In regions of high seismic risk, members resisting earthquake forces without transverse reinforcement conforming to Section 21.4.4 are permitted by this ACI 318–95 section to be designed for a reduced ϕ-factor of 0.5. The corresponding permission in Chapter 9 was deleted from ACI 318–95. So this section has now been deleted from ACI 318–99.

C.1.1.4. Changes have been made in this section to reflect the changes made in Section 9.3.4 of ACI 318–99.

C.1.2. This new section addresses the design of post-tensioned anchorage zones.

CHAPTER 21

The adoption of ACI 318-99 by reference into the 2000 IBC results in the following important differences between Section 1921, Reinforced Concrete Structures Resisting Forces Induced by Earthquake Motions, of the last two editions of the NBC and the SBC and the 1997 edition of the UBC on the one hand and the corresponding provisions of the 2000 IBC on the other:

9.3.4. This change, although made in Chapter 9, is placed here, because it is directly related to the new ACI 318-99 Section 21.7 discussed below. There is a new requirement that the strength reduction factor for shear in diaphragms shall not exceed the minimum strength reduction factor for shear used for vertical components of the primary lateral-force-resisting system. This is an attempt to prevent yielding in the diaphragm before yielding in elements of the lateral-force-resisting system. Also, the strength reduction factor of 0.85 for shear in joints has now been extended to shear in diagonally reinforced coupling beams. The requirements apply to structures that rely on special moment resisting frames or special reinforced concrete shear walls to resist earthquake effects.

21.0. The definitions of reinforcement ratios ρ_h and ρ_v have been clarified in a change that has been badly needed for quite some time.

21.1. A quantity termed "design displacement" has now been defined. The design displacement is an estimate of the maximum lateral displacement that is expected in the design-basis earthquake. The design displacement is calculated using static or dynamic linear-elastic analysis under code-specified actions considering effects of cracked sections, effects of vertical forces acting through lateral displacements, and modification factors to account for expected inelastic response. The design displacement generally is a few times larger than the displacement calculated from design-level forces applied to a linear-elastic model of the building.

In terms of the 2000 IBC, the design displacement is

$$\delta_x = C_d \delta_{xe} / I_E \qquad \text{(Equation 16-46)}$$

where:

C_d = deflection amplification factor given in the 2000 IBC Table 1617.6,

δ_{xe} = deflections determined by an elastic analysis of the lateral-force-resisting system under the code-prescribed seismic forces, and

I_E = occupancy importance factor determined in accordance with the 2000 IBC Section 1616.2

In terms of the 1997 UBC, the design displacement is the Maximum Inelastic Response Displacement

$$\Delta_M = 0.7 R \Delta_s$$

where:

R = response modification factor given in the 1997 UBC Table 16-N,

Δ_s = deflections determined by an elastic analysis of the lateral-force-resisting system under the code-prescribed seismic forces.

Under the definition of seismic hook, the use of a 90-degree hook instead of a 135-degree hook is now permitted in circular column hoops.

ACI 318–99 has also introduced terminology that defines framing types on the basis of anticipated levels of inelastic response in a manner that is compatible with terminology commonly used in model codes. Thus, three categories of structural walls have been defined: ordinary reinforced concrete structural wall, ordinary plain concrete structural wall, and special reinforced concrete structural wall. See earlier discussion on the 2000 IBC Section 1910.

21.2.1. For compatibility with terminology commonly used in recent editions of U. S. model codes other than the UBC, provisions applicable in regions of low, moderate and high seismic risk are now made applicable to structures assigned to low, intermediate and high seismic performance or design categories, respectively. Where the design seismic forces are computed using provisions for intermediate or special concrete systems, the requirements of Chapter 21 for intermediate or special systems, as applicable, must be satisfied, irrespective of the seismicity of the site where the structural system may be used. These sections also specify that in regions of moderate seismic risk, intermediate or special moment frames, or ordinary or special reinforced concrete structural walls must be used to resist forces induced by earthquake motions. In regions of high seismic risk, special moment frames, special reinforced concrete structural walls, and diaphragms and trusses complying with ACI 318–99 Sections 21.2 through 21.7 must be used to resist forces induced by earthquake motions. See earlier discussion of IBC Section 1910.

21.2.6. According to Section 21.2.6.1 of ACI 318–95, reinforcement resisting earthquake-induced flexural and axial forces in frame members or in wall boundary elements are permitted to be spliced using welded splices or mechanical connectors conforming to Section 12.14.3.3 or Section 12.14.3.4 (a full-welded splice or a full mechanical connection must be able to develop at least 125 percent of the specified yield strength, f_y, of the bar) "provided not more than alternate bars in each layer of longitudinal reinforcement are spliced at a section and the center-to-center distance between splices of adjacent bars is 24 inches or more measured along the longitudinal axis of the member." The staggering requirement, the entire text within quotes in the above sentence, was dropped from the 1997 UBC and has now been dropped from ACI 318–99. However, other requirements were added to the 1997 UBC, as indicated below.

Welded splices or mechanical splices that just meet the requirements of ACI 318 Section 12.14.3.3 or Section 12.14.3.4, respectively (which are now defined as Type 1 splices in the 1997 UBC as well as in ACI 318–99) are not allowed on billet steel A615 or low-alloy A706 reinforcement within an anticipated plastic hinge region, within a distance of one beam depth on either side of the plastic hinge region or within a joint, in Seismic Zones 2, 3 and 4. In those locations, in regions of moderate to high seismicity, only Type 2 splices are allowed. A Type 2 splice, in the 1997 UBC, is a mechanical connection that develops in tension the lesser of 95 percent of the ultimate tensile strength or 160 percent of the specified yield strength, f_y, of the bar.

ACI 318 Section 21.2.5.2 requires that for billet steel A615 Grades 40 and 60 reinforcement, the actual yield strength based on mill tests shall not exceed the specified yield strength by more than 18,000 psi, and that retests shall not exceed this value by more than an additional 3000 psi.

A similar requirement is already part of the ASTM specifications for low-alloy A706 reinforcement. However, even with these safeguards in place, steel that meets the above requirements can have an actual yield strength as much as 135 percent of the specified value. Thus, a splice that is capable of developing just 125 percent of the specified yield strength of the spliced reinforcing bars may not be sufficient to ensure yielding of the reinforcement prior to splice failure. This is what prompted the definition of the new Type 2 splice and the requirement that only these splices be allowed in regions of potential plastic hinging. Since A706 steel bars are incapable of developing 160 percent of the specified yield strength before they fail in tension, the 95 percent of ultimate tensile strength requirement was added.

In ACI 318–99, the definition of a Type 2 splice has been modified to the following: "Type 2 mechanical splices shall develop the specified tensile strength of the spliced bar." Locations where welded and Type 1 mechanical splices are not allowed have also been modified as follows: "within a distance equal to twice the member depth from the column or beam face or from sections where yielding of the reinforcement is likely to occur as a result of inelastic lateral displacements." Type 2 mechanical splices can be used at any location.

21.4.2.2. The so-called strong column-weak beam requirement (Figure A-6) has been changed in a number of significant ways. The check is now in terms of nominal rather than design moment strengths. The comparison of moment strengths is now permitted to be made at the face of the joint rather than at the center of the joint. When determining the nominal flexural strength of a girder section in negative bending (top in tension), the contribution of longitudinal reinforcement contained within an effective flange width of slab that acts monolithically with the girder (ACI 318–99 Section 8.10) is now required to be included. Example 3 illustrates the new code requirements for strong column-weak beam design.

21.4.3.2. This requires that closely spaced transverse reinforcement be provided along the length of longitudinal bar lap splices in columns. Text has been added to Commentary Section R21.4.3 to indicate that this is because of the uncertainty in moment distributions along the height, and the need for confinement of lap splices subject to stress reversals. Similar confinement has been required for lap splices of beam bars for quite some time (ACI 318 Section 21.3.2.3).

21.4.4.1. If the thickness of the concrete outside the confining transverse reinforcement in a column core exceeds 4 inches, additional transverse reinforcement is now required by this section. This change represents a slight modification of a requirement already in the 1997 UBC. The new ACI 318 Commentary Section R21.4.4.1 explains that an unreinforced shell may spall as a column deforms to resist earthquake effects. Separation of portions of the shell from the core caused by local spalling

$$(M_{ct} + M_{cb}) \geq (6/5)\,(M_{gl} + M_{gr})$$

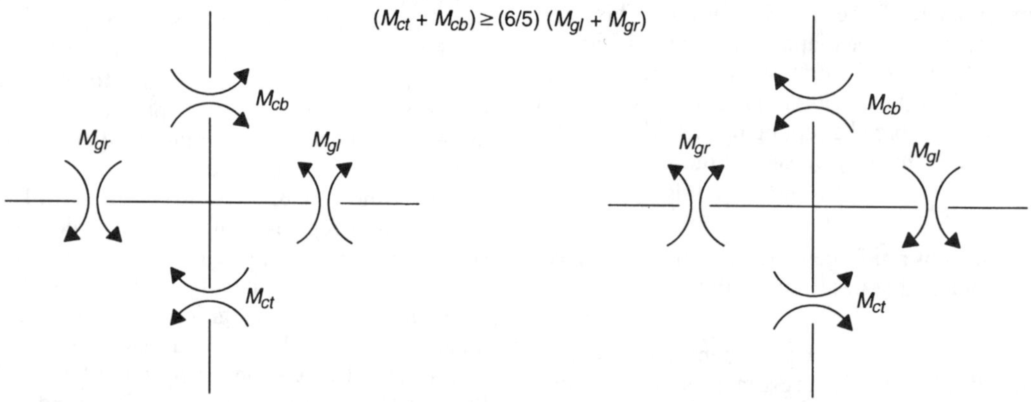

1. Subscripts *c* and *b* refer to column and girder, respectively.
Subscripts *l*, *r*, *t* and *b* refer to left support, right support, top of column, and bottom of column, respectively.

STRONG COLUMN-WEAK BEAM FRAME REQUIREMENTS

FIGURE A-6

constitutes a falling hazard. The additional reinforcement is intended to reduce this hazard.

21.4.4.2. This permits longitudinal spacing of transverse reinforcement in regions of potential plastic hinging to be increased from the previous maximum value of 4 inches to a variable, S_x, which may be as much as 6 inches in cases where horizontal spacing between hoop legs or cross ties is reduced from the maximum permitted spacing of 14 inches (Figure A-7). A new restriction has been added requiring that the transverse reinforcement spacing does not exceed 6 times the diameter of the longitudinal reinforcement, in order to prevent the compression buckling of such reinforcement.

21.6.5. A significant change has been made in the design procedure for shear walls in regions of high seismic risk (or assigned to high seismic performance or design categories), subjected to combined bending moments and axial forces.

Design requirements contained in ACI 318 through its 1995 edition for reinforced concrete shear walls in regions of high seismicity are considered by many to be overly conservative. According to these requirements, a shear wall must be provided with boundary elements at the ends if the extreme compressive fiber stress caused by the entire factored axial load tributary to the wall, and the entire factored overturning moment at the base of the wall equals or exceeds $0.2f'_c$ (f'_c = specified compressive strength of concrete). The stresses are calculated using a linearly elastic model of the shear wall and gross section properties. Boundary elements, where required, must be designed to carry the entire factored axial load tributary to the wall, and the entire factored overturning moment at the base of the wall by tension and compression in the boundary elements. In other words, the boundary elements are required to be designed ignoring the shear wall web. This gives rise to oversized boundary elements typically containing a large number of longitudinal reinforcing bars. The 1995 and prior editions of ACI 318 further require that these bars be tied and cross-tied at a maximum longitudinal spacing of 4 inches (or one-quarter the minimum plan dimension of the boundary element, whichever is smaller), with every other bar laterally supported by a corner of a tie or crosstie. All these requirements result in boundary elements that are uneconomical, and also difficult to construct.

The ACI 318 provisions so far have also been less than conservative with respect to shear. This is because shear walls with strong boundary elements have large flexural strengths, as a result of which they attract high shear forces in an earthquake. In view of this and the fact that the shear design of shear walls is based on shear forces obtained from analysis under code-prescribed seismic design forces, the strong boundary elements make brittle shear failure of shear walls in earthquakes more likely.

The 1994 UBC introduced new design provisions applicable in Seismic Zones 3 and 4 for shear walls under flexure and axial loads, in an attempt to remedy the problems indicated above. The 1994 provisions were revised in a number of important ways for the 1997 UBC.

ACI 318–99 has adopted a design procedure for shear walls in regions of high seismic risk (or in buildings assigned to high

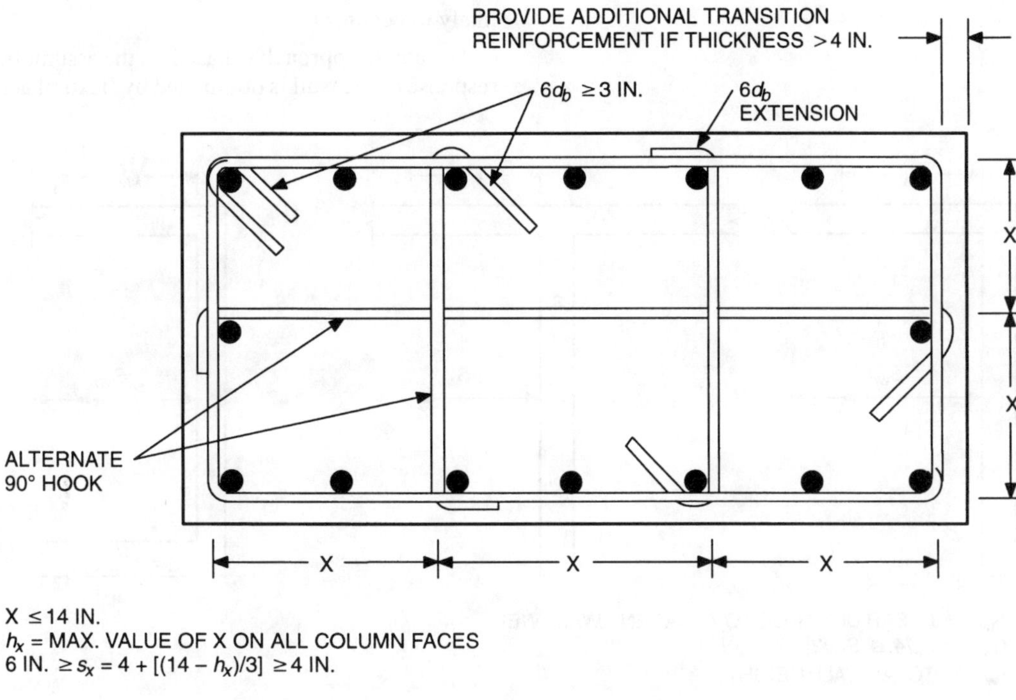

TRANSVERSE REINFORCEMENT IN COLUMNS OF SPECIAL MOMENT FRAMES

FIGURE A-7

seismic performance or design categories), subjected to combined bending moments and axial forces, that represents an evolution of the 1997 UBC design procedure. The ACI procedure uses a displacement-based design in which the neutral axis depth, rather than compressive strains in the concrete, is the quantity that drives the trigger for requiring confined boundary elements. The ACI procedure is significantly simpler and, based on limited studies, is expected to produce shear wall designs remarkably similar to those of the 1997 UBC, except possibly under high axial loads. For shear walls subjected to high axial loads, the ACI 318–99 procedure appears to be more conservative than the 1997 UBC procedure. More detailed studies still need to be carried out before definitive conclusions can be reached concerning comparisons between the two methods. By virtue of the adoption of ACI 318–99 by reference into the first edition of the IBC, the ACI 318–99 design procedure will also be the design procedure of the 2000 IBC for shear walls in buildings assigned to high seismic performance or design categories. A part of the shear wall design procedure of ACI 318–95 has also been retained in ACI 318–99 as an alternative as being conservative as well as applicable in many situations where the displacement-based approach is not truly applicable.

In a major departure from the past, Section 21.6.5.1 permits the entire section of a shear wall, including its web, to be designed under flexural and axial loads as a short column section, by Sections 10.2 and 10.3. Sections 10.3.6 on slenderness effects and 10.2.2 on nonlinear strain distribution do not apply.

Section 21.6.5.2 defines effective flange widths of flanged sections as shown in Figure A-8.

Section 21.6.6.2 requires parts of compression zones to be reinforced as special boundary elements if

$$c \geq \frac{\ell_w}{600(\delta_u/h_w)}$$

$\delta_u/h_w \geq 0.007$

where:

c = distance from extreme compression fiber to neutral axis per ACI 318-99 Section 10.2.7, calculated for the factored axial force and the corresponding nominal moment strength, consistent with the design displacement δ_u, resulting in the largest neutral axis depth

ℓ_w = length of entire wall or segment of wall considered in direction of shear force

δ_u = design displacement defined in Item 3 of this section

and

h_w = height of entire wall or segment of wall considered.

Typically, the reinforcement for a shear wall section is determined first for the combined effects of bending and axial load, and shear forces in accordance with the design load combinations. The distance, c, can then be obtained from a strain compatibility analysis for each load combination that includes seismic effects, considering sidesways to the left and to the right. The largest c is used in Equation 21-8 to determine if special boundary elements are required.

Where special boundary elements are required, they must extend horizontally from the extreme compression fiber a distance not less than the larger of $c - 0.1\ell_w$ and $c/2$ (Figure A-9). In the vertical direction, the special boundary elements must extend from the critical section a distance greater than or equal to the larger of ℓ_w or $M_u/4V_u$ where M_u and V_u are the factored overturning moment and the factored shear force at the base. This distance is based on upper bound estimates of plastic hinge lengths, and extends beyond the zone over which concrete spalling is likely to occur.

The above approach is based on the assumption that inelastic response of the wall is dominated by flexural action at a critical,

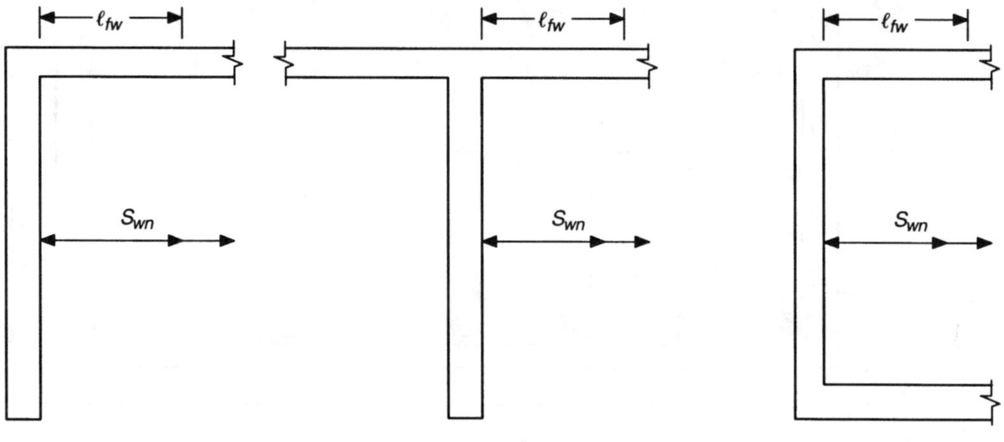

S_{wn} = CLEAR DISTANCE TO ADJACENT WALL WEB
ℓ_{fw} = $h_w/4 \leq S_{wn}/2$
h_w = TOTAL WALL HEIGHT

EFFECTIVE FLANGE WIDTHS FOR FLANGED SHEAR WALLS

FIGURE A-8

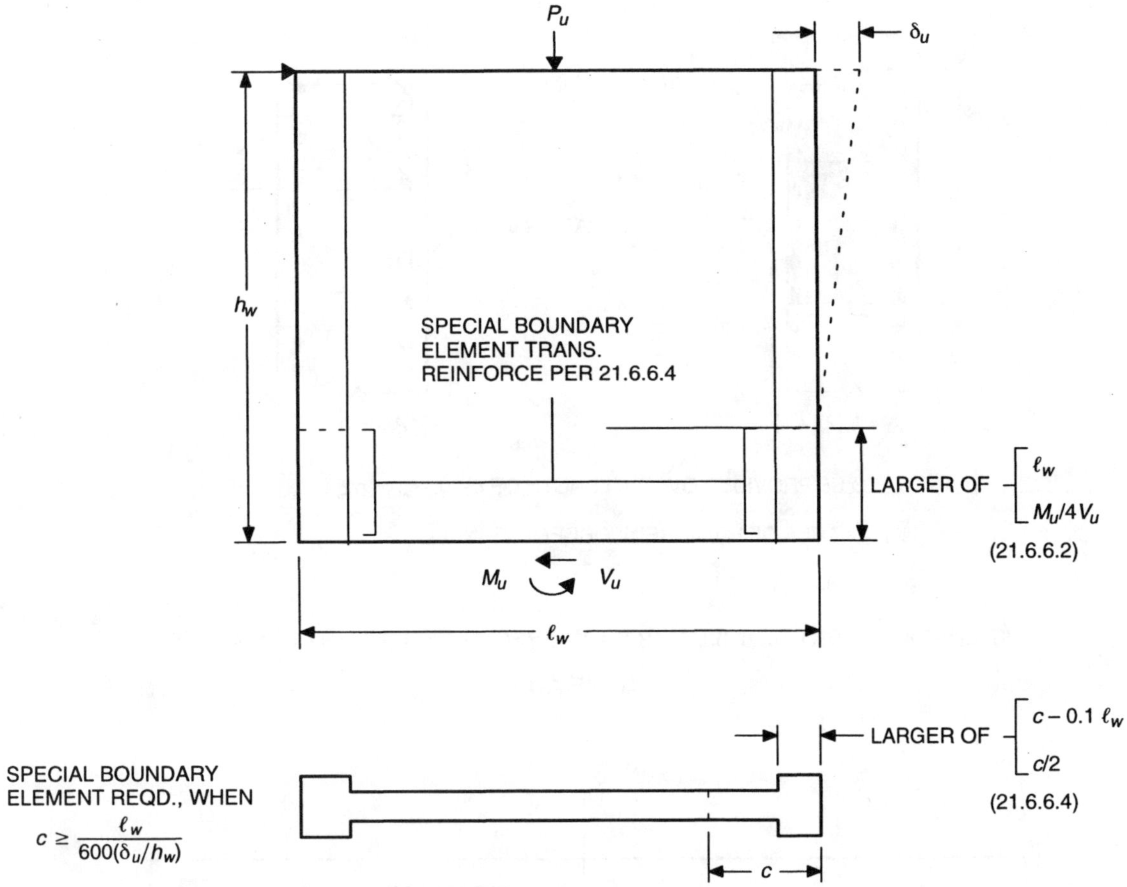

SHEAR WALL BOUNDARY ELEMENT REQUIREMENTS

FIGURE A-9

yielding section. The wall must be proportioned so that the critical section occurs where intended.

The ACI 318–95 trigger for requiring special boundary elements, based on elastically computed stresses under P_u and M_u, using gross cross-sectional properties at shear wall edges, has been retained as an alternative (Section 21.6.6.3) because it is conservative as well as applicable in many situations where the above displacement-based approach is not truly applicable. It is important to note, however, that special boundary elements, whether triggered by the neutral axis based criterion of Section 21.6.6.2 or the fictitious compression stress based criterion of Section 21.6.6.3, are to be proportioned and detailed according to the same criterion of Section 21.6.6.4. The prior requirement of having to design special boundary elements to carry the entire P_u and M_u is no longer part of ACI 318.

In flanged sections, the special boundary element must include the effective flange width in compression and must extend at least 12 inches into the web. Transverse reinforcement in a special boundary element must be special column-end transverse reinforcement required by ACI 318–99 Sections 21.4.4.1 through 21.4.4.3, except that Equation 21-3 does not apply. At the wall base, special boundary element transverse reinforcement must extend into the supporting element for one development length of the largest longitudinal bar in the special boundary element. If the special boundary element terminates on a footing or mat, the special transverse reinforcement must extend at least 12 inches into the footing or mat.

Horizontal reinforcement in the wall web must be anchored within the confined core of the special boundary element, to develop full f_y at the face of such element.

Mechanical and welded splices as well as lap splices are allowed in the longitudinal reinforcement of the boundary element.

Section 21.6.6.5 contains an additional important requirement. Where special boundary elements are not required, if the longitudinal reinforcement ratio at the wall boundary (Figure A-10) exceeds $400/f_y$, a non-special boundary element must be provided at that boundary. The horizontal and vertical extents of this element are the same as those of a special boundary element. The transverse reinforcement needs to satisfy only ACI 318–99 Sections 21.4.4.1(3) and 21.4.4.3. The maximum spacing of such reinforcement is 8 inches.

Where no special boundary element is required, the horizontal wall reinforcement must be anchored in one of two ways shown in Figure A-11. This requirement may be waived if the nominal shear stress in a shear wall section is less than $\sqrt{f'_c}$.

See Example 4 in Part 3 of this chapter.

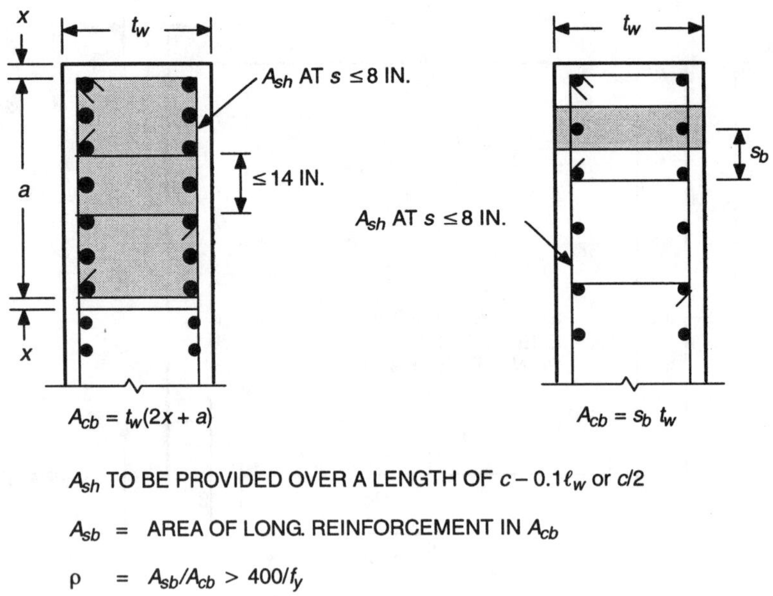

REINFORCEMENT DETAILS FOR "NON-SPECIAL" BOUNDARY ELEMENTS

FIGURE A-10

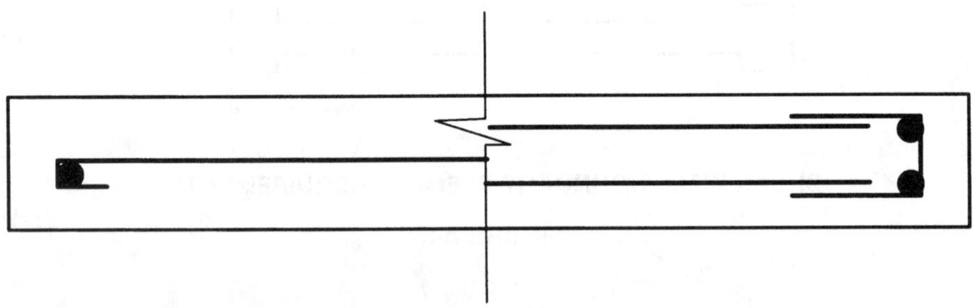

ANCHORAGE OF HORIZONTAL WALL REINFORCEMENT

FIGURE A-11

21.6.7. ACI 318–99 has adopted the 1997 UBC provisions on coupling beams with a few significant modifications. The 1997 UBC requires that coupling beams with $\ell_n/d<4$ and with factored shear force V_u exceeding $4\sqrt{f'_c}\ b_w d$ be reinforced with two intersecting groups of symmetrical diagonal bars. Experiments show that diagonal reinforcement is effective only if the bars are placed with a large inclination. Therefore, ACI 318–99 restricts diagonally-oriented reinforcement to coupling beams having aspect ratio $\ell_n/d<4$.

In the opinion of ACI committee 318, coupling beams with an aspect ratio, ℓ_n/d, between 2 and 4 are not deep enough to merit the mandatory requirement of diagonally-oriented reinforcement. Thus, ACI 318–99 specifies that coupling beams with $\ell_n/d<2$ and with V_u exceeding $4\sqrt{f'_c}\ b_w d$ must be reinforced with two intersecting groups of diagonally placed bars "symmetrical about the midspan unless it can be shown that loss of stiffness and strength of the coupling beams will not impair the vertical load carrying capacity of the structure, egress from the structure, or the integrity of the nonstructural components and their connection to the structure." The escape clause is incorporated from the 1997 NEHRP Provisions.[58]

Also, the 1997 UBC requires that reinforcement parallel and transverse to the longitudinal axis be provided and, as a minimum, conform to Sections 1910.5, 1911.8.9 and 1911.8.10. ACI 318–99 omits Section 10.5 (same as UBC Section 1910.5 — Minimum Reinforcement of Flexural members) from the corresponding list, because when diagonally-oriented reinforcement is used, the function of the additional reinforcement specified is to contain the concrete outside the diagonal cores in the event of damage caused by earthquake excitation.

The 1997 UBC requires that each diagonal consist of a minimum of four bars assembled in a core with a lateral dimension of each side not less than $b_w/2$ or 4 inches where b_w is the width of the coupling beam. ACI 318–99 requires the four bars to be assembled in a core having sides measured to the outside of transverse reinforcement of no less than $b_w/2$ perpendicular to the plane of the beam and $b_w/5$ in the plane of the beam and perpendicular to the diagonal bars (Figure A-12).

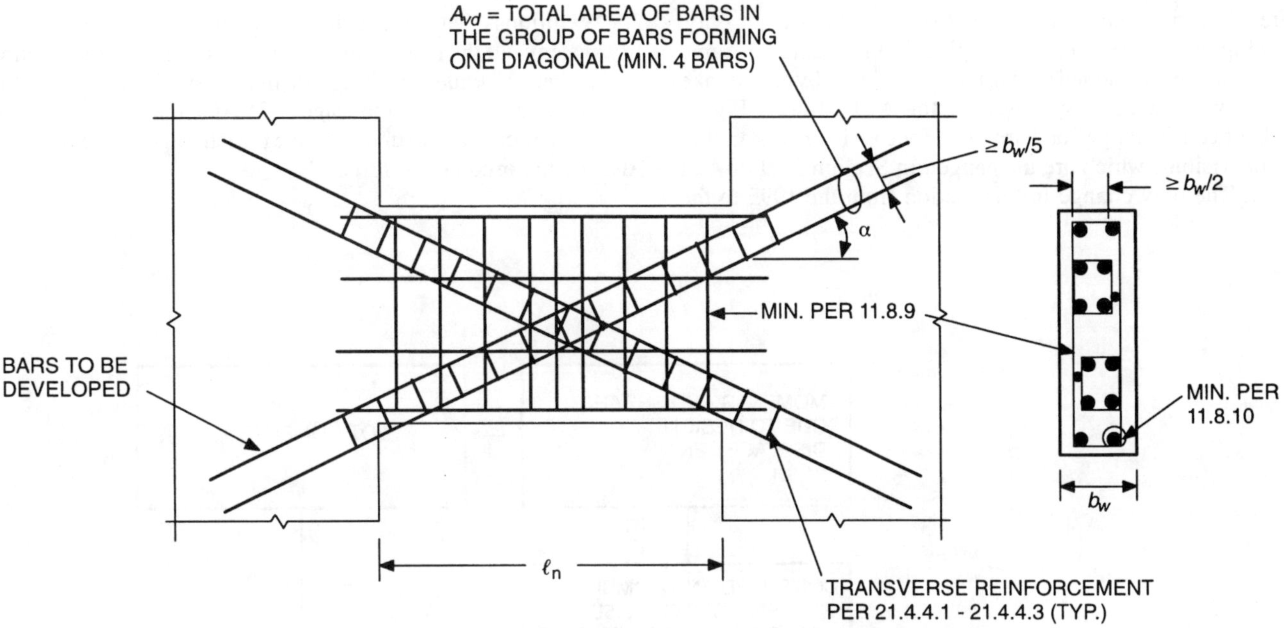

COUPLING BEAM WITH DIAGONALLY ORIENTED REINFORCMENT

FIGURE A-12

21.7. Diaphragm design provisions for structures in regions of high seismic risk (or assigned to high seismic performance or design categories) have been completely and extensively rewritten in ACI 318–99. The 1997 UBC allows a cast-in-place topping on a precast floor system to serve as the diaphragm, provided the cast-in-place topping acting alone is proportioned and detailed to resist the design forces. ACI 318–99 allows this design option, but also allows composite design of the cast-in-place topping and the precast floor system. There is a new requirement that reinforcement in the topping must resist the entire in-plane shear.

It is explained in ACI 318–99 Commentary Section R21.7.7 that according to typical construction practice, the topping slabs are scored immediately above the joints between the flanges of adjacent precast floor members to direct the paths of shrinkage cracks. As a result, critical sections of the diaphragm are cracked under service loads, and the contribution of the concrete to the shear strength of the diaphragm may have already been reduced before the design earthquake occurs.

There are specific limitations on diaphragm reinforcement in Section 21.7.5.1. Minimum reinforcement ratios for diaphragms correspond to the required amount of temperature and shrinkage reinforcement (ACI 318 Section 7.12). The maximum spacing of 18 inches is intended to control the widths of inclined cracks. Minimum average prestress requirements (Section 7.12.3) are considered to be adequate to limit the crack widths in post-tensioned floor systems; therefore, the maximum spacing requirements do not apply to these systems.

The minimum spacing requirement for welded wire fabric in topping slabs on precast floor systems is explained in the ACI 318 Commentary Section R21.7.5. Why the minimum spacing requirements do not apply to diaphragms reinforced with individual bars is also explained.

Section 21.7.5.2 imposes a maximum limit on stress due to design seismic forces in bonded prestressing tendons used as primary reinforcement in diaphragm chords or collectors. This is intended to avoid wide cracks in the boundary elements. Precompression from unbonded tendons is permitted to resist diaphragm design forces if a complete load path is provided.

The strength reduction factor for shear in diaphragms must not exceed the minimum strength reduction factor for shear used for vertical components of the primary lateral-force-resisting system, as mentioned in Item 1 of this section.

21.8. The new Section 21.8 giving requirements for foundations supporting buildings assigned to high seismic performance or design categories was added to ACI 318 in 1999. The section represents a consensus of a minimum level of good practice in designing and detailing concrete foundations including piles and drilled piers and caissons. It is generally desirable that inelastic response in strong ground shaking occurs above the foundations, as repairs to foundations can be extremely difficult and expensive. Section 1805.9 of the 2000 IBC requires that for structures assigned to SDC D, E and F, provisions of ACI 318 Sections 21.8.1 to 21.8.3 apply when not in conflict with the provisions of Section 1805. Section 1807.2.23.2, SDC D, E and F, similarly requires that the provisions of ACI 318 Section 21.8.4 apply when not in conflict with the provisions of Sections 1807 to 1811. In both cases Group R Division 3 or Group U Division 1 Occupancies of light frame construction two stories or less in height are exempt. In both Sections 1805.9 and 1807.2.23.2, a minimum value of 3000 psi is imposed on the specified compressive strength of concrete, to conform to the ACI 318 Chapter 21 restriction on the strength of concrete used in members resisting earthquake-induced forces.

21.9. The collapse of at least two parking structures during the 1994 Northridge earthquake could be attributed primarily to the failure of interior columns designed to carry gravity loads only. Following the experience, the detailing requirements for frame members not proportioned to resist forces induced by earthquake motions were extensively rewritten for ACI 318–95. Figure A-13 has been developed and provided for ease in understanding these provisions, which are unchanged in Section 21.9 of ACI 318–99. The only change in this section from the 1995 to the 1999 edition is that deformation compatibility between the gravity system and the lateral-force-resisting system is now required to be checked under the design displacement defined in Section 21.1 (see earlier discussion, page 257). ACI 318–95 required this check to be carried out under "twice the lateral displacements under the factored lateral forces."

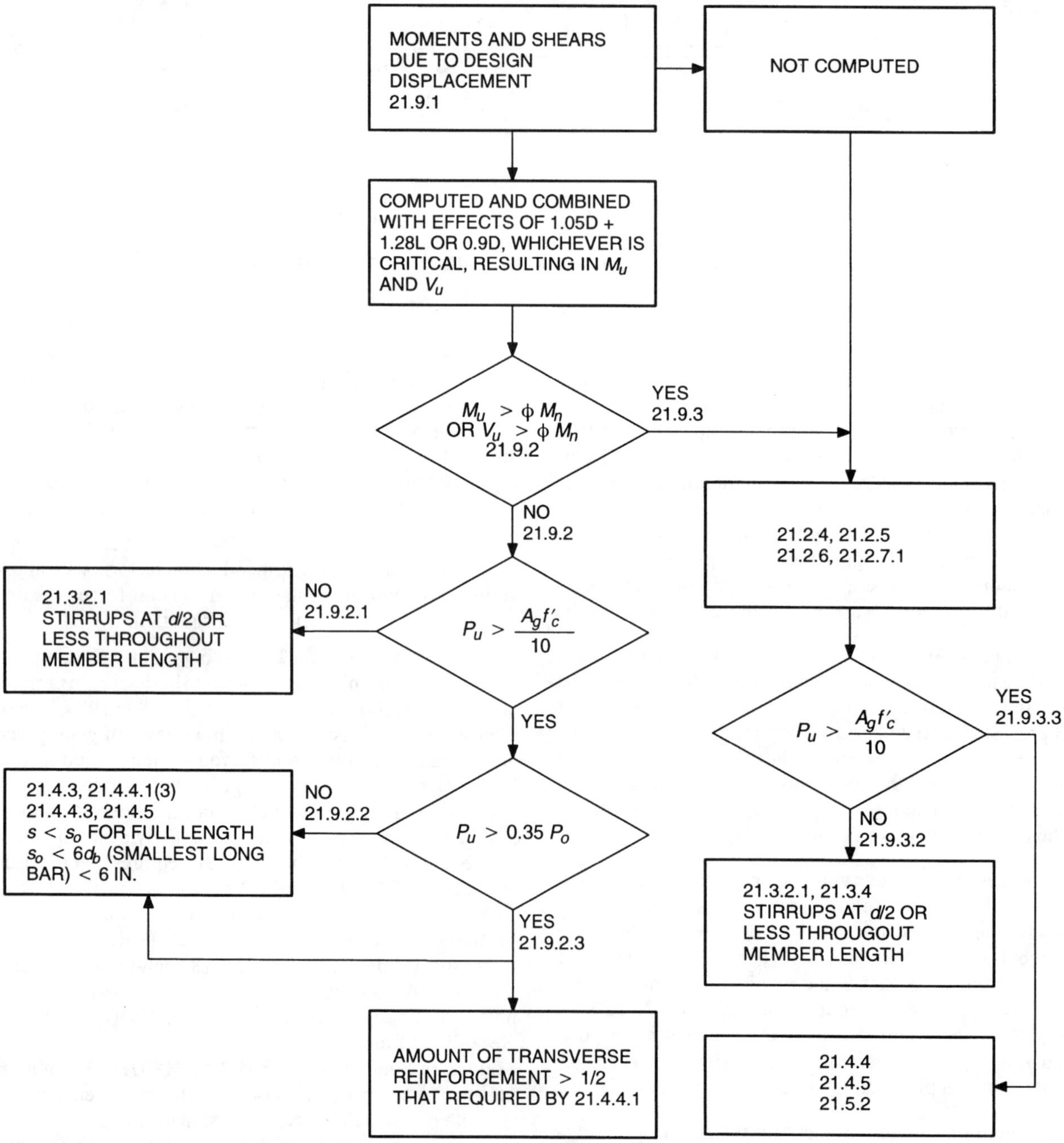

DESIGN "FLOW CHART" FOR DEFORMATION COMPATIBILITY

FIGURE A-13

CHAPTER 19—PART 3
DESIGN EXAMPLES

EXAMPLE 1. DESIGN EXAMPLE OF A 12-STORY PRECAST FRAME BUILDING USING STRONG CONNECTIONS

A typical floor plan and elevation of the example building are shown in Figures E1.1 and E1.2, respectively. Figures E1.1 and E1.2 clearly show the precast elements out of which the building is to be constructed. The relevant design data are given below.

Service Loads

Live Load = 50 psf

Superimposed Dead Load = 42.5 psf

Material Properties

Concrete: f'_c = 4 ksi [6 ksi for columns in the bottom six stories]

Unit Weight = 150 pcf

Member Dimensions

Transverse Beams:	24 × 26 in.
Longitudinal Beams:	24 × 20 in.
Columns:	24 × 24 in.
Slabs:	7 in.

Figures E1.1 and E1.2 depict the three connections detailed in this example:

1. A wet connection near midspan of an interior beam on the third floor level of the building. The beam is part of an interior longitudinal frame.
2. A column-to-column connection at mid-height between Levels 2 and 3 of an interior column stack that is part of an interior longitudinal frame.
3. A strong connection at the interface between a precast beam at the second floor level of the building that forms the exterior span of an exterior transverse frame, and the continuous corner column to which it is connected.

Grout sleeves for the mechanical connections are not shown in the sketches of the details. The designs did not consider reinforcement for construction loads (such as lifting load). The actual construction sequence may be left up to the contractor.

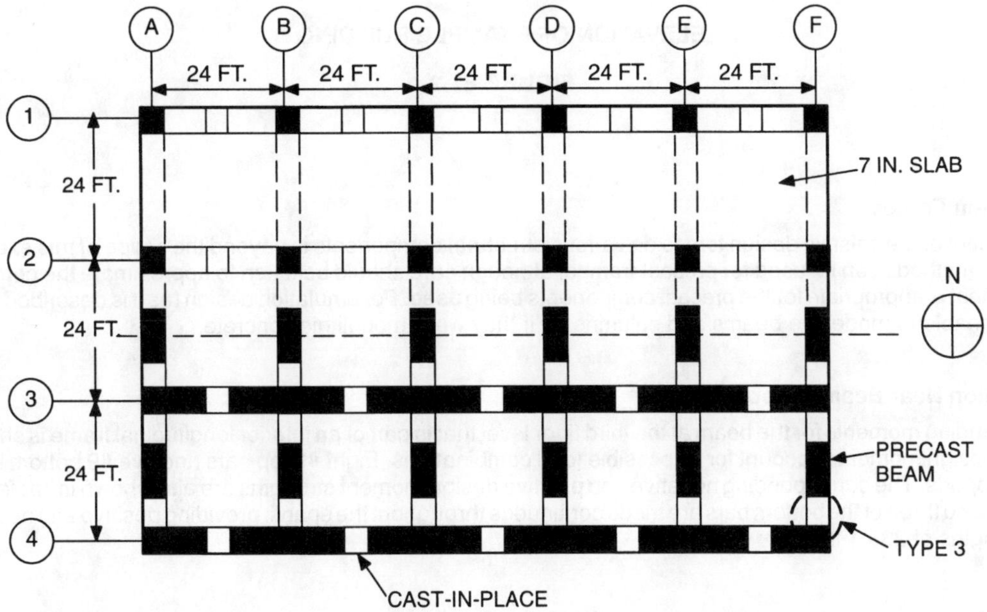

CONNECTION
TYPE 1: WET CONNECTION NEAR THE MIDSPAN (SEE FIGURE E1.2)
TYPE 2: COLUMN TO COLUMN CONNECTION AT MID-HEIGHT (SEE FIGURE E1.2)
TYPE 3: BEAM TO CONTINUOUS COLUMN STRONG CONNECTION

TYPICAL FLOOR PLAN OF EXAMPLE BUILDING

FIGURE E1.1

EXAMPLE 1—(continued)

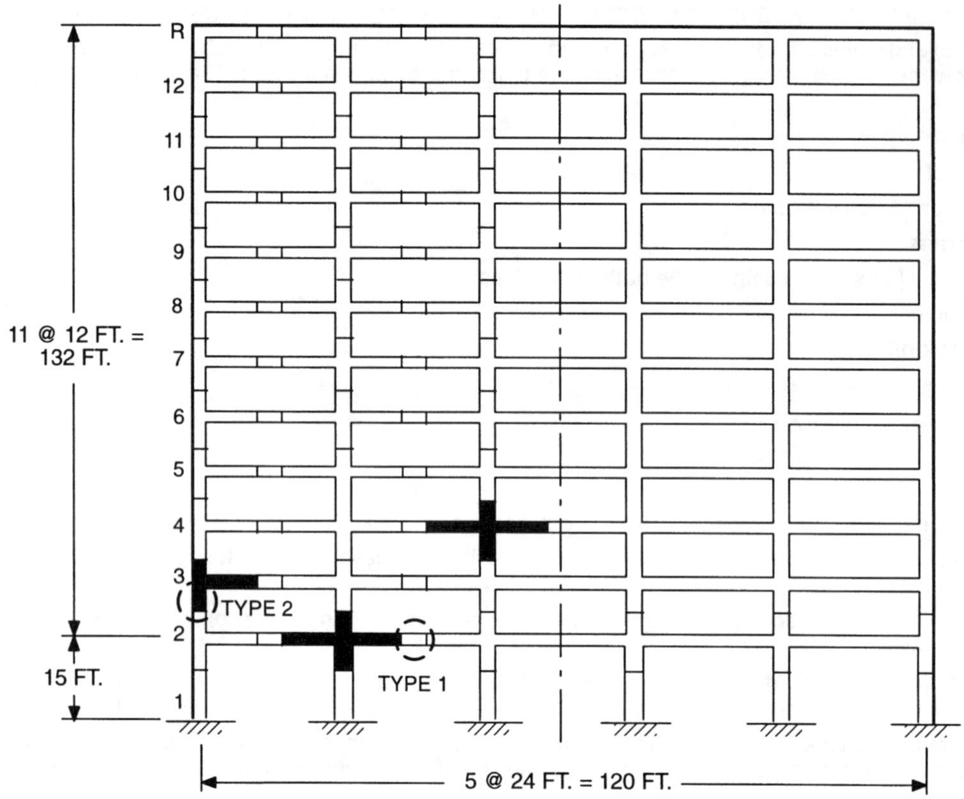

ELEVATION OF EXAMPLE BUILDING

FIGURE E1.2

Seismic Design Forces

The development of the seismic design forces on various structural components is beyond the scope of this example. Traditional analysis methods can be used for precast frames, although care should be taken to approximate the component stiffness in a way that is appropriate for the precast components being used. For emulation design (as it is described in this example) it is reasonable to model the beams and columns as if they were monolithic concrete.

Wet Connection Near Beam Midspan

The design bending moments for the beam at the third floor level that is part of an interior longitudinal frame is shown in Table E1.1. These design moments account for all possible load combinations. Eight #9 top bars and five #9 bottom bars are provided at all supports. The corresponding negative and positive design moment strengths are also shown in Table E1.1. Three of the top bars and three of the bottom bars are made continuous throughout the spans, providing positive and negative design moment strengths of 233.1 ft-kips.

TABLE E1.1. DESIGN FORCES FOR THE THIRD FLOOR BEAM FORMING PART OF AN INTERIOR LONGITUDINAL FRAME OF THE BUILDING

	M_u (ft-kips)	ϕM_n (ft-kips)
Negative	-510.8	-550.8
Positive	+311.7	+364.5

At the supports, $\phi M_n^+ = 364.5$ ft-kips > $\phi M_n^- /2 = 275.4$ ft-kips (OK) (ACI 318 Section 21.3.2.2). Also $(\phi M_n)_{min.} = 233.1$ ft-kips > $\phi M_n^- /4 = 137.7$ ft-kips (OK) (ACI 318 Section 21.3.2.2).

EXAMPLE 1—(continued)

Lap Splice Length — Per ACI 318 Section 12.2.2:

$$\frac{\ell_d}{d_b} = \frac{3}{40}\frac{f_y}{\sqrt{f'_c}}\frac{\alpha\beta\gamma\lambda}{\left(\frac{c+K_{tr}}{d_b}\right)}$$

$$\frac{c + K_{tr}}{d_b} \leq 2.5$$

$\alpha = 1.3$ for top bars; $\alpha = 1.0$ for other bars (ACI 318 Section 12.2.4)
$\beta = 1.0$ for non-epoxy-coated bars (ACI 318 Section 12.2.4)
$\gamma = 1.0$ for #7 and larger bars (ACI 318 Section 12.2.4)
$\lambda = 1.0$ for normal-weight concrete (ACI 318 Section 12.2.4)

From Fig. E1.3, $c = 2.56$ in.
$c/d_b = 2.28$; which makes it reasonable to take:

$$\frac{c + K_{tr}}{d_b} = 2.5$$

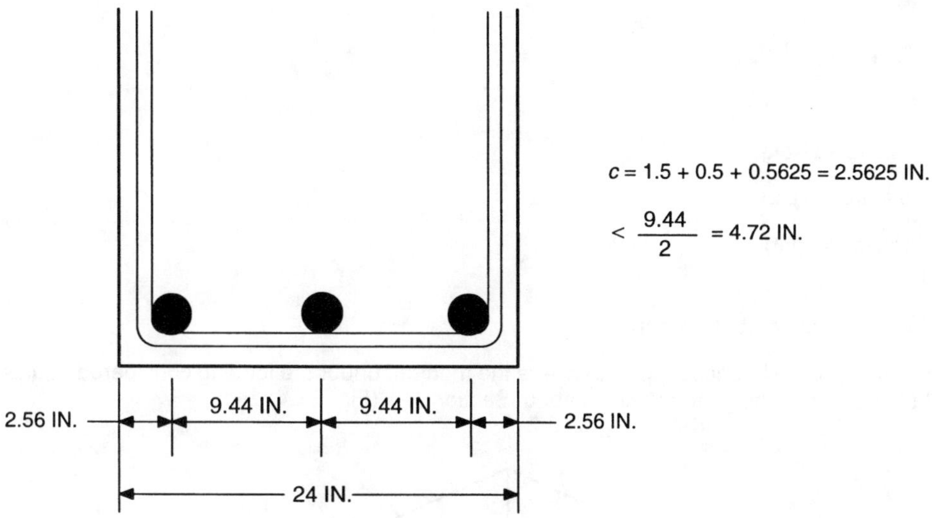

CROSS-SECTION OF BEAM DESIGNED

FIGURE E1.3

Thus:

$$\ell_d = \frac{3}{40}\frac{60000}{\sqrt{4000}}\frac{1}{2.5}d_b = 28.46d_b$$

= 32 in for bottom bars and
= $1.3 \times 28.46d_b$
= 41.62 in for top bars

However, it is shown later that 2 #9 bars are adequate beyond 9.29 ft from the faces of supports.

Thus, the top bar development length can be reduced by an excess reinforcement factor of $^2/_3$ (ACI 318 Section 12.2.5), yielding an $\ell_d = {}^2/_3 \times 41.62 = 27.75$ in.

Because all 3 top bars and all 3 bottom bars are spliced at the same location, Type B splices are to be used for both the top bars and the bottom bars. The Type B splice length = 1.3 × 32 = 41.6 in for the bottom bars. Provide the same 42-in (3 ft 6 in) splice lengths for both the top and the bottom bars.

EXAMPLE 1—(continued)

Reinforcing Bar Cutoff — M_{pr}^{+} and M_{pr}^{-} are calculated with $\phi = 1.0$ and $f_s = 75$ ksi, ignoring compression steel.

For five #9 bars:

$$a = \frac{A_s f_s}{0.85 f'_c b} = \frac{5(75)}{0.85(4)(24)}$$

$$= 4.6 \text{ in.}$$

$$M_{pr}^{+} = A_s f_s \left(d - \frac{a}{2}\right)$$

$$= \frac{5(75)}{12}\left(17.44 - \frac{4.6}{2}\right)$$

$$= 473.1 \text{ ft-kips}$$

since $d = 20 - 1.5$ (clear cover) $- 0.5$ (diameter of #4 stirrups) $- 0.5625$ (1/2 diameter of #9 bars) $= 17.44$ in.

For eight #9 bars:

$$a = \frac{8(75)}{0.85(4)(24)} = 7.35 \text{ in}$$

$$M_{pr}^{-} = \frac{8(75)}{12}\left(17.44 - \frac{7.35}{2}\right)$$

$$= 688.3 \text{ ft-kips}$$

$$w_D = 0.15 \times \frac{7}{12} \times 22 \text{ (slab weight)}$$

$$+ 0.0425 \times 24 \text{ (superimposed DL)}$$

$$+ \frac{0.15 \times 24 \times 20}{144} \text{ (beam weight)}$$

$$= 3.44 \text{ kips per ft}$$

$0.9w_D = 0.9 \times 3.44 = 3.10$ kips per ft at midspan

The distance from the face of the interior support to where the moment under the loading considered equals $\phi M_n^{-} = 233.1$ ft-kips is readily obtained by summing the moments about Section A-A (Fig. E1.4):

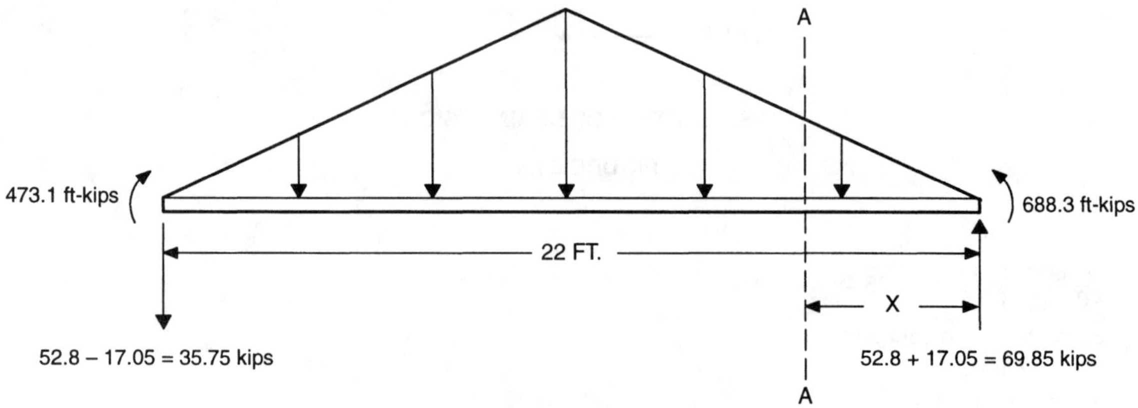

REINFORCING BAR CUTOFF
FIGURE E1.4

$$\frac{x}{2}\left(\frac{3.10x}{11}\right)\left(\frac{x}{3}\right) + 688.3 - 233.1 - 69.85x = 0$$

or, $0.04697x^3 - 69.85x + 455.2 = 0$ whence, $x = 6.72$ ft

Thus, 5 out of 8 #9 bars can be terminated at a distance of 6.72 ft + d = 8.17 ft from the faces of interior supports. Similar calculations can be made to show that all but 3 #9 top and 3 #9 bottom bars can be terminated short of the splice closure.

The wet connection near the beam midspan is illustrated in Fig. E1.5.

EXAMPLE 1—(continued)

Column-to-Column Connection at Mid-Height

The design forces for the interior column between Levels 2 and 3 (which is part of an interior longitudinal frame) are shown in Table E1.2.

TABLE E1.2. DESIGN FORCES FOR THE INTERIOR COLUMN BETWEEN THE SECOND AND THIRD FLOORS, FORMING PART OF AN INTERIOR LONGITUDINAL FRAME OF THE BUILDING

Axial load (kips)	Moment (ft-kips)		Shear (kips)
	Top	Bottom	
1609.8	-408.3	+467.5	70.7

Selection of Reinforcement — Consider 12 #10 bars.

Maximum axial load, P_u = 1609.8 kips (from Table E1.2).

The corresponding ϕM_n from PCACOL program = 659.1 ft-kips > M_u = 467.5 ft-kips (OK).

It can be verified using PCACOL or other design aids that 12 #10 bars are adequate for other axial load, bending moment combinations as well.

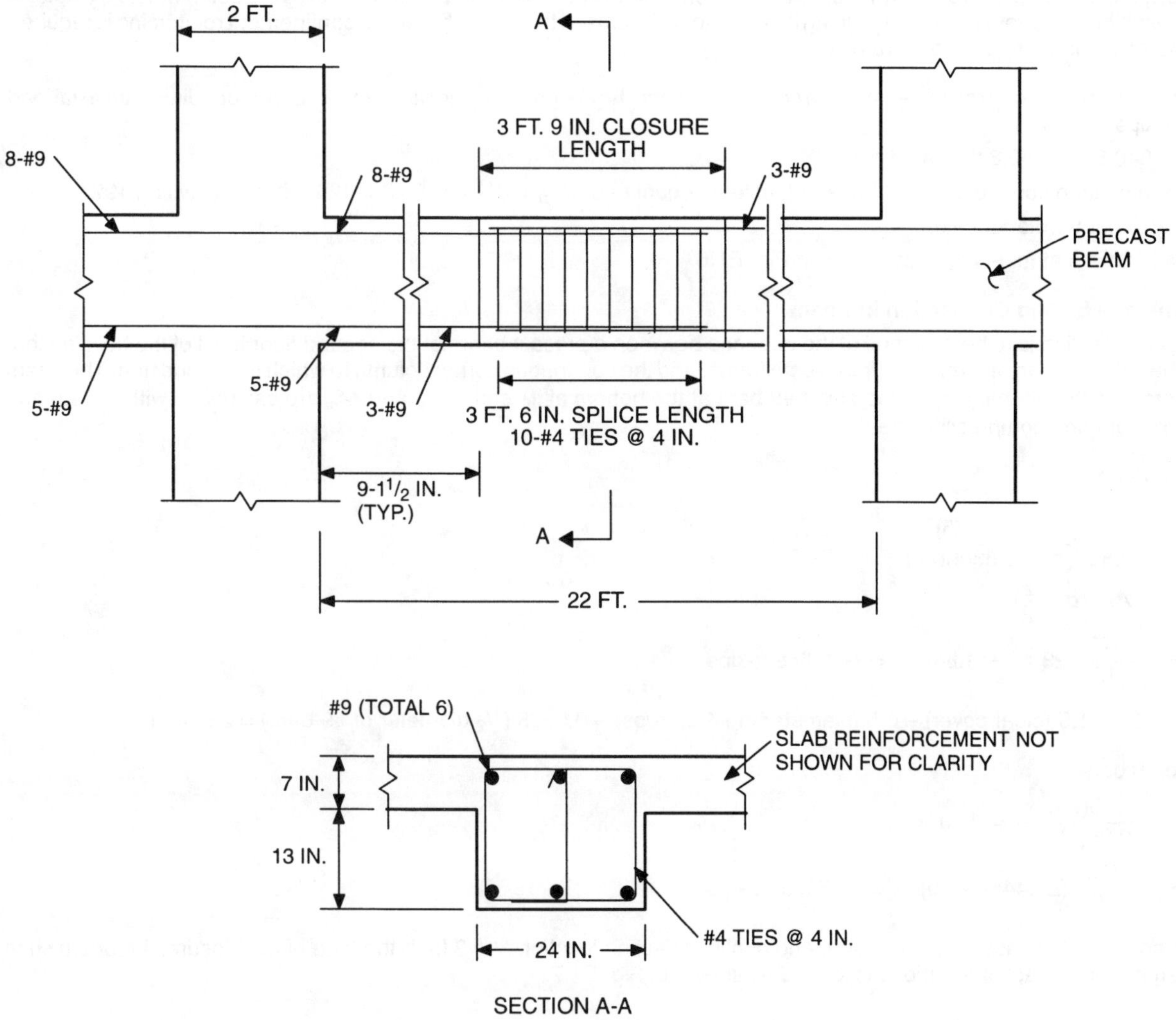

NOTE: Type 2 splices conforming to Section 1921.2.6.1.2 need not be staggered

BEAM-TO-BEAM WET CONNECTION NEAR MIDSPAN OF THIRD-FLOOR BEAM FORMING PART OF INTERIOR LONGITUDINAL FRAME

FIGURE E1.5

EXAMPLE 1—(continued)

$$\rho_g = \frac{A_{st}}{bh} = \frac{12(1.27)}{24 \times 24} = 0.0265$$

$\rho_{min} = 0.01 < \rho_g = 0.0265 < \rho_{max} = 0.06$ (OK, ACI 318 Section 21.4.3.1)

Verification of Strong Column, Weak Beam Requirement—Between the second and third floor levels, $\phi M_n = 840.6$ ft-kips corresponding to $P_u = 711.4$ kips.

Between the third and fourth levels, $\phi M_n = 836.1$ ft-kips corresponding to $P_u = 655.5$ kips

$\Sigma M_e = 840.6 + 836.1$

$= 1676.7$ ft-kips

From the preceding section, for beams framing in, $\phi M_n^- = 550.8$ ft-kips and $\phi M_n^+ = 364.5$ ft-kips

$\Sigma M_g = 550.8 + 364.5$

$= 915.3$ ft-kips

$\Sigma M_e = 1676.7 \text{ ft-kips} > {}^6/_5 \Sigma M_g = 1.2(915.3) = 1098.4$ ft-kips (OK) (ACI 318 Section 21.4.2.2)

The intent of this code provision is to prevent a story mechanism, rather than prevent local yielding in a column. The $^6/_5$ factor is clearly insufficient to prevent column yielding if the adjacent beams both hinge. Therefore, confinement reinforcing is required in the potential hinge regions of a frame column.

Minimum Connection Strength—M_{pr} for a column between the second and third floor levels, corresponding to an axial load of 711.4 kips

$\approx 1.25\ (840.6) = 1050.8$ ft-kips

Column-to-column connection must have ϕM_n at least equal to $0.4M_{pr} = 0.4 \times 1050.8 = 420.3$ ft-kips (Section 1921.2.7.4).

Twelve #10 bars are adequate.

Splice all 12 bars at mid-height, as shown in Fig. E1.6.

Column-Face Strong Connection in Beam

A strong connection is to be designed at the interface between a precast beam at the second floor level of the building that forms the exterior span of an exterior transverse frame, and the continuous corner column to which it is connected. The beam is reinforced with 5 #9 bars at the top and 4 #9 bars at the bottom at its ends. M_{pr}^+ and M_{pr}^- are calculated with $\phi = 1.0$ and $f_s = 75$ ksi ignoring compression steel.

For four #9 bars:

$$a = \frac{A_s f_s}{0.85 f'_c b} = \frac{4(75)}{0.83(4)(24)} = 3.68 \text{ in.}$$

$$M_{pr}^+ = A_s f_s \left(d - \frac{a}{2}\right)$$

$$= \frac{4(75)}{12}(23.44 - 1.84) = 539.9 \text{ ft-kips}$$

since $d = 26 - 1.5$ (clear cover) $- 0.5$ (diameter of #4 stirrups) $- 0.5625$ ($^1/_2$ diameter of #9 bars) $= 23.44$ in

For five #9 bars:

$$\alpha = \frac{5(75)}{0.85(4)(24)} = 4.60 \text{ in.}$$

$$M_{pr}^- = \frac{5(75)}{12}(23.44 - 2.30) = 660.5 \text{ ft-kips}$$

Assuming a 2-ft 6-in cast-in-place closure and nonlinear action location at $h/2$ from the face of the closure, the beam span between non-linear action locations is loaded as shown in Fig. E1.7.

EXAMPLE 1—(continued)

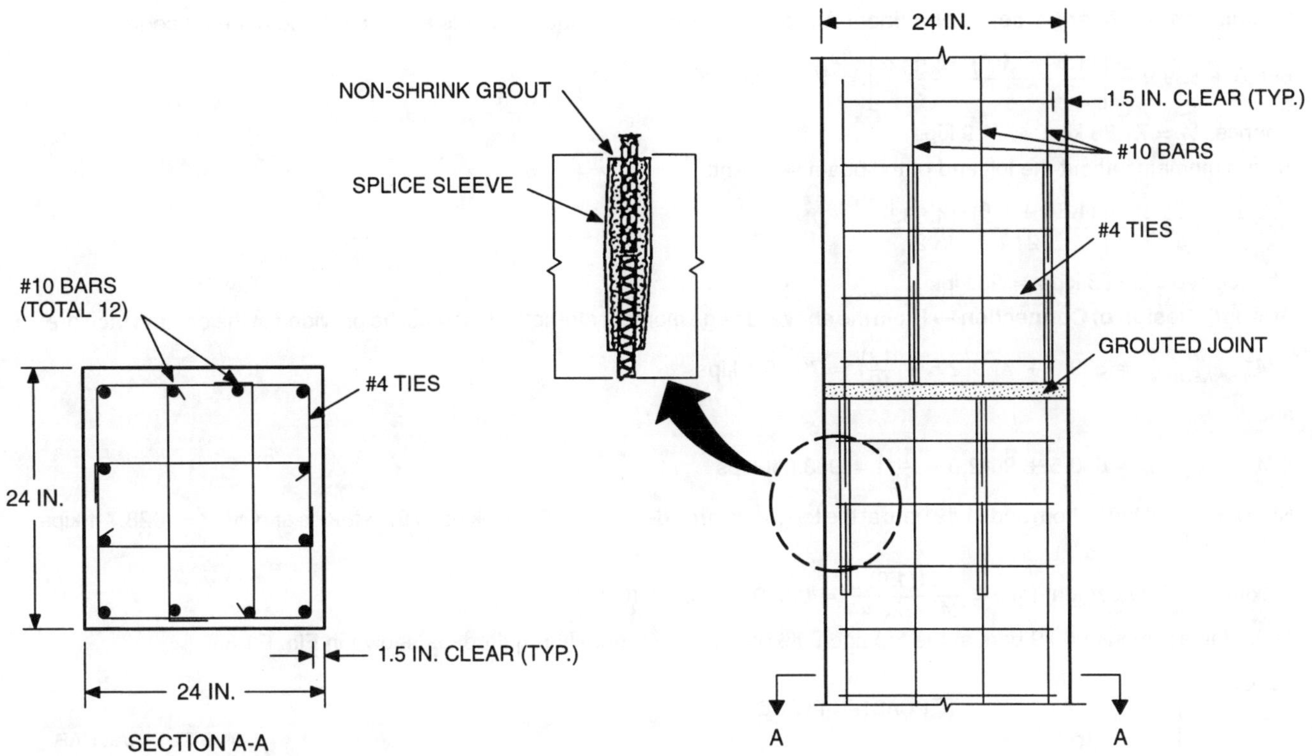

THERMITE WELDING MAY BE USED AT THE CONTRACTOR'S OPTION.

CENTER-TO-CENTER DISTANCE BETWEEN ALTERNATE SPLICED BARS = 24 IN. (MIN.)

NOTE: Type 2 splices conforming to Section 1921.2.6.1.2 need not be staggered.

COLUMN-TO-COLUMN WET CONNECTION AT MIDHEIGHT OF INTERIOR COLUMN BETWEEN SECOND AND THIRD FLOORS, FORMING PART OF INTERIOR LONGITUDINAL FRAME

FIGURE E1.6

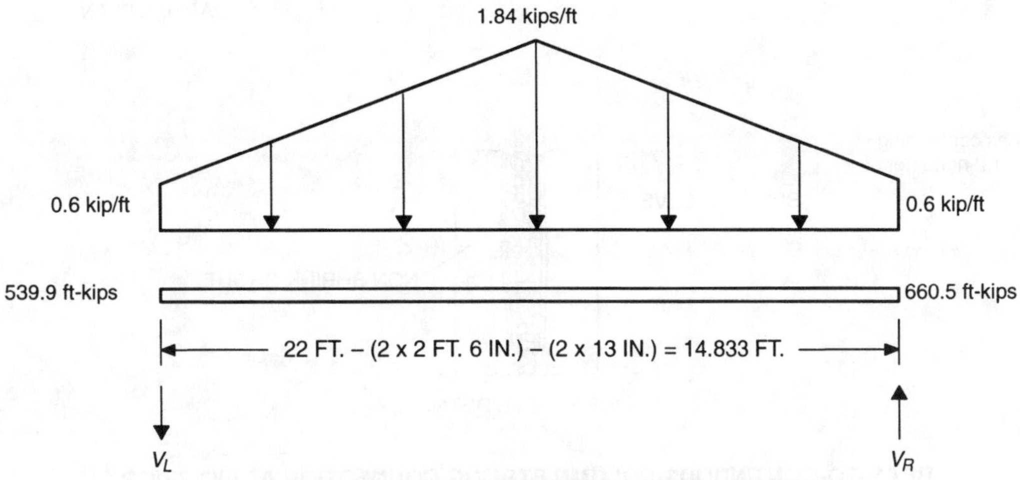

BEAM SPAN BETWEEN NONLINEAR ACTION LOCATIONS

FIGURE E1.7

EXAMPLE 1—(continued)

Calculation of Shear Forces at Nonlinear Action Locations — Taking moments about right end of beam segment:

$$660.5 + 539.9 - \left[\frac{(1.84 + 0.6)}{2}\frac{14.833^2}{2}\right] = V_L(14.833)$$

whence, $V_L = 71.88$ kips ≈ 71.9 kips

Taking moments about the left end of the beam segment:

$$539.9 + 660.5 - \left[\frac{(1.84 + 0.6)}{2}\frac{14.833^2}{2}\right] = V_R(14.833)$$

whence, $V_R = 89.98$ kips ≈ 90 kips

Strength Design of Connection — From the above, design moment strengths that must be provided at the column face are:

$$\phi M^+_{nCONNECTION} = 539.9 + 71.9\left(2.5 + \frac{13}{12}\right) = 797.5 \text{ ft-kips}$$

and

$$\phi M^-_{nCONNECTION} = 660.5 + 90\left(2.5 + \frac{13}{12}\right) = 983.0 \text{ ft-kips}$$

Nine #9 bars at the bottom and 11 #9 bars at the top would provide $\phi M_n^+ = 853.2$ ft-kips > 797.5 ft-kips and $\phi M_n^- = 1028.7$ ft-kips > 983.0 ft-kips

$$\text{Maximum reinforcement ratio} = \frac{11(1.0)}{24 \times 23.44} = 0.0196 < 0.025 \text{ (OK)}$$

Thus, the addition of 6 #9 bars at the top and 5 #9 bars at the bottom is required, as shown in Fig. E1.8.

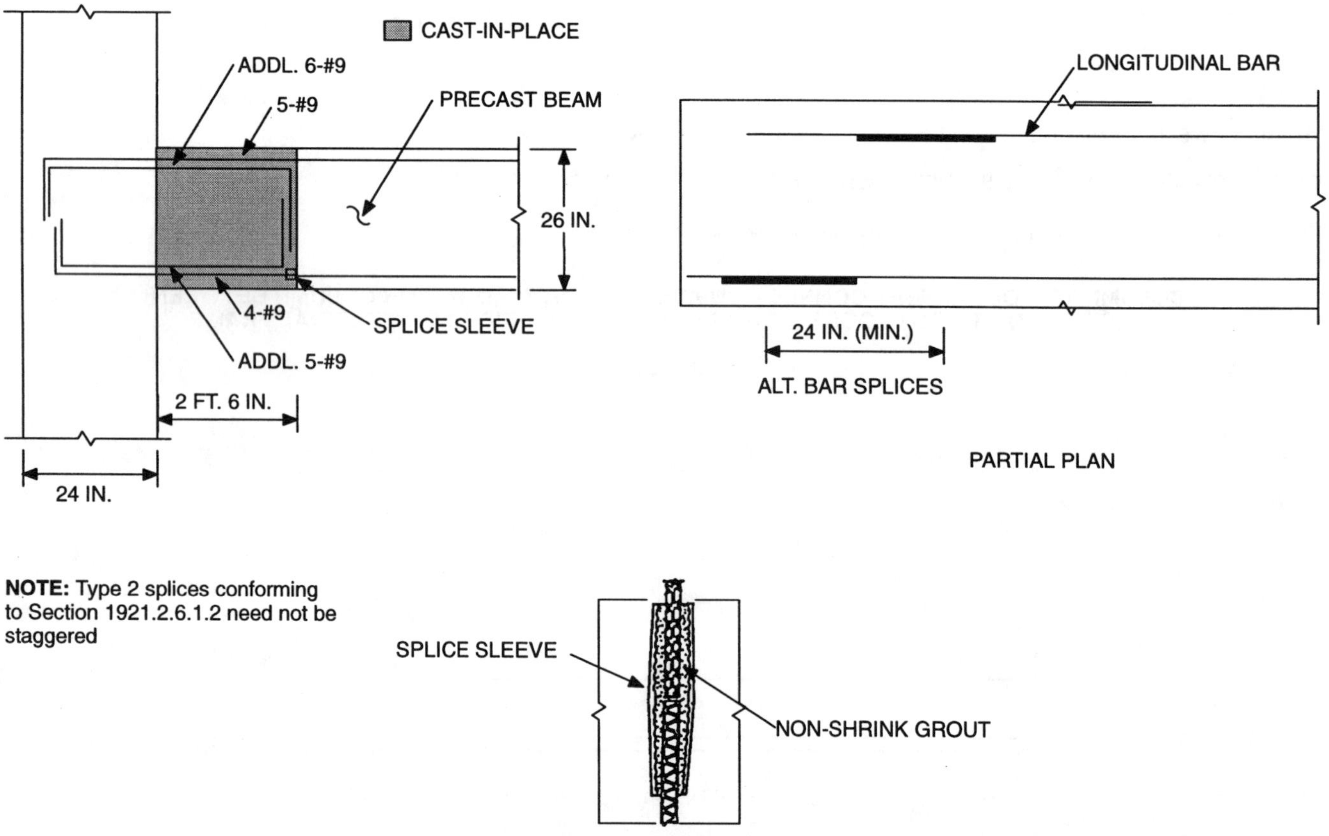

BEAM-TO-CONTINUOUS-COLUMN STRONG CONNECTION AT EXTERIOR SPAN OF TRANSVERSE FRAME AT SECOND FLOOR LEVEL

FIGURE E1.8

EXAMPLE 1—(continued)

Anchorage and splices — Per ACI 318 Section 21.5.4.1:

$$l_{dh} = \frac{f_y d_b}{65\sqrt{f'_c}} = \frac{(60000)(1.128)}{65\sqrt{4000}} = 16.46 \text{ in.}$$

Thus, the detail shown in Fig. E1.8 would conform to the requirements of ACI 318 Section 21.2.7.2.

Acknowledgement: This example has been adapted from:

Ghosh, S.K., Nakaki, S.D., and Krishnan, K., "Precast Structures in Regions of High Seismicity: 1997 UBC Design Provisions", PCI Journal, Vol. 42, No. 6, November-December 1997, pp. 76-93.

EXAMPLE 2. ALLOWABLE STRESS DESIGN CHECK ON ANCHOR BOLT

1-inch bolt $f'_c = 3500$ psi $P_s = 1500$ lbs $V_s = 2500$ lbs

Edge distance = 5 in. Spacing = 9 in.

Check acceptability

$P_t = 3250$ lbs	$V_t = 4500$ lbs	for $f'_c = 3000$ psi	for edge distance = 6 in. spacing = 12 in.
$= 3650$ lbs	$= 5300$ lbs	for $f'_c = 4000$ psi	
$= 3450$ lbs	$= 4900$ lbs	for $f'_c = 3500$ psi	

Reduction in edge distance $= 1 - 5/6 = 17\%$

Reduction in spacing $= 1 - 9/12 = 25\%$ governs

$P_t = 0.75 \times 3450 = 2588$ lbs

$V_t = 0.75 \times 4900 = 3675$ lbs

$(P_s/P_t)^{5/3} + (V_s/V_t)^{5/3} = (1500/2588)^{5/3} + (2500/3675)^{5/3}$

$= (0.58)^{5/3} + (0.68)^{5/3} = 0.40 + 0.53 = 0.93 < 1$ OK

EXAMPLE 3. RELATIVE STRENGTHS OF COLUMNS AND BEAMS AT JOINT

Given data:

Beams	=	34 x 24 in.	
Columns	=	40 x 40 in. (interior)	
c/c distance of columns	=	26 ft (in both directions)	
Factored axial load	=	4480 kips on column C1	(Fig. E3.1)
		4244 kips on column C2	(Fig. E3.1)
Service dead load	=	3.36 kip/ft	
Service live load	=	0.83 kip/ft	
Main reinforcements in columns	=	36 #10 bars	
Main reinforcements in beams	=	6 #8 bars (top)	
	=	3 #8 bars (bottom)	
Effective flange width	=	78 in.	(Fig. E3.2)

Other data are assumed as needed.
See Figs. E3.1 and E3.2 for details.

Figure E3.3 shows the P-M interaction diagram for the interior column.

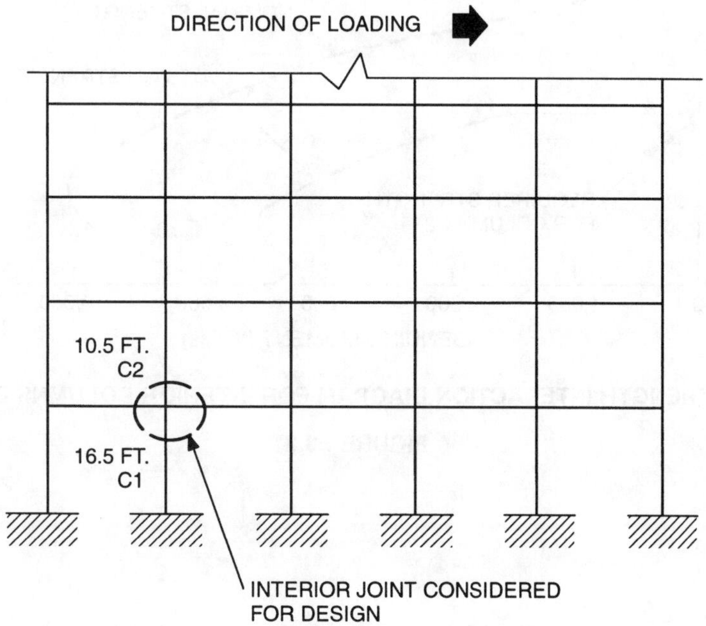

ELEVATION OF EXAMPLE BUILDING

FIGURE E3.1

EXAMPLE 3—(continued)

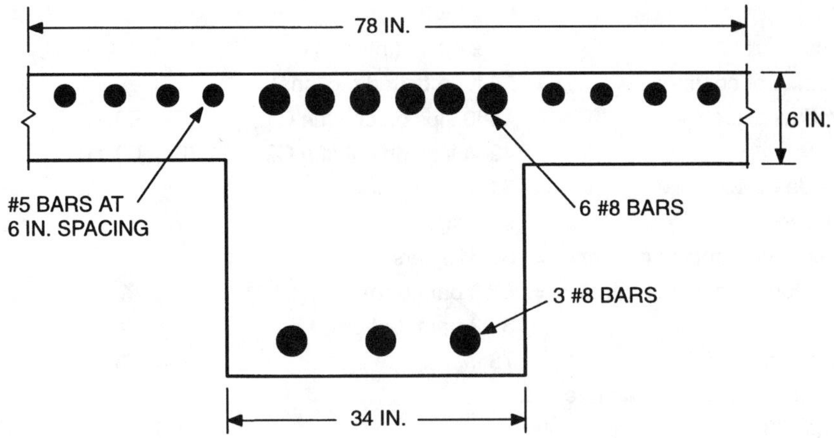

REINFORCEMENT DETAILS AT THE BEAM-SLAB CONNECTION

FIGURE E3.2

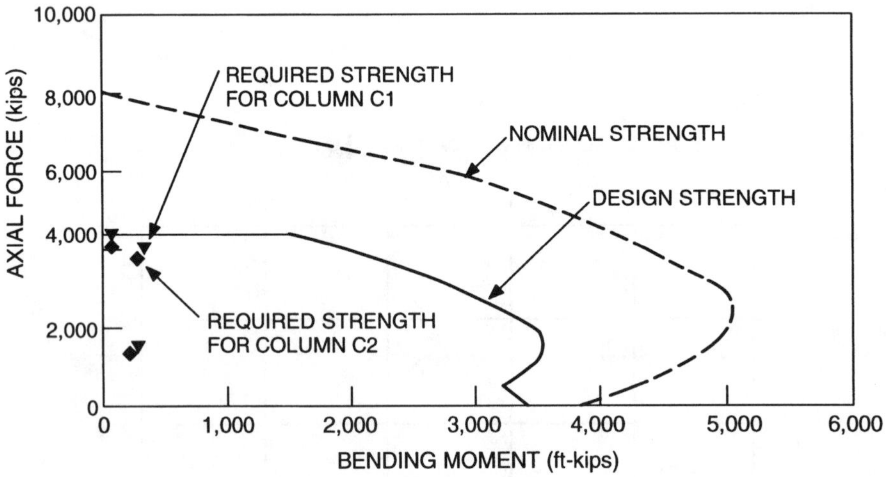

DESIGN STRENGTH INTERACTION DIAGRAM FOR INTERIOR COLUMNS C1 AND C2

FIGURE E3.3

Per ACI 318-99 Section 21.4.2.2

$\Sigma M_c \quad > 1.2\ \Sigma M_g$

where: ΣM_g is the sum of girder flexural strengths

ΣM_c is the sum of column flexural strengths corresponding to factored axial forces

Girders

Nominal strength, M_n^- = 828 ft-kips (considering slab reinforcement) (Fig. E3.2)

Nominal strength, M_n^+ = 248 ft-kips (with 3 #8 bars) (Fig. E3.2)

ΣM_g = 828 + 248 = 1076 ft-kips

EXAMPLE 3—(continued)

Columns:

M_n (lowest corresponding to different P_u) $\cong$ 3,400 ft-kips for Column C1 and 3,800 ft-kips for Column C2 (Fig. E3.3 — Nominal strength curve)

ΣM_c = 3,400 + 3,800 = 7200 ft-kips

Check strength:

$$\Sigma M_c/\Sigma M_g = \frac{7,200}{1,076} = 6.69 > 1.2 \qquad \text{OK}$$

Per ACI 318-95, the bending moments needed to be considered at the center of the joint, not at the joint faces. The moment at center of joint along the girder can be taken as follows:

Girders:

At joint faces

ϕM_{n1}^- = 432 ft-kips (with 6 #8, not considering any contribution from slab reinforcement) (Fig. E3.2)

ϕM_{n2}^+ = 223 ft-kips (with 3 #8 bars) (Fig. E3.2)

At joint centerline

$M_{gc}^+ = \phi M_n^+ + V_g \times c_1/2$ (Fig. E3.4)

$M_{gc}^- = \phi M_n^- + V_g \times c_1/2$ (Fig. E3.4)

where: $V_g = (\phi M_n^- + \phi M_n^+)/\ell_n + w_u \ell_n/2$

w_u = 0.75(1.4D+1.7L) = 0.75(1.4 x 3.36 + 1.7 x 0.83) = 4.58 k/ft

ℓ_n = 26 – 40/12 = 22.67 ft

V_g = (432 + 223)/22.67 + 4.58 × 22.67/2 = 80.8 kips

M_{gc}^+ = 432 + 80.8 × 40/(12 × 2) = 567 ft-kips

M_{gc}^- = 223 + 80.8 × 40/(12 × 2) = 368 ft-kips

ΣM_g = 567 + 368 = 935 ft-kips

Columns:

ϕM_n (lowest corresponding to different P_u) $\cong$ 1,500 ft-kips for Column C1 and 1,600 ft-kips for Column C2 (Fig. E3.3 — Design strength curve)

$M_{cb} = \phi M_{ncb} + V_{cb} \times d_1/2$ (Fig. E3.4)

$M_{ct} = \phi M_{nct} + V_{ct} \times d_1/2$ (Fig. E3.4)

where: $V_{cb} = (\phi M_{ncb})/0.5\ell_{nb}$

l_{nb} = 16.5 – 2.0 = 14.5 ft

V_{cb} = (1,500)/(0.5 × 14.5) = 206.9 kips

$V_{ct} = (\phi M_{nct})/0.5\ell_{nt}$

ℓ_{nt} = 10.5 – 2.0 = 8.5 ft

V_{cb} = (1,600)/(0.5 × 8.5) = 376.5 kips

M_{cb} = 1,500 + 206.9 × 24/(12 × 2) = 1707 ft-kips

M_{ct} = 1,600 + 376.5 × 24/(12 × 2) = 1976 ft-kips

ΣM_c = 1,707 + 1976 = 3683 ft-kips

Check strength:

$\Sigma M_c/\Sigma M_g$ = 3683/935 = 3.94 > 1.2 OK

EXAMPLE 3—(continued)

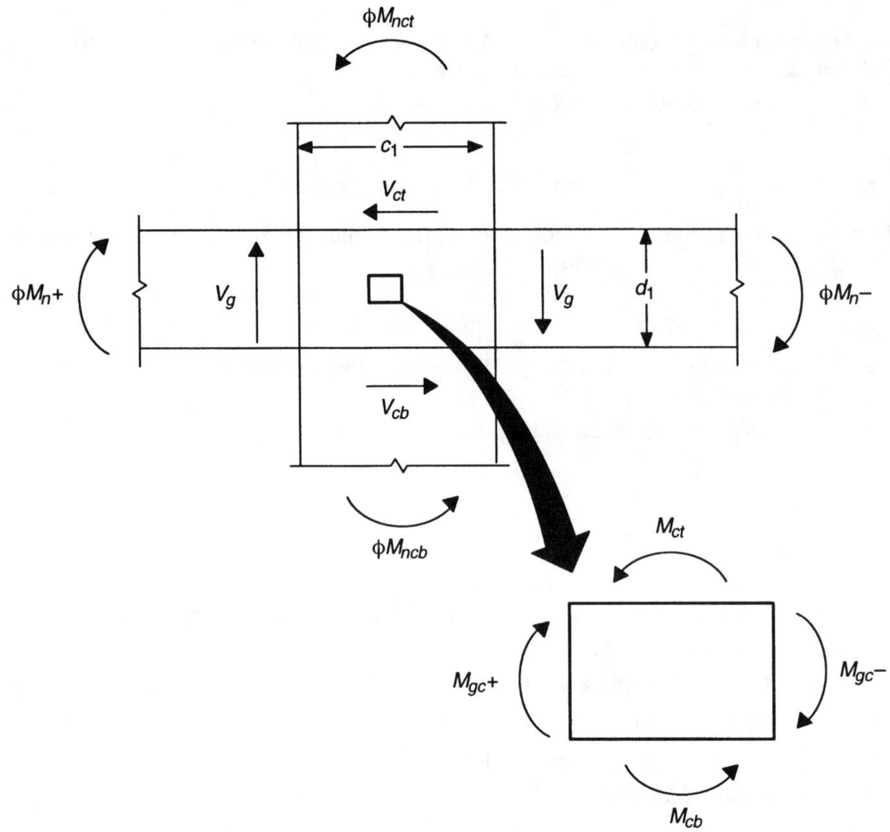

RELATIVE STRENGTH OF COLUMNS AND BEAMS AT JOINT PER ACI 318-95

FIGURE E3.4

EXAMPLE 4. DESIGN OF RC SHEAR WALL PER IBC 2000

Given Data:

Compressive strength of concrete f'_c = 4000 psi
Yield strength of reinforcements f_y = 60 ksi
Structural system: Building Frame with Special Reinforced Concrete Shear Walls
Site Class: D
S_{DS} = 1.33
S_{D1} = 0.93
C_d = 5.0
Use Group = I
R = 6
Importance Factor, I = 1.0
Redundancy factor, ρ = 1.0
Shear wall thickness, h = 12 in.
Seismic Design Category = E
Base shear, V = 1402 kips
Service-level axial dead load on shear wall = 316 kips
Service-level axial live load on shear wall = 34 kips
The forces due to lateral load are shown in Table E4.1
The displacement at the top of the building along the shear wall line was found to be 0.76 inch by elastic analysis under the code-prescribed forces.
Design displacement (δ_u) = 5.0 x 0.76 = 3.80 in
Note: A shear wall is a structural wall. The terms are used interchangeably here.

Shear Wall Design

The design of one of the shear walls at the base of the structure shown in Figures E4.1 and E4.2 is illustrated in this example. Similar procedures may be followed to design the shear wall at the other floor levels. The design of shear walls by IBC 2000 follows the procedure in ACI 318–99.

Design loads

Table E4.1 shows a summary of the axial force, shear force and bending moment at the base of the example shear wall based on different load combinations.

Required axial load strength, P_u = 520 kips
Required shear strength, V_u = 382 kips
Required flexural strength, M_u = 16,855 ft-kips

TABLE E4.1. SUMMARY OF DESIGN AXIAL FORCE, SHEAR FORCE AND BENDING MOMENT FOR SHEAR WALL BETWEEN GRADE AND LEVEL 2

Loads	Symbol	Axial Force (kips)	Shear Force (kips)	Bending Moment (ft-kips)
Dead Load	D	316	0	0
Live Load	L	34	0	0
Lateral Load	Q_E	38	382	16,855

Load Combinations				
1	$1.4D+1.7L$	500	0	0
2	$1.2D+(\rho Q_E+0.2S_{DS}D)+0.5L$	520	382	16,855
3	$0.9D-(\rho Q_E+0.2S_{DS}D)$	161	-382	-16,855

Load Combinations	Load Factors		
	D	L	Q_E
1	1.4	1.7	0
2	1.47	0.5	1
3	0.63	0	-1

EXAMPLE 4—(continued)

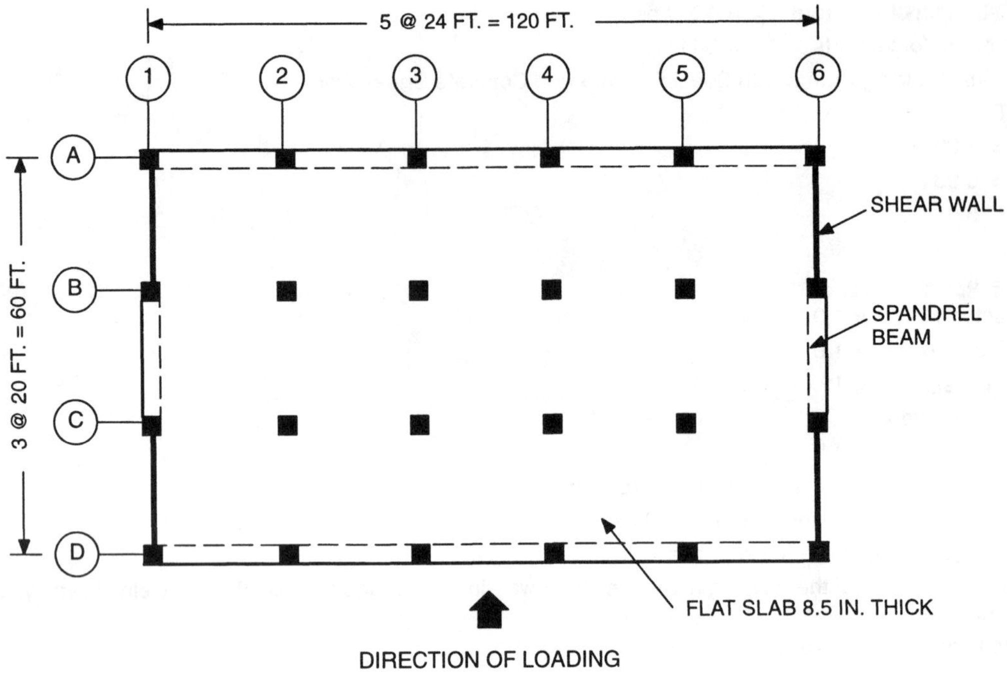

PLAN OF EXAMPLE BUILDING CONSIDERED

FIGURE E4.1

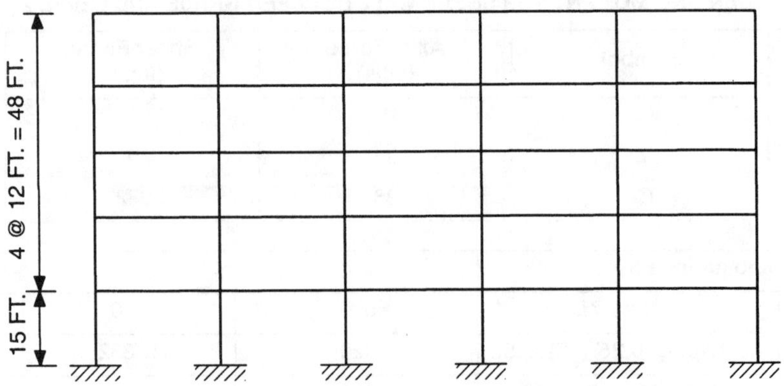

ELEVATION OF EXAMPLE BUILDING CONSIDERED

FIGURE E4.2

EXAMPLE 4—(continued)

Check strength under flexure and axial load

Draw P-M interaction diagram for the shear wall with assumed dimensions of wall and assumed longitudinal reinforcement in boundary elements and web. Check to see that all the points representing strength demand (from the three load combinations shown in Table 1) are within the design strength interaction diagram.

In this example, the shear wall dimensions and reinforcement, as shown in Figure E4.3, are considered.

Using 12 #8 bars in each boundary element, the reinforcement ratio in the elements is, (12 × 0.79)/(18 × 18) = 2.93%. This is high, but not excessive, and was judged to be acceptable.

Figure E4.4 shows the P-M interaction diagrams for the example shear wall. As can be seen, all the points representing required strength are within the design strength curve.

One other quantity needs to be determined at this stage. That is the neutral axis depth, *c*, corresponding to the maximum axial force (in the presence of lateral force).

P_u = 520 kips

c = 26 in. (using an in-house computer program)

Design for shear

Height of the shear wall, $h_w = 63$ ft

Length of the shear wall, $\ell_w = 20 + 18/12 = 21.5$ ft

$h_w/\ell_w = 63/21.5 = 2.93$

ACI 318 Section 21.6.4.4

V_u must not exceed $\phi 8A_{cv}\sqrt{f'_c}$

$A_{cv} = 12 \times (20 \times 12 + 18) = 3096$ in.^{2}

Take $\phi = 0.85$, since a wall with $h_w/\ell_w = 2.93$ is not going to be governed by shear in its failure mode.

$\phi 8A_{cv}\sqrt{f'_c} = 0.85 \times 8 \times 3096\sqrt{4000}/1000$

$= 1331$ kips > 382 kips (V_u) OK

ACI 318 Section 21.6.2.2

At least two curtains of reinforcement must be used if $V_u > 2A_{cv}\sqrt{f'_c}$

$2A_{cv}\sqrt{f'_c} = 2 \times 3096\sqrt{4000}/1000$

$= 392$ kips > 382 kips

Theoretically, 1 curtain needs to be provided. However, provide two curtains of reinforcement.

ACI 318 Section 21.6.2.1

For 2 #5 horizontal bars @ 18 inches o.c.

$\rho_n = \dfrac{2 \times 0.31}{12 \times 18} = 0.00287 > 0.0025$ OK

$s = 18$ in. ≤ 18 in. OK

Use 2 #5 horizontal bars @ 18 inches o.c.

EXAMPLE 4—(continued)

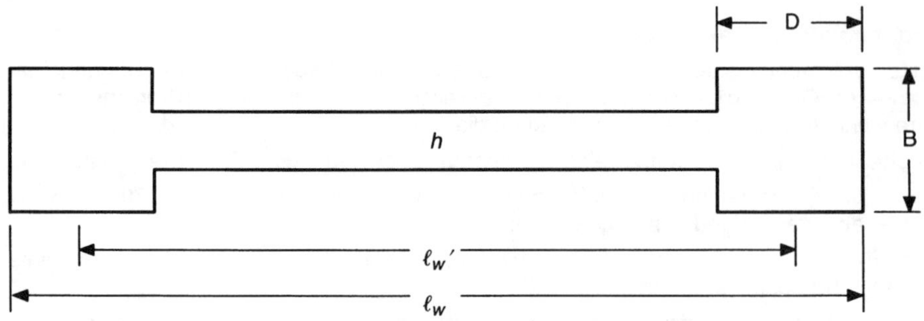

PLAN OF SHEAR WALL

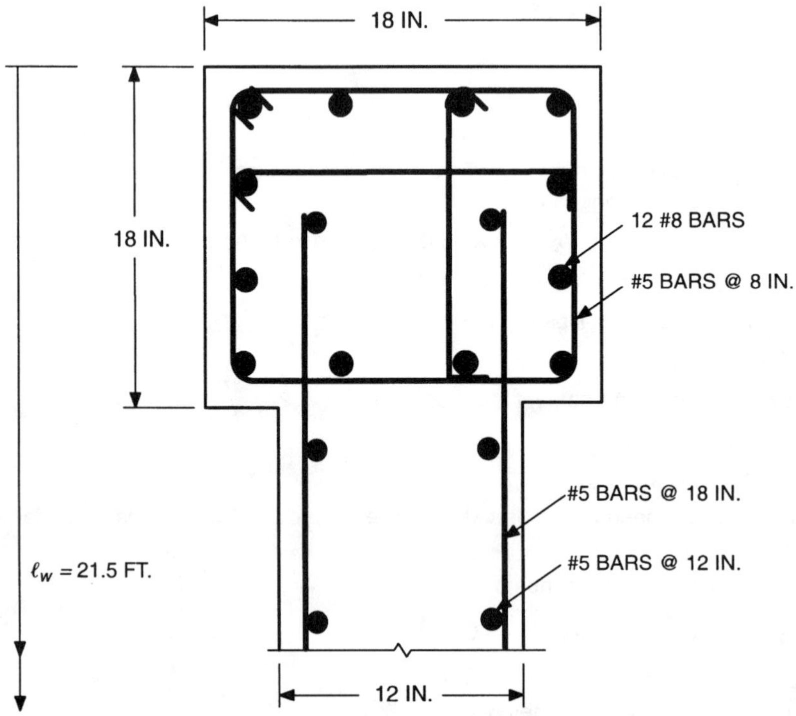

PLAN AND REINFORCEMENT DETAILS OF SHEAR WALL

FIGURE E4.3

ACI 318 Section 21.6.4.3

The vertical reinforcement ratio (ρ_v) must not be less than the horizontal reinforcement ratio (r_n) if the ratio $h_w/\ell_w < 2.0$. As $h_w/\ell_w = 2.93 > 2.0$, this clause is not applicable.

Provide 2 #5 vertical bars @ 12 inches o.c.

$\rho_v = 0.0043 > 0.0025$ (21.6.2.1) OK

ACI 318 Section 21.6.4.1

For $h_w/\ell_w = 2.93 > 2.0$

$\alpha_c = 2$

$V_n = A_{cv}(\alpha_c\sqrt{f'_c} + \rho_n f_y)$ (ACI 318 Equation 21-7)

$\phi V_n = 0.85 \times 3096[2\sqrt{4000} + 0.00287 \times 60,000]/1000$

$= 786$ kips > 382 kips OK

EXAMPLE 4—(continued)

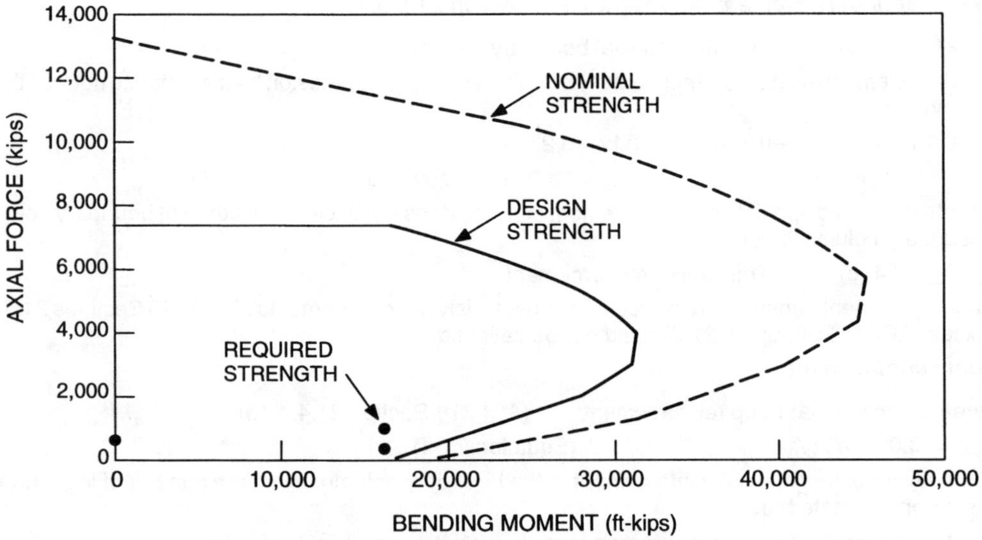

M-P INTERACTION DIAGRAM FOR SHEAR WALL C1-D1 (BETWEEN GRADE AND LEVEL 2)

FIGURE E4.4

Design for flexure and axial loads *(ACI 318 Section 21.6.5)*

ACI 318 Section 21.6.5.1

Shear walls and portions of such walls subject to combined flexural and axial loads shall be designed in accordance with Sections 10.2 and 10.3, i.e., the provisions applied to columns. Boundary elements and the wall web are considered effective.

Boundary Elements of Special RC structural walls *(ACI 318 Section 21.6.6)*

ACI 318 Section 21.6.6.1

The need for special boundary elements at the edges of shear walls needs to be evaluated in accordance with ACI 318 Section 21.6.6.2 (displacement-based approach) or ACI 318 Section 21.6.6.3 (stress-based approach). In this example, the displacement-based approach is followed.

ACI 318 Section 21.6.6.2(a) Displacement-Based Approach

Compression zones must be reinforced with special boundary elements where:

$$c \geq c_r = \frac{\ell_w}{600(\delta_u/h_w)} \quad \text{(ACI 318 Section Equation 21-8)}$$

As computed earlier,

c = 26 in.

ℓ_w = 21.5 ft

h_w = 63 ft

δ_u = 3.8 in along the wall line

δ_u/h_w = $3.8/(63 \times 12) = 0.005 < 0.007$ = > Use $\delta_u/h_w = 0.007$

$$c_r = \frac{21.5 \times 12}{600 \times 0.007} = 61.4 \text{ in.} > c = 26 \text{ in.}$$

Therefore, boundary zone details per ACI 318 Section 21.6.6.4 are not needed. However, for illustration purposes, the detailing will be shown in this example.

ACI 318 Section 21.6.6.2 (b) Height of special boundary element

The special boundary element reinforcement must extend vertically from the critical section a distance not less than the larger of ℓ_w or $M_u/4V_u$.

ℓ_w = 21.5 ft . . . governs

$$M_u/4V_u = \frac{16,855}{4 \times 382} = 11 \text{ ft}$$

EXAMPLE 4—(continued)

Shear wall Special Boundary Element Details *(ACI 318 Section 21.6.6.4)*

ACI 318 Section 21.6.6.4 (a) Length of special boundary element

Special boundary element must extend horizontally from the extreme compression fiber a distance not less than the larger of $c - 0.1\ell_w$ and $c/2$.

$c - 0.1\ \ell_w$ = $26 - 0.1 \times 21.5 \times 12 = 0.2$ in.

$c/2$ = $26/2$ = 13.0 in. . . . governs

Since the length of needed special boundary element (= 13 in) does not exceed the depth of boundary column (= 18 in), the entire boundary column is confined.

ACI 318 Section 21.6.6.4 (c) Transverse reinforcement

Special boundary element transverse reinforcement must satisfy the requirements of ACI 318 Sections 21.4.4.1 through 21.4.4.3, except ACI 318 Equation (21-3) need not be satisfied.

Boundary column confinement

Minimum area of rectangular hoop reinforcement (ACI 318 Section 21.4.4.1b)

$A_{sh} = 0.09\ s\ h_c f'_c / f_{yh}$ (Equation 21-4)

As there are 4 layers of longitudinal reinforcement in the boundary column, minimum number of legs (hoops and ties) needed to support alternate bars is 3.

Maximum horizontal spacing of hoop or crosstie legs, $h_x = (18 - 2 \times 2.5)/3 = 4.33$ in

According to Section 21.4.4.2, the spacing of transverse reinforcement must not exceed (a) one-quarter of the minimum member dimension, (b) six times the diameter of the longitudinal reinforcement, and (c) s_x, as defined by Equation (21-5).

s_x = 4 in. $\leq 4 + (14 - h_x)/3 \leq 6$ in. (Equation 21-5)

s_x = 4 in. ≤ 7.2 in. ≤ 6 in. ← Use $s_x = 6$ in

$s \leq 6$ in. ← governs

$\leq 6d_b = 6 \times 1.0$ = 6.0 in.

$\leq$ minimum plan dimension/4 = 4.5 in.

$h_c = 18 - 2 \times 1.5 - 5/8 = 14.4$ in.

$A_{sh} \geq 0.09 \times 4.5 \times 14.4 \times 4/60 = 0.39\ \text{in.}^2$

With one tie all around the longitudinal reinforcement and one crosstie in either direction (as shown in Fig. E.4.3),

A_{sh} provided $= 3 \times 0.31 = 0.93\ \text{in.}^2 > 0.39\ \text{in.}^2$ OK

REFERENCES

[1] *Uniform Building Code*, International Conference of Building Officials, Whittier, CA, 1997.

[2] *The BOCA National Building Code*, Building Officials and Code Administrators International, Country Club Hills, IL, 1993, 1996, 1999.

[3] *Standard Building Code*, Southern Building Code Congress International, Birmingham, AL, 1994, 1997, 1999.

[4] ACI Committee 318, *Building Code Requirements for Structural Concrete (ACI 318–99) and Commentary (ACI 318R–99)*, American Concrete Institute, Farmington Hills, MI, 1995, 1999.

[5] *Design and Control of Concrete Mixtures*, 13th Edition, Portland Cement Association, Skokie, IL, 1988.

[6] *Method of Test for Quality of Water to be Used in Concrete*, T26-79, American Association of State Highway and Transportation Officials, Washington, D. C., 1979.

[7] *Structural Welding Code – Reinforcing Steel*, ANSI/AWS D1.4–98, American Welding Society, Miami, FL, 1998.

[8] *International One- and Two-Family Dwelling Code*, International Code Council, Falls Church, VA, 1998 (formerly CABO One- and Two-Family Dwelling Code, Council of American Building Officials, Falls Church, VA, 1995).

[9] ACI Committee 201, *Guide to Durable Concrete*, ACI 301.2 R–92, American Concrete Institute, Detroit, MI, 1992. Also, *ACI Manual of Concrete Practice*, Part I.

[10] ACI Committee 222, *Corrosion of Metals in Concrete*, ACI 222 R–96, American Concrete Institute, Detroit, MI, 1996. Also, *ACI Manual of Concrete Practice*, Part I.

[11] ACI Committee 211, *Standard Practice for Selecting Proportions for Normal, Heavyweight, and Mass Concrete*, ACI 211.1–98, American Concrete Institute, Farmington Hills, MI, 1998. Also *ACI Manual of Concrete Practice*, Part I.

[12] ACI Committee 211, *Standard Practice for Selecting Proportions for Structural Lightweight Concrete*, ACI 211.2–91, American Concrete Institute, Detroit, MI, 1991. Also, *ACI Manual of Concrete Practice*, Part I.

[13] ACI Committee 304, *Guide for Measuring, Mixing, Transporting, and Placing Concrete*, ACI 304 R–89, American Concrete Institute, Detroit, 1989. Also, *ACI Manual of Concrete Practice*, Part 2.

[14] ACI Committee 309, *Guide for Consolidation of Concrete*, ACI 309 R–96, American Concrete Institute, Detroit, MI, 1996. Also, *ACI Manual of Concrete Practice*, Part 2.

[15] ACI Committee 308, *Standard Practice for Curing Concrete*, ACI 308–92, American Concrete Institute, Detroit, MI, 1992. Also, *ACI Manual of Concrete Practice*, Part 2.

[16] ACI Committee 517, *Accelerated Curing of Concrete at Atmospheric Pressure – State of the Art*, ACI 517.2R–80, American Concrete Institute, Detroit, MI, 1980.

[17] ACI Committee 306, *Cold Weather Concreting*, ACI 306 R–88, American Concrete Institute, Detroit, MI, 1988. Also, *ACI Manual of Concrete Practice*, Part 2.

[18] ACI Committee 305, *Hot Weather concreting*, ACI 305 R–91, American Concrete Institute, Detroit, MI, 1991. Also, *ACI Manual of Concrete Practice*, Part 2.

[19] ACI Committee 347, *Guide to Formwork for Concrete*, ACI 347 R–94, American Concrete Institute, Detroit, MI, 1994. Also, *ACI manual of Concrete Practice*, Part 2.

[20] Hurd, M. K., *Formwork for Concrete*, SP-4, 5th Edition, American Concrete Institute, Detroit, MI, 1989.

[21] Johnston, D. W., "Design and Construction of Concrete Formwork," Chapter 7, *Concrete Construction Engineering Handbook*, (E. G. Nawy, Editor-in-Chief), CRC Press, Boca Raton, FL, 1997, pp. 7.1-7.48.

[22] Ghosh, S. K, "Construction Loading in High-Rise Buildings," Chapter 8, *Concrete Construction Engineering Handbook*, (E. G. Nawy, Editor-in-Chief), CRC Press, Boca Raton, FL, 1997, pp. 8.1-8.60.

[23] ACI Committee 315, *ACI detailing Manual*, SP-66, American Concrete Institute, Detroit, MI, 1994.

[24] *Manual of Standard Practice*, 25th Edition, Concrete Reinforcing Steel Institute, Schaumburg, IL, 1990.

[25] *Structural Welded Wire Fabric Detailing Manual*, 1st Edition, Wire Reinforcement Institute, McLean, VA, 1985.

[26] Fanella, D. A., Munshi, J. A., and Rabbat, B. G., Ed., *Notes on ACI 318–99*, Portland Cement Association, Skokie, IL, 1999.

[27] Babaei, K., and Hawkins, N. M., "Field Bending and Straightening of reinforcing Steel," *Concrete International*, Vol. 14, No. 1, January 1992.

[28] Kemp, E. L., Brezny, F. S., and Unterspan, J. A., "Effect of Rust and Scale on the Bond Characteristics of Deformed Reinforcing Bars," ACI Journal, *Proceedings* Vol. 65, No. 9, September 1968. pp. 743-756.

[29] ACI Committee 408, *Bond Stress – The State of the Art*, ACI Journal, *Proceedings* Vol. 63., No. 11, November 1966, pp. 1161-1188.

[30] Deatherage, J. H., Burdette, E. G. and Chew, C. K., "Development Length and Lateral Spacing Requirements of Prestressing Strand for Prestressed Concrete Bridge Girders," *PCI Journal*; Vol. 39, No. 1, January – February 1994, pp. 70-93.

[31] Russell, B. W., and Burns, N. H., "Measured Transfer Lengths of 0.5 and 0.6 in. Strands in Pretensioned Concrete," *PCI Journal*, Vol. 41, No. 5, September – October 1996, pp. 44-65.

[32] Applied Technology Council, *Tentative Provisions for the Development of Seismic Regulations for Buildings*, ATC Publication ATC 3-06, NBS Special Publication 510, NSF Publication 78-8, U. S. Government Printing Office, Washington, D. C., 1978.

[33] Seismology Committee, Structural Engineers Association of California, *Recommended Lateral Force Requirements and Commentary*, Sixth and Seventh Editions, Sacramento, CA, 1996, 1999.

[34] Ghosh, S. K., "Design of Reinforced Concrete Buildings under the 1997 UBC," *Building Standards*, International Conference of Building Officials, May-June 1998, pp. 20-24.

[35] Ghosh, S. K., "Needed Adjustments in 1997 UBC," Proceedings, 1998 Convention, Structural Engineers Association of California, October 7-10, 1998, Reno-Sparks, Nevada, pp. T9.1-T9.15.

[36] *Strength Design Load Combinations for Concrete Elements*, IS 521, Portland Cement Association, Skokie, IL, 1998.

[37] Ishizuka, T., and Hawkins, N. M., *Effect of Bond Deterioration on the Seismic Response of Reinforced and Partially Prestressed Concrete and Ductile Moment Resistant Frames*, Report SM 87-2, Department of Civil Engineering, University of Washington, Seattle, 1987.

[38] Stanton, J., Stone, W. C., and Cheok, G. S., "A Hybrid Reinforced Precast Frame for Seismic Regions," *PCI Journal*, Vol. 42, No. 2, March-April 1997, pp. 20-32.

[39] Building Officials and Code Administrators International, *The BOCA National Building Code/1999 – Commentary*. Country Club Hills, IL, 1999.

[40] Southern Builing Code Congress International, *An Illustrated Commentary to the 1999 Edition of the Standard Building Code*, Birmingham, AL, 1999.

[41] Cook, R. F. *Strength Design of Anchorage to Concrete*, First Edition, Portland Cement Association, Skokie, Illinois, 1999.

[42] ACI Committee 349, "Code Requirements for Nuclear Safety Related Concrete Structures," ACI 349-97, *ACI Manual of Concrete Practice*, Part 4, 1999 (Appendix B - Steel Embedments, pp. 349-76 - 349-82).

[43] *PCI Design Handbook*, Fifth Edition, Precast/Prestressed Concrete Institute, Chicago, IL, 1999.

[44] Fuchs, W., Eligehausen, R., and Breen, J., "Concrete Capacity Design (CCD) Approach for Fastening to Concrete," *ACI Structural Journal*, Vol. 92, No. 6, November - December 1995, pp. 787-802.

[45] Eligehausen, R., and Balogh, T., "Behavior of Fasteners Loaded in Tension in Cracked Reinforced Concrete," *ACI Structural Journal*, Vol. 92, No. 2, May - June 1995, pp. 365-379.

[46] ACI Committee 506, *Specifications for Shotcrete*, ACI 506.2-95, American Concrete Institute, Detroit, MI, 1995.

[47] "Recommended Practice for Design, Manufacture and Installation of Prestressed Concrete Piling." *PCI Journal*, Vol. 38, No. 2, March-April 1993, pp. 14-41.

[48] *NEHRP (National Earthquake Hazards Reduction Program) Recommended Provisions for the Development of Seismic Regulations for New Buildings*, Building Seismic Safety Council, Washington, D. C., 1985, 1988, 1991, 1994, 1997.

[49] *Minimum Design Loads for Buildings and Other Structures*, ASCE 7–93, ASCE 7–95, and ASCE 7–98, American Society of Civil Engineers, New York, 1993, 1995, 2000.

[50] Standard Specifications for Highway Bridges, 16th Edition, American Association of State Highway and Transportation Officials, Washington, D. C., 1994.

[51] Gergely, P., and Lutz, L. A., "Maximum Crack width in reinforced Concrete Flexural members," *Causes, Mechanism and Control of Cracking in Concrete*, SP-20, American concrete Institute, Detroit, MI, 1989, pp. 87-117.

[52] Darwin, D., et al., "Debate: Crack Width, Cover, and Corrosion," *Concrete International*, Vol. 7, No. 5, May 1985, American Concrete Institute, Detroit, pp. 20-35.

[53] Oesterle, R. G., "The Role of Concrete Cover in Crack Control Criteria and Corrosion Protection," RD Serial No. 2054, Portland Cement Association, Skokie, IL, 1997.

[54] Beeby, A. W., "The Prediction of Crack Widths in Hardened Concrete, *The Structural Engineer*, Vol. 57A, No. 1, U. K., January 1979, pp. 9-17.

[55] Frosch, R. J., "Another Look at Cracking and Crack Control in Reinforced Concrete," *ACI Structural Journal*, Vol. 96, No. 3, May – June 1999, pp. 437-442.

[56] Athey, J. W., Ed., *Test Report on Slender Walls*, Southern California Chapter of the American Concrete Institute and Structural Engineers Association of Southern California, Los Angeles, CA, 1982.

[57] ACI-ASCE Committee 423, *Recommendations for Concrete Members Prestressed with Unbonded Tendons*, ACI 423.3 R-89, ACI Structural Journal, Vol. 86, No. 3, May-June 1989, pp. 301-318. Also, *ACI Manual of Concrete Practice*, Part 3.

[58] *Specifications for Unbonded Single Strand Tendons*, Revised 1993, Post-Tensioning Institute, Phoenix, AZ, 1993.

[59] Breen J. E., Burdet, O., Roberts, C., Sanders, D., Wollmann, G., and Falconer, B., *Anchorage Zone Requirements for Post-Tensioned Concrete Girders*, NCHRP Report 356, Transportation Research Board, Washington, D. C., 1994.

[60] Barth, F., "Unbonded Post-Tensioning in Building Construction," Chapter 12, *Concrete Construction Engineering Handbook*, (E. G. Nawy, Editor-in-Chief), CRC Press, Boca Raton, FL, 1997, pp. 12.1-12.55.

CHAPTER 20
ALUMINUM

Chapter 20 covers the requirements for quality, design, fabrication and erection of aluminum structures. The IBC references aluminum industry standards rather than transcribing the provisions directly into the code. One advantage to this approach is that the referenced standards can be easily updated by revising the year in Chapter 35, Referenced Standards, thereby keeping the code current with the latest available industry standard.

CHAPTER 21
MASONRY

The provisions in the IBC masonry chapter result from an amalgamation of the provisions from the 1997 *Uniform Building Code* (UBC),[1] the *National Building Code* (NBC),[2] the *Standard Building Code* (SBC),[3] the NEHRP *Recommended Provisions for Seismic Regulations for New Buildings and Other Structures,*[4] ACI 530-99/ASCE 5-99/TMS 402-99 *Building Code Requirements for Masonry Structures*[5] and from ACI 530.1-99/ASCE 6-99/TMS 602-99 *Specification for Masonry Structures.*[6] The 1997 UBC masonry provisions were the main resource for these provisions, although there are differences in content and format. The IBC adopts standards by reference. This has made the provisions more concise as many of the design provisions, test procedures, or material standards are not included in the body of the code but are incorporated by reference.

The UBC strength design provisions for masonry were developed over the period from 1986 through 1994 by the Masonry Joint Ad Hoc Committee, which was a joint committee of the Structural Engineers Association of California (SEAOC) Code and Seismology Committees. The provisions were introduced into various editions of the UBC as follows:

1. Masonry shear walls and slender wall out-of-plane designs appeared in 1988.
2. Revisions of shear wall confinement trigger mechanism from stress based to strain based and addition of wall-frame provisions appeared in 1991.
3. Reorganization of the chapter and addition of strength provisions for development, splices, anchorage, and for beams, piers, and columns appeared in 1994.

The masonry strength design provisions in the 1994 UBC were essentially complete. These provisions were essentially unchanged in the 1997 UBC. Many of the NEHRP provisions are based on the UBC strength provisions—some were incorporated in toto while others were modified and updated with the results of the latest research by Technical Coordinating Committee for Masonry Research (TCCMAR) and others. Co-author Robert Chittenden chaired SEAOC's Masonry Joint Ad Hoc Committee during the period 1990 through 2000. Some of the SEAOC committee members are also members of NEHRP Technical Subcommittee 5 (TS-5).

There are also the consensus masonry source documents produced by the Masonry Joint Standards Committee (MSJC), which is a joint committee of the American Concrete Institute (ACI), the American Society of Civil Engineers (ASCE), and The Masonry Society (TMS). These joint documents, formally known as ACI 530-99/ASCE 5-99/TMS 402-99 *Building Code Requirements for Masonry Structures*[5] and ACI 530.1-99/ASCE 6-99/TMS 602-99 *Specification for Masonry Structures*[6] are also referred to as the MSJC Code and the MSJC Specification. Some of the SEAOC committee members are also members of MSJC. Because of the cross membership and cross fertilization of ideas between committees, the provisions of the UBC, MSJC Code and NEHRP are converging.

Several of the source documents have extensive commentary. ACI 530-99/ASCE 5-99/TMS 402-99, ACI 530.1-99/ASCE 6-99/TMS 602-99 ACI 530-99, and NEHRP each have commentary incorporated directly into the document. The Masonry Society produces the *Commentary to Chapter 21 of the Uniform Building Code,*[7] and Building Officials & Code Administrators International, Inc., produce the commentary to the NBC entitled *The National Building Code/1999—Commentary Volume 2.*[8]

This Chapter will focus on the source of the provisions herein and modifications to those provisions that differ from the source documents rather than repeat extensive commentary from these other documents. Table 21-1 shows the source of various provisions in the IBC. The user is referred to the commentary for the cited source section for a more extensive background on the incorporated provisions.

Although the TMS Commentary is for the 1994 UBC, there were essentially no changes in the masonry provisions between the 1994 and 1997 UBC.

TABLE 21-1—IBC MASONRY PROVISION SOURCES

IBC SECTION NUMBER	IBC SECTION TITLE	SOURCE DOCUMENT[1]
2102	DEFINITIONS AND NOTATIONS	UBC Section 2101.4; ACI 530 Section 2.2
2103.1 2103.2 2103.3	Concrete masonry units Clay or shale masonry units Stone masonry units	NBC Section 2104.1 NBC Section 2104.2 NBC Section 2104.3
2103.5	Glass unit masonry	ACI 530, Section 2.2; ACI 530 Section 2.3D
2103.6	Second-hand units	NBC Section 2104.6
Table 2103.7(1)	Mortar Proportions	UBC Table 21-A, except footnotes changed to reference ASTM C 270
Table 2103.7(2)	Mortar Properties	ASTM C 270
2103.8	Surface-bonding mortar	NBC Section 2104.8
2103.9	Mortars for ceramic wall and floor tile	NBC Section 2104.4
2103.11	Metal reinforcement and accessories	NBC Sections 2104.9 (with updates); 2104.9.1, 2104.9.6
2104.1.1	Tolerances	NBC Section 2111
2104.1.2	Placing mortar and units	NBC Section 2111.1.2.1
2104.1.2.1	Bed and head joints	NBC Section 2111.1.2
2104.1.2.1.1	Open end units	NBC Section 2104.4.4.
2104.1.2.2	Hollow units	NBC Section 2111.1.2.2
2104.1.2.3	Solid units	NBC Section 2111.1.2.3
2104.1.2.4	Glass unit masonry	Similar to UBC Section 2110.2
2104.1.2.5	All units	NBC Section 2111.1.2.4
2104.1.3	Installation of wall ties	NBC Section 2111.1.3
2104.1.4	Chases and recesses	NBC Section 2112.1
2104.1.5	Lintels	NBC Section 2112.2
2104.1.6	Support on wood	NBC Section 2112.3
2104.1.7	Masonry protection	NBC Section 2111.1.7
2104.1.8	Weep-holes	NBC Section 2111.1.8
2104.2	Corbeled masonry	NBC Section 2111.2
2104.2.1	Molded cornices	NBC Section 2111.2.1
2104.3	Cold-weather construction	NBC Section 2111.3
2104.4	Hot weather construction	ACI 530.1 Section 1.8D
2104.5	Wetting of brick	NBC Section 2111.5
2105.2	Acceptance relative to strength requirements	UBC Section 2105.3.5
2105.4	Mortar testing	UBC Section 2105.4, with test reference changed from UBC standard to applicable ASTM standard
2105.5	Grout testing	UBC Section 2105.5, with test reference changed from UBC standard to applicable ASTM standard
2106.1.2.3	Response modification coefficients	NEHRP Table 5.2.2 source for R factors
2106.1.2.4	Design loads for shear walls	UBC Section 2107.1.7
2106.4	Seismic Design Category C	ACI 530 Section 1.13.5.1
2106.4.1	Design of elements that are not part of the lateral-force-resisting system	ACI 530 Section 1.13.5.2
2106.4.1.1	Load-bearing frames or columns	ACI 530 Section 1.13.5.2.1
2106.4.1.2	Masonry partition walls	ACI 530 Section 1.13.5.2.2
2106.4.1.3	Reinforcement requirements for masonry elements	ACI 530 Section 1.13.5.2.3

(continued)

TABLE 21-1—IBC MASONRY PROVISION SOURCES—(continued)

IBC SECTION NUMBER	IBC SECTION TITLE	SOURCE DOCUMENT[1]
2106.4.2	Design of elements that are part of the lateral-force-resisting system	ACI 530 Section 1.13.5.3
2106.4.2.1	Connections to masonry shear walls	ACI 530 Section 1.13.5.3.1
2106.4.2.2	Connections to masonry columns	ACI 530 Section 1.13.5.3.2
2106.4.2.3	Masonry shear walls	ACI 530 Section 1.13.5.3.3
2106.4.2.3.1	Minimum reinforcement requirements for masonry shear walls	ACI 530 Section 1.13.5.3.3
2106.5	Seismic Design Category D	UBC Section 2106.1.12.4 and some of those contained in UBC Section 2106.1.12.3
2106.5.2	Minimum reinforcement requirements for masonry walls	Similar to requirements in UBC Section 2106.1.12.4, Item 2.3
2106.5.3	Masonry shear walls	Similar to requirements in UBC Section 2106.5.3.1
2106.5.5	Material requirements	UBC Section 2106.1.12.4, Item 3
2106.5.6	Lateral tie anchorage	UBC Section 2106.1.2.4, Item 1
2106.6	Seismic Design Category E or F	Similar requirements to UBC Section 2106.1.12.4 Item 3 and Section 2106.1.12.3, Item 5
2106.6.1	Design of elements that are not part of the lateral-force-resisting system	UBC Section 2106.1.12.4, Item 2.4 and ACI 530 Section 1.13.7.2
2106.2	Design of elements that are part of the lateral-force-resisting system	ACI 530 Section 1.13.7.3
2108.1	General	Similar to requirements in UBC Section 2108.1.1
2108.2	Quality assurance provisions	Similar to requirements in UBC Section 2108.1.3
2108.3	Required strength	Similar to requirements in UBC Section 2108.1.3
2108.4.1.1	Flexure	UBC Section 2108.1.4.1.1
2108.4.1.2	Shear	NEHRP Table 11.5.3
2108.4.2.1	Walls with factored axial load stress of 0.05 f'_m or less	UBC Section 2108.1.4.2.1 and NEHRP Table 11.5.3
2108.4.2.2	Walls with factored axial load stresses greater then 0.05 f'_m	UBC Section 2108.1.4.2.2 and NEHRP Table 11.5.3
2108.4.3.1	Axial load and flexure	UBC Section 2108.1.4.3.1
2108.4.4.1	Flexure with or without axial load	UBC Section 2108.1.4.4.1
2108.4.4.2	Shear	UBC Section 2108.1.4.4.2
2108.4.5	Anchor bolts	NEHRP Section 11.3.12 and Table 11.5.3
2108.4.6.1	Development	UBC Section 2108.4.6.1
2108.4.6.2	Splice	UBC Section 2108.1.4.6.2
2108.5.1	Story drifts	NEHRP Section 11.5.4.1
2108.5.1.1	Cantilever shear walls	NEHRP Section 11.5.4.1.1
2108.5.2	Deflection–plain masonry members	NEHRP Section 11.5.4.2
2108.5.3	Deflection–reinforced masonry	NEHRP Section 11.5.4.3
2108.6	Headed and bent-bar anchor bolts	NEHRP Section 11.3.12n and Code Change S245, 1999 Code Change Cycle
2108.6.1	Axial strength of headed anchor bolts	NEHRP Section 11.3.12.1 with modifications
2108.6.1.1	Projected area of masonry	NEHRP Section 11.3.12.1.1 and Code Change S245, 1999 Code Change Cycle
2108.6.1.2	Effective embedment length of headed anchor bolts	NEHRP Section 11.3.12.1.2
2108.6.1.2.1	Minimum effective embedment length of headed anchor bolts	NEHRP Section 11.3.12.1.3

(continued)

TABLE 21-1—IBC MASONRY PROVISION SOURCES—(continued)

IBC SECTION NUMBER	IBC SECTION TITLE	SOURCE DOCUMENT[1]
2108.6.2	Axial strength of bent-bar anchor bolts	NEHRP Section 11.3.12.2 with modifications
2108.6.2.1	Projected area of masonry	NEHRP Section 11.3.12.2.1 and Code Change S245, 1999 Code Change Cycle
2108.6.2.2	Effective embedment length of bent-bar anchor bolts	NEHRP Section 11.3.12.2.2
2108.6.2.2.1	Minimum effective embedment length of bent-bar anchor bolts	NEHRP Section 11.3.12.2.3
2108.6.3	Shear length of headed and bent-bar anchor bolts	NEHRP Section 11.3.12.3 and Code Change S245, 1999 Code Change Cycle
2108.6.3.1	Projected area of masonry	NEHRP Section 11.3.12.3 and Code Change S245, 1999 Code Change Cycle
2108.6.3.2	Minimum effective embedment length	NEHRP Section 11.3.12.2.2
2108.6.4	Combined axial and shear strength of anchor bolts	NEHRP Section 11.3.12.4
2108.7.1	Modulus of elasticity of steel reinforcement	NEHRP Section 11.3.10.1
2108.7.2	Modulus of elasticity of masonry	NEHRP Section 11.3.10.2
2108.7.3	Modulus of rigidity of masonry	NEHRP Section 11.3.10.3
2108.7.4.1	Minimum compressive strength	NEHRP Section 11.3.10.4.1
2108.7.4.2	Maximum compressive strength	NEHRP Section 11.3.10.4.2
2108.7.5.1	Out-of-plane bending	NEHRP Section 11.3.10.5.1 for plain masonry and UBC Section 2108.2.4.6 for reinforced masonry
Table 2108.7.5	Modulus of rupture for out-of-plane bending	NEHRP Section 11.3.10.5.1
2108.7.5.2	In-plane bending	NEHRP Section 11.3.10.5.2
2108.7.6	Reinforcement strength	NEHRP Section 11.3.10.6
2108.8	Section properties	NEHRP Section 11.3.11
2108.9	Reinforced masonry	UBC Section 2107.2.1
2108.9.1	Design assumptions	UBC Section 2108.2.1.2
2108.9.2.1	Reinforcing bar size	UBC Section 2108.9.2.1 and NEHRP 11.4.2.1
2108.9.2.2	Joint reinforcement	NEHRP Section 11.4.2.2 modified by SEAOC and S249
2108.9.2.3	Clear distance between parallel bars	NEHRP Section 11.4.3.1
2108.9.2.4	Clear distance between vertical bars in columns and piers	UBC Section 2108.2.2.2 and NEHRP Section 11.4.3.2
2108.9.2.5	Clear distance between spliced bars	NEHRP Section 11.4.3.3
2108.9.2.6	Bundling of reinforcing bars	NEHRP Section 11.4.3.4
2108.9.2.7	Reinforcing bar cover	NEHRP Section 11.4.4.1
2108.9.2.8	Standard hooks	UBC Section 2108.2.2.4
2108.9.2.9	Minimum bend diameter for reinforcing bars	UBC Section 2108.2.2.5 and Table 21 G, and NEHRP Section 11.4.5.4.1 and Table 11.4.5.4.1
2108.9.2.11	Splices	UBC Section 2108.2.2.7 and Code Change S238, 1999 Code Change Cycle
2108.9.2.10	Development	UBC Section 2108.2.2.6
2108.9.2.12	Development of shear reinforcement	NEHRP Section 11.4.5.5
2108.9.2.13.1	Method A	NEHRP Section 11.6.2.2
2108.9.2.13.2	Method B	UBC Section 2108.2.5.6
2108.9.3	Design of beams, piers and columns	UBC Section 2108.2.3.1
2108.9.3.1	Design assumptions	UBC Section 2108.2.3.2
2108.9.3.2	Maximum reinforcement limits	NEHRP Section 11.4.2.2 modified by SEAOC and S249
2108.9.3.3	Required strength	UBC Section 2108.2.3.5
2108.9.3.5.1	Nominal axial and flexural strength	UBC Section 2108.2.3.6.1

(continued)

TABLE 21-1—IBC MASONRY PROVISION SOURCES—(continued)

IBC SECTION NUMBER	IBC SECTION TITLE	SOURCE DOCUMENT[1]
2108.9.3.5.2	Nominal shear strength	NEHRP Section 11.7.3.1
2108.9.3.6	Reinforcement	UBC Section 2108.2.3.7
2108.9.3.7	Seismic design provisions	UBC Section 2108.2.3.8
2108.9.3.8	Dimensional limits	UBC Section 2108.2.3.9
2108.9.3.9.1	Scope	UBC Section 2108.2.3.10.1
2108.9.3.9.2	Longitudinal reinforcement	UBC Section 2108.2.3.10.2
2108.9.3.9.3	Transverse reinforcement	UBC Section 2108.2.3.10.3
2108.9.3.9.4	Construction	UBC Section 2108.2.3.10.4
2108.9.3.10.1	Scope	UBC Section 2108.2.3.11.1
2108.9.3.10.2	Longitudinal reinforcement	UBC Section 2108.2.3.11.2 and Code Change S252, 1999 Code Change Cycle
2108.9.3.10.3	Transverse reinforcement	UBC Section 2108.2.3.11.3 and Code Change S255, 1999 Code Change Cycle
2108.9.3.11.1	Scope	UBC Section 2108.2.3.12.1
2108.9.3.11.2	Longitudinal reinforcement	UBC Section 2108.2.3.12.2
2108.9.3.11.3	Lateral ties	UBC Section 2108.2.3.12.3
2108.9.3.11.4	Construction	UBC Section 2108.2.3.12.4
2108.9.4.1	General	UBC Section 2108.2.4.1
2108.9.4.2	Maximum reinforcement	NEHRP Section 11.6.2.2
2108.9.4.3	Moment and deflection calculations	UBC Section 2108.2.4.3
2108.9.4.4	Walls with factored axial load stress of 0.05 f'_m	UBC Section 2108.2.4.4 except shear: NEHRP Section 11.7.3.1
2108.9.4.5	Walls with factored axial load stress greater than 0.05 f'_m	UBC Section 2108.2.4.5 except shear: NEHRP Section 11.7.3.1
2108.9.4.6	Deflection design	UBC Section 2108.2.4.6
2108.9.5.1	General	UBC Section 2108.2.5.1
2108.9.5.2	Reinforcement	UBC Section 2108.2.5.6
2108.9.5.3	Design strength	UBC Section 2108.2.5.3
2108.9.5.4	Axial strength	UBC Section 2108.2.5.4
2108.9.5.5	Shear strength	UBC Sections 2106.5.3.2 and 2108.4
2108.9.6.1	Special masonry moment frames (wall frames)	NEHRP 11.12.1
2108.9.6.2	Reinforcement	UBC Section 2108.2.6.2.4
2108.9.6.2.1	Moment strength	NEHRP 11.12.3.1
2108.9.6.2.2	Lap splices	UBC Section 2108.2.6.2.4
2108.9.6.2.3	Other splices	UBC Section 2108.2.6.2.4
2108.9.6.2.4	Yield strength	UBC Section 2108.2.6.2.4
2108.9.6.3.1	Compression force	UBC Section 2108.2.6.2.5
2108.9.6.3.2	Reinforcement ratio	UBC Section 2108.2.6.2.5
2108.9.6.3.3	Minimum clear span	UBC Section 2108.2.6.1.2
2108.9.6.3.4	Beam depth	UBC Section 2108.2.6.1.2
2108.9.6.3.5	Beam width	UBC Section 2108.2.6.1.2
2108.9.6.4.1	Spacing	UBC Section 2108.2.6.1.2
2108.9.6.4.2	Distribution	UBC Section 2108.2.6.1.2
2108.9.6.4.4	Reinforcement for each masonry unit	UBC Section 2108.2.6.2.5

(continued)

TABLE 21-1—IBC MASONRY PROVISION SOURCES—(continued)

IBC SECTION NUMBER	IBC SECTION TITLE	SOURCE DOCUMENT[1]
2108.9.6.5.1	Minimum shear strength	UBC Section 2108.2.6.2.8
2108.9.6.5.2	Hooks	UBC Section 2108.2.6.5.2, Item 2
2108.9.6.5.3	End region spacing	UBC Section 2108.2.6.5.2, Item 2
2108.9.6.5.4	Other maximum spacing	UBC Section 2108.2.6.5.2, Item 2
2108.9.6.5.5	Reinforcement ratio	UBC Section 2108.2.6.5.2, Item 2
2108.9.6.5.6	First bar location	UBC Section 2108.2.6.5.2, Item 2
2108.9.6.6.1	Maximum compression force	UBC Section 2108.2.6.2.7
2108.9.6.6.2	Parallel column dimensions	UBC Section 2108.2.6.1.2, but the UBC also limits the maximum depth of the column to 96 inches to match the limited research
2108.9.6.6.3	Height-to-depth ratio	UBC Section 2108.2.6.1.2
2108.9.6.6.4	Height-to-depth ratio	UBC Section 2108.2.6.1.2
2108.9.6.7.1	Minimum number	UBC Section 2108.2.6.2.6
2108.9.6.7.2	Distribution	UBC Section 2108.2.6.2.6
2108.9.6.7.4	Reinforcement ratio	UBC Section 2108.2.6.2.6
2108.9.6.8.1	Minimum shear strength	UBC Section 2108.2.6.2.8, but modified so that the plastic moment strength is calculated using 1.25 times the yield strength rather than 1.4 times as in the UBC
2108.9.6.8.2	Hooks	UBC Section 2108.2.6.2.6
2108.9.6.8.3	Spacing	UBC Section 2108.2.6.2.6
2108.9.6.8.4	Reinforcement ratio	UBC Section 2108.2.6.2.6
2108.9.6.9.1	Beam depth	UBC Section 2108.2.6.2.9
2108.9.6.9.2	Reinforcement details	UBC Section 2108.9.6.2.9
2108.10	Design of plain (unreinforced masonry) members	1997 NEHRP

[1]"NBC" refers to the *1999 National Building Code*; "NEHRP" refers to the 1997 *NEHRP Recommended Provisions for Seismic Regulations for New Buildings and Other Structures*; "UBC" refers to the 1997 *Uniform Building Code*.

SECTION 2101 GENERAL

The masonry provisions govern the materials, design, construction, and quality for masonry designed in accordance with working stress design, strength design, or empirical design, and for glass masonry and masonry veneers. This section contains the basic road map for the user. Section 2101.2 directs the user to specific sections depending on the design method or material being used. The requirements for construction documents provide the minimum information to be presented in those design drawings and specifications.

SECTION 2102 DEFINITIONS AND NOTATIONS

The sources for the definitions are UBC Section 2101.3 and NBC Section 2102.0. The sources for notation are UBC Section 2101.4 and ACI 530 Section 2.2.

SECTION 2103 MASONRY CONSTRUCTION MATERIALS

This section contains minimum requirements for masonry materials that are similar to UBC Sections 2102 and 2103. Rather than adopt UBC Standards, which are based on ASTM standards, the IBC adopts ASTM Standards and Specifications. Therefore, there are only minor differences in the specific requirements for masonry between the IBC and the UBC.

2103.4 Ceramic tile. References for ceramic tile mortar have been added based on requirements in other model codes. During the development of the IBC, it was often discussed whether architectural materials like ceramic tile belonged in structural chapters. For lack of a better place, the ceramic tile provisions were placed in Chapter 21 as in other model codes.

2103.5 Glass unit masonry. The requirement for treating surfaces of the glass block in contact with mortar is similar to UBC Section 2110.2.

2103.6 Second-hand units. Materials may be reused, provided that they meet all the code requirements for new materials. Note, however, that Section 104.9.1 restricts the use of used materials unless specifically approved by the building official. One should exercise caution in approving reuse of materials. The applicable material or design standards must be consulted to determine if re-use of used materials should be permitted. For example, glass block units may not be reused per IBC Section 2103.5.

This section allows the use of salvaged or "used" brick. Used bricks are often salvaged from the demolition of old buildings. Masonry units manufactured in the past may not have the same quality as masonry made to meet current standards. Caution should also be practiced when specifying used brick as a structural material. Even though the brick may appear clean, the pores in the bedding faces may be filled with cement paste, lime, and other deleterious microscopic particles that may reduce the absorption properties of the brick thereby adversely affecting the bond between the mortar and the masonry and reducing the mortar strength. Testing for the absorption rate of used masonry units in accordance with ASTM C 67 will give an indication of the bonding qualities of the used units with mortar. Used masonry units are best used as veneers where the units are not relied upon for structural strength.

Table 2103.7(1). Mortars proportioned in accordance with this table should have a cube strength in excess of that required by ASTM C 270 for the various mortar types. Type M mortar is high-strength mortar having a minimum average 28-day compressive strength of 2,500 psi. Type M is suitable for general use. Type M mortar is recommended where maximum compressive strength is required such as in unreinforced masonry below grade. Type S mortar is recommended where a high lateral strength is required and is specifically recommended for reinforced masonry. The minimum average compressive strength for Type S mortar is 1,800 psi. Type N mortar is a medium strength mortar having a minimum average compressive strength of 750 psi. Type N mortar may be used where high compressive or lateral strength is not required. Type N is generally used in exposed masonry above grade where exposed to weather. Type O mortar is a low strength mortar having a minimum average compressive strength of 350 psi. Type O mortar should only be used for non-bearing walls not exposed to severe weathering.

Table 2103.7(2). This table allows for the proportioning of mortar to meet the minimum requirements for 28-day compressive strength, minimum water retention, and maximum air content.

2103.8 Surface-bonding mortar. The specifications for pre-mixed mortar, masonry units, and other materials used in constructing dry-stack , surface bonded masonry, as well as the construction requirements, are referenced in this section.

2103.9 Mortars for ceramic wall and floor tile. See comments on Section 2103.4 regarding placement of provisions for architectural materials in structural chapters.

2103.10 Grout. Grout proportion requirements are shown in Table 2103.10. The minimum grout strength requirement of 2,000 psi set forth in the model codes has been removed from the code provisions since ASTM C 476 permits grout to comply with the minimum strength requirement of 2,000 psi, or to comply with the proportions shown in Table 2103.10. Grout batched in accordance with the proportions in Table 2103.1 will have a strength in excess of 2,000 psi.

2103.11 Metal reinforcement and accessories. Requirements for metal reinforcement and accessories reflect updates made in consensus standards. Deformed reinforcement must meet the requirements in IBC Section 2103.11.1. A new standard has been approved for joint reinforcement and is referenced in IBC Section 2103.11.2.

SECTION 2104 CONSTRUCTION

The provisions in IBC Section 2104 and the referenced standard, ACI 530.1/ASCE 6/TMS 602 provide minimum requirements to ensure the masonry is properly constructed consistent with the design methods used. More stringent construction requirements and referenced specifications than those contained in this code may be needed to satisfy aesthetic and architectural criteria. Such requirements should be written into the Construction Documents.

Many of the construction requirements that are contained in IBC Section 2104 are also contained in the MSJC Specification. The IBC Structural Subcommittee decided to not repeat many of these requirements in the IBC since they are already contained in the reference standard. The committee did, however, want certain minimum construction requirements related to placement of units and requirements for cold and hot weather construction. The committee's intent was that once users of the IBC become more familiar with the referenced standard as well, these construction provisions may be deleted since they are redundant. In this way, conflicts can be avoided between the IBC and the referenced standard.

2104.1 Masonry construction. This section cites the applicable code sections and references the construction provisions of ACI 530.1.

SECTION 2105 QUALITY ASSURANCE

The quality assurance provisions in the IBC were modeled after those in the 1997 UBC and the MSJC Code. Readers will find the requirements similar to those in the UBC, with a few exceptions as follows:

1. Compliance with the specified compressive strength of the masonry, f'_m, can no longer be verified by the Prism Test Record method that was permitted in the 1997 UBC. This procedure to ensure compliance was deleted because the masonry industry noted that it has rarely been used, and the requirements make it less likely to be used in the future. Moreover, such a procedure is not permitted in the MSJC Specification.

2. Design of masonry by the Working Stress Design Method using one half of the allowable stresses to avoid the requirements is no longer permitted. Although the UBC permits half stress design of masonry for uninspected masonry construction, this is not consistent with the MSJC, which requires a minimum level of inspection for all masonry structures.

The IBC requires full allowable stress for masonry designed by the Working Stress Design Method along with mandatory inspection. During the development of the IBC, it was noted that masonry damaged in past earthquakes and high wind events often showed extremely poor workmanship, which contributed greatly to the damage. Many of the failed masonry structures showed evidence of missing reinforcement, missing grout or missing connectors, and other improper construction techniques. Even when using half stresses for such designs, there would likely not be sufficient strength in poorly constructed masonry to support the expected wind loads or seismic demands. Special Inspection requirements have also been added in IBC Section 1707.5. IBC Section 2105 also requires testing of materials in accordance with ASTM Standards. Requirements for the frequency at which tests must be performed have been moved to Section 1706.6 with other testing requirements.

2105.1 General. This section has been adapted from ACI 530, Section 1.14.1 and ACI 530.1, Section 3.7B.

SECTION 2106 SEISMIC DESIGN

IBC Section 2106 contains the minimum design requirements for masonry structures in seismic areas. The section was based on requirements in the *1997 Uniform Building Code,* the MSJC Code, and the NEHRP Requirements. Requirements are broken down for various seismic risk categories, with requirements being cumulative for lower seismic risk to higher seismic risk. The categories used to designate seismic risk are now based on the concept of seismic design categories used in the 1997 NEHRP instead of seismic zones. Seismic design categories are based not only on the location of the structure in relation to known seismically active areas, but also according to building importance and classification of the soil beneath the structure. More detailed information on seismic design categories is contained in the commentary to Chapter 16 of the IBC and in the Commentary to the 1997 NEHRP Provisions.

2106.1 Seismic design requirements for masonry. General seismic design requirements are contained in this section. Basic seismic-force-resisting systems are described based on concepts from the 1997 NEHRP. Five shear wall types are included to indicate the expected performance of the walls with various construction techniques. These five shear wall types are assigned different seismic properties, such as response modification factors, *R*, based on the expected performance and ductility of the walls. Certain shear wall types are required in each seismic region, and unreinforced shear wall types are not permitted in intermediate and high seismic risk regions. Table 21-2 summarizes the requirements of each of the 5 masonry shear wall types.

2106.1.2 Alternate seismic design requirements for structures designed by the working stress design method. This section permits a designer to comply with the requirements of Section 1.13 of the 1999 MSJC Code since the provisions in Section 2106 are largely taken from this document. This section was added so that designers familiar with the MSJC Code could continue using the MSJC Code in its entirety and still comply with the IBC seismic requirements. This section, however, modifies and updates the MSJC Code provisions, as those MSJC provisions are based on earlier editions of ASCE 7 and NEHRP which do not include the IBC concepts of seismic design categories and the basic seismic-force-resisting systems. The modifications are covered in Sections 2106.1.2.1 through 2106.1.2.4.

2106.2 Seismic Design Category A. Minimum requirements for masonry in SDC A are contained in this section. Buildings classified in this low seismic risk category are permitted to be designed by any of the methods listed in IBC Chapter 21, and need only to meet minimal requirements for anchoring the structure to the elements providing lateral support. These requirements are similar in concept to those contained in 1997 UBC Sections 2106.1.7 and 2106.1.12.2.

TABLE 21-2. SHEAR WALL TYPES AND REQUIREMENTS

SHEAR WALL DESIGNATION	DESIGN METHODS	REINFORCEMENT REQUIREMENTS	MAY BE USED IN SEISMIC DESIGN CATEGORY
Ordinary plain masonry shear wall	Plain (unreinforced) masonry design per IBC Section 2107 (specifically MSJC Section 2.2) or Section 2108.1	None. Section must remain uncracked under design loads.	A and B
Detailed plain masonry shear walls	Plain (unreinforced) masonry design per IBC Section 2107 (specifically MSJC Section 2.2) or Section 2108.10	Per Section 2106.4.2.3.1. $A_{s\,min}$ = 0.20 in^2 each side openings, corners, wall ends, and 10′-0″ c.c. Section must remain uncracked under design loads.	A and B
Ordinary reinforced masonry shear walls	Reinforced masonry design per IBC Section 2107 (specifically MSJC 2.3) or Section 2108.9	As required by the design but a minimum per Section 2106.4.2.3.1. $A_{s\,min}$ = 0.20 in^2 each side openings, corners, wall ends, and 10′-0″ c.c maximum.	A, B, and C
Intermediate reinforced masonry shear walls	Reinforced masonry design per IBC Section 2107 (specifically MSJC Section 2.3) or Section 2108.9	As required by the design but a minimum per Section 2106.4.2.3.1. $A_{s\,min}$ = 0.20 in^2 each side openings, corners, wall ends, and 4′-0″ c.c. maximum.	A, B, and C
Special reinforced masonry shear walls	Reinforced masonry design per IBC Section 2107 (specifically MSJC Section 2.3) or Section 2108.9	As required by the design but a minimum per Section 2106.5.3.1. Sum of H and V $A_s \geq$ 0.002 A_{gross}, min 0.007 A_{gross} each direction, maximum spacing = 4′-0″ c.c	A, B, C, D, E and F

NOTE: The maximum spacing for reinforcement in an intermediate reinforced masonry shear wall is 4′-0″ c.c. This differs from the MSJC Code and NEHRP where the maximum spacing allowed is 10′-0″ c.c.

2106.3 Seismic Design Category B. The requirements for SDC B are slightly more restrictive than SDC A. The requirements are cumulative with each successive seismic design category. Masonry structures assigned to SDC B must meet all the requirements for SDC A in Section 2106.2 as well as the requirements for SDC B in Section 2106.3. As a minimum, these shear walls must comply with the requirements of either ordinary plain or ordinary reinforced masonry shear walls.

2106.4 Seismic Design Category C. This section parallels UBC Section 2106.1.12.3. Minimum reinforcing is required in order to provide some ductility and load transfer capability in masonry structures assigned to SDC C.

2106.4.2.2 Connections to masonry columns. Column reinforcement and tie requirements parallel those in the MSJC code and in UBC Section 2106.1.12.3, Item 1. Additionally, the tie requirements around anchor bolts are similar to those in UBC Section 2106.3.7.

2106.4.2.3.1 Minimum reinforcement requirements for masonry shear walls. Horizontal reinforcing requirements in masonry shear walls in this seismic design category are similar to those in UBC Section 2106.1.12.3. The maximum spacing of vertical reinforcement is permitted to be up to 10 feet in ordinary reinforced shear walls; however, the maximum spacing of vertical reinforcement for intermediate reinforced or special reinforced shear walls is 48 inches. Note that the maximum spacing for vertical reinforcing of an intermediate reinforced wall is 4 feet, which differs from the maximum spacing of 10 feet allowed in the MSJC Code for intermediate reinforced walls. This 10-foot spacing requirement, consistent with the requirements in the MSJC Code, was debated during the development of the IBC. The Structural Subcommittee agreed to use the requirements in the MSJC Code for the ordinary reinforced shear wall since there was insufficient evidence to determine the minimum reinforcing truly needed in areas of moderate seismic risk. Moreover, it was noted that because of the probable increase in force levels for masonry structures in this seismic design category, reinforcing more consistent with the requirements in the UBC would probably be required anyway. This would result in more reinforcement than the minimum which, for practical purposes, would be at closer spacing than the maximum spacing allowed by the MSJC. Hence the maximum 4-foot spacing for the intermediate shear wall.

2106.4.2.4 Discontinuous members. This is a new provision. These requirements for strength and toughness are intended to prevent local failure or collapse in elements supporting discontinuous portions of the lateral-force-resisting system. Inherent in the code philosophy is the assumption that the inelastic demands on the structure will be well distributed throughout the lateral-force-resisting system. The value of the response modification factor, *R,* is based on this assumption, as well as the assumption of sufficient ductility and overstrength to meet the maximum seismic demands. Elements used to redistribute or transfer the effect of overturning forces and shears from stiff discontinuous elements are susceptible to increased localized or concentrated inelastic demands, which violates the above assumption, and may not achieve the required ductility. The requirement for a minimum amount of transverse reinforcement at a maximum spacing increases the maximum usable masonry strain and ductility in the element so that the element may meet the maximum seismic demand and distribute the overturning forces and shears without failure.

2106.5 Seismic Design Category D. Structures in SDC D must comply with SDC C as well as the additional requirements of this section.

2106.5.1 Design requirements. The masonry element must be designed in accordance with either the strength design method or the working stress method and the requirements set forth in the remainder of Section 2106.5

2106.5.3 Masonry shear walls. Masonry shear walls in SDC D must comply with the special reinforced masonry shear wall requirements.

2106.5.3.2 Shear wall shear strength. In a plastic hinge zone, there is extensive cracking from flexure. Because of the extensive cracking, the capacity to develop shear resistance in the masonry is significantly reduced. Hence, the steel reinforcement should be designed to resist the entire shear force in plastic hinge zones, as required by this section. Note that this requirement applies to designs using either working stress design or strength design. There are no modifications in the IBC to the provisions in ACI 530, Section 2.3.5 to effect the requirements of this section. The strength method must be used to determine the necessary amount of steel and spacing to meet the intent of this section.

2106.5.4 Minimum reinforcement for masonry columns. The provisions in this section are based on the concept of UBC Section 2106.1.12.4, Item 1 and ACI 530, Section 1.13.6.5. However, the details for termination of the column ties are covered in Section 2106.5.6.

2106.6 Seismic Design Category E or F. Structures in SDC E and F must comply with the requirements for SDC D as well as the additional requirements outlined in this section. These are restrictions placed on the use of Type N mortar and masonry cement in the lateral-force-resisting system in this seismic design category. Additional restrictions are imposed on stack bond masonry in buildings assigned to these highest seismic risk categories.

2106.6.2.1 Masonry shear walls. Only special reinforced walls are allowed in SDC E or F.

SECTION 2107
WORKING STRESS DESIGN

2107.1 General. Section 2107 provides an overall reference to the working stress design method in MSJC Code with modifications that the Structural Subcommittee determined were appropriate. The subcommittee chose to use a reference to the MSJC Code because the basic philosophy of the IBC is to adopt consensus standards for design procedures by reference if a suitable consensus standard is available. The Subcommittee did this consistently, with the exception of Section 2108, since no consensus standard currently exists for the strength design of masonry.

The allowable stress design provisions in the referenced standard (MSJC Code) are based on the use of full design stresses only, assuming that structural masonry will receive some minimum level of inspection. These minimum levels of inspection have accordingly been incorporated into IBC Section 1707.5. Thus, the MSJC Code does not contain the half stress design procedure permitted by UBC 2107.1.2.

Other minor differences between the MSJC Code and the UBC do occur (e.g., slightly different modulus of elasticity values), but overall, the procedures and allowable values are quite consistent so that designers will easily be able to switch from UBC working stress design procedures to those in the MSJC Code.

2107.2 Modifications to ACI 530/ASCE 5/TMS 402. The Structural Subcommittee made several modifications to the MSJC Code. The modifications are discussed in the Sections 2107.2.1 through 2107.2.5 below.

2107.2.1 ACI 530/ASCE 5/TMS 402, Chapter 2. This modification requires special inspection in accordance with IBC Chapter 17 rather than the MSJC Code. The inspection requirements in Chapter 17 are more comprehensive than those required in the MSJC Code.

2107.2.2 ACI 530/ASCE 5/TMS 402, Section 2.1.4. This modification permits lightly loaded masonry columns in low seismic exposure buildings to be reinforced with a single vertical reinforcing bar as long as the column can safely support the code required loads and deformations. In the MSJC Code, columns are defined by geometry, not by applied load. Thus masonry members that have a certain geometry are classified as columns although they more closely resemble a flexural element with low axial load. Such "columns" are required by the MSJC Code to be reinforced with a minimum amount of vertical reinforcement and horizontal ties. Section 2107.2.2 exempts lightly loaded columns (such as those that support carport roofs, which experience primarily axial tension and flexure in high wind events) from these prescriptive requirements of the MSJC Code.

2107.2.3 ACI 530/ASCE 5/TMS 402, Section 2.1.8.6.1.1, Lap splices. This modification requires the reinforcing bar splice lengths to be consistent for all masonry design methods (working stress design and strength design). The existing splice lengths in the MSJC are based on developing the allowable stress in the bar by means of an assumed simplified bond mechanism. This method is unconservative for large bar sizes.

Both working stress and strength design methods assume that the reinforcing will have sufficient strength to resist the imposed forces. Splices of reinforcing bars must meet this same strength test; the same for development length. In seismic regions, the force in any particular bar is indeterminate, but may be at the yield strength of the bar. Required development and splice lengths are based on developing the yield strength of the reinforcing bar, including any apparent overstrength, without distress in the masonry as is done in the strength design method.

Provisions introduced in the 1994 UBC, Section 2108.2.2.6, contained more realistic requirements for development and splicing of reinforcing bars. These provisions were based on the research for development and splicing of reinforcing bars in concrete with adaptations as necessary to reflect that masonry does not have confinement reinforcement, as does concrete. Subsequent testing by the National Concrete Masonry Association validated the basic form of the equation used in the UBC but determined that the required splice length was conservative for small bars and unconservative for large bars. Hence, the equation was modified to include another factor that increased splice and development lengths for bar sizes No. 8 and larger, and reduced the length for bar sizes No. 5 and smaller. The upper limit was removed from the equation, and the limit on cover depth for purposes of computation of the required splice and development length was increased from $3d_b$ to $5d_b$.

The splice length or development length required by the equation in the code, including the ϕ factor, will develop 125 percent of the specified yield strength of the reinforcing bar. This allows for the likely overstrength of reinforcing bars and matches the requirements for welded or mechanical splices, which also must develop 125 percent of the specified yield strength of the bar.

The adopted modification is only for splices. Although the same length is also needed to develop the strength of the reinforcing bar, the requirement for development length is not in the IBC. Designers should use the same requirements for both development and splice lengths as is required for strength design. See IBC Section 2108.9.2.10.

2107.2.4 ACI 530/ASCE 5/TMS 402, maximum bar size. Placing large bars in masonry walls over-reinforces the section so that a brittle failure of the masonry is likely. At this time, there are no maximum reinforcement limits in working stress design provisions, although there is a committee exploring this issue. It is difficult to develop lap splices for large reinforcing bars in thin masonry walls. Research shows that when the reinforcing bar size number is larger than the nominal thickness of the wall, the splice will fail by splitting of the wall and pullout of the bar before the strength of the bar is developed in the splice. The research shows that a rough rule of thumb for maximum bar size is (n-1), where "n" is the nominal thickness of the wall. Hence, the limit on bar size to $^1/_8$ of the nominal thickness. This requirement parallels a similar requirement in Section 2108.9.1 for strength design.

2107.2.5 ACI 530/ASCE 5/TMS 402, splice for large bars. The working stress design method allows reinforcing bar sizes up to No. 11. As noted in Section 2107.2.4, these large bar sizes are difficult to splice without splitting the masonry. Mechanical connectors do not cause the splitting problem that occurs in lap splices. Hence, mechanical connectors are more appropriate for bar sizes larger than No. 8. This requirement parallels a similar requirement in Section 2108.9.2.11 for strength design.

SECTION 2108
STRENGTH DESIGN OF MASONRY

Section 2108 has detailed requirements for the strength design of masonry. The MSJC Code currently does not have a strength design procedure. A prime goal of the IBC Structural Subcommittee was to reference consensus design standards rather than include structural provisions within the IBC. However, to maintain the often preferred strength design method, the subcommittee chose to provide the extensive strength design provisions in this section. The subcommittee also encouraged the MSJC to work on the finalization of consensus provisions for strength design as soon as possible.

The provisions in Section 2108 were originally based on the UBC strength design provisions but the provisions for seismic design shear strength and anchor bolts were modified to more closely resemble the strength design provisions in the 1997 NEHRP provisions. As noted in the initial commentary, many of the NEHRP provisions are based on the UBC strength provisions but were modified and updated with the results of the latest research. Additional changes were made to reconcile the differences between the provisions in these two documents. The following describes new provisions and those provisions in the UBC that have undergone major revisions.

2108.4 Design strength. The guidelines for determining the design strength of a member are similar to those contained in UBC Section 2108.1.4. However, the limits of $0.04 f'_m$ on unfactored loads throughout Section 2108 have been modified to $0.05 f'_m$ on factored loads. This was done to make limits consistent throughout the chapter and clarify the requirements that must be met. The net effect on designs will be minor.

Design shear strengths along with corresponding strength reduction factors have been changed considerably based on requirements in the 1997 NEHRP. Therefore, the strength reduction factors in this section have been modified accordingly.

Similarly, anchor bolt provisions have been substantially revised based on the 1997 NEHRP and subsequent changes suggested by engineering groups. These changes reflect the dramatically superior performance of headed anchor bolts over the commonly used bent-bar anchor bolts (see Section 2108.6 analysis). The resulting strength reduction factors have accordingly been modified in this section.

2108.4.3.2 Shear. The strength reduction factor, ϕ, is 0.60 unless the wall is designed such that the nominal shear strength is greater than the shear corresponding to the nominal flexural strength. If the shear strength is less than the flexural strength, the wall is prone to a brittle shear failure. There is also more variability in the determination of shear strength than for flexural strength. Hence, the lower strength reduction factor is required for those cases where shear strength may govern the design.

2108.5 Deformation requirements. These deformation requirements are intended to ensure that masonry will be able to survive the deformations from seismic demands, as well as applied loads, without significant damage.

2108.5.1 Story drifts. Calculated story drifts must not exceed allowable story drifts.

2108.5.3 Deflection—reinforced masonry. Deflection calculations for reinforced masonry may be based on Equation 21-7 or a more exact procedure.

2108.6 Headed and bent-bar anchor bolts. Anchor bolt provisions have been substantially modified. During the development of the IBC, it was noted that the requirements in UBC Section 2108.6 were conservative; the requirements were factored-up values of the working stress values for anchor bolts with some adjustments. The 1997 NEHRP values, however, have not been substantiated as conservative for the edge or end distances equal to the minimum specified embedment. The NEHRP values appear to be based on isolated bolts. There is no available research to calibrate the anchor bolt strengths when the bolt is close to an edge and has minimum embedment.

The provisions adopted into the IBC somewhat split the difference between the conservative UBC values and the possibly nonconservative values in the 1997 NEHRP. In addition, the new provisions reflect the much more favorable performance of headed anchor bolts over bent-bar anchors in tension. The provisions specifically note that void areas either within or around the masonry are not to be taken into account when calculating the projected area of masonry. Similar to the concrete provision, the strength capacity of an anchor is reduced when the anchor is in zone of tensile cracking. The effect is particularly pronounced with shallow drilled-in anchors that rely on expansion to develop the anchor strength. An additional strength reduction factor of 0.7 is applied when anchors are embedded in a cracked tension zone.

2108.6.3 Shear strength of headed and bent-bar anchor bolts. The equation for the shear strength of headed and bent bar anchor bolts reflects the actual behavior during tests. The limit state for masonry is breakout of a surface approximately equal to one half of a right circular cone whether the anchor bolt is at an edge or far away from an edge.

2108.6.5 Anchor bolt placement. Although this section refers to the MSJC Code for edge distance, embedment, and spacing requirements, there are no minimum spacing or edge distance requirements in the MSJC Code. The only requirement in the MSJC Code is for a minimum effective embedment equal to the lesser of four times the bolt diameter, d_b, or 2 inches. The user should refer to UBC Section 2106.2.14 for minimum edge distance, embedment and spacing requirements.

2108.9.2 Reinforcement requirements and details.

2108.9.2.1 Reinforcing bar size. Note that this IBC Section allows a maximum bar size of No. 11 whereas both UBC and NEHRP limit maximum bar size to No. 9. Because the radial splitting forces increase with the square of the bar diameter, d_b, it is difficult to develop the strength of reinforcing bars larger than No. 9.

2108.9.2.2 Joint reinforcement. The use of joint reinforcement for use as shear reinforcement in high seismic risk areas is not recommended. There is no research showing that joint reinforcing is effective in resisting seismic demands. In addition, research by NIST has shown use of joint reinforcement in solid grouted walls, as often occurs in high seismic risk areas, is not practical because of the minimal area of the wires. Hence, the limitation on use in SDC C, D, and F.

2108.9.2.10 Development. Provisions for the development of reinforcement in masonry were based on the UBC and were updated based on new research findings. Equation 21-24 is similar in form to UBC Formula 8-13 with several minor modifications. The limit of 52 d_b has been removed based on new test results that show that this upper limit on splice length results in splices that cannot develop the strength of large bars. A new factor has also been added to reflect the need for longer lap lengths for large bar sizes. The limit on the depth of cover allowed for computation purposes has been increased from 3 d_b to 5 d_b. The tests showed that splices at these larger cover depths performed more favorably than those at the smaller cover depth, but did not experience a pullout type failure. A minor change has also been made to the numerical coefficient based on test results. The net result of these changes will be that for small bar sizes, lap lengths will be smaller than those required by the UBC while for larger bar sizes, lap lengths will be larger.

2108.9.2.11 Splices. The requirements for splices are the same as the requirements for development length. See the commentary in Section 2108.9.2.10.

2108.9.2.13 Maximum reinforcement percentages. The IBC adopts a major change to the method used to determine the maximum amount of reinforcement. UBC Section 2108.2.3.3 provided a method to determine a balanced reinforcing ratio, and other sections, such as UBC Section 2108.2.4.2, based the maximum permitted amount of reinforcement on this ratio. While this method was straightforward and generally conservative, the method was not appropriate for members subjected to high compressive loads. A typical interaction diagram for axial load and moment shows that high axial loads in combination with moments place the masonry member in the region above the balance point. Members in the region above the balance point have limited ductility and fail in a brittle manner with limited usable strain.

The new provisions in this section of the IBC account for axial load directly. Axial load effectively acts like additional reinforcement. The net effect of the method included herein is to reduce the amount of reinforcement allowed by the effects of the axial compressive load thus keeping the member in the ductile region below the balance point.

UBC Section 2108.2.5.6 contained mandatory requirements for boundary members of shear walls. The reinforcement limits of Section 2108.9.2.13.1 (Method A) in combination with the drift limits of Chapter 16, limit the maximum required strain from seismic demands to less than the maximum usable strain. Boundary elements are not needed if reinforcement limits are established in accordance with Method A. Higher reinforcement limits may also be used in accordance with the limits of Section 2108.2.13.2 (Method B). The reinforcement limits of Method B result in higher strains in the masonry that will exceed the maximum usable strain for unconfined masonry. When using Method B, boundary elements are necessary to provide sufficient confinement for the masonry to be considered confined masonry. See Figure 1 for the strain limits of unconfined and confined masonry.

2108.9.2.13.1 Method A. This method may be used only where drifts are limited to a maximum of 0.010 h_{sx} per Table 1617.3 and the maximum extreme fiber strain is less than the strain associated with maximum usable strain for unconfined masonry (see Figure 1). No confinement reinforcement is necessary in this case. See additional discussion above.

2108.9.2.13.2 Method B. This method may be used only where drifts are limited to a maximum of 0.013 h_{sx} per Table 1617.3. The maximum extreme fiber strain is greater than the strain associated with maximum usable strain for unconfined masonry but less than the the maximum usable strain for confined masonry (see Figure 1). Confinement reinforcement is necessary in this case. See the discussion above.

2108.9.3 Design of beams, piers and columns. Requirements for the design of beams, piers and columns are based on the requirements in UBC Section 2108.2.3 with two major differences. The first difference is the method by which the maximum reinforcing ratio is calculated. This method is described in the analysis of Section 2108.9.2.13. The second difference is the calculation of the nominal shear strength in Section 2108.9.3.5.2. As previously described, the nominal shear strength and related strength reduction values are based on the 1997 NEHRP provisions.

2108.9.3.2 Maximum reinforcement limits. Because there are no provisions for confinement reinforcement for beams, piers,

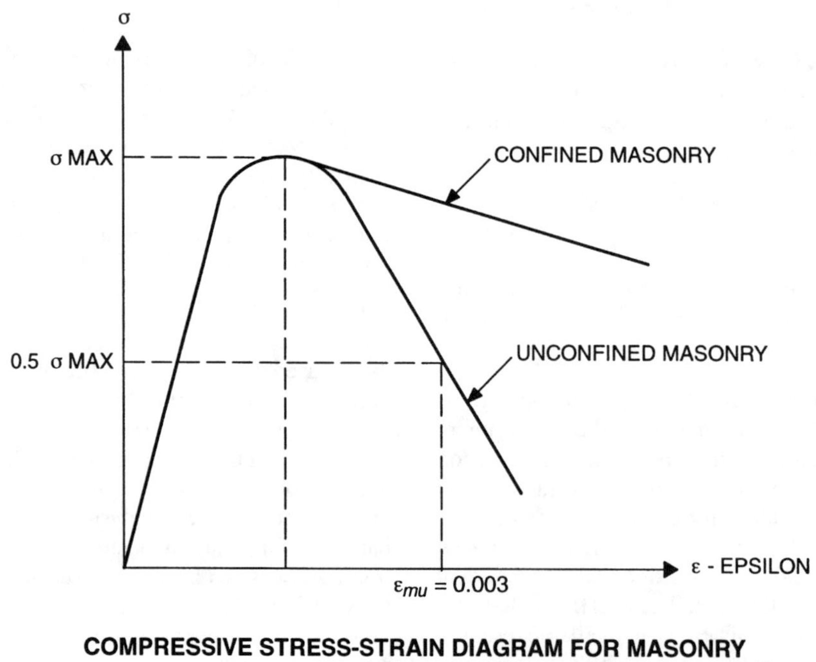

COMPRESSIVE STRESS-STRAIN DIAGRAM FOR MASONRY

FIGURE 1

or columns, the maximum reinforcement must be limited to Method A as specified in Section 2108.9.2.13.1. No confinement reinforcing is necessary when reinforcing is limited in accordance with Method A, as the maximum strains will not exceed the maximum usable strain for unconfined masonry.

2108.9.3.9 Beams.

2108.9.3.9.3 Transverse reinforcement. This has been modified from the UBC provision by requiring that the design shear, V_u, be based on either the moment associated with the maximum drift, δ_x, or the moment associated with the plastic moment capacity based on a yield strength equal to $1.25 f_y$.

2108.9.3.10 Piers.

2108.9.3.10.2 Longitudinal reinforcement. The UBC provision is modified to include the requirement that nominal flexural strength must exceed 1.5 times the cracking flexural strength.

2108.9.3.10.3 Transverse reinforcement. This has been modified from the UBC provision by requiring that the design shear, V_u, be based on either the moment associated with the maximum drift, δ_x, or the moment associated with the plastic moment capacity based on a yield strength equal to $1.25 f_y$.

2108.9.4 Wall design for out-of-plane loads. This section was based on UBC Section 2108.2.4 as noted earlier. The method to determine the maximum reinforcing ratio has been modified. Also, as noted earlier, the axial stress limit has been modified to $0.05 f'_m$ and is to be compared to factored loads. Additionally, the nominal shear strength is modified.

2108.9.4.4 Walls with factored axial load stress of $0.05 f'_m$ or less. These walls are often referred to as "slender." The provisions account for second order (P-delta) effects directly.

2108.9.5 Wall design for in-plane loads. This section is based on UBC Section 2108.9.5, but the nominal shear strength is based on the 1997 NEHRP requirements. As described in the analysis to Section 2108.9.2.13, boundary elements are no longer required if the requirements of Section 2108.9.2.13.1, Method A are met. Other minor modifications have also been made.

2108.9.5.2 Reinforcement. The provisions of this section are based on the UBC, except that in the IBC, the nominal moment capacity, M_n, must exceed the cracking moment, M_{cr}, by a factor of 1.5 for fully grouted walls or 3.0 for partially grouted walls. The cracking moment in a partially grouted wall is highly variable. Also the maximum reinforcement ratio, ρ, is determined by Section 2108.9.2.13. If the maximum reinforcement ratio, ρ, is determined by Section 2108.9.2.13.2, Method B, confinement reinforcement should be added to provide the necessary usable strain. See UBC 2108.2.5.6.

2108.9.6 Special masonry moment frames (wall frames).

2108.9.6.1. Calculations

2108.9.6.3 Wall frame beams.

2108.9.6.3.2. Reinforcement ratio. The reference to Section 2108.9.2.13 refers to Section 2108.9.2.13.1, Method A, as confinement reinforcement is not required. If the maximum reinforcement ratio, ρ, is determined by Section 2108.9.2.13.2, Method B, confinement reinforcement must be added to ensure the necessary usable strain.

2108.9.6.4 Longitudinal reinforcement for beams.

2108.9.6.4.3 Flexural strength. This is a new but worthwhile requirement that the nominal flexural strength must exceed 1.5 times the cracking flexural strength.

2108.9.6.5 Transverse reinforcement for beams.

2108.9.6.5.1 Minimum shear strength. Based on the UBC, but modified so that the plastic moment strength is calculated using 1.25 times the yield strength rather than 1.4 times as in the UBC.

2108.9.6.5.2 Hooks. The two full scale tests from which these provisions were derived both used one-piece transverse reinforcement in the beams. The researcher that performed the tests emphasized that the requirement for one-piece transverse reinforcing was critical to the performance of the frame. He felt that the strength and stiffness degradation that occurs during cyclic demands would increase at an unacceptable rate at very low levels of ductility without one-piece transverse reinforcing. The UBC requirement was for one-piece transverse reinforcing bars. This requirement was dropped when the UBC provisions were adapted into NEHRP. One-piece transverse reinforcing should be used to ensure ductile behavior.

2108.9.6.6. Wall frame columns.

2108.9.6.7 Longitudinal reinforcement for columns.

2108.9.6.7.3. Moment strength. This is a new requirement that the nominal flexural strength must exceed 1.5 times the cracking flexural strength.

2108.9.6.7.4 Reinforcement ratio. The reference to Section 2108.9.2.13 refers to Section 2108.9.2.13.1, Method A, as confinement reinforcement to achieve a higher usable strain is not required. The original research was based on a strong column–weak beam concept and all inelastic behavior was required to occur in the beams. Hence, the UBC requirement in Section 2108.2.6.2.7 that the nominal moment strength of the column must exceed 1.6 times the nominal moment strength of the beam to ensure strong column–weak beam mechanism. To achieve the strong column–weak beam mechanism implicit in these provisions, the column moment capacity should exceed the beam moment capacity, including the reinforcing in the floor slab, by at least a factor of 1.6.

2108.9.6.8 Transverse reinforcement for columns.

2108.9.6.8.1. The plastic moment strength is to be calculated using 1.25 times the yield strength rather than 1.4 times as in the UBC.

2108.9.6.9 Wall frame beam-column intersection.

2108.9.6.9.1 Beam depth. Loss of bond and slip of reinforcement because of cracking is a major problem in the beam-column joint in concrete special moment frames. Loss of bond and slip of reinforcement in a masonry wall frame is a worse problem. Concrete special moment frames have confining reinforcing that significantly increases the confined strength of the concrete and reduces the slip. There is no confinement in the joint of a masonry wall frame, only transverse reinforcement, which has a limited effect on confinement. The provisions to proportion the joint were established to reduce the amount of cracking in the joint and hence the slip of the reinforcing. The IBC provision does not include the UBC requirement that the joint shear forces be based on the assumption that the stress in all tension steel is equal to 1.4 times the specified yield stress. The purpose of this provision is to ensure that the inelastic behavior always occurs in the beams, not the column.

2108.10 Design of plain (unreinforced) masonry members. The requirements in this section for the strength design of plain (unreinforced) masonry were taken from the 1997 NEHRP.

SECTION 2109 EMPIRICAL DESIGN OF MASONRY

Section 2109 contains empirical design requirements for masonry that are nearly identical to those contained in the 1999 MSJC and that are similar to those in the 1997 UBC. This section also contains requirements for adobe masonry that are similar to those contained in the SBC and the *Uniform Code for Building Conservation* (UCBC).

SECTION 2110 GLASS UNIT MASONRY

Glass unit masonry provisions are similar to those contained in the UBC with additional updates and revisions based on the 1999 MSJC Code. See also the TMS commentary[7] and MSJC commentaries.[5, 6]

SECTION 2111 MASONRY FIREPLACES

These sections contain fireplace, heater, and chimney requirements from a variety of sources. It was a goal of the ICC to coordinate the provisions in the IBC with those in the *International Residential Code* (IRC). The resulting language coordinates the provisions between these two codes.

1997 UBC Section 2111 and Chapter 31 were used as references for these requirements, although many of the provisions may have been updated or revised. Users of the 1997 UBC will find consistent seismic anchorage requirements (from UBC Section 3102.4.3 in IBC Section 2111.3 and 2113.3), hearth requirements, firebox minimum dimensions, clearance requirements, flue sizing charts, etc. The format of the new provisions, however, is dramatically different and numerous changes were made to provide consistency between the IBC and the IRC.

REFERENCES

1. ICBO, 1997 *Uniform Building Code*, International Conference of Building Officials, Whittier, CA, 1997.
2. BOCA, *1999 National Building Code*, Building Officials & Code Administrators International, Inc. Country Club Hills, IL, 1999.
3. SBCCI, *1999 Standard Building Code*, Southern Building Code Congress International, Inc., Birmingham, AL, 1999.
4. NEHRP, *NEHRP (National Earthquake Hazard Reduction Program) Recommended Provisions for the Development of Seismic Regulations for New Buildings (and Other Structures)*, Building Seismic Safety Council, Washington, D.C., 1994 (1997).
5. ACI 530/ASCE 5/TMS 402, *Building Code Requirements for Masonry Structures*, American Concrete Institute, Farmington Hills, MI, 1995.
6. ACI 530.1/ASCE 6/TMS 602, *Specification for Masonry Structures*, American Concrete Institute, Farmington Hills, MI, 1995.
7. TMS, *Commentary to Chapter 21, Masonry, of the Uniform Building Code*, The Masonry Society.
8. BOCA, *The BOCA National Building Code—Commentary Volume 2*, Building Officials & Code Administrators International, Inc. Country Club Hills, IL, 1999.

BIBLIOGRAPHY

ASTM C270-96a, *Standard Specification for Mortar for Unit Masonry*, American Society for Testing and Materials, West Conshohocken, PA, 1996.

ICBO, *Handbook to the Uniform Building Code: An illustrative commentary*, International Conference of Building Officials, Whittier, CA, 1998.

ICC, *Proposed Changes to the Final Draft of the International Building Code*, International Code Council, January 1999.

ICC, *1998 Proposed Changes to the First Draft of the International Building Code*, International Code Council, April 1998.

SEAOC, *Recommended Lateral Force Requirements and Commentary*, Structural Engineers Association of California, Sacramento, CA, 1996.

UBC-IBC Structural Comparison & Cross Reference, International Conference of Building Officials, Whittier, CA, 2000.

CHAPTER 22
STEEL

SECTION 2201
GENERAL

2201.1 Scope. This chapter essentially gives the user a roadmap to the design standards appropriate to the various types of steel construction. Previous sections of the model codes often adapted only parts of the design standard, thus causing confusion. The 1997 *Uniform Building Code* started the transition step of adopting the design standards by reference similar to the *National Building Code* and the *Standard Building Code.*

SECTION 2202
DEFINITIONS AND NOMENCLATURE

2202.1 Definitions. These definitions are the minimum necessary.

2202.2 Nomenclature. The meaning of these symbols as used in this chapter is set forth.

SECTION 2203
IDENTIFICATION AND PROTECTION OF STEEL FOR STRUCTURES

2203.1 Identification. All steel must be identified for conformance to the specification and grade. Unidentified steel must be tested.

2203.2 Protection. Protection of structural steel and cold-formed steel structural members or panels from corrosion is required. Protection may be by painting or galvanizing.

SECTION 2204
STRUCTURAL STEEL CONSTRUCTION

Structural steel must be designed in accordance with the cited LRFD, ASD, or HSS specification. The *Specification for the Design of Steel Hollow Structural Sections* (Steel Hollow Structural Section 5) is a new standard specifically developed for the design of round, square, and rectangular steel tubular structural sections. Note that the section properties for the hollow structural sections (HSS) are approximately 90-95 percent of those printed in the Dimensions and Properties tables of the AISC *Manual of Steel Construction—Allowable Stress Design.*[1] The revised properties reflect the thicknesses resulting from the current fabrication practices of the HSS producers. Seismic design provisions are in Section 2212.

SECTION 2205
COLD-FORMED STEEL

2205.1 General. This section adopts the new *Specification for the Design of Cold-Formed Steel Structural Members—1996* published by the American Iron and Steel Institute. This new specification incorporates both load and resistance factor design and allowable stress design into a single specification. Seismic design provisions for light frame walls are in Section 2211. Cold formed stainless steel structures are designed in accordance with ASCE 8.

2205.2 Composite slabs on steel decks. Composite slabs covered by this section are those constructed of concrete over metal deck forms where the slab acts compositely through the mechanism of mechanical interlock of the aggregate with deformations in the deck and bond to the deck. The steel deck acts like reinforcing steel in the positive moment region of the span and reduces the need for additional reinforcing bars or mesh. Where the loads are high, mechanical shear connectors, such as welded studs, will also be required.

SECTION 2206
STEEL JOISTS

As in the model codes, steel joists are required to be designed, manufactured, and tested in accordance with the specifications published by the Steel Joist Institute (SJI).

Joists are used primarily as gravity-load-carrying members. When joists are incorporated into the lateral-force-resisting system as collectors, chords, and diaphragm ties (see Section 1620.2) care must be taken to ensure that the joists are specifically designed to function as such members. Normally, joists are designed only for gravity and wind uplift loads. A continuous load path is necessary for chords, collectors, and diaphragm ties, and their connections. The typical seat on a steel joist is eccentric to the chord and is not ordinarily designed to carry the axial force and resulting moment through the seat when functioning as a collector or chord. Hence, special seats must be designed and manufactured, or the load path must be directed through the chords by direct chord-to-chord connection; e.g., see Fisher[2] for methods of designing chord to chord connections.

SECTION 2207
STEEL CABLE STRUCTURES

2207.1 General. See the commentary in ASCE 19 for an explanation of the requirements for cable structures.

2207.2 Seismic requirements for steel cable. The modifications for seismic design originate in the NEHRP provisions and commentary.[3]

SECTION 2208
WELDING

This section does not directly adopt the *AWS Structural Welding Code.*[4, 5] Rather, it requires that welding be performed in accordance with the steel specification used for the design. This is done because the referenced standards either adopt different editions of an AWS D1.1 specification, adopt a different AWS specification or the referenced standards include their own welding requirements as in the Steel Joist Institute standards. For example, AISC ASD references AWS D1.1-88, AISC LRFD references AWS D1.1-92, and the AISI specification for cold formed steel references AWS D1.3-89.

Adoption of this approach has both positive and negative impacts. Positive impacts accrue from reduction in confusion as to what exactly are the requirements. However, the negative impact is that necessary changes and the results of the latest research are not incorporated respectively into the welding spec. For example, the valuable lessons on structural welding learned from the SAC Joint Venture investigations[6, 7] after the Northridge earthquake are not required by either the AISC ASD or AISC LRFD. The requirements of the referenced AWS D1.1 specification should be supplemented with additional welding requirements for structures classified as Seismic Design Category D, E, or F. For example, notch tough filler metals should be used for all welds in the lateral-force-resisting system as indicated in AISC Seismic Provisions, Supplement No. 1.[8]

SECTION 2209 BOLTING

The philosophy used for this section is similar to that used for welding requirements, because the design standards adopt different editions of different standards. Bolt standards are not adopted directly, but are referenced in the design standards of Sections 2204 and 2205. For example, AISC ASD adopts the *Specification for Structural Joints Using ASTM A325 or A490 Bolts* by the Research Council for Structural Connections (RCSC),[9] while AISC LRFD adopts *Load and Resistance Factor Design Specification for Structural Joints Using A325 or A490 Bolts* by RCSC.[10]

2209.2 Anchor bolts. The requirements are similar to previous model codes but the provision for oversize holes was deleted.

SECTION 2210 STEEL STORAGE RACKS

Use of the Rack Manufacturers Institute (RMI) specification is limited to the stated storage racks, which are the typical low to moderate height industrial racks mounted at grade as used in warehouse and warehouse retail applications. Seismic design of other types of racks not specifically included in the RMI specification must be in accordance with IBC Section 1622.3.4.

SECTION 2211 WIND AND SEISMIC REQUIREMENTS FOR LIGHT FRAMED COLD-FORMED STEEL WALLS

This is a new section giving design shear values for wood structural panel sheathing and gypsum board sheathing screwed to cold-formed steel studs, and detailing provisions for diagonal braced bays. The provisions give allowable shear and design shear values for resistance to wind and seismic forces for both allowable stress design (ASD) and load resistance factor design (LRFD). The provisions first appeared in the 1997 UBC and are modified herein. Except as noted below, the values given in the tables are nominal shear values that are adjusted by a resistance factor, ϕ, for LRFD, or divided by a safety factor, Ω, for ASD.

The nominal shear values given in the tables are for the following assemblies:

1. Gypsum board sheathing applied to nominal 20-gage studs with a maximum 2:1 height to width ratio.
2. $^{15}/_{32}$-inch structural I sheathing applied to nominal 20-gage studs with a maximum 2:1 height to width ratio.
3. $^{7}/_{16}$-inch rated sheathing (OSB) applied to nominal 20-gage studs with a 2:1 and 4:1 maximum height-to-width ratio.

The shear resistance values are based on testing documented in *Final Report—Shear Wall Values for Lightweight Steel Framing.*[11]

Wind shear values are based on monotonic testing, whereas the seismic values are based on cyclic testing that approximated the ATC-24 protocol.[12]

Other shear resistance values given in the tables for wood structural panel sheathing on thicker (nominal 16 gage) studs or sheathing oriented perpendicular to the studs, and for sheet steel, (t_{min} = 0.018 or 0.027 inch) are based on *Additional Shear Wall Values for Light Weight Steel Framing.*[13]

When using 4:1 aspect ratio walls, care must be taken to minimize slip between the hold-down anchor and the anchor bolt and slip between the hold-down anchor and the hold-down stud in order to limit the wall deflection. Any slip will result in additional deflection at the top af the wall equal to the cumulative slip magnified by four times. All structural and architectural elements should be checked for deformation compatibility if these high aspect ratio walls are used.

Note that the behavior of wood structural panels screwed to cold-formed steel studs is very different from the same panel nailed or stapled to wood studs. In an assembly of a wood structural panel on wood studs nailed with 8d or 10d nails to 2x studs, the behavior of the assembly is governed by the ductile bending of the nail in the stud. The nail behavior is ductile bending of the nail as defined by Mode III_s until low cycle fatigue failure or Mode IV. Mode III_s is fastener yielding in the (main) stud member along with bearing dominated yielding in the wood fibers of the (side) structural panel. Mode IV is fastener yielding in both the stud and structural panel with limited localized crushing of wood fibers. Refer to the NDS-1997.[14] Failure in cyclic testing is caused either by a low cycle fatigue failure of the nail or by tear out/tear through of the nail through the structural panel. Failure in earthquakes is generally from tear out/tear through of the nail through the structural panel and occasionally by splitting of the 2x wood members.

In an assembly of wood structural panels screwed to steel studs, the behavior of the assembly is governed by local distortion of the studs. The wood panels act as essentially rigid bodies, the screws are stiff and brittle, and the structural fuse is the bending and distortion in the steel stud. If the stud is too thick, the screws break in a brittle manner when subjected to monotonic or cyclic testing. The No. 8 waferhead screws tested performed satisfactorily with studs having an uncoated thickness of approximately 0.035 inch (nominal 20 gage). When the same size screws and structural panels were tested with studs having an uncoated thickness of approximately 0.055 (nominal 16 gage), the screws fractured in a brittle manner. The studs must have sufficient flexibility in the flange so as to not overpower the screw strength. Thus the requirement that the walls be constructed as assemblies without substitution.

The discussion above uses the term gage when referring to normal thickness. Although this is not strictly correct (the correct designation is by thickness), light-gage cold-formed steel members are commonly specified by gage rather than minimum thickness.

2211.1 General. The design of light-framed, cold-formed steel to resist wind and seismic loads must be in accordance with the AISI or ASCE 8 provisions and this section. Thicknesses, both maximum and minimum, are per Sections 2211.2.1 and 2211.7.4.

2211.2 Conditions of applications. Boundary elements are critical to the proper performance of the assembly. Note that the boundary elements must be designed and constructed in a manner that allows distortion of the flange or surface to which the screw is attached.

2211.2.1 Limitations for systems in Tables 2211.1(1), 2211.1(2), and 2211.1(3). The limitations in this section set forth the parameters of the materials and other requirements for the wall assembly.

2211.3 Wood structural panel sheathing.

2211.3.1 Shear values. The shear values for wind in Table 2211.1.1 are based on monotonic testing. Although this section allows shear values to be calculated using the principles of mechanics and approved fastener values, there has not been sufficient research to establish the appropriate cyclic values for screws in steel studs to use this approach for high seismic loads. Thus, calculated values are only allowed in Seismic Design Categories (SDC) A, B and C. Care should be taken that the stud has sufficient flexibility relative to the screw if shear values are calculated.

Note well the following limitations:

1. The shear values set forth in Tables 2211.1(1) and 2211.1(3) *may not be increased* for duration of load effects as is usually permitted for wood.
2. Except as noted in Table 2211.1 (1), Note c, the values for sheathing are not additive, nor may they be increased. If sheathing is installed on both sides of the wall, the shear values of *only one side* can be used to resist lateral forces.

2211.3.2 Orientation. Although the wood structural panels may be attached in either direction, all panel edges must be fully blocked per Section 2211.2.1 and, with one exception in Table 2211.1.1, the nominal shear values are the same regardless of orientation.

2211.3.3 Attachment. Screws are to be a minimum No. 8 with minimum head diameter of 0.292 inches and penetrate the steel framing member by at least three exposed threads.

2211.4 Gypsum board panel sheathing. Gypsum board sheathed walls are allowed only for wind loads. Gypsum board sheathed walls do not resist cyclic loads without significant strength and stiffness loss during cyclic tests. The brittle gypsum fractures at the edges and the paper tears and the nails then pull through the gypsum board. Hence they are not allowed to resist seismic ground shaking. Wind is a quasi-monotonic load the upper bound of which can be approximated by a Tippett Type II distribution. Hence, gypsum board sheathed walls may only be used to resist wind loads.

2211.4.1 Shear values. Note that gypsum board must be applied to both sides of the studs in order to use the shear values from Table 2211.1(2).

2211.4.2 Orientation. Panel edges not on a stud or track must be blocked in accordance with the table.

2211.4.3 Attachment. Attachment must be made with the designated screw required by the code.

2211.5 Sheet steel sheathing. Walls of this type have only limited cyclic test results.

2211.6 Design shear determination. A factor of safety, Ω, used as the divisor to adjust the nominal values to an allowable shear values is 2.5 for both wind and seismic. Where LRFD is used, the tabulated nominal shear values must be multiplied by the resistance factor, ϕ, of 0.55 to obtain the design shear value. Previous codes used a divisor of 3.0 for wind and 2.5 for seismic.

2211.7 Seismic Design Category D, E or F.

2211.7.1 Boundary elements. As shown in the test reports,[11, 13] the performance of boundary elements is critical to the performance of the wall assembly. The boundary elements of light framed braced bay members are required to meet the special seismic load combination of Section 1605.4 for the anticipated maximum seismic effects per Section 2211.7.3.

2211.7.2 Connections. Connections for these critical boundary elements must develop the lesser of the strength of the member or the force from the anticipated maximum earthquake effect.

2211.7.3 Braced bay members. The term "braced bay" includes bays braced by either wood structural panel sheathing or diagonal bracing. The intent of these provisions is to provide a braced panel that can develop the full strength of the wood structural panel sheathing or the diagonal brace. Boundary elements and anchorage must have the strength to resist the special seismic load combinations of Section 1605.4 for the anticipated maximum seismic effects.

2211.7.4 Wood structural panel sheathing. Openings in wood structural panels must be designed and detailed to transfer shear flows around the opening. See Section 2305.3.7 for methods to design and detail shear transfer around openings in wood structural panel shear walls. Studs, wall studs, and track are limited to a minimum and maximum thickness to match the tested configurations.

The shear values are based on testing of assemblies; i.e., a specific combination of stud, track wood structural panel and screw. In SDC D, E and F, the cited assembly must be constructed without substitution; i.e., a 16-gage stud cannot be substituted for a 20-gage stud, nor can the wood panel grade be changed in thickness or grade, nor can the screw type and size be changed.

In SDC D, E, and F, the uncoated stud base metal thickness is limited to a maximum of 0.048 inch, which is halfway between the minimum base metal thickness for 18 gage (0.043 inch) and 16 gage (0.054 inch). The intent is to limit the stud thickness to nominal 18 gage. Note, also that the design shear values may *only* be based on the values in Table 2211.1(3); i.e., the design shears must be substantiated by cyclic tests. Shear values are *not* permitted to be calculated by "rational" analysis.

SECTION 2212 SEISMIC REQUIREMENTS FOR STRUCTURAL STEEL CONSTRUCTION

Seismic requirements for structural steel structures are set forth in the AISC *Seismic Provisions for Structural Steel Building 1997.*[8] These AISC Seismic 1997 Provisions incorporate the latest requirements based on the NEHRP 1997[3] and the significant research results of the SAC Joint Venture investigation,[7, 15] which was initiated as a result of the extensive damage to welded steel moment frames in the Northridge earthquake. The AISC Seismic 1997 provisions present requirements for structural steel designed in accordance with the AISC LRFD specification in Part I, and the requirements for structural steel designed in accordance with the AISC ASD specification in Part III. Part III requirements mostly refer the user back to Part I requirements. Requirements for composite structural steel and concrete structures are in Part II. AISC Seismic 1997 contains an extensive commentary and bibliography. The user is referred to AISC Seismic 1997 and its commentary for a detailed discussion on the provisions.

2212.1 Seismic requirements for steel structures.

2212.1.1 Seismic Design Category A, B or C. Any system allowed by Sections 2204 through 2207 may be used on SDC A, B and C. The structure must be detailed and designed in accordance with AISC Seismic 1997 Part I or III for structural steel, or IBC Section 2211 for light framed walls, in order to use a response modification coefficient, R, greater than 3. Hence, a composite system would be required to use $R = 3$.

2212.1.2 Seismic Design Category D, E or F. Structures constructed of structural steel must be designed and detailed for ductile response in accordance with AISC Seismic 1997 Part I or III. Structures constructed of light framed walls must be designed and detailed in accordance with Section 2211.

SECTION 2213 SEISMIC REQUIREMENT FOR COMPOSITE CONSTRUCTION

The IBC contains the first concise technical provisions for combining structural steel and concrete in the lateral-force-resisting system. The use of composite construction in the lateral-force-resisting system has been growing in nonseismic areas, but its use in high seismic areas has been limited because of the lack of research documenting the behavior under cyclic seismic loading and accepted design requirements. Composite construction is commonly used in the gravity systems in all regions.

Because these are new requirements, it was felt necessary to require the designer to submit evidence to the building official substantiating the performance of the system in SDC B or above. Where the design relies on composite elements that are expected to undergo inelastic demands, the evidence must include cyclic tests in accordance with the test protocol and acceptance criteria set forth in AISC Seismic 1997. In SDC D, E or F, composite construction is not allowed except as permitted in Section 2213.2. Cyclic testing must be used to establish that the composite system has the ability to develop sufficient strength and to sustain the inelastic rotations necessary to resist the design earthquake with limited structural damage.

REFERENCES

1 AISC ASD–89, *Specification for Structural Steel Buildings—Allowable Stress Design*, American Institute for Steel Construction, Inc., Chicago, IL, 1989.

2 Fisher, James A., West, Michael, and Van de Pas, Julian, *Designing with Steel Joists, Joist Girders, and Steel Deck*, Vulcraft/Nucor, 1991.

3 NEHRP, *NEHRP (National Earthquake Hazard Reduction Program) Recommended Provisions for the Development of Seismic Regulations for New Buildings (and Other Structures)*, Building Seismic Safety Council, Washington, D.C., 1994 (1997).

4 AWS D1.1–98, *Structural Welding Code—Steel*, American Welding Society, Miami, FL, 1998.

5 AWS D1.3–98, *Structural Welding Code—Sheet Steel*, American Welding Society, Miami, FL, 1998.

6 SAC-95–02, *INTERIM GUIDELINES: Evaluation, Repair, Modification and Design of Steel Moment Frames*, SAC Joint Venture—A Partnership of the Structural Engineers Association of California, Applied Technology Council, and California Universities for Research in Earthquake Engineering, Sacramento, CA, 1995 (also known as FEMA 267).

7 SAC–96-03, *INTERIM GUIDELINES: Advisory No. 1*, SAC Joint Venture—A Partnership of the Structural Engineers Association of California, Applied Technology Council, and California Universities for Research in Earthquake Engineering, Sacramento, CA, 1996 (also known as FEMA 267A).

8 AISC Seismic–97, *Seismic Provisions for Structural Steel Buildings* (including Supplement No. 1, Feb 1999), American Institute for Steel Construction, Inc., Chicago, IL, April 1997.

9 RCSC–85, *Specification for Structural Joints Using A325 or A490 Bolts* (with 1988 Revisions), Research Council on Structural Connections, AISC, Chicago, Il 1988.

10 RCSC-94, *Load and Resistance Factor Design Specification for Structural Joints Using A325 or A490 Bolts,* Research Council on Structural Connections, AISC, Chicago, IL 1994.

11 Serrette, R., *Final Report—Shear Wall Values for Lightweight Steel Framing*, University of Santa Clara, Santa Clara, CA, 1996.

12 ATC–24, *Guidelines for Cyclic Seismic Testing of Components of Steel Structures*, Applied Technology Council, Redwood City, CA 1992.

13 Serrette, R., *Additional Shear Wall Values for Light Weight Steel Framing*, University of Santa Clara, Santa Clara, CA, 1997.

14 ANSI/AF&PA NDS-1997, *National Design Specification for Wood Construction (Revised)*, American Forest & Paper Association, Washington, D. C., 1997.

15 SEAOC, *Recommended Lateral Force Requirements and Commentary*, Structural Engineers Association of California, Sacramento, CA, 1996.

BIBLIOGRAPHY

AISC LRFD–98, *Load and Resistance Factor Design Specification for Structural Steel Buildings*, American Institute for Steel Construction, Inc., Chicago, IL, 1998.

AISC HSS, *Specification for the Design of Hollow Structural Sections*, American Institute for Steel Construction, Inc., Chicago, IL, 1998.

BOCA, *The BOCA National Building Code—Commentary Volume 2*, Building Officials & Code Administrators International, Inc. Country Club Hills, IL, 1999.

ICBO, *Handbook to the Uniform Building Code: An illustrative commentary*, International Conference of Building Officials, Inc., Whittier, CA, 1998.

ICC, *Proposed Changes to the Final Draft of the International Building Code*, International Code Council, January 1999.

ICC, *1998 Proposed Changes to the First Draft of the International Building Code*, International Code Council, April 1998.

SJI–1994, *Standard Specification, Load Tables, and Weight Tables for Steel Joists and Joist Girders*, Steel Joist Institute, Myrtle Beach, SC, 1994.

UBC-IBC Structural Comparison & Cross Reference, International Conference of Building Officials, Whittier, CA.

CHAPTER 23
WOOD

SECTION 2301
GENERAL

2301.1 Scope. This chapter is an amalgam of the 1997 *Uniform Building Code* (UBC, Ref. 31), the 1996 *National Building Code* (NBC, Ref. 14), and the 1997 *Standard Building Code* (SBC), with the addition of seismic provisions from the 1997 *National Earthquake Hazard Reduction Program Recommended Provisions for Seismic Regulations for New Buildings and Other Structures* (NEHRP, Ref. 34). The provisions were selected from these source documents based on technical merit, necessity, and clarity. New provisions were added where the needed provision did not exist.

The use of seismic design categories instead of seismic zones is a significant change from previous model codes. Seismic Design Categories (SDC) are determined by a combination of use of the structure, as defined by the Seismic Use Group (SUG), and the site seismic hazard. The site seismic hazard is a combination of the seismic risk with the site soil classification (see Section 1615). Seismic zones designations depend only on the location of the structure relative to areas of seismic hazard. See the extensive commentary in Section 1616.

The chapter is formatted into eight major sections that follow a logical format:

1. Section 2301—General
2. Section 2302—Definitions
3. Section 2303—Minimum Standards and Quality
4. Section 2304—General Construction Requirements
5. Section 2305—General Construction Requirements for Lateral-Force-Resisting Systems
6. Section 2306—Allowable Stress Design
7. Section 2307—Load and Resistance Factor Design
8. Section 2308—Conventional Light-Frame Construction

For allowable stress design, the user is referred to the 1997 National Design Specification for Wood Construction (NDS–97), published by the American Forest and Paper Association.[1] For load and resistance factor design, the user is referred to ASCE-16, Standard for Load and Resistance Factor Design (LRFD) for Engineered Wood Construction.[2]

Products addressed in Chapter 23 include boards, dimension lumber, posts, timbers, glued-laminated members and wood structural panels, including plywood, particleboard, fiberboard and hardboard. This chapter contains material specifications, quality requirements, design data and empirical provisions for minimum construction practices.

Wood and wood products are also regulated by other chapters in the code. Chapter 14 contains provisions for weather coverings for walls, as well as provisions for veneers and exterior trim. Wood and wood products used in fire-resistance-rated assemblies must comply with Chapter 7. Wood and wood products used as interior finish on walls, ceilings and floors must comply with Chapter 8. Wood roof coverings are regulated in Chapter 15.

2301.2 General design requirements. These provisions are applicable to wood used in combination with other materials. For example, a wood roof system may be combined with masonry walls.

2301.2.1 Allowable stress design. Allowable stress design (ASD) uses the load combinations of Section 1605.3 for the determination of strength. However, deformations and drifts are determined by using the strength level loads in accordance with the requirements of Section 1617.4.6 (E is not divided by 1.4 for deformation or drift). The special load combinations of Section 1605.4 are used for collector design for all structures assigned to SDC B through F, except wood frame buildings braced entirely by shear walls.

2301.2.2 Load and resistance factor design. Load and Resistance Factor Design (LRFD) has been added as a design method. The applicable load combinations are in Section 1605.2. Note that wood structures designed using LRFD are subject to the same general and lateral force provisions as structures designed using ASD. Section 2307 refers the user to AF&PA/ASCE 16[2] for the actual LRFD requirements and resistance values.

2301.2.3 Conventional light-frame wood construction. The conventional construction provisions are in both Sections 2304 and 2308.

2301.3 Nominal sizes. Nominal lumber sizes, for example, 2 inches by 4 inches, are the sizes usually referred to or specified in this chapter. Actual or net dimensions, which are always less than nominal dimensions, must be used in calculations to determine member sizes or stresses. The actual sizes of dimension lumber are set forth in DOC 20; the actual sizes for glued laminated lumber are set forth in the NDS.

SECTION 2302
DEFINITIONS

New definitions were added to clarify the provisions in other sections of this chapter. Many of the added definitions are for use with the new LRFD section. Several others have been added to clarify terms used in lateral-force-resisting systems.

COLLECTOR. The IBC recognizes both horizontal and sloped (or nearly horizontal) diaphragms. The definition of collector applies to both horizontal and sloped diaphragms. The word "horizontal" is used to differentiate from vertical elements such as a wall.

DIAPHRAGM. A diaphragm is a horizontal or nearly horizontal (sloped) structural element that transmits lateral forces to the vertical elements (walls or frames) of the lateral-force-resisting system. This clarifies that the term "diaphragm" should be used only for the horizontal (or sloping) element, not the vertical element.

DIAPHRAGM, BLOCKED. This definition has been revised to clarify that the adjacent sheathing panel edges must be supported on and fastened to common blocking members. The concept of a blocked diaphragm is to have continuity between the sheathing panel edges. A blocked diaphragm has significantly less deflection than an unblocked diaphragm because of the continuity of panel edges.

DIAPHRAGM, RIGID. Diaphragm can be classified as rigid, semi-rigid or flexible. Wood shear panel diaphragms are normally assumed to be flexible; concrete diaphragms are assumed to be rigid; and untopped steel deck diaphragms are assumed to be semi-rigid.

For the distribution of seismic or wind forces, the flexibility of the diaphragm relative to the flexibility of the vertical lateral-force-resisting elements (walls or frames) is the important parameter by which to classify the diaphragm. See commentary to Section 2305.2.5 for further discussion of diaphragm classification.

GRADE (LUMBER). References DOC PS 20, American Softwood Lumber Standard, listed under DOC (U.S. Department of Commerce) in Chapter 35. Voluntary Product Standard PS20–99 is published by the U.S. Department of Commerce.

NATURALLY DURABLE WOOD. Includes decay resistant woods, which are redwood, cedar, black locust and black walnut, and termite resistant woods, which are redwood and eastern red cedar.

Naturally durable wood is the heartwood of a durable listed species. Note that only the heartwood of redwood and Eastern red cedar are both decay and termite resistant.

TREATED WOOD. Includes both fire treated wood and wood treated to resist decay and termites.

SECTION 2303
MINIMUM STANDARDS AND QUALITY

2303.1 General. Structural lumber and wood structural panels are highly variable in strengths and other mechanical properties. The code requires that these materials (defined in the first paragraph of this section) conform to the applicable standards or grading rules specified in the code. Furthermore, the code requires that they be identified by a grade mark or be accompanied by a Certificate of Inspection issued by an approved agency. The grade mark is also required to be placed on the material by an approved agency (see labeling—Chapter 17). The proper use of a wood structural member cannot be determined unless it has been identified as to grade and species. Counterfeit grade stamps occasionally appear on lumber in the field, and it is important that designers and enforcement personnel be familiar with the grade-approved stamps. Examples of correct grade marks are shown in Figure 1.

Joist hangers are subject to the requirements of this chapter as well as the requirements in Chapter 22.

2303.1.1 Lumber. Lumber references the voluntary standard, *American Softwood Lumber Standard,* PS 20. NDS–97 references ASTM D 1990, ASTM D 245, ASTM D 2555, The Wood Handbook, the National Grading Rules for Dimensional Lumber, and PS20 for the classification, definition, methods of grading, and development of design values for lumber. The allowable wood stresses in NDS-97 are based on the IN-GRADE Testing Program conducted by the lumber industry, supplemented by testing in accordance with ASTM D 2555.

Approved end-jointed lumber is presumed equivalent to solid sawed lumber. The NDS permits the use of end-jointed lumber in Section 4.1.6 of that standard. The use of the term "approved" is intended to convey the need for quality control over the production of these glued products, and also to establish the qualification tests for the type of end joint used. The standards for proof testing of end-jointed lumber are outlined in guideline standards referenced in Part IV of Chapter 35. An example of end-jointed lumber is shown in Figure 2, which illustrates a finger-jointed end joint.

2303.1.2 Prefabricated wood I-joists. The shear, moment and stiffness capacities of prefabricated wood I-joists must be established in accordance with ASTM D 5055. This standard also specifies that application details, such as bearing length and web openings, are to be considered in determining the structural capacity. Wood I-joists are manufactured out of sawn or structural composite lumber flanges and structural panel webs and are bonded together with exterior adhesives to form an "I" cross section. Wood I-joists are structural members typically used in floor and roof construction. The standard requires I-joist manufactures to employ an independent inspection agency to monitor the procedures for quality assurance. The standard specifies that proper installation instructions accompany the product to the job site. The instructions are required to include weather protection, handling requirements and, where required, web reinforcement, connection details, lateral support, bearing details, web hole-cutting limitations, and any special conditions.

2303.1.3 Structural glued laminated timber. Glue laminated timbers (GLT) are manufactured in accordance with ANSI/AITC A 190.1–92, which references several other AITC Standards. ASTM D 3737 is the method for establishing allowable stresses for GLT. See AITC Timber Construction Manual.[3]

2303.1.4 Wood structural panels. Wood structural panels must conform to the voluntary product standards PS-1, for plywood, or PS-2, for oriented strand board (OSB) and other wood based panels.

Wood structural panels include all-veneer plywood; composite panels consisting of a combination of veneer and wood-based material; and mat-formed panels that contain wood fiber only, such as OSB, particleboard, and waferboard. The primary distinction between OSB and waferboard is that the wood fibers in OSB are generally all oriented in the same direction, while the wood fibers in waferboard are oriented randomly in all directions within the plane of the board. Plywood is defined as panels made by cross laminating three or more wood veneers and joining them together with glue.

The user is encouraged to obtain the referenced standards for additional technical information. It must be emphasized that the proper attachment of wood structural panels to the supporting structural frame is very important. The nailing schedules contained in the code and the manufacturer's recommendations

1. Panel Grade
2. Span Rating
3. Thickness
4. Exposure Durability Classification
5. Mill Number
6. Species Group Number
7. Product Standard PS-1-95 (or PS-2-92)
8. Product Standard PS 1 Grade Conformance Where Applicable
9. Tongue and Groove
10. Evaluation Service Report Number
11. FHA Use of Material Bulletin Number

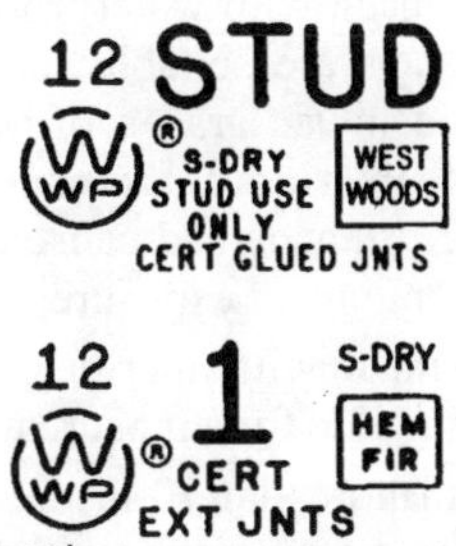

THE AWPB QUALITY MARK

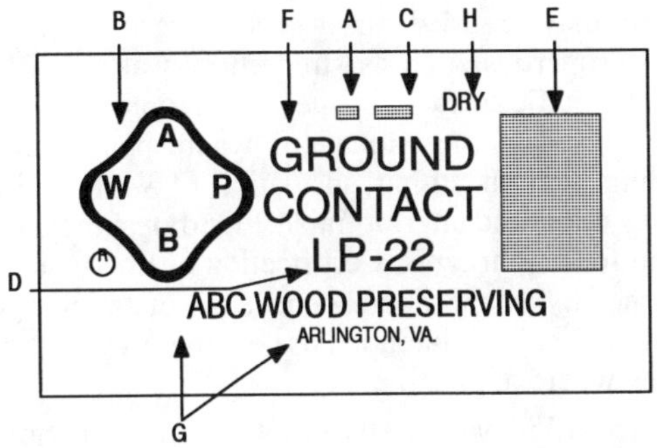

A. Year of treatment
B. American Wood Preservers Bureau Trademark
C. The preservative used for treatment
D. The applicable American Wood Preservers Bureau quality standard
E. Trademark of the agency supervising the treating plant
F. Proper exposure conditions
G. Treating company and plant location
H. Dry or KDAT if applicable

TYPICAL LUMBER GRADE STAMPS

FIGURE 1

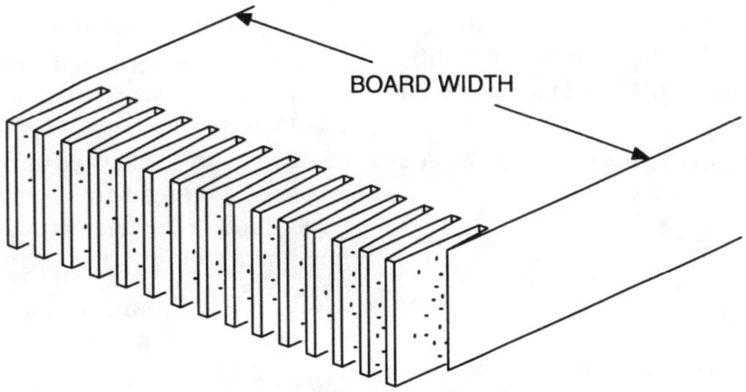

FINGER-JOINTED END JOINT

FIGURE 2

must be observed. The correct nail size and spacing is necessary to obtain the design strength of the wood structural panel system.

DOC PS-1 has been developed as a guide and specification for the manufacturing of plywood intended for industrial and construction uses. DOC PS-2 is a consensus standard that has been developed as a specification of product performance for various grades of wood structural panels. Provisions in DOC PS-1 and DOC PS-2 define the requirements for Structural I-grade panels, and give the requirements for sheathing and single floor-grade wood structural panels.

Wood structural panels manufactured in accordance with DOC PS-1 and DOC PS-2 are inspected and labeled to certify compliance by an approved agency, such as the American Plywood Association, Timber Engineering Company or Pittsburgh Testing Laboratories. The label identifies the grade and span ratings of the product. The inspection agencies maintain a continuous monitoring program designed to yield products that meet or exceed the applicable product standard. A number of tests, including deflection measurements, are required.

Besides the grades cited above, wood structural panels are also classified by exposure type:

1. Exterior—exterior type with a 100-percent waterproof glue line. Only the higher grades of veneers are allowed in exterior grades. Exterior rated panels are suitable for continuous exposure to weather.
2. Exposure 1—interior type made with waterproof exterior glue. Exposure 1 rated panels are suitable for extended construction exposure. The lower grades of veneers or strands used in the backs and interiors of Exposure 1 panels can affect the glue-line performance and cause delamination/deterioration during continuous exposure to weather.
3. Exposure 2—interior type made with interior glue. Exposure 2 rated panels are not suitable for exposure to weather.

Plywood is manufactured from more than 70 species of wood, which are divided into five groups in accordance with their stiffness and strength characteristics. Construction and industrial panel grades are generally identified under PS-1 in terms of face veneer grade or by a name indicating an intended use; e.g., APA-Rated Sturd-I-Floor. The plies may be of any species listed, except for panels designated Structural I and other special-use panels, which use only Group I species. The veneer grade defines the appearance in terms of natural, unrepaired growth characteristics (knots) and the number and size of repairs that may be made during manufacturing. The highest grades are N and A. The lowest grade is D. Grade D veneers may only be used for backs and inner plies of interior-use panels. Panels are also marked as sanded, unsanded and touchsanded.

OSB is manufactured from several species of wood. PS-2 sets forth performance requirements in terms of strength, stiffness, and durability. OSB is manufactured to meet the strength, stiffness, and durability requirements instead of being manufactured to a prescriptive recipe, as is plywood.

Wood structural sheathing and subflooring panels are classified as:

Rated Sheathing—Exterior

Rated Sheathing—Exposure 1

Rated Sheathing—Exposure 2

Structural I-Rated Sheathing—Exterior

Structural I-Rated Sheathing—Exposure 1

Wood structural panels intended for single-floor construction have limited voids in the inner plies in addition to the solid face veneer to prevent indentation caused by small concentrated loads. Single-floor panels intended for use under carpets and resilient flooring are classified as:

Rated Sturd-I-Floor Exterior

Rated Sturd-I-Floor Exposure 1

Rated Sturd-I-Floor Exposure 2

Rated Single Floor Exposure 2

Underlayment panels for use over subflooring are classified as:

Underlayment Interior

Underlayment Exposure 1

C-C Plugged Exterior

Siding is manufactured as panels or as lapped siding, and includes:

303-OL-MDO Exterior

303 Siding Exterior

Note that wood structural panels permanently exposed to weather, such as siding grades, must be exterior type. Panels that are interior type bonded with exterior glue (Exposure 1), are not allowed for siding applications.

2303.1.5 Fiberboard. Fiberboard is a smooth textured panel made up of natural fibers such as wood or cane. Fiberboard is used primarily as an insulating board and for decorative purposes, but may also be used as wall or roof sheathing under the provisions of this section. Unlike particleboard, the cellulosic components of the fiberboard are broken down to individual fibers and molded to create the bond between the fibers. Other ingredients may be added during processing to provide or improve certain properties such as strength or water resistance, or to achieve specific surface finishes for decorative products. Fiberboard is used in most locations where panels are necessary, including wall sheathing, insulation of walls and roofs, roof decking, doors and interior finish. Fiberboard may not, however, be used for diaphragms. Certification of fiberboard products is performed by an approved agency. The material is generally labeled to indicate an intended use, strength values and flame resistance where applicable.

Fiberboard may be used as roof or wall insulation, but is not intended for prolonged exposure to sunlight, wind, rain and snow. Where fiberboard is used as roof insulation, it must be protected with an approved roof covering to prevent water saturation and subsequent delamination and to avoid decay and destruction, caused by moisture, of the roofing bond.

Fiberboard is permitted without any fire-resistance treatment in the walls of all types of construction (Sections 707.4 and 723.1). When used in fire walls and fire separation walls, the fiberboard must be attached directly to a noncombustible base and protected by a tight-fitting, noncombustible veneer that is fastened through the fiberboard to the base. This will prevent the fiberboard from contributing to the spread of fire.

2303.1.6 Hardboard. Hardboard is used as exterior siding and in interior locations for paneling and underlayment.

2303.1.7 Particleboard. Particleboard is a generic term for construction panels and products manufactured from cellulosic materials, usually wood, in the form of discreet pieces and particles as distinguished from fibers. The particles are combined with synthetic resins and other binders and bonded together under heat and pressure.

Particleboard is used as underlayment, siding, and for shear walls. Particleboard used structurally for siding or shear walls must be stamped (labeled) M-S Exterior or M-2 Exterior. The "M" stands for medium density; the "2" designates the strength grade (grades range from 1 to 3); and "S" designates "special grade." Particleboard designated M-S is medium density and has physical properties between an M-1 and M-2 designation. Both must be made with exterior glue.

Although similar in characteristics to medium-density Grade 1 particleboard, the particleboard intended for use as floor underlayment is designated "PBU" and has stricter limits on permitted levels of formaldehyde emission than those placed on Grade M particleboard. The particleboard intended for use as floor underlayment is not commonly manufactured with exterior glue, which could emit higher levels of formaldehyde than that permitted for "PSU" grade floor underlayment by ANSI A 208.1.

Particleboard underlayment is often applied over a structural subfloor to provide a smooth surface for resilient-finish floor coverings or textile floor coverings. The minimum $^1/_4$-inch thickness is suitable for use over panel-type subflooring. Particleboard underlayment installed over board or deck subflooring that has multiple joints should have a thickness of $^3/_8$ inch. Joints in the underlayment should not be located over the joints in the subflooring.

All particleboard underlayment with thicknesses of $^1/_4$ inch through $^3/_4$ inch should be attached with minimum 6d annular threaded nails spaced 6 inches on center on the edges and 10 inches on center for intermediate supports.

2303.1.8 Preservative-treated wood. The applicable American Wood Preservers Association Standards are cited. Different preservative treatments are used depending on whether the wood is above ground or in contact with the ground. See commentary in Section 2304.11.

2303.1.8.1 Identification. All wood required to be preservative treated by Section 2304.11 must be stamped (labeled) with the information listed in the section. There are no exceptions.

2303.1.8.2 Moisture content. Preservative treatments used in above-ground locations are water-borne salts. These salts may leach unless the wood is dried below a moisture content of 19 percent (i.e., dry) and covered with a protective material.

2303.1.9 Structural composite lumber. Structural composite lumber (SCL) is covered in the code because of current widespread use. Structural capacities for SCL are set forth in evaluation reports by the model code agencies.

Reports prepared by approved agencies or evaluation reports published by the ICBO Evaluation Service may be accepted as part of the data needed by the building official to form the basis of approval of a material or product. Such research reports supplement the resources of the building official and eliminate the need for the official to conduct a detailed analysis on every new product. The building official is not obligated to approve the research reports issued by the model-code affiliated organizations, as the research reports are *advisory only* and are intended for technical reference.

2303.2 Fire-retardant-treated wood. Fire-retardant-treated wood (FRTW) is defined as plywood and lumber that has been pressure impregnated with chemicals to improve its flame-spread characteristics beyond that of untreated wood. The principal objective of impregnating wood with fire-retardant chemicals is to produce a chemical reaction at certain temperature ranges. This chemical reaction reduces the release of certain intermediate products that contribute to the flaming of wood, and also results in the increased formation of charcoal and water. Some chemicals are also effective in reducing the oxidation rate for the charcoal residue. Fire-retardant chemicals also reduce the heat release rate of the FRTW when burning over a wide range of temperatures. This section gives provisions for the treatment and use of FRTW. However, the fire-retardant chemicals are generally quite corrosive. Corrosion-resistant fasteners must be used with FRTW.

The effectiveness of the pressure-impregnated fire-retardant treatment is determined by subjecting the material to tests conducted in accordance with ASTM E 84, with the modification that the test is extended to 20 minutes rather than 15 minutes. Under this procedure, a flame-spread index is established during the standard 10-minute test period. The test is continued for an additional 20 minutes. During this added time period, there must not be any significant flame spread. At no time must the flame spread more than $10^1/_2$ feet past the centerline of the burners. These criteria have been correlated with large-scale fire tests.

2303.2.1 Labeling. Each piece of FRTW must be stamped (labeled). The labeling must show the performance of the material including the 20-minute ASTM E84 test. The labeling must state the strength adjustments, and conformance to the requirements for interior or exterior application.

The FRTW label must be distinct from the grading label to avoid confusion between the two. The grading label gives information about the properties of the wood before it is fire-retardant treated. The FRTW label gives properties of the wood after FRTW treatment. It is imperative that the FRTW label be presented in such a manner that it complements the grading label, and does not create confusion over which label takes precedence.

2303.2.2 Strength adjustments. Several factors can significantly affect the physical properties of FRTW. These factors are the pressure treatment and redrying processes used, and the extremes of temperature and humidity that the FRTW will be subjected to once installed. The design values for all FRTW must be adjusted for the effects of the treatment and environmental conditions, such as high temperature in attic installations and humidity. The design adjustment values must be based on an investigation procedure, which includes subjecting the FRTW to similar temperatures and humidities. The procedure must be approved by the building official. The FRTW tested must be identical to that which is produced. The building official reviewing the test procedure should consider the species and grade of the untreated wood and conditioning of wood, such as drying before the fire-retardant-treatment process. A fire-retardant wood treater may choose to have its treatment process evaluated by the National Evaluation Services.

The FRTW is required to be labeled with the design adjustment values. These design adjustment values can take the form of factors that are multiplied by the original design values of the untreated wood to determine its allowable stresses, or new allowable stresses that have already been factored down in consideration of the FRTW treatment.

2303.2.3 Exposure to weather. Some fire-retardant treatments are soluble when exposed to the weather or used under high-humidity conditions. When an FRTW product is to be exposed to weather conditions, it must be further tested in accordance with ASTM D 2898. The material is then subjected to the ASTM weathering test and retested after drying. There must not be any significant differences in the performance recorded before and after the weathering test.

2303.2.4 Interior applications. When an FRTW product is intended for use under high-humidity conditions, it must be further tested in accordance with ASTM D 3201. The material must demonstrate that when tested at 92-percent relative humidity, the moisture content of the FRTW does not increase to more than 28 percent. The label must show the test results.

2303.2.5 Moisture content. FRTW contains water-borne salts that are subject to leaching. The FRTW must be dried to the specified moisture contents after treating to minimize leaching. In addition, FRTW chemicals are quite corrosive to metal fasteners. Where the moisture content of the treated wood is too high, the corrosivity of the treated wood is even higher and contributes to greater corrosion of metal fasteners.

2303.2.6 Type I and II construction applications. Use of FRTW in Type I or II construction is limited to nonload-bearing partitions and exterior walls.

2303.3 Hardwood plywood. Hardwood plywood is not used for structural purposes.

2303.4 Trusses. Metal-plate-connected trusses are typically constructed out of nominal dimension lumber with the metal-plate connectors placed on either the narrow or wide dimension of the lumber (4-inch by 2-inch lumber for floor trusses versus 2-inch by 4-inch lumber for roof trusses). NDS–97 specifies the allowable design stresses for lumber while the Truss Plate Institute (TPI) *National Design Standard for Metal-Plate-Connected Wood Trusses* specifies how the allowable metal-plate design values are to be determined and how the maximum stresses in the truss elements are to be determined.

Adequate bracing for trusses is critical. Lateral bracing requirements (e.g. brace points, bracing size, or strength and stiffness) should be specified by the truss designer. Temporary bracing is to be left in place until permanent bracing is installed. All lateral bracing must be installed as assumed in the truss design so that the truss will have the same structural capacity for which it was designed.

The construction documents, drawings and specifications, must be prepared by a registered design professional and must be provided to and approved by the building official prior to installation into the structure. The items listed in the code are the minimum requirements.

Although the list states that the structure designer shall design the permanent bracing, the truss designer generally is the most knowledgeable concerning the required strength, stiffness and location of the bracing necessary to prevent buckling of the truss members. Bracing is necessary to resist buckling of the compression chord under maximum gravity loads, as well as the uplift condition of dead load plus wind. Bracing is usually necessary on the bottom chord at the first interior panel point to resist the wind uplift. The truss designer should specify either the strength and stiffness of braces, or the member size and grade of the braces (e.g., 2 by 4 DF #2) at the specified locations.

The truss designer should furnish complete calculations substantiating the size of all members and connector plate sizes. If the calculations are performed with a computer program, documentation should be provided that substantiates the basis of the program.

2303.5 Test standard for joist hangers and connectors. Section 1715.1 sets forth the test and acceptance criteria for joist hangers. Note that per Section 1715.1.4, only the design values based on the design limit states for the fasteners or the wood member may be increased for duration of load. If the hanger load is governed by the strength or deflection limit states of the steel, the design value may not be increased for duration of load. The evaluation reports and the manufacturer's catalogues must provide the limit state data in order for the structure designer to comply with this requirement.

2303.6 Nails and staples. This new section adds bending yield strength requirements for nails and staples. The bending yield strength requirements are those assumed in the NDS lateral strength tables, the UBC, NBC, and SBC fastener schedules, and the model code evaluation reports. These strengths are standardized within the nail industry for engineered fasteners and are set forth in ASTM F 1667. Note that the NDS–97 also requires that nails, staples, and spikes must meet Federal Specification FF-N-105B, (1997), *Wire, Cut and Wrought Nails, Staples, and Spikes*. This specification also sets dimensional limits.

SECTION 2304
GENERAL CONSTRUCTION REQUIREMENTS

2304.1 General. The requirements of this section apply to ASD, LRFD *and* conventional construction.

2304.2 Size of structural members. Net dimensions are set forth in NDS–97.

2304.3 Wall framing. Interior and exterior walls must be framed in accordance with conventional construction provisions unless a specific design is provided.

2304.3.1 Bottom plates. Sill plates must be at least nominal 2x even if calculations by ASD or LRFD show that a smaller size is acceptable. This requirement applies both to engineered (designed) structures and those constructed in accordance with conventional construction provisions.

2304.3.2 Framing over openings. Windows, doors, air-conditioning units and other service equipment require that openings be provided in wood-stud walls and partitions. Loads imposed above these openings must be transferred by a structural element above the opening to supports on both sides of the opening and then to a load-bearing wall or partition. In most wood frame structures, these structural elements are composed of two pieces of 2-inch dimensional lumber plus a spacer or plate, or a solid 4x member. These elements must be fastened in accordance with Table 2304.9.1. Based on the span and the loading, some openings may require trusses, laminated veneer lumber, glued-laminated members or steel beams. Headers may be engineered or selected from Tables 2308.9.5 and 2308.9.6. Header tables are also published in a number of technical documents. All other headers must be engineered in accordance with Sections 2308.9.5 and 2308.9.6. In all instances, the headers and their supports must be adequate to support the loads imposed (see Figure 3).

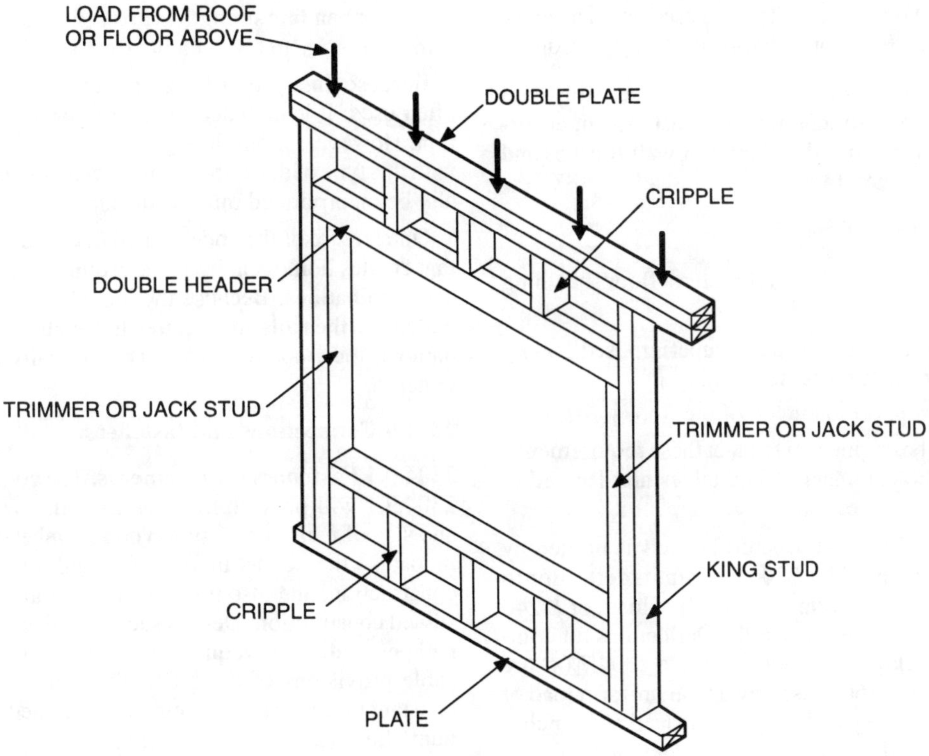

HEADERS OVER WALL OPENINGS

FIGURE 3

2304.4 Floor and roof framing. The framing of floors, joist and roof rafters must be either engineered (designed) or in accordance with the conventional construction provisions.

2304.5 Framing around flues and chimneys. Specific wording in the code requires wood framing to be a minimum of 2 inches from flues, chimneys, and fireplaces, and 6 inches from flue openings. This air space is required because the resistance of wood to ignition is lowered when it is subjected to low levels of heat for extended periods of time. The separations specified in this section and in the *International Mechanical Code* are intended to prevent the possibility of the wood being subjected to low heat for extended periods of time (see Section 2111.5). The openings between the wood and the masonry must be adequately fire blocked in accordance with Section 716.

It should be noted that 2 inches of masonry will not provide the same level of thermal resistance as 2 inches of air space. Therefore, adding 2 inches to the required thickness of a fireplace or chimney wall will *not* serve as an approvable alternative to the 2-inch clear air space requirement.

2304.6 Wall sheathing.

2304.6.1 Wall sheathing. Wall sheathing is intended to:

1. Protect the interior of the building from the weather. This may require the installation of a weather-resistant barrier beneath the exterior wall covering as discussed in Section 1403.3.

   As required by Section 1405.2, exterior wall coverings must provide weather protection for the structure. Although not explicitly required by the code, where wood structural panel products are used for exterior siding, such as plywood, particleboard or hardboard, joints should occur over framing members and be protected with continuous wood battens, tongue and groove joints, caulking, flashing, vertical or horizontal shiplaps or any other method approved by the building official that will make the joints resistant to water penetration. Alternatively, these panels may be applied over lumber and wood structural panel sheathing, in which case the double layers provide for an overlapping of joints and prevent direct penetration of water.
2. Be of sufficient strength to span between the studs or other structural members. The strengths or thicknesses of most of the exterior wall-covering materials listed in Table 2304.6.1 are based on a stud spacing of 16 inches on center. However, there are a few cases where the thickness is based on a 24-inch spacing.
3. Have sufficient durability to withstand, for the life of the building, the weathering effects of the elements to which they are exposed. Thus, where wood structural panels are used, the code requires that they be rated as exterior types. Other materials must be of a weather-resistant type of material, such as cedar shingles, or the material must be finished with a weather-resistant finish, such as exterior paint.

Provisions for other wall coverings are presented in Section 1405, and exterior plaster provisions are set forth in Section 2512.

2304.6.1.1 Wood structural panel sheathing. Wood structural panel sheathing used as an exterior wall finish must have an

Exterior designation. Wood structural panels used under an exterior finish must have an Exterior or Exposure 1 designation.

2304.6.2 Interior paneling. Interior paneling must comply with DOC PS-1 or PS-2. Wood structural panels installed in accordance with this section are considered interior wall finishes and cannot be used to resist lateral forces.

2304.7 Floor and roof sheathing.

2304.7.1 Structural floor sheathing. Structural floor sheathing serves two purposes:

1. Provides support for, and distributes superimposed gravity loads to the floor joists or trusses.
2. Provides lateral support to the top of the floor joists.

The sheathing may be engineered to meet these requirements, or be selected from the code tables. The tables are deemed to comply with the code requirements.

The maximum span for wood structural panels is limited by both strength and deflection. Table 2304.7 (3) limits deflection to $L/180$ under the tabulated uniform dead and live load, or $L/240$ under the tabulated uniform live load only. Deflections for combination subfloor/underlayment grades in Table 2304.7 (4) are based on a deflection of $L/360$ caused by a total uniform load of 100 psf except for $1^1/_8$-inch panels on joists spaced at 48 inches on center, which are rated at a deflection of $L/360$ at a uniform load of 65 psf. When using the tables, *all* the conditions set forth in the table must be met regarding loads, type, grade, species group, plies, blocking, direction of span, and other requirements. Sheathing systems that do not meet *all* the conditions must be engineered.

Wood structural panels in the Table 2304.7(3) are designated by the panel span rating (also called the panel identification index), instead of thickness. The rating consists of two numbers such as $^{32}/_{16}$. The first number is the allowable span for use as roof sheathing and the second is the allowable span for use as floor sheathing. Panels intended only for single floor grades are designated by one number, e.g., 16, but the panels may be used for roof sheathing with the spans listed in the table. The single floor grades have higher-grade faces than Structural I panels and may be preferable for aesthetic reasons as roof sheathing where visible from the underside.

Several thicknesses of structural panel are included under a single panel span rating. This is because different grades of interior and face veneers or strands may be used in different combinations. For example, a five-ply plywood panel will have a higher load rating than a four-ply panel with the same thickness. Conversely, the five-ply panel may be thinner than the four-ply panel yet have the same panel span rating. For example, a $^{15}/_{32}$-inch-thick four-ply panel will support the same total load as a $^{7}/_{16}$-inch-thick five-ply panel.

2304.7.2 Structural roof sheathing. See the discussion under Section 2304.7.1 Structural floor sheathing.

2304.8 Mechanically laminated floors and decks.

2304.8.1 General. A laminated lumber floor or deck designed in accordance with this section provides the equivalent of a solid-wood deck and may be designed as if it were a solid-wood deck of the same thickness. However, the code requires a conservative design for bending strength in that continuous spans are designed using the moment coefficients for a simple span.

Because this type of floor or deck is labor intensive, it is not often used. It is intended primarily for heavy-timber construction. However, strength is generally not a controlling criterion with this type of deck; therefore, lower grades of lumber can usually be incorporated into the design.

One feature of the code related to construction of these decks that creates homogeneity is the requirement for nailing of adjacent laminations. Because the laminations are thoroughly side nailed and the nails are required to penetrate two and a half laminations, the floor or deck acts essentially as a homogeneous material.

2304.9 Connections and fasteners.

2304.9.1 Fasteners requirements. The code intends that Table 2304.9.1 will provide minimum requirements for the number and size of nails connecting wood members. This table accommodates the constructor of nondesigned (conventional) construction, and also provides minimum requirements for designed construction. Details such as end and edge distances and nail penetration are required to be in accordance with the applicable provisions of the NDS–97. Where required, corrosion-resistant fasteners shall be either hot-dipped zinc-coated, aluminum alloy wire or stainless steel.

Table 2304.9.1 is comparable to the nailing tables in the other model codes. Footnote l, which requires 8d minimum nails for roof sheathing, corresponds to the 80 mph (fastest mile) entry in UBC Table 23-II-B-2 for wind uplift resistance.

Power driven fasteners, along with the typical sizes used, and staples are added to the table. The sizes designated in the table are common to all fastener manufacturers.

2304.9.2 Sheathing fasteners. Fasteners should be driven flush with the surface of the sheathing, but not overdriven. Overdriving of fasteners can significantly reduce the shear capacity and ductility of the diaphragm or shear wall. For three-ply material, the strength reduction is significant if the fastener is overdriven through one ply.

If no more than 20 percent of the fasteners around the perimeter of the panel are overdriven by $^1/_8$ inch or less, then no reduction in shear capacity need be considered. If more than 20 percent of the fasteners around the perimeter are overdriven by any amount, or if any fasteners are overdriven by more than $^1/_8$ inch, then additional fasteners must be driven to maintain the desired shear capacity, provided that the additional fasteners will not split the substrate, or the shear capacity be reduced. For every two fasteners overdriven, one additional fastener should be driven. Panels with more than 20 percent of the fasteners overdriven greater than $^1/_8$ inch should be replaced.

Also, if the actual panel thickness is greater than the design panel thickness needed to resist the design shear, the panel shear capacity may be adequate without the driving of additional fasteners. For example, if the design required a $^{15}/_{32}$-inch-thick panel, but a $^{19}/_{32}$-inch-thick panel with all fasteners overdriven by $^1/_8$ inch is used for the sheathing, the panel is adequate because the net thickness is $^{15}/_{32}$ inch.

2304.9.3 Joist hangers and framing anchors. Joist hangers and other framing hardware are usually evaluated by the model code agency's evaluation service. There are acceptance criteria for the performance of the hardware in terms of the strength limit states of the metal, wood, and fasteners, as well as deflection limit states.

Test requirements for joist hangers are found in Section 1715.1. Only the design values based on the strength limit states for the fasteners or wood member (Items 4 or 5 in Section 1715.1.2) are allowed to be increased for duration of load per the NDS. No increase is allowed for loads limited by steel strength or deflection. Evaluation Service reports and manufacturer's catalogs must provide the controlling limit strength of the connector in order for the designer to meet this requirement.

2304.9.4 Other fasteners. Fasteners not specifically cited in the code are subject to building official approval. See commentary for Section 1703.2.1 for acceptance of evaluation reports.

2304.9.5 Fasteners in preservative-treated and fire-retardant-treated wood. The water-borne salts in preservative-treated and fire-retardant-treated wood are corrosive. Fasteners must be corrosion resistant when used with these materials. Corrosion-resistant fasteners are made of type 304 or 316 stainless steel, silicon bronze, copper, or steel that has been hot-dipped or mechanically galvanized with a zinc coating of not less than 1.0 ounce per square foot.

Electro-galvanized steel fasteners do not qualify as corrosion resistant; the zinc coating typically is about 0.1 ounce per square foot. Electro-galvanized nails are suitable only for occasionally wet locations such as for nailing composition shingles.

2304.9.6 Load path. The load path must be continuous from the roof to the foundation. A continuous load path is necessary for good performance of the structure in response to superimposed loads, particularly wind loads and earthquake demands. For example, visualize what happens to the wind suction load on a low-slope roof. The upward force that is not offset by the dead load of the roof elements must be resisted by dead load elsewhere. Similarly, where the structure is subjected to earthquake demands, the inertial loads from the floor and roof diaphragms must be transferred to the lateral-force-resisting elements, e.g., wood shear walls. A positive, continuous load path is necessary to transfer all gravity and lateral loads from the roof and floors down to the foundation.

2304.9.7 Framing requirements. Columns must be provided with full end bearing to transfer the loads or connections designed to resist the full compressive load. Connections must also be able to resist lateral and net uplift loads.

2304.10 Heavy timber construction. The provisions contain general provisions for column continuity, transfer of loads from beams to columns, other connection criteria, and requirements for structural anchorage and continuity. Minimum element size requirements for Type IV construction are found in Section 602.4.

2304.11 Protection against decay and termites. The provisions adopted from the model codes were reorganized in the IBC for clarity. The provisions are grouped into the following areas:

1. Wood used above ground.
2. Laminated timbers exposed to weather.
3. Wood with ground contact.
4. Supports for appurtenances.
5. Termite protection.
6. Retaining walls.

The provisions of this section are intended to protect against decay and termite infestation. The provisions are based on the extensive material on biodeterioration of wood in the *Wood Handbook.*[4]

2304.11.2 Wood used above ground. Wood used above ground, if preservative treated, is usually treated with water-borne preservative such as ammoniacal copper arsenate (ACA) or chromated copper arsenate (CCA). The retention rates are lower than required for ground contact.

2304.11.2.1 Joists, girders and subfloor. There must be 18 inches clearance to joists and 12 inches clearance to wood girders if they are not of naturally durable or preservative-treated wood. See Figure 4.

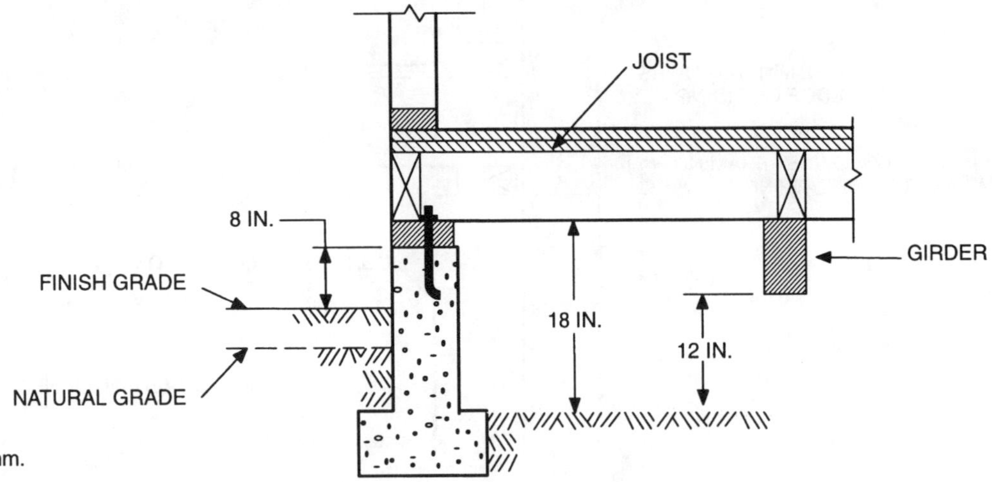

For SI: 1 inch = 25.4 mm.

UNDER-FLOOR CLEARANCE

FIGURE 4

2304.11.2.2 Framing. Framing, including sheathing (not siding), must have 8 inches of clearance from exposed earth if it is not naturally durable or preservative treated. See Figure 5.

2304.11.2.3 Sleepers and sills. Concrete and masonry slabs that are in direct contact with the earth are very susceptible to moisture because of absorption of ground water. This can occur on interior slabs as well as at the perimeter. This section is intended to prevent use of untreated wood that may decay under such conditions. Concrete that is fully separated from the ground by a vapor barrier is not considered to be in direct contact with earth.

2304.11.2.4 Girder ends. An airspace is required around the ends of wood girders to reduce the possibility of moisture that can contribute to decay of the member.

2304.11.2.5 Wood siding. Wood siding must have 6-inch clearance between the siding and earth unless of naturally durable or preservative-treated wood. Note that the clearance for wood sheathing under the siding is *8 inches* per Section 2304.11.2.2. In other words, siding can extend 2 inches below the foundation plate, or framing, whereas the sheathing must be terminated at the sill plate. See Figure 5.

2304.11.2.6 Posts or columns. This section is an amalgam of the requirements from the three model codes. See Figure 6.

2304.11.3 Laminated timbers. The portions of glue-laminated beams directly exposed to weather are subject to decay and should be of preservative-treated material or made from naturally durable wood.

2304.11.4 Wood in contact with the ground or fresh water. Note specifically the limiting adjective "fresh." This section only applies to wood in contact with the ground or fresh water. The water-borne preservatives used for fresh water are not suitable for brackish or salt water, where attack can also come from marine borers. See the discussion in the Section 1808.1 commentary, Wood piles. The preservative retention rates are higher for wood in ground contact than for above-ground uses.

The first paragraph of this code section allows wood in direct contact with the earth to be naturally durable. However, this only applies to wood in contact with the ground, not posts or columns. Posts and columns are required by Section 2304.11.4.1 to be preservative treated.

2304.11.4.1 Posts or columns. Posts or columns embedded in concrete or embedded in earth, such as columns in a pole-supported structure, have no opportunity to dry and are subject to decay. Hence, they must be of preservative-treated wood.

2304.11.4.2 Wood structural members. Where wood framing is used to support floors and roofs that are moisture permeable, such as a concrete slab over a patio or a patio slab over a garage, the framing must be of pressure-treated wood or approved naturally durable species, unless the slab is separated from the framing by a waterproof membrane.

Although these wood framing members are not necessarily in direct contact with the ground, their exposure to moisture is similar to that of wood in direct contact with the ground. Therefore, the wood framing must be of naturally durable wood, or it must be preservative treated in accordance with AWPA C2, C9 or C22.

2304.11.5 Supporting member for permanent appurtenances. Balconies, porches, and other appurtenances are exposed to weather conditions and may not have protective overhangs. Water can collect in the joints and on the surfaces creating alternating cycles of wetting and drying conducive to decay.

2304.11.6 Termite protection. Where termites are a significant hazard; for example, the southern states, floor framing must be preservative treated, naturally durable, or have some other approved method of termite protection.

2304.11.7 Wood used in retaining walls and cribs. Wood used in retaining walls, crib walls, bulkheads, and other walls that retain or support the earth must, with only a few exceptions, be of

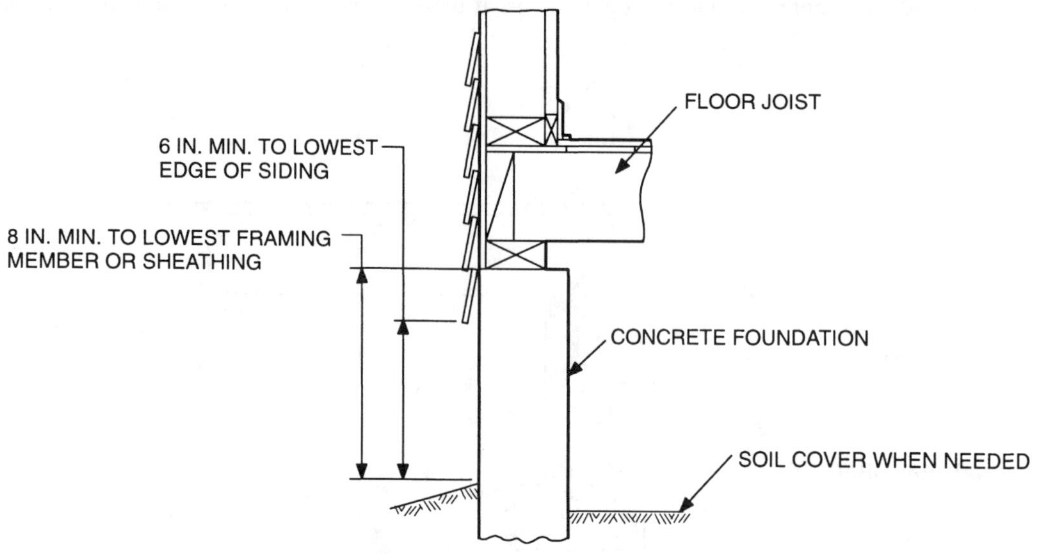

CLEARANCE BETWEEN WOOD FRAMING, WOOD SIDING AND EARTH

FIGURE 5

preservative-treated wood specified as ground-contact-treated wood.

2304.12 Wood supporting masonry or concrete. Wood structural members are subject to long-term creep, which increases the deflection, particularly where a high dead load is present. Thus, the code does not permit wood members to permanently support the dead load of masonry or concrete, since the deflection created by the long-term creep has the potential to cause severe cracking in the masonry or concrete.

The exceptions cover specific cases, such as supporting a structure on wood piles, which have been used successfully for over 100 years. Although Exception 1 permits masonry or concrete nonstructural floor or roof surfacing of not more than 4 inches in thickness to be supported by wood members, this exception is generally used for thinner materials up to about $1^1/_2$ inches in thickness. Thicker concrete or masonry floor surfacing can be accommodated, however, by rigid control of deflections. Exception 3 provides controls for the support of masonry veneer on a treated-wood foundation and for the support of interior wall veneer on wood floors with strict requirements for the design for deflection control.

SECTION 2305 GENERAL DESIGN REQUIREMENTS FOR LATERAL-FORCE-RESISTING SYSTEMS

These provisions are based on a combination of 1997 UBC Section 2315 and 1997 NEHRP Sections 12.1 through 12.4.

There are now separate sections for wood diaphragms (Section 2305.2) and wood shear walls (Section 2305.3). The term "diaphragm" refers exclusively to horizontal or nearly horizontal (sloping) elements such as floors and roofs; the term "shear walls" refers to vertical elements.

2305.1 General. Structures use wood diaphragms as part of the lateral-force-resisting system to resist wind, seismic, and other lateral loads. Wood diaphragms are often incorrectly assumed to be flexible. A wood diaphragm is usually flexible relative to a concrete diaphragm. A wood diaphragm, may be stiff relative to a wood or gypsum board shear wall. In this case the wood diaphragm is classified as rigid. However, a wood diaphragm is generally flexible relative to masonry or concrete shear walls.

Section 1602 defines a diaphragm as flexible when the maximum lateral deformation of the diaphragm is more than two times the average story drift determined by comparing the deflection of the diaphragm itself with the deflection of the adjoining vertical resisting elements. Conversely, a diaphragm is considered rigid when the diaphragm deflection is equal to or less than two times the average story drift. These definitions apply to all building materials, not just wood. Defining whether the diaphragm is classified as flexible or rigid is necessary to determine how the lateral forces and torsional moments will be distributed to the vertical elements of the lateral-force-resisting system. Flexible diaphragms are assumed to have insufficient stiffness to distribute torsional moments.

As an example, consider a 40-by-40 one-story SDC D, SUG I building having a wood roof diaphragm with no openings, 10-foot plate height, class D soils, and $S_5 = 0.75$. The lateral-force-resisting elements are a 5-foot-long wood structural panel shear wall on each side (2:1 aspect ratio). The shear in the walls would be moderate at approximately 330 pounds per linear foot; assume $^{15}/_{32}$-inch sheathing with nailing at 4-inch spacing.

The shear wall deflection (primarily nail slip plus $^1/_8$-inch allowance for anchorage deflection) is about 0.30 inch. The diaphragm deflection is approximately 0.15 inch, assuming $^3/_{16}$-inch slip in each chord splice. The total deflection is 0.45 inches. The deflection of the diaphragm relative to the deflection of the shear walls is $0.15/0.30 = 0.5 < 2$. Therefore, the

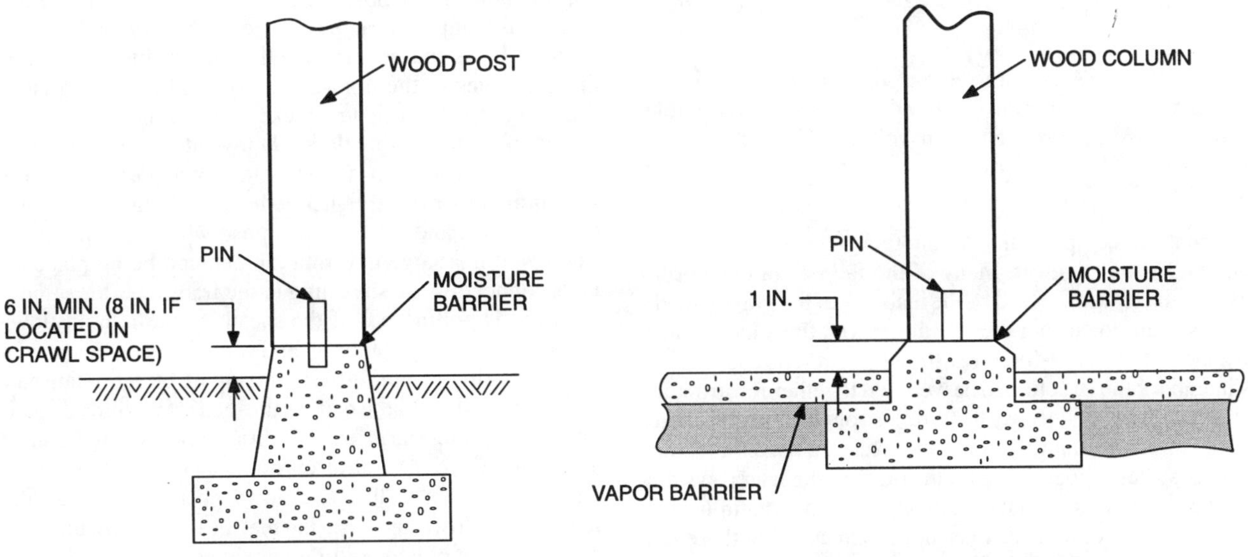

For SI: 1 inch = 25.4 mm.

POSTS AND COLUMNS

FIGURE 6

diaphragm is stiff relative to the shear walls and classified rigid for lateral-force distribution. Note that the shear wall deflection above is twice that of the diaphragm.

If the wood shear walls were replaced by a 4-foot-long 8-inch CMU wall solidly grouted, the deflection of the wall would be approximately 0.05 inch. The deflection of the diaphragm relative to the shear walls is 0.15/0.05 = 3 > 2. Therefore, the diaphragm is considered flexible for lateral force distribution.

This simple, but realistic, example demonstrates that the common assumption that all wood diaphragms are flexible is incorrect. As another example, consider a typical two-story garden office structure with a width of 40 feet and a length of 120 feet using wood diaphragms. Masonry shear walls are used in the transverse direction at each end, and a wood shear demising wall is placed across the width of the building at mid-length. In the longitudinal direction the walls are wood shear walls and glass curtain wall. Is the diaphragm flexible or rigid for purposes of distributing lateral forces? In the transverse direction, the diaphragms will likely be flexible relative to the shear walls, but in the longitudinal direction, the diaphragm will likely be rigid relative to the shear walls.

In previous model codes, wood-sheathed diaphragms have been considered to be flexible by many registered design professionals and building officials. This code, the 1997 NEHRP, and the 1997 UBC codes stipulate that the determination of diaphragm rigidity or flexibility for determinating the method to distribute forces is dependent on the relative stiffness and deformations of the horizontal and vertical resisting elements. Wood-sheathed diaphragms in structures with wood frame shear walls with various types of sheathing may be relatively rigid compared with the vertical resisting system and, therefore, capable of transmitting the torsional moment caused by the lateral forces. A relative deformation of the diaphragm of two or more when compared with the vertical resisting system deformation under the same force is used to define a diaphragm as being flexible.

See the 1999 SEAOC Blue Book[5] for a discussion of the many parameters necessary to classify the diaphragm as flexible or rigid. See also Example No. 1 in Volume II of the SEAOC Seismic Design Manual[6] for a demonstration of the necessary calculations.

Deformation compatibility is another area that must be considered by the engineer. Many of the failures in the Northridge earthquake were caused by the inability of the gravity load-carrying system to sustain the lateral deformations and strains undergone by the lateral-force-resisting system. The code provisions intend for the structure to be well tied together for structural integrity. The gravity system relies on the lateral-load-resisting system for stability. Since the structure acts as a whole, the gravity system "goes along for the ride" as the lateral system resists the wind or earthquake demands. The maximum usable strain in the gravity elements must not be exceeded or there is a high probability of collapse. The lateral resisting system must limit the deformations such that the maximum usable strains in the supported gravity system will not be exceeded. In other words, the deformation capability of the gravity system must be compatible with the deformations allowed by the lateral system. Thus, the term "deformation compatibility" is derived.

Deformation compatibility provisions appeared in previous model codes but were often ignored by registered design professionals and building officials. Deformation compatibility requirements were enhanced in the 1997 UBC and the 1997 NEHRP in response to the damage caused by the Northridge earthquake. Those provisions were used as the basis for the provisions in IBC Section 1617.6.4.3 for structures classified as SDC D, E or F.

Deformation compatibility of connections between structural elements should be considered such that the deformation of each element and connection comprising the lateral-force-system is compatible with the deformations of the other lateral-force-resisting elements and connections and with the deformations of the gravity system and connections thereto. Particular care should be used to determine that the deformations are compatible with any brittle nonstructural elements such as masonry veneers.

The registered design professional should visualize the deformed shape of the structure to ensure that the connections provide the necessary ductility to meet the probable deformation demand placed on the structure. Unlike steel or other metal structures, wood is not a ductile material and virtually all the ductility achieved in the structure is from the metal connections. The intended failure mechanism of wood structures must be through the connections, including the nailing of structural panels, otherwise the failure will be brittle in nature. The philosophy of strong elastic columns and yielding beams cannot be projected from steel to wood structures. To enable a wood structure to deform and dissipate energy during a seismic event, the connections must be the structural "fuse" in the structure and be ductile.

As an example of a compatibility issue, consider the deformation compatibility between a hold-down connector to the hold-down post and the edge nailing of shear wall sheathing to the hold-down post and adjacent bottom plate. Recent testing and observations from the Northridge earthquake have suggested that the hold-down post experiences notable displacement before significant load can be carried through the hold-down connector. This is caused, among other things, by the oversizing of the bolt holes in the hold-down post and the deformation and rotation of the hold-down bracket. Anchor bolts connecting the bottom plate to the foundation below attempt to carry the shear wall uplift in tension as the hold-down post moves up. The sheathing, however, is nailed to both the bottom plate, which is held in place, and the tie-down post, which is being pulled up. The result is a large deformation demand being placed on the nails connecting the sheathing to the framing. This often results in the nails pulling out of the sheathing at the hold-down post corner, or splitting of the sill, and sometimes results in an unzipping effect in the nailing. This unzipping effect is caused by the sequential failure of the nails as the load is transferred to adjacent nails. Unzipping can affect a significant portion of the sheathing. The most effective solution currently available is to limit the slip and deformation at the hold-down post by using a very stiff nailed hold-down and ensuring that the hold-down bolt is pretensioned. Use of bolted hold-downs should be avoided where high loads are placed on the hold downs and deformation compatibility becomes a problem. NEHRP recommends using only nailed hold-down connections.

NEHRP Section 12.3.4.4 requires the use of 3-inch by 3-inch by $^1/_4$-inch plate washers for all anchor bolts in shear walls regardless of seismic design category classification. The IBC requires 2-inch by 2-inch by $^3/_{16}$-inch plate washers only for structures classified SDC D, E and F. This requirement for plate washers is discussed further in the commentary for Section 2305.3.10.

2305.1.1 Shear resistance based on principles of mechanics. When calculating the shear resistance of diaphragms or shear walls by the principle of engineering mechanics for seismic demands, the values of fastener strength and sheathing resistance should be based on the results of cyclic tests. The capacity determined from cyclic tests is likely to be lower than the capacity determined from a monotonic test. When determining values based on this method, the user should be aware that there are currently no accepted rational methods to calculate deflections for diaphragms and shear walls sheathed with materials other than wood structural panels fastened with nails. Therefore, if a rational method is to be used, the capacity of the fastener in the sheathing material should be validated by acceptable test procedures employing cyclic forces and displacements. Validation must include correlation between the overall stiffness and capacity predicted by principles of mechanics and that observed from test results. A diaphragm or shear wall sheathed with dissimilar materials on the two faces should be designed as a single-sided diaphragm or wall using the capacity of the stronger material and ignoring the shear capacity of the weaker material.

2305.1.2 Framing. A diaphragm is a horizontal or nearly horizontal structural unit that acts as a deep beam or girder when flexible in comparison to its supports and as a plate when rigid in comparison to its supports. The analogy to a girder is appropriate since girders and diaphragms are made up as assemblies.[7, 8] Sheathing acts as the "web" to resist the shear in diaphragms and is stiffened by the framing members, which also provide support for gravity loads. Flexure is resisted by the edge or boundary elements acting like "flanges" to resist induced tension or compression forces. The flanges may be top plates, ledgers, bond beams, or any other continuous element at the perimeter of the diaphragm.

The flange (chord) can serve several functions at the same time, providing resistance to loads and forces from different sources. When it functions as the tension or compression flange of the girder, it is important that the connection to the web be designed to accomplish the shear transfer. Since most diaphragm flanges consist of many pieces, it is important that the splices be designed to transmit the tension or compression occurring at the location of the splice and to recognize that the direction of application of seismic forces can reverse. The splices should be designed to minimize slip in the connection. A significant proportion of the diaphragm deflection is caused by deformation in the chord splice from the axial load (see Equation 23-1, last term). It should also be recognized that the shear walls parallel to the flanges may be acting with the flanges to distribute the diaphragm shears. When seismic forces are delivered at right angles to the direction considered previously, the flange becomes a part of the reaction system. It may function to transfer the diaphragm shear to the shear wall(s), either directly or as a collector (drag strut) between segments of shear walls that are not continuous along the length of the diaphragm.

Similar to the analogy for diaphragms, shear walls may be considered deep vertical cantilever beams. The flanges are subjected to tension and compression while the webs resist the shear. It is important that the flange members, splices at intermediate floors, and the connection to the foundation be detailed and sized for the induced forces. The webs of diaphragms and shear walls often have openings. The transfer of forces around openings can be treated similarly to openings in the webs of steel girders. Members at the edges of openings have forces due to flexure and the higher web shear induced in them, and the resultant forces must be transferred into the body of the diaphragm beyond the opening, as required by this section. There is a similar requirement in Section 2305.1.3, Openings in shear panels, which states that "openings in shear panels which *materially* affect their strength shall be fully detailed on the plans and shall have their edges adequately reinforced to transfer all shearing stresses." Section 2305.3.7.2 allows unreinforced openings, provided the shear capacity is adjusted in accordance with Table 2305.3.7.2. For structures classified as SDC D, E or F, all openings greater than approximately 14 inches by 14 inches should be reinforced. The additional cost of straps and blocking is insignificant in comparison to the improved performance under cyclic demands.

Collectors and their connections are critical to performance of the lateral-force-resisting system. The collector must "collect" the shears in the diaphragm in areas where there is no shear wall and deliver those forces to the shear walls. Premature failure of a collector or its connection may cause a complete structural failure. Section 1620.1.6 (SDC B and above) requires that collectors, collector splices, and the connection of the collector to resisting elements have the strength to resist the special load combinations of IBC Section 1605.4; i.e., the maximum anticipated seismic force, E_m , unless the structure has light frame shear walls. In other words, the collectors, splices, and connections for a structure having a wood diaphragm and concrete tilt-up walls would have to be designed for the combinations using the maximum earthquake force, E_m, to remain essentially elastic. The collectors, splices, and connections for structures having a wood diaphragm and wood structural panel shear walls need only be designed to resist the load combinations of Section 1605.2 or 1605.3.

Chords and collectors must be placed close to the plane of the diaphragm in order to function in accordance with the assumed behavior as a deep beam flange. If the chord or collector is too far from the plane of the diaphragm, shear lag will prevent the chord or collector from acting in accordance with the assumed behavior. For example, a top plate at the top of a parapet 3 feet above the plane of the diaphragm will not be effective as a chord or collector.

2305.1.3 Openings in shear panels. Although the section requires that openings in shear walls that materially affect their strength have their edges reinforced, the phrase "materially affect their strength" is not defined in the code. Section 2305.3.7.2 permits openings in shear walls without force transfer design, provided certain restrictions are met. See commentary to Sections 2305.3.7.1 and 2305.3.7.2 for further discussion.

2305.1.4 Shear panel connections. Positive connections are required. The term "design forces" as used here may be confusing in regard to seismic loads. Design seismic forces determined in

Chapter 16 are strength level forces, *E*. When used for allowable stress design, the design force *E* is reduced in the ASD load combinations by 1.4 or *E*/1.4. See commentary to Section 2305.1.2 for forces required to attach collectors to shear walls.

Limiting the transfer of lateral forces by toenails or slant nails is necessary to minimize the failure mechanism of splitting caused by shrinkage of the blocking or closely spaced nails that provide a weakened plane. (See Figure 7).

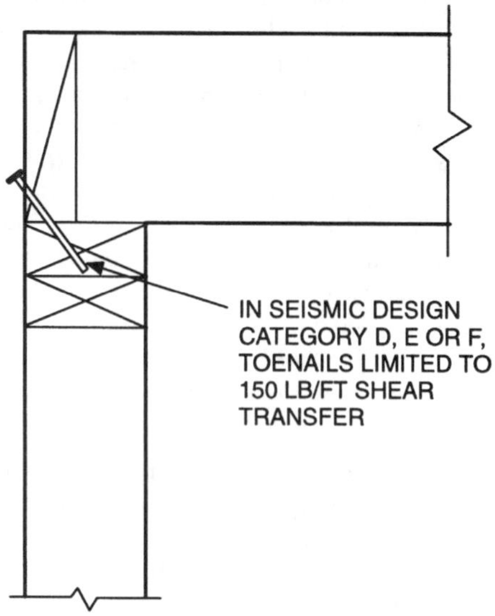

SLANT NAIL SHEAR TRANSFER

FIGURE 7

The shear value of 150 lb/ft was allowed based on the spacing of 8d nails at 6 inches on center using the 1991 NDS nail values. A slant nail factor of 1.0 was used because the orientation where the nail is driven perpendicular to grain for both members is slant nailing. Shears exceeding 150 lb/ft must be transferred by positive means such as face nailing to perpendicular blocking or framing anchors as shown in Figure 8. The limitation applies only to seismic forces in SDC D, E or F.

2305.1.5 Wood members resisting horizontal seismic forces contributed by masonry and concrete. Because of the significant differences in in-plane stiffness between wood and masonry or concrete systems, the use of wood members to resist the seismic forces produced by masonry and concrete is not allowed in structures greater than one story in height. This is because of the probable torsional response a structure will exhibit. There are two exceptions where wood can be used as part of the lateral-load-resisting system in conjunction with concrete or masonry. The first exception is when the wood is in the form of a horizontal truss or diaphragm and the lateral loads do not produce significant rotation of the horizontal member. The torsion caused by the offset between the center of mass (CM) and center of rigidity (CR) should be less than the code-assumed accidental torsion; that is, the offset between the CM and the CR should be less than 5 percent of the building dimension perpendicular to the direction of loading. The second exception is for structures of two stories or less in height. In this case, the capacity of the wood shear walls should be sufficient to resist the magnitude of loads imposed. Five restrictions are imposed on structures using the second exception to ensure that the structural response will not include significant rotational effects and the drift will not cause failure of the masonry or concrete portions of the structure.

2305.2 Design of wood diaphragms.

2305.2.1 General. The "permissible deflection" portion of the first sentence should limit the deflection the same as does the language in Section 2305.3.1 for wood shear walls. The intent of the provision is not to exceed the more restrictive of the permissible deflection of attached or distributing elements or the drift limits of Section 1617.3 less the deflections of the lateral-force-

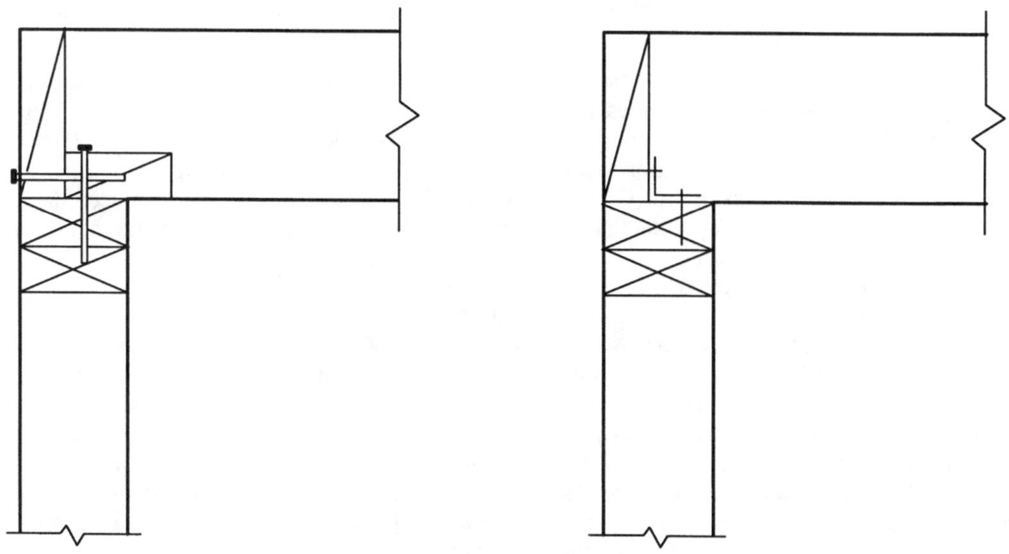

POSITIVE SHEAR TRANSFER

FIGURE 8

resisting system (shear walls). The drift limits noted in Section 1617.3 are total drifts, not element drifts.

2305.2.2 Deflection. The first paragraph refers to deformation compatibility. A complete discussion on deformation compatibility is found in Section 2305.1.

Equation 23-1, based on the results of monotonic diaphragm tests, is only for blocked wood structural panels that are uniformly nailed. Adjustments must be made if the nailing is not uniform. See ATC-7[8] for modifications to the coefficient for the third term for nail deformation in the equation. The major contributors to diaphragm deflection are nail deformation and chord splice slip.

There is currently no rational method to calculate the deflection of an unblocked diaphragm. Monotonic racking tests indicate that the deflection of an unblocked diaphragm may be on the order of three times the deflection of blocked diaphragm.

2305.2.3 Diaphragm aspect ratios. The limits on diaphragm aspect ratios are empirically based on observations of earthquake damage. Diaphragms with aspect ratios less than the tabular limits appear to perform satisfactorily in most cases. The tabular values are similar to the limits in the NEHRP, except NEHRP limits the aspect ratio for double diagonal sheathing to 3:1.

2305.2.4 Construction. Although not required explicitly by the code, the requirements of this section for exterior size and 4 by 8 panel size, except at boundaries and changes in framing, should also be applied to shear walls. Although it is not clearly outlined in this section, the minimum dimension of any sheet-type sheathing shall be 2 feet in any direction.

2305.2.4.1 Seismic Design Category F. Wood structural panels must be applied directly to the framing members; the use of gypsum wallboard between the wood structural panels and the framing members is prohibited because of the poor performance of nails in gypsum. NEHRP applies this restriction for fastening the wood structural panels directly to the diaphragm to structures assigned to SDC E as well as SDC F.

2305.2.5 Rigid diaphragms. Section 1602 defines a diaphragm as being flexible when the maximum lateral deformation of the diaphragm is more than two times the average story drift determined by comparing the maximum deflection of the diaphragm to the corresponding maximum deflection of the adjoining vertical elements of the lateral-force-resisting system. Conversely, a diaphragm will be considered rigid when the diaphragm deflection is equal to or less than two times the story drift.

For flexible diaphragms, seismic forces should be distributed to the vertical resisting elements according to tributary area or simple beam analysis. Although rotation of the diaphragm may occur because lines of vertical elements have different stiffnesses, the diaphragm is not considered stiff enough to redistribute seismic forces through rotation. The diaphragm can be visualized as a single-span beam supported on rigid supports.

For diaphragms defined as rigid, rotational or torsional behavior is expected and results in redistribution of seismic forces to the vertical-force-resisting elements. Requirements for distribution of horizontal shear and torsional shear are in Section 1617.4.4.1. Torsional response of a structure caused by irregular stiffness at any level within the structure can be a potential cause of failure. As a result, dimensional and diaphragm ratio limitations are provided for different categories of rotation. Additional requirements apply when the structure is deemed to have a torsional irregularity in accordance with Table 1616.5.1.

To understand limits placed on diaphragms acting in rotation, it is helpful to consider two different categories of diaphragms. Category I includes rigid diaphragms that rely on force transfer through rotation to maintain stability and are thus torsionally irregular. An example would be an open-front structure with shear walls on the remaining three sides. For this category of structures, applicable limitations are set forth for wood diaphragms:

- Wood diaphragms shall not be used to resist forces contributed by masonry or concrete in structures over one story (see exceptions in Section 2305.1.5).
- The length of the diaphragm normal to the opening shall not exceed 25 feet (to perpendicular shear walls), and diaphragm *l/w* ratios are limited to 1.0 for one-story structures and 0.67 for more than one story.
- Additional limitations are necessary when rotation is significant enough to be considered a torsional irregularity.

Category II includes rigid diaphragms that have two or more supporting shear walls in each of two perpendicular directions but, because the center of mass and center of rigidity do not coincide, redistribute forces to shear walls through rotation of the diaphragm. These can be further divided into Category IIA where the center of rigidity and mass are separated by a small portion of the structure's least dimension and the magnitude of the rotation is on the order of the accidental torsion specified in Section 1617.4.4.4. For this level of rotation, Section 2305.1.5 Exception 1 might be considered applicable and, as a result, no particular limitations would be placed on diaphragm rotation for Category IIA. Category IIB, rigid diaphragms with eccentricities larger than those discussed in Section 1617.4.4.4 should be subject to the following limitations for wood diaphragms:

- Diaphragm shall not be used to resist forces contributed by masonry or concrete in structures over one story.
- Additional limitations shall apply when rotation is significant enough to be considered a torsional irregularity.

Table 2305.2.3 provides limits for diaphragm ratios. Because flexible diaphragms have very little capacity for distributing torsional forces, further limitation of aspect ratios to less than the tabular maxima is used to limit diaphragm deformation such that rigid behavior will occur. The resulting deformation demand on the structure will then be limited. Where diaphragm ratios are further limited, exceptions permit higher ratios if calculations demonstrate that higher diaphragm deflections can be tolerated; i.e., deformation compatibility. In this case, it is important to determine the effect of diaphragm rigidity on the horizontal distribution and the ability of other structural and nonstructural elements to withstand the resulting element deformations.

Based on the above, open-front structures using wood diaphragms are severely limited in size to small buildings. The maximum dimensions are 25 feet deep by $37^1/_2$ feet wide. Similarly, structures with cantilevered diaphragms are allowed with the maximum dimension of the cantilever diaphragm limited to the lesser of two-thirds the diaphragm width or 25 feet. This limits the maximum plan dimension of the structure perpendicuilar to the cantilever to 37$^{1}/_{2}$ feet.

The last class of structures allowed in this section are those with limited torsional irregularities. The diaphragm aspect ratios are limited such that the diaphragm can be assumed rigid if using wood shear walls. These structures could not exceed one story in height if a masonry or concrete structure (see Section 2305.1.5) and the capacity of the wood diaphragm is presumed adequate for those demands.

2305.3 Design of shear walls.

2305.3.1 General. A shear wall is a vertical structural unit that acts as a deep beam. The analogy to a beam is appropriate since beams and shear walls are made up as assemblies. Sheathing acts as the web to resist the shear in the shear wall. The sheathing is stiffened by the framing members, which also provide support for gravity loads. Flexure is resisted by the edge or boundary elements acting like flanges to resist induced tension or compression forces. The flanges are often called hold-down posts or chords.

The flange (chord) functions as the tension or compression flange of the beam. It is important that the connection to the web be designed to accomplish the shear transfer. Since multi-story shear wall flanges consist of several pieces, it is important that the splices be designed to transmit the tension or compression occurring at the location of the splice and to recognize that the direction of application of seismic forces can reverse. The splices should be designed to minimize slip in the connection. A significant proportion of the shear wall deflection is caused by deformation in the chord splice from the axial load (see Equation 23-2, last term). It is important that the flange members, splices at intermediate floors, and the connection to the foundation be detailed and sized for the induced forces.

The webs of shear walls often have openings. The transfer of forces around openings can be treated similarly to openings in the webs of steel girders. Members at the edges of openings have forces due to flexure and the higher web shear induced in them, and the resultant forces must be transferred into the body of the diaphragm beyond the opening. Section 2305.3.7.2 permits unreinforced openings in shear walls (no force transfer design) with added restrictions outlined in the section.

Note that only wood structural panel shear walls may be used for structures assigned to SDC E or F. The uplift forces in the boundary elements must be resisted by either a portion of the structural dead load or by hold-downs. See the commentary in Section 2305.3.6 for a discussion of hold-down requirements and considerations.

2305.3.2 Deflection. The "permissible deflection" in the first paragraph is limited by the drift limits of Section 1617.3 and Table 1617.3. See footnote a to Table 1617.3 for deformation compatibility requirements for single-story buildings.

Equation 23-2 is limited to blocked wood structural panels with uniform nailing. There are currently no acceptable rational methods for determining the deflection of shear walls constructed of unblocked wood structural panels, single or double diagonally sheathed wood shear walls or shear walls constructed of particleboard, fiberboard, gypsum board, or plaster. Thus, if using these materials, one must use methods other than rational calculations to satisfy the requirements for deformation compatibility and determination of whether the diaphragm is flexible or rigid relative to the shear wall. Except for diagonal sheathing, use of these alternative materials should be limited to the seismic design categories shown in Table 1 below.

TABLE 1
PERMITTED SHEAR WALL MATERIAL

MATERIAL	SEISMIC DESIGN CATEGORY
Wood structural panel (Sec. 2305.3.1)	A, B, C, D, E, F
Diagonally sheathed lumber	A, B, C, D
Particleboard (Sec. 2306.4.3)	A, B, C
Fiberboard (Sec. 2306.4.4)	A, B, C
Gypsum board (Sec. 2306.4.5)	A, B, C, D[1]
Cement Plaster (Sec. 2306.4.5)	A, B, C, D[1]

[1]Allowable shear values must be reduced 50% in Seismic Design Category D.

Although their use is not restricted by this code, NEHRP Section 12.4.3.2 limits the use of particleboard, fiberboard, gypsum and plaster shear walls to conventional construction in structures assigned to SDC A, B or C. These alternative materials are not allowed in engineered construction in the NEHRP provisions.

The capacity of shear walls must be based on experimental results and the observations of performance during earthquakes. The 1997 NEHRP does not allow shear walls sheathed with other than wood or wood-based structural-use panels to resist seismic lateral forces in engineered construction. The 1997 NEHRP provisions were adopted as a result of relearning the lessons from past earthquakes through observations of performance of structures sheathed with these materials during the Northridge earthquake and laboratory testing.

2305.3.3 Shear wall aspect ratios. The shear wall aspect ratios, *h/w*, are limited to 2:1 in SDC D, E or F in light of the poor performance of walls with larger aspect ratios in the January 1994 Northridge earthquake and in recent tests.[9, 10] Limits for fiberboard walls are now in the table. The height-to-width ratio for both single or double diagonally sheathed shear walls should be limited to 2:1 in accordance with the NEHRP provisions.

2305.3.4 Shear wall height definition. See Figure 2305.3.4(a) to understand the definitions. These definitions were excerpted from the NEHRP provisions and are consistent with the dimensions illustrated in the model codes.

2305.3.5 Shear wall width definition. The NEHRP provisions recommend that the minimum width of a shear wall or shear wall segment be 2 feet. There are no cyclic test results for shear walls having a width less than 2 feet.

2305.3.6 Overturning restraint. Overturning moments must be resisted by anchorage devices that are referred to as "hold-downs," which are critical to the satisfactory performance of shear walls. The ultimate capacity of a shear wall is often controlled by the capacity of the hold-down rather than the capacity of the shear wall.

The allowable shear capacity of a shear wall is determined by dividing the minimum ultimate capacity by a safety factor of 2.5. Therefore, the ultimate capacity of the shear wall is at least 2.5 times the allowable shear. If the resistance from the combination of the hold-down capacity and the effective dead load is less than the boundary element uplift force associated with the ultimate shear capacity of the wall, then the wall capacity is limited by the hold-down capacity. The actual shear forces on the structure can easily be three times the allowable design force determined from the reduced base shear ($E/1.4$). Thus, the wall will likely be loaded to its ultimate shear capacity when subjected to the design earthquake. Although not explicitly required by the code, to match the capacity of the hold-downs to the strength of the shear wall and prevent a weak link in the load path, hold-downs should be sized based on the lesser of the force determined using the special load combinations of Section 1605.4, $\Omega_o E$, or the ultimate shear strength of the wall. The resistance of the hold-down may be based on the lesser of the ultimate capacity of the hold-down, the attachment of the hold-down to the boundary element, or the anchorage of the hold-down to the foundation or floor. The ultimate capacity for nails and bolts with $l/d \geq 4$ is approximately three times the allowable load. The ultimate capacity of an anchor bolt can be determined from the strength provisions for anchor bolts in ACI 318–97 using $\phi = 1.0$.

The code allows the deduction of effective dead load ($0.9D$) resistance from the uplift force determined from $E/1.4$. The hold-down is then designed for the net uplift force. This will result in under-capacity hold-downs as noted in the paragraph above. The uplift force should be determined using the capacity design approach for the shear force in the wall associated with $\Omega_o E$ prior to deduction of the effective dead load (0.9D). This will result in hold-downs with sufficient capacity to resist the ultimate shear capacity of the wall.

When using the above capacity approach, the foundation should, in turn, be designed for the ultimate capacity of the hold-down. The capacity of the foundation should be determined in accordance with ACI 318 using $\phi = 1.0$. Since most foundation widths and depths on low-rise buildings are determined by considerations other than foundation strength, this approach will seldom require any change in foundation dimensions, but may require a moderate increase in reinforcing steel.

Another issue for hold-down devices is the amount of deformation or slip allowed by the device. The purpose of the hold-down is to resist load and deflection in the form of uplift on the chord of the shear wall with zero slip. Hold-down devices should have zero slip relative to the chord before the uplift force is resisted. That is, the hold-down should resist uplift forces immediately, not only after a large amount of the force is resisted by the sheathing-to-plate nails because of slip.

Hold-down devices that permit significant vertical movement between the hold-down and the hold-down post can cause failure in the nails connecting the shear wall sheathing to the sill plate. High-tension forces and hold-down rotation caused by eccentricity may cause the bolts connecting the hold-down bracket to the hold-down post to pull through and split the hold-down post. Devices that permit such movement include heavily loaded one-sided bolted connections with small dimensions between elements resisting rotation due to eccentricity. Any device that uses over-drilled holes, such as most bolted connections, will also allow significant slip to occur between the device and the hold-down post before load is restrained. Both the NDS and the steel manual specify that bolt holes be over-drilled by not more than $^1/_{16}$ inch. This slip is what causes much of the damage to the nails connecting the sheathing to the sill plate. Friction between the hold-down post and the device cannot be counted on to resist load because relaxation in the wood will cause a loss of clamping and, therefore, a loss in friction over time. This is why all hold-down qualification tests should be conducted with the bolts "finger tight" as opposed to tightening with a wrench.

The hold-downs should exhibit zero slip as noted above. Examples of such devices are hold-downs attached to the hold-down post (chord) with nails and then bolted through the sill plate to the foundation or stud of a wall below with the anchor bolt tensioned to preload the hold-down.

Hold-downs should be qualified by cyclic testing. When nails, bolts, or similar types of fasteners are used to connect the device to the chord, cyclic tests using sequential phased displacement test procedures, or the equivalent, must be required to show that no loss in wall capacity, ductility, or stiffness is caused by the hold-down device. The bolts should be "finger tight" and friction between the tie-down device and the chord shall not be counted on to resist load. The tests shall also simulate the deformation patterns expected in a wall assembly during a seismic event and use full wall assemblies.

One other item of consideration concerning shear walls and hold-downs is the eccentric force induced in the hold-down post (chord). Hold-downs applied to one side of a chord can induce significant bending moments in the chord. The combined bending and tension in the chord can cause a brittle failure of the chord. Recent qualification testing of hold-downs for compliance with the City of Los Angeles interim standards[11] indicate that many manufactured hold-downs experienced a brittle failure of the chord at approximately two times the allowable loads; larger hold-downs (1-inch bolts) in some cases failed the chords prior to reaching the allowable load. The poor performance may be attributed to the manner in which the hold-downs were tested to establish allowable loads. Hold-down devices were typically tested in a steel jig rather than in an assembly resembling actual conditions. The allowable loads were based on the lower of the ultimate load divided by a factor of safety or the load calculated from the allowable bolt loads. To minimize the brittle chord failures, hold-downs should be qualified from assembly tests that resemble actual conditions of use, and chords should be designed for combined tension plus induced moment. Alternatively, consider use of one hold-down on each side of the chord. See Reference 11 for a thorough discussion of the phenomena related to hold-down eccentricity.

In consideration of the above, the uplift force should be calculated using the distance between the centerline of the hold-down anchor and the centroid of the compression chord.

2305.3.7 Shear walls with openings. There is very little cyclic test data for shear walls with openings. Most of the provisions in this section are based on the principles of engineering mechanics or limited monotonic testing.

2305.3.7.1 Force transfer around openings. The minimum width or a wall pier (shear wall segment) should be 24 inches as recommended by NEHRP. This is also consistent with the minimum panel width of 24 inches required by Section 2305.2.4. Boundary members should extend past the opening far enough to develop the forces into the shear wall. See ATC-7[8] for an example of the applicable mechanics and the methods suitable for reinforcement of the opening. The analysis uses a Vierendel truss analogy.

2305.3.7.2 No force transfer around openings. There are essentially three methods for designing shear walls in wood frame buildings: 1) the segmented approach simply ignores the openings and only includes full height segments that are designed for the allowable shear values and may require hold-downs at each end of each segment, 2) the method where wall piers are designed and detailed with force transfer around the openings, and 3) the perforated shear wall method that is described in Section 2305.3.7.2. The method used to design shear walls without force transfer around the openings is based on the perforated shear wall design method by AF&PA.[12]

The key features of the perforated shear wall approach are 1) the full height segments adjacent to the openings must comply with the aspect ratio limitations of Table 2305.3.3, 2) hold-downs need only be provided at the ends of the overall shear wall, not at the ends of each segment, 3) the capacity of the perforated shear wall is adjusted to be less than that of a segmented shear wall containing multiple segments, and 4) full height segments must be located at each end of the overall shear wall.

2305.3.8 Summing shear capacities. The capacities of dissimilar materials to either the same side, the opposite side, or in the same line are not cumulative because of incompatible stiffnesses and maximum usable strains. For example, the cracked stiffness of cyclically loaded gypsum is obviously much less than the stiffness of a wood structural panel subjected to the same seismic load. This holds true whether the dissimilar materials are in series or in parallel. Additionally, combinations of dissimilar materials have not been cyclically tested.

2305.3.9 Adhesives. The provisions are based on assemblies having energy dissipation capacities that were recognized in setting the *R* factors. For diaphragms and shear walls utilizing wood framing, the energy dissipation is almost entirely due to nail bending. Fasteners other than nails and staples have not been extensively tested under cyclic load application. When adhesives have been tested in assemblies subjected to cyclic loading, they have had a brittle mode of failure. For this reason, adhesives are prohibited for wood-framed shear wall assemblies and only the tabulated values for nailed or stapled sheathing are allowed. Analysis and design of shear wall sheathing applied with adhesives are beyond the scope of the provisions. If one wished to use shear wall sheathing attached with adhesives as an alternate method of construction in accordance with Section 104.11, caution should be used.[13, 14] The increased stiffness will result in larger forces being attracted to the structure. The anchorage connections and adjoining assemblies must, therefore, be designed for these increased forces. Because of the brittle failure mode, these walls should be designed to remain elastic, similar to unreinforced masonry. The use of adhesives for attaching sheathing for diaphragms increases their stiffness, and could easily change the diaphragm response from flexible to rigid.

2305.3.10 Sill plate size and anchorage in Seismic Design Category D, E or F. Specific requirements for sill plate, anchorage, and plate washers in SDC D, E or F are based on the 1997 NEHRP Provisions. Shear values are now given for both LRFD and ASD, since LRFD is an accepted method of design.

The exception is often used in retrofit work where it is not practical to remove existing plates, and in new residential construction where short sections of wall with design shears greater than 350 pounds per linear foot would require all the sill plates to be increased to 3-inch members because of detailing difficulties encountered when wood floor framing bears on intermixed 3x and 2x plates.

Splitting of the bottom plate of the shear walls has been observed in tests as well as in structures subjected to earthquakes. Splitting of plates remote from the end of the shear wall can be caused by the rotation of individual sheathing panels inducing upward forces in the nails at one end of the panel and downward forces at the other. With the upward forces on the nails and a significant distance perpendicular to the wall to the downward force produced by the anchor bolt, high cross-grain bending stresses occur. Splitting can be reduced or eliminated by use of square plate washers sufficiently stiff to reduce the eccentricity and by using thicker sill plates. Thicker sill plates (3 inches nominal, 65 mm) are required for all shear walls for which 3-inch nominal (65 mm) framing is required. This helps prevent failure of the sill plate due to high lateral loading and cross-grain bending.

SECTION 2306
ALLOWABLE STRESS DESIGN

2306.1 Allowable stress design. The *1997 National Design Specification*, NDS–97, is adopted by reference without amendments. A major change for UBC users is the load duration factor for seismic, which changes from 1.33 to 1.6. Although the 1.6 factor was substantiated for earthquake loads at the component level for nails and bolts, the earthquake design loads and detailing requirements for mitigating of strong ground shaking were calibrated with structures designed using a load duration factor of 1.33. As the recent Northridge and Kobe earthquakes have shown, the laboratory test results do not always correlate with the damage caused by real earthquakes.

2306.1.1 Joists and rafters. Although the section indicates that rafters may be designed using the span tables, the intent is that joists and rafters be permitted to be designed by the AF & PA Span Tables for Joists and Rafters.

2306.1.3 Treated wood stress adjustments. Several factors can significantly affect the physical properties of FRTW. These factors are the pressure treatment and redrying processes used, and the extremes of temperature and humidity that the FRTW will be subjected to once installed. The design values for all FRTW must be adjusted for the effects of the treatment and environmental conditions, such as high temperature and humidity in attic installations. The design adjustment values, must be based on an investigation procedure that includes subjecting the FRTW to similar temperatures and humidities, and which has been approved by the building official. The FRTW tested must be identical to that which is produced. The building official reviewing the test procedure must consider the species and grade of the untreated wood, and conditioning of wood, such as drying before the fire-retardant-treatment process. A fire-retardant wood treater may choose to have its treatment process evaluated by ICBO Evaluation Service.

The FRTW is required to be labeled with the design adjustment values. These design adjustment values can take the form of factors that are multiplied by the original design values of the untreated wood to determine its allowable stresses, or new allowable stresses that have already been factored down in consideration of the FRTW treatment.

2306.2 Wind provisions for walls.

2306.2.1 Wall stud bending stress increase. Allowable bending stresses, F_b, in wood studs resisting wind loads may be increased in accordance with Table 2306.2.1 in lieu of using the repetitive member factor increase of 1.15. This increase recognizes that the stud and sheathing act compositely with properly designed and installed fasteners. The wind pressures are transferred to the studs based on their relative stiffness to the sheathing. Since the minimum sheathing thickness is constant, the relative stiffness of the sheathing decreases as the stud depth increases; therefore, a higher proportion of load is carried by the stud as the stud depth increases.

2306.3 Wood diaphragms. Note that the term diaphragm is only applied to horizontal or sloping panel elements that resist lateral forces. Vertical panel elements that resist lateral forces are termed shear walls.

2306.3.1 Shear capacities modifications. The allowable shear capacities for wood diaphragms may be increased 40 percent for wind design only. The wind loads determined by ASCE 7 have increased and recent research has provided a better understanding of how structures are affected by wind. Code-prescribed wind loads have been refined since the tables were developed. The tables use a 2.8 factor of safety. Wind loads are essentially monotonic and bounded; hence, a safety factor of 2 is sufficient for wind loading, resulting in a 40-percent increase in the tabulated values.

2306.3.2 Wood structural panel diaphragms. Allowable shears for these diaphragms may be taken from the table, or calculated by the principles of mechanics. The APA publication *Design/Construction Guide—Diaphragms*[7] provides a good example of the necessary calculations. For structures in SDC D, E or F, the shear values should be based on cyclic tests or the tabular values and not calculated.

The values for allowable shear for nailed diaphragms are based on monotonic testing. The table also contains values for staples; these values are based on cyclic testing.

The minimum nail penetraton requirements have been reduced from previous model code requirements where 8d and 10d nails are used. Studies undertaken using the European Yield Method (EYM) for calculating nail lateral values showed that the penetrations indicated in the tables in the model codes are not necessary. The EYM methodology is included in the NDS. This change will now permit the use of flat-wise blocking in diaphragms and shear walls where 10d nails are used.

When the framing lumber is of a species other than Douglas Fir-Larch or Southern Pine, the tabular values must be adjusted to account for the fastener behavior in framing members of other lumber species. The adjustments must be made per Footnote 1, but the resulting value may not exceed the tabular value.

2306.3.3 Diagonally sheathed lumber diaphragms. Diagonally sheathed lumber diaphragms are seldom used in new construction, but are encountered in rehabilitation of older structures. The allowable shear values for diagonally sheathed lumber diaphragms are based on lateral design values for nails.

2306.4 Shear walls. Only wood structural panel shear walls are allowed in SDC E or F. Shear walls must be blocked (see Definitions).

2306.4.1 Wood structural panel shear walls. The allowable shear capacities for wood structural panel shear walls may be increased 40 percent for wind design only. The wind loads determined by ASCE 7 have increased and recent research has provided a better understanding of how structures are affected by wind. Code-prescribed wind loads have been refined since the tables use a factor of safety equal to 2.8. Wind loads are essentially monotonic and bounded; hence, a safety factor of 2.0 is sufficient for wind loading. This results in a 40 percent increase in the tabulated values.

Allowable shears for these shear walls may be taken from the table, or calculated by the principles of mechanics. For structures in SDC D, E or F, the shear values should be based on cyclic tests or the tabular values, and not calculated.

The values for allowable shear are based on monotonic racking tests using aspect ratios of 1:1. The tabular values were reduced by as much as 25 percent by some jurisdictions as a result of the extensive damage to wood structures observed from the Northridge earthquake. Preliminary results from cyclic testing of wood structural panel diaphragms being conducted by APA indicate that some tabular values may need to be reduced by as much as 10 percent.

The table also contains values for staples. The values for staples are based on cyclic testing.

When the framing lumber is of a species other than Douglas Fir-Larch or Southern Pine, the tabular values must be adjusted to account for the fastener behavior in framing members of other lumber species. The adjustments must be made per Footnote 1, but the resulting value may not exceed the tabular value.

Footnotes e and f require 3-inch or wider framing members at adjoining panel edges where nail spacing at the panel edges is 2 inches or less. Recent earthquakes have shown that highly loaded shear walls with close nail spacing sustained major damage because there was not adequate nail edge distance.

Footnote e applies to Seismic Design Categories D, E and F. All framing members receiving edge nailing, including sills and blocking, must be 3-inch nominal when the shear design value exceeds 350 pounds per lineal foot (ASD) or 490 pounds per lineal foot (LRFD). See the discussion of sill thickness in Section 2305.3.10.

2306.4.2 Lumber sheathed shear walls. Diagonally sheathed shear walls use the same detailing and load requirements as diagonally sheathed diaphragms covered in Sections 2306.3.4 and 2306.3.5.

2306.4.3 Particleboard shear walls. Particleboard shear walls should be used with care, as particleboard shear walls have not been cyclically tested. Note that type M-S or M-2, both with exterior glue, are the only panels allowed. Particleboard shear walls are not allowed in SDC D, E or F. NEHRP does not allow particleboard shear walls in engineered construction, but does permit them as a prescriptive braced panel in conventional construction.

2306.4.4 Fiberboard shear walls. Fiberboard shear walls should only be constructed with a height-to-width ratio of $1^1/_2$:1, e.g., an 8-foot-high wall must be 5 feet 4 inches long. Note that the shear values for fiberboard shear walls are based on monotonic testing of panels with a height-to-width ratio of $1^1/_2$:1.

Fiberboard shear walls should be used with care because they have not been cyclically tested. Fiberboard shear walls are not allowed in SDC D, E and F. NEHRP Section 12.4.3.2 does not allow fiberboard shear walls in engineered construction, but does permit them as a prescriptive braced panel in conventional construction.

2306.4.5 Shear walls sheathed with other materials. These tables for plaster and gypsum walls are relocated from Chapter 25. The detailed construction requirements for these walls are in Section 2306.4.5.1 and Chapter 25. Shear walls of these materials are rather brittle. The strength and stiffness of both plaster and gypsum shear walls decrease significantly under a limited number of cycles when subjected to seismic demands. Examination of the performance of structures subjected to strong shaking from the Northridge earthquake showed that these walls did not exhibit adequate strength or ductility. Therefore, these walls should be used to resist seismic demands only after careful consideration of the performance characteristics.

This section permits these gypsum and plaster shear walls to be used in SDC A, B or C with no reduction in allowable shear; however, this section permits these shear walls to be used in SDC D only with a 50-percent reduction in allowable shear, and prohibits their use in SDC E or F. NEHRP Section 12.4.3.2 does not allow use of these wall types for engineered construction, nor does it allow their use for bracing of cripple walls in either engineered or conventional construction. NEHRP does, however, allow the use of these walls for conventional construction with increased shear panel lengths.

SECTION 2307
LOAD AND RESISTANCE FACTOR DESIGN

The permitted use of the Load and Resistance Factor (LRFD) Standard for Engineered Wood Construction, AF&PA/ASCE 16,[2] has been adopted as a referenced standard and can be used for all wood design. The 1997 NEHRP Provisions uses this standard as the primary design procedure for engineered wood construction and adopted it by reference.

SECTION 2308
CONVENTIONAL LIGHT-FRAME CONSTRUCTION

Most of the seismic provisions noted in this section are based on Division IV of the 1997 UBC and the 1997 NEHRP Provisions. The NEHRP Provisions generally followed the requirements of the *International One- and Two-Family Dwelling Code,* with additions and modifications made to address seismic issues. New provisions were also added by the IBC Structural Committee as necessary.

2308.1 General. The provisions of Section 2308 provide prescriptive construction details and methods for light-frame wood construction. Typical details as required by the provisions are shown in Figures 9 through 13. Light-frame construction is characterized by 2x construction with walls of 2-inch nominal thickness studs at 16 or 24 inches on center, and roofs and floors of 2-inch nominal thickness rafters or joists at 12, 16, or 24 inches on center. Studs are typically 2 by 4 or 2 by 6. Construction that meets the prescriptive provisions of Section 2308 is deemed to comply with the intent of the code. See Section 2308.2 for the applicability of these conventional construction provisions.

It should be noted that IBC Section 101.2 has an exception that allows "one- and two-family dwellings and multiple single family dwellings (townhouses) not more than three stories high with separate means of egress" to be constructed to comply with the *International Residential Code* (IRC). One- and two-family dwellings that do not comply with the limitations prescribed by the IRC must be designed in accordance with the IBC. These buildings must either comply with the conventional construction provisions of Section 2308 or be designed in accordance with the engineering provisions.

The provisions of Section 2308 are based on experience gained over the last 60 years or more. In general, these types of provisions are reasonably easy to modify where experience shows they are inadequate. An example of such modification is the change in bracing requirements that resulted from experience gained in the 1971 San Fernando, 1987 Whittier, and the 1994 Northridge, California, earthquakes.

2308.2 Limitations. The structures to which conventional construction is applicable are described in this section. Additional requirements for structures classified as SDC B or C are in Section 2308.11, and for structures classified as SDC D or E, Section 2308.12. The provisions may not be used for structures classified as SDC F; engineering design is required for the SDC F structure.

Note that cripple walls exceeding 14 inches high in structures classified in any seismic design category are considered a story. (See Section 2308.9.4.1 and 2308.12.4.) Typical conventional construction for structures with cripple walls is to use post-and-beam construction to support the floor joists in the interior of the structure.

Since interior braced panel walls may not extend down to the foundation, all lateral loads must be transferred through the cripple walls to the foundation. The cripple walls are heavily loaded relative to the braced panel walls. The cripple walls thus are very important to satisfactory performance of the structure when subjected to lateral loads. By classifying the cripple walls as a story, higher bracing strength criteria are prescribed to resist the higher loads. See, for example, Table 2308.12.4.

2308.2.1 Basic wind speed greater than 100 mph (3-second gust). Where 3-second-gust wind speeds exceed 100 mph (this is approximately 80 mph fastest mile wind speed), special details are necessary to resist the higher wind pressures and ensure load path continuity. These details are presented in the referenced documents.

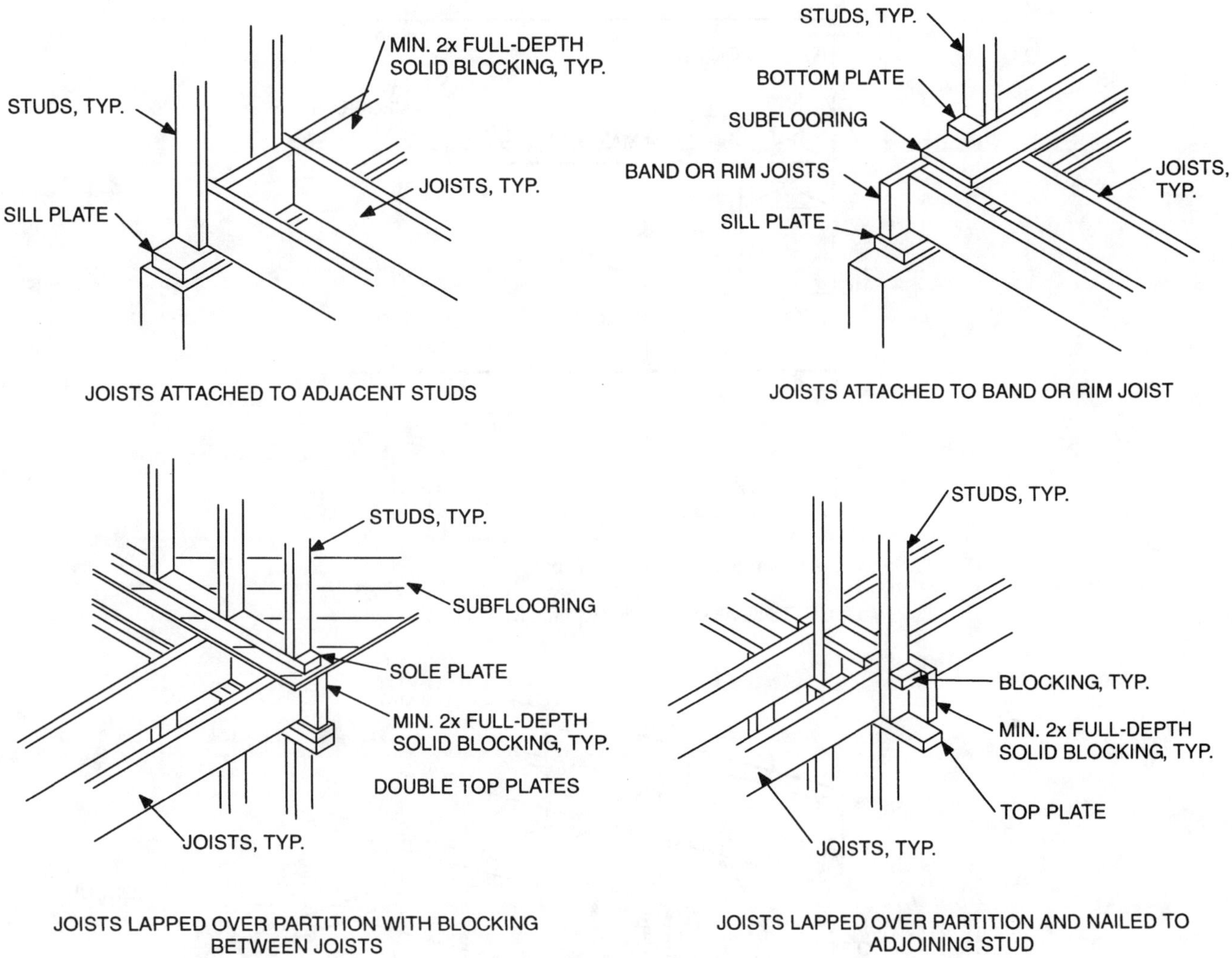

TYPICAL FRAMING DETAILS

FIGURE 9

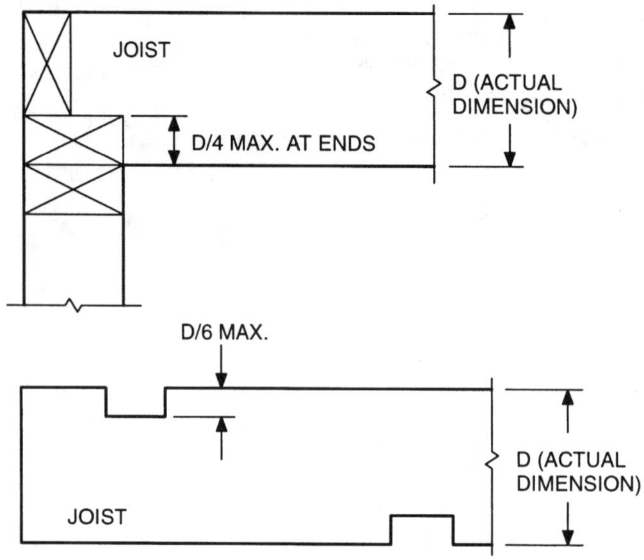

NOTE: Notching not permitted in middle $^1/_3$ of span

CUTTING AND NOTCHING LIMITATIONS

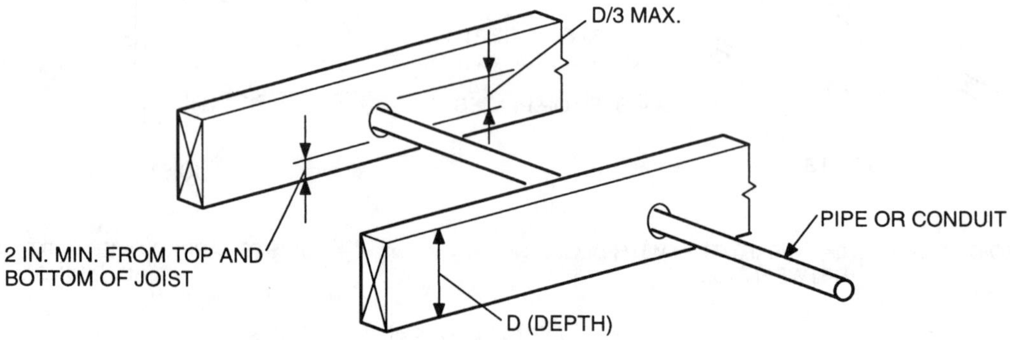

For SI: 1 inch = 25.4 mm.

BORED HOLES IN JOISTS

NOTCHING AND BORING LIMITATIONS—FLOOR JOISTS

TYPICAL DETAILS

FIGURE 10

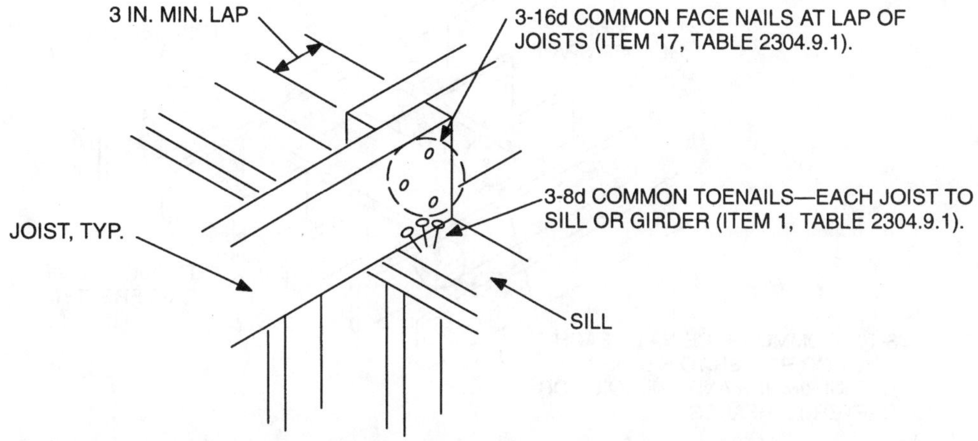

FLOOR OR CEILING JOIST LAPPING OVER BEAM, GIRDER OR PARTITION

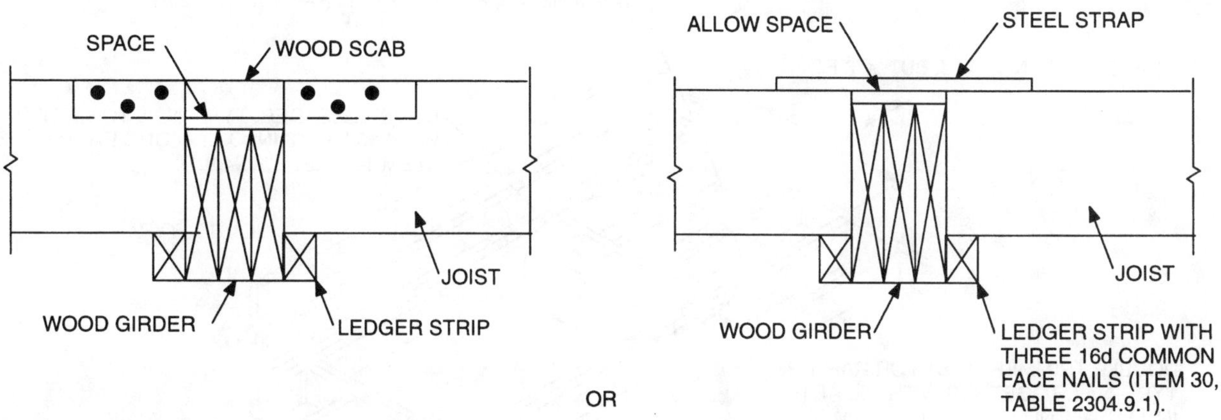

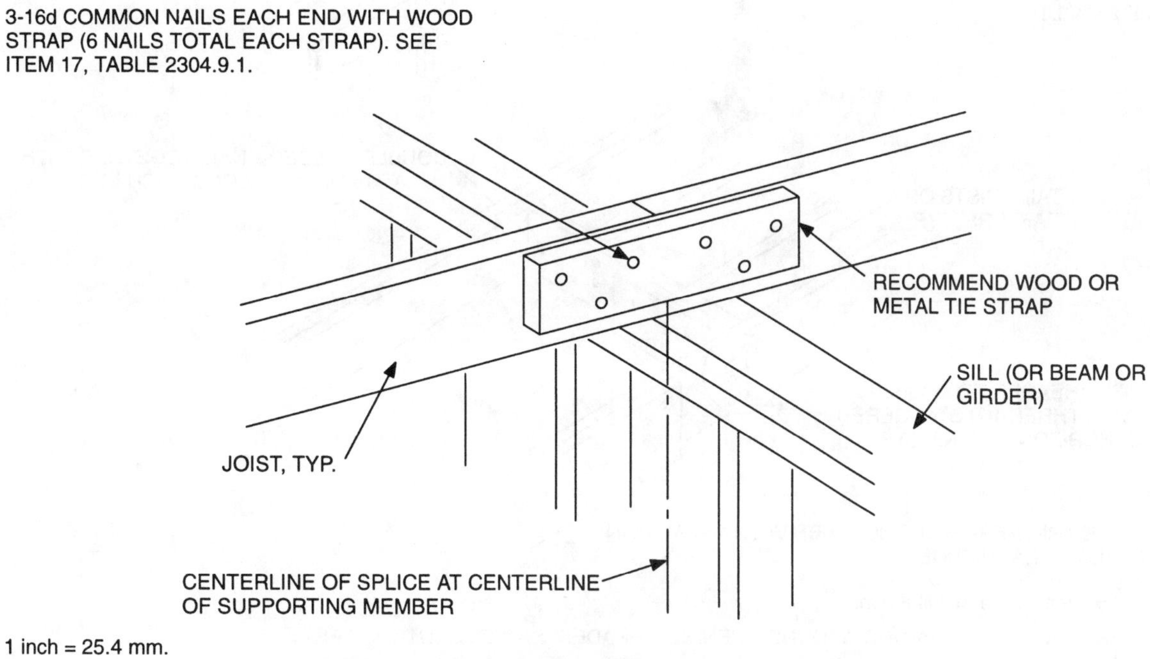

For SI: 1 inch = 25.4 mm.

TYPICAL DETAILS—FLOOR OR CEILING JOISTS

FIGURE 11

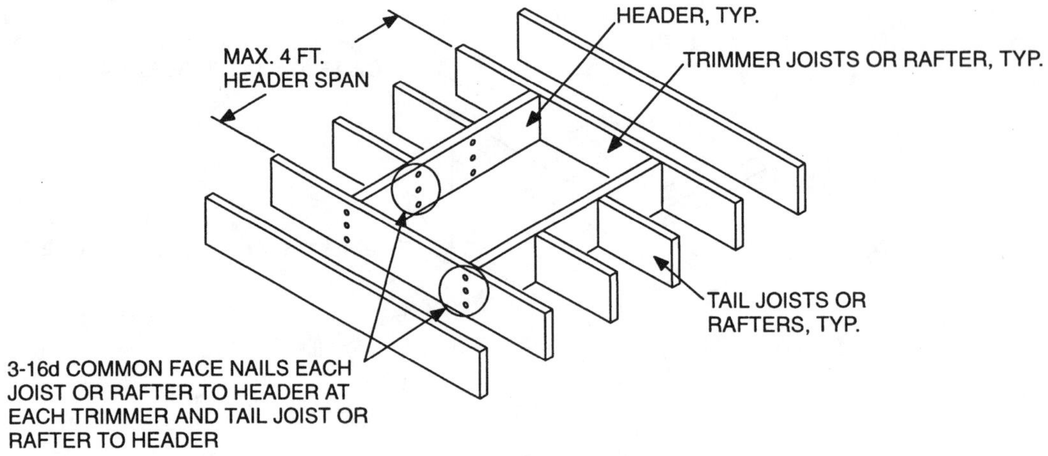

FRAMING AROUND OPENINGS—HEADER SPAN ≤ 4 FEET

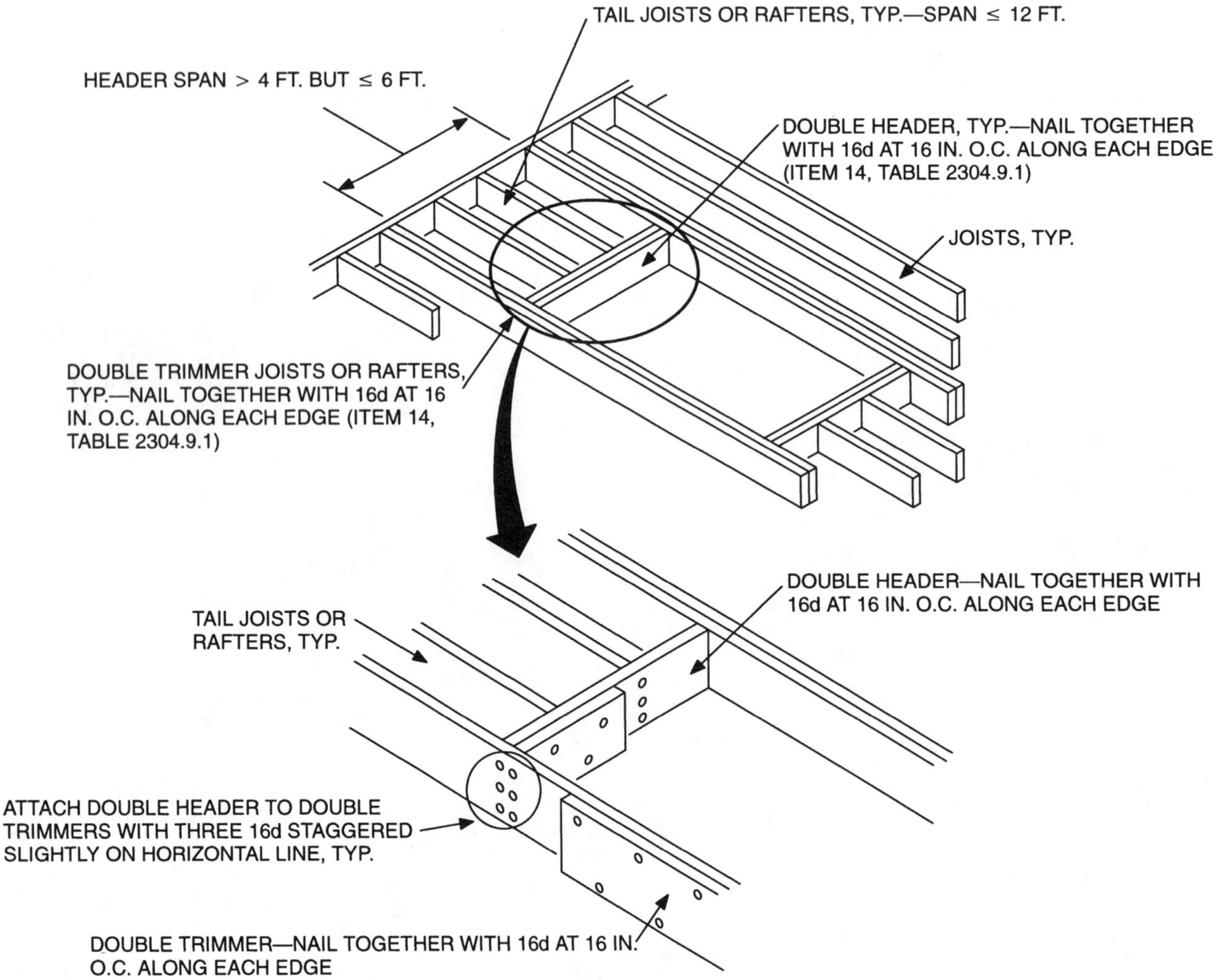

For SI: 1 inch = 25.4 mm, 1 foot = 304.8 mm.

FRAMING AROUND OPENINGS HEADER > 4 FEET BUT ≤ 6 FEET

TYPICAL DETAILS

FIGURE 12

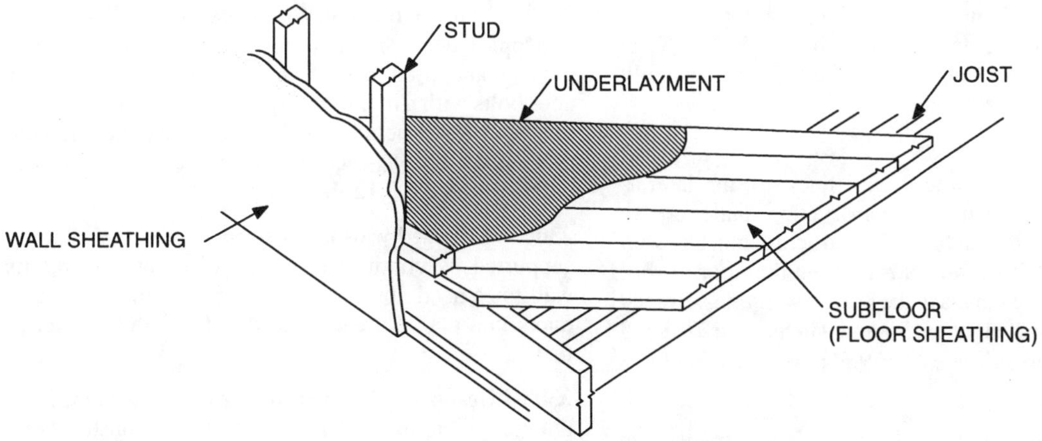

FLOOR SHEATHING AS SUBFLOORING

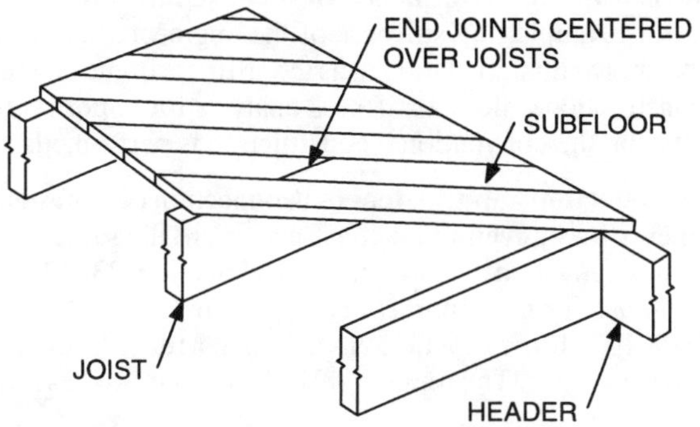

DIAGONAL SHEATHING AS SUBFLOOR

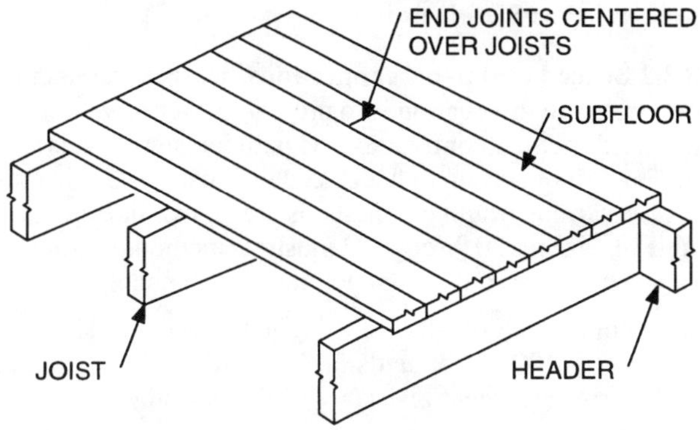

STRAIGHT SHEATHING AS SUBFLOOR

SUBFLOOR (FLOOR SHEATHING) ORIENTATION

LUMBER SUBFLOORING

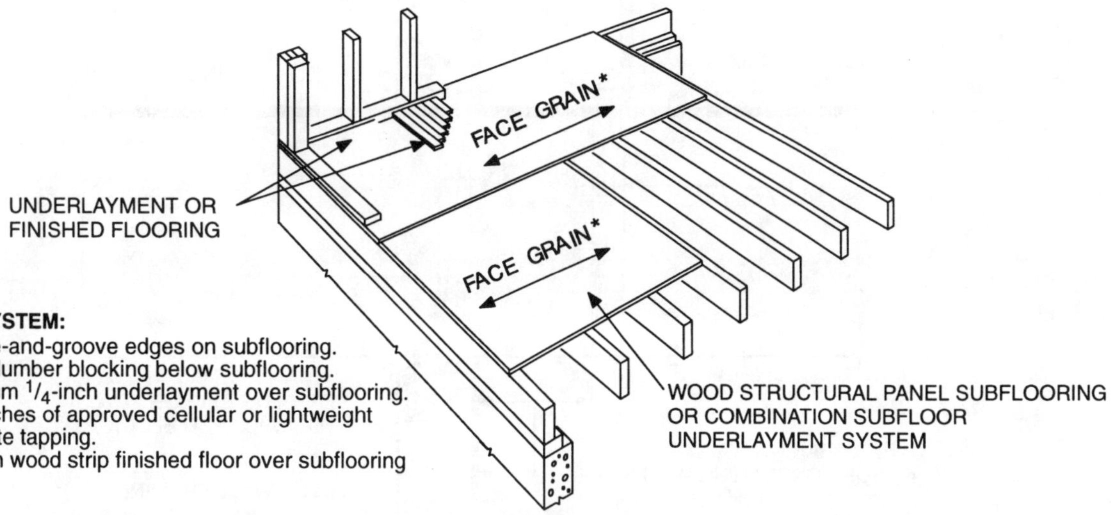

CHOICE OF SYSTEM:

1. Tongue-and-groove edges on subflooring.
2. 2-inch lumber blocking below subflooring.
3. Minimum $^1/_4$-inch underlayment over subflooring.
4. $1^1/_2$ inches of approved cellular or lightweight concrete tapping.
5. $^3/_4$-inch wood strip finished floor over subflooring

*Depending on the design loads, panel thickness and the panel span rating, the face grain (strength axis) of the wood structural panel may be oriented parallel or perpendicular to the supporting members below.

For SI: 1 inch = 25.4 mm.

PLYWOOD SUBFLOORING—TYPICAL DETAILS

FIGURE 13

2308.2.2 Buildings in Seismic Design Category B, C, D or E. Additional requirements for structures classified as SDC B, C, D or E are in Sections 2308.11 or 2308.12. The exceptions apply only to detached one- and two-family Group R-3 dwellings classified as SDC B or C.

2308.3 Braced wall lines. Braced wall lines are the lateral-resisting elements in conventional construction analogous to shear walls in engineered structures. The structure must be well connected to transfer the lateral loads through the floor or roof diaphragms to the braced panels in the braced wall lines. Braced wall panels may be any of eight types named in Section 2308.9.3 subject to the limitations in Table 2308.9.3(1) as well as Sections 2308.11 and 2308.12.

2308.3.1 Spacing. The 35-foot braced wall line spacing is from NEHRP. Section 2308.12 reduces the spacing to 25 feet for structures classified as SDC D or E.

2308.3.2 Braced wall panel connections. The general intent of the provisions in this section is to provide prescriptive requirements for achieving a continuous load path for lateral loads from the roof and floor system to the braced wall panels. Connection details for various framing conditions are shown in Figures 14 through 19. Figures 20 through 23 illustrate methods of transferring loads from the roof system to braced wall panels.

These connection details are designed to transfer shears of approximately 100-200 pounds per foot, which is compatible with the allowable shear resistance of the braced panels.

2308.3.3 Sill anchorage. Where braced wall lines are required to be supported by continuous footings (see Section 2308.3.4), sills must be anchored to the foundation with $^1/_2$-inch-diameter anchor bolts with a maximum spacing of 6 feet on center, or 4 feet on center for structures over two stories in height. Buildings in SDC E require $^5/_8$-inch-diameter anchor bolts in accordance with Section 2308.12.9.

2308.3.4 Braced wall line support. Braced wall lines must be supported by continuous footings except that interior braced wall lines need not be supported by continuous footings if the maximum plan dimension of the structure does not exceed 50 feet.

2308.4 Design of portions. Where a structure consists of a combination of engineered and conventional construction, only the engineered elements must be designed to the forces specified in Chapter 16. The performance of engineered elements should be compatible with the performance of a conventionally framed system. For example, the stiffness of the engineered elements should be approximately the same as the stiffness of the conventional construction unless a stiffness analysis for apportioning loads between the conventional construction is performed.

2308.5 Connections and fasteners. Connections and fastener requirements for conventional construction are the same as required for engineered construction. See Section 2304.9 and Table 2304.9.1 for minimum fastening requirements. Also see Table 2308.10.4.1 for rafter tie connections as a function of rafter slope and snow load. The number of 16d nails required as rafter

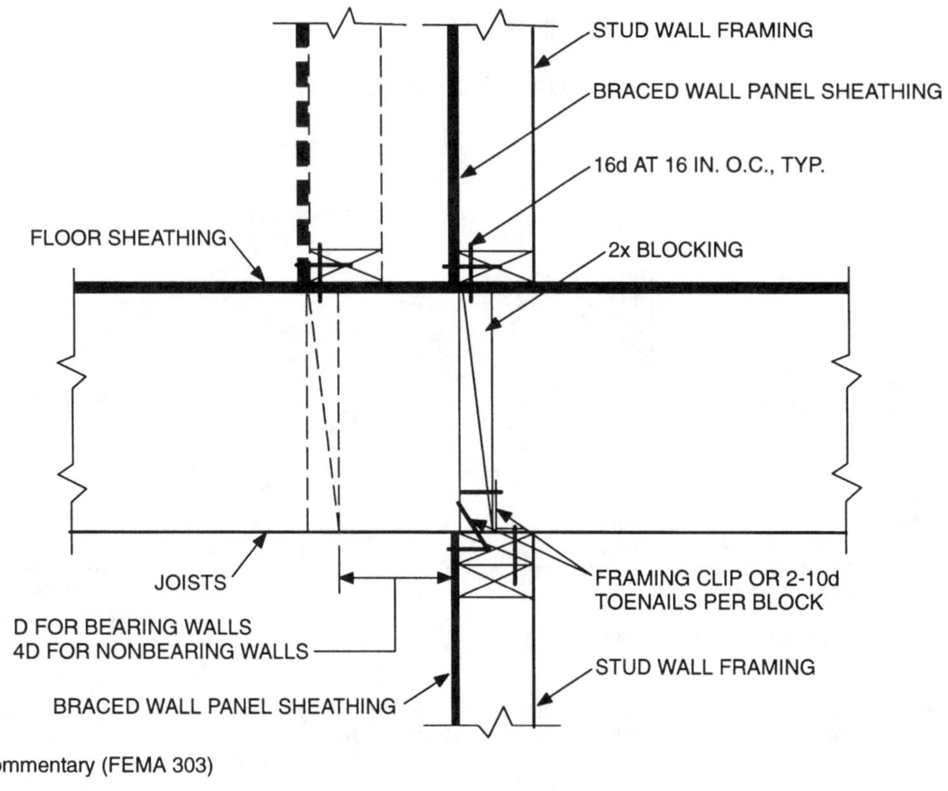

Source: 1997 NEHRP Commentary (FEMA 303)

INTERIOR BRACED WALL AT PERPENDICULAR JOIST

FIGURE 14

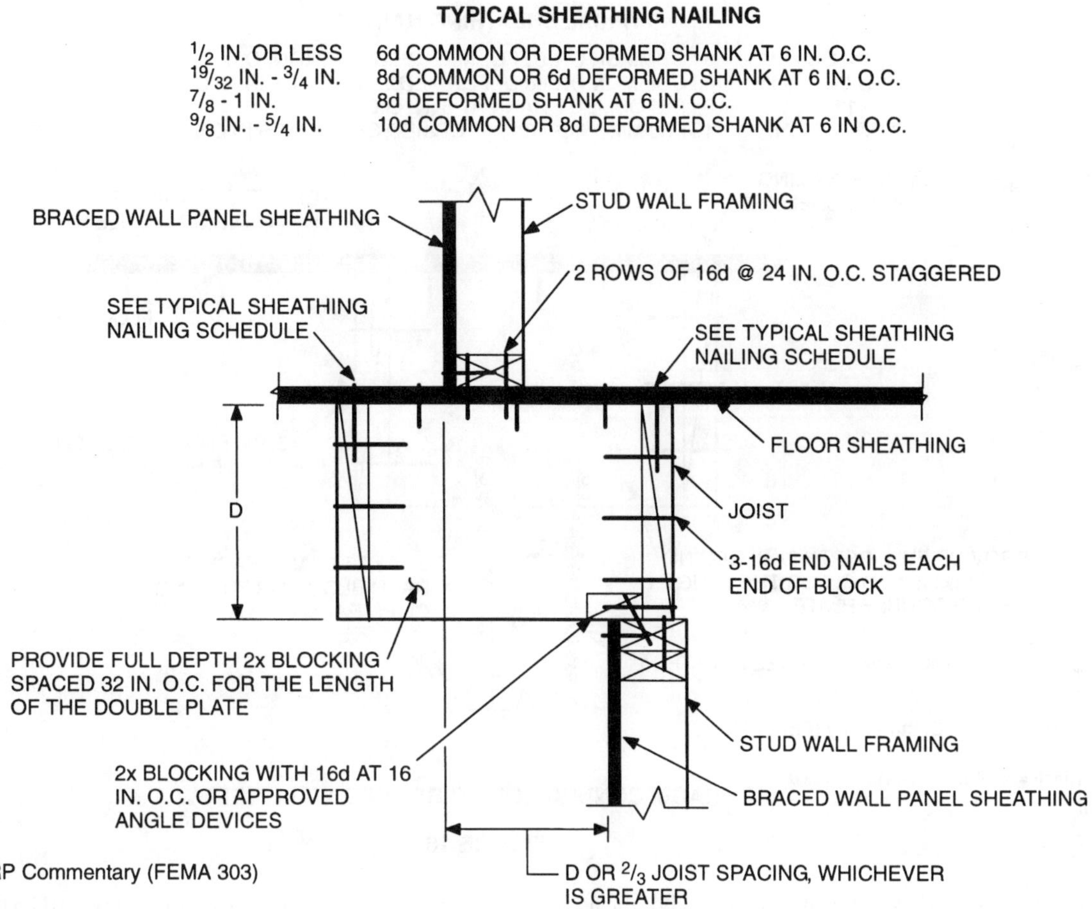

Source: 1997 NEHRP Commentary (FEMA 303)

For SI: 1 inch = 25.4 mm.

OFFSET AT INTERIOR BRACED WALL

FIGURE 15

tie connections per Table 2308.10.4.1 can be significantly greater than the minimum requirements of Table 2304.9.1.

2308.6 Foundation plates or sills. Prescriptive foundation plate and anchorage provisions are in Chapter 23. The provisions apply only to conventional construction, except the requirements in Section 2304 apply to both engineered construction and conventional construction.

2308.7 Girders. The design of girders to support floor loads requires so many variables the tables are practical only for simple cases. Most girders must be engineered. Figures 24 and 25 show acceptable details deemed to comply with the splice and tie requirements.

2308.8 Floor joists. Tables 2308.8(1) and 2308.8(2) are excerpted from the AF&PA Span Tables for Joist and Rafters. Joists selected from these tables are deemed to comply with code requirements for both strength and deflection. Note that Table 2308.8(1) is for a floor live load of 30 psf. Table 1607.1 allows a 30 psf floor live load in residential sleeping areas.

2308.8.1 Bearing. Figures 26 and 27 illustrate the bearing requirements.

2308.8.2 Framing details. Figure 28 depicts the provisions for support by solid blocking or other means, and joists framing into a girder.

Figure 29 illustrates the allowed notches or bored holes.

Figure 30 depicts the requirements for lapping and tying joists over a beam or partition.

2308.8.3 Framing around openings. Figure 31 depicts acceptable framing details for openings not greater than 4 feet. Figure 32 depicts acceptable framing for openings greater than 4 feet but not greater than 6 feet. Figure 33 shows framing and hangers for openings greater than 6 feet.

2308.8.4 Supporting bearing partitions. Figure 34 depicts the requirement for supporting bearing partitions.

2308.8.5 Lateral support. Figure 35 depicts the lateral support requirements.

2308.8.6 Structural floor sheathing. Flooring systems may consist of a subfloor on which may be placed an underlayment or a combination subfloor/underlayment system, upon which a finished floor-surfacing material may be applied. The finished floor-surfacing material may either be wood-strip flooring, tongue-and-groove flooring, various types of resilient floor

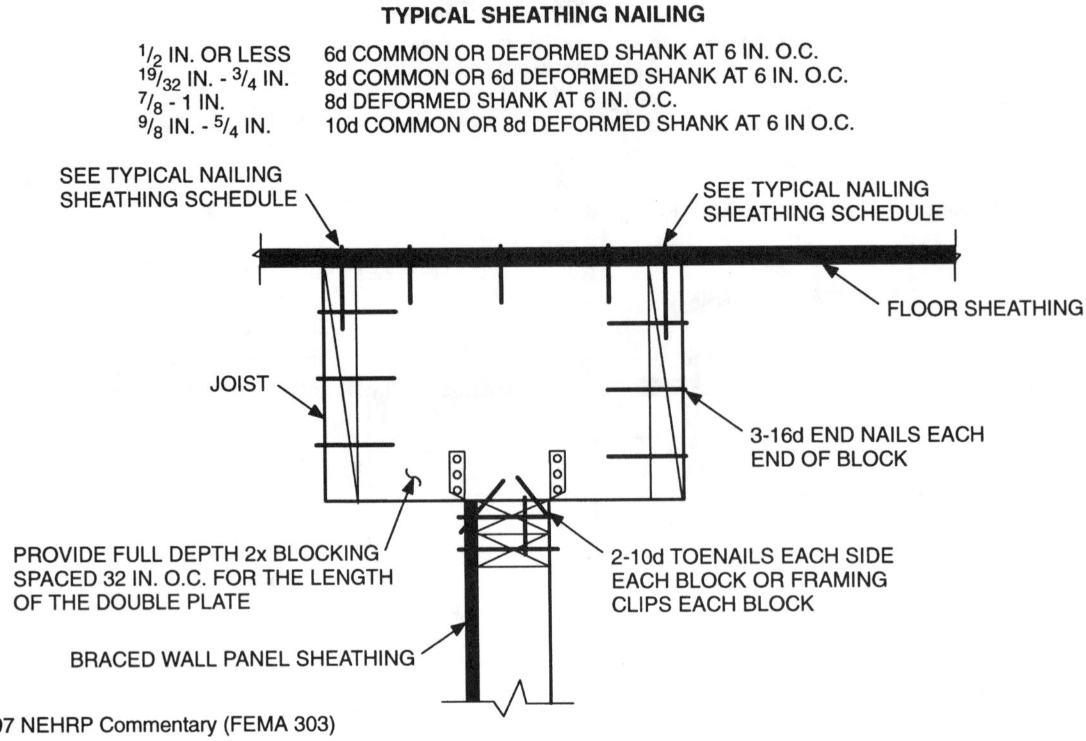

Source: 1997 NEHRP Commentary (FEMA 303)

For SI: 1 inch = 25.4 mm.

DIAPHRAGM CONNECTION TO BRACED WALL BELOW

FIGURE 16

coverings such as vinyl asbestos tile, or carpet. For the noncombined subfloor/underlayment system, underlayment is required to provide a smooth, even surface to which the finished flooring will be attached. However, in some cases, the underlayment is required to add strength to the subflooring.

Allowable spans for lumber subflooring are found in Tables 2304.7(1) and 2304.7(2). The span tables are based on the thickness of the floor sheathing, the orientation of the sheathing with respect to the joists (either perpendicular or diagonal) and the board grade of the lumber being used.

Wood structural panels may be manufactured for use as either structural subflooring or combination subfloor-underlayment. The allowable spans for structural subflooring and combination subfloor-underlayment are based on the wood structural panel's face grain (strength axis) parallel to supporting members or its being continuous over two or more spans with the face grain perpendicular to the supports. These qualifications are critical in determining the permissible spans. Most wood structural panels are considerably stronger when their face grain is perpendicular to the supports and continuous over two or more spans. Panels with multiple spans have greater capacity than when they are simply supported between two joists.

To create a stiffer floor and prevent or minimize squeaking of the floor system after the building has been in use, the subfloor may be glued to the joists. This gluing prevents the relative movement between the panel and the joist that takes place when loads are placed on the floor, and provides additional stiffness.

Particleboard can be used as underlayment, structural subflooring or as combined subfloor-underlayment. Where used as underlayment, the code permits Type PBU particleboard. Where particleboard is used as a structural subfloor or as combined subfloor-underlayment, the code specifies Type 2-M-W or 2-M-3 particleboard for structural subflooring and combination subfloor-underlayment, as they may be subject to wetting from rainfall until the building has been completely enclosed and weatherproofed. Therefore, the high durability and strength under high moisture conditions provided by Type 2-M-W or 2-M-3 particleboard are necessary.

Figure 13 depicts typical floor sheathing.

2308.9 Wall framing.

2308.9.1 Size, height and spacing. Figure 36 depicts stud requirements.

2308.9.2 Framing details. Top plate splices require eight 16d face nails each side of the joint. This double top plate splice has an allowable chord or collector force of approximately 1,100 pounds if using box nails. The allowable force for the single top plate is approximately 600 pounds. Single plate splices shall have at least twelve 8d nails with a 3-inch by 12-inch steel plate. NEHRP recommends this splice using 12 nails each side.

Figure 37 depicts the double top plate splice requirement; Figure 38 depicts the recommended single top plate splice.

2308.9.2.2 Top plates for studs spaced at 24 inches (610 mm). Figure 39 depicts the requirements for locating the joists or trusses.

2308.9.2.3 Nonbearing walls and partitions. This section allows for increased stud spacing on nonbearing walls, and studs may be turned with the long dimension parallel to the wall for

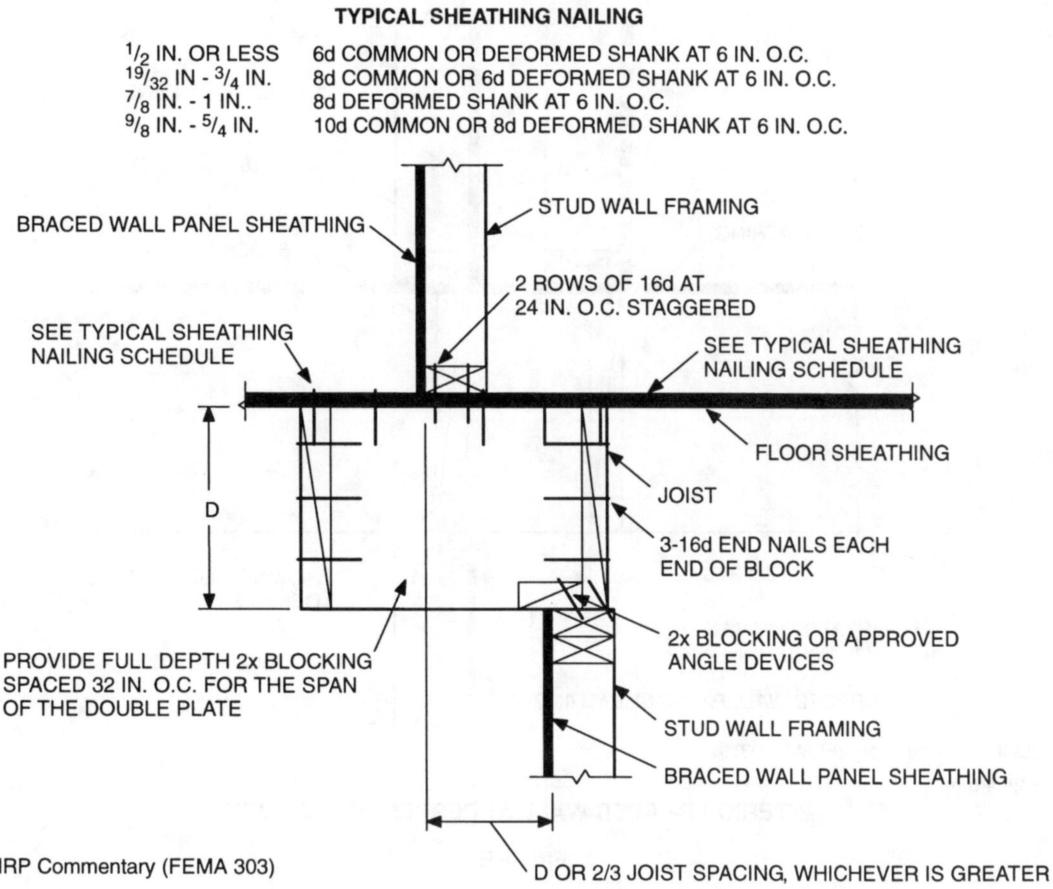

Source: 1997 NEHRP Commentary (FEMA 303)

For SI: 1 inch = 25.4 mm.

OFFSET AT INTERIOR BRACE WALL

FIGURE 17

construction of plumbing chases. Note that sheathing materials must be increased in thickness when wider stud spacing is used.

2308.9.3 Bracing. The bracing requirements for conventional construction are depicted in Figure 40. As required by Section 2308.3, braced wall lines are required at interior and exterior wall lines at the spacing of 25 or 35 feet depending on the seismic design category classification. Prescriptive requirements for eight allowable braced wall types are found in this section. Braced wall panels must start within 12.5 feet from the end of a braced wall line. Otherwise, a "designed" collector must be provided where the braced panel in a braced wall line is more than 12.5 feet from the end of the wall line. Figure 41 depicts this requirement.

Braced wall panels in a braced wall line must not be offset by more than 4 feet. Examples of acceptable locations for braced wall lines are illustrated in Figures 42 and 43.

Table 2308.9.3(1). This table is applicable only to structures classified as SDC A, B or C. Structures classified as SDC D or E have more stringent requirements set forth in Table 2308.12.4.

2308.9.3.1 Alternate bracing. Braced panels in Section 2308.9.3 may be replaced by the alternate braced panels of this section, which were developed to solve the problem of having narrow walls adjacent to garage door openings where the opening supports a floor above. Note that the alternate braced panel is an assembly—all the requirements must be met. The alternate braced panel requirements are illustrated in Figure 44.

2308.9.4 Cripple walls.

2308.9.4.1 Bracing. See commentary for Section 2308.2. Cripple walls (sometimes referred to as foundation stud walls or knee walls) are stud walls usually less than 8 feet in height that rest on the foundation plate and support the first immediate floor above.

The code requires a minimum height of 14 inches for cripple wall studs, and this minimum is based on the length necessary to properly fasten the studs to the foundation wall plate and the double-wall plate above. Where the 14-inch minimum is not possible, the code then requires that the cripple wall be framed with solid blocking. Under this circumstance, the cripple wall studs, even though shorter than 14 inches in length, should be installed with wall plates as required by Section 2308.9.2 and with the solid blocking tightly fitted between each stud. This solid blocking performs three purposes: it provides a level uniform bearing surface for the support of the floor above, it transmits lateral forces from the floor to the foundation and it reduces the "racking" effects of the studs during seismic or high-wind activity. Wood

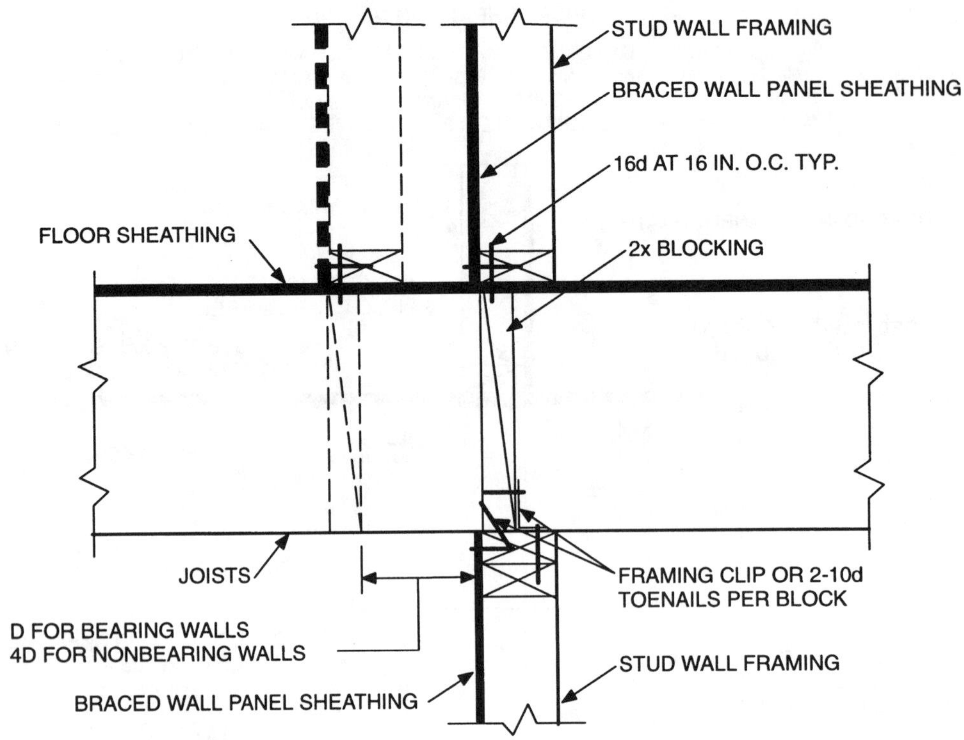

Source: 1997 NEHRP Commentary (FEMA 303)

For SI: 1 inch = 25.4 mm.

INTERIOR BRACED WALL AT PERPENDICULAR JOIST

FIGURE 18

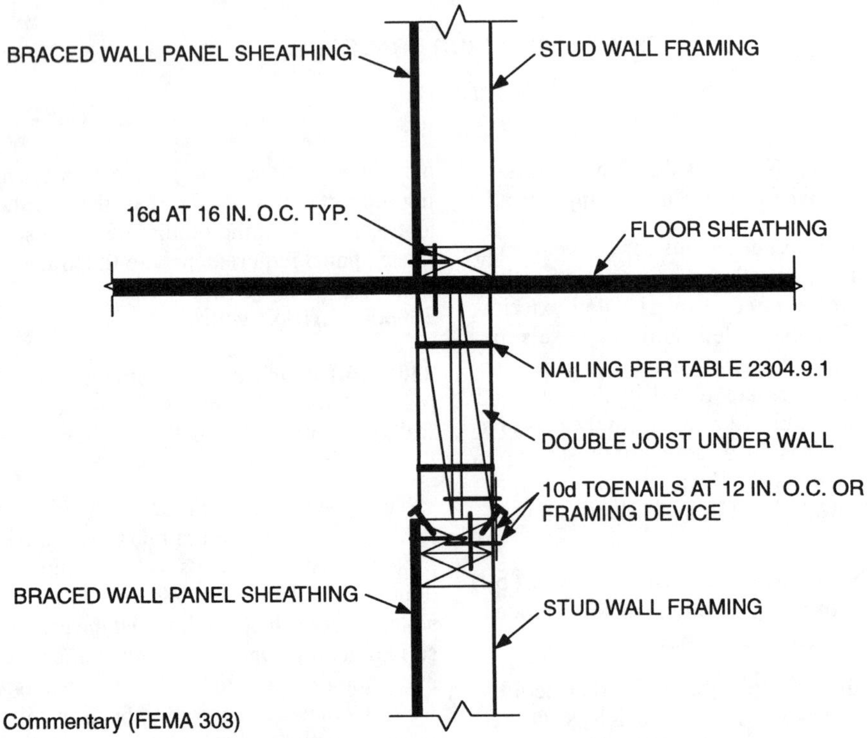

Source: 1997 NEHRP Commentary (FEMA 303)

For SI: 1 inch = 25.4 mm.

INTERIOR BRACED WALL AT PARALLEL JOIST

FIGURE 19

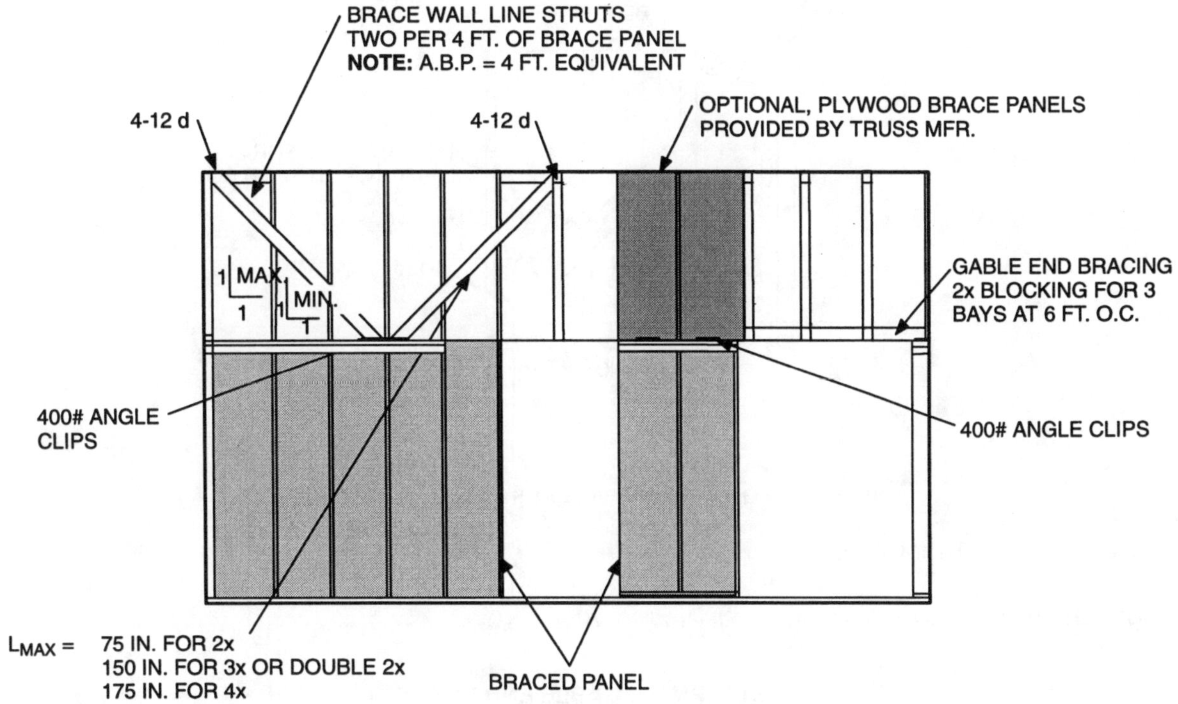

NOTE: 12d nails are 0.148 in. in diameter and $3^1/_4$ in long

Source: 1997 NEHRP Commentary (FEMA 303)

SUGGESTED METHOD FOR TRANSFERRING ROOF DIAPHRAGM LOADS TO BRACED WALL PANELS

FIGURE 20

structural panel sheathing may also be used to brace these walls, provided adequate nailing is present along the foundation sill and top plates.

Where cripple studs exceed 14 inches in height, the code has two requirements:

- Foundation stud walls having a stud height exceeding 14 inches shall be braced in accordance with Table 2308.9.3(1) or Table 2308.12.4.
- Foundation stud walls exceeding 4 feet in height must be framed with studs having the size required for an additional story.

Thus, for a building that would be considered to be two stories in height with a crawl space beneath the first story but having foundation stud walls with the studs more than 4 feet in height, the code would require that the studs be framed with either 3 by 4 or 2 by 6 members, as would be required for the first story of a three-story building.

2308.9.5 Openings in exterior walls.

2308.9.5.1 Headers. Headers in accordance with Table 2308.9.5 may be used only for one- and two-family dwellings for structures that fit the parameters of the table. Headers for all other structures must be engineered. Figure 45 illustrates header requirements.

2308.9.6 Openings in interior-bearing partitions. Headings in accordance with Table 2308.9.6 may be used only for one- and two-family dwellings for structures that fit the parameters of the table. Headers for all other structures must be engineered. See Figure 45.

2308.9.8 Pipes in walls. Figure 46 illustrates the requirements of this section.

2308.9.9 Bridging. Where stud partitions do not have adequate sheathing to brace the studs laterally in their weak or smaller dimension, and the studs have a height-to-least-thickness ratio exceeding 50, the studs are required to have bridging or solid blocking with a minimum nominal thickness of 2 inches and a width the same as the studs. This blocking should be installed at heights that reduce the height-to-least-thickness ratio below 50. Use of 2 by 4 studs will require placement of the blocking when the maximum height of the wall is over 6 feet 3 inches.

2308.9.10 Cutting and notching. Figure 47 illustrates acceptable cutting or notching of studs, and bored holes in studs.

2308.9.11 Bored holes. Figure 48 illustrates acceptable cutting or notching of studs, and bored holes in studs.

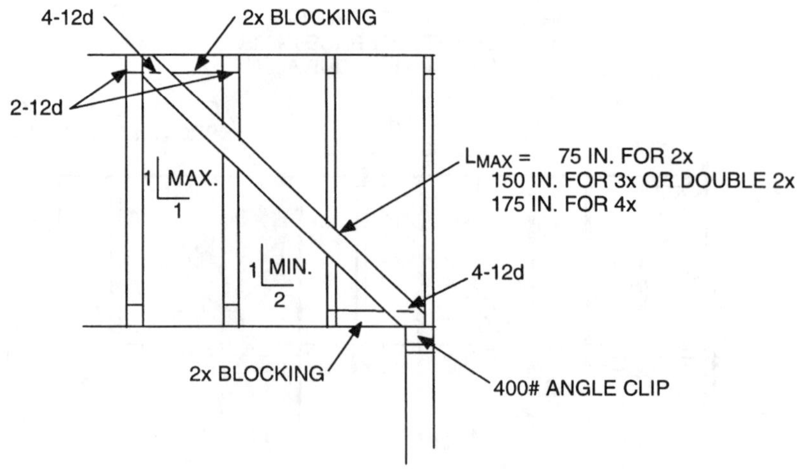

ALTERNATE GABLE END BRACE AT 6 FT. O.C.

For SI: 1 inch = 25.4 mm, 1 foot = 304.8 mm.

Source: 1997 NEHRP Commentary (FEMA 303)

ALTERNATE GABLE END BRACE

FIGURE 21

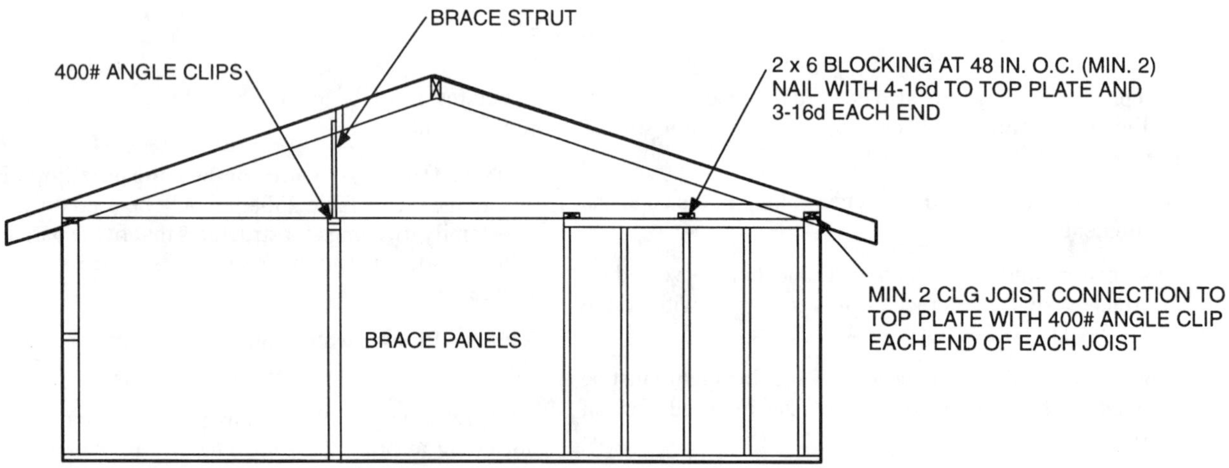

NOTE: Where braced wall lines align up with rafters, use 2 clg. joist as noted on each side of rafter and 400# angle clip at 48 inches o.c. Stagger each clip on each side of the ceiling joist so they are 24 inches o.c. at the plate

WALL PARALLEL TO TRUSS BRACING DETAIL

FIGURE 22

Source: 1997 NEHRP Commentary (FEMA 303)

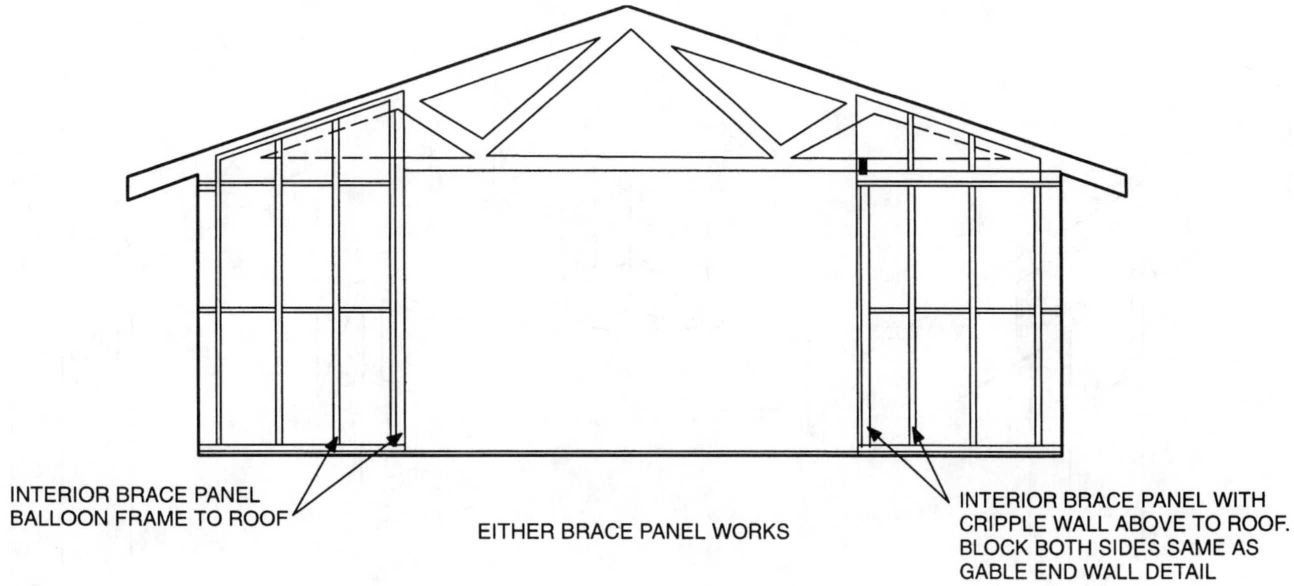

Source: 1997 NEHRP Commentary (FEMA 303)

WALL PARALLEL TO TRUSS ALTERNATE BRACING DETAIL

FIGURE 23

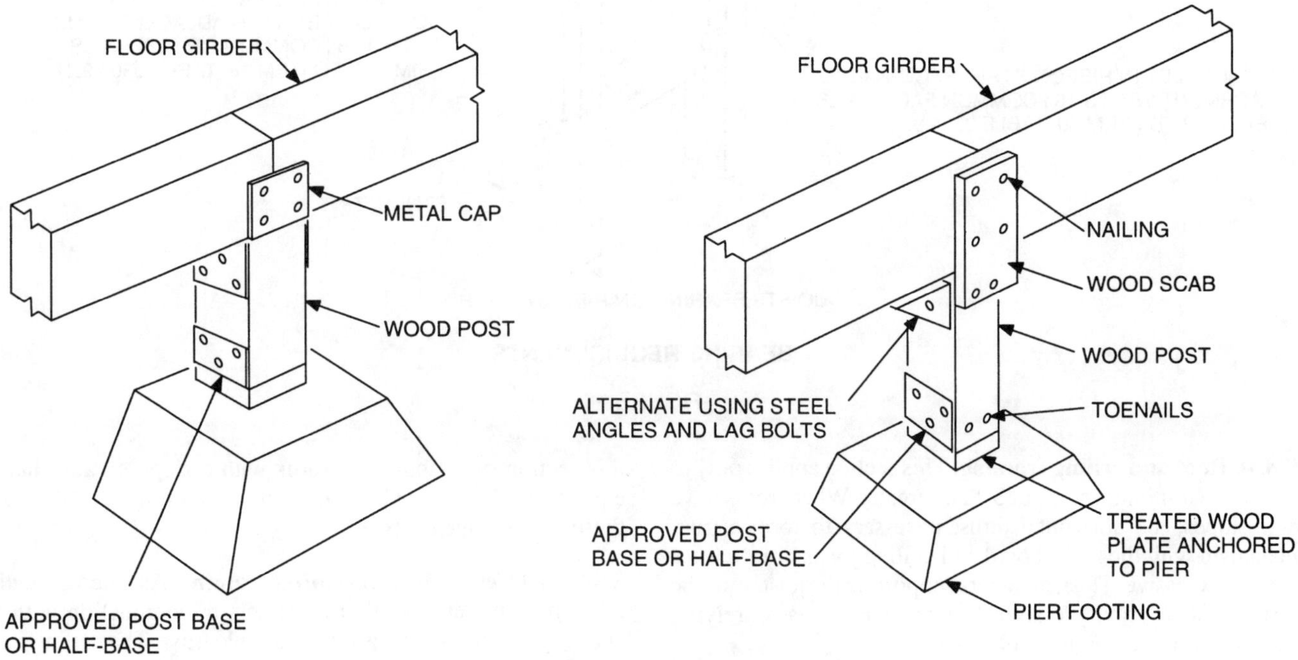

POST-TO-GIRDER CONNECTION

FIGURE 24

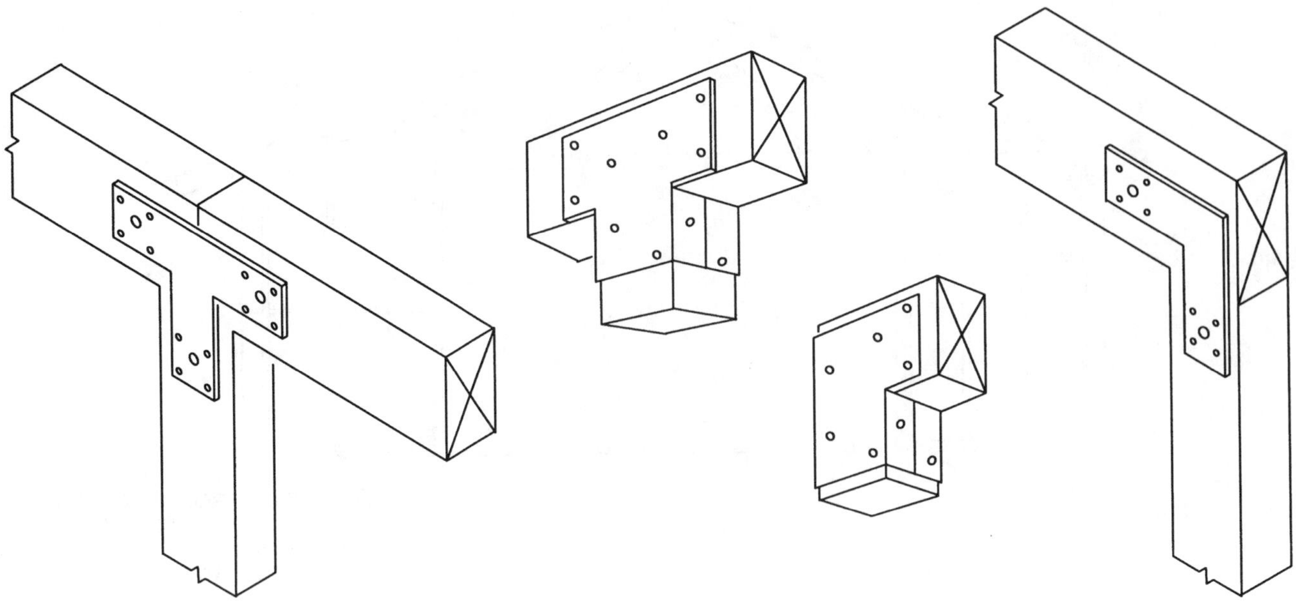

POST-TO-GIRDER CONNECTIONS

FIGURE 25

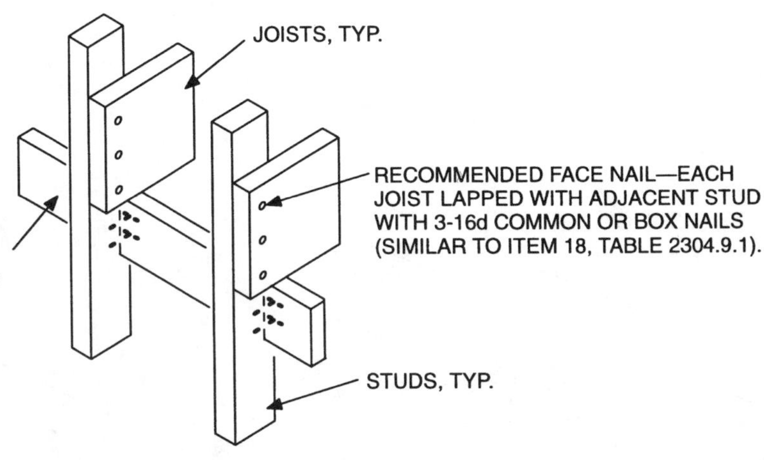

JOISTS BEARING ON RIBBON STRIP

BEARING REQUIREMENTS

FIGURE 26

2308.10 Roof and ceiling framing. This section applies only to roofs with a minimum slope of 3:12 or greater. Where roofs have lower slopes, the horizontal thrust necessary to form a truss mechanism with the ridge board and ceiling joists or rafter ties becomes excessive. Thus, members supporting the joists must be able to resist the gravity loads by beam action, instead of relying on truss action. See Figures 49 and 50.

2308.10.1 Wind uplift. Wind suction pressures can cause considerable uplift forces on roof assemblies. The uplift loads must be positively transferred into the structure below to mobilize sufficient gravity loads to resist the uplift. See also Section 2304.9.6, Load path, for additional commentary. Note that the uplift forces on roofs having slopes less than 3:12 will be larger than the forces for roofs with slopes ≥ 3:12. Hence, although this section only applies to roofs with a slope greater than or equal to 3:12, ties of at least the same strength should be used on these lower slope roofs.

2308.10.4 Ceiling joist and rafter framing. As noted in Section 2308.10 commentary, the roof rafters in conjunction with the ceiling joists or rafter ties form a simple truss. The ceiling joists or rafter ties resist the horizontal thrusts, as shown in Figure 50, in tension. Thus, the heel joint between the rafter and ceiling joist or rafter tie must have sufficient nails to transfer the force to the ceiling joist and the ceiling joist splice must have sufficient nails to resist the tension. Figure 51 illustrates the requirements. Nailing for the heel joint must be per Table 2308.10.4.1.

2308.10.5 Purlins. Figure 52 illustrates a purlin and strut.

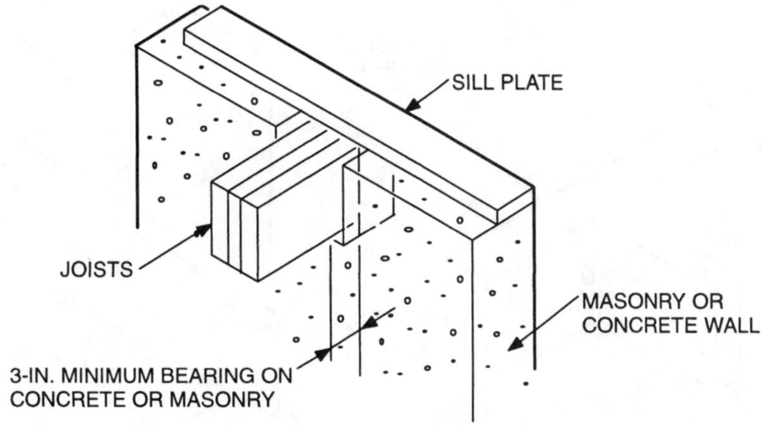

JOISTS BEARING ON CONCRETE OR MASONRY

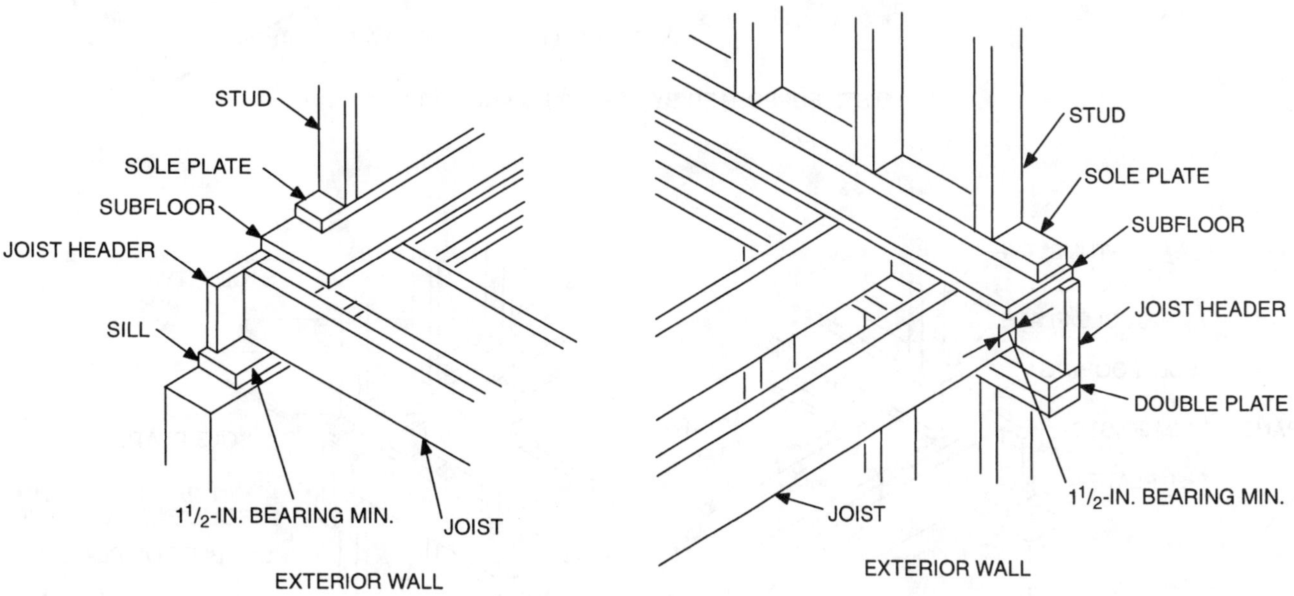

For SI: 1 inch = 25.4 mm.

JOISTS BEARING ON WOOD

BEARING REQUIREMENTS

FIGURE 27

2308.10.7 Wood trusses. All wood trusses must be engineered. The truss members and connections must not be altered by cutting, notching, drilling, etc. Additional loads, such as from adding mechanical equipment or changing roofing from composition roof to clay tile, may not be introduced without qualifying the truss for the additional load.

2308.10.8 Roof sheathing. The code requires that wood structural panels used for roof sheathing be bonded by exterior glue because moisture quite often gets beneath the roof covering. This causes delamination of plies or strands bonded with interior glue. Therefore, wood structural panels should be bonded with exterior glues to prevent delamination.

The wood structural panels should be labeled Exterior or Exposure 1.

2308.11 Additional requirements for conventional construction in Seismic Design Category B or C. These additional restrictions and requirements apply to structures classified as SDC B or C. The exceptions in Section 2308.11.2 are adapted from NEHRP. The term "structural use panel" is synonymous with "wood structural panel."

2308.11.3 Framing and connection details. Provisions for stepped footings are adopted from NEHRP Section 12.5.3.6. NEHRP recommends these provisions for all seismic design categories, but SDC A is exempted in the IBC.

2308.11.3.2 Stepped footings. Reference to IBC Figure 2308.11.3.2 helps clarify the intent of this section. The phrase "lowest floor framing" means the framing of the lowest floor

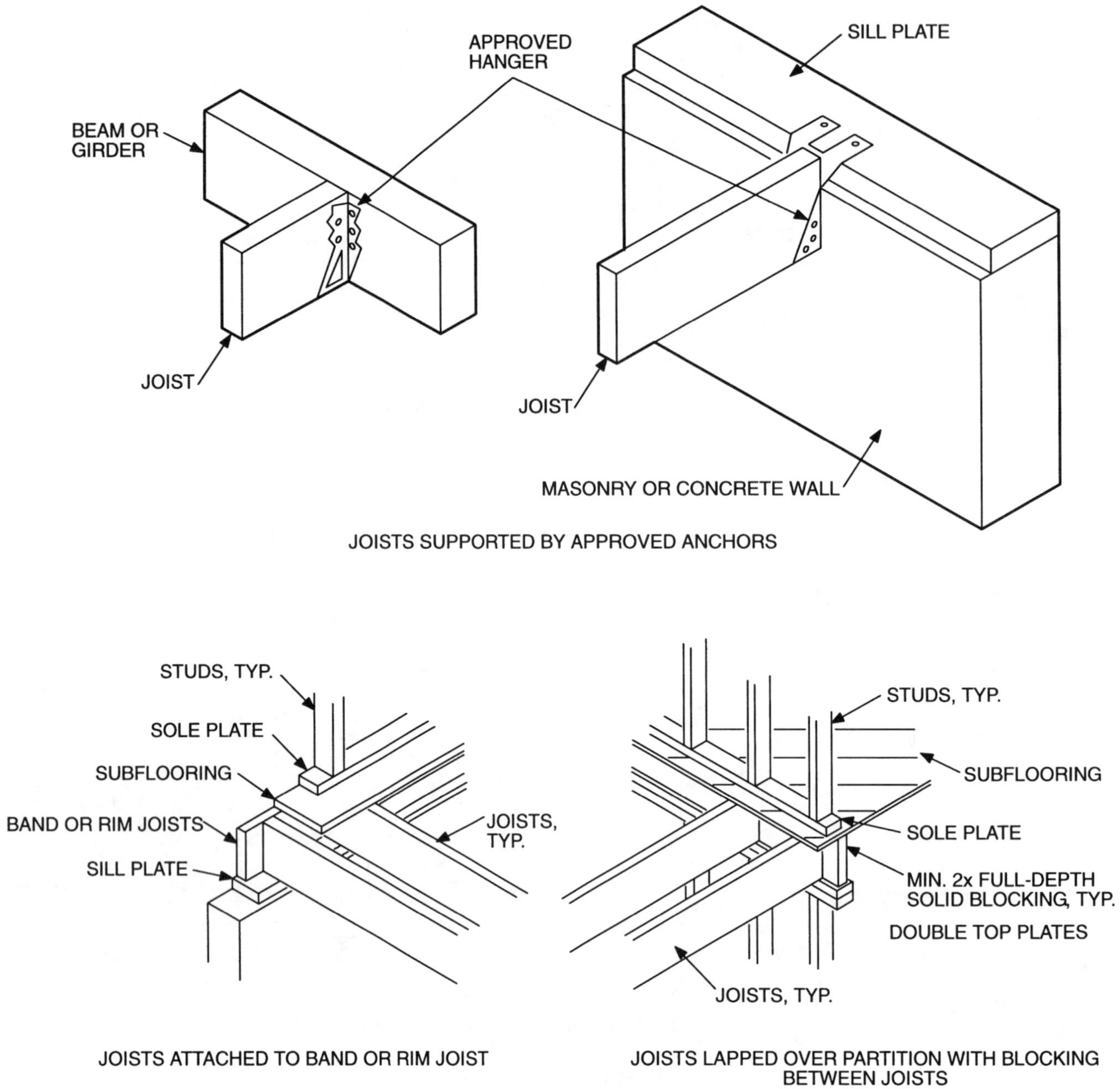

FRAMING DETAILS

FIGURE 28

bolted directly to the foundation as shown on the left side of IBC Figure 2308.11.3.2.

2308.11.3.3 Openings in horizontal diaphragms. Blocking and strapping are required to transfer shears around the opening. IBC Figure 2308.11.3.3 illustrates those requirements.

2308.12 Additional requirements for conventional construction in Seismic Design Category D or E. Additional restrictions and requirements are placed on structures classified as SDC D or E, as outlined in Sections 2308.12.1 through 2308.12.9. Conventional construction may not be used for structures classified as SDC F.

2308.12.1 Number of stories. Except for one- and two-family dwellings, structures using conventional construction are limited to one story. This limitation is based on the NEHRP provisions.

2308.12.2 Concrete or masonry. Masonry veneers cannot be used above the basement wall. This is also based on the NEHRP provisions.

2308.12.3 Braced wall line spacing. Braced wall line spacing is limited to 25 feet maximum in SDC D or E.

2308.12.4 Braced wall line sheathing. In accordance with Table 2308.12.4, braced wall panel lengths are increased

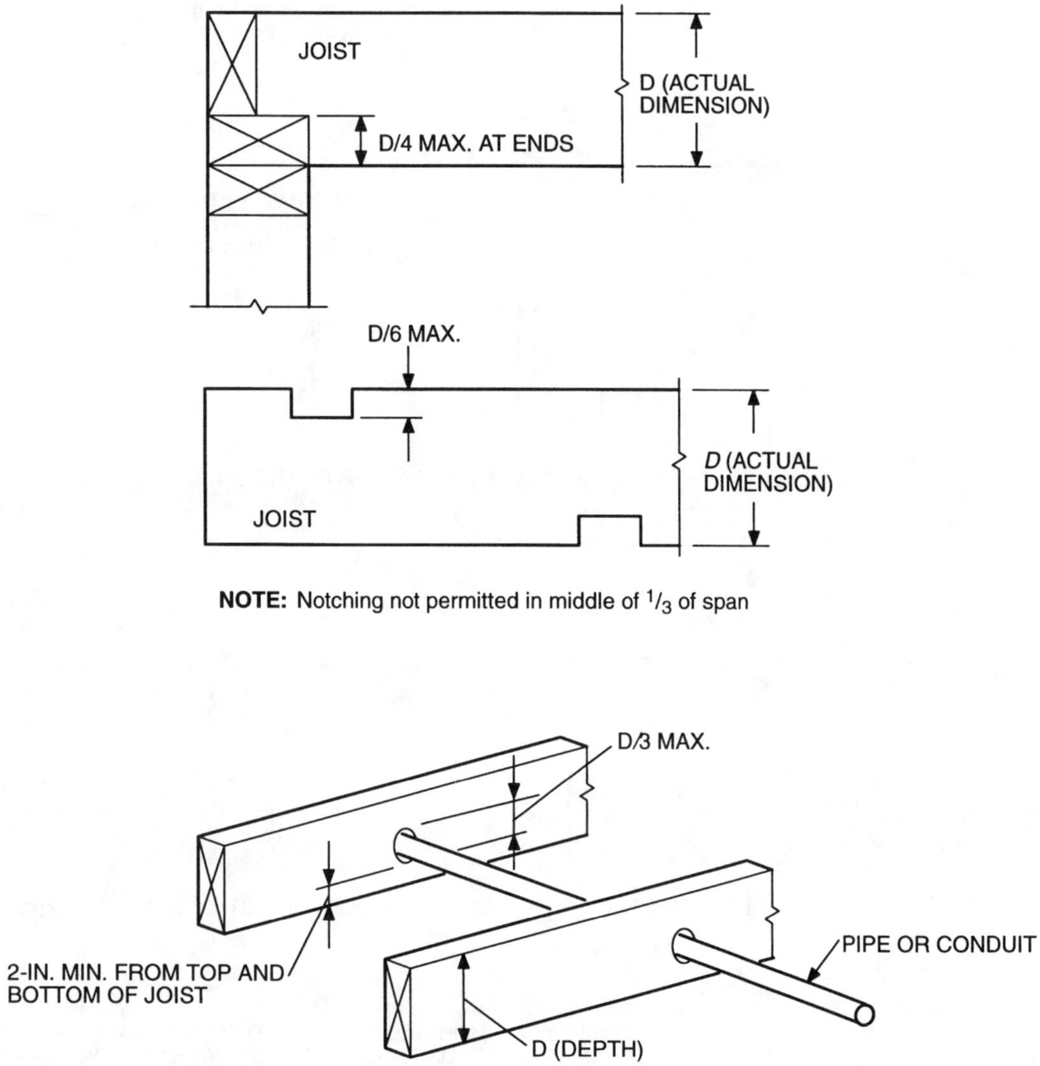

For SI: 1 inch = 25.4 mm.

CUTTING, NOTCHING, OR BORED HOLES

FIGURE 29

depending on the value of the short period spectral response acceleration, S_{DS}. Braced wall panels of materials other than the wood structural panels are allowed only for a one-story structure or the top story of a two-story structure. Conventional construction is not allowed for structures of more than two stories. The cripple wall in a two-story residence must be engineered, although the cripple wall in a one-story residence could use conventional construction. A one-story commercial structure with a cripple wall must be engineered because conventional construction is not allowed.

Braced wall panels must start no more than 8 feet from each end of a braced wall line. If the braced panel starts more than 8 feet from an end of the wall line, a collector must be designed and provided. See Figure 41 for illustration of this requirement.

The second paragraph requires the length of the cripple wall braced panels to be $1^1/_2$ times the value in Table 2308.12.4 if the interior braced wall lines are not on a continuous foundation, such as interior braced wall lines supported by post-and-beam construction on precast piers. Note that interior braced wall lines must be on continuous foundations per Section 2308.3.4, unless the structure is not more than 50 feet in any plan dimension. Thus, a structure 40 feet by 60 feet would require continuous footings under the interior braced wall lines, whereas a structure that was 40 feet by 50 feet could use post-and-beam construction for support of the interior wall lines.

2308.12.5 Attachment of sheathing. Wall sheathing must be attached by the specified nails or staples without substitution. Adhesives may not be used. Nails or staples yield when the braced panel is rocked by ground motions; the panel behaves in a ductile manner. A panel attached by adhesives behaves in a brittle manner.

2308.12.6 Irregular structures. Irregular structures in SDC D or E cannot use conventional construction. The figures in

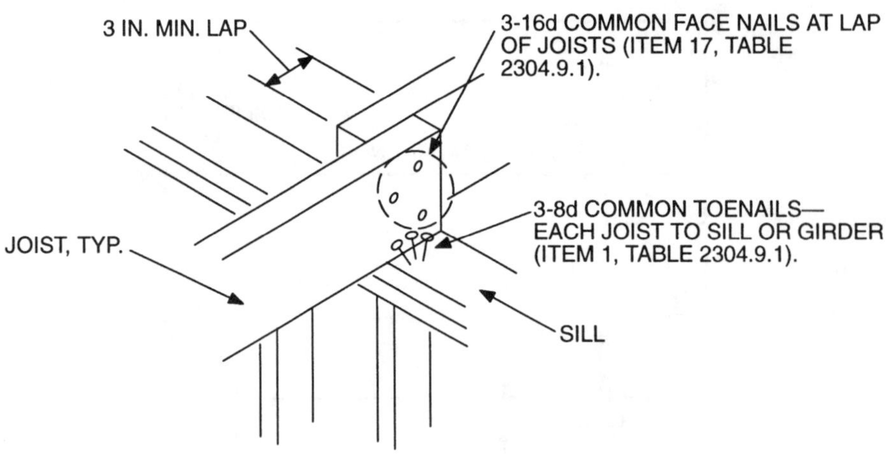

JOIST LAPPING OVER BEAM, GIRDER OR PARTITION

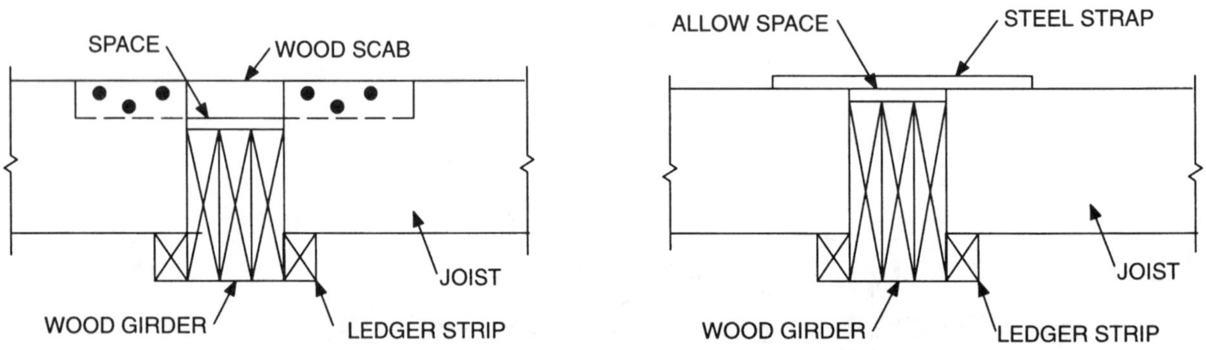

OR

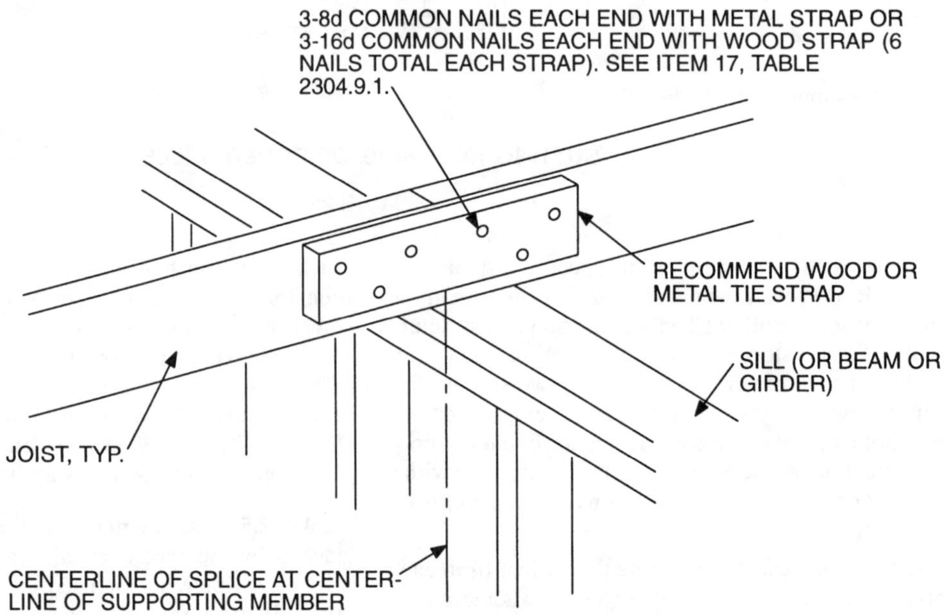

For SI: 1 inch = 25.4 mm.

FLOOR JOISTS TIED OVER WOOD BEAM, GIRDER OR PARTITION

FIGURE 30

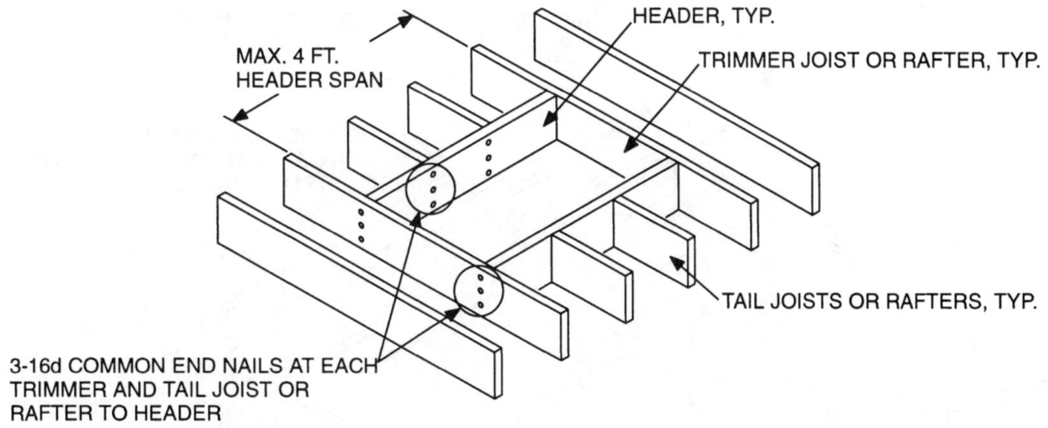

For SI: 1 foot = 304.8 mm.

FRAMING AROUND OPENINGS—HEADER SPAN ≤4 FEET

FIGURE 31

the IBC graphically describe the various conditions and greatly aid the user of the code.

The conditions describing irregular structures are from the 1997 NEHRP Provisions and are very similar to the UBC conditions, except that the NEHRP Provisions apply these restrictions to SDC C, D or E. Reference to IBC Figures 2308.12.6(1) through 2308.12.6(8) helps in understanding the intent of the requirements.

Structures with geometric discontinuities in the lateral-force-resisting system sustain more earthquake and wind damage than structures without discontinuities. They have also been observed to concentrate damage at the discontinuity location. For SDC D or E, this section translates applicable irregularities from Tables 1616.5.1 and 1616.5.2 into limitations on conventional light-frame construction. When a structure falls within the description of irregular, it is required that either the entire structure or the nonconventional portions be engineered in accordance with the engineered design provisions. While conceptually these are equally applicable to all seismic design categories, they are more significant in areas of high seismic risk, where damage caused by irregularities has repeatedly been observed in past earthquakes.

The engineered design of nonconventional portions in lieu of the entire structure is a common practice in some regions. The registered design professional is left to judge the extent of the portion to be designed. This often involves design of the nonconforming element, force transfer into the element, and a complete load path from the element to the foundation. A nonconforming portion will sometimes have enough of an impact on the behavior of a structure to warrant that the entire lateral-force-resisting system be based on engineered design.

Item 1. This limitation is based on Item 4 of Table 1616.5.1 and applies when braced wall panels are offset out-of-plane from floor to floor. In-plane offsets are discussed in Item 3. Ideally braced wall panels should always stack above each other from floor to floor with the length stepping down at upper floors since less length of bracing panel is required.

Because cantilevers and setbacks are very often incorporated into residential construction, the exception offers rules by which limited cantilevers and setbacks can be considered conventional. Floor joists are limited to 2 by 10 (actual $1^1/_2$ by $9^1/_4$ inches) or larger, and doubled at braced wall panel ends to accommodate the vertical overturning reactions at the end of braced wall panels. In addition, the ends of the cantilever are attached to a common rim joist to allow for redistribution of load. For rim joists that cannot run the entire length of the cantilever, the metal tie is intended to transfer vertical shear as well as provide a nominal tension tie. Limitations are placed on gravity loads to be carried by the cantilever or setback floor joists so that the joist strength will not be exceeded. The roof loads discussed are based on the use of solid sawn members where allowable spans limit the possible loads. Where engineered framing members such as trusses are used, gravity load capacity of the cantilevered or setback floor joists should be carefully evaluated.

Item 2. This limitation is based on Item 1 of Table 1616.5.1 and applies to open-front structures or portions of structures. The conventional construction bracing concept is based on using braced wall lines to divide a structure into a series of boxes of limited dimension, with the seismic force to each box being limited by the size. The intent is that each box be supported by braced wall lines on all four sides, limiting the amount of torsion that can occur. The exception, which permits portions of roofs or floors to extend past the braced wall line, is intended to permit construction such as porch roofs and bay windows, as illustrated in IBC Figure 2308.12.6(4). Walls that are not considered braced panels, i.e., with minimal lateral resistance, are allowed in areas where braced walls panels are prohibited. See the lower right-hand portion of IBC Figure 2308.12.6(4).

Item 3. This limitation is based on Item 4 of Table 1616.5.2 and applies when braced wall panels are offset in-plane. Ends of braced wall panels supported on window or door headers transfer large vertical reactions to headers that may

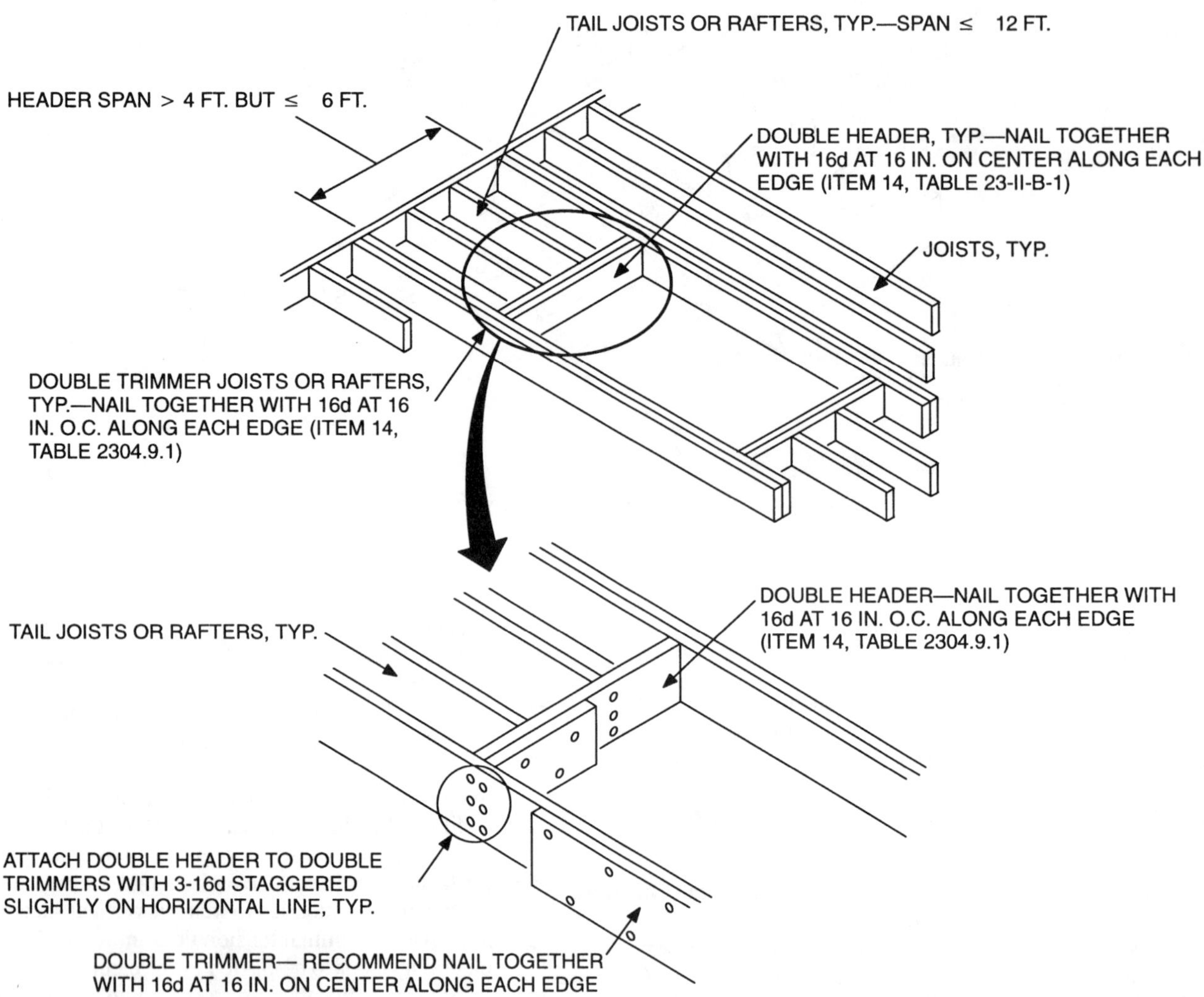

For SI: 1 inch = 25.4 mm, 1 foot = 304.8 mm.

FRAMING AROUND OPENINGS HEADER > 4 FEET BUT ≤ 6 FEET

FIGURE 32

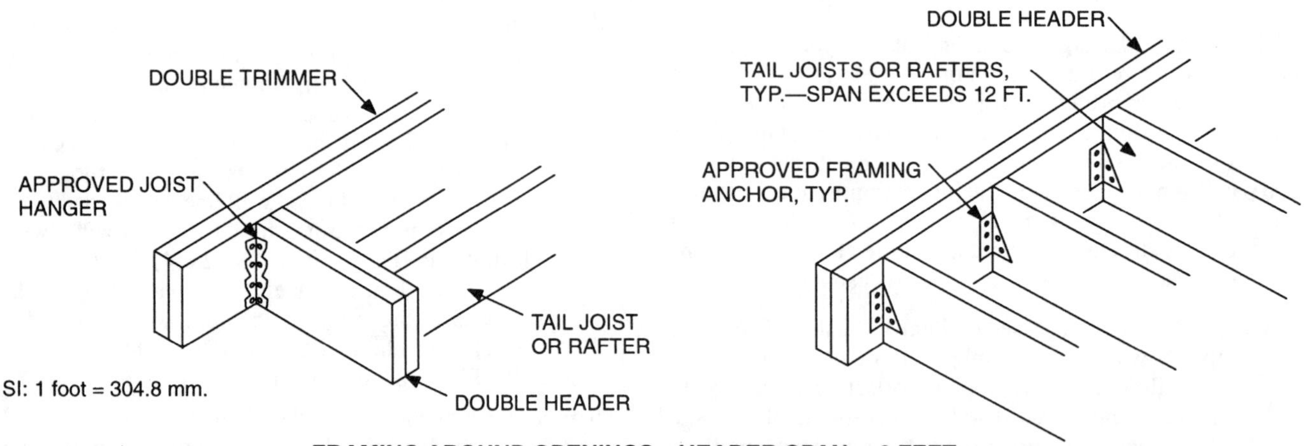

For SI: 1 foot = 304.8 mm.

FRAMING AROUND OPENINGS—HEADER SPAN >6 FEET

FIGURE 33

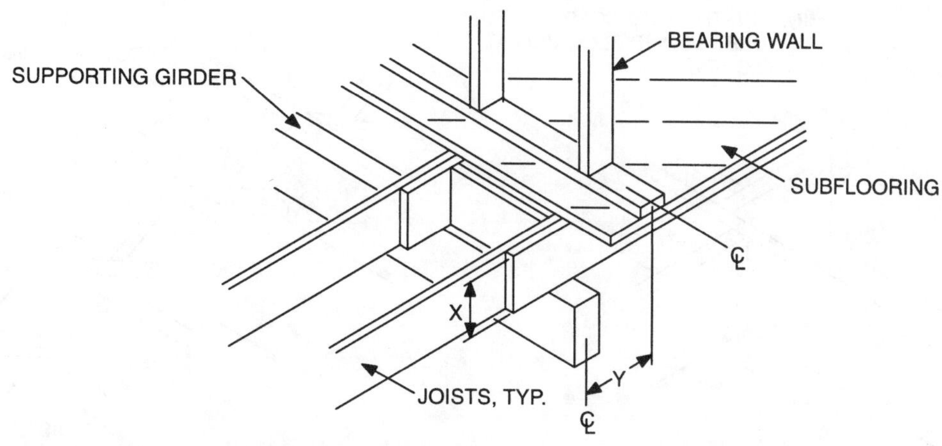

DISTANCE Y MUST NOT EXCEED DIMENSION X

SUPPORT OF BEARING PARTITION—PERPENDICULAR TO JOISTS

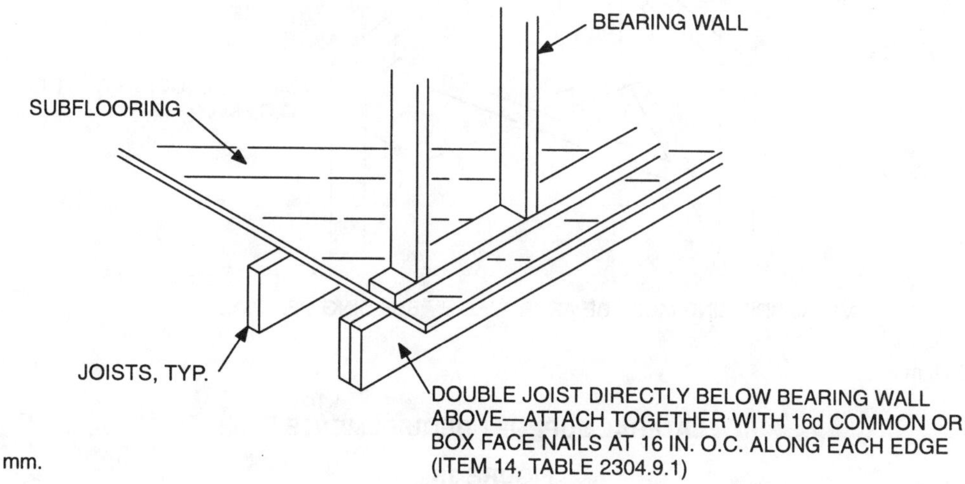

For SI: 1 inch = 25.4 mm.

SUPPORT OF BEARING PARTITION—PARALLEL TO JOISTS

SUPPORTING BEARING PARTITIONS

FIGURE 34

not be of adequate size to resist these reactions. The exception permits a 4-foot extension of the braced wall panel over a nominal 4 by 12 or larger header on the basis that the vertical reaction will not result in critical shear or flexure. All other header conditions require an engineered design. Walls that are not considered braced panels, i.e., with minimal lateral resistance, are allowed over openings.

Item 4. This limitation results from observation of damage that is somewhat unique to split-level wood frame construction. If floors on either side of an offset move in opposite directions because of earthquake or wind loading, the short bearing wall in the middle becomes unstable and vertical support for the upper joists can be lost, resulting in a collapse. If the vertical offset is limited to a dimension equal to or less than the joist depth, then a simple strap tie directly connecting joists on different levels can be provided, and the instability eliminated.

Item 5. This limitation is based on Item 5 of Table 1616.5.1 and applies to nonperpendicular braced wall lines. When braced wall lines are not perpendicular to each other, further evaluation is needed to determine force distributions and the required lateral-support system.

Item 6. This limitation is based on Item 3 of Table 1616.5.1 and attempts to place a practical limit on openings in floors and roofs. Because stair openings are essential to residential construction and have long been used without any report of life-safety hazards resulting, these are felt to be acceptable conventional construction. See Section 2308.11.3.3 for detailing requirements for permitted openings.

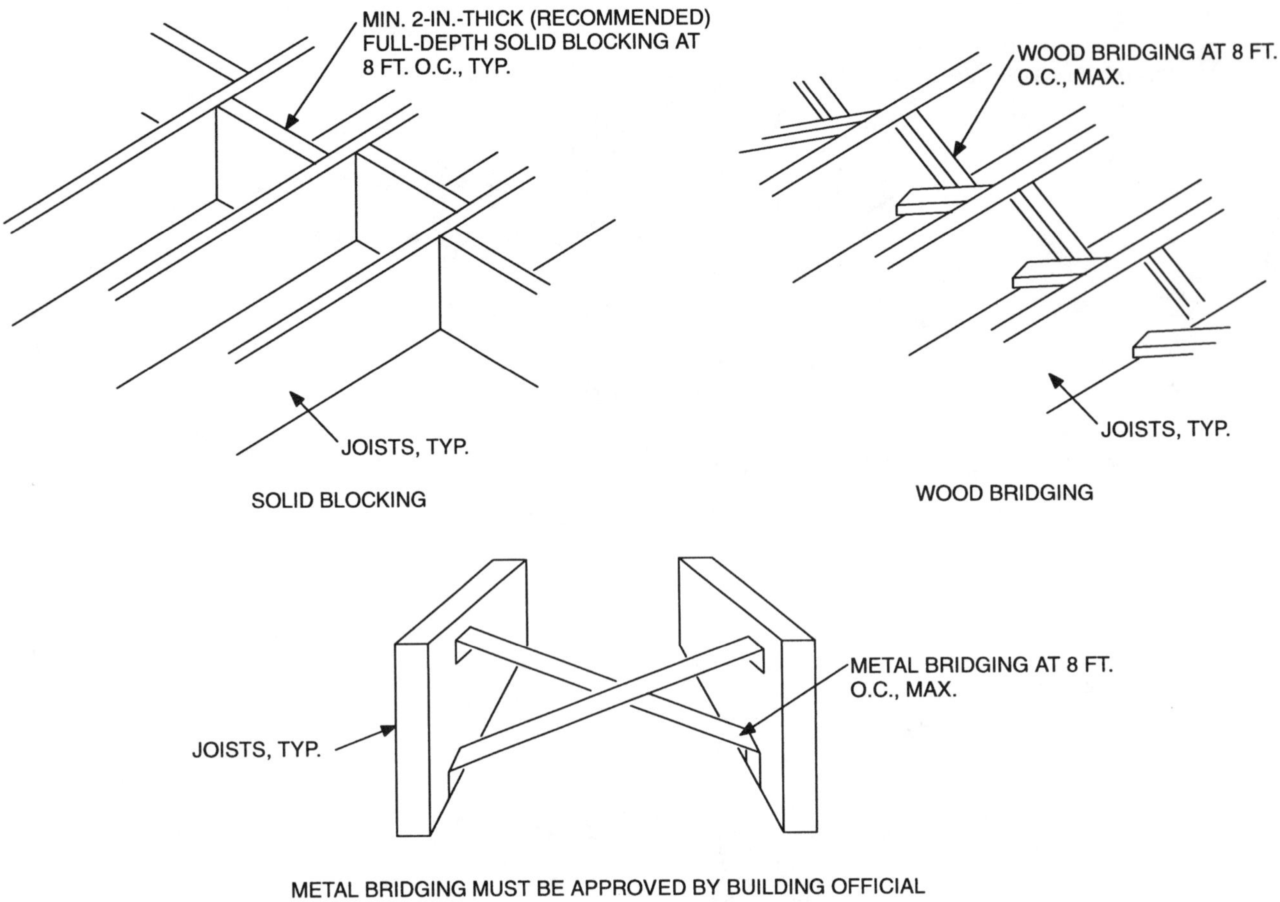

For SI: 1 foot = 304.8 mm.

LATERAL SUPPORT REQUIREMENTS

FIGURE 35

NEHRP also considers a structure irregular if there are differences of more than 6 feet in height of the shear panels in a single story. Where the heights of a braced wall panel vary significantly, the stiffness and thus the distribution of lateral forces will also vary. The usual assumption of a uniform shear/foot will not be correct. The net result is a possible torsional irregularity. For example, if a structure on a hill is supported on 2-foot-high braced cripple wall panes on one side and 8-foot-high panels on the other, torsion and redistribution of forces will occur. Even though the code does not currently require it, an engineered design is recommended to evaluate force distribution and provide adequate wall bracing and anchor bolting in this situation. This limitation applies specifically to walls from the foundation to the floor. While gable-end walls have similar variations in wall heights, this has not been observed to be a significant concern in conventional construction.

2308.12.7 Exit facilities. Positive anchorage to the main structure is required. Toenails and nails in withdrawal do not perform well when subjected to cyclic seismic demand. See commentary for Section 2305.1.4.

2308.12.8 Steel plate washers. This requirement originated in response to the extensive splitting of wood sills during the Northridge earthquake. The splitting of sills was caused by a variety of factors including typically oversize holes for anchor bolts in addition to splitting from insufficient edge distance in heavily loaded walls. Subsequent cyclic testing of wood shear panel assemblages showed that use of a 2-inch by 2-inch by $^{3}/_{16}$-inch, or larger, plate washer over the anchor bolts helps alleviate the splitting problem caused by anchor bolts. NEHRP recommends a 3-inch by 3-inch by $^{1}/_{4}$-inch washer, but some tests with 2-inch by 2-inch by $^{3}/_{16}$-inch plate washers have performed satisfactorily.

2308.12.9 Anchorage in Seismic Design Category E. Anchor bolts for SDC D are $^{1}/_{2}$-inch-diameter spaced at 48 inches on center and for SDC E are $^{5}/_{8}$-inch-diameter spaced at 48 inches on center. The larger diameter bolts are to transfer the increased load from the presumed increase in seismic demands.

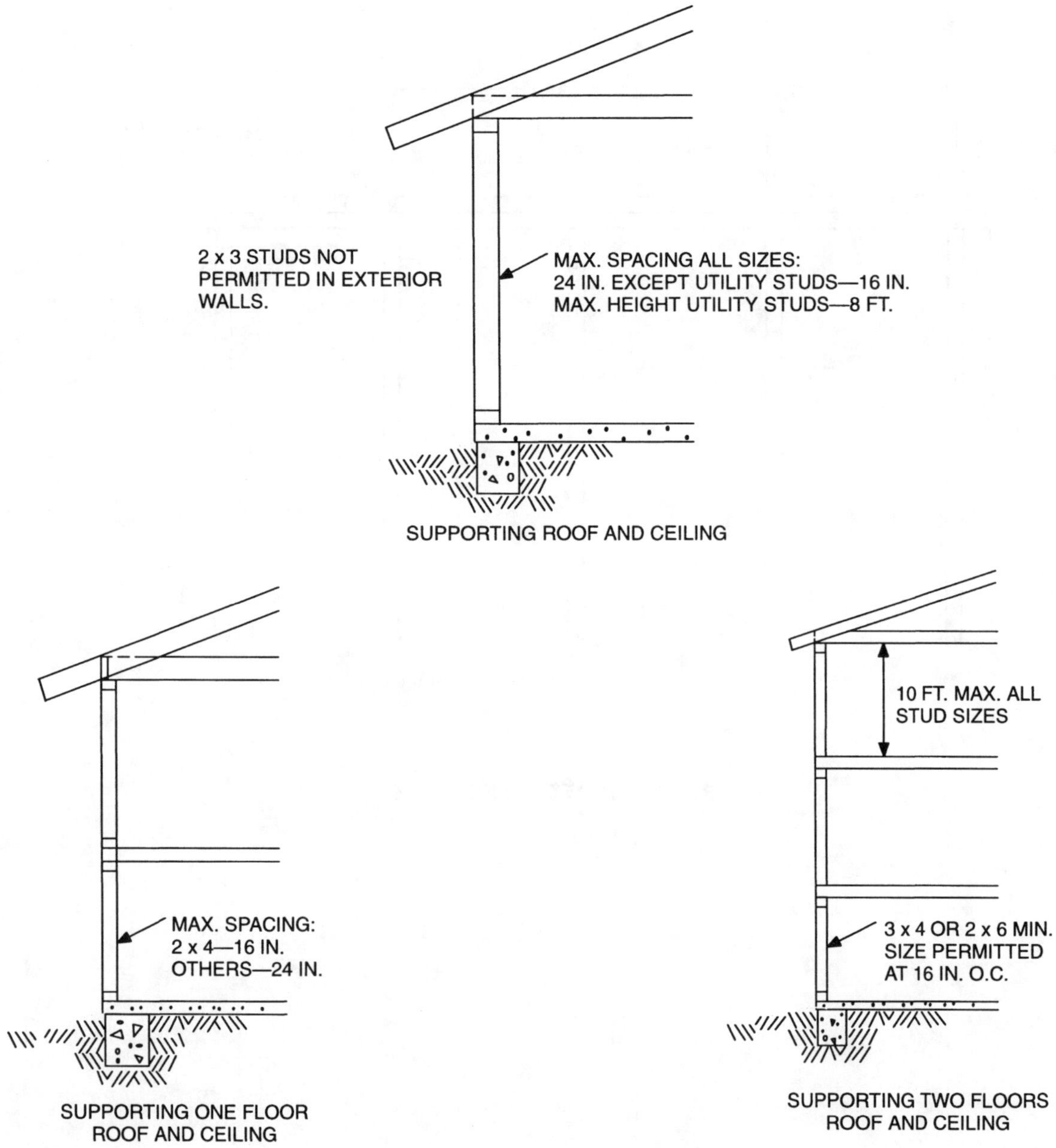

For SI: 1 inch = 25.4 mm, 1 foot = 304.8 mm.

STUD REQUIREMENTS

FIGURE 36

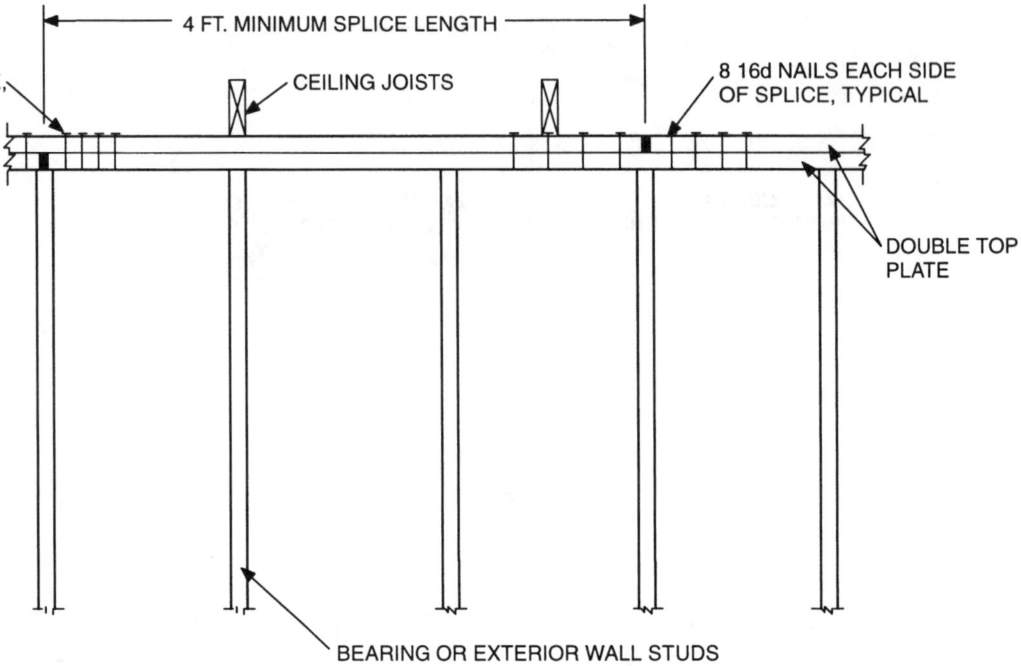

For SI: 1 foot = 304.8 mm.

DOUBLE TOP PLATE SPLICE

FIGURE 37

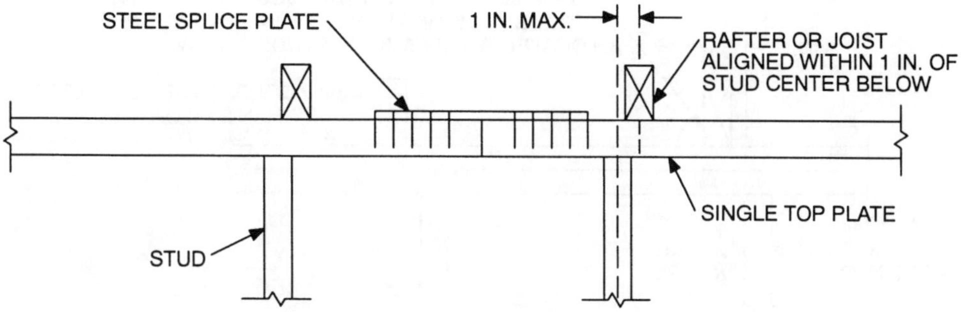

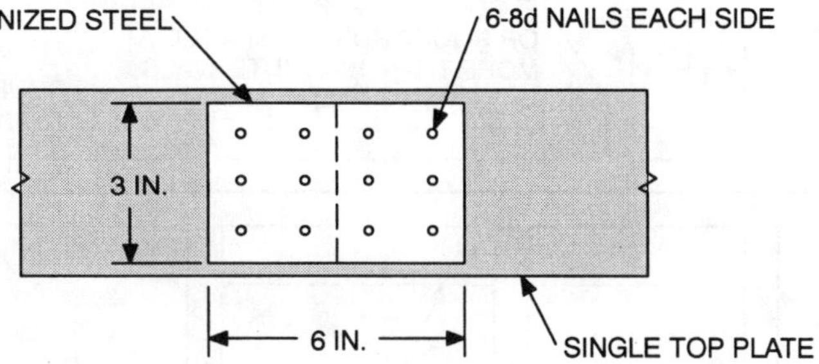

RAFTERS, JOISTS AND TRUSSES ARE CENTERED OVER THE STUDS WITH A TOLERANCE OF NOT MORE THAN 1 INCH.

For SI: 1 inch = 25.4 mm.

SINGLE TOP PLATE SPLICE—BEARING AND EXTERIOR WALLS

FIGURE 38

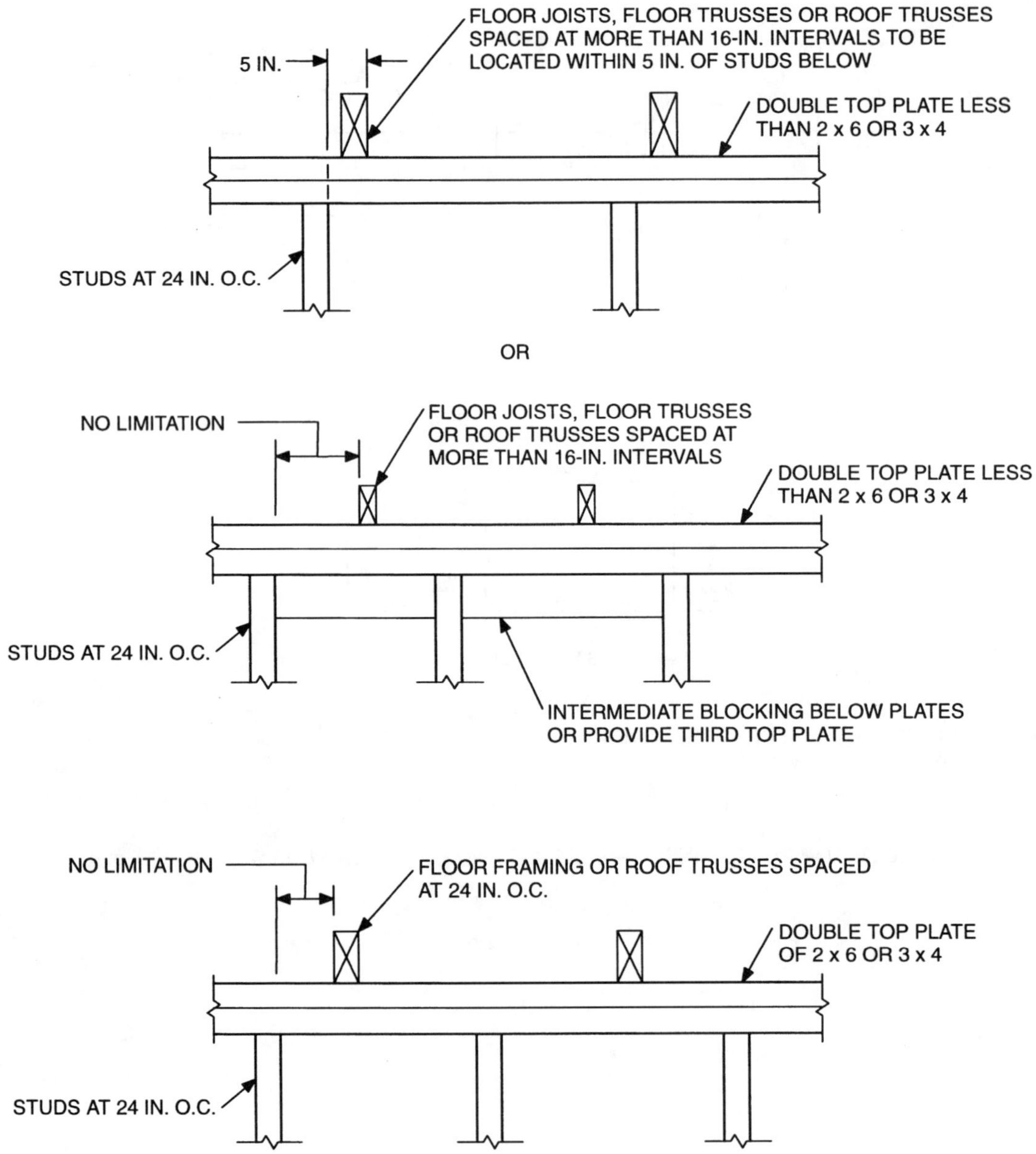

For SI: 1 inch = 25.4 mm.

TOP PLATE LIMITATIONS—BEARING

FIGURE 39

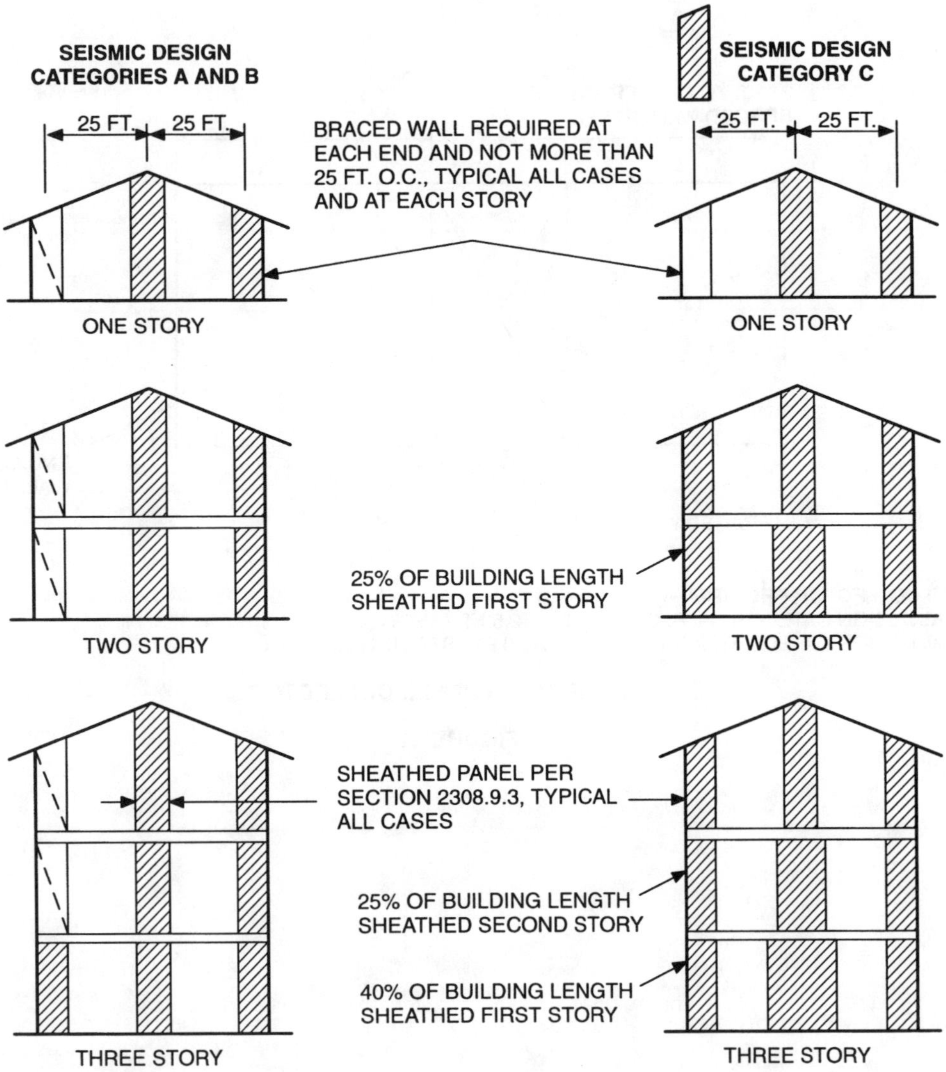

NOTE: Measurements are to centerline of panels, 25 feet on center.

For SI: 1 foot = 304.8 mm.

WALL BRACING PANEL[1]

FIGURE 40

[1]See Table 2308.12.4 for wall bracing requirements in Seismic Design Category D or E.

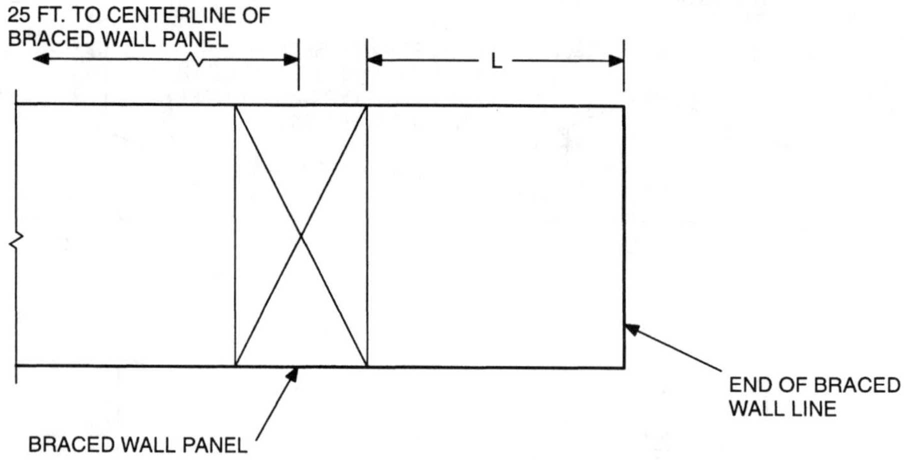

DESIGNED COLLECTOR REQUIRED IF:

SEISMIC DESIGN CATEGORY A, B, OR C	L > 12.5 FT. (SECTION 2308.9.3)
SEISMIC DESIGN CATEGORY D OR E	L > 8.0 FT. (SECTION 2308.12.4)

WALL BRACING PANEL COLLECTOR

FIGURE 41

SEISMIC DESIGN CATEGORY	MAXIMUM WALL SPACING (FEET)*
C, D OR E	25
B	35
A	NOT REQUIRED

*REFER TO TABLES 2308.9.3(1) AND 2308.12.4 FOR MINIMUM LENGTH OF WALL BRACING

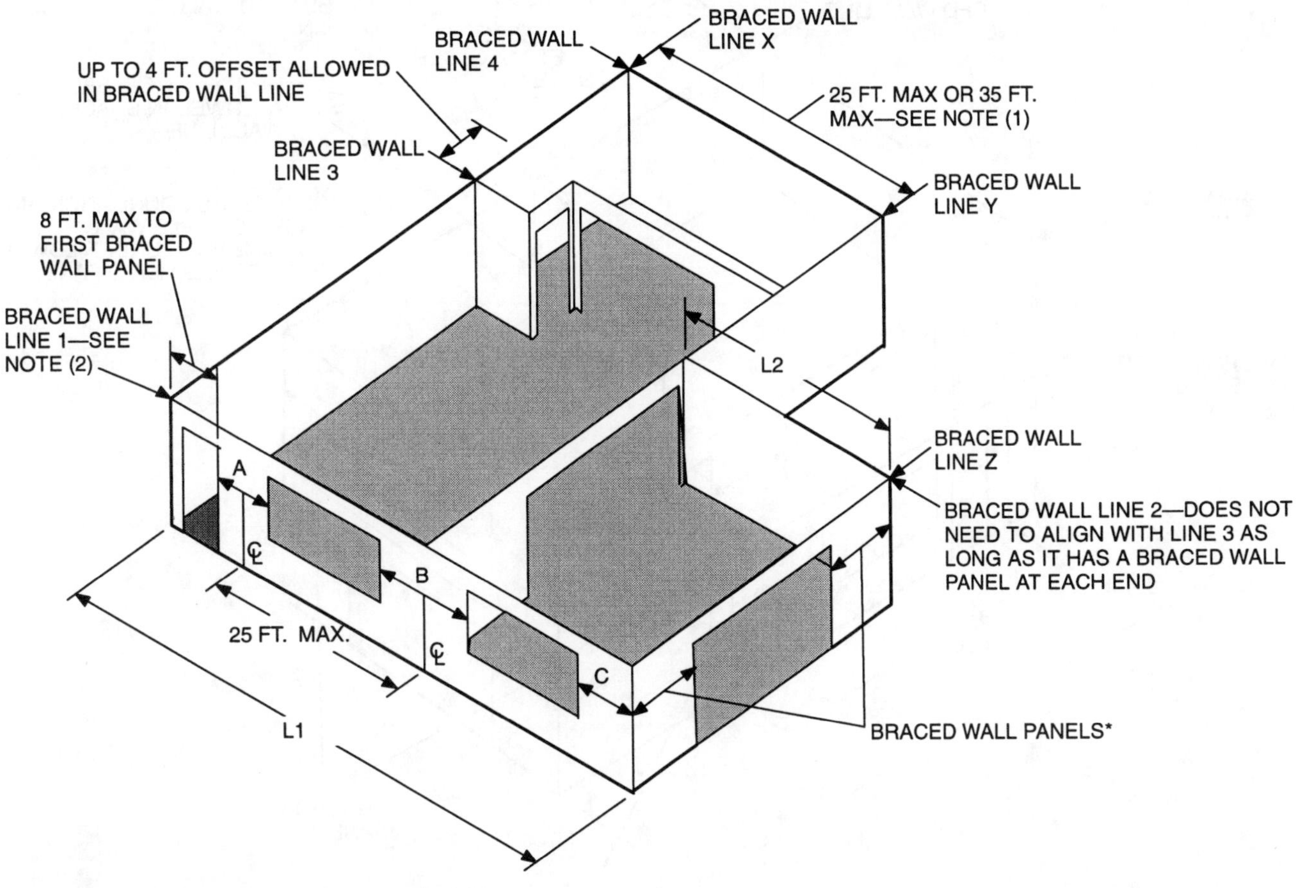

NOTES:
(1)Depending on Seismic Design Category
(2)Sum of braced wall panel lengths for braced wall line 1 = A + B + C

Source: 1997 NEHRP Commentary (FEMA 303)

ACCEPTABLE ONE-STORY BRACING EXAMPLE

FIGURE 42

SEISMIC DESIGN CATEGORY	MAXIMUM WALL SPACING (FEET)*
C, D OR E	25
B	35
A	NOT REQUIRED

*REFER TO TABLES 2308.9.3(1) AND 2308.12.4 FOR MINIMUM LENGTH OF WALL BRACING

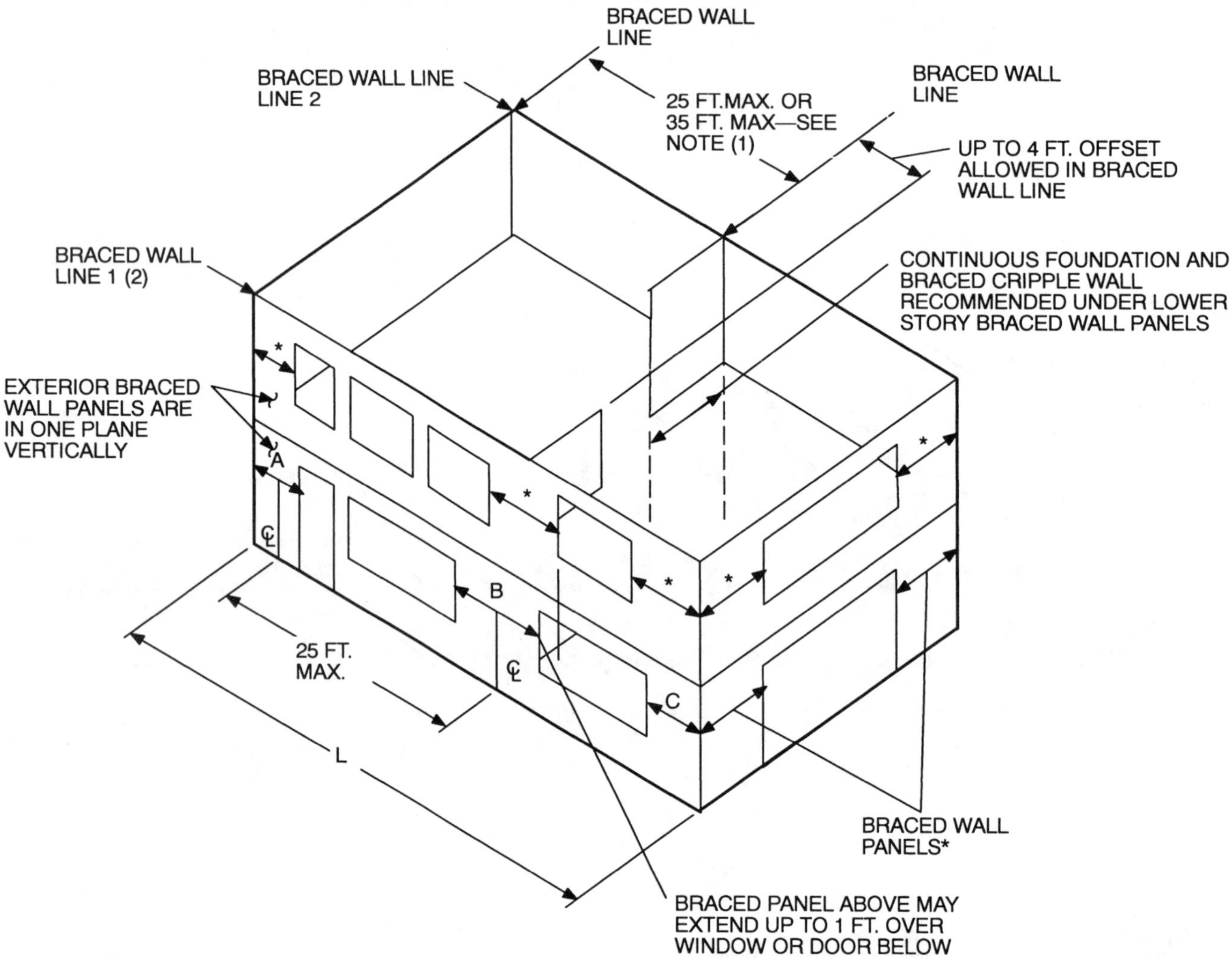

Source: 1997 NEHRP Commentary (FEMA 303)

NOTES:
(1) Depending on Seismic Design Category
(2) Sum of braced wall panel lengths for braced wall line 1 = A + B + C

ACCEPTABLE TWO-STORY BRACING EXAMPLE

FIGURE 43

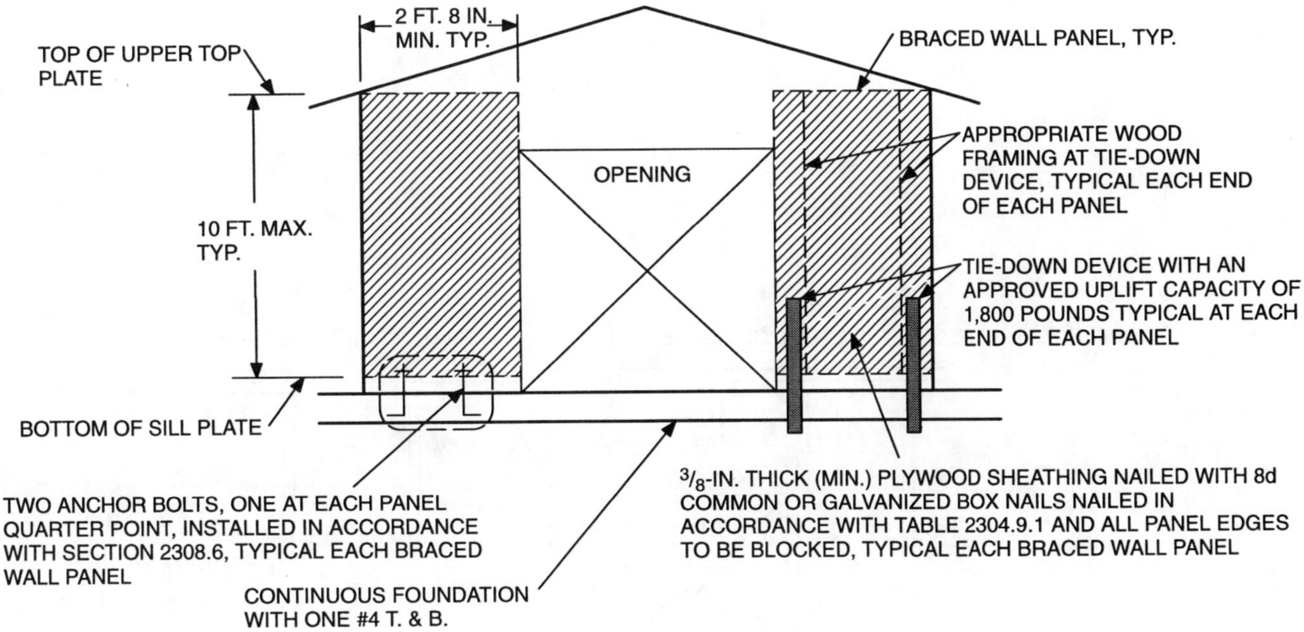

ONE-STORY BUILDING

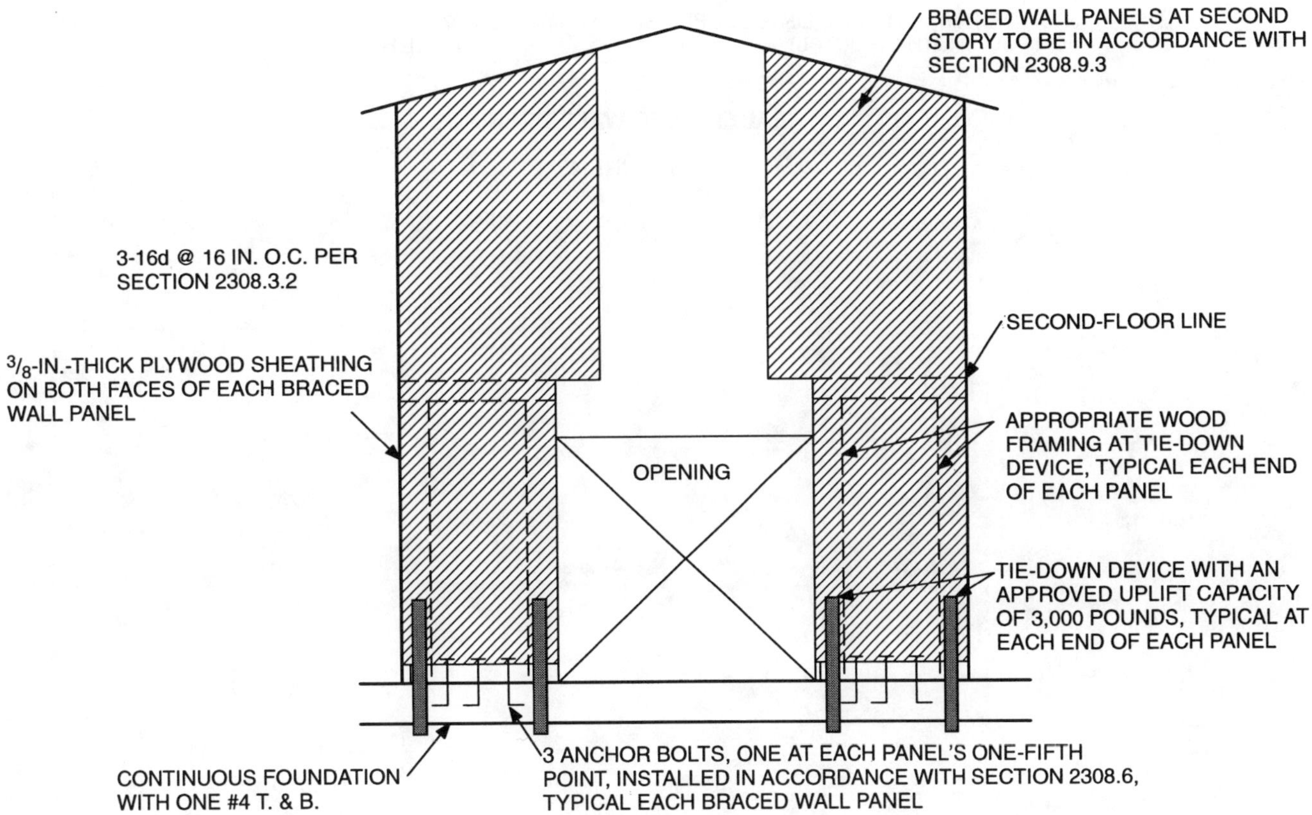

NOTE: Remaining items as noted for one-story building (Section 2308.9.3.1, Item 1).

TWO-STORY BUILDING

For SI: 1 inch = 25.4 mm, 1 foot = 304.8 mm, 1 pound = 4.45 N.

ALTERNATE BRACED PANELS

FIGURE 44

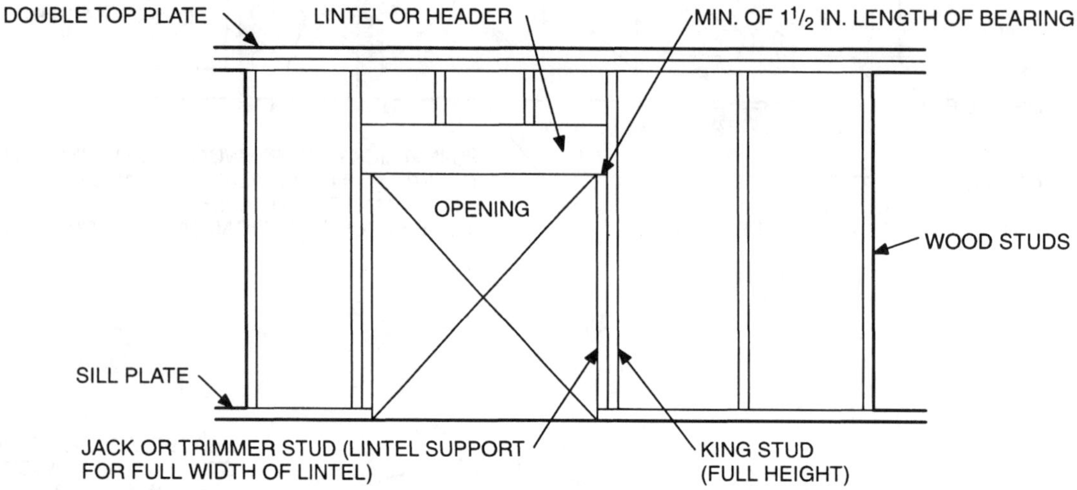

For SI: 1 inch = 25.4 mm.

HEADER OVER WALL OPENINGS

FIGURE 45

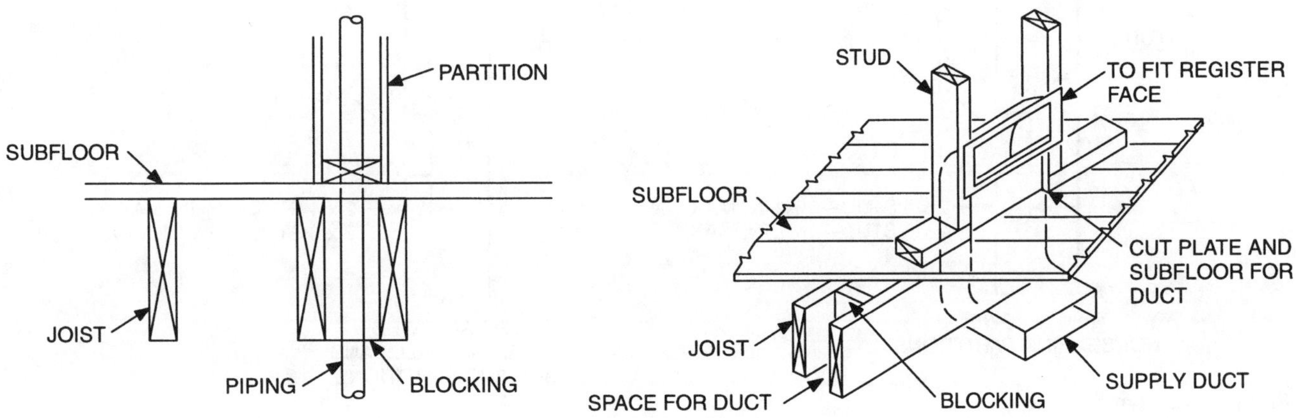

FLOOR FRAMING TO ACCOMMODATE PIPING AND DUCTWORK

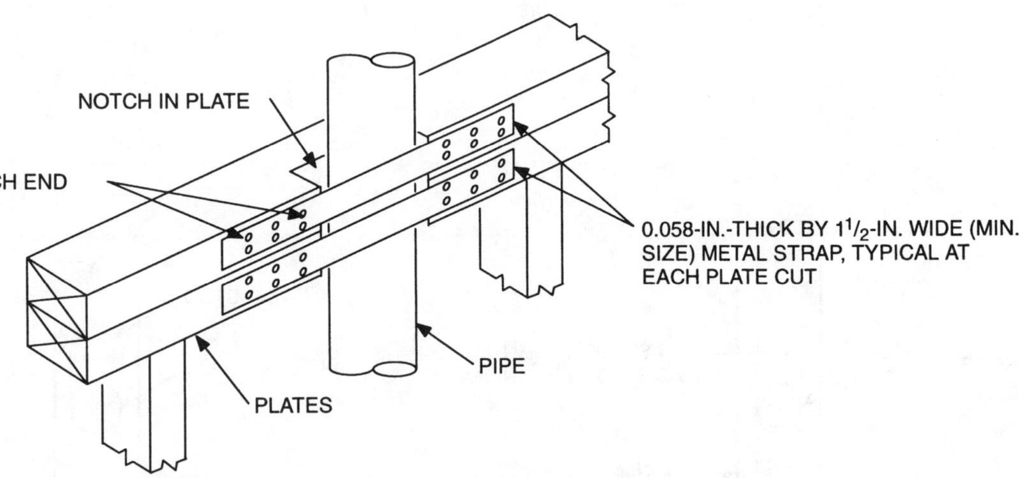

For SI: 1 inch = 25.4 mm.

PLATE FRAMING TO ACCOMMODATE PIPING

PIPES IN WALLS

FIGURE 46

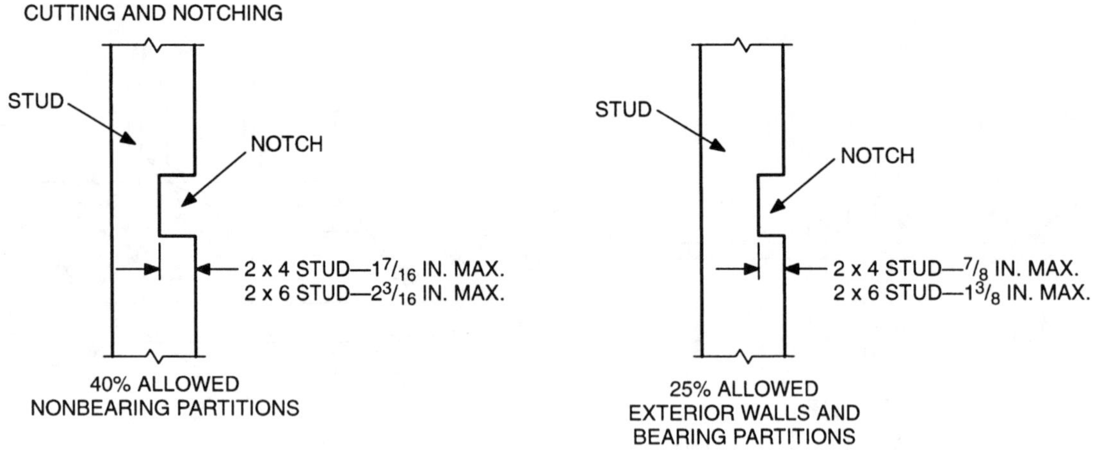

For SI: 1 inch = 25.4 mm.

CUTTING AND NOTCHING OF STUDS

FIGURE 47

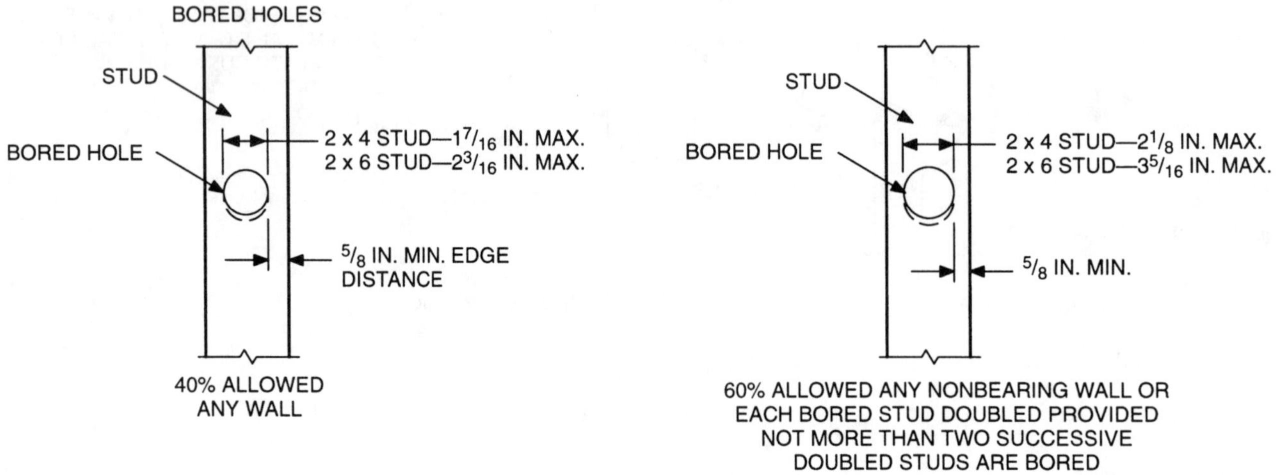

BORED HOLES IN STUDS

FIGURE 48

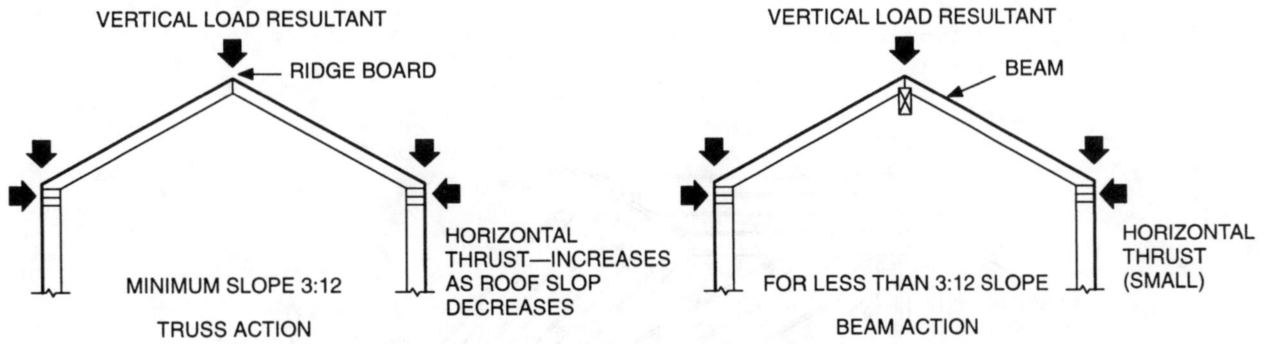

NOTE: For open beam or sloped ceilings, the ridge beam must be a designed member so that horizontal forces are reduced.

ROOF FRAMING

FIGURE 49

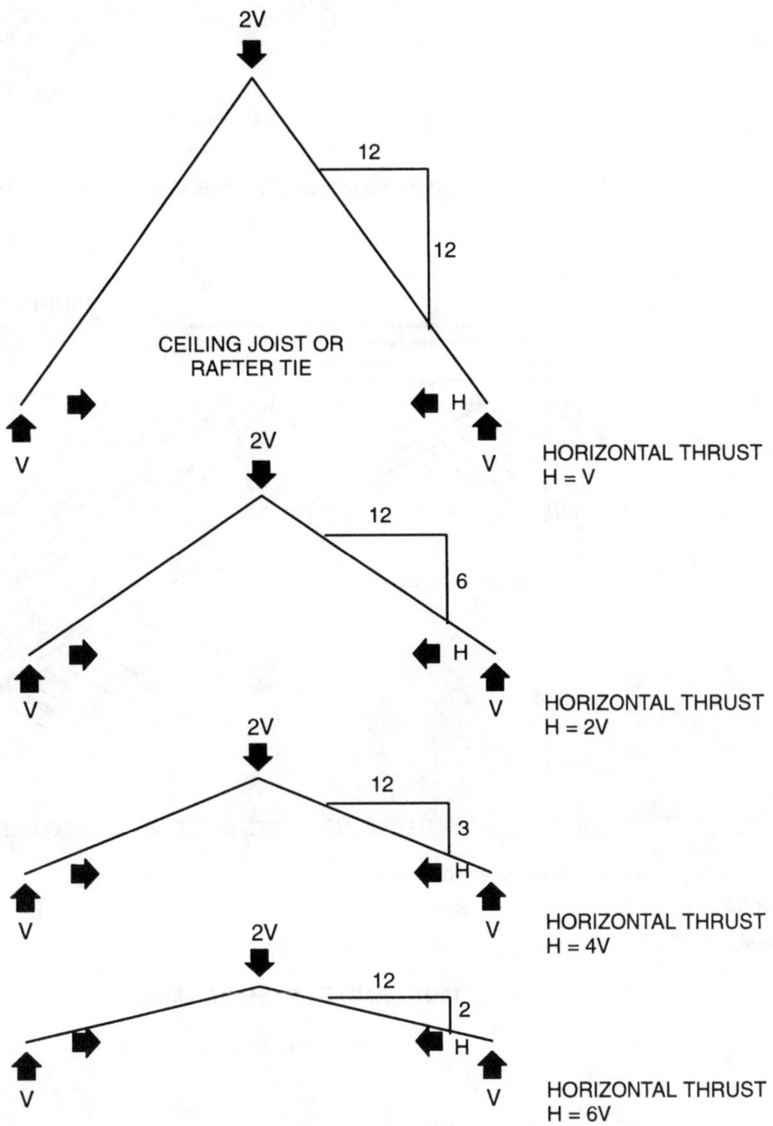

NOTE: Tension in ceiling joist and horizontal force in heel joint is equal to horizontal thrust.

ROOF FRAMING THRUSTS—TRUSS ACTION

FIGURE 50

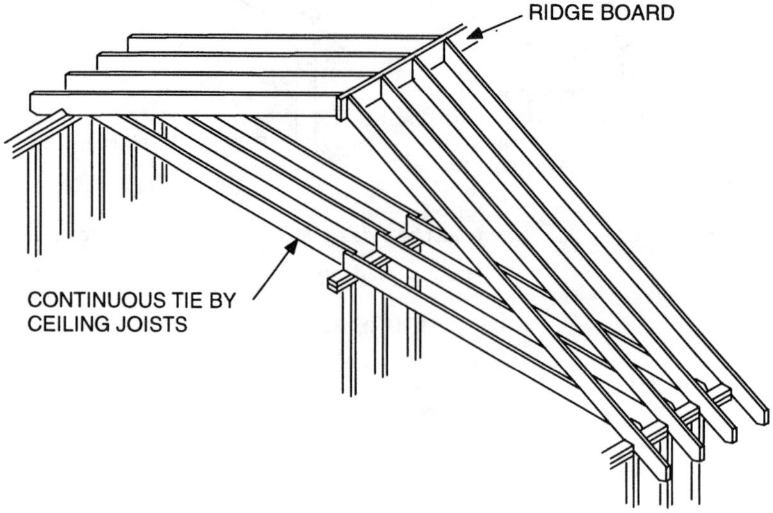

ROOF FRAMING WITH CEILING JOISTS PARALLEL TO RAFTERS

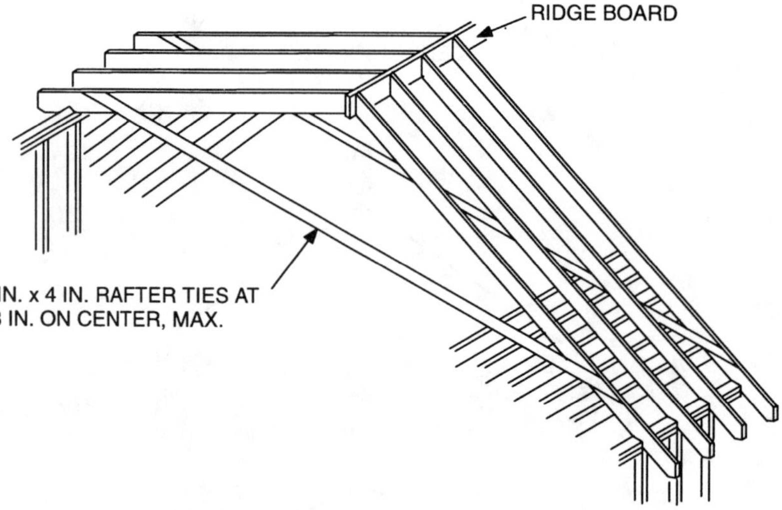

ROOF FRAMING WITH CEILING JOISTS NOT PARALLEL TO RAFTERS

NOTE: Locate ties as near as practical to the top of ceiling joists

See Tables 2304.9.1 and 2308.10.4.1 for nailing requirements.

For SI: 1 inch = 25.4 mm.

CEILING AND RAFTER FRAMING

FIGURE 51

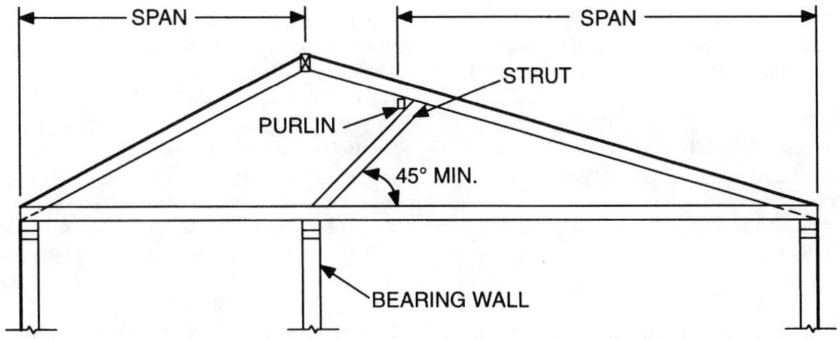

NOTE: Rafters must frame opposite each other at the ridge (Section 2308.10.4).

RAFTER AND PURLIN FRAMING

FIGURE 52

REFERENCES

1 AF&PA, *ANSI/NFoPA: NDS–1991, National Design Specification for Wood Construction*, American Forest & Paper Association, Washington, D.C.

2 ASCE-16, *Standard For Load and Resistance Factor For Engineered Wood Construction:* AF&PA/ASCE 16–95, American Society of Civil Engineers, 1995, New York, New York.

3 AITC, *Timber Construction Manual,* American Institute of Timber Construction, 1994, New York, New York, John Wiley and Sons, Inc.

4 FPL, Wood Handbook, Reprinted from Forest Productions Laboratory General Technical Report FPL-GTR-113 with the consent of the USDA Forest Service, Forest Products Laboratory, Forest Products Society, 1998.

5 SEAOC, *1999 Recommended Lateral Force Requirements and Commentary* (SEAOC Blue Book), Structural Engineers Association of California, 1999, ICBO, Whittier, CA.

6 SEAOC, *Seismic Design Manual, Volume II: Building Design Examples*, Structural Engineers Association of California, ICBO, Whittier, CA.

7 APA, *Design/Construction Guide—Diaphragms*, American Plywood Association, 1991, Tacoma, Washington.

8 ATC, *ATC-7: Guidelines for the Design of Horizontal Wood Diaphragms*, Applied Technology Council, 1981, Redwood City, California.

9 ATC, *ATC-R-1: Cyclic testing of Narrow Plywood Shear Walls*, Applied Technology Council, 1995, Redwood City, California.

10 White, M.W. and J.D. Dolan, "Seismic Response of Timber Shear Walls. Part I: Aspect Ratios." Paper submitted for publication in *ASCE Journal of Structural Engineering, 1996.*

11 Nelson, Rawn F., and Hamburger, Ronald O., "Hold Down Eccentricity and the Capacity of the Vertical Wood Member," *Structure*, 1999.

12 Stone, Jeffrey, Phillip Line and Brian Weeks (2000), Perforated Shear Wall Design, *Structural Engineer*, Civil Engineering News, INC., Alpharetta, GA.

13 Dolan, J.D., and M.W. White, *Design Considerations for Using Adhesives in Shear Walls*, ASCE Journal of Structural Engineering 118(12): 3473-3480, 1992.

14 Foschi, R.O., and A. Filiatrault, *Performance Evaluation of 3M Scotch Grip Wood Adhesive 5230 for the Static and Dynamic Design of Timber Shear Walls and Diaphragms,* Department of Civil Engineering Report, University of British Columbia, 1990, Vancouver, B.C.

BIBLIOGRAPHY

AF&PA, *Manual of Wood Construction: Load and Resistance Factor Design (LRFD),* American Forest & Paper Association. 1996, Washington, D.C.

APA, *Northridge California Earthquake, T94-5*, American Plywood Association, 1994. Tacoma, Washington.

APA, *Proposed Cyclic Testing Standard for Shear Walls*, American Plywood Association, 1996 Tacoma, Washington.

APA: Rose, J.D., *Preliminary Testing of Wood Structural Panel Shear Walls Under Cyclic (Reversed) Loading. Research Report 158*, American Plywood Association, 1996, Tacoma, Washington.

ASCE, *A Pre Standard Report American Society of Civil Engineers*, ASCE Committee on Wood Load and Resistance Factor Design for Engineered Wood Construction, 1988. New York, New York.

Breyer, Donald E., *Design of Wood Structures,* Third Edition, 1993, McGraw-Hill Book Company, New York, New York.

BOCA, *The BOCA National Building Code—Commentary Volume 2*, Building Officials & Code Administrators International, Inc. Country Club Hills, IL, 1999.

BOCA, *National Building Code*, Building Officials & Code Administrators International, Inc. Country Club Hills, IL, 1996.

CWC, *Wood Design Manual*, Canadian Wood Council, 1990, Ottawa, Canada.

CWC, *Wood Reference Handbook*, Canadian Wood Council, 1991, Ottawa, Canada.

CABO, *One- and Two-Family Dwelling Code*, Council of American Building Officials, 1995, Country Club Hills, Illinois.

DofANAF, *Seismic Design for Buildings,* TM5-809-10 (Tri-Services Manual), Department of the Army, Navy and Air Force, 1992, U.S. Government Printing Office, Washington, D.C.

Dolan, J.D., 1994, *Proposed Test Method for Dynamic Properties of Connections Assemblies with Mechanical Fasteners*, ASTM Journal of Testing and Evaluation 22(6): 542-547.

Dolan, J.D. and Johnson, A.C., *Monotonic Tests of Long Shear Walls with Openings*, Virginia Polytechnic Institute and State University, Timber Engineering Report No. TE-1996-001, 1996 Blacksburg, Virginia.

Dolan, J.D. and Johnson, A.C., *Cyclic Tests of Long Shear Walls with Openings*, Virginia Polytechnic Institute and State University, Timber Engineering Report No. TE-1996-002, 1996 Blacksburg, Virginia.

EERI, *Northridge Earthquake Reconnaissance Report, Chapter 6, Supplement C to Volume 11, pp 125 et seq., Earthquake Spectra*, Earthquake Engineering Research Institute, 1996.

Faherty, Keith F., and T.G. Williamson, *Wood Engineering and Construction Handbook*, 1989 McGraw-Hill, New York, New York.

FPL, *Wood: Engineering Design Concepts*, Forest Products Laboratory, 1986, Materials Education Council, The Pennsylvania State University, University Park, PA.

Goetz, Karl-Heinz, Dieter Hoor, Karl Moehler, and Julius Natterer, *Timber Design and Construction Source Book: A Comprehensive Guide to Methods and Practice*, McGraw-Hill, 1989, New York, New York.

Hoyle and Woeste, *Wood Technology and Design of Structures.* Iowa State University Press, 1989.

HUD, *HUD Minimum Property Standards, Vol. I, II, and III*, U.S. Department of Housing and Urban Development, 1984, United States Government Printing Office Washington, D.C.

ICBO, *Uniform Building Code*, International Conference of Building Officials, 1994, Whittier, CA.

ICBO, *Handbook to the Uniform Building Code: An illustrative commentary*, International Conference of Building Officials, Inc., Whittier, CA, 1998.

Keenan, F.J., *Limit States Design of Wood Structures*, Morrison Hershfield Limited, 1986.

NEHRP, *NEHRP (National Earthquake Hazard Reduction Program) Recommended Provisions for the Development of Seismic Regulations for New Buildings (and Other Structures)*, Building Seismic Safety Council, Washington, D.C., 1997.

NOAA, *San Fernando, California, Earthquake of February 9, 1971*, U.S. Department of Agriculture, National Oceanic and Atmospheric Administration, 1971, Washington, D.C.

Sherwood and Stroh, "Wood-Frame House Construction" in *Agricultural Handbook 73.* U.S. Government Printing Office, 1973,Washington, D.C.

Somayaji, Shan, *Structural Wood Design.* West Publishing Co., 1992, St. Paul, Minnesota.

Stalnaker, Judith J., and E.C. Harris, *Structural Design in Wood*, Second Edition, McGraw-Hill, 1996, New York, New York.

WWPA, *Western Wood Use Book*, Western Wood Products Association, Portland, Oregon, 1983.

Additional references are listed in John Peterson. 1983. "Bibliography on Lumber and Wood Panel Diaphragms," *Journal of Structural Engineering,* Vol. 109 No. 12. American Society of Civil Engineers, New York, New York.

APPENDIX 1

BACKGROUND TO SEISMIC STRENGTH DESIGN LOAD COMBINATIONS

Strength design for reinforced concrete was first introduced into the 1956 edition of ACI 318 *Building Code Requirements for Reinforced Concrete.*[1.1] From the 1971 through the 1995 edition of the ACI 318 standard, the strength design load combinations involving earthquake forces have remained unchanged at those shown in Item 1 of Table 1.1. The load combinations are meant to be used in conjunction with the strength reduction factors given in Chapter 9 of the ACI 318 standard. The *Uniform Building Code,* from its 1976 through its 1994 editions, modified the ACI strength design load combinations, for design in Seismic Zones 3 and 4, to those shown in Item 2 of Table 1.1. The strength reduction factors given in Chapter 9 of the ACI 318 standard were not modified in the UBC, thus increasing the margin of safety in comparison with ACI 318. When strength design for masonry was introduced into the UBC, the same seismic design load combinations as for concrete were adopted, along with strength reduction factors that were somewhat different from those of ACI 318 Chapter 9.

ANSI A58.1 (later ASCE 7) Standard *Minimum Design Loads for Buildings and Other Structures,*[1.2] in its 1982 edition, introduced a set of design load combinations that were different from those of ACI 318. The ANSI/ASCE load combinations were later adopted for steel load and resistance factor design (LRFD) and subsequently also for the strength design of wood. Strength design for masonry, whch has been under development for quite some time for incorporation into the ACI 530/ASCE 5/TMS 402 masonry standard,[1.3] is also expected to be based on the ANSI/ASCE load combinations. The ANSI/ASCE strength design load combinations, as given in the 1988 edition of the ASCE standard,[1.2] are shown in Item 3 of Table 1.1. ASCE 7-88 did not anticipate the application of these load combinations to the strength design of concrete or masonry structures.

ACI 318-95,[1.1] for the very first time, permitted the proportioning of concrete structural elements by the ASCE 7 load combinations (seismic as well as nonseismic) "if the structural framing includes primary members of other materials . . ." Thus a designer faced with the design of a building with a reinforced concrete shear wall core and steel framing outside of the core may choose to design the shear walls using the ASCE 7 rather than the ACI 318 load combinations. ASCE 7 gravity design load combinations provide lower design loads than the ACI 318 gravity design load combinations. While it is less clear how the design loads compare when it comes to gravity plus lateral load (wind or earthquake) combinations, out of a desire to preserve the margin of safety in going from the ACI 318 to the ASCE 7 load combinations, a set of strength reduction factors having slightly lower values than the Chapter 9 ϕ-factors were developed and listed in Appendix C of ACI 318-95. The ASCE 7 load combinations, if chosen, must be used with the strength reduction factors of Appendix C. ACI 318-99[1.1] did not change any of this.

In all the load combinations mentioned so far, the earthquake effect, *E*, is the effect of service-level earthquake forces as given, for instance, in UBC-1994.[1.4] ASCE 7-93[1.2] introduced strength design load combinations involving strength-level earthquake forces, as shown in Item 4 of Table 1.1. Under Section A.9.11, Supplementary Provisions for Reinforced Concrete, ASCE 7-93 states that the load combinations of ACI 318 are not applicable for the design of reinforced concrete to resist earthquake forces. Instead, ASCE 7 requires that: "The load combinations for earthquake load in [ACI 318] shall be replaced with the load combinations of [ASCE 7-93] multiplied by the factor of 1.1, which accounts for an incompatibility between the ϕ-factors of [ACI 318] and the load factors of this document." Being a load standard, ASCE 7 did not want to extend itself into a modification of strength reduction factors. The multiplier of 1.1 is intended to provide the same level of safety as that produced by the reduced ϕ-factors of Appendix C to ACI 318-95.

TABLE 1.1. SEISMIC STRENGTH DESIGN LOAD COMBINATIONS IN VARIOUS CODES AND STANDARDS

	(1) ACI 318-95, Ch. 9	(2) UBC-94	(3) ASCE 7-88
SERVICE LEVEL *E*	$U = 1.05D+1.28L+1.40E$	$U = 1.4\ (D + L + E)$	$U = 1.2D+1.5E+(0.5L$ or $0.2S)$
	$U = 0.9D + 1.43E$	$U = 0.9D \pm 1.4E$	$U = 0.9D - 1.5E$
	(4) ASCE 7-93 & 7-95	**(5) UBC-97**	**(6) NEHRP-97, IBC 2000**
STRENGTH LEVEL *E*	$U = 1.2D + 1.0E + 0.5L + 0.2S$	$U = 1.2D + 1.0E + (f_1L+f_2S)$	$U = 1.2D + 1.0E + (f_1L+f_2S)$
	$U = 0.9D + 1.0E$	$U = 0.9D \pm 1.0E$	$U = 0.9D \pm 1.0E$

Notes (1), (4) *E* can be positive or negative

(1), (2) *U* is to be used in conjunction with the appropriate ϕ-factor from ACI 318 Ch. 9

(4), (5) 1.1 *U* is to be used in conjunction with the appropriate ϕ-factor from ACI 318 Ch. 9

(6) *U* of NEHRP-97 is, and *U* of the IBC through its Final Draft was, required to be used in conjunction with the appropriate ϕ-factor from Appendix C to ACI 318-95.

(3) ACI 318-95 permits the use of ASCE 7-88 *U* in conjunction with the appropriate ϕ-factor from Appendix C for the design of concrete members in structures of mixed construction only.

The 1997 UBC[1.4] adopted the ASCE 7-95 load combinations (same as those in ASCE 7-93) with two minor modifications. Instead of a fixed live load factor of 0.5, the 1997 UBC prescribes a variable factor, f_1, which is to be taken as 1.0 for floors in places of public assembly, for live loads in excess of 100 psf, and for garage live load. Similarly, instead of a fixed snow load factor of 0.2, the 1997 UBC prescribes a variable factor, f_2, which is to be taken as 0.7 for roof configurations (such as saw tooth) that do not shed snow off the structure. The seismic strength design load combinations of the 1997 UBC are shown in Item 5 of Table 1.1. Exception 1 to Section 1612.2.1 of 1997 UBC specifies that load combinations that do not include seismic forces shall revert back to those of Section 1909.2 of ACI 318-95 for concrete design purposes. Exception 2 modifies load combinations that include seismic forces, for concrete and masonry design, to:

$U = 1.1\ [1.2D + 1.0E + (f_1 L + f_2 S)]$ UBC (12-5a)

$U = 1.1\ [0.9D \pm 1.0E]$ UBC (12-6a)

The multiplier of 1.1 is based on the ASCE 7-95 approach.

NEHRP-97[1.5] does include and the Final Draft of the International Building Code (IBC) did include the seismic strength design load combinations of the 1997 UBC. However, instead of adopting a multiplier of 1.1 on the design load, the IBC Final Draft, following NEHRP-97, required: "For load combinations which include earthquake loads, the design strength shall be computed using the strength reduction factor, ϕ, listed in Appendix C [of ACI 318-95]."

It was not realized until actual designs were undertaken using the 1997 UBC that the multiplier of 1.1 should have never been applied to the UBC load combination ($0.9D \pm 1.0E$), because this load combination is identical to the ACI load combination (9-3), modified for inclusion of earthquake effects:

$U = 0.9D \pm 1.43E$ ACI (9-3a)

or the 1994 UBC load combination:

$U = 0.9D \pm 1.4E$

if it is remembered that the E of the 1997 UBC is essentially 1.4 times the E of the 1994 UBC and ACI 318-95.

It is also questionable whether the 1.1 multiplier should apply to the load combination [$1.2D + 1.0\,E + (f_1\,L + f_2\,S)$]. While a comparison of the ACI and the ASCE 7 load combinations would readily reveal that ASCE 7 gravity load combinations definitely yield lower design loads than the ACI 318 load combinations, it is far from clear if the same is true of the ASCE versus ACI gravity and lateral load combinations. Table 1.2 shows a comparison between design loads yielded by the UBC Equation 12-5 and the corresponding gravity and earthquake load combination of ACI 318:

$U = 0.75\ [1.4D + 1.7L + 1.87E]$ ACI (9-2a)

It can be seen that the comparison depends on three variables: the earthquake-to-dead (*E/D*), the snow-to-dead (*S/D*), and the live-to-dead (*L/D*) load (or load effect) ratios. The 1997 UBC Equation 12-5 yields design loads that are over 10 percent lower than the corresponding design loads produced by ACI 318 Equation 9-2 (modified for earthquake effect) only when the live-to-dead load ratio exceeds 0.5, or even 0.6, which is not common in concrete structures.

The 1997 UBC Equation 12-5 would typically govern only the flexural design of moment frame beams. This is because the proportioning of reinforced concrete walls and columns is generally governed by the load combination yielding the minimum axial load in compression, or the maximum axial load in tension, which is typically Equation 12-6. A slight (up to 10 percent) underdesign of moment frame beams in flexure should be of no concern. Underdesign in shear would be a different matter, but that possibility is already precluded for beams of special as well as intermediate moment frames. A beam of a special moment frame must be designed for the maximum shear force that can develop in the beam, which is computed on the basis of moments equal to probable flexural strengths acting at the two ends. Also, the contribution of the concrete to shear strength is required to be neglected. A beam of an intermediate moment frame is also required to be designed for the maximum shear that can develop in it, which is computed on the basis of moments equal to nominal flexural strengths acting at the two ends.

In view of the above, it was recommended in References 1.6 and 1.7 that the 1.1 multiplier be not applied to the 1997 UBC Equation 12-5 or 12-6. In other words, Exception 2 to the 1997 UBC Section 1612.2.1 was recommended to be deleted.

For the same reasons as given above, the requirement of the Working, the First and the Final Drafts of the IBC that the reduced strength reduction factors of Appendix C of ACI 318, rather than those of Chapter 9, be used in conjunction with the seismic strength design load combinations of the IBC, was proposed for deletion. The proposal was accepted, and the acceptance is reflected in the First (2000) Edition of the IBC.

TABLE 1.2. A COMPARISON OF SEISMIC STRENGTH DESIGN LOAD COMBINATIONS OF ASCE 7-95 (UBC-97) AND ACI 318-95

$U(ACI) = 1.05D + 1.28L + 1.43E_w$

$U(ASCE - 7) = 1.2D + 0.5L + 0.2S + 1.0E$

$$\frac{U(ACI)}{U(ASCE-7)} = \frac{1.05 + 1.28(L/D) + 1.0(E/D)}{1.2 + 0.5(L/D) + 0.2(S/D) + 1.0(E/D)}$$

L/D	S/D=0.0	S/D=0.1	S/D=0.2	S/D=0.5	S/D=1.0
E/D=1					
0.25	1.02	1.01	1.00	0.98	0.94
0.40	1.07	1.06	1.05	1.02	0.99
0.50	1.10	1.09	1.08	1.05	1.02
0.60	1.13	1.12	1.11	1.08	1.04
0.75	1.17	1.16	1.15	1.13	1.08
E/D=2					
0.25	1.01	1.01	1.00	0.98	0.96
0.40	1.05	1.04	1.04	1.02	0.99
0.50	1.07	1.06	1.06	1.04	1.01
0.60	1.09	1.08	1.08	1.06	1.03
0.75	1.12	1.12	1.11	1.09	1.06
E/D=3					
0.25	1.01	1.01	1.00	0.99	0.97
0.40	1.04	1.03	1.03	1.01	0.99
0.50	1.05	1.05	1.04	1.03	1.01
0.60	1.07	1.07	1.06	1.05	1.03
0.75	1.10	1.09	1.09	1.07	1.05
E/D=4					
0.25	1.01	1.00	1.00	0.99	0.97
0.40	1.03	1.03	1.02	1.01	0.99
0.50	1.04	1.04	1.04	1.03	1.01
0.60	1.05	1.05	1.05	1.04	1.02
0.75	1.08	1.07	1.07	1.06	1.01

REFERENCES:

[1.1] ACI Committee 318, *Building Code Requirements for Structural* (previously Reinforced) Concrete (ACI 318) and Commentary (ACI 318R), American Concrete Institute, Detroit, MI, 1956, 1963, 1971, 1977, 1983, 1989, 1995, and Farmington Hills, MI, 1999.

[1.2] American Society of Civil Engineers, *ASCE Standard Minimum Design Loads for Buildings and Other Structures,* ASCE 7-88, ASCE 7-93, ASCE 7-95, ASCE 7-98 (also ANSI A58-55, ANSI A58.1-72, ANSI A58.1-82), New York, N. Y., 1990, 1993, 1995, and 2000, respectively.

[1.3] Masonry Standards Joint Committee, Building Code Requirements for Masonry Structures (ACI 530-95/ ASCE 5-95/ TMS 402-95), (ACI 530-99/ ASCE 5-99/ TMS 402-99) American Concrete Institute, Farmington Hills, MI (previously Detroit, MI), American Society of Civil Engineers, New York, N.Y., The Masonry Society, Boulder, CO, 1995, 1999.

[1.4] Pacific Coast Building Officials Conference (later the International Conference of Building Officials), *Uniform Building Code*, Long Beach, CA (later Whittier, CA), 1935, 1952, 1967, 1970, 1973, 1976, 1979, 1982, 1985, 1988, 1991, 1994, 1997.

[1.5] Building Seismic Safety Council, *NEHRP (National Earthquake Hazards Reduction Program)* Recommended Provisions for the Development of Seismic Regulations for New Buildings (and Other Structures), Washington, D.C., 1994, (1997).

[1.6] Ghosh, S.K., *Design of Reinforced Concrete Buildings under the 1997 UBC,* Building Standards, International Conference of Building Officials, May-June 1998, pp. 20-24.

[1.7] Ghosh, S.K., "Needed Adjustments in 1997 UBC," Proceedings, 1998 Convention, Structural Engineers Assocation of California, October 7-10, 1998, Reno-Sparks, Nevada, pp. T9.1-T9.15.

APPENDIX 2

BACKGROUND TO THE WIND LOAD PROVISIONS OF MODEL CODES AND STANDARDS

ASCE 7

The following is adapted largely from References 2.1 and 2.2.

The first major improvements in the standardized wind load provisions of this country occurred with the publication of ANSI A58.1-1972.[2.3] Unfortunately, however, the new provisions never gained wide acceptance by the model code bodies and practicing engineers, primarily because they represented a quantum jump in sophistication in comparison with the codes of practice of that time. The ANSI A58.1-1972 provisions were also flawed with ambiguities, inconsistencies in terminology, and a format that permitted certain provisions to be misinterpreted.

There was consensus among professional practitioners that the ANSI 1972 document needed revision and a new subcommittee of ANSI A58.1 was appointed in 1976 to accomplish this task. The subcommittee reviewed all available research data and deliberated on various proposals advanced to improve and simplify the provisions. The draft produced by the subcommittee was subjected to the ANSI consensus process. Upon conclusion of that process, the revision was published as ANSI A58.1-1982.[2.3] The revised standard contained an innovative approach to wind loads for components and cladding of buildings. Wind load specification was based on understanding the aerodynamics of wind pressure in building corners, eaves and ridge areas, as well as the effects of area averaging on pressures.

In 1985, the American Society of Civil Engineers (ASCE) assumed responsibility for the committee that establishes design loads for buildings and other structures. The ASCE Committee reviewed the wind load provisions of ANSI A58.1-1982 and made minor changes and clarifications that were incorporated in ASCE 7-88, published in 1990. A revised version of ASCE 7-88 was published in ASCE 7-93. However, the wind load provisions were not changed, and remained essentially the same as in ANSI A58.1-1982 until the publication of ASCE 7-95, which did make major changes in those provisions.

The most significant change in ASCE 7-95 was the use of 3-second gust speed, rather than the fastest-mile wind speed, as the basis of the basic wind speed used in design. The change necessitated revision of terrain and height factors, gust-effect factors and pressure coefficients for components and cladding. Additional significant changes and additions were as follows:

- Provisions were added for wind speed-up over isolated hills and escarpments (topographical effect).
- New provisions were added for full and partial loading on main wind-force resisting system of buildings with a mean roof height greater than 60 feet (torsional loading effect).
- An alternate procedure was added for determining external loads on main wind-force resisting systems of low-rise buildings.
- Internal pressure coefficients were increased for partially enclosed buildings located in hurricane-prone regions.
- Pressure coefficients for components and cladding were added for hipped, stepped, multispan, and sawtooth roofs.
- Velocity pressure exposure coeffecients were revised to be compatible with 3-second gust speed.
- Gust effect factor procedures were unified for flexible and non-flexible buildings and structures. A new procedure was provided for calculating a gust effect factor.
- Pressures for components and cladding of buildings with a mean roof height less than 60 feet were reduced for buildings sited in Exposure B.

Other changes in tables and figures and in the wind tunnel test procedure incorporated the latest available technical information. The basic format of the wind provisions remained the same as in ASCE 7-88.

The wind provisions of ASCE 7-98 contain several changes from those of ASCE 7-95 that are important to note:

1. The basic wind speed map in the 1998 standard has been updated based on a new and more complete analysis of hurricane wind speeds. The new analysis includes many more predictions for sites away from the coast and it includes the best available information regarding the rate at which hurricane winds degrade as they move inland. The most noticeable result is a significant reduction in wind speeds in inland Florida.
2. Wind directionality is now explicitly accounted for in the calculation of the wind loads; it is no longer just a component of the wind load factor. A new factor, K_d, has been introduced, which varies depending on the type of structure.
3. The format of the entire section has been changed to increase its ease of use. The wind provisions have been broken into three distinct methods. Method 1 "Simplified Procedure," is used for simple diaphragm buildings. Method 2 "Analytical Procedure," may be used for essentially any building or structure. Method 2 contains provisions for buildings of all heights including those commonly referred to as low-rise buildings. Method 3, "Wind Tunnel Procedure," includes provisions for conducting a wind tunnel test.
4. The definitions of Exposures C and D have changed slightly to allow the shorelines in hurricane prone regions to be classified as Exposure C rather than Exposure D. The commentary pertaining to the exposure categories has been expanded to provide more information and guidance to the user and now includes photographs to assist in the understanding of the different exposure categories.

FASTEST MILE VERSUS 3-SECOND GUST VELOCITY OF WIND

Wind is a turbulent flow, characterized by random fluctuations of velocity and pressure. If the instantaneous velocity of wind at a given point is recorded as a function of time on a chart, the result will look like that in Fig. 2.1.

Because of its fluctuating nature, wind velocity needs to be studied statistically. A statistical property is the mean or average. Because the intensity of wind changes constantly, different averages are obtained by using different averaging times. For instance, while a 5-minute average of the peak of a high wind may be 60 mph, the same wind averaged over an hour may be only 35 mph. This means that whenever a mean or average velocity of wind is desired, one must specify the averaging time.

The longest averaging time used for wind is a year, producing an annual or yearly average. For instance, the annual wind speed for Kansas City is about 11 mph. Although information on this speed is very important in wind energy utilization, it is useless for wind load on structures because in that case only high winds of short durations are of interest. The longest averaging time for high winds used in practice is one hour. In general, as the averaging time decreases, the maximum speed of the wind increases. Suppose V_T is the maximum wind speed based on an averaging time of T seconds, and V_H is the maximum hourly average. The relationship between V_T and V_H for open terrains is approximately given in Fig. 2.2. From the figure, the 1-second gust speed above open terrains is almost 1.6 times the maximum hourly wind speed.

The mean wind speed used in ANSI A8.1-1972, ANSI A58.1-1982, ASCE 7-88 and ASCE 7-93 is the "fastest-mile wind," which is the maximum, averaged over one mile of wind passing through a measuring instrument called an anemometer. The averaging time of the fastest-mile wind is:

$$T = \frac{3600}{V_{fm}}$$

where T is in seconds and the fastest-mile wind speed, V_{fm} is in mph. For instance, if V_{fm} = 60 mph, the averaging time is T=3600/60 = 60 seconds. If V_{fm} is 120 mph, T decreases to 30 seconds. From the foregoing, the averaging time of the fastest-mile wind used in the design of structures, which normally uses a wind speed between 60 and 120 mph, is from 30 to 60 seconds. A fixed 3 seconds is the averaging time for the 3-second gust speed accepted as the basic wind speed in ASCE 7-95 and ASCE 7-98.

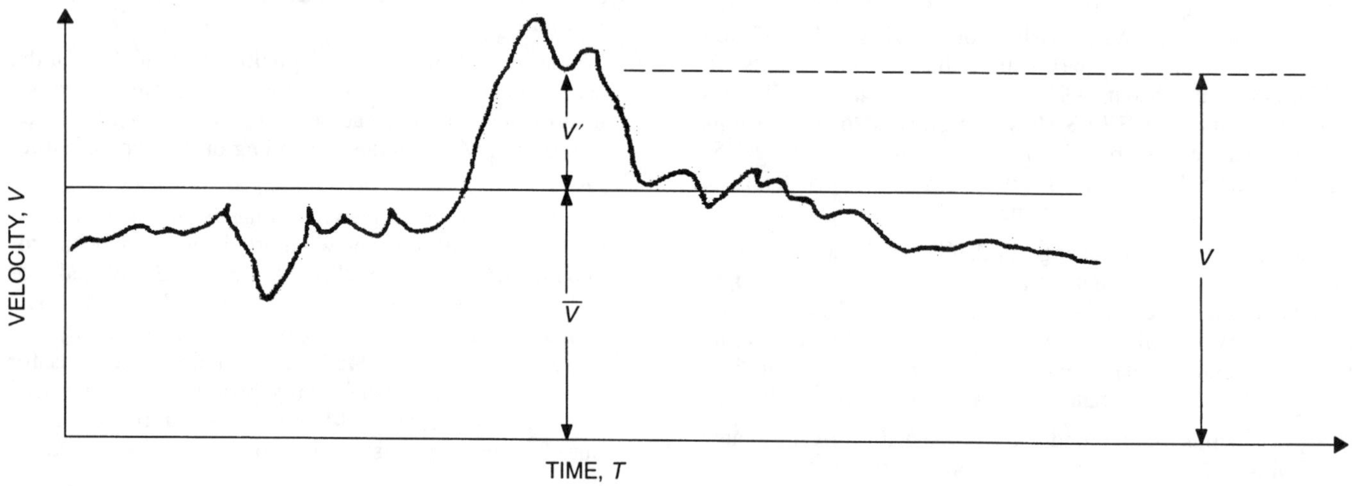

FLUCTUATIONS OF WIND VELOCITY

FIGURE 2.1

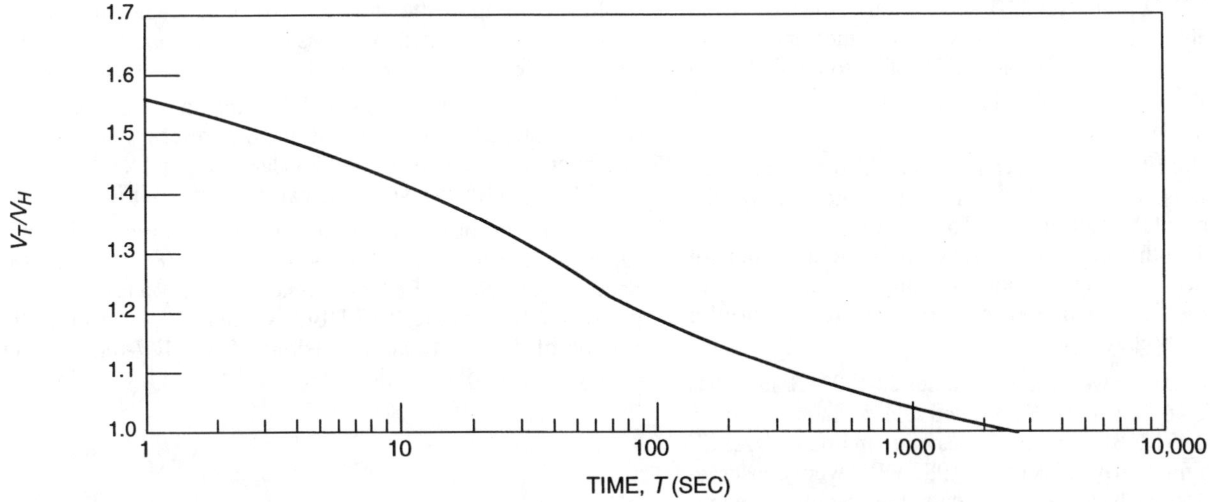

RELATIONSHIP BETWEEN HOURLY MEAN VELOCITY OF WIND AND VELOCITY OF WIND AVERAGED OVER A SHORTER PERIOD, *T*

FIGURE 2.2

BOCA / National Building Code[2.4]

The BOCA/NBC adopted the wind design provisions of ANSI A58.1-1972 in its 1978 edition, and retained them in the 1981 and 1984 editions. The revised wind design provisions of ANSI A58.1-1982 were adopted into the 1987 edition of the BOCA/NBC, and were retained in the 1990 edition. The 1993 edition of the BOCA/NBC adopted the wind design provisions of ASCE 7-1988, which have been retained in the 1996 and 1999 editions. The wind design provisions of ASCE 7-95 have not been adopted.

Standard Building Code[2.5]

SBCCI adoption of ANSI A58.1-1972 first happened in the 1977 revisions to the 1976 code, so 1979 was the first time it appeared in a full code edition. However, it was only to be used with one- and two-story buildings, and only with the wind speed map from the SBC. It stayed that way through the 1982 edition of the code. ANSI A 58.1-1982 was adopted into the 1985 edition of the SBC. For low-rise buildings (mean roof height ≤ 60 feet) the ANSI procedure was an alternate to the MBMA procedure. The 1988 SBC retained the same ANSI provisions, the ANSI procedure was an alternate to the other procedure for all building heights. ASCE 7-88 wind provisions were adopted into the 1991 SBC; the ASCE procedure was still an alternate to the other procedure. The same wind design provisions were retained in the 1994 SBC; the ASCE procedure was an alternate to the MBMA procedure for low-rise buildings. ASCE 7-95 wind design provisions have been adopted into the 1997 and 1999 *Standard Building Code.* The MBMA procedure is still an alternate for low-rise buildings (mean roof height ≤ 60 feet).

Uniform Building Code[2.6]

The following is adopted largely from Reference 2.7.

Through its 1979 edition, the *Uniform Building Code* wind design provisions were based on the ANSI standard A58-1955.[2.3]

In 1976, the International Conference of Building Officials (ICBO) appointed a task force of its General Design Code Development Committee to update its wind load provisions. This was because of strong pressure to upgrade the simplified UBC wind design provisions at the same time the other model code writing bodies were considering adopting ANSI A58.1-1972.

Practicing engineers on the West Coast considered the ANSI provisions too complicated for practical engineering and lobbied for a simplified method of calculating wind forces. They were accustomed to determining wind pressures that were dependent only on the height of the building and the basic wind speed. These pressures were applied against the area within the building's projected vertical or horizontal outline. In contrast, the ANSI provisions required the use of six graphs to evaluate coefficients used in determining wind pressures. These pressures were applied normal to the face of the wall or roof and depended on the slope of the roof, internal pressure and other factors.

The wind provisions published in the 1982 edition of the UBC were based on those of ANSI A58.1-1972, although the calculation procedure was simplified. The changes proposed for ANSI A58.1-1982 were known at that time. The important changes proposed for ANSI A58.1-1982 were incorporated into the 1982 UBC. Few changes were made in the 1985 and 1988 UBC wind provisions.

The 1991 UBC made many changes in substance and format in its wind design provisions. There were further minor changes in the 1994 edition of the code, and no changes at all in the 1997 edition.

The 1991 UBC required wind pressures to be calculated in a manner similar to that of ASCE 7-88, except that only four coefficients needed to be determined. To simplify the calculation procedure, certain assumptions were made about the building. These assumptions limit the applicability of the UBC procedure.

The 1991 UBC Figure No. 23-1 was similar to the basic wind speed map published in ASCE 7-88 except that the contours and Special Wind Regions in the states of Washington and Oregon were different. The same figure appears as Fig. 16-1 of the 1994 and the 1997 UBC.

In the 1991 edition, a new section was added that gathered many definitions, such as the three exposure categories, from the text and figures of the 1988 edition. To make the provisions consistent with the other code chapters, symbols and notations for wind were placed in a single location. Among the major new provisions was the addition of an exposure D terrain category for sites near large bodies of water.

Numerous changes were made to Tables 23-F, 23-G, and 23-H (Tables 16-F, 16-G, and 16-H, respectively, of later editions), bringing the 1991 UBC wind pressures more in line with ASCE 7-88. The original provisions of the 1982 UBC were conservative in their approaches and coefficients. For instance, they retained the traditional method of calculating wind forces, i.e., Method 2, and the pressure coefficients associated with basic wind speed were rounded up. Additionally, the forces associated with parts and portions, now called elements and components, were not keyed to tributary areas in the UBC.

The q_s and C_e factors were changed in the 1991 UBC to create a pressure profile equivalent to that of ASCE 7-88. The wind stagnation pressure, q_s, was extended to one decimal place instead of being rounded up to the next-highest integer.

The elements and components portions of Table 23-H (Table 16-H of later editions) were subdivided into coefficients at discontinuities and at areas away from these discontinuities. Pressures at discrete elements were now based on tributary areas 10 square feet or smaller, between 10 and 100 square feet, and up to 1000 square feet. The term "corner" was now more clearly defined.

Instead of having separate tables of Importance Factors for wind and for earthquake, these were combined into Table 23-L. Tables 23-K and 23-L of the 1991 UBC were later combined into Table 16-K of the 1994 and 1997 UBCs. A seismic importance factor, I_p, for parts and positions of a structure, not previously part of Table 23-L, was included in Table 16-K of later editions.

The provisions for Glass and Glazing in UBC Chapter 54 (later Chapter 24) were modified, and the prescriptive provisions of Appendix Chapters 24 and 25 (later Appendix Chapters 21 and 23, respectively) were also extensively modified.

It should be obvious from the foregoing brief background segments that the wind provisions of the 2000 IBC, adopting Section 6 of ASCE 7-98 by reference with only a few modifications, and those of the 1997 UBC, which represent a simplified version of the wind load provisions of ASCE 7-88, represent different stages of evolution, and thus different levels of sophistication.

REFERENCES

2.1 Mehta, K.C., Marshall, R.D., and Perry, D.C., *Guide to the Use of the Wind Load Provisions of ASCE 7-88,* American Society of Civil Engineers, New York, N. Y., 1991.

2.2 Mehta, K.C., and Marshall, R.D., *Guide to the Use of the Wind Load Provisions of ASCE 7-95,* American Society of Civil Engineers, New York, N. Y., 1998.

2.3 American Society of Civil Engineers, *ASCE Standard Minimum Design Loads for Buildings and Other Structures,* ASCE 7-88, ASCE 7-93, ASCE 7-95, ASCE 7-98 (also ANSI A58-55, ANSI A58.1-72, ANSI A58.1-82), New York, N. Y., 1990, 1993, 1995, and 2000, respectively.

2.4 Building Officials and Code Administrations International, *The BOCA National Building Code,* Country Club Hills, Illinois, 1978, 1981, 1984, 1987, 1990, 1993, 1996, 1999.

2.5 Southern Building Code Congress International, *Standard Building Code,* Birmingham, Alabama, 1979, 1982, 1985, 1988, 1991, 1994, 1997, 1999.

2.6 Pacific Coast Building Officials Conference (later the International Conference of Building Officials), *Uniform Building Code,* Long Beach, CA (later Whittier, CA), 1935, 1952, 1967, 1970, 1973, 1976, 1979, 1982, 1985, 1988, 1991, 1994, 1997.

2.7 Structural Engineers Association of Washington, *Wind Commentary to the Uniform Building Code 1991 Edition,* Seattle, Washington, 1993.

APPENDIX 3
BACKGROUND TO SEISMIC GROUND MOTION IN SEISMIC DESIGN

Introduction

Background to the seismic zoning map of the 1988 UBC was presented by the author in Reference 3.1. It was compiled from a number of readily available sources: a 1969 paper by Algermissen,[3.2] the commentary portions of ASCE 7-88,[3.3] ATC 3-06,[3.4] and the 1988 SEAOC Blue Book.[3.5] That information is expanded and brought up to date, relying largely upon the commentary to the 1997 NEHRP Provisions.[3.6]

Seismic Zones

The concept of seismic zones was first introduced into the 1935 edition of the *Uniform Building Code.*[3.7] The code included a map of the 11 western states, showing three different seismic zones of approximately equal seismic probability, with the most active being Zone 3, and the least active being Zone 1. The western coast of California was assigned to Zone 3, in part because of the historic seismicity of the region. Zone 2 included the central valley of California and extended into Nevada, Utah, Oregon and Montana. The remaining states were essentially in Zone 1. A seismic zonation factor equal to 1, 2, and 4, in Zones 1, 2, and 3, respectively, directly amplified the design base shear.

A seismic probability map of the United States was prepared in 1948 by Roberts and Ulrich with the advice of seismologists throughout the United States[3.8] and was issued by the Coast and Geodetic Survey (later the U.S. Geological Survey) in 1948. In 1949, the seismic probability map was revised such that the Charleston, South Carolina area was changed from Zone 3 to Zone 2, and a Zone 3 was set up for the Puget Sound region of Washington, which had formerly been included in Zone 2.[3.9] The revised map was adopted by the Pacific Coast Building Officials Conference (later ICBO) for inclusion in the 1952 edition of the *Uniform Building Code.*[3.7] Subsequent editions of the UBC, up to and including the 1967 edition, incorporated this map with no changes.

The seismic zone map adopted into the 1970 and 1973 editions of the UBC evolved from the work of Algermissen during the 1960s[3.2] and is based on the maximum recorded intensity of shaking without regard to the frequency with which such shaking might occur. As originally published, this map had four zones (0, 1, 2, and 3), so that several areas in the Eastern United States were in the same zone as California. During the 1970s the map was modified and eventually adopted into the 1976 edition of the UBC with a Zone 4 in parts of California and Nevada, and with the Z factor for the remaining Zone 3 areas reduced. The boundary between Zones 3 and 4 was determined by proximity to the major fault systems. The boundary was set at 25 miles from a fault considered capable of generating an earthquake of magnitude 7.0 or greater and 15 miles from a fault that could generate an earthquake of magnitude between 6.0 and 7.0. The distances were based on the Schnabel-Seed attenuation curve[3.10] and a value of 0.3g for the peak acceleration at the boundary on a rock site. The seismic zone map of 1976 UBC remained unchanged through the 1985 edition of that code.

ATC 3-06

Algermissen and Perkins in 1976 published a new contour map for peak ground acceleration on rock, based on a uniform probability of occurrence throughout the 48 contiguous states.[3.11] The probability that the contoured peak acceleration would not be exceeded was given as 90 percent in 50 years. In developing this map, the first step was to delineate zones within which earthquakes may occur and establish for each zone the frequency of earthquakes with different magnitudes. Attenuation equations were selected for both the eastern and the western parts of the country. These several parameters served as input to a computer program that computed the frequency for different peak accelerations at all points of a gridwork covering the 48 states.

The Seismic Risk Committee of ATC 3 modified the Algermissen-Perkins map to make it more suitable for use in a document resembling a model code.[3.4] The concept of Effective Peak Acceleration (EPA), related to the damageability of ground shaking, was introduced, and certain small zones of very high peak acceleration were eliminated, partly on the basis that their retention would constitute microzoning, which the committee had been instructed to avoid. The contours of the Algermissen-Perkins map were smoothed, so as to avoid the appearance of great precision, and in some locales the contours were shifted on the basis of more recent knowledge. The result was a map that retained the basic principles and trends of the Algermissen-Perkins map, but lacked the internal consistency of that map. It was estimated that the probability of not exceeding the contoured values of effective peak acceleration within 50 years was 80 percent to 95 percent. Maps of EPA for Alaska, Hawaii, Puerto Rico, and several territories were drawn using the best available information from various sources as guidance.

It was decided during the initial stages of development of ATC 3 that ground-shaking regionalization maps should take into account the distance from anticipated earthquake sources. This decision reflects the observation that the higher frequencies in ground motion attenuate more rapidly with distance than the lower frequencies. Thus, at distances of 60 miles or more from a major earthquake, flexible buildings may be more seriously affected than stiff buildings. To accomplish the objectives of the decision, it proved necessary to use separate ground motion parameters and, therefore, to prepare a separate map for each.

The two parameters used to characterize the intensity of design ground shaking were the Effective Peak Acceleration (EPA), and the Effective Peak Velocity (EPV). To best understand the meaning of EPA and EPV, they should be considered normalizing factors for construction of smoothed elastic response spectra for ground motions of normal duration. The EPA is proportional to spectral ordinates for periods in the range of 0.1 to 0.5 seconds, while the EPV is proportional to spectral ordinates at a period of about 1 second (Fig. 3.1). The constant of proportionality (for a spectrum corresponding to 5 percent of critical damping) is set at a value of 2.5 in both cases.

The EPA and EPV are related to peak ground acceleration and peak ground velocity, but are not necessarily the same as, or even proportional to, peak acceleration and velocity.

When very high frequencies are present in the ground motion, the EPA may be significantly less than the peak acceleration. This is consistent with the observation that chopping off the highest peak in an acceleration time history has very little effect upon the response spectrum computed from that motion, except at periods much shorter than those of interest in ordinary building practice. Furthermore, a rigid foundation tends to screen out very high frequencies in the free field motion. On the other hand, the EPV is generally greater than the peak velocity at large distances from a major earthquake. Ground motions increase in duration and become more periodic with distance. These factors tend to produce proportionately larger increases in that portion of the response spectrum represented by the EPV.

If an earthquake is of very short or very long duration, then it may be necessary to correct the EPA and EPV values to more closely represent the event. It is well documented that two motions having different durations but similar response spectra cause different degrees of damage—the damage being less for the shorter duration. In particular, there have been numerous instances where motions with very large accelerations and short duration have caused little or even no damage. Thus, when expressing the significance of a ground motion to design, it may be appropriate to decrease the EPA and EPV obtained from the elastic spectrum for a motion of short duration. On the other hand, for a motion of very long duration it may be appropriate to increase the EPA and EPV.

For ease in developing base shear formulas, it proved desirable to also express EPV by a dimensionless parameter (A_v), which is an acceleration coefficient. This parameter is referred to as the Effective Peak Velocity-Related Acceleration Coefficient. The relationship between EPV and A_v is given in Table 3-1 and may be expressed as follows:

$$A_v = \text{EPV (in./sec)} \times 0.4 / 12$$

TABLE 3-1. RELATIONSHIP BETWEEN EPV AND A_v

EFFECTIVE PEAK VELOCITY (in./sec)	VELOCITY-RELATED ACCELERATION COEFFICIENT, A_v
12	0.4
6	0.2
3	0.1
1.5	0.05

The ATC map for EPV was constructed by modifying the map for EPA. At all locations where a contour gives the highest EPA in a region, the EPV along that contour was set at the corresponding value of EPA. For example, the EPV was set at 12 in./sec along the contours for EPA = 0.4g. A study by McGuire,[3.12] based upon strong motion records from California, indicated that the distance required for EPV to decrease by a factor of 2 is about 80 miles. Thus, in the western part of the country, the contours for EPV = 6 in./sec were located about 80 miles outside the contours for EPV = 12 in./sec. Similarly, in Washington and Utah where the highest contour is at 0.2g, corresponding to EPV = 6 in./sec, the next contour for EPV = 3 in./sec was located about 80 miles away. The strong motion data available to McGuire were

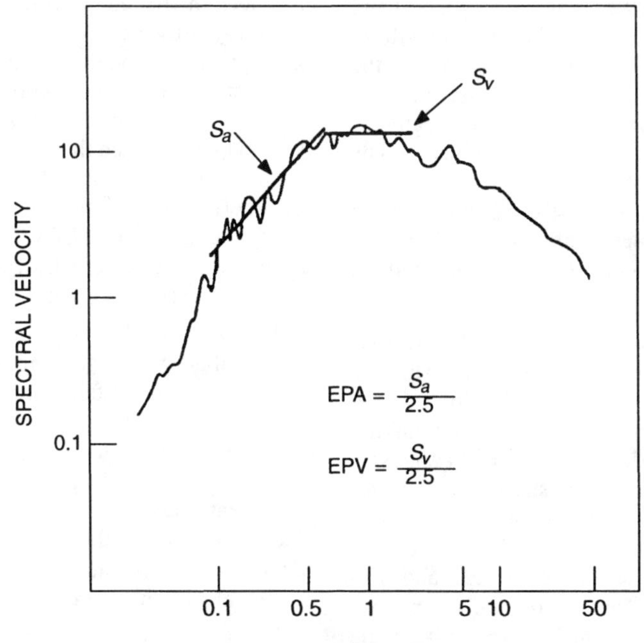

SCHEMATIC REPRESENTATION OF EFFECTIVE PEAK ACCELERATION AND EFFECTIVE PEAK VELOCITY

FIGURE 3.1

inadequate beyond a distance of about 100 miles. To estimate the attenuation of EPV beyond this distance, it was assumed that at large distances from an earthquake the logarithm of EPV would be linearly proportional to Modified Mercalli Intensity (MMI). Data from large earthquakes in California suggested that MMI decreased roughly linearly with distance, which would translate into EPV continuing to halve at equal increments of distance. Thus subsequent contours were also spaced at about 80 miles. For the midwest and east, reliance was placed entirely on information about the attenuation of MMI. Available studies indicated that MMI decays logarithmically with distance and that for the first 100 miles from a large earthquake the attenuation is roughly the same as in the west. The implication is that the distance required for EPV to halve increases with distance. Thus, starting from the contour for EPV = 6 in./sec centered on southeastern Missouri, the contour for EPV = 3 in./sec would be 80 miles away, and the contour for EPV = 1.5 in./sec would be about 160 miles beyond that. It was also stipulated that a contour for EPV should never fall inside the corresponding contour for EPA. After these various rules were applied to produce a set of contours for EPV, considerable smoothing was done and contours were joined where they fell close together. The EPV map had neither the detailed theoretical basis nor the internal consistency of the Algermissen-Perkins map for peak acceleration.

ANSI A58.1 – 1982

The ATC 3-06 map for Effective Peak Velocity-Related Acceleration Coefficient was selected as the basis for the zoning map in ANSI A58.1-1982.[3.3] The contour map was converted into a zoning map as follows.

A_v	Zone
> 0.4	4
0.2 to 0.4	3
0.1 to 0.2	2
0.05 to 0.1	1
< 0.05	0

There were several reasons for the choice of the map for EPV over that for EPA. First, the contours for EPA are very closely spaced in some regions. This is especially true in California and Nevada; use of the EPA map or the Algermissen-Perkins map would have meant that both states would be subdivided into five zones. Second, since only one map was to be used for the sake of simplicity, it seemed appropriate to use the more conservative map. Finally, use of the map for EPV meant a more modest change in the zonation of the country from that given in the 1979 UBC.[3.7]

The seismic zoning map in ANSI A58.1-1982, when compared with that in 1985 UBC, is seen to reduce the Z factor in many areas, especially in the eastern U.S.

UBC 1988 through 1997

The 1987 SEAOC Seismology Committee collaborated with a number of other organizations and individuals to produce a zone map of the United States for use in the 1988 UBC. There is only one zone map, but the philosophy embodying the two ATC maps was followed. In drawing the zone boundaries, both acceleration and velocity-related maps were consulted, and, if they disagreed, the one indicating the higher zone prevailed. The design base shear equation was modified so that the values of Z would correspond to the estimated values of effective peak acceleration. It was intended that the boundary between Zone 3 and Zone 4 correspond to a peak acceleration of 0.3g (or equivalent velocity) and the boundary between Zone 2 and Zone 3 correspond to 0.2g. The map is based principally on the ATC maps with modifications reflecting other sources of information, including the maps of acceleration and velocity published by Algermissen et al. in 1982.[3.13] The ATC maps and the maps by Algermissen et al. are based primarily on the historical record of earthquakes, which in California is short relative to the repeat time of major earthquakes even on the most active faults. To avoid the danger of missing areas that are potentially active but simply by chance have not shown activity during the short time of the historical record, geologic data were consulted, particularly data on fault slip rates. On the basis of geologic data, Zones 3 and 4 were extended in Southern California to encompass the Garlock fault. The modification was made with the intent to be consistent with the philosophy that the Z coefficient should correspond to ground motion values with a 10-percent probability of being exceeded in 50 years. The criterion was abandoned, however, in making many other modifications. It was abandoned in drawing the boundary between Zone 2 and Zone 3 in California and Oregon. The boundary was drawn so as to exclude Zone 2 from California in order to accommodate the desire to retain the structural detailing requirements of Zones 3 and 4 for the state. The criterion was also abandoned in the southwestern part of California and elsewhere to accommodate local opinion.

The 1988 seismic zoning map remained unchanged in the 1991 edition of the UBC. The 1994 UBC seismic zone map was somewhat different from the 1991 map. The notable changes from 1991 were as follows:

1. Parts of southern Arizona, including the city of Tucson, previously in Zone 1, were placed in Zone 2A.
2. Parts of the island of Oahu, including the city of Honolulu, previously in Zone 1, were placed in Zone 2A.
3. Western parts of the state of Oregon, previously in Zone 2B, were placed in Zone 3.
4. Western parts of the state of Washington, previously in Zone 2B, were placed in Zone 3.
5. The city of San Diego, previously in Zone 3, was placed in Zone 4.

Further changes in the seismic zones of the Hawaiian islands were made in the seismic zone map of 1997 UBC—the big island of Hawaii was assigned to Seismic Zone 4. Otherwise, the seismic zone map remained unchanged from the 1994 UBC.

NEHRP Provisions 1985-1994

The two maps developed during the ATC-3 project from a single map prepared by Algermissen and Perkins in 1976 were adopted into the 1985 edition of the NEHRP Provisions and were retained and used as the basis of seismic design through the 1994 edition.

In 1982, Algermissen and co-workers published a set of probabilistic maps for both acceleration and velocity using three different exposure times (thus three different levels of probability for excessive ground motions).[3.13] The basic procedure for generation of these new maps was not greatly different from that used for the 1976 map. The major difference was that the maps for ground velocity were prepared from basic data rather than being extrapolated from the acceleration map. The maps were thought to represent a step forward and a modified version was incorporated into the 1988 edition of the NEHRP Provisions through an appendix for trial use and evaluation. Presented in the ground motion maps of the contiguous United States were the expected maximum horizontal acceleration and velocity in rock for exposure times of 50 and 250 years (average return periods for the expected ground motions of 474 and 2372 years, respectively). The mapped accelerations have a 90-percent probability of not being exceeded in the appropriate exposure times.

Subsequently, attenuation equations became available that permitted construction of response spectra directly by means of separate attenuation equations for spectral ordinates for a number of periods. Use of response spectra in design avoids many of the problems associated with the peak response parameters that are in current widespread use. Because of these developments, interest turned toward formulation of design procedures that make use of these methods. Consequently, the use of the peak parameters was dropped from the "Appendix to Chapter 1" in the 1991 edition of the NEHRP Provisions in favor of furthering development of the spectral approach.

The hazard maps of the contiguous United States included for use with that appendix[3.14, 3.15] presented the spectral response accelerations at periods of 0.3 second and 1 second (as a percentage of the acceleration due to gravity), for an S_2 soil profile for exposure times of 50 and 250 years (average return periods of 474 and 2372 years, respectively). The mapped spectral response accelerations had a 90 percent probability of not being exceeded in the appropriate exposure times. More spectral ordinates could have been calculated, but Algermissen et al.[3.15] showed that the two ordinates mapped provided a reasonable approximation to a spectrum determined using all available ordinates.

Both the 50-year maps and the 250-year maps were updated by the USGS from the 1991 edition maps to reflect additional data and were included with the 1994 NEHRP Provisions. The Appendix to Chapter 1 of the 1994 NEHRP Provisions summarized unsuccessful attempts to develop so-called design value maps that were intended to replace the A_a and A_v maps in use since 1985. BSSC rejected the direct use of the 50-year spectral ordinate maps as design value maps for reasons stated in that appendix.

BOCA/NBC and SBC

The BOCA/*National Building Code* through its 1990 edition and the *Standard Building Code* through its 1991 edition adopted the national loading standard, ASCE 7 or ANSI A58.1, for seismic design purposes. The 1993 edition of the BOCA/NBC and the 1994 edition of the SBC directly adopted seismic design provisions based on the 1991 NEHRP Provisions. The 1996 and 1999 editions of the BOCA/NBC and the 1997 and 1999 editions of the SBC have retained 1991 NEHRP based provisions for seismic design. However, all four of these documents allow seismic design by ASCE 7-95 which has adopted seismic design provisions based on the 1994 NEHRP Provisions.

NEHRP Provisions 1997 and IBC 2000

As indicated above, the design ground motions in existing model codes and in the NEHRP Provisions through its 1994 edition are based on an estimated 90-percent probability of not being exceeded in 50 years (about a 500 year mean recurrence interval or return period). This has changed with the 1997 edition of the NEHRP Provisions and thus with IBC 2000.

Given the wide range in return periods for maximum-magnitude earthquakes in different parts of the Untied States (100 years in parts of California to 100,000 years or more in several other locations), the 1997 NEHRP Provisions focused on defining maximum considered earthquake ground motions for use in design. These ground motions may be determined in different manners depending on the seismicity of an individual region; however, they are uniformly defined as "the maximum level of earthquake ground shaking that is considered as reasonable to design buildings to resist." This definition facilitates the development of a design approach that provides approximately uniform protection against collapse throughout the United States.

It is widely recognized that the ground motion difference between 10-percent and 2-percent probabilities of being exceeded in 50 years in coastal California is typically smaller than the corresponding difference in inactive seismic areas such as the eastern and central United States. Figure 3.2, reproduced from the commentary to the 1997 NEHRP Provisions, plots the spectral acceleration at a period of 0.2 second, normalized at a 2-percent probability of being exceeded in 50 years (10 percent in 250 years), versus the annual frequency of being exceeded.

The figure shows that in coastal California, the ratio between the 0.2-second spectral accelerations for the 2- and 10-percent probabilities of being exceeded in 50 years is about 1.5, whereas the ratio varies between 2.0 and 5.0 in other parts of the United States. This is schematically represented for added clarity in Figure 3.3.

The question has therefore arisen as to whether the definition of ground motion based on a constant probability for the entire United States would result in similar levels of seismic safety for all buildings.

In addressing the question it was recognized that seismic safety is the result not only of the design earthquake ground motion definition, but also of such critical factors as proper site selection, structural design criteria, analysis procedures, adequacy of detailing and quality of construction.

The NEHRP 1997 seismic design provisions are based on the assessment that if a building experiences a level of ground motion 1.5 times the design level of the 1994 and prior Provisions, the building should have a low likelihood of collapse. Although quantification of this margin is dependent on the type of structure, detailing requirements, etc., the 1.5 factor was felt to be a conservative judgement.

As indicated above, in most U.S. locations, the 2-percent probability of ground motion values being exceeded in 50 years is more than 1.5 times those corresponding to a 10-percent probability within 50 years. This means that if the 10-percent probability of being exceeded in 50 years map were used as the design map and the ground motion corresponding to a 2-percent probability in 50 years were to occur, there would be a low confidence (particularly in the central and eastern U.S.) that buildings would not collapse because of these larger ground motions. Such a conclusion for most of the U.S. was not acceptable. The only location where the above results seemed to be acceptable was coastal California (ground motion corresponding to a 2-percent

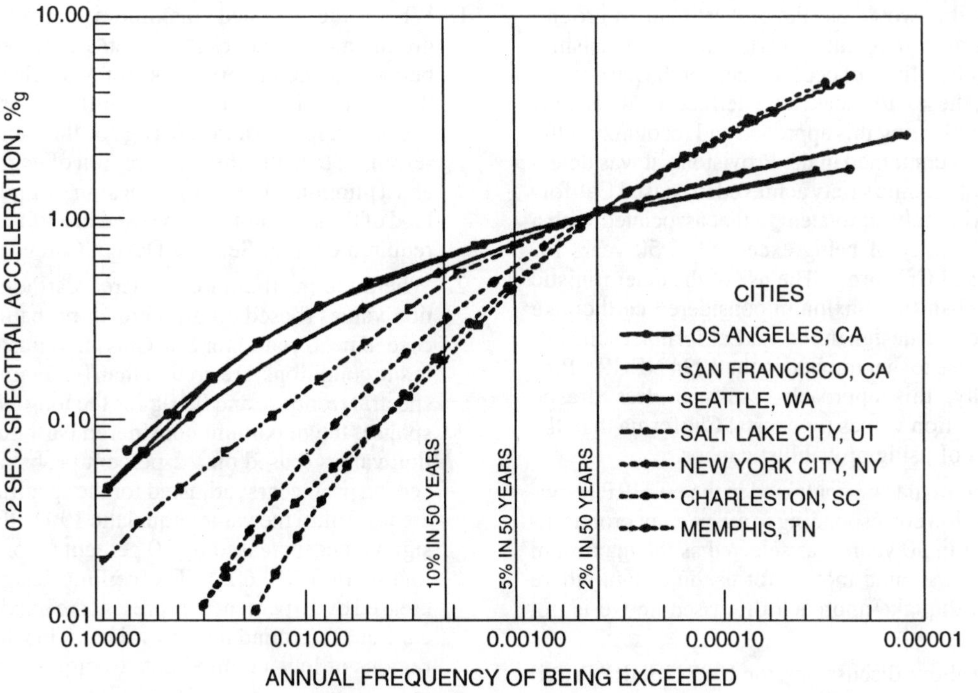

HAZARD CURVES FOR SELECTED CITIES

FIGURE 3.2

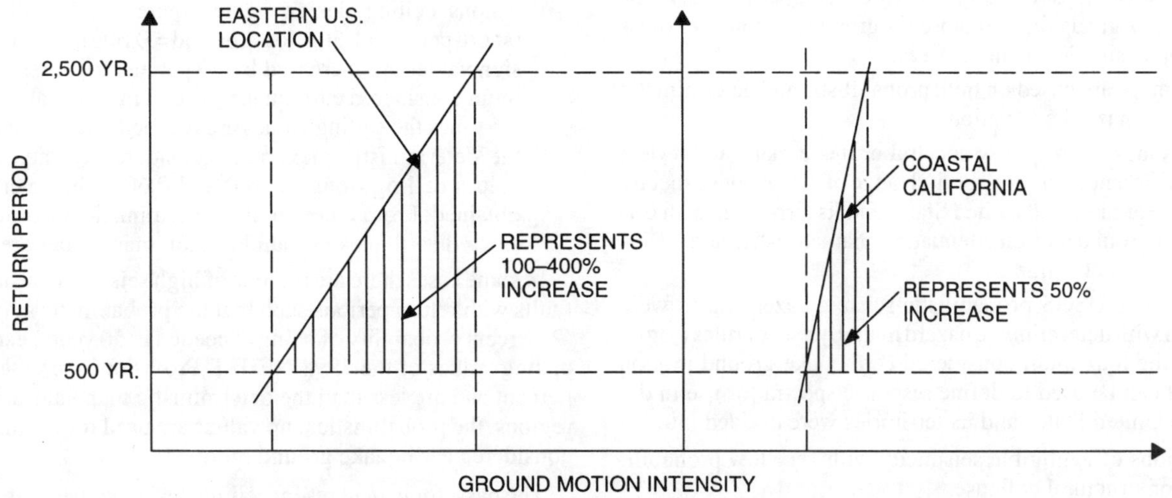

COMPARISON OF EARTHQUAKES WITH LONG AND SHORT RETURN PERIODS IN COASTAL CALIFORNIA AND EASTERN UNITED STATES

FIGURE 3.3

probability of being exceeded in 50 years is about 1.5 times that corresponding to a 10-percent probability in 50 years) where buildings have experienced levels of ground shaking equal to and above the design value.

Probabilistic seismic hazard maps from U.S. Geological Survey for Coastal California indicate that the ground motion corresponding to a 10-percent probability of being exceeded in 50 years is significantly different (in most cases larger) than the design ground motion values contained in the 1994 Provisions and in recent editions of the *Uniform Building Code*. One unique issue for coastal California is that the recurrence interval for the estimated maximum-magnitude earthquake is less than the recurrence interval represented by a 10-percent probability of being exceeded in 50 years. In other words, the recurrence interval for a maximum magnitude earthquake is 100 or 200 years versus 500 years.

Given that the maximum earthquake for many seismic faults in coastal California is fairly well known, a decision was made to develop a procedure that would use the best estimate of ground motion from maximum-magnitude earthquakes on seismic faults with higher probabilities of occurrence. For the purpose of the 1997 Provisions, these earthquakes are defined as "deterministic earthquakes." Following this approach and recognizing the inherent margin of 1.5 contained in the Provisions, it was determined that the level of seismic safety achieved in coastal California would be approximately equivalent to that associated with a 2- to 5-percent probability of being exceeded in 50 years for areas outside of coastal California. The use of the deterministic earthquakes to establish the maximum considered earthquake ground motions for use in design in coastal California results in a level of protection close to that implied in the 1994 NEHRP Provisions. Additionally, this approach results in less drastic changes to ground motion values for coastal California than the alternative approach of using probabilistic maps.

Based on the inherent margin contained in the NEHRP Provisions, the ground motion corresponding to a 2-percent probability of being exceeded in 50 years was selected as the maximum considered earthquake ground motion for use in design where the deterministic earthquake approach discussed above is not used.

To summarize the above discussions, the 1997 NEHRP Provisions maps reflect the following policy decisions that depart from past practice:

1. The maps define the maximum considered earthquake ground motion for use in design procedures,
2. The use of maps for design provides an approximately uniform margin against collapse for ground motions in excess of the design levels in all areas.
3. The maps are based on both probabilistic and deterministic seismic hazard evaluations.
4. The maps are response spectral ordinate maps and reflect the differences in short-period range of the response spectra for the areas of the United States and its territories with different ground motion attenuation characteristics and different recurrence times.

The various USGS probabilistic seismic hazard maps were combined with deterministic hazard maps by a set of rules (logic) to create the maximum considered earthquake ground motion maps that can be used to define response spectra for use in design. The United States and its territories were divided into:

1. Regions of negligible seismicity with very low probabilities of structural collapse,
2. Regions of low and moderate to high seismicity, and
3. Regions of high seismicity near known fault sources with short return periods.

The maximum considered earthquake ground motion maps for use in seismic design were developed by combining the regions as described below:

1. Where the mapped maximum considered earthquake ground motion values (based on a 2-percent probability of being exceeded in 50 years) for Site Class B, adjusted for the specific site conditions, are $\leq 0.25g$ for the short-period spectral response and $\leq 0.10g$ for the long-period spectral response, then the site is in a region of negligible seismicity and a minimum lateral force design of 1 percent of the dead load of the structure shall be used in addition to the detailing requirements for Seismic Design Category A structures.
2. Where the maximum considered earthquake ground motion values (based on a 2-percent probability of being exceeded in 50 years) for Site Class B, adjusted for the specific site conditions, are greater than 0.25g for the short-period spectral response and 0.10g for the long-period spectral response, the maximum considered earthquake ground motion values (based on a 2-percent probability of being exceeded in 50 years , adjusted for the specific site conditions) are used until the values equal the 1994 NEHRP ceiling design values increased by 50 percent (short-period = 1.50g, long-period = 0.60g). The ceiling design values are increased by 50 percent to represent the maximum considered earthquake ground motion values. This defines the sites in regions of low and moderate to high seismicity.
3. To shift from regions of low and moderate to high seismicity to regions of high seismicity with short return periods, the maximum considered earthquake ground motion values based on a 2-percent probability of being exceeded in 50 years are used until the values equal the 1994 NEHRP Provisions ceiling design values increased by 50 percent (short-period = 1.50g, long-period = 0.60g). The ceiling design values are increased by 50 percent to represent maximum considered earthquake ground motion values. When 1.5 times the ceiling values are reached, they are used until the deterministic maximum considered earthquake map values of 1.5g (long-period) and 0.60g (short-period) are obtained. From there on, the deterministic maximum considered earthquake ground motion map values are used.

In some cases there are regions of high seismicity near known faults with return periods such that the probabilistic map values (2-percent probability of being exceeded in 50 years) exceed the ceiling values of the 1994 NEHRP Provisions increased by 50 percent and are less than the deterministic map values. In these regions, the probabilistic map values are used for the maximum considered earthquake ground motions.

The basis for using present ceiling design values as the transition between the two regions is that experience has shown regularly configured, properly designed structures to have performed satisfactorily in past earthquakes.

The design level of ground motion is 1/1.5 or 2/3 times the maximum considered earthquake ground motion. Figure 3.4 schematically illustrates the definition of the design earthquake.

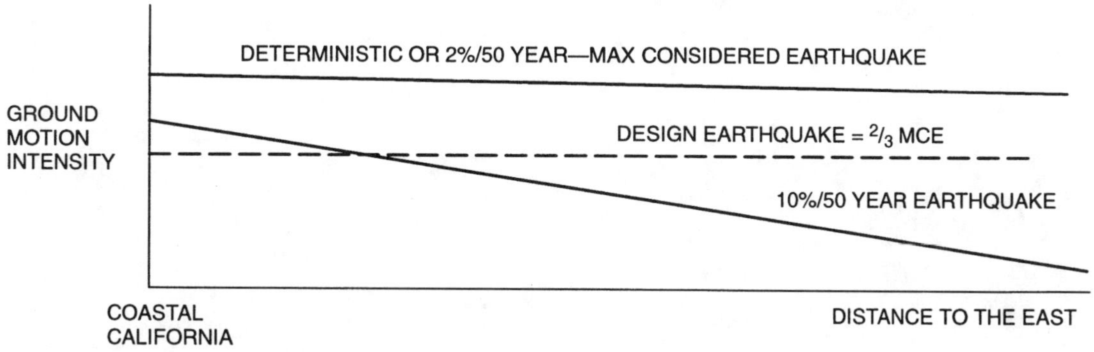

DEFINITION OF DESIGN EARTHQUAKE—SCHEMATIC

FIGURE 3.4

REFERENCES

[3.1] Ghosh, S.K., Domel, A.W., and Fanella, D.A., *Design of Concrete Buildings for Earthquake & Wind Forces,* Second Edition, Publication EB 113, Portland Cement Association, Skokie, IL, 1995

[3.2] Algermissen, S.T., "Seismic Risk Studies in the United States," "Proceedings of the Fourth World conference on Earthquake Engineering, Santiago, Chile, 1969, Vol. I., pp. A-1.14-A-1.27.

[3.3] American Society of Civil Engineers, *ASCE Standard Minimum Design Loads for Buildings and Other Structures,* ASCE 7-88 (formerly ANSI A58.1), New York, N.Y., 1990.

[3.4] Applied Technology Council, *Tentative Provisions for the Development of Seismic Regulations for Buildings,* ATC Publication ATC 3-06, NBS Special Publication 510, NSF Publication 78-8, U.S. Government Printing Office, Washington, D.C., 1978.

[3.5] Seismology Committee, Structural Engineers Association of California, *Recommended Lateral Force Requirements and Commentary,* San Francisco, CA, 1988.

[3.6] Building Seismic Safety Council, *NEHRP (National Earthquake Hazards Reduction Program) Recommended Provisions for the Development of Seismic Regulations for New Buildings and Other Structures,* Washington, D.C., 1997.

[3.7] Pacific Coast Building Officials Conference (later the International Conference of Building Officials), *Uniform Building Code,* Long Beach, CA (later Whittier, CA), 1935, 1952, 1967, 1970, 1973, 1976, 1979, 1982, 1985, 1988, 1991, 1994, 1997.

[3.8] Roberts, E.B., and Ulrich, F.P., "Seismological Activities of the U.S. Coast and Geodetic Survey in 1948," "Bulletin of the Seismological Society of America, Vol. 40, 1950, pp. 195-216.

[3.9] Roberts, E.B., and Ulrich, F.P., "Seismological Activities of the U.S. Coast and Geodetic Survey in 1949," Bulletin of the Seismological Society of America, Vol. 41, 1951, pp. 205-220.

[3.10] Schnabel, P.B., and Seed, H.B., "Acceleration in Rock for Earthquake in the Western United States," Bulletin of the Seismological Society of America, Vol. 63, 1973, pp. 501-516.

[3.11] Algermissen, S.T., and Perkins, D.M., *A Probabilistic Estimate of Maximum Acceleration in Rock in the Contiguous United States,* U.S. Geological Survey Open File Report 76-416, 1976, 45 pp.

[3.12] McGuire, R.K., *Seismic Structural Response Risk Analysis, Incorporating Peak Response Regression on Earthquake Magnitude and Distance,* Research Report R 74-51, Department of Civil Engineering, Massachusetts Institute of Technology, 1974, 371 pp.

[3.13] Algermissen, S.T., Perkins, D.M., Thenhaus, P.C., Hansen, S.L., and Bender, B.L., *A Probabilistic Estimate of Maximum Acceleration and Velocity in Rock in the Contiguous United States,* U.S. Geological Survey Open File Report 82-1033, 1982, 99 pp.

[3.14] Algermissen, S.T., Perkins, D.M., Thenhaus, P.C., Hansen, S.L., and Bender, B.L., *Probabilistic Earthquake Acceleration and Velocity Maps for the United States and Puerto Rico,* U.S. Geological Survey, Miscellaneous Field Studies Map MF-2120, 1990.

[3.15] Algermissen, S.T., Leyendecker, E.V., Bollinger, G.A., Donovan, N.C., Ebel, J.E., Joyner, W.B., Luft, R.W., and Singh, J.P., *"Probabilistic Ground-Motion Hazard Maps of Response Spectral Ordinates for the United States,"* Proceedings of the Fourth International Conference on Seismic Ordinates for the United States, Stanford University, Vol. II, 1991, pp. 687-694.

APPENDIX 4

CONSIDERATION OF SITE SOIL CHARACTERISTICS

Seismic Design Provisions Prior to the 1994 NEHRP

The 1976 edition of the *Uniform Building Code,*[4.1] the seismic design provisions of which were based on the 1974 edition of the SEAOC Blue Book,[4.2] represents the beginning of relatively modern seismic design provisions in the United States.

An S coefficient was introduced into the design base shear formula of the 1976 UBC and the 1974 SEAOC Blue Book to account for the variability of soil conditions. The commentary to Blue Book editions prior to 1974 pointed out that "The absence of a soil factor, S, should not be interpreted as meaning that the effect of soil conditions on building response is not important." There had in fact been consideration of the soil-dependence of the design base shear in early editions of the UBC. According to Reference 4.3, "it is interesting to note that early seismic design codes contained provisions for increased design lateral forces for buildings sited on poor soils – provisions that were to disappear in 1949 [this reference is to the 1949 UBC], only to be reintroduced in 1974 [this reference is to the 1974 Blue Book]."

The approach used in the 1974 Blue Book was to consider the possibility of resonance between the structure and the soil by comparing the natural period of vibration of the structure, T, and the fundamental period of the site, T_S. The following expression, introduced into the 1976 UBC from the 1974 Blue Book, was retained in *Uniform Building Code* editions through 1985[4.1] (Fig. 4.1):

Shortly after the 1974 Blue Book was completed, several studies appeared, which included some statistical treatment of strong motion response spectra recorded on different types of soil deposits.[4.4, 4.5, 4.6] By using these results it was possible to develop a more direct code formulation. Such a direct approach was adopted by ATC 3-06,[4.7] which considered three soil profile types to be different enough in seismic response to warrant separate seismic coefficients (S factors). The direct approach was adopted as an alternative to the site-structure resonance approach in the 1988 UBC.[4.1] Experience from the 1985 Mexico earthquake prompted the addition of a fourth soil profile type in the 1988 NEHRP Provisions[4.8] and the 1988 UBC. The four soil profile types are described in the 1994 NEHRP Commentary as follows:

1. Soil Profile Type S_1 – a soil profile with either 1) rock of any characteristic, either shale-like or crystalline in nature, that has a shear wave velocity greater than 2,500 ft/sec (762 m/sec), or 2) stiff soil conditions where the soil depth is less than 200 ft (61 m) and the soil types overlying the rock are stable deposits of sands, gravels, or stiff clays.
2. Soil Profile Type S_2 – a soil profile with deep cohesionless or stiff clay conditions where the soil depth exceeds 200 feet and the soil types overlying rock are the stable deposits of sands, gravels, or stiff clays.

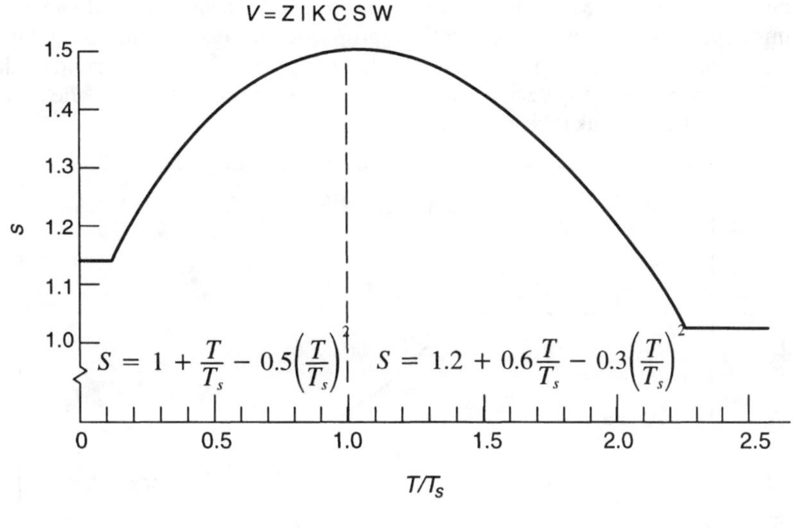

$S = 1.0 + T/T_S - 0.5\,(T/T_S)^2$ for $T/T_S \leq 1.0$ $\quad T \geq 0.3$ sec.

$= 1.2 + 0.6T/T_S - 0.3(T/T_S)^2$ for $T/T_S > 1.0$ $\quad 0.5 < T_S < 2.5$ sec.

> 1

$= 1.5$ when T_S is not properly established.

SITE COEFFICIENT, *S*, OF 1985 AND EARLIER UBC EDITIONS

FIGURE 4.1

3. Soil Profile Type S_3 – A soil profile containing 20- to 49-foot-thick soft-to-medium-stiff clays with or without intervening layers of cohesionless soils.
4. Soil Profile Type S_4 – A soil profile characterized by shear wave velocity of less than 500 ft/sec (152 m/sec) containing more than 40 feet (12 m) of soft clays or silts.

The above definitions are close to those of the 1994 UBC.

1994 NEHRP

The need for improvement in codifying site effects was discussed at a 1991 National Center for Earthquake Engineering Research [NCEER] workshop[4.9] that made several general recommendations. A committee was formed during that workshop to pursue resolution of pending issues and develop specific code recommendations. The committee collected information, guided related research, discussed the issues, and organized a November 1992 Site Response Workshop in Los Angeles.[4.10] This workshop discussed the results of a number of empirical and analytical studies and approved consensus recommendations that formed the basis of extensive modifications to the consideration of site effects in the 1994 NEHRP Provisions.[4.8] The basis is summarized here from the 1994 NEHRP Commentary.

In the 1985 Mexico and 1989 Loma Prieta earthquakes, low maximum rock accelerations of 0.05g to 0.10g were amplified by factors of about 1.5 to 4 at sites containing soft clay layers ranging in thickness from a few feet to more than a hundred feet and having depths of rock up to several hundred feet. The average amplification factor for soft soil sites tends to decrease as the rock acceleration increases – from 2.5 to 3 at low accelerations to about 1.0 for a rock acceleration of 0.4g. This effect is directly related to the nonlinear strain behavior of the soil.

Low peak accelerations can be amplified several times at soil sites, especially those containing soft layers and where the rock is very deep. On the other hand, larger peak accelerations can be amplified to a lesser degree and can even be slightly deamplified at very high rock accelerations. In addition to peak rock acceleration, a number of factors including soil stiffness and layering play a role in the degree of amplification. One important factor is the impedance contrast between soil and underlying rock.

Earthquake records on soft to medium clay sites subjected to low acceleration levels indicate that the soil/rock amplification factors for long-period spectral accelerations can be significantly larger than those for peak accelerations. Furthermore, the largest amplification often occurs at the natural period of the soil deposit. In Mexico City in 1985, the maximum rock acceleration was amplified four times by a soft clay deposit that would have been classified as S_4, whereas the spectral amplitudes were about 15 to 20 times larger than on rock at a period near 2 seconds. In other parts of the valley where the clay is thicker, the spectral amplitudes at periods ranging between 3 and 4 seconds were amplified about 15 times, but the damage was less due to the low rock motion intensity at these very long periods. Records obtained at some soft clay sites during the 1989 Loma Prieta earthquake indicated a maximum amplification of long-period spectral amplitudes on the order of three to six times. At least at one site, the largest soil/rock amplification appeared to occur at the natural period of the soil deposit, similar to the occurrence in Mexico City.

Two Factor Approach. To summarize the above discussion, soil sites generally cause a higher amplification of rock spectral accelerations at long periods than at shorter periods and, for a service level of shaking ($A_a \approx A_v \approx 0.4$), the shorter-period amplification or deamplification is small. However, short-period accelerations including the peak acceleration can be amplified several times, especially at soft sites subject to low levels of shaking. The latter evidence suggested a two-factor approach sketched in Fig. 4.2. In this approach, adopted in the 1994 NEHRP Provisions, the short-period plateau, of height proportional to A_a, is multiplied by a short-period site coefficient, F_a, and the curve proportional to A_v/T is multiplied by a long-period site coefficient, F_v. Both F_a and F_v depend on the site conditions and on the level of shaking, defined by the A_a and A_v coefficients, respectively.

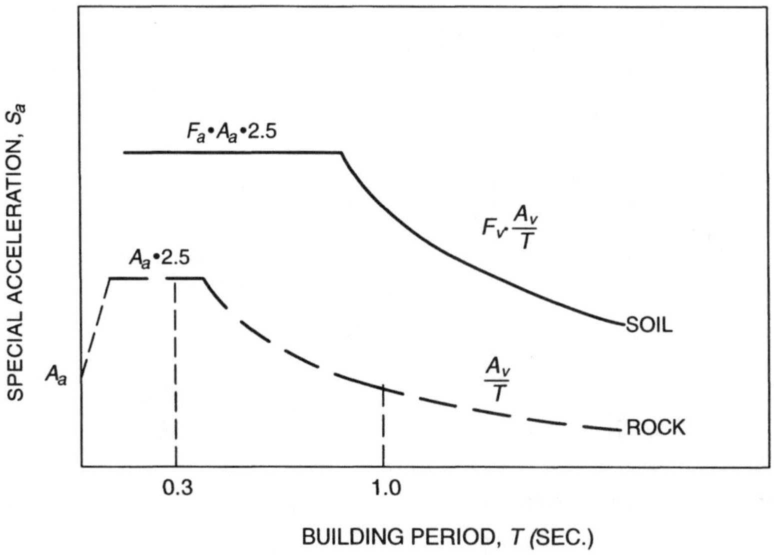

TWO-FACTOR APPROACH TO LOCAL SITE RESPONSE

FIGURE 4.2

Strong-motion records obtained from the Loma Prieta earthquake provided important quantitative measures of the in-site response of a variety of geological deposits to damaging levels of shaking. The data provided empirical estimates of the site coefficients F_a and F_v as a function of mean shear wave velocity for input ground motion near 0.1g. Extrapolation of amplification estimates at the 0.1g level as derived from the Loma Prieta data had, of necessity, to be based on laboratory and theoretical modeling considerations because few or no strong-motion records have been obtained at higher levels of motion, especially on soft soil deposits. Fortunately, it was found that the functional relationship between the logarithms of amplification and mean shear wave velocity is a straight line.

Site Class Definition. In view of the above, the site categories in the 1994 NEHRP Provisions are defined in terms of the average shear wave velocity in the top 100 feet of the profile, v_s. If the shear wave velocities are available for a site, they should be used.

However, in recognition of the fact that in many cases the shear wave velocities are not available, alternative definitions of the site categories are also included in the 1994 NEHRP Provisions. They use the standard penetration resistance for cohesionless soil layers and the undrained shear strength for cohesive soil layers. These alternative definitions are rather conservative since the correlation between site amplification and these geotechnical parameters is less certain than that with v_s. There will be cases where the values of F_a and F_v will be smaller if the site category is based on v_s rather than on geotechnical parameters. Also, the 1994 NEHRP Commentary cautions the reader not to interpret the site category definitions as implying any specific numerical correlation between shear wave velocity on the one hand and standard penetration resistance or shear strength on the other.

Studies have indicated that earthquake motions on outcrops of "hard rock" tend to be smaller than on outcrops of "regular rock" by 10 to 40 percent at both short and long periods (except at very small periods under about 0.2 second where the reverse may be true). On the basis of these studies and observations, the 1994 NEHRP Provisions incorporates the difference between "regular" rock, B, and "hard" rock of $v_s > 5000$ ft/sec by defining a new "hard rock" site category, A, and assigning to it site factors $F_a = F_v = 0.8$.

Dynamic Site Response Analysis

The following addition to the 2000 NEHRP Provisions Commentary has been proposed. While it may not become "official" for some time, it is being made available to the reader (with the permission of the Building Seismic Safety Council) because no guidance on the topic is readily available. Components of a dynamic site response analysis include: 1) modeling the soil profile; 2) selecting rock motions to input into the soil profile; and 3) conducting a site response analysis and interpreting the results.

1. Modeling the soil profile: Typically, a one-dimensional soil column extending from the ground surface to bedrock is adequate to capture first-order site-response characteristics. However, two- to three-dimensional models may be considered for critical projects when two or three-dimensional wave propagation effects may be significant (e.g., in basins). The soil layers in a one-dimensional model are characterized by their total unit weights, shear wave velocities from which low-strain (maximum) shear moduli may be obtained and by relationships defining the nonlinear shear stress-strain relationships of the soils. The required relationships for analysis are often in the form of curves that describe the variation of shear modulus with shear strain (modulus reduction curves) and by curves that describe the variation of damping with shear strain (damping curves). In a two- or three-dimensional model, compression wave velocities or moduli or Poissons ratios are also required. In an analysis to estimate the effects of liquefaction on soil site response, the nonlinear soil model must also incorporate the buildup of soil pore water pressures and the consequent effects on reducing soil stiffness and strength. Typically, modulus reduction curves and damping curves are selected on the basis of published relationships for similar soils.[4.11–4.16] Site-specific laboratory dynamic tests on soil samples to establish nonlinear soil characteristics can be considered where published relationships are judged to be inadequate for the types of soils present at the site. The uncertainty in soil properties should be estimated, especially the uncertainty in the selected maximum shear moduli and modulus reduction and damping curves.
2. Selecting input rock motions: Acceleration time histories that are representative of horizontal rock motions at the site are required as input to the soil model. Unless a site-specific analysis is carried out to develop the rock response spectrum at the site, the Maximum Considered Earthquake (MCE) response spectrum for Site Class B rock can be defined using the general procedure described in Section 4.1.2 (IBC Section 1615.1). For hard rock (Site Class A), the spectrum may be adjusted using the site factors in Tables 4.1.2.4a and b [IBC Tables 1615.1.2 (1) and 1615.1.2 (2)]. For profiles having great depths of soil above site class A or B rock, consideration can be given to defining the base of the soil profile and the input rock motions at a depth at which soft rock or very stiff soil of Site Class C is encountered. In such cases, the MCE rock response spectrum may be taken as the spectrum for Site Class C defined using the site factors in Tables 4.1.2.4a and b. Several acceleration time histories, typically at least four, recorded during earthquakes having magnitudes and distances that significantly contribute to the site seismic hazard should be selected for analysis. The U.S. Geological Survey results for de-aggregation of seismic hazard (website address: http://geohazards. cr.usgs.gov/eq/.) can be used to evaluate the dominant magnitudes and distances contributing to the hazard. Prior to analysis, each time history should be scaled so that its spectrum is at the approximate level of the MCE rock response spectrum in the period range of interest. It is desirable that the average of the response spectra of the suite of scaled input time histories be approximately at the level of the MCE rock response spectrum in the period range of interest. Because rock response spectra are defined at the ground surface rather than at a depth below a soil deposit, the rock time histories should be input to the analysis as outcropping rock motions rather than at the soil-rock interface.
3. Site response analysis and results interpretation: Analytical methods may be equivalent linear or nonlinear. Frequently

used computer programs for one-dimensional analysis include the equivalent linear program SHAKE[4.17] and nonlinear programs DESRA-2,[4.18] MARDES,[4.19] SUMDES,[4.20] D-MOD,[4.21] and TESS.[4.22] For analysis of liquefaction effects on site response, computer programs incorporating pore water pressure development (effective stress analyses) must be used (e.g., DESRA-2, SUMDES, D-MOD and TESS). Response spectra of output motions at the ground surface should be calculated and the ratios of response spectra of ground surface motions to input outcropping rock motions should also be calculated. Typically, an average of the response spectral ratio curves is obtained and multiplied by the MCE rock response spectrum to obtain the MCE soil design response spectrum. Sensitivity analyses to evaluate effects of soil property uncertainties should be conducted and considered in developing the design response spectrum.

REFERENCES

[4.1] Pacific Coast Building Officials Conference (later the International Conference of Building Officials), *Uniform Building Code*, Long Beach, CA (later Whittier, CA), 1935, 1952, 1967, 1970, 1973, 1976, 1979, 1982, 1985, 1988, 1991, 1994, 1997.

[4.2] Seismology Committee, Structural Engineers Association of California, *Recommended Lateral Force Requirements and Commentary,* San Francisco, CA, 1988.

[4.3] Applied Technology Council, *A Critical Review of Current Approaches to Earthquake-Resistant Design,* Publication ATC 34, Redwood City, CA, 1995.

[4.4] Mohraj, B.J., "A Study of Earthquake Response Spectra for Different Geologic Conditions," Bulletin of the Seismological Society of America, Vol. 66, No.3, June 1976, pp. 915-935.

[4.5] Seed, H.B., Ugas, C., and Lysmer, J., "Site Dependent Spectra for Earthquake-Resistant Design," Bulletin of the Seismological Society of America, Vol. 66, No.1, February 1976, pp. 221-224.

[4.6] Kiremidjian, A.S., and Shah, H.C., "Probabilistic Site Dependent Response Spectra," Journal of the Structural Division, Proceedings ASCE, Vol. 106, No. ST1, January 1980, pp. 69-86.

[4.7] Applied Technology Council, *Tentative Provisions for the Development of Seismic Regulations for Buildings,* ATC Publication ATC 3-06, NBS Special Publication 510, NSF Publication 78-8, U.S. Government Printing Office, Washington, D.C., 1978.

[4.8] Building Seismic Safety Council, *NEHRP (National Earthquake Hazards Reduction Program) Recommended Provisions for the Development of Seismic Regulations for New Buildings and Other Structures,* Washington, D.C., 1885, 1888, 1991, 1994, 1997.

[4.9] Whitman, R., Editor, *Proceedings of the Site Effects Workshop: October 2-24, 1991,* Report NCEER – 92-0006, National Center for Earthquake Engineering Research, Buffalo, New York, 1992.

[4.10] Martin, G.M., Editor, *Proceedings of the NCEER/SEAOC/BSSC Workshop on Site Response During Earthquakes and Seismic Code Provisions, November 18-20, 1992,* University of Southern California, Los Angeles, 1994.

[4.11] Seed, H.B., and Idriss, I.M., *Soil Moduli and Damping Factors for Dynamic Response Analyses,* Report No. EERC 70-10, University of California, Berkeley, Earthquake Engineering Research Center, 1970.

[4.12] Seed, H.B., Wong, R.T., Idriss, I.M., and Tokimatsu, K., "Moduli and Damping Factors for Dynamic Analyses of Cohesionless Soils," Journal of Geotechnical Engineering, ASCE, Vol. 112, No. 11, 1986, pp. 1016-1032.

[4.13] Sun, J.I., Golesorkhi, R., and Seed, H.B., *Dynamic Moduli and Damping Ratios for Cohesive Soils,* Report No. UCB/EERC-88/15, University of California, Berkeley, Earthquake Engineering Research Center, 1988.

[4.14] Vucetic, M., and Dobry, R., "Effect of Soil Plasticity on Cyclic Response," Journal of Geotechnical Engineering, ASCE, Vol. 117, No. 1, 1991, pp. 89-107.

[4.15] Electric Power Research Institute, *Guidelines for Determining Design Basis Ground Motions,* Report No. EPRI TR-102293, Electric Power Research Center, Palo Alto, California, 1993.

[4.16] Kramer, S.L., *Geotechnical Earthquake Engineering,* Prentice Hall, New Jersey, 1996.

[4.17] Idriss, I.M., and Sun, J.I., User's Manual for SHAKE91, Center for Geotechnical Modeling, Department of Civil and Environmental Engineering, University of California, Davis, 1992, 13 p. (plus Appendices).

[4.18] Lee, M.K.W., and Finn, W.D.L., DESRA-2, *Dynamic Effective Stress Response Analysis of Soil Deposits with Energy Transmitting Boundary including Assessment of Liquefaction Potential,* Soil Mechanics Series No. 36, Department of Civil Engineering, University of British Columbia, Vancouver, Canada, 1978, 60 p.

[4.19] Chang, C.-Y., Mok, C.M., Power, M.S., and Tang, Y.K., *Analysis of Ground Response at Lotung Large-Scale Soil-Structure Interaction Experiment Site,* Report No. NP-7306-SL, Electric Power Research Institute, Palo Alto, California, 1991.

[4.20] Li, X.S., Wang, Z.L., and Shen, C.K., SUMDES, *A Nonlinear Procedure for Response Analysis of Horizontally-Layered Sites Subjected to Multi-Directional Earthquake Loading,* Department of Civil Engineering, University of California, Davis, 1992.

[4.21] Matasovic, N., *Seismic Response of Composite Horizontally-Layered Soil Deposits,* Ph.D. Dissertation, Civil and Environmental Engineering Department, University of California, Los Angeles, 1993, 452 p.

[4.22] Pyke, R.M., *TESS: A Computer Program for Nonlinear Ground Response Analyses.* TAGA Engineering Systems & Software, Lafayette, California, 1992.

APPENDIX 5

IMPACT OF THE SEISMIC DESIGN PROVISIONS OF THE INTERNATIONAL BUILDING CODE

This appendix examines the potential impact of the First (2000) Edition of the *International Building Code* (IBC) on seismic design across the United States. This is done through a generalized comparison of detailing requirements and seismic design forces against the current code requirements in a number of specific locations. Several locations are chosen in the area of influence of each existing model code.

SEISMIC DESIGN CATEGORY — SEISMIC PERFORMANCE CATEGORY — SEISMIC ZONE

Comparison of IBC and BOCA/NBC

For a number of chosen specific locations in BOCA/NBC[5.1] territory, the effective peak acceleration coefficient, A_a, and the effective peak velocity-related acceleration coefficient, A_v (see Appendix 3), were determined from the contour maps of the BOCA/NBC (essentially the same as the contour maps of the 1991 NEHRP Provisions[5.2]). The seismic performance categories of standard-occupancy (Seismic Hazard Exposure Group I) structures at those locations were then determined from Table 5.1, and are listed in Table 5.2.

TABLE 5.1. SEISMIC PERFORMANCE CATEGORIES OF BOCA/NBC AND SBC

	SEISMIC HAZARD EXPOSURE GROUP		
VALUES OF A_v	I	II	III
$0.20 \le A_v$	D	D	E
$0.15 \le A_v < 0.20$	C	D	D
$0.10 \le A_v < 0.15$	C	C	C
$0.05 \le A_v < 0.10$	B	B	C
$A_v < 0.05$	A	A	A

For the same locations, the mapped (MCE) spectral response accelerations (for Site Class B) at short periods, S_S, and at 1-second period, S_1, were next determined from the contour maps included in the 2000 IBC (essentially the same as the contour maps of the 1997 NEHRP Provisions[5.2]). The design spectral response accelerations, S_{DS} and S_{D1}, were then determined for various site classes by applying the site coefficients of the 2000 IBC tables and the multiplier of two-thirds ($^2/_3$). With these S_{DS} and S_{D1} values, the seismic design categories assigned to standard-occupancy (Seismic Use Group I) structures on different site classes were established using 2000 IBC Tables 1616.3-1 and 1616.3-2. The higher SDC given by Table 1616.3-1 or 1616.3-2 for each site class at each location is listed in Table 5.2.

Table 5.3 shows approximate equivalency of the seismic performance categories (SPC) of the BOCA/NBC and the SBC, the seismic zones of the UBC, and the seismic design categories (SDC) of the IBC, in terms of detailing requirements and other restrictions that are triggered by the SPC, the seismic zone or the SDC.

TABLE 5.2. SEISMIC DESIGN CATEGORY (SDC) OF 2000 IBC vs. SEISMIC PERFORMANCE CATEGORY (SPC) OF 1999 BOCA/NBC

		2000 IBC				
		SITE CLASS				
	1999 BOCA/NBC	A	B	C	D	E
LOCATION	SPC	SDC				
Washington, D.C.	A	A	A	B	B	C
Chicago, IL	A	A	A	B	B	C
Baltimore, MD	A	A	A	B	B	C
Boston. MA	C	B	B	B	C	D
New York, NY	C	B	B	C	C	D
Cincinnati, OH	B	A	A	B	C	D
Philadelphia, PA	B	B	B	B	C	C
Richmond, VA	B	A	B	B	B	C

TABLE 5.3. APPROXIMATE EQUIVALENCY IN TERMS OF DETAILING REQUIREMENTS AND OTHER RESTRICTIONS

BOCA/NBC (1993, 1996, 1999), SBC (1994, 1997, 1999), NEHRP PROVISIONS PRIOR TO 1997	UBC THROUGH 1997	IBC 2000, NEHRP 1997
Seismic Performance Category	Seismic Zone	Seismic Design Category
A, B	0, 1	A, B
C	2A, 2B	C
D, E	3, 4	D, E, F

Note: This table does not imply that SPC A is equivalent to Zone 0, and SPC B to Zone 1. What it means to convey is that seismic detailing requirements in Zones 0 and 1 are generally equivalent to those for buildings assigned to SPC A or B.

A comparison of the soil-independent seismic performance categories and the soil-dependent seismic design categories for the various locations is instructive indeed. As can be seen from Table 5.2, in Cincinnati for instance, structures that are assigned to SPC B under the BOCA/NBC may have to be assigned to SDC A, B, C, or D under the IBC, depending upon soil conditions at the building site. The default Site Class D is of particular interest. If the soil conditions at a site are not known or, in other words, the average shear wave velocity or standard penetration resistance or unconfined shear strength has not been determined for the top 100 feet of a site, as required by Table 1615.1.1 of the 2000 IBC, design must be carried out assuming Site Class D. Table 5.2 shows that a standard-occupancy structure in Cincinnati on Site Class D would be assigned to IBC SDC C, thus requiring the equivalent of UBC Seismic Zone 2 detailing. A standard-occupancy structure at the same location on Site Class E would be assigned to IBC SDC D, thus requiring the equivalent of UBC Seismic Zone 3 or 4 detailing. Other restrictions triggered by higher seismic design categories would obviously also come into play. It should be noted, however, that comments here are made without specific knowledge of existing soil types at the various locations. For instance, Site Class E may or may not exist in and around Cincinnati.

Comparison of IBC and UBC

For a number of chosen, specific locations in UBC territory, the seismic zone was determined using the Seismic Zone map of the 1997 UBC.[5.3] The near-source factors, N_a and N_v, were also determined, if applicable. These are given in Table 5.4.

For the same locations, the seismic design categories assigned to standard-occupancy (Seismic Use Group I) structures, founded on the different site classes, were established as indicated above (see comparison of the IBC and BOCA/NBC), and are also given in Table 5.4.

Table 5.4 shows that in many of the Zone 3 and 4 locations examined, site-specific geotechnical investigation will be required on Site Class E. This is currently not required by the 1997 UBC. In Sacramento, on firmer soils, only the equivalent of Zone 2 detailing will be required under the 2000 IBC. This is because the seismicity at the location has been judged to be lower by the IBC. In many of the low-seismicity locations examined, for instance Denver (Seismic Zone 1) and Houston (Zone 0), the equivalent of Zone 2 detailing will be required to be done on Site Class E. It should be noted again that these comments are made without specific knowledge of existing soil types at the various locations. For instance, while it is known that Site Class A does not exist in California, Site Class B may or may not exist in and around Sacramento.

Comparison of IBC and SBC

For a number of chosen, specific locations in SBC territory, the effective peak acceleration coefficient, A_a, and the effective peak velocity-related acceleration coefficient, A_v, were determined from the contour maps of the SBC[5.4] (essentially the same as the contour maps of the 1991 NEHRP Provisions).

TABLE 5.4. SEISMIC DESIGN CATEGORY OF 2000 IBC vs. 1997 UBC SEISMIC ZONE

		2000 IBC				
		Site Class				
	1997 UBC	A	B	C	D	E
LOCATION	Zone	SDC				
West LA, (N_a = 1.3, N_v = 1.6)	4	E*	E*	E*	E*	**
San Francisco	4	D	D	D	D	**
Berkeley, (N_a = 1.5, N_v = 2.0)	4	E*	E*	E*	E*	**
Denver	1	A	A	A	B	C
Sacramento	3	B	C	D	D	D
St. Paul	0	A	A	A	A	B
Seattle	3	D	D	D	D	**
Portland	3	D	D	D	D	D
Houston	0	A	A	A	B	B

*F in the case of Seismic Use Group III buildings.

**Site-specific geotechnical investigation required per 2000 IBC.

TABLE 5.5. SEISMIC DESIGN CATEGORY OF 2000 IBC vs. SEISMIC PERFORMANCE CATEGORY OF 1999 SBC

LOCATION	1997 SBC SPC	2000 IBC SITE CLASS A (SDC)	B	C	D	E
Birmingham, AL	B	B	B	C	C	D
Atlanta, GA	B	A	B	B	C	D
Orlando, FL	A	A	A	A	B	B
Little Rock, AR	B	B	B	C	D	D
New Orleans, LA	A	A	A	A	B	B
Nashville, TN	B	B	B	C	D	D
Charlotte, NC	C	B	B	C	D	D
Charleston, SC	C	D	D	D	D	**

**Site-specific geotechnical investigation required per 2000 IBC.

The seismic performance categories of standard-occupancy (Seismic Hazard Exposure Group I) structures at these locations were then determined from Table 5.1, and are listed in Table 5.5.

For the same locations, the seismic design categories assigned to standard-occupancy (Seismic Use Group I) structures, founded on the different site classes, were established following the procedure outlined above under comparison of the IBC and BOCA/NBC. These are also given in Table 5.5.

A comparison of the soil-independent seismic performance categories and the soil-dependent seismic design categories for the various locations appear to indicate that the IBC may have a greater impact on seismic design and construction in cities in the SBC territory than elsewhere. In making these comparisons, the default Site Class D is of particular interest, as noted earlier under comparison of the IBC and BOCA/NBC. It may be seen that in the City of Atlanta, standard-occupancy structures are now in SPC B, requiring no special seismic detailing. Under the IBC, such structures will be assigned to SDC C, if founded on the default Site Class D, requiring the equivalent of UBC Seismic Zone 2 detailing. If founded on Site Class E, the same structures will be assigned to SDC D, requiring the equivalent of UBC Seismic Zone 3, 4 detailing. Other restrictions triggered by higher seismic design categories would obviously also come into play. In the City of Charlotte, standard-occupancy structures are now in SPC C, requiring the equivalent of Seismic Zone 2 detailing. Under the IBC, the same structures will be assigned to SDC D, if founded on default Site Class D or the softer Site Class E, thus requiring the equivalent of UBC Seismic Zone 3, 4 detailing. In the City of Charleston, SC, as in Charlotte, standard-occupancy structures are now assigned to SPC C, requiring the equivalent of UBC Seismic Zone 2 detailing. Under the IBC, the same structures will be assigned to SDC D, irrespective of the site class they are founded on, thus requiring the equivalent of UBC Seismic Zone 3, 4 detailing. This is because the seismicity at the location has been judged to be higher by the IBC.

It ought to be noted yet again that the above comments are made without specific knowledge of existing soil types at the various locations. For instance, Site Class E may or may not exist in and around Atlanta.

DESIGN BASE SHEAR

Comparison of IBC and BOCA/NBC

The ratio of the upper-bound (short-period) design base shears of the 2000 IBC and the BOCA/NBC (1993, 1996 and 1999 editions) is made up of three parts: 1) $S_{DS}/2.5A_a$, which is a function of the seismicity and the soil characteristics at a particular location, 2) the ratio of R-values of the BOCA/NBC and the IBC for the same structural system, and 3) the I-value of the IBC (I is not used in the 1993 through 1999 editions of the BOCA/NBC). For the specific locations in BOCA territory chosen for the comparisons of Table 5.2, the $S_{DS}/2.5A_a$ ratios for different site classes are given in Table 5.6. The values in Table 5.6 represent the ratios of the upper-bound design base shears of the 2000 IBC and the BOCA/NBC (1993, 1996 and 1999 editions), subject to modification by $R_{\text{BOCA}}/R_{\text{IBC}}$ (this ratio is dependent on the choice of the lateral-force-resisting system) and by I_{IBC}. The importance factor of the IBC will obviously boost the ratios of Table 5.6 by 25 percent for assembly buildings, and by 50 percent for essential facilities. The $R_{\text{BOCA}}/R_{\text{IBC}}$ ratio is not discussed here.

NR99 in Table 5.6 indicates no requirements for seismic design per BOCA/NBC-1993, 1996 and 1999. NR00 indicates no requirements for seismic design per the 2000 IBC (as is the case for structures assigned to SDC A). Ratios of design base shears are obviously meaningful only for cases where seismic design is required by both codes. The ratios are often smaller than 1.0 for the firmer Site Classes A, B, and C, indicating a decrease in the design base shear from the last three editions of the BOCA/NBC to the 2000 IBC. The ratios, however, are larger than 1.0, and sometimes substantially larger, for the softer Site Classes. For instance, in Richmond, VA, on Site Class E, the design base shear of the 2000 IBC is 3.66 times that of the BOCA/NBC. This increase in design forces goes together with a change from SPC B to SDC C for structures in Richmond, VA, that are founded on Site Class E. This comparison may be more complicated, however, depending on the structural system used. For instance, if the lateral-force-resisting system of a building consists of moment-resisting frames, going from SPC B to SDC C will require intermediate moment frames (IMF) as a minimum. Ordinary moment frames (OMF) will no longer be allowed. The R-values of 5.0 for the IMF versus 3.0 for the OMF will result in a 40-percent reduction in the design base shear.

TABLE 5.6. RATIO OF DESIGN BASE SHEARS — 2000 IBC TO 1999 BOCA/NBC

LOCATION	SITE CLASS				
	A	B	C	D	E
Washington, D.C.	NR99/00	NR99/00	NR99/00	NR99	NR99
Chicago, IL	NR99/00	NR99/00	NR99/00	NR99	NR99
Baltimore, MD	NR99/00	NR99/00	NR99/00	NR99	NR99
Boston, MA	0.59	0.73	0.88	1.13	1.65
New York, NY	0.71	0.89	1.07	1.32	1.80
Cincinnati, OH	NR00	NR00	1.18	1.57	2.45
Philadelphia, PA	0.88	1.10	1.32	1.69	2.47
Richmond, VA	NR00	1.52	1.83	2.40	3.66

NR99—Seismic design not required by 1999 BOCA/NBC

NR00—Seismic design not required by 2000 IBC except structure must resist lateral force equal to 1 percent of tributary weight applied at every floor level.

Comparison of IBC and UBC

The ratio of the upper-bound (short-period) design base shears of the 2000 IBC and the 1997 UBC is made up of three parts: 1) $S_{DS}/2.5C_a$, which is a function of the seismicity and the soil characteristics at a particular location, 2) the ratio of R-values of the UBC and the IBC for the same structural system, and 3) the ratio of I-values of the IBC and the UBC.

For the specific locations in UBC territory chosen for the comparisons of Table 5.4, the $S_{DS}/2.5C_a$ ratios for different site classes are given in Table 5.7. It may be noted that C_a of the 1997 UBC is very similar to the C_a of the 1997 NEHRP Provisions and the 2000 IBC (Appendix 3).

The values in Table 5.7 represent the ratios of the upper-bound design base shears of the 2000 IBC and the 1997 UBC, subject to modifications by R_{UBC}/R_{IBC} (this ratio is dependent on the choice of the lateral-force-resisting system) and by I_{IBC}/I_{UBC}. The ratio I_{IBC}/I_{UBC} is $1.5/1.25 = 1.2$ for Seismic Use Group III buildings and is equal to 1.0 for all other buildings. The R_{UBC}/R_{IBC} ratio is not discussed here.

Since the design base shear equations of the 2000 IBC and the 1997 UBC account for soils at the site of a structure in exactly the same manner, the ratios of Table 5.7 are basically reflective of changes in the seismic ground motions at the particular locations, as given by the seismic zone map of the UBC and the contour maps of the IBC. The major impact of the IBC, as reflected in Table 5.7, is that in all Zone 3 and 4 locations other than Sacramento, site-specific geotechnical analysis will be required to be performed on Site Class E, whereas such analysis is currently not required by the UBC.

TABLE 5.7. RATIO OF DESIGN BASE SHEARS — 2000 IBC to 1997 UBC

LOCATION	ZONE	SITE CLASS				
		A	B	C	D	E
West LA, $N_a = 1.3$	4	1.05	1.05	1.05	0.96	**
San Francisco	4	1.00	1.00	1.00	0.91	**
Berkeley, $N_a = 1.5$	4	0.88	0.89	0.89	0.81	**
Denver	1	0.93	0.85	0.89	0.90	0.91
Sacramento	3	0.53	0.53	0.56	0.59	0.67
St. Paul	0					
Seattle	3	1.33	1.33	1.21	1.11	**
Portland	3	1.07	1.07	0.97	0.91	**
Houston	0					

**Site-specific geotechnical investigation required per 2000 IBC.

TABLE 5.8. RATIO OF DESIGN BASE SHEARS — 2000 IBC TO 1999 SBC

LOCATION	SITE CLASS				
	A	B	C	D	E
Birmingham, AL	1.37	1.71	2.05	2.64	3.88
Atlanta, GA	NR00	0.77	0.92	1.23	1.90
Orlando, FL	NR99/00	NR99/00	NR99/00	NR99	NR99
Little Rock, AR	1.92	2.39	2.67	3.47	4.53
New Orleans, LA	NR99/00	NR99/00	NR99/00	NR99	NR99
Nashville, TN	0.85	1.07	1.28	1.65	2.43
Charlotte, NC	0.68	0.85	1.02	1.29	1.85
Charleston, SC	2.44	3.05	3.05	3.05	**

NR99—Seismic design not required by 1999 SBC

NR00—Seismic design not required by 2000 IBC except 1 percent of tributary weight applied at every floor level.

**Site-specific geotechnical investigation required per 2000 IBC.

Comparison of IBC and SBC

The ratio of the upper-bound (short-period) design base shears of the 2000 IBC and the SBC (1994, 1997 and 2000 editions) is also made up of three parts: 1) $S_{DS}/2.5A_a$, which is a function of the seismicity and the soil characteristics at a particular location, 2) the ratio of R-values of the SBC and the IBC for the same structural system, and 3) the I-value of the IBC (I is not used in the 1994 through the 1999 editions of the SBC). For the specific locations in SBC territory chosen for the comparisons of Table 5.5, the $S_{DS}/2.5A_a$ ratios for different site classes are given in Table 5.8. The values in Table 5.8 represent the ratios of the upper-bound design base shears of the 2000 IBC and the SBC (1994, 1997, and 1999 editions), subject to modification by R_{SBC}/R_{IBC} (this ratio is dependent upon the choice of the lateral-force-resisting system) and by I_{IBC}. The importance factor of the IBC will obviously boost the ratios of Table 5.8 by 25 percent for assembly buildings, and by 50 percent for essential facilities. The R_{SBC}/R_{IBC} ratio is not discussed here.

NR99 in Table 5.8 indicates no requirements for seismic design per SBC – 1994, 1997 or 1999. NR00 indicates no requirements for seismic design per the 2000 IBC (as is the case for structures assigned to SDC A). Ratios of design base shears are obviously meaningful only for cases where seismic design is required by both codes. The ratios are sometimes smaller than 1.0 for the firmer site classes A, B, and C, indicating a decrease in the design base shear from the last three editions of the SBC to the 2000 IBC. The ratios, however, are larger than 1.0, and quite often substantially larger, particularly for the softer site classes. When the ratios are significantly larger than 1.0 even for Site Classes A and B, as in the case of Birmingham, Little Rock, and Charleston, South Carolina, the seismicity of those locations has been upgraded from the older contour maps of the SBC to the newer contour maps of the IBC. It should be noted that the changes in design forces go together with the changes in seismic performance/design categories, as indicated in Table 5.5. For instance, a Class B site in Charleston, goes from SPC C to SDC D; at the same time, the seismic design force for the site goes up by a factor of 3.05. This comparison may be more complicated, however, depending on the structural system used. For instance, if the lateral-force-resisting system of a building consists of moment-resisting frames, going from SPC C to SDC D will require special moment frames (SMF) as a minimum. Intermediate moment frames (IMF) will no longer be allowed. The R-values of 8 for the SMF versus 5 for the IMF will result in a 37.5-percent reduction in the design base shear.

CONCLUDING REMARKS

Based on the information presented in this Appendix, the potential impact of the 2000 IBC on seismic design and construction across the country appears to be quite substantive. Limited comparative designs using the 2000 UBC, the 1997 UBC, and the 1991 NEHRP Provisions (as adopted into the last three editions of the BOCA/NBC and the SBC) have been carried out for reinforced concrete structures by S.K. Ghosh Associates Inc., and for steel, masonry and wood structures by J.R. Harris & Company through funding provided by the Federal Emergency Management Agency (FEMA) under a contract administered by the Building Seismic Safety Council (BSSC). A summary of the results is expected to be published by FEMA. Partial results of the comparative reinforced concrete designs have been published.[5.5]

ACKNOWLEDGMENT

Joseph J. Messersmith, Jr. of the Portland Cement Association carried out computations leading to the initial versions of Tables 5.2, 5.5, 5.6, and 5.8. His contribution is deeply appreciated.

REFERENCES

[5.1]Buildings Officials and Code Administrators International, *The BOCA National Building Code*, Country Club Hills, IL, 1993, 1996, 1999.

[5.2]Building Seismic Safety Council, *NEHRP (National Earthquake Hazards Reduction Program) Recommended Provisions for the Development of Seismic Regulations for New Buildings*, Washington, D.C., 1991, and *NEHRP Recommended Provisions for Seismic Regulations for new Buildings and Other Structures*, Washington, D.C., 1997.

[5.3]International Conference of Building Officials, *Uniform Building Code*, Whittier, CA, 1997.

[5.4]Southern Building Code Congress International, *Standard Building Code*, Birmingham, AL, 1994, 1997, 1999.

[5.5]Ghosh, S.K., and Khuntia, M., "Impact of Seismic Design Provisions of 2000 IBC: Comparison with 1997 UBC," Proceedings, 68th Annual Convention, Structural Engineers Association of California, Santa Barbara, CA, September 30-October 3, 1999.

INDEX

Related Products

2000 IBC Structural Q&A: Application Guide

This publication contains commonly asked questions that arise in the application of code provisions during design, plan review, construction, and daily code enforcement. Some answers include helpful illustrations that provide a clear understanding of the intent and meaning of the code text. An essential resource for engineers, architects, inspectors, building officials, plans examiners, instructors and students. *(119 pages)*

Item No. 124S2K

Seismic Design Handbook

Sponsored by ICBO and NCSEA, this new edition from Farzad Naeim includes three new chapters on seismic upgrading of existing structures, performance-based seismic engineering, and computer applications in seismic design. The book's substantial increase in size reflects the addition of many lessons learned from damaging earthquakes worldwide during the last decade. It includes a bonus CD-ROM containing the complete text along with ICBO's *UBC-IBC Structural Comparison & Cross Reference*, and FEMA's 273/274 and 302/303. An essential resource for civil, structural and geotechnical engineers; code officials and students. *(848 pages)*

Item No. SEIS03

Minimum Design Loads for Buildings and Other Structures (ASCE 7-98)

This revision is a replacement of ANSI/ASCE 7-95. This Standard provides requirements for dead, live, soil, flood, wind, snow, rain, ice, and earthquake loads, and their combinations that are suitable for inclusion in building codes and other documents. The major revision of this standard involves the section on wind loads, which has been greatly expanded to include the latest information in the field of wind load engineering. Additionally, requirements have been added for flood loads and ice loads. An appendix on serviceability requirements has also been added. Architects, structural engineers, and those engaged in preparing and administering local building codes will find the structural load requirements provided by this standard essential.

Item No. 347S98

UBC-IBC Structural Comparison & Cross Reference

A helpful tool that provides a comparative analysis between the structural provisions of the 1997 *Uniform Building Code* (UBC) and the 2000 *International Building Code* (IBC) with a cross-reference directory. Code sections, tables, and figures from the IBC are listed sequentially with an analysis of comparison to the UBC that can be used as a plan checking and field inspection aid. Readers can also locate IBC section numbers for similar provisions found in the UBC. *(232 pages)*

Item No. 101CCR

LRFD Manual for Engineered Wood Construction

The *LRFD Manual for Engineered Wood Construction,* 1996 Edition, provides a comprehensive guide for the design of engineered wood structures. Incorporated in this manual is the American Forest and Paper Association/ ASCE 16-95 Standard for Load and Resistance Factor Design for Engineered Wood Construction, along with five supplements and four guidelines. In addition, this manual contains several sections explaining provisions of the standard, including example problems. More than 40 details are included in the chapter on connections. Six case studies outlining the use of traditional and engineered wood products in commercial, industrial, and retail structures are also incorporated.

Item No. 344S96

1999 Masonry Standards Joint Committee Code, Specification and Commentaries

This new report includes *Building Code Requirements for Masonry Structures* (ACI 530-99/ASCE 5-99/TMS 402-99), *Specification for Masonry Structures* (ACI 530.1-99/ASCE 6-99/TMS 602-99) and accompanying commentaries.

Item No. 355S99

Building Code Requirements for Structural Concrete (318-99) and Commentary (318R-99)

Published by the American Concrete Institute, this new report covers drawings and specifications, inspection, materials, durability, concrete quality, strength evaluation of existing structures, and provisions for seismic design. It also includes a comprehensive commentary covering new or revised provisions.

Item No. 356S99

Recommended Lateral Force Requirements and Commentary (SEAOC Blue Book)

This new guide from the Structural Engineers Association of California (SEAOC) reviews recommended provisions for earthquake-resistant design of structures. Highlights include design requirements, structural tests and inspections, foundations, and recommended modifications to the 1997 UBC for reinforced concrete, reinforced masonry, structural steel and wood. *(440 pages)*

Item No. 000S99

1997 ASD/NDS Engineered Wood Construction Package

This 14-book set contains the following:

- 1999 ASD Manual
- Structural Lumber Supplement
- Structural-Use Panels Supplement
- Timber Poles and Piles Supplement
- Structural Connections Supplement
- Structural-Use Panel Shear Wall and Diaphragm Supplement
- Structural Glued Laminated Timber Supplement
- Wood I-Joists Guidelines
- Structural Composite Lumber Guidelines
- Metal Plate Connected Wood Trusses Guidelines
- Pre-Engineered Metal Connectors Guidelines
- 1997 National Design Specification (NDS) for Wood Construction
- 1997 NDS Supplement: Design Values for Wood Construction
- 1997 NDS Commentary

Item No. 35097

Allowable Stress Design (ASD) Manual of Steel Construction, Volume I, 9th Edition

This volume contains six parts: (1) Dimensions and Properties; (2) Beam and Girder Design; (3) Column Design; (4) Connections; (5) Specifications and Codes; and (6) Miscellaneous Data and Mathematical Tables. This book also incorporates the following other American Institute of Steel Construction (AISC) publications: S335 *Specification for Structural Steel Buildings* (and Commentary); S303 *Code of Standard Practice for Steel Buildings and Bridges;* S329 ASD *Specification for Structural Joints Using ASTM A325 and A490 Bolts;* and S343L ASD *Specification for Single-Angle Members. (1,144 pages)*

Item No. 345H00

2000 International Building Code

This long-awaited publication is based on years of combined experience and technical expertise of the three model code groups. The *International Building Code*® (IBC) features time-tested safety concepts, updated means of egress and interior finish requirements, comprehensive roof provisions, seismic engineering provisions, innovative construction technology, revamped structural provisions, reorganized occupancy classifications, and the latest industry standards in material design. The loose-leaf edition is in a durable seven-hole binder and includes sheet lifters imprinted with rulers and conversion charts. *(750 pages)*

Item No. 100S2K

2000 IBC Limited Millennium Hard Cover Edition

Serious code users will appreciate this high quality, premier publication that will stand up to the tests of time and use. Quantities are limited, so order yours today.

Item No. 100H2K

2000 IBC: ASTM Referenced Standards

An essential tool that will save code users time and help achieve compliance with the code. This comprehensive publication contains all ASTM Standards that are referenced by, but not included, the 2000 IBC. More than 230 standards in 1,432 pages!

Item No. 102S2K

IBC Turbo Tabs

You'll be surprised how easy it is to quickly find a code section using *Turbo Tabs*. With the section of the code printed on each Tab, you can flip through the code and find frequently used sections fast! *Turbo Tabs* are available for both soft cover and loose leaf codes. The soft-cover versions contain clear plastic, self-adhesive tabs that have the key sections of the codes printed in an easy-to-read format on them. The loose leaf versions contain full-page inserts with key sections printed on the tabs.

Item No. 310T2K

IBC CD-ROM

Navigate easily through the innovative 2000 *International Building Code* quickly and easily with this new CD-ROM. Search text, copy images from figures and tables, copy and paste code provisions into correspondence or reports, and more! Uses Acrobat® Reader.

Item No. 001C2K

Code Explorer—2000 International Code Collection CD-ROM

The latest addition to ICBO's exclusive series of CD-ROMs contains the complete searchable text of 10 International Codes! The International Building, Residential, Fire, Mechanical, Plumbing, Private Sewage Disposal, Property Maintenance, Fuel Gas, Energy Conservation and Zoning Codes are all on this valuable tool. It is powered by Autobook to provide tremendous multiple search capabilities, and hyperlinks between Codes and code sections. Copy and paste text or images, and add your own searchable notes directly to text in color or hide them!

Item No. 001X2K